THE
SOTHEBY'S
WINE
ENCYCLOPEDIA

THE
SOTHEBY'S
WINE
ENCYCLOPEDIA

TOM STEVENSON

LONDON, NEW YORK, MELBOURNE,
MUNICH, DELHI

FOURTH EDITION (2005)

DORLING KINDERSLEY

ART EDITOR Sue Metcalfe-Megginson

MANAGING ART EDITOR Marianne Markham

DTP DESIGNER Louise Waller

MAPS Encompass Graphics, Paul
Eames, David Roberts

PRODUCTION CONTROLLER Kevin Ward

EDITORS Joanna Benwell, Bill Evans,
Claire Nottage, Gary Werner

MANAGING EDITOR Deirdre Headon

DIGITAL CONTENT MANAGER Nina Blackett

AMERICANIZATION Margaret Parrish

INDEXER John Noble

Produced for Dorling Kindersley by

COOLING BROWN LTD.

CREATIVE DIRECTOR Arthur Brown

DESIGN Peter Cooling, Elaine Hewson,
Tish Jones, Elly King

SENIOR EDITOR Fiona Wild

COPY EDITOR Alyson Lacewing

Penguin Group (USA) Inc.,
375 Hudson Street, New York, New York 10014, USA
Penguin Group (Canada),
10 Alcorn Avenue, Toronto, Ontario, Canada M4V 3B2
(a division of Pearson Penguin Canada Inc.)
Penguin Books Ltd., 80 Strand, London WC2R 0RL, England
Penguin Ireland, 25 St Stephen's Green, Dublin 2, Ireland
(a division of Penguin Books Ltd.)
Penguin Group (Australia), 250 Camberwell Road, Camberwell,
Victoria 3124, Australia (a division of Pearson Australia Group Pty Ltd.)
Penguin Books India Pvt Ltd., 11 Community Centre,
Panchsheel Park, New Delhi - 110 017, India
Penguin Group (NZ), Cnr Airborne and Rosedale Roads, Albany,
Auckland, New Zealand (a division of Pearson New Zealand Ltd)
Penguin Books (South Africa) (Pty) Ltd., 24 Sturdee Avenue,
Rosebank, Johannesburg 2196, South Africa

Fourth edition published 2005
by Dorling Kindersley Limited,
80 Strand, London WC2R 0RL
First published in 1988 as Sotheby's World Wine Encyclopedia
Published in 1997 as The New Sotheby's Wine Encyclopedia

6 8 10 9 7 5

A CIP catalog record of this book is available from the British Library

ISBN 0-7566-1324-8

Color reproduction by Colorscan, Singapore
Printed and bound by SNP Leefung, China

See our complete catalog at
www.dk.com

CONTENTS

INTRODUCTION 7–47

Introduction 7
Using this book 8
The Taste of Wine 10
How to Assess a Wine 12
Terroir 14
Guide to Vineyard Soils 17
Viticulture 19
Annual Life cycle of the Vine 23
Vinification 25
The Choice of Oak 32
Grape Varieties 35
Glossary of Grape Varieties 36
Grape Variety Synonyms 43
Storing Wine 46
Serving Wine 47

The WINES of
THE WORLD 48–51
A World of Wine 50

The WINES of
FRANCE 52–259

France Introduction 54
Bordeaux 62
The Médoc 70
St.-Estèphe 81
Pauillac 84
St.-Julien 89
Margaux 92
Graves, Cérons,
Sauternes, and Barsac 97

Château Gruaud-Larose, St-Julien, France

Conca d'Oro estate, Vulture, Basilicata, Italy

The Libournais and Fronsadais 108
St.-Émilion 111
Pomerol 120
The Fronsadais and
St.-Émilion and Pomerol satellites 124
Bourg and Blaye 126
Entre-Deux-Mers 130

Burgundy 135
The Chablis District 140
Côte de Nuits and
Hautes-Côtes de Nuits 145
Côte de Beaune and
Hautes Côtes de Beaune 151
The Côte Chalonnaise 159
The Mâconnais 161
The Beaujolais 165

Champagne 169
Alsace 184

The Loire Valley 196
Pays Nantais 200
Anjou-Saumur 202
Touraine 207
Central Vineyards 211

The Rhône Valley 213
The Northern Rhône 215
The Southern Rhône 218

The Jura and Savoie 224
Southwestern France 228
Languedoc-Roussillon 235
Provence and Corsica 243
Vins de Pays 248

The WINES of
ITALY 260–299

Italy Introduction 262
Northwestern Italy 266
Northeastern Italy 275
West-Central Italy 282
East-Central Italy 289
Southern Italy and
the Islands 292

The WINES of
SPAIN 300–325

Spain Introduction 302
Rioja and Navarra 312
Penedés: Cava Country 318
Sherry Country 321

The WINES of
PORTUGAL 326–341

Portugal Introduction 328
Port: The Douro Valley 334
Madeira 340

The WINES of
GERMANY, AUSTRIA, AND SWITZERLAND 342–395

Germany Introduction 344
The Ahr 354
The Mittelrhein 356
Mosel 358
The Nahe 362
The Rheingau 364
Rheinhessen 368
The Pfalz 371
The Hessische-Bergstrasse 374
Franken 376

Rieschen Vineyard, Meersburg, Germany

Württemberg 379
Baden 381
Saale-Unstrut and Sachsen 385
Austria 387
Switzerland 392

The WINES of
NORTHWESTERN EUROPE 396–409

The British Isles 398
Luxembourg 404
Other Winemaking Countries of
Northwestern Europe 409

The WINES of
SOUTHEASTERN EUROPE 410–429

Bulgaria 412
Hungary 415
Romania 420
Slovakia and the Czech Republic 423
The Western Balkans 426
The Black and Caspian Seas 428

The WINES of
THE EASTERN MEDITERRANEAN 430–439

Greece 432
The Levant 437

The WINES of
THE AFRICAS 440–459

South Africa 442
North Africa 456
Other Winemaking Countries of Africa 458

The WINES of
THE AMERICAS 460–549

North America Introduction 462

Cabernet Sauvignon grapes, Chile

California 469
Mendocino County 479
Sonoma County 481
Napa County 487
The Central Coast (North) 495
The Central Coast (South) 498
The Central Valley 502
Other Appellations of California 504
The Pacific Northwest 507
The Atlantic Northeast 517
Other Winemaking Areas of the United States 527
Canada 532
Mexico 538
South America Introduction 540
Chile and Argentina 543

The WINES of
AUSTRALIA, NEW ZEALAND & ASIA 550–618

Australia Introduction 552
New South Wales 560
Victoria and Tasmania 567
South Australia 578
Western Australia 589
Queensland and Northern Territory 595
New Zealand 598
Asia 616

Wine and Food 619
Taste Chart 623
Guide to Good Vintages 626
Troubleshooter's Guide 628
Glossary 629
Index 641
Acknowledgments 664

Spring mustard flowers and vines, Napa Valley, California

GOOD NEWS AND BAD NEWS

THE GOOD NEWS IS THE NUMBER OF top-performing wine producers throughout the world, which has swollen out of all proportion when compared with earlier editions of this encyclopedia. Despite deleting hundreds of previously recommended producers, there are now in excess of 6,000 wineries recommended over the following pages. I have never upgraded the star ratings of so many producers in any revision than I have for the California chapter in this edition. And, proportionately, the number of increased ratings for wineries in Australia and, my self-confessed favorite, New Zealand, was not far behind.

The bad news is the low number of top-performing organic wine producers. To be frank, I had no idea just how bad the situation was when I first decided to use ◎ and ❸ symbols to identify recommended organic and biodynamic wine producers, but the relative rarity of these symbols throughout the book rang alarm bells. It is one thing if someone gifted like Olivier Humbrecht of Domaine Zind-Humbrecht in Alsace or Lalou Bize-Leroy of Domaine Leroy in Burgundy go organic or biodynamic. When great winemakers with exceptional *terroirs* "go green" they produce great organic or biodynamic wines. However, it is quite another matter when others less passionate about the quality of wine are organic. While they may well have a true passion for the environment, the majority of the world's organic producers clearly have no idea how to make a superior quality wine. And considering that many of them have been churning out their green gunge for years, they obviously could not care less. Just as worrying are the organizations that certify organic and biodynamic production, because it seems as if they could not care less either. It is not good enough to certify the method of production alone. They should acknowledge the importance of quality by introducing some sort of superior award on the label. Either that or the likes of Humbrecht and Bize-Leroy should set up international schools of organic and biodynamic excellence. Both ideas would be nice.

September 2005

USING THIS BOOK

Each chapter of the Encyclopedia is arranged on a country-by-country basis, within which each wine region is dealt with; any districts within regions are examined, as are any smaller winemaking areas in each district. Within each chapter, there are two basic types of page: general introductory text and taste guides. Introductory text has three regular features, "Label Language," "Recent Vintages," and "Factors Affecting Taste and Quality," which may be given at either the national or regional level (see below). Taste guides are variously entitled: "The Appellations of..."; "The Wine Styles of..."; and "The Wine Producers of...."

Where appropriate—in Bordeaux, for example—a listing of generic appellations provides an overview before the author deals with the more specific appellations. Various levels of information may be included in the Taste Guides, depending on the importance of a wine and/or its producer. Look for red, white, rosé, and sparkling tasting notes, with symbols denoting other information as detailed below right. When consulting the encyclopedia for a comment on a particular wine, look up the wine producer in the index. If you find that the producer is not listed, then look up the wine's appellation or style (by country or region).

COUNTRY AND REGION INTRODUCTION PAGES

CHAPTER INTRODUCTION
Full-spread chapter openers give readers a brief introduction to the region in question and a taste of what is to come.

COUNTRY MAP
Country maps show a country's main wine-producing regions, which are color-coded and cross-referenced, where appropriate, to regional maps.

COUNTRY INTRODUCTION
This gives a broad picture of the country in question. Much of the statistical and technical data is compartmentalized into boxes to avoid interrupting the flow of text while enabling readers seeking such information to zero-in on it quickly.

TABLES, CHARTS, AND BOXES
A wealth of statistical information is given in various charts, tables, and information boxes.

MAIN WINE REGION
If a country has major winemaking regions, each is given a full introduction.

REGIONAL MAP
Regional maps show a region's main winemaking areas, which are color-coded and cross-referenced, where appropriate, to district maps.

DISTRICTS AND TASTE GUIDES

WINE DISTRICTS
In France and California, each region's individual wine-producing districts are examined separately.

FACTORS AFFECTING TASTE AND QUALITY
In the introductory text for countries, regions, or districts, a tinted panel gives a quick-reference guide to the fundamental conditions that determine the quality and style of the wines produced in each area.

APPELLATIONS TEXT
Each winemaking area or appellation of a country, region, or district, whether legally defined or not, is listed and reviewed. The best producers in each appellation are listed. The symbols below form part of the text.

WINE STYLES
If a country or a region has a purely geographical system of appellations, then its wines may be described under the heading "The Wine Styles of…" The best-of-the-best wines of each wine style are listed.

DISTRICT MAP
These maps show color-coded winemaking areas, and, like some regional maps, also show intensive wine-producing zones and indicate the location of the best wine producers.

WINE PRODUCERS
The best and most famous wine producers in countries, regions, and districts are reviewed on Wine Producer pages. Star ratings are given where applicable, and particular wines are recommended.

ILLUSTRATIONS
Color photographs capture the flavor of each region.

STAR RATING SYSTEM

The Factors Affecting Taste and Quality boxes appear on the introductory pages of countries, regions, or districts. The taste guides (Appellations, Producers, and Wine Styles) follow these introductions.

FACTORS AFFECTING TASTE AND QUALITY

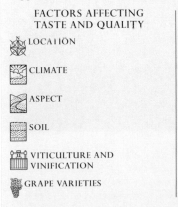

- LOCATION
- CLIMATE
- ASPECT
- SOIL
- VITICULTURE AND VINIFICATION
- GRAPE VARIETIES

TASTE GUIDE SYMBOLS

⊢⁓ When to drink for optimum enjoyment. This is usually given as a range (such as 3–7 years) from the date of the vintage. "Upon purchase" is for wines that should be both bought and drunk while young. "Upon opening" is for fortified wines that can keep for many years but, contrary to popular belief, do not keep well once opened.

Grape varieties used.

The very best wines in the author's experience.

Recommended producers, vineyards, and wines.

STAR RATING SYSTEM

Stars are given for a producer's general quality and do not necessarily apply to each wine produced. When a producer has neither stars nor a cross, this indicates an acceptable but not outstanding standard.

Half-stars indicate intermediate ratings

★ Wines that excel within their class or style.

★★ Very exceptional wines. The local equivalent of a Bordeaux super-second. See Glossary, p.638.

★★★ The best wines that money can buy, without any allowances made for limitations of local style and quality.

- A producer of organic wines.
- A producer of biodynamic wines.
- Wines of exceptional value for money, whether they are inexpensive or not.
- Wines that are inconsistent, or too rustic, or judgment has been reserved for a stated reason.
- Underperformers for their category or style.

THE TASTE OF WINE

The difference between tasting and drinking is similar to test-driving a car you may buy and the relish of driving it afterward. One is a matter of concentration, as you seek out merits and faults, while the other is a more relaxed and enjoyable experience. Almost anyone can learn to taste wine.

WHEN TASTING A WINE it is important to eliminate all distractions, especially comments made by others; it is all too easy to be swayed. The wine should be tasted and an opinion registered before any ensuing discussions. Even at professionally led tastings, the expert's job is not to dictate but to educate, to "lead from behind," putting into perspective other people's natural responses to smells or tastes through clear and concise explanation. The three "basics" of wine-tasting are sight, smell, and taste, known as "eye," "nose," and "palate."

THE SIGHT, OR "EYE," OF A WINE

The first step is to assess the wine's limpidity, which should be perfectly clear. Many wines throw a deposit, but this is harmless if it settles to yield a bright and clear wine. If it is cloudy or hazy, the wine should be discarded. Tiny bubbles that appear on the bowl or cling persistently to the edge of the glass are perfectly acceptable in a few wines, such as Muscadet *sur lie* and Vinho Verde, but probably indicate a flaw in most other still wines, particularly if red and from classic Old World regions.

The next step is to swirl the wine gently around the glass. So-called "legs" or "tears," thin sinewy threads of wine that run down the side of the glass, may appear. Contrary to popular belief, they are not indicative of high glycerol content, but are simply the effect of alcohol on wine's viscosity, or the way the wine flows. The greater the alcohol content, the less free-flowing, or more viscous, the wine actually becomes.

The color of wine

Natural light is best for observing a wine's color, the first clue to its identity once its condition has been assessed. Look at the wine against a white background, holding the glass at the bottom of the stem and tilting it away from you slightly. Red wines vary in color from *clairet*, which is almost rosé, to tones so dark and opaque that they seem black. White wines range from a colorless water-white to deep gold, although the majority are a light straw-yellow color. For some reason, there are very few rosé wines that are truly pink in color, the tonal range extending from blue-pink, through purple-pink, to orange-pink. Disregard any impression about a wine's color under artificial lighting because it will never be true—fluorescent light, for example, makes a red wine appear brown.

Factors affecting color

The color and tonal variation of any wine, whether red, white, or rosé, is determined by the grape variety. It is also influenced by the ripeness of the actual grapes, the area of production, the method of vinification, and the age of the wine. Dry, light-bodied wines from cooler climates are the lightest in color, while fuller-bodied or sweeter-styled wines from hotter regions are the deepest. Youthful red wines usually have a purple tone, whereas young white wines may hint of green, particularly if they are from a cooler climate. The aging process involves a slow oxidation that has a browning effect similar to the discoloration of a peeled apple that has been exposed to the air.

THE SMELL, OR "NOSE," OF A WINE

Whenever an experienced taster claims to be able to recognize in excess of 1,000 different smells, many wine lovers give up all hope of acquiring even the most basic tasting skills. Yet they should not be discouraged. Almost everybody can detect and distinguish over 1,000 different smells, the majority of which are ordinary, everyday odors. Ask anyone to write down all the

VISUAL EXAMINATION
Unless it has an extreme color or hue, the appearance of a wine is the least interesting aspect of a tasting note for most readers, which is why most authors use color descriptions sparingly. The eye is, however, one of the most important sensory organs for professional tasters, since even the most subtle shade or nuance can provide numerous clues to the wine's identity.

NOSING A WINE
As we smell most flavors, rather than taste them, a good sniff tells us a lot about a wine. But refrain from continuously sniffing, as this will dull your sense of smell. Take one good sniff, then pause for thought. Do not rush on to tasting the wine. Remember that no smells are specific to wine—they can all be compared to something familiar, but you need time to work out what they are.

smells they can recognize and most will be able to list several hundred without really trying. Yet a far greater number of smells are locked away in our brains waiting to be triggered.

The wine-smelling procedure is quite simple. Give the glass a good swirl, put your nose into the glass, and take a deep sniff. While it is essential to take a substantial sniff, it is not practicable to sniff the same wine again for at least two minutes. This is because each wine activates a unique pattern of nerve ends in the olfactory bulb; these nerve ends are like small candles that are snuffed out when activated and take a little time to reactivate. As a result, subsequent sniffs of the same smell can reveal less and less, yet it is perfectly feasible to smell different smells, therefore different wines, one after the other.

THE TASTE, OR "PALATE," OF A WINE

As soon as one sniffs a wine the natural reaction is to taste it, but do this only after all questions concerning the nose have been addressed. The procedure is simple, although it may look and sound rather strange to the uninitiated. Take a good mouthful and draw air into the mouth through the wine; this makes a gurgling sound, but it is essential to do it in order to magnify the wine's volatile characteristics in the back of the throat.

The tongue itself reveals very little; sweetness is detected on its tip, sourness or acidity on the sides, bitterness at the back and top, and saltiness on the front and sides. Apart from these four basic taste perceptions, we smell tastes rather than taste them. Any food or drink emits odorous vapors in the mouth that are automatically conveyed to the roof of the nasal passages. Here the olfactory bulb examines, discerns, and catalogs them—as they originate from the palate the natural inclination is to perceive them as tastes. For many of us it is difficult to believe that we taste with an organ located behind the eyes at the top of the nose, but when we eat ice cream too quickly, we painfully experience precisely where the olfactory bulb is, because the chilly aromas of the ice cream literally freeze this acutely delicate sensory organ. The texture of a wine also influences its taste; the prickly tactile sensation of carbon dioxide, for example, heightens our perception of acidity, while increased viscosity softens it.

SPITTING OUT
When tasting a large number of wines, each mouthful should be ejected after due assessment to prevent alcohol from affecting the ability to taste. Yet some wine will remain, even after spitting out, coating the inner surface of the mouth, where it is absorbed directly into the bloodstream. Contrary to popular belief, the more you taste the better you taste, but it is a race between the wine sharpening the palate and the alcohol dulling the brain!

QUALITY AND TASTE: WHY OPINIONS DIFFER

Whether you are a novice or a Master of Wine, it is always personal preference that is the final arbiter when you are judging wine. The most experienced tasters can often argue endlessly over the relative merits and demerits of certain wines.

We all know that quality exists, and more often than not agree which wines have it, and yet we are not able to define it. Lacking a solid definition, most experienced tasters would happily accept that a fine wine must have natural balance and finesse and show a definite, distinctive, and individual character within its own type or style. If we occasionally differ on the question of the quality of wine, should we disagree on what it tastes like? We may love or hate a wine, but surely the taste we perceive is the same?

Conveying specific taste characteristics from the mind of one person to that of another is difficult enough, whether one is writing a book or simply discussing a wine at a tasting. Much of this difficulty lies in the words we choose, but the problem is not confined to semantics. In a world of perfect communication, conveying impressions of taste would still be an inexact art because of the different threshold levels at which we pick up elementary tastes and smells, and because of the various tolerance levels at which we enjoy them. If individuals require different quantities of acidity, tannin, alcohol, sugar, esters, and aldehydes in a wine before actually detecting them, then the same wine has, literally, a different taste for each of us. In the unlikely event of people having the same threshold for every constituent and combination of constituents, disagreement would probably ensue because we also have different tolerance levels; therefore, some of us would enjoy what others dislike because we actually like the tastes and smells they dislike. Thresholds and tolerance levels vary enormously; the threshold for detecting sweetness, for example, varies by a factor of five, which explains the "sweet tooth" phenomenon, and there are an infinite number of tolerance levels. Apply this to every basic aroma and flavor, and it is surprising that we agree on the description of any wine.

MAGNIFYING THE TASTE OF A WINE
The tongue discerns only sweetness, sourness, bitterness, and saltiness. Every other "taste" we smell. By drawing air through a mouthful of wine, the volatilized aromas are taken into the back of the throat, where they are picked up by the olfactory bulb, which automatically analyzes them and transmits the information to the brain as various so-called flavors. (See also "Umami," Glossary p.639)

HOW TO ASSESS A WINE

It would be impossible to answer many of the following questions without a degree of experience. Likewise, it would be difficult to identify a particular wine, or type of wine, having never tasted it. But your knowledge will increase with every tasting.

SIGHT

Look at the color. Is it deep or pale? Is there a positive quality to it, a specific hue that reminds you of a particular grape variety, the growing climate, or the area of production? Is the color vivid and youthful, or is there browning that might suggest its age? What does the rim, or meniscus, indicate? Does it retain the intensity of colour to the rim of the glass, which suggests a high-quality product, or does it fade to an unimpressive, watery finish?

SMELL

If the first impression is very heady, is the wine fortified? (Classic fortified wines, such as port, sherry, and Madeira, do have easily recognizable characteristics, but it can still be difficult to distinguish between a robust wine with a naturally high alcohol level produced in a hot country and a fortified wine.) Does the wine have any distinctive aromas, or are they obscure or bland,

A SAMPLE TASTING

This chart provides a few examples from a whole range of the possible options that are open in the complex business of tasting. It also demonstrates that it is possible to approach the task systematically and rationally. When tasting it is important to keep your options open until you have assessed the sight, smell, and taste of the wine. At each stage you should be seeking to confirm at least one of the possibilities that has arisen during the previous stage. Be confident and do not be afraid to back your own judgement—it is the only way to learn.

SIGHT
The clear, well-defined garnet color of medium intensity suggests only moderately hot climatic origins. The tinge of purple on the meniscus could indicate youth.

SMELL
This is dominated by the distinctive pear-drop aroma of *macération carbonique*, hallmark of all but the best *cru* Beaujolais. Often mistaken for the varietal aroma of Gamay (from which Beaujolais is made), the aroma is characteristic of all wines fermented in this way. If this is a Beaujolais, the color suggests something more serious than a lighter basic Beaujolais or Nouveau.

TASTE
The balance between fruit, acidity, and alcohol confirms that this is Beaujolais. The good depth of spicy-grapey fruit beneath the pervasive pear-drop character indicates that it is better than average.

CONCLUSION
Grape variety Gamay
Region Beaujolais
Age 2 to 3 years old
Comment Beaujolais Villages

SIGHT
Water-white, this wine has obvious cool climatic origins, although the tiny bubbles collecting on the glass suggest it could be a Vinho Verde. But the palest usually have a tell-tale hint of straw color. Probably a modest *Qualitätswein* from the Mosel region of Germany.

SMELL
This is not Vinho Verde. Its crisp, youthful, sherbet aroma is typical Mosel Riesling. Considering its color, the nose would confirm that this is probably a *Qualitätswein*, or a *Kabinett* at most, of a modest vintage, but from a very good grower who is possibly as high up as the Saar tributary.

TASTE
Youthful, tangy fruit, the flower of the Riesling is still evident. More flavor than expected, and a nice dry, piquant finish with a hint of peach on the aftertaste.

CONCLUSION
Grape variety Riesling
Region Mosel
Age about 18 to 24 months
Comment *Kabinett*, top grower

SIGHT
Intense, almost black color that is virtually opaque. Obviously from a thick-skinned grape variety like the Syrah, which has ripened under a very hot sun. Australia's Swan Valley or France's Rhône Valley? California?

SMELL
As intense on the nose as on the eye. Definitely Syrah, and judging by its spicy aroma with hints of herbal scrub, almost certainly from the northern Rhône. Australia and California can now be ruled out. More massive than complex, it must be from an exceptional vintage.

TASTE
Powerful and tannic, the spicy-fruit flavor is rich with blackberries, blackcurrants, plums, and cinnamon. Beginning to develop, but has a long way to go. This is a high-quality Rhône Syrah, but without quite the class of Hermitage, or the finesse of Côte Rôtie.

CONCLUSION
Grape variety Syrah
Region Cornas, Rhône Valley
Age about 5 years old
Comment top grower, great year

SIGHT
The brick-red color and watery meniscus immediately suggest a young Bordeaux of *petit-château* quality. But first impressions can deceive—more evidence is needed.

SMELL
An attractive violet aroma with a restrained hint of soft, spicy fruit. Nothing contradicts my impressions, although the lack of blackcurrant suggests that the wine is a Bordeaux with a high proportion of Merlot rather than Cabernet Sauvignon.

TASTE
The palate perfectly reflects the nose. This is a medium-bodied, modest claret of no great age. However, the fruit is well rounded and the soft tannin structure indicates that in little more than another 2, possibly 3, years it will be at its peak.

CONCLUSION
Grape variety Merlot-dominated blend
Region Bordeaux
Age 2 years old
Comment *petit château* or good generic

or simply reticent? Does the wine smell as youthful or as mature as it appears to the eye? Is it smooth and harmonious, suggesting the wine is ready to drink? If so, should it be drunk? If it is not ready, can you estimate when it will be? Is there a recognizable grape variety aroma? Are there any creamy or vanilla hints to suggest that it has been fermented or aged in new oak? If so, which region ages such wine in oak? Is it a simple wine or is there a degree of complexity? Are there any hints as to the area of production? Is its quality obvious or do you need confirmation on the palate?

TASTE

This should reflect the wine's smell and therefore confirm any judgements that you have already made. Should. But human organs are fallible, not least the brain, so keep an open mind. Be prepared to accept contradiction as well as confirmation. Ask yourself all the questions you asked on the nose, but before you do, ask what your palate tells you about the acidity, sweetness, and alcoholic strength.

If you are tasting a red wine, its tannin content can be revealing. Tannin is derived from the grape's skin, and the darker and thicker it is, and the longer the juice macerates with the skins,

the more tannin there will be in the wine. A great red wine will contain so much tannin that it will literally pucker the mouth, while early-drinking wines will contain little.

If you are tasting a sparkling wine, on the other hand, its mousse, or effervescence, will give extra clues. The strength of the mousse will determine the style—whether it is fully sparkling, semi-sparkling, or merely *pétillant* – and the size of the bubbles will indicate the quality; the smaller they are, the better.

CONCLUSION

Just try to name the grape variety and area of origin, and give some indication of the age and quality of the wine. Wise tasters will not risk their credibility by having a stab at anything more specific, such as the producer or vineyard, unless he or she is 100 percent sure. In the Master of Wine examination, marks are given for correct rationale, even if the conclusion that is drawn is wrong, while it has been known for a candidate to name the wine in precise detail but, because of defective reasoning, to receive no score at all. Wine tasting is not a matter of guessing. It is about deduction, and getting it wrong should be encouraged because that is the only way to learn.

SIGHT
This distinctive yellow gold color retains its intensity to the rim. Various possibilities: a sweet wine, a full bodied dry wine, a mature wine, or something obscure like Retsina. If none of these, it could be a Gewürztraminer.

SMELL
Gewürztraminer! Full, rich, and spicy, the aroma hits you between the eyes and the first instinct is to think of Alsace. Usually you will be right, but bear in mind the possibility of a top grower in the Rheinpfalz or Austria. If the aroma were muted, it might be Italian; if exotic, Californian or Australian. This, however, seems to be a classic example of a ripe Alsace vintage of perhaps 4 years of age.

TASTE
A rich-flavored wine; full, fat, and fruity with well-developed spice and a soft, succulent finish. Evidently made from very ripe grapes.

CONCLUSION
Grape variety Gewürztraminer
Region Alsace
Age about 4 to 5 years old
Comment very good quality

SIGHT
Stunning color, more distinctive even than the Gewürztraminer, the old gold immediately suggests a full, rich, and probably very sweet wine. Sauternes springs to mind, but Austria, or even an oddity from Australia are also possible.

SMELL
This has the amazingly full, rich, and opulent nose of a botrytized wine. Anyone who dislikes sweet wine should smell a wine like this before giving up on it altogether. A touch of creamy-spicy oak rules out Austria and its maturity, probably between 10 and 15 years, probably disposes of Australia.

TASTE
Everything is here from peaches, pineapple, and cream to the honeyed aromatics of a fairly mature wine. Only a classic Sauternes can have such intense flavors, yet possess such great finesse.

CONCLUSION
Grape variety mostly Sémillon
Region Sauternes
Age about 15 years old
Comment *Premier cru*, great vintage

SIGHT
The orange-pink of this wine almost certainly pins it to Provence or Tavel, although, if the orange hue is not indicative of the style and vinification of the wine, it could be almost any over-the-hill rosé.

SMELL
Put the dunce's hat on and stand in the corner! The high-toned Pinot Noir aroma dismisses the firm conviction of a Tavel or Provence rosé. But what is it? It is not oxidized, so it cannot be an otherwise obvious wine that has gone over. Is the orange hue a clue to its origin? More information is needed; must taste the wine.

TASTE
Definitely Burgundian, but with a very distinctive, piquant Pinot Noir taste. At its peak now, but certainly not on the way down. By eliminating what it cannot be, only Rosé de Marsannay fits the bill.

CONCLUSION
Grape variety Pinot Noir
Region Burgundy
Age 4 to 5 years old
Comment medium quality

SIGHT
This sparkling wine has an attractive, lively, lemon-yellow color. Not young, but not old, its mousse is evident, but its power and size of bubble cannot be assessed without tasting. Its star-bright limpidity just makes it look like a fine wine.

SMELL
Its quality is immediately evident, with the autolytic characteristics of a wine with several years on its first cork (in contact with its lees prior to disgorgement), which eliminates every possibility other than a fine Champagne. It has the zippy tang of ripe Chardonnay grapes. This must be a Champagne *blanc de blancs* with a high proportion of wine from the Côte des Blancs.

TASTE
A gently persistent mousse of ultra-fine bubbles. The fresh, lively flavor has a long finish but needs five years more to reach perfection.

CONCLUSION
Grape variety Chardonnay
Region Champagne
Age about 5 years old
Comment top quality

TERROIR

The same grape grown in the same area can make two totally different wines, owing to seemingly inconsequential factors such as a different soil or aspect. And yet different grapes grown continents apart may produce two wines that are very similar.

THERE ARE CERTAIN, CONSTANT FACTORS that affect the taste and quality of wine. These include location; climate, which determines the ability to grow grapes; vintage, the vagaries of which can make or break a harvest; aspect, responsible for enhancing or negating local conditions; and soil. All these factors are discussed in more detail below and can be classified as elements of *terroir*. Also important, of course, are viticulture, because the cultivation techniques used can stretch or concentrate varietal character (*see* pp.19–22); vinification, which, like cooking methods, can produce a range of options from the same basic ingredient (*see* pp.25–31); the winemaker, the idiosyncratic joker in the pack; and grape variety—always the most important factor (*see* pp.35–45).

APPLE TREE IN CALVADOS, NORMANDY
Methods of vine-training are applicable to other cultivated fruits, as this spur-trained apple tree in Calvados illustrates.

LOCATION
The location of a vineyard is fundamental in determining whether its climate is suitable for viticulture. Virtually all the world's wine-producing areas, in both hemispheres, are located in the temperate zones between 30° and 50° latitude, where the annual mean temperature is between 10°C (50°F) and 20°C (68°F). The most northerly vineyards of Germany are at the outermost limit of this range, between 50° and 51° latitude (almost 53° if we include the scattered vineyards of former East Germany), but they survive because of the continental climatic influence, which assures hotter summers. The shorter days also retard the cane growth in favor of fruit maturity, allowing the grapes to ripen before the harsh continental winter. Interestingly, most of the world's finest wines are produced in west-coast locations, which tend to be cooler and less humid than east-coast areas. Forests and mountain ranges protect the vines from wind and rain. A relatively close proximity to forests and large masses of water can influence the climate through transpiration and evaporation, providing welcome humidity in times of drought, although they can also encourage rot. Thus some factors can have both positive and negative effects.

CLIMATE
Climate and weather are the most important factors that influence the growth of grapes for high-quality wines. Climate is determined by geographical location, whereas weather is the result of how nature decides to affect that climate on a daily basis. In other words, climate is what it should be, weather is what it is. A grower must select a region with an amenable climate and hope that nature does not inflict too many anomalies.

Although some vines survive under extreme conditions, most—and all classic—winemaking vines are confined to two relatively narrow climatic bands between 30° and 50° latitude and require a combination of heat, sunshine, rain, and frost.

HEAT
Vines will not provide grapes suitable for winemaking if the annual mean temperature is less than 50°F (10°C). The ideal

THE WORLD OF WINE
The most important areas of cultivation in both the northern and southern hemispheres lie mainly between latitudes 30° and 50°. However, there are a number of smaller winemaking areas closer to the equator. Indeed, equatorial vinifera *wines are produced in tiny quantities in Kenya and Peru.*

mean temperature is 57° to 59°F (14° to 15°C), with an average of no less than 66°F (19°C) in the summer and 30°F (-1°C) in the winter. In order for the vines to produce a good crop of ripe grapes, the minimum heat-summation, measured in "degree-days" with an average of above 50°F (10°C) over the growing season, is 1,800° (using °F to calculate) or 1,000° (using °C to calculate). Below are the degree-day totals over the growing season for a variety of vineyards from around the world.

AREA/REGION	DEGREE-DAYS FAHRENHEIT (CELSIUS)
Trier, Mosel, Germany	1,700 (945)
Bordeaux, France	2,375 (1,320)
McLaren Vale, South Australia	2,425 (1,350)
Russian River, California	3,600 (2,000)

SUNSHINE

While light is required for photosynthesis, the most important biological process of green plants, there is sufficient light for this even in cloudy conditions. For vinegrowing, however, sunshine is needed more for its heat than its light. Approximately 1,300 hours is the minimum amount of sunshine required per growing season, but 1,500 hours is preferable.

RAINFALL

A vine requires 27 inches (68 centimeters) of rain per year. Ideally, most of the rain should fall in the spring and the winter, but some is needed in the summer too. Vines can survive with less water if the temperature is higher, although rain in warm conditions is more harmful than rain in cool conditions. A little rain a few days before the harvest will wash the grapes of any sprays, and is therefore ideal if followed by sun and a gentle, drying breeze. Torrential rain, however, can split berries and cause fungus.

Below are annual rainfall figures for a variety of vineyards from around the world.

AREA/REGION	RAINFALL
McLaren Vale, South Australia	24 in (60 cm)
Trier, Mosel, Germany	26 in (65 cm)
Bordeaux, France	36 in (90 cm)
Russian River, California	53 in (135 cm)

PREPARING FOR RAIN
In southern Spain, furrows are dug horizontally between rows of vines to provide channels for any rain.

FROST

Surprising as it may seem, some frost is desirable, providing it is in the winter, since it hardens the wood and kills spores and pests that the bark may be harboring. However, frost can literally kill a vine, particularly at bud-break and flowering (*see p.23*).

VINTAGE

The anomalies of a vintage can bring disaster to reliable vineyards and produce miracles in unreliable ones. A vintage is made by weather, as opposed to climate. While the climate may be generally good, uncommon weather conditions can sometimes occur. In addition to this, the vintage's annual climatic adjustment can be very selective; on the edge of a summer hail storm, for example, some vineyards may be destroyed and produce no wine at all, while others are virtually unharmed and produce good wine. Vines situated between the two might be left with a partial crop of fruit that could result in wines of an exceptional quality if given a further two to three months of warm sunshine before the harvest, because reduced yields per vine produce grapes with a greater concentration of flavor.

CLIMATIC CONDITIONS

Favorable

• A fine, long summer with warm, rather than hot, sunshine ensures that the grapes ripen slowly. Such weather leads to a good acid–sugar balance.

• A dry, sunny fall is essential for ripening grapes and avoiding rot; but, again, it must not be too hot.

• The winter months from November to February (May to August in the southern hemisphere) are climatically flexible, with the vine able to withstand temperatures as low as -4°F (-20°C) and anything other than absolute flood or drought.

• Within the above parameters, the climate must suit the viticultural needs of specific grape varieties; for example a cooler climate for Riesling, hotter for Syrah, and so on.

Unfavorable

• Major dangers are frost, hail, and strong winds, all of which can denude a vine and are particularly perilous when the vine is flowering or the grapes are ripening and at their most susceptible.

• Rain and/or cold temperatures during the flowering may cause imperfect fertilization, which results in a physiological disorder called *millerandage*. The affected grapes contain no seeds and will be small and only partially developed when the rest of the cluster is fully matured.

• Persistent rain at, or immediately before, the harvest can lead to rot or dilute the wine, both of which can cause vinification problems.

• Sun is not often thought of as a climatic danger, but, just as frost can be beneficial to the vine, so sun can be harmful. Too much sun encourages the sap to go straight past the embryo grape clusters to the leaves and shoots. This causes a physiological disorder called *coulure*, which is often confused with *millerandage*. It is totally different, although both disorders can appear together due to the vagaries of climate. Most seeds suffering from *coulure* drop to the ground, and those that remain do not develop.

• Excessive heat during the harvest rapidly decreases the acid level of grape juice and makes the grapes too hot, creating problems during fermentation. It is especially difficult to harvest grapes at an acceptable temperature in very hot areas, such as South Africa. As a result, some wine estates harvest the grapes at night when the grapes are at their coolest.

ASPECT

The aspect of a vineyard refers to its general topography—which direction the vines face, the angle and height of any slope, and so on—and how this interrelates with the climate.

There are few places in the world where winemaking grapes—as opposed to table grapes—are successfully grown under the full effect of a prevailing climate. The basic climatic requirements of the vine are usually achieved by manipulating local conditions, keeping sunshine, sun strength, drainage, and temperature in mind.

SUNSHINE

South-facing slopes (north-facing in the southern hemisphere) attract more hours of sunshine and are therefore cultivated in cooler areas. In hotter regions, the opposite facing slopes tend to be cultivated.

SUN STRENGTH AND DRAINAGE

Because of the angle, vines on a slope absorb the greater strength of the sun's rays. In temperate regions the sun is not directly overhead, even at noon, and therefore its rays fall more or less perpendicular to a slope. Conversely, on flat ground the sun's rays are dissipated across a wider area, so their strength is diluted. (The plains are also susceptible to flooding and have soils that are usually too fertile, yielding larger crops of correspondingly inferior fruit). Lake- and river-valley slopes are particularly well suited for vines because they also receive rays reflected from the water.

A sloping vineyard also affords natural drainage. However, hilltop vines are too exposed to wind and rain and their presence, instead of a forest covering, deprives vines below of protection. Forested hilltops not only supply humidity in times of drought, but absorb the worst of any torrential rain that could wash away the topsoil below.

TEMPERATURE

While slopes are very desirable sites, it must be remembered that every 330 feet (100 meters) above sea level, the temperature falls 1.8°F (1°C). This can result in an extra 10 to 15 days being needed for the grapes to ripen and, because of the extra time, the acidity will be relatively higher. Thus a vineyard's altitude can be a very effective way of manipulating the quality and character of its crop. Riverside and lakeside slopes also have the advantages of reflected sunlight and the water acting as a heat reservoir, releasing heat at night that has been stored during the day. This not only reduces sudden drops in temperature that can be harmful, but also the risk of frost. However, depressions in slopes and the very bottoms of valleys collect cold air, are frost-prone, and retard growth.

SOIL

Topsoil is of primary importance to the vine because it supports most of its root system, including most of the feeding network. Subsoil always remains geologically true. Main roots penetrate several layers of subsoil, whose structure influences drainage, the root system's depth, and its ability to collect minerals.

The metabolism of the vine is well known, and the interaction between it and the soil is generally understood. The ideal medium in which to grow vines for wine production is one that has a relatively thin topsoil and an easily penetrable (and therefore well-drained) subsoil with good water-retaining characteristics. The vine does not like "wet feet," so drainage is vital, yet it needs access to moisture, so access to a soil with good water-retention is also important. The temperature potential of a soil, its heat-retaining capacity, and its heat-reflective characteristics affect the ripening period of grapes: warm soils (gravel, sand, loam) advance ripening, while cold soils (clay) retard it. Chalk falls between these two extremes, and dark, dry soils are obviously warmer than light, wet soils. High-pH (alkaline) soils, such as chalk, encourage the vine's metabolism to produce sap and grape juice with a relatively high acid content. The continual use of fertilizers has lowered the pH level of some viticultural areas in France, and these are now producing wines of higher pH (less acidity).

THE MINERAL REQUIREMENTS OF THE VINE

Just as various garden flowers, shrubs, and vegetables perform better in one soil type as opposed to another, so too do different grape varieties. Certain minerals essential to plant growth are found in various soils. Apart from hydrogen and oxygen (which are supplied as water) the most important soil nutrients are nitrogen, which is used in the production of a plant's green matter; phosphate, which directly encourages root development and indirectly promotes an earlier ripening of the grapes (an excess inhibits the uptake of magnesium); potassium, which improves the vine's metabolism, enriches the sap, and is essential for the development of the following year's crop; iron, which is indispensable for photosynthesis (a lack of iron will cause chlorosis); magnesium, which is the only mineral constituent of the chlorophyll molecule (lack of magnesium also causes chlorosis); and calcium, which feeds the root system, neutralizes acidity, and helps create a friable soil structure (although an excess of calcium restricts the vine's ability to extract iron from the soil and therefore causes chlorosis). For information on specific soil types, *see* pp.17–18.

TERRACED VINEYARDS OVERLOOKING THE RHINE
Vines beside bodies of water benefit from the sun's rays reflecting off the water, an advantage in areas where the climate is cooler.

HILLS NEAR SANCERRE
In the spring, vineyards give the rolling countryside in France's Loire Valley a speckled appearance. Most soils in the area are dominated by clay or limestone.

GUIDE TO VINEYARD SOILS

To the wine amateur, the details of geology are not always important; what matters is how soil affects the growth of vines. If one clay soil is heavier or more silty, sandy, or calcareous, that is relevant. But there is enough jargon used when discussing wine to think of mixing it with rock-speak.

Aeolian soil Sediments deposited by wind (e.g. loess).

Albariza White-surfaced soil formed by diatomaceous deposits, found in southern Spain.

Alluvial deposits (noun—alluvium) Material that has been transported by river and deposited. Most alluvial soils contain silt, sand, and gravel, and are highly fertile.

Aqueous rocks One of the three basic rock forms (*see* Rock). Also called sedimentary or stratified.

Arenaceous rocks Formed by the deposits of coarse-grained particles, usually siliceous and often decomposed from older rocks (e.g. sandstone).

Argillaceous soils This term covers a group of sedimentary soils, commonly clays, shales, mudstones, siltstones, and marls.

Basalt material accounts for as much as 90 percent of all lava-based volcanic rocks. It contains various minerals, is rich in lime and soda, but not quartz, the most abundant of all minerals, and it is poor in potash.

Bastard soil A *bordelais* name for medium-heavy, sandy-clay soil of variable fertility.

Boulbènes A *bordelais* name for a very fine siliceous soil that is easily compressed and hard to work. This "beaten" earth covers part of the Entre-Deux-Mers plateau.

Boulder *See* Particle size

Calcareous clay Argillaceous soil with carbonate of lime content that neutralizes the clay's intrinsic acidity. Its low temperature also delays ripening, so wines produced on this type of soil tend to be more acidic.

Calcareous soil Any soil, or mixture of soils, with an accumulation of calcium and magnesium carbonates. Essentially alkaline, it promotes the production of acidity in grapes, although the pH of each soil will vary according to its level of "active" lime. Calcareous soils are cool, with good water retention. With the exception of calcareous clays (*see* above), they allow the vine's root system to penetrate deeply and provide excellent drainage.

Carbonaceous soil Soil that is derived from rotting vegetation under anaerobic conditions. The most common carbonaceous soils are peat, lignite, coal, and anthracite.

Chalk A type of limestone, chalk is a soft, cool, porous, brilliant-white, sedimentary, alkaline

CHALK
Pristine white chalk on the Côtes des Blancs.

rock that encourages grapes with a relatively high acidity level. It also allows the vine's roots to penetrate and provides excellent drainage, while at the same time retaining sufficient moisture for nourishment. One of the few finer geological points that should be adhered to is that which distinguishes chalk from the numerous hard limestone rocks that do not possess the same physical properties.

Clay A fine-grained argillaceous compound with malleable, plastic characteristics and excellent water-retention properties. It is, however, cold, acid, offers poor drainage, and, because of its cohesive quality, hard to work. An excess of clay can stifle the vine's root system, but a proportion of small clay particles mixed with other soils can be advantageous.

Clayey-loam A very fertile version of loam, but heavy to work under wet conditions with a tendency to become waterlogged.

Cobble *See* Particle size

Colluvial deposits (noun—colluvium) Weathered material transported by gravity or hill-wash.

Crasse de fer Iron-rich hardpan found in the Libournais area of France. Also called *machefer*.

Crystalline May either be igneous (e.g. granite) or metamorphic.

Dolomite A calcium-magnesium carbonate rock. Many limestones contain dolomite.

Feldspar or **Felspar** One of the most common minerals, feldspar is a white- or rose-colored silicate of either potassium-aluminum or sodium-calcium-aluminum and is present in a number of rocks, including granite and basalt.

Ferruginous clay Iron-rich clay.

Flint A siliceous stone that stores and reflects heat, and is often associated with a certain "gun-flint" smell that sometimes occurs in wines, although this is not actually proven and may simply be the taster's auto-suggestion.

Galestro Rocky, schistous soil commonly found in most of Tuscany's best vineyards.

Glacial moraine A gritty scree that has been deposited by glacial action.

Gneiss A coarse-grained form of granite.

Granite A hard, mineral-rich rock that warms quickly and retains its heat. Granite contains 40 to 60 percent quartz and 30 to 40 percent potassium feldspar, plus mica or hornblende, and various other minerals. It has a high pH, which reduces wine acidity. Thus, in Beaujolais, it is the best soil for the acidic Gamay grape. It is important to note that a soil formed from granite is a mixture of sand (partly derived from a disintegration of quartz and partly from the decomposition of feldspar with either mica or hornblende), clay, and various carbonates or silicates derived from the weathering of feldspar, mica, or hornblende.

Gravel A wide-ranging term that covers siliceous pebble of various sizes that are loose, granular, airy, and afford excellent drainage. Infertile, it encourages the vine to send its roots down deep in search of nutrients. Gravel beds above limestone subsoils produce wines with markedly more acidity than those above clay.

GRAVEL
Château de France, Leognan, Gironde.

Greywacke Argillaceous rocks that could have been formed as recently as a few thousand years ago by rivers depositing mudstone, quartz, and feldspar. Commonly found in Germany, South Africa, and New Zealand.

Gypsum Highly absorbent, hydrated calcium-sulfate that was formed during the evaporation of seawater.

Gypsiferous marl A marly soil permeated with Keuper or Muschelkalk gypsum fragments, which improve the soil's heat-retention and water-circulation properties.

Hardpan A dense layer of clay that forms if the subsoil is more clayey than the topsoil at certain depths. Because hardpans are impermeable to both water and roots, they are not desirable too close to the surface, but may provide an easily reachable watertable if located deep down. A sandy, iron-rich hardpan known as ironpan is commonly found in parts of Bordeaux.

Hornblende A silicate of iron, aluminum, calcium, and magnesium, it constitutes the main mineral found in basalt, and is a major component of granite and gneiss.

Humus Organic material that contains bacteria and other microorganisms capable of converting complex chemicals into simple plant foods. Humus makes soil fertile. Without it, soil is nothing more than finely ground rock.

Igneous rock One of the three basic rock forms (*see* Rock), igneous rocks are formed from molten or partially molten material. Most igneous rocks are crystalline.

Ironpan A sandy, iron-rich hardpan.

Keuper Often used when discussing wines in Alsace, Keuper is a stratigraphic name for the Upper Triassic period, and can mean marl (varicolored, saliferous gray or gypsiferous gray) or limestone (ammonoid).

Kimmeridgian soil A grayish-colored limestone originally identified in, and so named after, the village of Kimmeridge in Dorset, England. A sticky, calcareous clay containing this limestone is often called Kimmeridgian clay.

Lignite The "brown coal" of Germany and the "black gold" of Champagne, this is a brown carbonaceous material intermediate between coal and peat. Warm and very fertile, it is mined and used as a natural fertilizer in Champagne.

Limestone Any sedimentary rock consisting essentially of carbonates. With the exception of chalk, few limestones are white, with gray- and buff-colored probably the most commonly found limestone in wine areas. The hardness and water retention of this rock varies, but being alkaline it generally encourages the production of grapes with a relatively high acidity level.

Loam A warm, soft, crumbly soil with roughly equal proportions of clay, sand, and silt. It is perfect for large-cropping wines of mediocre quality, but too fertile for fine wines.

Loess An accumulation of wind-borne, mainly silty material, sometimes calcareous, but usually weathered and decalcified. It warms up relatively quickly and also has good water-retention properties.

Machefer *See* **Crasse de fer**

Marl A cold, calcareous clay that delays ripening and adds acidity to wine.

Marlstone Clayey limestone that has a similar effect to marl.

Metamorphic rocks One of the three basic categories of rock (*see* **Rock**), it is caused by great heat or pressure, often both.

Mica A generic name encompassing various silicate minerals, usually in a fine, decomposed-rock format.

Millstone Siliceous, iron-rich, sedimentary rock.

Moraine *See* **Glacial moraine**

Mudstone A sedimentary soil similar to clay but without its plastic characteristics.

Muschelkalk Often used when discussing wines in Alsace, Muschelkalk is a stratigraphic name for the Middle Triassic period, and can mean anything from sandstone (shelly, dolomitic, calcareous, clayey, pink, yellow, or millstone) to marl (varicolored or fissile), dolomite, limestone (crinoidal or gray), and shingle.

Oolite A type of limestone.

Oolith A term used for small, round, calcareous pebbles that have grown through fusion of very tiny particles.

Palus A *bordelais* name for a very fertile soil of modern alluvial origin that produces medium-quality, well-colored, robust wines.

Particle size The size of a rock determines its descriptive name. No handful of soil will contain particles of a uniform size, unless it has been commercially graded, of course, so all such descriptions can only be guessed at, but it is worth noting what they should be, otherwise you will have nothing to base your guesses on. According to the Wentworth-Udden

scale, they are: boulder (greater than 256mm), cobble (64mm–256mm), pebble (4mm–64mm), gravel (2mm–4mm), sand (⅟₁₆mm–2mm), silt (⅟₂₅₆mm–⅟₁₆mm) and clay (smaller than ⅟₂₅₆mm). Notice that even by this precise scale, Wentworth and Udden have allowed overlaps, thus a ⅟₁₆mm particle might either be sand or silt and, of course, sub-divisions are possible within each group, as there is such a thing as fine, medium, or coarse sand and even gritty silt.

Pebble *See* **Particle size**

Perlite A fine, powdery, light, and lustrous substance of volcanic origin with similar properties to diatomaceous earth.

Porphyry A colored igneous rock with high pH.

Precipitated salts A sedimentary deposit. Water charged with acid or alkaline material, under pressure of great depth, dissolves various mineral substances from rocks on the seabed, which are then held in solution. When the water flows to a place of no great depth or is drained away or evaporates, the pressure is reduced, the minerals are no longer held in solution, and precipitate in deposits that may be just a few inches or several thousand yards deep. There are five groups: oxides, carbonates, sulfates, phosphates, and chlorides.

Pudding stones A term used for a large, heat-retaining conglomerate of pebbles.

Quartz The most common and abundant mineral found in various sizes and in almost all soils, although sand and coarse silt contain the largest amount. Quartz has a high pH, which reduces wine acidity, but quartz that is pebble-sized or larger, stores and reflects heat, which increases alcohol potential.

Red earth *See* **Terra rossa**

Rock A rock may be loosely described as a mass of mineral matter. There are three basic types of rock: igneous, metamorphic, and sedimentary (or aqueous or stratified).

Sand Tiny particles of weathered rocks and minerals that retain little water, but constitute a warm, airy soil that drains well and is supposedly phylloxera-free.

Sandstone Sedimentary rock composed of sand-sized particles that have either been formed by pressure or bound by various iron minerals.

Sandy-loam Warm, well-drained, sand-dominated loam that is easy to work and suitable for early-cropping grape varieties.

Schist Heat-retaining, coarse-grain, laminated, crystalline rock rich in potassium and magnesium, but poor in nitrogen and organic substances.

Scree Synonymous with colluvium deposits.

Sedimentary rock One of the three basic rock forms (*see* **Rock**), it includes arenaceous (e.g. sandstone), argillaceous (e.g. clay), calcareous (e.g. limestone), carbonaceous (e.g. peat, lignite, or coal), siliceous (e.g. quartz), and the five groups of precipitated salts, (oxides, carbonates, sulfates, phosphates, and chlorides). Sedimentary rocks are also called aqueous or stratified.

Shale Heat-retaining, fine-grain, laminated, moderately fertile sedimentary rock. Shale can turn into slate under pressure.

Shingle Pebble- or gravel-sized particle rounded by water-action.

Siliceous soil A generic term for acid rock of a crystalline nature. It may be organic (flint and kieselguhr) or inorganic (quartz) and have good heat retention, but no water retention unless found in a finely ground form in silt, clay, and

other sedimentary soils. Half of the Bordeaux region is covered with siliceous soils.

Silt A very fine deposit, with good water retention. Silt is more fertile than sand, but is cold and offers poor drainage.

Slate Hard, dark gray, fine-grain, platelike rock formed under pressure from clay, siltstone, shale, and other sediments. It warms up quickly, retains its heat well, and is responsible for many fine wines, most notably from the Mosel.

Steige A type of schist found on the north side of Andlau in Alsace, it has metamorphosed with the Andlau granite and is particularly hard and slaty. It has mixed with the granitic sand from the top of the Grand Cru Kastelberg and makes a dark, stony soil.

Stone This word should be used with rock types, such as limestone and sandstone, but is often used synonymously with pebble.

Stratified rock One of the three basic rock forms (*see* **Rock**), also called sedimentary or aqueous.

Terra rossa A red, claylike, sometimes flinty sedimentary soil deposited after carbonate has been leached out of limestone. It is often known as "Red earth."

Tufa Various vent-based volcanic rocks, the chalktufa of the Loire being the most important viticulturally speaking.

Volcanic soils Derived from two sources, volcanic soils are lava-based (the products of volcanic flow) and vent-based (material blown into the atmosphere). Some 90 percent of lava-based rocks and soils are comprised of basalt, while others include andesite, pitchstone, rhyolite, and trachyte. Vent-based matter has either been ejected as molten globules, cooled in the air, and dropped to Earth as solid particles (pumice), or as solid material and fractured through the explosive force with which it was flung (tufa).

PUDDING STONE
Large stones (galettes), Château de Beaucastel, in Châteauneuf-du-Pape.

TERRA ROSSA
The red soil of Wynns, Coonawarra, South Australia.

VITICULTURE

While it is the variety of grape that determines the basic flavor of a wine, it is the way in which the variety is grown that has the most profound effect on the quality of the wine.

IN VINE TRAINING, it is absolutely crucial to ensure that no cane ever touches the ground. Should a cane find its way to the ground, its natural inclination is to send out suckers that will put down roots. Within two or three years the majority of the grafted vine's (*see* Phylloxera, p.35) above-ground network would be dependent not on grafted roots, but on the regenerated root system of the producing vine. Not only would this have the effect of putting the vine at the mercy of phylloxera, but, ironically, that part of the vine still receiving its principal nourishment from the grafted hybrid rootstock would send out its own shoots and, unchecked by any sort of pruning, these would produce hybrid fruit. Therefore, the fundamental reason for training and pruning a vine is to avoid phylloxera and to ensure that the purity of the fruiting stock is maintained.

The manner in which a vine is trained will guide the size, shape, and height of the plant toward reaping maximum benefits from the local conditions of aspect and climate. Vines can be trained high to avoid ground frost, or low to hug any heat that may be reflected by stony soils at night. There may be a generous amount of space between rows to attract the sun and avoid humidity. On the other hand, vines may be intensively cultivated to form a canopy of foliage to avoid too much sun.

STYLES OF VINE TRAINING

Within the two basic systems of cane training and spur training, hundreds of different styles are employed, each developed for a reason, and all having their own advantages and disadvantages. In order to discern the style used in a particular vineyard, it is always best to look at the vines between late fall and early spring when the branches are not camouflaged with leaves. In the illustrations below, which are not drawn to scale, vines are shown as they appear during their winter dormancy, with the following season's fruiting canes shown in green. For cane-trained systems, a green-brown tint has been used to pick out the one-year-old wood used as next season's main branch.

Bush vine—*Spur-training system*

An unsupported version of the Gobelet system (*see* below left), the term "bush vine" originated in Australia, where a few old vineyards—usually planted with Grenache—are still trained in this fashion. Bush vines are traditional in Beaujolais (where both supported and unsupported methods are referred to as Gobelet) and they are commonly found throughout the most arid areas of the Mediterranean. Being unsupported, the canes often flop downward when laden with fruit, giving the vine a sprawling, straggly look. In the Beaujolais *crus*, the total number of canes on a vine is restricted to between three and five, but in other, less controlled, wine areas a bush vine may have as many as 10 canes. This method is only suitable for training low-vigor vines.

Chablis—*Spur-training system*

As the name implies, this style of vine training was originally developed in the Chablis district, although the method employed there now is, in fact, the Guyot Double. Champagne is the most important winemaking region to employ the Chablis system for training vines; there, it is used for more than 90 percent of all the Chardonnay grown. Either three, four, or five permanent branches may be cultivated, each one being grown at yearly intervals. This results in a three-year-old vine (the minimum age for AOC Champagne) having three branches, a four-year-old having four branches, and so forth. The distance between each

BASIC SYSTEMS OF VINE TRAINING

There are two basic systems of vine training, cane training and spur training, of which there are many local variations. Cane-trained vines have no permanent branch because all but one of the strongest canes (which will be kept for next season's main branch) are pruned back each year to provide a vine consisting of almost entirely new growth. Apart from the trunk, the oldest wood on a cane-trained vine is the main branch and that is only ever one year old. This system gives a good spread of fruit over a large area, and allows easier regulation of annual production, because the number of fruiting buds can be increased or decreased. With spur training there is no annual replacement of the main branch, thus a solid framework is formed. It is easy, therefore, to know which basic training system has been applied to a vine simply by looking at the main branch. Even if you cannot recognize the specific style of training, if the main branch is thin and smooth, you will know that it has been cane trained, whereas if it is thick, dark, and gnarled, it has been spur trained.

Will be next year's main cane (A)		Will be next year's main cane (A)
Beginning of season	Height of season	End of season

GUYOT—AN EXAMPLE OF CANE-TRAINING
In the winter, the main horizontal cane is cut off and the spare cane (A) is bent horizontally to be tied to the bottom wire, where it will become next season's main cane. Another shoot close to the trunk will be allowed to grow as next season's spare cane.

Beginning of season	Height of season	End of season

GOBELET—AN EXAMPLE OF SPUR-TRAINING
The main canes on a spur-trained vine are all permanent, and will only be replaced if they are damaged. Only the year-old shoots are pruned back.

vine in the same row determines the eventual life of the oldest branch because, when it encroaches on the next vine, it is removed and a new one cultivated from a bud on the main trunk.

The Chablis spur-training system is, in effect, little more than a slanting bush vine unsupported by a central post.

Cordon de Royat—*Spur-training system*

This is to Champagne's Pinot Noir what the Chablis system is to its Chardonnay and is nothing more complicated than a spur-trained version of Guyot Simple (*see below*). There is even a double variant, although this is rarely cultivated purely for its own ends, its primary reason for existence being to replace a missing vine on its blind side. When, after their winter pruning, they are silhouetted against the sky, Cordon de Royat vines look very

much like columns of gnarled old men in perfect formation; they all face forward, bent almost double, as if with one arm dug into the pit of the back and the other seeking the support of a stick.

Geneva Double Curtain—*Spur-training system*

This downward-growing, split-canopy system was developed by Professor Nelson Shaulis of the Geneva Experimental Station in New York State in the early 1960s to increase the volume and ripening of locally-grown Concord grapes. Since then, GDC, as it is often referred to, has been adopted all over the world (particularly in Italy). However, unlike Concord varieties, classic *vinifera* vines have an upward-growing tendency, which makes the system more difficult to apply. Successful results are obtained by shoot positioning, which can either be accomplished via a moveable wire (as in Scott Henry, *see opposite*), by hand, or even by machine. Yields from GDC are 50 percent higher than those from the standard VSP trellis (*see opposite*), and the system offers increased protection from frosts

(due to height above ground). It is ideal for full mechanization of medium- to high-vigor vineyards on deep fertile soils (low-vigor vines do not benefit).

Guyot—*Cane-training system*

Developed by Jules Guyot in 1860, both the double and simple forms shown here represent the most conservative style of cane training possible. It is the least complicated concept for growers to learn and, providing the number of fruiting canes and the number of buds on them are

restricted, Guyot is the easiest means of restraining yields. Even when growers abuse the system, it is still the most difficult vine-training method with which to pump up production. This

GUYOT DOUBLE

system is commonly used in Bordeaux, where the number of canes and buds are restricted by AOC rules (although, like most French bureaucratic systems, much depends on self-regulation. I have never seen an INAO inspector in the middle of a vineyard checking the variety of vines or counting them, let alone counting the number of canes or buds on canes!). Guyot is also used for some of the finest wines throughout the winemaking world, both Old and New.

GUYOT SIMPLE

Lyre—*Spur-training system*

Also known as the "U" system, the canopy is divided, so as to allow a better penetration of light (thereby improving ripeness levels) and air (thereby reducing the incidence of cryptogamic disorders). Although it was developed in Bordeaux, the Lyre system is more common in the New World where vine vigor is a problem, although not a major one. As with all split-canopy systems, the Lyre method is of no use whatsoever for low-vigor vineyards. Some growers have successfully adapted Lyre to cane training.

Minimal Pruning—*Spur-training system*

A wild, unruly mass that contains a central thicket of unpruned dead wood, by definition it has no disciplined form and is therefore impossible to illustrate. Some of the central thicket may be mechanically removed in the winter, but will still be a tangled mass. Initially, several canes are wrapped loosely around a wire, either side of the trunk, about 5 to 6 feet (1.5 to 2 meters) off the ground. The vine is then left to its own devices, although if necessary some of the summer shoots will be trimmed to keep the fruit off the ground. Some growers give up very quickly because yields can initially be alarmingly high and as the volume increases, so the quality noticeably deteriorates. However, if they are patient, the vine eventually achieves a natural balance, reducing the length of its shoots and, consequently, the number of fruiting nodes on them. Although mature minimally pruned vines continue to give fairly high yields, the quality begins to improve after two or three years. By the sixth or seventh year the quality is usually significantly superior to the quality achieved before minimal pruning was introduced—and the quantity is substantially greater. The ripening time needed by the grapes also increases, which can be an advantage in a hot climate, but disastrous in a cool one, particularly if it is also wet. Furthermore, after a number of years, the mass of old wood in the central thicket and the split-ends of machine-pruned cane ends surrounding it can make the vine vulnerable to various pests and diseases, especially rot and mildew, which is why minimally pruned vines in wet areas like New Zealand are more heavily pruned than they are in the hotter areas of Australia—such as Coonawarra and Padthaway—where minimal pruning first emerged and is still used to great effect.

Pendelbogen—*Cane-training system*

Also known as the "European Loop," or "Arc-Cane Training," this vine-training system, which is a variant of the Guyot Double (*see left*), is most popular in Switzerland and the flatter Rhine Valley areas of Germany and Alsace, although it can also be found in

Mâcon, British Columbia, and Oregon. By bending the canes in an arch, Pendelbogen has more fruit-bearing shoots than the Guyot Double system, thereby providing higher yields. The arching does promote better sap distribution, which helps the production of more fruit, but it can also reduce ripeness levels, making the prime motive for adopting Pendelbogen one of economy, not of quality.

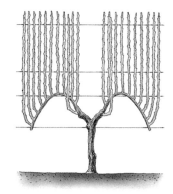

Scott Henry—*Cane-training system*

Developed by Scott Henry at the Scott Henry Vineyard in Oregon, this system effectively doubles the fruiting area provided by Guyot Double. It also offers a 60 percent increase in fruiting area over the standard VSP Trellis system (*see right*). Scott Henry not only provides larger crops, but riper, better fruit. And because the canopy is split and, therefore, less dense, the wines are less herbaceous, with smoother tannins. Increased yields and increased quality may seem unlikely, but Kim Goldwater of Waiheke Island has records to prove it; and as Goldwater Estate is consistently one of New Zealand's best red wines, that is good enough for me. When I have asked growers who have tried the Scott Henry method why they have given it up, they invariably reply "Have you ever tried to grow vine shoots downward? It doesn't work!" However, the downward-growing shoots actually grow upward for most of the season. They are separated from the other upward-growing shoots by a moveable wire that levers half the canopy into a downward position. The secret of this system's success is to move the wire no earlier than two or three weeks before the harvest, which gives the canes no time to revert and, with the increasing weight of the fruit, no inclination. In areas where grazing animals coexist with vines (as sheep do in New Zealand, for instance), the fact that both halves of the canopy are about 3 feet (1 meter) above the ground most of the time allows under-vine weeds and water shoots to be controlled without herbicides or manual labor, without fear of the crop being eaten in the process. Scott Henry is found mainly in the New World and is becoming increasingly popular.

Scott Henry—*Spur-training system*

When the Scott Henry cane-training system is adapted to spur training, each vine has two permanent spurs instead of four annual canes and produces either top canopies or bottom canopies, but not both. The vines are pruned at alternating heights to replicate the effect of cane training, and all canopies grow upward until those on the lower vines are eventually

levered downward to the position shown here. The detailed structure of the Scott Henry system is almost impossible to identify when the vines are shrouded in foliage.

Sylvos—*Spur-training system*

This is like Guyot Double, only the trunk is much longer—just over 6 feet (2 meters)—the main branches are permanent, and the fruiting canes are tied downward, not upward. Sylvos requires minimal pruning and is simple to maintain, lending itself to mechanization, but yields are low, unless pruned very lightly. *Vinifera* varieties do not like being forced downward, but shoot positioning has been introduced by growers in Australia (where it is called "Hanging Cane") and New Zealand. The system was originally conceived by Carlo Sylvos in Italy, where it is still very popular and is sometimes operated without a bottom wire, the canes falling downward under their own weight. The main disadvantage is the dense canopy, which makes the vines prone to bunch-rot.

Sylvos (Hawke's Bay variant)—*Spur-training system*

This version of the Sylvos system was developed by Gary Wood of Montana Wines in the early 1980s on a Hawke's Bay vineyard belonging to Mark Read. The difference between this and the similar Scott Henry system is that it has two main spurs instead of four. With alternate fruiting canes on the same spur trained upward then downward, the canopy is more open, and grape clusters are farther apart. This reduces bunch-rot significantly and facilitates better spray penetration. Yields are increased by as much as 100 percent. The only disadvantage is the longer ripening time needed, which is a risk in areas where late harvests have their dangers.

VSP Trellis—*Cane-training system*

The VSP or Vertical Shoot Positioned trellis is widely used, particularly in New Zealand, where it is commonly referred to as the "standard" trellising system. With the fruiting area contained within one compact zone on wires of a narrow span, it is ideally suited to mechanized forms of pruning, leaf removal, harvesting, and spraying, but it is prone to high vigor and shading. This is a very economic method and, when properly maintained, it is capable of producing wines of good, but not top, quality. VSP is only suitable for low-vigor vines. A spur-trained version with just two main spurs is commonly encountered in France and Germany.

VITICULTURAL SPRAYS

The use of sprays was once confined to protecting the vine against pests and diseases and for controlling weeds, but they now have additional uses. Foliar feeds supply nutrients direct to the vine, while other sprays halt the growth of foliage, rendering summer pruning unnecessary. Some sprays deliberately induce two disorders called *millerandage* and *coulure* to reduce the yield and, hopefully, increase the quality.

PRUNING

Important for controlling quantity, pruning is equally important for producing a good quality of fruit. As with any crop, be it grapes or prize roses, if the quantity is reduced, the quality is increased. Reducing the number of fruiting buds lowers the quantity of fruit.

FLOWERING

The most critical period of a vine's life is when it flowers—at this stage frost, hail, rain, wind, and excessively high or low temperatures could wipe out a crop before the growing season begins in earnest. Even quality-conscious growers usually leave a couple of extra buds on each vine in case of poor weather during flowering. It follows that if the weather permits a perfect flowering, even the best growers' vines end up with too many grape bunches.

MAN: THE JOKER IN THE PACK

The winemaker, and that includes the winegrower, can maximize or minimize the fruits of nature by his or her skill. Time and again I have seen that neighboring winemakers can make totally different quality wine using virtually the same raw product and the same technology. Chemical analyzes of the wines in question may be virtually indistinguishable, yet one wine will have all the definition, vitality, and expression of character that the other lacks. Why does this occur? No doubt there are valid reasons that science may one day establish, but in our current state of ignorance I can only say that it is always the winemakers with passion who are able to produce the finer, more characterful wines. Of course, many inferior wines are made by the misuse of up-to-date technology, but I have seen dedicated winemakers produce absolutely spellbinding wines using what I would consider to be totally inadequate or inferior equipment. Some winemakers have even been known to sleep by their vats during a particularly difficult fermentation, so that they are on hand to make any adjustments immediately if anything goes wrong. From the grower who never hesitates to prune the vine for low yields, yet always agonizes over the optimum time to harvest, to the winemaker who literally nurses the wines through each and every stage of fermentation and maturation and bottles at precisely the right time and at exactly the correct temperature, the human element is most seriously the joker in the pack when it comes to factors affecting the taste and quality of the wines produced.

INSPECTING MATURING WINE
Auguste Clape, one of the finest winemakers in France's Northern Rhône area, checks the progress of his oak-matured wine.

The weather is not often so kind in classic areas, but when it is, the perfect solution is to remove some of the embryo bunches. Most growers wait until the beginning of *véraison* (the ripening period), when the grapes start to take on color and begin to ripen, before cutting off unwanted bunches. By now the vine has already wasted much of its energy on developing the clusters about to be discarded, but their removal will help the remaining bunches of grapes to ripen.

THE TIMING OF THE GRAPE HARVEST

When to pick is one of the most crucial decisions a grower has to make each year. As grapes ripen, there is a reduction in their acidity (which is also converted from mostly malic acid to primarily tartaric acid) and an increase in sugar, color, various minerals, and essential aromatic compounds. The decision when to pick will vary according to the grape variety, the location of the vineyard, and the style of wine that is to be made. White wine generally benefits from the extra acidity of early-harvested grapes, but they also need the varietal aroma and richness that can only be found in ripe grapes. It is essential to get the balance right. Red wine requires relatively low acidity and profits from the increased color, sugar, and tannin content of grapes harvested later. The grower must also take the vagaries of the weather into account. Those who have the nerve to wait for perfectly ripe grapes every year can produce exceptional wines in even the poorest vintages, but run the risk of frost, rot, or hail damage. This can totally destroy not only an entire crop, but also an entire year's income. Those who never take a chance may always harvest healthy grapes, but in poor years the disadvantage of this approach is that the crop will be unripe and the wine mediocre.

MECHANICAL HARVESTING

Mechanical harvesting is a contentious subject. The advantages of mechanization are dramatically reduced labor costs and a quick harvest of the entire crop at optimum ripeness, but the vineyard has to be adapted to the machine chosen and the reception and fermentation facilities must be enlarged to cope with the greater amounts and quicker throughput, which is costly. Disadvantages relate to the efficiency of the machinery and the quality of the wine.

As the machines beat the vine trunks with rubber sticks, the grapes drop onto a conveyor along with leaves and other matter, most of which is ejected as the fruit is sorted on its way to the hold. Apart from the rubbish that inevitably remains with the harvested grapes—which is becoming less as machines become more sophisticated—the main disadvantage of mechanical harvesting is the inability of a machine to distinguish between the ripe and the unripe, and the healthy and the diseased or plain rotten (the first thing to drop from any plant when shaken).

Despite these inadequacies, many excellent red wines have been made from mechanically harvested grapes. From a practical point of view it would seem that this method of harvesting is better for red wine than it is for white, particularly sparkling, wine because it splits the grapes. This encourages oxidation and a loss of aromatics and, when harvesting black grapes for white sparkling wine, results in an undesirable coloration of the juice.

TRANSPORTING THE GRAPES

In the race against time to get the grapes from the vineyard to the winery, everything possible should be done to cosset the fruit. Ideally, the winery and the vineyards should be as close as possible and the grapes transported in plastic crates small enough to prevent damage from their own weight. The crates should be designed so that stacking one on top of the other does not crush the fruit. The fact that some of the best-value wines of Eastern Europe are dumped into huge skips and take hours to reach their destination is fine for red wine, but currently less useful for white. It splits the grapes, thereby encouraging oxidation and a loss of aromatics.

ANNUAL LIFE CYCLE OF THE VINE

The calendar of events by which any well-established vine seeks to reproduce, through the production of grapes, is outlined below, with a commentary on how the vine is cultivated to encourage the best grapes for winemaking. The vine's year starts and finishes with the end and approach of winter.

FEBRUARY Northern hemisphere
AUGUST Southern hemisphere

1. Weeping

Weeping is the first sign of the vine awakening after a winter of relative dormancy. When the soil at a depth of 10 inches (25 centimeters) reaches 50°F (10.2°C), the roots start collecting water and the sap in the vine rises, oozing out of the cane ends which were pruned in winter, in a manifestation called "weeping." This occurs suddenly, rapidly increases in intensity, and then decreases gradually. Each vine loses between half a quart and 11 pints (half and five-and-a-half liters) of sap. Weeping is the signal to prune for the spring growth. However, this poses a problem for the

As the soil warms up the vine awakes, pushing sap out of its cane ends.

grower because the vine, once pruned, is at its most vulnerable to frost. But waiting for the danger of frost to pass wastes the vine's preciously finite energy and retards its growth, delaying the ripening of the fruit by as much as 10 days, and thus risking exposure of the fruit to fall frosts later on.

MARCH to APRIL Northern hemisphere
SEPTEMBER to OCTOBER Southern hemisphere

2. Bud-break

In the spring, some 20 to 30 days after the vine starts to weep, the buds open. Different varieties bud-break at different times; there are early bud-breakers and the same variety can bud-break at different times in different years due to climatic changes. The type of soil can also affect the timing. Clay, which is cold, will retard the process, while sand, which is warm, will promote it. Early bud-break varieties are susceptible to frost in northerly vineyards (southerly in the southern hemisphere), just as late-ripeners are vulnerable

Buds begin to open at a time determined by variety and climate.

to fall frosts. In the vineyard, pruning continues into March (September in the southern hemisphere). The vines are secured to their training frames, and the earth that was plowed over the grafting wound to protect it in the winter is plowed back, aerating the soil and leveling off the ground between the rows.

APRIL to MAY Northern hemisphere
OCTOBER to NOVEMBER Southern hemisphere

3. Emergence of shoots, foliage, and embryo bunches

Embryo bunches, the vine's flowers, form.

Following bud-break, foliage develops and shoots are sent out. In mid-April (mid-October in the southern hemisphere), after the fourth or fifth leaf has emerged, tiny green clusters form. These are the flowers which, when they bloom, will develop into grapes. Commonly called embryo bunches, they are the first indication of the potential size of a crop. In the vineyard, spraying to ward off various vine pests, or cure diseases and other disorders, starts in May (November), and continues until the harvest. Many of these sprays are combined with systemic fertilizers to feed the vine directly through its foliage. These spraying operations are normally done by hand or tractor, but may sometimes be carried out by helicopter if the slopes are very steep or the vineyards too muddy to enter. At this time of year the vine can be affected by *coulure* or *millerandage* (see p.15).

MAY to JUNE Northern hemisphere
NOVEMBER to DECEMBER Southern hemisphere

4. Flowering of the vine

The 10 days in which the vine flowers is a vulnerable period.

The embryo bunches break into flower after the 15th or 16th leaf has emerged on the vine. This is normally about eight weeks after the bud-break and involves pollination and fertilization, and lasts for about 10 days. The weather must be dry and frost-free, but temperature is the most critical requirement. A daily average of at least 59°F (15°C) is needed to enable a vine to flower and between 68° and 77°F (20° and 25°C) is considered ideal. Heat summation, however, is more important than temperature levels, so the length of day has a great influence on the number of days the flowering will last. Soil temperature is more significant than air temperature, so the soil's heat-retaining capacity is a contributory factor. Frost is the greatest hazard, and many vineyards are protected by stoves or sprinkling systems.

5. Fruit set

After the flowering, the embryo bunches rapidly evolve into true clusters. Each fertilized berry expands into a grape, the first visible sign of the actual fruit that will produce the wine. This is called fruit set. The number of grapes per embryo bunch varies from variety to variety, as does the percentage that actually set into grapes. The panel below illustrates this. In the vineyard, spraying continues and summer pruning (cutting away some bunches) will concentrate the vine's energy on making fruit. In

Clearly recognizable grapes begin to form.

some vineyards this is the time for weeding, but in others the weeds are allowed to grow as high as 20 inches (50 centimeters) before they are mown and plowed into the soil to break up the soil and provide the vines with excellent green manure.

VARIETY	BERRIES PER EMBRYO BUNCH	GRAPES IN A RIPE CLUSTER	PERCENTAGE OF FRUIT SET
Chasselas	164	48	29%
Gewürztraminer	100	40	40%
Pinot Gris	149	41	28%
Riesling	189	61	32%
Sylvaner	95	50	53%

6. Ripening of the grapes

As the grape develops its fleshy fruit, very little chemical change takes place inside the berry until its skin begins to turn a different color—the process known as *véraison*. Throughout the grape's green stage, the sugar and acid content remains the same, but during August (January in the southern hemisphere), the ripening process begins in earnest. The skin changes color, the sugar content dramatically increases, and the hard malic acid diminishes as the riper tartaric acid builds up. Although the tartaric acid content begins to

The grapes begin to change color, the sign of true ripening.

decline after about two weeks, it always remains the primary acid. It is at this stage that the grape's tannins are gradually hydrolyzed. This is a crucial moment because only hydrolyzed tannins are capable of softening as a wine matures. In the vineyard, spraying and weeding continue, and the vine's foliage is thinned to facilitate the circulation of air and thus reduce the risk of rot. Be careful not to remove too much foliage, since it is the effect of sunlight on the leaves, not the grapes, that causes the grapes to ripen.

7. Grape harvest

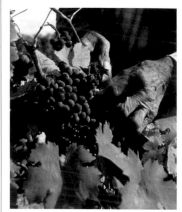

Grapes are picked at a time determined by the winemaker.

The harvest usually begins mid- to late September (mid- to late February in the southern hemisphere) and may last for a month or more, but, as is the case with all vineyard operations, the timing is earlier nearer to the equator and is dependent on the weather. Picking may, therefore, start as early as August (February) and finish as late as November (April). White grapes ripen before black grapes and must, in any case, be harvested that little bit earlier to achieve a higher acidity balance.

8. Grapes affected by Botrytis cinerea

Rotting grapes, soon to be harvested for sweet botrytized wine.

In November the sap retreats to the protection of the vine's root system. As a result, the year-old canes begin to harden and any remaining grapes, cut off from the vine's metabolic system, start to dehydrate. The concentrated pulp that they become is subject to severe cold. This induces complex chemical changes in a process known as *passerillage*. In specialist sweet-wine areas the grapes are deliberately left on the vine to undergo this quality-enhancing experience and, in certain vineyards with suitable climatic conditions, growers pray for the appearance of *Botrytis cinerea*, or "noble rot."

9. Eiswein

Grapes still on the vine may yet become wine.

In Germany and Canada you can see grapes on the vine in December and even January. In Germany this is often because the grower has hoped for *Botrytis cinerea*, or *Edelfäule* as it is called there, but it has failed to occur on some grapes. Should frost or snow freeze the grapes, they can be harvested to produced Eiswein, or Icewine, which is made in Canada. It is one of the world's most spectacular wines. Once the grapes are pressed the frozen water is skimmed off, leaving a super-concentrated unfrozen pulp to make Eiswein.

VINIFICATION

Although the internationalization of winemaking techniques is a topic that is always much discussed. Methods of production can still vary greatly not just from country to country, but from region to region, and quite commonly even from grower to grower within the same village.

IN WINEMAKING, much depends on whether traditional values are upheld or innovations are sought and, for the latter, whether the technology is available. Whatever the winemaker decides, certain principles will, essentially, remain the same. These are described below, followed by sections on styles of wine and the processes common or unique to each one.

THE DIMINISHING QUALITY FACTOR
The quality of the grapes when they are harvested represents the maximum potential of any wine that can be made from them. However, a winemaker will never be able to transfer 100 percent of this inherent quality to the wine, because deterioration sets in from the moment a grape is disconnected from the vine's metabolism. Furthermore, the very process of turning grapes into wine is necessarily a destructive one, so every action that the winemaker takes, however quality-conscious, will inevitably erode some of the wine's potential. Winemakers, therefore, can only attempt to minimize the loss of potential quality.

It is relatively easy to retain approximately 80 percent of the potential quality of a wine, but very difficult to claw back every percentile point after that. It is also relatively easy to double or even treble the basic grape quality by better selection of vineyard sites, improved training methods, the use of superior clones, correct rootstock, and a reduction in yields. As a result, research has now swung from the winery back to the vineyard.

That said, enological practices are still important and how they are employed will have a profound effect not only on quality, but also on the style of the wine produced.

PRINCIPLES OF VINIFICATION
With modern technology, good everyday-drinking wines can be made anywhere that grapes are grown. When such wines are not made, the reason is invariably a lack of equipment and expertise. Wines of a finer quality require vineyards that have a certain potential and winemakers with a particular talent. When not even good everyday-drinking wines are made from fine-wine vineyards, it is usually due to a combination of excessive yields and poor winemaking, and there is no excuse for either.

FERMENTATION
The biochemical process that transforms fresh grape juice into wine is called fermentation. Yeast cells excrete enzymes that convert natural fruit sugars into almost equal quantities of alcohol and carbonic gas. This process ceases when the supply of sugar is exhausted or when the alcoholic level reaches a point that is toxic for the yeast enzymes (usually 15 to 16 percent, although certain strains can survive at 20 to 22 percent). Traditionally, winemakers racked their wine from cask to cask (*see p.26*) until they were sure that fermentation had stopped, but there are now many other methods that halt fermentation artificially. These can involve the use of heat, sulfur dioxide, centrifugal filtration, alcohol, pressure, or carbonic gas.
- **Heat** There are various forms of pasteurization (for table wines), flash-pasteurization (for finer wines), and chilling operations that are used to stabilize wine. These operate on the basis that yeast cells are incapacitated at temperatures above 97°F (36°C), or below 26°F (-3°C), and that yeast enzymes are destroyed above 149°F (65°C). Flash-pasteurization subjects wines to a temperature of about 176°F (80°C) for between 30 seconds and one minute, whereas fully fledged pasteurization involves lower temperatures of 122 to 140°F (50 to 60°C) for a longer period.
- **Addition of sulfur dioxide or sorbic acid** Dosing with one or more aseptic substances will kill off the yeasts.
- **Centrifugal filtration or filtration** Modern equipment is now capable of physically removing all the yeasts from a wine, either by filtration (simply pouring the wine through a medium that prevents certain substances from passing through) or by centrifugal filtration (a process that separates unwanted matter from wine—or grape juice, if used at an earlier stage—by so-called "centrifugal force").
- **Addition of alcohol** Fortification raises the alcohol content to a level toxic to yeast.
- **Pressure** Yeast cells are destroyed by pressure in excess of eight atmospheres (the pressure inside a Champagne bottle is around six atmospheres).
- **Addition of carbonic gas (CO$_2$)** Yeast cells are killed in the presence of .5 oz per quart (15 g per l) or more of carbonic gas.

THE USE OF SULFUR
Sulfur is used in winemaking from the time the grapes arrive at the winery until just before the wine is bottled. It has several qualities, including antioxidant and aseptic qualities, that make it essential for commercial winemaking. To some extent, all wines are oxidized from the moment the grapes are pressed and the juice is exposed to the air, but the rate of oxidation must be controlled. This is where sulfur is useful, because it has a chemical attraction for the tiny amounts of oxygen that are present in wine. One molecule of sulfur will combine with two molecules of oxygen to form sulfur dioxide (SO$_2$), or fixed sulfur. Once it is combined with the sulfur, the oxygen is neutralized and can no longer oxidize the wine. More oxygen will be absorbed by wine during the vinification process, of course, and there will also be a small head of air between the wine and the cork after bottling. It is for this reason that wines are bottled with a set amount of free sulfur (the amount of the total sulfur content that is not fixed). On occasion a winemaker claims that sulfur is completely superfluous to the winemaking process, but whereas low-sulfur regimes are

---

YEAST THE FERMENTER

The yeasts used for fermentation may be divided into two categories: cultured yeasts and natural yeasts.

Cultured yeasts are nothing more than thoroughbred strains of natural wine yeasts that have been raised in a laboratory. They may be used because the juice has been cleansed of all organisms, including its yeasts, prior to fermentation; or because the winemaker prefers their reliability, or for a specific purpose, such as withstanding higher alcohol levels or the increased osmotic pressure that affects bottle-fermented sparkling wines.

Natural yeasts are to be found adhering to the *pruina*, a waxy substance that covers the skin of ripe grapes and other fruits. By the time a grape has fully ripened, the coating of yeasts and other micro-organisms, commonly referred to as the "bloom," contains an average of 10 million yeast cells, although only one percent—or just 100,000 cells—are so-called "wine-yeasts." A yeast cell is only microscopic, yet under favorable conditions it has the ability to split 10,000 sugar molecules every second during fermentation.

actually to be encouraged, wines produced without it are usually dire or have a very short shelf-life.

One famous wine that claimed not to use any sulfur was so long-lived that I had a bottle independently analyzed, only to find that it did contain sulfur. The quantity was small, but far too significant to have been created during fermentation (which is possible in tiny amounts). It was, therefore, an example of how effective a low-sulfur regime can be. Methods of reducing the level of SO_2 are well known, the most important being a very judicious initial dosage because a resistance to sulfur gradually builds up and, as a result, later doses always have to be increased.

Some wines can be over-sulfured and, although they are less common than they used to be, they are by no means rare. Over-sulfured wines are easily recognizable by their smell, which ranges from the slight whiff of a recently ignited match (which is the clean smell of free sulfur) to the stench of rotten eggs (which is H_2S, where the sulfur has combined with hydrogen—literally the stuff of stinkbombs). When H_2S reacts with ethyl alcohol or one of the higher alcohols, foul-smelling compounds called mercaptans are formed. They can smell of garlic, onion, burning rubber, or stale cabbage, depending on the exact nature of the compound. Mercaptans are extremely difficult for the winemaker to remove and can ruin a wine, which illustrates just how important it is to maintain a low-sulfur regime.

MALOLACTIC FERMENTATION

Malolactic fermentation is sometimes known as the secondary fermentation, but this is an inappropriate description. The malolactic, or "malo" (as it is sometimes called), is a biochemical process that converts the "hard" malic acid of unripe grapes into two parts "soft" lactic, or "milk," acid (so-called because it is the acid that makes milk sour) and one part carbonic gas. Malic acid is a very strong-tasting acid, which reduces during the fruit's ripening process. However, a significant quantity persists in ripe grapes, and, although reduced by fermentation, also in wine.

The quantity of malic acid present in a wine may be considered too much and the smoothing effect of replacing it with just two-thirds the quantity of the much weaker lactic acid is often desirable. This smoothing effect is considered vital for red wine, beneficial for fuller, fatter, more complex whites, and optional for lighter, crisper whites and certain styles of sparkling wine.

To ensure that the malo can take place, it is essential that specific bacteria are present. These are found naturally on grape skins among the yeasts and other microorganisms, but commercially prepared bacteria may also be used. To undertake their task, they require a certain warmth, a low level of sulfur, a pH of between 3 and 4, and a supply of various nutrients found naturally in grapes.

STAINLESS STEEL OR OAK?

The use of stainless steel and oak containers for fermentation and maturation is not simply dependent on the cost (*see right*). The two materials produce opposing effects on wine, so the choice is heavily dependent on whether the winemaker wants to add character to a wine or to keep its purity.

A stainless-steel vat is a long-lasting, easy-to-clean vessel made from an impervious and inert material that is ideally suited to all forms of temperature control. It has the capacity to produce the freshest wines with the purest varietal character. An oak cask has a comparatively limited life, is not easy to clean (it can never be sterilized), makes temperature control very difficult, and is neither impervious nor inert. It allows access to the air, which encourages a faster rate of oxidation, but also causes evaporation, which concentrates the flavour. Vanillin, the essential aromatic constituent of vanilla pods, is extracted from the oak by oxidation and, with various wood lactones and unfermentable sugars, imparts a distinctive, sweet and creamy vanilla nuance to wine. This oaky character takes on a smoky complexity if the wine is allowed to

STAINLESS-STEEL VATS
Stainless steel is the cornerstone of modern winemaking technology. The bands around each tank contain a coolant to regulate fermentation temperatures.

go through its malolactic fermentation in contact with the wood, and becomes even more complex, and certainly better integrated, if the wine has undergone all or most of its alcoholic fermentation in cask. Oak also imparts wood tannins to low tannin wine, absorbs tannins from tannic wine, and can exchange tannins with some wines. Oak tannins also act as catalysts, provoking desirable changes in grape tannins through a complex interplay of oxidations.

POST-FERMENTATION PROCEDURES

Numerous procedures can take place in the winery after fermentation and, where applicable, malolactic fermentation, have ceased. However, the five most basic procedures are racking, fining, cold stabilization, filtration, and bottling.

Racking

Draining the clear wine off its lees, or sediment, into another vat or cask is known as "racking" because of the different levels, or racks, on which the wine is run from one container into another. In modern vinification, this operation is usually conducted several times during vat or cask maturation. The wine gradually throws off less and less of a deposit. Some wines, such as Muscadet sur lie, are never racked.

Fining

After fermentation, wine may look hazy to the eye. Even if it does not, it may still contain suspended matter that threatens cloudiness in the bottle. Fining usually assists the clarification of wine at this stage. In addition, special fining agents may be employed to remove unwanted characteristics. When a fining agent is added to wine, it adheres to cloudy matter by physical or electrolytic attraction,

---

THE COST OF NEW OAK

Two hundred 59-gallon (225-liter) oak casks with a total capacity of 11,900 gallons (450 hectoliters) cost between four and 10 times the cost of a single 11,900-gallon (450-hectoliter) stainless-steel vat. After two years of much higher labor costs to operate and maintain the large number of small units, the volume of wine produced in the oak casks is 10 percent less because of evaporation, and the winemaker faces the prospect of purchasing another 200 casks.

creating tiny clusters (known as colloidal groups), which drop to the bottom of the vat as sediment. The most commonly encountered fining agents are egg white, tannin, gelatin, bentonite, isinglass, and casein. Winemakers have their preferences and individual fining agents also have their specific uses. Oositively charged egg white fines out negatively charged matter, such as unwanted tannins or anthocyanins, while negatively charged bentonite fines out positively charged matter, such as protein haze and other organic matter.

Cold stabilization

When wines are subjected to low temperatures, a crystalline deposit of tartrates can form a deposit in the bottle. Should the wine be dropped to a very low temperature for a few days before bottling, this process can be precipitated, rendering the wine safe from the threat of a tartrate deposit in the bottle. For the past 20 years, cold stabilization has been almost obligatory for cheap commercial wines, and it is now increasingly used for those of better quality as well. This recent trend is a pity because the crystals are, in fact, entirely harmless and their presence is a completely welcome indication of a considerably more natural, rather than heavily processed, wine.

Filtration

Various methods of filtration exist, and they all entail running wine through a medium that prevents particles of a certain size from passing through. Filtration has become a controversial subject in recent times, with some critics claiming that anything that removes something from wine must be bad. Depending on who you listen to, this "something" is responsible for a wine's complexity, body, or flavor. However, although it is undeniable that filtration strips something from a wine, if it is unfiltered, it will throw a much heavier deposit and do so relatively quickly. The mysterious "something" is, therefore, purged from all wines at some time or other, whether they are filtered or not, and whether the critics like it or not. Filtration, like so many things, is perfectly acceptable if it is applied in moderation. The fact that many of the world's greatest wines are filtered is a testament to this.

I prefer less or no filtration, as do most quality-conscious winemakers. This is not because of any romantic, unquantifiable ideal, it is simply because I prefer wine to be as unprocessed and as natural as possible. This is a state that can only be achieved through as much of a hands-off approach as the wine will allow. Generally the finer the wine, the less filtration required, as consumers of

FROM GRAPE TO GLASS

Virtually every ingredient of a fresh grape can be found in the wine it makes, although additional compounds are produced when wine is made and any sedimented matter is disposed of before it is bottled. The most significant difference in the two lists below is the disappearance of fermentable sugar and the appearance of alcohol, although the constituents will vary according to the variety and ripeness of the grape and the style of wine produced

THE "INGREDIENTS" OF FRESH GRAPE JUICE
Percentage by volume

73.5	Water	
25	Carbohydrates, of which:	
	20%	Sugar (plus pentoses, pectin, inositol)
	5%	Cellulose
0.8	Organic acids, of which:	
	0.54%	Tartaric acid
	0.25%	Malic acid
	0.01%	Citric acid (plus possible traces of succinic acid and lactic acid)
0.5	Minerals, of which:	
	0.25%	Potassium
	0.05%	Phosphate
	0.035%	Sulfate
	0.025%	Calcium
	0.025%	Magnesium
	0.01%	Chloride
	0.005%	Silicic acid
	0.1%	Others (aluminum, boron, copper, iron, molybdenum, rubidium, sodium, zinc)
0.13	Tannin and color pigments	
0.07	Nitrogenous matter, of which:	
	0.05%	Amino acids (arginine, glutamic acid, proline, serine, threonine, and others)
	0.005%	Protein
	0.015%	Other nitrogenous matter (humin, amide, ammonia, and others)
Traces	Mainly vitamins (thiamine, riboflavin, pyridoxine, pantothenic acid, nicotinic acid, and ascorbic acid)	

THE "CONTENTS" OF WINE
Percentage by volume

86	Water	
12	Alcohol (ethyl alcohol)	
1	Glycerol	
0.4	Organic acids, of which:	
	0.20%	Tartaric acid
	0.15%	Lactic acid
	0.05%	Succinic acid (plus traces of malic acid citric acid)
0.2	Carbohydrates (unfermentable sugar)	
0.2	Minerals, of which:	
	0.075%	Potassium
	0.05%	Phosphate
	0.03%	Calcium
	0.02%	Magnesium
	0.02%	Sulfate
	0.01%	Chloride
	0.005%	Silicic acid
	Traces	Aluminum, boron, copper, iron, molybdenum, rubidium, sodium, zinc
0.1	Tannin and color pigments	
0.045	Volatile acids (mostly acetic acid)	
0.025	Nitrogenous matter, of which:	
	0.01%	Amino acids (arginine, glutamic acid, proline, serine, threonine, and others)
	0.015%	Protein and other nitrogenous matter (humin, amide, ammonia, and others)
0.025	Esters (mostly ethyl acetate, but traces of numerous others)	
0.004	Aldehydes (mostly acetaldehyde, some vanillin, and traces of others)	
0.001	Higher alcohols (minute quantities of amyl plus traces of isoamyl, butyl, isobutyl, hexyl, propyl, and methyl may be present)	
Traces	Vitamins (thiamine, riboflavin, pyridoxine, pantothenic acid, nicotinic acid, and ascorbic acid)	

WATER INTO WINE

The individual flavoring elements in any wine represent barely two percent of its content. Although we can determine with great accuracy the amount and identity of 99 percent of these constituents, the mystery is that if we assembled them and added the requisite volume of water and alcohol, the result would taste nothing like wine, let alone like the specific wine we would be trying to imitate.

expensive wines expect sedimentation and are prepared to decant. Delicate reds, such as Pinot Noir, should be the least filtered of all, as I swear they lose fruit just by looking at them, and they certainly lose color—that, at least, is quantifiable. No wine with extended barrel-aging should ever require filtration—just a light, natural fining.

Each filtration is expensive and time-consuming, thus even producers of the most commercial, everyday wines (which even filtration critics accept must be filtered) should keep these operations to a minimum. The principle means of achieving this is by ensuring the best possible clarification by settling and racking. Fining (*see* p.26) should always take precedence, because it is both kinder on the wine and much cheaper than filtering. There are four basic types of filtration: Earth, Pad, Membrane, and Crossflow.

• **Earth Filtration** This system is primarily used after racking for filtering the wine-rich lees that collect at the bottom of the fermentation tank. A medium, usually kieselguhr (a form of diatomaceous earth), is continuously fed into the wine and used with either a Plate and Frame Filter or a Rotary Drum Vacuum Filter. Both types of filter are precoated with the medium, but in a Plate and Frame Filter, the wine and medium mix is forced, under pressure, through plates, or screens, of the medium, in a manner similar to that of any other filter. For the Rotary Drum Vacuum Filter, however, the precoat adheres to the outside of a large perforated drum by virtue of the vacuum that is maintained inside. The drum revolves through a shallow bath into which the wine is pumped and literally sucks the wine through the precoat into the center, where it is piped away. The advantage of this system is that on one side of the shallow bath there is a scraper that constantly shaves the coating on the drum to the desired thickness. The medium thus falls into the wine, with which it mixes, and is then sucked back onto, and through, the drum. It is a continuous process and a very economical one, since the amount of medium used is limited. In a Plate and Frame Filter, the medium is enclosed and eventually clogs up, requiring the operation to be stopped, and the equipment to be dismantled and cleaned before the process can resume.

• **Pad Filtration** Also called Sheet Filtration, this involves the use of a Plate and Frame Filter with a variable number of frames into which filter pads or sheets can slide. Before it was outlawed in the 1970s, these used to be made of asbestos. They now contain numerous filtration mediums, ranging from diatomaceous earth to regular cellulose pads, the latter of which are the most commonly used medium. Special filter formats include active carbon (to remove unwanted color, which is frowned upon for all but the most commercial, high-volume wines) and electrostatically charged pads. These are designed to attract any matter that is suspended in the wine, most of which will possess a negative or positive charge. It is claimed that these electrostatically charged pads are more effective in filtering out matter than the same pads without a charge.

• **Membrane Filtration** This is also called Millipore because the membranes contain microscopic holes capable of removing yeasts and other microorganisms. These holes account for 80 percent of the sheet's surface, so the throughput of wine can be extremely fast provided it has undergone a light prefiltration. Both filtration and prefiltration can now, however, be done at the same time with new Millipore cartridge filters. These contain two or more membranes of varying porosity, thus the coarser ones act as a screen for those with the most minuscule holes.

• **Crossflow Filtration** Originally designed to purify water, a crossflow filter varies from the others (with the exception of the Rotary Drum Vacuum Filter) because it is self-cleaning and never clogs up. The wine flows across the membrane, not into it, so only some of it penetrates. Most of it returns to the chamber from which it came and, because it flows very fast, takes with it any matter filtered out by the membrane.

BOTTLING

When visiting larger producers, automated bottling lines are the wine journalist's *bête noire*. They get faster and more complex each year and, having invested vast sums in the very latest bottling line, it is understandable that proprietors are keen to show off their new high-tech toy. However, as John Arlott once told me, as he resolutely refused to set foot in the bottling hall of Piper-Heidsieck, "I have not written a single word about bottling lines in my life and I'm not going to start now." They make a very dull experience and inevitably break down just as one's host boasts that it is the fastest bottling line in the world, but their smooth

HOW RED WINE IS MADE

HOPPER

CRUSHER/
DESTEMMER

PUMP

Some bunches fermented whole

REMONTAGE
Fermenting juice is pumped up and over the manta *of grapeskins*

PIGEAGE
The manta *is manually pushed under fermenting juice using poles*

FERMENTATION

operation most days of the week is essential if the wine is to remain as fresh as possible in the bottle. All that readers need to know is that the bottles should be sterile; that fully-automated lines cork, capsule, label, and box the wines; and that there is a device to detect any impurities before the bottles are boxed. All European systems print a lot number identifying the date each batch was bottled either on the label or directly onto the bottle using a laser. Therefore, in an emergency, a specific batch can be recalled, rather than the entire production having to be cleared from every wholesaler and retailer stocking a particular line.

RED WINES

On arrival at the winery the grapes are usually crushed and destemmed, although it was once accepted practice to leave the stems for a more tannic wine. However, stem tannins are too harsh and fail to soften as the wine matures. The modern winemaker can include a small quantity of stems if the grape variety requires extra structure or if the vintage needs firming up.

FERMENTATION

After the grapes are destemmed and lightly crushed, they are pumped into a vat where fermentation may begin as early as 12 hours or as late as several days later. Even wines that will be cask-fermented must start off in vats, whether they are old-fashioned oak *foudres* or modern stainless-steel tanks. This is because they must be fermented along with a *manta*, or cap, of grapeskins. To encourage fermentation, the juice may be heated and selected yeast cultures or partially fermented wine from another vat added. During fermentation, the juice is often pumped from the bottom of the vat to the top and sprayed over the *manta* to keep the juice in contact with the grapeskins. This ensures that the maximum color is extracted. Other methods involve the *manta* being pushed under the fermenting juice with poles. Some vats are equipped with crude but effective grids that prevent the *manta* from rising, others rely on the carbonic gas given off during fermentation to build up pressure, releasing periodically and pushing the *manta* under the surface; another system keeps the *manta* submerged in a "vinimatic," a sealed, rotating stainless-steel tank, based on the cement-mixer principle.

The higher the temperature during fermentation, the more color and tannin will be extracted; the lower the temperature, the better the bouquet, freshness, and fruit will be. The optimum temperature for the fermentation of red wine is 85°F (29.4°C). If it is too hot, the yeasts produce certain substances (decanoic acid, octanoic acids, and corresponding esters) that inhibit their own ability to feed on nutrients and cause the yeasts to die. It is, however, far better to ferment hot fresh juice than to wait two weeks (which is normal in many cases) to ferment cooler but stale juice. The fuller, darker, more tannic and potentially longer-lived wines remain in contact with the skins for anything between 10 and 30 days. Lighter wines, on the other hand, are separated from the skins after only a few days.

VIN DE GOUTTE AND VIN DE PRESSE

The moment the skins are separated from the juice, every wine is divided into two—free-run wine, or *vin de goutte*, and press wine, or *vin de presse*. The free-run juice runs out of the vat when the tap is opened. The remains—the *manta* of grapeskins, pips, and other solids—are put into a press to extract the very dark, extremely tannic "press wine." The free-run wine and the press wine are then pumped into separate vats or casks depending on the style of the wine being made. These wines then undergo their malolactic conversion separately and are racked several times, fined, racked again, blended, then fined and racked once more before bottling.

MACÉRATION CARBONIQUE

There are several variations of *macération carbonique*, a technique used almost exclusively for making red wine, involving an initial fermentation under pressure of carbonic gas. The traditional method, dating back at least 200 years, was to put the uncrushed grapes in a closed container, where after a while, a natural fermentation would take place inside the grapes. When the grapes eventually exploded, filling the container with carbonic gas, a normal fermentation continued and the grapes macerated in their own skins. Today the grapes are often placed in vats filled with carbonic gas from a bottle. *Macération carbonique* produces light wines with good color, soft fruit, and a "pear-drop" aroma.

WHITE WINES

Until fairly recently it could be said that two initial operations distinguished the white-winemaking process from the red one: first, an immediate pressing to extract the juice and separate the skins, and, second, the purging, or cleansing, of this juice. But for white wines of expressive varietal character the grapes are now often crushed and then macerated in a vinimatic for 12 to 48

PRESS

STAINLESS-STEEL TANK
(for maturation)

WOODEN BARRELS
(for malolactic fermentation and maturation)

FILTRATION   BOTTLING

Free-run juice

Free-run juice

Some wines not filtered or fined

hours to extract the aromatics that are stored in the skins. The juice that is run out of the vinimatic, and the juice that is pressed out of the macerated pulp left inside it, then undergoes cleansing and fermentation like any other white wine.

With the exception of wines macerated in a vinimatic, the grapes are either pressed immediately on arrival at the winery or lightly crushed and then pressed. The juice from the last pressing is murky, bitter, and low in acidity and sugar, so only the first pressing, which is roughly equivalent to the free-run juice in red wine, together with the richest elements of the second pressing, should be used for white-wine production. Once pressed, the juice is pumped into a vat where it is purged, or cleansed, which in its simplest form means simply leaving the juice to settle so that particles of grapeskin and any other impurities fall to the bottom. This purging may be helped by chilling, adding sulfur dioxide and, possibly, a fining agent. Light filtration and centrifugation may also be applied during this process.

After cleansing, the juice is pumped into the fermenting vat or directly into barrels if the wine is to be cask-fermented. The addition of selected yeast cultures occurs more often in the production of white wine because of the wine's limited contact with the yeast-bearing skins and the additional cleansing that reduces the potential amount of wine yeasts available.

The optimum temperature for fermenting white wine is 64°F (18°C), although many winemakers opt for between 50°F and 63°F (10°C and 17°C), and it is actually possible to ferment wine at temperatures as low as 39°F (4°C). At the lower temperatures, more esters and other aromatics are created, less volatile acidity is produced, and a lower dose of sulfur dioxide is required; on the other hand, the resulting wines are lighter in body and contain less glycerol.

With acidity an essential factor in the balance of fruit and, where appropriate, sweetness in white wines, many products are not permitted to undergo malolactic conversion and are not bottled until some 12 months after the harvest. Oak-matured wines which, incidentally, always undergo malolactic conversion, may be bottled between 9 and 18 months, but wines that are made especially for early drinking are nearly always racked, fined, filtered, and bottled as quickly as the process will allow in order to retain as much freshness and fruitiness as possible.

ROSÉ WINES

With the exception of pink Champagne, most of which is made by blending white wine with red, all good-quality rosés are produced either by bleeding, pressing, or limited maceration. A true-bled rosé is made from the juice that issues from black grapes pressed under their own weight. This is a sort of *tête de cuvée*, which, after fermentation, is a very pale *vin gris* color, but has a rich, fruity, and exquisitely fresh flavor. Pressed rosé is made by pressing black grapes until the juice takes on enough color. It, too, has a pale *vin gris* color, but lacks the true richness of a *tête de cuvée* rosé. Limited maceration is the most common method used in the production of rosé. During this process, rosé is made in exactly the same way as red wine, except that skin-contact is limited to what is sufficient to give the desired pink tint. (All shades of rosé exist, ranging from a barely perceptible hint of color to *clairet*, or almost red.) Some superior rosé wines that have been made using this last method are virtually by-products of red-wine production. In certain areas that lack the appropriate climate for deep red wines, some free-run juice might be run off in order to produce rosé, thus leaving a greater ratio of coloring pigment in the juice that remains.

SPARKLING WINES

When grape juice is fermented, sugar is converted into alcohol and carbonic gas. For still wines the gas is allowed to escape, but if it is prevented from doing so—by putting a lid on a vat or a cork in a bottle—it will remain dissolved in the wine until the lid or cork is removed. When the gas is released it rushes out of the wine in the form of bubbles. The production of all natural sparkling wines is based on this essential principle, using one of four different methods: *méthode champenoise*, bottle-fermented, *méthode rurale*, and *cuve close*. They can also be made by injecting the bubbles.

MÉTHODE CHAMPENOISE

Also referred to as *méthode traditionnelle* or *méthode classique* (France), *metodo classico* (Italy), and *Cap Classique* (South Africa), this term indicates a sparkling wine that has undergone a second fermentation in the bottle in which it is sold. A label may refer to a wine being "Individually fermented in this bottle," which is the beautifully simple American equivalent of *méthode champenoise*.

HOW WHITE WINE IS MADE

HOPPER

CRUSHER/ DESTEMMER

STAINLESS-STEEL TANK
(for prefermentation maceration of some aromatic wines)

Some bunches pressed whole

BOTTLE-FERMENTED

This refers to a wine produced through a second fermentation in a bottle, but (and this is the catch) not necessarily in the bottle in which it is sold. It may have been fermented in one bottle, transferred to a vat and, under pressure at 26°F (-3°C), filtered into another bottle. This is also known as the "transfer method."

MÉTHODE RURALE

This refers to the precursor of *méthode champenoise*, which is still used today, albeit only for a few obscure wines. It involves no second fermentation, the wine being bottled before the first alcoholic fermentation is finished.

CUVE CLOSE, CHARMAT, OR TANK METHOD

This is used for the bulk production of inexpensive sparkling wines that have undergone a second fermentation in large tanks before being filtered and bottled under pressure at 26°F (-3°C). Contrary to popular belief, there is no evidence to suggest that this is an intrinsically inferior method of making sparkling wine. It is only because it is a bulk production method that it tends to attract mediocre base wines and encourage a quick throughput. I genuinely suspect that a *cuve close* produced from the finest base wines of Champagne and given the autolytic benefit of at least three years on its lees before bottling might well be indistinguishable from the "real thing."

CARBONATION

This is the cheapest method of putting bubbles into wine and simply involves injecting it with carbon dioxide. Because this is the method used to make lemonade, it is incorrectly assumed that the bubbles achieved through carbonation are large and short lived. They can be, and fully sparkling wines made by this method will indeed be cheapskates, but modern carbonation plants have the ability to induce the tiniest of bubbles, even to the point of imitating the "prickle" of wine bottled *sur lie*.

FORTIFIED WINES

Any wine, dry or sweet, red or white, to which alcohol has been added is classified as a fortified wine, whatever the inherent differences of vinification may be. Still wines usually have a strength of 8.5 to 15 percent alcohol; fortified wines a strength of 17 to 24 percent. The spirit added is usually, but not always, brandy made from local wines. It is totally neutral, with no hint of a brandy flavor. The amount of alcohol added, and exactly when and how it is added, is as critical to the particular character of a fortified wine as is its grape variety or area of production. *Mutage*, early fortification, and late fortification are all methods that may be used to fortify wines.

MUTAGE

This is the addition of alcohol to fresh grape juice. This prevents fermentation and produces fortified wines, known as *vins de liqueurs* in France, such as Pineau des Charentes in the Cognac region, Floc de Gascogne in Armagnac, and Ratafia in Champagne.

EARLY FORTIFICATION

This is the addition of alcohol after fermentation has begun. This is often done in several small, carefully measured, timed doses spread over several hours or even days. The style of fortified wine being made will dictate exactly when the alcohol is added, and the style itself will be affected by the variable strength of the grapes from year to year. On average, however, alcohol is added to port after the alcohol level has reached 6 to 8 percent, and added to the *vins doux naturels* of France, such as Muscat de Beaumes de Venise, at any stage between 5 and 10 percent.

LATE FORTIFICATION

This is the addition of alcohol after fermentation has ceased. The classic drink produced by this method is sherry, which is always vinified dry, with any sweetness added afterward.

AROMATIZED WINES

With the exception of Retsina, the resinated Greek wine, aromatized wines are all fortified. They also all have aromatic ingredients added to them. The most important aromatized wine is vermouth, which is made from neutral white wines of 2 to 3 years of age, blended with an extract of wormwood (vermouth is a corruption of the German *wermut* meaning "wormwood"), vanilla, and various other herbs and spices. Italian vermouths are produced in Apulia and Sicily, and French vermouths in Languedoc and Roussillon. Chambéry is a delicate generic vermouth from the Savoie and Chambéryzette is a red-pink version flavored with alpine strawberries, but such precise geographical aromatized wines are rare. Most, in fact, are made and sold under internationally recognized brands such as Cinzano and Martini. Other well-known aromatized wines include Amer Picon, Byrrh, Dubonnet (both red and white), Punt e Mes, St.-Raphael, and Suze.

PRESS   WOODEN BARRELS

STAINLESS-STEEL FERMENTATION TANK

FERMENTATION

FILTRATION   BOTTLING

Some wines not filtered or fined

THE CHOICE OF OAK

I have seen the question only once in print, yet it is the most fundamental question that could possibly be asked: why oak? Why out of all the woods around the world is oak, and to any significant degree, only oak, used for barrel-making?

THE ANSWER IS THAT OTHER WOODS are either too porous or contain overpowering aromatic substances that unpleasantly taint the wine. It is not entirely true to say that only oak is used in winemaking. Chestnut, for example, is occasionally found in the Rhône and elsewhere, but it is so porous and so tannic that it is usually lined with a neutral substance, rendering the wood no different from any other lined construction material (such as concrete). A beech variety called *rauli* used to be popular in Chile until its winemakers, suddenly exposed to international markets, soon discovered they had become so used to the wood that they had not realized that it gave their wines a musty joss-stick character. Large, redwood tanks are still used in California and Oregon, but they are not greatly appreciated and, as the wood cannot be bent very easily, it is not practical for small barrels. Pine has a strong resinous character that the Greeks seem to enjoy, although they have had 3,000 years to acquire the taste. Most tourists try Retsina, but very few continue to drink it by choice when they return home. Moreover, it is made by adding resin, with no direct contact with the wood and, apart from an oddity called "Tea Wine," produced on La Palma in the Canary Islands, no wine to my knowledge is produced in barrels made of pine. Eucalyptus also has a resinous affect, acacia turns wine yellow, and hardwoods are impossible to bend and contain aromatic oils that are undesirable.

White oak, on the other hand, is easily bent, has a low porosity, acceptable tannin content, and mild, creamy aromatic substances that either have an intrinsic harmony with wine or, like the Greeks, we have grown accustomed to the effect.

LARGE OR SMALL?
The size of the cask is critical to its influence. The smaller it is, the larger the oak-to-wine ratio, and the greater an oaky flavor it imparts. A 53-gallon (200-liter) *barrique* has 1.5 times the internal surface area of oak for every quart of wine as a 132-gallon (500-liter) cask. Traditional sizes for *barriques* range from 54 gallons (205 liters) in Champagne, to 59 gallons (225 liters) in Bordeaux and Spain, 60 gallons (228 liters) in Burgundy, and 79 to 83 gallons (300 to 315 liters) in Australia and New Zealand.

AN OAK BARREL
The staves of a barrel are held together by metal hoops, which are sometimes positioned at slightly different distances, depending on the traditions of the cooper, or *tonnelier*, in question. There may be a red color between the two innermost hoops, but this is merely where some winemakers wish to conceal their own dribble marks

around the bung by dyeing the entire middle area with wine, which can look very impressive. When fermenting white wines, the bung is always uppermost and, even with a good ullage, or space, the hole may be left open during the most tumultuous period. It will be sealed with an air-lock valve when the fermentation process settles down to remain closed during the malolactic fermentation. After racking, when all wines mature for several months, the barrels are filled to the very top, and positioned so that the bung is to one side, visually reminding cellar-workers that the casks are full.

FERMENTING POSITION   MATURATION POSITION

Square barrels were even developed to increase the ratio of oak-to-wine. Although treated as a novelty, they were actually more practical and economical than normal casks. More practical because they made more efficient use of storage space and more economical because their straight sides could be reversed to create a new oak barrel from an old one. An Australian firm even built a square stainless-steel tank with two oak panels made from oak staves that could be replaced, reversed, and adjusted in size to give different oak-to-wine ratios. However, all such barrels became superfluous, with the advent and widespread use of oak chips.

CHIPS OFF THE OLD BLOCK
Using old oak barrels for the finest *barrique*-fermented or *barrique*-matured wines is a question of style rather than a consideration of cost. But for less expensive wines, it is almost entirely a question of economics, because barrels can double, for example, the cost of a *vin de pays*.

The use of new oak *barriques* for just a small percentage of a wine blend can add a certain subliminal complexity to it, although not the overt oakiness that so many people find attractive, yet so few are willing to pay very much for. Oak chips or shavings are the answer. Although generally believed to be a recent phenomenon, the use of oak chips was sufficiently widespread by 1961 to warrant statutory controls in the United States. In fact, as a by-product of barrel-making, today's ubiquitous chip probably has an equally long, if somewhat more covert, history. Oak chips have been one of the most potent weapons in the New World's armory, producing relatively inexpensive, but distinctly premium-quality, wines to conquer international markets. This has been particularly evident in Australia, where flying winemakers have not only perfected oak

Bung
Stave
Head
Middle stave
Hoop
Chimb

AMERICAN OAK DUST   FRENCH OAK CHIPS   AMERICAN OAK CHIPS
Light-toast   Medium-toast   High-toast

FRENCH OAK "APPELLATIONS"

Some winemakers swear by a particular variety of French oak, but most are suspicious of barrels that claim to be from one specific forest. Tronçais, for example, is one of the most famous oak forests, but the Tronçais forest supplies just 2 percent of all French oak and, if every barrel claiming to be from there actually did so, the forest would have disappeared long ago.

Perhaps the Bordelais, who are the most experienced in buying new French oak, realized this centuries ago, as they have traditionally purchased barrels made from "mixed staves" (i.e. various forests).

Most winemakers buy from a particular cooper because they like their barrels. This usually has less to do with their construction, than with the seasoning of the wood and the toasting of the barrels. Most barrels are not only made on a mix-and-match basis, but the mix of staves is likely to vary from year to year. This is because oak is sold by auction and coopers buy on quality, not name. It is more important who owns the forest than where it is located, because known sources, such as the *Office National des Forêts*, which is the only purveyor of *Haute Futaie* oak and who only sells *Haute Futaie* oak, can guarantee a consistency that a private proprietor, even with good wood, cannot. Therefore, some companies, such as Seguin Moreau, follow a policy of buying only *Haute Futaie* oak.

---

chip wines, but by the early 1990s had exported the techniques to virtually every winemaking country in the world. Some experiments have demonstrated that wine matured with oak chips used in old barrels is "virtually indistinguishable" from the same wine stored in new oak. The range of oak chip products is now very comprehensive, covering the entire range of oak varieties and different toast levels. Some are even impregnated with malolactic bacteria. If a wine label mentions oak, but not *barriques*, barrels, or casks, it is probably a clue that oak chips have been employed in the winemaking and, if the wine is cheap, you can bet on it.

ANYONE FOR TOAST?

Toasting is one operation in the barrel-making process that has a very direct effect on the taste of the wine. In order to bend the staves, heat is applied in three stages: warming-up (*pre-chauffrage*), shaping (*cintrage*), and toasting (*bousinage*), each of which browns, or chars, the internal surface of the barrel. However, it is only the last stage—*bousinage*—that determines the degree of toasting. During toasting, furanic aldehydes (responsible for "roasted" aromas) reach their maximum concentration, the vanilla aroma of vanillin is heightened, and various phenols, such as eugenol (the chief aromatic constituent of oil of cloves), add a smoky, spicy touch to the complexity of oak aromas in wine.

BOUSINAGE
The final barrel-firing operation puts a light, medium, or heavy toast on the inner surface.

There are three degrees of toasting; light, medium, and heavy. A light toasting is used by winemakers who seek the most natural oak character (although it is not as neutral as using staves that have been bent with steam); medium varies between a true medium, which suits most red wine demands, and the so-called medium-plus, which is the favorite for fermenting white wines; the third, a heavy toast, dramatically reduces the coconutty-lactones and leaves a distinctly charred-smoke character that can be overpowering unless used only as a small component in a blend. Furthermore, with time, the high carbon content of heavily toasted barrels can leach the color out of some wines, so they tend to be used for white wines (often big, brash Chardonnays), although heavy toast is best suited to maturing Bourbon whiskey.

THE DIFFERENT OAKS

Both American and European oaks are used for winemaking. The aromatics of fast-growing, wide-grained American white oak, *Quercus alba*, are more pungent, while there are more tannins, finer in texture, in slow-growing, tight-grained European brown oaks, *Quercus robur* (syn pedunculate oak), and *Quercus sessilis* (syn *Quercus petraea* and *Quercus rouvre*). Much of the appealing, if obvious, coconut character in American oak is also due to the very different barrel-making techniques used in the U.S.

Unlike European oak, American is sawn, not split. This ruptures the wood cells, releasing aromatic substances, especially vanillin and up to seven different lactones, which together explain the coconut aroma. American oak is also kiln-dried, which concentrates the lactones, while European oak is seasoned outside for several years, a process that leaches out some of the most aromatic substances, and reduces the more aggressive tannins. The whole process tends to accentuate the character of American oak, while subduing that of European oak.

Many French winemakers consider American oak vulgar. Even so, a little known fact is that in ultraconservative Bordeaux, at least 60 châteaux are experimenting with it. Coconut-flavored claret is by no means a foregone conclusion, but oak is expensive, a little sawn *Quercus alba* goes a long way, and a small percentage of American oak, either as barrels or mixed staves, could, in fact, significantly reduce the percentage of new oak needed each year.

EUROPEAN SPLIT VERSUS AMERICAN SAWN
After the bark has been stripped from a log destined for barrel-making, it will be split (in Europe) or sawn (in the United States) into quarters. The examples above clearly show that it is more economical to saw staves from a quarter, as opposed to splitting them. This is the major reason why American oak barrels cost half the price of European ones.

LIGHT TOAST   **MEDIUM TOAST**   **HEAVY TOAST**

REGIONAL OAK VARIETIES

For winemaking, the tighter the size of the oak grain, the better. The slower the tree grows, the tighter the grain—thus, cooler-climate European oak is older and tighter-grained than warmer-climate American oak. Of the European oaks, forest oak (*Quercus sessilis*) is preferred to solitary oak trees (*Quercus robur*) because its branches start higher and the trunk is longer and straighter. Solitary oaks grow faster and have a larger grain because they tend to grow in fertile soil where there is more water. *Quercus sessilis* is also preferred to *Quercus robur* because it is four times richer in aromatic components.

AMERICAN *Quercus alba*

This oak covers most of the eastern U.S. Some winemakers think that Minnesota and Wisconsin are the best, while others find them too tannic and consider Appalachian oak, particularly from Pennsylvania, to be superior. Other popular oaks are Ohio, Kentucky, Mississippi, and Missouri. All are white oaks, fast-growing, wide-grained, with lower tannin (except for Oregon) than any European brown oaks, but with higher, sweeter, more coconutty aromatics. *Quercus alba* is favored for traditional Rioja, Australian Shiraz, and California Zinfandel.

OREGON *Quercus gariana*

Although a white oak, *Quercus gariana* has a significantly tighter grain than *Quercus alba*. Relatively few barrels have been made from Oregon oak, and it has always been sawn, making it hard to evaluate the claim that it is similar to European oak. In 1996, however, barrels were made from split, open-air seasoned Oregon oak, so watch this space.

ALLIER *Quercus sessilis*

Tight-grained with well-balanced, medium tannin and aromatics, Allier is highly regarded.

ARGONNE *Quercus sessilis*

Tight-grained with low aromatics and tannin, this oak was used for Champagne before the advent of stainless-steel. Now seldom used.

AMERICAN OAK FORESTS

EUROPEAN OAK FORESTS

BOURGOGNE *Quercus sessilis*

Tight-grained with high tannin and low aromatics, most of this oak goes to Burgundian cellars.

LIMOUSIN *Quercus robur*

Wider-grained with high tannin and low aromatics, this oak used to be favored for Chardonnay, but is most widely used for brandy.

NEVERS *Quercus sessilis*

Tight-grained with well-balanced, medium tannin and aromatics, Nevers is highly regarded.

TRONÇAIS *Quercus sessilis*

The tightest-grained and, with Vosges, the highest tannin content, Tronçais grows in the Allier forest. It is highly suitable for long-term maturation, owing to its understated aromatics, and has been long sought after.

VOSGES *Quercus sessilis*

The tight grain, very high tannin content, and understated but slightly spicy aromatics make Vosges an especially well-balanced oak for winemaking. It is underrated, particularly in its home region of Alsace, where even though few winemakers use *barriques*, those who do ironically seem to experiment with virtually every French forest except the one that is actually on their own doorstep. Vosges is especially popular in California and New Zealand, where some winemakers think it is similar to Allier and Nevers. Vosges deserves to receive greater recognition.

BALKAN *Quercus robur*

Often called Slavonian or Yugoslav oak, the grain is tight, with medium tannin and low aromatics. Balkan oak is popular for large oval casks, particularly in Italy. Use is diminishing because of recent troubles.

PORTUGUESE *Quercus gariana*

Cooperage oak (*Quercus gariana*) is far less of a commercial concern in Portugal than stunted cork-industry oak (*Quercus suber*), but the former's medium-grain wood has good aromatic properties, making it preferable in Portugal itself, where it is much cheaper than French oak.

RUSSIAN *Quercus sessilis*

Tight-grained with low aromatics and easy to confuse with French oak under blind conditions, this was the major oak in Bordeaux during the 19th century and up until the 1930s. Thus all the great old vintages owe something to it. Thanks to investment from Seguin Moreau, which set up a cooperage in the Adygey region near the Black Sea, French producers have begun to use Russian oak again, although it is mysteriously just 10 percent cheaper than French.

GRAPE VARIETIES

The grape variety used for a wine is the most influential factor in determining its taste. The factors that determine the inherent flavor of any grape variety are the same as those that determine the varietal taste of any fruit. How they affect the taste of wine is outlined below.

SIZE

The smaller the fruit, the more concentrated the flavor will be. Thus most classic grape varieties, such as Cabernet Sauvignon and Riesling, have small berries, although some varieties that rely more on elegance than power of concentration, such as the Pinot Noir, may yield large berries. Many varieties are known as *petit-* or *gros-something*, and it is usually the *petit* that is the better variety—Petit Vidure is Cabernet Sauvignon; Gros Vidure, Cabernet Franc.

SKIN STRUCTURE

The skin contains most of the aromatic characteristics with which we associate the varietal identity of any fruit. Its construction and thickness is, therefore, of paramount importance. For example, the thick-skinned Sauvignon Blanc produces an aromatic wine that, when ripe, varies in pungency from "peach" in a warm climate to "gooseberry" in a cool climate, and when underripe varies in herbaceousness, ranging from "grassy" to "elderflower" and even "cat's pee." Meanwhile the thin-skinned Sémillon produces a rather neutral wine, although its thin skin makes it susceptible to noble rot and is thus capable of producing one of the world's greatest botrytized sweet wines, with mind-blowing aromatics.

SKIN COLOR AND THICKNESS

A dark-colored, thick-skinned grape, such as Cabernet Sauvignon, produces very deep-colored wines, while the lighter-colored, thin-skinned grapes, such as Merlot, produce a less intense color.

ACID–SUGAR RATIO AND PRESENCE OF OTHER CONSTITUENTS

The grape's sugar content dictates the wine's alcohol level and the possibility of any natural sweetness; together with the acidity level, this determines the balance. The proportions of a grape's other constituents, or their products after fermentation, form the subtle nuances that differentiate the varietal characters. Although soil, rootstock, and climate have an effect on the ultimate flavor of the grape, the genetics of the vine dictate the end result.

THE VITIS FAMILY

The vine family is a large and diverse family of plants ranging from the tiny pot-plant Kangaroo Vine to Virginia Creeper. The Wine Vine Tree, (*see below*), shows how the *Vitis vinifera*, the classic winemaking species, relates to the rest of the vine family. The *Vitis vinifera* is one of many belonging to the subgenus *Euvites*. Other species in this subgenus are used for rootstock.

PHYLLOXERA VASTATRIX—PEST OR BLESSING?

The vine louse—*Phylloxera vastatrix*—that devastated the vineyards of Europe in the late 19th century still infests the soils of nearly all the world's winegrowing regions. At the time, it was considered the greatest disaster in the history of wine, but with hindsight, it was a blessing in disguise.

Before phylloxera arrived, many of Europe's greatest wine regions had gradually been devalued because of increased demand for their wines. This led to bulk-producing, inferior varieties being planted, and vineyards being extended into unsuitable lands. As phylloxera spread, it became apparent that every vine had to be grafted onto phylloxera-resistant American rootstock. This forced a much-needed rationalization, in which only the best sites in the classic regions were replanted and only noble vines were cultivated, a costly operation that vineyard owners in lesser areas could not afford. The grafting took France 50 years, and enabled the *Appellation d'Origine Contrôlée* system to be set up. It is hard to imagine what regional or varietal identities might now exist if phylloxera had not occurred.

ROOTSTOCK

Hundreds of rootstock varieties have been developed from various vine species, usually *Vitis berlandieri*, *V. riparia*, or *V. rupestris*, because they are the most phylloxera-resistant. The precise choice of rootstock is dependent on its suitability to the vinestock on which it is to be grafted as well as on its adaptability to the geographical location and soil type. The choice can increase or decrease a vine's productivity, and thus has a strong effect on the quality of the wine produced from the grapes. Generally, the lower the quantity, the higher the quality.

VITIS VINIFERA *Several thousand varieties*

Aligoté • Cabernet Franc • Cabernet Sauvignon • Chardonnay • Chenin Blanc • Gamay • Gewürztraminer • Grenache • Merlot • Muscat Blanc • Nebbiolo • Pinot Gris • Pinot Meunier • Pinot Noir • Riesling • Sangiovese • Sauvignon Blanc • Sémillon • Sylvaner • Syrah • Touriga Nacional • Viognier • Zinfandel • Others

Vitis rotundifolia • *Vitis munsoniana* • *Vitis popenoei* • *Vitis vinifera* • *Vitis riparia* • *Vitis labrusca* • *Vitis berlandieri* • *Vitis amurensis* • *Vitis rupestris* • *Vitis cariboea* • *Vitis argentifolia* • Others

SUBGENUS MUSCADINIAE

SUBGENUS EUVITES *60 species, but only* Vitis vinifera *is important for winemaking*

GENUS VITIS *Of the 10 genera belonging to the Vitaceae family, only the genus* Vitis *is important for winemaking*

BOTANICAL FAMILY *Vitaceae (also called Ampelidaceae)*

THE WINE VINE TREE

The green line running from the ground traces the parentage of Vitis vinifera, *the species from which all classic winemaking grapes come. Although* Vitis vinifera *is the most important species of the subgenus* Euvites, *wine is made from grape varieties from other species, notably* Vitis labrusca, *native to North America.*

GLOSSARY OF GRAPE VARIETIES

There are thousands of winemaking grape varieties grown throughout the world. The varieties that are the most significant, to one degree or another, in the areas where they are cultivated are profiled over the following pages.

CROSSES AND HYBRIDS

A cross between grape varieties within one species is called a cross, whereas a cross between varieties from different species is called a hybrid. Cross the same grape varieties more than once and the odds are that the new strains produced will not be the same. Thus *Sylvaner x Riesling* is not only the parentage of the Rieslaner, but also the Scheurebe, two totally different grapes. It is also possible to cross a variety with itself and produce a different grape. In this glossary, the parentage of crosses and hybrids is always in italic.

CLONES AND CLONING

Within varietal limitations, intensive selection can produce a vine to suit specific conditions, such as to increase yield, resist certain diseases, or to thrive in a particular climate. Identical clones of this vine can then be replicated an infinite number of times by microbiogenetic techniques. Clones are named by number and initial. For instance, "Riesling clone 88Gm" is the 88th clone of the Riesling variety produced at Geisenheim (Gm), the German viticultural research station. A "localized" clone is a vine that has evolved naturally under specific conditions within a particular environment. These may be named first by grape variety and then by locality and referred to as subvarieties. However, the name of the original variety is often entirely forgotten with the passing of time, so that the variety acquires a new name altogether.

GRAPE COLOR

Most white wines are made from "white" grapes, which actually range from green to amber-yellow. On the other hand, most red or rosé wines are made from "black" grapes, which vary from red to blue-black. White wine can also be made from most black grapes because, with only a few exceptions (categorized as *teinturier*, literally "dyer," grapes) only the skin is colored, not the juice. But red wine can be made only from black grapes, because it is pigments in the skin, called anthocyanins, that give the wine its color. The acidity in the skin's sap also affects the color of its wine: high acid levels gives a ruddy color, while the lower the acidity the more purple, and eventually violet, the wine becomes.

WHITE GRAPE VARIETIES

Note Some pink-colored varieties, such as Gewürztraminer and Pinot Gris, are included in this section because the wine they make is essentially white.

ALBALONGA
A *Rieslaner x Sylvaner* cross developed and grown in Germany for its naturally high sugar level and early-ripening qualities.

ALIGOTÉ
See box, below.

ALTESSE
The finest of Savoie's traditional varieties, this grape makes delightfully rich and fragrant wines.

ALVARINHO
The classic Vinho Verde grape, although it might not rank as a classic grape variety *per se*.

ARINTO
The Arinto is one of Portugal's potentially excellent white grapes. Its use in the small district of Bucelas is to make a crisp, lemony wine that ages well.

ARNEIS
Literally meaning "little rascal," this Piedmontese grape was so named because of its erratic ripening. Once threatened by commercial extinction, this delicately aromatic variety is now extremely fashionable.

ASSYRTIKO
One of the better-quality indigenous varieties of Greece.

AUXERROIS
At home in Alsace, Luxembourg, and England, Auxerrois makes a fatter wine than Pinot Blanc, so suits cooler situations. Its musky richness has immediate appeal, but it is inclined to low acidity and blowsiness in hotter climates.

BACCHUS
A (*Riesling x Sylvaner*) x *Müller-Thurgau* cross that is one of Germany's more superior crosses.

BORRADO DES MOSCAS
A Dão grape, literally called "fly droppings," Borrado des Moscas retains high natural acidity at high alcohol levels, making it well suited to white winemaking in hot areas.

BOUVIER
A modest-quality variety in Austria and one which, as Ranina, produces the "Tiger's Milk" wine of Slovenia.

BUAL
The richest and fattest of Madeira's four classic grape varieties.

CHARDONEL
Known as "Chard in Hell" to many a wine judge forced to taste its wines, Chardonel is a *Seyval x Chardonnay* cross made by Cornell University in 1953, but not released until 1990. So far the wines produced have been more bland than even the most anonymous Chardonnay.

CHARDONNAY
See box, opposite.

CHASSELAS
Responsible for the best-forgotten Pouilly-sur-Loire wines (not to be confused with Pouilly-Blanc Fumé), this variety is at its modest best in Switzerland's Valais (where it is known as the Fendant) and Alsace. Primarily a good grape for eating.

CHENIN BLANC
See box, opposite.

CLAIRETTE
A sugar-rich, intrinsically flabby grape best known for its many wines of southern France. It is the Muscat though, not the Clairette, which is chiefly responsible for the "Clairette de Die" in the Rhône.

COLOMBARD
This produces thin, acidic wine ideal for the distillation of Armagnac and Cognac. It has also adapted well to the hotter winelands of California and South Africa, where its high acidity is a positive attribute.

CRUCHEN BLANC
Widely cultivated, this variety usually, but incorrectly, has the tag of Riesling attached to it, such as Cape Riesling and Clare Riesling.

DELAWARE
This American hybrid of uncertain parentage was developed in Frenchtown, New Jersey, and propagated in Delaware, Ohio, in the mid-19th century. Although grown in New York State and Brazil, it is far more popular in Japan.

ALIGOTÉ
This is a thin-skinned grape of unexceptional quality grown in Burgundy and Bulgaria. It makes tart wines of moderate alcoholic content, but in exceptionally hot years they can have good weight and richness. The variety's best wines come from certain Burgundian villages, especially Bouzeron, where the quality may be improved by the addition of a little Chardonnay.

CHARDONNAY

This is the greatest nonaromatic dry white wine grape in the world, despite the proliferation of cheap, identikit Chardonnay wines that are churned out around the world. This classic variety is responsible for producing the greatest white Burgundies and is one of the three major grape types used in the production of Champagne.

CHENIN BLANC

A variety that acquired its name from Mont-Chenin in the Touraine district in about the 15th century, it can be traced back to Anjou, around A.D. 845. The grape has a good acidity level, thin skin, and a high natural sugar content, making it very suitable for either sparkling or sweet wines, although some dry wines, notably Savennières, are made from it.

EHRENFELSER
A *Riesling* x *Sylvaner* cross, the Ehrenfelser has turned out to be a *cul-de-sac* in British Columbia, Canada, where it remains the preserve of a few die-hards.

ELBLING
This variety was once held in high esteem in Germany and France. The major Mosel grape in the 19th century, it is now mostly confined to the Ober-Mosel where its very acid, neutral flavor makes it useful for German *Sekt*. In Alsace it was *Knipperlé* and its former position was such that one of the *grand cru* Guebwiller slopes was named after it.

EMERALD RIESLING
A *Muscadelle* x *Riesling* cross, this grape was developed for cultivation in California by a Professor Olmo of UC-Davis fame as the sister to his Ruby Cabernet cross.

FABER
A *Weissburgunder* x *Müller-Thurgau* cross grown in Germany, where it produces a fruity wine with a distinctive light Muscat aroma.

FOLLE BLANCHE
Traditionally used for the distillation of Armagnac and Cognac, the Folle Blanche grape also produces the Gros Plant wine of the Loire Valley.

FORTA
A little of this *Madeleine Angevine* x *Sylvaner* cross is grown in Germany, where it produces good-quality grapes that are rich in sugar.

FREISAMER
A *Sylvaner* x *Pinot Gris* cross that is grown in Germany and produces a full, neutral, Sylvaner-like wine.

FURMINT
This strong, distinctively flavored grape is the most important variety used to make Tokaji in Hungary.

GARGANEGA BIANCO
The principal grape used in the production of Soave.

GEWÜRZTRAMINER
See box, below.

GLORIA
A *Sylvaner* x *Müller-Thurgau* cross grown in Germany, where it yields grapes that are rich in sugar, but make rather neutral wines.

GRENACHE BLANC
This is the white Grenache variant that is widely planted in France and Spain. It is an ancient Spanish variety with the potential to produce a good-quality, full-bodied wine.

GRÜNER VELTLINER
This is the most important wine grape in Austria, where it produces fresh, well-balanced wines, with a light, fruity, sometimes slightly spicy, flavor. Top-quality Grüner Veltliner from the Wachau can have a penetrating pepperiness.

GUTENBORNER
This *Müller-Thurgau* x *Chasselas* cross is grown in Germany and England. It produces grapes with intrinsically high sugar levels, but makes rather neutral wines.

HARSLEVELŰ
A Hungarian grape that is the second most important Tokaji variety. It produces a full, rich, and powerfully perfumed wine.

HUXELREBE
A *Chasselas* x *Muscat Courtillier* cross that is grown in Germany and England, and is capable of producing good-quality wine.

JACQUÈRE
The workhorse grape of the Savoie, the Jacquère is subject to rot, has a neutral flavor and high acidity.

JOHANNISBERG RIESLING
This is a synonym often used to distinguish a wine that is made from the true Riesling grape. Many people believe that the Riesling is at its classic best when grown in the Rheingau vineyards of Johannisberg, thus the synonym most probably evolved as a way of indicating that a wine contained Riesling grapes "as grown in Johannisberg."

KANZLER
A *Müller-Thurgau* x *Sylvaner* cross that produces a good Sylvaner substitute in the Rheinhessen.

KERNER
A *Trollinger* x *Riesling* cross that produces wines with a high natural sugar content and good acidity, but a very light aroma.

LEN DE L'EL
Flavorsome, naturally sugar-rich grape that is used in Gaillac.

MACABÉO
This is a Spanish variety used to "lift" a sparkling Cava blend and give it freshness. Bearing the name of Viura, it is also responsible for the "new wave" of fresh, unoaked white Rioja.

MADELEINE ANGEVINE
This is a *Précoce de Malingre* x *Madeleine Royale* cross that is grown quite successfully in England, where it produces a characteristically light-bodied, aromatic wine.

MANSENG
The Gros Manseng and Petit Manseng are grown in southwestern France, and are well known mainly for producing the legendary Jurançon Moelleux.

MARIENSTEINER
A *Sylvaner* x *Rieslaner* cross that is grown in Germany and is generally considered superior to the Sylvaner.

MARSANNE
This grape makes fat, rich, full wines and is one of the two major varieties used to produce the rare white wines of Hermitage and Châteauneuf-du-Pape.

MAUZAC
A late-ripening grape with good acidity, grown in southwestern France, Mauzac is flexible in the wines it produces, but is particularly suitable for sparkling wine.

MELON DE BOURGOGNE
This variety was transplanted from Burgundy to Nantais where it replaced less hardy vines after the terrible winter of 1709. Most famous for its production of Muscadet. When fully ripe, it makes very flabby wines, lacking in acidity, although curiously it can be successful in California's warmer climes.

MORIO-MUSKAT
This *Sylvaner* x *Pinot Blanc* cross is widely grown in the Rheinpfalz and Rheinhessen of Germany. It has always been intriguing how such neutral parents could produce such

GEWÜRZTRAMINER

At its most clear-cut and varietally distinctive in Alsace (where it is never spelled with an umlaut), this variety produces very aromatic wines that are naturally low in acidity. The Gewürztraminer's famous spiciness is derived from terpenes, which are found in the grape's skins. The grapes have to be ripe, otherwise the wine will just have a soft rose-petal character, and the wine must not be acid-adjusted or the spice will lack breadth and potential complexity.

MUSCAT À PETITS GRAINS

There are two versions of this variety—the Muscat Blanc à Petits Grains and the Muscat Rosé à Petits Grains—and some vines that seem to produce a motley crop somewhere between the two. Where one is cultivated, the other is often intermingled or growing close by. The two greatest products of the Petits Grains are the dry wines of Alsace and the sweet and lightly fortified Muscat de Beaumes de Venise, although in the production of the former the variety is giving way to the Muscat Ottonel.

a powerfully aromatic offspring, but now we know that the Traminer is one of Sylvaner's parents, the answer is obviously in the genes.

MÜLLER-THURGAU

This variety was bred at Geisenheim in 1882 by Professor Hermann Müller, who hailed from the canton of Thurgau in Switzerland, and was named after him by August Dern in 1891. It was originally believed to be a *Riesling* x *Sylvaner* cross, but not one single plant has ever reverted to Sylvaner, and the closest resemblance to it is the Rabaner, a *Riesling (clone 88Gm)* x *Riesling (clone 64Gm)*. This seems to confirm the theory that the Müller-Thurgau is, in fact, a self-pollinated Riesling seed. It is more prolific than the Riesling, has a typically flowery bouquet and good fruit, but lacks the Riesling's characteristic sharpness of definition. Although this variety has a justifiably important position in the production of cheap German *Tafelwein*, its cultivation in the classic Riesling vineyards of the Mosel does tend to devalue that

great wine region. It is widely planted in English and New Zealand vineyards, although in both cases the acreage devoted to it has shrunk markedly since the 1990s.

MULTANER

A *Riesling* x *Sylvaner* cross, a small amount of this variety is grown in Germany. However, the area planted is declining because the grapes need to be very ripe.

MUSCADELLE

A singular variety that has nothing to do with the Muscat family, although it does have a musky aroma and there is, confusingly, a South African synonym for the Muscat—the Muskadel. In Bordeaux, small quantities of this grape add a certain lingering "after-smell" to some of the sweet wines, but the Muscadelle is at its sublime best in Australia, where it is called the Tokay and produces a rich and sweet "liqueur wine."

MUSCAT

A family name for numerous related varieties, subvarieties, and localized

clones of the same variety, all of which have a distinctive musky aroma and a pronounced grapey flavor. The wines that are produced range from dry to sweet, still to sparkling, and fortified.

MUSCAT À PETITS GRAINS
See box, left.

MUSCAT D'ALEXANDRIE

An extremely important grape in South Africa, where it makes mostly sweet, but some dry, wines. In France, it is responsible for the fortified wine Muscat de Rivesaltes (a very tiny production of unfortified dry Muscat is also made in Rivesaltes), and the grape is also used for both wine and raisin production in California.

MUSCAT OTTONEL

An East European variety which, because of its relative hardiness, is now in the process of replacing the Muscat à Petits Grains in Alsace.

NOBLESSA

This is a low-yielding *Madeleine Angevine* x *Sylvaner* cross grown in Germany, which produces grapes with a high sugar level.

NOBLING

A *Sylvaner* x *Chasselas* cross grown in Baden, Germany, its grapes have high sugar and acidity levels.

ONDENC

A grape once widely planted in southwestern France and popular in Bergerac, it is now grown more in Australia than in France. Its acidity makes it useful for sparkling wines.

OPTIMA

Developed in 1970, this (*Riesling* x *Sylvaner*) x *Müller-Thurgau* cross is already widely grown in Germany because it ripens even earlier than the early-ripening Müller-Thurgau.

ORTEGA

A *Müller-Thurgau* x *Siegerrebe* cross that is grown in both Germany and

England, its aromatic grapes have naturally high sugar and make a pleasantly fragrant and spicy wine.

PALOMINO

The classic sherry grape variety.

PARELLADA

The major white grape variety of Catalonia, used for still wines and sparkling Cava, in which it imparts a distinctive aroma and is used to soften the firm Xarel-lo grape.

PERLE

A *Gewürztraminer* x *Müller-Thurgau* cross, this grape can survive winter temperatures as low as -22°F (-30°C), and produces a light, fragrant, and fruity wine, but in low yields.

PINOT BLANC

A variety that is perhaps at its best in Alsace, where it is most successful, producing fruity, well-balanced wines with good grip and alcohol content. Plantings of the true Pinot Blanc are gradually diminishing worldwide.

PINOT GRIS

See box, below left.

POULSARD

The Jura's famous grape with pink skin and pink juice can produce a fine and aromatic *vin gris*.

PROSECCO

This grape is responsible for producing a great deal of very ordinary Italian sparkling wine.

RABANER

This Riesling *(clone 88Gm)* x Riesling *(clone 64Gm)* cross has the dubious honor of being the variety that most resembles the Müller-Thurgau.

RABIGATO

This is the main white port grape variety. It is also known as Rabo da Ovelha, or "ewe's tail."

PINOT GRIS

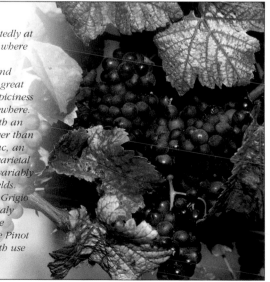

A variety undoubtedly at its best in Alsace, where it can produce succulent, rich, and complex wines of great quality, it has a spiciness seldom found elsewhere. When coupled with an acidity that is lower than that of Pinot Blanc, an absence of spicy varietal definition will invariably be due to high yields. This is why Pinot Grigio in northeastern Italy generally lacks the intensity of Alsace Pinot Gris, although both use the same clones.

RIESLING

The classic German grape produces a zesty, citrusy, intensely flavored wine of great minerally complexity, length, and longevity. When grown on certain soils, the terpenes in Riesling benefit from bottle-age and can, after several years, develop a bouquet reminiscent of gasoline. Alsace and Austria make most (not all) of the best dry Riesling. In Australia the wine from this grape has, by and large, a simplistic lime fruit character that is prone to going like gasoline in a relatively short while, but lacks the finesse and complexity of truly classic gasoline aromas.

REGNER

The parents of this *Luglienca Bianca* x *Gamay* cross are a curious combination. Why anyone would consider crossing a table grape with the red wine grape of Beaujolais to create a German white wine variety is a mystery. Predictably it produces sugar-rich grapes and mild, Müller-Thurgau-like wines.

REICHENSTEINER

This *Müller-Thurgau* x *Madeleine Angevine* x *Calabreser-Fröhlich* cross is grown in Germany and England. Its sugar-rich grapes produce a mild, delicate, somewhat neutral, Sylvaner-like wine.

RHODITIS

This grape is used as a supporting variety in the making of Retsina, a use only eclipsed by its suitability for the distilling pot!

RIESLANER

A *Riesling* x *Sylvaner* cross mainly grown in Franken, Germany, where it produces sugar-rich grapes and full-bodied, rather neutral wines.

RIESLING

See box, opposite.

RKATSITELI

A grape variety that is grown extensively in Russia, on a scale that would cover the vineyards of Champagne at least 10 times over. The Soviets consider it to be a high-quality wine grape; it is also grown in Bulgaria, China, California, and New York State.

ROBOLA

Confined to the island of Cephalonia, this is a good-quality Greek grape.

ROMORANTIN

An obscure variety that is confined to the Loire Valley, Romorantin can produce a delicate, attractive, and flowery wine if it is not overcropped.

ROUSSANNE

One of two major varieties used to produce the rare white wines of Hermitage and Châteauneuf-du-Pape in France's Rhône Valley, this grape makes the finer, more delicate wines, while those made from the Marsanne tend to be fatter and richer.

SACY

A minor grape variety that produces bland "stretching" wine and is grown in small quantities in the Chablis district. Its high acidity could make it very useful in the production of sparkling wines.

SAINT-ÉMILION

This is a synonym for the Ugni Blanc in France and for the Sémillon in Romania.

SAUVIGNON BLANC

See box, below.

SAUVIGNONASSE

This literally means "Sauvignon-like" and is, in fact, the Sauvignon Vert, which confusingly is no relation to the Sauvignon Blanc. According to Pierre Galet, this is the Tocai Friulano, although some find this hard to accept. The high-yielding Sauvignonasse is grown in Chile, where it used to masquerade as Sauvignon Blanc until the mid-1990s.

SAVAGNIN

This grape is a nonaromatic Traminer, and it is responsible for the sherry-like *vin jaune* of the Jura, of which the best known is Château Chalon. The Savagnin Rosé is the nonaromatic Traminer Rosé (from which the highly aromatic Gewürztraminer evolved) and this grape grows in the village of Heiligenstein, Alsace, where it is known as the Klevener de Heiligenstein.

SAVATIANO

This grape variety was used by the Greeks to make Retsina. A pure, unresinated Savatiano called Kanza is made in Attica, the heartland of Retsina.

SÉMILLON

In Sauternes and Barsac, this is the grape susceptible to "noble rot." Some say its aroma is reminiscent of lanolin, but as pure lanolin is virtually odorless, the comparison hardly conveys the Sémillon's distinctive bouquet. For dry wine, this grape is at its best in Australia, particularly the Hunter Valley, where its lime fruit takes to oak like a duck to water, whereas bottle-aged Sémillon can be sublime after several decades.

SCHEUREBE

A *Riesling* x *Sylvaner* cross, this is one of the best of Germany's new varieties. When ripe, it makes very good aromatic wines, but, if it is harvested too early, very herbaceous cat's-pee.

SCHÖNBURGER

A *Spätburgunder* x (*Chasselas Rosé* x *Muscat Hamburg*) cross, this grape is grown in Germany and England. It produces sugar-rich grapes that make wine with good aromatic qualities but low acidity.

SÉMILLON

See box, above.

SEPTIMER

A *Gewürztraminer* x *Müller-Thurgau* cross grown in Germany, where it is early-ripening and produces sugar-rich grapes that are made into aromatic wines.

SERCIAL

This classic grape of Madeira is reputed to be a distant relative of the Riesling. However, judging by its totally different leaf shape, this seems rather unlikely.

SEYVAL BLANC

This *Seibel 5656* x *Seibel 4986* hybrid is the most successful of the many Seyve-Villard crosses. It is grown primarily in New York State and England, where it produces attractive wines.

SIEGERREBE

This is a *Madeleine Angevine* x *Gewürztraminer* cross, a grape that is widely grown in Germany.

SYLVANER

See box, next page.

SYMPHONY

Plantations of this *Muscat d'Alexandrie* x *Grenache Gris* cross rapidly increased in California in the mid-1990s, althouth it was developed by Professor Olmo as long ago as 1940. The wine it makes is usually off-dry with a distinctly flowery-grapey Muscat aroma.

TORRONTÉS

Various different clones of this lightly aromatic grape are found throughout South America, but particularly in Argentina. No relation to the Spanish Torrontés (which is a local synonym for the Monastrell Blanco) or Torrontés Riojano (which is a local synonym for the Malvoisie).

TRAMINETTE

A *JS 23–416* x *Gewürztraminer* hybrid that was developed by Cornell University and released in 1996, since when it has become planted here and there throughout the Atlantic Northeast. Some American winemakers consider it superior to Gewürztraminer because of its significantly higher acidity, but this interferes with aromatics, which are more "spiky" than the Gewürztraminer's classic broad-spice bouquet. Notwithstanding this, there have been successes, even if they are few and far between. Generally perceived as a cool-climate grape, the Traminette's high acidity does however raise the question of whether it might not fare much better in the warmer climes of California.

TROUSSEAU GRIS

This grape is now more widely grown in California and New Zealand than in its traditional home of the northern Jura, France. It is yet another grape that has been erroneously tagged with the Riesling name in the New World but does not resemble that grape in the slightest.

UGNI BLANC

A variety that usually makes light, even thin, wines that have to be distilled, the Ugni Blanc is ideal for making Armagnac and Cognac. There are a few exceptions, but most wines are light, fresh, and quaffing at their very best.

SAUVIGNON BLANC

Sauvignon Blanc is at its best defined in New Zealand, particularly Marlborough, and is still a long way off achieving a similar level of quality and consistency in its home location of the Loire Valley. It is improving in Bordeaux, where it is also used in Sauternes and Barsac blends. Some exciting wines have begun to emerge from the Cape winelands, South Africa (ignoring those that are artificially flavored), but California remains hugely disappointing, even though its vines are the same Sauvignon Blanc clone as New Zealand.

SYLVANER
Originally from Austria, this variety is widely planted throughout Central Europe. It is prolific, early maturing, and yields the dry wines of Franken and Alsace. It is also widely believed to be the Zierfandler of Austria. Sylvaner has a tart, earthy, yet neutral flavor, which takes on a tomato-like richness in the bottle. This grape is now known to be the offspring of the Österreichisch Weiss and Traminer.

VIOGNIER
This individual, shy-bearing variety was until relatively recently confined to a tiny part of the Rhône Valley, where it produced the famous wines of Condrieu and Château Grillet. Although this variety crept out to Australia in the 1970s, the real explosion did not occur until the 1990s in Languedoc-Roussillon and California. At its best, Viognier has a lush, aromatic quality, with distinctive peachy character, but it is all too often over-oaked.

VERDELHO
A successful grape variety for making white wines in Australia, the Verdelho is possibly connected to the Verdello of Italy. Verdelho is best known, however, as a classic grape variety that is grown on Madeira for the production of the island's fortified wine (a Verdelho *tinto* also exists on the island).

VERDICCHIO
As well as being used to make Verdicchio wine, this grape is also employed for blending.

VILLARD BLANC
This *Seibel 6468 x Seibel 6905* hybrid is the widest cultivated of the Seyve-Villard crosses in France. Its slightly bitter, iron-rich wine cannot be compared with the attractive wine of the Seyve-Villard 5276 or Seyval Blanc grown in England.

VIOGNIER
See box, above.

WELSCHRIESLING
No relation whatsoever to the true Riesling, this variety is grown throughout Europe, producing ordinary medium-dry to medium-sweet white wines.

WÜRZER
A German variety with *Gewürz-traminer x Müller-Thurgau* origins.

XAREL-LO
A Spanish grape variety vital to the sparkling Cava industry, Xarel-lo makes firm, alcoholic wines.

BLACK GRAPE VARIETIES

AGIORGITIKO
An excellent indigenous Greek grape variety that is responsible for the rich and often oak-aged wines of Nemea.

ALICANTE BOUSCHET
A *Petit Bouschet x Grenache* cross, this is a *teinturier* grape, with vivid, red juice. It was a favorite during Prohibition, when the rich color of its juice enabled bootleggers to stretch wines with water and sugar. Although the cultivation of this grape has increased by 42 percent since 1995, Alicante Bouschet is used primarily for port-style wines today, and is seldom seen as a varietal table wine. The secret of a good Alicante Bouschet table wine is in achieving the tannins, structure, and mouthfeel that are compatible with its naturally inky-purple color. Many moons ago, Angelo Papagni's death-defying Alicante Bouschet was not to be missed, and Coturri and Jim Clendenen (with Il Podere dell'Olivos) have at times dabbled very successfully with this variety. Rainbow Ridge ("the first gay-owned winery in the country") has yet to demonstrate that its 2001 is more than a flash in the pan. Which leaves the organically minded Topolos as the only consistently high-quality producer of Alicante Bouschet nowadays.

BARBERA
A prolific Italian variety grown in Piedmont, the Barbera makes light, fresh, fruity wines that are sometimes very good.

BASTARDO
This is the classic port grape and is identified as the Trousseau, an ancient variety once widely cultivated in the Jura, France.

BLACK SPANISH
This grape is making something of a minor revival in Texas, where it was widely grown in the 1830s to make a portlike wine. This is, in fact, Lenoir or Jacquez, and contrary to those who believe it to be a natural *aestivalis-cinerea-vinifera* hybrid, 100 percent *vinifera*.

CABERNET FRANC
See box, right.

CABERNET PFEFFER
A grape of disputed origins. The French call this Pfeffer Cabernet (also called Fer Servadou), whereas the Americans have transposed the French name into Cabernet Pfeffer, which for Anglo-Saxons slips off the tongue easily and is more rational. There are various opinions as to its origins in the U.S., the most plausible being a 19th-century cross (but no one knows what with or who made the cross, and cannot be more precise than a 100-year-old span). Only two U.S. sources of this variety exist today: the 100-year-old Wirz Family vineyard in Monterey's Cienega Valley, California, and one of Casa Nuestra's vineyards in Oakville, where the vines were planted in the 1940s.

CABERNET SAUVIGNON
See box, opposite.

CARIGNAN
A Spanish grape grown extensively in southern France and California. One of its synonyms—Mataro—is a common name for the Mourvèdre, which also provides a well-colored wine, but one that is not quite as harsh. A Carignan Blanc and Gris also exist.

CARMENÈRE
An old *bordelais* variety that was almost extinct, until it was discovered in Chile posing as Merlot, and then in Franciacorta, where it was pretending to be

CABERNET FRANC
Cabernet Franc is grown throughout the world, but particularly in Bordeaux. It fares best as Bouchet in St-Émilion and at Pomerol, across the Dordogne River, where Cabernet Sauvignon is less well represented. Grown under neutral conditions, it might not be easy to distinguish any significant varietal differences between the two Cabernets, but, suited as they are to different situations, the Cabernet Franc tends to produce a slightly earthy style of wine that is very aromatic, but has less fine characteristics on the palate when compared to the Cabernet Sauvignon.

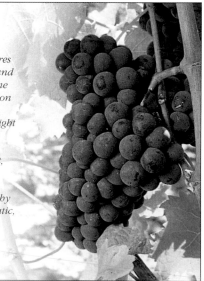

CABERNET SAUVIGNON

The noblest variety of Bordeaux, the Cabernet Sauvignon, rich in color, aroma, and depth, is vitally important to the classic Médoc wines. Many of its classical traits have been transplanted as far afield as California, Chile, and Australia. The complexities that this grape can achieve transcend simplistic comparisons to cedar, blackcurrants, or violets. The Cabernet Sauvignon's parents are now known to be Cabernet Franc and Sauvignon Blanc.

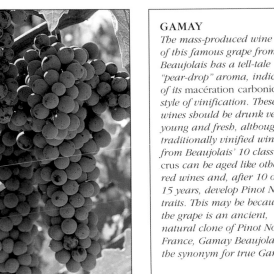

GAMAY

The mass-produced wine of this famous grape from Beaujolais has a tell-tale "pear-drop" aroma, indicative of its macération carbonique style of vinification. These wines should be drunk very young and fresh, although traditionally vinified wines from Beaujolais' 10 classic crus can be aged like other red wines and, after 10 or 15 years, develop Pinot Noir traits. This may be because the grape is an ancient, natural clone of Pinot Noir. In France, Gamay Beaujolais is the synonym for true Gamay.

Cabernet Franc (interestingly, one of Carmenère's synonyms is Grand Vidure, while one of Cabernet Franc's names is Gros Vidure). So far, the Carmenère produced in Franciacorta has more finesse than those in Chile, but overall there is a tendency to produce wines with a marked blackcurrant character that seldom develops complexity.

CÉSAR
A minor grape variety of moderate quality that is still used in some areas of Burgundy, most notably for Bourgogne Irancy.

CINSAULT
A prolific grape found mainly in southern Rhône and Languedoc-Roussillon vineyards, where it makes robust, well-colored wines. It is best blended, as happens at Châteauneuf-du-Pape, for example.

CONCORD
The widest-cultivated variety in North America outside of California, this variety has an extremely pronounced "foxy" flavor.

DOLCETTO
Underrated variety found in northwestern Italy, where it is often overcropped, but can be delightful when yields are restricted.

GAMAY
See box, above.

GRACIANO
An important variety used in the production of Rioja, where a small amount lends richness and fruit to a blend, Graciano could be the next pure varietal to grab the headlines.

GRENACHE
See box, right.

GROLLEAU
A prolific grape with a high natural sugar content, it is important for the bulk production of Anjou rosé, but rarely interesting in terms of quality.

KADARKA
Hungary's most widely cultivated grape variety is grown throughout the Balkans. It was once thought to be the same as the Zinfandel, but this theory no longer persists. It makes pleasant, light, and fruity wine.

LAMBRUSCO
An Italian variety, this is famous for its production of the medium-sweet, red, frothy wine of the same name in the Emilia-Romagna area.

LIMBERGER
An Austrian variety (also called Blaufränkisch) that makes a relatively simple, light red wine. This grape is also grown in the Atlantic Northeast, where it is more commonly referred to as Lemberger (a name that is also used elsewhere, erroneously, as a synonym for the Gamay).

MALBEC
This grape is traditionally used in Bordeaux blends in order to provide color and tannin. It is also grown in the Loire, Cahors, and Mediterranean regions, among many others, and was the grape responsible for the "black wine of Cahors"—a legendary name, if not wine, in the 19th century. However, Cahors is now made from a blend of grapes and is an infinitely superior wine to its predecessor.

MAZUELO
A variety grown in Rioja, it is believed to be the Carignan, although it bears little resemblance to it, and produces wines of light, yet rich, fruit and low alcohol.

MERLOT
See box, next page.

MONTEPULCIANO
A late-ripening variety that performs best in the Abruzzi region of Italy, where its wines are very deep in color, and can either be full of soft, fat, luscious fruit, or made in a much firmer, more tannic, style.

MONASTRELL
An underrated Spanish variety that is usually hidden in blends. However, it does have a full and distinctive flavor and could make individual wines of some appeal.

MONDEUSE
This variety may have originally hailed from Friuli in northeastern Italy, where it is known as the Refosco. It is now planted as far afield as the Savoie in France, parts of the U.S., including California, and in Switzerland, Italy, the Argentine, and Australia, where it is often an important constituent of the fortified port-type wines.

MOURVÈDRE
This excellent-quality grape has been used more than other lesser varieties in Châteauneuf-du-Pape blends in recent years. It is grown extensively throughout southern France, and, under the name of the Mataro, also in Spain. This is one of Australia's widest-cultivated black grapes, but a declining force in southern California.

NEBBIOLO
See box, next page.

NORTON
Also known as Cynthiana, although at one time Norton and Cynthiana were thought to be different varieties. Described accurately by some of its proponents as "The Real American Grape" because, unlike Zinfandel, Norton (or Cynthiana) is native to the U.S. It is pure *Vitis aestivalis*, not *vinifera*, but does not have any "foxy" character. Norton yields very small grapes with high pip ratio, necessitating *déstelage* to avoid excessively harsh tannins in the wine. Acidity is high, with an unusually high proportion of malic acidity, and the wine has the unnerving ability seemingly to "stain" glass! That said, it is the only wild grape capable of producing fine wine.

PAMID
This is the most widely cultivated of Bulgaria's indigenous black grape varieties. It makes light and fruity quaffing wine.

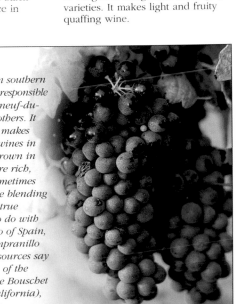

GRENACHE

The Grenache is grown in southern France, where it is partly responsible for the wines of Châteauneuf-du-Pape, Tavel, and many others. It is the mainstay of Rioja, makes port-style and light rosé wines in California, and is also grown in South Africa. Its wines are rich, warm, and alcoholic, sometimes too much so, and require blending with other varieties. The true Grenache has nothing to do with the Grenache de Logroño of Spain, which is, in fact, the Tempranillo or Tinto de Rioja. Some sources say the Alicante (a synonym of the Grenache) is the Alicante Bouschet (or plain Bouschet in California), but this too is misleading.

MERLOT

Merlot produces nicely colored wines, soft in fruit but capable of great richness. It is invaluable in Bordeaux, bringing fruity lusciousness and a velvet quality to wines that might otherwise be rather hard and austere. It is the chief grape in Château Pétrus, which is the top name in Pomerol.

PINOT MEUNIER

An important variety in Champagne, where vinified white gives more upfront appeal of fruit than the Pinot Noir when young, and is therefore essential for early-drinking Champagnes. Its characteristics are more immediate, but less fine and somewhat earthier than those of the Pinot Noir. The Pinot Meunier is extensively cultivated in the Marne Valley area of Champagne, where its resistance to frost makes it the most suitable vine. Now cropping up all over the place, and can make a red wine very similar to Pinot Noir.

PETIT VERDOT

A grape that has been used to good effect in Bordeaux because it is a late ripener, bringing acidity to the overall balance of a wine. Certain modern techniques of viticulture and vinification have rendered it less valuable, which might prove to be a pity, because it also produces a characterful, long-lived, and tannic wine when it is sufficiently ripe.

PETITE SIRAH

An ancient cross between Syrah and Peloursin, the Petite Sirah seems more at home in California than its native France.

PINEAU D'AUNIS

This grape is best known for its supporting role in the production of Rosé d'Anjou.

PINOTAGE

A *Pinot Noir* x *Cinsault* cross developed in 1925, it occupies an important position in South African viticulture, where its rustic and high-toned wine is greatly appreciated.

PINOT MEUNIER

See box, above.

PINOT NOIR

See box, below.

PORTUGIESER

The most widely planted black grape variety in Germany, it originates in the Danube district of Austria, not in Portugal as its name suggests. It makes very ordinary and extremely light red wine, so it is often used in bad years to blend with the too acidic white wine.

RONDINELLA

An Italian variety, secondary to the Corvina grape in terms of area planted, it is used in the production of Bardolino and Valpolicella.

ROTBERGER

A *Trollinger* x *Riesling* cross, the parents seem an odd couple, but the offspring is surprisingly successful, producing some excellent rosé wines.

RUBY CABERNET

An American *Carignan* x *Cabernet*

Sauvignon cross that originated in 1936, first fruited in 1940, and made its first wine in 1946.

SANGIOVESE

This is the principal variety used in Chianti. In a pure varietal form it can lack fruit and have a metallic finish.

SYRAH

See box, opposite.

TANNAT

This grape originated from the Basque region, and has the potential to produce deeply colored, tannic wines of great longevity (although there are certain modern methods of vinification that often change the traditional character of Tannat wines). The variety's best-known wines are the attractive red Madiran and Irouléguy. A little Tannat wine is used for blending purposes in and around the town of Cahors.

TEMPRANILLO

This is the most important variety in Rioja, where it is traditional to blend the grapes, although many pure

Tempranillo wines of excellent quality are made. It is capable of producing long-lived wines of some finesse and complexity. It is also an important variety in Argentina.

TOURIGA FRANCESA

This classic port grape is no relation of the Touriga Nacional. Its wine is less concentrated, but of fine quality.

TOURIGA NACIONAL

The finest port grape in the entire Douro, it produces fantastically rich and tannic wine, with masses of fruit, and is capable of great longevity and complexity.

VERDELHO TINTO

A classic Madeira grape.

XYNOMAVRO

Xyno means "acid" and "mavro" black, an indication of how dark and long-lived the wines of this excellent Greek variety can be.

ZINFANDEL

See box, opposite.

NEBBIOLO

Famous for its production of Barolo, this grape is also responsible, totally or in part, for the other splendid wines of Piedmont in Italy, such as Gattinara, Barbaresco, Carema, and Donnaz. It often needs to be softened by the addition of Bonarda grapes, which have the same role as Merlot grapes in Bordeaux. In fact, Merlot is used in Lombardy to soften Nebbiolo for the production of Valtellina and Valtellina Superiore wines, of which Sassella can be the most velvety of all.

PINOT NOIR

This is one of the classic varieties of Champagne, but its greatest fame lies in Burgundy. In the right place, and under ideal climatic conditions, the Pinot Noir can produce the richest, most velvet-smooth wines in the world. Depending on both climate and ripeness, its varietal flavor can range from cherries to strawberries. Great Pinot Noir is also made in California (notably Russian River and Santa Barbara), Oregon and Central Otago, New Zealand.

SYRAH

Because the name of this grape derived from Shiraz (which Australia has adopted), the capital of Fars, the idea has sprung up that this variety must have originated in Persia. We now know that it is pure French in its breeding, being the progeny of two minor varieties, the Mondeuse Blanche and Dureza. The Syrah makes fashionably dark-colored red wines in many countries.

ZINFANDEL

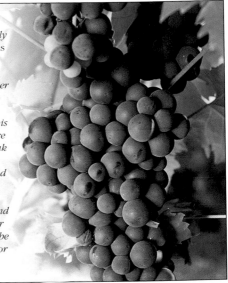

Once thought to be the only indigenous American Vitis vinifera grape, Zinfandel has now been positively identified by Isozyme "finger printing" as the Primitivo grape of southern Italy. However, the origins of this grape are Croatian, where it is known as the Crljenak Kastelanski. Depending on the vinification method used, Zinfandel can produce many different styles of wine, from rich and dark to light and fruity or nouveau style. They can be dry or sweet; white, rosé or red; dessert or sparkling.

GRAPE VARIETY SYNONYMS

Many varieties of grape are known by several different synonyms. The Malbec grape, for example, has at least 34 different names, including Pressac, Auxerrois, Balouzet, Cot, Estrangey, and Grifforin. This would not be too confusing if the synonyms applied, uniquely, to the same grape variety, but unfortunately this is not the case. The Malbec is a good example. A black grape, it is known as the Auxerrois in Cahors, but in Alsace and Chablis, the Auxerrois is a white grape, while in other parts of France, the Malbec is known as the Cahors!

SYNONYMS RELATING TO LOCALIZED clones or subvarieties are often regarded as singularly separate varieties in their own right. The Italian Trebbiano, itself a synonym for the French Ugni Blanc, has many subvarieties recognized by the Italian vine regulations. Also, many synonyms revolve around the name of another grape variety, although they are not necessarily related. Ampelographers distinguish between "erroneous" and "misleading" synonyms. The former refers to varieties that have mistakenly been given the name of another, totally different variety, whereas the latter refers to varieties whose names suggest, incorrectly, that they are related to another variety. For example, the Pinot Chardonnay, which is Chardonnay, is not remotely related to any Pinot variety whatsoever.

Albariño—Alvarinho
Alben—Elbling
Albig—Elbling
Alcaing—Macabéo
Alcabéo—Macabéo
Alicante—Grenache
Alicante Grenache—Grenache
Alva (in Portugal)—Elbling
Alzeyer Perle—Perle
Angélicant—Muscadelle
Angélico—Muscadelle
Aragad—Grenache
Aragonez—Tempranillo
Arnaison—Chardonnay
Aubaine—Chardonnay
Auvernat—Pinot Noir
Auvernat Blanc—Muscadelle
Auvernat Gris—Pinot Gris
Auvernat Gris—Pinot Meunier
Auxerrois—Malbec
Auxerrois Gris—Pinot Gris
Auxois—Pinot Gris

Baiyu—Rkatsitel
Balkan Kadarka—Kadarka
Balouzet—Malbec
Balzac—Mourvèdre
Banatski Rizling—Welschriesling
Beaunois—Chardonnay
Beaunois—Pinot Blanc
Beli Muscat—Muscat Blanc
    à Petits Grains
Beni Carlo—Mourvèdre
Béquin (in Bordeaux)—Ondenc
Bergeron—Roussanne
Bical Tinto—Touriga Nacional
Bidure—Cabernet Franc
Bidure—Cabernet Sauvignon
Biela Sladka Grasica—Welschriesling
Bigney—Merlot
Black Hamburg—Trollinger
Black Malvoisie—Cinsault
Blanc d'Anjou—Chenin Blanc
Blanc de Troyes—Aligoté
Blanc Doux—Sémillon

Blanc Fumé—Sauvignon Blanc
Blanc Select—Ondenc
Blanc Vert—Sacy
Blanche Feuille—Pinot Meunier
Blanc-lafitte—Mauzac
Blanquette—Clairette
Blanquette—Colombard
Blanquette—Ondenc
Blauburgunder—Pinot Noir
Blauer Limberger—Blaufränkisch
Blauer Malvasier—Trollinger
Blauer Spätburgunder—Pinot Noir
Blauer Trollinger—Trollinger
Blauer Zweigelt—Zweigelt
Blaufränkisch—Gamay
Bobal—Monastrell
Bois Dur—Carignan
Bordeleza Belcha—Tannat
Borgogna Crna—Gamay
Bötzinger—Sylvaner
Bouchet—Cabernet Franc
Bouchet—Cabernet Sauvignon
Bourdalès—Cinsault
Bourguignon Noir—Gamay
Bouschet Sauvignon—Cabernet Franc
Bouschet Sauvignon—Cabernet Sauvignon
Bouviertraube—Bouvier
Bovale—Monastrell
Breton—Cabernet Franc
Briesgaver—Elbling
Briesgaver Riesling—Elbling
Brown Muscat—Muscat Blanc
    à Petits Grains
Brunello (in Montalcino)—Sangiovese
Buisserate—Jacquère
Burger Elbling—Elbling
Burgundi Gamet—Gamay
Burgundi Kék—Gamay

Burgundi Lagtchi—Lagrein
Burgundi Mlc—Pinot Noir
Burgundi Nagyszemu—Gamay
Burgundske Sede—Pinot Gris
Burgundské Modré—Pinot Gris
Cabarnelle—Carmenère
Cabernet—Cabernet Franc
Cabernet Gris—Cabernet Franc
Cahors—Malbec
Calabrese—Sangiovese
Camobraque—Folle Blanche
Cape Riesling (in South Africa)—Cruchen Blanc
Carignan Noir—Carignan
Carignane—Carignan
Cariñena—Carignan
Carmelin—Petit Verdot
Carmenelle—Carmenère
Carmenet—Cabernet Franc
Catalan—Carignan
Catalan—Mourvèdre
Catape—Muscadelle
Cavalier—Len de l'El
Cencibel—Tempranillo
Chalosse—Folle Blanche
Chardonnay—Chasselas
Chardonnay—Pinot Blanc
Chasselas—Chardonnay
Chasselas Blanc—Chasselas
Chasselas Doré—Chasselas
Chaudenet Gras—Aligoté
Chenin Noir—Pineau d'Aunis
Chevier—Sémillon
Chevrier—Sémillon
Chiavennasca—Nebbiolo
Chira—Syrah
Christkindltraube—Gewürztraminer
Cinq-saou—Cinsault
Cinsaut—Cinsault
Clairette à Grains Ronds—Ugni Blanc

Clairette Blanc—Clairette
Clairette Blanche—Clairette
Clairette de Vence—Ugni Blanc
Clairette Ronde—Ugni Blanc
Clare Riesling (in Australia)—
    Cruchen Blanc
Clevner—Gewürztraminer
Clevner—Pinot Blanc
Codarka—Kadarka
Collemusquette—Muscadelle
Colombar—Colombard
Colombier—Colombard
Colombier—Sémillon
Cortaillod—Pinot Noir
Corvina Veronese—Corvina
Cot—Malbec
Cot à Queue Rouge—Pineau d'Aunis
Crabutet Noir—Merlot
Crna Moravka—Blaufränkisch
Crucillant—Sémillon
Cruina—Corvina
Crujillon—Carignan
Cugnette—Jacquère
Cuviller—Cinsault
Dannery—Romorantin
Dorin—Chasselas
Douce Noir—Dolcetto
Douzanelle—Muscadelle
Dreimanner—Gewürztraminer
Drumin—Gewürztraminer
Dusty Miller—Pinot Meunier
Edeltraube—Gewürztraminer
Elben—Elbling
Enragé—Folle Blanche
Enrageade—Folle Blanche
Entournerien—Syrah
Epinette Blanche—Chardonnay
Ermitage Blanc—Marsanne
Espagna—Cinsault
Espar—Mourvèdre
Esparte—Mourvèdre
Estrangey—Malbec
Estreito—Rabigato
Etaulier—Malbec
Etranger—Malbec
Farine—Sacy
Fauvet—Pinot Gris
Fehérburgundi—Pinot Blanc
Feiner Weisser Burgunder—
    Chardonnay
Fendant—Chasselas
Fendant Blanc—Chasselas
Fermin Rouge—Gewürztraminer
Fié dans le Neuvillois—
    Sauvignon Blanc
Flaischweiner—Gewürztraminer
Folle Enrageat—Folle Blanche
Formentin (in Hungary)—Savagnin
Franken—Sylvaner
Franken Riesling—Sylvaner
Frankenriesling—Sylvaner
Frankenthaler—Trollinger
Frankinja Crna—Gamay
Frankinja Modra—Gamay
Frankisch—Gewürztraminer
Frankovka—Limberger
Frankovka Modrá—Limberger
Frauentraube—Chasselas
Fréaux Hatif—a Gamay *teinturier*
French Colombard—Colombard
Frenscher—Gewürztraminer
Fromenté—Savagnin
Fromenteau Gris—Pinot Gris
Fromenteau Rouge—Gewürztraminer
Fromentot—Pinot Gris
Frontignac—Muscat Blanc à Petits Grains
Fumé Blanc—Sauvignon Blanc
Fuszeres—Gewürztraminer
Gaamez—Gamay
Gamai—Gamay
Gamay Beaujolais—Gamay
Gamay Blanc—Melon de Bourgogne
Gamay Blanc à Feuille Rond—
    Melon de Bourgogne
Gamay Castille—a Gamay *teinturier*

Gamay de Bouze—a Gamay *teinturier*
Gamay de Chaudenay—a Gamay
    teinturier
Gamay Fréaux—a Gamay *teinturier*
Gamay Noir—Gamay
Gamay Noir à Just Blanc—Gamay
Gamay Rond—Gamay
Gamay Teinturier Mouro—a Gamay
    teinturier
Gamé—Gamay
Gamza—Kadarka
Garnacha—Grenache
Garnacha Blanca—Grenache Blanc
Garnache—Grenache
Garnacho—Grenache
Garnacho Blanco—Grenache Blanc
Garnaxta—Grenache Blanc
Gelber Muscatel—Muscat Blanc
    à Petits Grains
Gelber Muscateller—Muscat Blanc
    à Petits Grains
Gelber Muskatel—Muscat Blanc à Petits
    Grains
Gelber Muskateller—Muscat Blanc
    à Petits Grains
Gelder Ortlieber—Elbling
Gentilduret Rouge—Gewürztraminer
Gentin à Romorantin—Sauvignon Blanc
Giboudot—Aligoté
Glera—Prosecco
Golden Chasselas—Chasselas
Gordo Blanco—Muscat d'Alexandrie
Goujan—Pinot Meunier
Gourdoux—Malbec
Graisse—Ugni Blanc
Graisse Blanc—Ugni Blanc
Granaccia—Grenache
Grand Picot—Mondeuse
Grande Vidure—Carmenère
Grasica—Welschriesling
Grassevina—Welschriesling
Grau Clevner—Pinot Blanc
Grauer Mönch—Pinot Gris
Grauerburgunder—Pinot Gris
Grauklevner—Pinot Gris
Gray Riesling—Trousseau Gris
Greffou—Roussanne
Grenache de Logroño—Tempranillo
Grenache Nera—Grenache
Grey Friar—Pinot Gris
Grey Pinot—Pinot Gris
Grey Riesling—Trousseau Gris
Grifforin—Malbec
Gris Cordelier—Pinot Gris
Gris Meunier—Pinot Meunier
Gris Rouge—Gewürztraminer
Gros Auxerrois—Melon de Bourgogne
Gros Blanc—Sacy
Gros Bouchet—Cabernet Franc
Gros Bouschet—Cabernet Franc
Gros Cabernet—Cabernet Franc
Gros Lot—Grolleau
Gros Monsieur—César
Gros Noir—César
Gros Noir Guillan Rouge—Malbec
Gros Plant—Folle Blanche
Gros Plant du Nantais—Folle Blanche
Gros Rhin—Sylvaner
Gros Rouge du Pays—Mondeuse
Gros Vidure—Cabernet Franc
Groslot—Grolleau
Grosse Roussette—Marsanne
Grosse Syrah—Mondeuse
Grossriesling—Elbling
Grossvernatsch—Trollinger
Gründel—Sylvaner
Grüner—Grüner Veltliner
Grüner Silvaner—Sylvaner
Grünfrankisch—Sylvaner
Grünling—Sylvaner
Grünmuskateller—Grüner Veltliner
Guenille—Colombard
Guépie—Muscadelle
Guépie-catape—Muscadelle
Guillan—Muscadelle

Guillan-musqué—Muscadelle
Gutedel—Chasselas
Haiden—Gewürztraminer
Hanepoot—Muscat d'Alexandrie
Harriague—Tannat
Heida—Gewürztraminer
Hermitage—Cinsault
Hermitage Blanc—Marsanne
Hignin—Syrah
Hignin Noir—Syrah
Hocheimer—Riesling
Hunter Riesling (in Australia)—Sémillon
Hunter River Riesling (in Australia)—
    Sémillon
Ilegó—Macabéo
Iskendiriye Misketi—Muscat
    d'Alexandrie
Island Belle—Campbell's Early
Italianski Rizling—Welschriesling
Italiansky Rizling—Welschriesling
Jacobain—Malbec
Johannisberg Riesling—Riesling
Johannisberger—Riesling
Kadarska—Kadarka
Kékfrankos—Blaufränkisch
Kékfrankos—Gamay
Klavner—Gewürztraminer
Klein Reuschling—Elbling
Kleinberger—Elbling
Kleiner Räuschling—Elbling
Kleinergelber—Elbling
Kleinweiner—Gewürztraminer
Klevener de Heiligenstein—
    Savagnin Rosé
Klevner—Pinot Blanc
Klevner—Pinot Noir
Knipperlé—Elbling
Kurztingel (in Austria)—Elbling
Lardot—Macabéo
Laski Rizling—Welschriesling
Laskiriesling—Welschriesling
Lemberger—Blaufränkisch
Lemberger—Gamay
Lemberger—Limberger
Len de lElh—Len de l'El
Lexia—Muscat d'Alexandrie
Limberger—Blaufränkisch
Limberger—Gamay
Limberger (in U.S.)—Lemberger
Liwora—Gewürztraminer
Luckens—Malbec
Lyonnaise Blanche—
    Melon de Bourgogne
Maccabeu—Macabéo
Mâconnais—Altesse
Madiran—Tannat
Magret—Malbec
Mala Dinka—Gewürztraminer
Malaga Morterille Noire—Cinsault
Malbeck—Malbec
Malmsey—Pinot Gris
Malvagia—Pinot Gris
Malvasia—Pinot Gris
Malvasia Rey—Tinta Amarela
Malvoisie—Pinot Gris
Manseng Blanc—Manseng
Marchigiano—Verdicchio
Mataro—Carignan
Mataro—Mourvèdre
Mausat—Malbec
Maussac—Mauzac
Mauzac—Malbec
Mauzac Blanc—Mauzac
Mavrud—Mavroud
Mazuelo—Carignan
Médoc Noir—Merlot
Melon—Melon de Bourgogne
Melon Blanc—Chardonnay
Melon d'Arbois—Chardonnay
Menu Pineau—Arbois
Meunier—Pinot Meunier
Modrý Portugal—Portugieser
Moisac—Mauzac
Molette Noir—Mondeuse
Monemrasia—Pinot Gris

Monterey Riesling (in California)—
    Sylvaner
Montonec—Parellada
Montonech—Parellada
Moravka Silvanske (in Czech Republic) –
    Sylvaner
Morellino—Sangiovese
Morillon—Pinot Noir
Morillon Taconé—Pinot Meunier
Morrastel—Graciano
Moscata—Muscat Blanc à Petits Grains
Moscata Bianca—Muscat Blanc à Petits
    Grains
Moscatel—Muscat Blanc à Petits Grains
Moscatel—Muscat d'Alexandrie
Moscatel Bravo—Rabigato
Moscatel de Alejandria—Muscat
    d'Alexandrie
Moscatel de Grano Menudo—Muscat
    Blanc à Petits Grains
Moscatel de Málaga—Muscat d'Alexandrie
Moscatel de Setúbal—Muscat
    d'Alexandrie
Moscatel Dorado—Muscat Blanc à Petits
    Grains
Moscatel Gordo—Muscat d'Alexandrie
Moscatel Gordo Blanco—Muscat
    d'Alexandrie
Moscatel Menudo Bianco—Muscat Blanc
    à Petits Grains
Moscatel Romano—Muscat d'Alexandrie
Moscatel Rosé—Muscat Rosé à Petits
    Grains
Moscatel Samsó—Muscat d'Alexandrie
Moscatello—Muscat Blanc à Petits
    Grains
Moscatello Bianco—Muscat Blanc
    à Petits Grains
Moscato—Muscat Blanc à Petits Grains
Moscato d'Asti—Muscat Blanc à Petits
    Grains
Moscato di Canelli—Muscat Blanc
    à Petits Grains
Mosel Riesling—Riesling
Moselriesling—Riesling
Mosttraube—Chasselas
Mourane—Malbec
Moustère—Malbec
Moustrou—Tannat
Moustroun—Tannat
Mueller-Thurgau—Müller-Thurgau
Müller Rebe—Pinot Meunier
Müller Schwarzriesling—Pinot Meunier
Müllerrebe—Pinot Meunier
Muscade—Muscadelle
Muscadel Ottonel—Muscat Ottonel
Muscadet—Chardonnay
Muscadet—Melon de Bourgogne
Muscadet—Muscadelle
Muscadet Doux—Muscadelle
Muscat—Muscat Blanc à Petits Grains
Muscat Canelli—Muscat Blanc à Petits
    Grains
Muscat Cknelli—Muscat Blanc
    à Petits Grains
Muscat d'Alsace—Muscat Blanc
    à Petits Grains
Muscat d'Alsace—Muscat Rosé
    à Petits Grains
Muscat de Frontignan—Muscat Blanc
    à Petits Grains
Muscat Doré—Muscat Blanc
    à Petits Grains
Muscat Doré de Frontignan—
    Muscat Blanc à Petits Grains
Muscat Fou—Muscadelle
Muscat Gordo Blanco—Muscat
    d'Alexandrie
Muscat Rosé à Petits Grains d'Alsace—
    Muscat Rosé à Petits Grains
Muscat Roumain—Muscat d'Alexandrie
Muscatel—Muscat Blanc à Petits Grains
Muscatel Branco—Muscat Blanc
    à Petits Grains

Muscateller—Muscat Blanc à Petits Grains
Muskadel—Muscadelle
Muskat—Muscat Blanc à Petits Grains
Muskateller—Muscat Blanc à Petits Grains
Muskat-Silvaner—Sauvignon Blanc
Muskotaly—Muscat Blanc à Petits Grains
Muskotály—Muscat Ottonel
Muskuti—Muscat Blanc
   à Petits Grains
Musquette—Muscadelle
Nagi-Burgundi—Pinot Noir
Nagyburgundi—Pinot Noir
Napa Gamay—Gamay
Naturé—Savagnin
Nebbiolo Lampia—Nebbiolo
Nebbiolo Michet—Nebbiolo
Nebbiolo Rosé—Nebbiolo
Nebbiolo Spanna—Nebbiolo
Negri—Malbec
Negron—Mourvèdre
Nerino—Sangiovese
Neuburské—Neuburger
Noir de Pressac—Malbec
Noir Doux—Malbec
Noiren—Pinot Noir
Oesterreicher—Sylvaner
Ojo de Liebre—Tempranillo
Olasz Rizling—Welschriesling
Olaszriesling—Welschriesling
Olaszrizling—Welschriesling
Oporto—Portugieser
Ormeasco—Dolcetto
Ortlieber—Elbling
Paarl Riesling (in South Africa)—
   Cruchen Blanc
Pansa Blanca—Xarel-lo
Panse Musquée—Muscat d'Alexandrie
Parde—Malbec
Perpignanou—Graciano
Petit Bouschet—Cabernet Sauvignon
Petit Cabernet—Cabernet Sauvignon
Petit Dannezy—Romorantin
Petit Gamai—Gamay
Petit Mansenc—Manseng
Petit Merle—Merlot
Petit Pineau—Arbois
Petit Rhin—Riesling
Petit Riesling—Riesling
Petit Verdau—Petit Verdot
Petite Sainte-Marie—Chardonnay
Petite Syrah—Petite Sirah
Petite-Vidure—Cabernet Sauvignon
Petit-Fer—Cabernet Franc
Picardin Noir—Cinsault
Picotin Blanc—Roussanne
Picoutener—Nebbiolo
Picpoul—Folle Blanche
Picpoule—Folle Blanche
Picutener—Nebbiolo
Pied de Perdrix—Malbec
Pied Noir—Malbec
Pied Rouge—Malbec
Pied-Tendre—Colombard
Pinat Cervena—Gewürztraminer
Pineau—Pinot Noir
Pineau Blanche de Loire—Chenin
   Blanc
Pineau de la Loire—Chenin Blanc
Pineau de Saumur—Grolleau
Pineau Rouge—Pineau d'Aunis
Pinot Beurot—Pinot Gris
Pinot Blanc—Chardonnay
Pinot Blanc (in California)—
   Melon de Bourgogne
Pinot Blanc Chardonnay—Chardonnay
Pinot Blanc Vrai Auxerrois—Pinot Blanc
Pinot Chardonnay—Chardonnay
Pinot de la Loire—Chenin Blanc
Pinot Grigio—Pinot Gris
Pinot Vérot—Pinot Noir
Piperdy—Malbec
Pisse Vin—Aramon
Plant Boisnard—Grolleau
Plant d'Arles—Cinsault
Plant d'Aunis—Pineau d'Aunis

Plant de Brie—Pinot Meunier
Plant Dore—Pinot Noir
Ploussard—Poulsard
Portugais Bleu—Portugieser
Portugalka—Portugieser
Prèchat—Malbec
Pressac—Malbec
Preto Martinho—Negra Mole
Primativo—Primitivo
Primitivo—Crljenak Kastelanski
Prolongeau—Malbec
Prugnolo (in Montepulciano)—
   Sangiovese
Ptinc Crveny—Gewürztraminer
Pugnet—Nebbiolo
Puiechou—Sauvignon Blanc
Punechon—Sauvignon Blanc
PX—Pedro Ximénez
Quercy—Malbec
Queue-Tendre—Colombard
Queue-Verte—Colombard
Rabo da Ovelha—Rabigato
Rabo da Ovelha Tinto—Tinta Amarela
Raisinotte—Muscadelle
Rajinski Rizling—Riesling
Rajnai Rizling—Riesling
Ranfoliza—Gewürztraminer
Ranina—Bouvier
Räuschling—Elbling
Rcatzitelli—Rkatsiteli
Rdeci Traminac—Gewürztraminer
Red Trollinger—Trollinger
Refosco—Mondeuse
Reno—Riesling
Resinotte—Muscadelle
Rezlink—Riesling
Rezlink Rynsky—Riesling
Rhein Riesling—Riesling
Rheingau Riesling—Riesling
Rheingauer—Riesling
Rheinriesling—Riesling
Rhine Riesling—Riesling
Riesler—Riesling
Riesling (in Australia)—Sémillon
Riesling du Rhin—Riesling
Riesling Italianski—Welschriesling
Riesling Italico—Welschriesling
Riesling Italien—Welschriesling
Riesling Renano—Riesling
Rieslinger—Riesling
Riesling-Sylvaner—Müller-Thurgau
Rislig Rejnski—Riesling
Rismi—Welschriesling
Rivaner—Müller-Thurgau
Rizling Rajinski Bijeli—Riesling
Rizling Vlassky—Welschriesling
Romain—César
Ronçain—César
Roriz—Tempranillo
Rössling—Riesling
Rossola—Ugni Blanc
Rotclevner—Gewürztraminer
Rotclevner—Pinot Noir
Rotedel—Gewürztraminer
Roter Nurnberger—Gewürztraminer
Roter Traminer—Gewürztraminer
Rotfranke—Gewürztraminer
Rotter Muscateller—Muscat Rosé
   à Petits Grains
Rotter Muskateller—Muscat Rosé
   à Petits Grains
Roussan—Ugni Blanc
Roussanne—Ugni Blanc
Rousselet—Gewürztraminer
Roussette—Altesse
Roussillon Tinto—Grenache
Roussillonen—Carignan
Royal Muscadine—Chasselas
Rulandské—Pinot Gris
Rulandské Bielé—Pinot Blanc
Rulandské Bílé—Pinot Blanc
Rulandské Modrý—Pinot Noir
Ruländer—Pinot Gris
Rulonski Szürkebarát—Pinot Gris
Rusa—Gewürztraminer

Rynski Rizling—Riesling
Ryzling Rynsky—Riesling
Ryzling Vlassky—Welschriesling
Ryzlink Rýnský—Riesling
Ryzlink Vlassky—Welschriesling
Saint-Emilion (in Romania)—Sémillon
Saint-Emilion—Ugni Blanc
Salvagnin—Savagnin
Sangiovese di Lamole—Sangiovese
Sangiovese Dolce—Sangiovese
Sangiovese Gentile—Sangiovese
Sangiovese Toscano—Sangiovese
Sanvicetro—Sangiovese
Sargamuskotaly—Muscat Blanc à Petits
   Grains
Sauvagnin—Savagnin
Sauvignon Jaune—Sauvignon Blanc
Sauvignon Vert (in California)—
   Muscadelle
Sauvignon Vert—Sauvignonasse
Savagnin Blanc—Savagnin
Savagnin Musqué—Sauvignon Blanc
Savagnin Noir—Pinot Noir
Savagnin Rosé—Gewürztraminer
Savignan Rosé—Traminer Rosé
Savignin—Pinot Noir
Savoyanche—Mondeuse
Scharvaner—Sylvaner
Schiava—Trollinger
Schiavagrossa—Trollinger
Schiras—Syrah
Schwartz Klevner—Pinot Noir
Schwarze Frankishe—Blaufränkisch
Schwarze Melonetraube—Gamay
Schwarzriesling—Pinot Meunier
Séme—Malbec
Semijon—Sémillon
Sémillon Muscat—Sémillon
Sémillon Roux—Sémillon
Sercial (in Australia)—Ondenc
Serenne—Syrah
Seretbhina (in Yugoslavia)—Elbling
Serine—Syrah
Serprina—Prosecco
Seyve-Villard—Seyval Blanc
Seyve-Villard 5276—Seyval Blanc
Shiraz—Syrah
Shyraz—Syrah
Silvain Vert—Sylvaner
Silván (in Czech Republic)—
   Sylvaner
Silvaner—Sylvaner
Silvaner Blanco—Sylvaner
Silvanske Zelené—Sylvaner
Sipon—Furmint
Sirac—Syrah
Sirah—Syrah
Sirrah—Syrah
Sirras—Syrah
Sonoma Riesling (in California)—Sylvaner
Soubirat-Parent—Malvasia
Spanna—Nebbiolo
Spätburgunder—Pinot Noir
Steen—Chenin Blanc
Surin—Sauvignon Blanc
Süssling—Chasselas
Svatovavrinecké—St. Laurent
Svätovavrinecké—St. Laurent
Syra—Syrah
Syrac—Syrah
Syras—Syrah
Szilváni (in Hungary)—Sylvaner
Szürkebarát—Pinot Gris
Talia—Ugni Blanc
Talijanski Rizling—Welschriesling
Tamyanka—Muscat Blanc
   à Petits Grains
Tanat—Tannat
Teinturier—Malbec
Tempranilla—Tempranillo
Tempranillo de la Rioja—Tempranillo
Termeno Aromatico—Gewürztraminer
Terranis—Malbec
Terrano—Mondeuse

Tinta Bairrada—Baga
Tinta Fina—Baga
Tinta Miuda—Graciano
Tinta Roriz—Tempranillo
Tinto—Mourvèdre
Tinto Aragonés—Grenache
Tinto de la Rioja—Tempranillo
Tinto de Toro—Tempranillo
Tinto Fino—Tempranillo
Tinto Madrid—Tempranillo
Tinto Mazuela—Carignan
Tokaier—Pinot Gris
Tokay (in Australia)—Muscadelle
Tokay—Pinot Gris
Tokay d'Alsace—Pinot Gris
Tokayer—Pinot Gris
Tokay-Pinot Gris—Pinot Gris
Touriga—Touriga Nacional
Tramin—Savagnin
Traminac—Gewürztraminer
Traminac Creveni—Gewürztraminer
Traminer—Gewürztraminer
Traminer Aromatico—Gewürztraminer
Traminer Aromatique—Gewürztraminer
Traminer Musqué—Gewürztraminer
Traminer Parfumé—Gewürztraminer
Traminer Rosé—Gewürztraminer
Traminer Rosso—Gewürztraminer
Traminer Roz—Gewürztraminer
Traminer Rozovy—Gewürztraminer
Tramini—Gewürztraminer
Tramini Piros—Gewürztraminer
Trebbiano (often with local place name
   appendaged)—Ugni Blanc
Tresallier—Sacy
Trincadeira—Tinta Amarela
Ugni Noir—Aramon
Ull de Llebre—Tempranillo
Uva di Spagna—Grenache
Uva Marana—Verdicchio
Veltliner—Grüner Veltliner
Veltlini (in Hungary)—Grüner Veltliner
Veltlinské Cervene—Roter Veltliner
Veltlinske Zelene—Grüner Veltliner
Verdet—Arbois
Verdone—Verdicchio
Verdot—Petit Verdot
Verdot Rouge—Petit Verdot
Vernatsch—Trollinger
Verneuil—Romorantin
Véron—Cabernet Franc
Vert Doré—Pinot Noir
Vidure—Cabernet Sauvignon
Vionnier—Viognier
Vitraille—Merlot
Viura—Macabéo
Wälschriesling—Welschriesling
Weiss Clevner—Pinot Blanc
Weiss Musketraube—Muscat Blanc
   à Petits Grains
Weissburgunder—Pinot Blanc
Weisse Muskateller—Muscat Blanc
   à Petits Grains
Weissemuskateller—Muscat Blanc
   à Petits Grains
Weisser Clevner—Chardonnay
Weisser Elbling—Elbling
Weisser Riesling—Riesling
Weisserburgunder (in Germany)—Melon
   de Bourgogne
Weissgipfler—Grüner Veltliner
White Frontignan—Muscat Blanc
   à Petits Grains
White Hermitage—Ugni Blanc
White Pinot—Chenin Blanc
White Riesling—Riesling
Wrotham Pinot—Pinot Meunier
Xarel-lo—Xarello
Zibibbo—Muscat d'Alexandrie
Zinfandel—Crljenak Kastelanski
Zinfandel—Primitivo
Zingarello—Primitivo
Zingarello—Zinfandel
Zuti Muscat—Muscat Blanc
   à Petits Grains

STORING WINE

Do you have to worry about how and where to store wine? Not really. More than 95 percent of wine is ready to drink straight from the shelf and most is actually consumed within 24 hours of purchase. If you do not have a cellar—and most people do not—then there really is no need to store wine. However, if you want to keep a few bottles for convenience, common sense will tell you to place it somewhere relatively cool and dark. On the other hand, if you are determined to built up a cellar of wine (and for the enthusiast, there is nothing more enjoyable), then there are some very important factors to consider, principally temperature and light.

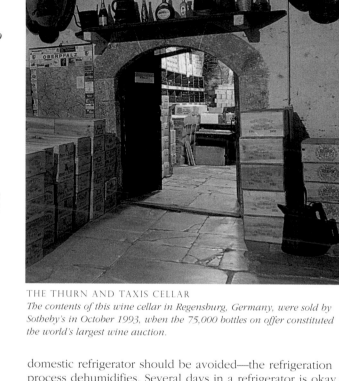

TEMPERATURE

While 52°F (11°C) is supposed to be the perfect storage temperature for wine, anything between 40°F and 65°F (5°C and 18°C) will in fact suffice for most styles of wines, providing there is no great temperature variation over a relatively short period of time. Higher temperatures increase the rate of oxidation in a wine, therefore a bottle of wine stored at 65°F (18°C) will gradually get "older" than the same wine stored at 52°F (11°C). However, a constant 59°F (15°C) is far kinder to a wine than erratic temperatures that often hit 52°F (11°C), but fluctuate between 40°F and 65°F (5°C and 18°C) from one day to the next. Such rapid changes in temperature cause the cork to shrink and expand, which can loosen the closure's grip on the inner surface of the bottle's neck, rendering the wine liable to oxidation through exposure to the air.

THE THURN AND TAXIS CELLAR
The contents of this wine cellar in Regensburg, Germany, were sold by Sotheby's in October 1993, when the 75,000 bottles on offer constituted the world's largest wine auction.

LIGHT

All wines are affected negatively by the ultraviolet end of the light spectrum, but some of the harmful photo-chemical effects this causes can be reversed by cellaring a light-affected wine in darkness for a few months. Brown or dead-leaf colored wine bottles offer more natural protection from ultraviolet light than those that are made of traditional green glass. But dark green is better than light green, whereas blue and clear are the most vulnerable (which is why Roederer Cristal is wrapped in protective yellow cellophane).

While it is perfectly okay to buy a wine for everyday drinking (or even for keeping a few months) off a well-lit supermarket shelf, if you want to keep a wine much longer, you should avoid any bottles displayed in sunlight or under artificial lighting. Ask instead for bottles of the same wine that are still in their cartons in the storeroom.

OTHER FACTORS

A certain humidity (between 60 and 70 percent) is essential to keep the cork moist and flexible, thereby avoiding oxidation. This is one reason why long-term storage in a

domestic refrigerator should be avoided—the refrigeration process dehumidifies. Several days in a refrigerator is okay, but much longer than this, and the cork will start to dry out. Wines should also be stored under vibration-free conditions, but this only becomes a significant factor over a long period for sparkling wines and mature wines with sediment.

The position in which a wine bottle is stored is also extremely important. Most wines should be stacked on their sides to keep their corks moist, and therefore fully swollen and airtight. Exceptions to this rule are sparkling wines and any wine that has been sealed with a screwtop lid. Champagne and any other sparkling wine may be safely stored in an upright position because the carbonic gas (CO_2) trapped in the space between the top of the wine and the base of the cork provides more-than-sufficient humidity to keep a sparkling-wine cork moist and swollen. Screwtop lids require no moistening, of course.

SYDMONTON COURT
The wine cellar in Sydmonton Court in Hampshire, England, is owned by Sir Andrew Lloyd Webber. He sold most of its contents in 1997 when he realized that he had far more wine than he could possibly drink in his lifetime.

SERVING WINE

Traditionally, white wines have been served chilled and red wines at room temperature, or chambré. *At higher temperatures, the odorous compounds found in all wines are more volatile, so the practice of serving full-bodied red wines* chambré *has the effect of releasing more aromatics into the bouquet.*

ONE MAJOR EFFECT OF CHILLING WINE is that more carbonic gas is retained at lower temperatures. This enhances the crispness and freshness and tends to liven the impression of fruit on the palate. It is thus vital to serve a sparkling wine sufficiently chilled, since this keeps it bubbling longer. However, the widespread use of refrigerators and central heating means that white wines are all too frequently served too cold, and red wines too warm.

Controversy surrounds the subject of the temperature at which wines are served. Over-chilling wine kills its flavor and aroma as well as making the cork difficult to remove because the wax on a cork adheres to the bottle. Over-warm wine, on the other hand, is bland to taste. The rough guide below is more than you need to know. I prefer not to complicate life with specific temperatures and simply think in terms of "putting a chill on" white or rosé wines and "taking the chill off" red wines.

WINE TYPE	SERVING TEMPERATURE
Sparkling (red, white, and rosé)	40–45°F (4.5–7°C)
White	45–50°F (7–10°C)
Rosé and light-bodied red	50–55°F (10–12.5°C)
Medium-bodied red	55–60°F (12.5–15.5°C)
Full-bodied red	60–65°F (15.5–18°C)

RAPID CHILLING AND INSTANT CHAMBRÉ
It is fine to chill wine in a refrigerator for a couple of hours, but not for much longer because the cork may stick. Unlike the cumulative effect of wide temperature variations, 10 or 15 minutes in the deep-freeze has never done a wine any harm. The belief that this practice "burns" a wine is unfounded; the cold creeps evenly into the bottle. The rapid-chill sheaths that can be kept in the freezer and slid over a bottle when needed are a great innovation.

Unlike cooling, warming a wine by direct heat is not an even process; whether standing a bottle by an open fire or putting it under a hot faucet, some of the wine gets too hot, leaving the rest too cold. The best way of "taking the chill off" is 60 to 90 seconds in a microwave on medium power.

DECANTING
With increasing age, many wines—especially red wines—throw a natural deposit of tannins and coloring pigments that collect in the base of the bottle. Both red and white wines, particularly white, can also shed a crystalline deposit due to a precipitation of tartrates. Although all these deposits are harmless, their appearance is distracting and decanting will be necessary to remove them.

Preparing the bottle and pouring the wine
Several hours prior to decanting, move the bottle into an upright position. So doing allows the sediment lying along the side of the bottle to fall to the bottom. Cut away the top quarter-inch so of the foil capsule. This could well reveal a penicillin growth or, if the wine is an old vintage, a fine black deposit, neither of which will have had contact with the wine, but to avoid any unintentional contamination when removing the cork it is wise to wipe the lip of the bottle neck and the top of the cork with a clean, damp cloth. Insert a corkscrew and gently withdraw the cork. Place a clean finger inside the top of the bottle and carefully remove any pieces of cork or any tartrate crystals adhering to the inside of the neck, then wipe the lip of the bottle neck with a clean, dry cloth.

Lift the bottle slowly in one hand and the decanter in the other and bring them together over a light source, such as a candle or torch, which will reveal any sediment as the wine is poured. Aim to pour the wine in a slow, steady flow so that the bottle does not jerk and wine does not "gulp for air." Such mishaps will disturb the sediment, spreading it through a greater volume of liquid.

Filtering dregs
Personally, I flout tradition by pouring cloudy dregs through a fine-grade coffee filter paper. I always attempt to decant the maximum volume, thereby filtering the minimum, and I have never been able to tell the difference between pure-decanted wine and that augmented by a small volume of filtered wine. In fact, none of my friends and colleagues who have doubted my assertion have been able to score higher than 50 percent in blind tastings.

ALLOWING WINE TO BREATHE
As soon as you open a bottle of wine, it will be "breathing" (exposed to the air). Wine "feeds" on the small amount of air trapped inside the bottle between the wine and the cork, and on the oxygen naturally absorbed by the wine itself. It is during this slow oxidation that various elements and compounds are formed or changed in a complex chemical process known as maturation. Allowing a wine to breathe is, in effect, creating a rapid, but less sophisticated, maturation. This artificial aging may be beneficial to certain still wines for several reasons, only some of which are known. The only generalization that tends to hold true is that breathing is likely to improve young, full-bodied, tannic red wines.

OPENING A BOTTLE OF CHAMPAGNE
• Remove the foil from the bulbous top end of the neck. Quite often there is a little foil tail sticking out, which you merely pull. Failing this, you may have to look for the circular imprint of the end of the wire cage, which will have been twisted, folded upward, and pressed into the neck. When you find this, simply pull it outwards—this will rip the foil, enabling you to remove a section from just below the level of the wire cage.
• Holding the bottle upright at an angle, keep one hand firmly on the cork to make sure it will not surprise you by shooting out, untwist the wire with the other hand, and loosen the bottom of the wire cage so that there is a good space all round. A good tip is not to remove the wire cage, not only because that is when most bottles fire their corks unexpectedly, but also because it acts as a good grip, which you need when a Champagne cork is stuck tight.
• Transfer your grip on the cork to the other hand, which should completely enclose the cork and cage, and, holding the base of the bottle with your other hand, twist both ends in opposite directions. As soon as you feel pressure forcing the cork out try to hold it in, but continue the twisting operation until, almost reluctantly, you release the cork from the bottle. The mark of a professional is that the cork comes out with a sigh, not a bang.

Keep a firm grip on the cork and cage while twisting

Twist the bottle and cork in opposite directions, backward and forward

The WINES of
THE WORLD

FROM A GLOBAL PERSPECTIVE, wine consumers are gradually moving upmarket in quality, from white wine to red, and from Old World to New. These shifts appear to be long term. Old World wine consumers drink considerably less than they did 15 years ago, whereas New World wine consumers drink significantly more. Ironically, the greatest decline in wine consumption is in the world's three largest wine-producing countries, France, Italy, and Spain, where younger generations are drinking more beer. However, wine consumption continues to increase in the U.K., Belgium, and the Scandinavian countries, which fit more into New World drinking patterns than Old. Wine consumption in Mediterranean countries fell by 40 percent in the past two decades of the 20th century, while wine production decreased by just 20 percent. The excess in Europe was not mopped up by growing exports, highlighting the most pressing problem at the beginning of the 21st century: surplus production. This excess production has supposedly been targeted by European Union policies, but not very successfully so far.

RIPENING CABERNET FRANC GRAPES
This traditional Bordeaux grape can now be found in sites all over the winemaking world.

A WORLD OF WINE

At just over 6.6 billion gallons (250 million hectoliters), world wine production has fluctuated very little over the past 10 years. It peaked at almost 8 billion gallons (300 million hl) in 2000, only slightly higher than it was a decade ago.

GOOD WINE WILL ALWAYS SELL, but almost every country produces more wine than it can consume or export. These surpluses are inevitably at the very lowest end of the quality spectrum. The situation is at its worst in, but not confined to, the European Union (EU), where the Common Agricultural Policy (CAP) has encouraged a dismal tradition of deliberate overproduction over the second half of the 20th century. Even though the wine regime under CAP was altered in 1999 to combat this practice, it has had little impact on growers, who find it much easier and more profitable to intentionally grow grapes that are not meant to be turned into wine. Intervention still exists; EU authorities continue to buy the surplus grapes and wines that achieve the minimum (intervention) prices. The grapes will be turned into rectified sugar for chaptalizing wines, while undrinkable wines are carted off for distillation (called "crisis distillation" under the new regulations). On average, global wine production exceeds demand every year, peaking at 1.4 billion gallons (53 million hl) of surplus wine in 1999 and 2000, with France and Italy claiming the dubious joint honor of providing some 80 percent of it.

For France, the main problem is straightforward overproduction in historically identifiable areas, which cynics might label as a legalized scam. Italy, on the other hand, has a serious problem of too much cheap wine competing for the same, declining market, which can be illustrated by the fact that the average price per quart of the entire Italian wine production is only 46 percent of the average price of French wine. In both countries and, indeed, throughout the entire EU, there is supposed to be a move toward drinking less in volume, more in quality, but a Bordeaux campaign to "drink less, drink better" was banned in 2004, after the National Association for the Prevention of Alcoholism took the Conseil Interprofessionnel des Vins de Bordeaux to court, and it was judged to be illegal because it "incited people to purchase wine."

BEWARE OF ALL-CONSUMING FACTS
Statistics for *per capita* wine consumption are notoriously unreliable. Even supposedly the same statistic (i.e., *per capita* consumption for the same country in the same year) can vary in different documents and tables from the same organization. There are many anomalies at work. The Luxembourgois, to quote one major reference, "leave everyone else standing" when it comes to wine consumption, but the Belgians and Germans use their country as a giant supermarket, buying wine, cigarettes, and gasoline in bulk because of the significantly lower taxes. The trade is so vast and Luxembourg's population so small that this cross-border trading distorts the imbibing prowess of the Luxembourgois, so precisely where they fit in the *per capita* scheme of things is debatable. In contrast, the population of France is so large that the trade makes no difference and would, in any case, be offset by cross-Channel transactions. Vacation islands with small populations, such as Cyprus, are prone to similar distortions, with much of the wine enjoyed by tourists rather than inhabitants. Small discrepancies may be due to the use of different 12-month periods, with some organizations using pure annual figures, while others use midyear to midyear and differing statistical adjustments. Such tables therefore generally provide a good overview, rather than a detailed picture.

INTERNATIONALIZATION?
Some critics are obsessed by what they see as a growing internationalization of wine. This is often ascribed to the spread of such ubiquitous grapes as Chardonnay and Cabernet Sauvignon, especially into new and emerging regions, and often at the expense of indigenous varieties. It is also attributed to a perceived homogenization in style due to technology, flying winemakers, and schools of enology, where winemakers are all taught to sing from the same sheet. Anyone who has to taste thousands of wines for a living gets "Chardonnayed out" far too frequently these days, but I believe there are good reasons not to be so pessimistic.

Those ubiquitous grapes
They were a necessary evil. It was not that long ago when it was a relief to taste a fresh young Chardonnay in parts of Languedoc-Roussillon, let alone Spain, southern Italy, Sardinia, Greece, and much more obscure wine-producing regions of the world. As recently as the early 1980s, it was almost impossible to discern whether many such areas had any potential whatsoever. Was the dire quality in these places caused by what were (then) unknown grape varieties, by the way that the vines were grown and harvested, a lack of experience of making wines of good quality, or the crude conditions under which the wines were produced? For anyone setting out to improve quality in these viticultural backwaters, the obvious place to start was in the vineyard and, equally obviously, Chardonnay was the best choice.

While Chardonnay might get a hard press these days, this was not always the case. If readers consult books and articles written a quarter of a century ago, they will discover Chardonnay to be universally revered as one of the greatest white wine grapes in the world. Furthermore, its ability to transplant varietal characteristics to myriad soils and climates throughout the world was considered uncanny and, if anything, served to confirm its nobility. Jancis Robinson waxed lyrical about Chardonnay in her seminal work *Vines, Grapes, and Wines* (1986), and even today only the most prejudiced wine drinker would deny that the best white Burgundies rank among the very greatest of dry white wines. If a winemaker in a lowly area of southern France, an Aegean island, or parts of China could not produce a half-decent wine out of the world's greatest, best-traveled grape variety, the vineyards in question would have been written off long ago.

Decline of indigenous varieties
Far from being under the threat of decline, these varieties owe their survival to the likes of Chardonnay and Cabernet Sauvignon muscling in on their areas of production. Had the so-called "international varieties" not achieved a certain success, these areas would have been grubbed up long ago. Between 1980 and 1994, the area under vine worldwide plummeted from over 25 million acres to less than 19 million (10 million to 8 million hectares), this loss almost entirely stemming from the Old World. Having demonstrated a suitability for viticulture via yardsticks like Chardonnay, local winemakers started to apply the standards learned to the indigenous varieties. In the New World, of course, there are virtually no indigenous grapes suited to winemaking, but again the experience with benchmark international varieties has encouraged growers in emerging wine areas to experiment with other European varieties. In both Old and New Worlds, there is too much ordinary Chardonnay being made, but it is only too much for critics and wine enthusiasts—if it were too much for most consumers, the wines would not exist. If they develop a deeper interest, the market will adapt—so perhaps wine critics should spend more time communicating.

Homogenization of style

Technology is what you make of it. It can enable vast volumes of technically correct wines to be produced with more fruit and fresher flavors, thus enticing greater numbers of consumers to explore finer wines, and that's not a bad thing. When the best technology is combined with the best traditions, it can also improve the quality and expressiveness of highly individual wines, and that's not bad either.

What about so-called flying winemakers? Are they responsible for homogenization in style? I cannot imagine how they can be, as they make less than one percent of one percent of the world's wine. What flying winemakers have done is to leave a certain level of cleanliness and competence in their wake, and to show winemakers in underperforming wineries what can be achieved. They have also created a reverse flow in terms of where winemakers go to seek practical experience. Over the past quarter century, New World winemakers had gone to Europe to pick up tips on fruit handling and winemaking techniques; now the most inquisitive Europeans go to Australia, New Zealand, or California to learn.

As for schools of enology, it used to be *de rigeur* to have the likes of Bordeaux, Dijon, or Montpellier on a winemaker's resumé, but now the university faculties at Roseworthy (Australia) and Davis are the fashion, as much in Europe as the New World itself. There might be a danger that these schools are producing technically correct enologists trained not to take risks, rather than winemakers whose passion is intimately entwined with the sort of risk-taking that can result in something truly special. However, ultimately, it is better for a winemaker to understand what he or she is doing, though even that statement has its exceptions, with many a self-taught winemaker who has never opened a book on enology producing some of the world's most stunning wines.

MULTINATIONALS

With all the talk of an international style dominating the range of wines we can buy, should we be worried by multinationals and other large companies increasing this homogenization by controlling production and sales? Again, the figures do not support commonly held beliefs. Indeed, because of the fragmented nature of the wine industry, the world's top 10 wine marketers combined account for less than 14 percent of global wine volume, in direct contrast to the world's top 10 brewers and the world's top 10 spirits companies, which account for 54 percent of their respective markets. The top 10 wine companies in 2003 were:

1. Constellation
2. E & J Gallo
3. Allied Domecq*
4. LVMH
5. Southcorp
6. Beringer Blass
7. Diageo
8. Castel Frères
9. Henkell & Co
10. Freixenet

taken over by Pernod-Ricard in April 2005

WORLD WINE PRODUCTION (THOUSAND HECTOLITERS)

COUNTRY (POSITION 10 YEARS AGO)	2003	2002	2001	2000	1999	1998	1997	1996	1995	1994
1. France (2)	47350	52000	55770	59740	60240	52670	53560	570500	54350	54640
2. Italy (1)	44090	44600	52290	54070	58070	54190	50890	587700	55700	59280
3. Spain (3)	36000	34440	30940	41790	32680	31180	33220	310000	20880	21000
4. USA (5)	23500	25400	23000	25000	20690	20500	22000	188800	18670	17550
5. Australia (9)	11800	12200	10770	8590	8510	7420	6170	67300	5030	5870
6. Argentina (4)	11200	12150	15840	12540	15890	12670	13500	126800	16440	18170
7. China (8)	10860	10800	10800	10500	10260	10640	9000	75000	7000	6200
8. Germany (6)	8290	10180	9080	10080	12290	10830	8500	86400	8510	10180
9. South Africa (7)	7610	7610	7610	6950	7970	7700	8120	87400	8340	9120
10. Portugal (8)	6800	6270	7430	6690	7810	3750	6120	97100	7260	6520
11. Chile (13)	5750	5750	5650	6670	4810	5480	4550	38200	3160	3600
12. Romania (11)	5460	5000	5500	5460	6500	5000	6690	76600	6720	5370
13. Greece (15)	4950	5000	4280	4600	3680	3830	3990	41100	3840	3050
14. Hungary (12)	4200	3800	5410	4300	3340	4330	4470	41900	3290	3690
15. Russia (17)	4100	3430	3430	3230	2903	2180	2230	2550	2150	2960
16. Brazil (16)	4000	3200	3200	3000	3190	2780	2740	31300	3130	3020
17. Austria (18)	3250	2600	2530	2340	2800	2700	1800	21100	2230	2650
18. Croatia (19)	2600	2200	2040	1890	2090	2280	2260	19600	1790	1890
19. Moldova (14)	2400	2100	1400	2020	1332	1700	3123	3598	4225	3350
Other	18370	19130	20210	24040	24260	24790	28030	271000	26900	22650
World	262580	267870	277160	293500	280010	255660	259810	269290	250230	252060

Source: COPS & CIES - Global Wine Markets, 1961–2003
Note: Columns may not total due to rounding

PER CAPITA CONSUMPTION—HIGHEST CONSUMING COUNTRIES (LITERS PER PERSON PER YEAR)

COUNTRY	2002	2001	2000	1999	1998	1997	1996	1995	1994	1993
1. Luxembourg (1)	60.9	59.4	65.1	62.8	62.1	61.5	60.5	55.2	51.0	65.0
2. France (2)	56.0	56.9	55.9	57.2	58.1	60.0	60.0	63.0	62.5	63.5
3. Italy (3)	51.0	50.0	51.0	51.5	52.0	53.5	54.2	55.7	57.8	60.4
4. Portugal (4)	43.0	47.0	46.0	48.0	51.0	54.5	56.6	58.1	58.9	60.0
5. Croatia (9)	42.1	43.2	42.0	47.0	50.8	45.1	35.8	48.2	48.1	38.6
6. Switzerland (6)	41.8	43.1	43.5	43.5	43.1	43.5	43.3	43.6	44.3	46.0
7. Argentina (7)	36.1	36.3	37.8	38.7	38.8	40.3	41.1	41.1	43.2	44.4
8. Hungary (13)	36.0	35.1	34.0	32.0	31.0	29.0	30.3	26.6	29.2	31.5
9. Greece (10)	33.9	34.0	34.0	35.2	32.0	34.9	34.0	34.5	33.8	35.2
10. Uruguay (15)	32.8	31.9	32.0	32.0	30.5	30.7	30.1	29.8	31.1	27.2
11. Denmark (16)	32.0	31.2	30.9	29.8	29.1	29.3	28.3	27.6	26.2	25.2
12. Slovenia (5)	31.2	31.1	35.4	28.3	41.5	51.9	56.2	47.6	47.7	47.8
13. Austria (11)	29.8	28.5	30.5	30.6	30.9	30.0	31.5	32.0	32.8	34.3
14. Spain (12)	29.6	30.0	32.0	34.0	35.6	35.1	30.3	30.6	32.2	34.1
15. Georgia (23)	28.7	31.9	33.2	37.1	15.9	15.9	12.9	17.7	17.8	17.9
16. Romania (14)	25.3	25.5	23.2	22.7	30.0	32.2	26.0	25.3	23.2	30.0
17. Belgium (24)	24.3	24.2	23.4	23.0	22.9	23.9	19.4	17.8	17.7	17.6
18. Germany (18)	24.2	24.0	23.1	23.0	22.8	23.0	23.1	22.2	22.6	22.6
19. Macedonia (17)	23.7	23.8	23.8	23.8	23.8	28.4	18.7	27.2	27.1	27.0
20. Finland (31)	23.5	21.9	20.6	19.5	17.5	15.6	13.1	11.5	8.8	8.3
21 Netherlands (26)	22.5	21.0	19.5	15.9	13.8	15.1	19.1	18.1	16.1	15.2
22. Bulgaria (19)	21.3	21.4	21.4	21.4	22.1	21.6	21.7	21.8	22.0	22.1
23. Australia (22)	21.2	20.5	20.5	20.4	19.7	19.5	19.0	18.3	18.4	18.6
24. United Kingdom (27)	17.6	17.0	15.3	17.2	16.9	15.8	14.9	14.3	14.5	13.3
25. New Zealand (25)	17.1	16.7	17.0	16.3	16.1	17.0	16.2	16.6	16.3	16.4
26. Sweden (28)	16.0	15.9	13.5	13.6	12.4	11.8	12.9	13.0	13.9	13.2
27. Cyprus (29)	16.0	15.2	14.6	11.1	11.5	11.2	11.0	11.8	11.9	11.7
28. Chile (20)	15.9	16.0	18.8	18.6	17.7	12.5	15.8	21.7	21.4	20.3
29. Moldova (8)	14.5	13.6	16.4	11.2	15.8	22.6	29.3	41.3	41.3	41.3
30. Yugoslavia (21)	13.0	13.1	14.2	14.1	19.9	27.7	23.1	19.1	19.3	19.2
31. Ireland (36)	13.0	12.8	11.6	9.8	8.6	7.5	6.7	6.0	5.5	5.3
32. Slovakia (34)	11.9	11.8	11.7	8.2	6.7	7.8	6.8	8.1	8.0	7.9
33. Norway (33)	11.3	10.9	10.3	9.9	9.6	9.3	9.0	8.7	8.4	8.1
34. South Africa (30)	9.5	9.2	9.0	9.1	8.9	9.3	9.7	9.2	9.7	9.4
35. Canada (31)	9.1	9.0	8.8	8.6	7.5	6.7	6.9	7.0	6.2	8.2
36 USA (35)	9.7	9.3	8.3	8.3	7.8	6.9	6.7	6.9	7.0	6.7

Sources: Australian Wine Bureau; Wine Institute (USA); Richard Cartier's *Wine Market Report*; CIES; OIV; IVV, Statec

The WINES of
FRANCE

FRENCH WINES ARE REGARDED AS THE BEST in the world, and a thread of this belief is even shared by France's fiercest New World competitors. Although the winemakers of Australia and California, for instance, no longer try to copy famous French wine styles, they still consider them benchmarks. The great French wine regions are a fortunate accident of geography, climate, and *terroir*. No other winemaking country in the world has such a wide range of cool climates; this factor has enabled France to produce the entire spectrum of classic wine styles—from the crisp sparkling wines of Champagne through the smooth reds of Burgundy to the rich sweet wines of Sauternes. Over many centuries of trial and error, the French have discovered that specific grapes are suited to certain soils and, through this, distinctive regional wine styles have evolved, so that every wine drinker knows what to expect from a bottle of Bordeaux, Burgundy, Champagne, or Rhône. This has been the key to success for French wines,

THE MOON RISING OVER CHÂTEAU LATOUR
The magnificent tower of Château Latour is bathed in moonlight, evoking the majesty of one of the world's greatest wines.

FRANCE

The success of French wine has been built on deservedly famous regions that have been enshrined by Appellation d'Origine Contrôlée (AOC) *laws, but the unwillingness to police this system in any meaningful sense has gradually debased historic reputations at the precise point in history when New World producers have been eager to establish their own wines.*

FRANCE HAS A TOTAL OF 2,153,800 acres (872,000 hectares) under vine, including 172,900 acres (70,000 hectares) for Cognac and 14,820 acres (6,000 hectares) for Armagnac, and produces an average of almost 630 million cases (57 million hectoliters) of wine every year. Since the mid-1980s, French wine production has dropped by 27 percent in response to a move away from the lower-quality end of the spectrum, as consumers have begun to drink less wine, but of better quality. How that quality is classified is the most contentious issue facing the French wine industry.

HOW FRENCH WINE IS CLASSIFIED
In 1935, when the Institut National des Appellations d'Origine (INAO) was established, France became the first nation to set up a countrywide system for controlling the origin and quality of its wines, although individual wine areas outside France had put in place quality controls much earlier (Chianti in 1716 and Rioja in 1560). INAO's task was to devise the geographical limits of appellations and to enforce the regulations governing them.

Appellation d'Origine Contrôlée (AOC)
There are now more than 470 separate AOCs, covering almost 1,210,300 acres (490,000 hectares), and producing just over 322 million cases (29 million hectoliters) of wine. The AOC laws regulate the grape varieties used, viticultural methods, harvest and yield restrictions, minimum alcohol content, and winemaking techniques for each area. Although the laws are supposed to control the quality of each wine by having it pass an official

CHÂTEAU GRUAUD-LAROSE
One of the largest and most consistent of Bordeaux's second growths, this estate was established by the Gruaud family in 1757; the chateau was built in 1875.

analysis and tasting, the latter of these has become something of a farce, since panels of tasting judges are composed of the very people who actually make the wine. Furthermore, the wines are not tasted and passed on a tank by tank basis, the absence of which is probably responsible for most of the very worst AOC wines on the shelf. Virtually all the producers I know admit that only those wines with faults—and obvious ones at that—are likely to be rejected, with no account taken of either quality or whether a wine reflects the character of the grapes used or expresses any particular regional style. Some were honest enough to explain that most people are too afraid to start the ball rolling on the issue of quality or style for fear that someone whose wine has already been rejected might seek revenge by rejecting other wines indiscriminately. It is little surprise, therefore, that only around 2 or 3 percent of wines fail to pass such sham tastings.

The tasting system is obviously deficient, as evidenced by the glut of very poor-quality AOCs that are put on the shelf every year. The best AOC wines are still the best, but without some sort of overhaul of the system (*see* Challenging Tradition, below), the onus remains very much on the knowledge of consumers to discern the reputation of individual producers.

On a more positive note, INAO has instituted tougher controls in the vineyards that could result in distillation of the entire crop of any grower who exceeds the *Plafond Limité de Classement* (PLC). The PLC is the absolute maximum yield for any AOC. This is usually set at 20 percent above the base yield, which may itself be adjusted upward on an annual basis by, normally, some 10–15 percent. INAO has formed local "work committees" to visit vineyards, to detect any aberrations. Essentially, but not exclusively, they will be looking for signs of overproduction, and if found, they will tell the grower (depending on the time of year) to prune, green-harvest, or thin the bunches. Later in the year, the grower could have his entire crop declassified if he has not done as requested. In future years, such an offender might not be given the opportunity to rectify any overcropping and could have his entire crop carted

FRENCH WINE AT A GLANCE

BY CLASSIFICATION

Appellation d'Origine Contrôlée (AOC or AC)
Exactly 58% of total French wine production—25% exported, 75% consumed within France

Vin Délimité de Qualité Supérieure (VDQS)
Less than 1% of total French wine production—17% exported, 83% consumed within France

Vin de Pays
Almost 31% of total French wine production—10% exported, 90% consumed within France

Vin de Table
Just over 10% of total French wine production—16% exported, 84% consumed within France

BY TYPE

Red wine
Just over 65% of total French wine production—30% exported, 70% consumed within France

White wine
21.5% of total French wine production—55% exported, 45% consumed within France

Rosé wine
6.5% of total French wine production—30% exported, 70% consumed within France

Sparkling wine
Just under 6% of total French wine production – 42% exported, 58% consumed within France

Fortified wine
Just under 1% of total French wine production—20% exported, 80% consumed within France

FRANCE

The colored areas on this map identify the 10 main wine-producing regions of France, where the areas of Appellation d'Origine Contrôlée, which cover 1.2 million acres (490,000 hectares), are concentrated. However, the country has almost 400,000 acres of vineyards in total, and many good, everyday-drinking wines are made in other parts of the country. See also Vin de Pays maps pp.248, 249.

DID YOU KNOW?

- There are over 147,000 vineyard owners in France, almost 110,000 of whom make and sell wine, of whom more than 58,000 are producers of AOC wines.

- 62 percent of all French vineyards are machine harvested.

- 1.6 percent of all French vineyards are farmed organically or biodynamically.

- 45 percent of all French wine is processed by 840 cave coopératives.

- Merlot is the most planted grape variety of any color in France.

- Ugni Blanc is the widest planted white grape variety in France.

Bordeaux
See also p63

Burgundy
See also p137

Champagne
See also p170, 172

Alsace
See also p186

The Loire Valley
See also p197

The Rhône Valley
See also p213

Jura and Savoie
See also p224

Southwest France
See also p228

Languedoc-Rousillon
See also p235

Provence and Corsica
See also p244

——— *Département* boundary

▲ Height above sea level (meters)

0   20   40   60   80   100 miles

0   50   100   150 km

off for distillation for inadequate pruning. Of course, the efficacy of this initiative will be dependent upon how tough the "work committees" actually are, and, like AOC tasting panels, these will be comprised of fellow winegrowers.

Vin Délimité de Qualité Supérieure (VDQS)

There are just over 33 VDQS wines, covering almost 17,000 acres (approximately 6,800 hectares), and producing an annual average of just over 4.8 million cases (438,000 hectoliters) under similar controls to those applied to AOC wines, but with yields that may be higher and alcoholic strengths that are often lower. The overall quality standard is not as high, although it may be argued in certain cases that the quality is easily comparable.

Since the emergence of the *vins de pays* category in the 1970s, there have been persistent rumors of the imminent demise of VDQS, but the INAO, which is the regulatory body for both AOC and VDQS wines, has found this category to be such a convenient staging post for potential AOCs that its removal is unlikely. VDQS wines promoted to AOC status include Coteaux du Tricastin (promoted in 1973), St.-Chinian (1982), Coteaux du Lyonnais (1984), Costières de Nîmes (1986), Côtes du Marmandais (1990), Marcillac (1990), Cheverny and Cour-Cheverny (1993), Coteaux Varois (1993), Côtes Roannaises (1994), Coteaux de Pierrevert (1998), Coteaux du Giennois (1998), Côtes de Toul (1998), Côtes du Forez (2000), and Sauvignon de St.-Bris (2003).

It would be a mistake, however, to think of all VDQS wines as purely transitory. It is not a guaranteed halfway house to full AOC status, as can be demonstrated by those wines that still retain VDQS classification 40 years after this category came into fruition, and the fact that the majority of surviving VDQS wines actually date from the 1960s and 1970s. It is not beyond imagination that the French might elevate these crusty old VDQS wines at some date in the future, but most potential new AOC wines will be selected from those VDQS wines that have come up through the nicely matured *vin de pays* ranks.

VINS DE PRIMEUR

We tend to think of Beaujolais Nouveau as the only *vin de primeur,* or "new wine," but there are no fewer than 55 different wines that are allowed by AOC regulations to be sold in the year they are harvested, and 25 of these must be labeled *primeur* or *nouveau*. They are made in a style that is at its peak in the first year of its life. So, for those who like drinking wine when it has only just stopped fermenting, why not look out for the following?

1. Anjou Gamay
2. Beaujolais (red or rosé)
3. Beaujolais Supérieur (red or rosé)
4. Beaujolais-Villages (red or rosé)
5. Beaujolais with village name but not *cru* (red or rosé)
6. Bourgogne (white only)
7. Bourgogne Aligoté (white only)
8. Bourgogne Grand Ordinaire (white only)
9. Cabernet d'Anjou (rosé)
10. Cabernet de Saumur (rosé)
11. Coteaux du Languedoc (red or rosé)
12. Coteaux du Lyonnais (red, white, or rosé)
13. Coteaux du Tricastin (red, white, or rosé)
14. Côtes-du-Rhône (red sold only as a *vin de café* or rosé)
15. Côtes du Roussillon (red, white, or rosé)
16. Côtes du Ventoux (red, white, or rosé)
17. Gaillac (red Gamay or white)
18. Mâcon (white or rosé)
19. Mâcon Supérieur (white only)
20. Macon-Villages (white only)
21. Macon with village name (white only)
22. Muscadet
23. Muscadet de Sèvre et Maine
24. Muscadet des Coteaux de la Loire
25. Muscadet Côtes de Grand-Lieu
26. Rosé d'Anjou
27. Tavel (rosé only)
28. Touraine Gamay (red only)
29. Touraine (rosé only)

The following wines may be sold from December 1 after the harvest without any mention of *primeur* or *nouveau*:

1. Anjou (white only)
2. Bergerac (white or rosé, but not red)
3. Blayais (white only)
4. Bordeaux (*sec, rosé*, or *clairet*)
5. Buzet (white or rosé)
6. Cabernet d'Anjou (rosé)
7. Cabernet de Saumur (rosé)
8. Corbières (white or rosé)
9. Costières de Nîmes (white or rosé)
10. Coteaux d'Aix-en-Provence (white or rosé)
11. Coteaux du Languedoc (white or rosé)
12. Coteaux Varois (white or rosé)
13. Côtes de Bourg (white only)
14. Côtes de Duras (white or rosé)
15. Côtes du Marmandais (white or rosé)
16. Côtes de Provence (white or rosé)
17. Côtes-du-Rhône (white or rosé)
18. Côtes du Ventoux (white or rosé)
19. Entre-Deux-Mers (white only)
20. Faugères (rosé only)
21. Graves (white only)
22. Graves de Vayres (white only)
23. Jurançon Sec
24. Minervois (white or rosé)
25. Montravel (white or rosé)
26. Muscadet
27. Muscadet de Sèvre et Maine
28. Muscadet des Coteaux de la Loire
29. Muscadet Côtes de Grand-Lieu
30. Premières Côtes de Blaye (white only)
31. Rosé d'Anjou
32. Rosé de Loire
33. St.-Chinian (rosé only)
34. Ste.-Foy-Bordeaux (white only)
35. Saumur (white only)
36. Touraine (white only)

Vin de pays

There are 153 *vin de pays*, or "country wine", appellations, covering 494,200 acres (200,000 hectares), and producing an annual average of almost 166 million cases (15 million hectoliters). Officially established in 1968, the *vins de pays* did not become a marketable reality until 1973, when the rules for production were fixed. They were created, quite simply, by authorizing some *vins de table* to indicate their specific geographic origin and, if desired, the grape varieties used, but the effect was more profound than that. For a long while, it was even obligatory for these wines to carry the term "Vin de Table" in addition to their *vin de pays* appellation, but this regulation was discontinued in 1989. Allowing producers of potentially superior table wine areas to declare, for the first time, the origin and content of their wines gave back a long-lost pride to the best growers, who started to care more about how they tended their vines and made their wines, and began to uproot low-quality varieties, replant with better ones, and restrict yields.

There are four categories of *vin de pays*, each with its own controls, but all regulated by the Office National Interprofessionnel des Vins (ONIVINS). Although every *vin de pays* must have a specified origin on the label, a wide range of grape varieties can be used and high yields are allowed. A certain flexibility on choice of grape varieties allows innovation, a character-building trait that has been denied winemakers under the AOC regime, but the high yields permitted have also caused many an unprincipled producer to jump on the relatively lucrative *vin de pays* bandwagon, thus the quality can vary greatly. This is, nevertheless, a most interesting category of wines, often infiltrated by foreign winemakers—usually Australian—producing some of the most exciting, inexpensive, and upfront-fruity wines.

Many *vins de pays* are, of course, bland and will never improve, but some will make it up the hierarchical ladder to VDQS and, possibly, then full AOC status. Certain individual producers, such as the Guiberts of Mas de Daumas Gassac and the Dürrbachs of Domaine de Trévallon, could not care less about AOC status, as they happen to be making wines under the less draconian *vin de pays* system. They already have reputations as good as those of the finest French appellations and demand even higher prices than some expensive AOC wines. For a description of the various *vin de pays* categories, a map showing the areas producing *vins de pays*, and profiles of every *vin de pays* along with their finest producers, see pp.248–259.

Vin de table

There are over 430,000 acres (175,000 hectares) of unclassified vineyards in France, producing an annual average of more than 75 million cases (nearly 5 million hectoliters) of *vins de table*, (although

BREAKDOWN OF FRENCH WINE PRODUCTION MEASURED IN HECTOLITERS

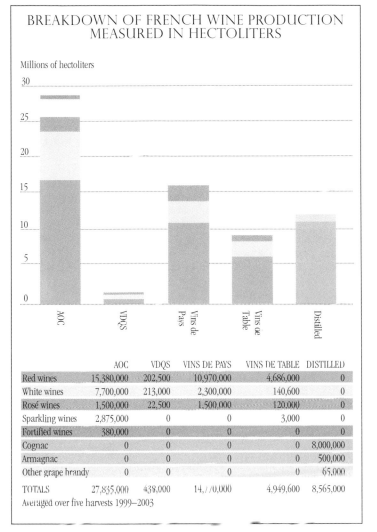

Millions of hectoliters

	AOC	VDQS	VINS DE PAYS	VINS DE TABLE	DISTILLED
Red wines	15,380,000	202,500	10,970,000	4,686,000	0
White wines	7,700,000	213,000	2,300,000	140,600	0
Rosé wines	1,500,000	22,500	1,500,000	120,000	0
Sparkling wines	2,875,000	0	0	3,000	0
Fortified wines	380,000	0	0	0	0
Cognac	0	0	0	0	8,000,000
Armagnac	0	0	0	0	500,000
Other grape brandy	0	0	0	0	65,000
TOTALS	27,835,000	438,000	14,770,000	4,949,600	8,565,000

Averaged over five harvests 1999–2003

FRENCH WINE PRODUCTION BY TYPE

Millions of hectoliters

Red 31,238,500
White 10,353,600
Rosé 3,142,500
Sparkling 2,878,000
Fortified 380,000

this also includes a variable volume of grape juice, grape concentrate, and wine vinegar). This compares with a production of 510 million cases (34 million hectoliters) 10 years ago, and is evidence of the trend away from the lower end of the market.

The official use of *vin de table* (also designated as *vin de consommation courante*, or wine for immediate consumption) is contrary to the common usage, particularly in New World countries, of table wine to refer to those that are neither fortified nor sparkling. In the latter sense, table wines are, or can be, quality wines, but in official French terms, *vins de table* are *vins ordinaires*, and are cheap in every sense of the word. They are not intended for keeping, and some cynics might argue that they are not fit for drinking either, since much of this wine is traditionally diluted with water before even the French can bring themselves to consume it.

Vins de table come under the auspices of ONIVINS, but there are no controls apart from negative ones, such as not being allowed to mention any grape names or indicate an origin more specific than France. The address of the producer seldom has any bearing on the origin of the wine, although some producers do try to fabricate a style in accordance with their local image. Thus a *négociant* based in Nuits-St.-Georges might attempt to make a *vin de table* with some sort of Burgundian character, but the consumer cannot be sure that any of the wines used will be from Burgundy, and the likelihood is that they will not. Some wine merchants pride themselves on the quality of their basic *vin de table* brand, but this is a dead-end category as far as being able to discover useful information, let alone rely on it, is concerned. However, there are always exceptions. These currently include:

Zind

Produced by Domaine Zind Humbrecht after the authorities finally made up their minds that Chardonnay should not be allowed in any AOC Alsace blend other than a Crémant d'Alsace. Not wishing to make a sparkling wine, Olivier Humbrecht MW was forced to sell the wine as a *vin de table*, which he has named simply Zind. He cannot put the year on this wine, so he numbers each *cuvée* starting with Z001. However, I can reveal that this is in fact the 2001 vintage, so Z002 is 2002, and so on. Humbrecht also cannot put the varietal content and origin on the label, but Zind is primarily Auxerrois (usually 50 percent of the blend, invariably from Clos Windsbuhl, Herrenweg, and Rotenberg), plus Pinot Blanc (15 percent, Herrenweg) and, of course, Chardonnay (35 percent, Clos Windsbuhl). The curious thing is that the maximum permitted yield for *vin de table* is 400 cases per acre (90 hectoliters per hectare), as opposed to 440 cases per acre (100 hectoliters per hectare) for the supposedly superior Alsace appellation. In addition, no *vin de table* is allowed to be chaptalized, whereas AOC Alsace is.

Libre Expression

Produced by Domaine Cazes, this rich, smooth white wine, which contains 16 percent alcohol, is effectively a late-harvest, nonfortified version of Rivesaltes, but one that finishes dry. It is vintaged, which is technically illegal, but by calling the wine "Libre Expression," the Cazes brothers are definitely making a statement.

Champagne 75,400 acres

Alsace 35,700 acres

Loire Valley 131,000 acres

Burgundy 121,000 acres

Bordeaux 296,000 acres

Rhône Valley 189,500 acres

Languedoc-Roussillon 101,300 acres

MAJOR AOC WINE-PRODUCING REGIONS *From this map, it is easy to discern the relative size of production of the seven most important wine regions of France.*

Muscat de Petit Grains Passerillé Vendange d'Octobre Elevée en Fûts de Chêne

Produced by Mas de Bellevue from old vines, on which the grapes have been left to shrivel. In the 2000 vintage (again illegally indicated), the only year I have tasted, at least half the grapes had been botrytized prior to *passerillage*.

CHALLENGING TRADITION

The French establishment has been slow to wake up to the fact that the AOC classification was not AOK, but they have started to think the unthinkable: change. When René Renou, the director of INAO (the man in charge of running the entire French appellation system), proposed a superappellation that would be bestowed on wines of "demonstrably superior quality," he shook the very foundations of French culture—tradition. This country produces both the best and the worst wines in the world because of its fixation with tradition, but whereas the French are always willing to preserve the best traditions, they are loath to banish the worst. Even when the need to do so is staring them in the face.

In 1995 Michel Bettane, one of France's top wine writers, was quoted as saying: "Today, *appellation contrôlée* guarantees neither quality nor authenticity." At the time, Alain Berger was the director of INAO, and when pressured he caused uproar by confessing that: "One can find on the market scandalously poor products with the *appellation contrôlée* halo." But was anything done? Of course not. For Renou to confirm the situation, and propose a solution, was a unique event. However, a fundamental shake-up to the system that gave birth to wine regimes throughout Europe threatened the moral authority of French wine, thus Renou's proposals have been met with hostility in some quarters, while in others they are viewed as absolutely necessary.

Those who support Renou are, essentially, a quality-conscious minority, while those who oppose include the worst of the worst, although the vast majority simply feel so safe with their traditions that they do not wish to rock the boat.

Initially, there was good news and bad news: the good news being that the Burgundians were for it, the bad being that the *bordelais* were not. However, the good news turned out to be bad, as evidenced by the supposedly pro-Renou Jean-François Delorme, who as president of the Bureau Interprofessionnel des Vins de Bourgogne (BIVB), commented: "Of course, all of Burgundy's AOCs would be super-AOCs." If all Burgundy were of the quality of Romanée Conti, Leroy, or Leflaive, no one would argue, but much too much is no better than *vin ordinaire*, while—as with every wine region—some wines can be almost undrinkable. So no, a pan-Burgundian application for super-AOCs would not be very super at all.

Being no fool, Renou allowed his historic proposal to "slip out" in London, where he could count on its radical goals receiving widespread objective approval, before presenting the plan in detail to the INAO's 80-member National Committee. He later provided more details about his superappellation, which he now called *Appellation d'Origine Contrôlée d'Excellence* (AOCE), and threw another monkey wrench in the traditionalist works by introducing the novel concept in the form of his proposed new *Site et Terroir d'Excellence* (STE) appellation.

On past experience, the odds always were that a compromise would be sought. That the goals would become so fudged, and the regulations so watered-down, that they will not simply be ineffective, but will probably be detrimental to the future of French wine. And that is precisely what has happened, but these new appellations and the reasons why they were rejected need exploring in more detail so that French wine lovers can at least know what Renou's good intentions were. Readers will then be able to appreciate how the French catastrophically missed this opportunity, and why the growers and government minister involved deserve to reap whatever ill fortune they have sown.

The BIVB was the first to support Renou's initiative, but Delorme's unrealistic position was disowned by its members, who turned out to be so hostile to the idea of AOCEs that

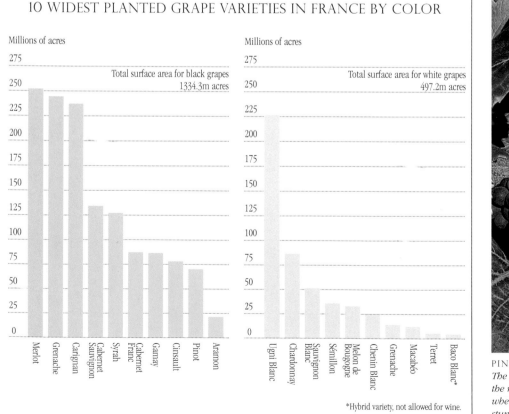

10 WIDEST PLANTED GRAPE VARIETIES IN FRANCE BY COLOR

Millions of acres

Total surface area for black grapes
1334.3m acres

Merlot, Grenache, Carignan, Cabernet Sauvignon, Syrah, Cabernet Franc, Gamay, Cinsault, Pinot, Aramon

Millions of acres

Total surface area for white grapes
497.2m acres

Ugni Blanc, Chardonnay, Sauvignon Blanc, Sémillon, Melon de Bourgogne, Chenin Blanc, Grenache, Macabéo, Terret, Baco Blanc*

*Hybrid variety, not allowed for wine.

PINOT NOIR GRAPES
The Holy Grail of red winemakers, the Pinot Noir is the most finicky of all black grapes to work with, but when successful, it can produce velvety red wines of stunning purity, finesse, and length.

Burgundy was given until "early 2005 at the latest" to present the INAO's president with modifications and solid proposals for putting such plans in place. They would not get the chance. The chop would come much earlier than that.

But what exactly did the Burgundians, and, in fact, growers from almost every wine region, object to? The AOCE designation would be granted only to areas that committed to a series of strict regulations in virtually every facet of vineyard management and winemaking, including lower yields, higher planting density, harvesting (manual or machines), aging (oak barrels or chips), grape varieties, wines judged by tasting panels, and so on. To become eligible for an AOCE, a minimum of 75 percent of the producers in an appellation would have to approve the tighter regulations, at which point any unwilling grower would be coerced to follow the majority and abide by the new regulations. INAO would review each appellation's status as an AOCE every five years.

There were two obvious flaws. First, if it is up to the wine producers of an appellation to decide by voting whether it is to be an AOC or AOCE, it cannot work. A truly famous wine that is offered the opportunity of claiming superappellation status is one thing, but an ordinary wine that assumes superappellation status simply because the majority of its growers vote for it would be pointless. Equally, if the growers of a truly famous wine did not grab such a chance with both hands, they would deserve to suffer the decline that would inevitably ensue, although there were many objectors who did not think that far ahead. In Chablis, for example, which is a truly famous wine region, one person with a short-term view is Jean Durup. He sits on the INAO National Committee, and was reported as saying that he didn't think the AOC would want to change its standards and adopt stricter rules because "we are the world's most famous white wine, and there is no crisis in Chablis." What would the next generation of Chablis growers think in 20 years' time, once the AOCE status of other white Burgundies had become well established? It would surely not be unreasonable for consumers at that juncture to assume that plain old Chablis AOC was simply not in the same class as Burgundy's AOCEs. The second potential flaw in the system was the panel tastings. If they were to be conducted by the producers themselves, the results would be as worthless as those for AOC wines.

SITE ET TERROIR D'EXCELLENCE

As for the brand new STE classification, this was a truly inspired concept and, as such, its demise has been an even greater tragedy. STE was designed to recognize the exceptional effort put in by serious, quality conscious producers in relatively modest or otherwise generally unambitious appellations. Individual wineries could receive the STE label if their wines are much better wines than those of most other producers in the appellation. Renou had intimated that INAO was likely to approve hundreds of STE wineries. What an opportunity the French have lost to fight back on the superpremium stage.

Jean-Michel Aubinel, who represents growers in Mâcon, clearly did not think so. He was reported as saying the scheme would entrench rivalry between neighboring properties, if applied to one and not the other. Well, that's the whole idea Monsieur: it is called competition. How else does anyone in any sphere strive to improve? But then, perhaps the AOC is meant only to guarantee mediocrity. Denis Dubourdieu of Château Reynon in Premières Côtes de Bordeaux was far more upbeat, pointing out that: "The STE concept appears to be the truly original point of the proposal. You can spend 20 years claiming you do better than most in one of Bordeaux's lesser-known satellite appellations, but the STE will give you status, and it will stimulate producers to make excellent wines." Well, Denis, my readers know about your top-performing wines, but it looks as though you'll have to spend another 20 years telling the rest of the world.

In conclusion, AOCEs and STEs would have reinvented and reinvigorated the French appellation system. Renou's proposals represented one of just four options. The second was to fudge them, the third was to do nothing at all, and the fourth was to scrap the "control-freak" element of French appellations altogether, bringing them more in line with New World thinking. There are good reasons why the fourth option should have been considered, such as: Why shouldn't people grow what they like, where they like? What does it matter what system of vine training a grower employs? Why try to control yields when the consumer will be the final arbiter of whether a producer will survive? Surely all that is necessary is the New World concept of truth in labeling: if a wine claims to be made from a particular variety, grown in a specific place, in a certain year, then that is what the wine should be. All good reasons—but there is a little Francophile part of me that wants to see the AOC concept survive, and to do that it needs reinventing from time to time. So what did they choose? The fudge, of course. The French cannot resist fudge, particularly when it comes sugar-wrapped.

At a three-hour crisis meeting between the French minister of agriculture, Hervé Gaymard, and representatives of the French wine industry on July 21, 2004, Renou's proposals were discarded because they made the French offer more complicated at a time when it needs to become more accessible (granted, separating the wheat from the chaff does tend to make the chaff less accessible!—T. S.). Gaymard stressed that there would be "tighter" controls for the production of AOC wines, to ensure that they were genuine *vins de terroir*, which represented "the top of the range," and were product-driven rather than consumer-driven (a flaw-free implementation of AOCE and STE would have achieved these very goals—T. S.). Gaymard's proposals were presented to each regional interprofessional bodies with a view to becoming effective with the 2006 harvest, along with a 50 percent increase in government aid for wine promotion overseas (the sugar coating—T. S).

FRENCH LABEL LANGUAGE

FRONT AND BACK LABEL DEFINITIONS

Année Literally year, this will refer to the vintage.

Appellation d'Origine Contrôlée Top official classification, commonly referred to as AOC, immediately above *Vin Délimité de Qualité Supérieure* (*see* p.54).

Barriques Small oak barrels of approximately 225 liters (59 gallons) capacity.

Blanc White.

Blanc de Blancs Literally "white of whites," a white wine made from white grapes, a term that is often, but not exclusively, used for sparkling wines.

Blanc de Noirs Literally "white of blacks," a white wine made from black grapes, a term that is often, but not exclusively, used for sparkling wines. In the New World, the wines usually have a tinge of pink, often no different from a fully-fledged rosé, but a classic *blanc de noirs* should be as white as possible without artificial means.

Brut Normally reserved for sparkling wines, *brut* literally means raw or bone dry, but in practice there is always some sweetness and so can at the most only be termed dry.

Cave coopérative Cooperative cellars where members take their grapes at harvest time, and the wines produced are marketed under one label. Basic products will often be blended, but top-of-the-range wines can be from very specific locations. A lot of cooperative wines can be ordinary, but the best cooperatives usually offer exceptional value.

Cépage This means grape variety, and is sometimes used on the label immediately prior to the variety, thus "Cépage Mauzac" means that the wine is made from the Mauzac grape variety.

Châtaignier Chestnut (occasionally used to make barrels).

Château Literally "castle" or "mansion," but whereas many wines do actually come from magnificent edifices that could truly be described as châteaux, many that claim this description are merely modest one-story villas, some are no more than custom-built *cuveries*, while a few are actually tin sheds! The legal connotation of a château-bottled wine is the same as for any domaine-bottled wine.

Chêne Oak (commonly used to make barrels).

Clairet A wine that falls somewhere between a dark rosé and a light red wine.

Climat A single plot of land with its own name, located within a specific vineyard.

Clos Synonymous with *climat*, except this plot of land is either enclosed by walls, or was once.

Côte, côtes Literally slope(s) or hillside(s) of one contiguous slope or hill, but in practical terms often no different from Coteau, Coteaux.

Coteau, Coteaux Literally slope(s) or hillside(s) in a hilly area that is not contiguous, but in practical terms often no different from Côte, Côtes.

Crémant Although traditionally ascribed to a Champagne with a low-pressure and a soft, creamy mousse, the term has now been phased out in Champagne as part of the bargain struck with other French sparkling wines that have agreed to drop the term *méthode champenoise*. In return they have been exclusively permitted to use this old Champagne term to create their own appellations, such as Crémant de Bourgogne, Crémant d'Alsace, etc.

Cru or **Crû** Literally means a growth or plot of land, this term usually implies that it has been officially designated in some way, such as a *cru bourgeois*, *cru classé*, *premier cru*, or *grand cru*.

Cru Bourgeois An officially designated growth below *cru classé* in the Médoc.

Cru Classé An officially classified vineyard in the Médoc and Provence.

Cuve A vat, *cuve* should not be confused with *cuvée*.

Cuve Close A sparkling wine that has undergone second fermentation in a vat, *cuve close* is synonymous with Charmat or Tank Method.

Cuvée Originally the wine of one *cuve* or vat, but now refers to a specific blend or product which, in current commercial terms, will be from several vats, this term is used most commonly, but not exclusively, in Champagne.

Dégorgé or **dégorgement** Found on some sparkling wines, this term will be followed by the date when the wine was disgorged of the yeast sediment that has built up during its second fermentation in bottle.

Demi-muid A large oval barrel, usually made of oak, with a capacity of 300 liters (79 gallons)—600 liters (158 gallons) in Champagne.

Demi-sec Literally semi-dry, but actually tastes quite sweet.

Domaine Closer to estate than vineyard, as a domaine can consist of vineyards scattered over several appellations in one region. The wine in the bottle must come from the domaine indicated on the label. Some former "châteaux" have changed to "domaine" in recent years.

Doux A sweet wine.

Encépagement The proportion of grape varieties in a blend or *cuvée*.

Elevage par X or **Eleveur X** Refers to the traditional function of a *négociant* (X), who has not made the wine initially, but purchased it, after which the *négociant* will age, possibly blend, bottle, and sell the wine.

Elevée en … Aged in ….

Elevée et mise en bouteille par X The wine was aged and bottled by X, but none or only part of the wine was produced by X.

Foudre A large wooden cask or vat.

Fûts Barrels, but not necessarily small ones.

Grand cru Literally "great growth," this term indicates the wine has come from a truly great vineyard (which, to put it in context, a lousy producer can make a hash of) in regions such as Burgundy and Alsace, where its use is strictly controlled. In Champagne, *grand cru* is much less meaningful, since it applies to entire villages, which might contain most of the best vineyards in the region, but where lesser vineyards also exist.

Grand vin This term has no legal connotation whatsoever, but when used properly in Bordeaux, *grand vin* applies to the main wine sold under the château's famous name, and will have been produced from only the finest barrels. Wines excluded during this process go into second, third, and sometimes fourth wines that are sold under different labels.

Lie French for lees: *sur lie* refers to a wine kept in contact with its lees.

Lieu-dit A named site, this term is commonly used for a wine from a specific, named site.

Médaille Medal: *médaille d'or* is gold medal, *médaille d'argent* is silver, and *médaille de bronze* is bronze.

Méthode Ancestrale A sweet sparkling wine from Limoux that is produced by a variant of *méthode rurale*, a process that involves no secondary fermentation, the wine being bottled before the first alcoholic fermentation has finished.

Méthode Classique One of the legal terms for a sparkling wine made by the *méthode champenoise*.

Méthode Champenoise Contrary to popular belief, this term is not banned in the EU. It is expressly reserved for Champagne, the producers of which seldom bother to use it. (I cannot say never because I saw it once!) *Méthode champenoise* is the process whereby an effervescence is produced through a secondary fermentation in the same bottle it is sold in.

Méthode Deuxième Fermentation, Traditionnelle, Méthode Traditionnelle Classique Legal terms for a sparkling wine made by the *méthode champenoise* (*méthode deuxième fermentation* is used only in Gaillac).

Millésime, millésimé Refers to the vintage year.

Mis en bouteille au domaine or **à la propriété** or **le château** Bottled at the domaine/property/

AOC

VDQS

VIN DE PAYS

CHAMPAGNE

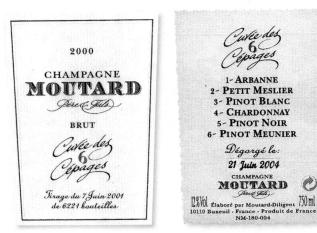

château indicated on the label (the wine must have been made exclusively from grapes grown there).

Mis en bouteille par ... Bottled by ... (not necessarily made by).

Mistelle Fresh grape juice that has been muted with alcohol before any fermentation can take place.

Moelleux Literally "soft" or "smooth," this term usually implies a rich, medium-sweet style in most French areas, except the Loire, where it is used to indicate a truly rich, sweet botrytis wine, thereby distinguishing it from *demi-sec*. This term is now obligatory in Alsace for wines that have a minimum residual sugar of 12g/l (9g/l for Riesling). If a wine has more than 6g/l of total acidity, the minimum residual sugar rises to 18g/l.

Monopole With one exception, this means that the wine comes from a single vineyard (usually a *grand cru*) that is under the sole ownership of the wine producer in question. The exception is Champagne Heidsieck & Co. Monopole, which is just a trading name.

Mousse The effervescence of a sparkling wine.

Mousseux Sparkling, found only on cheap fizz.

Négociant Literally a trader or merchant, this name is used by wine producers whose business depends on buying in raw materials. The name is derived from the traditional practice of negotiating with growers to buy grapes and/or wine, and with wholesalers and retailers to sell wine.

Négociant-éleveur Wine firm that buys in ready-made wines for *élevage*.

Négociant-Propriétaire A *négociant* who owns vineyards and probably offers a range of its own produced wines.

Non filtré The wine has not been filtered, thus liable to drop a sediment much earlier than most other wines, and should always be decanted.

Oeil-de-perdrix Literally "partridge eye" and refers to a rosé-colored wine.

Perlant Very slightly sparkling—less so than *pétillant*.

Pétillance, pétillant A wine with enough carbonic gas to create a light sparkle.

Premier cru Literally a "first growth," the status of a *premier cru* is beneath that of *grand cru* but only of relevance in areas where the term is controlled, such as Burgundy and Alsace. In Champagne, *premier cru* is much less meaningful, because it applies to entire villages, of which there are far too many, and in which much lesser vineyards also exist.

Produit Product, as in Product of ...

Propriétaire-Récoltant A grower-producer whose wine will be made exclusively from his own property.

Récolte Refers to the vintage year.

Réserve Ubiquitous and meaningless.

Rosé Pink.

Rouge Red.

Rubis Sometimes seen on rosé wines, particularly, but not exclusively, on darker styles.

Saignée A rosé wine produced by "bleeding" off surplus liquid from either the press or the fermenting vat.

Sec Dry, but in a sparkling wine this will have more sweetness than a *brut*.

Sélection de Grains Nobles A rare, intensely sweet, wine in Alsace made from selected botrytized grapes.

Sélection par X Selected, but not produced or bottled by X.

Supérieur As part of an appellation (e.g., Mâcon Supérieur as opposed to Mâcon plain and simple), this refers not so much to a superior quality than—possibly—a superior alcoholic strength, the minimum criteria being 0.5 percent ABV higher than the minimum for the same appellation without the Supérieur appendage).

Sur lie Refers to wines, usually Muscadets, that have been kept on their lees and have not been racked or filtered prior to bottling. This enhances the fruit of the normally bland Melon de Bourgogne grape used in Muscadet, often imparting a certain liveliness.

Tête de cuvée No legal obligation, but this term strongly suggests that a wine has been produced exclusively from the first flow of juice during the pressing, which is the highest in quality with the most acids, sugars, and minerals.

Tonneau A large barrel, traditionally four times the size of a *barrique*.

Trie Usually used to describe the harvesting of selected overripe or botrytized grapes by numerous sweeps (or *tries*) through the vineyard.

Union Coopérative A regional collective of local cooperatives.

Vendange tardive Late harvest; the term implies a sweet wine.

Vieilles Vignes Supposedly from old vines, implying lower yields and higher concentration, but no legal parameters apply, although most reputable producers would not dream of using the term unless the vines are at least 35 to 50 years old.

Vieillissement Aging.

Vigneron Literally a vineyard worker, but often used to denote the owner-winemaker.

Vigne Vine.

Vignoble Vineyard.

Vin d'une nuit A rosé or very pale red wine that is allowed contact with its grapeskins for one night only.

Vin de glace The French equivalent of *Eiswein* or Ice Wine.

Vin Wine.

Vin de l'Année Synonymous with *vin primeur*.

Vin de liqueur A fortified wine that is muted with alcohol before fermentation can begin.

Vin de paille Literally "straw wine," this is a complex sweet wine produced by leaving late-picked grapes to dry and shrivel while hanging from rafters over straw mats.

Vin de Pays Official classification, usually precedes the actual *vin de pays* name such as *Vin de Pays des Collines de la Moure, Vin de pays* is below VDQS and above *vin de table* (*see* p.56).

Vin de Table Lowest official classification, immediately below *vin de table* (*see* p.56).

Vin Délimité de Qualité Supérieure Official classification, commonly referred to as VDQS, below AOC and above *vin de pays* (*see* p.56).

Vin Doux Naturel A fortified wine, such as Muscat de Beaumes de Venise, that has been muted during fermentation, after it has achieved between 5 and 8 percent alcohol.

Vin gris A delicate, pale version of rosé.

Vin jaune The famous "yellow wine" of the Jura derives its name from the honey-gold color that results from its deliberate oxidation beneath a sherry-like flor. The resulting *vin jaune* is similar to an aged fino sherry, although *vin jaune* is not fortified.

Vin Mousseux Literally means sparkling wine without any connotation of quality one way or the other, but because all fine sparkling wines in France utilize other terms, it should be taken to mean a cheap, low-quality fizz.

Vin Nouveau Synonymous with *vin primeur*.

Vin primeur A young wine that is sold within weeks of the harvest, and meant to be drunk within the year. Beaujolais Primeur is the most commonly known example of this type of wine, but numerous other AOCs are allowed to be sold in this fashion (*see box*, p.56), as are all *vins de pays*.

BORDEAUX

Bordeaux is an area in an almost-perfect viticultural situation on the west coast of France and benefits from the ultimate marketing tool—a château-based classification system that was established 150 years ago.

THE NEW MILLENNIUM appears to be just as taxing for Bordeaux's reputation as the last decade of the 20th century turned out to be. Rain-drenched harvests toward the end of the 1990s challenged Bordeaux's claim to be the ultimate viticultural paradise, while the depressingly poor quality of its generic wines attracted almost as much bad publicity as the grossly inflated prices of modest vintages from the top châteaux. The weather might have improved in the first few years of the 21st century, but the quality of generic Bordeaux has remained abysmal, prices continue to rise almost in direct relation to the drop in sales—and then the unimaginable happened: the renowned US wine critic Robert Parker failed to appear for the *primeur* tastings in March 2003.

But all is not lost—Christian Delpeuch, the new head of the Conseil Interprofessionel des Vins de Bordeaux (CIVB), has mooted the possibility of declassifying some of the weaker Bordeaux wines into a wider *vin de pays*, which could then be bolstered by stronger wines from outside the region, but traditional to the southwest, such as the deep, dark Tannat. Delpeuch is the managing director of Ginestet, the region's biggest trader, and seems to have a good understanding of the more commercial end of Bordeaux's business. He has suggested the creation of a Vins des Cépages d'Aquitaine category for the Bordeaux region, under which varietal wines could be marketed. Far from detracting from the classic wines of Bordeaux, this would in fact improve their quality through stricter selection. And at the very top end of the market, the *bordelais* can once again sleep easy in their beds, as Robert Parker returned for the *primeur* tastings in 2004.

OVERVIEW

The Bordeaux appellation and the Gironde *département* are geographically one and the same. Moreover, the Gironde is the largest *département* in France, and Bordeaux is the largest source of quality wines in the world. There are more than 22,000 vineyard proprietors working in excess of 280,000 acres (120,000 hectares), producing over 71 million cases (6.4 million hectoliters) of Bordeaux wine (85 percent red, 3 percent rosé, and 12 percent white) under 57 different appellations every year. Of these 22,000 properties, no fewer than 10,000 are châteaux and domaines producing wine. Of these 10,000 wine-producing properties, some 6,000 make and market wine under their own name (75 percent of total production), while the remaining 4,000 wine-producing properties are members of 53 cooperative wineries in Bordeaux (representing 25 percent of production, a little of which is sold under the producing property name).

THE CHÂTEAU SYSTEM AND MERCHANT POWER

Prior to the concept of château wine estates, the land was worked on a crop-sharing basis. This feudal system slowly changed from the late 17th century onward. As the *Bordelais* brokers developed the habit of recording and classifying wines according to their *cru*, or growth (that is to say their geographical origin), and the prices they fetched, the reputations of individual properties became established.

The 19th century saw the rise of the *négociant*, or merchant, in Bordeaux. Many *négociants* were of English origin, and some firms were established by Scottish, Irish, Dutch, or German businessmen. The best château wines were not consumed by the French themselves; they were the preserve of other northern European countries. Thus foreign merchants had an obvious advantage over their French counterparts. Yearly, in spring, these *négociants* took delivery of young wines in cask from the various châteaux and matured them in their cellars prior to shipping. They were, therefore, responsible for their *élevage*, or upbringing, and came to be known as *négociants-éleveurs*, eventually becoming the middlemen found in every aspect of wine trading. Many foreign buyers found it more convenient to deal through a *négociant* than directly with the wine producer, and often they had no alternative, since a number of châteaux were owned by, or were exclusive to, certain *négociants*.

CHÂTEAU PALMER
This majestic turreted château is one of the finest in the Médoc.

THE MODERN BORDEAUX WINE TRADE

It was perhaps inevitable that the historically powerful and family-owned *négociant-éleveur* firms would eventually become a spent force. They lacked the resources required to finance adequately the huge increase in demand for Bordeaux in the 1960s, and those that did not founder during the oil crisis of the early to mid-1970s fell prey to the economic depressions of the following two decades.

As proud old firms were either taken over or went bankrupt, so the power shifted from the *négociants* to the châteaux, and in order to cope with a boom in world markets, many Bordeaux properties expanded their vineyards or added large, shiny new fermentation facilities. Many of these projects were financed with bank loans when interest rates were low. When sales slumped

VOLUME VS. REPUTATION

Very few Bordeaux wines are produced from great vineyards. As the table below illustrates, the famous appellations represent a relatively small amount of the bordelais vignoble, and the classified growths a minuscule proportion of that. Yet it could be argued that the reputation of Bordeaux has been built upon a fraction of its *cru classé* or *grand cru classé*—the best performers. Bordeaux is a great wine region, but not all bordeaux is great wine.

DISTRICTS	SURFACE AREA Expressed as a percentage of Bordeaux vineyards
Bordeaux (red)	36.8
Bordeaux Supérieur (red)	10.0
Médoc (red, non *cru classé*)	11.0
Médoc (red, *cru classé*)	2.4
Graves (red)	3.1
Saint-Émilion (red)	4.2
Saint-Émilion (red, *grand cru classé*)	0.8
Saint-Émilion satellites (red)	2.7
Pomerol (red)	0.7
Lalande de Pomerol (red)	1.0
Fronsac (red)	1.1
Various *côtes* (red)	14.4
Dry white	8.3
Sweet white	3.4

Médoc
See also pp71, 81, 85, 89, 92

Graves
See also p97

Pessac-Léognan
See also p97

Cérons
See also p97

Barsac
See also p97

Sauternes
See also p97

Blaye
See also p126

Bourg
See also p126

The Libournais District
See also pp108, 111, 120

St-Émilion
See also p111

Pomerol
See also p120

Entre-Deux-Mers
See also p130

— ·· — ·· — *Département* boundary

———— Delimited AOC region of Bordeaux

▲ Height above sea level (metres)

0   5   10   15 miles
0   5   10   15   20   25 km

BORDEAUX, *see also* p55
Sandwiched between the brandy
regions of Cognac to the north
and Armagnac to the south, the
Gironde *département, which
constitutes the AOC area of
Bordeaux, consists of the former
province of Guyenne and a part
of Gascony called Bazedais.*

and interest rates shot up, the repayments became unbearable. Consequently, aside from a few entrepreneurial owners, power then shifted from châteaux to investors—not only banks but insurance groups, pension funds, and the like.

In today's market, therefore, the *négoce* has much less influence than before, with its *élevage* role primarily restricted to branded wines. The *élevage* of fine *cru classé* wine is either handled by the individual château itself or dispensed with by selling wines ridiculously young through French supermarkets or through the worldwide *en primeur* trade (*see* p66). Additionally, a number of château owners have carved out little empires, collecting estates or developing their own *négociant* businesses.

THE CLASSIFICATION OF BORDEAUX WINES

Of all the Bordeaux classifications that exist, it is the 1855 Classification that is meant whenever anyone refers to "The Classification." It was commissioned by the Bordeaux Chamber of Commerce, which was required by the government of the Second Empire to present a selection of its wines at the 1855 Exposition Universelle in Paris. For their own ends, the brokers of the Bordeaux Stock Exchange traditionally categorized the most famous Bordeaux properties on the basis of the prices they fetched, so they were charged by the Chamber of Commerce to submit a "complete list of classified red Bordeaux wines, as well as our great white wines." The classifications listed above and to the right give the 19th-century names in the original form as listed by the brokers on April 18, 1855. The frequent absence of the word château has been followed, as has the circumflex in *crû*, and the use of *second crû* for red wines and *deuxième crû* for whites.

THE CLASSIC GRAPE VARIETIES OF BORDEAUX

Contrary to what one might expect, it is Merlot, not Cabernet Sauvignon, that is the most important grape variety in Bordeaux. Cabernet Sauvignon represents only 27 percent of black grapes cultivated in Bordeaux, whereas Merlot accounts for more than 58 percent. It is nearer the truth, therefore, to say that Cabernet Sauvignon gives backbone to Merlot, rather than to suggest that Merlot softens Cabernet Sauvignon (which is the old adage). Although Château Mouton-Rothschild contains no less than 90 percent Cabernet Sauvignon, it is an exception, as even on the Médoc's hallowed ground, where it is blasphemy to mention the name of Merlot, 40 percent of the vines grown are of that variety. Château Pétrus (*see* p123), one of the most expensive wines in

THE 1855 CLASSIFICATION OF THE WHITE WINES OF THE GIRONDE

PREMIER CRU SUPÉRIEUR
(Superior First Growth)
Yquem, Sauternes

PREMIER CRUS
(First Growths)
Latour Blanche, Bommes (now *Château La Tour Blanche*)
Peyraguey, Bommes (now two properties: *Château Lafaurie-Peyraguey* and *Château Clos Haut-Peyraguey*)
Vigneau, Bommes (now *Château Rayne-Vigneau*)
Suduiraut, Preignac
Coutet, Barsac
Climens, Barsac
Bayle, Sauternes (now *Château Guiraud*)
Rieusec, Sauternes (now *Château Rieussec*, Fargues)
Rabaud, Bomme (now two properties: *Château Rabaud-Promis* and *Château Sigalas-Rabaud*)

DEUXIÈME CRUS
(Second Growths)
Mirat, Barsac (now *Château Myrat*)
Doisy, Barsac (now three properties: *Château Doisy-Daëne*, *Château Doisy-Dubroca*, and *Château Doisy-Védrines*)
Pexoto, Bommes (now part of *Château Rabaud-Promis*)
D'arche, Sauternes (now *Château d'Arche*)
Filhot, Sauternes
Broustet Nérac, Barsac (now two properties: *Château Broustet* and *Château Nairac*)
Caillou, Barsac
Suau, Barsac
Malle, Preignac (now *Château de Malle*)
Romer, Preignac (now two properties: *Château Romer* and *Château Romer-du-Hayot*, Fargues)
Lamothe, Sauternes (now two properties: *Château Lamothe* and *Château Lamothe-Guignard*)

the world, contains 95 percent Merlot, without any Cabernet Sauvignon at all. Cabernet Sauvignon is a classic grape, quite possibly the greatest red-wine grape in the world, but its importance for Bordeaux is often overstated.

Sémillon is the most important white grape variety grown in Bordeaux. It is significant both in terms of its extent of cultivation and quality. This grape variety is susceptible to botrytis, the "noble rot" that results in classic Sauternes and Barsac. It is therefore considered to be the world's greatest sweet-wine grape. Sémillon also accounts for most of the fine dry white wines of Bordeaux, but these are relatively few and lack prestige. Sauvignon Blanc plays the supporting role in the production of sweet wines, and is used to a greater or lesser degree for dry wines. Many of the less expensive dry white wines are pure Sauvignon Blanc varietals.

VARIETAL CONTRIBUTIONS TO A CUVÉE

The Cabernet Sauvignon is the most complex and distinctive of all black Bordeaux grapes. It has a firm tannic structure, yet with time reveals a powerful, rich, and long-lasting flavor. Wines from this grape can have great finesse; their bouquets often possess a "blackcurrant" or "violets" character. Cabernet Franc has similar characteristics to Cabernet Sauvignon, but may also have a leafy, sappy, or earthy taste, depending on where it is cultivated. It does, however, shine through as the superior variety when grown in St.-Émilion and Pomerol, and can compete on even terms with its more famous cousin in parts of Graves. Merlot is soft, silky, and sometimes opulent. It is a grape that charms and can make wines with lots of juicy-rich and spicy fruit. Petit Verdot is a late-ripener with a naturally high acidity, while Malbec has a thick skin that is rich in color pigments. Small amounts of Petit Verdot and Malbec were traditionally used to correct the color and acidity of a blended wine. The cultivation and use of these two varieties for this purpose has been on the decline for the last 20 years owing to the various modern techniques of viticulture and vinification.

The white Sémillon grape provides a wine naturally rich in flavor and high in alcohol. It makes succulent, sweet white wines that are capable of great longevity. Its intrinsically low acidity

THE MERLOT GRAPE VARIETY
Almost twice as much Merlot as Cabernet Sauvignon grows in Bordeaux.

THE 1855 CLASSIFICATION OF THE RED WINES OF THE GIRONDE

PREMIERS CRUS
(First Growths)
Château Lafite, Pauillac
(now *Château Lafite-Rothschild*)
Château Margaux, Margaux
Château Latour, Pauillac
Haut-Brion, Pessac (Graves)

SECONDS CRUS
(Second Growths)
Mouton, Pauillac (now *Château Mouton-Rothschild* and a First Growth since 1973)
Rauzan-Ségla, Margaux
Rauzan-Gassies, Margaux
Léoville, St.-Julien (now three properties: *Châteaux Léoville-Las-Cases, Léoville-Poyferré,* and *Léoville-Barton*)
Vivens Durfort, Margaux (now *Château Durfort-Vivens*)
Gruau-Laroze, St.-Julien (now *Château Gruaud-Larose*)
Lascombe, Margaux (now *Château Lascombes*)
Brane, Cantenac (now *Château Brane-Cantenac*)
Pichon Longueville, Pauillac (now two properties: *Château Pichon-Longueville Baron* and *Château Pichon-Longueville-Comtesse-de-Lalande*)
Ducru Beau Caillou, St.-Julien (now *Château Ducru-Beaucaillou*)
Cos Destournel, St.-Estèphe (now *Château Cos d'Estournel*)
Montrose, St.-Estèphe

TROISIÈMES CRUS
(Third Growths)
Kirwan, Cantenac
Château d'Issan, Cantenac
Lagrange, St.-Julien
Langoa, St.-Julien (now *Château Langoa-Barton*)
Giscours, Labarde
St.-Exupéry, Margaux (now *Château Malescot-St. Exupéry*)
Boyd, Cantenac (now two properties: *Châteaux Boyd-Cantenac* and *Château Cantonac Brown*)
Palmer, Cantenac
Lalagune, Ludon (now *Château La Lagune*)
Desmirail, Margaux
Dubignon, Margaux (no longer in existence, but some of these original vineyards now belong to *Châteaux Malescot-St.-Exupéry, Château Palmer,* and *Château Margaux*)
Calon, St.-Estèphe (now *Château Calon-Ségur*)
Ferrière, Margaux
Becker, Margaux (now *Château Marquis d'Alesme-Becker*)

QUATRIÈMES CRUS
(Fourth Growths)
St.-Pierre, St.-Julien (now *Château St.-Pierre-Sevaistre*)
Talbot, St.-Julien
Du-Luc, St.-Julien (now *Château Branaire-Ducru*)
Duhart, Pauillac (at one time *Château Duhart-Milon Rothschild,* but now *Château Duhart-Milon,* although still Rothschild-owned)
Pouget-Lassale, Cantenac (now *Château Pouget*)
Pouget, Cantenac (now *Château Pouget*)
Carnet, St.-Laurent (now *Château La Tour-Carnet*)
Rochet, St.-Estèphe (now *Château Lafon-Rochet*)
Château de Beychevele, St.-Julien (now *Château Beychevelle*)
Le Prieuré, Cantenac (now *Château Prieuré-Lichine*)
Marquis de Thermes, Margaux (now *Château Marquis-de-Terme*)

CINQUIÈMES CRUS
(Fifth Growths)
Canet, Pauillac (now *Château Pontet-Canet*)
Batailley, Pauillac (now two properties: *Château Batailley* and *Château Haut-Batailley*)
Grand Puy, Pauillac (now *Château Grand-Puy-Lacoste*)
Artigues Arnaud, Pauillac (now *Château Grand-Puy-Ducasse*)
Lynch, Pauillac (now *Château Lynch-Bages*)
Lynch Moussas, Pauillac
Dauzac, Labarde
Darmailhac, Pauillac (now *Château d'Armailhac*)
Le Tertre, Arsac (now *Château du Tertre*)
Haut Bages, Pauillac (now *Château Haut-Bages-Libéral*)
Pédesclaux, Pauillac (now *Château Pédesclaux*)
Coutenceau, St.-Laurent (now *Château Belgrave*)
Camensac, St.-Laurent
Cos Labory, St.-Estèphe
Clerc Milon, Pauillac
Croizet-Bages, Pauillac
Cantemerle, Macau

few years ago. Early harvesting, prefermentation maceration on the grape skins to draw out the aromatics, and longer, cooler fermentation in stainless steel, have all combined to produce a far more interesting, medium-quality, dry white wine.

FERMENTATION AND MATURATION
Although some properties producing *crus classés* retain their wooden vats for the fermentation process (more because they lack the funds to reequip than for any idealistic reasons), hardly any of them actually invest in new oak vats, preferring those made of stainless steel. The one startling exception is Château Margaux. This great property has spent more money, following the advice of the legendary oenologist Professor Peynaud, than any other château in Bordeaux. This is puzzling because it was principally at his recommendation that virtually everyone else in Bordeaux invested in stainless steel.

ADDING VIN DE PRESSE
One technique that is more characteristic of red winemaking in Bordeaux than in any other region is the addition of a certain amount of *vin de presse*. This is produced after the wine has completed its alcoholic fermentation and has undergone malolactic conversion. The wine is drawn off its lees into casks and the residue of skin and pips at the bottom of the vat is pressed. Normally this requires two pressings: the first *vin de presse* is the best and represents about 10 percent of the total wine produced, the second provides a further 5 percent. *Vin de presse* is relatively low in alcohol, very dark, and extremely tannic. In a wine made for early drinking, *vin de presse* would be harsh and unpleasant, but with the structure of a classic oak-matured Bordeaux, it gives extra body and increases longevity.

THE VINIFICATION PROCESS
The proportion of grape varieties grown and the intrinsic potential of a château's terroir determine the basic quality and character of Bordeaux's finest wines. Manipulating the vinification process has, however, always been the method of honing the style of this region's best châteaux. Processes include adding up to 15 percent vin de presse; *grape-skin contact (which can be for up to a month); maturation, which used to take 3 to 5 years, but now takes 15 to 18 months; and a percentage of new oak, always the hallmark of Bordeaux's premiers crus.*

makes it less suitable for producing dry wines, but in exceptional circumstances the highest quality Sémillon does make a fine dry white wine—if matured in new oak. This enhances the aromatic character of the wine and gives it a firm structure without which it would be too "fat" and "flabby."

The Sauvignon Blanc in Bordeaux is soft, delicate, and easy to drink. It does not have the same bite as it does in the Loire vineyards of Sancerre or Pouilly-Fumé, but the varietal character is more pronounced today, with a crisper, fresher style, than it was a

BUYING EN PRIMEUR

WHAT IS BUYING EN PRIMEUR?
This is a method of investing in Bordeaux wines by buying the wine before it is bottled. It is no longer something I subscribe to. Every château in Bordeaux attempts to presell a certain amount of its wine production in the first year of the wine's life, although it will not be bottled and shipped until it is three or, perhaps, four years old.

APPROXIMATED BLENDS
The wines tasted by the trade and upon which *en primeur* offers are based will be approximated blends, which is to say that they will consist of several different casks in roughly the proportion of grape variety that will make up the final *grand vin*. Yet no matter how honest and accurate the winemaker tries to be, this can never be a true representation of the final wine. Winemakers do not know what the final proportions of grape varieties will be. Much depends on whether every

barrel matures as expected, and how strict the selection is when it comes to rejecting wines not fit for making *grand vin*.

WINE SALES BY MAIL ORDER
The first sales usually go on sale in the spring after the vintage, shortly after merchants from all over the world have spent a hectic week tasting hundreds of wines barely six months old. Cask samples (wine bottled from the cask) of the best wines are taken back to their home markets for tasting by the trade and key private buyers. This can be as early as March, although June is the most popular month and it is at around then that mail-order offers go out with vivid descriptions of the wines and how they are likely to mature.

WHY BUY EN PRIMEUR?
It is only worth buying a wine that you cannot touch for three or four years (and probably

should not drink for at least another three or four years after that), if you know it will be unavailable by any other means or, when it does become available, that it is likely to cost significantly more at that time.

WHICH WINES SHOULD YOU BUY?
Wine lovers are better advised to take up offers to buy *en primeur* wines such as Cornas from the Rhône, which never seem to be available when it is ready to drink. As far as investments are concerned, there is only one piece of advice I can give, and that is to stick to "blue-chip" wines in top vintages. It does not matter whether cask samples of Latour, Mouton, Pétrus, Yquem, and so on bear any resemblance to the final bottled product, they will always be a good investment, and from a wine drinker's point of view, there is no point in gambling on any other Bordeaux *en primeur*.

OAK CASK MATURATION

After fermentation and prior to bottling, all the best red Bordeaux are matured in 59-gallon (225-liter) Bordeaux oak casks called *barriques*. The duration of this operation and the percentage of new oak casks used should depend entirely on the quality and structure of the wine, and this will vary according to the vintage. The bigger the wine, the more new oak it can take and the longer maturation it will need. The greatest wines—all the *premiers crus*—require at least 18 to 24 months in 100 percent new oak to reach maturity. Other fine-quality Bordeaux wines do not need so much time, perhaps only 12 to 18 months, and do not benefit from 100 percent new oak; between 30 and 50 percent may be enough. If you get the chance, put your nose into a new oak cask before it has been used. The wonderful creamy-smoky, vanilla-and-charcoal aroma is the very essence of what should come through when a fine wine has been properly matured in oak.

PAST, PRESENT, AND FUTURE

During the early 1980s, the idea of "second wines"—always a factor in the production of the finest Bordeaux growths—began to catch on among the properties producing *crus bourgeois*, enabling

BARRELS IN A BORDEAUX CHAI
These new oak barriques at Château Langoa-Barton contain the wines of Château Léoville-Barton (Léoville-Barton has no chai of its own). Both properties belong to the Barton family (who are of British descent).

modest properties to make much better wines through stricter selection of their *grands vins*. Toward the end of the 1980s, "green harvesting," or crop-thinning, became *de rigueur* for all quality-conscious châteaux (even though the Romans considered such practices essential 2,000 years ago!).

However, the most significant advance in Bordeaux over the last 20 years came in 1994, when a decision was made to harvest grapes according to tannin ripeness, rather than sugar-acidity ripeness. Unripe tannins are not hydrolyzed; they are hard and will never soften, whereas ripe tannins are hydrolyzed, have a certain suppleness from day one, and will always soften. This phenomenon has long been known, but precisely when it occurs can vary from region to region, and year to year. In Bordeaux tannin ripeness has been under study since 1986 by Vincent Dupuch, who discovered that grapes deemed physiologically ripe in Bordeaux by their sugar-acidity ratio actually possessed a high proportion of unripe tannins.

In 1994, many *bordelais* harvested according to Dupuch's tannin ripeness parameters and were surprised to discover the optimum moment to pick was in fact much later than they had previously thought. This means not only that many Bordeaux wines will be riper, but also that by determining ripeness in this way, the winemaker is aware of the precise phenolic content, and this allows the fine-tuning of maceration and fermentation for each batch of grapes.

The 21st century will see a continuation in the rise of super-premium boutique wines, particularly from St.-Émilion. However, the increase in the density of vines to raise general standards in several Bordeaux appellations has been delayed. According to decrees issued in 1994, these new standards were to be fast-tracked, but this was fudged by new decrees in 1998, which let some areas off the hook, making higher-density planting not legally enforceable until 2025.

Meanwhile, the volume of dry white Bordeaux has dropped, leaving fewer producers making superior wines. Once the poorest cousin in Bordeaux, dry whites are better today than they have ever been. This applies across the board, from the lowliest Entre-Deux-Mers to the finest classified growth, even to the point where the 1993 Château Couhins-Lurton became the first Bordeaux *cru classé* to be sealed with a screwcap.

In a move to inform the public, and increase the region's profile among consumers of wines that do not include the Bordeaux name in the appellation (from Bourg to Blaye, and Fronsac to Pauillac, *et. al.*), all wines must include "Vin de Bordeaux" or "Grand Vin de Bordeaux" on the label.

RECENT BORDEAUX VINTAGES

2003 Unlike in the rest of France, this was not a drought year. In fact, precipitation levels were slightly above average. However, as in other French wine regions, 2003 was a very hot and sunny vintage, with exceptional ripeness. Exceptionally, acidification was permitted, but although initial concerns about low acid musts were widespread, relatively few producers bothered to add acid. This is a great Bordeaux vintage, with good to superb wines produced throughout the region, but favoring the Right Bank and improving the further north the vineyards are in the classic communal appellations of the Médoc. The most concentrated wines will be quite exotic and flamboyant. Great Sauternes were also produced.

2002 Hyped-up immediately after the vintage, when the wines were tasted the following spring, this vintage turned out to be far more variable than anyone had imagined. Essentially, it is a Cabernet year, not Merlot, thus some very high-quality Médocs were produced,

particularly in, but not restricted to, Pauillac. The further up the *cru classé* scale you go, the better the wines are, with Lafite a match for the greatest wines of any Bordeaux vintage. Excellent for Sauternes too.

2001 But for the outstanding 2000 vintage, everyone would have been hyping that of 2001 as one of Bordeaux's finest vintages across the board. Homogeneity (relevant to the intrinsic quality of the château, of course) is almost as widespread as in 2000, but the quality, although excellent, is not as great as that special year, while the style is more elegant, less concentrated. Another superb Sauternes vintage, and some of the best dry white *cru classé* wines produced in 10 years.

2000 God forgave the *bordelais* their transgressions and excesses of the recent past, and smiled on the world's foremost red wine region for the last vintage of the old millennium. He held back the rains until almost everyone had brought their harvest in.

The reds on both banks are beautifully colored, high in alcohol, with the weight and plumpness of a truly great year. This is a very special vintage indeed, producing wines of extraordinary concentration, except in Sauternes and Barsac, which were hit by rain during their late harvests—the results are not that bad, with quality equaling that of 1999.

1999 This is the year when almost everything that could go wrong did go wrong in Bordeaux. It was as if the last vintage of the 1990s was a testament to the climatic difficulties that masked this decade, with disease in the vineyards, rain at harvest, and a huge crop of unripe grapes. Very patchy, but most of the best wines were made in St.-Émilion, with some excellent Margaux and St.-Julien, and some Sauternes that can vie with the 1998s, though not the 1997s. It is in vintages such as 1999 that the difference in quality between Bordeaux as a whole and that found when tasting at the top 100 or so Bordeaux estates becomes so marked.

BORDEAUX'S BEST GENERIC BRANDS

Bordeaux has the greatest reputation for red wine in the world, but as in all regions, ordinary wines do exist. In fact, the majority of wines produced in any region is very ordinary, and Bordeaux is no exception. Remember that more than money separates Mouton Cadet from Château Mouton-Rothschild. While the former might be the most famous of all generic Bordeaux brands, it is merely the blended product of relatively inferior wines grown anywhere within the vast *departemental* appellation of Bordeaux, while the latter is a selection of one of the finest wines grown on a single estate—a *premier cru classé* in the small, communal AOC of Pauillac.

As a branded generic Bordeaux wine can be a disappointing introduction to the world's greatest wine region, the following brands are suggested as reliable choices:

DOURTHE NUMÉRO 1
Probably the best, largest-selling branded Bordeaux available.

LA COUR PAVILLON
One of the most reliable and underrated generic Bordeaux wines on the market at the moment. Made at Château Loudenne, this wine always displays good fruit, but possesses enough structure to keep for a while.

MAÎTRE D'ESTOURNEL
This has the same connection to Château Cos d'Estournel as "Mouton Cadet" has to Château Mouton-Rothschild, which is absolutely nonexistent as far as the wine is concerned, but both brands hope to sell on the back of their respective château name. There is however, a fundamental difference between the two, of course: "Maître d'Estournel" happens to be an expressive, early-drinking wine that can also take a few years in bottle, whereas "Mouton Cadet" is mutton posing as lamb.

MICHEL LYNCH
Produced by Michel Cazes of Château Lynch-Bages in an unashamedly up-front, fruity style. Red, white, and rosé are all thoroughly recommended.

PREMIUS EXIGENCE
Produced by Yvon Mau, the step up between the premium Premius and Premius Exigence is about as big as it can get for two wines sharing the same brand. The stricter selection of grapes and no-expense-spared handling shows through in the richer, oak-layered fruit.

SICHEL SIRIUS
This is as serious as it sounds. An excellent oak aged generic Bordeaux, it will improve for a further year or two in bottle.

THE APPELLATIONS OF GENERIC
BORDEAUX

There are more than 50 appellations in Bordeaux and every one has its generic wines, produced by a *négociant* or local *coopérative*.

BORDEAUX AOC

As with any large, and thus variable, appellation, the generic Bordeaux AOC is responsible for the good, bad, and ugly wines of the region. Overall, quality is of a decent standard, although the best wines are unlikely to fit the classic descriptions that have made the region famous. Wines carrying the generic appellation may come from any AOC vineyard in the entire Gironde. Some of the most interesting wines are from classic areas where the more specific appellation is confined to a precise style: such as a red Bordeaux produced by a château in Sauternes. If the wine is a brand, it should be ready to drink. If it is a château wine, the address should reveal its origin, and the price will be an indication of its quality and a guide to when it should be drunk.

RED Most are simply dry, luncheon claret styles, made for early drinking and usually softened by a high Merlot content.

🍇 Cabernet Sauvignon, Cabernet Franc, Carmenère, Merlot, Malbec, Petit Verdot

🍷 1–5 years

WHITE All medium-dry, basic white bordeaux contain at least 4 grams of residual sugar per liter, and have a certain sweetness. It is by far the most variable appellation category, with many dull wines. If the wine contains less than 4 grams of residual sugar per liter, the Bordeaux appellation must be qualified by "Sec." These dry whites are also variable, but most of the best wines of the appellation are found among them. They may be sold from December 1 without any mention of *primeur* or *nouveau*.

🍇 Sémillon, Sauvignon, Muscadelle plus up to 30% in total of Merlot Blanc, Colombard, Mauzac, Ondenc, Ugni Blanc

🍷 1–2 years

ROSÉ When made by individual properties, this medium-dry, medium-bodied wine can be attractive. These wines may be sold from December 1 following the harvest without any mention of *primeur* or *nouveau*.

🍇 Cabernet Sauvignon, Cabernet Franc, Carmenère, Merlot, Malbec, Petit Verdot

🍷 Immediately

BORDEAUX CLAIRET AOC

"Clairet" is a term that refers to a red wine that is light in body and color. It derives from *vin claret* in Old French, a term of respect; this suggests that Bordeaux achieved a reputation for limpidity before other wines.

ROSÉ Rich, dark rosé or failed, feeble red? The best examples of this medium-dry, medium-bodied wine come from the village of Quinsac in the Premières Côtes de Bordeaux.

🍇 Cabernet Sauvignon, Cabernet Franc, Carmenère, Merlot, Malbec, Petit Verdot

🍷 1–2 years

BORDEAUX ROSÉ AOC

The theory is that this appellation is reserved for wine deliberately produced as rosé, while "Bordeaux Clairet" is for a light-colored red wine. Both may simply be labeled "Bordeaux AOC." For technical details *see* Bordeaux AOC.

BORDEAUX SEC AOC

White bordeaux with less than 4 grams of residual sugar per liter (*see* Bordeaux AOC).

BORDEAUX SUPÉRIEUR AOC

Technically superior to Bordeaux AOC by only half a degree of alcohol, yet most of these wines do seem to have a greater consistency of quality, and, therefore, value. All generics are variable, but this one is less so than most.

RED These dry, light-bodied or medium- to full-bodied wines vary a lot but are generally fuller and richer than most red wines using the basic Bordeaux appellation.

🍇 Cabernet Sauvignon, Cabernet Franc, Carmenère, Merlot, Malbec, Petit Verdot

🍷 2–6 years

WHITE Dry or sometimes sweet, light- to medium-bodied white wines that are little seen.

🍇 Sémillon, Sauvignon, Muscadelle plus up to 30% in total Merlot Blanc, Colombard, Mauzac, Ondenc, Ugni Blanc; the proportion of Merlot Blanc must not exceed 15%

🍷 1–2 years

BORDEAUX SUPÉRIEUR CLAIRET AOC

This is a little-seen appellation: the wines are sold either as "Bordeaux Supérieur" or "Bordeaux Clairet."

ROSÉ Medium-dry and medium-bodied as Bordeaux Clairet, but with an extra half degree of alcohol.

🍇 Cabernet Sauvignon, Cabernet Franc, Carmenère, Merlot, Malbec, Petit Verdot

🍷 1–2 years

BORDEAUX SUPÉRIEUR ROSÉ AOC

This appellation has a small cast—and Château Lascombe's Rosé de Lascombes still tops the bill.

ROSÉ As few examples of these medium-dry, medium-bodied wines exist, it is possible to generalize and describe them as fuller, richer, and having more class than any Bordeaux Rosé AOC wines.

🍇 Cabernet Sauvignon, Cabernet Franc, Carmenère, Merlot, Malbec, Petit Verdot

🍷 1–2 years

CRÉMANT DE BORDEAUX AOC

This was introduced in 1990 to replace the old Bordeaux Mousseux AOC (which was phased out on December 31, 1995). Although preferable to a lot of poorly produced Loire sparkling wines, there is nothing special about Bordeaux bubbly. Changing the appellation has done nothing to change the product because, like its predecessor, Crémant de Bordeaux is merely a modest and inoffensive fizz. It lacks the spirit and expressiveness to stand out from the sea of far cheaper, but equally boring, sparkling wines that exist almost everywhere. I have tasted much better from areas far less suited to sparkling wine than Bordeaux.

SPARKLING WHITE Varies from dry to sweet and light- to medium-bodied, but is almost always bland.

🍇 Sémillon, Sauvignon, Muscadelle, Ugni Blanc, Colombard, Cabernet Sauvignon, Cabernet Franc, Carmenère, Merlot, Malbec, Petit Verdot

🍷 1–2 years

SPARKLING ROSÉ The authorities should have taken advantage of the introduction of a new appellation to allow the inclusion of white grapes for this style, as this would potentially have improved the quality.

🍇 Cabernet Sauvignon, Cabernet Franc, Carmenère, Merlot, Malbec, Petit Verdot

🍷 2–3 years

THE WINE PRODUCERS OF
BORDEAUX AND BORDEAUX SUPÉRIEUR

Although many of the following properties are located within more specific appellations, at least a certain portion of their wine production is sold as either Bordeaux or Bordeaux Supérieur, and it is those particular wines that have been recommended by the author in this section.

BORDEAUX

CHÂTEAU BALLUE-MONDON
Gensac

Soft and fruity "organic" claret.

CHÂTEAU DE BERTIN
Targon

Powerful Cabernet Sauvignon-dominated wines that age gracefully.

CHÂTEAU BERTINERIE
Cavignac

A serious rosé, pleasantly romantic, with delicately rich, floral fruit on the palate and a smooth finish.

CHÂTEAU BONHOSTE
St.-Jean-de-Blaignac
★ ❶

Classic white bordeaux at its best.

DOMAINE DU BRU
St.-Avit-St.-Nazaire

Refreshing clairet: light in color and body and easy to drink.

CHÂTEAU CARSIN
Rions

Popular in the UK, New World influenced.

CHÂTEAU COURTEY
St.-Macaire
★ V

These are intensely flavored old-style wines, possessing quite a remarkable bouquet.

CHÂTEAU FAUGAS
Cadillac

Well-balanced reds with attractive berry-fruit flavors.

CHÂTEAU DU GRAND MOUEYS
Capian

Consistently elegant red wines.

CHÂTEAU GRAND VILLAGE
Mouillac

Rich and easy Merlot-dominated, oak-aged red, and a good second wine under the "Beau Village" label.

CHÂTEAU DE HAUX
Haux

Gorgeously ripe and dry white wine, with very fresh and elegant fruit.

CHÂTEAU LAGROSSE
Tabanac
★ V

Elegant, ripe, and long, with lemony-rich, oaky fruit.

CHÂTEAU LAPÉYÈRE
Cadillac

Well-structured red, dominated by Cabernet Sauvignon.

CHÂTEAU DE LUGUGNAC
Pellegrue

Romantic 15th-century château making attractive, firm, and fleshy red that can show some finesse.

CHÂTEAU MARJOSSE
Branne
★ V

This is Pierre Lurton's home, where he makes lush and up-front reds with creamy-silky fruit and a beautiful dry white.

CHÂTEAU MORILLON
Monségur
★ V

Rich, fat, and juicy wines.

CLOS DE PELIGON
St-Loubès

Fine, full-bodied red with a hint of oak.

CHÂTEAU PLAISANCE
Capian

This château makes excellent, lightly rich Bordeaux Blanc Sec, made from 50-year-old vines and fermented in oak.

CHÂTEAU DE PLASSAN
Tabanac
★ V

The basic Bordeaux Blanc Sec has fresh, severe Sauvignon fruit, while the more expensive Bordeaux Blanc Sec, which is fermented and aged in oak, has lovely creamy fruit and a fine, lemony-vanilla finish.

CHÂTEAU POUCHAUD-LARQUEY
La Réole

Full and rich red with lots of fruit.

CAVE DE QUINSAC
La Tresne

Delicately colored, light-bodied, rosé-style wines sold as clairet.

CHÂTEAU RENON
Langoiran
★ V

This is a pleasantly fresh and floral Sauvignon-style wine.

CHÂTEAU REYNON
Cadillac
★ V

This is a star-performing château that produces cru classé dry white wine under the auspices of Denis Dubourdieu. The elite Vieilles Vignes cuvée is quite extraordinary, but everything produced here can be relied upon, right down to the aptly named "Le Second de Reynon." Also very good red.

CHÂTEAU ROC-DE-CAYLA
Targon

Easy-drinking, well-balanced reds with good fruit and some finesse.

LE ROSÉ DE CLARKE
Castelnau-de-Médoc

From Château Clarke, this has all the fragrance expected from a classic dry rosé.

CHÂTEAU THIEULEY
Créon
★ V

These are medium-bodied, elegant reds that possess more than just a hint of cask-aging. Also fine, fresh, floral, and fruity white wines.

CHÂTEAU TIMBERLAY
St.-André-de-Cubzac
★ V

Deep-colored, full of flavor, but not without a certain elegance.

BORDEAUX SUPÉRIEUR

CHÂTEAU DES ARRAS
St.-André-de-Cubzac
★ V

Deep-colored wines with good structure and lots of chunky fruit.

CHÂTEAU LA COMBE-CADIOT
Blanquefort
★ V

These well-colored wines have a big bouquet, and are oaky with delicious fruit.

CHÂTEAU FONCHEREAU
St.-Loubès
★ V

Well-structured, finely balanced vins de garde of extremely good quality.

CHÂTEAU FOUCHÉ
Bourg-sur-Gironde

This wine is firm yet has fat, juicy fruit and a smooth finish.

CHÂTEAU LA GRANGE-LES-TOURS
St.-André-de-Cubzac

Well-made, full, flavorsome wines.

CHÂTEAU GROSSOMBRE
Branne
★ V

Nicely concentrated, very good red wine which will improve for 12 to 18 months, and represents exceptional value.

CHÂTEAU LATOUR
Sauveterre-de-Guyenne

These medium-bodied wines have consistently good fruit, smooth flavor, and make a cheap way to get the "Latour" name on the table!

CHÂTEAU LAVILLE
St.-Loubès

Rich, tannic, and powerfully structured wines with spicy fruit.

MARQUIS DE BOIRAC
Castillon-la-Bataille

Super value coopérative wine with a big, oaky aroma and fruit to match.

CHÂTEAU MÉAUME
Coutras

Alan Johnson Hill used to be a UK wine merchant before settling north of Pomerol. Since then, he has gained a reputation for cleverly tailoring this red bordeaux to young British palates.

CHÂTEAU LA MICHELERIE
St.-André-de-Cubzac

Another property producing a big, tannic style of wine.

CHÂTEAU LES MOINES-MARTIN
Galgon

This is well-made wine for reasonably early drinking, with an attractive bouquet, round fruit, and fine balance.

CHÂTEAU DE PIERREDON
Sauveterre-de-Guyenne
★ V

Serious Cabernet Sauvignon-dominated bordeaux from the Haut-Benauge.

CHÂTEAU PUYFROMAGE
Lussac

Attractive, well-balanced, medium-bodied, and easy to drink.

ROSÉ DE LASCOMBES
Margaux

Refreshing, fruity rosé of excellent character, quality, and finesse.

CHÂTEAU SARRAIL-LA-GUILLAMERIE
St.-Loubès

Rich and fleshy wine that softens nicely with age.

CHÂTEAU DE SEGUIN
La Tresne

Look out for the Cuvée Prestige, which is rich and smoother than the basic Château Seguin.

CHÂTEAU TOUR-DE-L'ESPÉRANCE
Galgon

This is soft and smooth wine, full of fat, ripe, and juicy fruit, yet not without finesse.

CHÂTEAU TOUR PETIT PUCH
St.-Germain-du-Puch
★ V

Attractively colored, well-made, well-balanced wines, with a touch of spice.

CHÂTEAU DE LA VIEILLE TOUR
St.-Michel-Lapujade
★ V

Consistently rich and smooth, even in notoriously harsh vintages.

CHÂTEAU VIEUX MOULIN
Villegouge

These are well-rounded, long, and supple wines, which are of consistently fine quality.

THE MÉDOC

The style of wine alters more radically over short distances in the Médoc than in any other French red wine district. The wines are mild and unexceptional immediately to the northwest of Bordeaux, but from Ludon onward, they become progressively more characterful, acquire finesse, and—after Margaux—gain considerable body. Beyond St.-Estèphe, the firmness of body of the wines eventually turns to coarseness, and their finesse fades.

THE MÉDOC TAKES its name from the Latin phrase *medio aquae*—"between the waters"—referring to the Gironde estuary and the Atlantic Ocean. It is a long, thin strip of prized vines, extending northwest from the city limits of Bordeaux to the Pointe de Grave. At its center is the classic area of Bordeaux, where the vast majority of the most famous châteaux are located, and yet this was the last major district of Bordeaux to be cultivated. While winemaking in the Libournais district of St.-Émilion began as early as the Roman occupation, it was another thousand years before scattered plots of vines spread along the Médoc. Across the large, brown expanse of water called the Gironde, the Romans viewed Bourg and considered its hilly area far more suitable for growing vines. At that time the marshland of the Médoc was difficult to cross and impossible to cultivate. Today, the Médoc is the envy of winemakers the world over and Bourg is merely a source of inexpensive, if good-value, basic Bordeaux.

THE MÉDOC STYLE: VARIATIONS ON A THEME
The four famous communes of Margaux, St.-Julien, Pauillac, and St.-Estèphe, plus the two lesser-known but developing communes of Listrac and Moulis, are to be found in a region within the Médoc known as the Haut-Médoc, where the wines are fine, firm, and fleshy. The Haut-Médoc begins at the southern outskirts of the city of Blanquefort, along the northern reaches of the Graves district, where the wines are fairly neutral. The greatest wines of the Haut-Médoc are found in the area beginning at Ludon with Château la Lagune—the first *cru classé* encountered moving north from Blanquefort. Fine *crus bourgeois* are to be found in this area as well.

The wines at Margaux are soft and velvety and full of charm, although they are very much *vins de garde* and will improve well with age. The wines of St.-Julien are elegant with a very pure flavor. They have the delicate touch of Margaux, yet lean closer to Pauillac in body. The wines of Pauillac are powerful, often having a rich blackcurrant flavor with hints of cedar and tobacco. These

FACTORS AFFECTING TASTE AND QUALITY

LOCATION
The Médoc lies on the left bank of the Gironde estuary, stretching northwest from Bordeaux in the south to Soulac in the north.

CLIMATE
Two large masses of water on each side of the Médoc—the Atlantic and the Gironde—act as a heat-regulator and help provide a microclimate ideal for viticulture. The Gulf Stream generally gives the Médoc mild winters, warm summers, and long, sunny falls. The district is protected from westerly and northwesterly winds by the continuous coastal strip of pine forest that runs roughly parallel to the Médoc.

ASPECT
Undulating hillsides with knolls and gentle slopes are characteristic of the Médoc. The best vineyards can "see the river" and virtually all areas of the Haut-Médoc gradually slope from the watershed to the Gironde. Marshy areas, where vines cannot be grown, punctuate most communes.

SOIL
Similar topsoils lie over different subsoils in the Médoc. Its topsoils are typically outcrops of gravel, consisting of sand mixed with siliceous gravel of varying particle size. Subsoils may contain gravel and reach a depth of many feet, or may consist of sand, often rich in humus, and some limestone and clay.

VITICULTURE AND VINIFICATION
Only red wines can use the Médoc appellation. Mechanical harvesting is commonplace and all grapes are destalked prior to fermentation in tanks, or in vats increasingly made of stainless steel. Skin contact lasts for one to two weeks, although some châteaux have reverted to the once standard four weeks.

GRAPE VARIETIES
Primary varieties: Cabernet Sauvignon, Cabernet Franc, Merlot
Secondary varieties: Carmenère, Petit Verdot, Malbec

BARREL-MAKING AT
LAFITE ROTHSCHILD
Wines are aged in new oak at Château Lafite-Rothschild, although for a shorter length of time than in the past. The barrels are made with great care in a time-honored, traditional manner.

DISTRIBUTION OF MÉDOC CRUS CLASSÉS THROUGHOUT THE APPELLATIONS

APPELLATION	GROWTHS					
	1ST	2ND	3RD	4TH	5TH	TOTAL
Haut-Médoc	0	0	1	1	3	5
St.-Estèphe	0	2	1	1	1	5
Pauillac	3	2	0	1	12	18
St.-Julien	0	5	2	4	0	11
Margaux	1	5	10	3	2	21
TOTAL	4	14	14	10	18	60

are wines of great finesse, and Pauillac can be considered the greatest appellation of the Médoc. St.-Estèphe includes many minor growths of rustic charm and a few classic wines, and technology is changing the robustness of its spicy wines to richness.

Beyond St.-Estèphe lies the commune of St.-Seurin-de-Cadourne, whose wines are entitled to use the Haut-Médoc appellation, after which the appellation becomes simply AOC Médoc. This area, formerly known as the Bas-Médoc, has a lesser reputation than the Haut-Médoc. However, many exceptional wines are made here: the triangle formed by St.-Yzans, Lesparre, and Valeyrac contains such outstanding minor growths as Loudenne, Potensac, la Cardonne, Blaignan, les Ormes-Sorbet, la Tour-St-Bonnet, la Tour-de-By, and Patache d'Aux. In general the style is more simplistic than in the Haut-Médoc.

PROPORTION OF AOC AREA UNDER VINE REPRESENTED BY CRUS CLASSÉS

APPELLATION	ACRES	TOTAL (HA)	TOTAL IN HA	(ACRES)	CRUS CLASSÉS REPRESENTS
Médoc	3,240	(5,358)			No crus classés
Haut-Médoc	11,342	(4,590)	630	(255)	6% of AOC, 9% of crus classés
Listrac	1,641	(664)	–		No crus classés
Moulis	1,500	(607)	–		No crus classés
St.-Estèphe	3,099	(1,254)	558	(226)	18% of AOC, 8% of crus classés
Pauillac	2,988	(1,209)	2,081	(842)	70% of AOC, 30% of crus classés
St.-Julien	2,246	(909)	1,552	(628)	68% of AOC, 22% of crus classés
Margaux	3,464	(1,402)	2,110	(854)	61% of AOC, 31% of crus classés
TOTAL	39,520	(15,993)	6,931	(2,805)	8% of Médoc AOCs, 100% of crus classés

THE FIGHT FOR GRAVEL

The best soils for vine-growing also happen to be the most suitable for gravel quarrying. After WWII, in the absence of any legislation, gravel quarrying started in abandoned vineyards. Once the gravel was gone, the opportunity to reclaim the area as a vineyard was lost. There is plenty of gravel in the Gironde estuary itself, but it is more profitable to take it from an open pit. Quarrying companies will continue to plunder the Medoc's finite resources until the government agrees to protect them, but past administrations have shown little interest.

THE MÉDOC, *see also* p63
The Médoc, a narrow strip of land between the Gironde estuary and the Atlantic Ocean, stretches northwards from the city of Bordeaux to the Pointe de Grave. The climate is Bordeaux's mildest, moderated by both the estuary and the ocean.

CLASS STRUGGLE

According to the new bourgeois growths law of November 2000, the classification of wines of the Médoc is to be reassessed every 12 years. The first reassessment under this legislation took place in June 2003, and of the 490 châteaux that applied for consideration, only 245 were successful in gaining *cru bourgeois* status. The high failure rate reflects a seriousness often lacking in recent French classifications, and I believe that in most cases the judging panel got it right. However, some château owners objected to the outcome, none more so that Jean-François Mau, who was "outraged" by the exclusion of his Château Preuillac. Mau had purchased this property as recently as 1998, but the panel tasted wines only from the vintages of 1994 to 1999, which is why he was so critical of the process, stating "It is a huge injustice to be judged on the past and not present performance." My initial reaction was that Mau was wrong, that for a classification to be taken seriously, the successful châteaux must display a firm track record, and that he was impatient, as he will surely do much better in the next reclassification. But on reflection, I think the wines tasted could have had a more recent emphasis. Part of the criteria established by the November 2000 law take into account the reputation of any proposed bourgeois growth, and that has to be established over a period of time that—objectively—precludes the classification of Château Preuillac. But rather than tasting six vintages, the youngest of which is almost four years old, every single vintage since the last vintage tasted at the previous reclassification should be sampled. Nothing less will do, if this law is to stand the test of time. And, whereas it might not be right to classify according to the latest vintages only, the system could be made sufficiently flexible to award some form of commended classification for those châteaux that have made a profound and demonstrable effort to improve quality in recent years. This would not only be fair to new owners, and established ones who have renewed their efforts, but it would also perform a service for consumers, pointing them in the direction of Médoc wines that are improving with each vintage. This presumes, of course, that the Syndicat des Crus Bourgeois du Médoc is organized for the benefit of consumers, and not just its own glorification. The current 2003 classification consists of 9 *Crus Bourgeois Exceptionnels*, 87 *Crus Bourgeois Supérieurs*, and 151 *Crus Bourgeois* as follows:

CRUS BOURGEOIS EXCEPTIONNELS

Château Chasse-Spleen (Moulis-en-Médoc, Moulis-en-Médoc)
Château Haut-Marbuzet (Saint-Estèphe, Saint-Estèphe)
Château Labegorce Zédé (Soussans, Margaux)
Château Ormes-de-Pez (Saint-Estèphe, Saint-Estèphe)
Château de Pez (Saint-Estèphe, Saint-Estèphe)
Château Phélan Ségur (Saint-Estèphe, Saint-Estèphe)
Château Potensac (Ordonnac, Médoc)
Château Poujeaux (Moulis-en-Médoc, Moulis-en-Médoc)
Château Siran (Labarde, Margaux)

CRUS BOURGEOIS SUPÉRIEURS

Château d'Agassac (Ludon-Médoc, Haut-Médoc)
Château d'Angludet (Cantenac, Margaux)
Château Anthonic (Moulis-en-Médoc, Moulis-en-Médoc)
Château d'Arche (Ludon-Médoc, Haut-Médoc)
Château Arnauld (Arcins, Haut-Médoc)
Château d'Arsac (Arsac, Margaux)
Château Beaumont (Cussac-Fort-Médoc, Haut-Médoc)
Château Beau-Site (Saint-Estèphe, Saint-Estèphe)
Château Biston-Brillette (Moulis-en-Médoc, Moulis-en-Médoc)
Château Le Boscq (Saint-Estèphe, Saint-Estèphe)
Château Bournac (Civrac, Médoc)
Château Brillette (Moulis-en-Médoc, Moulis-en-Médoc)
Château Cambon La Pelouse (Macau, Haut-Médoc)
Château Cap-Léon-Veyrin (Listrac-Médoc, Listrac-Médoc)
Château La Cardonne (Blaignan, Médoc)
Château Caronne Sainte-Gemme (Saint-Laurent-Médoc, Haut-Médoc)
Château Castera (Saint-Germain-d'Esteuil, Médoc)
Château Chambert-Marbuzet (Saint-Estèphe, Saint-Estèphe)
Château Charmail (Saint-Seurin-de-Cadourne, Haut-Médoc)
Château Cissac (Cissac-Médoc, Haut-Médoc)
Château Citran (Avensan, Haut-Médoc)
Château Clarke (Listrac-Médoc, Listrac-Médoc)
Château Clauzet (Saint-Estèphe, Saint-Estèphe)
Château Clément Pichon (Parempuyre, Haut-Médoc)
Château Colombier-Monpelou (Pauillac, Pauillac)
Château Coufran (Saint-Seurin-de-Cadourne, Haut-Médoc)
Château Le Crock (Saint-Estèphe, Saint-Estèphe)
Château Dutruch Grand Poujeaux (Moulis-en-Médoc, Moulis-en-Médoc)
Château d'Escurac (Civrac, Médoc)
Château Fonbadet (Pauillac, Pauillac)
Château Fonréaud (Listrac-Médoc, Listrac-Médoc)
Château Fourcas Dupré (Listrac-Médoc, Listrac-Médoc)
Château Fourcas Hosten (Listrac-Médoc, Listrac-Médoc)
Château Furcas Loubancy (Listrac-Médoc, Listrac-Médoc)
Château du Glana (Saint-Julien-Beychevelle, Saint-Julien)
Château Les Grands Chênes (Saint-Christoly-de-Médoc, Médoc)
Château Gressier Grand Poujeaux (Moulis-en-Médoc, Moulis-en-Médoc)
Château Greysac (Bégadan, Médoc)
Château La Gurgue (Margaux, Margaux)
Château Hanteillan (Cissac-Médoc, Haut-Médoc)
Château Haut-Bages Monpelou (Pauillac, Pauillac)
Château La Haye (Saint-Estèphe, Saint-Estèphe)
Château Labegorce (Margaux, Margaux)
Château de Lamarque (Lamarque, Haut-Médoc)
Château Lamothe Bergeron (Cussac-Fort-Médoc, Haut-Médoc)
Château Lanessan (Cussac-Fort-Médoc, Haut-Médoc)
Château Larose Trintaudon (Saint-Laurent-Médoc, Haut-Médoc)
Château Lestage (Listrac-Médoc, Listrac-Médoc)
Château Lestage Simon (Saint-Seurin-de-Cadourne, Haut-Médoc)
Château Lilian Ladouys (Saint-Estèphe, Saint-Estèphe)
Château Liversan (Saint-Sauveur, Haut-Médoc)
Château Loudenne (Saint-Yzans-de-Médoc, Médoc)
Château Malescasse (Lamarque, Haut-Médoc)
Château de Malleret (Le Pian-Médoc, Haut-Médoc)
Château Maucaillou (Moulis-en-Médoc, Moulis-en-Médoc)
Château Maucamps (Macau, Haut-Médoc)
Château Mayne Lalande (Listrac-Médoc, Listrac-Médoc)
Château Meyney (Saint-Estèphe, Saint-Estèphe)
Château Monbrison (Arsac, Margaux)
Château Moulin à Vent (Moulis-en-Médoc, Moulis-en-Médoc)
Château Moulin de La Rose (Saint-Julien-de-Beychevelle, Saint-Julien)
Château Les Ormes Sorbet (Couquèques, Médoc)
Château Paloumey (Ludon-Médoc, Haut-Médoc)
Château Patache d'Aux (Bégadan, Médoc)
Château Paveil de Luze (Soussans, Margaux)
Château Petit Bocq (Saint-Estèphe, Saint-Estèphe)
Château Pibran (Pauillac, Pauillac)
Château Ramage La Batisse (Saint-Sauveur, Haut-Médoc)
Château Reysson (Vertheuil, Haut-Médoc)
Château Rollan de By (Bégadan, Médoc)
Château Saransot-Dupré (Listrac-Médoc, Listrac-Médoc)
Château Ségur (Parempuyre, Haut-Médoc)
Château Sénéjac (Le Pian-Médoc, Haut-Médoc)
Château Soudars (Saint-Seurin-de-Cadourne, Haut-Médoc)
Château du Taillan (Le Taillan-Médoc, Haut-Médoc)
Château Terrey Gros Cailloux (Saint-Julien-Beychevelle, Saint-Julien)
Château La Tour de By (Bégadan, Médoc)
Château La Tour de Mons (Soussans, Margaux)
Château Tour de Pez (Saint-Estèphe, Saint-Estèphe)
Château Tour du Haut Moulin (Cussac-Fort-Médoc, Haut-Médoc)
Château Tour Haut Caussan (Blaignan, Médoc)
Château Tronquoy-Lalande (Saint-Estèphe, Saint-Estèphe)
Château Verdignan (Saint-Seurin-de-Cadourne, Haut-Médoc)
Château Vieux Robin (Bégadan, Médoc)
Château Villegorge (Avensan, Haut-Médoc)

CRUS BOURGEOIS

Château Andron Blanquet
(Saint-Estèphe, Saint-Estèphe)

Château Aney (Cussac-Fort-
Médoc, Haut-Médoc)

Château d'Arcins (Arcins,
Haut-Médoc)

Château L'Argenteyre
(Bégadan, Médoc)

Château d'Aurilhac (Saint-Seurin-
de-Cadourne, Haut-Médoc)

Château Balac (Saint-Laurent-
Médoc, Haut-Médoc)

Château Barateau (Saint-Laurent-
Médoc, Haut-Médoc)

Château Bardis (Saint-Seurin-de-
Cadourne, Haut-Médoc)

Château Barreyres (Arcins,
Haut-Médoc)

Château Baudan (Listrac-Médoc,
Listrac-Médoc)

Château Beau-Site Haut-Vignoble
(Saint-Estèphe, Saint-Estèphe)

Château Bégadanet
(Bégadan, Médoc)

Château Bel Air (Saint-Estèphe,
Saint-Estèphe)

Château Bel Air (Cussac-Fort-
Médoc, Haut-Médoc)

Château Bel Orme Tronquoy-de-
Lalande (Saint-Seurin-de-
Cadourne, Haut-Médoc)

Château Bel-Air Lagrave (Moulis-
en-Médoc, Moulis-en-Médoc)

Château des Belles Graves
(Ordonnac, Médoc)

Château Bessan Ségur
(Civrac, Médoc)

Château Bibian (Listrac-Médoc,
Listrac-Médoc)

Château Blaignan
(Blaignan, Médoc)

Château Le Boscq
(Bégadan, Médoc)

Château Le Bourdieu
(Valeyrac, Médoc)

Château Le Bourdieu
(Vertheuil, Haut-Médoc)

Château de Braude (Macau,
Haut-Médoc)

Château du Breuil (Cissac-Médoc,
Haut-Médoc)

Château La Bridane (Saint-Julien-
Beychevelle, Saint-Julien)

Château des Brousteras (Saint-
Yzans-de-Médoc, Médoc)

Château des Cabans
(Bégadan, Médoc)

Château Cap de Haut
(Lamarque, Haut-Médoc)

Château Capbern Gasqueton
(Saint-Estèphe, Saint-Estèphe)

Château Chantelys (Prignac-en-
Médoc, Médoc)

Château La Clare
(Bégadan, Médoc)

Château La Commanderie
(Saint-Estèphe, Saint-Estèphe)

Château Le Coteau
(Arsac, Margaux)

Château Coutelin Merville
(Saint-Estèphe, Saint-Estèphe)

Château de La Croix

(Ordonnac, Médoc)

Château Dasvin-Bel-Air
(Macau, Haut-Médoc)

Château David (Vensac, Médoc)

Château Devise d'Ardilley
(Saint-Laurent-Médoc, Haut-Médoc)

Château Deyrem Valentin
(Soussans, Margaux)

Château Dillon (Blanquefort,
Haut-Médoc)

Château Domeyne (Saint-Estèphe,
Saint-Estèphe)

Château Donissan (Listrac-Médoc,
Listrac-Médoc)

Château Ducluzeau (Listrac-Médoc,
Listrac-Médoc)

Château Duplessis (Moulis-en-
Médoc, Moulis-en-Médoc)

Château Duplessis Fabre (Moulis-en-
Médoc, Moulis-en-Médoc)

Château Duthil (Le Pian-Médoc,
Haut-Médoc)

Château L'Ermitage (Listrac-Médoc,
Listrac-Médoc)

Château d'Escot (Lesparre-
Médoc, Médoc)

Château La Fleur Milon
(Pauillac, Pauillac)

Château La Fleur Peyrabon (Saint-
Sauveur, Pauillac)

Château La Fon du Berger (Saint-
Sauveur, Haut-Médoc)

Château Fontesteau (Saint-Sauveur,
Haut-Médoc)

Château Fontis (ffOrdonnac, Médoc)

Château La Galiane
(Soussans, Margaux)

Château de Gironville (Macau,
Haut-Médoc)

Château La Gorce (Blaignan,
Médoc)

Château La Gorre (Bégadan, Médoc)

Château Grand Clapeau Olivier
(Blanquefort, Haut-Médoc)

Château Grandis (Saint-Seurin-de-
Cadourne, Haut-Médoc)

Château Granins Grand Poujeaux
(Moulis-en-Médoc, Moulis-en-Médoc)

Château Grivière (Blaignan, Médoc)

Château Haut-Beauséjour (Saint-
Estèphe, Saint-Estèphe)

Château Haut-Bellevue (Lamarque,
Haut-Médoc)

Château Haut Breton Larigaudière
(Soussans, Margaux)

Château Haut-Canteloup (Saint-
Christoly-de-Médoc, Médoc)

Château Haut-Madrac (Saint-
Sauveur, Haut-Médoc)

Château Haut-Maurac (Saint-Yzans-
de-Médoc, Médoc)

Château Houissant (Saint-Estèphe,
Saint-Estèphe)

Château Hourbanon (Prignac-en-
Médoc, Médoc)

Château Hourtin-Ducasse (Saint-
Sauveur, Haut-Médoc)

Château Labadie (Bégadan, Médoc)

Château Ladouys (Saint-Estèphe,
Saint-Estèphe)

Château Laffitte Carcasset (Saint-
Estèphe, Saint-Estèphe)

Château Laffitte Laujac

(Bégadan, Médoc)

Château Lafon
(Prignac-en-Médoc, Médoc)

Château Lalande (Listrac-Médoc,
Listrac-Médoc)

Château Lalande (Saint-Julien-
Beychevelle, Saint-Julien)

Château Lamothe-Cissac
(Cissac-Médoc, Haut-Médoc)

Château Larose Perganson (Saint-
Laurent-Médoc, Haut-Médoc)

Château Larrivaux (Cissac-Médoc,
Haut-Médoc)

Château Larruau (Margaux, Margaux)

Château Laujac (Bégadan, Médoc)

Château La Lauzette-Declercq
(Listrac-Médoc, Listrac-Médoc)

Château Leyssac (Saint-Estèphe,
Saint-Estèphe)

Château Lieujean (Saint-Sauveur,
Haut-Médoc)

Château Liouner (Listrac-Médoc,
Listrac-Médoc)

Château Lousteauneuf
(Valeyrac, Médoc)

Château Magnol
(Blanquefort, Haut-Médoc)

Château de Marbuzet
(Saint-Estèphe, Saint-Estèphe)

Château Marsac Séguineau
(Soussans, Margaux)

Château Martinens
(Cantenac, Margaux)

Château Maurac (Saint-Seurin-de-
Cadourne, Haut-Médoc)

Château Mazails (Saint-Yzans-de-
Médoc, Médoc)

Château Le Meynieu (Vertheuil,
Haut-Médoc)

Château Meyre (Avensan,
Haut-Médoc)

Château Les Moines
(Couquèques, Médoc)

Château Mongravey (Arsac, Margaux)

Château Le Monteil d'Arsac (Arsac,
Haut-Médoc)

Château Morin (Saint-Estèphe,
Saint-Estèphe)

Château de Moulin Rouge
(Cussac-Fort-Médoc, Haut-Médoc)

Château La Mouline (Moulis-en-
Médoc, Moulis-en-Médoc)

Château Muret (Saint-Seurin-de-
Cadourne, Haut-Médoc)

Château Noaillac (Jau-Dignac-
Loirac, Médoc)

Château du Perier (Saint-Christoly-
de-Médoc, Médoc)

Château Le Pey (Bégadan, Médoc)

Château Peyrabon (Saint-Sauveur,
Haut-Médoc)

Château Peyredon Lagravette
(Listrac-Médoc, Listrac-Médoc)

Château Peyre-Lebade (Listrac-
Médoc, Haut-Médoc)

Château Picard
(Saint-Estèphe,
Saint-Estèphe)

Château Plantey (Pauillac, Pauillac)

Château Poitevin (Jau-Dignac-
Loirac, Médoc)

Château Pomys

(Saint-Estèphe, Saint-Estèphe)

Château Pontac Lynch
(Cantenac, Margaux)

Château Pontey (Blaignan, Médoc)

Château Pontoise Cabarrus (Saint-
Seurin-de-Cadourne, Haut-Médoc)

Château Puy Castéra (Cissac-Médoc,
Haut-Médoc)

Château Ramafort (Blaignan, Médoc)

Château du Raux (Cussac-Fort-
Médoc, Haut-Médoc)

Château La Raze Beauvallet
(Civrac, Médoc)

Château du Retout (Cussac-Fort-
Médoc, Haut-Médoc)

Château Reverdi (Listrac-Médoc,
Listrac-Médoc)

Château Roquegrave
(Valeyrac, Médoc)

Château Saint-Ahon (Blanquefort,
Haut-Médoc)

Château Saint-Aubin (Saint-
Sauveur, Médoc)

Château Saint-Christophe (Saint-
Christoly-de-Médoc, Médoc)

Château Saint-Estèphe
(Saint-Estèphe, Saint-Estèphe)

Château Saint-Hilaire
(Queyrac, Médoc)

Château Saint-Paul (Saint-Seurin-de-
Cadourne, Haut-Médoc)

Château Segue Longue
(Jau-Dignac-Loirac, Médoc)

Château Ségur de Cabanac (Saint-
Estèphe, Saint-Estèphe)

Château Semeillan Mazeau
(Listrac-Médoc, Listrac-Médoc)

Château Senilhac (Saint-Seurin-de-
Cadourne, Haut-Médoc)

Château Sipian (Valeyrac, Médoc)

Château Tayac (Soussans, Margaux)

Château Le Temple (Valeyrac, Médoc)

Château Teynac (Saint-Julien-
Beychevelle, Saint-Julien)

Château La Tonnelle
(Cissac-Médoc, Haut-Médoc)

Château Tour Blanche (Saint-
Christoly-de-Médoc, Médoc)

Château La Tour de Bessan
(Cantenac, Margaux)

Château Tour des Termes
(Saint-Estèphe, Saint-Estèphe)

Château Tour-du-Roc
(Arcins, Haut-Médoc)

Château Tour Prignac
(Prignac-en-Médoc, Médoc)

Château Tour Saint-Bonnet
(Saint-Christoly-de-Médoc, Médoc)

Château Tour Saint-Fort
(Saint-Estèphe, Saint-Estèphe)

Château Tour Saint-Joseph
(Cissac-Médoc, Haut-Médoc)

Château Trois Moulins
(Macau, Haut-Médoc)

Château Les Tuileries
(Saint-Yzans-de-Médoc, Médoc)

Château Vernous
(Lesparre, Médoc)

Château Vieux Château Landon
(Bégadan, Médoc)

Château de Villambis
(Cissac-Médoc, Haut-Médoc)

THE APPELLATIONS OF
THE MÉDOC

HAUT-MÉDOC AOC

This AOC encompasses the Médoc's four finest communes—Margaux, St.-Julien, Pauillac, and St.-Estèphe—as well as the less well-known Listrac and Moulis communes. Wines produced outside these six appellations but within the Haut-Médoc are not generally as thrilling, although infinitely superior to those of Médoc. Among these very reliable wines are a few great-value *crus classés* and many high-quality *crus bourgeois*, but although Haut-Médoc is a name to look out for on the label of château-bottled wines, it counts for little on a generic.

RED These dry wines have a generosity of fruit tempered by a firm structure, and are medium- to full-bodied.

🍇 Cabernet Sauvignon, Cabernet Franc, Merlot, Malbec, Petit Verdot, Carmenère

🍷 6–15 years (*crus classés*);
5–8 years (others)

LISTRAC-MÉDOC AOC

Significant funds have been invested in a number of high-performance châteaux in this commune, although its heavy clay soil does not have anything like as much potential as the gravel ridges found in the most famous Médoc appellations.

RED These dry, medium- to full-bodied wines have the fruit and finesse of St.-Julien combined with the firmness of St.-Estèphe. The most successful wines tend to have a large proportion of Merlot, which enjoys the Haut-Médoc's clay soil.

🍇 Cabernet Sauvignon, Cabernet Franc, Carmenère, Merlot, Malbec, Petit Verdot

🍷 5–10 years

MARGAUX AOC

The best Margaux are potentially the greatest wines in the whole of Bordeaux, but this is an appellation that covers five communes encompassing a great diversity of soil and some of its wines not unnaturally have a tendency to disappoint. Margaux benefits enormously from having a namesake château, which is unique in Bordeaux, and the fact that this property sets the most extraordinarily high standards has done no harm to the reputation and price of these wines generally. The phenomenal success of Château Margaux has, however, unfairly raised expectations of many lesser-quality châteaux in the area, but those critics who widely accuse proprietors of sacrificing quality for quantity could not be further from the truth. There are individual châteaux that overproduce and therefore fail to achieve their full potential, but excessive volume is not typically the problem with this appellation, since it has the

lowest yield per acre of the four famous Médoc AOCs.

RED Exquisite, dry, medium-bodied, and sometimes full-bodied, wines that can be deep-colored and fabulously rich, yet they have great finesse and a silky finish.

🍇 Cabernet Sauvignon, Cabernet Franc, Carmenère, Merlot, Malbec, Petit Verdot

🍷 5–20 years (*crus classés*);
5–10 years (others)

MÉDOC AOC

Technically, this appellation covers the entire Médoc, but most wines actually come from north of the Haut-Médoc in the area that was formerly called the Bas-Médoc. Its vineyards have undergone a rapid and extensive expansion since the mid-1970s.

RED The best of these dry, medium-bodied wines are similar in style to good Haut-Médocs, although the style is less sophisticated.

🍇 Cabernet Sauvignon, Cabernet Franc, Carmenère, Merlot, Malbec, Petit Verdot

🍷 4–8 years

MOULIS AOC OR MOULIS-EN-MÉDOC AOC

One of the two communal appellations located on the Atlantic side of the Médoc, Moulis-en-Médoc is smaller and potentially more interesting than its neighbor Listrac. Like Listrac, it has no *cru classé* châteaux, despite adjoining Margaux, the appellation that has the highest number of such properties in the Médoc.

RED These dry, medium-bodied, sometimes full-bodied, wines have more power than those of Margaux, but far less finesse.

🍇 Cabernet Sauvignon, Cabernet Franc, Carmenère, Merlot, Malbec, Petit Verdot

🍷 5–12 years

PAUILLAC AOC

This commune vies with Margaux as the most famous appellation, but is without doubt the most rock solid and consistent of Bordeaux AOCs, while its *premiers crus* of Latour, Lafite, and Mouton make it the most important.

RED Dark and virtually opaque, great Pauillac is a dry, powerfully constructed wine, typically redolent of blackcurrants and new oak. It might be unapproachable when young, but is always rich with fruit when mature. Although it does not have the grace of great Margaux, Pauillac

brings power and style together to produce wines of incomparable finesse for their size.

🍇 Cabernet Sauvignon, Cabernet Franc, Carmenère, Merlot, Malbec, Petit Verdot

🍷 9–25 years (*crus classés*);
5–12 years (others)

ST-ESTÈPHE AOC

The potential of St-Estèphe is exemplified by Cos d'Estournel, which is one of the best *deuxièmes crus* in the Médoc, but the strength of this appellation lies in its range of *crus bourgeois*. The area under vine is slightly less than that of Margaux, which has the largest area, but St.-Estèphe has far more unclassified châteaux, and even the best wines are wonderfully cheap.

RED If Pauillac is the stallion of the four famous appellations, St.-Estèphe must be the dray horse. These dry, full-bodied wines are big and strong, yet not without dignity. St-Estèphe demands affection and, with the rich fruit of a sunny year, deserves it. These most enjoyable, sweet-spice and cedary wines can have lots of honest, chunky fruit. Cos d'Estournel is the thoroughbred of the commune.

🍇 Cabernet Sauvignon, Cabernet Franc, Carmenère, Merlot, Malbec, Petit Verdot

🍷 8–25 years (*crus classés*);
5–12 years (others)

ST-JULIEN AOC

St Julien is the smallest of the four famous appellations and the most intensively cultivated, with almost 50 percent of the commune under vine. There are no first growths, but there are as many as five seconds, and the standard and consistency of style is very high. This AOC overlaps part of the commune of Pauillac, and, historically, châteaux Latour and Pichon-Longueville-Comtesse-de-Lalande could as easily have become St-Julien AOC as Pauillac AOC.

RED These are dry, medium-bodied, sometimes full-bodied, wines that have purity of style, varietal flavor, and can be long-lived. Well balanced and elegant, these wines fall somewhere between the lushness that is typical of Margaux and the firmer structure of Pauillac.

🍇 Cabernet Sauvignon, Cabernet Franc, Carmenère, Merlot, Malbec, Petit Verdot

🍷 6–20 years (*crus classés*);
5–12 years (others)

THE WINE PRODUCERS OF
THE MÉDOC

CHÂTEAU D'AGASSAC
AOC Haut-Médoc
Cru Bourgeois Supérieur
★✰♥

This is one of the best unclassified wines in the Haut-Médoc. The wine is matured in wood for 15 months, with one-third new oak.

RED Dark-colored, plummy wine, with a lot of soft, ripe fruit.

🍇 Cabernet Sauvignon 47%, Merlot 50%, Petit Verdot 3%

🍷— 4–10 years

Second wine: *Château Pomiès-Agassac*

CHÂTEAU D'AURILHAC
AOC Haut-Médoc Cru Bourgeois
★

A relative newcomer that has quickly developed a cult following. The grapes are machine harvested, and the wine is matured in wood for 12 months, with 35 percent new oak.

RED A flashy, huge, dark and dense wine with masses of fruit to balance the ripe tannins and extrovert oak.

🍇 Cabernet Sauvignon 56%, Merlot 38%, Cabernet Franc 3%, Petit Verdot 3%

🍷— 5–15 years

Second wine: *Château La Fagotte*

CHÂTEAU BEAUMONT
AOC Haut-Médoc
Cru Bourgeois Supérieur
✰♥

A large property that consistently produces wines of good quality. This wine is matured in wood for 12 months, with 30 percent new oak.

RED These are aromatically attractive wines with elegant fruit and supple tannin.

🍇 Cabernet Sauvignon 60%, Merlot 35%, Cabernet Franc 2%, Petit Verdot 3%

🍷— 4–8 years

Second wine: *Château d'Arvigny*

Other wine: *Tours de Beaumont*

CHÂTEAU BEL-AIR LAGRAVE
AOC Moulis, Cru Bourgeois
★✰♥

This growth was classified *cru bourgeois* in 1932, but not included in the Syndicat's 1978 list. The wine is matured in wood for 18 to 20 months, with 70 percent new oak.

RED These vividly colored wines have a fine bouquet and firm tannic structure.

🍇 Cabernet Sauvignon 60%, Merlot 35%, Petit Verdot 5%

🍷— 8–20 years

Second wine: *Château Peyvigneau*

CHÂTEAU BELGRAVE
AOC Haut-Médoc 5ème Cru Classé
★✰♥

Situated on a good gravel bank behind Château Lagrange, the wine, which is matured in wood for 24 months with up to 50 percent new oak, has improved consistently throughout the 1990s.

RED A good balance of blackcurrant fruit and ripe acidity, with much more supple tannin structure than used to be the case, and vanilla overtones of new oak.

🍇 Cabernet Sauvignon 55%, Merlot 32%, Cabernet Franc 12%, Petit Verdot 1%

🍷— 8–16 years

Second wine: *Diane de Belgrave*

CHÂTEAU BEL-ORME-TRONQUOY-DE-LALANDE
AOC Haut-Médoc Cru Bourgeois
★

This property has a confusingly similar name to Château Tronquoy-Lalande, St.-Estèphe. Steady improvement since the mid-1990s has turned the once four-square character of these wines into a more classically structured style. This wine is matured in wood for 12 to 14 months, with 10 percent new oak.

RED These are firm, fruity, classically structured wines.

🍇 Cabernet Sauvignon 35%, Merlot 55%, Cabernet Franc 10%

🍷— 7–15 years

CHÂTEAU BERNADOTTE
AOC Haut-Médoc
★✰♥

Consistently performing above its class, this château is situated on fine, gravelly ground that once had the right to the Pauillac appellation and formed part of a *cru classé*. The quality has improved since the property was purchased in 1996 by the redoubtable Madame Lencquesaing, who also owns Pichon-Longueville-Comtesse-de-Lalande. This wine is now matured in

wood for 12 months, with 30 percent new oak.

RED These wines are very stylish, with lush Cabernet fruit backed up by the creamy richness of new oak.

🍇 Cabernet Sauvignon 62%, Merlot 36%, Cabernet Franc and Petit Verdot 2%

🍷— 6–12 years

Second wine: *Château Le Fournas Bernadotte*

CHÂTEAU BISTON BRILLETTE
AOC Moulis
Cru Bourgeois Supérieur
★✰♥

This top-quality Moulis property ages its wines in wood for 12 to 15 months, with up to 35 percent new oak.

RED Wines that are very rich in color and fruit with a full, spicy-cassis character and a supple tannin structure.

🍇 Cabernet Sauvignon 55%, Merlot 40%, Malbec 2%, Petit Verdot 3%

🍷— 5–15 years

Second wine: *Château Biston*
Other wine: *Château Graveyron*

CHÂTEAU BOUQUEYRAN
AOC Moulis
✰♥

A big improvement in quality and value since this 32-acre (13-hectare) property was leased by Philippe Porcheron of nearby Château Rose Saint-Croix. Wines are matured in wood for 18 months with up to 50 percent new oak. La Fleur de Bouqueyran is a superior *cuvée*.

RED Lovely deep-colored, deep-flavored wines of not inconsiderable style and finesse.

🍇 Cabernet Sauvignon 41%, Merlot 57%, Petit Verdot 2%

🍷— 5–10 years

Second wine: *Les Tourelles de Bouqueyran*

CHÂTEAU LE BOURDIEU VERTHEUIL
AOC Haut-Médoc Cru Bourgeois

Situated between Vertheuil and St.-Estèphe, this château was classified *cru bourgeois* in 1932, but not included in the Syndicat's 1978 list. This wine is matured in wood for 12 months, with 30 per cent new oak.

RED Well-colored, full-bodied wines of robust character that are not lacking in charm.

🍇 Cabernet Sauvignon 60%, Merlot 25%, Cabernet Franc 10%, Petit Verdot 5%

🍷— 7–15 years

Second wine: *Château Haut-Brignays*

Other wines: *Château La Croix des Sablons, Château Victoria-Picourneau*

CHÂTEAU BRANAS GRANDPOUJEAUX
AOC Moulis
★✰♥

These excellent and rapidly improving wines are aged in wood for 18 months, with 100 percent new oak.

RED Thanks to an increase in Merlot, this wine has plenty of accessible fruit, charming aromatic properties, and increasing finesse.

🍇 Cabernet Sauvignon 50%, Merlot 45%, Petit Verdot 5%

🍷— 5–12 years

Second wine: *Clos des Demoiselles*

CHÂTEAU BRILLETTE
AOC Moulis
Cru Bourgeois Supérieur
★✰♥

This château's name reputedly derives from its glinting, pebbly soil. The wine is matured in wood for 12 months, with 40 percent new oak.

RED These are attractively colored wines of full but supple body, with delightful summer-fruit and vanilla aromas. Easily equivalent to *cru classé* quality.

🍇 Cabernet Sauvignon 40%, Merlot 48%, Cabernet Sauvignon 9%, Petit Verdot 3%

🍷— 5–12 years

CHÂTEAU CAMBON-LA-PELOUSE
AOC Haut-Médoc
Cru Bourgeois Supérieur
★

Under the same ownership as Château Grand Barrail-Lamarzelle-

Figeac, this estate was classified *cru bourgeois* in 1932, but not included in the Syndicat's 1978 list. This wine is matured in wood for 12 months, with 45 percent new oak.

RED Soft, medium- to full-bodied wines with fresh and juicy flavors.

🍇 Cabernet Sauvignon 30%, Merlot 50%, Cabernet Franc 20%

🍷 3–8 years

Other wine: *Château Trois Moulins*

CHÂTEAU CAMENSAC
AOC Haut-Médoc 5ème Cru Classé
★ ⓥ

Situated behind Château Belgrave, this property was renovated in the mid-1960s by the new owners, the Forner brothers, who are of Spanish origin, and later established Marquès de Cáceres in Rioja. Camensac began making wine equivalent to its classification in the late 1970s, and since 1995 has been performing beyond its class. It is matured in wood for 17 to 20 months, with 35–70 percent new oak.

RED Well-structured wine, with a medium weight of fruit and a certain amount of finesse.

🍇 Cabernet Sauvignon 60%, Merlot 40%

🍷 8–20 years

Second wine: *La Closerie de Camensac*

Other wine: *Le Bailly de Camensac*

CHÂTEAU CANTEMERLE
AOC Haut-Médoc 5ème Cru Classé
★ ☆ ⓥ

In 1980, new stainless-steel fermentation vats replaced the old wooden ones that had been responsible for some stingy vintages. Also discarded were all the old casks, so the 1980 vintage was uniquely matured in 100 percent new oak. The wine is normally matured in wood for 18 to 20 months, with one-third new oak. It is currently performing above its classification.

RED Deliciously rich wines of fine color, creamy-oaky fruit, beautiful balance, and increasing finesse.

🍇 Cabernet Sauvignon 50%, Merlot 40%, Cabernet Franc 5%, Petit Verdot 5%

🍷 8–20 years

Second wine: *Villeneuve de Cantemerle*

CHÂTEAU CAP-LÉON-VEYRIN
AOC Listrac
Cru Bourgeois Supérieur
★

Simply called Château Cap-Léon originally, the vines of this property are planted in two plots of clay-gravel soil over marl.

RED Deep-colored, full-bodied, richly flavored wines with high extract levels and a good balance of tannin.

🍇 Cabernet Sauvignon 35%, Merlot 60%, Petit Verdot 5%

🍷 5–12 years

CHÂTEAU LA CARDONNE
AOC Médoc
Cru Bourgeois Supérieur
★ ⓥ

This property was purchased by the Rothschilds of Lafite in 1973 and has since been expanded and renovated. This wine is matured in wood for 12 months, with 50 percent new oak.

RED These are attractive, medium-bodied wines with a good, grapey perfume and a silky texture, made in an elegant style.

🍇 Cabernet Sauvignon 45%, Merlot 50%, Cabernet Franc 5%

🍷 6–10 years

CHÂTEAU CARONNE-STE.-GEMME
AOC Haut-Médoc
Cru Bourgeois Supérieur
★ ☆ ⓥ

This property is situated south of Château Lagrange—a superb island of vines on a gravel plateau. Matured in wood for 12 months, with 25 percent new oak.

RED Full-bodied wines rich in flavor with undertones of creamy oak, and a supple, tannin structure.

🍇 Cabernet Sauvignon 65%, Merlot 33%, Petit Verdot 2%

🍷 8–20 years

Second wine: *Château Labat*

CHÂTEAU CASTÉRA
AOC Médoc
Cru Bourgeois Supérieur
★ ⓥ

The original château was reduced to ruins by the Black Prince in the 14th century. This wine is matured in wood for 12 months, with one-third new oak.

RED Soft-textured, medium-bodied wines best drunk relatively young.

🍇 Cabernet Sauvignon 45%, Merlot 45%, Cabernet Franc 7%, Petit Verdot 3%

🍷 4–8 years

Second wine: *Château Bourbon La Chapelle*

Other wines: *Château Moulin de Buscateau, La Chapelle du Castera*

CHÂTEAU CHANTELYS
AOC Médoc Cru Bourgeois
☆ ⓥ

Owner Christine Courrian Braquissac brings a gentle touch to the naturally firm wines of this district.

RED Well-colored, medium-bodied, gently rich-flavored wines of some elegance.

🍇 Cabernet Sauvignon 55%, Merlot 40%, Petit Verdot 5%

🍷 3–8 years

Second wine: *Château Gauthier*

CHÂTEAU CHARMAIL
AOC Haut-Médoc
Cru Bourgeois Supérieur
★ ⓥ

The wines from this château have improved dramatically since its excellent 1996 vintage, and continue to perform well in recent blind tastings. This wine is matured in wood for 12 months, with 30 percent new oak.

RED Rich, spicy, and long, with well-rounded, ripe tannins.

🍇 Cabernet Sauvignon 30%, Cabernet Franc 20%, Merlot 48%, Petit Verdot 2%

🍷 3–7 years

Second wine: *Château Tours de Charmail*

CHÂTEAU CHASSE-SPLEEN
AOC Moulis
Cru Bourgeois Exceptionnel
★ ★ ⓥ

The proprietor of this quality-conscious property also owns the *cru classé* Château Haut-Bages-Libéral and the excellent unclassified growth of Château la Gurgue in Margaux. The wine is matured in wood for 18 months with 40 percent new oak, and is usually of *cru classé* quality. Certainly, it well deserves being recently classified as one of only nine *crus bourgeois exceptionnels*.

RED Full-bodied wines of great finesse, vivid color, with a luxuriant, creamy-rich flavor of cassis and chocolate with warm, spicy-vanilla undertones. Easily equivalent to *cru classé* quality.

🍇 Cabernet Sauvignon 70%, Merlot 25%, Petit Verdot 5%

🍷 8–20 years

Second wines: *L'Oratoire de Chasse-Spleen, L'Ermitage de Chasse-Spleen, L'Orangeraie de Chasse-Spleen*

CHÂTEAU CISSAC
AOC Haut-Médoc
Cru Bourgeois Supérieur
★ ⓥ

Château Cissac is always good value, especially in hot years. It is fermented in wood and matured in cask with no *vin de presse*. This wine is matured in wood for 18 months, with up to 50 percent new oak.

RED These are deep-colored, well-

flavored, full-bodied wines made in a *vin de garde* style.

🍇 Cabernet Sauvignon 75%, Merlot 20%, Petit Verdot 5%

🍷 8–20 years

Second wine: *Château Les Reflets du Cissac*

Other wine: *Château Abiet*

CHÂTEAU CITRAN
AOC Haut-Médoc
Cru Bourgeois Supérieur

This substantial-sized property was once run by Château Coufran, then passed into Japanese ownership, under the Fujimoto company, which invested in improvements in the vineyard and winery. In 1997, it was taken back into French ownership, under the auspices of Groupe Taillan, and is run personally by Céline Villars. This wine is matured in wood for 12 to 14 months, with 40 percent new oak.

RED A once solid, if plodding, Médoc of robust character, the style has become more accessible since the mid-1990s, and since the new millennium has shown a true plumpness of fruit, with not inconsiderable finesse.

🍇 Cabernet Sauvignon 58%, Merlot 42%

🍷 5–15 years

Second wine: *Moulins de Citran*

CHÂTEAU LA CLARE
AOC Médoc Cru Bourgeois
☆ ⓥ

A well-established property that is receiving renewed attention of late. Approximately 30 percent of the wine is matured in wood for 23 months, with 5–10 percent new oak.

RED A rich, nicely colored, medium-bodied wine with some spicy finesse.

🍇 Cabernet Sauvignon 57%, Merlot 36%, Cabernet Franc 7%

🍷 4–8 years

Second wines: *Laveline, Gentilhomme*

CHÂTEAU CLARKE
AOC Listrac
Cru Bourgeois Supérieur
★ ⓥ

This estate's vines were dug up and its château pulled down in 1950. All was abandoned until 1973, when it was purchased by Baron Edmund de Rothschild. He completely restored the vineyard and installed an ultramodern winery. Since the 1981 vintage, it has become one of the Médoc's fastest-rising stars. The wine is fermented in stainless steel and matured in wood for 12 to 18 months, with up to 80 percent new oak.

RED Well-colored wines have a good measure of creamy-smoky oak, soft fruit, and increasing finesse.

🍇 Cabernet Sauvignon 40%, Merlot 60%

🍷 7–25 years

Second wine: *Château Granges des Domaines Edmond de Rothschild*

CHÂTEAU COUFRAN
AOC Haut-Médoc
Cru Bourgeois Supérieur
★🅥

These wines are matured in wood for 13 to 18 months, with 25 percent new oak.

RED Frank and fruity, this medium- to full-bodied wine has a chunky, chocolaty flavor, which is dominated by Merlot.

🍇 Cabernet Sauvignon 15%, Merlot 85%, Petit Verdot 5%

🍷 4–12 years

Second wine: *Domaine de la Rose-Maréchale*

CHÂTEAU DUTRUCH GRAND POUJEAUX
AOC Moulis
Cru Bourgeois Supérieur
★🅥

Dutruch is one of the best Grand Poujeaux satellite properties. It also makes two other wines from the specific-named plots "La Bernède" and "La Gravière." Matured in wood for 12 months, with 25 percent new oak.

RED These are fine, full-bodied wines of excellent color, fruit, and finesse.

🍇 Cabernet Sauvignon 45%, Merlot 50%, Petit Verdot 5%

🍷 7–15 years

Other wines: *La Bernède-Grand-Poujeaux, La Gravière-Grand-Poujeaux*

CHÂTEAU FONRÉAUD
AOC Listrac
Cru Bourgeois Supérieur

This splendid château has south-facing vineyards situated on and around a knoll, Puy-de-Menjon. This wine is matured in wood for 12 to 18 months, with one-third new oak.

RED Attractive medium- to full-bodied wines of good fruit and some style.

🍇 Cabernet Sauvignon 55%, Merlot 42%, Petit Verdot 3%

🍷 6–12 years

Second wine: *La Tourelle de Château Fonréaud*

CHÂTEAU FOURCAS DUPRÉ
AOC Listrac
Cru Bourgeois Supérieur
★🅥

A charming house, with vineyards situated on gravel over iron-pan

soil, which can excel in hot years. This wine is matured in wood for 12 months, with one-third new oak.

RED The good color, bouquet, and tannic structure of these wines is rewarded with rich fruit in good years.

🍇 Cabernet Sauvignon 44%, Merlot 44%, Cabernet Franc 10%, Petit Verdot 2%

🍷 6–12 years

CHÂTEAU FOURCAS HOSTEN
AOC Listrac Cru Bourgeois
★🅥

Under multinational ownership (French, Danish, and American) since 1972, the winemaking facilities here have been renovated. The wines are matured in wood for 12 months, with one-third new oak.

RED Deeply colored and full-bodied wines, rich in fruit and supported by a firm tannic structure, although the style is becoming more supple, and can even be quite fat in ripe years like 1982.

🍇 Cabernet Sauvignon 45%, Merlot 45%, Cabernet Franc 10%

🍷 8–20 years

Second wine: *Les Cèdres d'Hosten*

CHÂTEAU LES GRANDS CHÊNES
AOC Médoc
Cru Bourgeois Supérieur
★🅥

The quality here has been excellent since the mid-1990s, but has taken another step up since 1999, when the château was purchased by Bernard Magrez, one of the joint owners of Château Pape Clément. Magrez runs this property personally. The wine is matured in wood for 12 to 15 months, with one-third new oak (except for its "Prestige Cuvée," which utilizes 100 percent new oak).

RED Lush and charming, with opulent fruit and fine acidity balance.

🍇 Cabernet Sauvignon 65%, Merlot 30%, Cabernet Franc 5%

🍷 6–15 years

Other wine: ✓ *Château Les Grands Chênes Prestige Cuvée*

CHÂTEAU GRESSIER GRAND POUJEAUX
AOC Moulis
Cru Bourgeois Supérieur
★🅥

This château was classified *cru bourgeois* in 1932, but not in 1978. It has in recent years produced successful wines that compare well with good *crus classés*. This wine is matured in wood for 24 months, with one-third new oak.

RED Full-bodied wines with plenty of fruit and flavor. Well worth laying down.

🍇 Cabernet Sauvignon 50%, Merlot 30%, Cabernet Franc

10%, Petit Verdot 10%

🍷 6–12 years

CHÂTEAU GREYSAC
AOC Médoc Cru Bourgeois Supérieur
★🅥

Since it was purchased by the late Baron de Gunzbourg in 1973, the facilities of this château have undergone extensive modernization. The quality of the wine is excellent and its future promising. This wine is matured in wood for 12 months, with 25 percent new oak.

RED Stylish, medium-bodied wines with silky-textured, ripe-fruit flavors.

🍇 Cabernet Sauvignon 45%, Merlot 45%, Cabernet Franc 5%, Petit Verdot 5%

🍷 6–10 years

CHÂTEAU HANTEILLAN
AOC Haut-Médoc
Cru Bourgeois Supérieur
★🅥

Under the enthusiastic direction of Catherine Blasco, this large property produces a consistently fine wine, and her achievements have been consolidated by the new winemaking facilities. This wine is matured in wood for 12 months, with 30 percent new oak.

RED The wine has a fine color, spicy bouquet with underlying vanilla-oak tones, ripe fruit, and supple tannins.

🍇 Cabernet Sauvignon 50%, Merlot 41%, Cabernet Franc 5%, Petit Verdot 4%

🍷 6–12 years

Second wine: *Château Larrivaux Hanteillan*

CHÂTEAU LACOMBE-NOILLAC
AOC Haut-Médoc
★🅥

Jean-Michel Lapalu's property boasts some of the most northerly vines in the Médoc. The wine is matured in wood for 6 months, with 15 percent new oak.

RED Elegant, medium-bodied wines of surprising style and finesse for the location.

🍇 Cabernet Sauvignon 58%, Cabernet Franc 6%, Merlot 32%, Petit Verdot 4%

🍷 4–10 years

Second wine: *Château Les Traverses*
Other wine: *Château Les Traverses La Franque*

CHÂTEAU LA LAGUNE
AOC Haut-Médoc 3ème Cru Classé
★★🅥

Owned by the Ducellier family of Champagne Ayala, the immaculate vineyard of this fine château is the first *cru classé* encountered after leaving Bordeaux, and is situated on sand and gravel soil. The château itself was completely renovated in 2003. This wine is matured in wood

for 16 to 18 months, with 100 percent new oak.

RED These wines are deep-colored with complex cassis and stone-fruit flavors intermingled with rich, creamy-vanilla oak nuances. They are full-bodied but supple.

🍇 Cabernet Sauvignon 60%, Merlot 20%, Cabernet Franc 10%, Petit Verdot 10%

🍷 5–30 years

Second wine: *Moulin de Lagune*

CHÂTEAU DE LAMARQUE
AOC Haut-Médoc
Cru Bourgeois Supérieur
★🅥

This large and constantly improving property is owned and run by Pierre-Gilles and Marie-Hélène Gromand-Brunet d'Évry. The vineyard was systematically replanted in the 1960s and is currently at its optimum age for both quality and volume. While it will gradually decline in yield, the quality should continue to improve. The wine is matured in wood for 12 to 15 months, with one-third new oak.

RED This wine has the supple style of a modern Médoc, with plenty of real fruit flavor, and an enticingly perfumed bouquet.

🍇 Cabernet Sauvignon 46%, Merlot 25%, Cabernet Franc 24%, Petit Verdot 5%

🍷 5–12 years

Second wine: *D de Lamarque*
Other wines: *Réserve du Marquis d'Évry, Noblesse Oblige (saigné rosé)*

CHÂTEAU LAMOTHE-CISSAC
AOC Haut-Médoc
Cru Bourgeois
★🅥

An up-and-coming wine from one of Bordeaux's oldest properties, Lamothe-Cissac is matured in wood for 12 to 14 months, with 20 percent new oak. It has recently started to outperform Cissac.

RED Classically proportioned, Cabernet-dominated wines of excellent potential longevity.

🍇 Cabernet Sauvignon 70%, Merlot 26%, Petit Verdot 4%

🍷 4–16 years

CHÂTEAU LANESSAN
AOC Haut-Médoc Cru Bourgeois Supérieur
★★🅥

Supposedly missed out from the 1855 classification because the owner forgot to submit samples, or could not be bothered, this château was later classified *cru bourgeois* in 1932, but not included in the Syndicat's 1978 list. The grapes are machine harvested, and the wines are matured in wood for 15 months, with no claim of any new oak.

RED Big, intensely flavored wines of deep, often opaque, color and a quality that closely approaches that of a *cru classé*, requiring a similar minimum aging before its fruit shows through.

🍇 Cabernet Sauvignon 75%, Merlot 20%, Cabernet Franc 1%, Petit Verdot 4%

🍷 7–20 years

Second wine: *Domaine de Ste-Gemme*

CHÂTEAU LAROSE-TRINTAUDON
AOC Haut-Médoc Cru Bourgeois Supérieur
★ ☆ 🅥

This is the largest estate in the Médoc and was under the same ownership as Château Camensac until 1986, during which time vast sums were spent on renovation. The standard of these wines, which are matured in wood for 12 months with 25 percent new oak, is as high as it has ever been.

RED Medium-bodied, and sometimes full-bodied, wines with an elegantly rich flavor of juicy summer fruits, vanilla, and truffles, backed up by supple tannins. Larose-Perganson is more of a *tête de cuvée* than a second wine. Representing just 15 percent of the total production, this wine is exclusively from the oldest vines and the grapes are all handpicked, in contrast to Larose-Trintaudon, which is machine-picked.

🍇 Cabernet Sauvignon 65%, Merlot 30%, Cabernet Franc 5%

🍷 6–15 years

Second wine: *Larose Saint-Laurent*
Other wines: ✓ *Château Larose-Perganson, Les Hauts de Trintaudon*

CHÂTEAU LESTAGE-DARQUIER
AOC Moulis
★ 🅥

This is the least encountered of the many Poujeaux châteaux (formerly sold as Château Lestage-Darquier-Grand-Poujeaux), but well worth digging out. This wine is matured in wood for 9 to 12 months, with 100 percent year-old oak.

RED Densely colored wines, rich in bouquet and fruit, with a powerful structure.

🍇 Cabernet Sauvignon 50%, Merlot 45%, Cabernet Franc 2%, Petit Verdot 2%

🍷 8–20 years

CHÂTEAU LIVERSAN
AOC Haut-Médoc Cru Bourgeois Supérieur
★ 🅥

The estate of Château Liversan was purchased in 1984 by Prince Guy de Polignac, when it was inexorably linked with Champagne Pommery, but was first leased and then sold to the owners of Patache d'Aux. The vineyard is on fine, sandy gravel over a limestone subsoil, just under 2 miles (3 kilometers) from Lafite and Mouton-Rothschild. The wine is fermented in stainless steel and matured in wood for 12 months, with 25 percent new oak.

RED Rich and flavorful wines, of full body and some style. They are gaining in class with each vintage.

🍇 Cabernet Sauvignon 49%, Merlot 38%, Cabernet Franc 10%, Petit Verdot 3%

🍷 7–20 years

Second wine: *Les Charmes des Liversan*

CHÂTEAU LOUDENNE
AOC Médoc Cru Bourgeois Supérieur
★ 🅥

This pink-washed, Chartreuse-style château, with its lawns running down to the Gironde, once belonged to W. and A. Gilbey, who ran it in a style that harkened back to the last days of the British Empire. It was sold to Jean-Paul Lafragette in 1999. The wine is matured in wood for 15 to 18 months, with 25 percent new oak. Loudenne also produces a dry white wine that is attractive when drunk one to two years after the harvest.

RED Full-bodied wines with a spicy-blackcurrant bouquet, sometimes silky and hinting of violets, with underlying vanilla oak, a big mouthful of rich and ripe fruit, excellent extract, and great length.

🍇 Cabernet Sauvignon 45%, Merlot 45%, Cabernet Franc 7%, Malbec 2%, Petit Verdot 1%

🍷 5–15 years

Second wines: *Château Lestagne, Pavillon de Loudenne*

CHÂTEAU MALESCASSE
AOC Haut-Médoc Cru Bourgeois Supérieur
★ 🅥

Entirely replanted between 1970 and 1992, Château Malescasse was purchased midway through this process by the owner of Pontet-Canet and Lafon-Rochet, only to be sold to Alcatel Alsthon once completed. The wine is matured in wood for 16 months, with 30 percent new oak.

RED Firm, dependable, good-value claret, getting better with each vintage.

🍇 Cabernet Sauvignon 55%, Merlot 35%, Cabernet Franc 10%

🍷 4–8 years

Second wine: *Le Closerie de Malescasse*

CHÂTEAU DE MALLERET
AOC Haut-Médoc Cru Bourgeois Supérieur
★ 🅥

Château de Malleret is a vast estate, which incorporates a stud farm with two training racetracks and stables for both hunting and racing. The vineyard boasts 148 acres (60 hectares). This wine is matured in wood for 12 to 16 months, with up to 50 percent new oak.

RED Delightful wines of good bouquet, medium body, and juicy-rich fruit. Improving.

🍇 Cabernet Sauvignon 65%, Merlot 30%, Cabernet Franc 3%, Petit Verdot 2%

🍷 5–12 years

CHÂTEAU MAUCAILLOU
AOC Moulis Cru Bourgeois Supérieur
★ ★ ☆ 🅥

Château Maucaillou is consistently one of the best-value wines produced in Bordeaux. This wine is matured in wood for 18 months, with up to 80 percent new oak.

RED Deep-colored, full-bodied wine with masses of velvety-textured fruit, beautiful cassis and vanilla flavors, and supple tannins.

🍇 Cabernet Sauvignon 55%, Merlot 36%, Cabernet Franc 2%, Petit Verdot 7%

🍷 6–15 years

Second wine: *Château Cap de Haut-Maucaillou*
Other wine: *Château Duplessis-Fabre*

CHÂTEAU MAUCAMPS
AOC Haut-Médoc Cru Bourgeois Supérieur
★ 🅥

Situated between Macau itself and the *cru classé* Cantemerle to the south, this château makes superb use of its 37 acres (15 hectares) of fine, gravelly vineyards. This wine is matured in wood for 16 months, with up to 40 percent new oak.

RED Always a deep-colored, full-bodied wine with plenty of fruit flavor supported by supple tannins.

🍇 Cabernet Sauvignon 50%, Merlot 40%, Petit Verdot 10%

🍷 5–12 years

Second wine: *Clos de May*

CHÂTEAU LE MEYNIEU AOC
Haut-Médoc Cru Bourgeois
★ 🅥

This property is under the same ownership as Château Lavillotte, which is situated in St.-Estèphe. The deep-colored wine is not filtered before it is bottled.

RED This is a deep, dark, brooding wine of dense bouquet and solid fruit which promises much for the future.

🍇 Cabernet Sauvignon 62%, Merlot 30%, Cabernet Franc 8%

🍷 7–15 years

CHÂTEAU MOULIN-À-VENT
AOC Moulis Cru Bourgeois Supérieur

One-third of the property of Château Moulin-à-Vent overlaps the commune of Listrac, but its appellation is still Moulis. This wine is matured in wood for 20 months, with 25 percent new oak.

RED Medium-bodied wines with an elegant bouquet and a full flavor.

🍇 Cabernet Sauvignon 60%, Merlot 35%, Petit Verdot 5%

🍷 7–15 years

Second wine: *Moulin-de-St.-Vincent*

CHÂTEAU NOAILLAC
AOC Médoc Cru Bourgeois
★ 🅥

Under the same ownership as Château La Tour de By. The wine is matured in wood for up to 12 months, with 15 percent new oak.

RED Deliciously fruity style, underpinned by a discreet use of oak.

🍇 Cabernet Sauvignon 55%, Merlot 40%, Petit Verdot 5%

🍷 3–8 years

Second wines: *Moulin de Noaillac, La Rose Noaillac, Les Palombes de Noaillac*

CHÂTEAU LES ORMES-SORBET
AOC Médoc Cru Bourgeois Supérieur
★ 🅥

Owned by the Boivert family since 1764. The wine today is matured in wood for 18 to 20 months, with one-third new oak.

RED Once reputed for its characterful wines of substantial body, dense fruit, and positive flavor, this château has made an increasingly opulent style, with fine aromatics, since the early 1990s, fully justifying its 2003 *cru bourgeois supérieur* classification.

🍇 Cabernet Sauvignon 65%, Merlot 30%, Petit Verdot 2%, Carmenère 1%

🍷 4–15 years

Second wine: *Château de Conques*

CHÂTEAU PALOUMEY
AOC Haut-Médoc Cru Bourgeois Supérieur
★ 🅥

An old property that enjoyed fame in the 19th century, but was left rundown and forgotten until the current owner, Martine Cazeneuve, replanted it in 1990. The wine is matured in wood for 12 to 15 months, with one-third new oak.

RED Deliciously rich and ripe, fruit-driven style that is underpinned by a nicely restrained use of oak, with exceptional finesse for such young vines. Can only get better!

Cabernet Sauvignon 55%, Merlot 40%, Cabernet Franc 5%

4–8 years

Second wines: *Les Ailes de Paloumey, Château Haut-Carmaillet*

CHÂTEAU PATACHE-D'AUX
AOC Médoc
Cru Bourgeois Supérieur
★✩♥

This old property once belonged to the Aux family, descendants of the counts of Armagnac, but was purchased by a syndicate headed by Claude Lapalu in 1964. Although Patache-d'Aux is always reliable, it has performed particularly well since its stunning 1990 vintage. The wine is matured in wood for 12 months, with 25 percent new oak.

RED Stylish, highly perfumed, medium-bodied wine with very accessible fruit.

Cabernet Sauvignon 70%, Merlot 20%, Cabernet Franc 7%, Petit Verdot 3%

4–8 years

Second wine: *Le Relais de Patache-d'Aux*
Other wines: *Les Chevaux de Patache-d'Aux*

CHÂTEAU PEYRABON
AOC Haut-Médoc Cru Bourgeois
★✩♥

Virtually unknown until 1998, when it was purchased by Millesima (formerly Les Vins des Grands Vignobles), Château Peyrabon is matured in wood for 18 months, with one-third new oak.

RED Sturdy style, but not lacking in fruit, and usually very good value.

Cabernet Sauvignon 57%, Merlot 37%, Cabernet Franc 5%, Petit Verdot 1%

5–10 years

Second wines: *Lapiey, Château Le Fleur Peyrabon*
Other wines: *Château Pierbone, Domaine du Roman*

CHÂTEAU PLAGNAC
AOC Médoc

Owned by Domaines Cordier since 1972, this property has produced consistently good-value red Bordeaux since the end of that decade. The wine is matured in wood for 12 months.

RED Full-bodied and full-flavored, with some breed; lots of up-front Merlot fruit, and a smooth finish.

Cabernet Sauvignon 65%, Merlot 35%,

4–10 years

Second wine: *Château Haut de Plagnac*

CHÂTEAU PONTEY
AOC Médoc Cru Bourgeois
★✩♥

Owned by the Bordeaux *négociant* Quancard family, this château occupies an excellent location on a gravel plateau. The wines are matured in wood for 12 months, with one-third new oak.

RED These wines have always been cleverly constructed and brimming with lush, oaky fruit, but they are even more lush than before.

Cabernet Sauvignon 45%, Merlot 55%

3–12 years

Second wine: *Château Vieux Prezat*
Other wine: *Château Pontey Caussan*

CHÂTEAU POTENSAC
AOC Médoc
Cru Bourgeois Exceptionnel
★✩♥

This property is under the same ownership as Château Léoville-Las-Cases in St.-Julien, and its wines often aspire to *cru classé* quality, fully justifying the *cru bourgeois exceptionnel* classification in 2003. The wine is fermented in stainless steel, then matured in wood for 18 months, with 20 percent new oak.

RED Classy, full-bodied wines of a lovely, brick-red color, with lots of fruit and underlying chocolate and spice flavors.

Cabernet Sauvignon 60%, Merlot 25%, Cabernet Franc 15%

6–15 years

Second wine: *Château Lassalle*
Other wines: *Château Gallais-Bellevue, Goudy la Cardonne*

CHÂTEAUX POUJEAUX
AOC Moulis
Cru Bourgeois Exceptionnel
★★♥

After Chasse-Spleen, this château produces the best wine in Moulis and is easily the equivalent of a good *cru classé*. Hence, it was no surprise that it was classified as one of only nine *crus bourgeois exceptionnels* in 2003.

RED Full-bodied and deep-colored wine with a very expansive bouquet and creamy-rich, spicy fruit.

Cabernet Sauvignon 50%, Merlot 40%, Cabernet Franc 5%, Petit Verdot 2%

10–25 years

Second wine: *Château La Salle-de-Poujeaux*

CHÂTEAU PREUILLAC
AOC Médoc
★✩♥

Purchased in 1998 by Yvon Mau, who has sold his eponymously named *négociant* business to Freixenet in a bid to build up a portfolio of estate properties. Mau devoted a lot of money and attention to renovating this

property, reducing yields, and updating the vinification facilities, which is why he was so upset not to have been included in the 2003 *cru bourgeois* classification (*see* p72), although there is no doubt that it will succeed at the next reclassification in 2015. Certainly, if the current rate of improvement can be maintained, this château will do very well. The grapes are all handpicked, then sorted on tables, while the wines are fermented in stainless steel (2001 being the first such vintage), then matured in wood for 18 months, with 20 percent new oak.

RED The creamy cassis and chocolaty fruit in these wines is a testament to Mau's efforts. Preuillac used to be rather rustic, but now shows more finesse with each and every vintage.

Cabernet Sauvignon 54%, Merlot 44%, Cabernet Franc 2%

4–12 years

CHÂTEAU RAMAGE-LA-BATISSE
AOC Haut-Médoc
Cru Bourgeois Supérieur
★♥

This property has excelled itself since the late 1980s, making wines of remarkable quality–price ratio which are matured in wood for 14 months, with 50 percent new oak.

RED Rich, well-flavored, oaky wines that are immediately attractive in light years and ridiculously inexpensive *vins de garde* in the best vintages. Not unlike a poor man's Lynch-Bages (which, in turn, I have called a poor man's Latour!).

Cabernet Sauvignon 70%, Merlot 23%, Cabernet Franc 5%, Petit Verdot 2%

7–15 years

Second wine: *Le Terrey*
Other wine: *Château Dutellier*

CHÂTEAU ROLLAN DE BY
AOC Médoc
Cru Bourgeois Supérieur
★★

A new cult wine on the Bordeaux scene, it is matured in wood for 18 months, with 60 percent new oak. The wine has a string of blind

tasting victories. The Château Haut-Condessas is a super-selection, with 100 percent new oak.

RED Lots of up-front fruit, but long and classy, with plenty of finesse. Not big and, surprisingly, not overoaked.

Cabernet Sauvignon 20%, Merlot 70%, Petit Verdot 10%

4–12 years

Other wine: *Château Fleur de By*

CHÂTEAU ST-BONNET
AOC Médoc

Some 130 of this important estate's 210 acres are planted with vines (53 of 85 hectares). The wine is matured in wood for 18 months, with 25 percent new oak.

RED Full-flavored wines of promising quality and immediate aromatic appeal.

Merlot 50%, Cabernet Sauvignon 28%, Cabernet Franc 22%

5–10 years

CHÂTEAU ST-PAUL
AOC Haut-Médoc
Cru Bourgeois
★✩♥

Up-and-coming vineyard pieced together from parcels previously owned by two St.-Estèphe châteaux. This wine is matured in wood for 18 months, with 25 percent new oak.

RED Plump, fruit-driven reds of good class and finesse, with a long finish.

Cabernet Sauvignon 60%, Merlot 35%, Cabernet Franc 5%

4–12 years

CHÂTEAU SÉNÉJAC
AOC Médoc
Cru Bourgeois Supérieur
★✩♥

This property changed hands in 1999. The wine is matured in wood for 18 months, with 25 percent new oak (up to 100 percent for its prestige *cuvée* Karolus).

RED A firm, full-flavored wine of excellent longevity, Sénéjac is not, however, for the faint-hearted, especially in its rather stern youthful years. The Karolus is bigger, richer, and more concentrated.

Cabernet Sauvignon 60%, Merlot 25%, Cabernet Franc 14%, Petit Verdot 1%

5–15 years

Second wine: *Artique de Sénac*
Other wine: 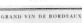 *Karolus*

CHÂTEAU SIGOGNAC
AOC Médoc
♥

Owned by Colette Bonny, this wine is matured in wood for 12 months, with 20 percent new oak.

RED Consistently good-value, lunchtime claret of some elegance.

🍇 Merlot 50%, Cabernet Sauvignon 28%, Cabernet Franc 22%

⌛ 3–8 years

Second wine: *Château La Croix du Chevalier*

CHÂTEAU SOCIANDO-MALLET
AOC Haut-Médoc Cru Bourgeois
★★ ⓥ

This property has been making a name for itself since 1970, when Jean Gautreau raised standards to near *cru classé* quality. The quality of Sociando-Mallet has continued to increase throughout the 1990s, when between 80 and 100 percent new oak became the norm. Its owners did not bother to submit wines for the 2003 reclassification, since it already achieves a higher price than a number of *cru classé* wines, but it is undoubtedly at least *cru bourgeois exceptionnel* in quality, if not in name.

RED These are powerfully built wines that are rich in color and extract. Often totally dominated by vanilla oak in their youth, they are backed up with plenty of concentrated cassis fruit.

🍇 Cabernet Sauvignon 55%, Merlot 42%, Cabernet Franc 2%, Petit Verdot 1%

⌛ 10–25 years

Second wine: *La Demoiselle de Sociando-Mallet*

CHÂTEAU SOUDARS
AOC Médoc
Cru Bourgeois Supérieur
★ ⓥ

Soudars was formed by the combination of several parcels of rock-strewn land that had become overgrown with brambles until Eric Miailhe took over the property in 1973 and spent several years clearing it. The wine is fermented in stainless steel, and matured in wood for 12 to 14 months, with up to 40 percent new oak.

RED Excellent, well-colored wines of good structure and accessible fruit.

🍇 Cabernet Sauvignon 44%, Merlot 54%, Cabernet Franc 1%

⌛ 5–10 years

Second wine: *Château Marquis de Cadourne*

CHÂTEAU LE TEMPLE
AOC Médoc Cru Bourgeois
★ ⓥ

Starting to live up to its reputation in the early 1900s, when it was known as "Lafite of the Bas-Médoc," this wine is matured in wood for 12 months, with 22 percent new oak.

RED Increasingly lush and fruit-dominant, without losing its classic, tannin structure.

🍇 Cabernet Sauvignon 60%, Merlot 35%, Petit Verdot 5%

⌛ 7–15 years

Second wine: *Château Bairac*
Other wine: *Château La Croix des Sablons*

CHÂTEAU LA TOUR DE BY
AOC Médoc Cru Bourgeois Supérieur
★ ⓥ

The tower of Tour de By was once a lighthouse. The wine is of very good quality; it is matured in wood for 16 months, with up to 30 percent new oak.

RED These deeply colored, full-bodied, richly flavored wines have good spicy fruit, backed up by a firm tannic structure.

🍇 Cabernet Sauvignon 60%, Merlot 36%, Cabernet Franc 4%

⌛ 6–12 years

Second wine: *Château La Roque-de-By*
Other wines: *Château Moulin de Roque, Château Moulin de la Roque*

CHÂTEAU LA TOUR-CARNET
AOC Haut-Médoc 4ème Cru Classé
★

This charming, 13th-century miniature moated castle has a well-kept vineyard. Its wines used to be lackluster, but have been transformed by the new owner, Bernard Magez of Pape-Clément, who purchased the property in 1999. The wine is now matured in wood for 12 to 18 months, with 60 percent new oak.

RED Much riper, more opulent fruit, with some lush new oak in a supporting role, this wine has the richness of flavor it used to lack, with improvements noticeable from one year to the next.

🍇 Cabernet Sauvignon 53%, Merlot 33%, Cabernet Franc 10%, Petit Verdot 4%

⌛ 5–15 years

Second wine: *Douves de Carnet*

CHÂTEAU TOUR HAUT-CAUSSAN
AOC Médoc Cru Bourgeois Supérieur
★ ★

An up-and-coming property owned by Philippe Courrian, who also makes wine in Corbières. The grapes are all hand-harvested, and the wine is matured in wood for 12 months, with one-third new oak.

RED Rich, well-colored wines with a great concentration of fruit and nicely integrated, creamy oak.

🍇 Cabernet Sauvignon 50%, Merlot 50%

⌛ 4–10 years

Second wine: *Château Landotte*

CHÂTEAU LA TOUR SAINT-BONNET
AOC Médoc
★

Situated on fine, gravely ridges, this property was known as Château la Tour Saint-Bonnet-Cazenave in the 19th century. This wine is matured in wood for 18 months, with 50 percent new oak.

RED Firm, full-flavored, well-colored wines of consistent quality.

🍇 Cabernet Sauvignon 45%, Merlot 45%, Malbec 5%, Petit Verdot 5%

⌛ 7–15 years

Second wine: *Château La Fuie-Saint-Bonnet*

CHÂTEAU VERDIGNAN
AOC Haut-Médoc Cru Bourgeois Supérieur
★ ⓥ

Since 1972, the property of the Miailhe family, who continue to improve the quality. The wine is fermented in stainless steel and matured in wood for 12 to 14 months, with 30 percent new oak.

RED Medium-bodied, fruity wines, made in a soft and silky style.

🍇 Cabernet Sauvignon 50%, Merlot 45%, Cabernet Franc 5%

⌛ 5–10 years

Second wine: *Château Plantey-de-la-Croix*

CHÂTEAU VILLEGORGE
AOC Haut-Médoc Cru Bourgeois Supérieur
★ ⓥ

This château was classified *cru bourgeois* in 1932. It was purchased by Lucien Lurton in 1973, but he then resigned from the Syndicat and, therefore, the château was not included in its 1978 list, although it is superior to a few that were. He was succeeded by his daughter, Marie-Louise, the present incumbent, who has continued improving the quality, achieving *supérieur* status in the 2003 reclassification. The wine is matured in wood for 10 to 24 months, with up to 30 percent new oak.

RED Full-bodied wines, with a lovely color, increasingly lush and opulent fruit, understated, creamy oak, and an increasing spicy finesse.

🍇 Cabernet Sauvignon 40%, Merlot 60%

⌛ 6–12 years

Second wine: *Reflet de Villegeorge*

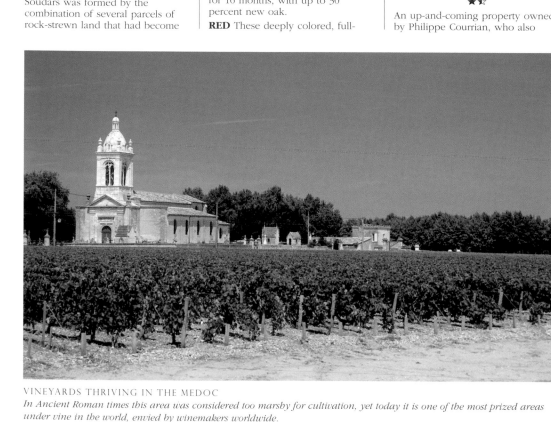

VINEYARDS THRIVING IN THE MEDOC
In Ancient Roman times this area was considered too marshy for cultivation, yet today it is one of the most prized areas under vine in the world, envied by winemakers worldwide.

SAINT-ESTÈPHE

Although St.-Estèphe can be considered the least sexy of the Médoc's famous four appellations, it has an abundance of high-quality bourgeois growths, which make it indubitably the "bargain basement" of Bordeaux wines.

WITH ONLY FIVE *CRUS CLASSÉS* covering a mere 6 percent of the commune, St.-Estèphe is a rich source of undervalued clarets, where the prices paid by wine drinkers are unlikely to be outbid by wine investors. Enthusiasts rather than speculators will benefit from the fact that no fewer than 4 of the Médoc's 9 *crus bourgeois exceptionnels* are to be found in this commune.

CHÂTEAU COS D'ESTOURNEL

St.-Estèphe might lack *crus classés*, but it is not lacking in class. If it had only one *cru classé*—the stunning, stylish Château Cos d'Estournel—St.-Estèphe would still be famous. The reputation of this château soared after Bruno Prats took over control in 1971. Essentially, this success can be put down to his maximizing the true potential of Cos d'Estournel's exceptional *terroir*, a superb, south-facing ridge of gravel with perfect

HARVEST, CHÂTEAU
COS D'ESTOURNEL
The bizarre eastern façade of this specially built winery overlooks the vineyards. The château was owned by perfectionist Bruno Prats before it was sold to the Bernard Taillan group in October 1998

FACTORS AFFECTING TASTE AND QUALITY

LOCATION
St.-Estèphe is the most northerly of the four classic communes of the Médoc. It is situated 11 miles (18 kilometers) south of Lesparre, bordering the Gironde.

CLIMATE
As for the Médoc (*see* p.00).

ASPECT
St.-Estèphe has well-drained, well-sited, softly sloping vineyards. The southeast-facing crest of gravel overlooks Château Lafite-Rothschild in Pauillac and is relatively steep for the Médoc.

SOIL
The topsoil is gravelly and more fertile than in communes farther south, with clay subsoil exposed in parts, consisting of clay beds, stony-clay, and limestone over iron-pan.

VITICULTURE AND VINIFICATION
Only the red wines have the right to the appellation in this commune. With increasing emphasis placed on the Merlot grape, which can now account for up to 50 percent of the vines cultivated in some châteaux, reduced use of *vin de presse*, and improved vinification techniques, these wines are becoming far more accessible in less sunny years. During the vinification, all grapes must be destalked, and duration of skin contact averages three weeks. Maturation in cask currently varies between 15 and 24 months.

GRAPE VARIETIES
Primary varieties: Cabernet Sauvignon, Cabernet Franc, Merlot
Secondary varieties: Carmenère, Malbec, Petit Verdot

drainage. Those vineyards on heavier soil with less gravel and more clay tend to produce more rustic wines.

MODERN ST.-ESTÈPHE

Most wines from St.-Estèphe have always been well structured, with natural longevity, but they now have more lushness of fruit, which allows the wines to be accessible when relatively young. It was once essential to buy only the greatest vintages and wait 20 years or more before drinking them. The increasing use of the Merlot grape as well as Cabernet Sauvignon and Cabernet Franc, and a tendency to favor vinification techniques that extract color and fruit in preference to the harsher tannins, provide richer, fruitier, and eminently drinkable wines in most vintages.

ST.-ESTÈPHE PROFILE

Appellation area
Covers parts of the commune of St.-Estèphe only

Size of commune
9,284 acres (3,757 ha)

AOC area under vine
3,099 acres (1,254 ha), 33% of commune

Surface area of *crus classés*
558 acres (226 ha), 6% of commune, 16% of AOC

Special comments
Approximately 12.5 acres (5 ha) of vineyards within St.-Estèphe are classified as AOC Pauillac

ST.-ESTÈPHE CRU CLASSÉ STATISTICS

***Crus classés* in AOC St.-Estèphe**
5 châteaux (by number: 8% of *crus classés* in the Médoc) with 558 acres (226 ha) of vineyards (by area: 8% of *crus classés* in the Médoc and 18% of this AOC)

1er crus classés
None

2ème crus classés
2 châteaux (by number: 14% of 2ème *crus classés* in the Médoc) with 299 acres (121 ha) of vineyards (by area: 15% of 2ème *crus classés* in the Médoc)

3ème crus classés
1 château (by number: 7% of 3ème

crus classés in the Médoc) with 119 acres (48 ha) of vineyards (by area: 11% of 3ème *crus classés* in the Médoc)

4ème crus classés
1 château (by number: 10% of 4ème *crus classés* in the Médoc) with 111 acres (45 ha) of vineyards (by area: 10% of 4ème *crus classés* in the Médoc)

5ème crus classés
1 château (by number: 6% of 5ème *crus classés* in the Médoc) with 30 acres (12 ha) of vineyards (by area: 2% of 5ème *crus classés* in the Médoc)

ST.-ESTÈPHE, *see also p63*
Of the Haut-Médoc's four best-known communes, St.-Estèphe is the most northerly, although the actual AOC area covers only part of the commune.

- ● *Cru Classé* château
- ● Other châteaux
- ● *Coopérative*
- — Communal boundary

Château Cos Labory

THE WINE PRODUCERS OF
SAINT-ESTÈPHE

CHÂTEAU ANDRON-BLANQUET
Cru Bourgeois
★ ⓥ

Under the same ownership as Château Cos Labory, the vineyards of this property are situated above the gravel crest of *cru classé* châteaux that overlook Château Lafite-Rothschild in Pauillac. This wine is matured in wood for 12 months, with 25 percent new oak.

RED An exceptionally well-made wine that consistently rises above its *petit château* status. Fermented and matured in cask, it has good fruit and a distinctive style.

🍇 Cabernet Sauvignon 40%, Merlot 35%, Cabernet Franc 25%

🍷 4–10 years

Second wine: *Château St.-Roch*
Other wine: *Château Blanquet*

CHÂTEAU BEAU-SITE
Cru Bourgeois Supérieur
★ ⓥ

This property should not be confused with Château Beau-Site Haut-Vignoble, a lesser St.-Estèphe. This wine is matured in wood for 16 to 18 months, with 50 percent new oak.

RED A stylish, medium-bodied, sometimes full-bodied, wine that often has an elegant finish reminiscent of violets.

🍇 Cabernet Sauvignon 70%, Merlot 30%

🍷 3–10 years

CHÂTEAU LE BOSCQ
Cru Bourgeois Supérieur
★ ⭒ ⓥ

This property has always produced good wine, but quality increased dramatically in the 1980s. It was taken over by Dourthe-Kressman in 1995.

RED Superbly aromatic, almost exotic, full-bodied wine that is elegant and rich with the flavor of summer fruits, and is nicely backed up with new oak.

🍇 Cabernet Sauvignon 42%, Merlot 51%, Petit Verdot 7%

🍷 5–12 years

Second wine: *Héritage de Le Boscq*

CHÂTEAU CALON-SÉGUR
3ème Cru Classé
★ ⭒ ⓥ

From the Gallo-Roman origins of this château grew the community of St.-Estèphe. The first wine estate in the commune, it used to boast "*Premier Cru de St.-Estèphe*" on its label until other producers objected. This wine is matured in wood for 18 months, with 50 percent new oak.

RED Full, fruity, well-structured wine that has a creamy, rich flavor. It is of consistently good quality and improves well in bottle.

🍇 Cabernet Sauvignon 50%, Merlot 35%, Cabernet Franc 10%, Petit Verdot 5%

🍷 3–20 years

Second wine: *Marquis de Ségur*

CHÂTEAU CAPBERN GASQUETON
Cru Bourgeois
★ ⓥ

This property is under the same ownership as Château Calon-Ségur. The vineyards are found north and south of the village of St.-Estèphe. This wine is matured in wood for 18 months, with 30 percent new oak.

RED Medium-weight, ripe, and fruity wine of consistent quality; it is mellowed by 24 months in wood.

🍇 Cabernet Sauvignon 50%, Merlot 35%, Cabernet Franc 15%

🍷 4–12 years

CHÂTEAU CHAMBERT-MARBUZET
Cru Bourgeois Supérieur
★ ⭒ ⓥ

Technically faultless, hand-harvested wine produced in limited quantities from the sister château of Haut-Marbuzet. Many would rate it easily equivalent to a *cru classé*. This wine is matured in wood for 18 months, with 50 per cent new oak.

RED Aromatically attractive, medium-bodied, sometimes full-bodied, wine. It is rich, ripe, and fruity, with plenty of caramel-oak and sufficient tannin to age well.

🍇 Cabernet Sauvignon 70%, Merlot 30%

🍷 3–10 years

Second wine: *Château Grand-Village Capbern*

CHÂTEAU COS D'ESTOURNEL
2ème Cru Classé
★★★★

This was one of the very first super-seconds to emerge and this was the achievement of one man, Bruno Prats, although he would claim it to be teamwork. In 1998 Prats was forced by French tax laws to sell out to Groupe Taillan, who in 2001 sold it on to Michel Reybier, a Geneva-based food manufacturer. Cos d'Estournel has no château as such, merely a bizarre façade to the winery with huge, elaborately carved oak doors that once adorned the palace of the Sultan of Zanzibar. Bruno Prats' son Jean-Guillaume manages the property for Reybier, and the wine is made in the same careful way that his father introduced. This involves some of the wine being fermented in stainless steel, but all of it is matured in cask for 18 to 24 months, with 100 percent new oak for big years, and up to 70 percent for lighter vintages.

RED A rich, flavorsome, and attractive wine of full body, great class, and distinction; without doubt the finest wine in St.-Estèphe. It is uniquely generous for the appellation and capable of amazing longevity, even in the poorest years. This is a complex wine with silky fruit and great finesse.

🍇 Cabernet Sauvignon 60%, Merlot 40%

🍷 8–20 years

Second wine: *Les Pagodes de Cos*

CHÂTEAU COS LABORY
5ème Cru Classé
★

Until the late 19th century, this property formed part of Château Cos d'Estournel. During the 1920s, it was purchased by distant cousins of Madame Audoy, the current owner. The wine is matured in wood for 15 to 18 months, with one-third new oak.

RED These wines used to be merely light and elegant with a certain degree of finesse, even when at their best. However, recent vintages have displayed a very welcome change to a distinctly fuller, fruitier, and fatter style.

🍇 Cabernet Sauvignon 55%, Merlot 35%, Cabernet Franc 5%, Petit Verdot 5%

🍷 5–15 years

Second wine: *Château Charme Labory*

CHÂTEAU LE CROCK
Cru Bourgeois Exceptionnel
★ ⭒ ⓥ

This property is under the same ownership as Château Léoville-Poyferré of St.-Julien, and was promoted to *exceptionnel* status in the 2003 reclassification. This hand-harvested wine is matured in wood for 18 months, with 20 percent new oak.

RED These dark-colored, substantial wines have surged in quality since 1995 under the personal guidance of Michel Rolland.

🍇 Cabernet Sauvignon 58%, Merlot 24%, Cabernet Franc 12%, Petit Verdot 6%

🍷 6–15 years

Second wine: *Château Croix Saint-Estèphe*
Other wine: *Château Fatin*

CHÂTEAU DOMEYNE
Cru Bourgeois
★ ⭒ ⓥ

This property was not classified *cru bourgeois* in 1932, nor was it listed by the Syndicat in 1978, but it certainly should have been. This wine is matured in wood for 18 months, with 40 percent new oak.

RED These are typically deep-colored, rich-flavored wines that have an excellent marriage of fruit and oak. They are smooth and well-rounded wines that can be drunk while fairly young.

🍇 Cabernct Sauvignon 60%, Merlot 35%, Cabernet Franc 5%

🍷 3–8 years

CHÂTEAU FAGET
★ ⭒ ⓥ

Château Faget was classified *cru bourgeois* in 1932, but was not included in the Syndicat's 1978 list. However, this *coopérative*-produced wine is now superior to some that were included. This hand-harvested wine is matured in wood for 12 months, with one-third new oak.

RED This is a well-made wine that gives a solid mouthful of flavor, and ages well.

🍇 Cabernet Sauvignon 60%, Merlot 30%, Cabernet Franc 10%

🍷 6–10 years

CHÂTEAU HAUT-MARBUZET
Cru Bourgeois Exceptionnel
★★ ⓥ

This is one of several properties belonging to Henri Duboscq. These wines receive 18 months in 100 percent new oak, which is extremely rare even for *cru classé* châteaux.

RED These full-bodied, deep-colored wines are packed with juicy fruit, backed up by supple tannin. They are marked by a generous buttered-toast and creamy-vanilla character.

🍇 Merlot 50%, Cabernet Sauvignon 40%, Cabernet Franc 10%

🍷 4–12 years

Second wine: *Tour de Marbuzet*

CHÂTEAU LA HAYE
Cru Bourgeois Supérieur
★ ⓥ

New equipment, 25 percent new oak casks every year, and a fair proportion of old vines combine to produce some exciting vintages at this property.

RED Always limpid, this medium-bodied, sometimes full-bodied, wine is rich in color and flavour, well balanced, and lengthy, with vanilla-oak evident on the finish.

Cabernet Sauvignon 50%,
Merlot 42%, Petit Verdot 8%

⌐⊶ 5–8 years

Second wine: *Fief de la Haye*

CHÂTEAU LAFON-ROCHET
4ème Cru Classé

When Guy Tesseron purchased this
vineyard, which is situated on the
borders of Pauillac, in 1959, he
embarked on a project to increase
the proportion of Cabernet
Sauvignon grapes used in the wine.
However, this proved to be a
mistake for Lafon-Rochet's *terroir*
and has been rectified in recent
years. The wine produced here is
matured in wood for 18 months,
with up to 50 percent new oak.

RED More fruit and finesse from
the mid-1990s onward.

Cabernet Sauvignon 55%,
Merlot 40%, Cabernet Franc 5%

⌐⊶ 5–12 years

Second wine: √ *Numero 2*

CHÂTEAU LAVILLOTTE
★★√

This star-performing *petit château*
gives good value. This wine is
matured in wood for 16 months,
with up to 40 percent new oak.

RED These are dark-colored wines
with a deep and distinctive
bouquet. Smoky, full-bodied,
intense, and complex.

Cabernet Sauvignon 72%,
Merlot 25%, Petit Verdot 3%

⌐⊶ 5–12 years

Second wine: *Château Aillan*

CHÂTEAU DE MARBUZET
Cru Bourgeois
★

Under the same ownership as Cos
d'Estournel, Marbuzet used to
include the wines rejected from the
grand vin of that "super-second."
However, all the wine from this
château has been produced
exclusively from its own 42-acre
(17-hectare) vineyard since 1994.
The wine is matured in wood for 12
to 14 months in used barrels.

RED These elegant, medium-
bodied, and sometimes full-bodied,
wines are well balanced and have
good fruit and a supple finish.

Cabernet Sauvignon 40%,
Merlot 60%

⌐⊶ 4–10 years

Second wine: *Château Charme
Labory*

LE MARQUIS DE SAINT-ESTÈPHE
★√

This wine is produced by the
conscientious Cave Coopérative
Marquis de Saint-Estèphe, who
mature it in wood for 12 months,
with a whopping 70 percent new
oak.

RED A consistently well-made,

good-value, usually medium-bodied
(although sometimes full-bodied)
wine, with increasingly more
noticeable oak.

Cabernet Sauvignon 65%,
Merlot 25%, Cabernet Franc
3%, Malbec 3%, Petit Verdot 4%

⌐⊶ 3–6 years

CHÂTEAU MEYNEY
Cru Bourgeois Supérieur
★√

This château is consistent in
managing to produce fine wines in
virtually every vintage.

RED These wines used to be big,
beefy, chunky, and chewy, and
required at least 10 years in bottle.
They have changed, and for the
better, acquiring a silky-textured
finesse and aging gracefully without
so many years in bottle.

Cabernet Sauvignon 67%,
Merlot 25%, Cabernet Franc
5%, Petit Verdot 3%

⌐⊶ 5–25 years

Second wine: *Prieuré de Meyney*

CHÂTEAU MONTROSE
2ème Cru Classé
★★√

This "youngest" of the *cru classé*
vineyards, this property grew out of
an inconsequential plot of vines
retained by a Mr. Dumoulin, the
former owner of Calon-Ségur, when
he sold that château in 1824. These
vines were on a 12–15 acre (5–6
hectare) plot of land called
l'Escargeon, which for some reason
he changed to Montrose the very
next year. There are rumors about
the origin of this new name, but no
one really knows the true story.
What we do know, however, is that
by 1855, Montrose had grown to
237 acres (96 hectares), as
Dumoulin bought and exchanged
parcels of land from and with his
neighbors. Despite the newfound
importance of Montrose, Calon-
Ségur was still considered by locals
to be its superior, thus there was
much surprise when Montrose was
classified as a *deuxième cru classé*,
above *troisième cru* Calon-Ségur.
The wines are matured in wood
for 19 months, with 50 percent
new oak.

RED The inhibiting factor at
Montrose had always been its
"stemmy" tannins. A vintage of
exceptional richness and fatness
was required to overcome the
aggressive character produced by
these tannins. The excellent 1994
gave me hope that this château has
started to harvest the grapes when
they are tannin-ripe (*see* p66) and
was applying more specific
maceration techniques. Happily,
my hopes were not dashed, and
Montrose's performance since the
mid-1990s has clearly demonstrated
that this wine is a true *deuxième
cru classé*.

Cabernet Sauvignon 65%,
Merlot 25%,

Cabernet Franc 10%

⌐⊶ 8–25 years

Second wine: √ *La Dame de
Montrose*

CHÂTEAU LES ORMES DE PEZ
Cru Bourgeois Exceptionnel
★★√

Owner Jean-Michel Cazes of
Château Lynch-Bages in Pauillac
installed new stainless-steel vats in
1981 and has raised the quality of
these wines from good to
sensational. Matured in wood for at
least 12 to 15 months, with 50
percent new oak, this relatively
cheap wine is easily equivalent to a
good *cru classé*.

RED Dark and fruity, yet capable of
aging with a herbal complexity.

Cabernet Sauvignon 65%,
Merlot 25%, Cabernet Franc
10%

⌐⊶ 3–15 years

CHÂTEAU DE PEZ
Cru Bourgeois Exceptionnel
★★√

This property was purchased by
Louis Roederer of Champagne in
1995. The wines are fermented in
wooden vats, then matured in small
casks for 18 months, with 40
percent new oak. These wines are
easily the equivalent of *cru classé*
quality.

RED Consistently one of the best
bourgeois growths in the entire
Médoc. A medium-bodied wine, it
has a rich fruit flavor and good
tannic structure, and can mature
into a sublime, cedary wine.

Cabernet Sauvignon 45%,
Merlot 44%, Cabernet Franc
8%, Petit Verdot 3%

⌐⊶ 6–20 years

CHÂTEAU PHÉLAN-SÉGUR
Cru Bourgeois Exceptionnel
★★√

This château was purchased in 1984
by its present owners, the Gardinier
family, one year after selling
Champagnes Pommery and Lanson.
In retrospect, it is quite clear to see
that there have been two steps up
in quality; the first in 1988 and the
second in 1999, with obvious
consolidation achieved during the

intervening decade, with serious
investment going into the
infrastructure of vineyard and
winery. Now one of the best-value
wines in the Médoc, this wine is
matured in wood for 16 months,
with 50 percent new oak.

RED Increasingly stylish wines of
good color and a certain plumpness
of fruit, without loss of true St.-
Estèphe structure. Unlike most other
success stories in the commune, this
has not been achieved by increasing
Merlot; the reverse, in fact.

Cabernet Sauvignon 60%,
Merlot 35%, Cabernet Franc 5%

⌐⊶ 5–10 years

Second wine: *Franck Phélan*
Other wine: *Croix Bonis*

CHÂTEAU POMYS
Cru Bourgeois
★√

This property was classified *cru
bourgeois* in 1932, but was not
included in the 1978 list, although it
is superior to a few that were. This
hand-harvested wine is matured in
wood for 15 months, with 30
percent new oak.

RED Substantial wines with good
fruit and tannin balance.

Cabernet Sauvignon 50%,
Merlot 35%, Cabernet Franc
15%

⌐⊶ 3–10 years

Other wine: *Château Saint-Louis*

CHÂTEAU TOUR DE PEZ
Cru Bourgeois Exceptionnel
★★√

The huge investments made since
this château changed hands in 1989
paid off in 2003 when it became
one of only nine *crus bourgeois
exceptionnels*. This wine is matured
in wood for 16 to 18 months, with
50 percent new oak.

RED Consistently elegant, medium-
bodied wine with good, plump,
fleshy fruit.

Cabernet Sauvignon 45%,
Cabernet Franc 10%, Merlot
40%, Petit Verdot 5%

⌐⊶ 3–7 years

Second wine: *T de Tour de Pez*
Other wines: *Château les Hauts de
Pez, Château L'Hereteyre Château
Haut-Coutelin*

CHÂTEAU TRONQUOY-LALANDE
Cru Bourgeois Supérieur
★√

Owned by Arlette Castéja-Texier
with active input from the Dourthe-
Kressman winemaking team.

RED This wine can be dark and
tannic, but as from the 1996
vintage it has displayed more
fruit and finesse.

Cabernet Sauvignon 45%,
Merlot 45%, Petit Verdot 10%

⌐⊶ 3–7 years

PAUILLAC

If any Bordeaux appellation can be described as "big, black, and beautiful," it is Pauillac—the commune most famous for the three premiers crus of Latour, Lafite, and Mouton. The wine is allowed to evolve very slowly, achieving an astonishing degree of finesse for its weight.

PAUILLAC IS, HOWEVER, an appellation of quite surprising contrasts. Although it boasts three-quarters of the Médoc's *premiers crus*, it also contains two-thirds of the region's *cinquièmes crus*. Very little lies between these two extremes, and *crus bourgeois* are, therefore, the exception rather than the rule. Cabernet Sauvignon is at its most majestic in Pauillac, and while the much-vaunted blackcurrant character of this grape may be elusive in many clarets, it is certainly very much in evidence in Pauillac. In this wine, the cassis character is always beautifully balanced by a tannic structure.

PAUILLAC CRU CLASSÉ STATISTICS

Crus classés in AOC Pauillac
18 châteaux (by number: 30% of *crus classés* in the Médoc) with 2,080 acres (842 ha) of vineyards (by area: 30% of *crus classés* in the Médoc and 70% of this AOC)

1er crus classés
3 châteaux (by number: 75% of *1er crus classés* in the Médoc) with 568 acres (230 ha) of vineyards (by area: 75% of *1er crus classés* in the Médoc)

2ème crus classés
2 châteaux (by number: 14% of *2ème crus classés* in the Médoc) with 222 acres (90 ha) of vineyards (by area: 11% of *2ème crus classés* in the Médoc)

3ème crus classés
None

4ème crus classés
1 château (by number: 10% of *4ème crus classés* in the Médoc) with 111 acres (45 ha) of vineyards (by area: 10% of *4ème crus classés* in the Médoc)

5ème crus classés
12 châteaux (by number: 67% of *5ème crus classés* in the Médoc) with 1,179 acres (477 ha) of vineyards (by area: 63% of *5ème crus classés* in the Médoc)

Note: Only Margaux has more *cru classé* châteaux than Pauillac, and no communal AOC has a greater concentration of *cru classé* vines.

CHÂTEAU LATOUR
Due to radical changes in vinification techniques introduced in the 1960s, Château Latour became the most consistent of Bordeaux's great premiers crus classés. *It produces the archetypal Pauillac wine, which is full of finesse.*

FACTORS AFFECTING TASTE AND QUALITY

⊗ LOCATION
Pauillac is sandwiched between St.-Estèphe to the north and St.-Julien to the south.

CLIMATE
As for the Médoc (see p.00

ASPECT
Pauillac consists of two large, low-lying plateaux, one to the northwest of the town of Pauillac, the other to the southwest. Exposure is excellent, and both drain down gentle slopes, eastward to the Gironde, westward to the forest, or north and south to canals and streams.

SOIL
Pauillac's two plateaux are massive gravel beds, reaching a greater depth than any found elsewhere in the Médoc. The water

drains away before the iron-pan subsoil is reached. St.-Sauveur consists of shallow sand over a stony subsoil to the west, and gravel over iron-pan (or more gravel) in the center and south.

🏛 VITICULTURE AND VINIFICATION
Only red wines have the right to the Pauillac appellation. Some vin de presse is traditionally used by most châteaux. Skin contact duration averages between 3 and 4 weeks, and maturation in cask currently varies between 18 and 24 months.

🍇 GRAPE VARIETIES
Primary varieties: Cabernet Sauvignon, Cabernet Franc, Merlot
Secondary varieties: Carmenère, Petit Verdot, Malbec

CAVEAU PRIVÉ, CHÂTEAU PICHON-LONGUEVILLE-COMTESSE-DE-LALANDE
One wall of the château's private cellars encapsulates a winemaking history, particularly of Bordeaux, stretching back nearly 200 years.

PAUILLAC PROFILE

Appellation area
Covers parts of the commune of Pauillac, plus 84 acres (34 ha) in St.-Sauveur, 40 acres (16 ha) in St.-Julien, 12.4 acres (5 ha) in St.-Estèphe, and 2.5 acres (1 ha) in Cissac

Size of commune
6,274 acres (2,539 ha)

AOC area under vine
2,988 acres (1,209 ha), 48% of commune

Surface area of crus classes
2,080 acres (842 ha), 3% of commune, 70% of AOC

PAUILLAC, see also p63
Blessed with three premiers crus, Lafite-Rothschild and Mouton-Rothschild in the north, and Latour to the south, Pauillac is sandwiched between St.-Estèphe and St.-Julien

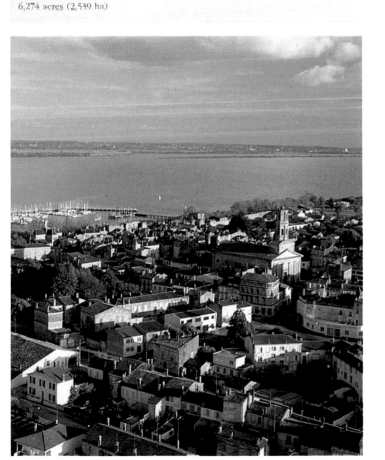

PAUILLAC
The town of Pauillac, the largest of the Médoc, sits on the west bank of the Gironde. Despite its size and position, it retains a quiet, rural character.

THE WINE PRODUCERS OF
PAUILLAC

CHÂTEAU D'ARMAILHAC
5ème Cru Classé
★★✫

Baron Philippe de Rothschild purchased Château Mouton d'Armailhac in 1933. In 1956 he renamed it Château Mouton Baron-Philippe. In 1975 it was changed to Mouton-Baronne-Philippe in honor of the baron's late wife. In 1991 it reverted to d'Armailhac, but without the Mouton tag because the baron believed the wine to be in danger of assuming second wine status due to the overwhelming prestige of Mouton-Rothschild. This property borders that of Mouton, and one of Baron Philippe's reasons for acquiring it was to provide an easier, more impressive access to the famous *premier cru*. The wines, which are matured in wood for 16 months, with 25 percent new oak, are produced with the same care and consideration. Despite this attention, I have criticized the "austere, light, and attenuated style" of Château d'Armailhac in the past, which "proves that even money cannot buy *terroir*," but within limits improvements can always be made, and by tweaking harvesting and vinification techniques, owners Baron Philippe de Rothschild S.A. produced the greatest wine this property has ever known in 2000. That was an extraordinary vintage, but the style shift and giant stride in quality continued in 2001, 2002, and 2003.

RED Since 2000, much riper tannins, and a more supple structure has given this wine more velvety fruit than previous vintages had established. The start of a new era.

🍇 Cabernet Sauvignon 52%, Merlot 26%, Cabernet Franc 20%, Petit Verdot 2%

🍷 6–15 years

CHÂTEAU BATAILLEY
5ème Cru Classé
★★✫ **Ⓥ**

This is a château that responds well to sunny years and produces underrated and undervalued wine.

The 1985 was possibly the best bargain in Bordeaux, and the 1986 is probably even better. This wine is matured in wood for 18 months, with 60 percent new oak.

RED This wine has sometimes been rustic and too assertive in the past, but now shows its class with fine, succulent fruit supported by a ripe tannic structure and a complex creamy-oak aftertaste.

🍇 Cabernet Sauvignon 70%, Merlot 25%, Cabernet Franc 3%, Petit Verdot 2%

🍷 10–25 years

Second wine: *Château Haut-Bages Monpelou*

CHÂTEAU CLERC MILON
5ème Cru Classé
★

This property was purchased by Baron Philippe de Rothschild in 1970. After more than a decade of investment and quite a few disappointing vintages along the way, it came good in 1981, achieved sensational quality in 1982, and now consistently performs well above its classification. This wine, which is matured in wood for 18 months with one-third new oak, is one worth watching.

RED A deep-colored, medium-bodied, sometimes full-bodied, wine with cassis-cum-spicy-oak aromas and rich berry flavors well balanced by ripe acidity.

🍇 Cabernet Sauvignon 70%, Merlot 20%, Cabernet Franc 10%

🍷 10–20 years

CHÂTEAU COLOMBIER-MONPELOU
Cru Bourgeois Supérieur
★ **Ⓥ**

In the third edition of *Bordeaux and its Wines*, published in 1874, this property was described as a *quatrième cru*. Of course, it was never classified as such, but its recent *cru bourgeois supérieur* achievement is about right. This wine is matured in wood for 16 months, with 40 percent new oak.

RED Rich, spicy, fruit with fine Cabernet characteristics, backed up by good, ripe tannic structure and vanilla-oaky undertones.

🍇 Cabernet Sauvignon 55%, Merlot 35%, Cabernet Franc 5%, Petit Verdot 5%

🍷 5–12 years

Other wines: *Château Grand Canyon, Château Pey la Rose, Château Coubersant, Château de Puy la Rose*

CHÂTEAU CORDEILLAN-BAGES
★

Jean-Michel Cazes of Château Lynch-Bages was the driving force behind the group of growers from the Médoc who renovated Château de Cordeillan, turning it into an extensive complex comprising a hotel, restaurant, and wine school. With only a very small production from just five acres of vineyard this hand-harvested wine that is produced by the Lynch-Bages winemaking team, is matured in wood for up to 15 months, with a massive 100 percent new oak.

RED As dark and as dense as might be expected from a wine produced with the Lynch-Bages influence, with smoky oak, tobacco plant, and violet aromas weaving their way through the chocolaty Cabernet fruit.

🍇 Cabernet Sauvignon 70%, Merlot 20%, Cabernet Franc 10%

🍷 3–8 years

CHÂTEAU CROIZET-BAGES
5ème Cru Classé
★ **Ⓥ**

Under the same ownership as Château Rauzan-Gassies of Margaux, and situated on the Bages plateau, Croizet-Bages is a classic example of a "château with no château." Its wine is matured in wood for 18 months and although not unattractive, it lacks class and rarely excites. Improvements started slowly in the mid-1990s, then stepped up a gear at the turn of the millennium.

RED Not one of the most deeply colored Pauillacs, this medium-bodied wine has always been easy-drinking, but has been more stylish since 1999, gaining both in gravitas and finesse.

🍇 Cabernet Sauvignon 37%, Cabernet Franc 30%, Merlot 30%, Malbec and Petit Verdot 3%

🍷 6–12 years

Second wine: *Enclos de Moncabon*

CHÂTEAU DUHART-MILON-ROTHSCHILD
4ème Cru Classé
★★✫

Another "château with no château," Duhart-Milon was purchased by the Lafite branch of the Rothschild family in 1962. Its wines prior to this date were almost entirely Petit Verdot, and so only in abnormally hot years did it excel with this late-ripening grape, which is traditionally cultivated for its acidity. Interestingly, in the near-tropical heat of 1947, Duhart-Milon managed to produce a wine that many considered to be the best of the vintage. The Rothschilds expanded these vineyards bordering Lafite and replanted them with the correct combination of varieties to suit the *terroir*. In 1994 Charles Chevalier arrived, and since 1996 he has moved these wines up a gear. The wine is matured for at least 18 months in wood, with 50 percent new oak.

RED These wines are elegantly perfumed, deliciously rich in creamy-oaky fruit, and have exceptional balance and finesse.

🍇 Cabernet Sauvignon 80%, Merlot 20%

🍷 8–16 years

Second wine: *Moulin de Duhart*

CHÂTEAU LA FLEUR-MILON
Cru Bourgeois

A "château with no château," La Fleur-Milon produces a wine accumulated from various parcels of vines bordering such prestigious properties as Lafite, Mouton, and Duhart-Milon. This wine is matured in wood for 18 months, with one-third new oak.

RED A consistently firm, solid, and decent kind of wine, which somehow fails to live up to the favored origins of its vines.

🍇 Cabernet Sauvignon 45%, Cabernet Franc 20%, Merlot 35%

🍷 4–10 years

Other wines: *Château Chanteclerc-Milon, Château Buisson-Milon*

CHÂTEAU FONBADET
Cru Bourgeois Supérieur
★ ❤

This growth was classified *cru bourgeois* in 1932, but was not included in the Syndicat's 1978 list, although it is superior to a few that were, and achieved due recognition in the 2003 reclassification. Many of the vines are in excess of 80 years old, with an average age of 50 years for the entire 50 acre (20-hectare) vineyard. This hand-harvested wine is matured in wood for 18 months, with 30 percent new oak. Great-value Pauillac.

RED This typical Pauillac has a deep, almost opaque color, an intense cassis, cigar-box, and cedarwood bouquet, a concentrated spicy, fruit flavor with creamy-oak undertones, and a long finish.

🍇 Cabernet Sauvignon 60%, Merlot 20%, Cabernet Franc 15%, Malbec and Petit Verdot 5%

🍷 6–15 years

Other wines: *Château Haut-Pauillac, Château Padarnac, Château Montgrand-Milon, Château Tour du Roc-Milon, Pauillac*

CHÂTEAU GRAND-PUY-DUCASSE
5ème Cru Classé
★ ★ ❤

Under the same owners as Château Rayne-Vigneau in Sauternes, this property produces an undervalued wine that comes from various plots scattered across half the commune. One of the best value, improving *cru classé* wines available, this wine is matured in wood for 18 to 24 months, with up to 40 percent

new oak.

RED Well-balanced, relatively early-drinking, medium-bodied, sometimes full-bodied, wine of classic Pauillac cassis character and more suppleness than is usual for this commune.

🍇 Cabernet Sauvignon 61%, Merlot 39%

🍷 5–10 years

Second wine: *Prélude à Grand-Puy Ducasse*

Other wine: *Château Artigues-Arnaud*

CHÂTEAU GRAND-PUY-LACOSTE
5ème Cru Classé
★ ★ ❤

Under the same ownership as Château Ducru-Beaucaillou, Grand-Puy-Lacoste is going from strength to strength under the skillful guidance of François-Xavier Borie. The wine is matured in wood for 18 months, with 50 percent new oak.

RED Deep-colored with complex cassis, cigar-box spice, and vanilla bouquet, with lots of fruit, length, and finesse.

🍇 Cabernet Sauvignon 75%, Merlot 25%

🍷 10–20 years

Second wine: *Lacoste-Borie*

CHÂTEAU HAUT-BAGES-LIBÉRAL
5ème Cru Classé
★

Under the same ownership as the bourgeois growth of Château Chasse-Spleen in Moulis and the excellent unclassified Château la Gurgue in Margaux, this dynamic property is currently producing sensational wines. They are matured for 16 months in wood, with up to 40 percent new oak.

RED Dark, full-bodied wines with masses of concentrated spicy-cassis fruit, great tannic structure, and ripe, vanilla oak. In a word—complete.

🍇 Cabernet Sauvignon 80%, Merlot 17%, Petit Verdot 3%

🍷 8–20 years

Second wine: *Chapelle de Bages*

CHÂTEAU HAUT-BATAILLEY
5ème Cru Classé
★ ❤

This property is under the same ownership as châteaux Grand-Puy-Lacoste and, in St.-Julien, Ducru-Beaucaillou. When the Borie family purchased Château Batailley in 1942, this part of the vineyard was given to one son, while the bulk of the property, including the château itself, was given to the other. The wine is matured in wood for 20 months, with one-third new oak.

RED Haut-Batailley is well-colored and medium-bodied and shows more elegance and finesse than Batailley, although it can lack the latter's fullness of fruit.

🍇 Cabernet Sauvignon 65%, Merlot 25%, Cabernet Franc 10%

🍷 7–15 years

Second wine: *Château La Tour l'Aspic*

Other wine: *Château La Couronne*

CHÂTEAU LAFITE-ROTHSCHILD
1er Cru Classé
★ ★ ★

Since 1994 this famous château, the vineyard of which includes a small plot in St.-Estèphe, has been run along traditional lines and with fastidious care by Charles Chevalier for Baron Eric of the French branch of the Rothschilds. The St.-Estèphe portion of the Lafite vineyard is allowed to bear the Pauillac appellation, having been part of the Lafite-Rothschild estate for several hundred years. A change of style occurred in the mid-1970s, when the decision was made to give the wines less time in cask, but under Chevalier they have gone into hyperdrive and are often the very best of the *premiers crus*. Well into

the first decade of the new millennium, Lafite is arguably the best performing of all *premiers crus*. This hand-harvested wine is matured in wood for 20 months, with 100 percent new oak.

RED Not the biggest of the *premiers crus*, but Lafite is nevertheless textbook stuff: a rich delicacy of spicy fruit flavors, continuously unfolding, supported by an array of creamy-oak and ripe tannins; a wine with incomparable finesse.

🍇 Cabernet Sauvignon 70%, Merlot 25%, Cabernet Franc 3%, Petit Verdot 2%

🍷 25–50 years

Second wine: ✓ *Carruades de Lafite*

Other wine: *Moulin des Carruades*

CHÂTEAU LATOUR
1er Cru Classé
★ ★ ★

The Pearson Group (which now owns the publisher of this book) was accused by the French of turning a Bordeaux *premier cru* into a dairy when temperature-controlled, stainless-steel vats were installed in 1964. These French critics conveniently ignored the fact that Château Haut-Brion had done the same three years earlier. Pearson actually owned just over half of Latour at the time and Harveys of Bristol owned a quarter. Together they paid less than three million dollars for almost 80 percent of this *premier cru*. It was a bargain, for although they invested heavily in renovating the vineyards and winery, Allied-Lyons (owners of Harvey's) paid almost $110 million in 1989 for Pearson's share, valuing the entire property at $180 million. Allied Lyons lost out, however, when in 1993 they needed to liquidate various shareholdings to finance takeovers and sold Latour to François Pinault, the French industrialist, for $130 million. Pinault appointed Frédéric Engerer, a graduate of one of France's top business schools, as the new young president of Latour. He has revolutionized working practices in both the vineyard and winery and with Frédéric Ardouin, his new, even younger winemaker at his side, the change in gear at Latour promised to be as dramatic as it was at Margaux. This hand-harvested wine is matured in wood for 18 months, with 100 percent new oak.

RED Despite its close proximity to the neighboring commune of St.-Julien, Latour is the archetypal Pauillac. Its ink-black color accurately reflects the immense structure and hugely concentrated flavor of this wine. If Lafite is the ultimate example of finesse, then Latour is the ideal illustration of how massive a wine can be while still retaining great finesse.

🍇 Cabernet Sauvignon 75%, Merlot 20%, Cabernet Franc and Petit Verdot 5%

🍷 15–60 years

Second wine: ✓ *Les Forts de Latour*

Other wine: *Pauillac de Latour*

CHÂTEAU LYNCH-BAGES

5ème Cru Classé
★★★ V

This château is sited on the edge of the Bages plateau, a little way out of Pauillac. It is on the southern fringe of the small town of Bages. Jean-Michel Cazes produces wines that some people describe as "poor man's Latour (or Mouton)." Well, that cannot be such a bad thing, but if I were rich, I would drink as many *cinquièmes crus* from this château as *premiers crus* from elsewhere. No expense was spared in building the new vinification and storage facilities at this château, and since 1980 the successes in off-vintages have been extraordinary, making it more consistent than some *deuxièmes crus*. This hand-harvested wine is matured in wood for 12 to 15 months, with 50 percent new oak.

RED An intensely deep purple-colored wine of seductive character that is packed with fruit and has obvious class. It has a degree of complexity on the nose, a rich, plummy flavor, supple tannin structure, and a spicy, blackcurrant and vanilla aftertaste.

🍇 Cabernet Sauvignon 75%, Merlot 15%, Cabernet Franc 10%

🍷 8–30 years

Second wine: ✓ *Château Haut-Bages-Avérous*

Other wine: *Blanc de Lynch-Bages* (rare "Médoc" white wine)

CHÂTEAU LYNCH-MOUSSAS

5ème Cru Classé
★

Owned by Emile Castéja of Borie-Manoux, this property has been renovated and the wines could well improve. The wine is matured in wood for 18 months, with 60 percent new oak.

RED After a false start in the mid-1980s, when an exceptionally stylish 1985 turned out to be exactly that (an exception), this château continued to produce light, rather insubstantial wines of no specific character or quality, but with better selection, riper fruit, less time in cask, and more than twice the

amount of new oak Lynch-Moussas used to receive, it has made significantly better wines since the mid-1990s.

🍇 Cabernet Sauvignon 75%, Merlot 25%

🍷 4–8 years

Second wine: *Château Haut-Madrac*

CHÂTEAU MOUTON-ROTHSCHILD

1er Cru Classé
★★★

The famous case of the only wine ever to be officially reclassified since 1855, Baron Philippe de Rothschild's plight ended with Mouton's status being justly raised to *premier cru* in 1973. Through promotion of Mouton's unique character, he was probably responsible for elevating the Cabernet Sauvignon grape to its present high profile. Part of his campaign to keep this château in the headlines was the introduction of a specially commissioned painting for the label of each new vintage. The hand-harvested wine is matured in wood for up to 22 months, with 100 percent new oak.

RED It is difficult to describe this wine without using the same descriptive terms as those used for Latour, but perhaps the color of Mouton reminds one more of damsons and the underlying character is more herbal, sometimes even minty. And although it ages just as well as Latour, it becomes accessible slightly earlier.

🍇 Cabernet Sauvignon 77%, Merlot 11%, Cabernet Franc 10%, Petit Verdot 2%

🍷 12–60 years

Second wine: *Le Petit Mouton de Mouton-Rothschild*

Other wines: *Aile d'Argent* (another rare "Médoc" white)

CHÂTEAU PEDESCLAUX

5ème Cru Classé

Little-seen *cru classé* produced from two very well-situated plots of vines, one bordering Lynch-Bages, the other between Mouton-

Rothschild and Pontet-Canet. Most of its exported production goes to Belgium. It is matured in wood for 18 months, with 50 percent new oak. Wine rejected for the *grand vin* is blended into the wine of Château Belle Rose, a *cru bourgeois* under the same ownership.

RED Full, firm, traditional style of Pauillac that is slow-maturing and long-lasting.

🍇 Cabernet Sauvignon 65%, Merlot 25%, Cabernet Franc 5%, Petit Verdot 5%

🍷 15–40 years

Second wine: *Château Haut-Pardanac*

CHÂTEAU PICHON-LONGUEVILLE BARON PICHON-LONGUEVILLE

2ème Cru Classé
★★☆

The smaller of the two Pichon vineyards and until very recently the less inspiring, although many experts reckoned the *terroir* of Pichon-Baron to be intrinsically superior to that of its neighbor, the star-performing Pichon-Comtesse. Indeed, 10 years ago, I even suggested that Madame de Lencquesaing should buy this château and cast her seemingly irresistible spell on what would inevitably be the still greater *terroir* of the two properties combined. Whether she had such an ambition, or even the cash to consider it, AXA-Millesimes got there first, and has been remarkably successful at conjuring the most incredible quality from Pichon-Baron. Essentially by reducing Cabernet Sauvignon in favor of Merlot and almost tripling the amount of new oak used, AXA has ensured that Pichon-Baron now lives up to its potential. The wine is matured in wood for 15 to 18 months, with 80 percent new oak.

RED Intensely colored, full-bodied wine with concentrated spicy-cassis fruit backed up by supple tannins, which are rich and heady with smoky-creamy oak and complexity. True super-second quality.

🍇 Cabernet Sauvignon 60%, Merlot 35%, Cabernet Franc 4%, Petit Verdot 1%

🍷 8–25 years

Second wine: ✓ *Les Tourelles de Longueville*

CHÂTEAU PICHON LONGUEVILLE COMTESSE-DE-LALANDE

2ème Cru Classé
★★☆

There is a limit to the quality of any wine and this is determined by the potential quality of its grapes. But at Pichon-Comtesse (as it is known), the formidable Madame de Lencquesaing demands the maximum from her *terroir*—and consistently gets it. The wine is matured in wood for 20 months, with 50 percent new oak.

RED This temptress is the Château Margaux of Pauillac. It is silky-textured, beautifully balanced, and seductive. A wine of great finesse, even in humble vintages.

🍇 Cabernet Sauvignon 45%, Merlot 35%, Cabernet Franc 12%, Petit Verdot 8%

🍷 10–30 years

Second wine: ✓ *Réserve de la Comtesse*

Other wines: *Les Gartieux*

CHÂTEAU PONTET-CANET

5ème Cru Classé
★★☆

The reputation of this château has suffered in recent decades, but many thought the situation would be reversed when Guy Tesseron purchased the property in 1975. The 1985 vintage gave a glimmer of hope, but it was not until 1995 that the breakthrough occurred, and the 1998 vintage is nothing less than outstanding. Definitely one to watch, this hand-harvested wine is matured in wood for 15 to 20 months, with 60 percent new oak.

RED Since the mid-1990s, these wines have been fruity and graceful with a rich, smooth, oaky touch.

🍇 Cabernet Sauvignon 68%, Merlot 20%, Cabernet Franc 10%, Malbec 2%

🍷 6–12 years

Other wine: *Les Hauts de Pontet*

CHÂTEAU LA TOUR-PIBRAN

★ V

This growth was classified *cru bourgeois* in 1932, but was not in the Syndicat's 1978 list, although it is superior to a few that were.

RED This wine has bags of blackcurranty fruit, yet retains the characteristic Pauillac structure and firm finish. The superb 1985 is not unlike a "mini-Mouton."

🍇 Cabernet Sauvignon 75%, Merlot 15%, Cabernet Franc 10%

🍷 6–16 years

SAINT-JULIEN

The commune's fame is disproportionate to its size, since it is smaller than any of the other three classic Médoc appellations—St.-Estèphe, Pauillac, or Margaux.

St.-Julien has no *premiers crus*, nor *cinquièmes crus*, although some châteaux sometimes produce wines that are undeniably of *premier cru* quality. The concentration of its 11 *crus classés* in the middle of the classification is St.-Julien's real strength, enabling this commune justly to claim that it is the most consistent of the Médoc appellations; these quintessential clarets have a vivid color, elegant fruit, superb balance, and great finesse.

It is perhaps surprising that wines from as far as 40 acres (16 hectares) inside St.-Julien's borders may be classified as AOC Pauillac, particularly in view of the perceived difference in style between these appellations. This illustrates the "gray area" that exists when communal boundaries overlap the historical borders of great wine estates, and highlights the existence and importance of blending, even in a region reputed for its single-vineyard wines. We should not be too pedantic about communal differences of style: if these borders of the Médoc followed local history, Château Latour, the most famous château of Pauillac, would today be in St.-Julien—and that makes me wonder how the wines of this commune might be described under such circumstances?

FACTORS AFFECTING TASTE AND QUALITY

LOCATION
St.-Julien lies in the center of the Haut-Médoc, 2.5 miles (4 kilometers) south of Pauillac.

CLIMATE
As for the Médoc (*see* p70).

ASPECT
The gravel crest of St.-Julien slopes almost imperceptibly eastward toward the village and drains into the Gironde.

SOIL
Fine, gravel topsoil of good-sized pebbles in vineyards within sight of the Gironde. Farther inland, the particle size decreases and the soil begins to mix with sandy loess.

The subsoil consists of iron-pan, marl, and gravel.

VITICULTURE & VINIFICATION
Only red wines have the right to the appellation. All grapes must be destalked. Some *vin de presse* may be used according to the needs of the vintage. Skin contact duration averages 2 to 3 weeks and most châteaux allow 18 to 22 months' maturation in cask.

GRAPE VARIETIES
Primary varieties: Cabernet Sauvignon, Cabernet Franc, Merlot
Secondary varieties: Carmenère, Malbec, Petit Verdot

ST.-JULIEN CRU CLASSÉ STATISTICS

Crus classés in AOC St.-Julien
11 châteaux (by number: 18% of *crus classés* in the Médoc) with 1,552 acres (628 ha) of vineyards (by area: 22% of *crus classés* in the Médoc and 68% of this AOC)

1er crus classés
None

2ème crus classés
5 châteaux (by number: 36% of *2ème crus classés* in the Médoc) with 786 acres (318 ha) of vineyards (by area: 40% of *2ème crus classés* in the Médoc)

3ème crus classés
2 châteaux (by number: 14% of *3ème crus classés* in the Médoc) with 170 acres (69 ha) of vineyards (by area: 16% of *3ème crus classés* in the Médoc)

4ème crus classés
4 châteaux (by number: 40% of *4ème crus classés* in the Médoc) with 396 acres (241 ha) of vineyards (by area: 51% of *4ème crus classés* in the Médoc)

5ème crus classés
None

ST.-JULIEN PROFILE

Appellation area
Covers part of the commune of St.-Julien only

Size of commune
3,840 acres (1,554 ha)

AOC area under vine
2,246 acres (909 ha), 59% of commune

Surface area of crus classés
1,552 acres (628 ha), 40% of commune, 68 of AOC

Special comments
Some 40 acres (16 ha) of St.-Julien are classified as AOC Pauillac

ST.-JULIEN-BEYCHEVELLE
The Médoc's most consistent appellation has two small villages as its major centers, St.-Julien-Beychevelle itself and, to the south, Beychevelle.

ST. JULIEN, *see also p63*
St. Julien lies south of Pauillac in the center of the Médoc. It has many distinguished châteaux.

THE WINE PRODUCERS OF
SAINT-JULIEN

CHÂTEAU BEYCHEVELLE
4ème Cru Classé
★★

The immaculate and colorful gardens of this château never fail to catch the breath of passers-by. Beychevelle also boasts one of the most famous legends of Bordeaux: its name is said to be a corruption of "*basse-voile*," the command to "lower sail." This arose because the Duc d'Épernon, a former owner who was also an admiral of France, apparently required the ships that passed through the Gironde to lower their sails in respect. His wife would then wave her kerchief in reply. This story, however, is not true. Épernon actually held the title of Baron de Beychevelle prior to being made the Amiral de Valette, and did not actually live at Beychevelle. I prefer the story of the sailors who lowered their pants and revealed their sterns, which shocked the duchess but made her children laugh. The wines are matured in wood for 20 months with 40 percent new oak.

RED Medium- to full-bodied wines of good color, ripe fruit, and an elegant oak and tannin structure. They can be quite fat in big years.

🍇 Cabernet Sauvignon 59%, Merlot 30%, Cabernet Franc 8%, Petit Verdot 3%

🍷 12–20 years

Second wine: ✓ *Réserve de l'Amiral*

Other wine: *Les Brulières de Beychevelle*

CHÂTEAU BRANAIRE-DUCRU
4ème Cru Classé
★ ⓥ

The vineyards of this château are situated farther inland than those of Beychevelle and Ducru-Beaucaillou and its soil contains more clay and iron-pan than theirs, so the wine here is fuller and can be assertive, although never austere. It is matured in wood for 18 months, with up to 50 percent new oak, and is remarkably consistent.

RED This is a quite full-bodied wine, which is richly flavored and can show a certain chocolate character in big years. It has a distinctive bouquet that sets it apart from other St.-Juliens.

🍇 Cabernet Sauvignon 75%, Merlot 20%, Cabernet Franc 5%

🍷 12–25 years

Second wine: *Duluc*

CHÂTEAU LA BRIDANE
Cru Bourgeois

The owners of this property have maintained a vineyard here since the 14th century.

RED Attractive, fruity, medium-bodied wine that is easy to drink.

🍇 Cabernet Sauvignon 55%, Merlot 45%

🍷 3–6 years

CHÂTEAU DUCRU-BEAUCAILLOU
2ème Cru Classé
★★★⯪

One of the super-seconds, the quality of this classic St.-Julien château, the flagship property of the Borie empire, is both legendary and inimitable. In both good years and bad it remains remarkably consistent and, although relatively expensive, the price fetched falls short of those demanded by *premiers crus*, making it a relative bargain. The wine is matured in wood for 20 months, with 50 percent new oak.

RED This wine has a fine, deep color that can belie its deft elegance of style. There is richness of fruit, complex spiciness of oak, great finesse, and exquisite balance.

🍇 Cabernet Sauvignon 65%, Merlot 25%, Cabernet Franc 10%

🍷 15–30 years

Second wine: *La Croix*

CHÂTEAU DU GLANA
Cru Bourgeois
★ ⓥ

This property is under the same ownership as Château Plantey in Pauillac and Château la Commanderie in St.-Estèphe.

RED Du Glana is normally an unpretentious and medium-weight wine, but it excels in really hot years, when it can be deliciously ripe and juicy.

🍇 Cabernet Sauvignon 68%, Merlot 25%, Petit Verdot 5%, Cabernet Franc 2%

🍷 3–6 years

CHÂTEAU GLORIA
★

Gloria excites opposite passions in wine drinkers: some consider it the equal of several *cru classé* wines—even superior in some cases—while others believe it earns an exaggerated price based on the reputation of merely a handful of vintages. Certainly the owners saw nothing to be gained by entering this wine for consideration in the 2003 reclassification, although it should have easily made *cru bourgeois supérieur* status had they done so. The wine is matured in wood for 12 months, with 40 percent new oak.

RED A deep plum-colored, full-bodied wine with masses of fruit and a rich, exuberant character.

🍇 Cabernet Sauvignon 65%, Merlot 25%, Cabernet Franc 5%, Petit Verdot 5%

🍷 12–30 years

Second wine: *Peymartin*

Other wine: *Haut-Beychevelle-Gloria*

CHÂTEAU GRUAUD-LAROSE
2ème Cru Classé
★★ ⓥ

This large property produces consistently great wines of a far more solid structure than most other St.-Julien wines. Anyone who has tasted the supposedly mediocre 1980 Sarget de Gruaud-Larose (made from the wines rejected from the *grand vin*) will realize the true potential of Château Gruaud-Larose in any year. If anything, the quality of Gruaud-Larose is still improving.

RED Full-bodied, rich, and plummy wine with masses of fruit. Its spicy blackcurrant flavor is supported by a structure of ripe tannins.

🍇 Cabernet Sauvignon 57%, Merlot 30%, Cabernet Franc 7%, Petit Verdot 4%, Malbec 2%

🍷 10–40 years

Second wine: ✓ *Sarget de Gruaud-Larose*

Other wines: *La Roseraie de Gruaud-Larose, Chevalier de Gruaud-Larose*

CHÂTEAU HORTEVIE
★⯪ ⓥ

There is no château as such on this property. This tiny vineyard's wine is made at Château Terrey-Gros-Caillou by Henri Pradère, the owner of both properties.

RED This is a silky-soft, rich, and succulent wine of excellent quality. This great-value wine is easily equivalent to *cru classé* quality.

🍇 Cabernet Franc and Cabernet Sauvignon 70%, Merlot 25%, Petit Verdot 5%

🍷 7–15 years

CHÂTEAU DE LACOUFOURQUE

This tiny 3-acre (1.25-hectare) vineyard is mentioned not because of its past performance but because it is unique in Bordeaux in being a 100 percent Cabernet Franc varietal, and it should be preserved.

RED This wine is sold in bulk as generic St.-Julien, which makes it impossible to make generalizations about its character.

🍇 Cabernet Franc 100%

CHÂTEAU LAGRANGE
3ème Cru Classé
★★★⯪ ⓥ

When the *Ban de Vendanges* was held at this Japanese-owned château in 1986, everyone realized that the Japanese were not simply content to apply state-of-the-art technology; they seriously intended to make Lagrange the best-quality wine in St.-Julien. They could very well succeed in this ambition. The formidable Bordeaux oenologist Professor Peynaud has dubbed Lagrange a "dream estate," and describes its vinification center as "unlike any other in the whole of Bordeaux." Each vat is, according to Peynaud, a "winemaking laboratory." The wine spends 18 months in wood, with up to 60 percent new oak.

RED A deeply colored wine with intense spicy-fruit aromas. It is full-bodied, silky-textured, and rich, with an exquisite balance and finish.

🍇 Cabernet Sauvignon 65%, Merlot 28%, Cabernet Franc and Petit Verdot 7%

🍷 8–25 years

Second wine: ✓ *Les Fiefs de Lagrange*

CHÂTEAU LALANDE-BORIE
★ ⓥ

Under the same ownership as the illustrious Château Ducru-Beaucaillou, Lalande-Borie is an inexpensive introduction to the wines of St.-Julien.

RED These are well-colored wines, dominated by rich, blackcurranty Cabernet Sauvignon flavors. Some vintages are fat and juicy, while others are more ethereal and tannic.

🍇 Cabernet Sauvignon 65%, Merlot 25%, Cabernet Franc 10%

🍷 5–10 years

CHÂTEAU LANGOA-BARTON

3ème Cru Classé
★ V

This beautiful château was known as Pontet-Langlois until 1821, when it was purchased by Hugh Barton, grandson of "French Tom" Barton, the founder of Bordeaux *négociant* Barton & Guestier, and is now run by Anthony Barton. Both Langoa-Barton and Léoville-Barton are made here using very traditional techniques. The wine is matured in wood for 24 months, with a minimum of one-third new oak.

RED Attractive, easy-drinking wine with good fruit and acidity. It is lighter than the Léoville and can sometimes taste a little rustic in comparison, but has gained a degree of extra elegance and finesse in recent years.

🍇 Cabernet Sauvignon 70%, Merlot 20%, Cabernet Franc 8%, Petit Verdot 2%

🍷 10–25 years

Second wine: ✓ *Lady Langoa* (a blend of Langoa-Barton and Léoville-Barton formerly sold simply as "St.-Julien")

CHÂTEAU LÉOVILLE-BARTON

2ème Cru Classé
★★☆ V

A quarter of the original Léoville estate was sold to Hugh Barton in 1826, but the château remained in the hands of the Léoville estate and is now called Château Léoville-Las Cases (*see below*). This wine is made by Anthony Barton at Langoa-Barton (*see above*). It is matured in wood for 24 months, with a minimum of one-third new oak. Although it is the better of the two Barton estates, it has been considered significantly beneath the standard set by Léoville-Las Cases—since the late 1980s, however, it has performed equally well. A great château in ascendancy.

RED Excellent wines of great finesse and breeding; they are darker, deeper, and richer than the Langoa-Barton, which is itself of very good quality. With maturity, a certain cedarwood complexity develops in this wine and gradually overwhelms its youthful cassis and vanilla character.

🍇 Cabernet Sauvignon 70%, Merlot 20%, Cabernet Franc 8%, Petit Verdot 2%

🍷 15–30 years

Second wine: ✓ *Lady Langoa* (a blend of Langoa-Barton and Léoville-Barton formerly sold simply as "St.-Julien")

CHÂTEAU LÉOVILLE-LAS CASES

2eme Cru Classé
★★★ ☆

The label reads "*Grand Vin* de Léoville du Marquis de Las Cases," although this wine is commonly referred to as "Château Léoville Las Cases." This estate represents the largest portion of the original Léoville estate. This is a great wine, and it certainly qualifies as one of the super-seconds, while "Clos du Marquis" is one of the finest second wines available and probably the best value St.-Julien. The *grand vin* spends 18 months in wood, with 50 percent new oak.

RED This dark, damson-colored, full-bodied, and intensely flavored wine is complex, classy, and aromatically stunning. A skillful amalgam of power and finesse.

🍇 Cabernet Sauvignon 65%, Merlot 19%, Cabernet Franc 13%, Petit Verdot 3%

🍷 15–35 years

Second wine: ✓ *Clos du Marquis*
Other wines: *Domaine de Bigarnon*

CHÂTEAU LÉOVILLE POYFERRÉ

2ème Cru Classé
★★ ☆

This property once formed a quarter of the original Léoville estate, and probably suffers from being compared to the other two châteaux, whose properties were also part of Léoville—Léoville-Barton and Léoville-Las Cases. Yet in the context of St.-Julien as a whole, it fares very well, and since

1982 it has had some extraordinary successes. Since the involvement of Michel Rolland from the mid-1990s, quality has gone up another notch. Wine is matured in wood for 18 months, with one-third new oak.

RED This wine has always been tannic, but is now much fuller in fruit, richer in flavor, and darker in color, with oaky nuances.

🍇 Cabernet Sauvignon 65%, Merlot 30%, Cabernet Franc 5%

🍷 12–25 years

Second wine: *Moulin-Riche*

CHÂTEAU MOULIN-DE-LA-ROSE

Cru Bourgeois Supérieur
★☆ V

This vineyard is well situated, being surrounded by *crus classés* on virtually all sides. Its wine is fermented in stainless steel and aged in cask for 18 months, with 25 percent new oak.

RED This attractively aromatic wine is unusually concentrated and firm for a minor St.-Julien, but rounds out well after a few years in bottle.

🍇 Cabernet Sauvignon 65%, Merlot 25%, Petit Verdot 8%, Cabernet Franc 2%

🍷 6–12 years

CHÂTEAU ST.-PIERRE

4ème Cru Classé
★★ V

This property was bought in 1982 by Henri Martin, who owns the *bourgeois* growth Château Gloria. The wine is matured in wood for between 18 and 20 months, with 50 percent new oak.

RED Once an astringent, coarse wine; now ripe, fat, and full of cedarwood, spice, and fruit.

🍇 Cabernet Sauvignon 70%, Merlot 20%, Cabernet Franc 10%

🍷 8–25 years

Second wine: *Saint-Louis-le-Bosq*
Other wine: *Clos d'Uza*

CHÂTEAU TALBOT

4ème Cru Classé
★★ V

Named after the English Commander who fell at the Battle of Castillon in 1453, this property remains under Cordier family ownership, while its sister château Gruaud-Larose now belongs to Groupe Taillan. To contrast the style

of these two St.-Juliens is justifiable, but to compare their quality is not: Château Talbot is a great wine and closer to the style of a classic St. Julien, but intrinsically it does not have the quality nor the consistency of Château Gruaud Larose. Talbot is matured in wood for between 15 and 18 months, with one-third new oak.

RED A graceful wine, medium-bodied, with elegant fruit, gently structured by ripe oak tannins and capable of considerable finesse.

🍇 Cabernet Sauvignon 66%, Merlot 24%, Cabernet Franc 3%, Petit Verdot 5%, Malbec 2%

🍷 8–30 years

Second wine: ✓ *Connétable Talbot*
Other wine: *Caillou Blanc*

CHÂTEAU TERREY-GROS-CAILLOU

Cru Bourgeois Supérieur
★★☆ V

This establishment is under the same ownership as Château Hortevie (whose wine it also makes), and is itself a top-performing property.

RED This beautifully colored, medium- to full-bodied wine always has rich fruit and is often equivalent to a good *cru classé*.

🍇 Cabernet Sauvignon 65%, Merlot 30%, Petit Verdot 5%

🍷 5–12 years

CHÂTEAU TEYNAC

Cru Bourgeois Supérieur
★☆ V

This fine gravel vineyard once formed part of *cru classé* Château Saint-Pierre.

RED Well-balanced, medium- to full-bodied wine with good spice and a firm tannin structure.

🍇 Cabernet Sauvignon 65%, Merlot 35%

🍷 6–10 years

MARGAUX

Situated in the south of the Médoc district, Margaux is the most famous of all Bordeaux appellations. While it bathes in the reflected glory of its name-sake premier cru, *it is also the largest and least consistent of the four classic Médoc appellations.*

WHILE THE OTHER THREE great Médoc AOCs—St.-Estèphe, Pauillac, and St.-Julien—are connected in one unbroken chain of vineyards, Margaux stands alone to the south, with its vines spread across five communes—Labarde, Arsac, and Cantenac to the south, Margaux in the center, and Soussans to the north. Margaux and Cantenac are the most important communes and, of course, Margaux contains the *premier cru* of Château Margaux itself. Cantenac has a slightly larger area under vine and no fewer than eight classified growths, including the star-performing Château Palmer, which was partly owned by the late Peter Sichel.

Margaux and Pauillac are the only appellations in the Médoc with *premier cru* vineyards, but only Margaux can boast vineyards in all five categories of the classification. It also has more *cru classé* châteaux than any other Médoc appellation, including an impressive total of 10 *troisièmes crus*.

FACTORS AFFECTING TASTE AND QUALITY

LOCATION
In the center of the Haut-Médoc, some 17 miles (28 kilometers) northwest of Bordeaux, encompassing the communes of Cantenac, Soussans, Arsac, and Labarde, in addition to Margaux itself.

CLIMATE
As for the Médoc (*see* p70).

ASPECT
One large, low-lying plateau centering on Margaux, plus several modest outcrops that slope west toward the forest.

SOIL
Shallow, pebbly, siliceous gravel over a gravel subsoil interbedded with limestone.

VITICULTURE AND VINIFICATION
Only red wines have the right to the appellation. All grapes must be destalked. On average, between 5 and 10 percent *vin de presse* may be used in the wine, according to the needs of the vintage. Skin contact duration averages 15 to 25 days, with the period of maturation in cask currently varying between 18 and 24 months.

GRAPE VARIETIES
Primary varieties: Cabernet Sauvignon, Cabernet Franc, Merlot
Secondary varieties: Carmenère, Malbec, Petit Verdot

MARGAUX CRU CLASSÉ STATISTICS

Crus classés in AOC Margaux
21 châteaux (by number: 35% of *crus classés* in the Médoc) with 2,110 acres (854 ha) of vineyards (by area: 35% of *crus classés* in the Médoc and 61% of this AOC)

1er crus classés
1 château (by number: 25% of *1er crus classés* in the Médoc) with 185 acres (75 ha) of vineyards (by area: 25% of *1er crus classés* in the Médoc)

2ème crus classés
5 châteaux (by number: 36% of *2ème crus classés* in the Médoc) with 670 acres (271 ha) of vineyards (by area: 34% of *2ème crus classés* in the Médoc)

3ème crus classés
10 châteaux (by number: 72% of *3ème crus classés* in the Médoc) with 754 acres (305 ha) of vineyards (by area: 72% of *3ème crus classés* in the Médoc)

4ème crus classés
3 châteaux (by number: 30% of *4ème crus classés* in the Médoc) with 259 acres (105 ha) of vineyards (by area: 22% of *4ème crus classés* in the Médoc)

5ème crus classés
2 châteaux (by number: 11% of *5ème crus classés* in the Médoc) with 242 acres (98 ha) of vineyards (by area: 13% of *5ème crus classés* in the Médoc)

CHÂTEAU MARGAUX
Margaux's celebrated premier cru *vineyards are matched by the grandeur of the building itself. Both the building and the wine are justifiably famous.*

MARGAUX, *SEE ALSO* P.00
Of the classic Médoc appellations, Margaux—the most famous—stands alone to the south, and can boast more cru classé *châteaux than any of the others.*

MARGAUX PROFILE

Appellation covers: parts of the communes of Arsac, Cantenac, Labarde, Margaux, and Soussans as follows.

REGION	SIZE OF COMMUNE	AOC AREA UNDER VINE	VINE AREA AS PROPORTION OF COMMUNE	VINE AREA AS PROPORTION OF APPELLATION
Arsac	7,954 acres (3,219 ha)	524 acres (212 ha)	7%	15%
Cantenac	3,502 acres (1,417 ha)	963 acres (387 ha)	27%	28%
Labarde	1,174 acres (475 ha)	279 acres (113 ha)	24%	8%
Margaux	2,083 acres (843 ha)	1,006 acres (407 ha)	48%	29%
Soussans	3,850 acres (1,558 ha)	699 acres (283 ha)	18%	20%
TOTAL	18,562 acres (7,512 ha)	3,464 acres (1,402 ha)	19%	100%

Total size of all five communes: 18,562 acres (7,512 ha)
Total AOC area under vine: 3,311 acres (1,402 ha) (19% of communes)
Surface area of crus classés: 2,110 acres (854 ha) (11% of communes, 64% of AOC)

AN OUTSTANDING WINE

If the massive Pauillac wines of Château Latour and Château Mouton are an object lesson in how it is possible to bombard the senses with power and flavor, and yet retain quite remarkable finesse, then the exquisite wines of Margaux at their very best are perfect proof that complexity does not necessarily issue from an intense concentration of flavor.

However, this is not to suggest that Margaux wines do not actually possess some concentration; indeed, Château Margaux has a particularly remarkable concentration of flavor, and it remains the quintessential wine of this appellation.

NEW CELLAR AT CHÂTEAU MARGAUX
Evidence of the investment made in Château Margaux since the late 1970s is the refurbished wine store and its full complement of new oak barrels.

SOUTIRAGE CHÂTEAU MARGAUX
As the wine matures in the barrel its clarity is checked regularly. It spends between 18 and 24 months in new oak.

CHÂTEAU CANTENAC BROWN
This third growth was originally part of Château Boyd, but after the Boyds and Browns—who were joined by marriage in the late 18th century—had a family crisis, the property was divided into Château Boyd-Cantenac and Château Cantenac Brown.

CHÂTEAU D'ANGLUDET
Angludet, home of the Sichel family, dates back to Bertrand d'Angludet, who in 1313 swore allegiance to Edward II of England. Owned by Sichel from 1960 till 1999, this property exudes its English heritage, with swans gliding on the brook at the bottom of the property.

THE WINE PRODUCERS OF
MARGAUX

CHÂTEAU D'ANGLUDET
Cru Bourgeois
★ ☆

This château is owned by the Sichel family, who are also part-owners of the star-performing Château Palmer. Since the late 1980s this château has established itself as *cru classé* quality. It will be interesting to see what the next decade brings. The wine is matured in wood for 12 months, with up to one-third new oak.

RED Vividly colored, medium- to full-bodied wines with excellent fruit, finesse, and finish—classic Margaux.

🍇 Cabernet Sauvignon 55%, Merlot 35%, Petit Verdot 10%

🍷 10–20 years

Second wine: *La Ferme d'Angludet*
Other wine: *Clairet d'Angludet*

CHÂTEAU D'ARSAC
AOC Margaux
Cru Bourgeois

Until recently this was the only property in Arsac not to benefit from the Margaux appellation. Since a change in ownership this estate has expanded its vineyards from just over 27 acres (11 hectares) to 252 acres (102 hectares), of which 100 (40 hectares) are now classified as Margaux. The wines are matured in wood for 12 to 18 months, with 20 percent new oak.

RED These are deep-colored, full-bodied wines.

🍇 Cabernet Sauvignon 80%, Merlot 15%, Cabernet Franc 5%

🍷 7–15 years

Second wine: *Château Ségur-d'Arsac*
Other wine: *Château Le Monteil-d'Arsac*

CHÂTEAU BEL-AIR MARQUIS D'ALIGRE
❶

Château Bel-Air Marquis d'Aligre was classified *cru bourgeois* in 1932, but was not included in the Syndicat's 1978 list, although it is superior to a few that were. The vineyard has limestone subsoil and only organic fertilizers are used.

RED Well-made wines of fine color, elegant fruit, with a distinctive style are produced by Château Bel-Air Marquis d'Aligre.

🍇 Merlot 35%, Cabernet Sauvignon 30%, Cabernet Franc 20%, Petit Verdot 15%

🍷 6–12 years

Second wine: *Château Bel-Air-Marquis-de-Pomereu*

CHÂTEAU BOYD-CANTENAC
3ème Cru Classé

Château Boyd-Cantenac is a property producing traditional-style wines from old vines. The wine is made at owner Mr. Guillemet's other property, Château Pouget, under the supervision of Professor Peynaud. It is matured in wood for 24 months, with 30 percent new oak and, in my opinion, would benefit from more Merlot and no Petit Verdot.

RED Full-bodied, firm wine of good color that needs a long time in bottle to soften. The mediocre 1980 was particularly successful.

🍇 Cabernet Sauvignon 70%, Merlot 20%, Cabernet Franc 5%, Petit Verdot 5%

🍷 12–20 years

CHÂTEAU BRANE-CANTENAC
2ème Cru Classé
★ ☆ ❶

This property is a superb plateau of immaculately kept vines situated on gravel over limestone and is owned and run by Henri Lurton. The wine is matured in wood for 18 months, with 25 to 30 percent new oak.

RED These stylish wines have a smoky-cream and new-oak bouquet, deliciously rich fruit, and finesse on the palate. They are top-quality wines, velvety and beautifully balanced.

🍇 Cabernet Sauvignon 70%, Cabernet Franc 15%, Merlot 13%, Petit Verdot 2%

🍷 8–25 years

Second wine: *Le Baron de Brane*
Other wines: *Domaine de Fontarney, Château Notton*

CHÂTEAU CANTENAC BROWN
3ème Cru Classé

Ever since I drank a 50-year-old half-bottle of 1926 Cantenac Brown in splendid condition, I have had a soft spot for this château, which has, frankly, been disproportionate to the quality of its wines. Despite heavy investment after being purchased by AXA, these wines have not noticeably improved, although in the late 1980s to early 1990s there was hope and some evidence that they might. The wines are matured in wood for 18 months, with one-third new oak.

RED This wine has always had a similar weight to Brane-Cantenac, but with a less velvety and generally more rustic style. The vintages of the 1980s have more finesse than those of the 1970s, but the quality and concentration took a sharp upward turn in 1989 and 1990.

🍇 Cabernet Sauvignon 65%, Merlot 25%, Cabernet Franc 10%

🍷 10–25 years

Second wine: *Canuet*
Other wine: *Lamartine*

CHÂTEAU CHARMANT

This property was not classified as a *cru bourgeois* in 1932, nor listed by the Syndicat in 1978, but it certainly deserves recognition today.

RED An elegant wine with plenty of fruit and a soft finish, it makes delightful drinking when young.

🍇 Cabernet Sauvignon 60%, Merlot 35%, Cabernet Franc 5%

🍷 3–8 years

CHÂTEAU DAUZAC
5ème Cru Classé
★

Now owned by MAIF and managed by Vignobles André Lurton, the quality of the wines from this château has steadily increased since the mid-1990s. The wine, which is matured in wood for 16 to 18 months with one-third new oak, is steadily improving.

RED Ruby-colored, medium-bodied, round, and attractively fruity wines that are easy to drink.

🍇 Cabernet Sauvignon 65%, Merlot 25%, Cabernet Franc 5%, Petit Verdot 5%

🍷 6–12 years

Second wine: *Labarde*
Other wine: *La Bastide*

CHÂTEAU DESMIRAIL
3ème Cru Classé
☆

A "château with no château" (because the building that was its château was purchased by Château Marquis d'Alesme-Becker), Desmirail has been on the ascent since its purchase by the Lurton family, but it still has some way to go before it becomes a true *troisième cru*. It is owned and run by Denis Lurton, while oenologist Professor Peynaud advises. The wine is matured in wood for 20 months, with 25 to 50 percent new oak.

RED A medium-bodied wine that is nicely balanced, with gentle fruit flavors and supple tannins. It is well-made and gradually gaining in finesse.

🍇 Cabernet Sauvignon 80%, Merlot 10%, Cabernet Franc 9%, Petit Verdot 1%

🍷 7–15 years

Second wine: *Château Baudry*
Other wine: *Domaine de Fontarney*

CHÂTEAU DEYREM-VALENTIN

This château was classified *cru bourgeois* in 1932, but was not included in the Syndicat's 1978 list, although it is superior to a few that were. Its vineyards adjoin those of Château Lascombes.

RED Honest, medium-bodied, fruity wine of some elegance.

🍇 Cabernet Sauvignon 45%, Merlot 45%, Cabernet Franc 5%, Petit Verdot 5%

🍷 4–10 years

CHÂTEAU DURFORT-VIVENS
2ème Cru Classé
★ ❶

Owned by Gonzague Lurton, who is married to Claire Villars, the administrator of châteaux Chasse-Spleen and Haut-Bages-Libéral. Dufort-Vivens has become one of the best-value *cru classé* wines of Margaux since the mid-1990s. This property matures its wine in wood for 18 to 20 months, with up to one-third new oak.

RED Higher tannic structure than Brane-Cantenac, but without the luxurious new-oak character, and with less fruit and charm. The 1985 was particularly rich and impressive.

🍇 Cabernet Sauvignon 82%, Cabernet Franc 10%, Merlot 8%

🍷 10–25 years

Second wine: *Second de Durfort*
Other wine: *Domaine de Curé-Bourse*

CHÂTEAU FERRIÈRE
3ème Cru Classé
★ ❶

When managed by Château Lascombes this was little more than second-label status, but it has gained in both exposure and quality since this property was purchased by the Villars family.

RED Quick-maturing wine of medium weight and accessible fruit.

🍇 Cabernet Sauvignon 75%, Merlot 20%, Petit Verdot 5%

🍷 4–8 years

Second wine: *Les Remparts de Ferrière*

CHÂTEAU GISCOURS
3ème Cru Classé
★★½

This property is situated in the commune of Labarde. It was purchased in 1952 by the Tari family, who have restored the château, the vineyard, and the quality of its wine to their former glory. In 1995 the château was sold to Eric Albada Jelgerms, a Dutch businessman who has at least maintained the quality and, arguably, improved it. The wine is matured in wood for 20 to 34 months, with 50 percent new oak.

RED Vividly colored wine, rich in fruit and finesse. Its vibrant style keeps it remarkably fresh for many years.

Cabernet Sauvignon 75%, Merlot 22%, Cabernet Franc 2%, Petit Verdot 1%

⌐— 8–30 years

Second wine: *La Sirène de Giscours*
Other wine: *Cantelaude*

CHÂTEAU LA GURGUE

This property was classified *cru bourgeois* in 1932, but not included in the Syndicat's 1978 list, although it is superior to a few that were. Its proprietor also owns the *cru classe* Haut-Bages-Libéral, and the *cru bourgeois* Chasse-Spleen.

RED Soft, elegant, medium-bodied wine of attractive flavor and some finesse.

Cabernet Sauvignon 70%, Merlot 25%, Petit Verdot 5%

⌐— 4–12 years

CHÂTEAU D'ISSAN
3ème Cru Classé
★★

This beautiful 17th-century château is frequently cited as the most impressive in the entire Médoc, and its remarkable wines, matured in wood for 18 months, with up to one-third new oak, are consistently just as spectacular.

RED This wine really is glorious! Its luxuriant bouquet is immediately seductive, its fruit is unbelievably rich and sumptuous. A great wine of great finesse.

Cabernet Sauvignon 85%, Merlot 15%

⌐— 10–40 years

Second wine: *Blason d'Issan*
Other wine: *De Candel*

CHÂTEAU KIRWAN
3ème Cru Classé
★★½ Ⓥ

Château Kirwan is a well-run and improving property owned by the Bordeaux négociant Schröder & Schÿler with Michel Rolland consulting. The wine is matured in wood for 18 to 24 months, with up to 50 percent new oak.

RED Deep-colored, full-bodied, rich and concentrated wines that are well-made and gaining in generosity, riper tannins, and new oak influence with each passing vintage.

Cabernet Sauvignon 40%, Merlot 30%, Cabernet Franc 20%, Petit Verdot 10%

⌐— 10–35 years

Second wine: *Les Charmes de Kirwan*

CHÂTEAU LABÉGORCE
★★ Ⓥ

This château was classified *cru bourgeois* in 1932, but not included in the Syndicat's 1978 list. Since Hubert Perrodo, a wine-loving oil tycoon, purchased Labégorce in 1989, the quality and price of its wines have increased steadily. The wine is matured in wood for 18 months, with up to one-third new oak.

RED Well-colored wine with good balance of concentration and finesse.

Cabernet Sauvignon 55%, Merlot 40%, Cabernet Franc 5%

⌐— 5–15 years

CHÂTEAU LABÉGORCE-ZÉDÉ
★★½ Ⓥ

Classified *cru bourgeois* in 1932, but not included in the 1978 list, although it is one of the best non-*cru classé* wines of the commune.

RED Fine flavor and great length, combined with a certain complexity, give the wines of this château a slight edge over those of Château Labégorce.

Cabernet Sauvignon 50%, Merlot 35%, Cabernet Franc 10%, Petit Verdot 5%

⌐— 5–15 years

Second wine: *Château de l'Amiral*

CHÂTEAU LASCOMBES
2ème Cru Classé
★★

Owned by Bass Group, the wines of this large property have always been good, yet they have improved dramatically under René Vanatelle. It was Vanatelle who recognized that only 125 of Lascombes' 208 acres (50 of 83 hectares) were of authentic *deuxième cru* potential. He therefore segregated the vineyard and sold the lesser wines as Château Segonnes. This accounted for the noticeable step up in quality in the 1980s. Then in 1997, the year before he retired, Vanatelle introduced a true second

wine, Chevalier des Lascombes, which has pushed standards up yet another notch, before handing over to Bruno Lemoine, formerly of Montrose. The wine is matured in wood for 14 to 20 months, with one-third new oak.

RED Full-bodied, rich, and concentrated wine with ripe fruit, a lovely cedarwood complexity, and supple tannin.

Cabernet Sauvignon 55%, Merlot 40%, Petit Verdot 5%

⌐— 8–30 years

Second wine: *Chevalier Lascombes*
Other wines: *Château Segonnes, Gombaud, Rosé de Lascombes, Vin Sec Chevalier Lascombes*

CHÂTEAU MALESCOT ST-EXUPÉRY
3ème Cru Classé
★

English-owned until 1955, when it was purchased by Roger Zuger, whose brother owns Château Marquis-d'Alesme-Becker. The wine is matured in wood for 18 months, with 20 percent new oak.

RED Richer, more complex wines have been produced since 1996.

Cabernet Sauvignon 50%, Merlot 35%, Cabernet Franc 10%, Petit Verdot 5%

⌐— 8–25 years

Second wines: *Château De Loyac, La Dame de Malescot*
Other wine: *Balardin*

CHÂTEAU MARGAUX
1er Cru Classé
★★★ Ⓥ

This is the most famous wine in the world and, since its glorious rebirth in 1978, the greatest. Its quality may occasionally be matched, but it is never surpassed. Purchased in 1977 for 72 million francs ($14.5 million) by the late André Mentzelopoulos, who spent an equal sum renovating it, this fabulous jewel in the crown of the Médoc is now run by his daughter, Corinne Mentzelopoulos. Both Château Margaux and its second wine, "Pavillon Rouge," are vinified in oak vats and matured for 18 to 24 months in 100 percent new oak.

RED If finesse can be picked up on the nose, then the stunning and complex bouquet of Château Margaux is the yardstick. The softness, finesse, and velvety texture of this wine belies its depth. Amazingly rich and concentrated, with an elegant, long, and complex finish supported by ripe tannins

and wonderful smoky-creamy oak aromas. This is as near perfection as we will ever get.

Cabernet Sauvignon 75%, Merlot 20%, Cabernet Franc and Petit Verdot 5%

⌐— 15–50 years

Second wine: *Pavillon Rouge du Château Margaux*
Other wine: *Pavillon Blanc du Château Margaux*

CHÂTEAU MARQUIS D'ALESME-BECKER
3ème Cru Classé

Like Château Malescot St.-Exupéry, this was English-owned until purchased by Jean-Claude Zuger, who also purchased the maison of neighboring Desmirail to act as its château. The wine is matured in wood for 12 months, with one-sixth new oak.

RED Austere and charmless wines from my point of view, although they have their admirers. They are well-made, but lack sufficient selection, although the terroir has potential.

Cabernet Sauvignon 40%, Merlot 30%, Cabernet Franc 20%, Petit Verdot 10%

⌐— 8–20 years

Second wine: *Marquise d'Alesme*

CHÂTEAU MARQUIS-DE-TERME
4ème Cru Classé

Situated next to Château Margaux, this once majestic estate developed the reputation for producing tight, tannic, one-dimensional wines, but its quality has picked up since the late 1970s and has been performing extremely well since 1983. The wine is matured in wood for 24 months, with one-third new oak.

RED Appears to be developing a style that is ripe and rich, with definite and delightful signs of new oak. The 1984 was quite a revelation.

Cabernet Sauvignon 60%, Merlot 30%, Petit Verdot 7%, Cabernet Franc 3%

⌐— 10–25 years

Second wine: *Terme des Goudat*

CHÂTEAU MARSAC-SÉGUINEAU

This property was classified *cru bourgeois* in 1932, but not included in the Syndicat's 1978 list, although it is superior to a few that were. The vineyards of this château include some plots that originally belonged to a *cru classé*.

RED Medium- to full-bodied wines of good bouquet and a soft style.

Cabernet Sauvignon 65%, Merlot 35%

⌐— 5–12 years

Second wine: *Château Gravières-de-Marsac*

CHÂTEAU MONBRISON
Cru Bourgeois
★ ☑

These vineyards used to be part of *cru classé* Château Desmirail; the wines were excellent 10 years ago, and now vie with those of true *cru classé* standard.

RED This château's second label offers a brilliant selection of beautifully deep-colored wines with spicy-oak, superrich juicy fruit, and a fine structure of supple tannin.

🍇 Merlot 35%, Cabernet Franc 30%, Cabernet Sauvignon 30%, Petit Verdot 5%

🍷 8–15 years

Second wine: *Château Cordat*

CHÂTEAU MONTBRUN

Château Montbrun was classified *cru bourgeois* in 1932, but not included in the Syndicat's 1978 list, although it is superior to a few that were. This used to be part of *cru classé* Château Palmer.

RED Beautifully made, ripe, and juicy, medium- to full-bodied, Merlot-dominated wines.

🍇 Merlot 75%, Cabernet Franc and Cabernet Sauvignon 25%

🍷 5–12 years

CHÂTEAU PALMER
3ème Cru Classé
★★★

Only Château Margaux outshines this property, jointly owned by Belgian, French, and British (the Sichel family) interests. Château Palmer 1961 and 1966 regularly fetch prices at auction that equal those fetched by the *premiers crus*. Judged at the very highest level, it could be more consistent. It is usually excellent, but not always astonishing—although when it is, it can stand shoulder to shoulder with *premiers crus* in a blind tasting. A true supersecond that promises to achieve even greater heights since the introduction of Alto Ego, a sort of superpremium of second wines, in 1998. The wine is matured in wood for 18 to 24 months, with one-third new oak.

RED Deep, almost opaque-colored wine with masses of cassis fruit and an exceedingly rich, intense, and complex construction of creamy, spicy, cedarwood, and vanilla flavrs, supported by a fine tannic structure.

🍇 Cabernet Sauvignon 50%, Merlot 40%, Cabernet Franc 7%, Petit Verdot 3%

🍷 12–35 years

Second wines: *Alto Ego, Réserve du Général*

CHÂTEAU PONTAC-LYNCH
★ ☑

This property was classified *cru bourgeois* in 1932, but not included in the Syndicat's 1978 list, although it is superior to a few that were. The vineyards are well-situated, and surrounded by *crus classés*.

RED Richly perfumed, deeply colored, full-bodied wines of good structure.

🍇 Cabernet Sauvignon and Merlot 47%, Cabernet Franc 45%, Petit Verdot 8%

🍷 6–15 years

Second wine: *Château Pontac-Phénix*

CHÂTEAU POUGET
4ème Cru Classé
❷

Under the same ownership as Boyd-Cantenac, this property houses the winemaking and storage facilities for both châteaux. The wine is matured in wood for 22 to 24 months, with 30 percent new oak.

RED Well-colored, full-bodied wine with good depth of flavor. Good, but not great, and could be more consistent.

🍇 Cabernet Sauvignon 70%, Merlot 17%, Cabernet Franc 8%, Petit Verdot 5%

🍷 10–25 years

CHÂTEAU PRIEURÉ-LICHINE
4ème Cru Classé
★

The late Alexis Lichine purchased Château Prieuré in 1951 and added his name to it. To develop the small rundown vineyard, he purchased various prized plots of vines from Palmer, Kirwan, Giscours, Boyd-Cantenac, Brane-Cantenac, and Durfort-Vivens—some 148 acres (60 hectares). The composite classification must be higher than its official status—the wines certainly are. Lichine's son Sacha ran the property until 1999, when he sold it to its current owners, the Ballande family. The wines are matured in wood for 19 months, with one-third new oak.

RED Well-colored, full-bodied wines, plummy and rich, with good blackcurrant fruit supported by supple tannins and a touch of vanilla-oak.

🍇 Cabernet Sauvignon 54%, Merlot 39%, Cabernet Franc 2%, Petit Verdot 5%

🍷 7–20 years

Second wine: *Château De Clairefont*

CHÂTEAU RAUZAN-GASSIES
2ème Cru Classé

Until the French Revolution of 1789, this property and Château Rauzan-Ségla were one large estate. The globe-trotting Professor Peynaud was brought in to steer this wine back on course in the early 1980s, but he failed miserably. Jean-Louis Camp, formerly of Loudenne, seems to be having more success. The wine is matured in wood for 17 to 20 months, with 20 percent new oak, although there is little evidence

of it on the palate.

RED The last vintage I really enjoyed was 1961; 1996 and particularly 1998 could herald an upturn in quality.

🍇 Cabernet Sauvignon 40%, Merlot 39%, Cabernet Franc 20%, Petit Verdot 1%

🍷 7–15 years

Second wine: *Enclos de Moncabon*

CHÂTEAU RAUZAN-SÉGLA
2ème Cru Classé
★★☆

The quality of this once-disappointing château began to lift in the 1980s due to significant investment in the property from its owner, the Bordeaux négociant house of Eschenauer, which also instigated a far stricter selection of the *grand vin*. In 1994 Rauzan-Ségla was sold to Chanel, the underbidder for Latour (sold by Allied-Lyons to the French industrialist François Pinault). Since then key personnel from the *premier cru* have been brought in to keep the improvements in full swing. The wine is matured in wood for 20 months, with 50 percent new oak, and is currently one of Bordeaux's top-performing *deuxièmes crus*.

RED In classic years, this wine is deep and dark, with a powerful tannic construction, and more than enough intensely flavored fruit to match. Lesser vintages are dark for the year, but much more lush, with softer tannins.

🍇 Cabernet Sauvignon 65%, Merlot 30%, Cabernet Franc 5%

🍷 15–30 years

Second wine: *Ségla*
Other wines: *Lamouroux*

CHÂTEAU SIRAN
★☆☑

Château Siran was classified *cru bourgeois* in 1932, but not included in the Syndicat's 1978 list, although it is superior to a few that were. The vineyard is well-situated, with immaculately manicured vines that border those of châteaux Giscours and Dauzac. The wine is matured in wood for 24 months, with one-third new oak, in air-conditioned cellars. Monsieur Miailhe, the owner, also likes to provide his guests with every facility.

RED Stylish, aromatic wines of good body, creamy-spicy fruit,

length, and obvious class. Easily equivalent to *cru classé* quality.

🍇 Cabernet Sauvignon 50%, Merlot 25%, Petit Verdot 15%, Cabernet Franc 10%

🍷 8–20 years

Second wine: *Château Bellegarde*
Other wines: *Château St-Jacques*

CHÂTEAU TAYAC
Cru Bourgeois

As Bernard Ginestet, whose family owned Château Margaux for 40 years, once wrote, "this is one of the largest of the smaller properties, and one of the smallest of the larger."

RED Firm, medium- to full-bodied wines of good character, although somewhat rustic; they tend to be coarse in lesser years.

🍇 Cabernet Sauvignon 65%, Merlot 25%, Cabernet Franc 5%, Petit Verdot 5%

🍷 6–12 years

CHÂTEAU DU TERTRE
5ème Cru Classé
★★☆

An underrated *cru classé*, this château has well-situated vineyards. It is under the same ownership as Giscours since 1998. The wine is matured in wood for 24 months, with 25 percent new oak.

RED Although the scent of violets is supposed to be common to Margaux wines, this is one of the few in which I pick it up. The wine is medium- to full-bodied, rich in fragrant fruit, and has excellent balance, with obvious class.

🍇 Cabernet Sauvignon 85%, Cabernet Franc 5%, Merlot 10%

🍷 8–25 years

CHÂTEAU LA TOUR DE MONS
Cru Bourgeois

These wines are aged in wood for 22 months, with 20 percent new oak and have improved enormously since the late 1980s. Easily equivalent to *cru classé* quality.

RED As richly flavored as ever, but without the tannins or acidity that used to be this wine's pitfall

🍇 Cabernet Sauvignon 45%, Merlot 40%, Cabernet Franc 10%, Petit Verdot 5%

🍷 10–30 years

Second wine: *Château Richeterre*

CHÂTEAU DES TROIS-CHARDONS
★☆☑

A tiny production of very high-quality wine from a château named after the current owner, a Monsieur Chardon, and his two sons.

RED Ultraclean, soft, fruity but serious wines of some finesse and well-defined Margaux character.

🍇 Cabernet Sauvignon 50%, Merlot 40%, Cabernet Franc 10%

🍷 6–15 years

GRAVES, CÉRONS, SAUTERNES, AND BARSAC

The finest red Graves wines are produced in Pessac-Léognan, good red and improving dry white wines in the center of Graves, and the great sweet wines of Sauternes and Barsac in the south. The emphasis in production is on classic red wines.

THE SILKY-SMOOTH red wines of the Graves district have been famous since the Middle Ages, when they were protected by local laws that punished those who dared to blend them with other Bordeaux wines. Château Haut-Brion was the only red wine outside the Médoc to be classified in 1855, and such was its reputation that it was placed alongside the *premiers crus* of Latour, Lafite, Mouton, and Margaux. Beneath Haut-Brion, there are a few great wines equivalent in quality to *deuxième* or *troisième cru*, but only a few.

The relative lack of superstars in Graves is offset by a higher base quality of wine and greater consistency of performance in the red wines at least. There are 43 communes in this appellation. Much the best are Léognan, Talence, and Pessac, after which Martillac and Portets are the most outstanding, followed by Illats and Podensac. All the greatest wines are therefore in the north of the Graves district, amid the urban sprawl of Bordeaux, and this presents something of a problem. The once-peaceful left bank of the Garonne is slowly and inexorably disappearing. As the city bursts outward, more rural vineyards are encircled by the concrete jungle, and many quite simply vanish. How many Bordeaux

aficionados who fly directly to the airport in Mérignac stop to consider the cost of such progress? In 1908 there were 30 winemaking properties in the commune of Mérignac; today there is just one—Château Picque-Caillou. The conurbated communes of Cadaujac, Gradignan, Léognan, Martillac, Mérignac, Pessac, Talence, and Villenave d'Ornon have lost 214 wine châteaux over the same period.

THE PROBLEM OF WHITE GRAVES SOLVED

Well almost! While the quality and reputation of the red wines have always been well established, white Graves had a serious identity problem that came to a crisis point in the mid-1980s. Although fine white Graves were being produced, most of it was in the northern communes, but they were tarred with the same brush as the worst white wines from farther south. It was not simply a north–south divide, there was also an identity problem— should they be making rich, oak-aged blends or light and fluffy Sauvignon Blanc? Paradoxically, the worst wines came from some of the best properties in the north, produced by winemakers who either did not know how to, or did not care to, clean up their act, as they continued to sell tired, oversulfured, oxidized, and flabby wines on the backs of their decaying reputations.

An official north-south divide, however, proved to be the solution for, since 1987, when the Pessac-Léognan AOC was introduced, things have never looked better for Graves. The Pessac-Léognan appellation is a single appellation for both red and white wines from the communes Cadaujac, Canéjan, Gradignan, Léognan, Martillac, Mérignac, Pessac, St. Médard-d'Eyrans, Talence, and Villenave d'Ornon. This has had the effect of giving the northern châteaux the official quality recognition

GRAVES, CÉRONS, SAUTERNES, AND BARSAC, *see also p63*
The winemaking area that includes Graves, Cérons, Sauternes, and Barsac forms a swathe that sweeps down from Bordeaux, parallel with the Garonne

VINES AT HAUT-BRION
Rose bushes at the end of each row act as a pest early-warning system.

THE CLASSIFICATION OF GRAVES

The only Graves property to be classified in 1855 was Château Haut-Brion. The Syndicat, for the defense of the Graves appellation, wanted to create its own classification, but was prevented from doing so until the 1921 law was changed in 1949. The first classification was not made until 1953, and this itself was later modified in 1959.

Distinction is made between red wines and white wines, but no attempt at ranking between the various growths is made—they all have the right to use the term *cru classé*. It can be seen from the 1,320 acres (535 hectares) of classified properties listed below that this represents not much more than 13 percent of the total 1,745 acres (4,350 hectares) of delimited vineyards planted in the Graves and Pessac-Léognan appellation.

RED WINES	COMMUNE	AREA CURRENTLY UNDER VINE	AREA CURRENTLY UNDER VINE
Château Bouscaut	Cadaujac	96 acres	(39 ha)
Château Carbonnieux	Léognan	124 acres	(50 ha)
Domaine de Chevalier	Léognan	82 acres	(33 ha)
Château de Fieuzal	Léognan	96 acres	(39 ha)
Château Haut-Bailly	Léognan	69 acres	(28 ha)
Château Haut-Brion	Pessac	106 acres	(43 ha)
Château La Mission -Haut-Brion	Pessac	52 acres	(21 ha)
Château Latour-Haut- Brion	Talence	12 acres	(5 ha)
Château La Tour- Martillac	Martillac	69 acres	(28 ha)
Château Malartic- Lagravière	Léognan	91 acres	(37 ha)
Château Olivier	Léognan	94 acres	(38 ha)
Château Pape-Clément	Pessac	74 acres	(30 ha)
Château Smith-Haut- Lafite	Martillac	109 acres	(44 ha)
TOTAL AREA UNDER VINE		1,075*ACRES	(435 HA)

WHITE WINES	COMMUNE	AREA CURRENTLY UNDER VINE	AREA CURRENTLY UNDER VINE
Château Bouscaut	Cadaujac	20 acres	(8 ha)
Château Carbonnieux	Léognan	104 acres	(42 ha)
Domaine de Chevalier	Léognan	12 acres	(5 ha)
Château de Fieuzal	Léognan	20 acres	(8 ha)
Château Couhins- Lurton	Villenave	13 ha	(32 acres)
Château Haut-Brion	Pessac	10 acres	(3 ha)
Château La Tour- Martillac	Martillac	25 acres	(10 ha)
Château Laville- Haut-Brion	Talence	10 acres	(4 ha)
Château Malartic- Lagravière	Léognan	17 acres	(7 ha)
TOTAL AREA UNDER VINE		250*ACRES	(100 HA)

*Note—These figures are not precise conversions of the hectare totals, but are column totals and differ because of rounding up.

VINEYARDS AT CHÂTEAU D'YQUEM
Here, the winter vineyard shows the characteristic sandy-pebbly clay topsoil and the system of wires and stakes that supports the vines. Yquem's clay subsoil contains 62 miles (100 kilometers) of terra-cotta pipes, which were laid down at the end of the 19th century to provide perfect drainage.

THE GLOWING TINTS OF CHÂTEAU D'YQUEM
Château d'Yquem vintages, stretching back from a bottle of the 1980. The younger wines are a rich gold with a greenish tinge, deepening to old gold and amber with the older vintages.

CHÂTEAU D'YQUEM: THE INNER COURTYARD
A huge stone well dominates the square central courtyard of this beautiful château, which comprises disparate elements dating from the 15th, 16th, and 17th centuries.

they both wanted and deserved. It was a bit slow to start off—after all, Pessac-Léognan hardly trips off the tongue and there were worries about its marketability. There is still a tendency to put Graves on labels, and use Pessac-Léognan to qualify the wine as if it were a higher classification of Graves, which for all practical purposes it is.

Once the châteaux realized that foreign markets were picking up on the superior connotation of Pessac-Léognan, use of the appellation soon became widespread. Whether by their own volition or due to peer pressure, many of the underperformers have become the most quality-conscious châteaux in the appellation, and it has spurred producers in the south to improve their wines. They do not like being considered inferior, and as they intend to prove they are not, the consumer can only gain.

CÉRONS

This is an area situated within the boundaries of Graves. It is the stepping stone between dry white Graves, and sweet white Sauternes and Barsac. The châteaux of Cérons have been given the official right to make both red and white Graves, Graves Supérieur (which may be dry but is usually sweet) and, of course, the sweet wine of Cérons—a wine that has enjoyed a modest reputation for nearly 200 years. In fact, only 20 percent of the production in this area is sold as Cérons since the appellation covers three communes, those of Illats, Podensac, and Cérons itself. Many of the vineyards comprise scattered plots, some of which are partially planted with acacias.

SAUTERNES AND BARSAC

The gap between ordinary sweet white wines and the great wines of Sauternes and Barsac is as wide as that between sweet and dry wines. What creates this gap is something called "complexity"—to

TRADITIONAL HORSE-DRAWN PLOW
At Château d'Yquem workhorses are used to help plow the topsoil between the rows, both after the harvest and again in March.

find out what that is, sample the aroma of a glass of mature Sauternes. The wines produced in Sauternes are not only the world's most luscious, but also the most complex wines. I have seen hardened men who resolutely refuse to drink anything sweeter than lemon juice go weak at the knees after one sniff of Château Suduiraut, and I defy the most stubborn and bigoted anti-sweet wine drinker not to drool over a glass of Château d'Yquem 1967. Astonishingly, there are dissenters, but for me Yquem is by far the best wine of these two appellations, Sauternes and Barsac. The battle for second place is always between the soft, luscious style of Suduiraut, and the rich, powerful character of Rieussec, with Climens, Nairac, and the nonclassified growths of Gilette and de Fargues in close pursuit. Guiraud has the potential to go right to the top, and with so many châteaux seriously improving, they could all end up chasing each other for the number two spot.

The "noble rot"

Yquem might be the ultimate sweet white wine, but many other great wines are made in these two small areas tucked away in the Bordeaux backwaters. What gives all these wines their hallmark of complexity is, literally, a lot of rot—namely "noble rot," or the fungal growth *Botrytis cinerea*. The low-lying hills of Sauternes and, to a lesser extent, of Barsac, together with a naturally warm but humid climate, provide a natural breeding ground for botrytis, the spores of which are indigenous to the area. They remain dormant in the vineyard soil and on vine bark until they are activated by suitable conditions—alternate moisture and heat (the early-morning mist being followed by hot, mid-morning sunshine). The spores latch on to the skin of each grape, replacing its structure with a fungal growth and feeding on moisture from within the grape. They also devour five-sixths of the grape's acidity and one-third of its sugar, but as the amount of water consumed is between one-half and two-thirds, the effect is to concentrate the juice into a sticky, sugar-rich pulp. A healthy, ripe grape with a potential of 13 percent alcohol is thus converted into a mangy-looking mess with a potential of between 17.5

percent and 26 percent. The spread of botrytis through a vineyard is neither orderly nor regular, and the harvest may take as long as 10 weeks to complete, with the pickers making various sorties, or *tries*, through the vineyard. On each *trie*, only the affected grapes should be picked, but care must be taken to leave some rot on each bunch to facilitate its spread. The longer the growers await the miraculous "noble rot," the more the vines are prone to the ravages of frost, snow, hail, and rain, any of which could destroy an entire crop

The viticulture of Sauternes and Barsac is the most labor-intensive of any region. The yield is very low, officially a maximum of 112 cases per acre (25 hectoliters per hectare), about half that in the Médoc, and the levels achieved in the best châteaux are much lower, around 67 to 90 cases per acre (15 to 20 hectoliters per hectare). At Yquem it is even less, the equivalent of one glass per vine. On top of all this, the vinification is, at the very least, difficult to handle, and maturation of a fine sweet wine demands a good proportion of very expensive new oak.

Variations in character

Not all the sugar is used up during fermentation, even when a wine of perhaps 14 to 15 percent alcohol is made. The remaining unfermented sugar, often between 50 and 120 grams per liter, gives the wine its natural sweetness. However, unlike Sauternes' German counterparts, its alcohol level is crucial to its character. Its strength, in harmony with the wine's sweetness, acidity, and fruit give it a lusciousness of concentration that simply cannot be matched. Its complexity is not, however, the effect of concentration, although an increased mineral level is no doubt an influence. Complexity is created by certain new elements that are introduced into the grape's juice during the metabolic activities of its botrytis—glycerol, gluconic acid, saccharic acid, dextrin, various oxidizing enzymes, and an elusive antibiotic substance called "botrycine."

It is easy to explain how these components of a botrytized wine that form its inimitably complex character can vary. When tasting wine from different *tries* at the same château, the intensity of botrytized character varies according to the "age" of the fungus when the grapes are harvested. Wines made from the same percentage of botrytized grapes collected at the beginning and end of the harvest are noticeably mute compared to those in the middle when the rot is at its most rampant. If it is not surprising that youthful *Botrytis cinerea* has an undeveloped character, the same cannot be said of late-harvested. Many people believe that the longer botrytis establishes itself, the more potent its effect, but this is not true.

CHÂTEAU DE FARGUES
The original family home of the Lur-Saluces family is now a ghostly ruin. The family moved to Yquem in 1785 upon its union with the De Sauvage family.

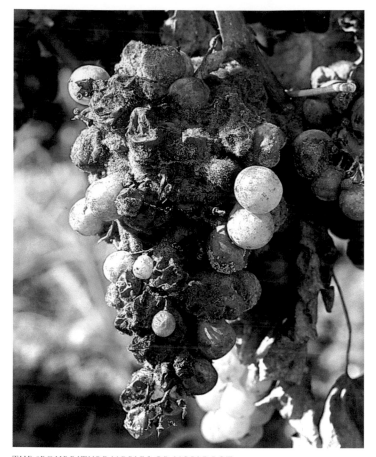

THE "POURRITURE NOBLE," OR NOBLE ROT
A bunch of Sémillon grapes ready for the first trie. *Some of the grapes are still unaffected by the fungus, some are affected and discolored but not shriveled, others are dried, withered, and covered with the fungus bloom.*

FACTORS AFFECTING TASTE AND QUALITY

LOCATION
The left bank of the Garonne river, stretching southeast from just north of Bordeaux to 6 miles (10 kilometers) east of Langon. Cérons, Sauternes, and Barsac are tucked into the southern section of the Graves district.

CLIMATE
Very similar to the Médoc, but fractionally hotter and with slightly more rainfall. In Sauternes and Barsac it is mild and humid, with an all-important fall alternation of misty mornings and later sunshine, the ideal conditions for "noble rot."

ASPECT
The suburbs of Bordeaux sprawl across the northern section of this district, becoming more rural beyond Cadaujac. Graves has a much hillier terrain than the Médoc, with little valleys cut out by myriad streams that drain into the Garonne. Some of the vineyards here are very steep. The communes of Sauternes, Bommes, and Fargues are hilly, but Preignac and Barsac, on either side of the Ciron—a small tributary of the Garonne—have gentler slopes.

SOIL
Traveling south through the district, the gravelly topsoil of Graves gradually becomes mixed with sand, then with weathered limestone and eventually with clay. The subsoil also varies, but basically it is iron-pan, limestone, and clay, either pure or mixed. Cérons has a stony soil, mostly flint and gravel, over marl; there is reddish clay-gravel over clay, or gravelly iron-pan in Sauternes, and clay-limestone over clay-gravel in Fargues. The gravel slopes of Bommes are sometimes mixed with heavy clay soils, while the plain is sandy clay with a reddish clay or limestone subsoil. Preignac is sand, gravel, and clay over clay-gravel in the south, becoming more alluvial over sand, clay, and limestone closer to Barsac. Where the classified growths of Barsac are situated, the soil is clay-limestone over limestone, elsewhere the topsoil mingles with sandy gravel.

VITICULTURE AND VINIFICATION
Some châteaux add a certain amount of *vin de presse* to the red wine. The *cuvaison* varies between eight and 15 days, although some Graves châteaux permit 15–25 days. Maturation in cask is generally between 15 and 18 months. The sweet white wines of Sauternes and Barsac are made from several *tries* of late-harvested, overripe grapes which, ideally, have "noble rot." Destalking is usually unnecessary. The fermentation of grape juice so high in sugar content is difficult to start and awkward to control, but it is usually over within two to eight weeks. The exact period of fermentation depends upon the style desired. Many of the best wines are matured in cask for one and a half to three and a half years.

GRAPE VARIETIES
Primary varieties: Cabernet Sauvignon, Cabernet Franc, Merlot, Sémillon, Sauvignon Blanc.
Secondary varieties: Malbec, Petit Verdot, Muscadelle

The rewards, the reality, and the future
A good Sauternes is the most arduous, expensive, and frustrating wine in the world to produce—and what is the winemaker's reward? Very little, I'm afraid. Aside from Château d'Yquem—not only the greatest Sauternes but the greatest wine *per se*—the wines of this region fail to realize their true worth. This is predictable in a world where the trend is toward lighter and drier styles of wine, and may have a positive effect for Sauternes *aficionados*, for it means a cheaper supply of their favorite wine. In the long term this is not a positive way to operate, and some proprietors simply cannot afford to go on. The Comte de Pontac uprooted all the vines at his *deuxième cru* Château de Myrat in Barsac, and even the ever-optimistic Tom Heeter, former owner of Château Nairac, once said "You have to be at least half-crazy to make a living out of these wines." I feel we certainly do not deserve the luscious wines of Sauternes and Barsac if we continue to ignore them, but if the authorities had more sense, and the owners more business acumen, these wines could literally become "liquid gold."

The only way ahead
The vineyards of Sauternes and Barsac should also be allowed to sell red and dry white wines under the Graves appellation. If this is a right accorded to modest Cérons, why not to its illustrious neighbors? Many châteaux already make red and dry white wines, but they are sold under the cheaper "Bordeaux" appellation. Tom Heeter was right, the proprietors must be half-crazy, because their motivation for producing these alternative products is to subsidize the cost of making their botrytized wine, when they should be trying to supplement their incomes. Given the incentive of a superior appellation, the châteaux should concentrate on making the finest red and dry white wines every year. Only when conditions appear favorable should some of the white grape crop be left on the vine, with fingers crossed for an abundance of *Botrytis cinerea*. Instead of these châteaux investing in new oak for modest vintages, they should utilize the casks for the red and the dry white. The result would be a tiny amount of the world's most luscious wine, maybe three or four years in 10. It would no longer be necessary to attempt the impossible task of selling an old-fashioned image to young wine drinkers; the limited supply would outstrip the current demand. After 30 years of watching this area's vain attempts to win over popular support for its wines, I have come to accept the view of Comte Alexandre de Lur-Saluces, proprietor of Château d'Yquem. When asked to justify the price of Yquem, he simply said his wines are not made for everyone; they are made for those who can afford them.

THE APPELLATIONS OF
GRAVES, CÉRONS, SAUTERNES, AND BARSAC

BARSAC AOC

The commune of Barsac is one of five that have the right to the Sauternes appellation. (The others are Preignac, Fargues, Bommes, and Sauternes itself.) Some generic wines sold in bulk may take advantage of this, but all individual properties are sold as Barsac. The wine must include overripe botrytized grapes harvested in *tries*.

WHITE Luscious, intensely sweet wines similar in style to Sauternes, but perhaps lighter in weight, slightly drier, and less rich. As in Sauternes, 1983 is one of the best vintages of the 20th century.

🍇 Sémillon, Sauvignon Blanc, Muscadelle

🍷 6–25 years for most wines; between 15–60 years for the greatest

CÉRONS AOC

These inexpensive wines from an area adjacent to Barsac are the best value-for-money sweet wines in Bordeaux. They must include overripe botrytized grapes harvested in *tries*.

WHITE Lighter than Barsac, but often just as luscious, the best of these wines can show true botrytis complexity.

🍇 Sémillon, Sauvignon Blanc, Muscadelle

🍷 6–15 years for most wines

GRAVES AOC

This appellation begins at the Jalle de Blanquefort, where the Médoc finishes and runs for 37 miles (60 kilometers) along the left bank of the Garonne. Almost two-thirds of the wine is red, and is consistently high in quality and value.

RED I was brought up on the notion that with full maturity a Graves reveals itself through a certain earthiness of character. Experience has taught me the opposite. The biggest Graves from hot years can have a denseness that may combine with the smoky character of new oak to give the wine a roasted or tobaccolike complexity, but Graves is intrinsically clean. Its hallmark is its vivid fruit, clarity of style, silky texture, and hints of violets.

🍇 Cabernet Sauvignon, Cabernet Franc, Merlot
Secondary grape varieties: Malbec, Petit Verdot

🍷 6–15 years

WHITE This is the disappointing half of the appellation: light- to full-bodied, from pure Sauvignon to pure Sémillon (with all proportions of blends in between, flabby to zingy, and unoaked to heavily oaked). Pay strict attention to the château profiles on the following pages. These wines may be sold from December 1 following the harvest without any mention of *primeur* or *nouveau*.

🍇 Sémillon, Sauvignon Blanc, Muscadelle

🍷 1–2 years for modest wines; 8–20 years for the best

GRAVES SUPÉRIEUR AOC

Some surprisingly good would-be Barsacs lurk beneath this appellation that is rarely seen, yet accounts for more than one-fifth of all white Graves produced.

WHITE This wine can be dry, but most is a sweet style, similar to Barsac.

🍇 Sémillon, Sauvignon Blanc, Muscadelle

🍷 6–15 years

PESSAC-LÉOGNAN AOC

Introduced in September 1987, this appellation covers the 10 best communes that have the right to the Graves AOC, and it is not by chance that it also encompasses 55 of the best estates, including all the *crus classés*. The technical requirements are similar to Graves except that the Carmenère may be used for red wines; white wines must contain at least 25 percent Sauvignon Blanc and a slightly stricter yield. If you are not sure which château to buy in the Graves, it is worth remembering this appellation and paying a premium for it.

RED Soft, silky reds of great violety elegance, and not lacking either concentration or length. Most have been aged in a percentage of new oak, which adds a smoky or tobaccolike complexity.

🍇 Cabernet Sauvignon, Cabernet Franc, Merlot, Malbec, Petit Verdot, Carmenère

🍷 6–20 years

WHITE The serious styles are invariably oaked these days, with oodles of flavor, often tropical and fruity, with a firm acid structure. These wines may be sold from December 1 following the harvest without any mention of *primeur* or *nouveau*.

🍇 A minimum of 25% Sauvignon Blanc, plus Sémillon, Muscadelle

🍷 Usually 3–8 years, but up to 20 years for the best

SAUTERNES AOC

The much hillier communes of Bommes, Fargues, and Sauternes produce the richest of all Bordeaux's dessert wines, while the châteaux in the lower-lying, flatter Preignac make wines very close in style to Barsac. The wine must include overripe botrytized grapes harvested in tries.

WHITE Golden, intense, powerful, and complex wines that defy the senses and boggle the mind. They are rich in texture, with masses of rich, ripe, and fat fruit. Pineapple, peach, apricot, and strawberry are some of the lush flavors that can be found, and the creamy-vanilla character of fruit and new oak matures into a splendid honeyed sumptuousness that is spicy and complex. Above all, these wines are marked by the distinctive botrytis character.

🍇 Sémillon, Sauvignon Blanc, Muscadelle

🍷 10–30 years for most wines; between 20 and 70 years for the greatest

---

THE GENERIC APPELLATIONS OF
GRAVES AND CÉRONS

CHÂTEAU D'ARCHAMBEAU
Illats
★☆ⓥ

Sited in Podensac, one of the communes of Cérons, this fine property is owned by Dr. Jean Dubourdieu, nephew of Pierre Dubourdieu of Doisy-Daëne, a *deuxième cru* in Barsac. He produces a fine-quality, fragrant, and attractively aromatic red wine, which has the typical silky Graves texture. The deliciously fresh, crisp, and fruity dry white Graves is better than some efforts by certain *cru classé* châteaux. His soft, fruity Cérons is *moelleux* with the emphasis more on perfume than richness.

Second wines: *Château Mourlet, Château La Citadelle*

CHÂTEAU LA BLANCHERIE
La Brède
◉★ⓥ

This fresh and lively dry white Graves is cool fermented, and has plenty of juicy fruit flavor balanced with ripe acidity.

CHÂTEAU LA BLANCHERIE-PEYRAT
La Brède
◉★ⓥ

The red wine of La Blancherie is sold under this label. It is a medium- to full-bodied wine that is matured in casks and has an engaging, spicy bouquet and a rich, fruity flavor.

CHÂTEAU BOUSCAUT
Cadaujac
Cru Classé (red and white)
★☆

Belongs to Sophie and Louis Lurton. The red wine is matured in wood for 18 months, with 25 percent new oak. The white wine is fermented and matured for up to six months in 100 percent new oak.

RED Until the 1980s this wine was big, tough, and tannic with little charm. Recent vintages have shown increasing suppleness, but the wine still struggles to find form. The second wine, Château Valoux, is a really excellent wine for its class.

🍇 Merlot 55%, Cabernet Sauvignon 35%, Cabernet Franc 5%, Malbec 5%

🍷 8–20 years

Second wine: *Château Valoux*

WHITE This dry, medium-bodied white wine has exotic fruit flavors supported by gentle oak.

🍇 Sémillon 70%, Sauvignon 30%

🍷 5–10 years

CHÂTEAU CARBONNIEUX
Léognan
Cru Classé (red and white)
★☆ⓥ

This is the largest wine estate in Graves. The white wine, the better known of the two styles, is cool-fermented in stainless steel and matured in 100 percent new oak for three months.

RED I frankly did not care for this wine until the splendid 1985

vintage, which seduced me with its creamy-oak nose, silky-textured fruit, and supple tannin, but similar joys have been few and far between.

🍇 Cabernet Sauvignon 55%, Merlot 30%, Cabernet Franc 10%, Malbec, and Petit Verdot 5%

🍷— 6–18 years

WHITE Once solid and uninspiring, this wine has really come into its own since the early 1990s. From this time Château Carbonnieux has been lush and creamy with well-integrated new oak and not a little finesse.

🍇 Sauvignon 60%, Sémillon 40%

🍷— 2–5 years

Second wine: *Château La Tour Léognan*

CHÂTEAU DE CARDAILLAN
Toulenne
★☆ⓥ

Under the same ownership as Château de Malle, this is a *deuxième cru* Sauternes in the commune of Preignac. This excellent property produces a technically brilliant red Graves with a voluptuous blackcurrant flavor, which develops quickly, yet ages well.

🍇 Cabernet Sauvignon 80%, Merlot 20%

CHÂTEAU LES CARMES-HAUT-BRION
Pessac
★

From 1584 until the French Revolution in 1789, this property belonged to the white friars Carmes, hence the name. This soft, Merlot-dominated wine has always been in the shadow of its more famous neighbor, Haut-Brion, and always will, but there has been a noticeable shift upward in quality.

CHÂTEAU DE CÉRONS
Cérons

This 17th-century château, which makes an attractively light, sweet white Cérons, is owned by Jean Perromat, owner of Mayne-Binet, de Bessanes, Ferbos, Ferbos-Lalanette in Cérons, and Prost in Barsac.

CHÂTEAU DE CHANTEGRIVE
Podensac
★ⓥ

This château produces a substantial quantity of an excellent, soft, and fruity red Graves (Cabernet Sauvignon 50 percent, Merlot 40 percent, Cabernet Franc 10 percent) that is matured in wooden vats for six months and then transferred to casks for a further 12 months with 20 percent new oak. It also produces an elegant, aromatic, cool-fermented dry white Graves that is produced entirely from the first pressing (Sémillon 60 percent, Sauvignon 30 percent, Muscadelle

10 percent). The proprietor also owns Château d'Anice.

Second wine: *Château Mayne-Lévêque*
Other wine: *Château Bon-Dieu-des-Vignes*

DOMAINE DE CHEVALIER
Léognan
Cru Classé (red and white)
★★★☆ⓥ

One of the top three Graves after Haut-Brion, this extraordinary property gives me more pleasure than any other in this AOC. It utilizes the most traditional methods to produce outstanding red and dry white wine. Fermenting red wine at a temperature as high as 89°F (32°C) might encourage some problems elsewhere, but under the meticulous care of those at the Domaine de Chevalier, this practice, designed to extract the maximum tannins and coloring material, is a positive advantage. The red wine is matured in wood for up to 24 months, with 50 percent new oak. The white wine is fermented and matured in wood for 18 months, with up to 25 percent new oak.

RED Deep-colored, medium-to-full or full-bodied wines, stunningly rich in fruit and oak, with intense cedarwood and tobacco overtones, yet subtle, seductive, and full of finesse. These are wines of great quality, longevity, and complexity.

🍇 Cabernet Sauvignon 65%, Merlot 30%, Cabernet Franc 5%

🍷— 15–40 years

WHITE Even better than the red, but produced in frustratingly small quantities, this star-bright, intensely flavored dry wine is almost fat with exotic fruit and epitomizes finesse.

🍇 Sauvignon 70%, Sémillon 30%

🍷— 8–20 years

CHÂTEAU CHICANE
Toulenne

Château Chicane is one of the châteaux that produce only red wine. It is typical of the large number of properties in the area that consistently make an excellent basic Graves. Here is an elegant, medium-bodied red wine, with a bouquet of violets, and heaps of clean, silky-smooth fruit.

CLOS FLORIDÈNE
Pujols-sur-Ciron
★★ⓥ

Owned by Bordeaux's white wine revolutionary, Denis Dubourdieu, who is producing a sensational dry white Graves (Sémillon 70 percent, Sauvignon 30 percent) from this small estate. The red Clos Floridène (Cabernet Sauvignon 80%, Merlot 20%) possesses an extraordinary combination of rich fruit and elegant new oak, and is the equivalent of a top *cru classé*.

Second wine: *Second de Floridène*

CLOS SAINT-GEORGES
Illats
★ⓥ

This property produces a small amount of red Graves, but is most famous for its scintillating sweet Graves Supérieur. A stunningly rich and flavorsome wine, full of botrytis complexity.

CHÂTEAU COUHINS
Villenave-d'Ornon
Cru Classé (white only)

The Institut National de La Récherche Agronomique (INRA) and Lucien Lurton share this estate. INRA produces a separate wine, which is cool fermented with no maturation in wood.

WHITE Clean, crisp, and fruity dry white wines that are well made.

🍇 Sauvignon 50%, Sémillon 50%

🍷— 2–4 years

Note Château also produces a red Graves, but it is not a *cru classé*.

CHÂTEAU COUHINS-LURTON
Villenave-d'Ornon
Cru Classé (white only)
★☆ⓥ

The highest-performing half of the Couhins estate owned by André Lurton. The wine is fermented and matured in 100 percent new oak.

WHITE Delicious dry wines that have all the advantages of freshness and fruitiness, plus the complexity of oak. Surprisingly fat for pure Sauvignon.

🍇 Sauvignon 100%

🍷— 3–8 years

Second wine: *Château Cantebau*

CHÂTEAU DE CRUZEAU
St.-Médard-d'Eyrans
★☆ⓥ

Situated on a high, south-facing crest of deep, gravel soil, this property belongs to André Lurton, owner of Château Couhins-Lurton, the high-performance white Graves *cru classé*. De Cruzeau makes 18,000 cases of full-bodied red Graves (Cabernet Sauvignon 60 percent, Merlot 40 percent) that is ripe and velvety with a spicy-cedarwood complexity.

This château also produces around 5,000 cases of a fine-quality white Graves (Sauvignon 90 percent, Sémillon 10 percent) that after some five years of maturation develops an intense citrous bouquet and flavor.

CHÂTEAU FERRANDE
Castres

A large property that, like so many in Graves, makes better red wine than white. The red wine (Cabernet Sauvignon 35 percent, Merlot 35 percent, Cabernet Franc 30 percent) is a consistently good-quality, chocolaty Graves that is matured in

wood for 15 to 18 months, with 10 to 15 percent new oak. The dry white Graves (Sémillon 60 percent, Sauvignon 35 percent, Muscadelle 5 percent) is somewhat less inspiring.

CHÂTEAU DE FIEUZAL
Léognan
Cru Classé (red only)
★★

This property occupies the highest and best exposed gravel crest in the commune. The vineyard and the château are immaculate, which is reflected in the style of its wines.

RED A deeply colored, full-bodied, rich, stylish wine with typical Graves silky texture and ample finesse.

🍇 Cabernet Sauvignon 60%, Merlot 30%, Malbec 5%, Petit Verdot 5%

🍷— 12–30 years

Second wine: *L'Abeille de Fieuzal*

Note De Fieuzal also produces a rich, exotic, and oaky dry white wine that is not *cru classé*, yet is one of the finest white Graves produced.

GRAND ENCLOS DU CHÂTEAU DE CÉRONS
Cérons
★☆ⓥ

This property, entirely enclosed by a wall, once formed the largest part of the estate of Château de Cérons. The wines produced here—far superior to those of Château de Cérons, and possibly the best of the appellation—are fat and rich, with good aging potential and some complexity. The proprietor also makes dry white wines at nearby Château Lamouroux.

DOMAINE DE LA GRAVE
Portets
★ⓥ

Formerly owned by maestro Peter Vinding-Diers, the Danish-born, Australian-trained winemaker who isolated the famous "RZ" yeast strain Vinding-Diers sold this property along with Landiras to Van Quikelberg in 1998. The wines are for medium-term consumption, with a very soft, vibrantly fruity, easy-to-drink red and a lovely oak-aged white.

CHÂTEAU HAURA
Illats

Château Haura produces wines under the Cérons appellation. Although not as consistent as it should be, it can sometimes produce a fine, honey-sweet wine with some distinction and concentration. The residence on this property is known as Château Hillot and red and dry white Graves are sold under this name that come from vines contiguous with those of Haura. The proprietor also owns Château Tucau in Barsac.

CHÂTEAU HAUT-BAILLY
Léognan
Cru Classé (red only)
★★✩ V

This château's well-kept vineyard is located on an excellent gravel crest bordering the eastern suburbs of Léognan. This red Graves is matured in wood for up to 20 months, with 50 percent new oak.

RED The class of fruit and quality of new oak is immediately noticeable on the creamy-ripe nose of this medium-bodied wine. Never block-busting stuff, but always elegant and stylish.

🍇 Cabernet Sauvignon 60%, Merlot 30%, Cabernet Franc 10%

🍷 12–25 years

Second wine: *Le Pardre de Haut-Bailly*

CHÂTEAU HAUT-BRION
Pessac
Cru Classé (red and white)
★★★

In 1663 this famous château was mentioned in Pepys's Diary as "Ho Bryan." It has been under American ownership since 1935, when it was purchased by Clarence Dillon, the banker. The parent company is called Domaine Clarence Dillon, and Dillon's granddaughter, the Duchesse de Mouchy, is the president. Jean Delmas is the technical director. The red wine is fermented in stainless steel and matured in wood for 24 to 27 months, with 100 percent new oak. The white wine is fermented and matured in 100 percent new oak.

RED This supple, stylish, medium- to full-bodied wine has a surprisingly dense flavor for the weight, and a chocolaty-violet character. The ideal commercial product, it develops quickly and ages gracefully.

🍇 Cabernet Sauvignon 55%, Merlot 25%, Cabernet Franc 20%

🍷 10–40 years

Second wine: ✓ *Bahans-Haut-Brion*

WHITE This is not one of the biggest white Graves, but it is built to last. It is sumptuous, oaky, and teeming with citrus and more exotic fruit flavors.

🍇 Sauvignon 50%, Sémillon 50%

🍷 5–20 years

CHÂTEAU LANDIRAS
Landiras

Mr. and Mrs. van Quikelberg purchased this property in 1998. Production is four-fifths white and potentially of *cru classé* quality.

CHÂTEAU LARRIVET-HAUT-BRION
Léognan
★★

Originally called Château Canolle, the name was at one point changed to Château Haut-Brion-Larrivet. Larrivet is a small stream that flows through the property, and Haut-Brion means "high gravel," referring to the gravel plateau west of Léognan on which the vineyard is situated.

Château Haut-Brion took legal action over the renaming, and since 1941 the property and its wines have been known as Château Larrivet-Haut-Brion. The red wine (Cabernet Sauvignon 55 percent, Merlot 45 percent), which is matured in wood for 18 months with 25 percent new oak, is certainly *cru classé* standard, being a well-colored and full-bodied Graves with good flavor, spicy-cedarwood undertones, and a firm tannic structure. The white wine (Sauvignon Blanc 85 percent, Sémillon 15 percent) has leapt in quality since 1996.

CHÂTEAU LAVILLE-HAUT-BRION
Talence
Cru Classé (white only)
★★

Since 1983, this small vineyard has been owned by Clarence Dillon, American proprietor of Château Haut-Brion. This "château with no château" is thought of as the white wine of La Mission. The wine is fermented and matured in oak.

WHITE Until 1982, the style was full, rich, oaky, and exuberant, tending to be more honeyed and spicy with a floral finesse since 1983. Both styles are stunning and complex.

🍇 Sauvignon 60%, Sémillon 40%

🍷 6–20 years

CHÂTEAU LA LOUVIÈRE
Léognan
★★ V

Part of André Lurton's Graves empire, this château has made a clear about-face since 1985 as far as the quality of its red wine goes. A string of dull, lifeless vintages has come to an end with the beautiful, deep, and vividly colored wines of the years 1985 and 1986. There was another step up in quality in the mid-1990s, since when this has been a truly splendid, full-bodied red Graves that is rich in spicy-blackcurrant fruit and new oak (Cabernet Sauvignon 70 percent, Merlot 20 percent, Cabernet Franc 10 percent). The white wines of Château La Louvière have always

been excellent, but even here there has been a gigantic leap in quality. These are exciting and complex wines that deserve to be among the very best *crus classés*.

Second wine: *Château Coucheroy*
Other wines: *"L" de Louvière* (dry white), *Château Les Agunelles, Château Cantebau, Château Clos-du-Roy, Château Le Vieux-Moulin*

CHÂTEAU MAGENCE
St.-Pierre-de-Mons
★✩ V

A good property making 5,000 cases of a supple, well-perfumed, red wine (Cabernet Sauvignon 40 percent, Cabernet Franc 30 percent, Merlot 30 percent) and 10,000 cases of attractive, aromatic, cool-fermented dry white Graves (Sauvignon 64 percent, Sémillon 36 percent).

CHÂTEAU MALARTIC-LAGRAVIÈRE
Léognan
Cru Classé (red and white)
★★

This 50-acre (20-hectare) vineyard forms a single block around the château. An underrated property, which has consistently produced much higher quality wines since the 1990s. The red wine is fermented in stainless steel at a low temperature (61°F/16°C), and matured in wood for 20 to 22 months, with one-third new oak. The white wine is now matured in 100 percent new oak for seven to eight months.

RED Rich, garnet-colored with an opulent sweet-oak nose, penetrating flavor, and supple tannin structure.

🍇 Cabernet Sauvignon 50%, Cabernet Franc 25%, Merlot 25%

🍷 7–25 years

WHITE Recent vintages of this once lackluster white Graves prove the worth of new oak. It is not difficult to mistake this honey-rich, ripe, and succulent wine for pure Sémillon.

🍇 Sauvignon 100%

🍷 5–12 years

CHÂTEAU MAYNE-BINET
Cérons

Proprietor Jean Perromat also owns several other châteaux, namely De Cérons, De Bessanes, Ferbos, and Ferbos-Lalanette in Cérons and Château Prost in Barsac. At Mayne-Binet he produces a fine sweet white Cérons.

CHÂTEAU MILLET
Portets
★ V (red only)

The red is a deep, dark-colored wine made in a traditional style with a dense flavor of concentrated spicy fruit. Although it has a firm tannin structure, this quickly rounds out with a few years in bottle. There is a dry white Graves, but it lacks the boldness and character of the red.

Other wine: *Château Du Clos Renon*

CHÂTEAU LA MISSION-HAUT-BRION
Pessac
Cru Classé (red only)
★★★

Under the ownership of Henri Woltner, this was the pretender to the throne of Graves. Little wonder, then, that Clarence Dillon of Haut-Brion snapped it up when the opportunity arose in 1983. The red wine is matured in wood for 24 months, with 50 percent new oak.

RED Despite different winemaking techniques, Dillon's La Mission is no less stunning than Woltner's. Both styles are deeper, darker, and denser than any other wine Graves can manage. They are essentially powerful wines that require great bottle-age, but they do lack finesse.

🍇 Cabernet Sauvignon 60%, Merlot 30%, Cabernet Franc 10%

🍷 15–45 years

Second wine: *La Chapelle de la Mission-Haut-Brion*

CHÂTEAU OLIVIER
Léognan
Cru Classé (red and white)
★

There has never been any doubt about this château's *terroir*, which has as much potential as any Graves *cru classé*, but it was one of the appellation's most disappointing producers until 1990. Since then progress has been agonizingly slow and patchy, but recent vintages have revived hopes that this remains a château to watch. The red wine is matured in wood for 18 months; the white wine up to three months, with 100 percent new oak.

RED The fruit is now easier-drinking and the oak, which used to be aggressive, more supple and creamy.

🍇 Cabernet Sauvignon 70%, Merlot 30%

WHITE This wine actually began to sparkle as early as 1985, with some quite outstanding vintages in the 1990s, since when has been an added freshness, real fruit flavor, and some positive character developing.

🍇 Sémillon 65%, Sauvignon 30%, Muscadelle 5%

🍷 3–7 years

CHÂTEAU PAPE-CLÉMENT
Pessac
Cru Classé (red only)
★★

After a disastrous period in the 1970s and early 1980s, Pape-Clément began to improve in 1985 and 1986, due to stricter selection of the *grand vin* and the introduction of a Second Wine. Some critics rate these two vintages highly, and they were very good wines, but when examined in the context of the enormous potential of this vineyard, my brain tells me they were not at all special, even if my heart wants them to be.

The trio of 1988, 1989, and 1990 wines turned out to be the best this château has produced since 1953, although they are nowhere near as great and still not special at the very highest level of Graves wine. However, even in the string of lesser vintages Bordeaux experienced in the early 1990s, Pape-Clément managed to produce good wines, and with 1995, 1996, 1998, and 1999, it has truly regained the reputation of its former glory years. The red wine from this château is matured in wood for 24 months, with a minimum of 50 percent new oak.

RED Medium-bodied wines of excellent deep color, a distinctive style, and capable of much finesse.

🍇 Cabernet Sauvignon 67%, Merlot 33%

Second Wine: Le Clémentin

Note This château also produces a little non-*cru classé* white Graves, made from equal proportions of Sémillon, Sauvignon, and Muscadelle.

CHÂTEAU RAHOUL
Portets

The wine produced by Château Rahoul is not quite as exciting as it was in the 1980s, when the property was home to—although never owned by—the maestro, Peter Vinding-Diers (see Domaine de la Graves and Château Landiras). However, both red and white wines are still reliable sources of very good value oak-aged Graves.

Second wine: *Château Constantin*

Other wine: *Petit Rahoul*

CHÂTEAU RESPIDE-MÉDEVILLE
Toulenne
★ ◊

Christian Médeville, the man responsible for Château Gilette, the rising star of Sauternes, produces excellent wines here using a totally different wine philosophy. Both the red and the white are fine examples of the best of modern vinification combined with new oak. The red is

a well-colored wine with rich, ripe fruit, some spice, and a creamy, new-oak aftertaste, good for early drinking. The white is a rich, creamy-vanilla concoction with soft, succulent fruit and a fat finish.

CHÂTEAU DU ROCHEMORIN
Martillac
★ ◊

Originally called "La Roche Morine," (the Moorish rock) this estate has a history that extends at least as far back as the eighth century, when Bordeaux was defended by the Moors from attacking Saracens. Another château belonging to André Lurton, Rochemorin produces a fine, elegant, fruity red Graves that is well0balanced and has a good spicy finish (Cabernet Sauvignon 60 percent, Merlot 40 percent). Rochemorin also produces a very clean and correct dry white Graves.

CHÂTEAU DE ROQUETAILLADE-LA-GRANGE
Mazères
★ ★ ◊

This is a very old property, that produces some 12,000 cases of an attractive, well-colored red Graves that has an aromatic bouquet and a delicious spicy-cassis flavor. This wine is made from Merlot 40 percent, Cabernet Sauvignon 25 percent, Cabernet Franc 25 percent, Malbec 5 percent, and Petit Verdot 5 percent. Its firm, tannic structure means it matures gracefully over 15 or more years. The white wine, which is made from Sémillon 80 percent, Sauvignon 20 percent, is less successful.

Second wine: *Château de Carolle*

Other wines: *Château de Roquetaillade-le-Bernet*

CHÂTEAU DU SEUIL
Cérons

Up-and-coming Graves property producing fine, elegant reds and fruity, oak-aged whites, both proving to be of increasingly excellent value.

CHÂTEAU SMITH-HAUT-LAFITTE
Martillac
Cru Classé (red only)
★ ★ ◊

This château has 124 acres (50 hectares) of fine vineyards. Michel Rolland consults on the reds and Christophe Olivier on the whites; reputation and quality are soaring. The red wine matures in wood for 18 months, with 50 percent new oak.

RED These wines are now in a richer style with creamy-oak undertones and up-front fruit,.

🍇 Cabernet Sauvignon 69%, Merlot 20% Cabernet Franc 11%

8–20 years

Second wine: *Les Hauts-de-Smith-Haut-Lafitte*

Note A white Graves is also made. It is not a *cru classé*, yet ironically now considered one of the finest white wines in Pessac-Léognan.

CHÂTEAU LA TOUR-HAUT-BRION
Talence Cru Classé (red only)
★ ★

This château is situated close to Château La Mission-Haut-Brion. By 1980 wine sold under the label of this château was merely regarded as the Second Wine of Château La Mission-Haut-Brion. All the grapes from both vineyards were vinified together, and the two wines made

by selection. However, after acquisition by Domaine Clarence Dillon in 1983, some 11 acres (4.5 hectares) of vines were delimited as Château La Tour-Haut-Brion, and from 1984 all its wines can be said to be from one specific site. The wine is matured in wood for 24 months, with 50 percent new oak.

RED This very dark, tannic, full-bodied wine is full of chocolaty, tannic fruit above an earthy-smoky bitterness of undeveloped extract. Despite its awesome attack of flavor it shows great finesse.

🍇 Cabernet Sauvignon 60%, Merlot 30%, Cabernet Franc 10%

20–40 years

CHÂTEAU LA TOUR-MARTILLAC
Martillac
Cru Classé (red and white)
★ ★

This property has its own herd of cattle to supply manure for the château's strictly "organic" wine. Its red wine is not as consistent as the very best Graves and tends to lack charm in cask. These factors make it an underrated wine. It is matured in wood for 18 to 22 months with one-third new oak. The white is fermented in stainless steel and matured in 100 percent new oak.

RED Not big or bold wines with immediate appeal; the reds are elegant with some finesse. The fruit in recent vintages has tended to be a bit plumper, but it is in bottle that these wines take on richness, developing creamy-oak flavor.

🍇 Cabernet Sauvignon 60%, Merlot 25%, Cabernet Franc 6%, Malbec 5%, Petit Verdot 4%

8–20 years

Second wine: *Château La Grave-Martillac*

WHITE The stunning 1986 vintage heralded a new era of exciting dry whites. This is very fresh, elegant wine, the fruit gently balanced by complex nuances of oak.

🍇 Sémillon 55%, Sauvignon 35%, Muscadelle 3%, old diverse varieties 7%

4–8 years

THE WINE PRODUCERS OF
SAUTERNES AND BARSAC

CHÂTEAU D'ARCHE
Sauternes
2ème Cru Classé
★ ◊

This property dates from 1530. It was known as Cru de Bran-Eyre until it was bought by the Comte d'Arche in the 18th century. It has been inconsistent. The wine sees up to 50 percent new oak.

WHITE The successful Château d'Arche is an elegantly balanced wine that is more in the style of

Barsac than Sauternes. It is sweet, rich, and has complex botrytis flavors, which often puts it on par with a *premier cru*, although it is less plump than most Sauternes. Easily equivalent to a classed growth in quality and the Crème de Tête is even better.

🍇 Sémillon 80%, Sauvignon 15%, Muscadelle 5%

8–25 years

Second wine: *Cru de Braneyre*

Other wine: *d'Arche-Lafaurie*

CHÂTEAU BASTOR-LAMONTAGNE
Preignac
★ ◊

A large property that deserves *deuxième cru* status. The wine is matured in wood for up to 36 months, with 10 to 15 percent new oak. Lighter years such as 1980, 1982, and 1985 lack botrytis but are successful in an attractive mellow, citrus style. Big years such as 1983 lack nothing: the wines are full,

rich, and stylish with concentrated botrytis flavor and ample class. 1989, 1990, 1996, 1997, 1998, and 1999 all very successful.

Second wine: *Les Remparts du Bastor*

CHÂTEAU BOUYOT
Barsac
★ ★ ◊

Jammy Fonbeney, the winemaker at this little-known property, is producing some stunning wines that deserve recognition. They have classic Barsac elegance, light in body, but not in flavor, with rich pineapple and creamy botrytis fruit, some spice, and fine length.

CHÂTEAU BROUSTET
Barsac 2ème Cru Classé
★ ✪

The wine produced at Château Broustet is matured in wood for 20 months with what was until recently just 10 percent new oak, but this increased to 40 percent after the 1986 vintage.

WHITE Château Broustet can be a delightful wine, with a fruit-salad-and-cream taste, a very elegant balance, and some spicy-botrytis complexity.

🍇 Sémillon 63%, Sauvignon 25%, Muscadelle 12%

⏳ 8–25 years

Second wine: *Château de Ségur*

CHÂTEAU CAILLOU
Barsac
2ème Cru Classé
★ ☆ ✪

This château gets its name from the *cailloux*, the stones that are brought to the surface during plowing. These have been used to enclose the entire 37-acre (15-hectare) vineyard and to provide hardcore for the tennis courts. Mr. Bravo, the owner, has run out of uses but he is still churning them up. This is not one of the better-known *deuxièmes crus*, but it consistently produces wines of a very high standard, and so deserves to be

WHITE A rich, ripe, and spicy-sweet Barsac with concentrated botrytis flavors underscored by refined oak. Not the fattest of Barsacs, but made in the richer rather than lighter style.

🍇 Sémillon 90%, Sauvignon 10%

⏳ 8–30 years

Second wine: *Petit-Mayne*

Other wines: *Cru du Clocher* (red), *Château Caillou Sec* (dry white), *Rosé St.-Vincent* (dry rosé)

CHÂTEAU DE LA CHARTREUSE
Preignac
★ ✪

This is the same stunning wine as Château Saint-Amande, but under a different exclusive label. *See also* Château Saint-Amande.

CHÂTEAU CLIMENS
Barsac
1er Cru Classé
★★★☆

Under the ownership of Bérénice Lurton, this property has long been considered one of the top wines of both appellations. The wine is matured in wood for 24 months with up to one-third new oak.

WHITE The fattest of Barsacs, yet its superb acidity and characteristic citrous style give it an amazingly fresh and zippy balance. This wine has masses of creamy-ripe botrytis fruit supported by good cinnamon and vanilla-oak flavors.

🍇 Sémillon 98%, Sauvignon 2%

⏳ 10–40 years

Second wine: *Les Cyprès de Climens*

CHÂTEAU CLOS HAUT-PEYRAGUEY
Bommes
1er Cru Classé
★★

Originally part of Château Lafaurie-Peyraguey, this property has long been owned by the Pauly family since 1934. A good dose of sulfur dioxide used to be the method of stopping fermentation at Clos Haut-Peyraguey and the bouquet was often marred by an excess of sulfur. Thankfully, this has not been evident since the 1985 vintage, when coincidentally, the wines began to benefit from some new oak. The wine is now matured in wood for 18 months, with up to 25 percent new oak.

WHITE This wine now flaunts a positively eloquent bouquet, and has a rich flavor with complex botrytis creamy-oak nuances—very stylish.

🍇 Sémillon 83%, Sauvignon 15%, Muscadelle 2%

⏳ 8–25 years

Second wine: *Château Haut-Bommes*

CHÂTEAU COUTET
Barsac
1er Cru Classé
★★

This château is usually rated a close second to Climens, but in fact it is capable of matching it in some vintages and its occasional production of tiny quantities of *tête de cuvée* called "Cuvée Madame" often surpasses it. It is fermented and matured for 24 months in cask with 30 to 50 percent new oak. The dry white "Vin Sec" is an AOC Graves and very disappointing.

WHITE This wine has a creamy vanilla-and-spice bouquet, an

initially delicate richness that builds on the palate, good botrytis character, and oaky fruit.

🍇 Sémillon 75%, Sauvignon 23%, Muscadelle 2%

⏳ 8–25 years (15–40 years for *Cuvée Madame*)

Other wines: *Cuvée Madame, Vin Sec du Château Coutet*

CHÂTEAU DOISY-DAËNE
Barsac
2ème Cru Classé
★★ ✪

Owner Pierre Dubourdieu cool ferments this wine in stainless steel until the desired balance of alcohol and sweetness is achieved, and then matures it in 100 percent new oak for a short while. The wine also undergoes various low-sulfur techniques. The result is a wine equal to a Barsac *premier cru*.

WHITE This is a wine of great floral freshness and elegance, with a delightful honeyed fragrance of deliciously sweet fruit, delicate botrytis character, hints of creamy oak, and perfect balance.

🍇 Sémillon 100%

⏳ 8–20 years

Second wine: *Château Cantegril*

Other wine: *Vin Sec de Doisy-Daëne*

CHÂTEAU DOISY-DUBROCA
Barsac
2ème Cru Classé

This property is run in conjunction with Climens, and is the smallest part of the original Doisy estate. But the wine, although consistent, is not in the same class as Doisy-Daëne, let alone Climens. It is matured in cask for 24 to 30 months with 25 percent new oak.

🍇 Sémillon 90%, Sauvignon 10%

⏳ 6–15 years

Second wine: *La Demoiselle de Doisy*

CHÂTEAU DOISY-VÉDRINES
Barsac
2ème Cru Classé
★ ☆ ✪

This is the original and largest of the three Doisy châteaux. It is owned by Pierre Castéja, the head of Bordeaux *négociant* Roger Joanne. The wine is matured in wood for 18 months with one-third new oak.

WHITE This wine was somewhat lackluster until 1983, since when it has exploded with character. Rich, ripe, and oaky, with a concentrated botrytis complexity.

🍇 Sémillon 80%, Sauvignon 20%

⏳ 8–25 years

Other wine: *Château La Tour-Védrines*

CHÂTEAU DE FARGUES
Fargues
★★

The eerie ruin of Château de Fargues is the ancestral home of the Lur-Saluces family. The small production of ultrahigh-quality wine is made by essentially the same fastidious methods as Yquem, including fermentation and maturation in 100 percent new oak. It is powerful and viscous, very rich, succulent, and complex, with a fat, toasty character (Sémillon 80 percent, Sauvignon 20 percent). Easily equivalent to a classed growth.

CHÂTEAU FILHOT
Sauternes
2ème Cru Classé
★

The beautiful Château Filhot was built between 1780 and 1850. This splendid château has a potentially great vineyard that consistently produces boring wine. Investment is required on a large scale in nearly every department. The proportion of Sémillon should be increased, the number of *tries* should be increased, the wine should contain more botrytized grapes and should be matured in cask, with some new oak.

WHITE At best these are well-made, simply fruity, and sweet.

🍇 Sémillon 60%, Sauvignon 37%, Muscadelle 3%

CHÂTEAU GILETTE
Preignac
★

Christian Médeville rejects modern marketing methods, preferring instead to keep his precious nectar (made from Sémillon 94 percent, Sauvignon 4 percent, Muscadelle 2 percent) in vats under anaerobic conditions for an amazing 20 years before bottling and selling it. The Crème de Tête is *premier cru* quality with a powerful bouquet and intense flavor of liquorice and peaches and cream, followed by a long barley-sugar aftertaste. The Crème de Tête deserves ★★, but I am less impressed with Château Gilette's regular bottlings (if, indeed, any bottling at this property can be so described!).

CHÂTEAU GUIRAUD
Sauternes
1er Cru Classé
★★

This property has been on the up since 1981, when the Narby family of Canada purchased it. The château and vineyards were in a very rundown state. Narby dug up much of the Sauvignon and planted Sémillon, then totally reequipped the winery and renovated the château. Only Yquem is on as high ground as Guiraud and since drainage is a key factor affecting the quality of the greatest Sauternes, where heavy clay soils dominate, the potential for this wine is very exciting and one that has been skillfully exploited with the help of Xavier Plantey, ex-manager of Château la Gaffelière. The wine is matured in wood for 30 months with at least 50 percent new oak. The first vintages of the dry white Vin Blanc Sec "G" were dull, but subsequent efforts have improved.

WHITE After two dismal decades, great Sauternes arrived at this château with the classic 1983 vintage, the first true botrytis wine under Narby's ownership. Guiraud is now plump with Sémillon fruit and fat with botrytis character. A deliciously sweet wine with luxuriant new oak, complexity, and considerable finesse.

🍇 Sémillon 70%, Sauvignon 30%

🍷 12–35 years

Second wine: *Le Dauphin*

Other wine: *Vin Blanc Sec "G"* (dry white)

CHATEAU HAUT-BOMMES
Bommes

The owner, Jacques Pauly, prefers to live here rather than at his *premier cru* Château Clos Haut-Peyraguey. Occasionally the wine used to excel for an unclassified growth; the recent improvements at Château Clos Haut-Peyraguey augur well for the future.

CHÂTEAU LES JUSTICES
Preignac
★ ✪

Under the same ownership as the star-performing Château Gilette, but here Christian Médeville gives his wines only four years of aging in vats. Les Justices is a consistent wine of excellent quality that is riper and fruitier than Gilette and the equivalent of a *deuxième cru*.

CHÂTEAU LAFAURIE-PEYRAGUEY
Bommes
1er Cru Classé
★★↟✪

As with Cordier properties, this wine shows remarkable consistency. It is matured in wood for between 18 and 20 months with up to 50 percent new oak.

WHITE The combination of botrytis and oak is like pineapples and peaches and cream in this elegant wine that keeps fresh and retains an incredibly light color in old age.

🍇 Sémillon 98%, Sauvignon 2%

🍷 8–30 years

CHÂTEAU LAMOTHE-DESPUJOLS
Sauternes
2ème Cru Classé

In 1961 the Lamothe vineyard was split in two. The section belonging to Jean Despujols has been the most disappointing half up until the 1985 vintage, but it has really come into its own since 1990.

WHITE Fuller, richer, and sweeter than previously expected, and in an oily, fuller-bodied style, with overtly attractive tropical fruit character.

🍇 Sémillon 70%, Sauvignon 20%, Muscadelle 10%

CHÂTEAU LAMOTHE-GUIGNARD
Sauternes
2ème Cru Classé
★ ✪

The Guignards are really trying to achieve something with their section of the Lamothe vineyard. It was called Lamothe-Bergey until the name was changed in 1981. The wine is matured in wood for 24 months with 20 percent new oak.

WHITE Rich, spicy, and concentrated wines of full body and good botrytis character.

🍇 Sémillon 85%, Muscadelle 10%, Sauvignon 5%

🍷 7–20 years

CHÂTEAU LIOT
Barsac
★ ✪

This wine is elegant, with light but fine botrytis character and creamy vanilla of new oak—probably the equivalent of a *deuxième cru* in quality and is excellent value. Owner Jean-Nicol David also produces Château Saint-Jean, a dry white Graves, and Château Pinsas, a fruity red Graves.

CHÂTEAU DE MALLE
Preignac
2ème Cru Classé

Dry white wine is produced under the "Chevalier de Malle" label, and red Graves from contiguous vineyards under the Château du Cardaillan label. While this vineyard does not shine every year (1989 and 1990 are its best-ever vintages), when it does, it can be superb value.

WHITE These are firm, well-concentrated wines often influenced more by *passerillage* than botrytis. Delicious, rich, and luscious.

🍇 Sémillon 75%, Sauvignon 22%, Muscadelle 3%

🍷 7–20 years

Second wine: *Château St.-Hélène*

Other wine: *Chevalier de Malle*

CHÂTEAU DU MAYNE
Barsac
✪

There is a good proportion of old vines at this property which adds concentration and weight to these wines, which are fatter than the norm for Barsac. Owned by the Sanders family of the splendid Château Haut-Bailly of Graves.

CHÂTEAU MÉNOTA
Barsac
✪

This quaint old property—with its historic towers and ramparts—has exported its wines to England since the 16th century. Château Ménota produces very good Barsac, despite the unusually high proportion of Sauvignon Blanc (60 percent).

CHÂTEAU NAIRAC
Barsac
2ème Cru Classé
★★↟

Tom Heeter established the practice of fermenting and maturing his wine in up to 100 percent new oak—Nevers for vanilla and Limousin for backbone—and his perfectionist ex-wife, Nicole Tari, has continued this format with great success.

WHITE These are rich and oaky wines that require ample aging to show true finesse. With enough bottle maturity the tannin and vanilla harmonize with the fruit, and the rich botrytis complexity emerges.

🍇 Sémillon 90%, Sauvignon 6%, Muscadelle 4%

🍷 8–25 years

CHÂTEAU PERNAUD
Barsac
★ ✪

This property was once part of the Sauvage d'Yquem estate. It was then owned by the Lur-Saluces family, but was abandoned after the oidium fungus devastated Bordeaux in the late 18th century. It has been completely replanted and renovated, and is now building up something of a reputation. This slightly richer style of Barsac (Sémillon 70 percent,

Sauvignon 25 percent, Muscadelle 5 percent) has a typically elegant balance and is certainly a wine to watch.

CHÂTEAU RABAUD-PROMIS
Bommes
1er Cru Classé
★★↟

The wines of this once-grand property used to be awful. It was sad to see the vineyard, château, and wine so neglected. What a joy to witness such a dramatic change. It began with the 1983; and the vintages are now something special.

WHITE A lovely gold-colored wine with full, fat, and ripe botrytis character on the bouquet and palate.

🍇 Sémillon 80%, Sauvignon 18%, Muscadelle 2%

🍷 8–25 years

CHÂTEAU RAYMOND-LAFON
Sauternes

As I wrote in the last edition, it is easy to understand how people can get carried away by the idea of a vineyard so close to Yquem as Raymond-Lafon, especially when its owner, Pierre Meslier, was régisseur at Yquem. This was, however, an overrated and overpriced wine in the mid-1980s, and although things have improved since the 1989 and 1990 vintages, it is performing at only *deuxième cru* level and is consequently overrated and overpriced. Now that the style has been cleaned up and plumped out, Raymond-Lafon (Sémillon 80 percent, Sauvignon 20 percent) is a nice Sauternes, but not worth three times the price of Rieussec or two-and-a-half times as much as Climens.

CHÂTEAU RAYNE-VIGNEAU
Bommes
1er Cru Classé
★

The quality of Rayne-Vigneau had plummeted to dismal depths until as recently as 1985. The wine is now matured in wood for 24 months with 50 percent new oak. It has a higher Sémillon content than the statistics would suggest, due to the 5,000 cases of dry Sauvignon Blanc that are sold as "Rayne Sec."

WHITE Château Rayne-Vigneau is now a very high-quality wine that has an elegant peachy ripeness to its botrytis character.

🍇 Sémillon 65%, Sauvignon 35%

🍷 8–25 years

Second wine: *Clos l'Abeilley*

Other wines: *Rayne Sec*

CHÂTEAU RIEUSSSEC
Fargues
1er Cru Classé
★★↟

This fine property promises to make even better wine since its acquisition by Domaines Rothschild in 1984. None of the Sauvignon produced here is used for Château Rieussec (it goes in the "R"), effectively making the wine 96 percent Sémillon. It is barrel-fermented and cask matured for 18 to 30 months with 50 percent new oak.

WHITE This wine is one of the richest and most opulent of Sauternes, with intense pineapple fruit and a heavily botrytized character.

Sémillon 75%, Sauvignon 22%, Muscadelle 3%

⌘ 12–35 years

Second wines: *Clos Labère, Mayne des Carmes*

Other wine: *"R" de Château Rieussec* (dry white)

CHÂTEAU DE ROLLAND
Barsac

The château of this estate has been turned into a hotel with a good restaurant, and is under separate ownership. The vineyard of Château de Rolland belongs to Jean and Pierre Guignard, who also own the excellent Château de Roquetaillade-la-Grange at Mazères in Graves. The wines (Sémillon 60 percent, Sauvignon 20 percent, Muscadelle 20 percent) are fresh and elegant with a particular emphasis on fruit.

CHÂTEAU ROMER
Fargues
2ème Cru Classé
?

The original Romer estate was divided in 1881, and at just 13 acres (five hectares) this is the smallest part. I have never come across the wine.

Sémillon 50%, Sauvignon 40%, Muscadelle 10%

CHÂTEAU ROMER-DU-HAYOT
Fargues
2ème Cru Classé
✪

Monsieur André du Hayot owns these 25 acres (10 hectares) of vines on a fine clayey-gravel crest that was once part of the original Romer estate. The wines are little seen, but represent very good value.

WHITE The 1980 and 1983 are in the fresh, not oversweet, fruit-salad and cream style, with light botrytis character and an elegant balance. More recent vintages have not been tasted.

Sémillon 70%, Sauvignon 25%, Muscadelle 5%

⌘ 5–12 years

CHÂTEAU ROUMIEU
Barsac
★ ✪

This property, which borders the classified growths of Climens and Doisy-Védrines, has produced luscious sweet wines of a richer than normal style in some vintages (Sémillon 90 percent, Sauvignon 10 percent).

CHÂTEAU ROUMIEU-LACOSTE
Barsac
★ ✪

A Dubourdieu property producing consistently fine Barsac (Sémillon 80 percent, Sauvignon 20 percent) with good botrytis concentration.

CHÂTEAU SAINT-AMANDE
Preignac
★ ✪

An elegant and stylish wine (Sémillon 67 percent, Sauvignon 33 percent) that is very attractive when young, yet some vintages have potentially excellent longevity and are often equivalent to a classed growth in quality. Part of the production of this property is sold under the Château de la Chartreuse label.

Second wine: *Château de la Chartreuse*

CHÂTEAU SIGALAS-RABAUD
Bommes
1er Cru Classé
★ ★

This is the largest part of the original Rabaud estate. The proprietor contracted Cordier to manage this property as from 1995 and the wines have already shown a marked improvement.

WHITE A stylish early-drinking wine with an elegant botrytis bouquet and deliciously fresh fruit on the palate.

Sémillon 85%, Sauvignon 15%

⌘ 6–15 years

CHÂTEAU SIMON
Barsac
2ème Cru Classé

A combination of modern and traditional methods produces a mildly sweet wine from Sémillon 70 percent, Sauvignon 30 percent. Most Sauternes and Barsacs are aged in Nevers or Limousin oak. Sometimes Allier is used, but at Simon they mature the wine in Merrain oak for two years.

CHÂTEAU SUAU
Barsac
2ème Cru Classé

The vineyard belongs to Roger Biarnès, who makes the wine at his Château Navarro in Cérons because the château is under different ownership. These wines do not have a particularly high reputation, but if the attractive wine produced in the very modest 1980 vintage is anything to go by it is worth giving them the benefit of the doubt.

WHITE The 1980 is an attractive, fresh, and fragrantly fruity wine with a gentle citrous-and-spice botrytis complexity.

Sémillon 80%, Sauvignon 10%, Muscadelle 10%

⌘ 6–12 years

CHÂTEAU SUDUIRAUT
Preignac
1er Cru Classé
★ ★ ★ ½

This splendid 17th-century château, with its picturesque parkland, effectively evokes the graceful beauty found in its luscious wines. Suduiraut's superb 245-acre (100 hectare) vineyard enjoys a good susceptibility to "noble rot," and adjoins that of Yquem. The wines went through an inconsistent patch in the 1980s, but have improved dramatically under the watchful eye of Jean-Michel Cazes's AXA insurance group. The wines are fermented and matured in cask for 24 months, with at least one-third new oak.

WHITE Soft, succulent, and sublime, this is an intensely sweet wine of classic stature. It is rich, ripe, and viscous, with great botrytis complexity that benefits from good bottle-age.

Sémillon 80%, Sauvignon 20%

⌘ 8–35 years

Second wine: *Castelnau de Suduiraut*

CHÂTEAU LA TOUR BLANCHE
Sauternes
1er Cru Classé
★ ★ ½

This property was placed at the head of the *premiers crus* in 1855, when only Yquem was deemed to be superior, but until relatively recently it failed to live up to this reputation. Even at its lowest ebb, few critics would have denied that these vineyards possessed truly great potential, but the wines were ordinary. This was made all the more embarrassing by the fact that the state-owned La Tour Blanche was a school of agriculture and oenology that was supposed to teach others how to make Sauternes. This depressing situation began to change, however, in the mid-1980s when Château la Tour Blanche started increasing the proportion of Sémillon, picking much riper grapes, and implementing stricter selection in both vineyard and chais. Fermentation is in wood (with up to 90 percent new oak but averaging 25 percent in most years), and the results have been exciting with excellent wines produced in 1988, 1989, 1990, (its greatest ever), 1994, 1995, 1996, 1997, and 1998.

WHITE These are now so rich they are almost fat and bursting with plump, ripe, juicy fruit and oodles of complex botrytis character.

Sémillon 78%, Sauvignon 19%, Muscadelle 3%

⌘ 8–20 years

Second wine: *Mademoiselle de Saint-Marc*

CHÂTEAU D'YQUEM
Sauternes
1er Cru Supérieur
★ ★ ★

This most famous of all châteaux belonged to the English crown from 1152 to 1453. It then passed into the hands of Charles VII, King of France. In 1593 Jacques de Sauvage acquired tenant's rights to the royal property and in 1711 his descendants purchased the fiefdom of Yquem. In 1785 it passed into the hands of the Lur-Saluces family. The *tries* tradition was kept alive at Yquem when it was long forgotten by other noble châteaux. Like Pétrus, one of Yquem's "secrets" is its pickers. They are all skilled; they know what to pick and, just as important, what to leave. The gap between *tries* can vary from three days to several weeks. Housing and feeding 120 pickers for several weeks of inactivity is not cheap.

The property has been run with passionate care by succeeding generations, although LVMH (which owns Moët & Chandon in Champagne) purchased a majority shareholding in 1999 (after three years of acrimony between members of the Lur-Saluces family). Alexandre Lur-Saluces lost his independence, but won a handsome contract to remain in his former home. He is still very much in charge.

In 1972 the harvest consisted of 11 *tries* spread over 71 days. In that year no wine was sold as Château d'Yquem. This is not to say that Yquem's fastidious attention to selection and quality does not pay off in some poor vintages. But in good years, because of the strict selection in the vineyard, the amount of wine that is finally used is as high as 80 to 90 percent. The wines are matured for up to 42 months with 100 percent new oak. Other *terroirs* in Sauternes and Barsac are potentially comparable, but, no matter how conscientious their owners, none makes the same sacrifices as Yquem.

WHITE This wine represents the ultimate in richness, complexity, and class. No other botrytis wine of equal body and concentration has a comparable finesse, breeding, and balance. Some of the characteristic aromas and flavors include peach, pineapple, coconut, nutmeg, and cinnamon, with toasty-creamy vanilla and caramel flavors of new oak.

Sémillon 80%, Sauvignon 20%

⌘ 20–60 years

Other wines: *"Y" de Château d'Yquem* (dry white)

THE LIBOURNAIS AND FRONSADAIS

The right bank of the Dordogne River, known as the Libournais district, is red-wine country. Dominated by the Merlot grape, the vineyards here produce deep-colored, silky- or velvety-rich wines of classic quality in the St.-Émilion and Pomerol regions, in addition to wines of modest quality, but excellent value and character, in the "satellite" appellations that surround them.

IN THE MID-1950S, many Libournais wines were harsh, and even the best AOCs did not enjoy the reputation they do today. Most growers believed that they were cultivating too much Cabernet Sauvignon and Malbec for their particular *terroir* and decided that they should plant more vines of Cabernet Franc. A few growers argued for the introduction of Merlot, which was allowed by the regulations, because it would give their wines the suppleness they desired. Even if they could have agreed on united action, changing the *encépagement* of an entire district would have been very a very long-term project, as well as being extremely expensive. However, in 1956, frost devastated the vineyards, forcing the Libournais growers into action. With poor, short crops inevitable for some years to come, prices soared, enabling them to carry out the massive replanting which, ironically, they could not have afforded prior to the crisis. This devastation led to the wholesale cultivation of Merlot and Cabernet Franc, which established a completely different style of wines, providing the catalyst for the spectacular postwar success of St.-Émilion and Pomerol.

THE GARAGISTE EFFECT

In 1979, Jacques Thienpont, owner of Pomerol's classy Vieux Château Certan, unintentionally created what would become the *"vin de garagiste"* craze, when he purchased a neighboring plot of land and created a new wine called Le Pin. With a very low yield, 100 percent Merlot, and 100 percent new oak, the decadently rich Le Pin directly challenged Pétrus, less than a mile away. It was widely known that Thienpont considered Vieux Château Certan to be at least the equal of Pétrus, and he could certainly claim it to be historically more famous, but Pétrus regularly got much the higher price, which dented his pride. So Le Pin was born, and although he did not offer his fledgling wine at the same price as Pétrus, it soon trounced it on the auction market. In 1999, a case of 1982 Le Pin was trading at a massive $19,000, while a case of 1982 Château Pétrus could be snapped up for a "mere" $13,000. By 2003, the Pétrus had traded up to a mind-boggling $26,000 and yet Le Pin sold for $44,000. Unfortunately, Jacques Thienpont died in 1985, long before his little experiment yielded such crazy prices. By the late 1980s, however, Le Pin's extraordinary financial success had became so obvious to a number of *vignerons* in neighboring St.-Emilion that they attempted to replicate it with small plots of land in their own appellation: Jean-Luc Thunevin with Château de Valandraud (first vintage 1991), Gérard and Dominique Bécot with Château La Gomerie (first vintage 1995), Von Neippberg with Château La Mondotte (first vintage 1996), Francis Gaboriaud with Château L'Hermitage (first vintage 1997), Alain and Françoise Raynaud with Château Quinault l'Enclos (first vintage 1997), and Château

THE LIBOURNAIS DISTRICT *See also* p63
This great red-wine area includes St.-Émilion, Pomerol, and their satellites. In the Libournais district, the Merlot grape reigns supreme, its succulent fruit essential to the local style.

Teyssier with Le Dôme (first vintage 1998). But it was Le Pin's cellar, which is truly a garage under a battered farmhouse, that inspired French wine writer Michel Bettane to coin the phrase "*vins de garage.*" It is interesting how this new breed of wines has polarized critics into opposite camps, as if there is something intrinsically right or wrong with producing wine on a small scale. Because that is all it is, and the *garagistes* are popping up in the Graves, the Médoc, and well beyond the borders of Bordeaux. While some consumers (all wealthy) are happy to pay any price demanded for these wines, others seem to take offense at the very mention of the word *garagiste*. Both positions are bizarre. Besides, where do you draw the line between a *vin de garage* and an honest *lieu-dit* wine? Oh dear Jacques and Michel: what have you started?

THE SATELLITE APPELLATIONS OF ST.-ÉMILION AND POMEROL

The wines of Lussac, Montagne, Parsac, Puisseguin, Sables, and St.-Georges were once sold as St.-Émilion, but in 1936 these outer areas were given their own AOCs. This was done to protect the image of the greatest St.-Émilion châteaux, but through the historical use of this famous name these areas won the right to attach the name of St.-Émilion to theirs. The tiny Sables area was later reclaimed by the St.-Émilion AOC, and in 1972 a new appellation, Montagne-St.-Émilion, was created. This appellation, which covered a large region, could be adopted by growers who had previously used either Parsac-St.-Émilion AOC or St.-Georges-St.-Émilion AOC, but the executive order that created Montagne-St.-Émilion AOC in 1972 did not disband either of these smaller appellations.

So, a situation arose in which growers could choose between two very similar AOCs. In 1993, however, Parsac-St.-Émilion was finally disbanded, since it was noticed that virtually all the producers of Parsac-St.-Émilion were not using the original AOC but opting for Montagne-St.-Émilion AOC. Many growers in St.-Georges-St.-Émilion, however, were still using the original appellation, and so disbanding this would not have been so simple. All five combined St.-Émilion AOCs would in fact benefit from merging, since they all produce wines of essentially similar nature, under identical regulations.

THE GENERIC APPELLATIONS OF
THE LIBOURNAIS AND FRONSADAIS

BORDEAUX SUPÉRIEUR CÔTES-DE-FRANCS AOC
See Bordeaux-Côtes-de-Francs AOC

BORDEAUX-CÔTES-DE-FRANCS AOC
This forgotten area's vineyards are contiguous with those of Puisseguin-St.-Émilion and Lussac-St.-Émilion, and have a very similar clay-limestone over limestone and iron-pan soil. The Bordeaux Supérieur version of these wines differs only in its higher alcohol level.

RED These are essentially robust, rustic, full-bodied wines that are softened by their high Merlot content.

🍇 Cabernet Franc, Cabernet Sauvignon, Malbec, Merlot

🍷 5–10 years

WHITE Little-seen dry, semisweet, and sweet wines of clean, fruity character.

🍇 Sauvignon Blanc, Sémillon, Muscadelle

🍷 5–10 years

BORDEAUX-CÔTES-DE-FRANCS LIQUOREUX AOC
This style of Bordeaux-Côtes-de-Francs wine must by law be naturally sweet and made from overripe grapes that possess at least 223 grams of sugar per liter. The wines must have a minimum level of 11.5 percent alcohol and 27 grams of residual sugar per liter.

WHITE Rich, genuinely *liquoreux* wines; only tiny amounts are made.

🍇 Sauvignon Blanc, Sémillon, Muscadelle

🍷 5–15 years

CANON-FRONSAC AOC
See Côtes-Canon-Fronsac AOC

CÔTES-CANON-FRONSAC AOC
Fronsac AOC and Côtes-Canon-Fronsac AOC will no doubt be the next wines to be "discovered" by budget-minded Bordeaux drinkers. The best of these wines are Côtes-Canon-Fronsac AOC, sometimes called Canon-Fronsac AOC. With lower yields and stricter selection, these wines could equal all but the best of St.-Émilion and Pomerol.

RED Full-bodied, deep-colored, rich, and vigorous wines with dense fruit, fine spicy character, plenty of finesse, and good length.

🍇 Cabernet Franc, Cabernet Sauvignon, Malbec, Merlot

🍷 7–20 years

CÔTES-DE-CASTILLON AOC
This is an attractive hilly area squeezed between St.-Émilion, the Dordogne River, and the Dordogne *département*. Its wine has long been appreciated for quality, consistency, and value. These wines used to be sold as Bordeaux and Bordeaux Supérieur wine until the 1989 vintage, when Côtes-de-Castillon received its own AOC status.

RED Firm, full-bodied, fine-colored wines with dense fruit and finesse.

🍇 Cabernet Franc, Cabernet Sauvignon, Carmenère, Malbec, Merlot, Petit Verdot

🍷 5–15 years

FRONSAC AOC
This generic appellation covers the communes of La Rivière, St.-Germain-la-Rivière, St.-Aignan, Saillans, St.-Michel-de-Fronsac, Galgon, and Fronsac.

RED These full-bodied, well-colored wines have good chunky fruit and a fulsome, chocolaty character. Not quite the spice or finesse of Côtes-Canon-Fronsac, but splendid value.

🍇 Cabernet Franc, Cabernet Sauvignon, Malbec, Merlot

🍷 6–15 years

LALANDE-DE-POMEROL AOC
This good-value appellation covers the communes of Lalande-de-Pomerol and Néac. No matter how good they are, even the best are but pale reflections of classic Pomerol.

RED Firm, meaty Merlots with lots of character but without Pomerol's texture and richness.

🍇 Cabernet Franc, Cabernet Sauvignon, Malbec, Merlot

🍷 7–20 years

LUSSAC-ST.-ÉMILION AOC
A single-commune appellation 5.5 miles (9 kilometers) northeast of St.-Émilion.

RED The wines produced on the small gravelly plateau to the west of this commune are the lightest, but have the most finesse. Those produced on the cold, clayey lands to the north are robust and earthy, while those from the clay-limestone in the southeast have the best balance of color, richness, and finesse.

🍇 Cabernet Franc, Cabernet Sauvignon, Carmenère, Malbec, Merlot

🍷 5–12 years

MONTAGNE-ST.-ÉMILION AOC

This appellation includes St.-Georges-St-Émilion, a former commune that is today part of Montagne-St.-Émilion. St.-Georges-St.-Émilion AOC and Montagne-St.-Émilion AOC are the best of all the appellations that append "St.-Émilion" to their names.

RED Full, rich, and intensely flavored wines that mature well.

🍇 Cabernet Franc, Cabernet Sauvignon, Malbec, Merlot

🍷 5–15 years

NÉAC AOC

This appellation has not been employed since the proprietors have been allowed to use the Lalande-de-Pomerol appellation. *See* Lalande-de-Pomerol AOC.

POMEROL AOC

The basic wines of Pomerol fetch higher prices than those of any other Bordeaux appellation. The average Merlot content of a typical Pomerol is around 80 percent.

RED It is often said that these are the most velvety-rich of the world's classic wines, but they also have the firm tannin structure that is necessary for successful long-term maturation and development. The finest also have surprisingly deep color, masses of spicy-oak complexity, and great finesse.

🍇 Cabernet Franc, Cabernet Sauvignon, Malbec, Merlot

🍷 5–10 years (modest growths); 10–30 years (great growths)

PUISSEGUIN-ST.-ÉMILION AOC

This commune has a clay-limestone topsoil over a stony subsoil and the wines it produces tend to be more rustic than those of the Montagne-St.-Émilion AOC.

RED These are rich and robust wines with a deep flavor and lots of fruit and color, but they are usually lacking in finesse.

🍇 Cabernet Franc, Cabernet Sauvignon, Carmenère, Malbec, Merlot

🍷 5–10 years

ST.-ÉMILION AOC

These wines must have a minimum of 10.5 percent alcohol, but in years when chaptalization (the addition of sugar to grape juice to increase alcohol content) is allowed, there is also a maximum level of 13 percent.

RED Even in the most basic St.-Émilions the ripe, spicy-juiciness of the Merlot grape should be supported by the firmness and finesse of the Cabernet Franc. The great châteaux achieve this superbly: they are full, rich, and concentrated, chocolaty and fruitcakey.

🍇 Cabernet Franc, Cabernet Sauvignon, Carmenère, Malbec, Merlot

🍷 6–12 years (modest growths); 12–35 years (great growths)

ST.-GEORGES-ST.-ÉMILION AOC

Along with the Montagne region of Montagne-St.-Émilion, this is the best parish of the outer areas.

RED These are deep-colored, plummy wines with juicy, spicy fruit, and good supporting tannic structure.

🍇 Cabernet Franc, Cabernet Sauvignon, Malbec, Merlot

🍷 5–15 years

SATELLITE APPELLATIONS IN THE ST.-EMILION AREA

It would make sound commercial sense if all the St.-Émilion satellites (Lussac-St.-Émilion, Puisseguin-St.-Émilion, and St.0-Georges-St. Émilion) were combined under the Montagne St.-Émilion appellation.

SAINT-ÉMILION

The Romans were the first to cultivate the vine in St.-Émilion, a small area that has exported its wines to various parts of the world for over eight hundred years. In the first half of the twentieth century it lapsed into obscurity, but in the last forty years it has risen like a phoenix.

ST.-ÉMILION AS WE KNOW IT is a phenomenon of the postwar era, but there are many reminders of this wine's ancient past—from the famous Château Ausone, named after the Roman poet Ausonius, to the walled hilltop village of St.-Émilion itself, which has survived almost unchanged since the Middle Ages. In contrast, the Union des Producteurs, the largest single-appellation *coopérative* in France, is a graphic illustration of the best in modern, technologically sophisticated wine production. Today, there are over a thousand *crus* within 6 miles (10 kilometers) of the village of St.-Émilion that may use this appellation.

THE APPEAL OF ST.-ÉMILION WINES

For those who find red wines too harsh or too bitter, St.-Émilion, with its elegance and finesse, is one of the easiest with which to make the transition from white to red. The difference between the wines of St.-Émilion and those of its satellites is comparable to the difference between silk and satin, whereas the difference between St.-Émilion and Pomerol is like the difference between silk and

velvet: the quality is similar, but the texture is not—although, of course, we must be humble about categorizing such complex entities as wine areas. It could justifiably be argued that the *graves* (gravelly terrain) that produces two of the very best St.-Émilions— Châteaux Cheval-Blanc and Figeac—has more in common with Pomerol than with the rest of the appellation.

CHÂTEAU FIGEAC
Without doubt in a class of its own within Class B of premiers grands crus classés, *Château Figeac has long fought to be classified with Ausone and Cheval Blanc.*

A LARGE PRODUCTION

If you look at the map of the entire Bordeaux region (*see* p63) you will be amazed by how small this appellation of a thousand châteaux really is. It is a surprising but regular occurrence that an appellation as small as St.-Émilion produces more wine than all the famous appellations of the Médoc combined—St. Estèphe, Pauillac, St.-Julien, and Margaux.

Château Cheval Blanc

Château Ausone

Château la Tour-Figeac

Château Canon

Château Troplong Mondot

Château Fonplégade

- Premier Grand Cru Classé (Class A)
- Premier Grand Cru Classé (Class B)
- Selected Grand Cru Classé
- Communal boundary

CHÂTEAU AUSONE
From its hilltop perch, this ancient château commands a spectacular view of the sweeping vineyards below.

THE CLASSIFICATION OF ST.-ÉMILION

St.-Émilion wines were first classified in 1958, with the intention that the classification be revised every 10 years according to the performance of properties during the previous decade. Three basic categories were established: *premier grand cru classé*, *grand cru classé*, and *grand cru*. Of the 12 châteaux that were classified *premiers grands crus classés*, Ausone and Cheval-Blanc were placed in a superior subsection. The rest were listed alphabetically, not qualitatively, as were the 64 *grands crus classés*. The classification was revised in 1969, 1985 (some six years late), and again in 1996—which brought the reclassification period back to that anticipated. Beware the distinction between *grand cru* (unclassified growths) and *grand cru classé* (classified growths) because the difference is considerable. In St.-Émilion, *grand cru* merely indicates a minimum alcoholic strength 0.5% higher than that required by the basic St.-Émilion appellation, and a slightly lower yield. Any producer may apply for a *grand cru*, and hundreds do so. It is not a classification, but merely an adjunct to the appellation, and would be more accurately conveyed as a new appellation called St.-Émilion Supérieur, since the difference between *grand cru* and *grand cru classé* is akin to that between basic Bordeaux and Bordeaux Supérieur.

ST.-ÉMILION CLASSIFICATIONS OF 1958, 1969, 1985, AND 1996
Incorporating vineyard soil classification

PREMIER GRAND CRU CLASSÉ CLASS A
1 Château Ausone
Soil: *Côte and St.-Émilion plateau*
22 Château Cheval Blanc
Soil: *Graves and ancient sand*

PREMIER GRAND CRU CLASSÉ CLASS B
3 Château l'Angélus [7]
Soil: *Pied de côte and ancient sand*
4 Château Beau-Séjour Bécot [1, 7]
Soil: *St.-Émilion plateau and côte*
5 Château Beauséjour (Duffau Lagarosse)
Soil: *Côte*
6 Château Belair Soil: *St.-Émilion plateau and côte*
7 Château Canon
Soil: *St.-Émilion plateau and côte*
8 Château-Figeac
Soil: *Graves and ancient sand*
9 Clos Fourtet
Soil: *St.-Émilion plateau and ancient sand*
10 Château la Gaffelière
Soil: *Côte, pied de côte*
11 Château Magdelaine
Soil: *St.-Émilion plateau, côte, and pied de côte*
12 Château Pavie
Soil: *Côte and St. Émilion plateau*
13 Château Trottevieille
Soil: *St.-Émilion plateau*

GRAND CRU CLASSÉ
14 Château l'Arrosée
Soil: *Côte*
15 Château Baleau (now Château Côte de Baleau) [1, 3]
Soil: *Côte and ancient sand*
16 Château Balestard la Tonnelle
Soil: *St.-Émilion plateau*
17 Château Bellevue
Soil: *Côte and St.-Émilion plateau*
18 Château Bergat
Soil: *Côte and St.-Émilion plateau*
19 Château Berliquet [2]
Soil: *Côte and pied de côte*
20 Château Cadet-Bon [1, 8]
Soil: *St.-Émilion plateau and côte*
21 Château Cadet-Piola
Soil: *St.-Émilion plateau and côte*
22 Château Canon-la-Gaffelière
Soil: *Pied de côte and sandy-gravel*
23 Château Cap de Mourlin
Soil: *Côte and ancient sand*

- Château la Carte [4]
Soil: *St.-Émilion plateau and ancient sand*
- Château Chapelle-Madeleine [5]
Soil: *Côte and St.-Émilion plateau*
24 Château le Châtelet [9]
Soil: *Côte and ancient sand*
25 Château Chauvin
Soil: *Ancient sand*
26 Château Clos des Jacobins
Soil: *Côte and ancient sand*
27 Château la Clotte
Soil: *Côte*
28 Château la Clusière
Soil: *Côte*
29 Château Corbin
Soil: *Ancient sand*
30 Château Corbin Michotte
Soil: *Ancient sand*
31 Château la Couspaude [1, 8]
Soil: *St.-Émilion plateau*
32 Château Coutet [1]
Soil: *Côte*
Château le Couvent [6]
Soil: *St.-Émilion plateau*
33 Couvent des Jacobins [3]
Soil: *Ancient sand and pied de côte*
34 Château Croque Michotte [9]
Soil: *Ancient sand and graves*
35 Château Curé Bon la Madeleine
Soil: *St-Émilion plateau and côte*
36 Château Dassault [3]
Soil: *Ancient sand*
37 Château la Dominique
Soil: *Ancient sand and graves*
38 Château Faurie de Souchard
Soil: *Pied de côte*
39 Château Fonplégade
Soil: *Côte*
40 Château Fonroque
Soil: *Côte and ancient sand*
41 Château Franc-Mayne
Soil: *Côte*
42 Château Grand Barrail Lamarzelle Figeac [9]
Soil: *Ancient sand*
43 Château Grand Corbin [9]
Soil: *Ancient sand*
44 Château Grand-Corbin-Despagne [9]
Soil: *Ancient sand*
45 Château Grand Mayne
Soil: *Côte and ancient sand*
46 Château Grandes Murailles [1, 8]
Soil: *Côte and ancient sand*
47 Château Grand-Pontet
Soil: *Côte and ancient sand*
48 Château Guadet St.-Julien
Soil: *St.-Émilion plateau*
49 Château Haut-Corbin

Soil: *Ancient sand*
50 Château Haut-Sarpe [5]
Soil: *St.-Émilion and St.-Christophe plateaux and côtes*
51 Château Jean Faure [1]
Soil: *Ancient sand*
52 Château Laniote [3]
Soil: *Ancient sand and pied de côte*
53 Château Larcis Ducasse
Soil: *Côte and pied de côte*
54 Château Larmande Soil: *Ancient sand*
55 Château Laroque [8]
Soil: *St.-Émilion plateau and côte*
56 Château Laroze
Soil: *Ancient sand*
57 Clos la Madeleine [9]
Soil: *St.-Émilion plateau and côte*
58 Château la Marzelle (now Château Lamarzelle)
Soil: *Ancient sand and graves*
59 Château Matras [3]
Soil: *Pied de côte*
60 Château Mauvezin
Soil: *St.-Émilion plateau and côte*
61 Château Moulin du Cadet
Soil: *Côte and ancient sand*
62 Clos de l'Oratoire [3]
Soil: *Pied de côte*
63 Château Pavie Décesse
Soil: *St.-Émilion plateau and côte*
64 Château Pavie Macquin
Soil: *St.-Émilion plateau, côte, and sandy gravel*
65 Château Pavillon-Cadet [9]
Soil: *Côte and ancient sand*
66 Château Petit-Faurie-de-Soutard
Soil: *Ancient sand and côte*
67 Château le Prieuré
Soil: *St.-Émilion plateau and côte*
68 Château Ripeau
Soil: *Ancient sand*
69 Château St.-Georges (Côte Pavie)
Soil: *Côte and pied de côte*
70 Clos St.-Martin
Soil: *Côte and ancient sand*
71 Château Sansonnet [9]
Soil: *St.-Émilion plateau*
72 Château la Serre
Soil: *St.-Émilion plateau*
73 Château Soutard
Soil: *St.-Émilion plateau and côte*
74 Château Tertre Daugay [3]
Soil: *St.-Émilion plateau and côte*
75 Château la Tour Figeac
Soil: *Ancient sand and graves*
76 Château la Tour du Pin Figeac (Owner: Giraud-Belivier)
Soil: *Ancient sand and graves*

77 Château la Tour du Pin Figeac (Owner: Moueix)
Soil: *Ancient sand and graves*
78 Château Trimoulet
Soil: *Ancient sand and graves*
- Château Trois-Moulins [4]
Soil: *St.-Émilion plateau and côte*
79 Château Troplong Mondot
Soil: *St.-Émilion plateau*
80 Château Villemaurine
Soil: *St.-Émilion plateau*
81 Château Yon-Figeac
Soil: *Ancient sand*

See opposite for an explanation of soil types.

Notes
[1] One *premier grand cru classé* and *six grands crus classés* demoted in the 1985 revision.
[2] This property was not in the original 1958 classification, nor was it included in the 1969 revision, but was awarded *grand cru classé* status in 1985.
[3] These properties were not in the original 1958 classification, but were awarded *grand cru classé* status in the 1969 revision.
[4] These two properties were merged with *premier grand cru classé* Château Beau-Séjour-Bécot in 1979. Wines bearing both labels can be found up to the 1978 vintage, and it is possible that they might reappear sometime in the future, particularly as the expansion of Château Beau-Séjour-Bécot vineyard was primarily responsible for its demotion in the 1985 classification.
[5] This property was merged with *premier grand cru classé* Château Ausone in 1970. Wines with this label can be found up to the 1969 vintage.
[6] This property changed hands prior to the 1985 revision and did not apply to be considered; it was not demoted, but simply ignored.
[7] Two properties were promoted to *premier grand cru classé* (B) in 1996.
[8] Four properties were promoted to *grand cru classé* in 1996.
[9] Eight properties were demoted to *grand cru* in 1996.

FACTORS AFFECTING TASTE AND QUALITY

LOCATION
St.-Émilion is on the right bank of the Dordogne, 80 miles (50 kilometers) east of Bordeaux.

CLIMATE
The climate is less maritime and more continental than that of the Médoc, with a greater variation in daily temperatures—there is also slightly more rain during spring, and substantially less during summer and winter.

ASPECT
The village of St.-Émilion sits on a plateau where vines grow at an altitude of 80–330 ft (25–100 m). These vineyards are quite steep, particularly south of the village where two slopes face each other. The plateau continues eastward in the form of hilly knolls. North and west of the village, the vineyards are on flatter ground.

SOIL
St.-Émilion's soil is extremely complex (see "The question of quality," left) and is part of the area known as "Pomerol-Figeac graves" that encompasses the châteaux Cheval Blanc and Figeac.

VITICULTURE AND VINIFICATION
Some of the vin de presse, usually the first pressing only, is considered necessary by many châteaux. Skin-contact usually lasts for 15–21 days, but may last up to four weeks. Some wines spend as little as 12 months in cask, but the average is nearer to 15–22 months.

GRAPE VARIETIES
Primary varieties: Cabernet Franc, Cabernet Sauvignon, Merlot
Secondary varieties: Malbec, Carmenère

THE QUESTION OF QUALITY

The diverse nature of St.-Émilion's soil has led to many generalizations that attempt to relate the quantity and character of the wines produced to the soils from which they come. Initially the wines were lumped into two crude categories, côtes (literally "hillside" or "slope") and graves (literally "gravelly terrain"). The term côtes was supposed to describe fairly full-bodied wines that develop quickly; the term graves, fuller, firmer, and richer wines that take longer to mature.

The simplicity was appealing, but it ignored the many wines produced on the stretch of deep sand between St.-Émilion and Pomerol, and those of the plateau, which has a heavier topsoil than the côtes. It also failed to distinguish between the eroded côtes and the deep-soiled bottom slopes. But most importantly, it ignored the fact that many châteaux are spread across more than one soil type (see the list of classified growths opposite) and that they have various other factors of terroir, such as aspect and drainage, which affect the character and quality of a wine (see Soil Survey of St.-Émilion, below).

The map below shows the positions of the 81 classified châteaux of St.-Émilion, listed with their soil types (see opposite). Châteaux la Carte, Chapelle-Madeleine, le Couvent, and Trois-Moulins are listed but do not appear on the map (see notes opposite).

SOIL SURVEY OF ST-ÉMILION

The map below shows the area covered by premier grand cru classé and grand cru classé châteaux. Each soil type is described (right) and color keyed on the map. The numbers of the châteaux are listed opposite.

Legend:
- Château
- Premier Grand Cru Classé vineyards
- Grand Cru Classé vineyards
- St-Christophe plateau
- Graves
- Ancient Sand
- Sandy-gravel
- St-Emilion plateau
- Bottom slopes
- Côtes
- Communal boundary

ST-CHRISTOPHE PLATEAU
Clay-limestone and clay-sand topsoil over limestone and terra rossa subsoil. Terra rossa is a red, claylike soil.

GRAVES
Deep gravel topsoil with a subsoil of large-grain sand over a very deep, hard, and impermeable sedimentary rock called molasse. The gravel is similar to that found in the Médoc.

ANCIENT SAND
Thick blanket of large-grain sand over a subsoil of molasse. The bulk of this sand extends northeast from the village of St.-Émilion toward Pomerol. Although this area seems to have a gentle slope all around it, and the sand is very permeable, the molasse below is flat and impermeable. The water collects, saturating root systems and increasing soil acidity. Some châteaux benefit greatly from underground drainage pipes.

SANDY-GRAVEL
Sandy and sandy-gravel topsoil over sandy-gravel, ferruginous gravel, and iron-pan.

ST-ÉMILION PLATEAU
Shallow clay-limestone and clay sand, shell debris, and silt topsoil over eroded limestone subsoil.

BOTTOM SLOPES
The gentler bottom slopes of the côtes have a deep, reddish-brown, sandy-loam topsoil over yellow sand subsoil.

CÔTES
The lower-middle to upper slopes of the côtes have a shallow, calcareous, clay-silty-loam topsoil with a high active lime content. Quite sandy on the middle slopes, the topsoil thins out higher up. The subsoil is mostly molasse, not the impermeable type found under the ancient sand and graves, but a weathered, absorbent molasse of limestone or sandstone.

THE WINE PRODUCERS OF
SAINT-ÉMILION

CHÂTEAU ANGÉLUS
Premier Grand Cru Classé (B)
★★

This is a large property with a single plot of vines on the south-facing *côtes*. At one time the château produced wines in the old "farmyard" style, but that ended with the 1980 vintage. Two-thirds of the wine is matured for 14 to 16 months in wood with 100 per cent new oak. This château is a rising star, and was promoted to *premier grand cru classé* (B) in 1996.

RED This is a soft, silky, and seductive wine. The luxury of new oak is having a positive effect on the quality, character, and aging potential of this wine.

🍇 Cabernet Franc 50%, Merlot 45%, Cabernet Sauvignon 5%

🍷 7–20 years

Second wine: *Carillon de l'Angélus*

CHÂTEAU L'ARROSÉE
Grand Cru Classé
★☆❤

This property sits on the *côtes* above the local *coopérative*. Through excellent selection of only its finest grapes, it has consistently produced wines that are a class above those of many of its peers.

RED This medium- to full-bodied wine has a lovely ruby color, a voluptuous bouquet, and soft, creamy-rich fruit backed up by supple oak tannin.

🍇 Merlot 50%, Cabernet Sauvignon 35%, Cabernet Franc 15%

🍷 5–15 years

Second wine: *Les Coteaux du Château l'Arrosée*

CHÂTEAU AUSONE
Premier Grand Cru Classé (A)
★★★

After gifted winemaker Pascal Delbeck took control of Château Ausone in 1975, this prestigious property produced wines of stunning quality, and it now deserves its superstar status. In 1997, after a power struggle between the two owners, Alain Vauthier took control

and fired Delbeck and hired Michel Rolland as consultant. The vineyard of Château Ausone has a privileged southeast exposure and its vines are fairly established at between 40 and 45 years of age. They are capable of yielding very concentrated wines, which are then matured in wood for between 16 and 22 months, with 100 percent new oak.

RED These rich, well-colored wines have opulent aromas and scintillating flavors. They are full in body, compact in structure, and refined in character, with masses of spicy-cassis fruit and creamy-oak undertones. These wines are the quintessence of class, complexity, and finesse.

🍇 Cabernet Franc 50%, Merlot 50%

🍷 15–45 years

CHÂTEAU BALESTARD LA TONNELLE
Grand Cru Classé
★

The label of this wine bears a 15th-century poem by François Villon that cites the name of the château. One-third of the wine is matured in 100 percent new oak for up to 24 months, one-third is aged in two-year-old barrels, and the remainder rests in stainless-steel vats until bottling, when it is all blended together.

RED The gentle, ripe aromas of this wine belie its staunchly traditional style. It is a full-bodied wine of great extract, tannin, and acidity that requires time to soften, but it has masses of fruit, and so matures gracefully.

🍇 Merlot 65%, Cabernet Franc 20%, Cabernet Sauvignon 10%, Malbec 5%

🍷 10–30 years

Second wine: *Les Tourelles de Balestard*

CHÂTEAU BEAUSÉJOUR
(Owner: Duffau-Lagarosse)
Premier Grand Cru Classé (B)
★★

These little-seen wines consistently underwhelmed critics until the 1980s, since when Château Beauséjour began to produce darker, fuller wines with more class, but I was not that impressed until the stellar class 2000 vintage.

RED Lovely rich wine, with concentrated fruit, and great potential longevity from 2000 onward.

🍇 Merlot 50%, Cabernet Franc 25%, Cabernet Sauvignon 25%

🍷 7–15 years

Second wine: *La Croix de Mazerat*

CHÂTEAU BEAU-SÉJOUR BÉCOT
Premier Grand Cru Classé (B)
★★

Since 1979, this property has almost doubled in size by merging with two *grands crus classés*, Château la Carte and Château Trois Moulins. In 1985, Beau-Séjour Bécot was the only *premier grand cru classé* to be demoted in the revision of the St.-Émilion classification. The demotion was not due to its quality or performance, but because of its expansion. However, the general application of such criteria would mean demoting nearly all the Bordeaux châteaux classified in 1855! The problem was that expansion within reasonable limits is allowed in the Médoc, but not in St.-Émilion. This has since been rectified and in 1996 this château was promoted and is once again a *premier grand cru classé* (B). The wine is fermented in stainless steel and matured in wood for 18 months, with 90 percent new oak.

RED Once lightweight and high-tone, this wine is now full, rich, and truly characterful. The silky Merlot fruit develops quickly, but is backed up with creamy new oak.

🍇 Merlot 70%, Cabernet Franc 15%, Cabernet Sauvignon 15%

🍷 7–25 years

Second wine: *La Tournelle des Moines*

CHÂTEAU BELAIR
Premier Grand Cru Classé (B)
★★

Pascal Delbeck, the gifted winemaker formerly of Château Ausone, lives here and makes the wine with the same care and attention that he used to apply at Ausone. The wine is matured in wood for 16 to 20 months. Up to half is aged in new oak, the rest in casks that have been used for one wine at Ausone. This is one of the very best *premiers grands crus*.

RED This is a deep-colored, full-bodied wine with a rich flavor of plums, chocolate, black cherries, and cassis. It has great finesse, an alluring style, and a scintillating, spicy-cedarwood complexity.

🍇 Merlot 60%, Cabernet Franc 40%

🍷 10–35 years

Second wine: *Roc Blanquet*

CHÂTEAU BELLEVUE
Grand Cru Classé

This small property was originally called "Fief-de-Bellevue" and belonged to the Lacaze family from 1642 to 1938. It is situated on the *côtes* and produces a wine that is seldom seen outside France.

RED No better than many unclassified St.-Émilions.

🍇 Merlot 67%, Cabernet Franc 16.5%, Cabernet Sauvignon 16.5%

🍷 5–10 years

CHÂTEAU BERGAT
Grand Cru Classé
❷

This small vineyard is managed by Philippe Castéja of Château Trottevieille. Its wine is rarely seen and I have never tasted it.

🍇 Merlot 50%, Cabernet Franc 40%, Cabernet Sauvignon 10%

CHÂTEAU BERLIQUET
Grand Cru Classé
★★☆

This was the only property to be upgraded to *grand cru classé* in the 1985 reclassification. With Patrick Valette consulting since 1997 there has been an upward trend in quality, and if this continues it would be difficult to deny Berliquet *premier grand cru classé* status during a future revision. The wine is made under the supervision of the local *coopérative*. It is fermented in stainless-steel vats and matured in wood for 18 months, with 30 percent new oak.

RED These are deep, dark, and dense wines with spicy-cassis fruit and good vanilla oak.

🍇 Merlot 70%, Cabernet Franc and Cabernet Sauvignon 30%

🍷 10–30 years

CHÂTEAU CADET-BON
Grand Cru Classé
★☆

This property was demoted from *grand cru classé* status in the 1985 reclassification, but after a period of progress Cadet-Bon was reinstated in the 1996 reclassification. Quality continues to improve.

🍇 Merlot 60%, Cabernet Franc 40%

CHÂTEAU CADET-PIOLA
Grand Cru Classé
★

With the exception of the vintages of 1980 and 1981, which were very light, this property usually shows great consistency and exquisite style. Up to 50 percent of the wine is matured in new oak.

RED These are full-bodied, intensely flavored wines with powerful, new-oak character and great tannic strength.

🍇 Merlot 51%, Cabernet Sauvignon 28%, Cabernet Franc 18%, Malbec 3%

🍷 12–25 years

Second wine: *Chevalier de Malte*

CHÂTEAU CANON
Premier Grand Cru Classé (B)
★★ ✔

Many years ago this château used to produce a second wine called "St.-Martin-de-Mazerat," which was the old parish name before Château Canon was absorbed by St.-Émilion. Excellent wines were made under Eric Forner and although he sold out in 1996 the quality has been maintained. In summer 2000 the new owners, Chanel Inc., bought the nearby property Curé Bon la Madeleine with INAO agreement to incorporate it into Canon from the 2000 vintage. So goodbye Curé Bon! The *grand vin*, fermented in oak vats and matured in wood for 20 months with 50 percent new oak, is one of the best of St.-Émilion's *premiers grands crus classés*.

RED These wines have a deep purple color, an opulent cassis bouquet, and are very rich and voluptuous on the palate with masses of juicy Merlot fruit and spicy complexity.

🍇 Merlot 55%, Cabernet Franc 40%, Cabernet Sauvignon 4%

🍷 8–30 years

Second wine: *Clos J. Kanon*

CHÂTEAU CANON-LA-GAFFELIÈRE
Grand Cru Classé
★★⯪

Owned since 1985 by Comte Von Neipperg, Château Canon-la Gaffelière is one of the oldest properties in St.-Émilion. Its wine was fermented in stainless-steel vats until wooden vats were installed in 1997, and the quality soared the very next year. Malolactic fermentation is carried out in barrel and the wines matured for 18 months, with up to 50 percent new oak.

RED This wine has been on form since 1998. It has been really plump, displaying vivid, concentrated, spicy fruit, finishing with creamy oak.

🍇 Merlot 65%, Cabernet Franc 30%, Cabernet Sauvignon 5%

🍷 8–20 years

Other wines: *Côte Mignon-la-Gaffelière*

CHÂTEAU CAP DE MOURLIN
Grand Cru Classé
★

Until 1982 there were two versions of this wine, one bearing the name of Jacques Capdemourlin and one that of Jean Capdemourlin. This property is run by Jacques. The wine is matured in wood for up to 24 months, with one-third new oak.

RED An improving, attractive, well-made, medium-bodied wine, with exquisitely fresh fruit, and a smooth finish.

🍇 Merlot 60%, Cabernet Franc 25%, Cabernet Sauvignon 12%, Malbec 3%

🍷 6–15 years

Second wine: *Mayne d'Artagnon*

CHÂTEAU LA CARTE
Grand Cru Classé

Since 1980, the vineyards of this property have been merged with those of *premier grand cru classé* Château Beau-Séjour-Bécot.

CHÂTEAU CHAPELLE-MADELEINE
Grand Cru Classé until 1996

Since 1971, these vineyards have been merged with those of *premier grand cru classé* Château Ausone.

CHÂTEAU CHAUVIN
Grand Cru Classé
★

This property's wine is matured in wood for 18 months, with one-third new oak. It is difficult to find, but its quality makes it deserving of better distribution.

RED When on form, Château Chauvin can have excellent color, an aromatic bouquet, full body, and plummy fruit. More hits than misses these days, as the wines are made with an increasing degree of finesse.

🍇 Merlot 60%, Cabernet Franc 30%, Cabernet Sauvignon 10%

🍷 4–10 years

Second wine: *Chauvin Variation*

CHÂTEAU CHEVAL BLANC
Premier Grand Cru Classé (A)
★★★

The unusual aspect of this great wine is its high proportion of Cabernet Franc, which harks back to the pre-1956 era. Switching to a majority of Merlot vines was advantageous for most Libournais properties but keeping a proportion of 60 percent Cabernet Franc was even better for Château Cheval Blanc. In 1998 this château was bought by two businessmen, Albert Frère from Belgium and Bernard Arnault, the head of LVMH. The wine is matured in wood for 20 months, with 100 percent new oak.

RED These wines have all the sweet, spicy richness one expects from a classic St.-Émilion property situated on *graves*.

🍇 Cabernet Franc 60%, Merlot 37%, Malbec 2%, Cabernet Sauvignon 1%

🍷 12–40 years

Second wine: *Le Petit Cheval*

CLOS FOURTET
Premier Grand Cru Classé (B)
★⯪ ✔

This property had an inconsistent record, but has steadily improved throughout the 1990s. The wines are matured in wood for 12 to 18 months, using 70 percent new oak.

RED Opulent and medium-bodied with silky Merlot fruit, gaining in complexity and finesse.

🍇 Merlot 60%, Cabernet Franc 20%, Cabernet Sauvignon 20%

🍷 6–12 years

Second wine: *Domaine de Martialis*

CHÂTEAU CLOS DES JACOBINS
Grand Cru Classé
★

Clos des Jacobins, which is kept in the impeccable style to which all the Cordier properties are accustomed, is impressive even during "off vintages."

RED These are rich, fat wines, bursting with chocolate and black-cherry flavors.

🍇 Merlot 85%, Cabernet Franc 10%, Cabernet Sauvignon 5%

🍷 8–25 years

CLOS DE L'ORATOIRE
Grand Cru Classé
★★

This property belongs to Stephan Von Neipperg, who should develop a cult following for this wine. The wine is matured in wood for 18 months, with one-third new oak.

RED These fine, full-flavored wines tend to have great concentration and style.

🍇 Merlot 75%, Cabernet Franc 25%

🍷 7–15 years

CLOS ST.-MARTIN
Grand Cru Classé

These wines are made at Château Côte Baleau alongside those of that property and those of Château Grandes Murailles. Of these three wines, only Clos St.-Martin retained *grand cru classé* status after the reclassification of 1985. It is aged in wood with 25 percent new barrels every four years.

RED Vivid color with ripe Merlot fruit, silky texture, and elegant style.

🍇 Merlot 75%, Cabernet Franc 25%

🍷 6–15 years

CHÂTEAU LA CLOTTE
Grand Cru Classé
❓

This property is under the same ownership as the Logis de la Cadène restaurant in St.-Émilion, where much of its wine is sold. The Libournais *négociant* Jean-Pierre Moueix takes three-quarters of the crop.

RED Although not as consistent as some *grands crus classés*, when successful this estate can make attractive and elegant wines with lots of soft, silky fruit that are a match for its peers.

🍇 Merlot 70%, Cabernet Franc 30%

🍷 5–12 years

CHÂTEAU LA CLUSIÈRE
Grand Cru Classé
❓

This is a small enclave within the property of Château Pavie and is under the same ownership as Pavie and Château Pavie Decesse. This wine is fermented in stainless-steel vats and matured in wood (two-year-old barrels from Château Pavie) for up to 24 months.

RED This wine has a certain elegance, but lacks finesse and has a high-tone style that does not appeal to me. To be fair, I must point out that those who appreciate this style often find la Clusière solid and characterful.

🍇 Merlot 70%, Cabernet Franc 20%, Cabernet Sauvignon 10%

🍷 5–10 years

CHÂTEAU CORBIN
Grand Cru Classé
❓

This property has the same owners as Château Grand Corbin—the Corbin estate, which is now divided into five separate properties bordering the Pomerol district. The wine is fermented in stainless steel and one-third of the production is matured in 100 percent new oak.

RED Deep-colored, full-bodied, and deliciously rich, but rather rustic for a classified growth.

🍇 Merlot 67%, Cabernet Franc and Cabernet Sauvignon 33%

🍷 6–12 years

Other wines: *Latour Corbin, Château Corbin-Vieille-Tour*

CHÂTEAU CORBIN MICHOTTE
Grand Cru Classé
★

This is one of five Corbin and two Michotte estates! This wine is fermented in stainless steel and some is matured in wood, with one-third new oak.

RED A dark, deeply flavored, full-bodied wine that has rich, juicy Merlot fruit and some finesse.

🍇 Merlot 65%, Cabernet Franc 30%, Cabernet Sauvignon 5%

🍷 6–15 years

Second wine: *Les Abeilles*

CHÂTEAU CÔTE DE BALEAU
Grand Cru Classé until 1985
★

This property was unjustly demoted from its *grand cru classé* status in the 1985 revision. Côte de Baleau deserves its former classification and is under the same ownership as Château Grandes Murailles and Clos St.-Martin, the former of which was also unfairly demoted. This wine is aged in wood and 25 percent of the barrels are renewed every four years.

RED Full, rich, and well-balanced wines that have good fruit, some fat, and an attractive underlying vanilla character.

🍇 Merlot 70%, Cabernet Sauvignon 20%, Cabernet Franc 10%

🍷 4–12 years

Second wine: *Des Roches Blanches*

CHÂTEAU LA COUSPAUDE
Grand Cru Classé
★

This property was demoted from its *grand cru classé* status in 1985 but, following a string of good vintages, was promoted back to its original classification in 1996, since when the quality has continued to improve. The wine is matured in wood, with up to 80 percent new oak.

RED This wine now has lots of upfront, juicy-Merlot fruit with an increasing amount of finesse.

🍇 Merlot 60%, Cabernet Franc and Cabernet Sauvignon 40%

🍷 3–7 years

Second wine: *Hubert*

CHÂTEAU COUTET
Grand Cru Classé until 1985
❓

This property was demoted from its *grand cru classé* status in 1985. It has a record of producing finer wines than la Couspaude (see previous entry), but, unfortunately, has the same lack of consistency.

RED Most vintages have a light but elegant style, with a firm tannin structure.

🍇 Cabernet Franc 45%, Merlot 45%, Cabernet Sauvignon 5%, Malbec 5%

🍷 4–8 years

COUVENT DES JACOBINS
Grand Cru Classé
★

The wine from the young vines of this property is not included in its *grand vin*, but is used to make a second wine called "Château Beau Mayne." One-third of the production is matured in wood, with 100 percent new oak.

RED The delicious, silky-seductive fruit in this consistently well-made wine is very stylish and harmonious.

CHÂTEAU CROQUE MICHOTTE
Grand Cru Classé until 1996
◉★

This property certainly deserves its *grand cru classé* status. The wine is fermented in stainless steel and matured in wood for between 18 and 24 months, with up to one-third new oak.

RED A delightful and elegant style of wine, brimming with juicy, soft, and silky Merlot fruit.

🍇 Merlot 80%, Cabernet Franc and Cabernet Sauvignon 20%

🍷 5–12 years

CHÂTEAU CURÉ BON LA MADELEINE
Grand Cru Classé

Surrounded by *premiers grands crus classés* such as Ausone, Belair, and Canon, this property has had an excellent record, but was absorbed by Château Canon in the summer of 2000.

CHÂTEAU DASSAULT
Grand Cru Classé
★☆

This property was promoted to *grand cru classé* in the 1969 revision of the 1954 St.-Émilion classification. It has an excellent record and more than deserves its classification. The wine is fermented in stainless steel and matured in wood for 12 months, with one-third of the casks being new oak, and undergoes as many as six rackings. With its beautifully understated Lafite-like label, Dassault's presentation is perfect.

RED Supremely elegant wines that always display a delicate marriage of fruit and oak in perfect balance, with fine acidity and supple tannin.

🍇 Merlot 65%, Cabernet Franc 20%, Cabernet Sauvignon 15%

🍷 8–25 years

Second wine: *Merissac*

CHÂTEAU LA DOMINIQUE
Grand Cru Classé
★★

This property, one of the best of the *grands crus classés*, is situated close to Château Cheval Blanc on the *graves* in the extreme west of St.-Émilion. The wine is fermented in stainless-steel vats that are equipped with grilles to keep the *marc* (residue of pips, stalks, and skin) submerged during the *cuvaison* (skin-contact fermentation). It is matured in wood for 24 months, with 50 percent new oak.

RED Very open and expressive wines that are plump and attractive, full of ripe, creamy fruit with elegant underlying oak.

🍇 Merlot 60%, Cabernet Franc 15%, Cabernet Sauvignon 15%, Malbec 10%

🍷 8–25 years

Second wine: *St.-Paul de la Dominique*

CHÂTEAU FAURIE DE SOUCHARD
Grand Cru Classé

Lackluster, underperformer.

RED As from 1986 the vintages have increased in color and concentration, but the wines are not special.

🍇 Merlot 65%, Cabernet Franc 26%, Cabernet Sauvignon 9%

🍷 4–7 years

Other wines: *Cadet-Peychez*

CHÂTEAU-FIGEAC
Premier Grand Cru Classé (B)
★★★

Some critics suggest that the unusually high proportion of Cabernet Sauvignon in the *encépagement* (varietal blend) of this great château is wrong, but owner Thierry de Manoncourt refutes this. He has bottles of pure varietal wines produced at Figeac going back 30 years. As far as I am concerned, his blended *grand vin* says it all every year. This château belongs with the elite of Ausone and its *graves* neighbor, Cheval Blanc. The wine is matured in wood for 18 to 20 months, with 100 percent new oak.

RED Impressively ripe, rich, and concentrated wines with fine color, a beautiful bouquet, stunning creamy-ripe fruit, great finesse, and a wonderful spicy complexity.

🍇 Merlot 30%, Cabernet Franc 35%, Cabernet Sauvignon 35%

🍷 12–30 years

Second wine: *La Grange Neuve*

CHÂTEAU FONPLÉGADE
Grand Cru Classé

Under the same ownership as Château la Tour du Pin Figeac, this property belongs to Armand Moueix, cousin of Jean-Pierre Moueix of Château Pétrus *et al*. The wine is matured in wood for 12 to 15 months, using one-third new oak.

RED I used to find this wine astringent and vegetal, earthy even, but then it appeared to pick up, only to lapse. There have been so many false starts in its perceived improvement that I no longer expect any consistency. Even though the best vintages (1982, 1990, 2000, and 2001) have been delightfully clean and attractive, literally bursting with the soft, ripe, juicy fruit flavors of raspberries and strawberries, mostly this is an

austere, tannic wine with attenuated fruit, and lacking style.

🍇 Merlot 60%, Cabernet Franc 35%, Cabernet Sauvignon 5%

🍷 5–12 years

Second wine: *Clos Goudichaud*

CHÂTEAU FONROQUE
Grand Cru Classé
★

Located just northwest of St.-Émilion itself, this secluded property has belonged to the négociant J.-P. Moueix since 1931. The wine is matured in wood for 24 months.

RED This is a deep-colored, well-made wine with a fine plummy character that shows better on the bouquet and the initial and middle palate than on the finish.

🍇 Merlot 70%, Cabernet Franc 30%

🍷 6–15 years

CHÂTEAU LA GAFFELIÈRE
Premier Grand Cru Classé (B)
★★☆

This property belongs to Comte Léo de Malet-Roquefort, who also owns the very old estate of Château Tertre Daugay, a *grand cru classé*. After a string of aggressive, ungenerous vintages, Gaffelière has produced increasingly excellent wines since the mid-1980s. The wine is matured in wood for 18 months, with 100 percent new oak.

RED These wines are concentrated and tannic, but they now have much more finesse, fat, and mouth-tingling richness than previously.

🍇 Merlot 65%, Cabernet Franc 20%, Cabernet Sauvignon 15%

🍷 12–35 years

Second wine: *Clos la Gaffelière*
Other wines: *Roquefort*

CHÂTEAU LA GOMERIE
Grand Cru
★★

Owned by Gérard and Dominique Bécot of Beau-Séjour-Bécot fame, I rather get the impression that the tiny production of this 100 percent Merlot vinified in 100 percent new oak is the vinous equivalent of giving the finger to the authorities. The unfair demotion of Beau-Séjour-Bécot in 1985 (rectified in 1996) was a cruel and unjustified blow to the Bécots, who had improved the quality of their wine. By producing an unclassified superpremium St.-Émilion that demands and receives a higher price than its own *premier grand cru classé*, the Bécots have demonstrated that the classification is meaningless.

RED Masses of rich, ripe Merlot fruit dominate this wine, despite its 100 percent new oak. A stunning wine that deserves its cult following.

🍇 Merlot 100%

🍷 4–18 years

CHÂTEAU GRAND-CORBIN-DESPAGNE

Grand Cru Classé until 1996
★ ✔

This part of the Corbin estate was bought by the Despagne family—hence the name. It was demoted in the 1996 St.-Émilion Classification. The wine is fermented in stainless steel and matured in wood for up to 18 months, with some new oak.

RED A well-colored wine of full and rich body with plenty of creamy fruit and oak, supported by supple tannin.

🍇 Merlot 90%, Cabernet Franc 10%

🍷 7–25 years

Second wine: *Reine-Blanche*

CHÂTEAU GRANDES MURAILLES

Grand Cru Classé
★

This property was demoted from its *grand cru classé* status in 1985, unjustly I think. The wines produced here are better and more consistent than those of many châteaux that were not demoted at that time. Château Grandes Murailles was, however, promoted back to its previous status in the 1996 St.-Émilion Classification. It is under the same ownership as Château Côte de Baleau and Clos St.-Martin, the former of which was also unfairly demoted. The wine is fermented in stainless-steel vats and matured in wood for 20 months, using up to 25 percent new oak.

RED These elegant, harmonious wines have good extract and a supple tannin structure that quickly softens. They are a delight to drink when relatively young, although they also age gracefully.

🍇 Merlot 60%, Cabernet Franc 20%, Cabernet Sauvignon 20%

🍷 5–20 years

CHÂTEAU GRAND MAYNE

Grand Cru Classé
★ ☆ ✔

This château ferments its wine in stainless-steel vats and ages it in wood with 80 percent new oak.

RED This is a firm, fresh, and fruity style of wine that had a rather inconsistent reputation until the 1990s, when the wines have had much more richness than in previous years.

🍇 Merlot 50%, Cabernet Franc 40%, Cabernet Sauvignon 10%

🍷 4–10 years

Second wine: *Les Plantes du Mayne*

Other wines: *Cassevert, Château Beau Mazerat*

CHÂTEAU GRAND-PONTET

Grand Cru Classé
★ ☆ ✔

Since 1980 this property has been under the same ownership as

Château Beau-Séjour Bécot. The wine is matured in wood for 12–18 months with 50 percent new oak.

RED After a string of very dull vintages, this property is now producing full-bodied wines of fine quality and character. They are fat and ripe, rich in fruit and tannin, with delightful underlying creamy-oak flavors.

🍇 Merlot 60%, Cabernet Franc and Cabernet Sauvignon 40%

🍷 6–15 years

CHÂTEAU GUADET ST.-JULIEN

Grand Cru Classé

This property consistently produces wines that well deserve their status. They are matured in wood for 18 to 20 months, using up to one-third new oak.

RED These are wines that show the silky charms of Merlot very early, and then tighten up for a few years before blossoming into finer and fuller wines.

🍇 Merlot 75%, Cabernet Franc and Cabernet Sauvignon 25%

🍷 7–20 years

CHÂTEAU HAUT-CORBIN

Grand Cru Classé
★

This wine is matured in wood for 24 months, with up to 20 percent new oak. Same ownership as Canteneste, with a string of good vintages since the 1990s.

🍇 Merlot 70%, Cabernet Franc and Cabernet Sauvignon 30%

Second wine: *Vin d'Edouard*

CHÂTEAU HAUT-SARPE

Grand Cru Classé
★

Although not one of the top performers, this château certainly deserves its status. The wine is matured in wood for 20 to 22 months, using 25 percent new oak.

RED Elegant, silky, and stylish medium-bodied wines that are best appreciated when young.

🍇 Merlot 70%, Cabernet Franc 30%

🍷 4–8 years

CHÂTEAU JEAN FAURE

Grand Cru Classé until 1985

This property was demoted from its *grand cru classé* status in 1985. I have not tasted vintages beyond 1983. The wine is matured in wood for 24 months, with 25 percent new oak.

RED These wines have good color and easy, attractive, supple fruit.

🍇 Cabernet Franc 60%, Merlot 30%, Malbec 10%

🍷 3–8 years

CHÂTEAU L'HERMITAGE

★

Owned by Véronique Gaboriaud, a friend of *garagiste* Jean-Luc

Thunevin, this well-sited property produces just 750 cases annually, with wines matured in 100 percent new oak.

RED So succulent and luscious is the fruit, and so supple the tannins, that this wine is accessible from a remarkably youthful age, yet will still improve.

🍇 Merlot 60%, Cabernet Sauvignon 40%

🍷 5–15 years

CHÂTEAU LAMARZELLE

Grand Cru Classé
☆

Under the same ownership as Grand Barrail Lamarzelle Figeac, this property preserved its classification in 1996, while the other château was demoted.

RED Forward, fruity wines that have improved throughout the 1990s.

🍇 Cabernet Franc 80%, Merlot 20%

🍷 3–7 years

CHÂTEAU LANIOTE

Grand Cru Classé
☆

An old property that incorporates the Holy Grotto where St.-Émilion lived in the 8th century. The wine is fermented and matured in wood with 25 percent new oak.

RED Stylish medium-bodied wines, with plenty of fresh, elegant fruit.

🍇 Merlot 70%, Cabernet Franc 20%, Cabernet Sauvignon 10%

🍷 6–12 years

CHÂTEAU LARCIS DUCASSE

Grand Cru Classé
★ ☆

This property, whose vineyard is situated on the Côte de Pavie, matures its wine in vat and wood for 24 months.

RED Fuller, richer wines in the 1990s, particularly in the best years.

🍇 Merlot 65%, Cabernet Franc and Cabernet Sauvignon 35%

🍷 4–8 years

CHÂTEAU LARMANDE

Grand Cru Classé
★ ☆

Consistently one of the best *grands crus classés* in St.-Émilion, fermented in stainless-steel vats and matured in wood for 12 to 18 months, with 35 to 50 percent new oak.

RED These superb wines are typified by their great concentration of color and fruit. They are rich and ripe with an abundance of creamy cassis and vanilla flavors that develop into a cedarwood complexity.

🍇 Merlot 65%, Cabernet Franc 30%, Cabernet Sauvignon 5%

🍷 8–25 years

Second wine: *Le Cadet de Larmande*

Other wines: *Des Templiers*

CHÂTEAU LAROQUE

Grand Cru Classé
★

Made a *grand cru classé* in 1996, this is one of three *grands crus classés* châteaux that are not situated in the commune of St.-Émilion itself.

RED As smooth and fruity as might be expected, with good tannic edge and increasing oak influence.

🍇 Merlot 80%, Cabernet Franc 15%, Cabernet Sauvignon 5%

🍷 4–16 years

Second wine: *Les Tours de Laroque*

CHÂTEAU LAROZE

Grand Cru Classé
★ ♠

This 19th-century château was named Laroze after a "characteristic scent of roses" was found in its wines. The wine is matured in wood for one to three years.

RED The wine does have a soft and seductive bouquet, although I have yet to find "roses" in it. It is an immediately appealing wine of some finesse that is always a delight to drink early.

🍇 Merlot 50%, Cabernet Franc 45%, Cabernet Sauvignon 5%

🍷 4–10 years

CHÂTEAU MAGDELAINE

Premier Grand Cru Classé (B)
★★ ✔

This could be considered the Pétrus of St.-Émilion. It is the grandest St.-Émilion estate in the Jean-Pierre Moueix Libournais empire, but as fine as the *terroir* is, and as much as Moueix does to extract maximum quality, the wine falls short of Pétrus. The wine matures in wood for 18 months, with a third new oak.

RED These well-colored wines have excellent concentration, yet great finesse and a certain delicacy. The flavor is multilayered with a long, elegant, and complex finish.

🍇 Merlot 80%, Cabernet Franc 20%

🍷 10–35 years

CHÂTEAU MATRAS

Grand Cru Classé
★

This wine is matured in tank for 12 months, followed by 12 months in one-third new oak. A fine 1990.

RED Opulent, silky fruit.

🍇 Cabernet Franc 60%, Merlot 40%

🍷 6–15 years

CHÂTEAU MAUVEZIN
Grand Cru Classé
❷

This property deserves its *grand cru classé* status. The wine is fermented and matured in new oak.

RED The style usually has been aromatic and supple with some oaky finesse.

🍇 Cabernet Franc 50%, Merlot 40%, Cabernet Sauvignon 10%

🍷 7–15 years

CHÂTEAU MONBOUSQUET
Grand Cru
★★☆

This was hypermarket owner Gérard Perse's first venture into wine and he openly admits that he bought the property because of its beauty, rather than out of any detailed analysis of its viticultural potential. That said, he has, with the help of consultant Michel Rolland, taken this château to unbelievable heights and, having done so, set about analyzing what could and should be purchased in St.-Émilion from a purely viticultural perspective. He set his sights on Pavie and Pavie Décesse, which he purchased in 1998 and 1997. Monbousquet remains his home.

RED Voluptuous, velvety, and hedonistic, these wines lack neither complexity nor finesse, but they are so delicious to drink that their more profound qualities easily slip by. Or should that be slip down?

🍇 Cabernet Sauvignon 10%, Cabernet Franc 40%, Merlot 50%

🍷 4–15 years

CHÂTEAU MONDOTTE
Grand Cru
★★

Since the 1996 vintage, Stephan Von Neipperg's unclassified *vin de garage* has surpassed the quality and price of his excellent *grand cru classé* Château Canon-la-Gaffelière. Low yield, 100 percent oak, and ludicrous prices.

RED Extraordinary color, density, and complexity for a wine that is not in the slightest bit heavy and makes such charming and easy drinking.

🍇 Cabernet Franc 10%, Merlot 90%

🍷 5–20 years

CHÂTEAU MOULIN DU CADET
Grand Cru Classé
❶★Ⓥ

This château, which is farmed by the Libournais *négociant* J.-P. Moueix, is consistently one of the best *grands crus classés*. The wine is matured in wood for 18 months, with a small proportion of new oak.

RED These wines have good color, a fine bouquet, delightfully perfumed Merlot fruit, excellent finesse, and some complexity. They are not full or powerful, but what they lack in size, they more than make up for in style.

🍇 Merlot 85%, Cabernet Franc 15%

🍷 6–15 years

CHÂTEAU PAVIE
Premier Grand Cru Classé (B)
★★Ⓥ

This top-performing château was purchased in 1998 along with Pavie Décesse and La Clusière by Gérard Perse. Perse used to own a group of hypermarkets, but his love of fine wine began to take over his working life in 1993, when he purchased Monbousquet. The link between Pavie under its previous owners, the Valette family, and now is Michel Rolland, who has been retained as consultant. Although Pavie has produced some of the greatest wines of St.-Émilion in recent decades, the obvious advantage for Rolland is that Perse has poured a small fortune into new installations. The wine is matured in wood for 18 to 24 months, with 100 percent new oak.

RED Great, stylish wines packed with creamy fruit and lifted by exquisite new oak. Fabulous concentration since 1998, without losing any finesse, although I will keep an open mind about the 2003 for a decade or so!

🍇 Merlot 60%, Cabernet Franc 30%, Cabernet Sauvignon 10%

🍷 8–30 years

CHÂTEAU PAVIE DÉCESSE
Grand Cru Classé
★★☆

This property was under the same ownership as Château Pavie when the Valette family were the owners, and still is under Perse. Although it is not one of the top *grands crus classés*, it is consistent and certainly worthy of its status.

RED Huge seachange in color, quality, and concentration in the 1998 and 1999 vintage.

🍇 Merlot 60%, Cabernet Franc 25%, Cabernet Sauvignon 15%

🍷 6–12 years

CHÂTEAU PAVIE MACQUIN
Grand Cru Classé
★★☆

This property was named after Albert Macquin, a local grower who pioneered work to graft European vines on to American rootstock.

These wines have noticeably improved throughout the 1990s, when Nicolas Thienpont of Vieux Château Certan has overseen the production.

RED Much richer, with more fruit and new oak in recent years.

🍇 Merlot 75%, Cabernet Franc and Cabernet Sauvignon 25%

🍷 4–8 years

CHÂTEAU PETIT-FAURIE-DE-SOUTARD
Grand Cru Classé
★★☆

This excellent property used to be part of the neighboring Château Soutard, but is now run by Jacques Capdemourlin, who also runs Château Cap de Mourlin and Château Balestard la Tonnelle. Half of its production is matured in wood for up to a year.

RED This wine has soft, creamy aromas on the bouquet, some concentration of smooth Merlot fruit on the palate, a silky texture, and a dry, tannic finish. It is absolutely delicious when young but gains a lot from a little bottle-age.

🍇 Merlot 60%, Cabernet Franc 30%, Cabernet Sauvignon 10%

🍷 3–8 years

CHÂTEAU PIPEAU
Grand Cru
★Ⓥ

Up and coming château, Pipeau is matured in wood for 18 months, with 50 percent new oak.

RED Rich, stylish, and quite striking wines that are full of fruit, underpinned by creamy-smoky oak, and easier to drink younger than most St.-Émilions.

🍇 Merlot 80%, Cabernet Franc 10%, Cabernet Sauvignon 10%

🍷 4–10 years

CHÂTEAU LE PRIEURÉ
Grand Cru Classé
☆

This property is under the same ownership as Château Vray Croix de Gay in Pomerol and Château Siaurac in Lalande-de-Pomerol. The wine produced here is matured in wood for 18 to 24 months, with 25 percent new oak.

RED Light but lengthy wines of some elegance that are best enjoyed when young and fresh.

🍇 Merlot 60%, Cabernet Franc 30%, Cabernet Sauvignon 10%

🍷 4–8 years

Second wine: *L'Olivier*

QUINAULT L'ENCLOS
Grand Cru
★Ⓥ

Increasingly impressive since being purchased by Dr. Alain Raynaud in 1997, this wine is matured in wood for 18 months, with 100 percent new oak.

RED Exceptionally concentrated

and complex.

🍇 Merlot 80%, Cabernet Franc 10%, Cabernet Sauvignon 5%, Malbec 5%

🍷 6–20 years

CHÂTEAU ST.-GEORGES (CÔTE PAVIE)
Grand Cru Classé
★

Owned by Jacques Masson, this small property's vineyard is well situated, lying close to those of châteaux Pavie and la Gaffelière. The wine is fermented in stainless steel and matured in wooden casks for 24 months.

RED This is a delicious, medium-bodied wine with plump, spicy-juicy Merlot fruit, made in an attractive early-drinking style that does not lack finesse.

🍇 Merlot 50%, Cabernet Franc 25%, Cabernet Sauvignon 25%

🍷 4–8 years

CHÂTEAU SANSONNET
Grand Cru Classé until 1996
❷

Supposedly purchased in 1999 by François d'Aulan, the former owner of Piper-Heidsieck and the master puppeteer behind numerous wine-related deals ever since. One of my spies reports that the previous owner is still there. If d'Aulan is serious about taking this château on, then we can expect some investment and improvement. However, if it's just part of one of his deals, don't hold your breath.

RED This wine is inconsistent and many vintages lack concentration, but the 1982, which is very light for the year, is supple and attractive.

🍇 Merlot 60%, Cabernet Franc 20%, Cabernet Sauvignon 20%

🍷 3–7 years

CHÂTEAU LA SERRE
Grand Cru Classé
★Ⓥ

This is another property that is improving tremendously in quality. It occupies two terraces on St.-Émilion's limestone plateau, one in front of the château and one behind. The wine is fermented in lined concrete tanks and matured in wood for 16 months with a small proportion of new oak.

RED This wine initially charms, then goes through a tight and sullen period, making it reminiscent of Château Guadet St.-Julien. Their styles, however, are very different. When young, this is quite a ripe and plump wine, totally dominated by new oak. In time, the fruit emerges to form a luscious, stylish wine of some finesse and complexity.

🍇 Merlot 80%, Cabernet Franc 20%

🍷 8–25 years

Second wine: *Menuts de la Serre*

CHÂTEAU SOUTARD
Grand Cru Classé
★☆ⓥ

The large and very fine château on this estate was built in 1740 for the use of the Soutard family in the summer. Vines have grown here since Roman times. The wine of Soutard is matured in wood for 18 months, with up to one-third new oak casks.

RED This dark, muscular, and full-bodied wine is made in true *vin de garde* style, which means it improves greatly while aging. It has great concentrations of color, fruit, tannin, and extract. With time it can also achieve great finesse and complexity.

🍇 Merlot 65%, Cabernet Franc 30%, Cabernet Sauvignon 5%

🍷 12–35 years

Second wine: *Clos de la Tonnelle*

CHÂTEAU TERTRE DAUGAY
Grand Cru Classé
★

This property was purchased in 1978 by Comte Léo de Malet-Roquefort, the owner of *premier grand cru classé* Château la Gaffelière. The wine of Château Tertre Daugay, which is matured in wood with one-third new oak, is excellent and is getting better by the vintage.

RED These wines are rich, plump, and fruity with a fine bouquet, ripe underlying oak, great finesse, and surprising longevity.

🍇 Merlot 60%, Cabernet Franc 30%, Cabernet Sauvignon 10%

🍷 7–20 years

Second wine: *De Roquefort*
Other wines: *Moulin du Biguey*

CHÂTEAU TERTRE RÔTEBOEUF
★★

François Mitjavile's cult wine is yet more proof that the only important classification is made by the consumer. This was considered to be outrageously expensive before Mondotte. The price has not gone down, but in France you can get four or five bottles of Tertre-Rôteboeuf for the cost of one bottle of Mondotte.

RED Huge, oaky, complex, and cultish: the Leonetti of St.-Émilion!

🍇 Cabernet Franc 20%, Merlot 80%

🍷 5–20 years

CHÂTEAU LA TOUR FIGEAC
Grand Cru Classé
★☆

This property was attached to Château Figeac in 1879 and today it is one of the best of the *grands crus classés*. The wine is matured in wood for 18 months, with one-third new oak.

RED These are fat and supple wines with a very alluring bouquet and masses of rich, ripe cassis fruit gently supported by smoky-creamy oak.

🍇 Merlot 60%, Cabernet Franc 40%

🍷 4–8 years

CHÂTEAU LA TOUR DU PIN FIGEAC
(Giraud-Bélivier)
Grand Cru Classé
❓

This property is run by André Giraud, who also owns Château le Caillou in Pomerol. Unfortunately, these wines have never impressed me and so I am unable to recommend them.

🍇 Merlot 75%, Cabernet Franc 25%

CHÂTEAU LA TOUR DU PIN FIGEAC
(Moueix)
Grand Cru Classé
★☆

This property is one of the best of the *grands crus classés*. It is now part of the Armand Moueix stable of châteaux. The wine is matured in wood for 12 to 15 months, with one-third new oak.

RED These consistently well-made wines always show a beautiful balance of spicy-juicy Merlot fruit, creamy oak, and supple tannin.

🍇 Merlot 60%, Cabernet Franc 30%, Cabernet Sauvignon and Malbec 10%

🍷 6–15 years

CHÂTEAU TRIMOULET
Grand Cru Classé

This is an old property overlooking St. Georges–St. Émilion. The wine is matured in wood for 12 months, with 100 percent new oak.

RED This well-colored wine has an overtly ripe and fruity aroma, lots of creamy-oaky character, a fruit flavor, and supple tannin.

🍇 Merlot 60%, Cabernet Franc 20%, Cabernet Sauvignon 20%

🍷 7–20 years

CHÂTEAU TROIS-MOULINS
Grand Cru Classé

These vineyards have been incorporated with those of Château Beau-Séjour Bécot since 1979.

CHÂTEAU TROPLONG MONDOT
Grand Cru Classé
★★

This property is owned by Claude Valette and is run by his daughter Christine. Half the production is matured in wood for 18 months with 80 percent new oak.

RED Since the introduction of temperature-controlled fermentation and a second wine in 1985, some critics have believed the quality of this wine to be on a par with that of a *premier grand cru classé*, but for me, Troplong Mondot came on board with the sensational 1988, 1989, 1990, 1992, and 1996 (those in between being merely excellent!).

🍇 Merlot 65%, Cabernet Franc and Malbec 20%, Cabernet Sauvignon 15%

🍷 4–8 years

Second wine: *Mondot*

CHÂTEAU TROTTEVIEILLE
Premier Grand Cru Classé (B)
★☆

This property has the reputation of producing a star wine every five years or so, interspersed by very mediocre wines indeed, but has been made very consistent since 1985, and now makes true *premier grand cru classé* quality wine every year. The wine is matured in wood for 18 months, with up to 100 percent new oak.

RED The quality has dramatically improved since the mid-1980s. It has fabulous Merlot-fruit richness with new oak and the power of a true *premier grand cru classé*.

🍇 Merlot 50%, Cabernet Franc 40%, Cabernet Sauvignon 10%

🍷 8–25 years (successful years only)

CHÂTEAU VALANDRAUD
Grand Cru
★★

Owned by Jean-Luc Thunevin, Château Valandraud is one of St.-Émilion's best-known *vins de garage*, although it has grown from its original small plot of 1½ acres to 11 acres (0.6 hectares to 4.5 hectares), making it more of a *parc de stationnement*.

RED Wines that even Gary Figgins of Leonetti in Washington state might complain were too oaky!

🍇 Merlot 70%, Cabernet Franc 30%

🍷 6–25 years

CHÂTEAU VILLEMAURINE
Grand Cru Classé

Château Villemaurine belongs to Robert Giraud, which is a *négociant* concern owning not only this property, but also some 20 other *petits châteaux* in various Bordeaux districts. The wine is matured in wood for 18 to 24 months, with 50 percent new oak.

RED These are full-bodied wines of excellent, spicy Merlot fruit, good underlying oak, and firm structure.

🍇 Merlot 70%, Cabernet Sauvignon 30%

🍷 8–25 years

Other wines: *Maurinus, Beausoleil*

CHÂTEAU YON-FIGEAC
Grand Cru Classé
★

This is an important property situated near Pomerol. The wine is matured for 18 months with 100 percent new oak.

RED This wine was merely attractive and easy-to-drink until 1997, since when it has shown admirable concentration of rich, spicy fruit of increasing complexity and finesse.

🍇 Merlot 80%, Cabernet Franc 20%

🍷 6–20 years

THE BEST OF THE REST

With more than a thousand châteaux in this one district, it not practical to feature every recommendable wine, thus I list here the best of the rest: châteaux that consistently make wine that stands out for either for quality or value, sometimes both. Those marked with a star sometimes produce wines that are better than many grands *crus classés*.

Château Bard-Haut
Château du Barry
*Château Belregard-Figeac
*Château Carteau Côtes Daugay
*Château Le Castelot
*Château Le Châtelet
Château Cheval Noir
*Château la Commanderie
*Château Destieux
*Château Faugères
Château de Ferrand
*Château la Fleur

*Château Fleur Cardinale
*Château Fleur-Cravignac
Château la Fleur Pourret
*Château Fombrauge
Château Franc Bigoroux
Château Grand Barrail Lamarzelle-Figeac
Château Grand Champs
*Château la Grave Figeac
*Château Haut Brisson
*Château Haut Plantey
*Château Haut-Pontet
*Haut-Quercus

Clos Labarde
Château Lapelletrie
*Château Laroque
*Château Magnan la Gaffelière
Château Martinet
Clos des Menuts
*Château Monbousquet
*Château Moulin-St.-Georges
Château Patris
*Château Pavillon Figeac
*Château Petit-Figeac
Château Petit-Gravet

*Château Petit Val
Château Peyreau
*Château Pindefleurs
*Château Plaisance
Château de Pressac
Château Puy Razac
Château Roc Blanquant
*Château Rolland
*Château Rolland-Maillet
Château Sansonnet
*Château Teyssier
Château Tour St.-Christophe

POMEROL

The most velvety and sensuous clarets are produced in Pomerol, yet the traveler passing through this small and rural area, with its dilapidated farmhouses at every turn, few true châteaux and no really splendid ones, must wonder how this uninspiring area can produce such magnificently expensive wines.

THE PROSPERITY OF RECENT YEARS has enabled Pomerol's properties to indulge in more than just an extra lick of paint, but renovation can only restore, not create, and Pomerol essentially remains an area with an air of obscurity. Even Château Pétrus, which is the greatest growth of Pomerol and produces what for the last 20 years has been consistently the world's most expensive wine, is nothing more than a simple farmhouse.

There has been no attempt to publish an official classification of Pomerol wines, but Vieux Château Certan was considered to be its best wine in the 19th century. Today, however, Pétrus is universally accepted as the leading growth. It commands prices that dwarf those of wines such as Mouton and Margaux, so could not be denied a status equivalent to that of a *premier cru*. Indeed, Le Pin has become considerably more expensive than Pétrus itself. If, like the 1885 classification, we classify Pomerol according to price, next would come Lafleur, followed by a group including L'Evangile, La Fleur Pétrus, La Conseillante, Trotanoy, and a few others, all of which can cost as much as a Médoc First Growth. It is difficult to imagine, but Pomerol was ranked as an inferior sub-appellation of St.-Émilion until it obtained its independent status in 1900. Even then it was a long hard struggle, since even Pétrus did not become sought after until the mid-1960s.

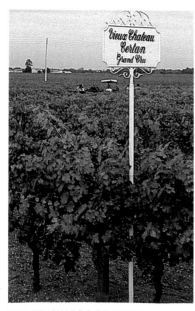

THE VINEYARDS OF VIEUX CHÂTEAU CERTAN
After Château Pétrus, this is one of the best wine-producing properties in Pomerol. A quaint signpost marks the boundary of the vineyard.

POMEROL, *see also* p108
The sleepy area of Pomerol and Lalande-de-Pomerol fans out above the riverside town of Libourne. None of the so-called "châteaux" is particularly imposing: among the most attractive are Château Nénin and Vieux Château Certan.

- The best château
- Other outstanding châteaux
- Selected great châteaux
- Communal boundary

THE WINE PRODUCERS OF
POMEROL

CHÂTEAU BEAUREGARD
★★☆

An American architect who visited Pomerol after World War I built a replica of Beauregard called "Mille Fleurs" on Long Island, New York. Quality changed dramatically at Beauregard in 1985, two years before the arrival of Michel Rolland, who followed 1985's superb wine with others and was generally responsible for turning this château around. The wine is matured in wood for 24 months with 60 percent new oak.

RED Firm, elegant, and lightly rich wine with floral-cedarwood fruit.

🍇 Merlot 48%, Cabernet Franc 44%, Cabernet Sauvignon 6%, Malbec 2%

🍷 5–10 years

Second wine: *Le Benjamin de Beauregard*

CHÂTEAU BONALGUE

This small property lies on gravel and sand northwest of Libourne. The wine is matured in wood.

RED This medium- to full-bodied wine has always been of respectable quality with a frank attack of refreshing fruit flavors, a supple tannin structure, and a crisp finish.

🍇 Merlot 65%, Cabernet Franc and Cabernet Sauvignon 30%, Malbec 5%

🍷 5–10 years

Second wine: *Burgrave*

CHÂTEAU LE BON PASTEUR

This good and steadily improving wine is matured in wood for 24 months, with 35 percent new oak.

RED These intensely colored, full-bodied, complex wines are packed with cassis, plum, and black-cherry flavors.

🍇 Merlot 75%, Cabernet Franc 25%

🍷 8–25 years

CHÂTEAU BOURGNEUF-VAYRON
★☆Ⓥ

This property is situated close to Château Trotanoy. It has an honorable, if not exciting, record and a 25-acre (10-hectare) vineyard.

RED Made in a quick-maturing style with soft fruit and a light herbal finish.

🍇 Merlot 85%, Cabernet Franc 15%

🍷 4–8 years

CHÂTEAU LA CABANNE
★

This is a fine estate producing increasingly better wine. The wine is matured in wood for 18 months, with one-third new oak.

RED These medium-bodied, sometimes full-bodied, wines have fine, rich, chocolaty fruit.

🍇 Merlot 60%, Cabernet Franc 30%, Malbec 10%

🍷 7–20 years

Second wine: *Domaine de Compostelle*

CHÂTEAU CERTAN DE MAY DE CERTAN
★★

This can be a confusing wine to identify because the "De May de Certan" part of its name is in very small type on the label and it is usually referred to as "Château Certan de May." It is matured in wood for 24 months, with 50 percent new oak.

RED This is a firm and tannic wine that has a powerful bouquet bursting with fruit, spice, and vanilla.

🍇 Merlot 65%, Cabernet Franc 25%, Cabernet Sauvignon and Malbec 10%

🍷 15–35 years

CHÂTEAU CLINET
★★

This wine, which is matured in wood with one-third new oak, has undergone a revolution in recent years. It used to disappoint those looking for the typically fat, gushy-juicy style of Pomerol, and critics often blamed this on the wine's high proportion of Cabernet Sauvignon. The 1985 vintage was more promising (a touch plumper than previous vintages, with more juicy character), so Clinet's previous lack of typical Pomerol character was evidently not entirely due to the blend of grape varieties, although the vineyard has since undergone a radical change in varietal proportions. There was talk of a turnaround in quality beginning with the 1986 vintage, but it was not until the stunning 1989 and 1990 vintages that we really saw this wine take off. There has, however, been inconsistency, going through phases of better, and not so good, quality, although currently on the up.

RED Château Clinet is now producing exceedingly fine, rich, ripe wine with ample, yet supple tannin structure mixed with oaky tannins to produce a creamy-herbal-menthol complexity.

🍇 Merlot 75%, Cabernet Sauvignon 15%, Cabernet Franc 10%

🍷 7–20 years

CLOS DU CLOCHER
★★☆Ⓥ

This belongs to the Libournais négociant Audy. The wine is rotated in thirds between new oak, one-year-old casks, and vat, and is one of the most undervalued Pomerols.

RED These are deliciously deep-colored, attractive, medium-bodied, sometimes full-bodied, wines that have plenty of plump, ripe fruit, a supple structure, intriguing vanilla undertones, and plenty of finesse.

🍇 Merlot 80%, Cabernet 20%

🍷 8–20 years

Second wine: *Esprit de Clocher*
Other wine: *Château Monregard-Lacroix*

CLOS L'ÉGLISE
★★

There are several "Église" properties in Pomerol. The wine from this one is matured in wood for 24 months, with some new oak.

RED A consistently attractive wine with elegant, spicy Merlot fruit and firm structure; it is eventually dominated by violet Cabernet perfumes.

🍇 Merlot 55%, Cabernet Sauvignon 25%, Cabernet Franc 20%

🍷 6–15 years

Second wine: *La Petite Église*

CLOS RENÉ
★Ⓥ

This property is situated just south of l'Enclos on the western side of the N89. The wine is matured in wood for 24 months with up to 15 percent new oak. An underrated wine, it represents good value.

RED These wines have a splendid spicy-blackcurrant bouquet, plenty of fine plummy fruit on the palate, and a great deal of finesse. They are sometimes complex in structure, and are always of excellent quality.

🍇 Merlot 60%, Cabernet Franc 30%, Malbec 10%

🍷 6–12 years

Other wine: *Moulinet-Lasserre*

CHÂTEAU LA CONSEILLANTE
★★★☆

If Pétrus is rated a "megastar," this property must be rated at least a "superstar" in the interests of fairness. The wine is matured in wood for 20 to 24 months, with 50 percent new oak.

RED This wine has all the power and concentration of the greatest wines of Pomerol, but its priorities are its mindblowing finesse and complexity.

🍇 Cabernet Franc 45%, Merlot 45%, Malbec 10%

🍷 10–30 years

CHÂTEAU LA CROIX
★

This property's wine is matured in wood for 20 to 24 months.

RED These attractive wines are quite full bodied, yet elegant and quick-maturing, with fine, spicy Merlot fruit.

🍇 Merlot 60%, Cabernet Sauvignon 20%, Cabernet Franc 20%

🍷 5–10 years

Second wine: *Le Gabachot*

CHÂTEAU LA CROIX DE GAY
★

This property is situated in the north of Pomerol on sandy-gravel soil, and the wine is matured in wood for 18 months, with up to 100 percent new oak.

RED Used to be somewhat lightweight, but attractive, with easy-drinking qualities, the fruit in Croix de Gay has plumped-up in recent vintages.

🍇 Merlot 80%, Cabernet Sauvignon 10%, Cabernet Franc 10%

🍷 4–8 years

Other wines: *Château le Commandeur, Vieux-Château-Groupey*

CHÂTEAU LA CROIX-ST-GEORGES
★

Under the same ownership as Château La Croix-de-Gay, this wine is matured in wood for 18 months, with 100 percent new oak.

RED Rich, soft and seductive.

🍇 Merlot 95%, Cabernet Franc 5%

🍷 4–10 years

Other wines: *Château le Commandeur, Vieux-Château-Groupey*

CHÂTEAU DU DOMAINE DE L'ÉGLISE

This is the oldest estate in Pomerol. The wine is matured in wood for 18 to 24 months, with one-third new oak.

124 FRANCE

THE WINE PRODUCERS OF THE FRONSADAIS AND THE
SAINT-ÉMILION AND POMEROL SATELLITES

CHÂTEAU D'AIGUILHE
AOC Bordeaux-Côtes-de-Castillon
★☆ⓥ

Purchased in 1998 by Stephan Von Neipperg, who has restored the property. One to watch.

Second wine: *Seigneurs d'Aiguihle*

CHÂTEAU DES ANNEREAUX
AOC Lalande-de-Pomerol

Attractive, fruity, medium-bodied wines of some elegance.

CHÂTEAU BARRABAQUE
AOC Côtes Canon-Fronsac
★☆ⓥ

Situated on the mid-*côte*, this 70 percent Merlot has really shone since the late 1990s.

CHÂTEAU BEL-AIR
AOC Puisseguin-St.-Émilion

This property makes generous, fruity, early-drinking wines.

CHÂTEAU DE BEL-AIR
AOC Lalande-de-Pomerol
★ⓥ

One of the best of the appellation, this property has fine, sandy gravel.

CHÂTEAU BELAIR-MONTAIGUILLON
AOC St.-Georges-St.-Émilion
★ⓥ

Consistently rich, deliciously fruity. The best wine selected from old vines and matured in cask, including some new oak, is sold as Château Belair-St.-Georges.

CHÂTEAU DE BELCIER
AOC Bordeaux-Côtes-de-Francs and Bordeaux Supérieur Côtes-de-Francs

This property produces fruity wines that can claim the Côtes de Castillon or Côtes de Francs appellations.

CHÂTEAU CALON
AOC Montagne-St.-Émilion and AOC St.-George-St.-Émilion
★☆

This château is under the same ownership as the *grand cru classé* Château Corbin-Michotte. The wine is good quality, with a juicy style, and very Merlot in character. Part of this vineyard falls within the St.-George-St.-Émilion area and this produces the best wine.

CHÂTEAU CANON
AOC Côtes Canon-Fronsac
★★☆ⓥ

This is one of several Fronsadais properties formerly owned, and still managed by, J.-P. Moueix. It was sold to a member of the Carrefour family in September 2000. It produces the best wine in this appellation from 100 percent Merlot.

CHÂTEAU CANON DE BREM
AOC Côtes Canon-Fronsac
★☆ⓥ

No longer owned by J.-P. Moueix, Château Canon de Brem was sold to a member of the Carrefour family in September 2000. It produces fine, firm, and flavorsome *vins de garde* that are deep-colored and powerful, yet complex and spicy.

Second wine: *Château Pichelèbre*

CHÂTEAU CANON MOUEIX
AOC Côtes Canon-Fronsac
★☆ⓥ

Sold to a member of the Carrefour family in September 2000, this property was known as Château Pichelèbre until 1985, when it was purchased by J.-P. Moueix. Although under new ownership, it is still managed by J.-P. Moueix; whether the name remains is uncertain.

CHÂTEAU CAP DE MERLE
AOC Lussac-St.-Émilion

Château Cap de Merle is wine guru Robert Parker's best Lussac performer for the 1981, 1982, and 1983 vintages.

CHÂTEAU CARLES
AOC Fronsac
★ⓥ

The producer's primary wine is attractive and juicy, but it is the 1.5 blockbusting 95 percent Merlot selection which is sold as Château Haut Carles that really stands out here.

Other wine: *Château Haut Carles*

CHÂTEAU CASSAGNE-HAUT-CANON
AOC Côtes Canon-Fronsac

Château Cassagne-Haut-Canon produces a selection of rich, full, fat, fruitcake-flavored wines that are especially attractive when they are still young.

CHÂTEAU DE CLOTTE
AOC Bordeaux-Côtes-de-Castillon and AOC Bordeaux Supérieur Côtes-de-Castillon
★☆ⓥ

This property has the right to both the Côtes-de-Castillon and Côtes-de-Francs appellations, but uses only the former.

CHÂTEAU LA CROIX CANON
AOC Côtes Canon-Fronsac
★☆ⓥ

Another former Moueix property that has sold to a member of the Carrefour family and yet remains managed by the established team. Attractive, Merlot-dominated wines are full of juicy fruit.

CHÂTEAU DU COURLAT
AOC Lussac-St.-Émilion

These are spicy-tannic wines with good fruit flavors

CHÂTEAU COUSTOLLE VINCENT
AOC Côtes Canon-Fronsac

Château Coustolle Vincent's wines are well-flavored, and matured in up to 20 percent new oak.

CHÂTEAU DALEM
AOC Fronsac
★☆ⓥ

These soft and velvety wines develop quickly but have finesse and are among the very best of their appellation.

CHÂTEAU DE LA DAUPHINE
AOC Fronsac

This property has been sold to a member of the Carrefour family, but is still run by the Moueix team, which produces fresh and fruity wines that mature in oak, 20 percent of which is new.

CHÂTEAU DURAND LAPLAIGNE
AOC Puisseguin-St.-Émilion
★ⓥ

The excellent-quality wine produced by Château Durand Laplaigne is grown using clay-and-limestone soil, with a strict selection of grapes and modern vinification techniques.

CHÂTEAU LA FLEUR DE BOÜARD
AOC Lalande-de-Pomerol

Very good wines, getting much better since this property was purchased by the owner of Angelus in 1998.

Second wine: *Château La Fleur St.-Georges*

CHÂTEAU FONTENIL
AOC Fronsac
★★☆ⓥ

This rich, velvety 90 percent Merlot high-flyer has heavy helpings of new oak and is from Michel Rolland's own property.

CHÂTEAU GRAND ORMEAU
AOC Lalande-de-Pomerol
★ⓥ

A rich and lusciously fruity wine that is matured in 50 percent new oak, Grand Ormeau is very classy for its appellation.

Second wine: *Château d'Haurange*

CHÂTEAU GRAND-BARIL
AOC Montagne-St.-Émilion

Attractive, fruity wine made by the agricultural school in Libourne.

CHÂTEAU GUIBEAU-LA FOURVIEILLE
AOC Puisseguin-St.-Emilion
★★☆ⓥ

Much investment has gone into this property, the wines of which are now considered to be the best in Puisseguin.

Second wines: *Le Vieux Château Guibeau, Château La Fourvieille*

CHÂTEAU HAUT-CHAIGNEAU
AOC Lalande-de-Pomerol
★ⓥ

Look out for Château Le Sergue 1.5, which is selected from this property's best wines and matured in 80 percent new oak. A poor man's Mondotte?

Other wines: *Château Le Sergue*

CHÂTEAU HAUT-CHATAIN
AOC Lalande-de-Pomerol
★☆ⓥ

Fat, rich, and juicy wines with definite hints of new-oak vanilla are made by Château Haut-Chatain.

CHÂTEAU LES HAUTS CONSEILLANTS
AOC Lalande-de-Pomerol

Château les Hauts-Conseillants is another fine Néac property.

Other wines: *Château les Hauts-Tuileries* (export label)

CHÂTEAU HAUT-TUQUET
AOC Bordeaux-Côtes-de-Castillon and AOC Bordeaux Supérieur Côtes-de-Castillon

This wine is consistently good.

CHÂTEAU JEANDEMAN
AOC Fronsac

This château produces fresh, fruity wine with good aroma.

CHÂTEAU JUNAYME

AOC Côtes Canon-Fronsac

★ ✓

Well-known wines of finesse.

CHÂTEAU DES LAURETS

AOC Puisseguin-St.-Émilion

The appellation's largest property.

Other wines: *Château la Rochette, Château Maison Rose*

CHÂTEAU DE LUSSAC

AOC Lussac-St.-Émilion

Château de Lussac produces well-balanced, early-drinking wine.

CHÂTEAU DU LYONNAT

AOC Lussac-St.-Émilion

The appellation's largest property.

Other wines: *La Rose Perruchon*

CHÂTEAU MAISON BLANCHE

AOC Montagne-St.-Émilion

Château Maison Blanche produces attractive wine that is easy to drink.

CHÂTEAU MAQUIN-ST.-GEORGES

AOC St.-Georges-St.-Émilion

This wine is 70 percent Merlot.

Other wines: *Château Bellonne-St Georges*

CHÂTEAU MAUSSE

AOC Côtes Canon-Fronsac

Wines with good aroma and flavor.

CHÂTEAU MAYNE-VIEIL

AOC Fronsac

Easy-drinking wines with good Merlot spice and fruit.

CHÂTEAU MAZERIS

AOC Côtes Canon-Fronsac

There is an unusually high proportion of Cabernet Sauvignon in these wines.

CHÂTEAU MILON

AOC Lussac-St.-Émilion

★ ✓

A château that produces a fine-quality, full, yet fragrant, wine.

CHÂTEAU MONCETS

AOC Lalande-de-Pomerol

★ ✓

This Néac property makes a fine, rich, and elegant Pomerol look-alike.

CHÂTEAU MOULIN HAUT-LAROQUE

AOC Fronsac

Well-perfumed, rather fat wines with lots of fruit and good tannin.

CHÂTEAU MOULIN NEUF

AOC Bordeaux-Côtes-de-Castillon and AOC Bordeaux Supérieur Côtes-de-Castillon

★ ✓

These wines regularly win medals.

CHÂTEAU LA PAPETERIE

AOC Montagne-St.-Émilion

Wines with a rich nose and a big fruit-filled palate.

CHÂTEAU DU PONT DE GUESTRES

AOC Lalande-de-Pomerol

★ ✓

This château produces full, ripe, fat wines of good quality.

CHÂTEAU PUYCARPIN

AOC Bordeaux-Côtes-de-Castillon and AOC Bordeaux Supérieur Côtes-de-Castillon

This property produces a well-made red, and a little dry white.

CHÂTEAU DU PUY

AOC Bordeaux-Côtes-de-Francs and AOC Bordeaux Supérieur Côtes-de-Francs

Red wines from this property are rustic and overtly fruity.

CHÂTEAU PUYGUERAUD

AOC Bordeaux-Côtes-de-Francs and AOC Bordeaux Supérieur Côtes-de-Francs

Aromatically attractive wines with good color and supple fruit.

CHÂTEAU DE LA RIVIÈRE

AOC Fronsac

★ ✿ ✓

Magnificent wines that are built to last: they are rich, tannic, and fruity, and matured in up to 40 percent new oak.

CHÂTEAU ROBIN

AOC Bordeaux-Côtes-de-Castillon and AOC Bordeaux Supérieur Côtes-de-Castillon

✿ ✓

Château Robin produces award-winning red wines.

CHÂTEAU LA ROCHE-GABY

AOC Côtes Canon-Fronsac

★ ✓

Château La Roche-Gaby produces intensely flavored, attractive, and well-structured wines, which are designed to have a long life.

CHÂTEAU ROCHER-BELLEVUE

AOC Bordeaux-Côtes-de-Castillon and AOC Bordeaux Supérieur Côtes-de-Castillon

✿ ✓

A good St-Émilion look-alike that

regularly wins medals.

Other wines: *La Palène, Coutet-St.-Magne*

CHÂTEAU ROUDIER

AOC Montagne-St.-Émilion

★ ✿ ✓

Quality wines that are well-colored, richly flavored, finely balanced, and long and supple.

CHÂTEAU SIAURAC

AOC Lalande-de-Pomerol

Fine, firm, and fruity wines.

CHÂTEAU ST.-GEORGES

AOC St.-Georges-St.-Émilion

★ ✿ ✓

Super quality wine of great finesse.

CHÂTEAU STE-COLOMBE

AOC Bordeaux-Côtes-de-Castillon

★ ✓

This château was purchased in 1999 by Gérard Perse of Pavie *et al* and Alain Reynaud of La Croix-de-Gay. These wines look very promising indeed.

CHÂTEAU TARREYO

AOC Bordeaux-Côtes-de-Castillon and AOC Bordeaux Supérieur Côtes-de-Castillon

Château Tarreyo (Gascon for "knoll of stones") is sited on a limestone mound, as its name suggests.

CHÂTEAU THIBAUD-BELLEVUE

AOC Bordeaux-Côtes-de-Castillon and AOC Bordeaux Supérieur Côtes-de-Castillon

Medium-bodied, fruity red wine.

CHÂTEAU TOUMALIN

AOC Côtes Canon-Fronsac

Fresh, fruity wine from a property under the same ownership as Château La Pointe in Pomerol.

CHÂTEAU TOUR-DU-PAS-ST.-GEORGES

AOC St.-Georges-St.-Émilion

✿ ✓

An excellent and inexpensive *entrée* into the world of *premier cru* claret.

CHÂTEAU DES TOURELLES

AOC Lalande-de-Pomerol

✿ ✓

Fine wines with vanilla undertones.

CHÂTEAU TOURNEFEUILLE

AOC Lalande-de-Pomerol

★ ✿ ✓

This rich, long-lived wine is the best of the appellation.

CHÂTEAU DES TOURS

AOC Montagne-St.-Émilion

✿ ✓

The largest property in the

appellation. The wine is big, full, and fleshy, yet soft and easy to drink.

CHÂTEAU LA VALADE

AOC Fronsac

★ ✿ ✓

Elegant, aromatic, and silky-textured wines, which are made exclusively from Merlot grapes.

CHÂTEAU LA VIEILLE CURE

AOC Fronsac

★ ✿

Very fresh and velvety with delightful floral, summer fruit aromas, these wines are at the very top of their appellation. The 1998 is stunning.

VIEUX-CHÂTEAU-ST.-ANDRÉ

AOC Montagne-St.-Émilion

★ ✿ ✓

A soft, exciting wine, full of cherry, vanilla, and spice flavors.

CHÂTEAU LA VILLARS

AOC Fronsac

★ ✓

Soft, fat, and juicy wines of excellent quality, one-third of which are matured in new oak.

CHÂTEAU VRAY-CANON-BOYER

AOC Côtes Canon-Fronsac

This château produces a fruity, medium-bodied wine that is attractive for early drinking from 90 percent Merlot grapes.

BOURG AND BLAYE

Ninety-five percent of the wine produced in Bourg and Blaye is good-value red. Tiny Bourg makes more wine than its five-times-larger neighbor, Blaye, and most of the vines grown in Blaye come from a cluster of châteaux close to the borders of Bourg.

AS ONE WOULD EXPECT of an area that has supported a settlement for 400,000 years, Bourg has a close-knit community. Comparatively recently, the Romans used neighboring Blaye as a *castrum*, a fortified area in the defense system that shielded Bordeaux. According to some sources, the vine was cultivated in Bourg and Blaye as soon as the Romans arrived. Vineyards were certainly flourishing here long before those of the Médoc, just on the other side of the Gironde.

Bourg is a compact, heavily cultivated area with pretty hillside vineyards at every turn. The vine is less important in Blaye, which has other interests, including a caviare industry based at its ancient fishing port where sturgeon is still a major catch. The south-facing vineyards of Blaye are mostly clustered in the countryside immediately bordering Bourg and, despite the similarity of the countryside, traditionally produce slightly inferior

FACTORS AFFECTING TASTE AND QUALITY

LOCATION
The vineyards fan out behind the town of Bourg, which is situated on the right bank of the confluence of the Dordogne and the Garonne, some 12.5 miles (20 kilometers) north of Bordeaux. Blaye is a larger district that unfolds beyond Bourg.

CLIMATE
These two areas are less protected than the Médoc from westerly and northwesterly winds, and have a higher rainfall.

ASPECT
Bourg is very hilly with vines cultivated on steep limestone hills and knolls up to a height of 260 ft (80 m). In the southern section of Blaye the country is rich and hilly, with steep slopes overlooking the Gironde that are really just a continuation of those in Bourg. The northern areas are gentle and the hills lower, with marshes bordering the viticultural areas.

SOIL
In Bourg the topsoil is clay-limestone or clay-gravel over a hard limestone subsoil, although in the east the subsoil sometimes gives way to gravel and clay. The soil in Blaye is clay or clay-limestone over hard limestone on the hills overlooking the Gironde, getting progressively sandier going east.

VITICULTURE AND VINIFICATION
There are many grape varieties here, some of which are far too inferior or unreliable to contribute to the quality of these wines, particularly the whites. Bourg produces the best reds, Blaye the best whites, but there is relatively little white wine made in both appellations—even Blaye is 90 percent red and Bourg is in excess of 99 percent red. Very few *petits châteaux* in both areas can afford the use of casks, let alone new ones, and much of the wine in Bourg is made by one of its five *coopératives*.

GRAPE VARIETIES
Primary varieties: Cabernet Franc, Cabernet Sauvignon, Merlot, Sauvignon Blanc, Sémillon
Secondary varieties: Malbec, Prolongeau, Cahors, Béguignol (Fer), Petit Verdot, Merlot Blanc, Folle Blanche, Colombard, Chenin blanc, Muscadelle, Ugni Blanc

Château
Intensive vine-growing zone
Blaye
Bourg
Height above sea level (metres)

0 1 2 3 4 5 miles
0 2 4 6 8 km

THE TOWN OF BLAYE
The attractive fishing port of Blaye with, in the foreground, the ruins of its ancient citadel guarding against the approach of marauders from the sea.

BOURG AND BLAYE, see also p63
Most of the best growths of Bourg and Blaye are clustered behind the respective ports that give this wine-producing area its name. Bourg, the smaller area, has a higher concentration of vineyards and generally produces the better wines.

wines to those of Bourg. The D18 highway appears to be a barrier beyond which the less intensely cultivated hinterland takes on a totally different topography, where the more expansive scenery is dotted with isolated forests.

THE POTENTIAL OF BOURG AND BLAYE

To the Romans, these south-facing vineyards overlooking the Gironde seemed the ideal place to plant vines. Indeed, the quality achieved today in these vineyards would have surpassed the most optimistic hopes of those past masters of the vine. However, by today's expectations, Bourg and Blaye have been relegated to a viticultural backwater. This is a pity, since there are some exciting quality wines being made here. Perhaps when the world has woken up to the gems in Canon-Fronsac, more curious consumers might turn their attention to the better producers in this district. As soon as wine lovers are prepared to pay higher prices for these wines, so its proprietors will be able to restrict yields, improve vinification techniques, and indulge in a percentage of new oak.

CHENIN BLANC IN BORDEAUX

The Chenin Blanc of Loire fame (or infamy, as the case may be) is allowed in the white wines of Bourg, albeit restricted to a maximum of 10 percent. However, in the AOCs of Blayais and Côtes de Blaye (but not Premières Côtes de Blaye), this interloper from the north has a free run, or could have, if a producer wanted to market a pure Chenin Blanc varietal wine. I have never been a fan of Chenin Blanc in the Loire, except in those idyllic vintages when the sublime *moelleux* style can be produced in quantity, and it is very hard not to produce liquid magic. The problem with Chenin in the Loire is that it grows like a weed, but rarely has the degree of sunshine this grape likes to luxuriate in. Combine that with the inclination of far too many growers to overyield and season it with those who have less than clinically clean vinification habits, and it is clear why Loire Chenin, particularly dry Loire Chenin, has such a poor reputation. On the other hand, even cheap, mass-produced Chenin Blanc wines in the New World have lovely ripe, tropical fruit flavors. Not all of them, of course, the New World has its good, bad, and ugly too, but I believe that the longer hours of warmer sunshine in Bordeaux could produce some excellent dry Chenin wines. A pure Chenin Blanc Bordeaux would be a novelty.

VINEYARDS ALONG THE DORDOGNE AT BOURG
The Romans planted these south-facing vineyards, believing this to be a far more ideal place to grow vines than on the other side of the confluence of the Dordogne and Garonne estuaries where, understandably, they failed to realize the possibilities of the Médoc concealed beyond its virtually impenetrable marshes.

CHÂTEAU SEGONZAC, ST.-GENÈS-DE-BLAYE
A short distance from the fortress of Blaye, these sweeping vineyards belong to Château Segonzac, a wine estate created in 1887 by Jean Dupuy, the owner of the Petit Parisiane, the largest-circulation newspaper in the world at the time.

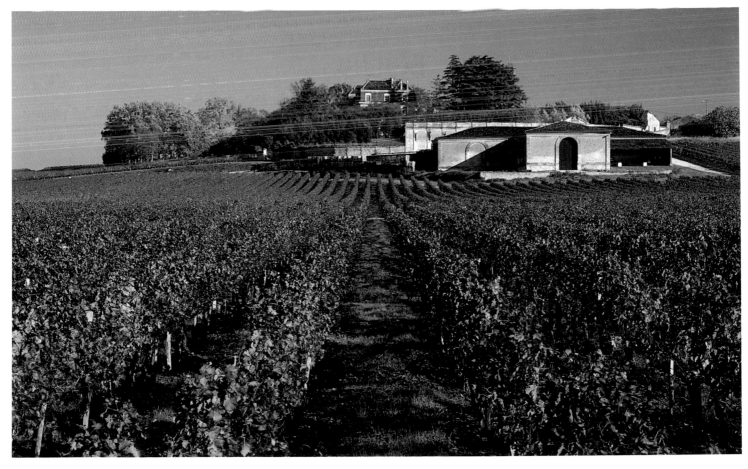

of oak-aged reds under Laroche Bel Air.

CHÂTEAU LATOUR
St.-Martin-du-Puy
AOC Entre-Deux-Mers

From this ancient château, parts of which date back to the 14th century, 10,000 cases of attractive, well-balanced, smooth red Bordeaux Supérieur are produced every year. This château's technically sound wines often win prizes and enable its devotees to claim that they can afford to drink Château Latour every day, at minimum expense.

CHÂTEAU LATOUR
Camblanes-et-Meynac
AOC Premières-Côtes-de-Bordeaux and AOC Cadillac

This is another everyday-drinking claret with this prestigious name.

CHÂTEAU LAUNAY
Soussac
AOC Entre-Deux-Mers

This large property produces 40,000 cases of a fresh dry white wine and 15,000 cases of a red wine sold under the "Haut-Castanet" label.

Other wines: *Bradoire, Château Dubory, Château Haut-Courgeaux, Château La Vaillante*

CHÂTEAU LAURETTE
Cadillac
AOC Ste.-Croix-du-Mont
✫

This property is under the same ownership as Château Lafue and runs along similar lines.

CHÂTEAU LOUBENS
Cadillac
AOC Ste.-Croix-du-Mont
★

This château produces rich, liquorous, superbly balanced sweet white wines. Dry white wines are sold as "Fleur Blanc," and a little red wine is also made.

Other wine: *Fleur Blanc de Château Loubens*

CHÂTEAU LOUPIAC-GAUDIET
Loupiac
AOC Loupiac

Fine, honey-rich sweet wines hinting of crystallized fruit are produced here.

CHÂTEAU LOUSTEAU-VIEIL
Cadillac
AOC Ste.-Croix-du-Mont
★

This property produces richly flavoured, high-quality sweet wines.

CHÂTEAU MACHORRE
St.-Martin-de-Sescas
AOC Côtes-de-Bordeaux-St.-Macaire
✫

The sweet white wine of this château has an attractive, fresh, fruit-salad flavor and is one of the best examples of the appellation. Very respectable red and dry Sauvignon wines are also produced, which are sold under the Bordeaux appellations.

CHÂTEAU DES MAILLES
Cadillac
AOC Ste.-Croix-du-Mont

Some outstanding sweet wines are produced at Château des Mailles, but the wines can occasionally be disappointing.

CHÂTEAU LA MAUBASTIT
AOC Ste.-Foy-de-Bordeaux

Some 5,000 cases of white and 2,000 of red, both "organic" wines, are sold under the Bordeaux appellation.

CHÂTEAU MORLAN-TUILIÈRE
St.-Pierre-de-Bat
AOC Entre-Deux-Mers-Haut-Benauge and Bordeaux Haut-Benauge

One of the best properties of the area, producing a vibrant, crystal-clear Entre-Deux-Mers-Haut-Benauge, a Bordeaux Supérieur in the *moelleux* style, and a fairly full-bodied red AOC Bordeaux.

CHÂTEAU MOULIN DE LAUNAY
Soussac
AOC Entre-Deux-Mers

Despite the vast quantity produced, the dry white wine is crisp and fruity, and of a very fine standard. A little red is also produced.

Other wines: *Plessis, Château Tertre-de-Launay, Château de Tuilerie, Château la Vigerie*

CHÂTEAU MOULIN DE ROMAGE
AOC Ste.-Foy-de-Bordeaux

This château produces equal quantities of "organic" red and white.

DOMAINE DU NOBLE
Loupiac
AOC Loupiac

This property consistently produces fine botrytized wines that combine sweetness and strength with elegance and a fresh, long finish.

CHÂTEAU PETIT-PEY
St.-André-du-Bois
AOC Côtes-de-Bordeaux-St.-Macaire

Good, sweet white St.-Macaire and agreeably soft red AOC Bordeaux are made at this property.

CHÂTEAU PEYREBON
Grézillac
AOC Entre-Deux-Mers

Produces red and white wine in almost equal quantities. The dry white is fine and flavorsome.

CHÂTEAU PEYRINES
Mourens
AOC Entre-Deux-Mers-Haut-Benauge and Bordeaux Haut-Benauge
★★✫

The vineyard of this château has an excellent southern exposure and produces fruity red and white wines.

CHÂTEAU DE PIC
Le Tourne
AOC Premières-Côtes-de-Bordeaux

The basic red is a lovely, creamy-sweet, easy-drinking, fruity wine. A superb oak-aged red under the *Cuvée* Tradition label is also made.

CHÂTEAU PICHON-BELLEVUE
Vayres
AOC Graves de Vayres

The red wines are variable, but the dry whites are delicate and refined.

CHÂTEAU PLAISANCE
Capian
AOC Premières-Côtes-de-Bordeaux

The *Cuvée* Tradition, in which the wine is aged in oak and is unfiltered, gives rich, ripe fruit with supple tannin structure and smoky oak.

Other wines: *De l'Esplanade, Château Florestin*

CHÂTEAU DE PLASSAN
Tabanac
AOC Premières-Côtes-de-Bordeaux

The basic red has a lot of character, with cherry-minty undertones in riper years. However, the fuller, more complex *cuvée spéciale* is worth paying for, particularly if you want a wine to accompany food.

CHÂTEAU PONTETTE-BELLEGRAVE
Vayres
AOC Graves de Vayres

This property has a reputation for subtly flavored, dry white wines.

CHÂTEAU PUY BARDENS
Cambes
AOC Premières-Côtes-de-Bordeaux

This top-performing château produces reds with sweet, ripe, fat fruit and a soft, velvety finish.

CHÂTEAU LA RAME
Cadillac
AOC Ste.-Croix-du-Mont

One of the top wines of the appellation, La Rame can have fruit, with cream and honey flavors.

CHÂTEAU REYNON-PEYRAT
Béguey
AOC Premières-Côtes-de-Bordeaux

This property produces a superb, oak-aged Premières Côtes red wine, and two dry white wines under the Château Reynon label.

CHÂTEAU RICAUD
Loupiac
AOC Loupiac

The wines of Château Ricaud are once again the best in the Loupiac appellation. They suffered a significant decline under the previous proprietor, but have at last recovered, and now display great class under new ownership.

CHÂTEAU DE LA SABLIÈRE-FONGRAVE
Gornac
AOC Entre-Deux-Mers-Haut-Benauge and Bordeaux Haut-Benauge

Sold as a Bordeaux Supérieur, the red wine of Château de la Sablière-Fongrave is fairly robust and requires time in bottle to soften. A much better quality dry white is produced and sold under the Entre-Deux-Mers appellation.

CHÂTEAU TANESSE
Langoiran
AOC Premières-Côtes-de-Bordeaux and AOC Cadillac

A Cordier property, Château Tanesse produces a decent Cabernet-dominated red, and fine-quality, Sauvignon-style dry white.

CHÂTEAU DES TASTES
Cadillac
AOC Ste.-Croix-du-Mont
★ⓥ

The sweet white wine is truly exciting; luxurious in texture, with creamy-rich flavors showing the classic complex character of botrytis.

CHÂTEAU TERFORT
Cadillac
AOC Ste.-Croix-du-Mont
✫

A small amount of excellent sweet white wine is produced by Château Terfort.

CHÂTEAU THIEULEY
La Sauve
AOC Entre-Deux-Mers
✫

Château Thieuley is owned by Professor Courselle, a former Médoc professor of viticulture and oenology. His dry white combines good fruit flavor with a fine Sauvignon style, while the red is good and silky.

CHÂTEAU DE TOUTIGEAC
Targon
AOC Entre-Deux-Mers-Haut-Benauge and Bordeaux Haut-Benauge
✫ⓥ

Château de Toutigeac is a well-known property that produces full, rich red wine. It is made for early drinking, and is the best the château produces.

BURGUNDY

Villages with double-barreled names are the key to Burgundy's greatest wines. This is because these villages hijacked the names of their most famous vineyards, so that humble village wines could sell on the backs of the finest grands crus. The village of Gevrey was the first to do this when in 1848 it took the name of its Chambertin vineyard to become Gevrey-Chambertin. You cannot become a Burgundy expert overnight, but if you remember the second part of every double-barreled Burgundian village is one of its best vineyards, you will instantly know some of Burgundy's greatest wines.

VIRÉ, MÂCONNAIS
Viré is the most ubiquitous of Mâcon's village appellations, but makes consistently fine wines. There are moves to upgrade this village and Clessé to superior appellations.

SAY "BURGUNDY" AND most people think of the famous wines of the Côtes de Nuits and Côtes de Beaune, but Burgundy in fact stretches from Chablis in the north, which is close to the Aube vineyards of Champagne, down to Beaujolais in the south, in the Rhône *département*. In fact, the Côtes de Nuits and Côtes de Beaune account for less than 10 percent of Burgundy, while Beaujolais represents almost half of the region's entire production.

Burgundy still produces the world's greatest Chardonnay and Pinot Noir wines, and the only Gamay wines ever to achieve classic status, but it is increasingly debased by a growing number of lackluster, sometimes quite disgusting, supermarket wines that rely solely upon the reputation of the famous Burgundian names, which their producers abuse to sell low-quality wines at high prices.

Burgundy, or *Bourgogne* as it is known in French, is an area rich in history, gastronomy, and wine, but unlike the great estates of Bordeaux, the finest Burgundian vineyards are owned by a proliferation of smallholders. Prior to 1789, the church owned most of the vineyards in Burgundy, but these were seized and broken up as a direct result of the Revolution, which was as much antichurch as antiaristocracy. While in Bordeaux, although some of the large wine estates were owned by the aristocracy, many were owned by the *bourgeoisie*, who, because of their long association with the English, were antipapist, and so escaped the full wrath of the Revolution. In Burgundy the great vineyards were further fragmented by inheritance laws, which divided the plots into smaller and smaller parcels. Consequently, many *crus*, or growths, are now owned by as many as 85 individual growers. The initial effect of this proprietorial carve-up was to encourage the supremacy of le négoce. Few commercial houses had been established prior to the mid-18th century because of the difficulty of exporting from a land-locked area, but with better transportation and no opposition from land-owning aristocracy, merchant power grew rapidly. A network of brokers evolved in which dealers became experts on very small, localized areas.

As ownership diversified even further, it became a very specialized, and therefore rewarding, job to keep an up-to-date and comprehensive knowledge of a complex situation. The brokers were vital to the success of a *négociant*, and the *négoce* himself was essential to the success of international trade and therefore responsible for establishing the reputation of Burgundy.

RECENT BURGUNDY VINTAGES

2003 The year of the never-ending heatwave took its toll on Burgundy, where hopes and hype were high, but the results are of variable quality at best, with reds generally showing huge, exaggerated flavors, high alcohol levels, and low acidity in the Côte d'Or. This is not a year for true connoisseurs of Pinot Noir, who adore the elegance and finesse of this great grape. This is one of those vintages where variability is the savior, and some delightful exceptions are to be found in the Côte de Nuits. Most white wines are heavy, alcoholic, and lacking in both freshness and acidity (some of Michel Laroche's Chablis *grands crus* being among the exceptions).

2002 A very good vintage where a lovely ripeness of fruit has given the reds a slight edge over the excellent whites. One of the most interesting aspects of this vintage is how well the relatively modest village wines have excelled, especially in the hands of top growers.

2001 Despite the initial bad press, this was a good, albeit variable, vintage. I seem to have had better, fresher, more elegant whites than some other critics, although 2001 is a long way short of being a special year for either color. Not quite as good as the variable 2000 vintage, but not as bad as initially feared, the quality generally gets better the farther north the appellation.

2000 This was a good to very good year in Chablis and the Côte de Nuits, where attractive, plump, early-drinking wines were made. The Côte de Beaune and Chalonnaise suffered rot following a bad storm in September, but there will be little pockets of joy where the best producers have rigorously discarded any rot-affected grapes and selected only the healthiest fruit.

1999 A large crop of high-quality reds, although rain caused some dilution in the Côte de Nuits, where the quality is not as regular as elsewhere. The whites lack acidity and crispness in the generic appellations, but are rich and concentrated from the best growers in the top *crus*.

VINEYARD AND CHÂTEAU OF RULLY
With the most northerly AOC vineyards of the Côte Chalonnaise, Rully produces excellent dry Chardonnay wines and some pleasant red wines as well.

Valley Shiraz turned out to be a fault, so has "*ça sent la merde*." Hanson now admits: "I certainly oversimplified the case when I wrote in 1982 that great Burgundy smells of shit... if I perceive decaying vegetable and animal smells, I now mostly find them unacceptable".

While the California wineries of Santa Barbara, Carneros, and Russian River lead the way in the search for the winemaker's Holy Grail—successful Pinot Noir—and individual wineries in other parts of California, and in Oregon and New Zealand, are not far behind, rarely can anyone outside Burgundy manage to produce a deep-colored, full-bodied example of Pinot Noir and still retain its varietal purity, finesse, and elegance. Even in Burgundy it does not come easy and cannot be attempted on grapes coming from anywhere but the best *cru* vineyards. It is, however, a relatively common occurrence.

Chardonnay is so ubiquitous it is probably cultivated in every wine-producing country in the world. Australian versions of this varietal are consistent and drinkable, even at the lowest level, but more expensive Chardonnays exist in Australia, just as they do in New Zealand, South Africa, Chile, California, Oregon, and lots of other places. This is why it is easy to forget just how different great white Burgundy is. When it is right, good white Burgundy is in a class of its own, and the incomparable richness, complexity, and longevity of the very greatest *grands crus* must be experienced to be believed.

THE GENERIC APPELLATIONS OF
BURGUNDY

BOURGOGNE AOC

Many writers consider Bourgogne AOC to be too basic and boring to warrant serious attention, but for me it is the most instructive of all Burgundy's appellations. If a producer cares about the quality of the *Bourgogne*, how much more effort does that producer put into making higher-quality wines? I delight in finding a delicious, easy-to-drink *Bourgogne*, and I often get more of a kick discovering one that will improve for several years than I do from a superior appellation that should age well, considering its famous name and high price. Light-red/dark-rosé wines may be sold as Bourgogne Clairet AOC, but the style is outmoded and the appellation rarely seen.

RED Despite the grape varieties that may be used to make this wine, the only *Bourgogne* worth seeking out is that with the flavor and aroma of pure Pinot Noir. Many producers indicate the grape variety on the label.

🍇 Pinot Noir, Pinot Gris, Pinot Liébault plus, in the Yonne district, César, Tressot, and Gamay (if from one of the original nine *crus* Beaujolais—but not Régnié)

🍷 *2–5 years*

WHITE There are a lot of boring white wines made under this appellation, and unless you

have access to something more interesting like the wine from J.-F. Coche-Dury or another top grower, it is probably safer to buy an inexpensive Mâcon AOC. The once overperforming Bourgogne Blanc Clos du Château du Meursault, which was often better than Château du Meursault itself (which is Meursault AOC), is now one of Burgundy's underperformers (along with Château de Meursault!). These wines may be sold as *primeur* or *nouveau* as from the third Thursday of November following the harvest.

🍇 Chardonnay, Pinot Blanc

🍷 *1–4 years*

ROSÉ The wines produced under this appellation are acceptable, but they are never special—it is the least exciting category of *Bourgogne*.

🍇 Pinot Noir, Pinot Gris, Pinot Liébault, plus, in the Yonne district, César and Tressot

🍷 1–4 years

✓ **Bourgogne Rouge** *Robert Arnoux • Ghislaine Barthod • Bertagna • Jean-Marc Boillot • Pascal Bouley • Carré-Courbin • Sylvain Cathiard • Château de Chamilly • Philippe Charlopin • Christian Clerget • J.-F. Coche-Dury • de la Combe • Joseph Drouhin • Alex Gambal • Anne Gros • Henri Jayer • Michel Juillot • Pierre Labet • Labouré-Roi • Michel Lafarge • Marie-Hélène Laugrotte • Dominique*

Laurent • Olivier Leflaive • Lucien Lemoine • Leroy ❸ *Hubert Lignier • Catherine et Claude Maréchal* (Cathérine, Gravel) *• Jean-Philippe Marchand • Mauperthuis* (Grande Réserve) *• Denis Mortet • Lucien Mouzard • de Perdrix • des Pitoux • de la Pousse d'Or • Daniel Rion & Fils • Michel & Patrice Rion • Nicolas Rossignol • Emmanuel Rouget • Tollot-Beaut • Vallet Frères • A. & P. de Villaine* ❶ *• de la Vougeraie* ❸ (Terres de Familles)

Bourgogne Blanc *Jean-Baptiste Béjot • Simon Bize & Fils • Jean-Marc Boillot • Jean-Marc Brocard* (Cuvée Jurassique) *• J.-F. Coche-Dury • Coste-Caumartin • Alex Gambal • Patrick Javillier • François Jobard • Labouré-Roi • Michel Lafarge • Hubert Lamy • Leflaive* ❸ *• Olivier Leflaive • Lucien Lemoine • Lorenzon • Catherine et Claude Maréchal • Bátrice & Gilles Mathias • Pierre Morey* ❸ *• Antonin Rodet • Georges Roumier • Michel Rouyer* (Domaine du Petit-Béru) *• Tollot-Beaut • Henry de Vézelay • A. & P. de Villaine* ❶

Bourgogne Rosé *Abbaye du Petit Quincy • Philippe Defrance • Elise Villiers*

Note For other more local generic wines *see*:
Chablis Bourgogne Chitry AOC, Bourgogne Coulanges-la-Vineuse AOC, Bourgogne Côtes d'Auxerre AOC, Bourgogne Côte Saint-Jacques AOC, Bourgogne Épineuil AOC, Bourgogne Vézelay AOC (p.137)

• **Côte de Nuits** and **Hautes-Côtes de Nuits** Bourgogne Hautes-Côtes de Nuits AOC, Bourgogne Le Chapitre AOC, Bourgogne Montrecul AOC (p.140)

• **Côte de Beaune** and **Hautes-Côtes de Beaune** Bourgogne La Chapelle Notre-Dame AOC, Bourgogne Hautes-Côtes de Beaune AOC (p.140)

• **Côte Chalonnaise** Bourgogne Côte Chalonnaise AOC, Bourgogne Côtes du Couchois AOC (p.153)

BOURGOGNE ALIGOTÉ AOC

The finest Bourgogne-Aligoté wines come from the village of Bouzeron in the Mercurey region, which has its own appellation (*see also* Bouzeron

AOC, p.160). With the exception of the wines below, the remaining Aligoté can be improved by adding *crème de cassis*, a local blackcurrant liqueur, to create an aperitif known as a "Kir."

WHITE Dry wines that are usually thin, acid, and not very pleasant: bad examples are even worse and are becoming widespread. When good, however, Aligoté can make a refreshing change from Burgundy's ubiquitous Chardonnay wines. However, even among the top producers, this grape seems to inflict its own inconsistency. Any one of the following recommended producers could make the greatest Aligoté of the vintage one year, then turn out something very ordinary the next year. Bourgogne Aligoté may be sold as *primeur* or *nouveau* from the third Thursday of November following the harvest.

🍇 Aligoté and a maximum of 15% Chardonnay

🍷 1–4 years

✓ *d'Auvenay* **B** • *Bersan* • *Marc Brocard* • *Arnaud Ente* • *Naudin-Ferrand* • *de la Folie* • *Alex Gambal* • *Ghislaine et Jean-Hugues Goisot* • *François Jobard* • *Daniel Largeot* • *Catherine et Claude Maréchal* • *Edmond Monot* • *Alice et Olivier Moor* • *Jacky Renard* • *Thévenot-le-Brun & Fils* • *A. & P. de Villaine* **O**

BOURGOGNE GRAND-ORDINAIRE AOC

In English-speaking markets the *"Grand"* sounds very grand indeed, and the fact that it qualifies *"Ordinaire,"* not *"Bourgogne,"* seems to get lost in the translation. Light-red/dark-rosé wines may be sold as Bourgogne Clairet Grand-Ordinaire AOC, but the style is outmoded and the appellation is rarely encountered.

RED These are mostly inferior wines made from the Gamay grape, but there are some interesting Pinot Noir-dominated versions.

🍇 Pinot Noir, Gamay, plus, in the Yonne district, César and Tressot

🍷 2–6 years

WHITE These dry wines are even more dismal than standard-issue *Bourgogne blanc*. Buy Mâcon blanc instead! These wines may be sold as *primeur* or *nouveau* as from the third Thursday of November following the harvest.

🍇 Chardonnay, Pinot Blanc, Aligoté, Melon de Bourgogne, plus, in the Yonne district, Sacy

🍷 1–4 years

ROSÉ The Hautes-Côtes *coopérative* produces a dry, light but elegant wine under this appellation, Rosé d'Orches.

🍇 Pinot Noir, Gamay, plus, in the Yonne district, César and Tressot

🍷 1–3 years

✓ *Jean-Paul Brun* (Terres Dorées) • *Edmond Cornu & Fils* • *Michel Lafarge* • *Emmanuel Rouget*

BOURGOGNE MOUSSEUX AOC

Since December 1985 this appellation has been limited to, and remains the only outlet for, sparkling red Burgundy.

SPARKLING RED A favorite fizzy tipple in the pubs of prewar Britain. This wine's sweet flavor is very much out of step with today's sophisticated consumers.

🍇 Pinot Noir, Gamay, plus, in the Yonne district, César and Tressot

🍷 Upon purchase

BOURGOGNE ORDINAIRE AOC

See Bourgogne Grand-Ordinaire AOC

BOURGOGNE PASSE-TOUT-GRAINS AOC

Made from a *mélange* of Pinot Noir and Gamay grapes, *passe-tout-grains* is the descendant of an authentic peasant wine. A grower would fill his vat with anything growing in his vineyard and ferment it all together. Thus *passe-tout-grains* once contained numerous grape varieties. The Pinot Noir and Gamay varieties were, however, the most widely planted, and the wine naturally evolved as a two-grape product. Up until 1943 a minimum of one-fifth Pinot Noir was enforced by law; now the minimum is one-third.

RED Many *passe-tout-grains* used to be drunk too early, as the better-quality examples require a few years of bottle-aging to show the aristocratic influence of their Pinot Noir content. With an increase in Pinot Noir production and

more modern vinification techniques, more producers have begun making softer, less rustic *passe-tout-grains*, which are easier to drink when young. They remain relatively modest wines.

🍇 Pinot Noir plus a maximum of one-third Gamay and a combined maximum of 15% Chardonnay, Pinot Blanc, and Pinot Gris

🍷 2–6 years

ROSÉ This dry, pink version is worth trying.

🍇 A maximum of one-third Gamay plus Pinot Noir and Pinot Liébault

🍷 1–3 years

✓ *Robert Chevillon* • *Edmond Cornu & Fils* • *Michel Lafarge* • *Laurent Ponsot* (former Volpato old vines) • *Lejeune* • *Daniel Rion & Fils*

CRÉMANT DE BOURGOGNE AOC

This appellation was created in 1975 to supersede the Bourgogne Mousseux AOC, which failed to inspire a quality image because the term *"mousseux"* also applied to cheap sparkling wines. Bourgogne Mousseux is now for red wines only. The major production centers for Crémant de Bourgogne are the Yonne, Region de Mercurey, and the Mâconnais. There are already many exciting wines, and the quality is certain to improve as more producers specialize in cultivating grapes specifically for sparkling wines, rather than relying on excess or inferior grapes, as was traditional in Burgundy.

SPARKLING WHITE Dry but round, the styles range from fresh and light to rich and toasty.

🍇 Pinot Noir, Pinot Gris, Pinot Blanc, Chardonnay, Sacy, Aligoté, Melon de Bourgogne, and a maximum of 20% Gamay

🍷 3–7 years

SPARKLING ROSÉ Until now the best pink Crémant produced outside of Champagne has come from Alsace. Good examples are made in Burgundy, but have not realized their potential.

🍇 Pinot Noir, Pinot Gris, Pinot Blanc, Chardonnay, Sacy, Aligoté, Melon de Bourgogne, and a maximum of 20% Gamay

🍷 2–5 years

✓ *Caves de Bailly* • *André Bonhomme* • *Paul Chollet* • *André Delorme* • *Roux Père* • *Caves de Viré*

THE CHABLIS DISTRICT

Chablis is one of Burgundy's two classic white-wine areas, yet this island of vines is closer to Champagne than to the rest of Burgundy, and its Chardonnay grape is grown on soils and under climatic conditions that are more champenois *than* bourguignon.

THE TOWN OF CHABLIS
Above the town of Chablis, the vines face southeast and southwest, clinging to hills along the banks of the Serein, a small tributary of the Yonne. These are the grand cru *vineyards that make this district's finest wines.*

LIKE CHAMPAGNE, CHABLIS owes much of its success to a cool and uncertain northern climate that puts viticulture on a knife-edge. This is a source of constant worry and not a little diabolical wine, but when everything comes together just right, Chablis can produce the most electrifying Chardonnay in the world.

Known as the "Golden Gate," this area has the advantage of being the inevitable first stop for anyone visiting the Burgundy region by car, whether directly from Paris or via Champagne. Situated in the Yonne *département*, much of which once formed part of the ancient province of Champagne, Chablis gives the distinct impression of an area cut off not simply from the rest of Burgundy but from the rest of France. Indeed, the great *négociants* of the Côte d'Or rarely visit Chablis and have never made any significant penetration into what appears to be a closed-shop trade.

▒ Intensive vine-growing zone	▓ Chablis 1er Cru
▓ Chablis	● Villages entitled to add their name to Bourgogne AOC
▒ Petit Chablis	▲ Height above sea level (meters)
▓ Saint-Bris	
▓ Chablis Grand Cru	0 2 4 miles / 0 2 4 6 km

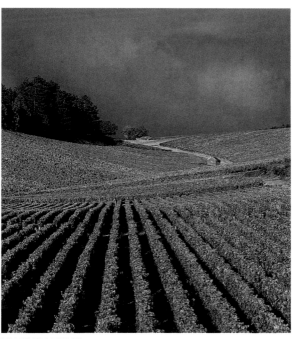

FOURCHAUME
Just north of Chablis itself, Fourchaume is one of only two premier cru slopes that face southwest. The other is Montée de Tonnerre. It is probably no coincidence that, out of a total of 17 Chablis premiers crus, these vineyards are always among the top three.

CHABLIS DISTRICT
Overlooked by its grands crus and surrounded by premiers crus, Chablis lies at the center of its eponymous wine-producing area, which is geographically and climatically closer to Champagne than to the rest of Burgundy.

FACTORS AFFECTING TASTE AND QUALITY

LOCATION
Chablis is halfway between Beaune and Paris, 19 miles (30 kilometers) from the southernmost vineyards of Champagne, but 60 miles (100 kilometers) from the rest of Burgundy.

CLIMATE
This area has a semicontinental climate with minimal Atlantic influence, which results in a long, cold winter, a humid spring, and a fairly hot, very sunny summer. Hail storms and spring frosts are the greatest hazards.

ASPECT
All the *grands crus* are located on one stretch of southwest-facing slopes just north of Chablis itself, where the vineyards are at a height of between 490 to 660 feet (150 and 200 meters). Apart from the southwest-facing slopes of Fourchaume and Montée de Tonnerre, the *premier cru* slopes face southeast.

SOIL
This area is predominantly covered with calcareous clay, and the traditional view is that of the two major types, Kimmeridgian and Portlandian, only the former is suitable for classic Chablis; but this is neither proven nor likely. Geologically they have the same Upper Jurassic origin. Any intrinsic geographical differences should be put down to aspect, microclimate, and the varied nature of the sedimentary beds that underlie and interbed with the Kimmeridgian and Portlandian soils.

VITICULTURE AND VINIFICATION
The vineyards in Chablis have undergone rapid expansion, most particularly in the generic appellation and the *premiers crus*, both of which have doubled in size since the early 1970s. Mechanical harvesting has now found its way to the *grands crus* slopes of Chablis, but smaller producers still pick by hand. Most Chablis is fermented in stainless steel, but oak barrels are making a comeback, although too much new oak fights against the lean, austere intensity of the Chardonnay grown in this district.

GRAPE VARIETIES
Primary varieties: Chardonnay
Secondary varieties: Pinot Noir, Pinot Blanc, Pinot Gris (*syn.* Pinot Beurot), Pinot Liébault, Sauvignon Blanc, Gamay, César, Tressot, Sacy, Aligoté, Melon de Bourgogne

THE VARYING STYLES OF CHABLIS

The traditional description of Chablis is of a wine of clear, pale color with a green hue around the rim. It is very straight and positive, with an aggressive, steely character, very direct attack, and a high level of acidity that needs a few years to round out. This description, however, rarely applies, as much has changed in the way these wines are made at both ends of the quality spectrum.

Thirty years ago most Chablis did not undergo malolactic fermentation. The wines that resulted had a naturally high acidity, and were hard, green, and ungenerous in their youth, although they often matured into wines of incomparable finesse. Now, most Chablis wines undergo malolactic fermentation and cold stabilization, which is used to precipitate tartrates (although some wines fermented or matured in small oak casks do not), making the wine fuller, softer, and rounder.

At the top end of the market, there are two distinctly different schools. Some wines are fermented in stainless steel and bottled early to produce the most direct and attacking style, while others are fermented in wood and matured in casks with an increasing amount of new oak. Writers often describe the unoaked, stainless-steel-fermented Chablis as traditional, but these vats were introduced in the 1960s, so it cannot be a well-established tradition. The oak barrel is much older, of course, and thus far more traditional, but what the critics really mean is that new oak has never been a feature of Chablis winemaking, therefore the crisp, clean style of Chablis fermented in stainless steel is closer to the original style: traditional by default. Obviously, the most authentic style of Chablis is the wine that is made in old or, more accurately, well-used casks. The traditional Chablisienne cask, known as a *feuillette*, is only half the size of a normal Burgundian barrel, thus has twice the effect, but not being new oak, this would be an oxidative effect, not creamy-vanilla or other aromatics. However, the more rapid oxidative effect of the *feuillette* does explain why the wines were traditionally bottled early, retaining the minerality of the fruit, and invariably imparting a slight spritz, further separating the style of these wines from Chardonnay produced in the Côte d'Or.

What makes the divide between oaked and unoaked Chablis even wider is the fact that the leaner, more mineral style of wine produced in this district can fight against the effects of new oak, whereas the fatter, softer, more seductive wines of the Côte d'Or embrace it with open arms. Recognizing that some people enjoy new oak characteristics, the recommendations in this book include producers of the best oaky Chablis. However, the trend for new oak peaked sometime in the late 1990s. Today, even producers known for the oakiest Chablis have been holding back, to promote the minerality meant to be expressive of the *terroir*.

There has always been a certain inconsistency about Chablis, which is only to be expected given its uncertain climate, and this has never deterred its devotees. However, things have gone from bad to worse over the past 15 years, and it is not the weather that has always been to blame—it is the increasing yields by greedy producers and sloppy winemaking. There are still great joys to be had with the best and most passionately produced of Chablis, from the lowliest appellation to the greatest *grands crus*, but wine buyers must be increasingly vigilant.

OTHER WINES OF YONNE

Other than Chablis, the two best-known wines of the Yonne are the red wines of Bourgogne Irancy AOC and the white Saint-Bris AOC, made from the Sauvignon Blanc grape—a trespasser from the Loire. Other grapes peculiar to the Yonne are the César and Tressot, which are black, and the Sacy, which is white. None is permitted in any Burgundian appellation other than AOC Bourgogne from Yonne, and they are not even widely cultivated here. César is the most interesting of these varieties, albeit rather rustic. It is a low-yielding vine that produces a thick, dark, tannic

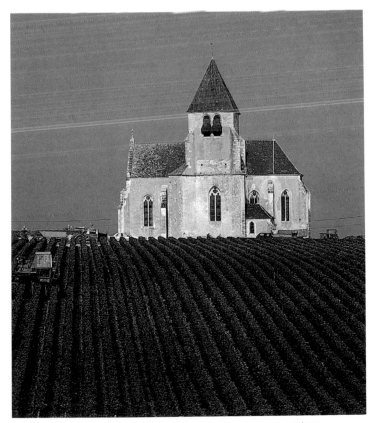

MACHINE-HARVESTING AT DOMAINE STE.-CLAIRE IN PRÉHY
Machine-harvesting, which can lower the quality of white wines in particular, is widespread in Chablis, even on the grands crus. *The technique is most appropriate at Préhy, where the vineyards are of lesser quality.*

Mazelots César, Les Bessys, Côte-de-Moutier) • *Roger Delalogue* • *Christophe Ferrari* (*rouge* only) • *Félix* • *Saint-Germain* (La Bergère)

PETIT CHABLIS AOC

A depreciatory appellation that covers inferior soils and expositions within the same area as generic Chablis, with the exception of Ligny-le-Châtel, Viviers, and Collan. Although I have found four more reliable producers than last time, this appellation should be downgraded to VDQS or uprooted. The rumor is that it will be phased out, but do not misunderstand: this does not mean that they will uproot the vines, simply that this inferior land will instead produce Chablis, albeit of a *petit vin* quality.

WHITE Aside from the occasional pleasant surprise, most are mean and meager dry wines of light to medium body. The producers below provide most of the pleasant surprises.

🥂 Chardonnay

🍷 2–3 years

☑ *Jean-Marc Brocard* • *Jean Durup* • *Vincent Gallois* • *Thierry Hamelin* • *Francine & Olivier Savary*

SAINT-BRIS AOC

This wine is as good as most Sauvignon Blanc AOCs, and considerably better than many other white AOCs made from lesser grape varieties. Ten years ago I did not believe it possible that Sauvignon de St.-Bris would ever overcome Burgundy's Chardonnay-chauvinism to rise to the ranks of Appellation Contrôlée, but in 2003, Sauvignon de St-Bris VDQS was promoted to Saint-Bris AOC (retrospectively applied to the 2001 vintage).

WHITE Fine wet-grass or herbaceous aromas, full smoky-Sauvignon flavors, and a correct, crisp, dry finish. Made from the rare Sauvignon Gris, Ghislaine & Jean-Hugues Goisot's Cuvée du Corps de Garde Gourmand Fié Gris is the best, most consistent, and most unusual wine in this appellation, while the same producer's "straight" Sauvignon is easily the top thoroughbred Sauvignon Blanc.

🥂 Sauvignon Blanc, Sauvignon Gris

🍷 2–5 years

☑ *Jean-Marc Brocard* • *Robert Defrance* • *Félix* • *Ghislaine & Jean-Hugues Goisot* • *Erick Lavallée* • *Jacky Renard*

🥂 Chardonnay

🍷 6–20 years

☑ **Blanchot** *Billaud-Simon* (Vieilles Vignes) • *Michel Laroche* • *Raveneau* • *Domaine Vocoret* **Bougros** *William Fèvre* • *Joseph Drouhin* • *de la Maladière* • *Michel Laroche* **Les Clos** *Billaud-Simon* • *La Chablisienne* • *René & Vincent Dauvissat* • *Jean-Paul Droin* • *Joseph Drouhin* • *Caves Duplessis* • *William Fèvre* • *Michel Laroche* • *de la Maladière* • *Domaines des Malandes* • *Louis Michel* • *J. Moreau* (lieu-dit Clos des Hospices) • *Pinson* • *Raveneau* • *Servin* **Grenouilles** *La Chablisienne* (Château Grenouilles) • *Louis Michel* **La Moutonne** *Long-Depaquit* **Les Preuses** *Billaud-Simon* • *Joseph Drouhin, René & Vincent Dauvissat* • *William Fèvre* **Valmur** *Jean Collet* • *Jean-Paul Droin* • *William Fèvre* • *Olivier Leflaive* • *Raveneau* **Vaudésir** *Billaud-Simon* • *La Chablisienne* • *Jean-Paul Droin* • *Joseph Drouhin* • *William Fèvre* • *Michel Laroche* • *des Malandes* • *Louis Michel*

CHABLIS PREMIER CRU

Premiers crus: Les Beauregards, Beauroy, Berdiot, Chaume de Talvat, Côte de Jouan, Côte de Léchet, Côte de Vaubarousse, Fourchaume, Les Fourneaux, Montée de Tonnerre, Montmains, Mont de Milieu, Vaillons, Vaucoupin, Vau-de-Vey (or Vaudevey), Vau Ligneau, and Vosgros. Unlike the *grands crus*, the 17 *premiers crus* of Chablis are scattered among the vineyards of 15 surrounding communes, and the quality and style is patchy. Montée de Tonnerre is the best *premier cru* throughout the different producers and across the many vintages. One of its *lieux-dits*, Chapelot, is considered by many to be the equivalent of a *grand cru*. After Montée de Tonnerre, Côte de Léchet, Les Forêts (which is a *climat* within Montmains), Fourchaume, Mont de Milieu, and Vaillons vie for second place.

WHITE Dry wines that can vary from light- to fairly full-bodied, but should always be finer and longer-lasting than wines of the basic Chablis appellation, although without the concentration of flavor expected from a *grand cru*.

🥂 Chardonnay

🍷 4–15 years

☑ **Les Beauregards** *Jean-Marc Brocard* **Beauroy** *Sylvain Mosnier* **Berdiot** *None* **Chaume de Talvat** *None* **Côte de Jouan** *Michel Cobois* **Côte de Léchet** *Jean-Paul Droin* • *Jean Defaix* • *Sylvain Mosnier* **Côte de Vaubarousse** *None* **Fourchaume** *Billaud-Simon* • *La Chablisienne* • *de Chantemerle* • *Jean-Paul Droin* • *Gérard Duplessis* • *Jean Durup* • *William Fèvre* (Côte de Vaulorent) • *Lamblin & Fils* • *Michel Laroche* (Vieilles Vignes) • *des Malandes* • *Louis Michel* • *Francine & Olivier Savary* **Les Fourneaux** *Jean-Pierre Grossot* • *Louis & Anne Moreau* **Montée de Tonnerre** *Billaud-Simon* • *Jean-Paul Droin* (Vieilles Vignes) • *Caves Duplessis, William Fèvre* • *Louis Michel* • *Raveneau* (including Chapelot and Pied d'Aloue *lieux-dits*) • *Guy Robin* **Montmains** *La Chablisienne* • *René & Vincent Dauvissat* (La Forest [sic] *lieu-dit*) • *Jean-Paul Droin, Caves Duplessis* • *des Malandes* • *des Marronniers* • *Louis Michel* • *Georges Pico, Pinson* • *Raveneau* (Butteaux *lieu-dit*) • *Guy Robin* (Butteaux *lieu-dit*) • *Robert Vocoret* (La Fôret *lieu-dit*) **Mont de Milieu** *Barat* • *Billaud-Simon* (especially Vieilles Vignes) • *La Chablisienne* • *Jean Collet* • *Jean-Pierre Grossot* • *de Meulière* • *Pinson* **Vaillons** *Barat* • *Billaud-Simon* • *R. & V. Dauvissat* (Séchet *lieu-dit*) • *Jean Defaix* • *Jean-Paul Droin* • *Gérard Duplessis* • *Michel Laroche* (Vieilles Vignes) • *François Raveneau* **Vaucoupin** *Jean-Pierre Grossot* **Vau-de-Vey** *Jean Durup* • *Michel Laroche* **Vau Ligneau** *Thierry Hamelin* • *Louis & Anne Moreau* **Vosgros** *Jean-Paul Droin* • *Gilbert Picq*

IRANCY AOC

Irancy was promoted from Bourgogne Irancy to full village AOC status in its own right in 1999. This red-wine-only appellation encompasses 395 acres (160 hectares) in Irancy and neighboring villages of Cravant and Vincelottes.

RED Irancy is supposed to be the "famous" red wine of Chablis, but it is not really that well known and is not even the best local red wine. Michel Lorain's Côte Saint-Jacques Clos des Capucins, and Domaine de l'Abbaye du Petit Quincy's Côte de Grisey Cuvée Juliette are both consistently superior to the best Irancy, though the latter do possess a certain richness of fruit that most examples of this modest appellation lack. Original Irancy was a pure César wine: Anita and Jean-Pierre Colinot make the most interesting example (Les Mazelots César).

🥂 Pinot Noir, Pinot Gris, César

🍷 1–3 years

☑ *Léon Bienvenu* • *Benoît Cantin* (Cuvée Emiline) • *Roger Delaloge* • *Anita & Jean-Pierre Colinot* (Palotte, Les Mazelots, Les

CÔTE DE NUITS AND HAUTES-CÔTES DE NUITS

The Côte de Nuits is essentially a red-wine area (with one or two extraordinary whites), and with 22 of Burgundy's 23 red grands crus, it is the place par excellence for Pinot Noir.

THE CÔTE D'OR, or "golden slope," is the departmental name for both the Côte de Nuits and the Côte de Beaune. Firmness and weight are the key words to describe the wines produced here, and these characteristics intensify as the vineyards progress north. A string of villages with some of the richest names in Burgundy—Gevrey-Chambertin, Chambolle-Musigny, Vosne-Romanée, and Nuits-St.-Georges—these slopes ring up dollar signs in the minds of merchants throughout the world. Ironically, the most famous appellations also produce some of Burgundy's worst wines.

CÔTE DE NUITS AND HAUTES-CÔTES DE NUITS, see also p137
The best vineyards of the Côte de Nuits form a tighter, more compact strip than those of the Côte de Beaune, (see also p151), and the wines produced are, coincidentally, tighter, with more compact fruit.

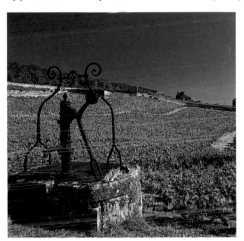

CLOS ARLOT
OF DOMAINE
DE L'ARLOT
Purchased in 1987 by the dynamic AXA group, Domaine de l'Arlot is one of the most consistent, high-quality producers in Nuits-St.-Georges, making textbook Pinot Noir and, from its monopole Clos Arlot, minuscule amounts of sublime white wine

FACTORS AFFECTING TASTE AND QUALITY

LOCATION
The Côte de Nuits is a narrow, continuous strip of vines stretching from Dijon to just north of Beaune, with the Hautes-Côtes de Nuits in the southwestern hinterland.

CLIMATE
Semicontinental climate with minimal Atlantic influence, which results in a long, cold winter, a humid spring, and a fairly hot, very sunny summer. Hail is its greatest natural hazard and heavy rain is often responsible for diluting the wines and causing rampant rot.

ASPECT
A series of east-facing slopes that curve in and out to give some vineyards northeastern, some southeastern aspects. The vines grow at an altitude of between 740 and 1,150 feet (225 to 350 meters) and, aside from Gevrey-Chambertin and Prémeaux-Prissey, those vineyards that have the right to the village and higher appellations rarely extend eastward beyond the RN 74 road.

SOIL
A subsoil of sandy-limestone, which is exposed in places but usually covered by a chalky scree mixed with marl and clay particles on higher slopes and richer alluvial deposits on lower slopes. Higher slopes sometimes have red clay.

VITICULTURE AND VINIFICATION
The vines are trained low to benefit from heat reflected from the soil at night. For red wines, the grapes are almost always destemmed and the juice is kept in contact with the skins for between eight and 10 days. Less than three percent of the wine produced is white, but this is mostly high quality and traditionally cask fermented. The best wines are matured in oak.

GRAPE VARIETIES
Primary varieties: Pinot Noir, Chardonnay
Secondary varieties: Pinot Gris (known locally as Pinot Beurot), Pinot Liébault, Pinot Blanc, Aligoté, Melon de Bourgogne, Gamay

CONFRÉRIE DES CHEVALIERS DU TASTEVIN

After the three terrible vintages of 1930, 1931, and 1932, and four years of world slump following the Wall Street Crash of 1929, Camille Rodier and Georges Faiveley formed the Confrérie des Chevaliers du Tastevin to revive Burgundy's fortunes. They named the brotherhood after the traditional Burgundian *tastevin*, a shallow, dimpled, silver tasting-cup with a fluted edge.

The first investitures took place on November 16, 1934, in a cellar in Nuits-St.-Georges; the Confrérie now boasts thousands of members in numerous foreign chapters and averages 20 banquets a year at Château du Clos de Vougeot. Until the late 1980s, wines bearing the distinctive Tastevinage label used to be a useful means of quickly identifying wines within basic appellations that have risen above their modest status, but the selection gradually became less rigorous, with some decidedly underperforming wines slipping through. In recent years, however, there appears to be more consistency, once again making the Tastevinage label worth watching out for.

On average only one-third of the wines submitted for the Tastevinage receive the coveted label. No charge is made for entering. The minimum quantity for commercial availability is just 900 bottles, and there is no maximum. The wines are tasted blind, and most importantly, the tasters include hoteliers, restaurateurs, sommeliers, wine merchants, and wine press, as well as producers. A wine can also be rejected on the basis of laboratory analysis alone (if, for example, it has elevated levels of volatile acidity). Another plus point is the random checks that are carried out at the point of sale on all markets.

VINEYARDS OF CLOS DE VOUGEOT ON THE COTE DE NUITS
The Château du Clos de Vougeot has played a big part in the region's wine industry for many years. However, the 124 acres (50 hectares) of vineyards surrounding the château are split into more than 80 plots.

✓ *Robert Arnoux • Sylvain Cathiard • J.-J. Confuron • Joseph Drouhin • Follin-Arbelet • Alain Hudelot-Noëllat • Lucien Lemoine • Leroy* ❸ *• de la Romanée-Conti*

RUCHOTTES-CHAMBERTIN AOC
Grand Cru

This is the second-smallest of the nine *grands crus* of Gevrey-Chambertin. It is situated above Mazis-Chambertin and is the last *grand cru* before the slope turns to face north.

RED Normally one of the lighter Chambertin look-alikes, but top growers like Roumier and Rousseau seem to achieve a bagful of added ingredients in their splendidly rich wines.

🍇 Pinot Noir, Pinot Gris, Pinot Liébault

🍷 8–20 years

✓ *Frédéric Esmonin • Mugneret-Gibourg • Christophe Roumier • Georges Roumier • Armand Rousseau*

LA TÂCHE AOC
Grand Cru

One of Vosne-Romanée's six *grands crus*, this fabulous vineyard belongs to the world-famous Domaine de la Romanée-Conti (DRC), which also owns the Romanée-Conti *grand cru*.

RED While this wine is indeed extremely rich and very complex, it does not in comparative terms quite have the richness of Richebourg, nor the complexity of Romanée-Conti. It does, however, have all the silky texture anyone could expect from the finest of burgundies, and no other wine surpasses La Tâche for finesse.

🍇 Pinot Noir, Pinot Gris, Pinot Liébault

🍷 12–30 years

✓ *de la Romanée-Conti*

VOSNE-ROMANÉE AOC

This is the most southerly of the great villages of the Côte de Nuits. Some Vosne-Romanée vineyards are in neighboring Flagey-Echézeaux. This village includes the Romanée-Conti vineyard.

RED Sleek, stylish, medium-bodied wines of the purest Pinot Noir character and with the silky texture so typical of the wines of this village.

🍇 Pinot Noir, Pinot Gris, Pinot Liébault

🍷 10–15 years

✓ *Robert Arnoux • Sylvain Cathiard • Bruno Clavelier • Engel • Confuron-Contédidot • Bernard Dugat-Py* (Vieilles Vignes) *• Forey Père & Fils • Jean Grivot • Anne Gros • Michel Gros • Méo-Camuzet • Mugneret-Gibourg • Perrot-Minot • Emmanuel Rouget • Fabrice Vigot*

VOSNE-ROMANÉE PREMIER CRU AOC

Premiers crus: Les Beaux Monts, Les Beaux Monts Bas*, Les Beaux Monts Hauts*, *Les Brûlées*, Les Chaumes, La Combe Brûlées, *La Croix Rameau*, Cros-Parantoux, Les Gaudichots, Les Hauts Beaux Monts, *Aux Malconsorts*, En Orveaux*, *Les Petits Monts*, Clos des Réas, *Aux Reignots*, *Les Rouges du Dessus* *, Les Suchots. *These *premier cru* vineyards of Vosne-Romanée are actually in Flagey-Echézeaux.

RED These are well-colored wines with fine aromatic qualities that are often reminiscent of violets and blackberries. They have a silky texture and a stylish flavor that is pure Pinot Noir. The best *premiers crus* to look out for are: Les Brûlées, Cros-Parantoux, Les Petits-Monts, Les Suchots, and Les Beaumonts (an umbrella name for the various Beaux Monts, high and low).

🍇 Pinot Noir, Pinot Gris, Pinot Liébault

🍷 10–20 years

✓ *de l'Arlot • Robert Arnoux • Albert Bichot* (Clos Frantin) *• Sylvain Cathiard • Confuron-Cotétidot • Engel • Jean Grivot • Alain Hudelot-Noëllat • S. Javouhey • Henri Jayer • Lamarche • Lucien Lemoine • Leroy* ❸ *• Vicomte Liger-Belair • Méo-Camuzet • Gérard Mugneret • Perrot-Minot • Nicolas Potel • Daniel Rion & Fils • Michelle & Patrice Rion • Emmanuel Rouget*

VOUGEOT AOC

The modest village wines of Vougeot are a relative rarity, this appellation covering less than 12 acres (5 hectares), which is less than one-tenth of the area encompassed by the Clos de Vougeot *grand cru* itself.

RED Little-seen, fine-flavored, well-balanced wines that are overpriced due to their scarcity. It is better to buy a *premier cru*.

🍇 Pinot Noir, Pinot Gris, Pinot Liébault

🍷 8–20 years

WHITE A rarity.

✓ *Bertagna • Mongeard-Mugneret*

VOUGEOT PREMIER CRU AOC

Premiers crus: Les Crâs, Clos de la Perrière, Les Petits Vougeots, La Vigne Blanche.

The *premiers crus* are located between Clos de Vougeot and Musigny and, from a *terroir* point of view, should produce much better wines.

RED Can be nicely colored, medium bodied, and have an attractive flavo°r with a good balance and a certain finesse.

🍇 Pinot Noir, Pinot Gris, Pinot Liébault

🍷 10–20 years

WHITE A clean, rich, and crisp wine of variable quality, called Clos Blanc de Vougeot, is produced by L'Héritier Guyot from the *premier cru* of La Vigne Blanche.

🍇 Chardonnay, Pinot Blanc

🍷 4–10 years

✓ *Bertagna* (Clos de la Perrière *monopole*) *• Lamarche • de la Vougeraie* ❸ (Clos du Prieuré *monopole*)

CÔTE DE BEAUNE AND HAUTES-CÔTES DE BEAUNE

Pinot Noir in the Côte de Beaune is renowned for its softness and finesse, characteristics that become more evident as one progresses south through the region, but with seven of Burgundy's eight white grands crus this is really Chardonnay country, and the wines produced are the richest, longest-lived, most complex, and stylish white wines in the world.

ENTERING THE CÔTE DE BEAUNE from the Nuits-St. Georges end, the most immediately visible viticultural differences are its more expansive look and the much greater contrast between the deep, dark, and so obviously rich soil found on the inferior eastern side of the RN 74 road and the scanty patches of pebble-strewn thick drift that cover the classic slopes west of the road.

CÔTE DE BEAUNE VINEYARDS
The slopes of the Côte de Beaune vineyards are generally a little gentler than those of the Côte de Nuits. In both areas, Pinot Noir and Chardonnay vines are planted, but it is here that Chardonnay is king.

LADOIX-SERRIGNY
Situated to the west of Aloxe-Corton, parts of Ladoix-Serrigny are encompassed by that village's appellations, including the grands crus of Corton and Corton-Charlemagne.

CÔTE DE BEAUNE AND HAUTES-CÔTES DE BEAUNE *See also p137*
The Côte d'Or is a hilly ridge that follows the trajectory of the Autoroute du Soleil. Most of the village and Hautes-Côtes appellations are clustered between Nuits-St.-Georges in the north and Chagny in the south.

Map legend:
- Communal appellations villages or towns
- Maranges
- Intensive vine-growing zone
- Hautes-Côtes de Beaune
- Côte de Beaune-Villages
- Blagny
- Communal appellation boundary
- ▲ Height above sea level (metres)

0   1   2   3 miles
0   2   4 km

BLAGNY PREMIER CRU AOC

Premiers crus: La Garenne (or Sur la Garenne), Hameau de Blagny (in Puligny-Montrachet), La Jeunelotte, La Pièce sous le Bois, Sous Blagny (in Meursault), Sous le Dos d'Ane, Sous le Puits.

RED These rich wines have even more grip and attack than basic Blagny.

🍇 Pinot Noir, Pinot Gris, Pinot Liébault

🍷 10–20 years

✓ *Robert Ampeau* • *François Jobard* • *Larue* (Sous le Puits) • *Leflaive* ⓑ • *Matrot*

BLAGNY-CÔTE DE BEAUNE AOC

Alternative appellation for Blagny. *See* Blagny AOC.

BOURGOGNE LA CHAPELLE NOTRE-DAME AOC

One of three Bourgogne *lieux-dits* created in 1993. La Chapelle Notre Dame is located in Serrigny, which is just east of Ladoix. Red, white, and rosé may be produced according to the same grapes and rules as for Bourgogne AOC (*see* p.133). P. Dubreuil-Fontaine has produced a wine from this *lieu-dit* for many years. It has always been decent, not special, but capable of improving in bottle. André and Jean-René Nudant also makes a light, fresh red from this appellation.

BOURGOGNE HAUTES-CÔTES DE BEAUNE AOC

This appellation is larger and more varied than Hautes-Côtes de Nuits. Half-red/half-rosé wines may be sold as Bourgogne Clairet Hautes-Côtes de Beaune AOC, but the style is outmoded and the appellation rarely encountered.

RED Ruby-colored, medium-bodied wines with a Pinot perfume and a creamy-fruit finish.

🍇 Pinot Noir, Pinot Gris, Pinot Liébault

🍷 4–10 years

WHITE Not very frequently encountered, but Guillemard-Dupont's pure Pinot Beurot (Pinot Gris) is rich, dry, and expressive. Its grape variety makes it a very pale white, red, or rosé according to the regulations!

🍇 Chardonnay, Pinot Blanc

🍷 1–4 years

ROSÉ Pleasantly dry and fruity wines with some richness and a soft finish.

🍇 Pinot Noir, Pinot Gris, Pinot Liébault

🍷 1–3 years

✓ *Contat-Grange* • *Jean Joliot & Fils* • *Didier Montchovet* • *Claude Nouveau* • *Naudin-Ferrand*

CHARLEMAGNE AOC
Grand Cru

This white-only *grand cru* of Aloxe-Corton overlaps Pernand-Vergelesses and is almost, but not quite, identical to the *grand cru* of Corton-Charlemagne.

CHASSAGNE-MONTRACHET AOC

These village wines have a lesser reputation than those of Puligny-Montrachet.

RED Firm, dry wines with more color and less softness than most Côte de Beaune reds.

🍇 Pinot Noir, Pinot Gris, Pinot Liébault

🍷 10–20 years

WHITE An affordable introduction to the great wines of Montrachet.

🍇 Chardonnay, Pinot Blanc

🍷 5–10 years

✓ *Bernard Colin & Fils* • *Fontaine-Gagnard* • *Jean-Noël Gagnard* • *Marquis de Laguiche* • *Bernard Morey* • *Jean-Marc Morey* • *Ramonet*

CHASSAGNE-MONTRACHET PREMIER CRU AOC

Premiers crus: Abbaye de Morgeot, Les Baudines, *Blanchot Dessus*, Les Boirettes, Bois de Chassagne, Les Bondues, La Boudriotte, Les Brussonnes, En Cailleret, La Cardeuse, Champ Jendreau, Les Champs Gain, La Chapelle, Clos Chareau, Les Chaumées, Les Chaumes, Les Chenevottes, Les Combards, Les Commes, Ez Crets, Ez Crottes, *Dent de Chien*, Les Embrazées, Les Fairendes, Francemont, La Grande Borne, La Grande Montagne, Les Grandes Ruchottes, Les Grands Clos, Guerchère, Les Macherelles, *La Maltroie*, Les Morgeots, Les Murées, Les Pasquelles, Petingeret, Les Petites Fairendes, Les Petits Clos, Clos Pitois, Les Places, Les Rebichets, En Remilly, La Romanée, La Roquemaure, Clos St.-Jean, Tête du Clos, Tonton Marcel, Les Vergers, *Vide Bourse*, Vigne Blanche, Vigne Derrière, En Virondot.

RED The wines of Chassagne-Montrachet have the weight of a Côte de Nuits and the softness of a Côte de Beaune.

🍇 Pinot Noir, Pinot Gris, Pinot Liébault

🍷 10–25 years

WHITE Flavorsome dry wines, but lacking the finesse of those in the neighboring appellation of Puligny.

🍇 Chardonnay, Pinot Blanc

🍷 6–15 years

✓ *Guy Amiot & Fils* • *Roger Belland* (Morgeot Clos Pitois *monopole*) • *Bernard Colin & Fils* • *Marc Colin* • *Vincent Dancer* • *Michel Colin-Deléger* (due to a split in this domaine, look out for Bruno Colin and Philippe Coil) • *Fontaine-Gagnard* • *Jean-Noël Gagnard* • *Gagnard-Delagrange* • *Vincent Girardin* • *Gabriel et Paul Jouard* • *Vincent et François Jouard* • *Louis Latour* • *Olivier Leflaive* • *Lucien Lemoine* • *Château de la Maltroye* • *Bernard Moreau & Fils* • *Marc Morey* • *Michel Niellon* • *Ramonet* • *Roux* • *Verget*

CHASSAGNE-MONTRACHET-CÔTE DE BEAUNE AOC

Alternative appellation for red wines only. *See* Chassagne Montrachet AOC.

CHEVALIER-MONTRACHET AOC
Grand Cru

This is one of Puligny-Montrachet's four *grands crus*.

WHITE Fatter and richer than Bienvenues-Bâtard-Montrachet, this wine has more explosive flavor than Bâtard-Montrachet.

🍇 Chardonnay

🍷 10–20 years

✓ *d'Auvenay* ⓑ • *Bouchard Père & Fils* • *Vincent Dancer* • *Georges Déléger* • *Vincent Girardin* • *Louis Jadot* • *Leflaive* ⓑ • *Marc Morey* • *Michel Niellon*

CHOREY-LÈS-BEAUNE AOC

This satellite appellation of Beaune produces exciting, underrated wines.

RED Although next to Aloxe-Corton, Chorey has all the soft and sensuous charms that are quintessentially Beaune.

🍇 Pinot Noir, Pinot Gris, Pinot Liébault

🍷 7–15 years

WHITE Less than one percent of the wines produced in this village are white.

✓ *Arnoux Père & Fils* • *Maillard Père & Fils* • *Maurice Martray* • *Tollot-Beaut*

CHOREY-LÈS-BEAUNE CÔTE DE BEAUNE AOC

Alternative appellation for red wines only. *See* Chorey-lès-Beaune AOC.

CORTON AOC
Grand Cru

This is one of the *grands crus* of Aloxe-Corton (it extends into Ladoix-Serrigny and Pernand-Vergelesses). Corton is the only *grand cru* in the Côte de Beaune that includes red and white wines and thus parallels the Côte de Nuits *grand cru* of Musigny. The following 20 *climats* may hyphenate their names (with or without the prefix) to the Corton appellation: Les Bressandes, Le Charlemagne, Les Chaumes, Les Chaumes et la Voierosse, Les Combes, Le Corton, Les Fiètres, Les Grèves, Les Languettes, Les Maréchaudes, Les Miex, Les Meix Lallemand, Les Paulands, Les Perrières, Les Pougets, Les Renardes, Le Rognet-Corton, Le Clos de Roi, Les Vergennes, La Vigne au Saint. So it is possible to get a red Corton-Charlemagne. Beware: Corton is one of the least dependable *grands crus* for quality. When it is great, it is wicked, but production is vast (38,850 to 42,180 cases/3,500 to 3,800 hectoliters per year)—more than twice the volume of the huge, overproducing Clos de Vougeot, and over one-quarter of all the red *grand cru* wine produced in both the Côte de Nuits and Côte de Beaune.

RED These wines may sometimes appear intense and broody in their youth, but, when fully mature, a great Corton has such finesse and complexity that it can stun the senses.

🍇 Pinot Noir, Pinot Gris, Pinot Liébault

🍷 12–30 years

WHITE A medium- to full-bodied wine with a fine, rich flavor.

🍇 Chardonnay

🍷 10–25 years

✓ *Arnoux Père & Fils* • *Bouchard Père & Fils* • *Chevalier Père & Fils* (Rognet) • *Vincent Girardin* • *Antonin Guyon* • *Louis Jadot* • *Leroy* ⓑ • *Bonneau du Martray* • *Faiveley* • *Michel Juillot* • *Prince Florent de Mérode* • *Jacques Prieur* • *Rapet Père & Fils* • *Comte Daniel Senard* • *Tollot-Beaut*

CORTON-CHARLEMAGNE AOC
Grand Cru

Domaine Michel Juillot

CORTON-CHARLEMAGNE
GRAND CRU
APPELLATION CONTRÔLÉE

2003

Michel et Laurent Juillot
Viticulteurs à Mercurey, Saône-et-Loire, France
Produit de France

13,5% vol.   75 cl

This famous *grand cru* of Aloxe-Corton extends into Ladoix-Serrigny and Pernand-Vergelesses. Although the best Corton-Charlmagne is incomparable, there is so much produced that consumers can pay a lot of money for relatively disappointing wine. At an average of 25,300 cases (2,280 hectoliters), the production of Corton-Charlemagne represent more than two out of every three bottles of all the *grand cru* white wines produced in both the Côte de Nuits and Côte de Beaune.

WHITE At its natural best, this is the most sumptuous of all white Burgundies. It has a fabulous concentration of rich, buttery fruit flavors, a dazzling balance of acidity, and delicious overtones of vanilla, honey, and cinnamon.

🍇 Chardonnay

🍷 5–25 years

✓ *Bertrand Ambroise • Bonneau du Martray • Bouchard Père & Fils • J.-F. Coche-Dury • Joseph Drouhin • Genot Boulanger • Vincent Girardin • Antonin Guyon • Louis Jadot • Patrick Javillier • Michel Juillot • Louis Latour • Olivier Leflaive • Lucien Lemoine • Jacques Prieur • Rapet Père & Fils • Remoissenet Père & Fils • Christophe Roumier*

CÔTE DE BEAUNE AOC

Wines that are entitled to the actual Côte de Beaune appellation are restricted to a few plots on the Montagne de Beaune above Beaune itself.

RED These are fine, stylish wines that reveal the purest of Pinot Noir fruit. They are produced in the soft Beaune style.

🍇 Pinot Noir, Pinot Gris, Pinot Liébault

🍷 10–20 years

WHITE Little-seen, dry basic Beaune.

🍇 Chardonnay, Pinot Blanc

🍷 3–8 years

✓ *Lycée Agricole & Viticole de Beaune*

CÔTE DE BEAUNE-VILLAGES AOC

While AOC Côte de Nuits-Villages covers red and white wines in a predominantly red-wine district, AOC Côte de Beaune-Villages applies only to red wines in a district that produces the greatest white Burgundies!

RED Excellent-value fruity wines, made in true soft Beaune style.

🍇 Pinot Noir, Pinot Gris, Pinot Liébault

🍷 7–15 years

✓ *Bernard Bachelet & Fils • Coron Père & Fils • Lequin Roussot*

CRIOTS-BÂTARD-MONTRACHET AOC
Grand Cru

The smallest of Chassagne-Montrachet's three *grands crus*.

WHITE This wine has some of the weight of its great neighbors and a lovely hint of honey-and-toast richness, but it is essentially the palest and most fragrant of all the Montrachets.

🍇 Pinot chardonnay (*sic*)

🍷 8–20 years

✓ *Joseph Belland • Blain-Gagnard • Vincent Girardin*

LADOIX AOC

Parts of Ladoix-Serrigny have the right to use the Aloxe-Corton Premier Cru appellation or the *grands crus* of Corton and Corton-Charlemagne. Ladoix AOC covers the rest of the wine produced in the area.

RED Many wines are rustic versions of Aloxe-Corton, but there are some fine grower wines that combine the compact fruit and structure of a Nuits with the softness of a Beaune.

🍇 Pinot Noir, Pinot Gris, Pinot Liébault

🍷 7–20 years

WHITE Just 5 percent of the production is white and it is not very well distributed.

🍇 Chardonnay, Pinot Blanc

🍷 4–8 years

✓ *Capitain-Gagnerot • Edmond Cornu & Fils • François Gay & Fils • Maurice Martray • Prince Florent de Mérode*

LADOIX PREMIER CRU AOC

Premiers crus: Basses Mourottes, Bois Roussot, Les Buis, Le Clou d'Orge, La Corvée, Les Gréchons, *Hautes Mourottes*, Les Joyeuses, La Micaude, En Naget, *Rognet et Corton*.

These *premiers cru* vineyards were expanded from 35 to 59 acres (14 to 24 hectares) in 2000.

RED These wines are decidedly finer in quality and deeper in color than those with the basic village appellation.

🍇 Pinot Noir, Pinot Gris, Pinot Liébault

🍷 7–20 years

WHITE Prince Florent de Mérode of de Serrigny makes the only white Ladoix Premier Cru I know: Ladoix Hautes Mourottes blanc.

✓ *Capitain-Gagnerot • Edmond Cornu & Fils • Prince Florent de Mérode • Naudin-Ferrand • André Nudant & Fils • G. & P. Ravaut*

LADOIX CÔTE DE BEAUNE AOC
See Ladoix AOC

Alternative appellation for red wines only.

MARANGES AOC

In 1989 Maranges AOC replaced three separate appellations: Cheilly-lès-Maranges AOC, Dézize-lès-Maranges AOC, and Sampigny-lès-Maranges AOC, a trio of villages sharing the once moderately famous *cru* of Marange, which is on a well-exposed hillside immediately southwest of Santenay. The red wines may also be sold as Côte de Beaune AOC or Côte de Beaune-Villages AOC. Production used to be erratic, with most of the wine (including much of that qualifying for *premier cru*) sold to *négociants* for blending into Côte de Beaune-Villages, but two or three dedicated growers are beginning to get the name around.

RED Wines with a very pure Pinot perfume, which are developing good color and body.

🍇 Pinot Noir, Pinot Gris, Pinot Liébault

🍷 2–7 years

WHITE Rarely produced in any of the three villages and never in Dézize-lès-Maranges, as far as I am aware, although it is allowed.

✓ *Fernand Chevrot • Contat-Grange • Jaffelin • René Martin • Edward Monnot • Claude Nouveau*

MARANGES CÔTE DE BEAUNE AOC

Alternative appellation for red wines only. *See* Maranges AOC.

MARANGES PREMIER CRU AOC

Premiers crus: Clos de la Boutière, La Croix aux Moines, La Fussière, Le Clos des Loyères, Le Clos des Rois, Les Clos Roussots.

Some of these *climats* officially designated as *premiers crus* are a bit of a puzzle. Clos de la Boutière, for example, was originally just plain old La Boutière, and Les Clos Roussots once adjoined a *premier cru* called Les Plantes de Marange, but was never classified as one itself. According to maps prior to the merging of the three appellations, Les Plantes de Marange, Maranges, and En Maranges were the authentic names of the most important vineyards in the area classified as *premier cru*, but they have since adopted less repetitive *lieux-dits*, and such revisionism is probably justified from a marketing aspect.

RED The best examples are well colored, with a good balance of fruit, often red fruits, and a richer, longer finish than those wines bearing the basic Maranges appellation.

🍇 Pinot Noir, Pinot Gris, Pinot Liébault

WHITE Rarely encountered.

🍇 Chardonnay, Pinot Blanc

✓ *Bernard Bachelet & Fils • Fernand Chevrot • Contat-Grangé • Edward Monnot • Claude Nouveau*

MEURSAULT AOC

While the greatest white Côte de Beaune is either Montrachet or Corton-Charlemagne, Meursault is probably better known and is certainly more popular

RED This is often treated as a novelty, but it is a fine wine in its own right, with a firm edge.

🍇 Pinot Noir, Pinot Gris, Pinot Liébault

🍷 8–20 years

WHITE Even the most basic Meursault should be deliciously dry with a nutty-buttery-spice quality added to its typically rich flavor.

🍇 Chardonnay, Pinot Blanc

🍷 5–12 years

✓ *Robert Ampeau • d'Auvenay* **B** *• Bouchard Père & Fils • Boyer-Martenot • Alain Coche-Bizouard • J.-F. Coche-Dury • Jean-Philippe Fichet • Henri Germain* (Limozin) *• Albert Grivault • Patrick Javillier • François Jobard • Rémy Jobard • Comte Lafon* **B** *• Michelot* (any Michelot, hyphenated or otherwise, with a Meursault address) *• François Mikulski • Pierre Morey* **B** *• Guy Roulot*

MEURSAULT PREMIER CRU AOC

SANTENAY-CÔTE DE BEAUNE AOC

Alternative appellation for red wines only. *See* Santenay AOC.

SAVIGNY AOC

See Savigny-lès- Beaune AOC

SAVIGNY PREMIER CRU AOC

See Savigny-lès-Beaune Premier Cru AOC

SAVIGNY-CÔTE DE BEAUNE AOC

Alternative appellation for red wine only. *See* Savigny-lès-Beaune AOC.

SAVIGNY-LÈS-BEAUNE AOC

This village has gifted winemakers producing very underrated and undervalued wines.

RED Delicious, easy-to-drink, medium-bodied wines that are very soft and Beaune-like in style.

🍇 Pinot Noir, Pinot Gris, Pinot Liébault

🍷 7–15 years

WHITE Some excellent dry wines with good concentration of flavor, a smooth texture and some finesse, but they are difficult to find.

🍇 Chardonnay, Pinot Blanc

🍷 4–10 years

✓ *Robert Ampeau • Simon Bize & Fils • Bouchard Père & Fils • Camus-Brochon • Philippe Delagrange* (white) • *Maurice Giboulot • Girard-Vollot • Pierre Guillemot • Lucien Jacob • Maréchal-Caillot • Parent • Jean-Marc Pavelot • du Prieuré • Rollin Père & Fils • Tollot-Beaut*

SAVIGNY-LÈS-BEAUNE PREMIER CRU AOC

Premiers crus: Aux Clous, Aux Fournaux, Aux Gravains, Aux Guettes, Aux Serpentières, Bas Marconnets, Basses Vergelesses, Clos la Bataillères (*or* Aux *or* Les Vergelesses), Champ Chevrey (*or* Aux Fournaux), Les Charnières, Hauts Jarrons, Les Hauts Marconnets, Les Jarrons (*or* La Dominode), Les Lavières, Les Narbantons, Petits Godeaux, Les Peuillets, Redrescut, Les Rouvrettes, Les Talmettes

RED These wines have a very elegant, soft, and stylish Pinot flavor that hints of strawberries, cherries, and violets. The best are: Les Lavières, La Dominode, Aux Vergelesses, Les Marconnets, and Aux Guettes.

🍇 Pinot Noir, Pinot Gris, Pinot Liébault

🍷 7–20 years

WHITE Domaine des Terregelesses produces a splendidly rich, dry Les Vergelesses.

🍇 Chardonnay, Pinot Blanc

🍷 5–15 years

✓ *Simon Bize & Fils • Bouchard Père & Fils • Camus-Brochon • Chandon de Briailles •*

Chanson Père & Fils • Bruno Clair • Maurice Ecard • François Gay & Fils • Machard de Gramont • A.-F. Gros (Clos des Guettes) *• Louis Jadot • Leroy* Ⓑ *• Albert Morot* (La Bataillère aux Vergelesses) *• Olivier Père & Fils* (Les Peuillets) *• Pavelot • des Terregelesses* (Les Vergelesses) *• Tollot-Beaut*

SAVIGNY-LÈS-BEAUNE-CÔTE DE BEAUNE AOC

Alternative appellation for red wines only. *See* Savigny-lès-Beaune AOC.

VOLNAY AOC

Volnay ranks in performance with such great *crus* as Gevrey-Chambertin and Chambolle-Musigny. It is the most southerly red-wine-only appellation in the Côte d'Or, and the only great wine village located above its vineyards.

RED These wines are not cheap, but they are firm and well colored with more silky finesse than should be expected from a village appellation.

🍇 Pinot Noir, Pinot Gris, Pinot Liébault

🍷 6–15 years

✓ *Marquis d'Angerville • Michel Lafarge • Régis Rossignol*

VOLNAY PREMIER CRU AOC

Premiers crus: Les Angles, Les Aussy, La Barre, Bousse d'Or (or Clos de la Bousse d'Or), Les Brouillards, En Cailleret, Les Caillerets, Cailleret Dessus (part of which may be called Clos des 60 Ouvrées), Carelles Dessous, Carelle sous la Chapelle, Clos de la Caves de Ducs, En Champans, Chanlin, En Chevret, Clos de la Chapelle, Clos des Chênes (or Clos des Chânes), Clos de Ducs, Clos du Château des Ducs, Frémiets (or Clos de la Rougeotte), La Gigotte, Les Grands Champs, Lassolle, Les Lurets, Les Mitans, En l'Ormeau, Pitures Dessus, Pointes d'Angles, Robardelle, Le Ronceret, Taille Pieds, En Verseuil (or Clos du Verseuil), Le Village.

RED No *grands crus*, but its silky-smooth and fragrant *premiers crus* are great wines, showing

tremendous finesse. The best are: Clos des Chêne, Taille Pieds, Bousse d'Or, Clos de Ducs, the various *climats* of Cailleret, Clos des 60 Ouvrées, and En Champans.

🍇 Pinot Noir, Pinot Gris, Pinot Liébault

🍷 8–20 years

✓ *Marquis d'Angerville • Jean-Marc Boillot • Jean-Marc Bouley* (Les Carelles) *• Antonin Guyon • Louis Jadot • Michel Lafarge • Comte Lafon* Ⓑ *• Olivier Leflaive • Leroy* Ⓑ *• Hubert de Montille • Nicolas Potel • de la Pousse d'Or • Régis Rossignol*

VOLNAY-SANTENOTS PREMIER CRU AOC

This confusing appellation is in Meursault, not Volnay, although it does run up to the boundary of that village. It dates back to the 19th century, when the Meursault *lieu-dit* of Les Santenots du Milieu became famous for its red wines. White wines cannot be called Volnay-Santenots and must be sold as Meursault or, if produced from the two-thirds of this vineyard farthest from the Volnay border, they may be sold as Meursault Premier Cru AOC or Meursault-Santenots. The right to the Volnay-Santenots appellation was accorded by Tribunal at Beaune in 1924.

RED These wines, which are not often found, are similar to Volnay with good color and weight, but can lack its silky elegance.

🍇 Pinot Noir, Pinot Gris, Pinot Liébault

🍷 8–20 years

✓ *Robert Ampeau • Comte Lafon* Ⓑ *• Leroy* Ⓑ *• Matrot • François Mikulski • Jacques Prieur • Prieur-Brunet*

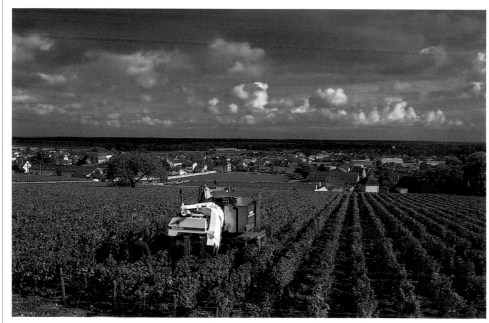

GRAND CRU VINEYARD CORTON CLOS DES VERGENNES
The tiny vineyard of Corton Clos des Vergennes is under single ownership and the wines are distributed by Moillard-Grivot.

THE CÔTE CHALONNAISE

This is a simple district in wine terms, with just five appellations, two exclusively white and three red or white. Despite the fact that many of the wines are little known, their quality in all appellations is very good, and the value for money is even better.

THE CÔTE CHALONNAISE, or Région de Mercurey, as it is sometimes called, was once the forgotten area of Burgundy, perceived as too serious for its own good. Because its flavorsome reds and buttery whites have more in common with the wines of the Côte de Beaune than elsewhere, merchants categorized them as inferior or pretentious. Perhaps the Côte Chalonnaise need not have been forgotten had merchants thought of it more as a superior Mâconnais than as an inferior Côte de Beaune. However, over the last 10 years, as merchants across the world have become more willing to seek out lesser-known wines, the area has built up a reputation as one of Burgundy's best sources of quality wines.

EXCELLENT NÉGOCIANTS

The Burgundy drinker is blessed with a fine choice of *négociants* in the Côte Chalonnaise, including Chandesais, Delorme, and Faiveley. There is a good *coopérative* at Buxy, and an increasing number of talented growers. This area produces fine Crémant de Bourgogne and, in Bouzeron, has the only single-village appellation of Aligoté wine.

THE CÔTE CHALONNAISE, *see also* p137
The vine-growing zones form three separate "islands" west of Chalon, between the Côte de Beaune to the north and the Mâconnais to the south.

FACTORS AFFECTING TASTE AND QUALITY

LOCATION
These three islands of vines are situated to the west of Châlon-sur-Saône, 217 miles (350 kilometers) southeast of Paris, between the Côte de Beaune in the north and the Mâconnais in the south.

CLIMATE
Slightly drier than that of the Côte d'Or, with many of the best slopes protected from the worst ravages of frost and hail.

ASPECT
This is a disjointed district in which the great plateau of the Côte d'Or peters out into a complex chain of small hills with vines clinging to the most favorable slopes, at an altitude of between 750 and 1,050 feet (230 to 320 meters), in a far more sporadic fashion than those in the Côte d'Or.

SOIL
Limestone subsoil with clay-sand topsoils that are sometimes enriched with iron deposits. At Mercurey there are limestone ooliths mixed with iron-enriched marl.

VITICULTURE AND VINIFICATION
The wines are produced in an identical way to those of the Côte de Beaune, with no exceptional viticultural or vinification techniques involved, *see* p152.

GRAPE VARIETIES
Primary varieties: Pinot Noir, Chardonnay
Secondary varieties: Pinot Gris (syn. Pinot Beurot), Pinot Liébault, Pinot Blanc, Aligoté, Melon de Bourgogne, Gamay

---

THE APPELLATIONS OF
THE CÔTE CHALONNAISE

BOURGOGNE CÔTE CHALONNAISE AOC

As from the 1990 vintage, basic Bourgogne made exclusively from grapes harvested in the region may bear this specific appellation.

RED A. & P. de Villaine's Digoine has outstanding fruit and finesse for such a modest appellation.

Only Michel Goubard's Mont-Avril comes close in richness, and can be truly excellent, but is not in the same class. Both are terrific value.

Pinot Noir, Pinot Liébault, Pinot Gris

1–3 years

WHITE Normally softer and fuller than a Mâcon, but not particularly rich in fruit, except for A. &

P. de Villaine's Clous, which is the best white wine in the appellation, and Venot's La Corvée, the number two.

Chardonnay, Pinot Blanc

Upon purchase

ROSÉ Seldom encountered and not special; no reason though why it should not be successful.

despite the smoothing effect of modern vinification techniques, these wines will always be of rustic quality with a characteristic hard edge. I well remember a blind tasting I once organized as editor of *The Sunday Telegraph Good Wine Guide*. All that the tasters knew was that the wines were produced from the Gamay grape and were thus most probably Beaujolais. British Master of Wine Christopher Tatham simply wrote "Limestone's the trouble!" about one wine. It turned out to be the only non-Beaujolais wine; it was Mâcon Rouge, which meant that limestone was indeed the problem. Such an accurate observation under blind conditions highlights how inappropriate the Gamay is in the Mâconnais.

It is possible to make a pure Pinot Noir Mâcon *rouge*, but because the market assumes that this appellation is pure Gamay, there is little incentive for producers to plant the more noble grape. It is, however, far more suitable and capable of producing wines of some finesse in the limestone vineyards of the Mâconnais. Perhaps it is time to introduce a Mâcon Rouge Pinot Noir appellation, or maybe producers should print the grape variety boldly on the label of the existing appellation?

BERZÉ-LE-CHÂTEL, SAÔNE-ET-LOIRE, MÂCONNAIS
The massive fortifications of Berzé-le-Châtel, the seat of the first feudal barony of Mâcon, boast 13 medieval towers.

THE APPELLATIONS OF
THE MÂCONNAIS

MÂCON AOC

Most wines from this district-wide appellation are produced in the area north of the Mâcon-Villages area.

RED Better vinification techniques have improved these essentially Gamay wines, but Gamay is still a grape that does not like limestone.

🍇 Gamay, Pinot Noir, Pinot Gris

🍷 2–6 years

WHITE These are basic-quality Chardonnay wines that are also fresh, frank, tasty, and dry; easy to drink and superb value. They may be sold as *primeur* or *nouveau* from the third Thursday of November following the harvest.

🍇 Chardonnay, Pinot Blanc

🍷 1–4 years

ROSÉ These lightweight wines have an attractive, pale raspberry color and light fruit flavor, and are more successful than their counterparts. They may be sold as *primeur* or *nouveau* from the third Thursday of November after the harvest.

🍇 Gamay, Pinot Noir, Pinot Gris

🍷 1–3 years

✓ *Bénas Frères* • *E. Brocard* (red) • *Desvignes* • *des Deux Roches* (Pierreclos red & Chavigne red) • *Maurice Gonon* (red) • *Guffens-Heynen* • *Jean Thévenet* • *Henri Lafarge* (Braye red) • *Saumaize-Michelin* (Les Bruyères red) • *Valette*

MÂCON SUPÉRIEUR AOC

All of France's so-called "*Supérieur*" appellations merely demand extra alcohol (usually one degree more than the basic appellation), which does not necessarily make a superior wine.

RED Aside from those listed, these well-colored, medium-bodied wines are nothing special.

🍇 Gamay, Pinot Noir, Pinot Gris

🍷 3–8 years

WHITE It is curious that almost a quarter of Mâcon Supérieur is white. The wines could just as easily sell as Mâcon AOC plain and simple. These wines may be sold as *primeur* or *nouveau* from the third Thursday of November following the harvest.

🍇 Chardonnay, Pinot Blanc

🍷 1–4 years

ROSÉ These are attractively colored wines with a fresh and tasty fruit flavor.

🍇 Gamay, Pinot Noir, Pinot Gris

🍷 1–2 years

✓ *Paul Beaudet* (Terres Rouges) • *Père Tienne* (Elevé en Fût)

MÂCON-SUPÉRIEUR (VILLAGE NAME) AOC

See Mâcon (village name) AOC

MÂCON-VILLAGES AOC

This white-only appellation covers 41 villages, 8 of which also fall within the Beaujolais-Villages appellation (*see* p.167); four of these have the additional right to the Saint-Véran AOC (*see* p.164). If the wine comes from a single village, it may replace the "Villages" part of this appellation with the name of that specific village (*see* the list below for details of all 41 villages).

WHITE These are some of the world's most delicious, thirst-quenching, easy-drinking, dry Chardonnay wines. They also represent tremendous value. These wines may be sold as *primeur* or *nouveau* commencing from the third Thursday of November following the harvest.

🍇 Chardonnay, Pinot Blanc

🍷 1–4 years

✓ **Mâcon-Villages** (*without a named village*) Gonon • *René Michel* (Vieilles Vignes)

THE 41 VILLAGES OF MÂCON-VILLAGES

The single-village version of Mâcon-Villages AOC covers the white wines from 41 villages (originally 43 villages, but Mâcon-Clessé and Mâcon-Viré were replaced by Viré-Clessé in 1999, *see* Viré-Clessé AOC):

MÂCON-AZÉ AOC

This village has a good *coopérative*, and its wines a reputation for fatness and consistency.

✓ *Cave d'Azé* (Cuvée Jules Ricard) • *Georges Blanc* (d'Azenay) • *des Grand Bruyères* • *Duvergey-Taboureau* (de la Garonne)

MÂCON-BERZÉ-LE-CHÂTEL AOC

The only wine I have tasted here has been Paul Beaudet's Château de Berzé.

MÂCON-BERZÉ-LE-VILLE AOC

I have not encountered these wines.

MÂCON-BISSY-LA-MÂCONNAISE AOC

Rijckaert's delicious wine is the only Mâcon-Bissy-La-Mâconnaise I have encountered.

✓ *Jean Rijckeart*

MÂCON-BURGY AOC

I have very rarely encountered these wines, but elegant examples from de Chervin demonstrate its potential.

✓ *de Chervin* • *Verget*

MÂCON-BUSIÈRES AOC

Rarely encountered.

✓ *du Terroir de Jocelyn*

MÂCON-CHAINTRE AOC

Chaintre is home to Georges Duboeuf's older brother, Roger. Since this village is one of five that form the appellation of Pouilly-Fuissé, its wines are entitled to two appellations.

✓ *Cave Coopérative de Chaintre* • *Roger Duboeuf* • *des Granges* • *Valette*

MÂCON-CHÂNES AOC

This village is also part of the Beaujolais-Villages and Saint-Véran areas, so its wines have a choice of three appellations.

✓ *de Lalande* (Les Serraudières)

MÂCON-LA CHAPELLE-DE-GUINCHAY AOC

This village is also part of the Beaujolais-Villages area and its wines therefore have the right to both appellations.

MÂCON-CHARDONNAY AOC

These wines have a certain following due in part, no doubt, to the novelty of their name. The *coopérative*, however, produces fine wines.

✓ *Cave de Lugny* (L'Originel)

MÂCON CHARNAY-LÈS-MÂCON AOC

Excellent wines produced east of Pouilly-Fuissé.

✓ *E. Chevalier & Fils • Jean Manciat • Manciat-Poncet • Didier Tripoz* (Clos des Tournons)

MÂCON-CHASSELAS AOC

Unfortunately, Chasselas is also the name of a table grape known for producing inferior wines, thus growers here usually sell their wines as basic Mâcon or as Saint-Véran. The only Mâcon-Chasselas I have come across was a decent, but not special red wine from Château de Chasselas.

MÂCON-CHEVAGNY-LÈS-CHEVRIÈRES AOC

Reasonable wines, but not easy to find.

✓ *Groupement de Producteurs de Prissé*

MÂCON-CLESSÉ AOC

This appellation lapsed as of 2002. *See* Viré-Clessé AOC.

MÂCON CRÊCHES-SUR-SAÔNE AOC

I have not encountered these wines.

MÂCON-CRUZILLE AOC

These are rare wines from a tiny hamlet in the extreme north of the *villages* appellation area.

✓ *Demessy* (Château de Messy) • *Guillot-Broux* 🅱

MÂCON DAVAYÉ AOC

Some excellent wines are made here, although they are usually sold as Saint-Véran AOC.

✓ *des Deux Roches • Lycée Viticole de Davayé*

MÂCON-FUISSÉ AOC

This village is one of five communes that form Pouilly-Fuissé AOC.

✓ *Cordier • de Fussiacus • Yves Giroux • Le Moulin du Pont • La Soufrandise • Jean-Paul Thibert*

MÂCON-GRÉVILLY AOC

A village with a good reputation, Mâcon-Grévilly is located in the extreme north of the *villages* appellation area.

✓ *Guillot-Broux* 🅱

MÂCON-HURIGNY AOC

I have not encountered these wines.

MÂCON-IGÉ AOC

The wines from this village are not very often seen, but have a good reputation.

✓ *Les Vignerons d'Igé*

MÂCON-LEYNES AOC

This village is also part of the Beaujolais-Villages and Saint-Véran AOCs and its wines therefore have a choice of all three appellations.

✓ *André Depardon*

MÂCON-LOCHÉ AOC

This village also has the right to the Pouilly-Loché and Pouilly-Vinzelles AOCs, and its wines therefore have a choice of all three appellations.

✓ *Caves des Grands Crus Blancs • Château de Loché*

MÂCON-LUGNY AOC

Louis Latour has done much to promote the wines of this village.

✓ *Louis Latour • Cave de Lugny • du Prieuré*

MÂCON-MILLY-LAMARTINE AOC

Dominique Lafon makes a delicious Milly-Lamartine, particularly from the Clos du Four.

✓ *Comte Lafon* 🅱

MÂCON-MONTBELLET AOC

Rarely encountered wines that develop well after a couple of years in bottle.

✓ *Henri Goyard* (de Roally) • *Jean Rijckaert* (En Pottes Vieilles Vignes)

MÂCON-PÉRONNE AOC

These wines seem to be fuller on the nose and stronger on the palate than those of most villages, but with less charm, although their producers say this is because they take longer than most Mâcon to "come around."

✓ *Maurice Josserand • de Lanques* (Les Berthelots) • *des Légères • Cave de Lugny • du Mortier • Daniel Rousset*

MÂCON-PIERRECLOS AOC

Guffens-Heynen is by far the best producer here.

✓ *Guffens-Heynen • Henri de Villamont*

MÂCON-PRISSÉ AOC

This village is also part of the Saint-Véran area and its wines therefore have a choice of two appellations.

✓ *Groupement de Producteurs de Prissé • de Thibert Père & Fils*

MÂCON-PRUZILLY AOC

This village is situated in the Beaujolais-Villages area and its wines therefore have a choice of two appellations.

MÂCON-LA ROCHE VINEUSE AOC

These underrated wines of Mâcon-La Roche Vineuse are produced on west- and south-facing slopes north of Pouilly-Fuissé, the potential of which is pushed to the very limits by Olivier Merlin, one of Mâcon's greatest winemakers.

✓ *Olivier Merlin • Groupement de Producteurs de Prissé • Verget*

MÂCON-ROMANÈCHE-THORINS AOC

The village of Mâcon-Romanèche-Thorins is also part of the Beaujolais-Villages area, so its wines have a choice of two appellations. Most of its production is red.

MÂCON-SOLOGNY AOC

The village of Mâcon-Sologny lies just north of Pouilly-Fuissé AOC and produces a fresh, crisp, herbaceous wine.

✓ *Ets Bertrand • Cave de Sologny*

MÂCON-SOLUTRÉ AOC

This village is one of the five communes of Pouilly-Fuissé and also forms part of the Saint-Véran area. Its wines therefore have a choice of three appellations.

✓ *André Depardon • Jean-Michel & Beatrice Drouhin • Chantal & Dominique Vaupré*

MÂCON-ST.-AMOUR-BELLEVUE AOC

Mâcon-St. Amour Bellevue is a village famous for its *cru* Beaujolais St.-Amour and also forms part of the Beaujolais-Villages and Saint-Véran areas. Some of its vineyards therefore have a choice of four appellations and this one is the least appealing.

MÂCON-ST. GENGOUX DE-SCISSÉ AOC

I have not encountered these wines.

MÂCON-ST.-SYMPHORIEN-D'ANCELLES AOC

As Mâcon-St.-Symphorien-d'Ancelles is also part of the Beaujolais-Villages area, its wines therefore have the advantage of a choice between two appellations.

MÂCON ST.-VÉRAND AOC

This village is in an area that is also part of the Beaujolais-Villages and the similarly spelled Saint Véran areas and its wines therefore have a choice of all three appellations.

MÂCON-UCHIZY AOC

More commonly seen than a few years ago, the wines from this village, which is adjacent to Chardonnay, are usually of a good, thirst-quenching quality.

✓ *Raphaël et Gard Sallet* (Clos des Ravières) • *Paul & Philebert Talmard*

MÂCON-VERGISSON AOC

This village of Mâcon-Vergisson is one of five communes that form the Pouilly-Fuissé AOC. Its wines are richer than most, and can be aged a few years in bottle.

✓ *Daniel Barraut • Michel Forest • Verget*

MÂCON-VERZÉ AOC

Rarely encountered.

✓ *du Clos Gandin*

MÂCON-VINZELLES AOC

This village also has the right to Pouilly-Vinzelles AOC and its wines therefore have a choice of two appellations.

✓ *Caves des Crus Blancs*

hasten to add that it is not harmful. The amount of antipathy, even in Burgundy, to this style of Gamay is revealed by Anthony Hanson, who, in his book *Burgundy*, quotes Jean-Marie Guffens as describing the fermentation method used in much Beaujolais as "carbonic masturbation."

The profit generated by Beaujolais Nouveau is considerable, but the wine itself should not be taken too seriously by anyone. No producer of Beaujolais Nouveau claims it is a fine wine. Such a claim would destroy the carefully marketed image of a young, unpretentious wine intended to be consumed in copious quantities. Beaujolais Nouveau should be fun and used to promote a greater awareness of wine *per se*, just as Liebfraumilch can attract new wine drinkers, although readers should be aware that these "lollipop" wines are not good-quality Gamay, whereas the best *crus* of Beaujolais are the world's greatest Gamay wines.

THE APPELLATIONS OF
THE BEAUJOLAIS

BEAUJOLAIS AOC

This generic Beaujolais appellation accounts for half the wine produced in the district and more than half of this is sold as Beaujolais "Primeur." The basic quality of these wines means that they cannot be bought from the great *négociants* of the Côte d'Or, although *cru* Beaujolais can be.

RED Due to their method of vinification, most of these wines have a "pear-drop" character to their fruitiness. The best also have a delightful freshness and frankness that beg for the wine to be consumed in large quantities.

🍇 Gamay, Pinot Noir, Pinot Gris

🍷— 1–3 years

WHITE Less than half of one percent of the production of this basic appellation consists of dry white wine, and the specialized producers of this usually make very fine wines. Pierre Charmet's Beaujolais *blanc* is aromatic and peachy.

🍇 Chardonnay, Aligoté

🍷— 1–3 years

ROSÉ Fresh, "pretty," and fruity.

🍇 Gamay, Pinot Noir, Pinot Gris

🍷— 1–3 years

✓ *Jean-Paul Brun* (Terres Dorées) • *Jean-Jacques Martin* (white) • *Cave Sain-Bel* (Les Bruyères) • *Cave Saint-Vérand* (Vieilles Vignes) • *Terres Morel* • *Vissoux* (Traditionnelle)

BEAUJOLAIS NOUVEAU AOC

See Beaujolais Primeur AOC

BEAUJOLAIS PRIMEUR AOC

More than half of all the Beaujolais produced is sold as *vin de primeur*, a wine made by intensive semicarbonic maceration methods that enable it to be consumed in export markets from the third Thursday of each November. "Beaujolais Nouveau" is synonymous with "Beaujolais Primeur" and the former is the name more often seen on export market labels, while the latter is more popular on the French market itself. Beaujolais Nouveau is supposed to be a fun wine, but the merrymaking wears a bit thin when it smells like nail polish and tastes of bubble gum. What else can you expect from something that was swinging from the vine just a few weeks before? "Lollipop" wine is how it is known in the trade. There is no such thing as good-quality Beaujolais Nouveau, and that is "official." While organizing tastings for the preparation of the 2005 revised edition of this book, the Union Interprofessionnelle des Vins du Beaujolais (UIVB) conveyed to me that it was eager to assist. One of the challenges I gave the UIVB was to show me, if such wines existed, a serious-quality Beaujolais Nouveau from a producer with a successful track record with this style, rather than the exception. Of all the wines the UIVB submitted for my

consideration, there was not one Beaujolais Nouveau or Primeur. It was not as if it were bad timing, as the UIVB had the 2003 vintage to choose from, and that was supposed one of the best vintages ever for *nouveau*. The only conclusion I can draw is that even the local authorities consider that there is no such thing as good-quality Beaujolais Nouveau. This regulations for this AOC should be totally overhauled, or it should be banned altogether. If the regulations are overhauled, then the one thing that must be tackled above everything else is the method of production. With today's technology, there are numerous ways to make a serious-quality red wine drinkable within weeks without inducing the pear-drop aroma of full-scale carbonic maceration. As one of several tools, carbonic maceration can have a positive effect, but its use has to be restricted to no more than 10 to 20 percent of the wine, so that the grape is allowed to express itself (many consumers unwittingly believe that pear drops are the varietal aroma of Gamay!). If the authorities and, ultimately, producers are not willing to take this on, then Beaujolais Nouveau will continue being a joke, and not a very funny one at that. For real Beaujolais and great Gamay, then readers must be prepared to pay for the wines recommended under any of the other appellations.

BEAUJOLAIS SUPÉRIEUR AOC

Only 1 percent of all Beaujolais wines carry this appellation. It is very rare to find a

Beaujolais Supérieur that is superior in anything other than strength to basic Beaujolais AOC, since this appellation merely indicates that the wines contain an extra 1 percent alcohol. Red and rosé Beaujolais Supérieur may be sold as *primeur* or *nouveau* from the third Thursday of November following the harvest.

RED By no means superior to Beaujolais AOC—buy basic Beaujolais for fun or *cru* Beaujolais for more serious drinking.

🍇 Gamay, Pinot Noir, Pinot Gris

🍷 3–8 years

WHITE Barely 5 percent of this tiny appellation produces white wine. Fine as it may be, it has no intrinsic superiority over the quaffing quality of basic Beaujolais *blanc*.

🍇 Chardonnay, Aligoté

🍷 1–3 years

ROSÉ I have not encountered any pink versions of this appellation.

✓ *Cave Beaujolais du Bois-d'Oingt* • *Cave Saint-Vérand*

BEAUJOLAIS-VILLAGES AOC

The 38 villages that may add their names to the Beaujolais AOC (*see* Beaujolais [village name] AOC) also have the right to this appellation and must use it if the wine is a blend of wines from two or more villages.

RED If you find a good example, these wines are well coloured with a rich Gamay flavor and should have all the superiority that Beaujolais Supérieur wines mysteriously lack.

🍇 Gamay, Pinot Noir, Pinot Gris

🍷 3–8 years

WHITE Very little encountered, but more Villages *blanc* is produced than Beaujolais *blanc*. These wines may be sold as *primeur* or *nouveau* from the third Thursday of November following the harvest.

🍇 Chardonnay, Aligoté

🍷 1–3 years

ROSÉ Seldom encountered, but the Cave Beaujolais du Bois-d'Oingt makes an attractive wine. These wines may be sold as *primeur* or *nouveau* from the third Thursday of November following the harvest.

🍇 Gamay, Pinot Noir, Pinot Gris

🍷 1–3 years

✓ *Accoeur* • *Philippe Deschamps* • *des Duc* • *Stephane Gardette* • *Jean-Claude Lapalu* (Vieilles Vignes) • *Manoir du Pavé* • *Sermezy* • *Michel Tête* (Clos du Fief)

BEAUJOLAIS (VILLAGE NAME) AOC

Of the 38 villages that may add their names to this appellation, very few do. One reason is that all or part of 15 of these villages (asterisked below) qualify for one of the superior *cru* Beaujolais appellations and it makes no sense to use a less famous name to market the wines. Another is that eight of the villages are entitled to the Mâcon-Villages AOC (marked "M") and four of these are also within the St.-Véran AOC (*see also* p.164), marked "S. V.," which overlaps with Mâconnais and Beaujolais; some of these villages, of course, produce more white wine than red. These village names are also underexploited because,

apart from a few that are famous (the best wines of which will claim *cru* Beaujolais status), the rest are either unknown or more suggestive of Mâcon than Beaujolais, thus it is easier to sell them as nothing more specific than Beaujolais-Villages. The wines may be sold as *primeur* or *nouveau* from the third Thursday of November following the harvest.

The following is a complete list of villages that may use the appellation: Arbuisonnas; Les Ardillats; Beaujeu; Blacé; Cercié*; Chânes (M., S.-V.); La Chapelle-de-Guinchay* (M.); Charentay; Chénas; Chiroubles*; Denicé; Durette; Emeringes*; Fleurie*; Jullié*; Juliénas*; Lancié; Lantignié; Leynes (M., S.-V.); Marchampt; Montmelas; Odenas; Le Perréon; Pruzilly* (M.); Quincié*; Régnié*; Rivolet; Romanèche-Thorins* (M) St-Amour-Bellevue* (M., S.-V.); St.-Étienne-des-Ouillères; St.-Étienne-la Varenne*; St.-Julien; St.-Lager; St.-Symphorien-d'Ancelles (M.); St.-Vérand (M., S.-V.); Salles; Vaux; Vauxrenard; Villié-Morgon*

RED When you find good examples, they should be richly flavored Gamay wines that are similar in quality to nonspecific Beaujolais-Villages, but with more personality.

🍇 Gamay, Pinot Noir, Pinot Gris

🍷 3–8 years

WHITE I have rarely encountered these wines.

🍇 Chardonnay, Aligoté

🍷 1–3 years

ROSÉ Rarely encountered, and uninspiring when they are.

🍇 Gamay, Pinot Noir, Pinot Gris

🍷 1–3 years

BROUILLY AOC
Cru Beaujolais

The largest and most southerly of the 10 *cru* villages, this is the only one, with Côte de Brouilly, to permit grapes other than Gamay.

RED Most Brouilly are serious wines, even if they do not rank among the best *cru* Beaujolais. They are not quite as intense as Côte de Brouilly wines, but they are full, fruity, and supple, if a little earthy. They should be rich and can be quite tannic.

🍇 Gamay, Chardonnay, Aligoté, Melon de Bourgogne

🍷 2–7 years (4–12 years for *vin de garde* styles produced in the very best vintages)

✓ *de la Chanaise* (Château du Prieuré) • *Daniel Guillet* • *Jean-Claude Lapalu* (Vieilles Vignes) • *Joseph Pellerin* • *Château Thivin*

CHÉNAS AOC
Cru Beaujolais

The smallest of the *cru* Beaujolais, situated on the slopes above Moulin-à-Vent. These slopes used to be occupied by oak trees, and so its

name derives from *chêne*, the French for oak.

RED Although most Chénas cannot match the power of the wines from neighbouring Moulin-à-Vent, they are nevertheless in the full and generous mold, and wines made by gifted growers such as Jean Benon and Champagnon are seductively rich and powerful, the former oaked, the latter not.

🍇 Gamay

🍷 3–8 years (5–15 years for *vin de garde* styles produced in the very best vintages)

✓ *Jean Benon* (especially Vieillis en Fût de Chêne) • *Champagnon* • *des Duc* (Chante Grilles) • *Hubert Lapierre* (Vieilles Vignes)

CHIROUBLES AOC
Cru Beaujolais

Situated high in the hills above the Beaujolais plain, the terrace of Chiroubles produces the most fragrant of all the *cru* Beaujolais.

RED These light-bodied wines have a perfumed bouquet and a deliciously delicate, crushed grape flavor. They are charming to drink when young, but exceptional examples can improve with age.

🍇 Gamay

🍷 1–8 years (5–15 years for *vin de garde* styles produced in the very best vintages)

✓ *Alain Passot* • *Bernard Méirat* • *Céline & Gilles Méziat* (Petit Puits) • *Maison des Vignerons de Chiroubles* (Cuvée Vidame de Rocsain) • *Château de Raousset*

CÔTE DE BROUILLY AOC
Cru Beaujolais

If there were such things as *grands crus* in Beaujolais, Côte de Brouilly would undoubtedly be classified as the *grand cru* of Brouilly (the vineyards of which practically surround those of this appellation).

RED A fine Côte de Brouilly is full, rich, and flavorsome. Its fruit should be vivid and intense, with none of the earthiness that may be found in a Brouilly.

🍇 Gamay, Pinot Noir, Pinot Gris

🍷 3–8 years (5–15 years for *vin de garde* styles produced in the very best vintages)

✓ *Jean-Paul Brun* (Terres Dorées) • *Georges Duboeuf* • *Franchet* • *Griffon* • *Château Thivin* (especially Cuvée Zacharie) • *Bernadette et Gilles Vincent*

COTEAUX DU LYONNAIS AOC

This is not part of the true Beaujolais district, but it falls within its sphere of influence and certainly utilizes classic Beaujolais grapes. In May 1984, this wine was upgraded from VDQS to full AOC status.

RED Light-bodied wines with fresh Gamay fruit and a soft balance. These wines may be sold as *primeur* or *nouveau* from the third Thursday of November following the harvest.

exciting. Perhaps they just need more time on yeast? They are worth keeping an eye on, even if I cannot give them *carte blanche* approval below. And Feuillatte's newfound quality has continued into the 1997 vintage, so it is good to know that the surge in quality was not a flash in the pan due more to vintage than intrinsic improvements.

✓ *Cuvée Speciale* (**V**) • *Palmes d'Or* (**V**) • *Palmes d'Or Rosé* (**V**)

FLEURY
43 Grande rue
10250 Courteron
ⓑ★ⓥ

One of the more readily available biodynamic Champagnes on export markets, Fleury was nothing more than acceptable until the 1996 vintage, when this grower produced a classic *barrique*-fermented Champagne with a mind-blowing barrage of aromas and flavors.

✓ *Fleur de l'Europe Brut* (**NV**) • *Brut* (**V**)

GARDET & CIE
13 rue Georges Legros
51500 Chigny-les-Roses
★ⓥ

This Champagne used to be sold as Georges Gardet in the UK and Charles Gardet in France, but the emphasis is now on Gardet plain and simple. Gardet has always prided itself on the longevity of its wines, but I prefer the vintage almost before it is even released, although the greatest Gardet I have ever tasted was the 1964 in 1995. A very welcome addition to the range is the succulent new *blanc de blancs*, the first vintage of which was 1990.

✓ *Brut Spécial* (**NV**) • *Brut* (**V**) • *Blanc de Blancs* (**V**)

RENÉ GEOFFROY
150 rue du Bois-des-Jots
51480 Cumières
★ⓥ

The Geoffroy family has been growers in Cumières since 1600 and conscientiously harvests grapes in *tries*. The Champagne, which does not go through malolactic fermentation and may be matured in oak *foudres*, is classic, long-lived, and capable of great complexity.

✓ *Cuvée Prestige* (**NV**) • *Cuvée de Réserve Brut* (**NV**) • *Cuvée Sélectionnée Brut* (**V**) • *Brut Rosé* (**NV**)

PIERRE GIMONNET
1 rue de la République
51530 Cuis
★★ⓥ

This excellent grower's vineyards are all planted with Chardonnay, hence every wine is a *blanc de blancs*, which is a very rare phenomenon, even among growers on the Côte des Blancs. Quality is exceptionally high and prices very reasonable.

✓ *Entire range*

PAUL GOERG
4 Place du Mont Chenil
51130 Vertus
★ⓥ

This small but superior *coopérative* produces very fine and elegant yet rich, concentrated Champagnes.

✓ *Blanc de Blancs* (**NV**) • *Brut* (**V**) • *Cuvée Lady C* (**V**)

GOSSET (GM)
69 rue Jules Blondeau
51160 Aÿ-Champagne
★★★ⓥ

Established in 1584, Gosset is the oldest house in the region, but for still wines, not sparkling. In 1992, Gosset became the first new *grande marque* for more than 30 years, then in 1994, after 400 years of family ownership, the house was sold to the Cointreau family, and is under the direct control of Béatrice Cointreau. The *chef de caves* and oenologist remain the same, as do the winemaking techniques. I have always rated the Grande Réserve, the Grand Millésimé, and the Grand Millésimé Rosé as three of the consistently greatest Champagnes available, and they have since been accompanied by the prestige vintage *brut* and rosé under the Celebris label.

✓ *Entire range* (except Brut Excellence)

HENRI GOUTORBE
11 rue Jeanson
51160 Aÿ-Champagne
★★ⓥ

With 37 acres (15 hectares) of vineyards and half a million bottles in stock, this is one of the larger wine growers. Henri Goutorbe produces some rich, classic, and well-structured Champagnes that become very satisfying with age.

✓ *Entire range*

GRAND CHAMPAGNE NAPOLEON
2 rue de Villiers-aux-Bois
51130 Vertus
★

This small, low-profile quality-conscious house is run by Etienne Prieur, whose brother Vincent makes the wines in one of the tiniest Champagne cellars I've seen. The Carte Or is richer and more mature than the Carte Vert, with some biscuity complexity.

✓ *Carte Or* (**NV**)

ALFRED GRATIEN
30 rue Maurice-Cerveaux
51201 Epernay
★★ⓥ

This house is part of Gratien, Meyer, Seydoux & Cie, who also sell a range of Loire traditional method wines under the Gratien & Meyer brand. Alfred Gratien is one of the most traditionally produced Champagnes available. The old vintages never fail to amaze, as they

are brilliant in quality and retain a remarkable freshness for decades. The nonvintage wine is beautifully fresh with mature reserves coming through on the palate, making it a wine to drink now, yet one that will improve with age.

✓ *Vintage Brut*

CHARLES HEIDSIECK (GM)
12 allée du Vignoble
51061 Reims
★★ⓥ

Charles Heidsieck is part of Rémy-Cointreau's Champagne group, which also includes Piper-Heidsieck. The superb quality of the house of Charles Heidsieck was guided by the masterly hand of Daniel Thibault until his untimely demise in 2002. As his creation of Mis en Cave demonstrated, Thibault was one of Champagne's greatest winemakers. Mis en Cave is still the best-value, most consistent Champagne in the richly flavored style, regularly achieving a standard few vintage Champagnes can match. Thibault will be a hard act to follow, but for a few years he had been grooming Régis Camus, the former *chef de caves* at Jacquart, to do just that. Due to the long lead time required before a Champagne reaches the shelf, it will not be until the year following publication of this edition of the encyclopedia that we will begin to know whether he is succeeding. This Champagne is rated on the hope that he is.

✓ *Entire range*

HENRIOT
3 place des Droits-de-l'Homme
51100 Reims
★

Under family ownership since 1994, when Joseph Henriot left Clicquot, the house he had famously performed a reverse-takeover on prior to the formation of LVMH. Henriot's son, Stanislaus, is now in day-to-day control, while Odilon de Varenne has moved from Deutz to take over as *chef de caves*. Aside from the fact that the Enchanteleurs is more often than not released far too late, there is not much to criticize here.

✓ *Cuvée des Enchanteleurs* (**V**) • *Brut Millésime* (**V**) • *Blanc de Blancs Brut* (**NV**)

JACQUART
5 rue Gosset
51066 Reims
★★ⓥ

This CRVC (Coopérative Régionale des Vins de Champagne) *coopérative* cleverly converted its primary brand into a *négociant-manipulant* Champagne by making its members shareholders. The quality of Jacquart is always acceptable at the very least, and some vintages, such as the 1985, can be outstanding, while the 1987 turned out to be one of the four best wines of that year.

✓ *Cuvée Mosaïque Brut* (**V**) • *Cuvée Mosaïque Blanc de Blancs* (**V**) • *Cuvée Mosaïque Rosé* (**V**) • *Brut de Nominée* (**NV**) • *Cuvée Onctueuse Rosé* (**NV**)

JACQUESSON & FILS
68 rue du Colonel Fabien
51310 Dizy
★★★☆

This small, family-owned house is run by the Chiquet brothers, two of the most charming people you are likely to meet. Michael McKenzie of Mayfair Cellars is a shareholder. Jacquesson makes utterly sublime Champagnes, on the same quality level as Billecart-Salmon, but in a bigger, fuller style. Both houses make Champagnes of complexity and finesse, but Jacquesson has more complexity, while Billecart-Salmon has more finesse. Jacquesson has pioneered various quality-enhancing practices in the vineyards, while in the winery it has turned Champagne's traditional nonvintage concept on its head by not attempting any consistency in style. Rather than smooth out the differences presented by each harvest, the new concept is to produce the best possible nonvintage Champagne each year. It is something that no large *grande marque* would dare contemplate, but it is a very clever move for a small house, as it effectively creates a second vintage wine and one that is easier to make, given the flexibility of blending in wine from other years. The first new nonvintage was named Cuvée No. 728 and was 2000-based, Cuvée No. 729 is 2001-based, and so on. Another innovation is a whole raft of single-vineyard Champagnes, the best of which will take several vintages to discern, although the 1998 Le Clos de Jacquesson, a pure Pinot Meunier Champagne, has been the most exciting so far. And the 2003 Oiry Champ Braux *vin clair* was so delicious that I ordered a case bottled as a still wine!

✓ *Entire range*

ANDRÉ JARRY
Rue Principale
51260 Bethon
★ⓥ

Excellent Champagne in a style that is midway between the classic character of Champagnes from the Marne *département* and the exotic character of Sézannais Champagnes, full of biscuity richness yet with an aftertaste of vanilla and peaches.

✓ *Cuvée Special* (**NV**)

KRUG & CO. (GM)
5 rue Coquebert
51051 Reims
★★★

Krug puts quality first and makes Champagne in its own individual style, regardless of popular taste or production costs. With the possible exception of Salon, this sort of quality is not equalled by any other

Champagne house, although it could be if they were willing to sell tiny quantities at very high prices. If everyone did this, it would be a disaster—Champagne has to be affordable—but that at least one house does is not just laudable, it is very important for Champagne.

✓ *Entire range*

LANSON INTERNATIONAL
22 rue Maurice-Cerveaux
51205 Epernay
★ **V**

One of the region's largest producers, yet Lanson International (formerly Marne et Champagne) has been relatively unknown because its wines are sold under some 200 low-key labels. Its presence has been more noticeable, however, since its acquisition of Lanson and Besserat de Bellefon. Quality, even under the most obscure label or buyers'-own-brands, can be very good, particularly if cellared for an additional 12 months, but the best-quality Champagnes are to be found under the Alfred Rothschild (restricted to the French market), Pol Gessner, Eugène Cliquot, Geismann & Co., and Gauthier labels. Other top-selling brands include Pol Albert, Bourgeois, Baron de Brou, De Bracieux, Colligny Père & Fils, Delacoste & Fils, Laurence Duvivier, Leprince-Royer, Georges Martel, Mary Marthi, Veuve Pasquier & Fils, Roger Perreau, Roger Perrov, Marquis de Prevel, and Veuve Guérin.

LANSON PÈRE & FILS (GM)
12 boulevard Lundy
51056 Reims
★★ **V**

This house was purchased in 1991 by Marne et Champagne (now Lanson International), a low-profile firm specializing in *sous marque* and own-label Champagnes. Lanson famously eschewed malolactic, excelling at classic, slow-maturing, biscuity vintage Champagnes, but the deal did not include the vineyards that this *grande marque* had relied upon, so the jury was out for a while. Even when Lanson had vineyards, the vintages were sometimes ordinary at best when released, but devotees got to know a good vintage when they saw one (some stunning old vintages *en magnum* are still commercially available: 1989, 1988, 1981, 1979, 1976). When the 1993 was first released, it was a creditable wine, but not special, and this was put down to the good, but not exceptional, year. However, it attained much more gravitas with an additional 12 months on yeast, and today the magnums with 4 years postdisgorgement aging are unbelievably classic in quality. The 1995 was obviously excellent from the start, but the 1996 is singularly special—the greatest value, classic quality Champagne of that very particular year. Lanson is back!

✓ *Entire range*

GUY LARMANDIER
30 rue du Général Koenig
51130 Vertus
★

Guy and François Larmandier have a well-earned reputation for finely balanced wines of surprising depth and obvious finesse.

✓ *Blanc de Blancs Cramant* (**NV**)

LARMANDIER-BERNIER
43 rue du 28 août
51130 Vertus
★

These high-quality *blanc de blancs* Champagnes are made by Pierre Larmandier, the president of the Young Winegrowers of Champagne.

✓ *Entire range*

LAURENT-PERRIER (GM)
Avenue de Champagne
51150 Tours-sur-Marne
★★ **V**

This house used to head a sprawling vinous empire until its outposts in Burgundy and Bordeaux were sold off to concentrate Laurent-Perrier's efforts and finances on its Champagne holdings, including De Castellane, Delamotte, Lemoine, and Salon, and in 2003 it took over Château Malakoff (Champagnes Beaumet, Jeanmaire, and Oudinot, plus the Michelin-starred La Briqueterie in Vinay). Michel Fauconnet took over as *chef de caves* in early 2004.

✓ *Entire range* (except Ultra Brut)

LECLERC BRIANT
67 rue de la Chaude-Ruelle
51204 Epernay
B V

Pascal Leclerc can come up with the odd Champagne to dumbfound people, such as his blood-red Rubis Rosé des Noirs, which excels in some vintages. When he does, they represent excellent value for money, but there could be more consistency here. His Les Authentiques range of single-vineyard Champagnes was a brilliant marketing concept, but the wines, while enjoyable enough when launched, have failed to display any consistent and distinctive *terroir* character. A *cuvée* called Divine is the best of the range, despite its gaudy label.

✓ *Divine* (**PC**)

LILBERT FILS
223 rue du Moutier
51200 Cramant

This house is a consistent producer of firm *blancs de blancs* that show finesse and age gracefully.

✓ *Entire range*

MAILLY GRAND CRU
28 rue de la Liberation
51500 Mailly-Champagne
★★☆ **V**

I have never been so impressed by this mono-*cru* cooperative than I

am now. The quality and innovation has been on a roll for a few years.

✓ *Cassiopée* (**NV**) • *Brut Millésime* (**V**) • *Cuvée des Echansons* (**V**) • *Cuvée l'Intemporelle* (**V**) • *Cuvée du 60e Anniversaire* (**V**)

HENRI MANDOIS
66 rue du Gal-de-Gaulle
51200 Pierry
★★☆ **V**

The house style of Henri Mandois is for elegant Champagnes that have a very satisfying length of attractive, creamy fruit, and a fine balance. Most *cuvées* peak at between five and six years of age and do not attain great complexity. However, they do represent great value and give much satisfaction. Jimmy Boyle's favorite Champagne!

✓ *Entire range*

SERGE MATHIEU
Les Riceys
10340 Avirey-Lingey
★★ **V**

Mathieu, a small grower in the Aube, consistently produces excellent Champagnes that are beautifully focused, have much finesse, and a real richness of fruit for such light and elegantly balanced wines.

✓ *Entire range*

MERCIER (GM)
75 avenue de Champagne
51200 Epernay
V

Mercier, established by Eugène Mercier in 1858, was the original owner of the Dom Pérignon brand, although it never utilized it and, in a strange twist of fate, sold it to Moët & Chandon in 1930. Moët liked the product so much that it bought Mercier, albeit some 40 years later. Mercier is still the best-selling brand in France, no matter how hard the parent company tries to make Moët number one, although Moët is way ahead in global sales. There are rumors that LVMH wants shot of Mercier like it did Canard-Duchêne (the reasoning being that it would increase the vineyards-to-sales ratio, the average price of LVMH brands, and gross profit percentage), and it would not surprise me if this house were to be snapped up by Lanson International.

✓ *Brut* (**V**)

DE MERIC
17 rue Gambetta
51160 Aÿ-Champagne
★ **V**

De Meric, whose wines are made by Christian Besserat, ranges from the simple but elegant and fruity nonvintage Brut to the sublime and very special Cuvée Catherine de Medicis, with various fine and fragrant *cuvées* in between.

✓ *Blanc de Blancs* (**NV**) • *Rosé* (**NV**) • *Cuvée Catherine de Medicis* (**PC**)

LE MESNIL
Union des Propriétaires Récoltants
51390 Le Mesnil-sur-Oger
V

If only all the Champagnes produced by this cooperative were as stunning as those recommended below.

✓ *Vigne Sélectionnée Blanc de Blancs* (**V**) • *Réserve Sélection, Blanc de Blancs* (**V**) • *Sublime* (**V**)

MOËT & CHANDON (GM)
20 avenue de Champagne
54120 Epernay
★★☆

The largest Champagne house by a mile, Moët is also the leading company in the LVMH group, which also includes Mercier, Krug, Ruinart, Pommery, and Veuve Clicquot. When first released, the soft style of Brut Impérial makes it amenable to everyone and offensive to no one, but after a further 12 months bottle-age, it mellows into a much fuller, toasty-rich Champagne that has won many a competitive tasting. Between the unfairly criticized nonvintage and the universally praised Dom Pérignon, the vintage Brut Impérial and Brut Impérial Rosé have both been ignored and underrated. With sales of Dom Pérignon approaching two million bottles, and a group ethos that is pushing the premium *cuvée* envelope (by cutting out lower-priced brands, increasing the vineyard-to-sales ratio, and introducing innovative, premium-priced *cuvées*), the obvious move would be to add another 247 acres (100 hectares) to the 494 (200 hectares) currently reserved for this most famous of Champagnes, invest in a showcase winery exclusively devoted to Dom Pérignon, and develop a range of wines under this label, which is already perceived as a brand in its own right.

✓ *Brut Impérial* (**V**) • *Dom Pérignon* (**PC**) • *Dom Pérignon Rosé* (**PC**)

MONCUIT
11 rue Persault-Maheu
51190 Le Mesnil-sur-Oger
★ **V**

Some years (or disgorgements of apparently the same wine) can have overly dominant buttery-malo aromas, while others are fresh and crisp, with lively rich fruit that is tasty and satisfying. Usually matures into a creamy-biscuity style.

✓ *Cuvée Nicole Moncuit Vieille Vigne* (**V**)

G. H. MUMM & CO. (GM)
29 & 34 rue du Champ-de-Mars
51053 Reims
★

Now owned by the Anglo-Spanish Allied-Domecq group, Mumm has successfully pulled its act together under the direction of Jean-Marie Barellière, whose masterstroke was to put a young winemaker by the name of Dominique Demarville in charge of a large *grande marque* house in 1998, after trying him out for three years. Demarville was so successful, so quickly and so efficiently, that Barellière promoted him to Wines and Vines Director for both Mumm and Perrier-Jouet. Demarville continues to improve the quality, returning Mumm to its authentic house-style freshness, light balance, fragrance, and elegance, although he knows he still has a way to go before he can be satisfied.

✓ *Brut Rosé* (**NV**) • *Demi-Sec* (**NV**) • *Mumm de Cramant* (**NV**) • *Cordon Rouge* (**V**)

BRUNO PAILLARD
avenue du Champagne
51100 Reims
★★✰ Ⓥ

Bruno Paillard is Champagne's fastest-rising star. He opts for elegance rather than body or character, and his Première Cuvée is not just elegant, it is one of the most consistent nonvintage Champagnes on the market. This house belongs personally to Bruno Paillard and is not part of the BCC group, which he heads. Look out for the excellent new vintaged *blanc de blancs*.

✓ *Entire range*

PALMER & CO.
67 rue Jacquart
51100 Reims
★★ Ⓥ

Palmer is generally acknowledged to be one of the highest-quality and most reliable *coopératives* in Champagne, on top of which it has a growing reputation for the excellent Champagnes sold under its own label and is particularly well known for its mature vintages.

✓ *Entire range*

PANNIER
23 rue Roger Catillon
02400 Château-Thierry
★✰ Ⓥ

For some time now this coopérative has been able to produce some very good vintage Champagne, especially its prestige *cuvée* Egérie de Pannier, but the basic Brut Tradition was always forthright. This changed with the 1990-based Brut Tradition. Although this was and still is Pannier's best *cuvée*, due no doubt to the year in question, it also marked a general increase in finesse and this promises better quality ahead.

✓ *Brut Tradition* (**NV**) • *Brut Vintage* (**V**) • *Egérie de Pannier* (**V**)

JOSEPH PERRIER (GM)
69 avenue de Paris
51005 Châlons-sur-Marne
★ Ⓥ

This house is still run by Jean-Claude Fourmon, even though he has sold a 51 percent share in the business to his cousin Alain Thienot via an ephemeral interest by Laurent-Perrier. The style of these Champagnes is rich and mellow, although the difference when switching from one *cuvée* or vintage to the next can be quite severe, and the wines need to be laid down for 12 months or so.

✓ *Cuvée Royale* (**NV**) • *Cuvée Royale Rosé* (**NV**) • *Cuvée Royale Blanc de Blancs* (**NV**) • *Cuvée Royale* (**V**) • *Cuvée Joséphine* (**PC**)

PERRIER-JOUET (GM)
26/28 avenue de Champagne
51200 Epernay
★★✰

Now owned by Allied-Domecq, along with its sister house Mumm. The straight vintage here has always been one of Champagne's longest-lived, and this standard has been maintained by the current *chef de caves*, Hervé Deschamps.

✓ *Grand Brut* (**V**) • *Belle Époque Brut* (**PC**) • *Belle Époque Rosé* (**PC**) • *Belle Époque Blanc de Blancs* (**PC**)

PHILIPPONNAT
13 rue du Pont
51160 Mareuil-sur-Aÿ
★★✰

Part of the BCC group, under the day-to-day control of Charles Philipponnat, a direct descendant and a sharp player in the grape-buying business. Philipponnat has built new facilities, with space for up to 500 barrels. Clos des Goisses is already 35 to 45 percent wood and will stay that way; vintages are 15 to 20 percent wood and will increase to about 30 to 35 percent; nonvintage is 5 to 10 percent and will increase to 20 to 25 percent. Clos des Goisses remains Philipponnat's jewel in the crown—one of the greatest Champagnes available, Clos des Goisses is a fully south-facing vineyard on a very steep incline overlooking the Marne canal.

✓ *Grand Blanc* (**V**) • *Clos des Goisses* (**PC**) • *Abel Lepitre* (Cuvée No. 134, Brut Millésime)

PIPER-HEIDSIECK (GM)
51 boulevard Henri Vasnier
51100 Reims
★★✰ Ⓥ

After working his miracles on Charles Heidsieck, the late Daniel Thibault upgraded the quality of Piper-Heidsieck without upsetting the supremacy of its sister brand. He achieved this by pouring more fruit into the blend and sourcing much of it from the warm Aube vineyards, giving the wine a soft but simple, fruity aroma, and very tempting fruit on the palate. New *chef de caves* Régis Camus launched a quartet of delicious new *cuvées* in 2004, the same year that the 1996 vintage (made by Thibault) scooped the Champagne Trophy at the first Decanter World Wine Awards.

✓ *Rosé Sauvage* (**NV**) • *Divin Blanc de Blancs* (**NV**) • *Brut Millésimé* (**V**) • *Cuvée Rare* (**PC**) • *Sublime* (**NV**)

PLOYEZ-JACQUEMART
51500 Ludes
★ Ⓥ

Although the prestige *cuvée* L. d'Harbonville has always been excellent, it has jumped up a class since the 1989 vintage, when it was first fermented in small oak barrels and not put through its malolactic fermentation. This made it even more succulent and mouthwatering than usual, with ample *dosage* to balance its electrifying acidity.

✓ *Entire range*

POL ROGER & CO. (GM)
1 rue Henri Lelarge
51206 Epernay
★★★✰ Ⓥ

If I were to choose just one house from which to source a vintage Champagne to lay down, there is no question that I would choose Pol Roger. There are always exceptions, of course, but, generally speaking, these Champagnes last longer and remain fresher than those of any other house, however justified their great reputations may be, and I base this opinion on tasting a good number of vintages spanning back a century or more at many houses.

✓ *Entire range*

POMMERY (GM)
5 place Général Gouraud
51053 Reims
★★

Owned by Vranken, Pommery has been on a roll since 1995, which is no mean feat for such a light and elegant Champagne with a production of almost seven million bottles, because the lighter the wine's style, the more difficult it is to maintain the quality as production increases.

✓ *Entire range*

LOUIS ROEDERER (GM)
21 boulevard Lundy
51100 Reims
★★★✰ Ⓥ

Louis Roederer is the most profitable house in Champagne, and should be an object lesson for those houses that count success in terms of the number of bottles they sell. The keys to real success in Champagne are an impeccable reputation, which guarantees a premium price; sufficient vineyards to guarantee consistent quality for a production large enough to rake in the money; and the self-discipline required not to go beyond that level. Jean-Claude Rouzaud knows that if he goes too far beyond Roederer's current production of 2.5 million bottles, he will be unable to guarantee the quality he demands and his brand would soon lose the cachet of relative exclusiveness. He does not, however, like to see his capital lie idle, which is why he would rather take over Deutz than increase his own production. Jean-Baptiste Lecaillon has slipped seamlessly into the position of *chef de cave* previously occupied by the talented Michel Pansu.

✓ *Entire range*

RUINART (GM)
4 rue de Crayères
51053 Reims
★★

Established in 1729 by Nicolas Ruinart, this is the oldest commercial producer of sparkling Champagne. This house was taken over in 1963 by Moët & Chandon, but has managed to maintain the image of an independent, premium-quality Champagne in spite of it being part of LVMH, the largest Champagne group, and tripling its production in the meantime. The house style tends to develop very toasty aromas.

✓ *Entire range*

SALON (GM)
5 rue de la Brèche
51190 Le Mesnil-sur-Oger
★★★

Owned by Laurent-Perrier, located next door to Delamotte (also owned by Laurent-Perrier), Salon is one of the greatest Champagnes available, and possibly the rarest, since only one *cuvée* is produced and it is exclusively vintage, thus it is not produced every year. The wine does not usually undergo malolactic fermentation, is often kept on its sediment for 10 years or more, and continues to benefit from at least an equal amount of aging after disgorgement.

✓ *"S"* (**V**)

JACQUES SÉLOSSE
22 rue Ernest Vallée
51190 Avize
★★

Anselme Sélosse has found a niche in the market for *barrique*-fermented, nonmalolactic wines that receive minimal *dosage* and usually require several years extra postdisgorgement cellarage to show their full potential, by which time they have lost much of the finesse that would have been present with a normal *dosage*. Generally far too much raw oak for my liking, but there is no denying the quality of the wine underneath, and rated for those who like the style.

✓ *Entire range* (but with care)

TAITTINGER (GM)
9 place Saint-Nicaise
51061 Reims
★★

This house uses a high proportion of Chardonnay in its nonvintage Brut Réserve, making it one of the most elegant and delicate of *grande marque* Champagnes. Comtes de Champagne *blanc de blancs* is one of the greatest Champagnes produced.

✓ *Entire range*

ALAIN THIENOT
14 rue des Moissons
51100 Reims
★ ✔

A very savvy financier who has quietly built up a significant group (including Joseph Perrier, Canard-Duchêne, George Goulet, and Marie Stuart), Alain Thienot also produces good-value, fruit-driven Champagnes under his own label, ranging from a successful pouring-quality nonvintage, through good-quality vintage *brut* and rosé, to an excellent Cuvée Stanislas.

✓ *Brut Rosé* (**V**) • *Grand Cuvée Brut* (**V**) • *Cuvée Stanislas* (**V**)

UNION CHAMPAGNE
7 rue Pasteur
51190 Avize
★

Champagne de St.-Gall is this cooperative's primary brand, with Cuvée Orpale its prestige *cuvée*. There are two ranges, Grands Crus and Premiers Crus, and wines in the former range are not always superior. The quality of Champagnes released by this cooperative has improved considerably over the last five years or so.

✓ *Grands Crus Millésime* (**N**) • *Cuvée Orpale* (**PC**)

DE VENOGE
30 avenue de Champagne
51200 Epernay
★ ✔

Part of BCC (Boizel-Chanoine Champagne) group, this remains a good-value, well-made brand, but its one top-quality Champagne, the often truly excellent Cuvée des Princes, looks ridiculous in its novelty, tear-shaped bottle.

✓ *Blanc de Noirs* (**V**) • *Brut* (**V**) • *Cuvée des Princes* (**PC**)

VEUVE CLICQUOT-PONSARDIN (GM)
12 rue du Temple
51054 Reims
★★☆

The quality and image of this producer is surprisingly high and upmarket for such a large house. The Clicquot style is not just big, but beautiful. This is achieved by the excellence of its Pinot Noir vineyards on the Montagne de Reims, with Bouzy often dominating the selection of grapes from these vineyards, and the relatively hands-off approach to winemaking. The fermentation temperature is not excessively low at Veuve Clicquot-Ponsardin, there is no filtering before blending, and only a light filtration prior to bottling, with reserves stored on their lees.

✓ *Entire range*

VEUVE A. DEVAUX
Domaine de Villeneuve
10110 Bar-sur-Seine
★ ✔

This was the most dynamic cooperative in Champagne from the late 1980s and throughout the 1990s, producing richer, crisper, fruitier Champagnes than some Marne-based cooperatives with a large percentage of *grand cru* vineyards. The quality took a dip at the turn of the millennium, but is now back on track.

✓ *Grande Réserve Brut* (**NV**) • *Cuvée D Brut* (**NV**) • *Blanc de Noirs* (**NV**) • *Cuvée Distinction Rosé* (**V**) • *D. de Devaux* (**V**)

VILMART
4 rue de la République
51500 Rilly-la-Montagne
★★★☆

The top *cuvées* became too oaky, but Vilmart has now gone through this heavy-handed phase, and emerged all the better for it as from the 1996 vintage.

✓ *Entire range*

VRANKEN
42 avenue de Champagne
51200 Epernay
✿

The house of Vranken is owned by Belgian Paul Vranken, whose ideas on quality I do not share but who undoubtedly has one of the most clever commercial brains in the region. His brands include Charles Lafitte, René Lallement, Demoiselle, Vranken, Barancourt, and Heidsieck & Co. Monopole, but his masterstroke was the purchase of Pommery in 2002. Marne et Champagne bought Lanson at the top of the market, and watched its assets dwindle, whereas Vranken bought Pommery at the bottom of the market, and watched his assets grow. He paid €150–180 million ($180–215 million), which was some €50 ($60 million) less than LVMH was asking. Although sales inevitably sank after the millennium blip, Vranken knew they were about to rise, and very quickly saw the value of Pommery jump €50 million ($60 million). In addition, Pommery sells at a premium compared to other Vranken brands, thus his group's profit margin increased overnight. Some critics believed the Belgian business maestro would have to sell more bottles of Pommery to meet his bank repayments, and the only way he could do that would be by cutting prices, but he has in fact increased both sales and price. Vranken also owns subsidiaries in Portugal (Port: Quinta do Convento, Quinta do Paco, and São Pedro) and Spain (Cava: Senora, and Vranken).

BEST OF THE REST

The following producers have produced at least some wines of excellence since the early 2000s.

Ch de l'Auche (CM, Janvry)
Barnaut (RC, Bouzy)
Baron Albert
   (NM, Charly-sur-Marne)
Besserat de Bellefon (NM, Epernay)
Henri Billiot (RM, Ambonnay)
H. Blin (RC, Vincelles)
Brice (NM, Aÿ-Champagne)
Louise Brison
   (RC, Noé-les-Mallets)
P. Brugnon (RM, Rilly-la-Montagne)
Roger Brun (RC, Aÿ-Champagne)
Le Brun de Neuville
   (CM, Bethon)
Christian Bourmault (RM, Avize)
Guy Cadel (RM, Mardeuil)
Pierre Callot (RM, Avize)
Guy Charbaut
   (RM, Mareuil-sur-Aÿ)
Guy Charlemagne
   (RM, Le Mesnil-sur-Oger)
J. Charpentier
   (RM, Villers-sous-Châtillon)
Collard Chardelle
   (RM, Viller-sous-Châtillon)
Chartogne-Taillet (RC, Merfy)
Raoul Collet
   (CM, Aÿ-Champagne)
Delouvin Nowack (RM, Vandières)
Doquet-Jeanmaire (RM, Vertus)
Didier Doué (RM, Montguex)
Charles Ellner (NM, Epernay)
Gatinois (RM, Aÿ-Champagne)
Henri Giraud
   (NM, Aÿ-Champagne)
Michel Gonet (RM, Avize)
Gosset Brabant
   (RM, Aÿ-Champagne)
George Goulet (NM, Epernay)
Goussard & Dauphin
   (RM, Avirey-Lingey)
Jacquinot (NM, Epernay)
Pierre Jamain
   (RM, La Celle-sous-Chantemerle)
R. C. Lemaire
   (RM, Villers-sous-Châtillon)
Lancelot-Pienne (RM, Cramant)
Lenoble (NM, Damery)
Michel Loriot (RM, Festigny)
A. Margaine
   (RM, Villers-Marmery)
Rémy Massin
   (RM, Villé-sur-Arce)
Milan (RM, Oger)
Jean Moutardier (RM, Le Breuil)
Pierre Paillard (RM, Bouzy)
Fabrice Payelle
   (RM, Ambonnay)
Pehu-Simonet (RM, Verzenay)
Petit-Camusat
   (RM, Noé-les-Mallets)
Alain Robert
   (RM, Le Mesnil-sur-Oger)
Tarlant (RM, Oeuilly)
De Telmont (NM, Epernay)
Tribaut (RM, Hautvillers)
J. L. Vergnon
   (RM, Le Mesnil-sur-Oger)
Jean Vesselle (RM, Bouzy)
Maurice Vesselle (RM, Bouzy)

MORE GREEN CHAMPAGNES

In addition to the few Champagnes listed in this directory that are biodynamic or organic, there are also the following. No negative inference of quality should be taken from the fact that they are not featured among the recommended Champagne producers. The truth is that there are over 12,500 brands, and I have no experience of the Champagnes produced by many of the following.

Biodynamic
Champagne Françoise Bedel (Crouttes-sur-Marne)
Champagne Benoît Lahaye (Bouzy)
Champagne Thierry Demarne (Villé-sur-Arce)
Champagne David Léclapart (Trépail)
Champagne Réaut-Noirot (Courteron)
Champagne Ruffin (Avenay)
Champagne Schreiber (Courteron)
Champagne Vouette & Sorbée (Buxieres-sur-Arce)

Organic
Champagne Jacques Beaufort (Ambonnay)
Champagne Bénard-Pitois (Mareuil-sur-Aÿ)
Champagne Jean Bliard (Hautvillers)
Champagne Vincent Bliard (Hautvillers)
Champagne Serge Faust (Vandières)
Champagne José Ardinat (Vandières)
Champagne Roger Fransoret (Mancy)
Champagne Vincent Laval (Cumières)
Champagne Lefèvre (Bonneil)
Champagne Régis Poirrier (Venteuil)

ALSACE, see also p.55
The appellation itself encompasses the départements of Bas-Rhin and Haut-Rhin (left). Outside the appellation to the northwest, in what was the province of Lorraine, are two other areas classified VDQS, Vin de Moselle and Côtes de Toul (above).

FORTIFIED CHURCH OF STE.-HUNA, HUNAWIHR
One of the best wine villages in Alsace, Hunawihr is most famous for its Clos Ste.-Hune vineyard, from which Trimbach consistently produces great Riesling.

best export markets. This is because the phenomenon applies primarily to the best producers and vineyards, particularly *grands crus*. These are the wines that make the headlines, are reviewed and entered into competitions. However, putting the problem into perspective does not help those who buy the best Alsace wines, or order a Riesling in a restaurant to go with fish only to find it is as sweet as Sauternes.

The simple solution would have been to introduce an obligatory dry wine designation, but in 2004 the opposite was accomplished when it was ruled that wines with a minimum of 12 grams per liter (9 grams per liter for Riesling) of residual sugar must be labeled "*moelleux*." If a wine has more than 6 grams per liter of total acidity, then the minimum residual sugar rises to 18 grams per liter (12 grams per liter for Riesling). The trouble with defining minimum residual sugar content for a sweet designation is that it does not mean that all those wines that do not qualify are in fact dry. The introduction of *moelleux* has reduced, not

solved, the dilemma facing Alsace consumers, but when it comes to French bureaucracy, this is about as good as it gets.

THE WINES OF LORRAINE

Viticulture in these parts dates back to Roman times, and when the *départements* of Meurthe-et-Moselle and Moselle formed part of the old Province of Lorraine, their vineyards covered some 74,000 acres (30,000 hectares). This area was more than twice that of neighboring Alsace today. They currently cover a mere 222 acres (90 hectares), virtually all of which are in the Meurthe-et-Moselle *département*. The viticultural outcrops of the Moselle are particularly sparse and make a sorry sight compared to their former glory; today it is the *Route de la Mirabelle* (damson road), not the *Route du Vin* (wine road), that is flourishing. Growing damsons, it would seem, is far less risky than growing vines, although most people find that working in the industrialized town of Metz is more profitable.

THE GRANDS CRUS OF
ALSACE

In the 2001 revised edition of this encyclopedia, I wrote: "The original *grand cru* legislation was introduced in 1975, but it was not until 1983 that the first list of 25 *grand cru* sites appeared. Three years later a further 23 were added, and there are now 50, although this number is the subject of much controversy, not least because it excludes what is acknowledged as one of the most famous, truly great *crus* of Alsace—Kaefferkopf in Ammerschwihr. While the *grands crus* will be of long-term benefit to both Alsace and the consumer, the limitation of *grand cru* to pure varietal wines of just four grapes—Muscat, Riesling, Pinot Gris, and Gewurztraminer—robs us of the chance to drink the finest quality Pinot Noir, Pinot Blanc, Sylvaner, and Chasselas.

"Even if these wines might not be in the same league as the big four, it seems wholly unreasonable to prevent their cultivation for AOC Alsace Grand Cru when market forces dictate that most growers will, in any case, plant the four classic varieties in their most prized *grand cru* sites because they fetch the highest prices. If, however, a grower on a *grand cru* is determined to make the best possible wine from any of the less lucrative varieties or, indeed, to produce a classic blend, why should we, the buyers, be prevented from knowing where the grapes came from because the law prevents the grower from mentioning *grand cru* on the label of such wines?"

I have been aware of these shortcomings since the publication of *The Wines of Alsace* (1993), so it was particularly heartening when in 2000 various impeccable sources informed me that the *grand cru* appellation would shortly be opened up to include varieties other than the so-called noble grapes. In 2004 Zotzenberg became the first (for Sylvaner), followed by Altenberg de Bergheim (for a blend of grapes), and, having cleared that hurdle, the INAO

was forced to give the go-ahead for *grand cru* application.

It will not stop there. There is talk of allowing Pinot Noir for Steinklotz, and if Steinklotz is classified for Pinot Noir, then Vorbourg cannot be far behind. The ball will just keep rolling because if Sylvaner from Zotzenberg, why not Chasselas from Hengst? There will be fears that these wines will dilute the status of *grand cru*, and that may indeed happen, but it does not matter. In the long term, it is the market that dictates status, not a decree. Reputations have to be earned, not bestowed. That is why the cheapest wine from Zind-Humbrecht is more expensive than some producers' *grands crus*. The classification Alsace Grand Cru was late in coming, but happened in a rush, leapfrogging any thought of an intermediate *premier cru* appellation, and the delimitation of many sites was a joke. However, the market is already starting to separate the chaff from the wheat and the same will happen to classified wines made from less classic varieties and grape blends.

Under the same law that permits local *syndicats* of growers to press for different wine styles under their own particular *grand cru*, they are also permitted to impose more stringent quality criteria on a growth-by-growth basis. Where the *syndicats* have actually done this, you will find the new specifications listed below. Where there are no new specifications, the criteria laid down in the *grand cru* decree applies, and that is as follows. Riesling and Muscat: maximum yield of 66hl/ha (basic limit of 55hl/ha plus 11hl/ha PLC); minimum ripeness equivalent to 11% at time of harvest, and chaptalization up to 1.5% allowed. Pinot Gris and Gewurztraminer: maximum yield of 66hl/ha (basic limit of 55hl/ha plus 11hl/ha PLC); minimum ripeness equivalent to 12.5% at time of harvest, and chaptalization up to 1.5% allowed. Note that all ripeness levels are expressed as percent ABV.

ALTENBERG DE BERGBIETEN
Bergbieten

An exceptional growth, but not a truly great one. Its gypsum-permeated, clayey-marl soil is best for Gewurztraminer, which has a very floral character with immediate appeal, yet can improve for several years in bottle. The wines are now allowed to be blended from different varieties. The local *syndicat* has renounced the PLC, limiting the yield to an absolute maximum of 55hl/ha. It has also outlawed all chaptalization, and has increased the minimum

ripeness of Riesling and Muscat from 11% to 12%, and that of Pinot Gris and Gewurztraminer from 12.5% to 14%.

♟ *Etienne Loewe* • *Frédéric Mochel*

ALTENBERG DE BERGHEIM
Bergheim

This Altenberg has been a true *grand cru* since as long ago as the 12th century, and its calcareous clay soil is best suited to Gewurztraminer, which is tight and austere in youth, but gains in depth and bouquet with

aging. This *cru* will apply for classification of wines made from a blend of grapes.

♟ *Marcel Deiss* **Ⓑ** • *Louis Freyburger* **Ⓑ**

ALTENBERG DE WOLXHEIM
Wolxheim

Even though it was appreciated by Napoleon, this calcareous clay *cru* cannot honestly be described as one of the greatest growths of Alsace, although it has a certain reputation for its Riesling.

♟ *Zoeller*

BRAND
Turckheim

This *cru* might legitimately be called Brand New, the original Brand being a tiny *cru* of little more than 7½ acres (3 hectares). In 1924 it was expanded to include surrounding sites: Steinglitz, Kirchthal, Schneckenberg, Weingarten, and Jebsal, each with its own fine reputation. By 1980 it had grown to 74 acres (30 hectares) and it is now almost double that. This confederation of *lieux-dits* is one of the most magnificent sites in the entire region, and the quality of the wines consistently excites me—great Riesling, Pinot Gris, and Gewurztraminer. The local *syndicat* has reduced chaptalization of Riesling and Muscat from the allowable 1.5% to 1%, and that of Pinot Gris and Gewurztraminer from 1.5% to 0.5%. It has also increased the minimum ripeness of Riesling and Muscat from 11% to 11.5%, and that of Pinot Gris and Gewurztraminer from 12.5% to 13.5%.

♈ *Albert Boxler* • *Dopff Au Moulin* • *JosMeyer* ❸ • *Preiss-Zimmer* • *Zind-Humbrecht* ❸

BRUDERTHAL
Molsheim

Riesling and Gewurztraminer—reputedly the best varieties—occupy most of this calcareous clay *cru*. I have tasted good, fruity Riesling from Bernard Weber, which was elegant, but not really top stuff. Gérard Neumeyer used not to impress me at all, but his genuinely dry 2001 Pinot Gris was one of the best Bruderthal I have tasted. The local *syndicat* has renounced all chaptalization. It has also increased the minimum ripeness of Riesling and Muscat from 11% to 12%, and that of Pinot Gris and Gewurztraminer from 12.5% to 13%.

♈ *Alain Klingenfus* • *Gérard Neumeyer*

EICHBERG
Eguisheim

This calcareous clay *cru* has the lowest rainfall in Colmar and produces very aromatic wines of exceptional delicacy, yet great longevity. Famous for Gewurztraminer, which is potentially the finest in Alsace, Eichberg is also capable of making superb long-lasting Riesling and Pinot Gris. The local *syndicat* has reduced chaptalization of Riesling from 1.5% to 1%, and outlawed it completely for Pinot Gris and Gewurztraminer. It has also increased the minimum ripeness of Riesling from 11% to 11.5%, and Pinot Gris and Gewurztraminer from 12.5% to 13%. The chaptalization and minimum ripeness of Muscat remain the same.

♈ *Charles Baur* ❸ • *Emile Beyer* • *Léon Beyer* (not sold as such, Beyer's Cuvée des Comtes d'Eguisheim is 100% pure Eichberg) • *Paul Ginglinger* • *Albert Hertz*

ENGELBERG
Dahlenheim and Scharrachbergheim

One of the least-encountered *grands crus*, this vineyard gets long hours of sunshine and is supposed to favor Gewurztraminer and Riesling; but few of the wines I have tasted suggest anything special.

♈ *Jean-Pierre Bechtold*

FLORIMONT
Ingersheim and Katzenthal

Mediterranean flora abounds on the sun-blessed, calcareous clay slopes of this *cru*—hence its name, meaning "hill of flowers"—the excellent microclimate producing some stunning Riesling and Gewurztraminer.

♈ *François Bohn* • *René Meyer* • *Bruno Sorg*

FRANKSTEIN
Dambach-la-Ville

Not so much one vineyard as four separate spurs, the warm, well-drained, granite soil of this *cru* is best suited to the production of delicate, racy Riesling, and elegant Gewurztraminer. J. Hauller used to be by far and away the best producer of Frankstein, for both the Riesling and Gewurztraminer.

♈ *Charles & Dominique Frey* ❸ • *Ruhlman* • *Schaeffer-Woerly*

FROEHN
Zellenberg

This *cru* sweeps up and around the southern half of the hill upon which Zellenberg is situated. The marly-clay soil suits Muscat, Gewurztraminer, and Pinot Gris, in that order, and the wines are typically rich and long-lived. The local *syndicat* has outlawed all chaptalization, and increased the minimum ripeness of Riesling and Muscat from 11% to 12%, and that of Pinot Gris and Gewurztraminer from 12.5% to 13.5%.

♈ *J. .P & J. F. Becker* ❸

FURSTENTUM
Kientzheim and Sigolsheim

This estate is best for Riesling, although the vines have to be well established to take full advantage of the calcareous soil. Gewurztraminer can also be fabulous—in an elegant, more floral, less spicy style—and Pinot Gris excels even when the vines are very young. The local *syndicat* has reduced all chaptalization from the allowable 1.5% to 0.5%. It has also increased the minimum ripeness of Riesling and Muscat from 11% to 11.5%, and Pinot Gris and Gewurztraminer from 12.5% to 13%.

♈ *Paul Blanck* ◉ • *Bott-Geyl* • *Albert Mann* • *Weinbach/Faller*

GEISBERG
Ribeauvillé

Geisberg has been well documented since as long ago as 1308 as Riesling country par

excellence. The calcareous, stony-and-clayey sandstone soil produces fragrant, powerful, and long-lived wines of great finesse. Trimbach owns vines here, and in a contiguous plot with vines in Osterberg, the whole of which produces the superb Riesling Cuvée Frédéric Émile. The local *syndicat* has reduced the chaptalization of Riesling, Pinot Gris, and Gewurztraminer from 1.5% to 0.5%. It has also increased the minimum ripeness of Riesling from 11% to 11.5%, and that of Pinot Gris and Gewurztraminer from 12.5% to 13%. The chaptalization and minimum ripeness of Muscat remain the same.

♈ *Robert Faller* • *André Kientzler*

GLOECKELBERG
Rodern and St-Hippolyte

This clay-granite *cru* is known for its light, elegant, and yet persistent style of wine, with Gewurztraminer and Pinot Gris the most successful varieties. The local *syndicat* has halved the PLC, thereby reducing the absolute maximum yield allowed to 60.5hl/ha.

♈ *Koberlé-Kreyer*

GOLDERT
Gueberschwihr

Dating back to the year 750, and recognized on export markets as long ago as 1728, Goldert derives its name from the color of its wines, the most famous of which is the golden Gewurztraminer. The Muscat grape variety also excels on the calcareous clay soil, and whatever the varietal the style of wine is rich and spicy with a luscious creaminess.

♈ *Ernest Burn* (Clos St-Imer) • *Zind-Humbrecht* ❸

HATSCHBOURG
Hattstatt and Voegtlinshoffen

Gewurztraminer from this south-facing, calcareous marl soil slope excels, but Pinot Gris and Riesling are also excellent.

♈ *Buecher-Fix* • *André Hartmann* • *Lucien Meyer*

HENGST
Wintzenheim

Hengst Gewurztraminer is a very special, complex wine, seeming to combine the classic qualities of this variety with the orange zest and rose-petal aromas more characteristic of the Muscat grape variety. But Hengst is a very flexible *cru*. Besides Gewurztraminer, its calcareous marl soil also produces top-quality Muscat, Riesling, and Pinot Gris. The local *syndicat* has renounced all chaptalization. It has also increased the minimum ripeness of Riesling and Muscat from 11% to 12%, and that of Pinot Gris and Gewurztraminer from 12.5% to 13%.

♈ *JosMeyer* ❸ • *Albert Mann* • *Zind-Humbrecht* ❸

KAEFFERKOPF
Ammerschwihr

Although not technically a *grand cru*, this is one of the greatest Alsace *crus*, superior to many of the officially nominated sites, and after a long haggle, will shortly be classified. Possibly even by the time this edition is published. Kaefferkopf was legally delimited in 1932. However, the bureaucrats refused to recognize all of it because it is not geologically uniform. Furthermore, they refused to recognize the traditional Kaefferkopf practice of blending varieties—usually Riesling and Gewurztraminer. However, after the brilliant, but fanatical Jean-Michel Deiss bulldozed his way through this bureaucratic nonsense with his sensational, succulently sweet, classic blends under the Altenberg de Bergheim Grand Cru, INAO had no option but to agree that Kaefferkopf blends may be classified as a *grand cru*. However, bureaucrats being what they are, they only did this on the proviso that the borders of Grand Cru Kaefferkopf should not be as large as the 1932 delimitation. This desire to keep *grands crus* as small, authentic, and as geologically homogenous as possible would be admirable if it had been applied to all the other 49 *grands crus*, but some *grands crus* are geologically less uniform and have swollen well beyond their historical boundaries. Brand, for example, is 20 times its original designated size. After unreasonably withholding *grand cru* status from the growers on Kaefferkopf for so long, and unreasonably allowing the growers on what is now Brand to get away with murder, the decent thing would have been to recognize the 1932 delimitation.

🏆 *J. B. Adam* (Jean-Baptiste) • *Marcel Freyburger* Ⓑ • *Meyer-Fonné* (Nicolas) • *Martin Schaetzel* Ⓑ • *Maurice Schoech*

KANZLERBERG
Bergheim

Although this tiny *cru* adjoins the western edge of Altenberg de Bergheim, the wines of its gypsum-permeated, clayey-marl *terroir* are so different from those of the Altenberg growth that the vinification of the two sites has always been kept separate. The wines have the same potential longevity, but the Kanzlerbergs are fuller and fatter. Kanzlerberg has a reputation for both Riesling and Gewurztraminer, but their ample weight can be at odds with their varietal aromas when young, and both wines require plenty of bottle age to achieve their true finesse. The local *syndicat* has renounced the PLC, limiting the yield to an absolute maximum of 55hl/ha. It has also outlawed all chaptalization, and increased the minimum ripeness of Riesling and Muscat from 11% to 12%, and that of Pinot Gris and Gewurztraminer from 12.5% to 14%.

🏆 *Louis Freyburger* Ⓑ • *Sylvie Spielmann* Ⓑ

KASTELBERG
Andlau

One of the oldest vineyards in Alsace, Kastelberg has been planted with vines since the Roman occupation. Situated on a small hill next to Wiebelsberg, Andlau's other *grand cru*, the very steep, schistous *terroir* has long proved to be an excellent site for racy and delicate Riesling, although the wines can be very closed when young and require a few years to develop their lovely bottle aromas. Kastelberg wines remain youthful for 20 years or more, and even show true *grand cru* quality in so-called "off" years.

🏆 *Guy Wach*

KESSLER
Guebwiller

Though a *cru* more premier than grand (the truly famous sites of Guebwiller being Kitterlé and Wanne, the latter not classified), the central part of Kessler is certainly deserving of *grand cru* status. Here, the vines grow in a well-protected, valleylike depression, one side of which has a very steep, south-southeast facing slope. Kessler is renowned for its full, spicy, and mellow Gewurztraminer, but Riesling can be much the greater wine. The local *syndicat* has renounced the PLC, limiting the yield to an absolute maximum of 55hl/ha. It has also outlawed all chaptalization, and increased the minimum ripeness of Riesling and Muscat from 11% to 11.5%, and that of Pinot Gris and Gewurztraminer from 12.5% to 13.5%.

🏆 *Dirler-Cadé* Ⓑ • *Schlumberger*

KIRCHBERG DE BARR
Barr

The true *grands crus* of Barr are Gaensbroennel and Zisser, but these have been incorporated into the calcareous marl *terroir* of Kirchberg, which is known for its full-bodied yet delicate wines that exhibit exotic spicy fruit, a characteristic that applies not only to Pinot Gris and Gewurztraminer but also to Riesling.

🏆 *Stoeffler* Ⓞ

KIRCHBERG DE RIBEAUVILLÉ
Ribeauvillé

One of the few *lieux-dits* that has regularly been used to market Alsace wine over the centuries. It is famous for Riesling, which typically is firm, totally dry, and long-lived, developing intense gasoline characteristics with age. Kirchberg de Ribeauvillé also produces great Muscat with a discreet, yet very specific, orange-and-musk aroma, excellent acidity, and lots of finesse. The local *syndicat* has reduced the chaptalization of Riesling, Pinot Gris and Gewurztraminer from 1.5% to 0.5%. It has also increased the minimum ripeness of Riesling from 11% to 11.5%, and that of Pinot Gris and Gewurztraminer from 12.5% to 13%. The chaptalization and minimum ripeness of Muscat remain the same.

🏆 *André Kientzler* • *Jean Sipp* • *Louis Sipp*

KITTERLÉ
Guebwiller

Of all the grape varieties that are grown on this volcanic sandstone *terroir*, it is the crisp, gasolinelike Riesling that shows greatest finesse. Gewurztraminer and Pinot Gris are also very good in a gently rich, supple, and smoky-mellow style. The local *syndicat* has renounced

the PLC, limiting the yield to an absolute maximum of 55hl/ha. It has also outlawed all chaptalization, and has increased the minimum ripeness of Riesling and Muscat from 11% to 11.5%, and that of Pinot Gris and Gewurztraminer from 12.5% to 13.5%.

🏆 *Schlumberger*

MAMBOURG
Sigolsheim

The reputation of this *cru* has been documented since 783, when it was known as the "Sigoltesberg." A limestone *coteau*, with calcareous clay topsoil, Mambourg stretches for three-quarters of a mile (over a kilometer), penetrating farther into the plain than any other spur of the Vosges foothills. Its vineyards, supposedly the warmest in Alsace, produce wines that tend to be rich and warm, mellow and liquorous. Both the Gewurztraminer and the Pinot Gris have plenty of smoky-rich spice in them. The local *syndicat* has reduced chaptalization of Riesling, Pinot Gris and Gewurztraminer from 1.5% to 0,5% and increased the minimum ripeness of Riesling from 11% to 12%, and that of Pinot Gris and Gewurztraminer from 12.5% to 13%.

🏆 *Jean-Marc Bernhard* • *Marcel Deiss* Ⓑ • *Daniel Fritz* • *Pierre Sparr* • *Marc Tempé* Ⓑ

MANDELBERG
Mittelwihr and Beblenheim

Mandelberg—"almond tree hill"—has been planted with vines since Gallo-Roman times, and used as an appellation since 1925. Its reputation has been built on Riesling, although today more Gewurztraminer is planted; high-quality Pinot Gris and Muscat is also produced. The local *syndicat* has renounced the PLC, limiting the yield to an absolute maximum of 55hl/ha. It has also outlawed chaptalization for Pinot Gris and Gewurztraminer, increasing the minimum ripeness for these two grapes from 12.5% to 13%. The minimum ripeness for Riesling and Muscat remains at 11%, and the possibility of chaptalization is retained exclusively for these two varieties.

🏆 *Hartweg* • *Frédéric Mallo* • *André Stentz* Ⓞ

MARCKRAIN
Bennwihr and Sigolsheim

Markrain is the east-facing slope of the Mambourg, which overlooks Sigolsheim. The soil is a limestone-marl with oolite pebbles interlayering the marl beds. It is mostly planted with Gewurztraminer, with some Pinot Gris and a few Muscat vines. The Bennewihr *coopérative* usually makes a decent Pinot Gris under the Bestheim label. The local *syndicat* has reduced the chaptalization of Pinot Gris and Gewurztraminer from an allowable 1.5% to 1%, and increased the minimum ripeness of these grapes from 12.5% to 13%. The chaptalization and minimum ripeness of Riesling and Muscat remain the same.

🏆 *Bestheim*

MOENCHBERG
Andlau and Eichhoffen

Moenchberg—"monk's hill"—was owned by a Benedictine order until 1097, when it was taken over by the inhabitants of Eichhoffen. With its clayey-marl soil, excellent exposure to the sun, and very hot, dry microclimate, this *cru* has built up a reputation for firm, intensely fruity, and very racy Riesling. Excellent though it is, often achieving a rich gingerbread character when mature.

🍇 Gewurztraminer

🍷 3–10 years (20–30 years for great examples)

✓ *Barmès-Buecher* **Ⓑ** • *Charles Baur* **Ⓑ** • *Léon Beyer* • *Paul Blanck* **Ⓞ** • *Bott-Geyl* • *Albert Boxler* • *Camille Braun* (Cuvée Annabelle) • *Brobecker* (Cuvée Spéciale) • *Hugel & Fils* (Jubilée) • *André Kientzler* • *Meyer-Fonné* (Réserve Particulière) • *Muré* **Ⓞ** (Clos St-Landelin) • *Rolly Gassmann* • *Georges et Claude Humbrecht* (Vieilles Vignes) • *Martin Schaetzel* **Ⓑ** • *A. Scherer* • *François Schmitt* (Pfingstberg) • *Jean Sipp* • *Bruno Sorg* (Pfersigberg) • *Sylvie Spielmann* **Ⓑ** • *Antoine Stoffel* • *F. E. Trimbach* • *Weinbach/Faller* • *Zind-Humbrecht* **Ⓑ** • **VT** *J. B. Adam* • *Léon Beyer* • *Léon Boesch* **Ⓞ** • *René Fleith-Eschard* • *Louis Freyburger* **Ⓑ** (Kanzlerberg) • *Geschikt* • *Hugel & Fils* • *Jean Huttard* (Burgreben) • *Roger Jung* • *André Kientzler* • *Ostertag* **Ⓑ** • *Pierre Meyer* • *Maurice Schoech* • *André Thomas* **Ⓑ** • *Weinbach/Faller* • *Zind-Humbrecht* **Ⓑ** • **SGN** *Léon Beyer* (especially Quintessence) • *Paul Blanck* **Ⓞ** • *Léon Boesch* **Ⓞ** • *Albert Boxler* • *Dirler-Cadé* **Ⓑ** • *Hugel & Fils* • *André Kleinknecht* **Ⓑ** • *Albert Mann* • *Muré* **Ⓞ** (Clos St.-Landelin) • *Rolly Gassmann* • *Seppi Landmann* • *Damien Schlegel* • *Schlumberger* (Cuvée Anne) • *Sick-Dreyer* • *F. E. Trimbach* • *Weinbach/Faller* • *Zind-Humbrecht* **Ⓑ**

GUTEDEL AOC

Synonym under which Chasselas may be marketed. *See* Chasselas AOC

KLEVENER DE HEILIGENSTEIN AOC

An oddity in Alsace for three reasons: first, the wine is made from a grape variety that is native to the Jura farther south and not found anywhere else in Alsace; second, of all the famous village appellations (Rouge d'Ottrott, Rouge de Rodern, etc.), it is the only one specifically defined in the regulations; third, it is the only grape confined by law to a fixed area within Alsace (the village of Heiligenstein). It is not to be confused with Klevner, a common synonym for the Pinot Blanc.

WHITE Dry, light-bodied wines of a subdued, spicy aroma, and delicate, fruity flavor. Sadly, no wines worth recommending.

🍇 Savagnin Rosé

🍷 2–4 years

KLEVNER AOC

See Pinot Blanc AOC

MOSELLE VDQS

This VDQS was called Vins de Moselle until 1995, when it became simply Moselle. Although many restaurants list German Mosel as "Moselle," the river and the wine it produces are called Mosel in Germany, only becoming Moselle when crossing the border into France (and Luxembourg). Gamay is limited by law to a maximum of 30 percent of the surface area of this appellation. A maximum of 12.5 percent alcohol is applied to prevent producers from overchaptalizing.

RED Château de Vaux produces a surprisingly good Pinot Noir.

🍇 Gamay, Pinot Meunier, Pinot Noir

🍷 Upon purchase

WHITE There has been an improvement in these wines, particularly the Pinot Gris.

🍇 Auxerrois, Müller-Thurgau, Pinot Blanc, Pinot Gris, Riesling, Gewurztraminer

🍷 Upon purchase

✓ *Michel Maurice* (Pinot Gris) • *Oury-Schreiber* • *Château de Vaux* (Pinot Noir Les Hautes Bassières)

MUSCAT AOC

The best Muscat wine, some growers believe, is made from the Muscat d'Alsace, a synonym for both the white and pink strains of the rich, full Muscat à Petits Grains. Others are convinced that the lighter, more floral Muscat Ottonel is best. A blend of the two is probably preferable. These wines are better in average years, or at least in fine years that have good acidity, rather than in truly great vintages.

WHITE Dry, aromatic wines with fine floral characteristics that often smell of orange-flower water and taste of peaches. A top-quality Muscat that is expressive of its *terroir* is a great wine.

🍇 Muscat Blanc à Petits Grains, Muscat Rosé à Petits Grains, Muscat Ottonel

🍷 Upon purchase

✓ *Jean Becker* • *Emile Beyer* • *Ernest Burn* (Clos St.-Imer) • *Pierre Henri Ginglinger* **Ⓑ** • *Roger Jung* • *André Kientzler* • *Frédéric Mochel* • *Muré* **Ⓞ** (Clos St.-Landelin) • *Rolly Gassmann* • *Sylvain Hertzog* • *Bruno Sorg* • *Sylvie Spielmann* **Ⓑ** • *Weinbach/Faller* • *Zind-Humbrecht* **Ⓑ** (Goldert) **VT (or VT style)** *Jean-Marc et Frédéric Bernhard* • *Barmès-Buecher* **Ⓑ** **SGN (or SGN style)** *Claude Bleger* • *Fernand Engel* **Ⓞ** • *Romain Fritsch* • *Albert Mann* (Le Tri)

PINOT AOC

JOSMEYER

ALSACE PINOT BLANC
APPELLATION ALSACE CONTRÔLÉE
Mise du Printemps®
2003
mis en bouteille par JOSMEYER & FILS, à F 68920 WINTZENHEIM
ALC.12LBY10   PRODUCT OF FRANCE   750 ml

Not necessarily pure Pinot Blanc, this white wine may be made from any of the Pinot grape varieties, including Auxerrois (often confused with Pinot Blanc but in fact a totally separate variety). Most Pinot wines are a blend of Pinot Blanc and Auxerrois; the farther north the vines are cultivated, the more Auxerrois is used to plump out the Pinot Blanc. Zind is included under Zind-Humbrecht below because this luscious, effectively dry blend of 50 percent Auxerrois, 35 percent Chardonnay, and 15 percent Pinot Blanc used to be sold under the Pinot designation. When the authorities enforced the regulations that state Chardonnay may only be used in Crémant d'Alsace, not a still wine under the AOC, Zind-Humbrecht was forced to sell the wine as *vin de table*. Since it

is not allowed to indicate a vintage on a *vin de table* (the European Union wine regime obviously does not believe in greater transparency), Olivier Humbrecht used a code, and it does not take a genius to figure out that Z001 stands for 2001, or that the next NV will be numbered Z002, and so on. The funny thing is that the maximum permitted yield for *vin de table* is 90 hectoliters per hectare as opposed to 100 hectoliters per hectare for the Alsace appellation, and chaptalization is banned. Silly us for thinking that an AOC is supposed to be superior to a *vin de table*!

WHITE Some Pinot wines are occasionally spineless, but lackluster examples are not as common as they used to be, as it is the plump and juicy *cuvées* that have made this the fastest-growing category of Alsace wine.

🍇 Pinot Blanc, Auxerrois, Pinot Noir (vinified white), Pinot Gris

🍷 2–4 years

✓ *J. B. Adam* • *Camille Braun* • *C. V. Cléebourg* • *Pierre Frick* **Ⓞ** (Précieuse) • *JosMeyer* **Ⓑ** • *Koeberlé-Kreyer* • *Albert Mann* • *CV Pfaffenheim* • *Rolly Gassmann* • *Sylvie Spielmann* **Ⓑ** • *Zind-Humbrecht* **Ⓑ** (including Zin *vin de table*)

PINOT BLANC AOC

This designation should only be used if the wine is made from 100 percent Pinot Blanc. *See also* Pinot AOC

PINOT GRIS AOC

CLOS ST LANDELIN

PINOT GRIS 2002
René Muré

This designation is now the most common way of marketing wine from the rich Pinot Gris grape. For hundreds of years, it has been known locally as Tokay d'Alsace. Legend had it that the Pinot Gris was brought back to Alsace from Hungary by Baron Lazare de Schwendi in the 1560s, and as Tokay or Tokaji was the only famous Hungarian wine, it was assumed that this was the grape Tokay was made from, and the name stuck. But they got it all wrong: this grape came to Alsace from Burgundy, Schwendi had nothing to do with it, and Pinot Gris has nothing to do with Tokay/Tokaji. In the 1980s, the Hungarians wanted their name back, and initially the French agreed, but after counterarguments from Alsace producers, alleging over 400 years' use of the name, the French reneged, and agreed instead to change the name from Tokay d'Alsace to Tokay-Pinot Gris, with vague promises that they might drop the Tokay at some time in the future. That did not happen, but the fall of communism did, and with Hungary's entry to the European Union, the French were forced to honor their partner's historic appellation, so all bottles will have to be labeled Pinot Gris, with no reference to Tokay, no later than the end of 2006.

WHITE This full-bodied, off-dry wine is decadently rich, but has excellent acidity, and its fullness of flavor never tires the palate. A young Pinot Gris can taste or smell of banana, sometimes be smoky, with little or no spice, but as it matures it increasingly develops a smoky-spice, toasty-creamy richness, finally achieving a big, honeyed walnut-brazil complexity with good bottle age. Top Alsace Riesling can be much finer, but the variety is so sensitive to soil conditions and handling that the quality is nowhere near as consistent as Pinot Gris across the board.

🍇 Pinot Gris

🍷 5–10 years

☑ *Lucien Albrecht • Barmès-Buecher* **B** *• J. P. & J. F. Becker* **B** *(Froehn) • Albert Boxler • C. V. Cléebourg • Robert Faller (Bénédicte) • C. V. de Hunawihr (Rosacker) • André Kientzler • Henri Klée • Albert Mann • Mittnacht-Klack • Muller-Koeberle • Ostertag* **B** *• Antoine Stoffel • Bernard Weber (Finkenberg) • Weinbach/Faller • Zind-Humbrecht* **B** *• VT Lucien Albrecht • Joseph Cattin • Jean-Marie Koehly • Marc Kreydenweiss • Hugel & Fils • Vignobles Reinhart • Zind-Humbrecht* **B** *• SGN J B Adam • Léon Beyer (Quintessence) • Albert Boxler • Marcel Deiss* **B** *• Louis Freyburger* **B** *(Altenberg de Bergheim) • Hugel & Fils • Marc Kreydenweiss • Koberlé-Kreyer • Kuentz-Bas • Albert Mann (Altenbourg Le Tri) • F. E. Trimbach • Weinbach/Faller • Zind-Humbrecht* **B** *• Pierre Paul Zink (Barrique)*

PINOT NOIR AOC

Not so long ago, Pinot Noir d'Alsace was synonymous in style with rosé, but the trend has swung hard over toward a true red wine. After a steep learning curve, during which many wines were overextracted, lacked elegance, were prone to rapid oxidation, and bore the most ungainly caramelized characteristics, Alsace winemakers have now managed to master the handling of oak and red-wine techniques. Alsace producers are now allowed to use a fatter bottle of almost Burgundian proportions for Pinot Noir instead of the Flûte d'Alsace, the use of which has been enshrined in law since 1959. This is a positive move, and although strictly confined to Pinot Noir, I hear rumors that it will be used for other Pinot varieties, which would also be good.

RED Most are unsatisfactory (overextracted, too tannic, or too oaky—sometimes all three), but Marcel Deiss's Burlenberg is in a different class and is comparable to a good Burgundy. A step down, but still good, is Domaine Weinbach Réserve in a good year, and the most commercial of all, Hugel Jubilée Pinot Noir, with its special selection Le Neveaux, is a serious contender for Deiss's crown. And that is about it. You can find perhaps another four or five wines each year that are delightful on the nose, but do not live up to the promise on the palate. Why is it that although both Alsace and Germany started at the same time (mid-1980s) to develop Pinot Noir as a serious red wine style (as opposed to rosé), only Germany has succeeded? The cadre of top-performing German Pinot Noir producers includes the likes of Deutzerhof, Kreuzberg, Huber, Johner, Knipser, Philipp Kuhn, Bernhart, Fürst, August Kesseler, and Aldinger, yet the only Alsace producer who would not be shown up in such company is Deiss, and the very best of Hugel's wines.

🍇 Pinot Noir

🍷 2–6 years (12 years for exceptional *cuvées*)

ROSÉ At its best, this dry, light-bodied wine has a deliciously fragrant aroma and flavor, which is reminiscent of strawberries, raspberries, or cherries. Seldom seen on export markets, but still commonly encountered by the *pichet* in local *winstubs*.

🍇 Pinot Noir

🍷 1–2 years

☑ *Marcel Deiss* **B** *(Burlenberg) • Hugel & Fils (Jubilée Le Neveux) • Weinbach/Faller (Réserve)*

RIESLING AOC

Of all Alsace grape varieties, Riesling is the most susceptible to differences in soil: clay soils give fatness and richness; granite Riesling is also rich, but with more finesse; limestone adds obvious finesse but less richness; and volcanic soil gives a well-flavored, spicy style.

WHITE In youth, fine Rieslings can show hints of apple, fennel, citrus, and peach, but can be so firm and austere that they give no hint of the beautiful wines into which they can evolve.

🍇 Riesling

🍷 4–20 years

☑ *J B Adam • Lucien Albrecht (Clos Schild) • Barmès-Buecher* **B** *• Léon Baur* **B** *• Léon Beyer • Paul Blanck* **O** *(Furstentum, Schlossberg) • Albert Boxler (Sommerberg Vieilles Vignes) • Albert Hertz • JosMeyer* **B** *(Hengst) • Mader • Albert Mann (Schlossberg) • Frédéric Mochel • Muré* **O** *(Clos St.-Landelin) • Rolly Gassmann • Martin Schaetzel* **B** *• Roland Schmitt • Schoffit • Jean Sipp • Louis Sipp • Sipp-Mack • Bruno Sorg • Sylvie Spielmann* **B** *•*

Bernard Schwach • F. E. Trimbach (Cuvée Frédéric Emile, Clos Ste.-Hune, Réserve) • Weinbach/Faller • Wunsch & Mann • Zind-Humbrecht **B** *• VT Jean Becker • Hugel & Fils • JosMeyer* **B** *• André Kientzler • Weinbach/Faller • Zind-Humbrecht* **B** *• SGN Hugel & Fils • Fernand Engel* **O** *• André Kientzler • F. E. Trimbach • Weinbach/Faller • Zind-Humbrecht* **B**

SYLVANER AOC

Hugh Johnson once described the Sylvaner as "local tap-wine," and this is how it should be served—direct from the stainless-steel vat, with all the zip and zing of natural carbonic gas (normally filtered out during the bottling process). Like the Muscat, it does not suit heat, and is a wine to buy in cooler years. Most attempts at late-harvest or botrytized styles (which cannot legally be sold as either VT or SGN) are diabolical. This does not mean that people should give up, just that they should not try to palm off these failures on the public. Better to add their tiny quantity to a much larger volume of an Edelzwicker—or whatever they like to call it—and sell more bottles of a turbo-charged basic appellation at a much smaller premium, as this might result in better reviews and a better profit. Alsace producers should take a lesson from Angelo Publisi of Ballandean winery (*see p.596*), who replicates the VT style by cutting the fruit-bearing canes just after *véraison*. This cuts the grape off from the vine's metabolism and the effect is much the same as when the leaves drop and sap returns to the roots after the first snap of winter. The resulting wine is consistently fabulous.

WHITE Sylvaner is an unpretentious, dry, light- to medium-bodied wine, with fragrance rather than fruitiness. It is generally best drunk young, but, like the Muscat, exceptionally long-living examples can always be found.

🍇 Sylvaner

🍷 Upon purchase

☑ *Agathe Bursin • JosMeyer* **B** *(Rouge—sic) • Rolly Gassmann • Weinbach/Faller • Zind-Humbrecht* **B**

VIN D'ALSACE AOC

Alternative designation for Alsace AOC.

MORE GREEN ALSACE

In addition to the Alsace producers recommended above, and which are either biodynamic or organic, there are also the following. No negative inference of quality should be taken from the fact that they are not featured among my recommended Alsace producers. There are a number that have been recommended in other editions, and still make some fine wines, but have been culled out to make room for others.

Biodynamic
Geschickt (Ammerschwihr)
Jean Ginglinger (Pfaffenheim)
Pierre-Paul Humbrecht (Pfaffenheim)
Marc Kreydenweiss (Andlau)
Jean Schaetzel (Ammerschwihr)
Trapet Alsace (Beblenheim)
Valentin Zusslin Fils (Orschwihr)

Organic
Yves Amberg (Epfig)
Yannick et Jean Baltenweck (Ribeauvillé)
Maurice Barthelme (Wettolsheim)
Rémy Biwand (Mackenheim)
Lucien et Théo Dietrich (Sigolsheim)
Yves Dietrich (Sigolsheim)
André Durrmann (Andlau)
Eblin-Fuchs (Zellenberg)

Gilg (Wettolsheim)
Philippe & Fernand Heitz (Molsheim)
Annick Hummel (St-Léonard Boersch)
Bernard Hummel (St-Léonard Boersch)
Martin Jund (Colmar)
Clément Klur (Katzenthal)
Mathieu Knecht (Dambach la Ville)
Pierre Martin (Scherwiller)
Mischler (Bennwihr)
Mittnacht Frères (Hunawihr)
Charles Muller & Fils (Traenheim)
François-Joseph Munsch (Jungholtz)
André Rohrer (Mittelbergheim)
Albert Staehle (Wintzenheim)
Philippe Vorburger (Voegtlinshoffen)
Odile & Danielle Weber (Eguisheim)

THE LOIRE VALLEY

In winemaking terms, the Loire Valley is best imagined as a long ribbon with crisp white wines at either end and fuller wines of all types in the middle. It is the home of Sauvignon Blanc, the only wine area in the world that specializes in Cabernet Franc and, in truly great vintages, makes some of the most sublime and sumptuous botrytized wines.

THE LOIRE IS THE LONGEST RIVER in France. From its source in the Cévennes Mountains, it flows 620 miles (1,000 kilometers) through 12 *départements*. The variations in soil, climate, and grape varieties found along its banks and those of its tributaries are reflected in the wide range of wines grown in the four major wine-producing districts. Red, white, and rosé; still, *pétillant*, and fully sparkling wines are produced in 87 different appellations ranging in style from bone dry to intensely sweet.

THE LOIRE'S MOST IMPORTANT GRAPE

The Chenin Blanc grape produces four distinctly different styles of wine—dry, semisweet, sweet, and sparkling. This is due to traditional practices that have been forced on growers by the vagaries of climate. This grape has abundant natural acidity and, if it receives enough sun, a high sugar content. But the Loire is considered a northern area in viticultural terms, and the vine grower must contend with late frosts, cold winds, and variable summers. Given a sunny year, the grower's natural inclination is to make the richest wine possible with this sweet and tangy grape; but in many vintages, only a medium or a dry style can be achieved. This variation in style is the root of the Loire's problems because it is difficult to build a reputation on uncertainty. If you take into account overproduction, the all too often debilitating effect of rot, and the lack of almost any

VINEYARDS AT VOUVRAY
In sunny years the area just to the east of Tours produces sweet, slow-maturing wines, valued for their longevity.

RECENT LOIRE VINTAGES

2003 The vintage par excellence for Cabernet Franc and other Loire reds, which have an intensity of color and flavor seldom seen in the Loire, with a plumpness of fruit and, thanks to low acid levels, a seductively soft finish. Some very rich, incredibly sweet wines have been made, but through *passerillage*, not botrytis. Be very wary of all dry whites, with the possible exception of Muscadet, which might not be Muscadet as we know it, but has made some tremendous wines for those who like to see a more Burgundian style.

2002 Top-class vintage for all styles in all districts, the wines have great ripeness levels, but pack more acidity than the 2003s.

2001 A very good year for dry whites, but not for reds, although some of the best growers in Bourgueil and Chinon made some good wines. Sweet whites possess lots of botrytis, thus great finesse.

2000 With heavy rain and cold temperatures in July, along with widespread mildew, this was a problematic year with extremely variable results. Contrary to expectations, the reds have good color and represent one of the Loire's successes. They have an easy-drinking suppleness, but are not for keeping. However, it is the Sauvignon wines of the Central Loire that stand out. Good Muscadet was made, with fruit as well as acidity for a change, but very few sweet wines of any note.

1999 A difficult year that produced some surprisingly good, soft, and supple reds (Alphonse Mellot's red Sancerre in particular). The whites have good acidity. Tread carefully.

Legend:
- Pays Nantais *See also p200*
- Anjou-Saumur *See also p202*
- Touraine *See also p207*
- Central Vineyards *See also p211*
- Haut-Poitou
- Châteaumeillant
- Saint-Pourçain
- Côtes d'Auvergne
- Côtes Roannaises
- Côtes du Forez
- *Département* boundary
- Delimited VDQs regions
- ▲ Height above sea level (meters)

0   5   10   15 miles
0   10   20   30 km

THE LOIRE VALLEY, *see also* p.55

The longest river in France claims a larger number of appellations than any other classic wine region, commencing with Muscadet on the Atlantic side, and traveling upriver to Anjou-Saumur, Touraine, the Central Vineyards, and the little-known Upper Loire appellations.

selection criteria for picking grapes for all styles of wine except those produced from late-harvested or botrytized grapes, then add an alarming spread of sloppy winemaking, you have all the reasons why, for me, the Loire has become the least exciting of all French wine regions.

With the exception of wines such as the best Savennières, dry Chenin Blanc wines are all too often thin, harsh, and acidic. These wines do little to enhance the reputation of the Loire, but they do have similar characteristics to the wines of Champagne in that they are disappointing when still, yet appear glamorous when sparkling. It is little wonder, then, that as the Champagne trade rapidly evolved in the 19th century, so the seeds of a sparkling-wine industry were sown in Saumur, and today the Loire boasts the largest such market outside of Champagne itself.

THE LOIRE NEAR SANCERRE
In this area the ground rises well above the river and the neighboring vineyards.

DID YOU KNOW?

• The Loire is the last wild river in Europe and designated a World Heritage Site by the United Nations Educational, Scientific, and Cultural Organization (UNESCO).

• As a wild river, the water level can vary by several yards within a few days, and its islands slowly move from year to year.

• The Loire Valley is known as the "Garden of France."

• The Loire Valley is the second-largest sparkling wine region in France (although Crémant d'Alsace is the second-largest individual appellation).

To suggest that the Chenin Blanc is fit only for fizzing up is to do the grape a great injustice. First, it is not in fact suited to the classic *brut* style of sparkling wine, as its aromatic qualities tend to fight rather than absorb the subtle effects of second fermentation. Second, it is this very character that makes Chenin Blanc one of the world's greatest wine grapes when botrytized. However, it is not the grape that is intrinsically disappointing when vinified as a still wine, but merely the methods employed by the grower and winemaker.

Chenin Blanc has been given pride of place in the Anjou-Saumur district, but unfortunately its cultivation has spread to unsuitable areas over the past 25 years. Producers more interested in making money than building a fine reputation have taken advantage of the Chenin Blanc's natural inclination to overcrop. It is a grape that should be harshly pruned, but most growers lack the courage to do this, and when the weather is unsettled it is these same growers who are the first to harvest. The heavier the crop, the less ripe the grapes, and the less ripe the grapes, the more washed out the flavors.

However, there are quality-conscious growers in the Loire, who restrict their yield and allow the grapes to ripen, yet still agonize over whether to risk the weather for one more day's maturity. It is from such top-performing growers as Domaine Baumard in the Coteaux du Layon, Clos Naudin and Huet in Vouvray, and Dominique Moyer in Montlouis that we get Chenin Blanc wines that dazzle our palates.

FROM SOURCE TO SEA

For some inexplicable reason, most references restrict the Loire to its four major districts of Pays Nantais, Anjou-Saumur, Touraine, and Central Vineyards. Although some books incorporate the outlying areas of Fiefs Vendéens and Haut-Poitou, few mention the appellations of the Upper Loire, yet the wines of Côtes du Forez, Côte Roannaise, Côtes d'Auvergne, St.-Pourçain, and Châteaumeillant are equally legitimate members of the Loire's family of wines. And whereas the most famous appellations could and should rank among the most exciting wines of the world, there are so many underachievers that the major districts have become a minefield for wine lovers, while growers in the lesser-known areas of the Upper Loire have everything to prove.

THE GENERIC AND OUTLYING APPELLATIONS OF
THE LOIRE VALLEY

CHÂTEAUMEILLANT VDQS

Borders the Cher and Indre, around Bourges. Although only red-wine grapes are grown, white wine of some standing used to be made here, and its production is still permitted.

RED The Gamay grape usually dominates the red wines, which should be drunk as young as possible.

🍇 Gamay, Pinot Gris, Pinot Noir

🍷 6–12 months

ROSÉ The best Châteaumeillant wines. They are fresh, grapey, and delicately balanced.

🍇 Gamay, Pinot Gris, Pinot Noir

🍷 6–12 months

✓ *Du Chaillot* • *CV Châteaumeillant* • *Valérie et Frédéric Dallot* • *De Pavillon*

CÔTES D'AUVERGNE VDQS

Côtes d'Auvergne is located south of Saint-Pourçain and west of Côtes du Forez on the edge of the Massif Central. This is the most remotely situated of all the outer areas that fall officially within the Loire region. The wines from certain villages are superior and have therefore been given the right to use the following communal appellations: Côtes d'Auvergne-Boudes (villages of Boudes, Chalus, and St.-Hérant); Côtes d'Auvergne-Chanturgues (villages of Clermont-Ferrand and Cézabat [part]); Côtes d'Auvergne-Châteaugay (villages of Châteaugay and Cézabat [part]); Côtes d'Auvergne-Corent (villages of Corent, Les Martres-de-Veyre, La Sauvetat, and Veyre-Monton); and Côtes d'Auvergne-Madargues (village of Riom).

RED The best of these dry, light-bodied, and fruity wines carry the Chanturgues appellation. Most are made from Gamay, a grape that has traditionally been grown in the area, and are very much in the style of Beaujolais.

🍇 Gamay, Pinot Noir

🍷 1–2 years

WHITE These dry, light-bodied wines made from Chardonnay have been overlooked but can be more accessible than the same variety grown in more classic areas of the Loire, thus they are surely a marketable commodity in view of Chardonnay's upmarket status.

🍇 Chardonnay

🍷 1–2 years

ROSÉ These are dry, light-bodied wines with an attractive cherry flavor. They are made in the village of Clermont-Ferrand, and carry the Chanturgues appellation.

🍇 Gamay, Pinot Noir

🍷 Within 1 year

✓ *Vignoble de l'Arbe Blanc* • *Pradier* • *Gilles Persilier*

CÔTES DU FOREZ AOC

Similar to Beaujolais, this wine is produced in the Loire *département* adjacent to Lyon, and was upgraded from VDQS to AOC in 2000. The wines are improving through the efforts of the *coopérative* and a few quality-conscious growers, but they could be better.

RED These are dry, light-bodied wines with some fruit. They are best drunk young and at a cool temperature.

🍇 Gamay

🍷 Upon purchase

ROSÉ Simple, light-bodied, dry rosés that make attractive, unpretentious picnic wines.

🍇 Gamay

🍷 Upon purchase

✓ *Gilles Bonnefoy* (La Madone) • *Les Vignerons Foreziens* • *Odile Verdier et Jacky Logel*

CÔTE ROANNAISE AOC

Red and rosé wines made from a localized Gamay clone called Gamay Saint-Romain. Grown on south- and southwest-facing slopes of volcanic soil on the left bank of the Loire some 25 miles (40 kilometers) west of the Mâconnais district of Burgundy. This appellation was promoted from VDQS to full AOC status in 1994.

RED Some of these dry, medium- to full-bodied wines are produced using a form of *macération carbonique*, and a few are given a little maturation in cask. The result can vary between well-colored wines that are firm and distinctive, and oaky and fruity Beaujolais-type versions for quaffing when young.

🍇 Gamay

🍷 1–5 years

ROSÉ Dry, medium-bodied, well-made wines that are crisp and fruity.

🍇 Gamay

🍷 2–3 years

✓ *Alain Baillon* (Cuvée Monplaisir) • *Paul et Jean-Pierre Benetère* (Vieilles Vignes) • *Des Pothiers* • *De la Rochette* (Vieilles Vignes) • *Robert Serol* (Cuvée Troisgros)

CRÉMANT DE LOIRE AOC

Of all the Loire's sparkling wines, this is probably the most underrated, yet it has the greatest potential because it can be blended from the wines of Anjou-Saumur and Touraine and from the widest range of grape varieties.

SPARKLING WHITE The better-balanced *cuvées* of these dry to semisweet, light- to medium-bodied wines are normally a blend of Chenin Blanc in the main, with a good dash of Cabernet Franc and Chardonnay. The best Chardonnay clones are yet to be established in the Loire, but at least Chardonnay is widely utilized for sparkling wines, whereas Pinot Noir is not—this is a mystery, as it is a proven variety in the region.

🍇 Chenin Blanc, Cabernet Franc, Cabernet Sauvignon, Pineau d'Aunis, Pinot Noir, Chardonnay, Arbois, Grolleau Noir, and Grolleau Gris

🍷 1–3 years

SPARKLING ROSÉ The best of these light- to medium-bodied wines are *brut*, and usually contain a high proportion of Cabernet Franc and Grolleau Noir grapes. Cabernet Franc makes the most distinctive wine. A pure Pinot Noir *crémant* rosé would be interesting to taste.

🍇 Chenin Blanc, Cabernet Franc, Cabernet Sauvignon, Pineau d'Aunis, Pinot Noir, Chardonnay, Arbois, Grolleau Noir and Gris

⏳ Most are best consumed upon purchase, although some benefit if kept 1–2 years.

✓ *Baumard* • *Yves Lambert* • *Château de Montgueret* • *De Nerleux* • *Château de Putille* • *C. V. de Saumur*

HAUT-POITOU VDQS

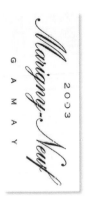

Situated 50 miles (80 kilometers) southwest of Tours, the Poitiers district produces wines that have achieved a remarkable reputation despite its hot, dry climate, and flat land that is more suited to arable farming than to viticulture. The local *cave coopérative* was responsible for this achievement, partly because of its high tech establishment, which turned out clean wines during the late 1980s, when the rest of the Loire was going through its worst dirty wine period, and partly due to clever marketing. However, things went wrong on the financial side, Georges Duboeuf bought 40 percent of the cooperative, and it now operates as a *négociant*.

RED This is a wine to watch: although the really successful reds have until now been in short supply and confined mainly to Cabernet, there is a feeling that a general breakthrough is imminent. The quality of the entire appellation is likely to rise significantly, and there is promise of some exciting, pure varietal reds.

🍇 Pinot Noir, Gamay, Merlot, Malbec, Cabernet Franc, Cabernet Sauvignon, and a maximum of 20% each of Gamay de Chaudenay and Grolleau

⏳ Within 3 years

WHITE Dry, light- to medium-bodied, varietal wines. Those made from pure Sauvignon are softer and more floral than most of their northern counterparts, yet retain the freshness and vitality that is so important to this grape variety.

🍇 Sauvignon Blanc, Chardonnay, Pinot Blanc, and up to a maximum of 20% Chenin Blanc

⏳ Within 1 year

ROSÉ These dry, light- to medium-bodied wines are fresh and fruity.

🍇 Pinot Noir, Gamay, Merlot, Malbec, Cabernet Franc, Cabernet Sauvignon, and a maximum of 20% each of Gamay de Chaudenay and Grolleau

⏳ Within 3 years

✓ *Ampelidæ* • *Du Centaure* • *C. V. Haut-Poitou*

ORLÉANS VDQS

Although made an appellation as recently as 2000, vines have been growing in this area since the 10th century. Legend has it that vines were originally brought from the Auvergne, hence the local synonyms of Auvernat Rouge for Pinot Noir and Auvernat Blanc for Chardonnay. The delimited area consists of 494 acres (200 hectares) in scattered parcels, of which 395 acres (160 hectares) are currently planted, encompassing the outskirts of Orléans, where the soil is silty, and 11 neighboring villages, stretching from the chalky soils of Saint Hilaire, and red, sandy-stony soils of Sologne, near Mézières, to clayey soils elsewhere.

RED Successful wines have good color and just about enough fruit to balance the tannins, affording a more supple finish. Montigny-Piel's Clos Saint-Fiacre stands out as the best wine of this appellation in all its color formats.

🍇 Minimum of 60% Pinot Meunier, plus Pinot Noir and Pinot Gris

⏳ Within 3 years

WHITE The least exciting wines so far, although it is very early days for these dry white wines, which must possess no more than 4 grams per liter of residual sugar.

🍇 Minimum of 60% Chardonnay, plus Pinot Gris

⏳ Within 1 year

ROSÉ The few encountered have been fresh, easy drinking with Meunier-cum-Pinot character, expressed more as red summer fruits than as cherries.

🍇 Minimum of 60% Pinot Meunier, plus Pinot Noir and Pinot Gris

⏳ Within 3 years

✓ *Montigny-Piel* (Clos Saint-Fiacre)

ORLÉANS-CLÉRY VDQS

This subappellation was granted in 2002, and is restricted to red wines produced in Cléry-Saint-André and four neighboring villages southwest of Orléans, but confusingly from entirely different grapes from the main appellation.

RED The local *coopérative* (Grand Maison) makes a good wine from 25-year-old vines, which is old for this rediscovered part of the Loire, but most Cabernet-based wines from this area suffer too much from a herbaceous character.

🍇 Minimum of 75% Cabernet Franc, plus Cabernet Sauvignon planted before October 2002

⏳ Within 3 years

✓ *Jacky Legroux* • *C. V. de la Grand Maison*

PINEAU DES CHARENTES AOC

A *vin de liqueur* produced in the Cognac region, which is between the Loire and Bordeaux (thus not really the Loire Valley, but it has to go somewhere!).

WHITE Few manage to rise above the typically dull, oxidative *vin de liqueur* style that goes *rancio* with age.

🍇 Cabernet Franc, Cabernet Sauvignon, Colombard, Folle Blanche, Jurançon Blanc, Meslier Saint-François, Merlot, Merlot Blanc, Montils, Sauvignon Blanc, Sémillon, Ugni Blanc

⏳ Upon opening

ROSÉ Few manage to rise above the typically dull, oxidative *vin de liqueur* style that goes *rancio* with age.

🍇 Cabernet Franc, Cabernet Sauvignon, Malbec, Merlot

⏳ Upon opening

✓ *Barbeau & Fils* (Tres Vieux Rosé Grand Réserve) • *Chais du Rouissoir* (Rosé) • *Vinet* (Félix-Marie de la Villière Blanc)

ROSÉ DE LOIRE AOC

A dry rosé wine introduced in 1974 to exploit the international marketing success of Rosé d'Anjou and to take advantage of the trend for drier styles. The result has been very disappointing on the whole, although the few producers (recommended below) who have really tried demonstrate that very good-quality dry rosé can be made throughout the Loire.

ROSÉ Dry, light- to medium-bodied rosé from the Loire that could (and should) be the most attractive wine of its type—a few growers try, but most do not. These wines may be sold from December 1 following the harvest without any mention of *primeur* or *nouveau*.

🍇 Pineau d'Aunis, Pinot Noir, Gamay, Grolleau, and at least 30% Cabernet Franc and Cabernet Sauvignon

⏳ Upon purchase

✓ *De Chanteloup* • *Lecheteau* • *De Montgilet* • *Château de Passavant*

ST-POURÇAIN VDQS

The wines of Saint-Pourçain have a long and impressive history for what is, after all, an obscure VDQS, with vineyards first planted not by the Romans, as elsewhere in the Loire Valley, but by the Phoenicians. The Saint-Pourçain area covers 19 communes southeast of the Bourges appellations of the Central Vineyards in the Allier *département*. The growers are quite ambitious, and many people think that these wines have a particularly promising future. There are 1,235 acres (500 hectares) of vineyards.

RED Dry, light- to medium-bodied wines, but they can vary from very light Beaujolais look-alikes to imitations of Bourgogne Passetoutgrains, depending on the grape varieties in the blend.

🍇 Gamay, Pinot Noir, and up to a maximum of 10% Gamay Teinturier

⏳ 1–2 years

WHITE Dry, light- to medium-bodied wines. The Tresallier grape (which is known as the Sacy in Chablis), when blended with Chardonnay and Sauvignon, produces a crisp, toasty, full-flavored wine that does have some merit. Very little is known about the Saint-Pierre-Doré, except that locals say it makes a "filthy wine," according to Master of Wine Rosemary George in *French Country Wines*.

🍇 A maximum of 50% Tresallier and 10% Saint-Pierre-Doré, plus Aligoté, Chardonnay, and Sauvignon Blanc

⏳ 1–2 years

ROSÉ Crisp, dry, light- to medium-bodied wines that have a fragrance that is reminiscent of soft summer fruits. The rosés are generally more successful than the red wines of the area, but both styles are particularly refreshing and thirst-quenching.

🍇 Gamay, Pinot Noir, and up to a maximum of 10% Gamay Teinturier

⏳ 1–2 years

✓ *De Bellevue* • *Jallet* (Les Ceps Centenaires) • *C. V. de Saint-Pourçain* (Cuvée Réserve) • *Cave Touzain*

PAYS NANTAIS

Nantais is Muscadet country. The Sèvre-et-Maine district produces the richest Muscadet, while Côtes de Grandlieu, granted its own appellation in 1994, and the Coteaux de la Loire to the north produce wines with extra acidity.

SOUTHEAST OF NANTES are the vineyards of Muscadet. The best are those of the Sèvre-et-Maine district, named after two rivers, which is much hillier than the surrounding countryside and protected from northwesterly winds by Nantes itself. Sèvre-et-Maine accounts for one-quarter of the general appellation area, yet 85 percent of all Muscadet produced. Only in unusually hot or dry years, when they contain extra natural acidity, can Muscadet grapes grown farther north in the Coteaux de la Loire sometimes surpass those of Sèvre-et-Maine.

THE MUSCADET GRAPE AND ITS WINES
It is uncertain when the Muscadet grape, also known as the Melon de Bourgogne and the Gamay Blanc, was first planted in the area. There is a plaque at Château de la Cassemichère that claims that the first Muscadet vine was transplanted there from Burgundy in 1740. But Pierre Galet, the famous ampelographer (vine botanist), tells us that "following the terrible winter of 1709, Louis XIV ordered that the replanting of the frozen vineyards of Loire-Atlantique be with Muscadet blanc."

The wine produced from the Muscadet grape is neutral in flavor and bears no hint of the muskiness that some believe its name implies. Traditionally, it is harvested early to preserve acidity, and yet, in doing so, the grower risks making a wine that lacks fruit. But if the wine is left in contact with its sediment and bottled *sur lie*, this enhances the fruit, adds a yeasty roundness, and, by retaining more of the carbonic gas created during fermentation, imparts a certain liveliness and freshness.

There have always been rare examples of exceptionally ripe Muscadet, which tend to age like a modest Burgundy after a few years in bottle. More recently, however, there has been a trend among quality-conscious growers to pick riper grapes (which is a significant risk, given the weather), in order to produce fuller, richer wines. This practice has come under attack from more conservative growers, who believe that there should not only be a maximum alcoholic strength for the finished wine (currently 12 percent after any chaptalization), but also a high minimum total acidity.

I have some sympathy with these traditionalists, since the Melon de Bourgogne grape is intrinsically incapable of competing with Chardonnay at even modest levels, thus most of the wines produced in this manner, while being extraordinary for Muscadet, make disappointing "Burgundy." Furthermore, I like the way that a correctly lean structure and naturally high acidity yield a certain nervosity of fruit in good Muscadet. However, good Muscadet represents perhaps one out of every 10 bottles, and it is a lack—sometimes a total absence—of fruit that is the pitfall of the rest. The *sur lie* process cannot conjure fruit out of thin air. But, despite their initial concentration on richness rather than fruit, the new winemakers should be encouraged, as they need to experiment in every direction if they are to find a reliable way to impart a feather-light fruit and freshness to these wines. There is no need for traditionalists to worry about the classic Muscadet style being perverted by a few; they have already done much worse by allowing the majority to all but destroy its classic quality. They should give the rebels the chance to do better; they will not want a reputation for poor man's Burgundy, but rather for rich man's Muscadet.

FACTORS AFFECTING TASTE AND QUALITY

LOCATION
The Pays Nantais lies in the coastal area and the westernmost district of the Loire Valley, with vineyards occupying parts of the Loire-Atlantique and the Maine-et-Loire *départements*.

CLIMATE
Mild and damp, but winters can be harsh and spring frosts troublesome. Summers are generally warm and sunny, although they are also rainy.

ASPECT
Some of the vineyards are found on the flat land around the mouth of the Loire southwest of Nantes. There are rolling hills in the Sèvre-et-Maine and Coteaux de la Loire, with the best vineyards on gentle riverside slopes. Some of the smaller valleys are actually too steep for viticulture, and the vines in these areas occupy the hilltops.

SOIL
The best vineyards of the Sèvre-et-Maine are light and stony, with varying proportions of sand, clay, and gravel above a granitic, schistous, and volcanic subsoil that is rich in potassium and magnesium. The Coteaux de la Loire is more schistous, while the Côtes de Grandlieu is schistous and granitic, and vineyards in the generic Muscadet appellation have sand with silt. These soils provide good drainage, essential here.

VITICULTURE AND VINIFICATION
The Muscadet is a frost-resistant, early-ripening grape that adapts well to the damp conditions of the Pays Nantais. It is harvested early (mid- to late September) to preserve its acidity, although a number of growers have started to reduce yields and pick riper. The best Muscadet is left in vat or barrel on its sediment—*sur lie*—until it is bottled. This imparts a greater depth and fruitiness, and a faint prickle of natural carbonic gas.

GRAPE VARIETIES
Primary varieties: Muscadet, Folle Blanche
Secondary varieties: Cabernet Franc, Cabernet Sauvignon, Gamay, Gamay de Chaudenay, Gamay de Bouze, Négrette, Pinot Noir, Groslot Gris, Chardonnay, Chenin Blanc

PAYS NANTAIS. *see also* p.196
The finest wines in the Pays Nantais are produced to the east of Nantes in Sèvre-et-Maine and Coteaux de la Loire.

THE APPELLATIONS OF
PAYS NANTAIS

COTEAUX D'ANCENIS VDQS

These varietal VDQS wines, which come from the same area as Muscadet Coteaux de la Loire, should be promoted to full AOC status.

RED Bone-dry to dry, and light- to medium-bodied wines that include Cabernets, made from both Cabernet Franc and Cabernet Sauvignon grapes. Surprisingly, they are not as successful as the juicy Gamay wines that represent no less than 80 percent of the total production of this appellation.

🍇 Cabernet Sauvignon, Cabernet Franc, Gamay, and up to a combined total of 5% Gamay de Chaudenay and Gamay de Bouze

⌒ 2 years

WHITE Dry to medium-dry, light-bodied wines. The Pinot Gris, also sold as "Malvoisie," is not as alcoholic as its Alsatian cousin, yet can possess a light richness that will linger in the mouth. The Chenin Blanc, known locally as "Pineau de la Loire," is rarely very special.

🍇 Chenin Blanc, Pinot Gris

⌒ 12–18 months

ROSÉ Bone-dry to dry, light- to medium-bodied wines, some of which are fresh, firm, and lively. Gamay is the most popular grape variety.

🍇 Cabernet Sauvignon, Cabernet Franc, Gamay, and up to a combined total of 5% Gamay de Chaudenay and Gamay de Bouze

⌒ 2 years

✓ *CV des Terroirs de la Noëlle* • *Guindon* • *Du Haut Fresne*

FIEFS VENDÉENS VDQS

A *vin de pays* until 1984, this appellation has been steadily improving and deserves its VDQS status. The regulations controlling the grape varieties permitted for this appellation are unique. They determine the proportion of each variety that must be cultivated in the vineyard, yet they do not limit the percentages of grapes contained in the final blend; thus blends and pure varietals are allowed.

RED The communes of Vix and Mareuil-sur-Lay-Disais produce the best wines. They are dry, medium-bodied, and firm, but not long-lived. They can have a grassy character, derived from the Cabernet Franc, which is the predominant grape grown in both these villages.

🍇 A minimum of 50% Gamay and Pinot Noir plus Cabernet Franc, Cabernet Sauvignon, Négrette, and up to a maximum of 15% Gamay de Chaudenay

⌒ Within 18 months

WHITE Bone-dry to dry, light-bodied wines which, apart from those of Vix and Pissotte, are of limited quality. This could be because the Chenin Blanc rarely ripens properly in a northerly coastal area. If some of the other permitted grape varieties were grown over a much wider area, quality might improve.

🍇 A minimum of 50% Chenin Blanc, plus Sauvignon Blanc and Chardonnay. A maximum of 20% Melon de Bourgogne in the communes of Vix and Pissotte and a maximum of 30% Groslot Gris in the coastal vineyards around Les Sables d'Olonne.

⌒ Upon purchase

ROSÉ Dry, light- to medium-bodied wines. The best wines of Vix and Mareuil-sur-Lay-Disais are soft, delicate, and underrated.

🍇 A minimum of 50% Gamay and Pinot Noir plus Cabernet Franc, Cabernet Sauvignon, Négrette, and a maximum of 15% Gamay de Chaudenay. A maximum of 30% (was as high as 30% until 1994) Groslot Gris in the coastal vineyards around Les Sables d'Olonne.

⌒ Within 18 months

✓ *Coirer* (Pissotte Sélection) • *Des Dames* (Les Aigues Marines) • *Saint Nicolas* (Brem Reflets)

GROS PLANT VDQS OR
GROS PLANT NANTAIS VDQS

Gros Plant is the local synonym for the Folle Blanche—one of the grapes used to make Cognac.

WHITE Gros Plant is normally so dry, tart, and devoid of fruit and body that it seems tough and sinewy to taste. I would rather drink lemon juice than 99 percent of the Gros Plant that I have had, but if yields are limited and the wine bottled *sur lie*, it can have sufficient depth to match its inherent bite.

🍇 Gros Plant

⌒ Usually upon purchase

✓ *De la Boitaudière* (Sur Lie) • *Guy Bossard* Ⓑ (De l'Ecu) • *La Haut-Vrignais* (Sur Lie)

MUSCADET AOC

This basic appellation covers the whole Muscadet area, yet the wines produced under it account for only 10 percent of the total production.

WHITE Bone-dry, light-bodied wines that, with very few exceptions, are ordinary at best, and often lack balance. Not one basic Muscadet has impressed me in recent years. These wines may be sold as *primeur* or *nouveau* as from the third Thursday of November following the harvest.

🍇 Muscadet

⌒ Upon purchase

MUSCADET DES
COTEAUX DE LA LOIRE AOC

The Coteaux de la Loire is the most northerly wine area on the French coast, above which it is almost impossible to grow grapes of sufficient ripeness for winemaking.

WHITE Bone-dry, light-bodied wines of variable quality, usually lacking in fruit, but can be the best balanced of all Muscadets in very hot years.

🍇 Muscadet

⌒ Upon purchase

✓ *Guindon* • *Du Moulin Giron* • *De la Varenne*

MUSCADET CÔTES DE
GRANDLIEU AOC

Delimited as recently as 1994, this area west of Sèvre-et-Maine once represented 73 percent of the basic Muscadet appellation. The wines now fetch a nice premium above that received when they were merely perceived as generic Muscadets and, while some deserve elevated price and status, many plainly do not.

WHITE Bone-dry, light-bodied wines that initially displayed considerable variation in quality, but the best are now showing a fine, floral-minerality of fruit.

🍇 Muscadet

⌒ Upon purchase

✓ *Du Fief Guerin* • *Gandais Père & Fils* • *Les Hautes Noëlles*

MUSCADET DE
SÈVRE-ET-MAINE AOC

Classic Muscadet from a small area containing most of the best wines. Some 45 percent of this appellation is bottled and sold as *sur lie*, having remained in contact with its sediment for at least one winter before bottling. There are so many groupings of Muscadet estates that I have decided to list them separately where I can.

WHITE Bone-dry to dry, light-bodied wines. The best should have fruit, acidity, and elegance, but although they can be reminiscent of a modest white Burgundy and exceptional wines can survive considerable aging, they seldom improve and always trade off finesse for depth.

🍇 Muscadet

⌒ 2 years, although some may last 3–4 years

✓ *Guy Bossard* Ⓑ (De l'Ecu) • *De la Braudière* • *Michel Bregeon* • *De la Chauvinière* • *Chasseloir* • *Coing de Saint-Fiacre* • *Comte Leloup de Chasseloir* • *Jean Douillard* • *Gandais Père & Fils* • *Grand Fief de la Cormeraie* • *La Haute Févrie* • *De la Louvetrie* • *Des Petites Cossardières* • *De la Quilla* • *Château des Roi* • *Abbaye de Ste Radegonde* • *Sauvion* Ⓞ

MUSCADET SUR LIE AOC

Until recently there were no controls and unscrupulous producers would simply describe an ordinary filtered wine as *sur lie* and thereby demand a higher price. Since 1994, however, this term may be applied to only one of the three subappellations (Coteaux du Loire, Côtes de Grandlieu, and Sèvre-et-Maine) and may not be used on any wines bearing the generic Muscadet AOC. Quite what the logic is to this is uncertain, since Gros Plant VDQS is permitted to use *sur lie* and it is even more inferior than the generic Muscadet appellation. The lesser the wine, the more need for a *sur lie* boost, thus rather than limiting its use, more emphasis should be placed on stricter controls.

At the moment Muscadet *sur lie* must remain in contact with its sediment for one winter, and may not be bottled before the third week of March following the harvest, with a second bottling period of mid-October to mid-November for fuller styles. The wine must also be bottled directly off its lees, and must not be racked or filtered, but there is still no regulation on the size and type of vessel in which the wine should be kept *sur lie*. Some growers would like the term applied only to wines kept in wooden barrels, arguing that the effect of keeping a wine in contact with its lees in huge vats is negligible, but at the very least vats over a certain size should be equipped with paddles to circulate the lees.

ANJOU-SAUMUR

Anjou-Saumur is a microcosm of the entire Loire Valley, with almost every grape available in the Loire producing virtually every style of wine imaginable—from dry to sweet, red through rosé to white, and still wines to sparkling.

SAUMUR IS THE LOIRE'S SPARKLING-WINE CENTER, where tourists flock in the summer, visiting the numerous cellars hewn out of the solid tufa subsoil. The magnificent white tufa-stone castle that overlooks the town was built in the 14th century. It is regarded as one of the finest of the Loire châteaux, and is used by the Confrérie des Chevaliers du Sacavins (one of Anjou's several wine fraternities) for various inaugural ceremonies and celebrations.

VINEYARDS, COTEAUX DU LAYON
In favorable sites, the vines are sometimes attacked by "noble rot." The area is famous for its sweet white wines.

THE WINES OF ANJOU

Rosé still represents as much as 45 percent of Anjou's total wine output, even though it is on the decline. The figure was 55 percent in the late 1980s. However, although rosé remains this district's most popular wine, it has a down-market image and is essentially a blend of minor grapes; thus its commercial success has not propelled a specific variety to fame. Anjou's most celebrated grape is the Chenin Blanc used to make white wines. This vine has been cultivated in the area for well over a thousand years. It has many synonyms, from "Pineau de la Loire" to "Franc-blanc," but its principal name, Chenin Blanc, stems from Mont-Chenin in 15th-century Touraine. Under other names it can be traced as far

back as the year 845, to the abbey of Glanfeuil (south of the river in the Anjou district). The distinctive tang of the Chenin Blanc grape comes from its inherently high tartaric acid content and this, combined with a naturally high extract, makes for unacceptably tart and often bitter styles of dry and medium-dry white. Exceptions to this rule are few and mostly confined to the four sun-blessed, southeast-facing slopes of Savennières. Anjou growers go by the rule rather than the exception, and the common practice has always been to leave the harvest of this variety until as late as

ANJOU-SAUMUR,
see also p.196–7
Boasting sparkling wine, and more, from Saumur, and a range of wines from Angers's environs, Anjou-Saumur produces most types of wine found in the Loire as a whole.

BOTTLING AT
SAUMUR-CHAMPIGNY
The appellation produces some of the Loire Valley's finest red wines from Cabernet Franc.

possible. This invites the risk of rain, but by going over the vines several times in the time-honored tradition of *tries*, picking only the ripest and healthiest grapes on each and every sweep of the vineyard, a miraculous wine may be made. Although this is a time-consuming, labor-intensive operation, the unique quality of overripe grapes produced can result in the most succulent and immaculately balanced of sweet wines. Unlike poor and boring dry Chenin Blanc wines that only deteriorate with age, these treasures are vinous investments that are capable of great maturity and can achieve wonderfully complex honeyed characteristics.

THE SPARKLING SAUMUR INDUSTRY

With the rapid growth of the Champagne market in the 19th century, producers in the Loire began to copy effervescent winemaking practices, believing that here, at last, was a potential outlet for the surplus of thin, tart Chenin Blanc wines with which even the most quality-conscious growers were often lumbered. Saumur eventually turned into the largest French sparkling-wine industry outside Champagne. In many parts of the Loire the Chenin Blanc grape has the perfect acidity for a quality sparkling wine, although devotees of the true yeasty character of Champagne can find its bouquet sweet and aromatic, maintaining that its flavor is too assertive to be properly transmuted by the traditional method. However, the wines are hugely popular, and the mixture of Chardonnay and other neutral varieties can greatly improve the overall blend. The most ardent admirer of Champagne has been known to fall prey to the charms of a superior pure Chenin Blanc bubbly from this region, and even

TUFA SUBSOIL CELLARS
The tufa-stone not only dominates the architecture; the subsoil is ideal for the sparkling-wine cellars.

THE TOWN OF SAUMUR
The 14th-century castle, one of the finest in the Loire, towers above the bustling town of Saumur, the buildings distinguished by the brilliant white tufa-stone typical of the area.

I have been known to be besotted by Bouvet-Ladubay's luxuriously ripe, oak-fermented Trésor.

THE REGION'S RED WINES

It is in Anjou, especially south of Saumur, that the Cabernet Franc emerges as the Loire's best red-wine grape. However, beyond neighboring Touraine, its cultivation rapidly diminishes. The Loire is the largest wine region in France, yet surprisingly it boasts just three classic red wines—Saumur-Champigny, Bourgueil, and Chinon—to which we might now add Anjou-Villages. It is no coincidence that most of the vineyards producing these wines are clustered together in a compact area around the confluence of the Vienne and the Loire—two rivers that long ago established the gravel terraces so prized for growing Cabernet Franc today.

FACTORS AFFECTING TASTE AND QUALITY

LOCATION
West-central district with mostly left-bank vineyards situated between Angers and Saumur.

CLIMATE
A gentle Atlantic-influenced climate with light rainfall, warm summers, and mild falls, but frost is a problem in Savennières.

ASPECT
Soft, rolling hills which hold back the westerly winds. The best sites are the south-facing rocky hillsides of Savennières and the steep-sided valley of the Layon River.

SOIL
In the west and around Layon, the soil is schist with a dark, shallow topsoil that stores heat well and helps ripen the grapes, but some colder clay-soil areas produce heavier wines. The chalk-tufa soil in the east of the district around Saumur produces lighter wines, while the shale and gravel in Saumur-Champigny favors Cabernet Franc.

VITICULTURE AND VINIFICATION
The Chenin Blanc is a particularly slow-ripening grape that is often left on the vine until November, especially in the Coteaux du Layon. The effect of the fall sun on the dew-drenched, overripe grapes can encourage "noble rot," particularly in Bonnezeaux and Quarts-de-Chaume. In good years, pickers go through the vineyards several times, selecting only the ripest or most rotten grapes—a tradition known as *tries*. Most wines are bottled in the spring following the vintage, but wines produced from such richly sweet grapes take at least three months to ferment and, for this reason, might not be bottled until the following fall.

GRAPE VARIETIES
Primary varieties: Chenin Blanc, Cabernet Franc, Gamay, Grolleau
Secondary varieties: Chardonnay, Sauvignon Blanc, Cabernet Sauvignon, Malbec, Pineau d'Aunis

THE APPELLATIONS OF
ANJOU-SAUMUR

ANJOU AOC

The Anjou district encompasses the vineyards of Saumur; thus Saumur may be sold as Anjou, but not vice versa. The red wines are by far the best, the whites the worst, and the rosé wines, although waning in popularity, remain the most famous. Because "mousseux" has "cheap bubbly" connotations, the wines officially designated as Anjou Mousseux appellation are often marketed simply as "Anjou."

RED Dry, medium- to full-bodied wines, made mostly from pure Cabernet Franc or with a touch of Cabernet Sauvignon. These delightful wines are best drunk young, although the odd oak-aged wine of surprising complexity can be found.

🍇 Cabernet Franc, Cabernet Sauvignon, Pineau d'Aunis

🍷— 1–3 years

✓ *Des Baumard • Bouvet-Ladubay* (Non Pareils) *• Château de Fesles • Richard Leroy • Le Logis du Prieuré • D'Orgigné • Des Sablonnettes* (Genêts) *• Saint Arnoul • De la Sansonnière • Château Soucherie* (Champ aux Loups) *• De Terrebrune*

WHITE Although these wines vary from dry to sweet and from light- to full-bodied types, there are too many aggressively acid-dry or simply mediocre medium-sweet Chenin Blanc wines in the appellation. Some improvement has been made by growers maximizing the 20 percent Chardonnay and Sauvignon allowance, while Jacques Beaujeu and a few others use oak to smooth out Chenin's jagged edges, and Ogereau even ferments *en barrique*. These wines may be sold from December 1 following the harvest without any mention of *primeur* or *nouveau*.

🍇 A minimum of 80% Chenin Blanc and a maximum of 20% Chardonnay and Sauvignon Blanc

🍷— Upon purchase

✓ *Philippe Delesvaux • Les Grandes Vignes* (Varenne de Combre) *• Ogereau • Château de Passavant* ⦿ *• Jo Pithon • Du Regain • Du Roy René* (Les Pierres) *• Richou • Château La Varière*

ROSÉ Once a marketing miracle, Anjou Rosé or Rosé d'Anjou sells less well in today's increasingly sophisticated markets. There is nothing intrinsically wrong with a wine that happens to be pink with some sweetness, although you would be forgiven for thinking this is exactly why some critics turn up their

noses at these wines. I prefer dry rosés, but I enjoy medium-sweet rosés when they are very fresh and fruity. The trouble with so many of these medium-sweet, light- to medium-bodied, coral-pink wines is that, while they can be delicious in the early spring following the vintage, an alarming number quickly tire in the bottle. The moral is, therefore, that even when you have found an Anjou rosé you like, never buy it by the case. These wines may be sold as *primeur* or *nouveau* from the third Thursday of November following the harvest or from December 1 without any mention of *primeur* or *nouveau*.

🍇 Predominantly Grolleau, with varying proportions of Cabernet Franc, Cabernet Sauvignon, Pineau d'Aunis, Gamay, Malbec

🍷— Upon purchase

✓ *C. V. de la Loire* (Elysis) *• Château La Varière*

ANJOU COTEAUX DE LA LOIRE AOC

This rare, white-only appellation is situated southwest of Angers. Production is small and will dwindle even further as vineyards are replanted with Cabernet for the increasingly popular Anjou Rouge appellation. The minimum natural richness of the grapes at harvest is 221 grams per liter (the same as Sauternes), with a minimum residual sugar in the finished wine of 17 grams per liter.

WHITE Although currently produced in dry through to medium styles, this was originally legally defined in 1946 as a traditionally sweet wine. Today, producers following the trend for drier styles are hampered by out-of-date regulations that set the alcoholic strength too high and the yield too low.

🍇 Chenin Blanc

🍷— Within 1 year

✓ *Musset Roullier*

ANJOU GAMAY AOC

Gamay is only allowed in Anjou AOC wines if the name of the grape is added to the appellation on the label.

RED Dry to medium-dry, light-bodied wines that are rarely of great interest. These wines may be sold as *primeur* or *nouveau* as from the third Thursday of November following the harvest.

🍇 Gamay

🍷— Upon purchase

✓ *De la Charmoise • Roy René* (La Creusette)

ANJOU MOUSSEUX AOC

This traditional method wine is softer, but less popular than its Saumur equivalent, although it may come from the communes within Saumur itself.

SPARKLING WHITE These dry to sweet, light- to medium-bodied wines desperately need a change of regulation to allow a little Chardonnay in the blend. The Chardonnay's fatter, more neutral character would enable producers to make a more classic, less frivolous style of sparkling wine.

🍇 A minimum of 60% Chenin Blanc plus Cabernet Sauvignon, Cabernet Franc, Malbec, Gamay, Grolleau, Pineau d'Aunis

🍷— 1–2 years

SPARKLING ROSÉ If you want to know what Anjou Rosé tastes like with bubbles, try this light- to medium-bodied wine, which is mostly sold as *demi-sec*.

🍇 Cabernet Sauvignon, Cabernet Franc, Malbec, Gamay, Grolleau, Pineau d'Aunis

🍷— Upon purchase

ANJOU PÉTILLANT AOC

A little-used appellation for gently sparkling traditional method wines with a minimum of nine months' bottle age, which must be sold in ordinary still-wine bottles with regular corks.

SEMI-SPARKLING WHITE These are dry to *demi-sec*, light-bodied sparkling wines. Considering the variable quality of Anjou Blanc, many producers might be better advised to fizz it up and sell it under this appellation.

🍇 A minimum of 80% Chenin Blanc and a maximum of 20% Chardonnay and Sauvignon Blanc

🍷— Upon purchase

SEMI-SPARKLING ROSÉ Dry to medium, light-bodied wines which are rarely encountered outside the area and may be labeled "Anjou Pétillant," "Anjou Rosé Pétillant," or "Rosé d'Anjou Pétillant."

🍇 Grolleau, Cabernet Franc, Cabernet Sauvignon, Pineau d'Aunis, Gamay, Malbec

🍷— Upon purchase

ANJOU ROSÉ AOC

See Anjou AOC

ANJOU-VILLAGES AOC

This superior, red-wine-only appellation was first delimited in 1986, but it did not come into effect until 1991. If you buy from the best growers, you will get some of the finest red wines that the Loire has to offer.

RED The very best wines can be deeply colored with a creamy-raspberry aroma and flavor.

🍇 Cabernet Franc, Cabernet Sauvignon

🍷— 2–6 years

✓ *Patrick Baudoin • De la Bergerie • Château Pierre Bise • Des Griottes • L. & F. Martin • De la Motte • Ogereau • De la Poterie • De Putille • Des Quattre Quarres • Michel Robineau • Des Saulaies • Château La Varière*

ANJOU–VILLAGES BRISSAC AOC

This village was singled out under the Anjou-Villages appellation in 1998 and backdated for wines from 1996 onward. It covers the area of Brissac-Quincé and nine surrounding communes.

✓ *Davieu* (Château de Brissac) *• De Haute-Perche • Du Prieuré • Richou • Des Rochelles* (La Croix de Mission) *• Château La Varière*

BONNEZEAUX AOC

Grown on three south-facing river slopes of the commune of Thouarcé in the Coteaux du Layon, this is one of the undisputed great sweet wines of France. The grapes must be harvested in *tries* with the pickers collecting only the ripest, often botrytis-affected fruit, which can take up to two weeks. In 2003 the minimum natural richness of the grapes at harvest was increased from 204 to 238 grams per liter (compared to 221 grams per liter for Sauternes), and the minimum residual sugar increased from 17 to 34 grams per liter.

WHITE Intensely sweet, richer, and more full-bodied than Quarts-de-Chaume, the other great growth of the Layon Valley, this wine can have pineapple and liquorice fruit when young, often achieving a beautiful honeyed-vanilla complexity with age.

🍇 Chenin Blanc

🍷 Up to 20 years or more

✓ *Philippe Delesvaux • Château de Fesles • Godineau/Des Petit Quarts • Claude Robin (Floriane) • De la Sansonnière • De Terrebrune • Château La Varière*

CABERNET D'ANJOU AOC

This appellation includes Saumur, and it was a *saumurois* named Taveau who, in 1905, was the first person to make an Anjou Rosé from Cabernet grapes. Despite its classic Cabernet content and an extra degree of natural alcohol, this is not as superior to Anjou Rosé as it should be because bulk sales at cheap prices have devalued its reputation.

ROSÉ Good examples of these medium to medium-sweet, medium-bodied wines produced by the best domaines have a clean and fruity character with aromas of raspberries. These wines may be sold as *primeur* or *nouveau* from the third Thursday of November following the harvest or from December 1 without any mention of *primeur* or *nouveau*.

🍇 Cabernet Franc, Cabernet Sauvignon

🍷 Upon purchase

✓ *La Croix des Loges • C. V. de la Loire (Elysis) • Des Petite Grouas • De Preville*

CABERNET DE SAUMUR AOC

All Cabernet de Saumur wines have the right to claim the appellation Cabernet d'Anjou, but those sold as Saumur are usually finer in quality.

ROSÉ A delicate, medium sweet, light to medium-bodied wine with a hint of straw to its pink color and a distinctive raspberry aroma. These wines may be sold as *primeur* or *nouveau* from the third Thursday of November following the harvest or from December 1 without any mention of *primeur* or *nouveau*.

🍇 Cabernet Franc, Cabernet Sauvignon

🍷 Upon purchase

✓ *Du Val Brun*

CHAUME 1ER CRU DES COTEAUX DU LAYON AOC

This new appellation covers the south-facing vineyards on the *butte* de Chaume, and has been a long time in receiving recognition, as the original application dates back almost 50 years. The grapes must have a minimum natural sugar of 238 grams per liter (compared to 221 grams per liter for Sauternes) and are harvested by successive *tries*, with a maximum yield of 110 cases per acre (25 hectoliters per hectare) and a minimum residual sugar in the finished wine of 34 grams per liter. Because of the natural air-drainage on these slopes, *passerillage* is more widespread than *Botrytis cinerea*.

WHITE Big, rich, lusciously sweet wines that will make their mark in years to come.

🍇 Chenin Blanc

🍷 5–15 years

✓ *Château Pierre Bise • Michel Blouin • Cady • Du Petit Metris • Du Rocher • De la Soucherie*

COTEAUX DE L'AUBANCE AOC

These wines are made from old vines grown on the schistous banks of the Aubance River. To be entitled to this appellation growers must use grapes that are well ripened and harvested by *tries*, a labor-intensive system that is not cost-effective, thus until recently most growers produced Cabernet d'Anjou. A new generation of growers has transformed this appellation such that in 2003 the minimum natural sugar of the grapes at harvest was increased from 204 to 230 grams per liter (compared with 221 grams per liter for Sauternes) or 294 grams per liter for Coteaux l'Aubance "Sélection de Grains Nobles," as indicated on the label. The minimum residual sugar was increased from 17 to 34 grams per liter.

WHITE A few growers still make this rich and semisweet, medium- to full-bodied wine of excellent longevity and exceptional quality.

🍇 Chenin Blanc

🍷 5–10 years

✓ *De Bablut ● • Davieu • De Montgilet (Clos Prieur) • Richou*

COTEAUX DU LAYON AOC

This appellation, which overlaps Anjou Coteaux de la Loire in the northwest and Saumur in the southeast, has been famous for its sweet white wines since the fourth century. In favorable sites the vines are sometimes attacked by "noble rot," but in all cases the grapes must be extremely ripe and harvested by *tries* to a minimum of 12 percent alcohol from a maximum 132 cases per acre (30 hectoliters per hectare). Due to the relatively low price this appellation commands, harvesting by *tries* is viable only for the top domaines. In 2003 the minimum natural richness of the grapes at harvest was increased from 204 to 221 grams per liter (the same as Sauternes) or 294 grams per liter for Coteaux du Layon "Sélection de Grains Nobles." The minimum residual sugar was also increased from 17 to 34 grams per liter.

WHITE Green-gold- to yellow-gold-colored, soft-textured, sweet, medium- to full-bodied wines, rich in fruit, and potentially long lived.

🍇 Chenin Blanc

🍷 5–15 years

✓ *Patrick Baudoin • Baumard (le Paon) • Château Pierre Bise • Philippe Delesvaux • Dhomme • Château de Fesles (Château de la Roulerie) • De la Gerfauderie (Les Hauts de la Gerfauderie) • Ogereau (Prestige) • Du Petit Val (Simon) • Du Portaille (Planche Mallet) • Du Regain (Le Paradis) • Des Sablonnettes (La Bohème)*

COTEAUX DU LAYON VILLAGES AOC

Historically, these six villages have consistently produced the cream of all the wines in the Coteaux du Layon, and thus have the right to add their names to the basic appellation. In 2003 the minimum natural sugar of the grapes at harvest was increased from 204 to 238 grams per liter (compared to 221 grams per liter for Sauternes) or 294 grams per liter for Coteaux du

Layon Villages "Sélection de Grains Nobles." The minimum residual sugar was also increased from 17 to 34 grams per liter.

WHITE Sweet wines that are medium- to full-bodied. According to the "Club des Layon Villages," Beaulieu has a soft, light aroma; Faye has a scent reminiscent of brushwood; Rablay is big, bold, and round; Rochefort is full-bodied, tannic, and matures well; St.-Aubin has a delicate aroma that develops; and St.-Lambert is robust yet round.

🍇 Chenin Blanc

🍷 5–15 years

✓ **Beaulieu** *Château de Breuil • Château Pierre Bise •* **Faye** *Château de Fresne* (Clos de Cocus), *Richard Leroy •* **Rablay** *Des Sablonnettes ● •* **Rochefort** *De la Motte •* **St.-Aubin** *Des Barres, Philippe Delesvaux, Jo Pithon, De la Roche Moreau •* **St.-Lambert** *Ogereau, Jo Pithon, Du Roy René* (Les Cartelles), *Michel Robineau*

COTEAUX DU LAYON-CHAUME AOC

In many ways, there is very little that separates this single-village appellation from Coteaux du Layon, although it does have a lower maximum yield of 110 cases per acre (25 hectoliters per hectare) instead of 132 cases per acre (30 hectoliters per hectare), which itself is very low.

WHITE Sweet, medium- to full-bodied, fine, viscous wines that usually rank above most basic Coteaux du Layon

🍇 Chenin Blanc

🍷 5–15 years

✓ *Château de Fesles (Château de la Roulerie Aunis) • Des Forges (Les Onnis) • Château de la Guimonière • L. & F. Martin • Du Petit Metris*

COTEAUX DE SAUMUR AOC

After the ban in 1985 on the use of the term *méthode champenoise* for wines produced or sold in the European Union (see p.169), there were moves to develop this little used appellation as the principal still wine of the Saumur district in order to promote Saumur AOC as an exclusively sparkling wine. That idea has, it seems, ground to a halt.

WHITE Relatively rare, semisweet, medium- to full-bodied wines that are richly flavored and worth seeking out.

🍇 Chenin Blanc

🍷 5–10 years

✓ *Champs Fleuris (Sarah) • De Nerleux • De Saint Just (La Valboisière)*

QUARTS-DE-CHAUME AOC

These wines are grown on the plateau behind the village of Chaume in the Coteaux-du-Layon commune of Rochefort-sur-Loire. The vineyards of Quarts-de-Chaume used to be run by the abbey of Ronceray, whose landlord drew a quarter of the vintage as rent. In 2003 the minimum natural sugar of the grapes at harvest was increased from 204 to 238 grams per liter (compared to 221 grams per liter for Sauternes), and the minimum residual sugar increased from 17 to 34 grams per liter.

WHITE These are semisweet to sweet, medium- to full-bodied wines. Although harvested by *tries* and produced in the same manner as Bonnezeaux, Quarts-de-Chaume comes from a more northerly area and as a result is slightly lighter in body. It also tends to have a touch less sweetness.

🍇 Chenin Blanc

🍷 Up to 15 years or more

☑ *Des Baumard • Château de Bellerive • De Laffourcade • Château de la Roche Moreau • Château Pierre Bise • Château La Varière*

ROSÉ D'ANJOU AOC
See Anjou AOC

ROSÉ D'ANJOU PÉTILLANT AOC
See Anjou Pétillant AOC

SAUMUR AOC

Saumur, situated within the borders of the Anjou appellation, is regarded as the pearl of Anjou. Its wine may be sold as Anjou, but Anjou does not automatically qualify as Saumur. Unless made from Cabernet grapes, all rosé wines must adopt the Anjou Rosé appellation. Like Anjou, its white wines are variable, yet its red wines are excellent.

RED These fine, bone-dry to dry, medium- to full-bodied wines are often similar to the red wines of Anjou, although they can vary from light and fruity to deep-colored and tannic.

🍇 Cabernet Franc, Cabernet Sauvignon, Pineau d'Aunis

🍷 1–10 years according to style

☑ *Du Bois Mignon* (La Belle Cave) • *Du Collier • De Fiervaux • De Château-Gaillard ❸ • Filliatreau • Guiberteau • Des Hautes Vignes • Langlois-Château* (Vieilles Vignes) • *Des Nerleux • Château de Passavent • Des Raynières • C. V. de Saumur* (Reserve) • *Château Yvonne*

WHITE Varying from bone-dry to sweet and from light- to full-bodied, these wines have a style more akin to Vouvray than Anjou, due to the limestone and the tufa soil. In poor-to-average years, however, a Saumur is easily distinguished by its lighter body, leaner fruit, and a tartness of flavor that can sometimes have a metallic edge on the aftertaste. These wines may be sold as from December 1 following the harvest without any mention of *primeur* or *nouveau*.

🍇 A minimum of 80% Chenin Blanc and a maximum of 20% Chardonnay and Sauvignon Blanc

🍷 Upon purchase

☑ *Du Collier • Guiberteau* (Le Clos) • *Château de Hureau • Langlois-Château* (Vieilles Vignes) • *Des Roches Neuves • Clos Rougeard • C. V. de Saumur • Château de Villeneuve*

SPARKLING WHITE Although the production per acre of this wine is one-third more than for its Anjou equivalent, Saumur is—or at least should be—better in quality and style due to its Chardonnay content and the tufa-limestone soil. Most wines are made in a true, bone-dry, *brut* style, although the full gamut is allowed and wines up to *demi-sec* sweetness are relatively common. The vast majority of these wines have a tart greengage character, lack finesse, and do not pick up bottle aromas. The wines indicated below have an elegance sadly lacking in most Saumur, and possess gentler, more neutral fruit, which will benefit from a little extra time in bottle, although after a while all these wines tend to age rather than mature gracefully. The creamy-rich *barrique*-fermented Bouvet Trésor

is the one significant exception as not only is it just the best sparkling wine in the Loire, it can be compared to very good-quality Champagne, although it is in a very different style.

🍇 Chenin Blanc plus a maximum of 20% Chardonnay and Sauvignon Blanc, and up to 60% Cabernet Sauvignon, Cabernet Franc, Malbec, Gamay, Grolleau, Pineau d'Aunis, and Pinot Noir

🍷 3–5 years

☑ *De Beauregard • De la Bessière • Bouvet-Ladubay* (Mlle Ladubay, Trésor) • *De Brizé • Gratien & Meyer* (Flamme) • *C. V. de Saumur* (Spéciale)

SPARKLING ROSÉ An increasing number of pink Saumurs are pure Cabernet Franc and an increasing number are showing very well. However, the aggressive potential of this grape can quickly turn a thrilling raspberry-flavored fizz into something hideous. Pure Cabernet Sauvignon rosés can be much smoother, less overt, and not as intrinsically Saumur as a Cabernet Franc *cuvée*.

🍇 Cabernet Sauvignon, Cabernet Franc, Malbec, Gamay, Grolleau, Pineau d'Aunis, Pinot Noir

🍷 Upon purchase

☑ *Bouvet-Ladubay* (Trésor) • *Gratien & Meyer* (Flamme)

SAUMUR-CHAMPIGNY AOC

Many people believe that the vineyards southeast of Saumur entitled to add the village name of Champigny to their appellation produce the best red wines in the Loire.

RED Bone-dry to dry, full-bodied wines with a distinctive deep color and full and fragrant raspberry aromas, often tannic and long-lived.

🍇 Cabernet Franc, Cabernet Sauvignon, Pineau d'Aunis

🍷 5–10 years

☑ *Du Bois Moze Pasquier • La Bonnelière • Des Champs Fleuris • Filliatreau • Château du Hureau* (Lisagathe) • *René-Noël Legrand • Petit Saint Vincent • De Rocfontaine* (Vieilles Vignes) • *Des Roches Neuves • Clos Rougeard • De Saint Just • Château de Villeneuve • Château Yvonne*

SAUMUR MOUSSEUX AOC

This is the technically correct appellation for all fully sparkling white and rosé Saumur wines made by the traditional method, but producers have shied away from the down-market term *mousseux*, selling the wines simply as Appellation Saumur Contrôlée. There is no allowance for this in the regulations, but it is a widespread practice. A significant amount of red traditional method wine is also produced, but this cannot claim AOC status. *See also* Saumur AOC

SAUMUR D'ORIGINE AOC

When the European Union banned the term *méthode champenoise*, this marketing term was developed by the producers of sparkling Saumur to promote and advertise their wines. *See also* Saumur AOC

SAUMURZ PÉTILLANT AOC

Little-used appellation for gently sparkling, traditional method wine with a minimum of nine months' bottle age, which must be sold in ordinary still-wine bottles with regular corks.

SEMI-SPARKLING WHITE These dry to *demi-sec*, light-bodied, and fruity wines are not

dissimilar to the fine wines of the Montlouis Pétillant appellation and should be revived.

🍇 A minimum of 80% Chenin Blanc and a maximum of 20% Chardonnay and Sauvignon Blanc

🍷 Upon purchase

SAVENNIÈRES AOC

When this small portion of Anjou Coteaux de la Loire produced only sweet wines, the AOC regulations set a correspondingly low maximum yield. This concentrates the wines on four southeast-facing slopes of volcanic debris that produce the world's greatest dry Chenin Blanc.

WHITE Bone-dry to dry wines of great mineral intensity, Savennières can be some of the longest-lived dry white wines in the world. Most critics believe that the single greatest Savennières is Nicolas Joly's Clos de la Coulée de Serrant and, while I agree that it is one of the greatest wines of the Loire, I think that Baumard's Clos du Papillon (not to be confused with Clos du Papillon from other growers) consistently displays greater elegance and finesse. Over the past 15 years or so, a few producers have resurrected the semisweet style that used to be more popular in Savennières in the first half of the 20th century.

🍇 Chenin Blanc

🍷 5–8 years (10–15 years for Clos de la Coulée de Serrant)

☑ *Des Baumard • Du Closel* (Clos du Papillon) • *Château de Fesles* (Château de Varennes) • *Nicolas Joly* (Clos de la Coulée de Serrant) • *De la Monnaie • Château Pierre Bise • Pierre Soulez*

SAVENNIÈRES COULÉE-DE-SERRANT AOC

One of just two single-vineyard designations authorized for Savennières, Coulée-de-Serrant is 17 acres (7 hectares) and a mono-*cru*, solely owned by Nicolas Joly of Château de la Roche-aux-Moines. Many consider this to be the single-greatest Loire dry white wine. *See also* Savennières AOC

SAVENNIÈRES ROCHE-AUX-MOINES AOC

The second and largest of the two single-vineyard designations authorized for Savennières, Roche-aux-Moines is 42 acres (17 hectares) and owned by three producers: Nicolas Joly of Château de la Roche-aux-Moines, Pierre and Yves Soulez of Château de Chamboureau, and Madame Laroche of au Moines. *See also* Savennières AOC

VINS DU THOUARSAIS VDQS

Michel Gigon is the sole producer of Vins du Thouarsais, a wine that could once boast over a hundred growers.

RED Dry, light- to medium-bodied, fruity reds, sometimes reminiscent of cherries and other stone fruit.

🍇 Cabernet Franc, Cabernet Sauvignon, Gamay

🍷 1–2 years

WHITE A lighter-bodied but far more fragrant version of dry and semisweet Anjou Blanc.

🍇 Chenin Blanc plus up to 20% Chardonnay

🍷 Upon purchase

ROSÉ This is a splendid dry, light-bodied or light- to medium-bodied picnic wine.

🍷 Upon purchase

☑ *Michel Gigon*

TOURAINE

Wines bearing Touraine appellations are prolific and capable of giving good value, but for the most part they are not great. However, there are notable exceptions, such as the wines from Vouvray and the less well-known but equally elite wines of Montlouis, Bourgueil, and Chinon.

THE WINEGROWING DISTRICT around Tours dates back to Roman times, as does the town itself. The Cabernet Franc, known locally as Breton, was flourishing in the vineyards of the abbey of Bourgueil 1,000 years ago and, as recently as 500 years ago, the Chenin Blanc—today's predominant Touraine grape—acquired its name from Mont Chenin in the south of the district.

TOURAINE'S WINE REGIONS
With the possible exception of Saumur-Champigny, the best red wines in the Loire come from the appellations of Chinon and Bourgueil, which face each other across the Loire River, just west of Tours. Made predominantly from Cabernet Franc, good vintages aged in oak may be complex and comparable to claret, while the more everyday wines have the aromas of fresh-picked raspberries and can be drunk young and cool. To the east, Vouvray and Montlouis produce rich, sweet, long-lived *moelleux* wines from overripe Chenin Blanc grapes in sunny years. North of Tours, the wines produced in Jasnières are from the same grape, but the dry style is distinctly different. Jasnières is a singular white subappellation within a wider red, white, and rosé AOC called the Coteaux du Loir. The "Loir" is not a typographical error for "Loire," but a tributary of the great river. Also grown on the banks of the Loir, Coteaux du Vendômois produces the full spectrum of still-wine styles, as does Cheverny to the east, including a distinctive dry white wine from the obscure Romorantin grape. Touraine Sauvignon Blanc makes an attractively priced, unassuming alternative to Sancerre, while the fruity Gamay makes easy-drinking reds and rosés. Chenin Blanc is still the dominant

variety here and, as in Anjou-Saumur, the tradition has been to produce naturally sweet wines in great years when these grapes are full of sugar, but lighter, not completely dry styles are more usual. The surplus of less-than-overripe grapes, like that in Anjou-Saumur, is traditionally utilized for sparkling wines.

TOURAINE, *see also* p.197
Surrounded by different appellations, the ancient city of Tours is the focal point of an area rich in the variety of its wines.

FACTORS AFFECTING TASTE AND QUALITY

LOCATION
East-central district with most of its vineyards in the *département* of Indre-et-Loire, but they extend into Loir-et-Cher, Indre, and Sarthe.

CLIMATE
Touraine falls under some Atlantic influence, but the climate is less maritime than in the Nantes district and Anjou-Saumur. Protected from northerly winds by the Coteaux du Loir. Warm summer, low October rainfall.

ASPECT
Attractively rolling land, flatter around Tours itself, hillier in the hinterland. Vines are planted on gently undulating slopes, which are often south-facing, at between 130 to 330 feet (40 and 100 meters) above sea level.

SOIL
Clay and limestone over tufa subsoil east of Tours around Vouvray and Montlouis. Tufa is chalk boiled by volcanic action. It is full of minerals, retains water, and can be tunneled out to make large, cool cellars for storing wine. Sandy-gravel soils in low-lying Bourgueil and Chinon vineyards produce fruity, supple wines; the slopes or *coteaux* of sandy-clay produce firmer wines.

VITICULTURE AND VINIFICATION
White-wine fermentation takes place at low temperatures and lasts for several weeks for dry wines, several months for sweet wines. The reds undergo malolactic fermentation. Some Bourgueil and Chinon is aged for up to 18 months in oak casks before bottling.

GRAPE VARIETIES
Primary varieties: Chenin Blanc, Cabernet Franc, Sauvignon Blanc, Grolleau
Secondary varieties: Cabernet Sauvignon, Pinot Noir, Meslier, Gamay, Gamay Teinturier, Pineau d'Aunis, Romorantin, Arbois, Chardonnay, Malbec

Legend:
- Villages which are entitled to add their name to the Touraine appellation
- Intensive vine-growing zone
- Touraine
- Coteaux du Loir
- Coteaux du Vendômois
- Cheverny and Cour-Cheverny
- Valençay
- Jasnières
- Saint-Nicolas-de-Bourgueil
- Bourgueil
- Chinon
- Vouvray
- Montlouis
- ▲ Height above sea level (meters)

0   5   10 miles
0   10   20 km

THE APPELLATIONS OF
TOURAINE

BOURGUEIL AOC

Most of the vines are grown on a sand-and-gravel plateau, or *terrasse*, by the river. The wines have a pronounced fruity character and are delicious to drink when less than six months old. Those grown on the south-facing clay and tufa slopes, or *coteaux*, ripen up to 10 days earlier and produce more full-bodied, longer-lived wines.

RED Bone-dry to dry, medium-bodied, lively wines, full of soft-fruit flavors, which are often aged in cask. They are very easy to drink when less than six months old; many close up when in bottle and need time to soften. Wines from the *terrasse* vineyards are best drunk young, while those from the *coteaux* repay keeping.

🍇 Cabernet Franc with up to 10% Cabernet Sauvignon

🍷 Within 6 months or after 6 years

ROSÉ Bone-dry to dry, light- to medium-bodied wines that are very fruity with aromas of raspberries and blackberries and good depth of flavor. They deserve to be better known.

🍇 Cabernet Franc with up to 10% Cabernet Sauvignon

🍷 2–3 years

✓ *Yannick Amirault* (Les Quartier Vieilles Vignes) • *Breton* • *Des Chesnaies* (Prestige) • *De la Chevalerie* (Busardières) • *De la Cotelleraie* • *Delaunay Père & Fils* • *Vignoble de la Grioche* (Santenay) • *Des Ouches* • *Du Petit Bondieu* (Le Petit Mont) • *Guy Saget* (L'Echallerie) • *De la Taille au Loups*

CHEVERNY AOC

Upgraded from VDQS to full AOC status in 1993. These good-value, crisp, and fruity wines deserve their promotion and should be better known. Cheverny is usually made and marketed as a pure varietal wine, the most interesting of which, Romorantin, has been awarded its own AOC for the best vineyards around Cour-Cheverny itself. *See also* Cour-Cheverny AOC

RED Dry, light- to medium-bodied wines. The smaller growers mostly produce pure Gamay wines of very acceptable quality, although the addition of 10 percent or more Pinot Noir gives a smoother wine. Gamay Teinturier de Chaudenay, which has colored juice, is no longer permitted.

🍇 Between 40 and 65% Gamay, plus Pinot Noir, Cabernet Franc, Malbec. Cabernet Sauvignon is no longer permitted.

🍷 1–2 years

WHITE Dry, light-bodied, modest wines with a fine, flowery nose, delicate flavor, and crisp balance. Now primarily a Sauvignon Blanc wine, as Romorantin may not be used and the amount of Sauvignon in these wines has been regulated since 1993.

🍇 Between 65 and 80% Sauvignon Blanc, plus Chardonnay, Chenin Blanc, and Arbois

🍷 1–2 years

ROSÉ Only small quantities are produced, but the wines are agreeably dry and light-bodied and very consistent in quality. Since acquiring full AOC status, Cabernet Franc, Cabernet Sauvignon, and Malbec have been allowed for

the production of these wines, which has boosted the quantity even further.

🍇 At least 50% Gamay, plus Cabernet Franc, Cabernet Sauvignon, Malbec, Pineau d'Aunis, and Pinot Gris

🍷 1–2 years

✓ *De la Desoucherie* • *De la Gaudronnière* (Tradition) • *Du Moulin* • *Sauger & Fils*

CHINON AOC

The appellations of Chinon and Bourgueil produce the best red wine in Touraine using the Cabernet Franc grape, known locally as Breton. Chinon wines are generally lighter and more delicate than those of Bourgueil, but those from the tufa hill slopes have greater depth and flavor and age well.

RED Bone-dry to dry, light- to medium-bodied wines that are lively, soft, and delicate. Most growers use small oak casks for aging and produce wines of very good quality.

🍇 Cabernet Franc with up to 10% Cabernet Sauvignon

🍷 2–3 years

WHITE A tiny production of clean, dry, light- to medium-bodied wines that are strangely aromatic for Chenin Blanc with an intriguing perfumed aftertaste.

🍇 Chenin Blanc

🍷 1–2 years

ROSÉ These are dry, fairly light-bodied, smooth, and fruity wines which, like Bourgueil rosés, are very easy to drink and deserve to be better known.

🍇 Cabernet Franc with up to 10% Cabernet Sauvignon

🍷 2–3 years

✓ *Philippe Alliet* • *Château de l'Aulée* (Artissimo) • *Bernard Baudry* • *Guy Saget* (Marie de Beauregard) • *Breton* • *Château de Coulaine* • *Couly-Dutheil* (Clos de l'Echo) • *Charles Joguet* • *J. L. Page* (Sélection Clément Martin) • *Jean-Marie Raffault* (Le Puy) • *De Saint-Louand* (Réserve de Trompegueux) • *Serge et Bruno Sourdais*

COTEAUX DU LOIR AOC

This is an area that had extensive vineyards in the 19th century. Production has since declined and these generally unexciting wines come from the Loir, which is a tributary of, and not to be confused with, the Loire.

RED These are dry, medium-bodied wines that can have a lively character and good extract in sunny years.

🍇 Minimum of 30% Pineau d'Aunis with Gamay, Pinot Noir, Cabernet Franc, and Cabernet Sauvignon

🍷 1–2 years

WHITE Bone-dry to dry, light-bodied wines that are high in acidity that can be mean and astringent.

🍇 Chenin Blanc

🍷 As early as possible

ROSÉ Dry, fairly light-bodied wines, a few of which are fruity and well balanced.

🍇 Pineau d'Aunis, Cabernet Franc, Gamay, and Malbec with up to 25% Grolleau

🍷 Within 1 year

✓ *De Bellivière* • *Jean-François Maillet* (Réserve d'Automne)

COTEAUX DU VENDÔMOIS AOC

Situated on both banks of the Loir, upstream from Jasnières, this steadily improving wine was upgraded to full AOC status in 2001, when the *encépagement* changed.

RED Dry, fairly light-bodied wines that are full of soft-fruit flavors and very easy to drink.

🍇 Minimum of 40% Pineau d'Aunis plus 10–40% Gamay, Pinot Noir, and Cabernet Franc, with a maximum of 20% Gamay reducing to 10% in 2016 (Cabernet Sauvignon is no longer permitted)

🍷 1–2 years

WHITE Dry, fairly light-bodied wines which, when made from pure Chenin Blanc, have a tendency to be very astringent. Growers who blend Chardonnay with Chenin Blanc produce better-balanced wines.

🍇 Primarily Chenin Blanc with up to 20% Chardonnay

🍷 Within 1 year

ROSÉ Fresh and fragrant, Coteaux du Vendômois is one of the most appealing, yet little seen, of the Loire's dry rosés.

🍇 Pineau d'Aunis (Gamay is no longer permitted)

🍷 1–2 years

✓ *Patrice Colin* • *Du Four à Chaux* • *C. V. de Villiers-sur-Loir*

COUR-CHEVERNY AOC

Cheverny gained this special single-village appellation exclusively for Romorantin when it was upgraded in 1993 from a VDQS to an AOC, but it lost its right to produce sparkling wine. Romorantin is grown in the best sites around Cour-Cheverny. *See also* Cheverny AOC

WHITE These are dry, light-bodied, modest wines, which have a fine, flowery nose, delicate flavor, and crisp balance.

🍇 Romorantin

🍷 1–2 years

✓ *De la Desoucherie* • *De la Gaudronnière* (Le Mur de Gaudronnière) • *Du Moulin*

JASNIÈRES AOC

This is the best area of the Coteaux du Loir—the wines produced here can, in hot years, achieve a richness that compares well with those of Savennières in Anjou (*see* p.206).

WHITE Medium-bodied wines that can be dry or sweet. They are elegant and age well in good years, but they can be unripe in poor years.

🍇 Chenin Blanc

🍷 2–4 years

✓ *De Bellivière* • *J. Martellière* (Poète)

MONTLOUIS-SUR-LOIRE AOC

All Montlouis appellations were renamed Montlouis-sur-Loire AOC from November 2003. Like Vouvray, Montlouis produces wines that can be dry, medium-dry, or sweet depending on the vintage and, like those of its more famous neighbor, the greatest wines of Montlouis are the sweetest, most botrytis-rich wines often sold as *moelleux*. The wines are very similar in style to those of Vouvray, but Montlouis is terribly underrated, whereas Vouvray is often overrated. I would rank Moyer's 1959 and the 1947 Montlouis alongside even the greatest vintages of Château d'Yquem Sauternes.

WHITE Light- to medium-bodied wines that can be dry or sweet. They are softer and more forward than the wines of Vouvray but can have the same honeyed flavor in fine years. Sweet Montlouis is aged in cask, but the best medium-dry styles are clean-fermented in stainless steel.

🍇 Chenin Blanc

🍴 1–3 years for medium-dry, up to 10 years for sweeter wines

✓ *Laurent Chatenay • François Chidaine • De la Croix Melier • Alex Mathur (Dionys) • Dominique Moyer • De la Taille au Loups*

MONTLOUIS-SUR-LOIRE MOUSSEUX AOC

In poor vintages the grapes are used to make traditional method sparkling versions of Montlouis. The medium-dry (*demi-sec*) styles of the AOC are very popular in France.

SPARKLING WHITE These light- to medium-bodied wines can be *brut, sec, demi-sec*, or *moelleux*. The last two styles are made only in years that are particularly sunny.

🍇 Chenin Blanc

🍴 Upon purchase

✓ *Alain Joulin • Thierry et Daniel Mosny*

MONTLOUIS-SUR-LOIRE PÉTILLANT AOC

Gently effervescent, Montlouis Pétillant is one of the most successful, yet least encountered, and underrated, slightly sparkling French white wines.

SEMI-SPARKLING WHITE Light- to medium-bodied wines that can be dry or sweet. Very consistent in quality, with a rich, fruity flavor balanced by a delicate *mousse* of fine bubbles.

🍇 Chenin Blanc

🍴 Upon purchase

✓ *Levasseur • Dominique Moyer*

ST.-NICOLAS-DE-BOURGUEIL AOC

This is a commune with its own appellation in the northwest corner of Bourgueil. The soil is sandier than that of surrounding Bourgueil and the wines are lighter but certainly equal in terms of quality. These are some of the finest red wines in the Loire.

RED Bone-dry to dry, medium-bodied wines that age well and have greater finesse than the wines of Bourgueil.

🍇 Cabernet Franc with up to 10% Cabernet Sauvignon

🍴 After 5–6 years

ROSÉ A small amount of dry, medium-bodied rosé with firm, fruity flavor is produced.

🍇 Cabernet Franc with up to 10% Cabernet Sauvignon

🍴 Upon purchase

✓ *Yannick Amirault • Max Cognard (Estelle,*

Malagnes) • *Sebastian David • Frédéric Malibeau (Coutures, Eclipse) • Jacques et Vincent Malibeau (La Gardière Vieilles Vignes) • Clos des Quarterons (Vieilles Vignes) • Du Rochouard (Pierre du Lane)*

TOURAINE AOC

A prolific appellation with sparkling wines in dry and medium-dry styles, plus sweet white, red, and rosé still wines from all over Touraine. Most are pure varietal wines and the label should indicate which grape they have been made from. *See also* Touraine Mousseux AOC and Touraine Pétillant AOC

RED Dry, light- to medium-bodied wines of little interest, which cannot be enhanced by the fact that the lackluster Grolleau grape has been used in Touraine *rouge* since 1994. Those made from Gamay are fresh and fruity, and may be sold as *primeur* or *nouveau* from the third Thursday of November following the harvest.

🍇 Gamay, Cabernet Franc, Cabernet Sauvignon, Malbec, Pinot Noir, Pinot Meunier, Pinot Gris, Pineau d'Aunis, and Grolleau

🍴 Within 3 years

WHITE These are bone-dry to dry, medium-bodied wines; when made from pure Sauvignon, they are fresh, aromatic, and fruity. Good Touraine Sauvignon is better than average Sancerre. Chardonnay has been restricted in Touraine *blanc* since 1994. These wines may be sold from December 1 following the harvest without any mention of *primeur* or *nouveau*.

🍇 Chenin Blanc, Sauvignon Blanc, Arbois, and a maximum of 20% Chardonnay

🍴 1–2 years

ROSÉ Dry, light- to medium-bodied wines, while those made from Pineau d'Aunis are drier and more subtle than Anjou rosé. They may be sold as *primeur* or *nouveau* from the third Thursday of November following the harvest.

🍇 Cabernet Franc, Gamay, Grolleau, and Pineau d'Aunis with up to 10% Gamay Teinturier de Chaudenay or Gamay de Bouze

🍴 1–2 years

✓ *De la Charmoise (also those simply labeled Henry Marionnet) • Des Corbillères • De la Garrelière ❷ • Henri Marionnet • Michaud • Dominique Percereau • De la Puannerie • Du Pre Baron (Sauvignon L'Elegante) • Clos Roche Blanche • Les Vaucorneilles (Gamay)*

TOURAINE AMBOISE AOC

Modest white wines and light reds and rosés are produced by a cluster of eight villages surrounding, and including, Amboise. The vines are grown on both sides of the Loire adjacent to the Vouvray and Montlouis areas.

RED Dry, light-bodied wines that are mostly blended. Those containing a high proportion of Malbec are the best.

🍇 A minimum of 60% Gamay, plus 10–30% Cabernet Franc and Malbec, with an optional maximum of 10% Cabernet

Sauvignon until 2010, when it will no longer be allowed

🍴 2–3 years

WHITE These bone-dry to dry, light-bodied Chenin Blancs are usually uninspiring; the rosés are superior.

🍇 A minimum of 60% Chenin Blanc, plus a maximum of 30% Sauvignon Blanc, and a maximum of 15% Chardonnay

🍴 Upon purchase

ROSÉ These dry, light-bodied, well-made wines are mouth-watering.

🍇 A minimum of 80% Gamay, plus Cabernet Franc and Malbec

🍴 Within 1 year

✓ *Dutertre • Guy Saget • Lionel Truet (Grande Foucaudière)*

TOURAINE AZAY-LE-RIDEAU AOC

Good-quality wines from eight villages on each side of the Indre River, a tributary of the Loire.

WHITE Delicate, light-bodied wines that are usually dry but may be *demi-sec*.

🍇 Chenin Blanc

🍴 1–2 years

ROSÉ Attractive, refreshing, truly dry (maximum of 3 grams per liter residual sugar) wines that are coral-pink and often have a strawberry aroma.

🍇 A minimum of 60% Grolleau, plus Malbec, Gamay, Cabernet Franc, and Cabernet Sauvignon (the last two must not total more than 10% of the entire blend)

🍴 1–2 years

✓ *J.L. Page • Pibaleau Père & Fils*

TOURAINE MESLAND AOC

Wines from the vineyards of Mesland and the five surrounding villages on the right bank of the Loire. The reds and rosés of this appellation are definitely well worth looking out for.

RED These dry, medium- to full-bodied wines are the best of the AOC and can be as good as those of Chinon or Bourgueil.

🍇 A minimum of 60% Gamay, plus 10–30% Cabernet Franc and Malbec, with an optional maximum of 10% Cabernet Sauvignon until 2010, when it will no longer be allowed

🍴 1–3 years

WHITE Dry, light-bodied wines with a high acidity that is only tamed in the best and sunniest years.

🍇 A minimum of 60% Chenin Blanc, plus a maximum of 30% Sauvignon Blanc, and a maximum of 15% Chardonnay

🍴 1–2 years

ROSÉ These dry, medium-bodied wines have more depth and character than those of Touraine Amboise.

🍇 A minimum of 80% Gamay, plus Cabernet Franc and Malbec

🍴 1–3 years

✓ *De la Briderie ❷ • Château Gaillard*

TOURAINE MOUSSEUX AOC

Very good-value traditional method red, white, and rosé wines. While the grapes for the white and rosé can come from the entire Touraine AOC area, those for red Touraine Mousseux may come from only the following areas: Bourgueil, St.-Nicolas-de-Bourgueil, or Chinon.

SPARKLING RED Dry, light- to medium-bodied wines that are fruity and refreshing.

🍇 Cabernet Franc

🍷 Upon purchase

SPARKLING WHITE These light- to medium-bodied wines are made in dry and sweet styles, and the quality is consistent due to the large production area, which allows for complex blending.

🍇 Primarily Chenin Blanc but may also include Arbois and up to 20% Chardonnay and a combined maximum of 30% Cabernet, Pinot Noir, Pinot Gris, Pinot Meunier, Pineau d'Aunis, Malbec, and Grolleau

🍷 Upon purchase

SPARKLING ROSÉ Light- to medium-bodied wines that are attractive when *brut*, though a bit cloying if sweeter.

🍇 Cabernet Franc, Malbec, Noble, Gamay, and Grolleau

🍷 1–2 years

✓ *Blanc Foussy* (Robert de Schlumberger, Veuve Oudinot) • *Jean-Pierre Laissement* (Rosé) • *Monmousseau* (JM)

TOURAINE NOBLE-JOUÉ AOC

A rosé-only appellation, this AOC was created in 2001 in recognition of the *vin gris* produced that was modestly famous in the 19th century, but its vineyards were gradually swallowed by the creeping urbanization southwest of Tours.

ROSÉ Yet to reestablish a reputation, the best of these wines so far have been fresh, light-bodied, elegantly fruity wines with smoky-floral minerality.

🍇 A minimum of 40% Pinot Gris, plus at least 20% Pinot Gris and a minimum of 10% Pinot Noir

🍷 Upon purchase

✓ *Bernard Blondeau*

TOURAINE PÉTILLANT AOC

Refreshing, slightly effervescent white and rosé wines made from the same grape varieties as Touraine Mousseux. None are exported.

SEMI-SPARKLING RED Medium-dry, light-bodied wines that are not very popular.

🍇 Cabernet Franc

🍷 Upon purchase

SEMI-SPARKLING WHITE Well-made, refreshing, light-bodied wines, in dry and sweet styles.

🍇 Chenin Blanc, Arbois, Sauvignon Blanc, and up to 20% Chardonnay

🍷 Upon purchase

SEMI-SPARKLING ROSÉ Attractive, light, quaffing wines that are made in dry and sweet styles.

🍇 Cabernet Franc, Malbec, Noble, Gamay, and Grolleau

🍷 Upon purchase

VALENÇAY AOC

Situated in the southeast of Touraine around the Cher River, these vineyards produce well-made, attractive wines. Promoted from VDQS to AOC in 2003, when the *encépagement* changed. Rarely seen outside France.

RED Dry, light-bodied, fragrant wines that can be very smooth and full of character. The Malbec, known locally as Cot, is particularly successful.

🍇 30–60% Gamay, with at least 30% in total of Pinot Noir and Malbec, plus optional

Cabernet Franc and Cabernet Sauvignon, which together must not exceed 10% of the entire blend (20% up to the 2003 vintage)

🍷 1–2 years

WHITE Simple, dry, light-bodied wines that are improved by the addition of Chardonnay.

🍇 A minimum of 70% Sauvignon Blanc, plus Arbois and Chardonnay

🍷 1–2 years

ROSÉ Dry to medium-dry, light-bodied wines that can be full of ripe soft-fruit flavors.

🍇 30–60% Gamay, with at least 30% in total of Pinot Noir and Malbec, plus an optional maximum of 30% Pinot d'Aunis, with or without Cabernet Franc and Cabernet Sauvignon, which together must not exceed 20% of the entire blend

🍷 Upon purchase

✓ *Chantal et Patrick Gibault* • *Jean-François Roy*

VOUVRAY AOC

These white wines may be dry, medium-dry, or sweet depending on the vintage. In sunny years, the classic Vouvray that is made from overripe grapes affected by the "noble rot" is still produced by some growers. In cooler years, the wines are correspondingly drier and more acidic, and greater quantities of sparkling wine are produced.

WHITE At its best, sweet Vouvray can be the richest of all the Loire sweet wines. In good years, the wines are very full bodied, rich in texture, and have the honeyed taste of ripe Chenin Blanc grapes.

🍇 Chenin Blanc but may also contain Arbois

🍷 Usually 2–3 years; the sweeter wines can last up to 50 years

✓ *Des Aubuisières* (Giraudières) • *Champalou* (Le Clos du Portail Sec) • *Philippe Foreau* (Clos Naudin) • *De la Haute Borne* (Tendre) • *Huet* • *Clos de Nouys* • *Pichot* • *De la Taille au Loups* • *Vigneau Chevreau* ◉ • *Alain Robert* (La Sablonnière)

VOUVRAY MOUSSEUX AOC

These sparkling wines are made from overripe grapes. In years when the grapes do not ripen properly they are converted into sparkling wines using the traditional method and blended with reserve wines from better years.

SPARKLING WHITE Medium- to full-bodied wines made in both dry and sweet styles. They are richer and softer than sparkling Saumur but have more edge than sparkling Montlouis.

🍇 Chenin Blanc and Arbois

🍷 Non-vintage 2–3 years, vintage *brut* and *sec* 3–5 years, vintage *demi-sec* 5–7 years

✓ *Marc Brédif* • *Champalou* • *Champion* • *Clos de l'Epinay* (Tête de Cuvée) • *Philippe Foreau* • *Domaine de la Galinière* (Cuvée Clément) • *Sylvain Gaudron* • *Huet* • *Laurent et Fabrice Maillet* • *Château de Moncontour* (Cuvée Prédilection)

VOUVRAY PÉTILLANT AOC

These are stylish and consistent semi-sparkling versions of Vouvray, but very little is produced.

SEMI-SPARKLING WHITE Medium- to full-bodied wines made in dry and sweet styles. They should be drunk young.

🍇 Chenin Blanc and Arbois

🍷 Upon purchase

✓ *Gilles Champion* • *Jean-Charles Cathelineau* • *Huet*

MORE GREEN WINES

In addition to the Loire producers recommended in this book that are either biodynamic or organic, there are also the following. They include a number that have been recommended in other editions, and still make some fine wines, but have been culled out to make room for others.

PAYS NANTAIS
Biodynamic

St. Nicolas (Brem sur Mer)

Organic

Chevolleau-Goulpeau (Aubigny), *De La Louvetrie* (La Haye-Fouassière), *De la Parentière* (Vallet), *Bruno Dejardin* (Rosnay)

ANJOU-SAUMUR
Biodynamic

De la Charmeres se (Faye d'Anjou), *De la Sansonnière* (Thouarcé), *Château La Tour Grise* (Le Pûy Notre Dame)

Organic

Laurent Charrier (Doué la Fontaine), *Collegiale des de Loire* (Le Puy Notre Dame), *Cousin Leduc* (Martigne Briand), *De Dreuillé* (Champ-sur-Layon), *De l'Echalier* (Rablay-sur-Layon), *Elliau* (Vaudelany), *Foucault* (Chacé), *Château Fouquet* (Dampierre-sur-Loire), *Des Frogères* (Chacé), *I. & J. Godineau Pithon* (St-Lambert du Lattay), *Anne Hacquet* (Beaulieu-sur-Layon), *Hauret* (Martigné Briand), *Henquinet-Pilhon* (Champ-sur-Layon), *Michel Joseph* (Chacé), *Du Layon* (St.-Georges du Layon), *Gérard Leroux* (Les Verchers-sur-Layon), *Manoir de la Tête Rouge* (Le Puy Notre Dame), *De Mosse* (St.-Lambert du Lattay), *Nouteau-Cerisier Père & Fils* (Faye d'Anjou), *Du Pas St. Martin* (Doué la Fontaine), *Régnier-David* (Meigné), *Rochais* (Rochefort-sur-Loire), *De Rochambeau* (Soulaines-sur-Aubance), *Rochard* (Chanzeaux), *Ste.-Barbe* (Saumur), *Patric Thomas* (St.-Georges-sur-Layon), *Val Brun* (Parnay), *Du Vieux Tuffeau* (Le Puy Notre Dame), *Vintrou* (St. Jean des Mauvrets).

TOURAINE
Biodynamic

De Pontcher (Thesée)

Organic

Clos Roches Blanches (Mareuil-sur-Cher), *Philippe Tessier* (Cheverny), *Michelle Thibault* (Bourgueil), *Du Clos Tue Boeuf* (Les Montils), *Breton* (Restigné), *Yves Lecocq* (Bourgueil), *Loquineau* (Cheverny), *De la Mabillière* (Vernou-sur-Brenne), *Joseph Moreau* (Vallères), *Du Mortier* (St. Nicolas de Bourgueil), *Château de la Roche* (Cheillé), *Les Cailloux du Paradis* (Soings en Sologne), *Alain Courtault* (Thésée), *Joël Courtault* (Thésée—in conversion to biodynamic), *Denis Père et Fils* (Civray de Touraine), *Des Deux Saintes* (St. Aubin le Dépeint), *Georget* (La Brosse-Touvois), *Guion* (Le Pontarin)

CENTRAL VINEYARDS
Organic

Claude Prugnard (Orcet), *Clos St. Jean*, *Clos de la Chapelle* (St. Jean St. Maurice), *Carroget Gautier* (Anetz), *Christian Chaput* (Prompsat), *Joël Lapalue* (St. Jean St. Maurice)

CENTRAL VINEYARDS

In this district of scattered vineyards, all the classic wines are dry variations of the Sauvignon Blanc, but there are some discernible differences between the best of them—the concentration of Sancerre, the elegance of Pouilly Fumé, the fresh-floral character of Menetou-Salon, the lightness of Reuilly, and the purity of Quincy.

CHÂTEAU DU NOZET, POUILLY-SUR-LOIRE
This 19th-century château at Pouilly-sur Loire is the home of Patrick de Ladoucette, the baron of Pouilly.

THE CENTRAL VINEYARDS are so called because they are in the center of France, not the center of the Loire Valley. This is a graphic indication of how far the Loire Valley extends and, while it might not be a surprise to discover the vineyards of Sancerre are quite close to Chablis, it does take a leap of the imagination to accept that they are nearer to the Champagne region than to Tours. And who could discern by taste alone that Sancerre is equidistant between the production areas of such diverse wines as Hermitage and Muscadet?

Best known of all the towns in this district is Orléans, famous for its liberation by Joan of Arc from the English in 1429. The other important town is Bourges, which is situated in the south between the wine villages of Reuilly, Quincy, and Menetou-Salon, and was once the capital of the Duchy of Berry.

THE REGION'S SAUVIGNON BLANC WINES

The Sauvignon Blanc is to the Central Vineyards what Muscadet is to the Pays Nantais. It produces the classic wine of the district, which, like Muscadet, also happens to be both white and dry. But two dry white wines could not be more different in style and taste. In the best Muscadet *sur lie* there should be a yeasty fullness, which can sometimes be misread as the Chardonnay character of a modest Mâcon. In Central Vineyard Sauvignons, however, whether they come from Sancerre or Pouilly—or even from one of the lesser-known, but certainly not lesser-quality, villages around Bourges—the aroma is so striking it sometimes startles. The rasping dryness of the wine's flavor catches the breath and can come from only one grape variety.

A BURGUNDIAN INFLUENCE

Historically, this district was part of the Duchy of Burgundy, which explains the presence of Pinot Noir vines. After the scourge of *phylloxera*, the area under vine shrank. That brought back into production was mostly replanted with Sauvignon Blanc, which began to dominate the vineyards, although isolated spots of Pinot Noir were maintained. Some of the wines these produce today can be good, although they are extremely delicate in style; and however fine the quality, they are but a shadow of great Burgundian Pinot.

CENTRAL VINEYARDS, *see also* p.197
The most easterly of the Loire's vineyards, and the most central of France, the Central Vineyards are famous for wines made from the Sauvignon Blanc grape.

FACTORS AFFECTING TASTE AND QUALITY

LOCATION
The most easterly vineyards of the Loire are situated in the center of France, chiefly in the *départements* of Cher, Nièvre, and Indre.

CLIMATE
More continental than areas closer to the sea; the summers are shorter and hotter and the winters longer and colder. Spring frosts and hail are particular hazards in Pouilly. Harvests are irregular.

ASPECT
Chalk hills in a quiet, green landscape. Vines occupy the best sites on hills and plateaus. At Sancerre they are planted on steep, sunny, sheltered slopes at an altitude of 660 feet (200 meters).

SOIL
The soils are dominated by clay or limestone, topped with gravel and flinty pebbles. When mixed with chalk-tufa, gravelly soils produce lighter, finer styles of Sauvignon wines; when combined with Kimmeridgian clay, the result is firmer and more strongly flavored.

VITICULTURE AND VINIFICATION
Some of the vineyard slopes in Sancerre are very steep, so cultivation and picking are done by hand. Most properties are small and use the traditional wooden vats for fermentation, but some growers have stainless-steel tanks.

GRAPE VARIETIES
Primary varieties: Sauvignon Blanc, Pinot Noir
Secondary varieties: Chasselas, Pinot Blanc, Pinot Gris, Cabernet Franc, Chenin Blanc, Gamay

THE APPELLATIONS OF
CENTRAL VINEYARDS

CÔTES DU GIEN COSNE-SUR-LOIRE AOC

Of the 16 communes that produce Coteaux du Giennois, only eight are entitled to add Cosne-sur-Loire to the appellation. It was promoted from VDQS to AOC in 1998.

RED Dry, bright ruby-colored wines. Often full-tasting, but rarely with the body to match and sometimes quite tannic.

🍇 Gamay, Pinot Noir—since 1992, neither variety may exceed 80% of the total blend

🍷 1–2 years

WHITE These are dry, medium-bodied, curiously aromatic white wines that develop a full, toasty flavor with a little bottle age.

🍇 Sauvignon Blanc

🍷 1–2 years

ROSÉ Light-salmon-colored wines, slightly fuller bodied than the Coteaux du Giennois made a little further to the north, but equally capable of the same citrous fragrance.

🍇 Gamay, Pinot Noir—since 1992, neither variety may exceed 80% of the total blend

🍷 1–4 years

✓ *Alain Paulat* ◉

COTEAUX DU GIENNOIS AOC

This appellation could boast nearly a thousand growers at the turn of the 20th century when it was 40 times its current size. Promoted from VDQS to AOC in 1998.

RED Dry, light-bodied red wines that often have less color than many rosés.

🍇 Gamay, Pinot Noir—since 1992, neither variety may exceed 80% of the total blend

🍷 1–2 years

WHITE These very basic, dry, light-bodied wines lack interest. Chenin Blanc can no longer be used to make this wine.

🍇 Sauvignon Blanc

🍷 1–2 years

ROSÉ Light-salmon-colored, light-bodied wines that can have a fragrant citrous character.

🍇 Gamay, Pinot Noir—since 1992, neither variety may exceed 80% of the total blend

🍷 1 year

✓ *Emile Balland* • *De Beaurois* • *De Villegeai*

MENETOU-SALON AOC

This underrated appellation covers Menetou-Salon and the nine surrounding villages.

RED These are dry, light-bodied, crisp, and fruity wines with fine varietal aroma. They are best drunk young, although some oak-matured examples can age well.

🍇 Pinot Noir

🍷 2–5 years

WHITE Bone-dry to dry wines. They are definitely Sauvignon in character, but the flavor can have an unexpected fragrance.

🍇 Sauvignon Blanc

🍷 1–2 years

ROSÉ Extremely good-quality, dry, light-bodied aromatic wines, full of straightforward fruit.

🍇 Pinot Noir

🍷 Within 1 year

✓ *Georges Chavet & Fils* • *De Loye* • *Henry Pellé*

POUILLY BLANC FUMÉ AOC
See Pouilly Fumé AOC

POUILLY FUMÉ AOC

This used to be the world's most elegant Sauvignon Blanc wine, but too many wines of ordinary and often quite dire quality have debased this once-great appellation. In Pouilly-sur-Loire and its six surrounding communes, only pure Sauvignon wines have the right to use "Fumé" in the appellation name, a term that evokes the grape's gunsmoke character.

WHITE Great Pouilly Fumé is rare but when found, its crisp, gooseberry flavor will retain its finesse and delicacy in even the hottest years.

🍇 Sauvignon Blanc

🍷 2–5 years

✓ *Bouchié-Chatellier* • *Jean-Claude Châtelain* • *Didier Dagueneau* • *Château Tracy*

POUILLY-SUR-LOIRE AOC

This wine comes from the same area as Pouilly Fumé, but it is made from the Chasselas grape, although Sauvignon Blanc is allowed for blending. Chasselas is a good dessert grape but makes very ordinary wine.

WHITE Dry, light-bodied wines. Most are neutral, tired, or downright poor.

🍇 Chasselas, Sauvignon Blanc

🍷 Upon purchase

✓ *Guy Saget*

QUINCY AOC

These vineyards, on the left bank of the Cher, are situated on a gravelly plateau. Although located between two areas producing red, white, and rosé wines, Quincy produces only white wine, from Sauvignon Blanc.

WHITE Bone-dry to dry, quite full-bodied wines in which the varietal character of the Sauvignon Blanc is evident. There is a purity that rounds out the flavor and seems to remove the rasping finish usually expected in this type of wine.

🍇 Sauvignon Blanc

🍷 1–2 years

✓ *Bailly* • *De Ballandors* • *Mardon* • *De Puy-Ferrand* • *Philippe Portier* • *Silice de Quincy*

REUILLY AOC

Due to the high lime content in the soil, Reuilly produces wines of higher acidity than those of neighboring Quincy.

RED These are dry, medium-bodied wines. Some are surprisingly good, although often tasting more of strawberries or raspberries than the more characteristic redcurrant flavor associated with Pinot Noir.

🍇 Pinot Noir, Pinot Gris

🍷 2–5 years

WHITE These are bone-dry to dry, medium-bodied wines of good quality with more of a grassy than a gooseberry flavor, yet possessing a typically austere dry finish.

🍇 Sauvignon Blanc

🍷 1–2 years

ROSÉ This bone-dry to dry, light-bodied wine is a pure Pinot Gris wine, although it is simply labeled Pinot.

🍇 Pinot Gris

🍷 2–5 years

✓ *Aujard*[1] • *Claude Lafond* • *De Seresnes*[1] *Jean-Michel Sorbe*[1] • *Pascal Desroches* (Clos des Varennes)

[1]Also particularly recommended for red or rosé

SANCERRE AOC

This appellation is famous for its white wines, although originally its reds were better known. Recently the reds and rosés have developed greater style.

RED These wines have been more variable in quality than the whites, but the consistency is improving rapidly. They are dry, light- to medium-bodied wines, with a pretty floral aroma and a delicate flavor.

🍇 Pinot Noir

🍷 2–3 years

WHITE Classic Sancerre should be bone dry, highly aromatic, and have an intense flavor, sometimes tasting of gooseberries or even peaches in a great year. However, too many growers overproduce, never get the correct ripeness, and make the most miserable wines.

🍇 Sauvignon Blanc

🍷 1–3 years

ROSÉ Attractive, dry, light-bodied rosés with strawberry and raspberry flavors.

🍇 Pinot Noir

🍷 Within 18 months

✓ *Henri Bourgeois* • *Pascal Cotat* • *Lucien Crochet*[1] • *Vignoble Dauny* ◉ • *André Dezat*[1] • *Fouassier* (Clos Paradis, Les Grands Groux) • *Gitton* • *Alphonse Mellot* • *Henry Natter* • *Vincent Pinard* • *Christian Thirot* (Des Vieux Pruniers)

[1]Also particularly recommended for red or rosé

VINS DE L'ORLÉANAIS VDQS

These wines have been made for centuries, but only one-third of the appellation is worked now.

RED Dry, medium-bodied, fresh, and fruity wines that are given a short maceration, producing a surprisingly soft texture. They are usually sold as pure varietal wines: the Pinot can be delicate, the Cabernet Franc is fuller.

🍇 Pinot Noir, Pinot Meunier, Cabernet Franc

🍷 1–2 years

WHITE Very small quantities of interesting wines are made from Chardonnay, known locally as Auvernat Blanc. Dry, medium-bodied, and surprisingly smooth and fruity.

🍇 Chardonnay (*syn.* Auvernat Blanc), Pinot Gris (*syn.* Auvernat Gris)

🍷 1–2 years

ROSÉ The local speciality is a dry, light- to medium-bodied rosé known as Meunier Gris—an aromatic *vin gris* with a crisp, dry finish.

🍇 Pinot Noir, Pinot Meunier, Cabernet Franc

🍷 Within 1 year

✓ *Clos St.-Fiacre* • *Vignerons de la Grand'Maison*

THE RHÔNE VALLEY

Famous for its full, fiery, and spicy-rich red wines, the Rhône Valley also produces small quantities of rosé and white, and even some sparkling and fortified wines. Although essentially red-wine country, and great red-wine country at that, the Rhône has experienced a kind of revolution in white-wine production. There has been a growing number of exotic, world-class white wines in various appellations since the late 1980s, when just a few began to emerge in Châteauneuf-du-Pape.

STRETCHING FROM VIENNE TO AVIGNON, the Côtes-du-Rhône appellation occupies a 125-mile (200-kilometer) length of the Rhône River. Beyond this great region other Rhône wines exist, and some are not even French. The banks of this mighty European river are clad with vines all the way from the Valais vineyards of Visp in Switzerland, just 30 miles (50 kilometers) from the Rhône's glacial origins in the Alps, to the *vin de pays* vineyards of the Bouches-du-Rhône, set amid the Rhône delta just west of Marseilles, where the river finally and sluggishly runs into the Mediterranean.

Only a tiny patch of vineyards in the very north of this region is in fact located within the Rhône *département* (which is a geographic misnomer as it actually accounts for 70 percent of Burgundy's output). Comparing the contrasting characters of Rhône

LA LANDONNE VINEYARD, CÔTE RÔTIE
Syrah grapes are harvested on the steep slopes of Guigal's top-performing La Landonne vineyard in the Côte Brune area of Côte Rôtie, above Ampuis.

NORTHERN RHÔNE
SOUTHERN RHÔNE

THE RHÔNE VALLEY,
see also p.55
Viticulturally the Rhône Valley covers a large area of southern central France, from Vienne into the heart of Provence.

Côtes-du-Rhône
See also pp215, 218

Côtes-du-Rhône-Villages
See also p218

Clairette de Die
See also p214

Châtillon-en-Diois
See also p214

Coteaux du Tricastin
See also p218

Coteaux de Pierrevert
See also p218

Côtes du Lubéron
See also p218

Côtes du Ventoux
See also p218

Côtes du Vivarais
See also p218

——— Département boundary

▲ Height above sea level (meters)

0   10   20 miles

0   10   20   30   40 km

CÔTE BRUNE ON THE CÔTE RÔTIE, NORTHERN RHÔNE
The Côte Brune is an area of the Côte Rôtie where the rust color of the soil is visible evidence of iron-rich elements in its granitic sandy soil.

and Burgundy wines produced within the one *département* can have a humbling effect on all those who glibly talk about regional styles. For example, what could be further apart than a rich, classic Condrieu and a fresh, light Mâcon, or an intense, ink-black Côte Rôtie and a quaffing, cherry-colored Beaujolais? Yet all of these wines are produced in the same *département* and could thus be described as coming from the same region.

BEAUMES-DE-VENISE, SOUTHERN RHÔNE
Home to one of the most elegant and consistent fortified Muscat wines in the world, Beaumes-de-Venise also produces a soft, peppery red wine under the Côtes-du-Rhône-Villages appellation.

RECENT RHÔNE VINTAGES

2003 Another classic region turned upside-down by the dramatic heat wave, with unprecedented high sugar and low acidity levels that provided the potential for great red wines only from those skilled enough to cope with the challenge. There will be many more flashes of brilliance that will have the critics raving about big, black monsters, only to find the wines will shed their fruit relatively quickly to end up with the alcohol showing through. The northern Rhône probably has the edge over the south, but where the wines are properly balanced, the greatest reds from all over the region will probably be a match for the best Rhônes from any vintage in living memory. There will always be exceptions, but generally you can forget the whites and rosés.

2002 A washout, literally.

2001 Some good northern reds, particularly in Côte-Rôtie, but September rain meant that many lack finesse, leaving them overall average at best. Much better, potentially long-lived reds in the south.

2000 A brilliant year for reds in both the northern and southern Rhône, with the wines showing excellent color and tannin structure, and lush fruit. The whites, however, are fat and blowsy.

1999 Soft, juicy, well-colored reds in the Northern Rhône have the edge over the southern reds, although those in the south who picked late have made wines to rival their northern cousins.

A REGION DIVIDED

In terms of grape varieties, the Rhône divides neatly into two—the Syrah-dominated north and the Grenache-influenced south—although there are those who confuse the issue by separating the southernmost section of the northern district and calling it the Middle Rhône. The north and south differ not only in terrain and climate, but also contrast socially, culturally, and gastronomically.

THE NORTHERN RHÔNE

The Northern Rhône is dominated by the ink-black wines of Syrah, the Rhône's only truly classic black grape. A small amount of white wine is also produced and, in the south of the district, at St.-Péray and Die, sparkling wines are made.

THE NORTHERN RHÔNE might be the gateway to the south, but it has more in common with its northern neighbor, Burgundy, than it does with the rest of the Rhône, even though its wines cannot be compared with those from any other area. Indeed, it would be perfectly valid to isolate the north as a totally separate region called the Rhône, which would, therefore, allow the Southern Rhône to be more accurately defined as a high-quality extension of the Midi.

THE QUALITY OF THE NORTHERN RHÔNE

The ink-black classic wines of Hermitage and Côte Rôtie stand shoulder to shoulder with the *crus classés* of Bordeaux in terms of pure quality, and the greatest Hermitage and Côte Rôtie deserve the respect given to *premiers crus* such as Latour, Mouton, or Lafite. Cornas can be even bigger and blacker than Hermitage or Côte Rôtie, and the top growers can rival the best of wines from its better-known neighbors. While the fine, dry white wines of Condrieu and (potentially) Château Grillet are unique in character, the presence of such a style in this part of France is not as surprising as that of the sparkling white wines of St.-Péray and Die, particularly the latter, which Francophiles would describe as a superior sort of Asti!

FACTORS AFFECTING TASTE AND QUALITY

LOCATION
The narrow strip of vineyards that belong to the Northern Rhône commences at Vienne, just south of Lyon, and extends southward to Valence.

CLIMATE
The general effect of the Mediterranean is certainly felt in the Northern Rhône, but its climate has a distinctly continental influence. This results in the pattern of warmer summers and colder winters, which is closer to the climate of southern Burgundy, to the north, than to that of the Southern Rhône. The climatic factor that the area does have in common with the southern half of the Rhône is the Mistral, a bitterly cold wind that can reach up to 90 miles (145 kilometers) per hour and is capable of denuding a vine of its leaves, shoots, and fruit. As a result, many Mistral-prone vineyards are protected by poplar and cypress trees. The wind can, however, have a welcome drying effect in humid harvest conditions. The average summertime temperature is just two degrees Fahrenheit lower than in the south.

ASPECT
The countryside is generally less harsh than that of the southern Rhône, with cherry, peach, chestnut, and other deciduous trees in evidence. The valley vineyards are cut far more steeply into the hillsides than they are in areas farther south.

SOIL
The Northern Rhône's soil is generally light and dry, granitic and schistous. More specifically, it is made up of: granitic-sandy soil on the Côte-Rôtie (calcareous-sandy on the Côte Blonde and ruddy, iron-rich sand on the Côte Brune);

granitic-sandy soil at Hermitage and Condrieu with a fine overlay of decomposed flint, chalk, and mica, known locally as *arzelle*; heavier soil in Crozes-Hermitage with patches of clay; granitic sand with some clay between St.-Joseph and St.-Péray, getting stonier toward the southern end of the region, with occasional outcrops of limestone; and limestone and clay over a solid rock base in the area that surrounds Die.

VITICULTURE AND VINIFICATION
Unlike the Southern Rhône, most Northern Rhône wines are produced entirely or predominantly from a single grape variety, the Syrah, despite the long list of grapes that are occasionally used (*see* Secondary varieties, *below*). Viticultural operations are labor-intensive in the northern stretch of the district and, due to the cost, the vineyards were once under the threat of total abandonment. Since that threat we pay much more for Côte Rôtie, but at least it has remained available. Vinification techniques are very traditional and, when wines are aged in wood, there is less emphasis on new oak than is given in Bordeaux or Burgundy, although chestnut casks are sometimes used.

GRAPE VARIETIES
Primary varieties: Syrah, Viognier
Secondary varieties: Aligoté, Bourboulenc, Calitor, Camarèse, Carignan, Chardonnay, Cinsault, Clairette, Counoise, Gamay, Grenache, Marsanne, Mauzac, Mourvèdre, Muscardin, Muscat Blanc à Petits Grains, Pascal Blanc, Picardan, Picpoul, Pinot Blanc, Pinot Noir, Roussanne, Terret Noir, Ugni Blanc, Vaccarèse

- Côtes du Rhône
- Côte Rôtie
- St-Joseph
- Condrieu
- Crozes-Hermitage
- Cornas
- St-Péray
- Clairette de Die
- Châtillon-en-Diois
- ▲ Height above sea level (metres)

0   5   10 miles
0   5   10 km

THE NORTHERN RHÔNE,
see also p.213
At the heart of this region the towns of Tain and Tournon face each other across the river.

AMPUIS UNDER SNOW
These southeast-facing vineyards of Côte Rôtie form a dramatic stretch of scenery on the west bank of the Rhône, 5 miles (9 kilometers) south of Vienne.

THE APPELLATIONS OF
THE NORTHERN RHÔNE

CHÂTEAU GRILLET AOC

Château Grillet has remained under the same family ownership (Neyret-Gachet) since 1830, and is one of only two single-estate appellations in France, the other being Romanée-Conti. Although it is often described as one of the world's great white wines, this is a legacy from more than a century ago. Château Grillet has not achieved anything like its full potential for at least the last few decades. There is no doubt that its sun-blessed terraces could produce Viognier of a singularly outstanding quality, but there is no inkling the proprietors can be bothered to pursue such a course. Who could blame them when Château Grillet could charge two or three times the price of Condrieu? But the price of some of the best Condrieu are now snapping at its heels, and unless there is a dramatic increase in quality, Château Grillet will drop in price. In today's more transparent market, fine wine consumers are no longer willing to drink labels.

WHITE This is, potentially, a wine of great finesse and complex character, but not one to keep in bottle as long as some would have you believe.

🍇 Viognier

⏳ 3–7 years

CHÂTILLON-EN-DIOIS AOC

This wine was raised to full AOC status in 1974, although it is hard to comprehend what merited such an elevation then or now.

RED Light in color and body, thin in fruit, with little discernible character.

🍇 Gamay, plus up to 25% Syrah and Pinot Noir

WHITE Sold as pure varietal wines, the light and fresh, gently aromatic Aligoté is as good as the richer, fuller, and rather angular Chardonnay.

🍇 Aligoté, Chardonnay

ROSÉ I have not encountered any.

🍇 Gamay, plus up to 25% Syrah and Pinot Noir

🍾✓ Didier Cornillon (Clos de Beylière)

CLAIRETTE DE DIE AOC

This dry sparkling wine is being phased out in favor of Crémant de Die from 1999 in what must be a classic example of Gallic logic—removing the name Clairette from an appellation of a wine that must be made from 100 percent Clairette grapes, yet retaining it for one (see below) that does not have to contain any!
See also Crémant de Die AOC

CLAIRETTE DE DIE MÉTHODE DIOISE ANCESTRALE AOC

Formerly sold as Clairette de Die Tradition, this wine may contain Clairette, but it is not the primary grape. What makes it so different, however, is that it is produced from one fermentation only, as opposed to the two required by Crémant de Die, the old Clairette de Die Mousseux, and most other sparkling wines.

In the *Méthode Dioise Ancestrale*, the wine first undergoes a long, cold part-fermentation in bulk and when bottled must contain a minimum of 55 grams of residual sugar per liter and no *liqueur de tirage*. Fermentation continues inside the bottle, but when disgorged the wine must still retain at least 35 grams of residual sugar per liter. The wine undergoes *transvasage* (meaning it is filtered into a fresh bottle) and is corked without any addition of a *liqueur d'expédition*.

SPARKLING WHITE A very fresh, deliciously fruity, gently sparkling wine of at least *demi-sec* sweetness, with a ripe, peachy flavor.

🍇 At least 75% Muscat à Petits Grains (this went up in 1993 from a minimum of 50%), plus Clairette

⏳ Upon purchase

🍾✓ Buffardel Frères • C. V. du Diois (Clairdie, Clairdissime)

CONDRIEU AOC

This is the greatest white-wine appellation in the entire Rhône Valley, with more up-and-coming young talent among its producers than anywhere else in the world. Initially the trend was to produce sweet and medium-sweet wines, but Condrieu has tended to be a distinctly dry wine for a couple of decades now. When the vintage permits, late-harvested sweeter wines are produced, and these styles are very much part of Condrieu's recent revival as one of the undisputed great white wines of the world.

WHITE These pale-gold-colored wines are essentially dry, but can have such an exotic perfume that you might easily think they are sweet when you first breathe in their heavenly aroma. The bouquet is fine, floral, and fruity, with heady, opulent aromas that can include may-blossom, honeysuckle, violets, roses, peaches, lime, and apricot, and in especially rich vintages there can also be some youthful honey wafting through. The fruit on the palate is always very perfumed and can give the impression of sweetness, even when completely dry. A great Condrieu has a beguiling balance of fatness, freshness, and finesse that produces an elegant, peachy-apricoty coolness of fruit on the finish. Do not be fooled into cellaring these wines—the dry ones in any case—as their greatest asset is the freshness and purity of fruit, which can only be lost over the years.

🍇 Viognier

⏳ 4–8 years

🍾✓ Yves Cuilleron (Les Ayguets) • Delas (Clos Boucher) • E. Guigal (La Doriane) • Vignobles du Monteillet (Les Grandes Chaillées) • Alain Paret (Lys de Volan) •

André Perret (Clos Chanson) • Georges Vernay • François Villard (Le Grand Vallon)

CORNAS AOC

The sun-trap vineyards of Cornas produce the best value of all the Rhône's quality red wines, but you have to buy it as soon as it is released as it is always sold far too young, so there is none left when it starts to show its true potential.

RED Ink-black, full-bodied, strong-flavored, pure Syrah wines with lots of blackcurrant and blackberry fruit, lacking only a little finesse if compared to a great Hermitage or Côte Rôtie.

🍇 Syrah

⏳ 7–20 years

🍾✓ Thierry Allemand • Auguste Clape • Jean-Luc Colombo • Courbis (Les Eygats) • Eric & Joël Durand • Patrick Lesec • Paul Jaboulet Aîné • Tardieu-Laurent (Vieilles Vignes)

CÔTE RÔTIE AOC

The terraces and low walls of the "burnt" or "roasted" slopes of Côte Rôtie must be tended by hand, but the reward is a wine of great class that vies with Hermitage as the world's finest example of Syrah.

RED A garnet-colored wine of full body, fire, and power, made fragrant by the addition of Viognier grapes. The result is a long-living and complex wine with nuances of violets and spices, and great finesse.

🍇 Syrah, plus up to 20% Viognier

⏳ 10–25 years

◉✓ Patrick & Christophe Bonnefond • Clusel-Roch ◉ • Cuilleron-Gaillard-Villard (Les Essartailles) • Delas (Seigneur de Maugiron) • Jean-Michel Gerin (Champin le Seigneur) • E. Guigal • Paul Jaboulet Aîné • Joseph Jamet • Patrick Jasmin • Michel Ogier • René Rostaing • Vidal-Fleury (La Chatilonne) • François Villard (La Brocarde)

COTEAUX DE DIE AOC

This new appellation was created in 1993 to soak up wines from excess Clairette grape production that were formerly sold under previous sparkling-wine appellations.

WHITE Perhaps it is unfair to prejudge a wine that has had so little time to establish itself, but it is hard to imagine a quality wine made from this grape. In effect, Coteaux de Die is the still-wine version of Crémant de Die. It is easy to see why such a bland dry wine needs bubbles to lift it, yet so few make the transition successfully.

🍇 Clairette

⏳ Upon purchase

🍾✓ Jean-Claude Raspail

CÔTES DU RHÔNE AOC

Although generic to the entire region, relatively little Côtes du Rhône is made in this district, where the only difference in technical criteria is that Syrah may replace Grenache as the principal red wine variety.

CRÉMANT DE DIE AOC

This dry sparkling wine was introduced in 1993 to replace Clairette de Die Mousseux, which was phased out by January 1999. Like the old Clairette de Die Mousseux appellation, Crémant de Die must be made by the traditional method, but whereas the former could include up to 25 percent Muscat à Petit Grains, the latter must be made entirely from Clairette.

SPARKLING WHITE It is too early to make a definitive pronouncement, but it looks as if Crémant de Die will be every bit as neutral and lackluster as Clairette de Die.

🍇 Clairette

⏱ 1–3 years

☑ Carod

CROZES-ERMITAGE AOC
See **Crozes-Hermitage AOC**

CROZES-HERMITAGE AOC

Crozes-Hermitage is produced from a relatively large area surrounding Tain, hence the quality is very variable, but a good Crozes-Hermitage will always be a great bargain.

RED These well-colored, full-bodied wines are similar to Hermitage, but they are generally less intense and have a certain smoky-rustic-raspberry flavor that only deepens into blackcurrant in the hottest years. The finest wines do, however, have surprising finesse, and make fabulous bargains.

🍇 Syrah, plus up to 15% Roussanne and Marsanne

⏱ 6–12 years
    8–20 years for top wines and great years

WHITE These dry white wines are improving and gradually acquiring more freshness, fruit, and acidity.

🍇 Roussanne, Marsanne

⏱ 1–3 years

☑ *Chapoutier* ⓑ *(Les Varonnières)* • *Yann Chave* (Tête de Cuvée) • *Les Chenets* • *C. V. des Clairmonts* (Pionniers) • *du Colombier* (Gaby) • *Combier* ⓞ *(Clos des Grives)* • *Alain Graillot* • *Paul Jaboulet Aîné* (Thalabert) • *des Remizières*[1] (Emilie)

ERMITAGE AOC
See **Hermitage AOC**

HERMITAGE AOC

One of the great classic French red wines, produced entirely from Syrah grapes in virtually all cases, although a small amount of Marsanne and Roussanne may be added. The vines are grown on a magnificent south-facing slope overlooking Tain.

RED These wines have a deep and sustained color, a very full body, and lovely, plummy, lip smacking, spicy, silky, violety, blackcurrant fruit. A truly great Hermitage has boundless finesse, despite the weighty flavor.

🍇 Syrah, plus up to 15% Roussanne and Marsanne

⏱ 12–30 years

WHITE These big, rich, dry white wines have a full, round, hazelnut and dried-apricot flavor. The wines have improved recently but are generally no more than curiosities.

🍇 Roussanne, Marsanne

⏱ 6–12 years

☑ *M Chapoutier*[1] ⓑ (Ermite, Méal, L'Orée, Pavillon) • *Jean-Louis Chave*[1] • *Emmanuel Darnaud* • *Delas* (Les Bessards) • *Alain Graillot* • *E. Guigal* (Ex Voto) • *Paul Jaboulet Aîné* (La Chapelle) • *des*

Remizières[1] (Emilie) • *Marc Sorrel* (Gréal) • *Tardieu-Laurent* (Vieilles Vignes)

[1]Particularly recommended for white as well as red.

HERMITAGE VIN DE PAILLE AOC

In the first edition of this book (1988), I wrote "In 1974 Gérard Chave made the last *vin de paille* of Hermitage, a wine that is now confined to the Jura vineyards of eastern France. Monsieur Chave declares he made the wine for 'amusement.' Considering its success, it is extraordinary that some enterprising grower has not taken advantage of this appellation."

Chapoutier has since made several vintages of Hermitage *vin de paille* on a commercial basis—or as near commercial as you can get with this style of wine—and other producers include Michel Ferraton, Jean-Louis Grippat, and Guigal. Even the local *coopérative* has churned some out. At one time all Hermitage *blanc* was, in effect, *vin de paille*, a style that dates back in this locality to at least 1760. Marc Chapoutier apparently drank the last wine of that vintage in 1964 when it was 204 years old. The traditional *vin de paille* method in Hermitage is not as intensive as the one revived relatively recently in Alsace, in which the grapes are dried out over straw beds until more than 90 percent of the original juice has evaporated before they are pressed, as even Chave's legendary 1974 was made from grapes bearing as much as a third of their original juice, but some of the results have been equally stunning. Despite decades between production, this wine still has its own AOC.

WHITE Some *vins de paille* are rich and raisiny whereas others—the best—have a crisp, vivid freshness about them, with intense floral-citrous aromas and a huge, long, honeyed aftertaste. After his famed 1974 vintage, Chave made a 1986 and at least a couple more vintages since. His *vin de paille* is reputed to be the greatest, but is practically unobtainable and certainly not available on the open market. This wine is made in the most commercial quantity, yet this still amounts to hardly anything, since the wine is hard to find and very expensive. Jean-Louis Grippat made a *vin de paille* in 1985 and 1986, neither of which I have had the privilege to taste, but John Livingstone-Learmonth describes them as "not quite like late-harvest Gewürztraminer" in his seminal work *The Wines of the Rhône*.

🍇 Roussanne, Marsanne

⏱ Up to 30 years

☑ *Chapoutier* ⓑ

L'ERMITAGE AOC
See **Hermitage AOC**

L'HERMITAGE AOC
See **Hermitage AOC**

ST.-JOSEPH AOC

At last, some truly exciting wines are being produced under this appellation. St.-Joseph has now replaced Cornas as the bargain-seeker's treasure trove.

RED The best wines are dark, medium to full-bodied, with intense blackberry and blackcurrant fruit aromas and plenty of soft fruit, whereas mediocre St.-Joseph remains much lighter bodied with a pepperiness more reminiscent of the Southern Rhône.

🍇 Syrah, plus up to 10% Marsanne and Roussanne

⏱ 3–8 years

WHITE At their best, clean, rich, and citrous-resinous dry wines.

🍇 Marsanne, Roussanne

⏱ 1–3 years

☑ *Chapoutier* ⓑ (Les Granits) • *Chave* • *Courbis*[1] (Les Roys) • *Pierre Coursodon* (Le Paradis Saint-Pierre) • *Yves Cuilleron* • *Pierre Gaillard* • *Gonon*[1] (Les Oliviers) • *E. Guigal* (Vignes de la Hospices) • *Vignobles du Monteillet* (Fortior) • *Tardieu-Laurent* (Vieilles Vignes) • *François Villard* (Reflet)

[1]Particularly recommended for white as well as red

ST.-PÉRAY AOC

This white-wine-only village appellation is curiously out of step with the rest of the area.

WHITE Firm and fruity, with good acidity for a wine from the south of the region, but unfortunately it usually lacks charm. Even the best growers within this region, recommended below, struggle to produce anything of interest.

🍇 Marsanne, Roussanne

⏱ 1–3 years

☑ *J.-F. Chaboud* • *Bernard Gripa* • *Jean Lionnet* • *Alain Voge*

ST.-PÉRAY MOUSSEUX AOC

This is a traditional method sparkling wine made from the wrong grapes grown on the wrong soil. The growers would be advised to rip the whole lot up and replant with black grapes for a red Côtes du Rhône.

SPARKLING WHITE An overrated, dry sparkling wine with a coarse *mousse*.

🍇 Marsanne, Roussanne

THE SOUTHERN RHÔNE

While the mellow warmth of the Grenache is found in most Southern Rhône wines, this region is in fact a blender's paradise, with a choice of up to 23 different grape varieties.

THE SOUTHERN RHÔNE is a district dominated by herbal scrubland, across which blows a sweet, spice-laden breeze. This is a far larger district than the slender northern *côtes*, and its production is, not unnaturally, much higher. Allowing the north a generous 10 percent of the generic Côtes du Rhône appellation, the southern Rhône still accounts for a staggering 95 percent of all the wines produced in the region.

WINES OF THE MIDI OR PROVENCE?

At least half of the Southern Rhône is in what was once called the Midi, an area generally conceded to cover the *départements* of the Aude, Hérault, and Gard. This is never mentioned by those intent on marketing the Rhône's image of quality, because the Midi was infamous for its huge production of *vin ordinaire*. The Rhône River marks the eastern border of the Midi and its most famous appellations are geographically part of Provence. But, viticulturally, these areas do not possess the quasi-Italian varieties that dominate the vineyards of Provence and may, therefore, be more rationally defined as a high-quality extension of the Midi.

THE SOUTHERN RHÔNE, *see also p.213*
The wider southern part of the Rhône Valley area stretches its fingers down toward Provence and eastwards to the Alps.

FACTORS AFFECTING TASTE AND QUALITY

LOCATION
The Southern Rhône starts at Viviers, south of Valence, and runs south to Avignon.

CLIMATE
The Southern Rhône's climate is unmistakably Mediterranean and its vineyards are far more susceptible to sudden change and abrupt, violent storms than are those of the Northern Rhône.

ASPECT
The terrain in the south is noticeably Mediterranean, with olive groves, lavender fields, and herbal scrub amid rocky outcrops.

SOIL
The limestone outcrops that begin to appear in the south of the Northern Rhône become more prolific and are often peppered with clay deposits, while the topsoil is noticeably stonier. Châteauneuf-du-Pape is famous for its creamy-colored drift boulders, which vary according to location. Stone-marl soils persist at Gigondas and weathered-gray sand in Lirac, Tavel, and Chusclan. The soils also incorporate limestone rubble, clay-sand, stone-clay, calcareous clay, and pebbles.

VITICULTURE AND VINIFICATION
The vines are traditionally planted at an angle leaning into the wind so that the Mistral may blow them upright when they mature. The south is a district where blends reign supreme. However, pure varietal wines are gaining ground. Traditional methods of vinification are used on some estates, but modern techniques are common.

GRAPE VARIETIES
Primary varieties: Carignan, Cinsault, Grenache, Mourvèdre, Muscat Blanc à Petits Grains, Muscat Rosé à Petits Grains
Secondary varieties: Aubun, Bourboulenc, Calitor, Camarèse, Clairette, Clairette Rosé, Counoise, Gamay, Grenache Blanc, Grenache Gris, Macabéo, Marsanne, Mauzac, Muscardin, Oeillade, Pascal Blanc, Picardan, Picpoul Blanc, Picpoul Noir, Pinot Blanc, Pinot Noir, Roussanne, Syrah, Terret Noir, Ugni Blanc, Vaccarèse, Vermentino (known locally as Rolle), Viognier

Map legend:
- Villages entitled to add their name to the Côtes du Rhône Villages appellation
- Côtes du Vivarais *crus* entitled to be included in the appellation
- Côtes du Rhône Villages
- Côtes du Rhône
- Côtes du Vivarais
- Coteaux du Tricastin
- Châteauneuf-du-Pape
- Haut-Comtat
- Lirac
- Gigondas
- Beaumes-de-Venise
- Tavel
- Côtes du Ventoux
- Coteaux de Pierrevert
- Côtes du Lubéron
- Height above sea level (metres)

0   5   10 miles
0   10   20 km

THE APPELLATIONS OF
THE SOUTHERN RHÔNE

BRÉZÈME CÔTES DU RHÔNE AOC

A regulatory curiosity, Brézème is not one of the 16 Côtes du Rhône Villages, which may attach their name only to the end of that appellation, but an anomalous village that through a peculiarity in the AOC laws is allowed to put its name before the basic Côtes du Rhône appellation (although some prefer to place it after, in much larger letters). The story dates back to the mid-1800s, when the wines from Brézème almost rivaled those of Hermitage, and sold for nearly as much. In 1943, when Brézème was first allowed to add its own name to the Côtes du Rhône AOC, the vineyards amounted to a mere 25 acres (10 hectares). Shortly afterward, most of the vineyards were abandoned and the village was all but forgotten. By 1961 there were barely 2½ acres under cultivation, yet remarkably a few producers continued to make Brézème. According to Eric Texier, one of the most respected growers was a Monsieur Pouchoulin, who was known as the "Grandfather of Brézème." Texier, a former nuclear engineer, took over Pouchoulin's vines, which are all Syrah and range from 60 to 100 years old. Thanks to Pouchoulin and others like him, the Brézème AOC was extended to include 208 acres (84 hectares) and, with renewed interest in the wine, plantings have increased by a further 55 acres (22 hectares), with more vines going in each year.

RED This pure Syrah wine has been likened to a Crozes-Hermitage, but some *cuvées* (Lombard's Grand Chêne and Eugène, for example) are aged in a percentage of new oak and are not at all like a Northern Rhône wine.

🍇 The full spectrum of Côtes du Rhône grapes is allowed, but Syrah is the only red wine grape grown

⌛ 3–10 years

WHITE Texier produces a pure Viognier and a pure Roussanne.

🍇 The full spectrum of Côtes du Rhône grapes is allowed, but only Marsanne, Roussanne, and Viognier are grown

⌛ 3–10 years

✓ *Jean-Marie Lombard* • *Eric Texier* (Syrah, Viognier)

CHÂTEAUNEUF-DU-PAPE AOC

The name Châteauneuf-du-Pape dates from the time of the dual papacy in the 14th century. The appellation is well known for its amazingly stony soil, which at night reflects the heat stored during the day, but the size, type, depth,

and distribution of the stones varies enormously, as does the aspect of the vineyards. These variations, plus the innumerable permutations of the 13 grape varieties that may be used, account for the diversity of its styles. In the early 1980s, some growers began to question the hitherto accepted concepts of *encépagement* and vinification; winemaking in Châteauneuf-du-Pape is still in an evolutionary state. The steady decline of the traditionally dominant Grenache has speeded up as more growers are convinced of the worth of the Syrah and Mourvèdre. The Cinsault and Terret Noir are still well appreciated, and the Counoise is beginning to be appreciated for its useful combination of fruit and firmness. The use of new oak is under experimentation and it already seems clear that it is better suited to white wine than red.

The regulations for this appellation have a unique safeguard designed to ensure that only fully ripe grapes in the healthiest condition are utilized: between 5 and 20 percent of the grapes harvested within the maximum yield for this AOC are rejected and may be used to make only *vin de table*. This process of exclusion is known as *le rapé*.

RED Due to the variations of *terroir* and almost limitless permutations of *encépagement*, it is impossible to describe a typical Châteauneuf-du-Pape, but there are two categories—the traditional, full, dark, spicy, long-lived style and the modern, easy-drinking Châteauneuf-du-Pape, the best of which are unashamedly upfront and brimming with lip-smacking, juicy-jammy fruit. Both are warmer and spicier than the greatest wines of Hermitage and Côte Rôtie.

🍇 Grenache, Syrah, Mourvèdre, Picpoul, Terret Noir, Counoise, Muscardin, Vaccarèse, Picardan, Cinsault, Clairette, Roussanne, Bourboulenc

⌛ 6–25 years

WHITE Early harvesting has reduced sugar levels and increased acidity, while modern vinification techniques have encouraged a drop in fermentation temperatures, so these wines are not as full as those produced previously. They can still be very rich, albeit in a more opulent, exotic fruit style, with a much fresher, crisper finish. The very best white Châteauneuf-du-Pape is generally agreed to be Château de Beaucastel Vieilles Vignes.

🍇 Grenache, Syrah, Mourvèdre, Picpoul, Terret Noir, Counoise, Muscardin, Vaccarèse, Picardan, Cinsault, Clairette, Roussanne, Bourboulenc

⌛ 1–3 years (4–6 years in exceptional cases)

✓ *Paul Autard* (Côte Ronde) • *Barville* • *Château de Beaucastel*[1] ⓞ • *de Beaurenard* (Boisrenard) • *Benedetti*[1] • *Bois de Boursan* (Felix) • *Bousquet des Papes* • *La Boutinière* • *Clos du Caillou* • *Les Cailloux* (Centenaire) • *Réserve des Célestins* • *Chapoutier* ⓑ (Barbe Rac, Croix de Bois) • *de la Charbonnière* • *Gérard Charvin* • *de Cistia* • *Font de Michelle* • *Château de la Gardine* • *Grand Veneur* • *de la Janasse* • *Lafond Roc-Epine* • *Patrick Lesec* • *de Marcoux* ⓑ • *Font de Michelle* (Etienne Gonet) • *Monpertuis* • *Château Mont-Redon* • *de la Mordorée* (Reine des Bois) • *de Nalys* • *Château la Nerthe*[1] • *de Panisse* • *Clos des Papes* • *du Pegaü* • *Château Rayas*[1] • *Roger Sabon* • *Clos St. Michel* (Grand Clos) • *de la Solitude* • *Tardieu-Laurent* (Vieilles Vignes) • *Pierre Usseglio* • *de la Vieille Julienne* • *du Vieux Télégraphe* • *de Villeneuve*

[1]Particularly recommended for white as well as red

COTEAUX DE PIERREVERT AOC

This appellation consists of some 990 acres (400 hectares) and was upgraded from VDQS to full AOC status in 1998.

RED Dull, uninspiring wines with little original character to commend them.

🍇 Carignan, Cinsault, Grenache, Mourvèdre, Oeillade, Syrah, Terret Noir

⌛ 2–5 years

WHITE Unspectacular, light, dry white wines with more body than fruit.

🍇 Clairette, Marsanne, Picpoul, Roussanne, Ugni Blanc

⌛ 1–3 years

ROSÉ Well-made wines with a blue-pink color and a crisp, light, fine flavor.

🍇 Carignan, Cinsault, Grenache, Mourvèdre, Oeillade, Syrah, Terret Noir

⌛ 1–3 years

✓ *La Blaque* (Réserve) • *Vignobles de Regusse* (Bastide des Oliviers)

COTEAUX DU TRICASTIN AOC

Established as a VDQS in 1964, Tricastin was upgraded to full AOC status in 1973.

RED Very good wines, especially the deeply colored, peppery Syrah wines that are a delight after a few years in bottle. These wines may be sold as *primeur* or *nouveau* from the third Thursday of November following the harvest.

🍇 Grenache, Cinsault, Mourvèdre, Syrah, Picpoul Noir, and a maximum of 20% Carignan; and 20% (in total) of Grenache Blanc, Clairette, Bourboulenc, and Ugni Blanc

⌛ 2–7 years

WHITE Although I was unable to recommend Tricastin *blanc* in the first edition of this book (1988), the variety of grapes permitted has since been expanded to include Roussanne, Marsanne, and Viognier, which has enabled some producers to make richer, crisper, more interesting wines.

Grenache Blanc, Clairette, Picpoul, Bourboulenc, and a maximum of 30% (in total) of Ugni Blanc, Roussanne, Marsanne, and Viognier

ROSÉ A small production of fresh and fruity dry rosé that occasionally yields an outstandingly good wine. These wines may be sold as *primeur* or *nouveau* as from the third Thursday of November following the harvest.

Grenache, Cinsault, Mourvèdre, Syrah, Picpoul Noir, and a maximum of 20% Carignan; and 20% (in total) of Grenache Blanc, Clairette, Bourboulenc, and Ugni Blanc

Upon purchase

✓ *Bour* • *des Estubiers* • *de Grangeneuve* • *de Montine* • *Saint-Luc*

CÔTES DU LUBÉRON AOC

The wine of Côtes du Lubéron was promoted to full AOC status in February 1988. Much of the credit must go to Jean-Louis Chancel: his vineyards at Château Val-Joanis are still young, but the promise is such that this property has been described as the jewel in Lubéron's crown.

RED These are bright, well-colored wines with plenty of fruit and character, improving with every vintage.

A blend of two or more varieties to include a minimum of 60% Grenache and Syrah (in total)—of which Syrah must represent at least 10%; a maximum of 40% Mourvèdre; 20% (each) of Cinsault and Carignan; and 10% (either singly or in total) of Counoise, Pinot Noir, Gamay, and Picpoul

3–7 years

WHITE As white Lubéron has no established style or reputation, it seems bureaucratic nonsense to be so precise about the percentage of each grape variety that may or may not be included in its production. There was a feeling that some sort of quality and style was about to emerge in these wines in the late 1980s when Lubéron was merely a VDQS. Even then the regulation concerning grape varieties was unnecessarily complicated. Since its upgrade to full AOC status, the regulations have become even more confusing, and I doubt if it is a coincidence that Lubéron *blanc* has completely lost its way over the same period.

A blend of two or more varieties, which can include Grenache Blanc, Clairette, Bourboulenc, Vermentino, a maximum of 50% Ugni Blanc, and up to 20% (of the blend) of Roussanne and/or Marsanne

1–3 years

ROSÉ These attractively colored, fresh, fruity wines are much better quality than most Provence rosé.

A blend of two or more varieties to include

a minimum of 60% Grenache and Syrah (in total)—of which Syrah must represent at least 10%; a maximum of 40% Mourvèdre; 20% (each) of Cinsault and Carignan; 20% (in total) of Grenache Blanc, Clairette, Bourboulenc, Vermentino, Ugni Blanc, Roussanne, and Marsanne; plus 10% (either singly or in total) of Counoise, Pinot Noir, Gamay, and Picpoul

Upon purchase

✓ *de la Bastide de Rhodarès* • *Château la Canorgue* • *de la Citadelle* • *Château Constantin-Chevalier* (Fondateurs) • *de Fontenille* (Prestige) • *Cellier de Marrenon* (Grand Lubéron) • *de Mayol* • *de la Royere* • *Château Thouramme* ◉ • *Château Val Joanis*

CÔTES DU RHÔNE AOC

A generic appellation that covers the entire Rhône region, although the vast majority of wines are actually produced in the Southern Rhône. There are some superb Côtes du Rhônes, but there are also some disgusting wines. The quality and character varies to such an extent that it would be unrealistic to attempt any generalized description. The red and rosé may be sold as *primeur* or *nouveau* from the third Thursday of November following the harvest, although the reds can be sold only unbottled as *vin de café*. Red, white, and rosé wines can go on sale from December 1 without mention of *primeur* or *nouveau*.

RED The red wines are the most successful of this basic appellation, and often represent the best choice when dining in a modest French restaurant with a restricted wine list. Top *négociants* like Guigal consistently produce great-value Côtes du Rhône, but those below are all capable of very special quality.

A minimum of 40% Grenache (except in the Northern Rhône, where Syrah may be considered the principal variety), plus Syrah and/or Mourvèdre, with up to 30% in total of any of the following: Camarèse, Carignan, Cinsault, Clairette Rosé, Counoise, Grenache Gris, Muscardin, Vaccarèse, Picpoul Noir, Terret Noir, and no more than 5% in total of any of the following white varieties: Clairette, Grenache Blanc, Marsanne, Picpoul, Roussanne, Bourboulenc, Ugni Blanc, Viognier

3–10 years

WHITE These wines have improved tremendously in the past 5–10 years and continue to do so in encouraging fashion.

Bourboulenc, Clairette, Grenache Blanc, Marsanne, Roussanne, Viognier, and up to 20% Ugni Blanc and/or Picpoul

1–3 years

ROSÉ Many of the best rosés are superior in quality to those from more expensive Rhône appellations.

A minimum of 40% Grenache (except in the Northern Rhône, where Syrah may be considered the principal variety), plus Syrah and/or Mourvèdre, with up to 30% in total of any of the following: Camarèse, Carignan, Cinsault, Clairette Rosé, Counoise, Grenache Gris, Muscardin, Vaccarèse, Picpoul Noir, Terret Noir, and no more than 5% in total of any of the following white varieties: Clairette, Grenache Blanc, Marsanne, Picpoul, Roussanne, Bourboulenc, Ugni Blanc, Viognier

1–3 years

✓ *Max Aubert* (dè la Présidente) • *Castan* • *Coudoulet de Beaucastel* • *Cuilleron-Gaillard-Villard* • *Fond Croze* • *Château de Fontsegune* • *Grand Veneur* • *Clos de l'Hermitage* • *Paul Jaboulet Aîné* • *Clos des Magnaneraie* • *Clos Martin* • *Château de Montfaucon* • *Château Mont-Redon* • *Rigot* • *des Roches Fortes* (Prestige) • *Xavier Vignon*

CÔTES DU RHÔNE VILLAGES AOC

Compared with the generic Côtes du Rhône, these wines generally have greater depth, character, and quality. The area covered by the appellation is entirely within the Southern Rhône. If the wine comes from one commune only, then it has the right to append that name to the appellation.

Gigondas, Cairanne, Chusclan, and Laudun were the four villages that formed the original Côtes du Rhône Villages appellation. Gigondas achieved its own AOC in 1971, but other villages have been added from time to time. Vacqueyras became an AOC in its own right in 1990.

The wines recommended immediately below the criteria for rosé carry the Côtes du Rhône Villages appellation without any specified village, followed by separate entries for each of the 16 villages that are currently allowed to add their name to this AOC.

RED These wines are mostly excellent.

A minimum of 50% Grenache, plus a minimum of 20% Syrah and/or Mourvèdre, with up to 20% in total of Camarèse, Carignan, Cinsault, Clairette Rosé, Counoise, Grenache Gris, Muscardin, Vaccarèse, Picpoul Noir, Terret Noir

3–10 years

WHITE These wines are improving—Vieux Manoir du Frigoulas is the best.

Bourboulenc, Clairette, Grenache Blanc, Marsanne, Picpoul, Roussanne, Viognier

🍷 1–3 years

ROSÉ These wines can be very good.

A minimum of 50% Grenache, plus a minimum of 20% Syrah and/or Mourvèdre; up to 20% in total of Camarèse, Carignan, Cinsault, Clairette Rosé, Counoise, Grenache Gris, Muscardin, Vaccarèse, Picpoul Noir, Terret Noir; no more than 20% in total of any of the following white varieties: Bourboulenc, Clairette, Grenache Blanc, Marsanne, Picpoul, Roussanne, Viognier; and a maximum of 20% Ugni Blanc and/or Picpoul

🍷 1–3 years

✓ *Les Aphillanthes • Bouche • Le Clos du Caillou • Château la Gardine • Château d'Hugues • de la Janasse* (Terre Argile) *• Mas de Libian • du Petit-Barbras* (Le Chemin de Barbras Sélection) *• La Réméjeanne* (Eglantiers) *• Dominique Rocher* (Monsieur Paul) *• St.-Anne • Saint Estève d'Uchaux* (Vieilles Vignes) *• C. V. de St. Hilaire d'Ozilhan* (Saveur du Temps) *• Viret* (Emergence)

THE 16 VILLAGES OF THE CÔTES DU RHÔNE VILLAGES

These single-villages versions of the above appellation wines can add their village name to the Côtes du Rhône Villages appellation.

CÔTES DU RHÔNE BEAUMES-DE-VENISE AOC

Famous for its delectable, sweet Muscat wine, Beaumes-de-Venise also produces a pleasant red wine with a good peppery-raspberry fruit flavor. Dry white and rosé wines are produced under the generic AOC.

✓ *La Chapelle Notre Dame d'Aubune • Durban*

CÔTES DU RHÔNE CAIRANNE AOC

Since Vacqueyras was promoted to its own AOC, Cairanne is now the top village in the appellation. It is an excellent source of rich, warm, and spicy red wines that age very well.

✓ *d'Aeria • Daniel et Denis Alary • Les Grand Bois* (Mireille) *• Les Hautes Cances • de l'Oratoire St.-Martin • Marcel Richaud* (L'Ebrescade)

CÔTES DU RHÔNE CHUSCLAN AOC

One of two single-village appellations whose wines actually come from more than one commune, Chusclan may also be made from vines growing in Bagnols-sur-Cèze, Cadolet,

Orsan, and St.-Etienne-des-Sorts. These villages are situated just north of Lirac and Tavel, two famous rosé appellations, and make an excellent rosé. However, most of the wines are red, and produced in a good, quaffing style. The white is fresh, lively, and reliable.

✓ *C. V. de Chusclan* (Esprit de Terroir) *• Château Signac*

CÔTES DU RHÔNE LAUDUN AOC

Laudun, one of the appellation's four original villages, produces the other wine (*see* Côtes du Rhône Chusclan AOC) that can be made from vines grown outside the village indicated—in this case from St.-Victor-Lacoste and Tresques – and excels in making fine, fresh, and spicy red wines. It also makes the best white wines in the Côtes du Rhône Villages appellation, and a small amount of quite delightful rosé wines.

✓ *Château St.-Maurice*

CÔTES DU RHÔNE RASTEAU AOC

This village is best known for its sweet Rasteau "Rancio" (*see below*), yet it produces nearly four times as much dry red, white, and rosé as it does Rasteau. Its red is the best: deep-colored, full, and rich, with a spicy warmth, Rasteau *rouge* is a wine that can improve for up to 10 years.

✓ *de Beaurenard* (Argiles Bleus) *• Bressy-Masson • La Courançonne* (Magnificat) *• des Escaravailles* (La Ponce) *• La Soumade* (Confiance) *• Tardieu-Laurent*

CÔTES DU RHÔNE ROAIX AOC

Neighboring the vineyards of Séguret, Roaix produces a similar dark-colored red wine that requires two or three years in bottle to mellow. A little rosé is also produced.

✓ *C. V. de Roaix-Séguret*

CÔTES DU RHÔNE ROCHEGUDE AOC

Only the red wine of Rochegude may claim the Côtes du Rhône Villages appellation. I have encountered only the local *coopérative* wine, but it is good quality, well colored, soft, and plummy. As at Beaumes-de-Venise, the white and rosé is sold as generic Côtes du Rhône.

✓ *C. V. de Rochegude*

CÔTES DU RHÔNE ROUSSET-LES-VIGNES AOC

The neighboring villages of Rousset-les-Vignes and St.-Pantaléon-les-Vignes possess the most northerly vineyards of this appellation, close to the verdant Alpine foothills. With the coolest climate of all the Côtes du Rhône villages, the wines are light, but soft and quaffable. Most of the production is monopolized by the local *coopérative*.

✓ *La Bouvade*

CÔTES DU RHÔNE SABLET AOC

This village's soft, fruity, and quick-maturing red and rosé wines are consistent in quality, and are always good value.

✓ *de Piaugier* (Montmartel)

CÔTES DU RHÔNE ST.-GERVAIS AOC

The valley vineyards of St.-Gervais are not those of the great river itself, but belong to the Cèze, one of its many tributaries. The red wines are deliciously deep and fruity, and the whites are fresh and aromatic with an excellent, crisp balance for wines from such a southerly location.

✓ *Clavel* (L'Étoile du Berger) *• C. V. de St.-Gervais* (Prestige) *• Sainte-Anne*

CÔTES DU RHÔNE ST.-MAURICE AOC OR CÔTES DU RHÔNE ST.-MAURICE-SUR-EYGUES AOC

Light, easy-drinking red and rosé wines. Production is dominated by the local *coopérative*.

✓ *C. V. des Coteaux St.-Maurice*

CÔTES DU RHÔNE SÉGURET AOC

Séguret produces red wine that is firm and fruity with a good, bright, deep color. A little white and rosé is also made but they seldom excel.

✓ *de Mourchon* (Grande Réserve) *• Eric Texier*

CÔTES DU RHÔNE ST.-PANTALÉON-LES-VIGNES AOC

The neighboring villages of St.-Pantaléon-les-Vignes and Rousset-les-Vignes possess the most northerly vineyards of this appellation. With the coolest climate of all the Côtes du Rhône villages, the wines are light, but soft and quaffable. Production is monopolized by the local *coopérative*, which has yet to make anything special.

CÔTES DU RHÔNE VALRÉAS AOC

These are fine red wines with plenty of fruit flavor. A little rosé is also made.

✓ *Clos Petite Bellane • Comte Louis de Clermont-Tonnerre • des Grands Devers • Le Val des Rois*

CÔTES DU RHÔNE VINSOBRES AOC

This village consistently produces good-quality, firm red wines. It also produces a small amount of passable rosé.

✓ *des Ausellons • du Corriançon • du Moulin* (Charles Joseph) *• Perrin*

CÔTES DU RHÔNE VISAN AOC

These red wines have good color and true *vin de garde* character. Fresh, quaffing white wines are also made.

✓ *de la Coste Chaude • Olivier Cuilleras*

CÔTES DU VENTOUX AOC

The limestone subsoil of the Côtes du Ventoux appellation produces a lighter wine than is normal for the Rhône.

RED These fresh and fruity, easy-to-drink reds are the best wines in this AOC. The wines may be sold as *primeur* or *nouveau* from the third Thursday of November following the harvest.

Grenache, Syrah, Cinsault, and Mourvèdre, plus up to 30% Carignan, and a maximum of 20% (in total) of Picpoul Noir, Counoise, Clairette, Bourboulenc, Grenache Blanc, Roussanne, and—until the 2014 vintage—Ugni Blanc, Picpoul Blanc, and Pascal Blanc

🍷 2–5 years

WHITE A little white is produced, but it is seldom anything more than of minimal interest. These wines may be sold as *primeur* or *nouveau* from the third Thursday of November following the harvest.

🍇 Clairette, Bourboulenc, plus up to 30% (in total) of Grenache Blanc, Roussanne, and—until the 2014 vintage—Ugni Blanc, Picpoul Blanc, and Pascal Blanc

ROSÉ The fresh character and deliciously delicate fruit of these wines can be pure joy on a hot sunny day. They may be sold as *primeur* or *nouveau* from the third Thursday of November following the harvest.

🍇 Grenache, Syrah, Cinsault, and Mourvèdre, plus up to 30% Carignan, and a maximum of 20% (in total) Picpoul Noir, Counoise, Clairette, Bourboulenc, Grenache Blanc, Roussanne, and—until the 2014 vintage—Ugni Blanc, Picpoul Blanc, and Pascal Blanc

🍷 Upon purchase

✓ *La Ferme Saint Pierre* (Roi Fainéant) • *Le Murmurium* • *Château Talaud* • *Les Terrasses d'Eole* (Lou Mistrau) • *Château Valcombe* • *de la Verrière* • *Xavier Vignon* (Xavier)

CÔTES DU VIVARAIS AOC

The *côtes* of Vivarais look across the Rhône River to the *coteaux* of Tricastin. Its best *cru* villages (Orgnac, St.-Montant, and St.-Remèze) may add their names to the Côtes du Vivarais appellation, and of these, the wines of the village of Orgnac stand out. Promoted from VDQS to AOC in 1999.

RED These light, quaffing reds are by far the best wines in the district.

🍇 Since 1995 Mourvèdre, Picpoul, Aubun, and Carignan have been banned, and this wine must now contain a minimum of 90% (in total) of Syrah and Grenache; the Syrah must account for at least 40% and Grenache at least 30%, with Cinsault and Carignan optional

🍷 1–3 years

WHITE These wines were always dull and disappointing, but with the recent improvement in the *encépagement*, standards have undoubtedly improved, and Vivarais *blanc* may very well prove to be interesting in the future.

🍇 Since 1995 Bourboulenc, Macabéo, Mauzac, Picpoul, and Ugni Blanc have been banned, and this wine must now be made from at least two varieties of the three recommended grapes—Clairette, Grenache, and Marsanne—with no single variety accounting for more than 75% of the total

🍷 1–3 years

ROSÉ These pretty pink, dry wines can have a ripe, fruity flavor and are generally better than the whites.

🍇 Since 1995 Mourvèdre, Carignan, Picpoul, and Aubun have been banned, and this wine must now be made from at least two of the three recommended grapes—Syrah, Grenache, and Cinsault—with no single variety accounting for more than 80% of the total

🍷 1–3 years

✓ *Les Chais du Vivarais*

GIGONDAS AOC

Gigondas produces some of the most underrated red wines in the Rhône Valley.

RED The best have an intense black-red color with a full, plummy flavor.

🍇 A maximum of 80% Grenache, plus at least 15% Syrah and Mourvèdre, and a maximum of 10% (in total) of Clairette, Picpoul, Terret Noir, Picardan, Cinsault, Roussanne, Marsanne, Bourboulenc, Viognier, Counoise, Muscardin, Vaccarèse, Pinot Blanc, Mauzac, Pascal Blanc, Ugni Blanc, Calitor, Gamay, and Camarèse

🍷 7–20 years

ROSÉ Good-quality, dry rosé wines.

🍇 A maximum of 80% Grenache and a maximum of 25% (in total) of Clairette, Picpoul, Terret Noir, Picardan, Cinsault, Roussanne, Marsanne, Bourboulenc, Viognier, Counoise, Muscardin, Vaccarèse, Pinot Blanc, Mauzac, Pascal Blanc, Ugni Blanc, Calitor, Gamay, and Camarèse

🍷 2–5 years

✓ *La Bouissière* • *Brusset* (Le Grand Montmirail, Les Hauts des Montmirail) • *du Cayron* • *de la Gardette* • *Les Goubert* (Florence) • *Grapillon d'Or* (Elevé en Vieux Foudres) • *de Longue-Toque* • *Gabriel Meffre* (Château Raspail) • *L'Oustau Fauquet* (Secret de la Barrique) • *Saint Cosme* • *Saint-Damien* (Les Souteyrades) • *de St.-Gayan* (Fontmaria) • *Sainte Anne* • *Santa Duc* • *La Tourade*

LIRAC AOC

This appellation was once the preserve of rosé, but the production of red is now on the increase.

RED In really great years, the Syrah and Mourvèdre can dominate despite the quite small quantities used, which produces a more plummy wine with silky-spicy finesse.

🍇 A minimum of 40% Grenache and 25% (in total) of Syrah and Mourvèdre, plus up to 10% Carignan and no limit on the amount of Cinsault (although this used to be restricted to 20%, and I suspect this

relaxation is due to clerical error when the regulations were rewritten in 1992)

🍷 4–10 years

WHITE A fragrant, dry white wine, the best of which has improved since 1992, when Marsanne, Roussanne, and Viognier were permitted for use in this appellation. The cheapest wines have declined in quality because the amount of Clairette allowed has been doubled. Macabéo and Calitor are no longer permitted.

🍇 Up to 60% (each) of Bourboulenc, Clairette, and Grenache Blanc; plus up to 25% (each) of Ugni Blanc, Picpoul, Marsanne, Roussanne, and Viognier (but these secondary varieties must not represent more than 30% of the blend in total)

🍷 1–3 years

ROSÉ Production is declining in favor of red wine, but these dry rosés can have a delightful summer-fruit flavor that is fresher than either Tavel or Provence.

🍇 A minimum of 40% Grenache and 25% (in total) of Syrah and Mourvèdre, plus up to 10% Carignan, no limit on the amount of Cinsault (but *see* red wine grapes above), and up to 20% (in total) of Bourboulenc, Clairette, Grenache Blanc, Ugni Blanc, Picpoul, Marsanne, Roussanne, and Viognier

🍷 1–3 years

✓ *Château d'Aquéria* • *Lafond Roc-Epine* • *Maby* (La Fermade) • *de la Mordorée*

MUSCAT DE BEAUMES-DE-VENISE AOC

These wines from Muscat de Beaumes-de-Venise are the most elegant of the world's sweet fortified Muscat wines. Very little sweet Muscat was made before World War II. When the AOC was granted in 1945, the wine was classified as a *vin doux naturel*. The process by which this is made entails the addition of pure grape spirit, in an operation called *mutage*, after the must has achieved 5 percent alcohol by natural fermentation. The final wine must contain at least 15 percent alcohol, plus a minimum of 110 grams per liter of residual sugar. The Coopérative des Vins & Muscats, which was established in 1956, accounts for a formidable 90 percent of the wine produced. It is often said that this wine is always nonvintage, but in fact 10 percent is sold with a vintage on the label.

WHITE/ROSÉ The color varies between the rare pale gold and the common light apricot-gold, with an aromatic bouquet more akin to the perfume of dried flowers than fruit. You should expect Muscat de Beaumes-de-Venise to have hardly any acidity, which surprisingly does not make it cloying, despite its intense sweetness, but does enable it to be one of the very few wines to partner ice cream successfully.

🍇 Muscat Blanc à Petits Grains, Muscat Rosé à Petits Grains

🍷 1–2 years

✓ *de Coyeux* • *de Durban* • *Paul Jaboulet Aîné* • *Gabriel Meffre* (Laurus) • *Pigeade* • *de St.-Saveur* • *Vidal-Fleury*

RASTEAU AOC

This appellation was first created in the early 1930s, and was promoted to full AOC status on January 1, 1944. Rasteau was the first of the Rhône's two *vin doux naturel* appellations. In popularity and quality it is, however, second to Muscat de Beaumes-de-Venise.

RED A rich, sweet, coarse, grapey-flavored concoction with plenty of grip, a rather awkward spirity aroma, and a pithy, apricot-skin aftertaste.

🍇 A minimum of 90% Grenache (Gris or Blanc), plus up to 10% (in total) of Clairette, Syrah, Mourvèdre, Picpoul, Terret Noir, Picardan, Cinsault, Roussanne, Marsanne, Bourboulenc, Viognier, Carignan, Counoise, Muscardin, Vaccarèse, Pinot Blanc, Mauzac, Pascal Blanc, Ugni Blanc, Calitor, Gamay, and Camarèse

🍷 1–5 years

WHITE/TAWNY/ROSÉ This wine can be white, tawny, or rosé depending on the technique used and on the degree of aging. It does not have the grip of the red, but has a mellower sweetness.

🍇 A minimum of 90% Grenache (Gris or Blanc), plus up to 10% (in total) of Clairette, Syrah, Mourvèdre, Picpoul, Terret Noir, Picardan, Cinsault, Clairette, Roussanne, Bourboulenc, Viognier, Carignan, Counoise, Muscardin, Vaccarèse, Pinot Blanc, Mauzac, Pascal Blanc, Ugni Blanc, Calitor, Gamay, and Camarèse

🍷 1–5 years

✓ *des Escaravailles*

RASTEAU "RANCIO" AOC

These wines are similar to those of the Rasteau AOC (*see above*), except they must be stored in oak casks "according to local custom," which often means exposing the barrels to sunlight for a minimum of two years, which allows the wines to develop the "rancio" character.

TAVEL AOC

Tavel is the most famous French dry rosé, but only the very best domaines live up to its reputation. In order to retain freshness, Tavel's alcoholic level is restricted to a maximum of 13 percent.

MORE GREEN SOUTHERN RHÔNE

In addition to the producers recommended in this directory that are either biodynamic or organic, there are also the following. No negative inference of quality should be taken from the fact that they are not featured among my recommended producers. There are a number that have been recommended in other editions, and still make some fine wines, but have been cut out to make room for others.

Biodynamic

Pierre André (Courthézon), *Château de Bastet* (Sabran), *des Estubiers* (Les Granges Gontardes), *Grande Bellane* (Domaine de la Grande Bellane), *Gaïa* (Saint-Marcellin), *Patrick Pélisson* (Goult), *Eric Saurel* (Sarrians), *St. Apollinaire* (Vaison-La-Romaine)

Organic

des Adrès (Villedieu), *Arbre aux Soleils* (Faucon), *des Auzières* (Roaix), *de Balazut* (St. Paulet de Caisson), *des Carabiniers* (Roquemaure), *Catherine Le Goeuil* (Cairanne), *des Cèdres* (St. Nazaire), *Le Clos de Caveau* (Vacqueyras), *Clos du Joncuas* (Gigondas), *des Coccinelles* (Domazan), *Château de la Croix des Pins* (Mazan), *Jean David* (Séguret), *Michel Delacroix* (Theziers), *Duseigneur* (St. Laurent des Arbres), *de la Gautière* (La Penne-sur-Ouvèze), *Goisbault* (Saze), *Grange de Louiset* (Flassans), *Herbouze* (St. Alexandre), *de la Jasse* (Violès), *de Lumian* (Valreas), *Monastère de Solan* (La Bastide d'Engras), *C. V. du Nyonsais* (Nyons), *de la Roche Buissière* (Faucon St. Honorat (Domazan), *St. Pons* (Villars), *Terres de Solence* (Mazan), *C. V. des Vignerons de Vacqueyras* (Vacqueyras), *Val de Morcasse* (Montfrin), *Le Van* (Bedoin), *du Vieux Chêne* (Camaret-sur-Aigues), *La Vigneronne* (Vaison la Romaine)

ROSÉ Some properties still cling to the old-style vinification methods and, frankly, this means the wines are too old before they are sold. The top domaines in the appellation make clean-cut wines with freshly scented aromas and fine fruit flavors, which are invariably good food wines.

🍇 Grenache, Cinsault, Clairette, Clairette Rosé, Picpoul, Calitor, Bourboulenc, Mourvèdre, and Syrah (none of which may account for more than 60% of the blend), plus a maximum of 10% Carignan

🍷 1–3 years

✓ *Château d'Aquéria* • *Come des Rieu* • *de la Mordorée* (La Dame Rousse)

VACQUEYRAS AOC

Formerly one of the single-village wines under the AOC Côtes du Rhône-Villages, Vacqueyras was elevated to full AOC status in 1990, without any mention of Côtes du Rhône or Côtes du Rhône-Villages, and is now theoretically on a par with Gigondas. The vines are spread over two communes, Vacqueyras and Sarrians, growing in the foothills of the Dentelles de Montmirail.

RED The best are dark, rich, and robust, with a warm, black-pepper spiciness.

🍇 At least 50% Grenache, plus up to 20% in total of Syrah and/or Mourvèdre, plus no more than 10% in total of any of the following: Camarèse, Carignan, Cinsault, Clairette Rosé, Counoise, Grenache Gris, Muscardin, Vaccarèse, Picpoul Noir, Terret Noir

🍷 4–12 years

WHITE This is the least successful style of the appellation; most tend to be either flabby or so dominated by modern, cool vinification methods that they are simply fresh and could come from anywhere.

🍇 Grenache Blanc, Clairette, and Bourboulenc, plus up to 50% in total of Marsanne, Roussanne, and Viognier

🍷 2–3 years

ROSÉ Can be lovely, fresh, and fruity.

🍇 At least 60% of Grenache, plus a minimum of Mourvèdre and/or Cinsault, with an optional maximum 10% of any of the following: Camarèse, Carignan, Cinsault, Clairette Rosé, Counoise, Grenache Gris, Muscardin, Vaccarèse, Picpoul Noir, Terret Noir

🍷 2–3 years

✓ *des Amouriers* • *de la Brunely* (Elevé en Fût de Chêne) • *de la Charbonnière* • *La Fourmone* • *Les Grands Cyprès* • *de la Monardière* (Vieilles Vignes) • *Le Sang des Cailloux* (Lopy) • *Tardieu-Laurent* (Vieilles Vignes) • *Xavier Vignon* (Povidis)

THE JURA AND SAVOIE

White wines dominate the production from these picturesque vineyards set amid the ski slopes of the French Alps. Sparkling wines are the specialty of Savoie, while Jura can boast the rare, sweet vins de paille and the amazingly long-lived vins jaunes.

THE JURA IS DOMINATED by the town of Arbois, a little alpine community reigned over by the winemaker Henri Maire. His infamous sparkling "Vin Fou," or "Mad Wine," has no appellation and comes in various different *cuvées*, of which some are better than others, but many taste the same. Despite the light-hearted approach to its consumption, "Vin Fou" has performed one admirable function: it has introduced wine drinkers to the district of Jura and Savoie and its many better wines. This could not have been achieved by the *vins de paille* and *vins jaunes*, due to their scarcity and high price. The very sweet *vin de paille*, or "straw wine," is so called because the grapes were traditionally dried on straw mats to concentrate the juice into a syrup. The *vin jaune*, or

"yellow wine," derives its name from the color that results from its deliberate oxidation under a yeast *flor* when matured in casks that are not topped up for six years. This region also produces a number of more ordinary wines, often pure varietals, that are seldom exciting. The Jura's other claim to fame is, of course, as the birthplace of Louis Pasteur (1822–1895), who for all intents and purposes invented oenology, having been requested by Napoléon III to investigate the changes already observed during the maturation of wine. Born in the Arbois, where a small museum dedicated to him exists today, Pasteur's discoveries included the vital role of yeast during fermentation—totally unsuspected in his day, but without the knowledge of which the branch of chemistry called oenology would not exist. His vineyard, just outside Arbois, is now owned by the firm of Henri Maire.

The vineyards in the area between Lake Geneva and Grenoble, known as the Savoie, should be far more of a success than they are. I cannot imagine a better way to promote these wines than through the Savoie's winter-sports business. The only obstacle to their greater success is the failure of foreign wine merchants to import the wines in sufficient quantities.

THE SAVAGNIN CONSPIRACY

The Savagnin grape is none other than the Traminer or, to be more precise, the nonspicy Traminer as found in Tramin, Italy, and Heiligenstein in Alsace, where it is sold as Klevener de Heiligenstein. At best it has very delicate aromatics, but more often than not it is quite bland. In the Jura, however, it has

CHÂTEAU-CHALON VINEYARDS
This commune produces the most famous of all the vins jaunes from 100 percent Savagnin. Best drunk very old, the wine takes its name from its deep honey-gold color.

THE JURA AND SAVOIE,
see also p.55
This region lies parallel to Burgundy, between Beaune and the southern limits of the Beaujolais. There are two mountain ranges.

	Villages entitled to add their names to the Rousette de Savoie AOC
	Villages entitled to add their names to the Vin de Savoie appellation
	Villages entitled to add their names to the Rousette du Bugey appellation
	Crus entitled to add their names to the Vin du Bugey appellation

	Côtes du Jura
	Arbois
	Château-Chalon
	L'Étoile
	Vin de Savoie and Rousette de Savoie
	Crépy
	Vin du Bugey and Rousette du Bugey
	Seyssel
---	International boundary
---	Département boundary
▲	Height above sea level (meters)

0   10   20 miles

0   10   20   30   40 km

RECENT JURA AND SAVOIE VINTAGES

2003 A benchmark year for red wines in both regions, and for *vins de paille* in the Jura, but dry whites were problematic. There is a question mark over the *vins jaunes*, although the Jura has never experienced such Jerez-like heat, thus the quality could surprise everyone.

2002 Much better in the Jura than in the Savoie. Although the harvest in Savoie was saved by good weather in the last few weeks, the best wines were early drinking, and would have been at their best as *après ski* before this edition was due to be published. All styles were good in the Jura.

2001 Although there are a handful of well-made wines, these are the exceptions to what is an easily forgettable vintage.

2000 Early-maturing wines of average to quite good quality at best.

1999 A top-class vintage in the Jura in all styles, and the first year that this author noticed Savagnin made in a fresh, light, dry style with absolutely none of the oxidation that has been traditionally and erroneously associated with its varietal character. The Savoie was not very successful, and any half-decent wines should have been drunk long ago.

FACTORS AFFECTING TASTE AND QUALITY

LOCATION
Running down the mountainous eastern border of France, the Jura and Savoie are parallel to the Burgundy region.

CLIMATE
The climate is continental, with hot summers and cold winters. The close proximity of the Jura and the Savoie mountain ranges can provoke sudden changes, although these may sometimes be mitigated by the calming effect of lakes Geneva and Bourget.

ASPECT
The vineyards of the Jura are situated on the lower slopes of the Jura mountains. The vines grow at an altitude of 820–1,640 feet (250–500 meters). The Savoie vineyards lie lower than those of the Jura.

SOIL
The limestone of the Jura is generally mixed with clay over a subsoil of compacted marl. There are limestone and marl topsoils over a base of sandy and gravelly marls at Arbois and Château Chalon and a limestone scree, calcareous sand, and claylike sand with alluvial deposits at Bugey and Seyssel.

VITICULTURE AND VINIFICATION
The Jura is famous for two special techniques: the viticultural practice responsible for *vin de paille* and the vinification procedure required to make *vin jaune*. For *vin de paille*, wicker trays or wire mesh may be used, but in most cases bunches of grapes are hung from the rafters of heated huts, after which the shriveled-up, highly concentrated, raisinlike grapes produce an amber-colored sweet wine of great potential longevity. *Vin jaune* is produced entirely from the Savagnin grape, which, after a normal fermentation, is left to age in wooden barrels for six years with no topping off. A yeast *flor* develops similar to that generated during the production of *fino* sherry and the results are not dissimilar. Light dry Jura white wines made from the traditional Savagnin grape used to be distinctly oxidized due to the common practice of blending in any *vin jaune* that failed to make the grade, but some producers have begun to make at least a few of these wines without any declassified *vin jaune*, thus in a totally fresh, nonoxidative style.

GRAPE VARIETIES
Aligoté, Cabernet Franc, Cabernet Sauvignon, Chardonnay (*syn.* Melon d'Arbois or Gamay Blanc), Chasselas, Chasselas Roux, Chasselas Vert, Etraire de la Dui, Frühroter Veltliner (*syn.* Malvoisie Rosé or Veltliner Rosé), Gamay, Gringet (close relation to Savagnin), Jacquère, Joubertin, Marsanne, Molette, Mondeuse, Mondeuse Blanche, Persan, Pinot Blanc, Pinot Noir (*syn.* Gros Noiren), Poulsard (*syn.* Ploussard), Roussette, Roussette d'Ayze, Savagnin (*syn.* Naturé), Serène, Trousseau, Verdesse

always had a tendency to oxidize. Or so we were told. Every time I tasted a pure Savagnin produced in a light table wine style, it always had at least a niggling oxidative hint. And every time I asked the producer, whether in the Jura or at tastings in London, why this should be so in a grape variety that is not oxidative elsewhere, I was always told "*C'est le Savagnin, il est un vin typé.*" And now I know that each time, every producer I spoke to lied. It is not the Savagnin. It is the *vin jaune* that fails to receive certification, or has been weeded out somewhere along its six-year route to certification, and that they have disposed of by blending it into their dry white table wines.

While I fully support a certification process that prevents inferior wines from bearing the *vin jaune* designation, and I understand the dilemma of producers faced with stocks of yellow, oxidized wine they are unable to sell as *vin jaune*, the answer is not to spoil fresh, light table wines. The only rational solution is to create a *vin de pays* for the *vin jaune* style. Consumers will understand that the *vin de pays* version is not supposed to be of the same standard and, indeed, this would be reflected in the price. However, although cheaper than *vin jaune* proper, a *vin de pays* "*vin jaune*" would probably attract a premium over the price of the Jura's light table wines, and without the rejected *vin jaune*, the light table wines would be fresher, crisper, cleaner, and fruitier, the sales and price of which could only increase. Better profits for producers, and better wines for consumers. A result all round, I would have thought. And no need to tell lies.

THE APPELLATIONS OF
THE JURA AND SAVOIE

ARBOIS AOC
This is the best-known appellation of the Jura, from in and around the town of Arbois.

RED Trousseau wines are rich, and sometimes coarse, and Pinot wines are light and rustic.

Trousseau, Poulsard, Pinot Noir

2–8 years

WHITE Light, fresh Chardonnays are best; pure Savagnin can be delicately aromatic when not blended with declassified *vin jaune*, good examples of which are world renowned.

Savagnin, Chardonnay, Pinot Blanc

1–3 years

ROSÉ Famous for its firm and distinctive dry rosé wines made in the pale *vin gris* style.

Poulsard, Trousseau, Pinot Noir

1–3 years

✔ *Daniel Dugois • Raphaël Fumey & Adeline Chatelain • Michel Gahier* (Trousseau Grands Vergers) *• Labet Père & Fils • Henri Maire* (Montbief Chardonnay) *• De la Pinte* ◉ (Terre Rouge) *• Jacques Puffeney • Cave de la Reine Jeanne • Jean Rijckaert • André & Mireille Tissot* ◉ *• Jacques Tissot • De la Tournelle*

ARBOIS MOUSSEUX AOC
This is a traditional method sparkling wine seldom seen outside Arbois.

SPARKLING WHITE These fresh, dry sparkling wines show more potential than quality.

Savagnin, Chardonnay, Pinot Blanc

1–3 years

✔ *Foret • Fruitière Vinicole d'Arbois*

ARBOIS PUPILLIN AOC

This is a single-commune appellation for red, white, rosé, *vin jaune*, and *vin de paille* made to the same specification as Arbois AOC. *See* Arbois AOC, Arbois Vin de Paille AOC, and Arbois Vin Jaune AOC.

✓ *Désiré Petit & Fils* (Vin de Paille) • *De la Renardière*

ARBOIS VIN JAUNE AOC

For details of production and style, *see* Château-Chalon AOC.

✓ *De la Pinte* ◉ • *Jacques Puffeney* • *Rolet* • *André & Mireille Tissot* ◉ • *Jacques Tissot*

ARBOIS VIN DE PAILLE AOC

This wine is made from grapes that are dried to concentrate the juice, followed by a long fermentation and up to four years in wood.

WHITE These are very sweet wines with an old-gold color, complex bouquet, and a rich, nutty flavor.

🍇 Poulsard, Trousseau, Savagnin, Chardonnay

⏱ 10–50 (or more) years

✓ *Rolet* • *André & Mireille Tissot* ◉

BUGEY VDQS

Formerly called Vin de Bugey, the criteria for these wines has changed substantially since the decree of January 2004, particularly the *encépagement*. The village of Machuraz no longer has the right to add its name to this appellation. However, the following villages may still add their name: Manicle (for Chardonnay or Pinot Noir), Montagnieu (Mondeuse), Virieu-le-Grand (white only).

RED Fresh wines that range from the fruity Pinot to the rich Mondeuse.

🍇 Gamay, Mondeuse, Pinot Noir

⏱ 2–8 years

WHITE Off-dry, fresh, light, and gently fruity.

🍇 A minimum of 50% Chardonnay, plus optional Aligoté, Altesse, Jacquère, Mondeuse Blanche, and Pinot Gris

⏱ 1–3 years

ROSÉ Light and refreshing dry wines.

🍇 Gamay, Mondeuse, Pinot Noir

⏱ 1–3 years

✓ *Monin* (Mondeuse: Les Griots, Les Perrailles)

BUGEY CERDON VDQS

This appellation was a confusing mess until January 2004. Prior to this date, the wines could be still or sparkling, dry or sweet, and white or red. If sparkling they had to be white, but could be described as *mousseux* or *pétillant*, and had to be made by the traditional method. Now they must be rosé only, and made by *méthode ancestrale*, with a minimum

of 40 grams per liter of residual sugar, which puts it at the top side of *demi-sec*, thus could easily become *doux*. The appellation is restricted to Cerdon and seven surrounding villages.

SPARKLING ROSÉ Should be fresh and luscious, but true Cerdon Rosé Méthode Ancestrale has yet to establish a track record.

🍇 Gamay, Poulsard

⏱ Within 1 year

✓ *Daniel Boccard* • *Christian Bolliet*

CHÂTEAU-CHALON AOC

The Jura's *vins jaunes* possess a unique style and Château-Chalon (which is the name of a commune) is its most legendary exponent. It is normally fermented, then left to age in sealed wooden barrels for six years with no topping up. During this time, a *flor* develops—a skin of yeast that floats on top of the wine. The changes induced by the *flor* give the acetaldehyde-dominated *vin jaune* a resemblance to a *fino* sherry, but the fact that it is not fortified (whereas sherry is) and is made from a different grape produces its unique character.

WHITE *Vin jaune* is something of an acquired taste and should be drunk when very old. The vast array of complex nuances of bouquet eventually subdue and transmute the sherrylike smell of acetaldehyde. It has a dry flavor.

🍇 Savagnin

⏱ 10–100 years

✓ *Baud Père & Fils* • *Berthet-Bondet* • *Philippe Butin* • *Durand-Perron* • *Jean Macle*

CÔTES DU JURA AOC

This generic appellation contains some of the most widely encountered Jura wines. Its larger area of production gives it an edge over Arbois, the better-known AOC within its boundaries.

RED Usually light in color and body, with elegant fruit and a little finesse.

🍇 Poulsard, Trousseau, Pinot Noir

⏱ 2–8 years

WHITE Simple dry whites that make an ideal accompaniment to the local *raclette* cheese dish.

🍇 Savagnin, Chardonnay

⏱ 1–3 years

ROSÉ These dry rosés have a fine and fragrant *vin gris* style, with solid fruit.

🍇 Poulsard, Trousseau, Pinot Noir, Pinot Gris, Savagnin, Chardonnay

⏱ 1–3 years

✓ *Château d'Arlay* • *Daniel & Pascal Chalandard* (Cuvée Siloé) • *Charbonnier* • *Ganevat* (Florine Ganevat Chardonnay, Julien Ganevat Pinot Noir) • *Grand Frères* (Tradition) • *Labet* • *Jean Macle* • *Pignier* ⓑ (Trousseau) • *Jean Rijckaert* • *Rolet* (Chardonnay) • *André & Mireille Tissot* ◉

CÔTES DU JURA MOUSSEUX AOC

Probably Jura's best sparkling-wine appellation.

SPARKLING WHITE These wines have a persistent *mousse* of tiny bubbles, excellent balance, surprising finesse, and great potential.

🍇 Savagnin, Chardonnay, Pinot Blanc

⏱ 1–3 years

✓ *Château Gréa*

CÔTES DU JURA VIN JAUNE AOC

For details of production and style, *see* Château-Chalon AOC.

✓ *Château d'Arlay* • *Philippe Butin*

CÔTES DU JURA VIN DE PAILLE AOC

These wines are made from grapes that are dried to concentrate the juice, after which fermentation is long and the wine is given up to four years in wood.

WHITE These very sweet wines have old-gold, honey-gold, and amber-gold colors; a full, distinctive, and complex bouquet; a powerfully rich and nutty flavor; and a surprisingly crisp finish, with a raisiny, apricot-skin aftertaste.

🍇 Poulsard, Trousseau, Savagnin, Chardonnay

⏱ 10–50 (or more) years

✓ *Berthet-Bondet* • *Denis & Marie Chevassu* • *Richard Delay* • *Château Gréa* • *Labet* • *Morel-Thibaut* • *Désiré Petit & Fils* • *Pignier* ⓑ *Père & Fils* • *Philippe Vandelle*

CRÉMANT DU JURA AOC

This appellation was introduced in 1995. It can be used for any wine conforming to *vin mousseux* AOCs of the Côtes du Jura, Arbois, and L'Étoile, and may be applied retrospectively to any of these wines from 1991 onward. Part of the *"crémantization"* of French traditional method appellations, once most sparkling wines in the region are marketed as Crémant du Jura, the unwieldy bunch of *mousseux* appellations (*see below*) will be quietly dropped.

✓ *Richard Delay* • *Grand Frères* (Prestige) • *De Montebourgeau* • *Désiré Petit & Fils* (Cuvée Désiré) • *Rolet Père & Fils* (Coeur de Chardonnay) • *Jacques Tissot*

CRÉPY AOC

These wines are well known to the skiing set, who enjoy them after a day on the *piste*.

WHITE Light, dry, and fruity wines, with a floral aroma and a slight spritz.

🍇 Chasselas Roux, Chasselas Vert

⏱ 1–3 years

✓ *Goutte d'Or* (Tête de Cuvée)

L'ÉTOILE AOC

These wines are named after the star-shaped fossils found in the local limestone.

WHITE Light, dry white wines whose aromas reveal the scents of alpine herbs and bracken.

🍇 Chardonnay, Poulsard, Savagnin

⏱ 1–3 years

✓ *Baud Père & Fils*

L'ÉTOILE MOUSSEUX AOC

Not quite up to the standard of Côtes du Jura Mousseux, but this traditional method wine has more potential than Arbois Mousseux.

SPARKLING WHITE De Montbourgeau makes a fine-quality, dry, sparkling wine.

🍇 Chardonnay, Poulsard, Savagnin

⏱ 1–3 years

✓ *Château de l'Étoile*

L'ÉTOILE VIN JAUNE AOC
See **Château-Chalon AOC**

🍇 Savagnin

⌛ 10–100 years

✓ *Château de l'Étoile • Claude & Cédric Joly*

MACVIN AOC OR MACVIN DU JURA AOC

Macvin, a *vin de liqueur*, is made by adding *marc* (local brandy distilled from the residue of skins) to grape juice, preventing fermentation.

RED Typical dull *vin de liqueur* aroma, sweet and grapey.

🍇 Poulsard, Trousseau, Pinot Noir

⌛ Upon purchase or never

WHITE This has a typical dull *vin de liqueur* aroma, and is sweet and grapey. This is the most oxidative Macvin style.

🍇 Chardonnay, Poulsard, Savagnin

⌛ Never!

ROSÉ Typical dull *vin de liqueur* aroma, sweet and grapey.

🍇 Poulsard, Trousseau, Pinot Noir

⌛ Upon purchase or never

✓ *Labet*

ROUSSETTE DU BUGEY VDQS

The following villages may add their name to this appellation, if harvested within an extremely low yield: Anglefort, Arbignieu, Chanay, Lagnieu, Montagnieu, and Virieu-le-Grand.

WHITE Light, fresh, and agreeable off-dry wines with few pretensions.

🍇 A minimum of 50% Roussette, plus (until 2008) Chardonnay

⌛ 1–3 years

✓ *Jean Peillot*

ROUSSETTE DE SAVOIE AOC

The following villages have the right to add their name to this appellation, if the wine is 100 percent Roussette: Frangy, Marestel (or Marestel-Altesse), Monterminod, and Monthoux.

WHITE Drier than Roussette de Bugey, these wines have fine, tangy fruit.

🍇 Roussette, Mondeuse Blanche, plus up to 50% Chardonnay

⌛ 1–3 years

✓ *Dupasquier • Château de Monterminod • André & Michel Quenard • De Saint-Germain*

SEYSSEL AOC

This is a favorite après-ski wine.

WHITE These are fragrant, dry, refreshing wines.

🍇 Roussette

⌛ 1–3 years

✓ *Maison Mollex*

SEYSSEL MOUSSEUX AOC

It was Varichon & Clerc that first carved a niche for Seyssel Mousseux in the export market.

SPARKLING WHITE With a full, yeasty nose, fine *mousse*, and elegant flavor, the Royal Seyssel Private Cuvée is a yardstick for other producers.

🍇 Molette, Chasselas, plus a minimum of 10% Roussette

⌛ 1–3 years

✓ *Maison Mollex • Royal Seyssel*

VIN DE SAVOIE AOC

The wines in this generic appellation are produced to a high standard. The following villages have the right to add their name to the appellation: Abymes, Apremont, Arbin, Ayze, Chautagne, Chignin, Chignin-Bergeron (white Roussanne only), Cruet, Jongieux, Marignan (Chasselas white only), Marin, Montmélian, Ripaille (Chasselas white), St.-Jean de la Porte, St.-Jeoire Prieuré, and Sainte-Marie d'Alloix.

RED Blends and single-variety wines, the blended wines are usually better.

🍇 Gamay, Mondeuse, Pinot Noir, plus a maximum of 10% (in the Savoie *département*) of Cabernet Franc, and Cabernet Sauvignon, Persan, and (in the Isère *département*) Etraire de la Dui, Joubertin, Persan, and Serène

⌛ 2–8 years

WHITE These dry wines are the best of the AOC, with Abymes, Apremont, and Chignin the best villages. All are fine, rich, and complex.

🍇 Aligoté, Altesse, Jacquère, Mondeuse Blanche, Roussette, Veltliner Précoce, plus a maximum of 10% (in the Ain and Haute-Savoie *départements*) of Chasselas, Gringet, Roussette d'Ayze, and (in the Isère *département*) Marsanne and Verdesse

⌛ 1–3 years

ROSÉ Attractive, light, and fruity, dry to off-dry rosés made for early drinking.

🍇 Gamay, Mondeuse, Pinot Noir, plus a maximum of 10% (in the Savoie *département*) of Cabernet Franc, and Cabernet Sauvignon, Persan, and (in the Isère *département*) Etraire de la Dui, Joubertin, Persan, and Serène

⌛ 1–3 years

✓ *Pierre Boniface, Dupasquier, De L'Idylle* (Mondeuse), *Louis Magnin* (Jacquère, Rousse), *Jean Perrier & Fils* (Mondeuse Vieilles Vignes), *De Rouzan* (Gamay), *De Saint-Germain* (Chardonnay) • **Best single-*cru* wines: Abymes** *Frédéric Giachino;* **Apremont** *Philippe Betemps;* **Arbin** *Genoux, Louis Magnin, Charles Trosset* (Mondeuse); **Chignin** *André & Michel Quénard, Raymond Quénard* (Mondeuse); **Chignin-Bergeron** *Gilles Berlioz* ◉, *Louis Magnin, André & Michel Quénard, Philippe Ravier, Jean Vullien;* **Jongieux** *Edmond Jacquin & Fils;* **Montmélian** *Louis Magnin*

VIN DE SAVOIE AYZE PÉTILLANT OR MOUSSEUX AOC

These are very promising, single-commune, traditional method wines, but unfortunately are seldom encountered.

SEMI-SPARKLING WHITE Wispy-light wines with an Alpine-fresh, clean taste.

🍇 Gringet, Roussette, plus up to 30% Roussette d'Ayze

⌛ 1–3 years

VIN DE SAVOIE MOUSSEUX AOC

These are very consistent and undervalued generic traditional-method wines. The Savoie does not have a large-scale sparkling-wine industry as such, although it most certainly has the potential to build one. The tradition of making the effervescent wines in this part of eastern France dates back to 1910, when two growers, Messieurs Varichon and Clerc, joined together to make sparkling wine in Seyssel from the Roussette grape, the wines of which were naturally *pétillant*, just as the Swiss wines made from the Chasselas, just across Lake Geneva, were, and still are, today.

SPARKLING WHITE These dry and delicately fruity wines have a fragrant aroma, fine acidity, and a good balance.

🍇 Aligoté, Roussette, Jacquère, Chardonnay, Pinot Gris, Mondeuse Blanche, plus (in the Ain and Haute-Savoie *départements*) Chasselas, (in the Haute-Savoie and Isère *départements*) Molette, (in the Haute-Savoie *département*) Gringet and Roussette d'Ayze, (in the Isère *département*) Marsanne and Verdesse

⌛ 1–2 years

✓ *Maison Mollex • Des Rocailles*

VIN DE SAVOIE PÉTILLANT AOC

A very consistent and undervalued generic traditional method wine.

SEMI-SPARKLING WHITE Attractive, early-drinking dry wines with a gentle, light *mousse* and a fragrant flavor.

🍇 Aligoté, Roussette, Jacquère, Chardonnay, Pinot Gris, Mondeuse Blanche, plus Chasselas (in the Ain and Haute-Savoie *départements*), Gringet, Rousset d'Ayze (in the Haute-Savoie *département*), Marsanne, and (in the Isère *département*) Verdesse

⌛ Within 1 year

✓ *Perrier & Fils • Varichon & Clerc*

SOUTHWEST FRANCE

This region encompasses numerous small, scattered areas that combine to produce an impressively wide range of excellent-value wines with diverse, but quite discernible, stylistic influences from Bordeaux, Spain, Languedoc-Roussillon, and the Rhône.

AT THE HEART OF THE REGION lies Gascony, the great brandy district of Armagnac. It was from here that d'Artagnan set out in around 1630 to seek fame and fortune in the King's Musketeers. The narrow tracks upon which his eventful journey began still wind their lonely way around wooded hills and across bubbling brooks. Aside from brightly colored fields of cultivated sunflowers, surprisingly little has changed since Alexandre Dumas painted such a vivid and colorful picture of these parts, for they remain sparsely populated to this day. Time passes slowly even in the towns, where

the main square is usually completely deserted all day long, except during the five o'clock rush hour, which can last for all of 10 minutes.

THE DIVERSITY OF THE APPELLATIONS

The Southwest does not have a single wine of truly classic status, yet it probably offers more value for money and is a greater source of hidden bargains than any other French region. From the succulent, sweet Jurançon *moelleux* and Monbazillac to the fine wines of Bergerac, Buzet, and Marmandais, the revitalized "black wines" of Cahors, the up-and-coming Frontonnais, the tannic Madiran, and the highly individual Irouléguy of the Basque country, this part of France represents tremendous potential for knowing wine drinkers.

Perhaps because it is a collection of diverse areas, rather than one natural region, the appellations of the Southwest seem at first numerous and confusing—even within one area there appear to be needless duplications. In Bergerac, for example, the dry white wines and red wines are reasonably easy to understand, since there are three dry appellations (Bergerac, Bergerac sec, and

SOUTHWEST FRANCE, *see also* p.55
This diverse region bridges the southwest corner of France. While it is mostly subject to the climatic influence of the Atlantic, areas such as Gaillac are also affected by the Mediterranean.

Bergerac	Cahors	Madiran
Pécharmant	Buzet	Côtes de St.-Mont
Côtes du Frontonnais	Gaillac	—— Other AOC and VDQS areas
Côtes de Duras	Irouléguy	-·-·- *Département* boundary
Côtes du Marmandais	Jurançon	▲ Height above sea level (meters)

0   10   20   30   40 miles
0   10   20   30   40   50   60 km

CÔTES DE BUZET VINEYARDS
*This good-value Bordeaux satellite is barely 9 miles
(15 kilometers) from the Gironde* département.

Montravel) and three red-wine appellations (Bergerac, Côtes
de Bergerac, and Pécharmant), but there is a veritable galaxy of
sweet and semi-sweet appellations (Bergerac, Bergerac Moelleux,
Montbazillac, Côtes de Montravel, Haut-Montravel, Rosette, and
Saussignac). When such a small and relatively minor area as
Bergerac can develop so many different appellations, it is little
wonder that a large and famous region such as Bordeaux has
evolved into 50-odd appellations. It would surely be simpler to
have a single Bergerac appellation to which certain villages might
be allowed to add a communal name; if the same logic were
applied throughout this region, more of its wines could achieve
marketing success, rather than attracting only occasional attention
as hidden bargains. With a more cohesive image and some
enterprising wineries straddling the many different appellations,
Southwest France should be at least as exciting as Languedoc-
Roussillon has recently become. Flying winemakers have
occasionally come to roost here in the past few years, but it will
take a permanent New World winery for the exciting potential
of Southwest France to be fully recognized.

RECENT SOUTHWEST FRANCE VINTAGES

2003 As elsewhere in France, a vintage that was too hot and too early,
with some reds and late-picked sweet whites the only likely standouts.

2002 Good to exceptional quality in Cahors particularly, but also
Bergerac and Buzet. Variable elsewhere.

2001 The best year all around since 1998.

2000 Good reds, particularly in Madiran, and an excellent year for
sweeter Jurançon.

1999 Extremely variable for all styles.

FACTORS AFFECTING TASTE AND QUALITY

LOCATION
The southwest corner of
France, bordered by Bordeaux, the
Atlantic, the Pyrenees, and the
Mediterranean vineyards of
Languedoc-Roussillon.

CLIMATE
The climate of southwestern
France is Atlantic-influenced, with
wet winters and springs, warm
summers, and long, sunny falls. The
vineyards of Cahors, Fronton, and
Gaillac are subject to the greater
heat but more changeable
characteristics of the Mediterranean.

ASPECT
Mostly east- and east-through-
to-south-facing slopes, affording
protection from the Atlantic, in a
varied countryside that can range
from rolling and gently undulating
to steep and heavily terraced.

SOIL
This collection of diverse areas
has, not unexpectedly, a number of
different soils: sandy-and-calcareous
clay over gravel in the best vineyards
of Bergerac; sandy soils on the Côte
de Duras; calcareous and alluvial
soils in the *côtes* of Buzet and
Marmandais; gravel-clay and gravel
crests over marly bedrock in the
hilly hinterland of Cahors, and
alluvial soils peppered with pebbly
quartz, limestone, and gravel over a
calcareous bedrock in the Lot Valley;
limestone, clay-and-limestone, and
gravel at Gaillac; sandy soils in
Madiran, Tursan, and Irouléguy; and
stony and sandy soils in Jurançon.

VITICULTURE AND
VINIFICATION
The viticultural traditions and
vinification techniques of Bergerac,
Buzet, Marmandais, and, to some
extent, Cahors, are similar to those
of Bordeaux. Other districts of this
composite region have very much
their own distinctive, individual
practices: Béarn, Gaillac, and
Jurançon produce almost every
style of wine imaginable by many
vinification techniques, among them
the *méthode rurale* (known locally
as the *méthode gaillaçoise*).
Although the winemaking
technique in these areas is
generally very modern, the Basque
district of Irouléguy remains stoutly
traditional, allowing only the
introduction of Cabernet Sauvignon
and Cabernet Franc to intrude upon
its set ways.

GRAPE VARIETIES
Abouriou, Arrufiac, Baroque,
Cabernet Franc, Cabernet
Sauvignon, Camaralet, Castet,
Chardonnay, Chenin Blanc,
Cinsault, Clairette, Claret de Gers,
Claverie, Colombard, Courbu Blanc,
Courbu Noir, Cruchinet, Duras, Fer,
Folle Blanche, Fuella, Gamay, Gros
Manseng, Jurançon Noir, Lauzet,
Len de l'El, Malbec (*syn.* Cot),
Manseng Noir, Mauzac, Mauzac
Rosé, Mérille, Merlot, Milgranet,
Mouyssaguès, Muscadelle, Négrette,
Ondenc, Petit Manseng, Picpoul,
Pinot Noir, Raffiat, Roussellou,
Sauvignon Blanc, Sémillon, Syrah,
Tannat, Ugni Blanc, Valdiguié

THE APPELLATIONS OF
SOUTHWEST FRANCE

BÉARN AOC

This modest AOC shines in the local Basque area. Wines made in Bellocq, Lahontan, Orthez, and Saliès are allowed to add the communal designation Bellocq to the appellation.

RED Fresh, light, and fruity wines with a good balance, but lacking depth.

🍇 A maximum of 60% Tannat, plus Cabernet Franc, Cabernet Sauvignon, Fer, Manseng Noir, Courbu Noir

🍷 1–4 years

WHITE Light, dry, and aromatic wines.

🍇 Petit Manseng, Gros Manseng, Courbu Blanc, Lauzet, Camaralet, Raffiat, Sauvignon Blanc

🍷 1–2 years

ROSÉ Simple, fruity, dry rosés with a fresh floral aroma.

🍇 Tannat, Cabernet Franc, Cabernet Sauvignon, Fer, Manseng Noir, Courbu Noir

🍷 1–2 years

✓ *Bouscassé* (Rosé) • *C. V. de Jurançon* (Larribère)

BÉARN-BELLOCQ AOC
See Béarn AOC

BERGERAC AOC

Adjoining Bordeaux, Bergerac produces wines that are sometimes mistaken for the modest appellations of its more famous neighbor. Its wines were shipped to London as early as 1250. Supplies dried up after the Hundred Years' War, which ended with the Battle of Castillon, and Castillon-la-Bataille marks the ancient English-French boundary between Bergerac and Bordeaux.

RED The best reds have a good garnet or ruby color, fine fruit, and an elegant balance.

🍇 Cabernet Sauvignon, Cabernet Franc, Merlot, Malbec, Fer, Mérille

🍷 2–8 years

WHITE Mostly dry Bordeaux-style wines, but semisweet wines with up to 54 grams per liter of residual sugar are permitted. Until 1993, such wines had to be described as *moelleux*; however, as this is no longer compulsory, we will not know whether some of these wines are *moelleux* or not. Bergerac Blanc may be sold from December 1 following the harvest without any mention of *primeur* or *nouveau*.

🍇 Sémillon, Sauvignon Blanc, Muscadelle, Ondenc, Chenin Blanc, and up to 25% Ugni Blanc (on the proviso that the quantity of Sauvignon Blanc used is at least equal)

🍷 1 3 years

ROSÉ These are light, easy, and attractive dry wines. They may be sold from December 1 following the harvest without mention of *primeur* or *nouveau*.

🍇 Cabernet Sauvignon, Cabernet Franc, Merlot, Malbec, Fer, Mérille

🍷 1–3 years

✓ *de l'Ancienne Cure* • *Julienne* (Casnova des Conti) • *Château Les Justices* • *Château Laulerie* • *Château Miaudoux* (Inspiration) • *Château Le Payral* (Héritage) • *Château Pion* • *Julien de Savignac* (Rosé) • *Château*

Tour des Gendres • *Les Verdots* (Les Verdots selon David Fourtout)

BERGERAC SEC AOC

These white wines are distinguished from Bergerac Blanc by having to be dry, with no more than 4 grams per liter of residual sugar.

WHITE Dry Bordeaux-style wines. They may be sold from December 1 following the harvest without any mention of *primeur* or *nouveau*.

🍇 Sémillon, Sauvignon Blanc, Muscadelle, Ondenc, Chenin Blanc, and up to 25% Ugni Blanc (on the proviso that the quantity of Sauvignon Blanc used is at least equal)

🍷 1–3 years

✓ *de l'Ancienne Cure* • *Château Cailevet* (Accent) • *Château Miaudoux* • *Château de Panisseau* (Divin) • *Michel Roche* (Le Top de Mazière) • *Julien de Savignac* (Les Jardins de Cyrano) • *Château Tour des Gendres* • *Château Tourmentine* (Barrique) • *Les Verdots* (Les Verdots selon David Fourtout)

BUZET AOC

Formerly known as Côtes de Buzet, this supervalue Bordeaux satellite is located on the northern edge of the Armagnac region.

RED The best are always very good, with considerable finesse and charm.

🍇 Merlot, Cabernet Sauvignon, Cabernet Franc, Malbec

🍷 3–10 years (15 in exceptional cases)

WHITE These dry whites are the least interesting wines in this appellation. They may be sold from December 1 following the harvest without any mention of *primeur* or *nouveau*.

🍇 Sémillon, Sauvignon Blanc, Muscadelle

🍷 1–3 years

ROSÉ Ripe, fruity, dry rosés. They may be sold from December 1 following the harvest without any mention of *primeur* or *nouveau*.

🍇 Merlot, Cabernet Sauvignon, Cabernet Franc, Malbec

🍷 1–4 years

✓ *Baron d'Albret* • *C. V. de Buzet* • *Château Sauvagnères*

CAHORS AOC

The once-famous "black wine" of Cahors got its name from the Malbec grape, which, prior to phylloxera, produced dark, inky-colored wines. But the vines did not graft well to the earliest American rootstocks and Cahors fell into decline. Compatible rootstocks were developed, and with the introduction of the Merlot and Tannat, Cahors has started to claw back its reputation. The sheer number of good producers now makes Cahors one of the most reliable red-wine appellations in France. Vieux Cahors must be aged in oak for at least three years.

RED Most Cahors wines have a deep color with a blackcurrant tinge. They are full of fruit and have a good, plummy, Bordeaux-like taste, with a silky texture and a distinctive violet-perfumed aftertaste.

🍇 A minimum of 70% Malbec, plus up to 30% (in total) of Merlot and Tannat—Jurançon Noir has not been permitted since 1996

🍷 3–12 years (20 in exceptional cases)

✓ *Château de Clasou* • *Château la Caminade* (Commandery, Esprit) • *Château de Cèdre* • *de la Coustarelle* • *Croix du Mayne* (Elevé en Fûts de Chêne) • *C. V. Côtes d'Olt* • *Château Gautoul* • *des Grauzils* • *Château Haut Monplaisir* (Pur Plaisir) • *Clos d'Un Jour* • *Château Lacapell Cabanac* (Prestige Elevé en Fûts de Chêne) • *Château Lagrezette* • *Château Lamartine* (Expression, Particulière) • *Primo Palatum du Prince* • *Château La Reyne* (Vente d'Ange) • *Clos Triguedina*

COTEAUX DU QUERCY VDQS

Located just south of the Cahors area, and a *vin de pays* since 1976, Coteaux du Quercy was promoted to VDQS in 1999, when its *encépagement* changed (formerly Gamay- and Merlot-dominated wines).

RED Richly colored, full-bodied wines, the best of which have plenty of morello cherry and blackberry fruit.

🍇 Cabernet Sauvignon, Cabernet Franc, Merlot, Malbec, Fer, Mérille

🍷 1–4 years

ROSÉ Soft, easy-drinking, fresh, and fruity rosé, with a maximum of 3 grams per liter residual sugar, thus truly dry.

🍇 Cabernet Sauvignon, Cabernet Franc, Merlot, Malbec

🍷 Upon purchase

✓ *de Merchien*

CÔTES DE BERGERAC AOC

Geographically, there are no *côtes*; the only difference between this appellation and Bergerac is an extra degree of alcohol. The appellation Côtes de Bergerac Moelleux was withdrawn in 1993 (wines from this appellation must now be sold as Bergerac or Bergerac Moelleux), thus any wine bearing Côtes de Bergerac must now be red.

RED Should be richer than Bergerac AOC.

🍇 Cabernet Sauvignon, Cabernet Franc, Merlot, Malbec, Fer, Mérille

🍷 3–10 years

✓ *Château La Bard Les Tendoux* (Elevé en Fûts de Chêne) • *Château Les Mailleries*

(Dany Moelleux) • *Château Masburel* • *Marlene & Alain Mayet* (Révelation du Bois de Pourquie) • *Château Tour des Verdots*

CÔTES DU BRULHOIS VDQS

Elevated from *vin de pays* in November 1984, this appellation encompasses vineyards along the Garonne immediately west of Buzet.

RED Decent, if unexciting, Bordeaux-like wine, though more rustic in style.

🍇 Cabernet Franc, Cabernet Sauvignon, Fer, Merlot, Malbec, Tannat

🍷 2–4 years

ROSÉ Fresh, easy-to-drink dry wine.

🍇 Cabernet Franc, Cabernet Sauvignon, Fer, Merlot, Malbec, Tannat

🍷 1–3 years

✓ *Château Grand Chêne* (Elevé en Fûts de Chêne)

CÔTES DE DURAS AOC

An appellation of increasing interest.

RED Light Bordeaux-style wines.

🍇 Cabernet Sauvignon and Franc, Merlot, Malbec

🍷 2–3 years

WHITE Clean, crisp, and dry wines, except for those designated *moelleux*, which must have a minimum of 4 grams per liter of residual sugar, although most good *moelleux*, such as Château Lafon, contain much more than this and are definitely sweet. With the exception of *moelleux*, these wines may be sold from December 1 following the harvest without any mention of *primeur* or *nouveau*.

🍇 Sauvignon Blanc, Sémillon, Muscadelle, Mauzac, Chenin Blanc, Ondenc, and up to 25% Ugni Blanc (provided that the quantity of Sauvignon Blanc used is at least equal)

🍷 1–3 years

ROSÉ These attractively colored, dry, crisp, fruity rosés are firm and fresh. They may be sold from December 1 following the harvest without any mention of *primeur* or *nouveau*.

🍇 Cabernet Sauvignon, Cabernet Franc, Merlot, Malbec

🍷 1–3 years

✓ *des Allegrets* (Elevé en Fûts de Chêne) • *Duc de Berticot* (Elevé en Fûts de Chêne) • *Château la Grave Bechade* (Alexandre Elevé en Fûts de Chêne) • *Château Laplace* • *Château Moulière* • *Château La Petite Bertrande* (Elevé en Fûts de Chêne) • *Château La Petit Malrome* (Sarah Elevé en Fûts de Chêne)

CÔTES DU FRONTONNAIS AOC

Situated just west of Gaillac. The wines of two villages, Fronton and Villaudric, are allowed to add their own names to the appellation.

RED These medium- to full-bodied wines have excellent color and violet-perfumed fruit.

🍇 50–70% Négrette, up to 25% (in total) of Malbec, Mérille, Fer, Syrah, Cabernet Franc, and Cabernet Sauvignon, plus a maximum of 15% Gamay, Cinsault, and Mauzac

🍷 2–8 years

ROSÉ Overtly fruity wines.

🍇 50–70% Négrette, up to 25% (in total) of Malbec, Mérille, Fer, Syrah, Cabernet Franc, and Cabernet Sauvignon, plus a maximum

of 15% Gamay, Cinsault, and Mauzac

🍷 1–3 years

✓ *Château Baudare* • *Château Bellevue la Forêt* • *Château Bouissel* • *Château Devès* (Allegro) • *Château Laurou* (Elevé en Fûts de Chêne) • *Château Plaisance* • *Château le Roc*

CÔTES DU FRONTONNAIS FRONTON AOC

See Côtes du Frontonnais AOC

CÔTES DU FRONTONNAIS VILLAUDRIC AOC

See Côtes du Frontonnais AOC

CÔTES DU MARMANDAIS AOC

This successful Bordeaux imitation, upgraded from VDQS to AOC in 1990, is situated on the border of Bordeaux itself; its vines grow on both sides of the Garonne, on the left-bank Côtes de Cocumont and the right-bank Côtes de Beaupuy. Few French people outside the region know anything about these wines, but the English have shipped them since the 14th century.

RED Fresh, clean, and impeccably made wines.

🍇 A maximum of 75% (in total) of Cabernet Franc, Cabernet Sauvignon, and Merlot, plus up to 50% (in total) of Abouriou, Malbec, Fer, Gamay, and Syrah

🍷 2–5 years

WHITE These dry white wines are soft and delicious. They may be sold from December 1 following the harvest without any mention of *primeur* or *nouveau*.

🍇 At least 70% Sauvignon Blanc, plus Ugni Blanc and Sémillon

🍷 1–2 years

ROSÉ Ripe and dry wines. They may be sold from December 1 following the harvest without any mention of *primeur* or *nouveau*.

🍇 A maximum of 75% (in total) of Cabernet Franc, Cabernet Sauvignon, and Merlot, plus up to 50% (in total) of Abouriou, Malbec, Fer, Gamay, and Syrah

🍷 1–2 years

✓ *CV de Cocumont* (Beroy) • *Château La Gravette* (Elevé en Fûts de Chêne) • *Elian da Ros*

CÔTES DE MILLAU VDQS

Upgraded to VDQS in 1994 from *vin de pays* status (Gorges et Côtes de Millau), this appellation has yet to establish any characteristic style or reputation. There is no intrinsic reason why it should not, but with just 124 acres (50 hectares) under vine and one dominant *coopérative* (Aguessac), it will not be easy.

RED *Vin primeur* is a specialty.

🍇 A blend of at least two varieties, including a minimum of 30% Gamay and Syrah, plus Fer, Duras, and up to 20% Cabernet Sauvignon

WHITE Very little is made and I have not encountered any.

🍇 Chenin Blanc, Mauzac

ROSÉ Very little is made and I have not encountered any.

🍇 A blend of at least two varieties, including a minimum of 50% Gamay, plus Syrah, Cabernet Sauvignon, Fer, and Duras

✓ *C. V. des Gorges du Tarn* (Maitre des Sampettes) • *du Vieux Noyer*

CÔTES DE MONTRAVEL AOC

This wine must have a minimum residual sugar of 8 grams per litre and a maximum of 54 grams per liter in order to meet the requirements of the appellation. Any red wines produced here are sold as Bergerac AOC.

WHITE These fat, fruity wines are usually produced in a *moelleux* style.

🍇 Sémillon, Sauvignon Blanc, Muscadelle

🍷 3–8 years

✓ *Château du Bloy* • *Château Lespinassat* (Vieilles Vignes) • *Château Masburel*

CÔTES DE SAINT-MONT VDQS

Situated within the Armagnac region, the vineyards of this appellation extend northward from Madiran. Wine production is dominated by the local *coopérative*.

THE DORDOGNE RIVER, SEEN FROM THE TOWN OF DOMME
Southwest France includes appellations lying just east of Bordeaux, such as Côtes de Duras and Bergerac on the Dordogne, as well as areas of vineyard close to the Spanish border.

RED Well-colored wines of good flavor and medium body. They are not dissimilar to a lightweight Madiran, although they could become deeper, darker, and more expressive if the *coopérative* were prepared to reduce yields and produce better-quality wine.

🐝 At least 70% Tannat, plus Cabernet Sauvignon, Cabernet Franc, Merlot, and Fer (which must constitute one-third of all the grapes other than the Tannat)

🍷 2–5 years

WHITE Fruity, dry wines with a tangy finish.

🐝 At least 50% Arrufiac, Clairette, and Courbu, plus Gros Manseng and Petit Manseng

🍷 1–2 years

ROSÉ Dry wines with a clean, fruity flavor.

🐝 At least 70% Tannat, plus Cabernet Sauvignon, Cabernet Franc, Merlot, and Fer (which must constitute one-third of all grapes other than the Tannat)

🍷 1–3 years

✓ *Producteurs Plaimont* • *Château Saint-Go* (Elevé en Fûts de Chêne)

FLOC DE GASCOGNE AOC

This *vin de liqueur* is produced in the Armagnac region.

WHITE Few manage to rise above the typically dull, oxidative *vin de liqueur* style that goes *rancio* with age.

🐝 A minimum of 70% Colombard, Gros Manseng, and Ugni Blanc, plus Baroque, Folle Blanche, Petit Manseng, Mauzac, Sauvignon Blanc, and Sémillon

🍷 Upon opening

ROSÉ Few manage to rise above the typically dull, oxidative *vin de liqueur* style that goes *rancio* with age.

🐝 A minimum of 50% Tannat, plus Cabernet Franc, Cabernet Sauvignon, Fer Servadou, Malbec, and Merlot

🍷 Upon opening

✓ *C. V. du Muscat de Lunel* (Prestige) • *Saint Pierre de Paradis* (Vendange d'Automne)

GAILLAC AOC

These vineyards, among the oldest in France, have only recently begun to make their mark. In order to emphasize local styles, there has been a concerted move away from classic grapes toward different native varieties. Gaillac Liquoreux and Gaillac Moelleux are no longer permitted appellations, but such wines are still available under the Gaillac Doux appellation. The Gaillac Sec Perlé denomination for slightly *pétillant* dry white wines has been dropped (although Gaillac Perlé still seems to flourish), and the sparkling wines of Gaillac are now segregated by their method of production (*see* Gaillac Mousseux AOC and Gaillac Mousseux Méthode Gaillaçoise AOC). The required *encépagement* has always been confusingly complex, but became even more so with the new regulations introduced in 2001.

RED Wines made mostly in the fresh, soft but light *macération carbonique* style. They may be sold as *primeur* or *nouveau* from the third Thursday of November following the harvest.

🐝 At least 60% Duras, Fer, Gamay, and Syrah, of which Duras, Fer, and Syrah (or any two of these) must represent at least 30% of the entire blend; furthermore, there must be at least 10% each of Duras and Fer, plus optional Cabernet Franc, Cabernet Sauvignon, and Merlot

🍷 1–3 years

WHITE Dry and fresh, these wines may be sold as *primeur* or *nouveau* as from the third Thursday of November following the harvest.

🐝 At least 15% of Len de l'El or Sauvignon Blanc (or a blend of the two), plus Mauzac, Mauzac Rosé, Muscadelle, Ondenc, and Sémillon

🍷 Upon purchase

ROSÉ Easy to drink, light, fresh, and dry rosés.

🐝 At least 60% Duras, Fer, Gamay, and Syrah, of which Duras, Fer, and Syrah (or any two of these) must represent at least 30% of the entire blend; furthermore. there must be at least 10% each of Duras and Fer, plus optional Cabernet Franc, Cabernet Sauvignon, and Merlot

🍷 1–2 years

✓ *Causse Marines* (Délires d'Automne) • *Manoir de l'Émeille* (Tradition) • *d'Escausses* (La Vigne l'Oubli) • *de Gineste* (Aurore, Grand Cuvée) • *de Larroque* (Privilège d'Autan) • *Château de Lastours* • *Château Lecusse* (Spéciale) • *Château Montels* • *Paysels* (Tradition) • *Robert Plageoles* • *René Rieux* (Concerto) • *des Terrisses* (Saint-Laurent) • *Château La Tour Plantade*

GAILLAC DOUX AOC

These are naturally sweet wines that must contain a minimum of 70 grams per liter of residual sugar.

WHITE Sweet to very sweet wines of ripe-peach, or richer, character.

🐝 At least 15% (each or in total) of Len de l'El and Sauvignon Blanc, plus Mauzac, Mauzac Rosé, Muscadelle, Ondenc, and Sémillon

🍷 5–15 years

✓ *Barreau* (Caprice d'Automne) • *Château Palvie* (Les Secrets) • *Peyres-Combe* (Flaveurs d'Automne) • *Robert Plageoles* • *Rotier* (Renaissance) • *Sanbatan* (Muscadelle) • *de Vayssette* (Maxime) • *Les Vergnades*

GAILLAC MOUSSEUX AOC

This is a sparkling wine made by the traditional method. Expect to see a phasing out of the term *mousseux* on these and other Gaillac sparkling-wine appellations.

SPARKLING WHITE These wines are fresh and fragrant with a fine sparkle.

🐝 At least 15% (each or in total) of Len de l'El and Sauvignon Blanc, plus Mauzac, Mauzac Rosé, Muscadelle, Ondenc, and Sémillon

🍷 1–3 years

SPARKLING ROSÉ Attractive, fresh, fruity wines.

🐝 At least 60% Duras, Fer, Gamay, and Syrah, of which Duras, Fer, and Syrah (or any two of these) must represent at least 30% of the entire blend; furthermore, there must be at least 10% each of Duras and Fer, plus optional Cabernet Franc, Cabernet Sauvignon, and Merlot

🍷 1–2 years

✓ *Manoir de l'Emeille* • *René Rieux*

GAILLAC MOUSSEUX MÉTHODE GAILLAÇOISE AOC

Sparkling wines made by the *méthode rurale*, involving just one fermentation, with no addition of a *liqueur de tirage*. The wine is bottled before the fermentation stops and no *liqueur d'expédition* is added prior to distribution, thus any residual sweetness is entirely from the original grape sugars. Styles include *brut* and *demi-sec*. A *doux* is also available, but is governed by stricter rules and is given its own appellation (*see below*).

SPARKLING WHITE These very fresh, fragrant, and grapey wines have a fine natural sparkle.

🐝 At least 15% (each or in total) of Len de l'El and Sauvignon Blanc, plus Mauzac, Mauzac Rosé, Muscadelle, Ondenc, and Sémillon

🍷 1–3 years

SPARKLING ROSÉ These wines are attractive, fresh, and deliciously fruity.

🐝 At least 60% Duras, plus Fer, Gamay, Syrah, Cabernet Sauvignon, Cabernet Franc, Merlot

🍷 1–2 years

GAILLAC MOUSSEUX MÉTHODE GAILLAÇOISE DOUX AOC

This is a sparkling wine made by the *méthode rurale* (*see above*) from riper grapes (minimum of 11 percent) than those of any other Gaillac sparkling-wine appellation, and with at least 45 grams per liter of residual natural sugar.

SPARKLING WHITE Not as exotic as, say, Clairette de Die Méthode Dioise Ancestrale, but delicious, grapey, and fragrant all the same.

🐝 At least 15% (each or in total) of Len de l'El and Sauvignon Blanc, plus Mauzac, Mauzac Rosé, Muscadelle, Ondenc, and Sémillon

🍷 1–3 years

SPARKLING ROSÉ I have never come across a Gaillac Doux rosé, but if the white is anything to go by, it would be an interesting wine.

🐝 At least 60% Duras, Fer, Gamay, and Syrah, of which Duras, Fer, and Syrah (or any two of these) must represent at least 30% of the entire blend; furthermore, there must be at least 10% Cabernet Franc, Cabernet Sauvignon, and Merlot

🍷 1–2 years

GAILLAC PREMIÈRES CÔTES AOC

These are dry white wines that come from 11 communes. The grapes must be riper than for ordinary Gaillac AOC and the wine must conform to the technical requirements of Gaillac Doux in all but sweetness.

✓ *Robert Plageoles* • *Château de Salettes*

HAUT-MONTRAVEL AOC

This wine must have a minimum residual sugar of 8 grams and a maximum of 54 grams per liter to meet the requirements of the appellation. Any red wines produced here are sold as Bergerac AOC.

WHITE Fat, fruity, and *moelleux* wines.

🐝 Sémillon, Sauvignon Blanc, Muscadelle

🍷 3–8 years

✓ *Château Puy-Servain*

IROULÉGUY AOC

The local *coopérative* dominates this Basque appellation, which makes some of the most distinctive red wines in Southwest France. Surprisingly, however, the production of rosé outweighs that of red.

RED These deep, dark, tannic wines have a rich and mellow flavor, with a distinctive earthy-and-spicy aftertaste.

Tannat, plus at least 50% (in total) of Cabernet Sauvignon and Cabernet Franc

4–10 years

WHITE These modest dry whites are the least interesting of this appellation.

Courbu, Manseng

ROSÉ This salmon-colored, very fruity dry rosé is best drunk very young and fresh.

Tannat plus at least 50% (in total) of Cabernet Sauvignon and Cabernet Franc

Upon purchase

✓ *Arretxea* ⊚ • *Etxegaraya*

JURANÇON AOC

The sweet version of this wine from the Pyrénées-Atlantiques was used at Henri de Navarre's christening in 1553 and is often sold today as *vendanges tardives* or *moelleux*. Most production is, however, tart, dry, and nervy, and sold as Jurançon Sec (*see below*).

WHITE The best wines have a fine, spicy, and tangy bouquet and flavor, and can hint of pineapples and peaches, candied peel, and cinnamon.

Petit Manseng, Gros Manseng, Courbu, plus up to 15% (in total) of Camaralet and Lauzet

5–20 years

✓ *Bru-Baché* • *Cauhapé* • *Clos Lapeyre* • *Primo Palatum* • *Clos Thou* • *Clos Uroulat*

JURANÇON SEC AOC

This wine has to meet the same requirements as Jurançon AOC, but less residual sugar is allowed, and the grapes may be less ripe. It is best drunk young. These wines may be sold from December 1 following the harvest without any mention of *primeur* or *nouveau*.

WHITE If any wine in the world habitually has a certain nervousness, it has to be Jurançon Sec.

Most lack any individual character that would make them stand out from other dry whites, and none has the complexity and richness of Jurançon's late-harvest wines, but the best can have an intensity that hints of grapefruit.

Petit Manseng, Gros Manseng, Courbu, plus up to 15% (in total) of Camaralet and Lauzet

2–5 years

✓ *Capdevieille* (Brise Océane) • *Cauhape* (Sève d'Automne) • *du Cinquau* • *C. V. de Jurançon* (Grain Sauvage) • *Lapeyre* • *Larredya* • *Nigri* • *Primo Palatum*

MADIRAN AOC

One of the most individually expressive appellations in Southwest France, but there are as many disappointments as successes. Many domaines are trying new oak, and there is a trend toward more Cabernet Franc.

RED You literally have to chew your way through the tannin in these dark, rich, and meaty wines when young.

At least 40% Tannat, plus Cabernet Franc, Cabernet Sauvignon, and Fer

5–15 years

✓ *Berthoumieu* • *Château Bouscassé* • *Château Labranche-Laffont* • *Château Laffitte-Teston* • *Laffont* • *Château Montus* • *Plaimont* (Arte Benedicte) • *Primo Palatum* • *Château de Viela*

MARCILLAC AOC

This rarely encountered wine from the northeastern borderlands was upgraded from Vin de Marcillac VDQS to Marcillac AOC in 1990, when greater focus was placed on the local Fer and Gamay—Jurançon Noir, Mouyssaguès, and Valdiguié were disallowed.

RED Rough and rustic when young, these wines soften with age.

At least 90% Fer, plus Cabernet Franc, Cabernet Sauvignon, and Merlot

3–6 years

ROSÉ Full, ripe, and attractive dry rosés that have expressed more individual style since the minimum Fer content has tripled.

At least 90% Fer, plus Cabernet Franc, Cabernet Sauvignon, and Merlot

1–3 years

✓ *C. V. de Ladrecht*

MONBAZILLAC AOC

An excellent value Sauternes-style appellation at the heart of Bergerac, these wines date back to 1080, when vines were planted by the abbey of St.-Martin on a hill called Mont Bazilhac.

WHITE These intensely sweet, rich wines are of a very high quality.

Sémillon, Sauvignon Blanc, Muscadelle

7–20 years

✓ *de l'Ancienne Cure* (Abbaye, L'Extase) • *Château Caillavel* • *Château Fonmorgues* • *Grande Maison* ⊚ (Cuvée du Château) • *Château Tirecul La Gravière*

MONTRAVEL AOC

The largest of the three Montravel appellations and the only one where the white wine can (and must) be dry.

RED Elegant, ruby-colored reds that are very much in the Bergerac style. These wines may be sold from December 1 following the harvest without any mention of *primeur* or *nouveau*.

A minimum of 50% Merlot, plus Cabernet Franc, Cabernet Sauvignon, and Malbec

2–8 years

WHITE Dry, crisp, and aromatic Sauvignon-dominated wines. These wines may be sold from December 1 following the harvest without any mention of *primeur* or *nouveau*.

A minimum 25% each of Sémillon and Sauvignon Blanc, plus optional Muscadelle (Chenin Blanc, Ondenc, and Ugni Blanc are no longer allowed)

1–2 years

✓ *Château du Bloy* (Le Bloy) • *Château Laulerie* • *Moulin Caresse* (Cent pour 100) • *Château Pagnon* • *Château Pique-Sègue* • *Portes du Bondieu* • *Château Puy-Servain* (Marjolaine)

PACHERENC DU VIC-BILH AOC

New oak is being increasingly used in this white-only appellation, which covers the same area as Madiran.

WHITE Exotic floral aromas, a fruit salad of flavors, Pacherenc du Vic-Bilh is made in off-dry (sold as *sec*), medium-sweet (*moelleux*), and sweet (*doux*) styles.

A minimum of 30% Arrufiac, which with Courbu and Petit Manseng must represent at least 60% of the entire blend, plus Gros

Manseng and a maximum of 10% in total of
Sauvignon Blanc and Sémillon

⟜ 3–7 years

✓ *Château Boussacé • Berthoumieu •
Château Labranche-Laffont • Château
de Viela*

PÉCHARMANT AOC

These are the finest red wines of Bergerac; all
but one (Saint-Saveur) of the communes in this
appellation are also within the Rosette AOC.

RED All the characteristics of Bergerac, but
with a greater concentration of color, flavor,
and tannin.

🍇 Cabernet Franc, Cabernet Sauvignon,
Merlot, Malbec

⟜ 4–12 years

✓ *Château Beauportail • Château de Biran
(Prestige de Bacchus) • Château Champarel
• Château Hugon (Elevé en Fûts de Chêne)*

ROSETTE AOC

A white-wine-only appellation. The wines must
contain 8 to 54 grams per liter of residual sugar.
Any red wines are sold as Bergerac AOC.

WHITE Soft and delicately fruity with a sweet,
waxy flavor.

🍇 Sémillon, Sauvignon Blanc, Muscadelle

⟜ 4–8 years

✓ *Château de Contancie*

SAUSSIGNAC AOC

A sweet-wine appellation; it must have a
minimum of 18 grams per liter of residual sugar.
Any red wines are sold as Bergerac AOC.

WHITE The best can be very rich, fat, and full.

🍇 Sémillon, Sauvignon Blanc, Muscadelle,
Chenin Blanc

⟜ 5–15 years

✓ *Château Le Chabrier • Château Eyssards
(Flavie) • Château Grinou (Elevé en Fûts
de Chêne) • Château La Maurigne (La
Maurigne) • Château Miaudoux*

TURSAN VDQS

The reds rely on the Tannat, the same
primary grape used in Madiran; the whites
are essentially Baroque, a variety more at
home in Tursan. There was a change of
encépagement as from 2003.

RED Rich and chewy, or finer-flavored and
aromatic, depending on the dominant grape.

🍇 A minimum of 30% Tannat and 30% Cabernet
Franc, plus (until 2010) a maximum of 10%
Cabernet Sauvignon and Fer

WHITE The *coopérative* traditionally makes a
full-bodied white with a solid, somewhat rustic,
rich flavor, but it is gradually being influenced
by the growing reputation of the wine made
under the relatively new Château de Bachen
label, Baron de Bachen, which is far more
aromatic and elegant.

🍇 A minimum of 30% Baroque, plus a maximum
of 50% (in total) of Gros Manseng and Petit
Manseng, of which Petit Manseng must not
represent more than 20% of the entire blend;
no more than 30% Sauvignon Blanc and 20%
Chenin Blanc (Claverie, Raffiat, Claret du
Gers, and Clairette no longer allowed)

⟜ 2–5 years

ROSÉ An unpretentious dry wine with good,
juicy, fruit flavor.

🍇 A minimum of 50% Cabernet Franc and
10–30% Tannat, plus a maximum of 40%
Cabernet Sauvignon and Fer

⟜ 1–3 years

✓ *Michel Guérard (Baron de Bachen) •
C. V. de Landais (Haute Carte)*

VINS D'ENTRAYGUES AND DU FEL VDQS

This area overlaps the Aveyron and Cantal
départements in the northeast of the region,
but only a tiny amount is made. The wines
are rarely encountered and never exported.

RED Light, rustic wines that are best consumed
locally because they need all the local ambience
they can get.

🍇 Cabernet Franc, Cabernet Sauvignon, Fer,
Gamay, Jurançon Noir, Merlot, Mouyssaguès,
Négrette, Pinot Noir

⟜ 1–2 years

WHITE Light, dry, and crisp wines for
unpretentious quaffing.

🍇 Chenin Blanc, Mauzac

⟜ Upon purchase

ROSÉ Light, fresh, and dry rosés.

🍇 Cabernet Franc, Cabernet Sauvignon, Fer,
Gamay, Jurançon Noir, Merlot, Mouyssaguès,
Négrette, Pinot Noir

⟜ 1–2 years

✓ *Jean-Marc Viguer*

VINS D'ESTAING VDQS

This area is contiguous with the southern tip
of the above VDQS and production is even
more minuscule.

RED These wines are light bodied, attractive,
and fruity.

🍇 Fer, Gamay, Abouriou, Jurançon Noir,
Merlot, Cabernet Franc, Cabernet Sauvignon,
Mouyssaguès, Négrette, Pinot Noir, Duras,
Castet

⟜ 1–3 years

WHITE These are unpretentious, dry white
wines with a crisp flavor and a rustic,
tangy style.

🍇 Chenin Blanc, Roussellou, Mauzac

⟜ 1–2 years

ROSÉ These pleasant dry wines are probably
the most interesting in the appellation.

🍇 Fer, Gamay, Abouriou, Jurançon Noir,
Merlot, Cabernet Franc, Cabernet Sauvignon,
Mouyssaguès, Négrette, Pinot Noir, Duras,
Castet

⟜ Upon purchase

✓ *C. V. d'Olt (Prestige)*

VINS DE LAVILLEDIEU VDQS

Situated south of Cahors, this VDQS is a
northern extension of the Frontonnais, with
vines growing on a *boulbènes* soil that is
similar to that of Bordeaux's Entre-Deux-Mers
district. Production is dominated by the local
coopérative, and the wines are seldom seen
outside the locality.

RED Nicely colored, medium-bodied wines with
a fresh, fruity flavor.

🍇 A minimum of 80% (in total) of Mauzac,
Mérille, Cinsault, Fuella, and Négrette
(which must account for at least 35%), plus
up to 20% (in total) of Syrah, Gamay,
Jurançon Noir, Picpoul, Milgranet, and Fer

⟜ 3–6 years

WHITE Dry, crisp, aromatic wines.

🍇 Mauzac, Sauvignon Blanc, Sémillon,
Muscadelle, Colombard, Ondenc, Folle
Blanche

⟜ 1–3 years

✓ *C. V. de Lavilledieu du Temple*

LANGUEDOC-ROUSSILLON

The 1990s saw an influx of Australian winemakers, who have since played a not insignificant role in the raising of standards; but the sale in 2003 of the Australian-owned Domaine de la Baume could signal a swing back to a more homegrown stimulus. Domaine de la Baume is not significant in terms of the total production of this region, but there is no denying that its purchase by BRL Hardy in 1990, at the beginning of Australia's inexorable success on export markets, gave local wine producers a psychological boost.

VINEYARDS AT BAGES
The Mediterranean coastal vineyards of the Côtes du Roussillon, around Perpignan, are reputed to be some of the hottest in France.

IN A STRANGE WAY, the presence of a top Australian group was viewed as a seal of approval for local winemakers, just as the presence of Moët & Chandon in Australia had been seen by that country's sparkling winemakers. It was all a matter of timing: Australian wines were surging, French wines were slowing down, and the south was all potential, with very few wineries taking advantage of it. And *vins de pays* were not, as yet, a force to be reckoned with. BRL Hardy, or Hardy's as it was known then, was leading the Australian charge on global exports, and yet it saw sufficient promise in a small domaine in an

LANGUEDOC-ROUSSILLON, *see also* p.55
This is the largest wine-producing region in France, with vineyards stretching from the Camargue to the Spanish border, including what used to be the Midi.

- • Villages entitled to add their names to the Coteaux du Languedoc appellation
- • Villages entitled to add their names to the Côtes du Roussillon appellation

Minervois

Coteaux du Languedoc

Costières de Nîmes

Corbières

Fitou

Côtes du Roussillon

Côtes du Roussillon Villages

Maury

Collioure and Banyuls

Limoux

Other AOC regions

—— Département boundary

▲ Height above sea level (meters)

0   10   20   30 miles

0   10   20   30   40   50 km

ınknown part of France to be sidetracked into purchasing it outright. The next few years saw the rise of *vins de pays*, particularly Vin de Pays d'Oc, including those of Domaine de la Baume, which became a commercial success on the UK market, against the tide for most other inexpensive French wines. During this time, there was an internationalization of grape varieties and wine styles in the south of France, and, barring some unfortunate experiments in the late 1970s and the 1980s, this development was far from regrettable.

Some French producers had started putting their own houses in order long before the BRL Hardy purchased Domaine de la Baume. Indeed, a number of domaines began bottling their own wines in the late 1970s, when the government's *vins de pays* program was encouraging quality-conscious growers to reduce yields. The problem was that there were never enough "quality-conscious" growers. But those who were formed a new generation of elite winemakers. They combined modern technology with the best traditional practices, including the use of some aging with new oak, to create exciting new wines in the early 1980s. As other growers observed the vastly increased prices that their pioneering neighbors were attracting, more of them switched from selling in bulk to domaine-bottling, and it was this potential that attracted the Australians.

It was thus the French who created the newfound pride in this region, but it was the Australians who grabbed the limelight, focusing international attention on the fabulous potential. It is almost possible to give consumers an iron-clad guarantee that if they buy ultrapremium *cuvées* from Languedoc-Roussillon they will not only be delighted with the wines, but they will also be cheaper than and far superior to medium-priced wines bearing the most famous French appellations.

When BRL Hardy sold Domaine de la Baume to Les Grands Chais in 2003, the Australians left this wine region in a far better commercial position than they found it 13 years earlier; so the French in general, and Les Grands Chais in particular, have no excuse if they fail to take Languedoc-Roussillon to the next level of success. That will require a twin philosophy that does not restrict the planting of classic grapes and yet encourages a resurgence of the most interesting local varieties.

RECENT LANGUEDOC-ROUSSILLON VINTAGES

2003 Higher-altitude appellations, such as Pic-St.-Loup, have fared best, but it will be a mishmash of good, bad, and ugly elsewhere, with a very small scattering of stunning reds.

2002 The year of the floods, with only those areas that escaped (essentially western and southern extremities, and higher-altitude vineyards) managing to produce a decent quality.

2001 The best year all around since 1998, with excellent quality achieved in all styles.

2000 A good, but not great, year in which Roussillon generally fared better than Languedoc.

1999 An average year except for Corbières and Minervois, which excelled and in some cases produced wines of the decade.

FACTORS AFFECTING TASTE AND QUALITY

LOCATION
A crescent of vineyards situated in southern France between the Rhône to the east and the Pyrenees to the southwest.

CLIMATE
The Mediterranean-influenced climate is generally well suited to the cultivation of the vine, although it is subject to occasional stormy weather. Two winds dominate: the cold and parching Mistral, which blows down from the heights of the Alpine glaciers, and the wet and warm Marin, which comes in from the sea and can cause rot at harvest time. There are many microclimates in this collection of isolated vine-growing areas.

ASPECT
Famous for its unending tracts of flat, *vin ordinaire* vineyards that stretch across the vast plains; the best sites of Languedoc-Roussillon, however, mostly occupy south-, southeast-, and east-facing *garrigues* and hillsides, or nestle beneath protective overhanging cliffs.

SOIL
In general terms, the plains and valleys have rich alluvial soils, while the hillsides are schist or limestone and the *garrigues*, or former moorlands, are comprised of stony, carbonaceous soils over fissured limestone. However, specific situations vary enormously.

VITICULTURE AND VINIFICATION
This remains the great *vin ordinaire* region of France, where everything is mechanized and the vines of the plain are farmed like wheat or corn. There is a trend toward developing single-domaine vineyards that have potentially expressive *terroirs*, growing classic varieties and combining various traditional methods with modern techniques. Limoux still practices the ancient *méthode rurale*—in Blanquette Méthode Ancestrale AOC (*see below*)—although the majority of the wines are pure traditional method and sold under the new *crémant* appellation.

GRAPE VARIETIES
Aspiran Noir, Aspiran Gris, Aubun (*syn.* Counoise), Bourboulenc (known in some areas as Malvoisie or Tourbat), Cabernet Franc, Cabernet Sauvignon, Carignan, Carignan Blanc, Cinsault, Clairette, Duras, Fer, Grenache, Grenache Blanc, Grenache Gris, Lladoner Pelut, Listan Negra (the black version of Spain's Palomino), Malbec, Macabéo, Marsanne, Merlot, Mourvèdre, Muscat d'Alexandrie, Muscat Blanc à Petits Grains, Muscat Doré de Frontignan, Muscat Rosé à Petits Grains, Négrette, Oeillade, Picpoul, Picpoul Noir, Roussanne, Syrah, Terret, Terret Noir, Ugni Blanc, Vermentino (*syn.* Rolle).

THE APPELLATIONS OF
LANGUEDOC-ROUSSILLON

Note In the following entries, a wine described as a *vin doux naturel* (or VDN) is made from very ripe grapes and fortified with pure grape spirit after its fermentation has reached 5 or 6 percent. It has the natural sweetness of the grape. To be labeled "Rancio" a VDN must be stored in oak casks "according to local custom," which often means exposing the barrels to direct sunlight for a minimum of two years. This imparts the distinctive *rancio* flavor that is so prized in Roussillon. Depending on the color of the original wine, the wine technique used, and how long it has been aged, the style of the wine produced varies; it can be red, white, rosé, or tawny.

BANYULS AOC

The most southerly appellation in France, the vineyards of this *vin doux naturel* are literally a stone's throw from those of Spain. The vines are grown on precipitous slopes of schist where man and mule have great difficulty in maintaining a foothold, mechanization is out of the question, yields are extremely low, and ripeness very high. You will often see "rimage" on labels; this word is derived from the Catalan *rime*, or "grape," and refers to the vintage.

RED This is the deepest and darkest of all VDNs. A rich, sweet, red Banyuls (without too much barrel-age) has a chocolaty, bottled-fruitiness, which is the nearest France gets to the great wines of Portugal's Douro region. It lacks the fire of a great port, but has its own immense charm. After 15 to 20 years in bottle a great Banyuls develops a curious but wonderful complexity that falls somewhere between the porty-plummy, dried-fruit spice of a mature vintage port and the coffee-caramel, nutty-raisiny smoothness of a fine old tawny.

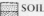 10–40 years

WHITE/ROSÉ/TAWNY Like all VDNs that may be made in red, white, and rosé style, they can all turn tawny with time, particularly "rancio" wines.

All wines: a minimum of 50% Grenache, plus Grenache Gris, Grenache Blanc, Macabéo, Tourbat, Muscat Blanc à Petits Grains, Muscat d'Alexandrie, and a maximum 10% (in total) of Carignan, Cinsault, and Syrah

⌇— 10–20 years

✓ *Le Dominican* (Hanicotte) • *C. V. l'Étoile* (Extra Vieux) • *Du Mas Blanc* • *De la Tour Vieille* • *Du Traginer* ◉ (Rimage Mis Tardive)

BANYULS GRAND CRU AOC

The requirements are the same as for Banyuls AOC, but a minimum of 75 percent Grenache is required. The grapes must be destemmed and macerated for a minimum of five days and the wine matured in oak for at least 30 months. The wines are similar in character to those of the basic, although not at all ordinary, Banyuls appellation, but in terms of classic port styles, they veer more toward the tawny than vintage.

✓ *L'Abbé Rous* (Christian Reynal) • *L'Étoile* (Réserve) • *Cellier des Templiers*

BANYULS GRAND CRU "RANCIO" AOC
See Banyuls Grand Cru AOC

BANYULS "RANCIO" AOC
See Banyuls AOC

BLANQUETTE DE LIMOUX AOC

Although this always has been a surprisingly good traditional method wine for such sunny southern vineyards, the best Blanquette de Limoux have improved by leaps and bounds over the past decade, moving away from a somewhat rustic bubbly to a much finer style, although not to the degree of finesse possible in a Crémant de Limoux. Some may regret its loss of individuality (more so for the Crémant appellation) and this is to a certain extent a true loss, but Limoux must adopt a more refined style if it is to compete in the international premium sparkling-wine market. Although we should not overstate the case, the best of these wines still retain a sufficiently distinctive style to stand out in any blind tasting. This has been assured by the Mauzac component, which rose from optional to a minimum of 90 percent when the Crémant appellation was introduced.

SPARKLING WHITE These wines used to have the distinctive aroma of fresh-cut grass, but are now developing finer, more flowery, autolytic aromas.

🍇 Mauzac, Chardonnay, Chenin Blanc

⌇— 1–3 years (up to 12 for vintages)

✓ *Antech* (Flascon des Maïstre) • *Robert* (Dame Robert, Maistre Blanquetïers) • *Sieur d'Arques* (Aimery Princesse)

BLANQUETTE MÉTHODE ANCESTRALE AOC

Formerly called Vin de Blanquette, but still produced by the ancient *méthode rurale*, this wine was apparently invented by the monks at the abbey of St.-Hilaire in 1531.

SPARKLING WHITE These succulently sweet sparkling wines are a hedonist's dream and should be far more commercially available. The ancient *méthode rurale* should be perfected so that prestige *cuvées* can be sold at a premium,

allowing Limoux to capitalize on its historical value and individual wines' reputation.

🍇 Mauzac

✓ *Sieur d'Arques* (Dame d'Arques)

CABARDÈS AOC

An obscure appellation north of Carcassonne, these wines were once sold as Côtes du Cabardès et de l'Orbiel VDQS, but this hardly tripped off the tongue, thus the shortened form was in common usage long before the appellation was promoted to full AOC status in 1999, when the *encépagement* changed.

RED The best wines have elegant fruit and a leaner, more Bordeaux-like balance than most of the warmer, spicy-ripe southern French reds.

🍇 At least 40% Grenache and Syrah, plus a minimum of 40% Cabernet Franc, Cabernet Sauvignon, and Merlot (Aubun and Carignan are no longer allowed)

⌇— 3–8 years

ROSÉ A rich, fruity, well-colored rosé.

🍇 At least 40% Grenache and Syrah, plus a minimum of 40% Cabernet Franc, Cabernet Sauvignon, and Merlot (Aubun and Carignan are no longer allowed)

⌇— Between 2–3 years

✓ *Château de La Bastide* (L'Esprit) • *Claude et Michelle Carayol* (Cabrol Vent d'Est) • *Château de Pennautier* (L'Esprit) • *Château Ventenac* (Le Caila)

CLAIRETTE DE BELLEGARDE AOC

When compared with all the best *vins de pays*, this appellation, which is dedicated to the lowly, intrinsically flabby Clairette grape, does not deserve to be a VDQS, let alone an AOC.

WHITE Unimpressive dry white wines.

🍇 Clairette

⌇— Before Christmas of the year of production

CLAIRETTE DU LANGUEDOC AOC

The appellation of Clairette du Languedoc covers three basic wine types. These are natural, fortified, and *rancio*. The *rancio* must be aged in sealed casks for at least three years, and can be produced in both natural and fortified styles.

WHITE The natural wine is fuller and richer than Bellegarde, but has more alcohol and less sweetness in its *rancio* form. The fortified version is off-dry to medium-sweet, with a resinous flavor that is stronger in *rancio* character than the natural white.

🍇 Clairette

⌇— 1–3 years for naturally fermented wines, 8–20 years for fortified wines and *rancio* wines

✓ *Saint Rome* (Moelleux)

CLAIRETTE DU LANGUEDOC "RANCIO" AOC
See Clairette du Languedoc AOC

COLLIOURE AOC

An obscure but exciting appellation for unfortified wines from normally harvested grapes grown in Banyuls, the eponymous wine of which is made from only the ripest, late-picked (but not botrytized) grapes. The *encépagement* changed in 2003.

RED These deep, dark, and powerful wines have a full and concentrated fruit flavor, with a soft, spicy aftertaste.

🍇 At least 60% (in total) of Grenache, Mourvèdre, and Syrah (no variety may exceed 90%), plus Cinsault and no more than 30% Carignan (Grenache Gris is no longer allowed)

⌇— 2–10 years

WHITE These wines had to be sold as Vin de Pays de la Côte Vermeille until 2002, when white Collioure was first allowed.

🍇 Minimum of 70% in total of Grenache Blanc and/or Grenache Gris, plus a maximum of 30% in total (and individually a maximum of 15%) of Malvoisie, Macabeo, Marsanne, Rousanne, and Velmentino

⌇— 1–3 years

ROSÉ I have not encountered these wines.

🍇 At least 60% (in total) of Grenache, Mourvèdre, and Syrah (no variety may exceed 90%), plus Cinsault and no more than 30% Carignan (Grenache Gris is no longer allowed)

⌇— Upon purchase

✓ *Château des Abelles* • *Du Mas Blanc* (Les Junquets) • *Mas Cornet* • *Celliers des Templiers* (Abbaye de Valbonne) • *De la Tour Vieille* (Puig Oriol) • *Du Traginer* (Octobre)

CORBIÈRES AOC

When this appellation was elevated to full AOC status in December 1985, its area of production was practically halved to its current realm of 57,000 acres (23,000 hectares). The top estates often use *macération carbonique*, followed by 12 months or so in new oak and the results can be stunning. The only problem appears to be the difficulty of projecting any characteristic style, especially as there is such a great diversity of *terroirs* in the appellation.

This has led to the unofficial formation of 11 internal zones: Boutenac (central-north of Corbières, Mourvèdre apparently does well); Durban (wedged between the two hilly halves of Fitou, this zone is cut off from any Mediterranean influence); Fontfroide (extending from the northern tip of Durban to the western outskirts of Narbonne, this zone has a very low rainfall and is well suited to Mourvèdre); Lagrasse (protected limestone valley vineyards immediately west of Boutenac); Lézignan (a low plateau of gravelly vineyards in the most northerly zone of Corbières); Montagne d'Alaric (northerly zone just west of Lézignan, with vines growing on well-drained slopes of gravel over limestone); Quéribus (most southerly zone, with vineyards on high, stony slopes); St.-Victor (the very heart of Corbières); Serviès (the northwestern perimeter, the wettest zone, with calcareous-clay soils particularly well suited to Syrah); Sigean (the coastal strip of Corbières, where Syrah performs best); Termenès (the western perimeter, between Serviès and Quéribus, with the highest vineyards in the appellation). The *encépagement* changed in 2003.

RED These wines have an excellent color, a full, spicy-fruity nose, and a creamy-clean, soft palate that often hints of cherries, raspberries, and vanilla.

🍇 A minimum of 50% of Grenache, Lladoner Pelut, Mourvèdre, and Syrah, plus Carignan, Picpoul Noir, Terret, and a maximum of 20% Cinsault (Macabéo and Bourboulenc are no longer allowed)

🍷 2–5 years (3–8 years in exceptional cases)

WHITE Soft, almost clinically clean, dry wines that have acquired a more aromatic character in recent vintages—Château Meunier St.-Louis is probably the best example—but many of the wines should be more expressive. There have been some successful experiments with oak fermentation. These wines may be sold from December 1 following the harvest without any mention of *primeur* or *nouveau*.

🍇 Bourboulenc, Grenache Blanc, Macabéo, Marsanne, Roussanne, and Vermentino, plus a maximum of 10% Clairette, Muscat Blanc à Petit Grains, Picpoul, and Terret

🍷 1–3 years

ROSÉ The best of these dry wines have an attractive color and a pleasant, floral aroma, but are nothing special.

🍇 A minimum of 50% of Grenache, Lladoner Pelut, Mourvèdre, and Syrah, plus Carignan, Picpoul Noir, Terret Noir, a maximum of 20% Cinsault, and no more than 10% Bourboulenc, Grenache Blanc, Macabéo, Marsanne, Roussanne, and Vermentino, plus a maximum of 10% Clairette, Muscat Blanc à Petit Grains, Picpoul, and Terret

🍷 1–3 years

✓ *Clos de L'Anhel* • *Des Chandelles* • *Clos Canos* (Les Cocobirous) • *Desmoiselles* (Blanc de Blancs) • *C. V. de Gruissan* (Elevé en Fûts de Chêne) • *Château de Mansenoble* (Marie-Annick, Réserve) • *C. V. du Mont Ténarel d'Octaviana* (Sextant) • *Château de Romilhac* (Privilège) • *Rouire-Ségur* (Vieilles Vignes) • *Château la Voulte-Gasparets* (Romain Pauc)

COSTIÈRES DE NÎMES AOC

Formerly a VDQS called Costières du Gard, these wines have never been special, but most have been better than many a lackluster wine from far more famous appellations, and in this respect Costières de Nîmes well deserved its promotion to AOC status in 1986. But since then the grape varieties permitted for all three styles—red, white, and rosé—have altered so radically that you have to wonder why they bother to have any controls whatsoever.

RED Simple, light, fruity wines are the norm, yet the best are round, aromatic, and spicy.

🍇 A maximum of 40% (each) Carignan and

Cinsault, a minimum of 25% Grenache, and at least 20% (in total or each) of Mourvèdre and Syrah

🍷 2–3 years (average wines), 3–8 years (better *cuvées*)

WHITE Fresh, soft, but uninspiring. These wines may be sold from December 1 following the harvest without any mention of *primeur* or *nouveau*.

🍇 Bourboulenc, Clairette, Grenache Blanc (maximum 30%), Ugni Blanc, plus Macabéo, Marsanne, Roussanne, and Vermentino

🍷 1–2 years

ROSÉ Good-value dry wine with a delightful color and ripe fruit. These wines may be sold from December 1 following the harvest without any mention of *primeur* or *nouveau*.

🍇 A maximum of 40% (each) of Carignan and Cinsault, a minimum of 25% Grenache, at least 20% (in total or each) of Mourvèdre and Syrah, plus up to 10% (in total) of Clairette, Grenache Blanc, Bourboulenc, Ugni Blanc, Marsanne, Roussanne, Macabéo, and Rolle

🍷 Within 1–2 years

✓ *Château Amphoux* (Les Galion des Crêtes Elevé en Fûts de Chêne) • *Barbe-Caillette* (Haut Jovis) • *Château Grande Cassagne* • *Château Lamargue* (Aegidiana) • *Château La Tour de Beraud* • *Château Tuilerie* (Carte Blanche) • *Château de Valcombe* (Garence)

COTEAUX DU LANGUEDOC AOC

This appellation consists of a collection of areas strung out across three *départements*, which gives rise to a variation in style, but the quality is remarkably consistent. After a decade of exciting red wine developments, it is now the time for white wines to buzz.

RED Full and honest red wines that make excellent everyday drinking. These wines may be sold as *primeur* or *nouveau* from the third Thursday of November following the harvest.

🍇 A minimum of 50% Grenache (itself limited to maximum of 40%), Lladoner Pelut, Mourvèdre, and Syrah (these last two must represent at least 10% of the entire blend), no more than 40% of either Carignan or Cinsault, plus a maximum of 10% (in total) Counoise, Grenache Gris, Terret, and Picpoul Noir

🍷 1–4 years

WHITE Getting better by the day, some wonderfully fresh, aromatic, dry white wines are being made by the appellation's younger *vignerons*, often with a little new oak and not infrequently from very old vines. These wines may be sold from December 1 of the vintage indicated without any mention of *primeur* or *nouveau*.

🍇 Bourboulenc, Clairette, Grenache Blanc, Picpoul, Marsanne, Roussanne, Vermentino, plus a maximum of 30% Macabéo, Terret Blanc, Carignan Blanc, and Ugni Blanc (growers may no longer plant Carignan Blanc, Macabéo, or Ugni Blanc)

ROSÉ These dry wines have good fruit and are far more enjoyable than many a pricey Provence rosé. These wines may be sold as *primeur* or *nouveau* from the third Thursday of November following the harvest.

🍇 A minimum of 50% Grenache (itself limited to maximum of 40%), Lladoner Pelut, Mourvèdre, and Syrah (these last two must

represent at least 10% of the entire blend), no more than 40% of either Carignan or Cinsault, plus a maximum of 10% (in total) Bourboulenc, Carignan Blanc, Clairette, Counoise, Grenache Blanc, Grenache Gris, Macabéo, Picpoul, Picpoul Noir, Marsanne, Roussanne, Terret Blanc, Terret Noir, Ugni Blanc, and Vermentino

🍷 1–2 years

✓ *De l'Aiguelière* • *Mas de Bayle* (Grande Cuvée) • *Château Chenaie* (Le Douves Blanches) • *Château La Clotte-Fontaine* (Mouton) • *Château des Crès Ricards* (Les Hauts de Milési) • *Dupéré-Barrera* (Chien de Prairie) • *Château Daurion* (Prestige Elevé en Fûts de Chêne) • *C. V. La Fontesole* (Prieuré Saint-Hippolyte) • *De Ganoupiac* (Les Cresses) • *Château Gres Saint Paul* (Antonin) • *Mas Haut-Buis* (Costa Caoude) • *Virgile Joly* (Virgile) • *Château de Lascaux* (Les Secrets) • *Mas Lumen* (La Sylve) • *Paul Mas* • *Château de Montpezat* (La Pharaonne) • *Château de la Négly* (L'Ancely) • *Peyre Rose* ◉ • *Prieuré St.-Jean de Bébian* • *De Roquemale* • *C. V. de Saint-Saturnin* • *Mas de la Seranne* (Les Griottiers) • *Le Clos du Serres* (Le Florilège) • *De Serres Cabanis* (Bos de Canna) • *Les Souls* • *Château Le Thou* (Georges et Clem)

COTEAUX DU LANGUEDOC (VILLAGE NAME) AOC

Except where stated, the wines bearing the names of the following villages conform to the requirements of Coteaux du Languedoc AOC.

LES ASPRES AOC

New red-wine-only appellation as from the 2004 vintage, Les Aspres must be produced from at least three varieties, with a minimum of 50 percent Grenache, Mourvèdre, and Syrah (the last two varieties must represent at least 20 percent of the entire blend), plus a maximum of 20 percent Carignan. Too early to provide a critique.

CABRIÈRES AOC

This is a single commune of steep schistous slopes in the center of the Clairette du Languedoc subappellation. Cabrières's production is dominated by the local *coopérative*. This village produces mostly rosé: a fine, firm, and racy wine that contains more Cinsault than other Languedoc rosés. A little red is also produced, and its *vin vermeil*, so-called because of its vivid vermilion color, is best known.

✓ *Du Temple* (Jacques de Molay)

LA CLAPE AOC

These red, white, and rosé wines come from vineyards on a limestone outcrop extending across five communes of the Aude *département* where the appellations of Coteaux du Languedoc and Corbières overlap. One of only two whites allowed under the Coteaux du Languedoc Villages appellation, it must be made from at least 60 percent Bourboulenc and Grenache Blanc. White La Clape can be full, fine, and golden or firm, with an attractive Mediterranean spice, and is generally more expensive than the red. But the latter is easily best, with its full, rich flavor and *vin de garde* style. The rosé is refreshing, light, and well worth seeking out.

✓ *Ferri Arnaud* (Romain Elevé en Fûts de Chêne) • *Château de la Négly* (La Falaise) •

Château Pech Redon • Château Rouquette-sur-Mer (Henry Lapierre)

COTEAUX DE LA MÉJANELLE AOC
See La Méjanelle AOC

COTEAUX DE ST.-CHRISTOL AOC
See St.-Christol AOC

COTEAUX DE VÉRARGUES AOC
See Vérargues AOC

GRÈS DE MONTPELLIER AOC
New red-wine-only appellation as from the 2002 vintage, Grès de Montpellier effectively encompasses the Coteaux du Languedoc Villages designations of St.-Christol, St.-Drézéry, St.-Georges-d'Orques, and Vérargues. It must be produced from at least 70 percent in total of Grenache (itself a minimum of 20 percent), Mourvèdre, Syrah, and up to 30 percent Carignan. Too early to provide a critique.

LA MÉJANELLE AOC
This appellation, which may also be sold as Coteaux de la Méjanelle, covers four communes in an area once part of the Rhône delta—river-smoothed boulders litter the vineyards.

Rosé is permitted, but La Méjanelle produces mostly red wines of a dark, rich, and well-structured *vin de garde* style. Château de Flaugergues consistently ranks at the best.

✓ *Château de Flaugergues* (Sommelière)

MONTPEYROUX AOC
This village is located on schistous hills next to St.-Saturnin, just north of the Clairette du Languedoc subappellation. The style of all but the best of these red and rosé wines is firm and somewhat rustic, but they are honest and pleasing, and those recommended below rank among the finest in Languedoc.

✓ *D'Aupilhac* • *Des Grecaux* (Hêméra) • *Château de Lancyre* (Vieilles Vignes)

PICPOUL-DE-PINET AOC
Covering six communes, this white-wine-only appellation must be made, as the name suggests, from 100 percent Picpoul, which in Pinet produces a lively young wine that quickly tires, and thus must be drunk as young as possible. Gaujal is undoubtedly the best.

✓ *Château Font-Mars* • *C. V. de Florensac* (Ressac Prestige) • *Des Lauriers*

PIC-ST.-LOUP AOC
Red and rosé wines from 12 communes in Hérault and one in Gard, all in the vicinity of the *pic*, or peak, of Pic St.-Loup, including some high-altitude locations that must rank among the coolest vineyards in southern France. Permitted grape varieties for Pic-St.-Loup break from the norm—red wines must be made from a blend of at least two of the following: Grenache, Mourvèdre, and Syrah (no minimum or maximum restrictions), plus up to 10 percent Carignan and Cinsault (Counoise, Grenache Gris, Terret Noir, Picpoul Noir, and Lladoner Pelut are not allowed). The grapes for rosé are the same, except that Carignan is excluded and as much as 30 percent Cinsault may be used.

✓ *Devois du Claus* (Elevé en Fûts de Chêne) • *Foulaquier* (Les Chalades) • *Mas Gourdou* (Les Roches Blanches) • *De l'Hortus* •

Clos Marie • *Morties* (Que Sera Sera) • *Château Taurus-Montel* (Prestige Elevé en Fûts de Chêne)

QUATOURZE AOC
These sandy-soil vineyards just south of Narbonne overlap the Corbières appellation, but the wines, mostly red with some rosé, are rather stern and four-square, although the best can fill out and soften up with a few years in bottle. I have tasted nothing recommendable from this village since the last edition.

ST.-CHRISTOL AOC
Just north of Lunel, the calcareous-clay soil of St.-Christol produces ripe, spicy, well-balanced red and rosé wines that may also be sold as Coteaux de St.-Christol AOC. The local *coopérative* dominates production.

✓ *De la Coste* (Sélectionné) • *Guinand* (Elevé en Fûts de Chêne) • *Gabriel Martin* • *C. V. de St.-Christol*

ST.-DRÉZÉRY AOC
Both red and rosé wines are allowed under this village appellation north of Montpellier, but I have encountered only reds, and those have been of a very modest quality.

ST.-GEORGES-D'ORQUES AOC
Just west of Montpellier, the St.-Georges-d'Orques appellation extends over five communes and produces mostly red wines of very good color, plenty of fruit, and no little finesse for this unpretentious Languedoc appellation. A small quantity of rosé is also made, the best having a bouquet of dried flowers and some summer fruits on the palate.

✓ *Château de l'Engarran* (Quetton Saint-Georges) • *Château Icard* (Elevé en Fûts de Chêne) • *Les Quatre Pilas*

ST.-SATURNIN AOC
Named after the first bishop of Toulouse, these red and rosé wines come from three communes in the foothills of the Cévennes Mountains, just west of Montpeyroux, where deep-colored, fine, and full-flavored red wines are possible, if not always evident. Production is dominated by the *coopératives* of St.-Félix-de-Lodez and St.-Saturnin, the former specializing in a pleasant, slightly *pétillant* rosé, while the latter makes a *vin d'une nuit*, a light-bodied red that has been macerated for only one night.

✓ *Lucian* • *C. V. de St-Saturnin*

VÉRARGUES AOC
Vérargues produces large quantities of quaffing, but otherwise unexceptional, red and rosé wines from nine communes, four of which also constitute the Muscat de Lunel appellation. They are also sold as Coteaux de Vérargues AOC.

✓ *Château du Grès-St.-Paul*

CÔTES DE LA MALEPÈRE VDQS
Between the Razès *coopérative* and Domaines Virginie (Des Bruyère), this is becoming one of the fastest-rising, value-for-money, superb-quality appellations in Languedoc-Roussillon. Should be made an AOC.

RED Well-colored wines of medium to full body, with elegant, deliciously spicy fruit.

🍇 A minimum of 50% Merlot, at least 20% Cabernet Franc and Malbec, plus optional

Cabernet Sauvignon, Cinsault, Grenache, and Lladoner Pelut (Syrah is no longer allowed)

🍷 3–7 years

ROSÉ These attractive dry wines are totally different from the reds, due to the greater use and mellow effect of Grenache.

🍇 A minimum of 70% Cabernet Franc, Cinsault, and Grenache, plus optional Cabernet Sauvignon, Malbec, Merlot, and Syrah (Lladoner Pelut is no longer allowed, and growers must not plant any now Syrah)

🍷 1–3 years

✓ *Château de Barthe* • *Girard* (Neri) • *Château Guilhem* (Prestige) • *Château Guiraud*

CÔTES DU CABARDÈS ET DE L'ORBIEL VDQS
See Cabardès AOC

CÔTES DU ROUSSILLON AOC
Situated south of Corbières, this large appellation began to shrug off the sort of reputation that typified the wines of the Midi long before Languedoc. Although the latter region tends to grab most of the headlines these days, Roussillon still offers a tremendous choice of richly flavored wines of exciting value and quality.

RED The best of these wines have a good color and a generosity of southern fruit, with the tiniest hint of vanilla and spice. They may be sold as *primeur* or *nouveau* from the third Thursday of November following the harvest.

🍇 A blend of at least three of the following varieties, no two of which may exceed 90% of the total: Carignan (60% maximum), Cinsault, Grenache, Lladoner Pelut, Macabéo (10% maximum), Mourvèdre, and Syrah (there must be at least 20% of Syrah and/or Mourvèdre)

🍷 3–8 years

WHITE The best of these floral wines were fat, and all too often lacked acidity, prior to the change of *encépagement* in 2002. (So was 2003, but that was the vintage, rather than the varietal mix.) They may be sold as *primeur* or *nouveau* from the third Thursday of November following the harvest.

🍇 At least 50% of Grenache, Macabéo, and Tourbat, plus a minimum of 20% Marsanne, Roussanne, and Vermentino (all varieties obligatory)

🍷 1–2 years

ROSÉ Fresh and attractive dry wines, these rosés may be sold as *primeur* or *nouveau* from the third Thursday of November following the harvest.

🍇 A blend of at least three of the following varieties, no two of which may exceed 90% of the total: Carignan (60% maximum), Cinsault, Grenache, Lladoner Pelut, Macabéo (10% maximum), Mourvèdre, and Syrah (furthermore, there must be at least 20% of Syrah and/or Mourvèdre)

🍷 1–2 years

✓ *Alquier* (Des Filles) • *Mas Amiel* • *Mas des Baux* (Soleil) • *De Casenove* • *C. V. Catalans* • *Mas Crémat* (Dédicace, La Llose) • *Cazes Frères* ⓑ • *Jaubert-Noury* (Château Planères) • *Joliette* ⓞ (André Mercier) • *Lafage* (Le Vignon) • *Du Mas Rous* (Elevé en Fûts de Chêne) • *Mosse* (Tradition) •

C. V. de Passa (Mas d'en Badie) • *Piquemal* • *Primo Palatum* • *Pujols* (La Montadella) • *Château de Rey* (Les Galets Roulés) • *Sarda-Malet* • *Sol-Payre* (Scelerata Ame Noire)

CÔTES DU ROUSSILLON VILLAGES AOC

This appellation encompasses exclusively red wines from 25 villages along the Agly River and its hinterland, in the best area of the Côtes du Roussillon. The *encépagement* changed in 2003.

RED Just as good value as basic Côtes du Roussillon, the best can have even more character and finesse.

A blend of at least three of the following varieties, no two of which may exceed 90% of the total: Carignan (60% maximum), Cinsault, Grenache, Lladoner Pelut, Macabéo (10% maximum), Mourvèdre, and Syrah (furthermore, there must be at least 30% of Syrah and/or Mourvèdre)

3–10 years

✓ *Château Aymerich* (Général Joseph Aymerich) • *Château de Caladroy* (La Juliane) • *Clot de L'Oum* (Saint Bart Vieilles Vignes) • *Clos des Fées* • *Força Real* (Hauts de Força) • *Gardiés* • *Haute Coutume* (Schistes de Trémoine) • *Mas de Lavail* (Tradition) • *Château Planezes* (Eleve en Fûts de Chêne) • *Des Schistes* (Tradition)

CÔTES DU ROUSSILLON VILLAGES CARAMANY AOC

This supervalue red wine conforms to the requirements of Côtes du Roussillon Villages, except for a minimum Syrah content and the stipulation that the Carignan must be vinified by *macération carbonique*. (This strange criterion stems from the fact that, in 1964, the local *coopérative* claimed to be the first in France to use this technique.)

RED Simply the fullest, richest, and longest-living wines of Roussillon, despite the *macération carbonique*, which just goes to prove how useful that process can be when used to lift the natural fruit of a wine instead of dominating it with pear-drop aromas.

As for Côtes du Roussillon Villages except that there must be at least 25% Syrah

3–15 years

✓ *C. V. Catalans*

CÔTES DU ROUSSILLON VILLAGES LESQUERDE AOC

This relatively recent (1996) red wine district is restricted to vines growing in the villages of Lansac, Lesquerde, and Rasiguères. It conforms to the requirements of Côtes du Roussillon Villages, except for some of the *encépagement* and the stipulation that the Carignan must be vinified by *macération carbonique* (see Côtes du Roussillon Caramany for explanation).

RED Rich, well-colored wines that deserve their own village designation.

As for Côtes du Roussillon Villages except that Macabéo is not allowed, and there must be at least 30% Syrah and Mourvèdre

3–15 years

✓ *Semper* (Voluptas) • *C. V. de Tautavel* (Tradition)

CÔTES DU ROUSSILLON VILLAGES TAUTAVEL AOC

This relatively recent (1997) red wine district is restricted to vines growing in the villages of Tautavel and Vingrau. It conforms to the requirements of Côtes du Roussillon Villages, except for some of the *encépagement*, the stipulation that at least 50 percent of the Carignan content must be vinified by *macération carbonique* (see Côtes du Roussillon Caramany for explanation), and the fact that the wines may not be released for sale prior to October 1 following the year of harvest.

RED Rich, well-colored wines that deserve their own village designation.

As for Côtes du Roussillon Villages except that Macabéo is not allowed, and there must be at least 20% Grenache and Lladoner Pelut, and no more than 50% Carignan

3–15 years

✓ *Des Chênes* (La Carissa) • *Fontanel* (Prieuré Elevé en Fûts de Chêne)

CÔTES DU ROUSSILLON VILLAGES LATOUR-DE-FRANCE AOC

This is a fine-value red wine that conforms to the requirements of Côtes du Roussillon Villages. Virtually the entire production of Latour-de-France used to be sold to, and through, the national French wine-shop group Nicolas, which was a great advantage when this village obtained its own appellation, as its seemingly cheeky name was already known the length and breadth of the country.

RED Full in color and body, these fine-value wines have a fruity flavor.

3–15 years

✓ *De L'Ausseil* (La Capitelle)

CRÉMANT DE LIMOUX AOC

This provisional sparkling wine was introduced in 1989 to allow producers to decide the future name of their appellation: Blanquette de Limoux or Crémant de Limoux. The former relied primarily on the Mauzac grape and, upon introducing the Crémant appellation, at least 90 percent content of this local variety became compulsory. In contrast, the newly created Crémant de Limoux had a minimum content of Chenin Blanc, albeit a more modest percentage. The choice was not merely about a name, but what direction and style the wine should follow. It was thought that Mauzac-based Blanquette de Limoux would take the slow lane while Chardonnay-influenced Crémant would be in the fast lane. By law, they should have made this decision by the end of 1994, but Crémant de Limoux did not take off as anticipated. Just a year before the deadline, only one-twentieth of Limoux's sparkling-wine harvest had adopted the Crémant appellation. The lawmakers face a dilemma, since two names are being used for one wine and there is much less support for the new appellation than expected. However, both styles deserve to exist.

SPARKLING WHITE Chardonnay tends to be the main base, with just enough Mauzac retained to assure a certain style, and Chenin Blanc is used as a natural form of acid adjustment. The wines are generally more refined than Blanquette de Limoux, and the best have a finesse that the more traditional products cannot match.

A maximum of 90% in total of Chardonnay and Chenin Blanc, including at least 20% of the latter, plus a maximum of 20% in total of Mauzac and Pinot Noir, with the latter restricted to no more than 10%

✓ *De l'Aigle* • *Sieur d'Arques* • *Veuve Tailhan*

FAUGÈRES AOC

Although fair-sized, Faugères is an obscure and overlooked appellation, probably due to the fact that it was formerly known for *eau-de-vie* and fortified Muscat, with red wine a postwar development. Despite the similarity between the schistous, hillside vineyards and grape varieties here and in neighboring St.-Chinian, the two appellations make distinctly different wines.

RED These rustic wines have a deep color and are heavy with the spicy, warm flavors of Cinsault and Carignan.

3–10 years

ROSÉ Small production of attractively colored, ripe, and fruity dry rosés. These wines may be sold as from December 1 following the harvest without any mention of *primeur* or *nouveau*.

A maximum of 40% Carignan, and no more than 20% Cinsault, plus at least 20% Grenache and/or Lladoner Pelut, a minimum of 15% Syrah, and at least 5% Mourvèdre (furthermore, Grenache, Lladoner Pelut, Mourvèdre, and Syrah represent at least 50% of the entire blend)

3–10 years

✓ *Alquier* • *Château des Estanilles* • *Abbaye de Sylva Plana*

FITOU AOC

When it was made an AOC in 1948, Fitou was fast asleep, but wine buyers beat a path to its desolate door in the early 1980s, making it the fastest-rising star in the Mediterranean firmament. It seems to have returned to its dozing state. The *encépagement* changed in 2001.

RED Even at the lowest level, these wines have a fine color and a spicy warmth of Grenache that curbs and softens the concentrated fruit and tannin of low-yielding Carignan.

A minimum of 30% Carignan, plus Mourvèdre, Syrah, and at least 30% Grenache and Lladoner Pelut, within this Carignan, Grenache, and Lladoner Pelut must account for at least 70% of the entire blend; and until 2007 there must be at least 10% Cinsault, while as from 2008 there must be at least 10% Mourvèdre (Macabéo and Terret Noir are no longer allowed)

3–6 years (4–10 years in exceptional cases)

✓ *Bertrand Bergé* • *Château des Erles* • *C. V. de Mont Tauch* (Seigneur de Don Neuve) • *Château de Nouvelles* • *De la Rochelière* (Noblesse du Temps) • *De Roland*

FRONTIGNAN AOC

See **Muscat de Frontignan AOC**

GRAND ROUSSILLON AOC

The largest appellation producing the least amount of wine, Grand Roussillon is a VDN that encompasses 100 communes, yet produces as little as 330 cases (30 hectoliters) of wine per year. This has nothing to do with low yields or a strict selection process—the appellation is apparently used as a sort of *sous marque* or dumping ground for the inferior wines produced by the better VDNs within its boundaries.

Muscat d'Alexandrie, Muscat Petits Grains, Grenache (Gris, Blanc, and Noir), Macabéo, Tourbat, plus up to 10% (in total) of Carignan, Cinsault, Syrah, and Listan

GRAND ROUSSILLON "RANCIO" AOC
See Grand Roussillon AOC

LIMOUX AOC

Until 1993, Mauzac was the only grape allowed for the still-wine version of Blanquette de Limoux, but new regulations reduced this to a minimum of 15 percent and allowed the inclusion of Chardonnay and Chenin Blanc. At the same time, Limoux became the first French AOC to insist upon barrel fermentation and some fabulous successes quickly established an enviable reputation for the Chardonnay-dominated wines of this appellation. The only question now is will Limoux have equal success with Chenin Blanc? A new red Limoux was introduced in 2004.

RED Newly introduced in 2004.

Minimum of 50% Merlot, plus Cabernet Franc, Cabernet Sauvignon, Carignan, Grenache, malbec and Syrah. The Carignan must not exceed 10% and is due to be phased out by 2010. there must be at least three varieties, no two of which may exceed 90% of the total blend.

3–6 years

WHITE Although every wine must contain at least 15 percent Mauzac, you will encounter supposedly pure Chardonnay and Chenin Blanc varietal wines (and Mauzac, of course). This is explained by the European Union law that requires that a pure varietal wine must contain at least 85 percent of the grape named. Chardonnay varietals are sherbetty-fresh with a zesty style at minimum; the best are beautifully rich, with succulent, lemony-oaky fruit and mouth watering acidity. The pure Mauzac from Rives-Blanques makes me wonder whether it would not be better for producers to focus on this, their local grape, rather than resign themselves to making yet another Chardonnay in a world awash with that variety. This was not initially my view. Tasted when first released, the Chardonnay clearly outshines the Mauzac, thus it is little wonder that the Cuvée Occitania vacuums up so many medals for Rives-Blanques. However, follow them in bottle for just 12 months, and the Mauzac evolves into the more expressive wine.

A minimum of 15% Mauzac, plus Chardonnay and Chenin Blanc

1–2 years

D'Antugnac (Gravas) • Rives-Blanques (Dédicace) • Sieur d'Arques (Toques et Clochers)

MAURY AOC

Despite the long list of possibilities, these fortified wines are mostly pure Grenache, a fact that is recognized by the gradual increase in the compulsory percentage of this grape—the minimum was just 50 percent 10 years ago.

RED/WHITE/ROSÉ/TAWNY Pale and intricate wines, they have a combination of tangy, toasty, berry flavors and nutty-raisiny richness.

At least 75% Grenache (a minimum of 70% for pre-2000 vintages), a maximum of 10% Macabéo (15% for pre-2000 vintages), plus Grenache Gris, Grenache Blanc, Muscat à

Petits Grains, Muscat d'Alexandrie, Tourbat, and a combined maximum of 10% of Carignan, Cinsault, Syrah, and Listan Negra

10–30 years

Mas Amiel • Jean-Louis Lafage (Prestige Vieilli en Fûts de Chêne) • Pouderoux

MAURY "RANCIO" AOC
See Maury AOC

MINERVOIS AOC

North of Corbières and adjoining the western extremity of the Coteaux du Languedoc, the rocky Minervois area has the typically hot and arid air of southern France. Elevated to full AOC status in February 1985, its vineyards are divided into zones. As in Corbières, these are not official, but one day they may in part or whole join La Livinière, which was recognized as a *cru* in its own right in 1999. The zones are: L'Argent Double (rough, rugged vineyards amid rocky outcrops in the arid heart of Minervois); La Clamoux (a cooler western area with a touch more rainfall than most Minervois zones, with Grenache and Syrah doing well, particularly on the higher-altitude vineyards); La Clause (rugged, mountain climate and stony, *terra rosa* soil combine to produce rather rustic *vins de garde* in the north of Minervois); Les Côtes Noires (under a harsh mountain climate, these high-altitude vineyards situated in the northwestern corner of Minervois are better suited to the production of white wine rather than of red); Le Petit Causse (when it can get enough moisture, Mourvèdre does well on these baking-hot, sheltered, limestone slopes in the arid heart of Minervois—La Livinière is located at the heart of Le Petit Causse); Les Serres (very dry, stony vineyards over limestone subsoil, mostly planted with Carignan). The *encépagement* for red and rosé changed in 2003.

RED At worst, these wines are rough and ready for an AOC, but some of the best domaines also produce *vins de pays* that are better than the Minervois of other properties, thus their Minervois can be very good indeed.

A minimum of 40% Grenache, Lladoner Pelut, Mourvèdre, and Syrah (these last two must represent at least 10% of the entire blend, and at least 20% as from 2006), plus optional Aspiran Noir, Carignan, Cinsault, Picpoul Noir, and Terret Noir

1–5 years

WHITE Less than one percent of Minervois is white. A simple, dry, and fruity wine fermented at cooler temperatures than was once standard, it is now fresher and more aromatic.

Bourboulenc, Grenache Blanc, Macabéo, Marsanne, Roussanne, Vermentino, plus not more than 20% Clairette, Muscat à Petits Grains (itself limited to a maximum of 10%), Picpoul, and Terret Blanc

Within 1 year

ROSÉ Most of these are good-value wines with a pretty pink color and a dry, fruity flavor.

A minimum of 40% Grenache, Lladoner Pelut, Mourvèdre, and Syrah (these last two must represent at least 10% of the entire blend, and at least 20% as from 2006), plus optional Aspiran Noir, Carignan, Cinsault, Picpoul Noir, and Terret Noir, with no more than 10% Bourboulenc, Clairette, Grenache Blanc, Macabéo, Marsanne, Roussanne,

Muscat à Petits Grains, Picpoul, Terret Blanc, and Vermentino

Within 1 year

Des Aires Hautes • Borie de Maurel (Sylla) • Le Cazal (Le Paps de Zarat) • Château d'Oupia (Oppius) • Primo Palatum • Du Roc (Passion) • La Tour Buisse

MINERVOIS LA LIVINIÈRE AOC

Located in Le Petit Causse, the central-northern zone of Minervois, La Livinière was in 1999 the first *cru* in this appellation to be recognized in its own right. The vines grow on the best areas of the Petit Causse, the sheltered, limestone cliffs that skirt the foot of the Montagne Noir at a height of 460 feet (140 meters).

RED Where there is sufficient finesse to match the structure of these wines, they represent some of Minervois's best *vins de garde*.

A minimum of 40% Grenache, Lladoner Pelut, Mourvèdre, and Syrah (these last two must represent at least 10% of the entire blend, and at least 20% as from 2006), plus optional Aspiran Noir, Carignan, Cinsault, Picpoul Noir, and Terret Noir

2–10 years

Clos de l'Escandil • C. V. des Crus de Haut-Minervois (Gaïa) • Château Faiteau

MUSCAT DE FRONTIGNAN AOC

It is claimed that the Marquis de Lur-Saluces visited Frontignan in 1700 and it inspired him to make sweet wines at Château d'Yquem in Sauternes, but Muscat de Frontignan is no longer botrytized—it is a fortified wine. Muscat de Frontignan may either be a *vin doux naturel* (VDN) or a *vin de liqueur* (VDL). In the latter, the spirit is added to the grape juice before any fermentation whatsoever can take place. If the label does not differentiate between the two, the small green tax mark on the cap should bear the letters VDN or VDL.

WHITE The VDNs are delightful, golden-colored, raisiny rich, sweet, and delicious wines that have a succulent, honeyed aftertaste with a somewhat fatter style than those of Beaumes, although many lack its finesse. The VDLs are much sweeter.

Muscat Doré de Frontignan

1–3 years

Château des Aresquiers • Château de la Peyrade

MUSCAT DE LUNEL AOC

Situated on limestone terraces northeast of Montpellier, this undervalued VDN approaches Frontignan in terms of pure quality.

WHITE/ROSÉ Lighter than Frontignan, these wines nevertheless have fine, fragrant Muscat aromas of great delicacy and length.

🍇 Muscat Blanc à Petits Grains, Muscat Rosé à Petits Grains

⏳ 1–3 years

✓ *Lacoste* (Clos Bellevue, Passerillé) • *C. V. du Muscat de Lunel* (Prestige)

MUSCAT DE MIREVAL AOC

This is a little-seen VDN appellation.

WHITE Light and sweet wines that can have a better balance and (relatively) more acidity than those from neighboring Frontignan. Mireval wines can have more elegance, although they may lack the raisiny-rich concentration.

🍇 Muscat Blanc à Petits Grains

⏳ 1–3 years

✓ *Château d'Exindre* (Vent d'Anges) • *Du Mas Neuf*

MUSCAT DE RIVESALTES AOC

This appellation should not be confused with the blended Rivesaltes VDNs that bear no mention of the Muscat grape.

WHITE/ROSÉ Rich, ripe, grapey-raisiny wines that are very consistent in quality.

🍇 Muscat Blanc à Petits Grains, Muscat d'Alexandrie

⏳ 1–3 years

ⓑ✓ *Cazes Frères* ⓑ • *Des Chênes* • *Cornelianum* • *Jean Estavel* (Prestige) • *Lafage* • *Laporte* • *Château de Nouvelles* • *Sarda-Malet* • *Des Schistes* • *Arnaud de Villeneuve*

MUSCAT DE ST.-JEAN-DE-MINERVOIS AOC

This tiny subappellation of Minervois produces a little *vin doux naturel* that used to be grossly underrated but has gained excellent distribution on export markets over the past seven years.

WHITE/ROSÉ These golden wines have a balanced sweetness and an apricot flavor.

🍇 Muscat Blanc à Petits Grains, Muscat Rosé à Petits Grains

⏳ 1–3 years

✓ *De Barroubio* • *La Muscat* (Petit Grain)

RIVESALTES AOC

This appellation represents half of the *vin doux naturel* produced in France. Optional legally defined terms include *ambré* for an oxidative style of tawny colored Rivesaltes; *tuilé* for an oxidative red; and *grenat* for a reductive-style red that must not be bottled any later than March 1 of the second year. *Hors d'age* requires a minimum of five years' aging.

RED/ROSÉ The warm, brick-red glow of these wines belies their astringent-sweet, chocolate, and cherry-liqueur flavor and drying, tannic finish.

🍇 A minimum of 50% (for oxidative style) or 75% (for reductive style) Grenache, plus Grenache Blanc, Grenache Gris, Tourbat, with a maximum of 10% Carignan, Cinsault, Palomino, and Syrah

⏳ 10–40 years

WHITE/TAWNY Because much of the red version can be lightened after lengthy maturation in wood, all Rivesaltes eventually merge into one tawny style with time. The whites do not, of course, have any tannic astringency and are more oxidative and raisiny, with a resinous, candied-peel character.

🍇 Grenache Blanc, Grenache Gris, Macabéo, Muscat Blanc à Petits Grains, Muscat d'Alexandrie, Muscat Romain, Tourbat (the Muscat varieties must not exceed 20% of the entire blend in total or separately)

⏳ 10–20 years

✓ *Du Mas Alart* (Ambré Hors d'Age) • *Des Chênes* • *Cazes Frères* ⓑ • *Gardies* • *Château de Nouvelles* (Tuilé) • *Sarda-Malet* (La Carbasse) • *Château de Sau* (Ambré Hors d'Age) • *Terrassous* (Ambré Vinifié en Fûts de Chêne) • *Arnaud de Villeneuve* (Ambré Hors d'Age)

RIVESALTES "RANCIO" AOC

See Rivesaltes AOC

ST.-CHINIAN AOC

Upgraded from VDQS in May 1982, the excellent-value appellation of St.-Chinian is the nearest that native southern French grapes come to resembling Bordeaux. Similar grapes from comparable schistous hillsides in neighboring Faugères make an entirely different, far more rustic wine that lacks the finesse of St.-Chinian, let alone Bordeaux. As from 2004, two *crus* have been awarded their own designation: St.-Berlou and St.-Chinian Roquebrun, but it is too early to make a critique. Moves are under way to introduce a white style of St.-Chinian.

RED Relatively light in color and weight, these wines have an elegance that belies their Mediterranean origin.

🍇 At least 50% in total of Grenache, Lladoner Pelut, Mourvèdre, and Syrah, plus a maximum of 40% Carignan and no more than 30% Cinsault

⏳ 2–6 years

ROSÉ Dry and delicately fruity rosés with an attractive, fragrant bouquet and flavor. May be sold from December 1 following the harvest without any mention of *primeur* or *nouveau*.

🍇 At least 50% in total of Grenache, Lladoner Pelut, Mourvèdre, and Syrah, plus a maximum of 40% Carignan and no more than 30% Cinsault

⏳ 1–3 years

✓ *Clos Bagatelle* • *Berloup* (Vignes Royales) • *Mas Canet Valette* • *De Canimals Le Haut* • *Mas Champart* • *Château La Dournie* • *Fontaine Marcousse* • *Des Jougla* (Vieihs Arrasics) • *Navare* (Olivier)

VIN DE FRONTIGNAN AOC

See Muscat de Frontignan AOC

MORE GREEN WINES

In addition to the producers recommended in this directory that are either biodynamic or organic, there are also the following. No negative inference of quality should be taken from the fact that they are not featured among my recommended producers. There are a number that have been recommended in other editions, and still make some fine wines, but have been culled out to make room for others.

Biodynamic

Beau-Thorey (Corconne), *De Bila-Haut* (Latour de France), *De Combebelle* (Villespassans), *Jean-Claude Daumond* (Vendargues), *De Fontedicto* (Caux), *De Malaïgue* (Uzés), *Des Perrières* (Manduel), *Le Petit Domaine de Gimios* (St Jean de Minervois), *St Julien* (Azille), *Sylvain Saux* (Lauraguel)

Organic

Cabanis (Beauvoisin), *De Caillan* (Bessan), *De Camplazens* (Combaillaux), *Château de Caraguilhes* (St Laurent de la Cabrerisse), *De Clairac* (Cazouls lès Béziers), *Combes-Giraud* (Valros), *Costeplane* (Cannes et Clairan), *CV les Côteaux de Creissan* (Creissan), *Jean Bigou* (Rouvenac), *Blanquette Beirieu* (Roquetaillade), *Bourguet* (Béziers), *Alain Bousquet* (St Etienne de Gourgas), *Couderc* (Neffies), *Mas Coutelou* (Puimisson), *Du Farlet* (Meze), *La Fon de Lacan* (St Pargoire), *Jacques Frélin Vignobles* (Villeneuve lès Béziers), *Grand Bourry* (Le Cailar), *La Grangette* (Castelnau de Guers), *De Gressac* (Verfeuil), *Mas de Janiny* (St Bauzille de la Sylve), *Mas Jullien* (Jonquières), *CV La Clairette* (Bellegarde), *La Tour* (Beaucaire), *Du Lac* (Montescot), *CV Languedoc Roussillon* (Montpellier), *Bernard Legoy* (Condat-en-Combrailles), *CV Les Gres* (Vendargues), *De Litenis* (St Jean de Fos), *Lou Pas d'Estrech* (St Christol de Rodières), *Loupia* (Pennautier), *Louvet/Cellier du Languedoc Vins Distribution* (Narbonne), *Château Maris* (La Livinière), *Maurel Vedeau* (Servian), *Antoine Maurel* (Conques-sur-Orbiel), *De Mayrac* (Couiza), *De Montabuc* (St Jean de Minervois), *Croix de Bel-Air* (Marseillan), *De Montjouy* (Florensac), *CV de Montpeyroux* (Montpeyroux), *Ochre Rouge* (Dions), *Château du Parc* (Pezenas), *Pastouret* (Bellegarde), *Château Pech-Latt* (Lagrasse), *De Petit Roubié* (Pinet), *Château des Auzines* (Auzines), *Bannières* (Castries), *Du Mas Barjac* (Monteils), *Bassac* (Puissalicon), *De Malavieille* (Merifons), *Peyre-Rose* (St Pargoire), *De Picheral* (Mus), *Château Roubia* (Roubia), *La Solana* (Festes), *Des Soulié* (Assignan), *St Alban* (Neffies), *Château St Auriol* (Lézignan-Corbières), *De St Blaise* (Cessenon), *Ste Marie des Pins* (Verzeille), *Des Syles* (Béziers) *La Triballe* (Guzargues), *De Valescure* (Aimargues), *Abbaye de Valmagne* (Villeveyrac), *Château Ventaiolle* (Ventenac-Cabardes), *Château Veredus* (Cruscades), *Zumbaum-Tomasi* (Claret), *De l'Ametlier* (Pézenas), *Anthéa* (Sallès d'Aude), *La Batteuse* (Antugnac), *Château Bel Air La Côte* (Beauvoisin), *Château Belaussel* (Lagrasse), *Belles Croix Robin* (Guzargues), *Château Bousquette* (Cessenon-sur-Orb), *De Brau* (Villemoustaussou), *De Buzarens* (Assas), *Arnaudiés* (Ceret), *Batlle-Jacquet* (Fourques), *Carle-Courty* (Millas), *Henri-Albert Foxonet* (Toulouges), *Joliette* (Espira de l'Agly), *Franck Jorel* (St Paul de Fenouillet), *Château de L'Ou* (Montescot), *Laguerre* (St Martin de Fenouillet), *Le Casot de Mailloles* (Banyuls-sur-Mer), *Lenan* (Trouillas), *Nivet-Galinier* (Toulouges), *Jean-Michel Paraire* (Fourques), *Olivier Pithon* (Calce), *De la Rourède* (Fourques), *Du Soula* (St Martin de Fenouillet), *Clos St Martin* (Bompas)

PROVENCE AND CORSICA

If any wine does not travel, it has to be Provence rosé. But this probably has more to do with the romance surrounding the wine than with the wine itself. The best Provençal wines are red, and they can be truly splendid.

YOU CAN FORGET MOST PROVENCE ROSÉ. It may come in an exotically shaped bottle, but exotic is the last word that could be used to describe its dull, flabby contents. They have been making wine here for more than 2,600 years, and by the time the Romans arrived, in 125BC, it was already so good that they immediately exported it back to Rome. But ask yourself this question: do you think that wine was a rosé? Of course not; Provence rosé is a relatively recent phenomenon and, some would cynically say, one that was deliberately designed to swindle the gold-draped *nouveau riche* who flock here.

Rosé still represents more than half of all Provençal production, although sales have declined in recent years, as the once-

CORSICAN VINEYARDS
These vineyards of Domaine de Valrose at Borgo, near the east coast, are typical of the Corsican landscape. The east-coast plains are backed by dramatic mountains, and palm trees proliferate.

FACTORS AFFECTING TASTE AND QUALITY

LOCATION
Provence is situated in the southeast of France, between the Rhône delta and the Italian border. A farther 68 miles (110 kilometers) southeast lies Corsica.

CLIMATE
Winters are mild, as are springs, which can also be humid. Summers are hot and stretch into long, sunny falls. A vine requires 1,300 hours of sunshine in one growing season—1,500 hours is preferable, but in Provence, it luxuriates in an average of 3,000 hours. The close proximity of the Mediterranean, however, is also capable of inducing sharp fluctuations in the weather. Rain is spread over a limited number of days in fall and winter.

ASPECT
The vineyards run down hillsides and on to the plains.

SOIL
The geology of Provence is complex. Many ancient soils have undergone chemical changes and numerous new soils have been created. Sand, red sandstone, and granite are, however, the most regular common denominators, with limestone outcrops that often determine the extent of superior *terroirs*: the Var *département* has mica-schist, chalky scree, and chalky tufa as well as granite hillsides; there are excellent flinty-limestone soils at Bandol; and pudding stones (conglomerate pebbles) that are rich in flint at Bellet. The south of Corsica is mostly granite, while the north is schistous, with a few limestone outcrops and deposits of sandy and alluvial soils in between.

VITICULTURE AND VINIFICATION
All the vines used to be planted in *gobelet* fashion, but most are now trained on wires. The recent trend toward Cabernet Sauvignon has stopped, although many excellent wines are still made from this grape. The current vogue is to reestablish a true Provençal identity by relying exclusively (where possible) on local varieties, and the laws have been changed to encourage this particular evolution. Much of the rosé has been improved by modern cool-vinification techniques, although most remains tired and flabby.

GRAPE VARIETIES
Aragnan, Aramon, Aramongris, Barbarossa, Barbaroux, Barbaroux Rosé, Bourboulenc, Braquet, Brun-Fourcat, Cabernet Sauvignon, Calitor (*syn.* Pecoui-touar), Carignan, Castets, Chardonnay, Cinsault (*syn.* Plant d'Arles), Clairette, Clairette à Gros Grains, Clairette à Petits Grains, Clairette de Trans, Colombard, Counoise, Doucillon, Durif, Fuella, Grenache, Grenache Blanc, Marsanne, Mayorquin, Mourvèdre, Muscat d'Aubagne, Muscat Blanc à Petits Grains, Muscat de Die, Muscat de Frontignan, Muscat de Hambourg, Muscat de Marseille, Muscat Noir de Provence, Muscat Rosé à Petits Grains, Nielluccio, Panse Muscade, Pascal Blanc, Petit-Brun, Picardan, Picpoul, Pignerol, Sauvignon Blanc, Sémillon, Sciacarello, Syrah, Téoulier (*syn.* Manosquin), Terret Blanc, Terret Gris (*syn.* Terret-Bourret), Terret Noir, Terret Ramenée, Tibouren (*syn.* Tibourenc), Ugni Blanc, Ugni Rosé, Vermentino (*syn.* Rolle)

exclusive resorts become more accessible to the sophisticated middle classes, who recognize how dull these wines are. Quality improved in the 1980s, but has reached a plateau and, without resorting to actually acidifying the wines, modern vinification techniques will never be able to rid them of the dusty flabbiness that is their sunny southern heritage.

THE TRUE CLASSIC WINES OF PROVENCE
For most people, Provence evokes the beaches of St.-Tropez or the rich, *bouillabaisse*-laden aromas of backstreet Marseille, but there are other experiences to be had in this sun-blessed corner of southern France. For while the wines of Provence may not have the classic status of Burgundy or Bordeaux, the reds, such as the magnificent Bandol, the darkly promising Bellet, and the aptly named Cassis, have an abundance of spice-charged flavors that show more than a touch of class. Silly-shaped bottles are being discarded by the more serious winemakers who find the classic,

RECENT PROVENÇAL AND CORSICAN VINTAGES

2003 The year of the heatwave meant extremely variable results in Provence, where even the best reds are all too often overalcoholic and lacking in elegance.

2002 Wet at best, floods at worst, with few exceptional wines in Provence (a good rosé year!), but good in Corsica for Vin de Corse (particularly, though not exclusively, for whites), Patrimonio, and Muscat du Cap Corse.

2001 A dry year produced well-colored Provençal red wines of good to very good quality.

2000 Very good quality all around.

1999 Average to good for Bandol, better for other reds.

Legend:

- Villages entitled to add their names to the Vin de Corse (*see* Corsica map) or the Coteaux d'Aix-en-Provence appellation (*see* Provence map)
- Coteaux d'Aix-en-Provence
- Côtes de Provence
- Coteaux Varois
- Cassis
- Palette
- Bandol
- Bellet
- Vin de Corse
- Patrimonio
- Ajaccio
- Muscadet du Cap Corse
- *Département* boundary
- ▲ Height above sea level (meters)

0 10 20 miles
0 10 20 30 40 km

PROVENCE AND CORSICA,
see also p.55
Although part of this wine-producing area is an island and part is on the French mainland, both of these sun-soaked regions are subject to the same capricious Mediterranean weather conditions, although frost is rare in both.

THE CRUS CLASSÉS OF PROVENCE

Provence is the only region outside Bordeaux to boast a cru classé system. The cru classé concept was conceived by Napoléon III, hence the 1855 classification. One hundred years later, 14 domaines in the Côtes de Provence somehow managed to arrange their own classification, endorsed by ministerial decree on July 20, 1955. These domaines were selected on the basis of the following criteria: ancestral inheritance; family ownership; historic buildings and reputation; the soil, vineyard, winery, and cellar; the wine produced; and the quality sought for more than one century. The crus classés of Côtes de Provence are:

- Château de Brégançon (Bormes les Mimosas): 124 acres/50ha • Clos Cibonne (Le Pradet): 34½ acres/14ha
- Château du Galoupet (La Londe): 163 acres/66ha • Domaine du Jas d'Esclans (La Motte): 156 acres/63ha
- Château de Mauvanne (Hyères): 124 acres/50ha • Château Minuty (Gassin): 161 acres/65ha • Clos Mireille (La Londe): 131 acres/53ha
- Domaine de Rimauresq (Pignans): 91 acres/37ha • Château de Roubine (Lorgues): 173 acres/70ha • Château Ste. Marguerite (La Londe): 62 acres/25ha • Château de St. Martin (Taradeau): 94 acres/38ha • Château St. Maur (Cogolin): 119 acres/48ha • Château Ste. Roseline (Les Arcs-sur-Argens): 222 acres/90ha • Château de Selle (Taradeau): 151 acres/61ha

understated lines of Bordeaux- and Burgundy-style bottles better reflect the quality of their wines.

The top estates of the Riviera produce red wines of a far more serious caliber than might be expected from an area better known for its play than its work. Maximum yields are low, however, and the potential for quality can be high. The smaller AOCs of Bandol, Bellet, and Palette are restricted to a maximum of 180 cases per acre (40 hectoliters per hectare), which is very modest for a region that could easily average more than double this amount. Even the all-embracing AOCs of Côtes de Provence and Coteaux d'Aix-en-Provence are absolutely full of fine vineyards capable of producing the exciting red wine that must surely be Provence's future.

CORSICA—"THE ISLE OF BEAUTY"

In Corsica, the advent of France's *vin de pays* system meant that around one-third of the island's vineyards were uprooted and put to better use. If the *vin de pays* system was intended to encourage the production of superior-quality wines from the bottom of the market upward, then here at least it has been successful, for this island is no longer the generous contributor to Europe's "wine-lake" it used to be.

The days when Corsica's wines were fit only for turning into industrial spirit are long gone, but nor is this a potentially fine wine region. Just 15 percent of its vineyards are AOC, and these yield barely more than 5 percent of Corsica's total wine production. Although this is a fair and accurate reflection of its true potential, most critics agree that even within the modest limits of *vin de pays* production there should be many more individually expressive domaines. What has restricted their numbers is, however, something few are willing to talk about—intimidation and extortion by the local Mafia, which has caused more than one brave new Corsican venture to founder.

THE APPELLATIONS OF
PROVENCE AND CORSICA

Note * denotes producers who are particularly recommended for rosé.

AJACCIO AOC

This is a predominantly red-wine appellation on the west coast of Corsica.

RED When successful, this will inevitably be a medium-bodied Sciacarello wine with a good bouquet.

🍇 At least 60% (in total) of Barbarossa, Nielluccio, Vermentino, and Sciacarello (the last of which must account for at least 40%), plus a maximum of 40% (in total) of Grenache, Cinsault, and Carignan (the last of which must not exceed 15%)

WHITE Decently dry and fruity, the best have a good edge of Ugni Blanc acidity.

ROSÉ Average to good-quality dry rosé with a typical southern roundness.

🍇 As for the red

🍷 All wines: 1–3 years

✓ *Comte Abbatucci* (Faustine Abbatucci) • *Comte Peraldi*

BANDOL AOC

The red wine of this Provence appellation is a true *vin de garde* and deserves recognition. The white wine *encépagement* changed in 2003.

RED The best of these wines have a dark purple-black color, a deep and dense bouquet, masses of spicy-plummy Mourvèdre fruit, and complex after-aromas that include vanilla, cassis,

cinnamon, violets, and sweet herbs.

🍇 A blend of at least two of the following: Mourvèdre, Grenache, and Cinsault, of which a minimum of 50% Mourvèdre is obligatory, plus no more than 15% in total or 10% individually of Syrah and Carignan

🍷 3–12 years

WHITE These dry wines are now fresher and more fragrant than they were, but they are nothing special compared with the reds.

🍇 A minimum of 20% (50% as from 2011) Clairette, plus 40% (60% as from 2011) of Bourboulenc and/or Ugni Blanc (Sauvignon Blanc is no longer allowed)

🍷 Within 1 year

ROSÉ Well-made, attractive dry rosés, with body, structure, and a fine individual character.

🍇 As for red but no minimum Mourvèdre content

🍷 1–2 years

✓ *Château des Baumelles* • *Bunan* (Moulin des Costes Charriage, Château la Rouvière, Mas de la Rouvière) • *Dupéré-Barrera* (India) • *du Gros'Noré* • *de l'Hermitage* • *de la Laidière* • *Lafran-Veyrolles* • *Château de Pibarnon* • *Château Pradeaux* • *Château Ste.-Anne* ⦿ • *des Salettes* • *La Suffrene* (Les Lauves) • *Tempier* • *Terrebrune* • *Vannières*

LES BAUX DE PROVENCE AOC

Excellent red and rosé wines, sold under the subappellation of Coteaux d'Aix-en-Provence Les Baux until 1995, when they were given their own AOC and the requirements changed.

RED Deep, dark, and rich, with creamy-spicy cherry and plum flavors.

🍇 A minimum of 60% Grenache, Mourvèdre and Syrah, no two varieties of which must account for more than 90% of the entire blend, plus a maximum 30% in total of one or more of the following: Carignan, Cinsault and Counoise, with a maximum of 20% Cabernet Sauvignon

🍷 4–10 years

ROSÉ De la Vallongue is rich and ripe.

🍇 A minimum of 60% Cinsault, Grenache, and Syrah, no two varieties of which must account for more than 90% of the entire blend, plus a maximum of 30% in total of one or more of the following: Carignan, Counoise, and Mourvèdre, with a maximum of 10% Cabernet Sauvignon

🍷 1–2 years

✓ *Hauvette* ⦿ • *Mas Sainte-Berthe* (Louis David) • *de la Vallongue** ⦿

BELLET AOC

This tiny Provence appellation is cooled by Alpine winds and produces exceptionally fragrant wines for such a southerly location.

ROSÉ Fine, floral, dry rosés that are exceptionally fresh and easy to drink.

🍇 Braquet, Fuella, Cinsault, plus up to 40% (in total) of Grenache, Rolle, Ugni Blanc, Mayorquin, Clairette, Bourboulenc, Chardonnay, Pignerol, and Muscat à Petits Grains

🍷 1–2 years

RED These wines have a good color and structure, with a well-perfumed bouquet.

🍇 Braquet, Fuella, Cinsault, plus up to 40% (in total) of Grenache, Rolle, Ugni Blanc, Mayorquin, Clairette, Bourboulenc, Chardonnay, Pignerol, and Muscat à Petits Grains

🍷 4–10 years

WHITE Fine, firm yet fragrant, and highly aromatic, dry white wines of unbelievable class and finesse.

Rolle, Ugni Blanc, Mayorquin, plus up to 40% Clairette, Bourboulenc, Chardonnay, Pignerol, and Muscat à Petits Grains

⏱ 3–7 years

✓ *Château de Bellet* • *Clos Saint-Vincent* (Clos)

CASSIS AOC

This is a decent but overpriced Provence appellation located around a beautiful rocky bay, a few miles east of Marseille. In all but a few enterprising estates, these vineyards are on the decline.

RED These solid, well-colored red wines can age, but most do not improve.

Grenache, Carignan, Mourvèdre, Cinsault, Barbaroux, plus up to 10% (in total) of Terret Noir, Terret Gris, Terret Blanc, Terret Ramenée, Aramon, and Aramon Gris

WHITE These dry white wines have an interesting bouquet of herby aromas of gorse and bracken, but are usually flabby and unbalanced on the palate. However, Bagnol and St.-Magdeleine produce excellent, racy whites for such southerly vineyards, and Ferme Blanche can be almost as good.

Ugni Blanc, Sauvignon Blanc, Doucillon, Clairette, Marsanne, Pascal Blanc

ROSÉ Pleasantly fresh, dry rosés of moderately interesting quality.

Grenache, Carignan, Mourvèdre, Cinsault, Barbaroux, plus up to 10% (in total) of Terret Noir, Terret Gris, Terret Blanc, Terret Ramenée, Aramon, and Aramon Gris

⏱ All wines: 1–3 years

✓ *du Bagnol* • *Clos Val Bruyère*

CORSE AOC

Alternative appellation, *see* Vin de Corse AOC

COTEAUX D'AIX-EN-PROVENCE AOC

This large appellation has many fine estates, several of which have been replanted and reequipped.

RED The best are deeply colored *vins de garde* with lots of creamy-cassis, spicy-vanilla, and cherry flavors, capable of some complexity.

Grenache, plus a maximum of 40% of

Cinsault, Counoise, Mourvèdre, Syrah, Cabernet Sauvignon, and Carignan (the last two of which must not exceed 30%)

⏱ 3–12 years

WHITE Dry and fruity white wines that are of moderate quality, and are certainly improving. These wines may be sold from December 1 following the harvest without any mention of *primeur* or *nouveau*.

A maximum of 70% (each) of Bourboulenc, Clairette, Grenache Blanc, Vermentino, up to 40% Ugni Blanc and no more than 30% (each) of Sauvignon Blanc and Sémillon

⏱ Upon purchase

ROSÉ Fine-quality dry rosés that are light in body, but bursting with deliciously fresh and ripe fruit. These wines may be sold from December 1 following the harvest without any mention of *primeur* or *nouveau*.

As for red, plus up to 10% (in total) of Bourboulenc, Clairette, Grenache Blanc, Vermentino, Ugni Blanc, Sauvignon Blanc, and Sémillon

⏱ 1–2 years

✓ *des Béates* ❽ (Terra d'Or) • *Château de Beaupré* • *Château de Calissanne* • *de Camaissette* (Amadeus) • *Jean-Luc Colombo* (Pin Couchés) • *Hauvette* ◉ • *Château Pigoudet* (La Chapelle) • *Château St-Jean**

COTEAUX VAROIS AOC

Upgraded from *vin de pays* to VDQS in 1985 and to AOC in 1993, this appellation covers an area of pleasant country wines in the center of Provence. The *encépagement* changed in 2001.

RED The best have good color, a deep fruity flavor, and some finesse.

At least two of the following must represent 80 to 90% of the entire blend: Cinsault, Grenache, Mourvèdre, and Syrah, plus optional Cabernet Sauvignon, Carignan, and Tibouren (permitted since 2001)

WHITE Soft and fresh at best.

A minimum of 30% Vermentino, plus Clairette, Grenache Blanc, a maximum of 30% Sémillon, and no more than 25% Ugni Blanc

ROSÉ These attractive, easy-to-drink, dry rosés offer better value than some of the more famous, pretentious wines of Provence.

At least two of the following must represent 80 to 90% of the entire blend: Cinsault, Grenache, Mourvèdre, and Syrah, plus optional Cabernet Sauvignon, Carignan, and Tibouren (permitted since 2001), and no more than 10% Clairette, Grenache Blanc, Sémillon, Ugni Blanc, and Vermentino

⏱ All wines: 1–3 years

✓ *des Chaberts* (Prestige) • *de Garbelle* (Les Barriques de Barbelle) • *Château Lafoux* • *de Ramatuelle* • *Château Thuerry* (Les Abeillons) • *Château Trians*

CÔTES DE PROVENCE AOC

While this AOC is famous for its rosés, it is the red wines of Côtes de Provence that have real potential, and they seem blessed with good vintages, fine estates, and talented winemakers. Inferior wines are made, but drink the best and you will rarely be disappointed. The major drawback of this all-embracing appellation is its very size. There are, however, several areas with peculiarities of soil and specific microclimates that would make a Côtes

de Provence Villages AOC a logical evolution and give the most expressive growers something to aim for.

RED There are too many exciting styles to generalize, but the best have a deep color and many show an exuberance of silky Syrah fruit and plummy Mourvèdre. Some have great finesse, others are more tannic and chewy. The southern spicy-cassis of Cabernet Sauvignon is often present and the Cinsault, Grenache, and Tibouren grapes also play important roles.

The following must represent at least 70% (80% as from 2015) of the entire blend: Cinsault, Grenache, Mourvèdre, Syrah, and Tibouren, but no two varieties may account for more than 90%; plus optional Barbaroux Rosé, Cabernet Sauvignon, Calitor, and Carignan, with no more than 10% of Clairette, Sémillon, Ugni Blanc, and Vermentino

⏱ 3–10 years

WHITE Moderate but improving soft, dry, fragrant, and aromatic wines. These wines may be sold from December 1 following the harvest without any mention of *primeur* or *nouveau*.

Clairette, Sémillon, Ugni Blanc, and Vermentino

⏱ 1–2 years

ROSÉ Mediterranean sun is integral to the enjoyment of these wines, which are without doubt made to accompany food, but even the best fail to perform against other rosés under blind conditions; their low acidity makes them seem flat and dull. These wines may be sold from December 1 following the harvest without any mention of *primeur* or *nouveau*.

The following must represent at least 70% (80% as from 2015) of the entire blend: Cinsault, Grenache, Mourvèdre, Syrah, and Tibouren, but no two varieties may account for more than 90%; plus optional Barbaroux Rosé, Cabernet Sauvignon, Calitor, and Carignan, with no more than 10% of Clairette, Sémillon, Ugni Blanc, and Vermentino

⏱ 1–2 years

✓ *Clos d'Alari* (Manon) • *Château des Anglades* (Collection Privée) • *Château de l'Aumerade* (Louis Fabre) • *Château Barbeyrolles* • *de la Bastide Neuve* (d'Antan) • *Ludovic de Beauséjour* (Bacarras) • *de la Courtade* • *Château Coussin Sainte-Victoire* (César) • *Dupéré-Barrera* (En Caractère) • *Domaines Gavoty* • *du Grand Cros* (Nectar) • *de Jalle* (La Bouïsse) • *de La Lauzade* • *de la Malherbe** • *Château Maravenne* • *Château Minuty* (Prestige) • *Commanderie de Peyrassol** • *Château Requier** (Tête de Cuvée) • *de Rimauresq* • *La Rouvade* (Prestige) • *Saint-André de Figuière* • *St.-Baillon* • *Château Sainte-Roseline* • *Château Sarrins** • *Château de Selles** (also Clos Mireille) • *Château de la Tour l'Evêque** • *Vignerons Presqu'Ile St.-Tropez* (Château de Pampelonne, Carte Noire) • *Vannières* • *Vitis Alba* (Elevé en Fûts de Chêne)

MUSCAT DU CAP CORSE AOC

When I first wrote this book in 1988, Corsica's only truly classic wine, the succulent sweet Muscat of Cap Corse, was not even recognized, let alone awarded the AOC status it deserved, and it took five more years to get it on the statute books. The Muscat du Cap Corse appellation overlaps Vin de Corse Coteaux du Cap Corse and five of the seven communes that comprise the Patrimonio AOC.

WHITE The wines of Clos Nicrosi (in particular) demonstrate that Corsica has the ability to produce one of the most fabulous Muscats in the world. These wines are so pure and succulent, with wonderful fresh aromas that they have very little to gain through age.

🍇 Muscat Blanc à Petits Grains

🍷 Upon purchase

✓ *Clos Nicrosi • Leccia • Orenga de Gaffory*

PALETTE AOC

The ridiculously long list of permissible grapes here illustrates one of the worst excesses of the AOC system. What is the point of such a large number of diverse grape varieties? Ignoring the fact that it includes some low-quality ones that should, if anything, be banned, it is obvious that no specific style could possibly result from the infinite permutation of varieties and percentages this AOC permits. Why not simply have an appellation that guarantees that Palette is from Palette? Despite this farce, Palette is one of the best in Provence. It can be considered the equivalent of a *grand cru* of Coteaux d'Aix-en-Provence, standing out from surrounding vineyards by virtue of its calcareous soil. Three-quarters of this appellation is occupied by just one property—Château Simone.

RED Though not in the blockbusting style, this is a high-quality wine with good color and firm structure, and can achieve finesse.

🍇 At least 50% (in total) of Mourvèdre, Grenache, and Cinsault, plus Téoulier, Durif, and Muscat (any variety planted), Carignan, Syrah, Castets, Brun-Fourcat, Terret Gris, Petit-Brun, Tibouren, Cabernet Sauvignon, and up to 15% (in total) of Clairette (any variety planted), Picardan, Ugni Blanc, Ugni Rosé, Grenache Blanc, Muscat (any variety planted), Picpoul, Pascal, Aragnan, Colombard, and Terret-Bourret

🍷 7–20 years

WHITE Firm but nervy dry wine with a pleasantly curious aromatic character.

🍇 At least 55% (in total) of Clairette (any

variety planted), plus Picardan, Ugni Blanc, Ugni Rosé, Grenache Blanc, Muscat (any variety planted), Picpoul, Pascal, Aragnan, Colombard, and a maximum of 20% Terret-Bourret

🍷 Upon purchase

ROSÉ A well-made but not exceptional wine, which is perhaps made too seriously for its level of quality.

🍇 At least 50% (in total) of Mourvèdre, Grenache, and Cinsault, plus Téoulier, Durif, and Muscat (any variety planted), Carignan, Syrah, Castets, Brun-Fourcat, Terret Gris, Petit-Brun, Tibouren, Cabernet Sauvignon, and up to 15% (in total) of Clairette (any variety planted), Picardan, Ugni Blanc, Ugni Rosé, Grenache Blanc, Muscat (any variety planted), Picpoul, Pascal, Aragnan, Colombard, and Terret-Bourret

🍷 1–3 years

✓ *Château Crémade • Château Simone*

PATRIMONIO AOC

This is a small appellation situated west of Bastia in the north of Corsica. The *encépagement* changed in 2002.

RED Some fine-quality red wines of good color, body, and fruit are made.

🍇 At least 90% Nielluccio, plus Grenache, Sciacarello, and Vermentino

WHITE Light and dry wines of a remarkably fragrant and floral character for Corsica.

🍇 Vermentino

ROSÉ Good-value dry rosés that have a coral-pink color and an elegant flavor.

🍇 At least 75% Nielluccio, plus Grenache, Sciacarello, and Vermentino

🍷 All wines: 1–3 years

✓ *Aliso-Rossi • de Catarelli • Gentile* (Sélection Noble) • *Giacometti* (Cru des Agrigates) • *Leccia • Orenga de Gaffory • Pastricciola • Clos Teddi*

VIN DE BANDOL AOC

See Bandol AOC

VIN DE BELLET AOC

See Bellet AOC

VIN DE CORSE AOC

Vin de Corse is a generic appellation covering the entire island. The *encépagement* changed in 2003.

RED These honest wines are full of fruit, round, and clean, with rustic charm.

🍇 At least 50% Grenache, Nielluccio, Sciacarello, and Grenache Noir, plus a maximum of 50% Barbarossa, Carignan, Cinsault, Mourvèdre, Syrah, and Vermentino (Carignan and/or Vermentino must not exceed 20% of the entire blend)

WHITE The best are well-made, clean, and fresh, but not of true AOC quality.

🍇 At least 75% Vermentino, plus optional Ugni Blanc

ROSÉ Attractive, dry, fruity, easy-to-drink wines.

🍇 At least 50% Grenache, Nielluccio, Sciacarello, and Grenache Noir, plus a maximum of 50% Barbarossa, Carignan, Cinsault, Mourvèdre, Syrah, and Vermentino (Carignan and/or Vermentino must not exceed 20% of the entire blend)

🍷 All wines: 1–3 years

✓ *Andriella • Casablanca • Clos Colombu • CV de L'Ile de Beauté* (Réserve du Président) • *Maestracci • Musoleu* (Monte Cristo) • *Clos de L'Orlea • Clos Poggiale*

VIN DE CORSE CALVI AOC

Lying north of Ajaccio, this subappellation of Vin de Corse AOC requires the same grape varieties and meets the same technical level.

✓ *Colombu • Maestracci • Renucci*

VIN DE CORSE COTEAUX DU CAP CORSE AOC

A subappellation of Vin de Corse, this requires the same varieties, except that Codivarta may be used with Ugni Blanc in support of Vermentino.

VIN DE CORSE FIGARI AOC

Situated between Sartène and Porto Vecchio, Vin de Corse Figari is a subappellation of Vin de Corse AOC and requires the same grape varieties and technical level.

✓ *de Petra Bianca* (Vinti Legna)

VIN DE CORSE PORTO VECCHIO AOC

The southeastern edge of Corsica, around Porto Vecchio, is a subappellation of Vin de Corse AOC and requires the same grape varieties and technical level.

VIN DE CORSE SARTENE AOC

South of Ajaccio, this subappellation of Vin de Corse AOC requires the same grape varieties and conforms to the same technical level.

✓ *Clos d'Alzeto • Saparale*

VINS DE PAYS

This category of wine includes some of the most innovative and exciting wines being produced in the world today, yet most of the 153 vin de pays *denominations are superfluous and confusing. The success of the* vin de pays *system lies not in creating more appellations, but in freeing producers from them, which allows the most talented individuals to carve out their own reputations.*

VINS DE PAYS, OR "COUNTRY WINES," are supposed to be unpretentious, but many are better than average-quality AOC wines and the best rank as some of the finest wines that France can produce. This was never the intention; a *vin de pays* was merely meant to be a quaffing wine that should display, in a very rudimentary sense, the broadest characteristics of its region's greatest wines. However, because of this modest aim, *vin de pays* had fewer restrictions than higher appellations. This encouraged the more creative winemakers to produce wines that best expressed their *terroir* without being hampered by an overregulated AOC system and, in so doing, they managed to equal and occasionally surpass the quality of the more famous local appellations. As news of these exciting *vins de pays* hit the headlines of the international wine press, so the thought of shedding the shackles of AOC restrictions attracted a new generation of winemakers, including a number of Australians. The combination of French and foreign winemakers opened up the *vin de pays* system, turning it into something its creators had never imagined.

COUNTRY ORIGINS
The expression "Vin de Pays" first appeared in the statute books in a decree dated February 8, 1930. The law in question merely allowed wines to refer to their canton of origin provided they attained a certain alcoholic degree; for example "Vin de Pays de Canton X." These cantons were not controlled appellations as such: there was no way of

enforcing a minimum standard of quality, and the relatively small amounts of these so-called *vins de pays* were often the product of inferior hybrid grapes. It was not until 1973 that the concept was officially born of *vins de pays* that were a superior breed of *vins de table*, originating from a defined area and subject to strict controls. By 1976, a total of 75 *vins de pays* had been established, but all the formalities were not worked out until 1979, and between 1981 and 1982 every single existing *vin de pays* was redefined and another 20 created. Currently there are 153, although the number fluctuates as *vins de pays* are upgraded to VDQS, when new *vins de pays* are created, or, as has happened recently, when some *départements* are denied the right to produce a *vin de pays* (see Vins de Pays at a Glance, p.250).

Officially, a *vin de pays* is a *vin de table* from a specified area that conforms to quality-control laws that are very similar to those regulating AOC and VDQS wines, although obviously not quite as strict. *Vin de pays* came of age in 1989, prior to which all such wines had to carry the additional descriptor *Vin de Table Français* or *Vin de Table de France*. From time to time, *vins de pays* are upgraded to VDQS, which itself has become a staging post for AOC status. The last *vin de pays* to be promoted was Coteaux du Quercy, in 1999, which is now a VDQS, and others are expected to follow.

VARIETY IS THE SPICE OF LIFE FOR VIN DE PAYS
While the universally recognized great wines produced in the most famous regions of France remain, very much, in a cozy market of their own, their volume in global terms is minute, and

DOMAINE DE LA BAUME
This property was made famous by BRL Hardy, one of Australia's largest wine companies. Believing the French had not exploited varietal wines and seeing an opening in the market for Australian-made French wines, Hardy purchased Domaine de la Baume on the outskirts of Béziers just in time for the 1990 harvest.

Vin de pays d'Oc

Département boundary

Zonal *Vin de pays* boundary

Regional boundary

0   10   20   30   40 miles
0   20   40   60 km

VIN DE PAYS, MAP A,
see also p.249 (opposite)
Languedoc-Roussillon encompasses the greatest concentration of zonal vins de pays *and is dominated by the regional* Vin de Pays d'Oc, *by far the most successful* vin de pays.

the average-quality AOC wines have been losing the export battle against the New World, particularly "Brand Australia." It was left to the up-and-coming *vins de pays* to fight a rear-guard action, while the AOC regions sort out their problems of perennial mediocrity (if indeed they can). However, even with fewer restrictions than AOCs, *vins de pays* have had to fight with one hand behind their back. The first and most important disadvantage was that *vins de pays* were marketing wines under names such as Coteaux du Littoral Audois or Comté Tolosan, while the opposition was simply selling Chardonnay or Cabernet Sauvignon. While

the varietal concept might cause a "sense of place" crisis for the New World's finer wines, when they try to ride the export surf into Europe, it matters not one bit in the US, and the *vins de pays* are not up against such wines. At the price point of most *vins de pays* and their New World opponents, the appellation *per se* is irrelevant. All readers of this encyclopedia will drink such wines, and delight in searching out those that are the best and most interesting, but the vast majority of consumers do not know or even care about appellations. They see

VIN DE PAYS, MAP B,
see also p.248 (opposite)
This map shows all the regional and départemental vins de pays, plus those zonal appellations that are situated beyond the boundaries of the Languedoc-Roussillon region.

Vins de pays du Jardin de la France

Vin de pays du Comté Tolosan

Vin de pays d'Oc

Vin de pays Comtés Rhodaniens

Port de Méditerranée

Regional boundary
Sub-regional *Vins de pays* boundary
Département Vins de pays boundary
Zonal *Vin de pays* boundary
Sub-zonal *Vins de pays* boundary

VINS DE PAYS AT A GLANCE

153 VIN DE PAYS DENOMINATIONS IN TOTAL
Or 167 if the subregional and subzonal *vins de pays* are included. From virtually zero production in 1973 to an annual average of almost 166 million cases (15 million hectoliters), *vins de pays* now represent over 30 percent of the total French wine production, and this expansion is continuing.

TYPES OF VINS DE PAYS
There are three basic categories of *vins de pays*: regional, *départementale*, and zonal. Although no official quality differences exist between these, it is not an unreasonable assumption that the zonal *vins de pays* may sometimes show more individual character than the much larger *vins de pays départementaux* or all-encompassing regional *vins de pays*, but this is not always so.

A grower within a specific zone may find it easier to sell wine under a more generic *vin de pays*, which explains why so many individual wines are to be found under the vast Vin de Pays d'Oc denomination. Also, the geographical size of a *vin de pays* can be deceptive, with many *départements* producing relatively little wine compared with some more prolific, relatively minute, zonal *vins de pays*. In the Loire few producers bother with the *départementale* denominations.

REGIONAL VINS DE PAYS (45 percent of total *vin de pays* output)
There are five of these wide-ranging appellations: Comté Tolosan; Comtés Rhodaniens; Jardin de la France (which includes a further two subregional denominations); Oc; and Portes de Méditerranée. Each encompasses two or more *départements*. They represented only 12 percent of *vin de pays* production in 1990, yet Vin de Pays d'Oc alone accounts for 26 percent today.

DÉPARTEMENTALE VINS DE PAYS (28 percent of total *vin de pays* output)
These cover entire *départements*, and although 52 are officially in use, some are effectively redundant as producers have opted for one of the more widely supported regional appellations, which are often easier to promote. In theory every *département* in France can claim a

vin de pays under its own *départementale* denomination, but to avoid confusion with AOC wines the following were in 1995 expressly forbidden from exercising this right: the Marne and Aube (in Champagne), the Bas-Rhin and Haut-Rhin (in Alsace), the Côte-d'Or (in Burgundy), and the Rhône (which encompasses Beaujolais but is likely to cause confusion with the Côtes du Rhône AOC). Jura, Savoie, and Haut-Savoie have also been disenfranchised.

ZONAL VINS DE PAYS (27 percent of total *vin de pays* production)
There are now 96 zonal *vins de pays*, plus 12 subzonal denominations, although many of the former and some of the latter are seldom encountered.

VINS DE CÉPAGE
After a widespread authorization of pure varietal *vins de pays* in 2000, regulations for which lagged well behind the actual production, this category has taken off to such an extent that it now accounts for half of all the *vins de pays* produced each year, with 80 percent sold under one of five regional *vins de pays*, of which 70 percent is Vin de Pays d'Oc.

VINS DE PAYS PRIMEUR
Since 1990, all *vin de pays* denominations have been permitted to produce these wines, which may be marketed from the third Thursday of October following the harvest (much earlier than Beaujolais Nouveau). The regulations allow for red and white wines to be made as *vins primeurs*, but strangely not rosé, although by the very nature of their production many reds are lighter than some rosés, so it is a somewhat moot point. White wines are vinified by cool-fermentation techniques and red wines by one of three methods: *macération carbonique* (see Glossary), part-*macération carbonique* (some of the grapes are crushed and mixed with the whole bunches), and "short-classic" (traditional vinification with minimum skin contact). Cool-fermented whites and *macération carbonique* reds are dominated by amylic aromas (pear drops, banana, nail polish). "Short-classic" rarely provides enough fruit, depth, or color, whereas part-*macération carbonique* can be very successful in enhancing the fruitiness of a wine without drowning it in amylic aromas, but it has to be expertly applied.

74.2%

10.2%

15.6%

Chardonnay on two or three bottles, and grab one. Why? Probably because they have had it before, and it was okay, or for no other reason than the label looks nicer than the others—but the reason is immaterial. What is important is that in making their choice, they—that is, the vast majority—have gone straight past the Coteaux du Littoral Audois *et al.*

This is the old story of customers proclaiming, "I don't want Chablis, I want Chardonnay," and the French authorities have agonized about how to get around the problem. The French being French could not bring themselves to allow *vins de pays* to be sold as pure varietal wines. Instead, in 1996, they tried to divert consumer attention from single-varietal names with the twin-varietal concept, enabling producers to market wines as Cabernet-Merlot, Chardonnay-Sémillon, and so on. Although some very good wines were produced, the idea never really took off. It is fine in a New World country, where the varietal wine concept is all, and a twin-varietal is simply seen as a logical move, but for the *vins de pays* it was like learning to run before they could walk.

The French realized this, and in 2000 issued wide-sweeping decrees authorizing varietal wines for almost all *vins de pays*. It was still an unfair fight because the regulations insisted that such wines be made from 100 percent of the variety indicated, whereas New World imports merely had to comply with the European Union minimum of 85 percent. At the price point of most *vins de pays* and New World varietals, the flexibility to strengthen or soften a variety to one degree or another in a given year is a major advantage. Another advantage the opposition had was to use oak chips. It is one thing to expect a *cru classé* château to use casks rather than chips (although I cannot see why it actually has to be illegal), but it is impossible for *vins de pays* to compete at the same price as the New World wines if the French have to use oak casks or nothing. With casks, they cannot even get the wine on

the shelf at the same time, let alone the same price. Fortunately, Hervé Gaymard, the French Minister of Agriculture, finally agreed that it was unfair, and in July 2004 authorized producers to use oak chips and to blend up to 15 percent of another variety and vintage into a single-varietal *vin de pays*.

VIN DE PAYS DES CÉPAGES DE FRANCE

At the same meeting, one thing that Gaymard refused to authorize was the proposed Vin de Pays des Cépages de France. The faction proposing this have only themselves to blame. Cross-regional blending is a good idea; the error was simply in the naming of the *vin de pays*, which doomed it to failure from the start. Those who objected in principle to cross-regional blending, including a number of UK shippers, claimed that it would "almost certainly become a dumping ground, especially in the current climate of oversupply." That was part of the attraction, from my viewpoint. How else do the classic AOC regions raise the quality of their most basic wines without some form of selection, i.e. dumping, of lesser quality wines? Furthermore, wines might be "dumped" by Bordeaux for different, sometimes opposite, reasons from the Rhône or Roussillon, and blending the two, together with wines from nonclassic areas, could produce something superior to its individual parts. And even when it does not, the shippers have nothing to fear because no one is making them buy the wines.

Where the cross-regional *vin de pays* went wrong was in naming it Vin de Pays des Cépages de France, sourcing the wine from anywhere in France, and expecting European Union legislation to be modified to allow this through. All they had to do was to draw a line from Vannes on the west coast to Roubaix on the Belgian border, name the wine Vin de Pays des Cépages de Sud-Est France (deliberate shades of southeastern Australia), and it would have been passed without anyone blinking an eye.

THE VINS DE PAYS OF
FRANCE

AGENAIS
Zonal *vin de pays* Map B, No.1

These red, white, and rosé wines are produced from a combination of classic *bordelais* grapes and some rustic regional varieties, including the Tannat and Fer. Although more than three-quarters of the output is red, it is the rosé made primarily from Abouriou that is best known.

✓ *de Cazeaux* (Tradition)

AIGUES
Zonal *vin de pays* Map A, No.2

Created as recently as 1993, this *vin de pays* roughly corresponds to the Coteaux du Lubéron, and has a similar range of grape varieties.

AIN
Départementale *vin de pays* Map B

This *départementale vin de pays* encompasses unclassified vineyards in southern Burgundy, and has relatively recently come into usage, but the level of production remains insignificant. Pure varietal wines have been allowed since 2000.

✓ *Jean-Christophe Pellerin* (Chardonnay Cep d'Argent)

ALLIER
Départementale *vin de pays* Map B

Relatively recent *départementale vin de pays* for red and rosé wines, primarily from Cabernet Franc, Cabernet Sauvignon, Gamay, and Grolleau, but also Abouriou, Pinot d'Aunis, and Pinot Noir. Whites primarily from Chardonnay, Chenin Blanc, and Sauvignon Blanc, but also Arbois, Folle Blanche, Grolleau Gris, Melon de Bourgogne, and Pinot Blanc. Pure varietal wines have been allowed since 2000.

ALLOBROGIE
Zonal *vin de pays* Map B, No.3

This is the *vin de pays* equivalent of the Vin de Savoie, although it extends beyond the borders of that AOC into cattle country, where the existence of vines is very sporadic. The wines are similar to Vin de Savoie, if somewhat lighter and more rustic in style. Almost 90 percent of production is white, made primarily from Jacquère, Chardonnay, and Chasselas, although Altesse, Mondeuse Blanche, Roussanne, and Molette can also be used. The balance of the production is essentially red and may be made from Gamay, Mondeuse, and Pinot Noir, with rosé accounting for less than 1 percent. Pure varietal wines have been allowed since 2000.

✓ *Demeure-Penet* (Jacquère)

ALPES DE HAUTE-PROVENCE
Départementale *vin de pays* Map B

Most of these wines come from the Durance Valley in the east of the *département*. Production is mostly red, made from Carignan, Grenache, Cinsault, Cabernet Sauvignon, Merlot, and Syrah. Rosé accounts for 15 percent and white made from Ugni Blanc, Clairette, Chardonnay, and Muscat for just 7 percent. Pure varietal wines have been allowed since 2000.

✓ *La Madeleine* (Cabernet Sauvignon) • *de Régusse* (Muscat Moelleux, Pinot Noir Elevé en Fûts de Chêne)

ALPES-MARITIMES
Départementale *vin de pays* Map B

Some 70 percent of production is red and 30 percent rosé, made from Carignan, Cinsault, Grenache, Ugni Blanc, and Vermentino grapes, mostly from the communes of Carros, Mandelieu, and Mougins. White wines may also be produced. Pure varietal wines have been allowed since 2000.

✓ *de Toasc* (Lou Vin d'Aqui)

ARDÈCHE
Départementale *vin de pays* Map B

Red and white wines, from a range of Rhône and *bordelais* grapes, are produced on a limited scale. Pure varietal wines have been allowed since 2000.

✓ *de Champal* (Viognier Arzelle)

ARGENS
Zonal *vin de pays* Map A, No.4

This denomination covers part of the Côtes de Provence and almost half the wines are rosé of a similar style and quality to those of the Vin de Pays du Var. Half the production is red, which is rich, tannic, and spicy, made from Carignan, Cinsault, Syrah, Roussanne du Var, Mourvèdre, and Cabernet Sauvignon. A little white is also produced.

ARIÈGE
Départementale *vin de pays* Map B

Recent *départementale vin de pays* with a small production of red, white, and rosé wine, Ariège is in the very south of France, at the foot of the Pyrenees, overlapping the notional borders of Southwest France and Languedoc-Roussillon. Pure varietal wines have been allowed since 2000.

AUDE
Départementale *vin de pays* Map B

Although still the second or third largest *vin de pays*, this used to boast almost exactly the same output as Vin de Pays d'Oc in 1993, but while the production of the latter appellation has more than tripled, Vin de Pays de L'Aude has virtually stood still. Nevertheless, a lot of fresh and fruity wine is made here, most of which is red, with just 5 percent each of rosé and white. Mediterranean grape varieties dominate. Pure varietal wines have been allowed since 2000.

✓ *de La Bouysse* ❸ (Merlot) • *de Fontannelles* (Poête Renaissance)

AVEYRON
Départementale *vin de pays* Map B

Since most of the wines produced in this *département*, which is situated between Cahors and Hérault, used to claim the Vin de Pays des Gorges et Côtes de Millau (now Côtes de Millau VDQS) appellation, it will be interesting to see how many *vin de pays* producers utilize this denomination or prefer to use the wider Comté Tolosan appellation. Pure varietal wines have been allowed since 2000.

BALMES DAUPHINOISES
Zonal *vin de pays* Map B, No.5

In the denomination of Balmes Dauphinoises, dry white, made from Jacquère and Chardonnay, accounts for 60 percent of production, and red, made from Gamay and Pinot Noir, accounts for 40 percent. Rosé may also be produced.

BÉNOVIE
Zonal *vin de pays* Map A, No.6

This denomination is located at the eastern extremity of the Coteaux du Languedoc and overlaps part of the Muscat-de-Lunel area. Almost 80 percent of the production is a light, fruity red, made predominantly from Carignan, Grenache, Cinsault, and Syrah, although Merlot and Cabernet Sauvignon may also be used. A fair amount of attractive rosé is made, mostly by the *saignée* method, plus a small quantity of Ugni Blanc-based dry white. Pure varietal wines have been allowed since 2000.

✓ *des Hospitaliers* (Merlot)

BÉRANGE
Zonal *vin de pays* Map A, No.7

Production in Bérange is 75 percent red, 20 percent rosé, and 5 percent white, made from a range of grape varieties very similar to those used in the Coteaux du Languedoc and neighboring Bénovie.

BESSAN
Zonal *vin de pays* Map A, No.8

This tiny, single-village denomination just east of Béziers is best known for its dry, aromatic rosé, which now accounts for 65 percent of production. Just 10 percent red is made, with simple Ugni Blanc-based white accounting for the balance.

BIGORRE
Zonal *vin de pays* Map B, No.9

Mostly full, rich, Madiran-type red wine is made here, plus a little good crisp, dry white. Rosé may also be produced.

BOUCHES-DU-RHÔNE
Départementale vin de pays Map B

This denomination has one of the largest *vin de pays* productions in the country, some 80 percent of which is red and most of that comes from the Coteaux d'Aix-en-Provence area. These wines are warm, spicy, and often quite powerfully structured from Carignan, Grenache, Cinsault, Cabernet Sauvignon, Merlot, and Syrah. The production of rosé is just 12 percent, which is a reasonable proportion for the style, and also in view of the absence of the mystique of a name (it cannot have Provence on the label). The quality is invariably much better than most of the AOC rosé from this area. A little white is also made from Ugni Blanc, Clairette, Bourboulenc, Vermentino, Chardonnay, and Chasan (a slightly aromatic Listan and Chardonnay cross). Domaine de Trévallon is not only the finest wine of the appellation, but one of the greatest *vins de pays*, producing a quality easily equal to some of best *crus classés* of Bordeaux. Pure varietal wines have been allowed since 2000.

✓ *Hauvette* ◉ • *de l'Île St.-Pierre* (Chardonnay) • *La Michelle* (Rouge) • *Jean-Paul Luc* (Minna Vineyard Rouge) • *de Trévallon*

BOURBONNAIS
Zonal vin de pays Map B, No.10

This is a rarely seen *vin de pays* from a white-only area of unclassified vines in the Loire Valley.

CALVADOS
Départementale vin de pays Map B

Growers are legally entitled to produce a *vin de pays* named after the *département* in which the vines are located, but after all the fuss about *départementale* names that could be construed to come from a classic wine region, it is surprising to see Calvados approved. Although a *départementale vin de pays*, the area of vines is very small, located at Grisy, west of St. Pierre-sur-Dives. The wines are varietal (Auxerrois, Pinot Gris, Melon, and Müller-Thurgau) made by Gérard Samson under the Arpents du Soleil label. Pure varietal wines have been allowed since 2000.

CASSAN
Zonal vin de pays Map A, No.11

This area is in the Coteaux du Languedoc north of Béziers and overlaps part of Faugères. Almost three-quarters of the wine is red and full bodied, from Carignan, Cinsault, Grenache, Cabernet Sauvignon, Merlot, and Syrah. The balance is split between a well-flavored rosé and a crisp, dry white made primarily from Ugni Blanc, although Clairette and Terret may also be used. Since 2000, however, it has been permissible to market wines as pure varietals, without any specification in the new regulation as to what those varieties may be, hence the Tempranillo below.

✓ *de La Tour Penedesses* (Tempranillo Mas de Couy Elevé en Fûts de Chêne)

CATHARE
Zonal vin de pays Map A, No.12

This area overlapping the Aude and Ariège *départements* was made a *vin de pays* in 2001. Red wines are made from the following: Merlot, Cabernet Franc, Cabernet Sauvignon, and Merlot, one or more of which must represent 50 to 70 percent of the entire blend, plus at least two of the following must account for 30

to 50 percent: Arinarnoa, Caladoc, Carignan, Cinsaut, Chenanson, Eiodola, Grenache, Malbec, Marselan, Pinot Noir, Pinot Gris, Pinot Blanc, Portan, and Syrah. For white wine, there should be 60 to 80 percent of Chardonnay and/or Sauvignon Blanc, plus 20 to 40 percent Bourboulenc, Chasan, Chenin Blanc, Grenache, Grenache Blanc, Macabéo, Marsanne, Mauzac, Roussanne, Sémillon, Ugni Blanc, Vermentino, and Viognier. Rosé is made from Merlot, Cabernet Franc, Cabernet Sauvignon, and Syrah, one or more of which must represent 50 to 70 percent of the entire blend, plus one or more of the following, which must account for 30 to 50 percent: Caladoc, Cinsaut, Chanson, Grenache, and Portan.

✓ *de Sautes* (Signature Cathare)

CAUX
Zonal vin de pays Map A, No.13

This *vin de pays* produces a good, typical dry and fruity rosé in a Languedoc style from vines growing north of Béziers. Some 40 percent of the output is red, and a little white and rosé are also made. Pure varietal wines have been allowed since 2000.

✓ *Causses de Nizzas* (Carignan Vieilles Vignes)

CESSENON
Zonal vin de pays Map A, No.14

This appellation produces red wines of a rustic St.-Chinian style, plus a little rosé.

CÉVENNES
Zonal vin de pays Map A, No.15

This new appellation is an amalgamation of four former *vins de pays*, now subzones: Coteaux Cévenols (15a), Coteaux du Salavès (15b), Côtes du Libac (15c—originally Serre du Coiran), Mont Bouquet (15d), and Uzège (15e), each of which may add its subzonal name to the Vin de Pays des Cévennes. Most of the wines are red; 15 percent are rosé, with *saignée* rosé a specialty. Pure varietal wines have been allowed since 2000. Very small quantities of white *vin primeur* are also produced. Production is mostly of an honest, fruity Languedoc style. Pure varietal wines have been allowed since 2000.

✓ *Clos de La Roque* (Pinot Noir)

CHARENTAIS
Zonal vin de pays Map B, No.16

The dry white wines are really good, even though 50 percent of the grapes used are Ugni Blanc. It seems that this lowly variety and, indeed, the Colombard make light but very fresh, crisp, and tangy wine in the Charente, which is not only well suited to distilling Cognac, but makes a cheap, cheerful, quaffable wine. Some red and rosé wines from Gamay and *bordelais* grapes are also made. The following subzonal areas are allowed to add their names to Vin de Pays Charentais: Île d'Oléron (16a), Île de Ré (16b), and Saint Sornin (16c). Pure varietal wines have been allowed since 2000.

✓ *de La Chauvillière* (Chardonnay) • *Gardrat* (Colombard) • *Chai du Roussoir* (Cabernet Terroir de Fossiles) • *Terra Sana*

CHARENTE
Départementale vin de pays Map B

Hardly used *départementale vin de pays*, most producers preferring the wider-known Vin de

Pays Charentais. Pure varietal wines have been allowed since 2000.

CHARENTE-MARITIMES
Départementale vin de pays Map B

Hardly used *départementale vin de pays*, most producers preferring the wider-known Vin de Pays Charentais. Pure varietal wines have been allowed since 2000.

CHER
Départementale vin de pays Map B

Mostly Touraine-like, Gamay-based red wine, plus a small amount of dry rosé in a light *vin gris* style. Since 1997, an increasing amount of dry white Sauvignon Blanc has been made by the cooperative at Venesmes, which makes a wine comparable to a rustic Sancerre or Menetou-Salon. Pure varietal wines have been allowed since 2000.

CILAOS
Zonal vin de pays Map B, No.17

The most remote of all French wines, the Vin de Pays de Cilaos was created in January 2004 for vines growing on the island of Réunion, a French protectorate in the Indian Ocean, 420 miles (680 kilometers) east of Madagascar. Grape varieties already grown include Chenin Blanc, Pinot Noir, and Malbec, with plans to plant Gros Manseng, Pinotage, Syrah, and Verdelho. The styles produced are red, white, rosé, and, because the tendency is for grapes to overripen rather too easily, *moelleux*. The only wine producer currently is the local cooperative, which in January 2004 harvested 28 tons of grapes. "Cilaos" means "the place you never leave."

CITÉ DE CARCASSONNE
Zonal vin de pays Map A, No.18

Red wines account for over 90 percent of production, rosé 5 percent, and white wine barely 1 percent. The wines come from 11 communes around Carcassonne. Pure varietal wines have been allowed since 2000. If blended, red and rosé wines must include at least 20 percent of one or more of the following: Cabernet Franc, Cabernet Sauvignon, Malbec, Merlot, Pinot Noir, and Syrah, plus a maximum of 40 percent Alicante Bouschet, Arinarnoa, Caladoc, Carignan, Chenanson, Cinsaut, Egiodola, Grenache, Marselan, and Portan. Red *vin de primeur* is restricted to Chenanson, Cinsaut, Merlot, Portan, and Syrah. White wine blends may be made from any of the following: Bourboulenc, Carignan Blanc, Chardonnay, Chasan, Chenin Blanc, Clairette, Colombard, Grenache Blanc, Macabéo, Marsanne, Mauzac, Muscat d'Alexandrie, Muscat à Petits Grains Blanc, Picpoul, Roussanne, Sauvignon Blanc, Sémillon, Terret, Turbat, Ugni Blanc, and Viognier.

✓ *Auzias*

COLLINES DE LA MOURE
Zonal vin de pays Map A, No.19

More than 80 percent of production is basic red, made from a choice of Carignan, Cinsault, Grenache, Syrah, Cabernet Sauvignon, and Merlot, the last two of which are often vinified separately. A light, dry rosé accounts for about 15 percent of production, but very little white is made and it is mostly from Ugni Blanc. Although late-harvest rather than a *vin doux naturel*, it should still come as no surprise that this *vin de pays* denomination roughly corresponds to the AOCs Muscat de Mireval and Muscat de Frontignan.

✓ *Montlobre* (La Chapelle) • *de Mujolan* (Mas de Mante Vertige)

COLLINES RHODANIENNES
Zonal *vin de pays* Map B, No.20

A large denomination at the center of Comtés Rhodaniens, this *vin de pays* straddles five *départements* (Rhône, Isère, Drôme, Ardèche, and Loire) and produces primarily red wines from Gamay, Syrah, Merlot, and Pinot Noir. Some extremely small quantities are made of rosé and white, the latter coming from an interesting choice of Chardonnay, Marsanne, Roussanne, Viognier, Jacquère, Aligoté, and Clairette. With the range of body, fatness, aromatic complexity, and acidity that a successful blend of these varieties could bring, there is ample scope for Collines Rhodaniennes to develop a first-rate reputation for white wines. Pure varietal wines have been allowed since 2000.

✓ *Cuilleron-Gaillard-Villard* (Sotanum) • *François Villard* (Syrah)

COMTÉ DE GRIGNAN
Zonal *vin de pays* Map B, No.21

Virtually all the production of Comté de Grignan is red and most of that Grenache-dominated, although Syrah, Cinsault, Gamay, Carignan, Merlot, and Cabernet Sauvignon are also allowed. Rosé accounts for just 1 percent, and white is virtually nonexistent.

COMTÉ TOLOSAN
Regional *vin de pays* Map B

Modest quantities of mostly red wines are produced, with some rosé and a tiny amount of white (of which Daubert and Ribonnet stand out). The white wines should be made from the same grape varieties permitted for Armagnac (Blanc Dame, Colombard, Folle Blanche, Graisse, Jurançon Blanc, Mauzac, Mauzac Rosé, Meslier St.-François, Ugni Blanc, and until 2010 Baco Blanc). Red wine grapes are not specified beyond "what is growing"! Certainly the white wines are the most successful. Domaine de Ribonnet makes a very good stab at the Australian Chardonnay-Sauvignon Blanc style. Pure varietal wines have been allowed since 2004.

✓ *Baudave* (Rouge) • *François Daubert* (Madrigal sur le Mauzac) • *Plaimont* (Rive Haute Sauvignon Blanc) • *de Ribonnet*

COMTÉS RHODANIENS
Regional *vin de pays* Map B

Created in 1989, Comtés Rhodaniens encompasses eight *départements* and its name

can be given only to wines that have already qualified as a zonal *vin de pays*. It is the smallest of the five regional *vins de pays*, with just one-tenth of the production of the second-smallest regional *vin de pays* (Comté Tolosan), and a mere one-thousandth of the largest (Oc).

✓ *C. V. Ardechois*

CORRÈZE
Départementale vin de pays Map A

Mostly reds from Cabernet Franc, Merlot, and Gamay, grown on the stony, limestone *coteaux* of Branceilles, the vineyards of which flourished in the 19th century, but were restored as recently as the 1990s. Pure varietal wines have been allowed since 2000.

✓ *Mille et Une Pierre* (Elevé en Fûts de Chêne)

CÔTE VERMEILLE
Zonal *vin de pays* Map A, No.22

Mostly red and rosé, these wines are the *vin de pays* equivalent of Collioure, which in turn is the table-wine equivalent of Banyuls.

✓ *Vial Magnères*

COTEAUX DE L'ARDÈCHE
Zonal *vin de pays* Map B, No.23

This large denomination has a very significant output and is particularly well known for its dark, spicy red wine, which accounts for 80 percent of the total production. Often Syrah dominated, this wine may also include Cabernet Sauvignon, Carignan, Cinsault, Grenache, Gamay, and Merlot. Louis Latour's Chardonnay put this *vin de pays* on the map during the 1990s, and the same firm's stunning Pinot Noir is proving to be an even greater success. Just over 10 percent of this denomination's total output is rosé, and just under 10 percent is white, the latter made from Bourboulenc, Marsanne, Viognier, Roussanne, Marsanne, Sauvignon Blanc, and Ugni Blanc. About 30 percent of all wines produced are sold as pure varietal.

✓ *C. V. Ardechois* • *de Bournet* (Chris) • *Mas d'Intras* • *Louis Latour* • *des Louanes* (L'Encre de Sy)

COTEAUX AUXOIS
Zonal *vin de pays* Map B, No.24

This zonal *vin de pays* has replaced the *départementale* denomination Côte d'Or (which some growers want to utilize for a new AOC), and may produce red and rosé wines from one or more of Gamay, Pinot Gris, and Pinot Noir; while white wines are made from one or more of Aligoté, Auxerrois, Chardonnay, Pinot Gris, Melon de Bourgogne, Sauvignon Blanc, and Sauvignon Gris.

✓ *C. V. de Flavigny* (Chardonnay Fûts de Chêne)

COTEAUX DES BARONNIES
Zonal *vin de pays* Map B, No.25

Almost 90 percent of Coteaux des Baronnies wines are red and almost 10 percent rosé, made from Cabernet Sauvignon, Cinsault, Syrah, Grenache, Pinot Noir, Gamay, and Merlot. Less than 2 percent is white, with varietal wines generally increasing. Pure varietal wines have been allowed since 2000.

✓ *du Rieu Frais* (Cabernet Sauvignon) • *La Rosière* (Merlot)

COTEAUX DE BESSILLES
Zonal *vin de pays* Map A, No.26

Fresh, light, rustic-style wines from the Coteaux du Languedoc immediately north of Pinet. Production is two-thirds red, one-quarter rosé, and the balance white. Pure varietal wines have been allowed since 2000.

✓ *St.-Hilaire* (Vermentino)

COTEAUX DE LA CABRERISSE
Zonal *vin de pays* Map A, No.27

Mostly red wine, as might be expected from what is after all the heart of Corbières, with 10 percent rosé and just 3 percent white, including some *vins primeurs*. There is a wide range of grape varieties permitted, particularly for the red, which may be made from Carignan, Grenache, Cinsault, Syrah, Mourvèdre, Terret Noir, Cabernet Sauvignon, Cabernet Franc, Merlot, and the Teinturier grape Alicante Bouschet. White grapes include Terret, Grenache Blanc, Clairette, Ugni Blanc, and Macabéo.

COTEAUX DE CEZE
Zonal *vin de pays* Map A, No.28

This is a large denomination with a modest output of roughly 80 percent red and 20 percent rosé, with a minuscule amount of white.

COTEAUX CHARITOIS
Zonal *vin de pays* Map B, No.29

Basic white wines and light reds (Pinot Noir) from the Loire Valley.

✓ *du Puits de Compostelle* (Pinot Noir Elevé en Fûts de Chêne)

COTEAUX DU CHER ET DE L'ARNON
Zonal *vin de pays* Map B, No.29

The reds and *vin gris* are made from Gamay, and dry white from Sauvignon Blanc.

COTEAUX DE COIFFY
Zonal *vin de pays* Map A, No.31

A relatively new and as yet untested *vin de pays* from way up north, between Champagne and Alsace, in the southeastern corner of the Haute-Marne *département*. Red and rosé from Gamay and Pinot Noir; whites from Aligoté, Arbane, Auxerrois, Chardonnay, Pinot Blanc, Pinot Gris, and Petit Meslier. Pure varietal wines have been allowed since 2001.

✓ *C. V. les Coteaux de Coiffy* (Auxerrois)

COTEAUX D'ENSÉRUNE
Zonal *vin de pays* Map A, No.31

This *vin de pays* west of Béziers used to produce two-thirds red and one-third rosé, but red wines now account for almost 90 percent of the output, made from a typical range of Languedoc grapes. Just 10 percent rosé is produced, but hardly any white. However, Jeanjean makes a nice, soft, fruity dry white from Ugni Blanc, Marsanne, and Chardonnay.

✓ *Jeanjean*

COTEAUX FLAVIENS
Zonal *vin de pays* Map A, No.33

From hills named after the Roman Emperor Flavius, this *vin de pays* just south of Nîmes in the Costières de Nîmes produces a full, warm-hearted red which accounts for 85 percent of the output. Most of the rest is rosé, and just a small amount of white is made. Carignan, Grenache, Cinsault, Cabernet Sauvignon, Merlot, and Syrah are the main grape varieties used.

COTEAUX DE FONTCAUDE
Zonal *vin de pays* Map A, No.34

This area overlaps much of Saint-Chinian in the eastern section of the Coteaux du Languedoc. Almost 80 percent of the wines are red, and these are made in a light, fresh but interesting style from Carignan, Cinsault, Grenache, Cabernet Sauvignon, and Syrah. Rosé and a little white are also to be found.

COTEAUX DE GLANES
Zonal *vin de pays* Map B, No.35

This appellation produces mainly red wines, which are Gamay or Merlot dominated, plus a little rosé.

COTEAUX DU GRÉSIVAUDAN
Zonal *vin de pays* Map B, No.36

Red and rosé Savoie-style wines made from Gamay, Pinot, and Etraire de la Dui (a local grape variety), and Jacquère-based dry whites.

COTEAUX DE LAURENS
Zonal *vin de pays* Map A, No.37

Some 85 percent of these wines are a red *vin de pays* equivalent of Faugères, made mostly from Carignan, Cinsault, Syrah, and Grenache, but some of the better wines also include Cabernet Sauvignon and Merlot. A small amount of rosé and even less white is made.

✓ *de La Commanderie de St.-Jean*

COTEAUX DU LIBRON
Zonal *vin de pays* Map A, No.38

Situated around Béziers itself, this *vin de pays* produces mainly red wines, made from Carignan, Grenache, Cinsault, Cabernet Sauvignon, Merlot, and Syrah. Some 12 percent of the output is rosé, and less than 7 percent white, the latter being made mainly from Ugni Blanc, with a touch of Terret and Clairette. Pure varietal wines have been allowed since 2000.

✓ *de la Colombette* • *de Pierre-Belle* (Réserve)

COTEAUX DU LITTORAL AUDOIS
Zonal *vin de pays* Map A, No.39

This area corresponds geographically to the unofficial Sigean zone of Corbières, where Syrah performs best and is used, not surprisingly, in many of these *vins de pays*, of which red wine accounts for no less than 98 percent of the total output. Other black grape varieties permitted include Carignan, Grenache, Cinsault, Merlot, and Cabernet Sauvignon. Minuscule amounts of rosé and white are produced; the latter is made mainly from Grenache Blanc and Macabéo, but can also include Ugni Blanc, Terret, and Clairette.

COTEAUX DE MIRAMONT
Zonal *vin de pays* Map A, No.40

Red wines from a typically Mediterranean range of *bordelais* and southern-Rhône grapes dominate this denomination, which bridges the Côtes de La Malepère and Corbières. Rosé and white together account for less than 5 percent of output, including some *vins primeurs*.

✓ *Foncalieu*

COTEAUX DE MONTÉLIMAR
New zonal *vin de pays* Map B, No.41

This *vin de pays* was established in September 2004, and encompasses vineyards between Montélimar and Dieulefit in the Drôme *département*, just north of the Coteaux de Tricastin AOC. Pure varietal wines are allowed. Red and rosé must be made from one or more of the following: Cabernet Sauvignon, Carignan, Cinsault, Gamay, Grenache, Marselan, Merlot, Pinot Noir, and Syrah. White wines from one or more of Chardonnay, Clairette, Grenache Blanc, Marsanne, Muscat à Petits Grains, Roussanne, Sauvignon Blanc, and Viognier.

COTEAUX DE MURVIEL
Zonal *vin de pays* Map A, No.42

Just next to the Saint-Chinian area, this *vin de pays* produces some very good reds, which account for 85 percent of the output, made from Carignan, Cinsault, Grenache, Cabernet Sauvignon, Merlot, and Syrah. There are a number of rosés, but very few whites.

✓ *de Ciffre* (Val Taurou) • *de Ravanès* (Les Gravières du Taurou Grande Réserve)

COTEAUX DE NARBONNE
Zonal *vin de pays* Map A, No.43

Mostly soft red wines, and just 4 percent in total of white and rosé, come from this coastal edge of Corbières where the vines overlap with those of Coteaux du Languedoc.

✓ *Hospitalet*

COTEAUX DE PEYRIAC
Zonal *vin de pays* Map A, No.44

Full and rustic red wines, made from local grape varieties augmented by the Syrah, Cabernet, and Merlot, account for more than 80 percent of the production of this *vin de pays* in the heart of Minervois. The remainder is mostly rosé, with less than 1 percent white.

COTEAUX DU PONT DU GARD
Zonal *vin de pays* Map A, No.45

The Pont du Gard is a stunningly beautiful, three-tier Roman aqueduct from the 1st century BCE. Its bottom tier is still strong enough to support modern traffic 2,000 years later, but the wines of Coteaux du Pont du Gard, though mostly rich and powerful reds, are built for a considerably shorter life span. A small amount of white and rosé is also produced, with *vins primeurs* a local specialty.

✓ *Mas de Forton* • *Leyris Mazière*

COTEAUX DU SALAGOU
Zonal *vin de pays* Map A, No.46

Production is 80 percent red and 20 percent rosé, from a range of typical Languedoc grapes.

COTEAUX DE TANNAY
Zonal *vin de pays* Map B, No.47

This relatively new *vin de pays* area east of Sancerre was created in 2001. White wines are made from Chardonnay or Melon de Bourgogne. Red and rosé come from Gamay and Pinot Noir, plus up to 20 percent of Gamay Teinturier de Bouze and Gamay de Chaudenay. Pure varietal wines are allowed.

✓ *Cyrille Raty* (Chardonnay)

COTEAUX ET TERRASSES DE MONTAUBAN
Zonal *vin de pays* Map B, No.48

Red and rosé wines from the Pays de La Garonne.

✓ *de Montels* (Louise)

COTEAUX DU VERDON
Zonal *vin de pays* Map B, No.49

This *vin de pays* in the northern hinterland of Côtes de Provence and Coteaux Varois was created as recently as 1992 and has no restriction on the grape varieties that may be used.

✓ *La Colline de Vignoble* (Merlot-Cabernet Sauvignon)

CÔTES DU BRIAN
Zonal *vin de pays* Map A, No.50

An area in Minervois, Côtes du Brian produces 90 percent red, from Carignan for the most part, although Grenache, Cinsault, Cabernet Sauvignon, Merlot, and Syrah may also be used. The balance of the production is principally rosé, with very few white wines. Pure varietal wines have been allowed since 2000.

CÔTES CATALANES
Zonal *vin de pays* Map A, No.51

Much enlarged following the absorption of and merger with the former *vins de pays* of Catalan, Coteaux de Fenouillèdes, and Vals d'Agly. This nonsensical exercise of bureaucratic expediency has angered many, not least those in the Coteaux de Fenouillèdes, who were just beginning to make a name for themselves when their *vin de pays* was suppressed in September 2003. Furthermore, the inhabitants of the Fenouillèdes are not Catalan, nor do they speak Catalan. Hopefully some sense and sensitivity will prevail. In the meantime, I list the best wines according to their old *vin de pays* below. Pure varietal wines have been allowed since 2000.

✓ **Coteaux de Fenouillèdes** *Gauby* ❸ (Le Soula), *Salvat* (Fenouil Rouge) • **Catalan** *Mas Baux* (Grenache Velours Rouge), *Mosse* ◉ (La Carignan) • **Côtes Catalanes** *Boudau* (Le Petit Clos Rosé, Muscat Sec), *Cazes Frères* ❸, *de Pézilla, Arnaud de Villeneuve* (Muscat Moelleux) • **Vals d'Agly** *des Chênes* ❸

CÔTES DU CÉRESSOU
Zonal *vin de pays* Map A, No.52

Typically light and fruity Languedoc wines are produced in fairly large amounts; 60 percent is red, 15 percent white, and 25 percent rosé.

CÔTES DU CONDOMOIS
Zonal *vin de pays* Map B, No.53

Production includes 60 percent red, dominated by the Tannat grape, and 40 percent white, from the Colombard or Ugni Blanc. A little rosé is also produced.

✓ *Plaimont* (Prestige du Condomois)

CÔTES DE GASCOGNE
Zonal *vin de pays* Map B, No.54

These deliciously tangy, dry white wines are the undistilled produce of Armagnac. Those made from the Colombard grape are the lightest, while those from the Ugni Blanc are fatter and more interesting. Manseng and Sauvignon Blanc are also used to good aromatic effect in some blends. Less than 20 percent of production is red and barely 1 percent rosé. Pure varietal wines have been allowed since 2000.

√ *Alain Brumont* (Les Menhirs) • *des Cassagnoles* (Gros Manseng Sélection) • *de Joy* (Sauvignon Gros Manseng) • *de Lartigue* • *Plaimont* • *du Tariquet* (Les Premières Gries)

CÔTES DE LASTOURS
Zonal *vin de pays* Map A, No.55

This area roughly corresponds to the Cabardès VDQS and produces mostly red wines from a similar range of grapes. Just 4 percent rosé and 3 percent white (Mauzac, Chenin, Chardonnay, and Ugni Blanc) is made, with *vins primeurs* a local specialty.

√ *Baron d'Ambres*

CÔTES DE MONTESTRUC
Zonal *vin de pays* Map B, No.56

Production includes reds, made from Alicante Bouschet, Cabernets, Malbec, Merlot, and Jurançon Noir, and white wines, made from the Colombard, Mauzac, and Ugni Blanc.

CÔTES DE PÉRIGNAN
Zonal *vin de pays* Map A, No.57

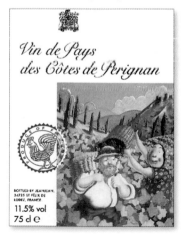

This area is within the southern extremity of the Coteaux du Languedoc, just north of La Clape AOC and incorporating some of La Clape's northern slopes. Almost 90 percent is red wine that is similar, if more rustic, in style to the wines of La Clape and made from a similar range of grape varieties, but with Grenache, Syrah, and Cinsault dominating. The fresh, dry rosé can be good quality and flavorsome too. Just 1 percent of white wine is made, mainly from Clairette and Ugni Blanc, but Terret and Macabéo are also permitted. *Vin primeur* is also made.

√ *de La Negly* (Palazy Rosé)

CÔTES DE PROUILLE
Zonal *vin de pays* Map A, No.58

These red, white, and rosé wines produced by the Côtes de Prouille appellation come from the Aude *département*.

CÔTES DU TARN
Zonal *vin de pays* Map B, No.59

Côtes du Tarn is the *vin de pays* equivalent of Gaillac: some 60 percent is red, 30 percent white, and the rest rosé. These wines are made from *bordelais* and southwestern grape varieties, plus, uniquely for France, the Portugais Bleu. Gamay is often used for Côtes du Tarn Primeur, while together with Syrah it makes an appealing, delicate *saignée* rosé. Pure varietal wines have been allowed since 2000.

√ *Guy Fontaine* (Les Vignes des Garbasses Syrah) • *Sabrelle* (Chardonnay)

CÔTES DE THAU
Zonal *vin de pays* Map A, No.60

A small denomination west of Béziers, producing almost equal quantities of red, white, and rosé from all the usual Languedoc varieties. These wines used to be used for vermouth until the upswing in *vin de pays*.

√ *de Marie-Anais* (Syrano)

CÔTES DE THONGUE
Zonal *vin de pays* Map A, No.61

Just south of Faugères, this appellation produces mostly red wine, from grapes including Grenache, Cinsault, Cabernet Sauvignon, Merlot, Syrah, and Carignan, with *vins primeurs* of the last three varieties a speciality. Emphasis is placed on pure varietal wines of all styles. Some 15 percent rosé and 10 percent white is also made in this up-and-coming *vin de pays*. Pure varietal wines have been allowed since 2000.

√ *C. V. d'Alignan du Vent* (Icare, Montarels) • *Clos de l'Arjolle* • *de la Croix Belle* (Cascaillou, No.7 Rouge) • *Deshenrys* (Lissac) • *Mont d'Hortes* (Sauvignon) • *Montplézy* (Félicité)

CÔTES DU VIDOURLE
Zonal *vin de pays* Map A, No.62

Wedged between the Coteaux du Languedoc and Costières de Nîmes, more than 80 percent of the wines produced are red, from Carignan, Grenache, Cinsault, Cabernet Sauvignon, Merlot, Cabernet Franc, and Syrah. About 15 percent rosé is made, but white is seldom seen.

CREUSE
Départementale vin de pays Map B

Recent, little-used *départementale vin de pays* right in the center of France. Red and rosé wines are made primarily from Cabernet Sauvignon, Cabernet Franc, Merlot, Tannat, although Abouriou, Fer Servadou, and Malbec are sometimes used. White wines are primarily from Chenin Blanc, Sauvignon Blanc, and Sémillon, although Chardonnay, Colombard, Gros Manseng, and Muscadelle are occasionally used. Pure varietal wines have been allowed since 2000.

CUCUGNAN
Zonal *vin de pays* Map A, No.63

A tiny denomination of essentially red wines in the midst of the Côtes du Roussillon Villages

district, produced from Rhône varieties boosted by Cabernet Sauvignon and Merlot. Rosé may be made, but it seldom is, although there is an average of 1 percent dry white from Mauzac, Chenin Blanc, Chardonnay, and Ugni Blanc.

DEUX-SÈVRES
Départementale vin de pays Map B

Simple wines of a frank nature, from the vineyards with the richest soil (and thus the poorest for wine production) in the Nantais. Pure varietal wines have been allowed since 2000.

√ *Bouvet-Ladubay* (Non Pareils)

DOUBS
Départementale vin de pays Map B

Recent *départementale vin de pays* with minute production, Doubs is in the very east of France, between the Jura and Alsace. Pure varietal wines have been allowed since 2000.

DRÔME
Départementale vin de pays Map B

Red, white, and rosé wines are produced from typical Rhône varieties augmented by Gamay, Cabernet Sauvignon, and Merlot. More than 90 percent of the output is red and similar in style to Coteaux du Tricastin AOC. A small amount of decent rosé is made, but white wines represent barely 1 percent. Pure varietal wines have been allowed since 2000.

√ *Le Plan* (Rouge) • *Sud-Est Appellations* (Syrah)

DUCHÉ D'UZÈS
Zonal *vin de pays* Map A, No.64

In theory, this area is in the southern half of Vin de Pays des Cévennes, but in practice the two *vins de pays* are virtually identical. This was recognized by the decree in 1995, in which Duché d'Uzès overlaps all but 10 of the 131 villages in Vin de Pays des Cévennes.

FRANCHE COMTÉ
Zonal *vin de pays* Map B, No.65

A vast area overlapping the Jura and Savoie, Franche Comté produces fresh, clean, crisp, but otherwise unremarkable red and rosé wines. Only the white, made from Chardonnay, Pinot Gris, and Pinot Blanc, is of any note. Wines produced in the village of Champlitte have the right to add the subzonal name Coteaux de Champlitte (65a) to the Franche Comté *vin de pays*.

√ *Vignoble Guillaume* (Collection Réservée)

GARD
Départementale vin de pays Map B

A large production of mostly red wines made from Carignan, Grenache, Cinsault, Cabernet Sauvignon, Merlot, and Syrah. Some 15 percent of the output is a clean, fruity rosé, and the mainly Ugni Blanc-based white wines account for less than 3 percent (with Viognier a growing niche within this small percentage). Pure varietal wines have been allowed since 2000.

√ *Mas de Aveylands* • *Mas de Bressades* • *de Campuget* (Viognier Prestige) • *des Cantarelles* • *de Guiot* • *Saint-Antoine*

GERS
Départementale vin de pays Map B

Mostly white wines, similar in style to Côtes de Gascogne. Pure varietal wines have been allowed since 2000.

✓ *Patrick Azcué* • *Château Bouscassé*

GIRONDE
Départementale vin de pays Map B

Red and white wines made in isolated areas not classified for the production of Bordeaux. Pure varietal wines have been allowed since 2000.

HAUTE GARONNE
Départementale vin de pays Map B

Robust red and rosé wines made from Jurançon Noir, Négrette, and Tannat grapes grown in old vineyards south of Toulouse, with a little Merlot, Cabernet, and Syrah. A minuscule amount of dry white is made, and total production of all styles is very small, but De Ribonnet has put this denomination on the viticultural map and is in a class apart from all the other producers. Pure varietal wines have been allowed since 2000.

✓ *de Ribonnet*

HAUTE MARNE
Départementale vin de pays

Located adjacent to Champagne's Aube and Burgundy's Côte d'Or, it is not surprising that Le Muid Montsaugeonnais has made some pretty good Pinot Noir. Pure varietal wines have been allowed since 2000.

✓ *Le Muid Montsaugeonnais* (Pinot Noir Elevé en Fûts de Chêne)

HAUTERIVE
Zonal vin de pays Map A, No.66

Formerly called Vin de Pays d'Hauterive en Pays d'Aude, this appellation was renamed in 2004, when it was merged with the former *vins de pays* of Coteaux de Termenès, Côtes de Lézignan, and Val d'Orbieu. Production is primarily red, made from a range of typical Languedoc and southwestern grapes in the Corbières. A little *vin primeur* is made, as well as small amounts of white and rosé.

HAUTES-ALPES
Départementale vin de pays Map B

Very little wine is produced under this denomination, which is the *département* just south of the Savoie. Pure varietal wines have been allowed since 2000.

✓ *de Trésbaudon* (Rouge)

HAUTE-SAÔNE
Départementale vin de pays Map B

Rarely used, this is a minor *départementale vin de pays* for red, white, and rosé wines from unclassified vineyards in the south of Burgundy. Pure varietal wines have been allowed since 2000.

HAUTE-VALLÉE DE L'AUDE
Zonal vin de pays Map A, No.67

Mostly dry whites, from Chardonnay, Chenin, Mauzac, and Terret grapes grown in the Limoux district. A quarter of the output is red, from *bordelais* grapes, with just 3 percent rosé. Pure varietal wines have been allowed since 2000.

✓ *de l'Aigle* (Chardonnay Les Aigles, Pinot Noir

Terres Rouges) • *Marc Ramires* (Prieuré d'Antugnac)

HAUTE-VALLÉE DE L'ORB
Zonal vin de pays Map A, No.68

A limited amount of red, white, and rosé, primarily from Pinot Noir, Chardonnay, and Viognier. Pure varietal wines have been allowed since 2000.

✓ *Marc Ramires* (Prieuré d'Antugnac) • *de Roquebrun* (Orb Rouge)

HAUTE-VIENNE
Départementale vin de pays Map B

Rarely used, minor *départementale vin de pays* for red, white, and rosé wines east of the Cognac region. Pure varietal wines have been allowed since 2000.

HAUTS DE BADENS
Zonal vin de pays Map A, No.69

These red and rosé wines are produced in a rustic Minervois style.

HÉRAULT
Départementale vin de pays Map B

Red wine accounts for 85 percent of production and is increasing. The choice of grapes is quite wide, but most blends are based on Carignan, Cinsault, Grenache, and Syrah, boosted by a small proportion of *bordelais* varieties. About 10 percent rosé and 5 percent white wine is produced, the latter made from Clairette, Macabéo, Grenache Blanc, and Ugni Blanc. Production is vast, over 11 million cases (one million hectoliters), making it the second or third largest *vin de pays*, together with Vin de Pays de l'Aude. Improved viticultural and vinicultural techniques have transformed what was once the heart of Midi mediocrity into delicious, brilliant-value wine in some cases. Pure varietal wines have been allowed since 2000.

The most famous wine bearing this modest *vin de pays* denomination is, of course, Mas de Daumas Gassac. Situated northwest of Montpellier at Aniane, this property has been dubbed "the Lafite of the Languedoc," but when Aimé and Véronique Guibert purchased it, wine was the last thing on their minds. That was, however, before the visit of Professor Enjalbert, the Bordeaux geologist and author, who discovered Daumas Gassac had a rare, fine,

powdery volcanic soil that is an incredible 65 feet (20 meters) deep. Enjalbert predicted that it would yield a world-class wine if cultivated as a *grand cru*, and that is exactly what Aimé Guibert set out to do. I am not convinced about the rosé, and the white has been far too flabby in recent vintages, but the red is the equivalent of a Bordeaux *cru classé*. Even in lighter vintages, when Guibert gets slated by the critics, I think his red has a rare elegance that is missed just because it is not as big as people expect.

✓ *Mas de Daumas Gassac* (Rouge) • *de la Fadèze* • *C. V. Frontignan* (Abeillon) • *La Grange des Pères* • *Mas de Janiny* (Cabernet Sauvignon) • *Les Quatre Pilas* (Mouchère)

ÎLE DE BEAUTÉ
Zonal vin de pays Map B, No.70

With AOC wines accounting for just 15 percent of Corsica's wine output, its one all-encompassing (though technically not *départementale*) *vin de pays* has a huge impact on the perceived quality of this island's wine. Almost 60 percent of this *vin de pays* is red and 25 percent rosé, both made from a wide range of grapes, including many indigenous Corsican varieties, some of which may be related to certain Italian grapes. Grape varieties used include: Aleatico (red Muscat-like variety), Cabernet Sauvignon, Carignan, Cinsault, Grenache, Merlot, Syrah, Barbarossa, Nielluccio (the widest-planted on the island and said to be related to Sangiovese), Sciacarello (echoes of Provence's Tibouren), and Pinot Noir. A lot of effort is made to promote Corsican Pinot Noir, but at the time of writing this seems to be totally misguided. The best show decent varietal aroma, but lack an elegance of fruit and do not possess the essence of Pinot on the palate. Maybe someone will make good Corsican Pinot Noir, but it is a variety that requires a lot more care and attention in the vineyard and winery than is evident in any example I have tasted so far. Nielluccio has a reputation for good rosé, but as Orenga de Gaffory of Patrimonio in Corsica has shown, it also has the ability to produce a very fine red wine.

White wines from Chardonnay, Ugni Blanc, Muscat, and Vermentino are usually more demonstrative of clean, anaerobic handling and very cool fermentation than they are of any expression of *terroir*. Pure varietal wines have been allowed since 2000.

✓ *Casabianca* (Nectar d'Automne) • *du Mont Saint-Jean* (Aleatico, Pinot Noir) • *de Patrapiana* (Nielluciu) • *de Saline* • *Terra Viecchia* (Rouge)

INDRE
Départementale vin de pays Map B

Red, white, and rosé wines, including a pale *vin gris* style, from traditional Loire grape varieties are produced under this appellation. Pure varietal wines have been allowed since 2000.

INDRE-ET-LOIRE
Départementale vin de pays Map B

From vineyards east of Tours, this *vin de pays* is 80 percent red, made primarily from Gamay, although Cabernet Franc and Grolleau are also used. A little white, but even less rosé, is made. Pure varietal wines have been allowed since 2000.

ISÈRE
Départementale vin de pays Map B

Hardly used *départementale vin de pays*, most producers preferring one of a number of zonal appellations for the unclassified vineyards in this part of the northern Rhône Valley. Mostly red wine, a smattering of white, but no rosé. Pure varietal wines have been allowed since 2000.

JARDIN DE LA FRANCE
Regional *vin de pays* Map B

This *vin de pays* produces red, white, and rosé wines from 14 *départements* covering most of the Loire Valley. It would seem, from the wines most commonly encountered, that the majority of this vast output must be dry white, dominated by either Chenin Blanc or Sauvignon Blanc, but, according to the statistics, 60 percent is red. Generally a disappointing appellation, with the thin, acid Chardonnays being the most depressing, but the Cabernet Sauvignon from Pierre & Paul Freuchet is surprisingly soft and perfumed for this northerly denomination. Pure varietal wines have been allowed since 2000.

✓ *Paul Boutinot* (Signature Chardonnay) • *Adéa Consules* (Ligeria) • *Bruno Cormerais* (Elevé en Fûts de Chêne) • *de la Couperie* (Clyan Elevé en Fûts de Chêne) • *Manoir La Perrière* (Chardonnay) • *Henry Marionnet* (Provinage) • *du Petit Château* (Chardonnay) • *Château de La Ragotière* • *de la Saulze* (Gamay Rosé)

LANDES
Départementale vin de pays Map B

Red, white, and rosé wines are produced under this appellation. Approximately 80 percent is red, and the grapes used are traditional southwestern varieties. Pure varietal wines have been allowed since 2000.

✓ *Duprat Frères* (Cabernet-Tannat)

LOIRE-ATLANTIQUE
Départementale vin de pays Map B

Red and rosé wines, including a pale *vin gris*, are made from Gamay and Grolleau, while Folle Blanche and Melon de Bourgogne are used for white, with some interesting developments using Chardonnay. Pure varietal wines have been allowed since 2000.

LOIRET
Départementale vin de pays Map B

This appellation produces a small amount of red and rosé, including a pale *vin gris* style, made from Gamay. A Sauvignon Blanc white is also made. Pure varietal wines have been allowed since 2000.

LOIR-ET-CHER
Départementale vin de pays Map B

Red, white, and rosé wines, including a pale *vin gris*, are made from traditional Loire grape varieties, mostly from around Blois in the Cheverny area. Almost half the production is red and the rest white, but a touch more of the former is made, with very little rosé. Pure varietal wines have been allowed since 2000.

LOT
Départementale vin de pays Map B

Most wines in this *département* are red, and claim either the regional Comté Tolosan denomination or Vin de Pays des Coteaux de Glanes. Pure varietal wines have been allowed since 2000.

✓ *des Ardailloux* (Chardonnay Tradition)

LOT-ET-GARONNE
Départementale vin de pays Map B

This denomination is seldom seen, as the wines in this *département* are mostly red and sold as Vin de Pays du Comté Tolosan, but a tiny amount of white wine is produced under the Vin de Pays du Lot-et-Garonne label. Pure varietal wines have been allowed since 2000.

✓ *C. V. des Coteaux du Mézinais* (Gros Manseng Moelleux)

MAINE-ET-LOIRE
Départementale vin de pays Map B

Production is 85 percent red, and white and rosé account for the rest, made from traditional Loire grape varieties in the Anjou-Saumur district. Substantial quantities are produced, but most are sold from the back door. Pure varietal wines have been allowed since 2000.

✓ *Gaillard* ⓑ

MARCHES DE BRETAGNE
Subregional *vin de pays* Map B, No.71

Wines from the Marches de Bretagne subregion have the right to add this name to the Vin de Pays du Jardin de la France. Production includes red and rosé wines, made predominantly from Abouriou, Gamay, and Cabernet Franc, plus a little white from Muscadet and Gros Plant.

MAURES
Zonal *vin de pays* Map B, No.72

This denomination has a very large production and covers most of the southern part of the Côtes de Provence. Almost half the wines are rosé of a similar style and quality to those of the *Vin de Pays du Var*. The rest is red, which is rich, warm, and spicy, while white wine accounts for just 5 percent of total output. Pure varietal wines have been allowed since 2000.

✓ *Borrely-Martin* (Le Carre de Laure) • *Dupéré-Barrera* (Nowat Syrah) • *Marouine* (Carignan Vieilles Vignes)

MEUSE
Départementale vin de pays Map B

This *vin de pays* produces red and rosé wines, including a pale *vin gris*, from Pinot Noir and Gamay. Some white wine from Chardonnay, Aligoté, and Auxerrois is also made. Pure varietal wines have been allowed since 2000.

✓ *de Coustille* (Pinot Gris) • *Laurent Degenève* (Auxerrois)

MONT BAUDILE
Zonal *vin de pays* Map A, No.73

Production is mostly red wine, from a typical Languedoc range of grapes grown in the foothills of the Causses de Larzac. Rosé and white account for less than 15 percent of the total output, although crisp, dry whites are on the increase.

✓ *d'Aupilhac*

MONT-CAUME
Zonal *vin de pays* Map B, No.74

Effectively the *vin de pays* of Bandol—it is indeed the red wines that are the best here, including some truly outstanding wines, such as Bunan's classic Cabernet Sauvignon. However, the main varieties for most red and rosé wines (which account for 45 percent of the total production) are Carignan, Grenache, Cinsault, Syrah, and Mourvèdre. A little white is produced, but it is of little interest. Pure varietal wines have been allowed since 2000.

✓ *Bunan* (Cabernet Sauvignon, Mourvèdre) • *Gauby* (Ginestre)

MONTS DE LA GRAGE
Zonal *vin de pays* Map A, No.75

These red and rosé wines are produced in a basic Languedoc style, often beefed up with Syrah grapes. White wines must be truly dry (less than 2.5 grams per liter residual sugar). Pure varietal wines have been allowed since 2000.

✓ *de la Bergerie d'Amilhac* (Syrah) • *Le Bosc* (Syrah) • *Condamine Bertrand* (Petit Verdot Gourmandise) • *de la Fadèze* (Merlot Elevé en Fûts de Chêne) • *Grange des Rouquette* (Agrippa) • *de Malleport* (Alexandre) • *Mas Montelle* (Jéricho) • *de Montlobre* (Tête de Cuvée) • *de Saint-Louis* • *du Soleil* (Solstice Merlot Réserve Barrique) • *des Soulie* (Merlot) • *de Terre Mégère* (Cabernet Sauvignon) • *Vigne Blanche* (Cabernet Sauvignon)

NIÈVRE
Départementale vin de pays Map B

Red, white, and rosé wines, production of which is mostly confined to the areas of Charité-sur-Loire, La Celle-sur-Nièvre, and Tannay. Pure varietal wines have been allowed since 2000.

OC
Regional *vin de pays* Map B

This vast appellation is the most successful of all *vins de pays*, commercially and qualitatively. It sells well because of the simplicity of its name, which even English speakers have no difficulty pronouncing, and it encompasses most of the best *vins de pays* produced in France. The "Oc" of this regional *vin de pays* is southern dialect for "yes," it being "oui" elsewhere in France; thus, Languedoc, the "tongue of Oc." Some 70 percent of production is red, with the balance split equally between white and rosé. Even though most of the finest *vins de pays* are produced here, the volume of output is so vast that the quality will inevitably be variable. What has enabled so many truly fine wines to emerge in this denomination is the role of the so-called *cépages améliorateurs*. These grapes, such as Cabernet Sauvignon, Merlot, Syrah, Chardonnay, and Sauvignon Blanc, are not traditional in the region, but add greatly to the quality and finesse of more rustic local varieties. They also make excellent varietal wines. Viognier is on the increase as a varietal wine and makes a good-value, juicy-fruity (sometimes creamy-oaky), more exotic alternative to Chardonnay.

The quest for Pinot Noir du Vin de Pays d'Oc has been less satisfactory. The best so far are the oaky renditions from Clovallon and Joseph de Bel Air, and the strawberry-milkshake-flavored concoction from Virginie. They might succeed, but even these three are very far from doing so, and the efforts of others have been totally alien to any knowledgeable drinker's concept of this grape. Some of Domaine de La Baume's wines are organic.

✓ *de l'Aigle* (Chardonnay Les Aigles) • *des Aires Hautes* • *Astruc* (Chardonnay Réserve) • *de la Baume* • *Condamine Bertrand* (Cigalus, Elixir Rouge) • *Jean-Marc Boillot* (de la Truffière) • *des Bons Auspices* (Emparitz Cabernet Sauvignon) • *Chantovent* (Chardonnay Dolmen des Fées) • *Jean-Louis Denois* • *Le Fort* (Blanche Chardonnay) • *Foncalieu* (Bouquet d'Oriane, Enseduna Réserve Syrah) • *de Gourgazaud* • *La Grange des Quatre Sous* • *de Granoupiac* (Merlot) • *James Herrick* • *Lalande* (Pinot Noir) • *Michel Laroche* (La Croix Chevalière) • *Paul Mas* (La Forge Merlot) • *Mas Neuf* • *Gabriel Meffre* (Galet Vineyards) • *Montlobre* (Tête de Cuvée Rouge) • *de l'Orviel* (Chardonnay) • *Primo Palatum* (Chardonnay) • *Peirière* (Elevé en Fûts de Chêne: Cabernet Sauvignon, Merlot, Syrah) • *Michel Picard* (Chardonnay) • *Antonin Rodet* (Syrah) • *St.-Hilaire* • *Skalli* (Réserve F: Cabernet Sauvignon or Merlot) • *du Soleil* (La Chasse du Pape: Chardonnay, Viognier, or Syrah) • *de Terre Mégère* • *C. V. des Trois Terroirs* (L'Esprit du Midi Viognier, XL Les Grès) • *Vedeau* (Chardonnay Terre d'Amandiers) • *Arnaud de Villeneuve* (Grenache, Syrah) • *Virginie* (Castel Chardonnay Réservée, Gold Label Cabernet Merlot Réserve) • *Les Yeuses* (Cuvée La Soure)

PAYS DE RETZ
Subregional *vin de pays* Map B, No.77

This denomination may be added to the Vin de Pays du Jardin de la France. Best known for its rosé made from the Grolleau Gris (typified by Domaine du Parc), although red wines are also made from Grolleau, Gamay, and Cabernet Franc and account for as much as 70 percent of production. A tiny amount of white from Grolleau Gris can be found. Pure varietal wines have been allowed since 2000.

✓ *du Parc* (Grolleau)

PÉRIGORD
Zonal *vin de pays* Map B, No.77

This name replaced the *départementale* Vin de Pays of Dordogne for vines growing on the *causse* or limestone region of Périgord, where vineyards flourished in the 19th century. Now there are just 45 acres (18 hectares), producing 35% rosé, 10% Perigord Noir, and 50% Tradition (an oak-matured red wine). The balance is sold as *vin primeur*. The subzonal Vin de Domme (77a) is allowed to add its name to this *vin de pays*.

✓ *C. V. des Coteaux du Céou* (Vin de Domme Tradition)

PETITE CRAU
Zonal *vin de pays* Map B, No.78

A small *vin de pays* just south of Avignon, production is almost 80 percent red and 20 percent rosé from mostly Carignan, Grenache, Cinsault, and Syrah. Most rosé wines are made from, or dominated by, the Cinsault using the *saignée* method. Insignificant amounts of white from Ugni Blanc and Clairette are also produced. Pure varietal wines have been allowed since 2000.

✓ *C. V. de Laure* (Cabernet Pétrarque et Laure)

PORTES DE MÉDITERRANÉE
Regional *vin de pays* Map B

A vast regional *vin de pays*, but merely a modest production.

✓ *La Blaque* (Pinot Noir)

PÉZENAS
Zonal *vin de pays* Map A, No.79

Just south of Cabrières AOC, this single-village denomination produces mostly red wines. The grapes permitted are typical for Languedoc, with pure varietal wines on the increase, particularly Merlot, Cabernet Sauvignon, and Syrah. Rosé and white account for about 10 percent each, with crisp, dry whites on the increase, including a tiny amount sold as *vins primeurs*.

PRINCIPAUTÉ D'ORANGE
Zonal *vin de pays* Map B, No.80

This is a full red wine, made predominantly from Rhône grape varieties grown around Orange, north of Avignon, in an area that bridges Châteauneuf-du-Pape and Côtes-du-Rhône Villages. Just 4 percent rosé and barely 1 percent white is made.

✓ *Font Simian*

PUY-DE-DÔME
Départementale *vin de pays* Map B

Red, white, and rosé wines of simple, rustic quality are made under this appellation. A *puy* is a volcano stack, a number of which are found in the Puy-de-Dôme *département*. Pure varietal wines have been allowed since 2000.

PYRÉNÉES-ATLANTIQUES
Départementale *vin de pays* Map B

Two-thirds red and one-third white wine from traditional southwestern grape varieties is produced under this appellation. Pure varietal wines have been allowed since 2000.

PYRÉNÉES-ORIENTALES
Départementale *vin de pays* Map B

From the most southerly French *département*, bordering Spain's Andorra region, much of the *vin de pays* in the Pyrénées-Orientales comes from the same area as the AOC Côtes-du-Roussillon and Vin de Pays Catalan. Most of the production consists of full, fruity reds, with just 10 percent rosé and 5 percent white. Pure varietal wines have been allowed since 2000.

✓ *The Fifteen* (Grenache)

SABLES DU GOLFE DU LION
Zonal *vin de pays* Map A, No.81

A very go-ahead *vin de pays* situated along the Mediterranean coast of Gard, Hérault, and Bouches-du-Rhône, where the vines are mostly ungrafted and grown on on an amazing sandbar with seawater on both sides. Production is, unusually, two-thirds rosé, including a large proportion in pale *vin gris* style, plus 30 percent red and a small amount of white wine. Pure varietal wines have been allowed since 2000.

✓ *Bosquet-Canet* (Cabernet Sauvignon) • *du Petit Chaumont* (Chardonnay) • *Listel* (Jarras Gris de Gris)

SAINT BAUME
New zonal *vin de pays*

Too recent to map, this *vin de pays* was established in September 2004 and encompasses vineyards in the villages of Bras, Brignoles, La Celle, Mazaugues, Méounes-lès-Montrieux, Nans-les-Pins, Néoules, Ollières, Plan-d'Aups, Riboux, La Roquebrussanne, Rougiers, Saint-Maximin, Saint-Zacharie, Signes, and Tourves in the Var *département*. No grape varieties are specified, but pure varietal wines are allowed.

SAINT-GUILHEM-LE-DÉSERT
Zonal *vin de pays* Map A, No.82

Formerly called Vin de Pays des Gorges de L'Hérault, this denomination is in Coteaux du Languedoc and overlaps most of the Clairette du Languedoc appellation, yet less than 10 percent of its wines are white, with Ugni Blanc and Terret supporting Clairette. They are, however, better known than the reds, which account for over 80 percent of output. Some rosés are also made.

✓ *d'Aupilhac* (Plos des Baumes)

SAINT-SARDOS
Zonal *vin de pays* Map B, No.83

This *vin de pays* produces wines from a typical hodgepodge of grape varieties, with reds and rosés from Cabernet Franc, Cabernet Sauvignon, Gamay, Syrah, and Tannat, plus a maximum of 30 percent in total of Gamay Teinturier de Bouze and Teinturier de Chaudenay, both of which have colored juice; while whites are made from Chardonnay, Mauzac, Muscadelle, Sauvignon Blanc, and Sémillon.

✓ *C. V. de Saint-Sardos* (Gilles de Morban Rouge)

SAINTE-MARIE-LE-BLANCHE
Zonal *vin de pays* Map A, No.84

This *vin de pays* area straddles the border between Côte d'Or and Saône-et-Loire. Those in the Côte d'Or are just a few miles east of Beaune, and used to have the right to the Vin de Pays de la Côte d'Or until it was suppressed in 1998. Pure varietal wines are allowed. Red wines are made from one or more of Gamay, Pinot Gris, and Pinot Noir, while white wines are made from one of the following: Aligoté, Auxerrois, Chardonnay, Melon de Bourgogne, Pinot Blanc, and Pinot Gris.

✓ *Vincent Sauvestre* (Chardonnay)

SAÔNE-ET-LOIRE
Départementale vin de pays Map B

Rarely exported *départementale vin de pays* for mostly red and white wines from unclassified vineyards in the Burgundy region. Pure varietal wines have been allowed since 2000.

SARTHE
Départementale vin de pays Map B

Red, white, and rosé wines may be made, although production of this *vin de pays départementale* is minuscule and, as far as I am aware, limited to just one grower in Marçon. Pure varietal wines have been allowed since 2000.

SEINE-ET-MARNE
Départementale vin de pays Map B

Recently created, rarely used, minor *départementale vin de pays* for red, white, and rosé wines from unclassified vineyards in between Champagne and Paris. Red and rosé wines from Gamay and Pinot Noir, white wines from Aligoté, Auxerrois, Chardonnay, and Sauvignon Blanc. Pure varietal wines have been allowed since 2000.

TARN
Départementale vin de pays Map B

Relatively minor *départementale vin de pays* for red, white, and rosé wines produced outside the well-known Côtes du Tarn *vin de pays*. Pure varietal wines have been allowed since 2000.

✓ *C. V. de Labastide de Lévis* (Les Trois Bastides)

TARN-ET-GARONNE
Départementale vin de pays Map B

Red wine accounts for 90 percent of the tiny production of this appellation, although some rosé and a minuscule amount of white is also made. Most of these vines are west of Montauban, in an area that can also claim the Vin de Pays Saint-Sardos, which overlaps part of a southwest VDQS called Vins de Lavilledieu. The grape varieties are similar to those for Lavilledieu, except for the fact that they can also include Merlot, Cabernet, and Tannat. Pure varietal wines have been allowed since 2000.

TERROIRS LANDAIS
Zonal *vin de pays* Map B, No.85

These are red, white, and rosé wines from four separate subzonal areas in Aquitaine, each of which may be appended to this *vin de pays* denomination: Les Coteaux de Chalosse (85a—the largest area in the south of the Landes *département*, where vines grow in and around Dax and Murgon); Les Côtes de l'Adour (85b—from vines around Aire-sur-Adour and Geaune); Les Sables de l'Océan (85c—the romantic-sounding "Sands of the Ocean" refers to vines growing in the sand dunes around Messanges); and Les Sables Fauves (85d—the "Wild Sands" is a tiny enclave of vines west of Eauze). Reds and rosés are made from Tannat supported by *bordelais* varieties, while whites are primarily Ugni Blanc plus Colombard, Gros Manseng, and Baroque.

✓ *Michel Guérard* (Rouge de Bachen)

THÉZAC-PERRICARD
Zonal *vin de pays* Map A, No.86

This is a small *vin de pays* adjoining the western extremity of Coteaux du Quercy, producing Cahors-like reds from Cabernet Franc, Cabernet Sauvignon, Gamay, Malbec, Merlot, and Tannat.

✓ *C. V. de Thézac-Perricard* (Vin du Tsar Le Bouquet)

TORGAN
Zonal *vin de pays* Map A, No.87

As this is geographically the *vin de pays* equivalent of Fitou AOC, it is no surprise to discover that 98 percent of its wines are red. They are, in fact, made from a very similar range of grapes as that used to make Fitou, but certain other grapes are also permitted, including *bordelais* varieties and the Teinturier Alicante Bouschet. Rosé may be made, but seldom is, and the minuscule amount of aromatic dry white may be made from Clairette, Macabéo, and Marsanne. This *vin de pays* used to be known as Coteaux Cathares.

✓ *C. V. du Mont Tauch* (de Gardie)

URFÉ
Zonal *vin de pays* Map B, No.88

Red wine is made in modest quantities. White and rosé may also be produced.

VAL-DE-CESSE
Zonal *vin de pays* Map A, No.89

These are mostly red wines, plus 10 percent rosé, and 5 percent white from local grape varieties in the Minervois area.

VAL-DE-DAGNE
Zonal *vin de pays* Map A, No.90

This area overlaps part of the Côtes de Malepère and produces almost entirely red wines from a choice of Carignan, Grenache, Terret Noir, Merlot, Cabernet Sauvignon, Cabernet Franc, and the Teinturier Alicante Bouschet. Very little rosé and white is made.

VAL DE MONTFERRAND
Zonal *vin de pays* Map A, No.91

Mostly red wines, but rosé accounts for 25 percent of production, and white for 15 percent in this denomination, which encompasses the *garrigues* below the Cévennes. The usual Languedoc grapes are used. *Vin primeur* and *vin d'une nuit* are local specialities produced in relatively large quantities.

✓ *Mas de Martin* (Roi Patriote)

VALLÉE DU PARADIS
Zonal *vin de pays* Map A, No.92

Mostly red wines from an area that overlaps Corbières and Fitou, made from Carignan, Syrah, Grenache, Cinsault, Cabernet Sauvignon, and Merlot. Very little white wine is made (usually as *vin primeur*) and even less rosé. A heavenly name, even to English-speakers' ears, which no doubt helps it on export markets, which account for almost half its sales.

✓ *Jeanjean*

VAR
Départementale vin de pays Map B

This denomination is one of the largest producers of *vins de pays*. Covering the vast majority of the Côtes de Provence AOC, it not surprisingly produces a large quantity of rosé:

no less than 45 percent, in fact. The wines are usually made by the *saignée* method and range from a very pale *vin gris* style, through orange to almost cherry red. The quality is equally as variable. The big, rich, spicy reds are much better and of a more consistent quality, often using Syrah, Mourvèdre, and Cabernet Sauvignon to boost the Grenache, Cinsault, Carignan, and Roussane du Var, on which the rosés mainly rely. Some white wines are also made, but represent just 5 percent of production. They are not usually very exciting, and are mostly made from Ugni Blanc, Clairette, Bourboulenc, and Vermentino. The white from Rabiega is one of the exceptions, relying on Chardonnay for body and Viognier and Sauvignon Blanc to lift the Ugni Blanc base. Pure varietal wines have been allowed since 2000.

✓ *de Garbelle* (Vermentino) • *Château Sarrins* • *Château Thuerry* (L'Exception)

VAUCLUSE
Départementale vin de pays Map B

Three-quarters of output of this *vin de pays* is red, similar to basic Côtes-du-Rhône. Rosé can be fresh, and accounts for just 10 percent of output; white is generally the least interesting. Pure varietal wines have been allowed since 2000.

✓ *de la Citadelle* (Cabernet Sauvignon) • *Fondacci* (Chasan) • *Fontaine du Clos* (Chardonnay) • *de Marotte*

VAUNAGE
Zonal *vin de pays* Map A, No.93

Light red wines made in typical Languedoc style.

VENDÉE
Départementale vin de pays Map B

Red, white, and rosé wines are produced in small quantities, in a similar style to Fiefs Vendéens (which was a *vin de pays* until it was promoted to VDQS status in December 1984). Pure varietal wines have been allowed since 2000.

VICOMTÉ D'AUMELAS
Zonal *vin de pays* Map A, No.94

Overlapping part of Cabrières, this *vin de pays* produces mostly red wines of a simple, fresh, fruity style, from traditional southwestern grape varieties, such as the typical Languedoc grape. Just over 10 percent of wines are rosé, and a tiny amount of crisp, dry white is produced.

VIENNE
Départementale vin de pays Map B

This appellation produces red, white, and rosé wines, most of which are grown in and around the Haut-Poitou district. Pure varietal wines have been allowed since 2000.

✓ *Ampelidae*

VISTRENQUE
Zonal *vin de pays* Map A, No.96

This appellation produces red and rosé wines, which are made in very small quantities. White wine may also be produced.

YONNE
Départementale vin de pays Map B

The Yonne is a white-only appellation, and its production of wines is quite small. Pure varietal wines have been allowed since 2000.

The WINES of
ITALY

THE WINES OF ITALY ARE RICH IN POTENTIAL but lack focus; consequently, the country's image is muddled, when it should really be diverse. In Italy, vines are so easy to grow that one even expects them to shoot up from cracks in the sidewalk after a Mediterranean squall. Furthermore, the number of interesting indigenous grape varieties is greater than can be found in any other major winemaking country of the world, including France. However, there are no wine regions, great or otherwise, in Italy—just provinces that abut each other. Consumers cannot visualize Italian wines in the maps of their minds as they can French wines. Vine varieties and the types of wine they make not only merge within provinces, but also overlap their boundaries, blurring the already confused picture. Despite this, Italy, like France, makes a quarter of the world's wines, and Italian exports are healthy. If and when Italy manages to project a coherent image of distinct regional styles, France will have a rival to worry about.

HILLSIDE VINES ABOVE FUMANE, VENETO
*The town of Fumane is situated in one of five valleys
that comprise the historic Valpolicella Classico area.*

ITALY

This country churns out new appellations as if there is no tomorrow, with far too many that are far too obscure. The trend also continues to promote ordinary DOCs to even-less-than-ordinary DOCGs. Italy has an extraordinary and exceptional potential to make some of the greatest wines in the world, yet seems even more inept than France at running its wine industry.

IT IS STAGGERING TO THINK that a quarter of the world's wine is Italian yet, despite 4,000 years of Italian winemaking history, the Italian wine industry remains in a state of flux. Italy's enormous wine production has given many discerning wine drinkers a misleading impression of the country's true quality

MONTALCINO
With its famous Brunello vines in the foreground, Montalcino basks in Tuscan sunshine. Viticulturally, the surrounding area is highly prestigious; its tannic red wines generally need at least 10 years' maturation.

potential. Italy can, and does, make many fine wines, but they have always been surrounded by so much *vin ordinaire* that finding them is a hit-and-miss affair. Like Italy, France churns out a huge volume of wine and its production can include a fair amount of plonk, but the names of great French wines roll off the tongue of even the uninitiated, and, rightly or wrongly, France has managed to get away with it, whereas Italy never has. Yet Italy has at least as much potential in terms of the diversity of its *terroir* and a plethora of native grape varieties. The key problem is identity: in Italy vines grow in every corner, whereas in France they are mostly confined to half a dozen major regions and each of these has its own recognizable style and reputation.

ITALY'S LAW OF MEDIOCRITY
Italy's DOC legislation was introduced in 1963, but this law was fundamentally flawed because it failed to establish a small number of easily identifiable regions, each bearing an umbrella name and style. It also actively encouraged increased volume by officially recognizing the most productive grape varieties and classifying the highest-yielding areas on the edges of famous appellations. The late 1950s and early 1960s were crucial in the development of the modern wine industry in Europe, and Italy's DOC system

encouraged its largest bottlers to move out of the low-yielding, hilly, *classico* areas, which make better wines than the higher-yielding plains but are the more difficult and expensive to maintain. From this point, the Italian wine industry became increasingly dominated by mass production; most wineries became passionless factories and the quality of Italy's most famous wines sank as fast as the volume of production increased.

At first, out of respect for Senator Paolo Desana, who fathered the DOC concept, Italy ignored foreign criticism of its new wine regime. But by the early 1980s, its greatest wine names were so devalued that many of its best wines were being sold as *vini da tavola*, which made a mockery of the DOC system. In the end, even the most conservative Italians had to admit something must

be done. Over the next 10 years, successive agricultural ministers tried to overhaul Italy's wine laws, but failed because of the political clout of the industrial bottlers, who had a lot to gain by flooding the market with cheap wines. When agricultural minister Giovanni Goria declared his intention to press for even more radical changes than any of his predecessors had, few took him seriously. No one would have bet a single lira on Goria's success, yet within 10 weeks of his appointment, a "New Disciplinary Code for Denomination of Wines of Origin" had been ratified by the Senate.

GORIA'S LAW

In February 1992 Law 164, now known simply as Goria's Law or the Goria Law, replaced Desana's wine regime. When the law first

ITALY
As might be expected of a nation so geographically and culturally diverse, Italy produces a vast array of different types of wine. Away from the mainland, the islands of Sicily and Sardinia both have thriving wine industries.

Northwest Italy
see also pp266,267

Northeast Italy
see also p275

West-Central Italy
see also pp282,283

East-Central Italy
see also p289

Southern Italy and the Islands
see also pp292, 295

— Provincia boundary

▲ Height above sea level (meters)

came into force, much attention was focused on the introduction of a brand new category called IGT (*Indicazioni Geografiche Tipiche*). The equivalent of French *vins de pays*, IGTs were supposed to form a buffer between the DOCs and *vini da tavola*, Goria having denied the latter the right to bear any geographical provenance other than Italy itself. Each IGT would come from an officially recognized zone of production, but could not claim to be anything more specific, such as the product of a village, microzone, estate, or single vineyard. Under Law 164 all such specific origins were restricted to DOC or DOCG wines.

In the euphoric first few months of this new law, it was predicted that there would be 150 to 200 IGTs, accounting for some 130 million cases (12 million hectoliters) of wine, which should—according to Goria's own plans—rise to 40 percent of the total Italian wine output, representing 10 percent of world production. For almost five years, no applications were received for IGT status. Without the right to mention the specific origins of these wines, yet being obliged to meet similar criteria to a DOC, why would producers bother, when they might as well opt for DOC or simply make *vino da tavola*? This is why the major thrust of Goria's groundbreaking law was considered, even in Italy, to have been stillborn. Then, with the 1996 harvest, the applications poured in, and there are now no fewer than 118 classified IGTs, in addition to the 309 DOCs and 30 DOCGs.

NEW RESPECT FOR THE DOCS?
Did the Goria Law successfully reconfigure the fundamentally flawed DOCs and DOCGs? The answer is yes and no. "No" because Italy's wines will never achieve their true potential until, like those of France, they can be encapsulated within half a dozen major regions of recognizable style (*see* DOC's Lack of Specificity below) and reputation. Goria did not even attempt to tackle this problem. Furthermore, Italy's greatest wines will never receive the international acclaim they deserve until their delimited areas are reduced to the original hilly *classico* districts, about which Goria also did nothing.

Until Goria's Law, many wines were denied the *vini da tavola* status because Italy's appellation system defined the characteristics of each DOC, and in so doing did not take into account the foreign grapes and nontraditional vinification methods that most premium *vini da tavola* came to employ. Giovanni Goria had the sense to realize that any system that did not recognize some of the country's finest wines is a discredited system. He thus made it easier for such wines to be accepted within established DOCs.

To qualify for DOC status, the wine or wines must have a history of at least five years' production. Any DOC with a further

five years of recorded production can apply for a DOCG, providing it has acquired a "reputation and commercial impact both at home and at an international level."

DOC'S LACK OF SPECIFICITY
Part of the problem of Italian wines being unable to project a readily discernible image is the number of ways in which a single DOC wine may be interpreted. An appellation system should project and protect a recognizable style (and, one hopes, quality) through detailed regulations, or it should simply make sure the provenance of a wine is as stated—guaranteeing where it comes from, even if it is a blend of different areas. The very last thing that any wine regime should do is insist on an intricate recipe of grape-variety percentages and precise geographical limitation, then say it can be dry, off-dry, medium sweet, sweet, still, *passito*, *frizzantino* (slightly sparkling), *frizzante* (semi-sparkling), or *spumante* (fully sparkling). All this does is foster the uncertain image with which Italian wines have long been lumbered.

ALL THAT SPARKLES
No country has as many sparkling wine appellations as Italy, with its optional "may be *spumante*" clauses littering over 100 of its DOCs, including some of its truly greatest red wines. However, despite so many possibilities, Italy had no specific appellation for dry sparkling wine until 1995 when Franciacorta, the first and still the only appellation to insist on the traditional method, was given DOCG status. The rest of Italy's little-known, half-forgotten sparkling wine appellations are all *cuve close*. Bottle-fermentation does not guarantee quality, but it does encourage producers in the right direction, which is why it is a mistake for any dry sparkling DOC wine to be produced by any other process. Until all DOC *cuve close* is outlawed, no Italian dry sparkling wine will be taken seriously and Franciacorta's efforts to establish the country's first classic *brut* appellation will be frustrated.

FUTURE SIMPLICITY
The solution to Italy's wine worries is very simple. Map out no more than half-a-dozen truly classic Italian wine regions, reduce the number of DOCs within these regions to a maximum of 100, all limited to historically authentic areas, and the most famous styles (no more multiple choice appellations!), with tough regulations and qualifying tastings performed by an independent

RIONERO, BASILICATA
A 17th-century farm building on the Conca d'Oro estate in Vulture, where Fratelli d'Angelo produces a great red wine called Aglianico del Vulture.

ITALIAN LABEL LANGUAGE

ABBOCCATO Slightly sweet

AMABILE Sweeter than *abboccato*

AMARO Bitter or very dry

ANNATA This means "year" and often precedes or follows the vintage date. At least 85 percent of the wine must be from the vintage indicated. *See also Vendemmia*

ASCIUTTO Bone dry

AUSLESE German term used in the Alto Adige for wines from selected grapes

AZIENDA, AZIENDA AGRICOLA, AZIENDA AGRARIA, OR AZIENDA VITIVINICOLA Estate winery

BIANCO White

CANTINA SOCIALE OR COOPERATIVA A cooperative winery

CASCINA North Italian term for a farm or estate

CASA VINICOLA A commercial winery

CERASUOLO Cherry red, used for vividly colored rosés

CHIARETTO Wines falling between very light red and genuine rosé

CLASSICO The best or most famous part of a DOC zone

CONSORZIO A group of producers who control and promote wine, usually insisting on higher standards than DOC regulations enforce

DENOMINAZIONE DI ORIGINE CONTROLLATA, OR DOC There are more than 250 DOCs, but some are multiple-varietal appellations covering as many as 12 different wines, resulting in more than 600 DOC names. This is similar, and just as worthless as, the French AOC system, as both merely guarantee mediocrity. The producer's name is still the best assurance of quality.

DENOMINAZIONE DI ORIGINE CONTROLLATA E GARANTITA, OR DOCG Theoretically the highest-quality official denomination, but encompasses a lot of very ordinary wine, as well as isolated pockets of truly fine wine. Again, the producer's name is the best assurance of quality.

DOLCE Very sweet

FATTORIA Farm

FERMENTAZIONE NATURALE Method of producing sparkling wine by natural refermentation in a tank or bottle

FIORE Term meaning "flower." Often part of a name, it indicates quality, as it implies that the first grape pressing has been used.

FRIZZANTE Semi-sparkling, the equivalent of *pétillant*

FRIZZANTINO Very lightly sparkling

IMBOTTIGLIATO ALL'ORIGINE Estate-bottled

INDICAZIONE GEOGRAFICA TIPICA, OR IGT The Italian equivalent of a French *vin de pays*

LIQUOROSO Usually fortified and sweet, but may also be dry wine that is simply high in alcohol

LOCALITÀ, RONCO, OR VIGNETO Indicates a single-vineyard wine

MESSO IN BOTTIGLIA NELL'ORIGINE Estate-bottled

METODO CLASSICO OR METODO TRADIZIONALE The Italian for traditional method

PASSITO Strong, often sweet wine made from semidried grapes

PASTOSO Medium-sweet

PRODUTTORE ALL'ORIGINE Estate-bottled

RAMATO Copper-colored wine made from Pinot Grigio grapes that are briefly macerated on their skins.

RECIOTO Strong, sweet wine made from semidried grapes

RIPASSO Wine refermented on the lees of a *recioto* wine

RISERVA OR RISERVA SPECIALE DOC or DOCG wines that have been matured for a statutory number of years (the *speciale* is older)

ROSATO Rosé

ROSSO Red

SECCO Dry

SEMI-SECCO Medium-sweet

SPUMANTE Fully sparkling

STRAVECCHIO Very old wines aged according to DOC or DOCG rules

SUPERIORE When part of the appellation, this usually refers to a longer minimum aging period before the wine can be sold

TALENTO A registered trademark signifying a sparkling wine made by the traditional method

TENUTA Estate

UVAGGIO Wine blended from various grape varieties

VECCHIO Old

VENDEMMIA This means "harvest" and often precedes or follows the vintage date. At least 85 percent of the wine must be from the vintage indicated. *See also Annata*

VIGNA OR VIGNETO Vineyard

VIN SANTO OR VINO SANTO Traditionally sweet, occasionally dry, white wine made from *passito* grapes stored in sealed casks, and not topped up for several years

VINO Wine

VINO NOVELLO Italian equivalent of Beaujolais Nouveau

VINO DA PASTO Ordinary wine

VINO DA TAVOLA Literally "table wine," this is Italy's most basic category, but as well as including most of the country's plonk, it also includes some of its greatest wines, although many of the latter are gradually developing their own appellations

body with no vested interests. Set up a panel of experts to determine the 12 truly greatest wines to receive DOCG status, and set that in stone, so that no expansion can ever dilute the DOCG reputation. Within each DOCG, an Italian equivalent of *grand cru* and *premier cru* classification should be made. Then I would dispose of all the 118 IGTs except for the 12 regional IGTs (Basilicata, Toscana, Sicilia, etc.), and increase their number to 20, which would cover the entire country. There should be no other type of IGT. To balance this restriction, I would encourage the greatest flexibility in IGT regulations, including the use of single-village, single-estate, and individual site names. I would even allow the use of obsolete DOCs and IGTs (providing they are not classified as such, and their names are printed at no more than one-third the size of the regional IGT), so that no producer could claim that he had been prevented from selling his wine under the appellation for which it had become known, however obscure or meaningless that might have been to the outside world. The bureaucrats might squeal at the thought of such a thing, but it really does not matter. What matters is that these IGTs would have a recognizable name and therefore offer some sense of place for drinkers in other countries. Just as important, a flexible IGT could be used both to preserve traditional values and promote innovation. And, finally, the clever part: the Italians should steal René Renou's concept of *Site et Terroir d'Excellence* (STE—see p.58). If the French authorities are too stupid to adopt such an ingenious idea, then the Italians should demonstrate what an opportunity they have missed. With the number of regional IGTs and DOCGs fixed, there must be another means of rewarding true standout quality, if any new system is to avoid the current wine regime's guarantee of mediocrity, and a nice big STE stamp on the label of an IGT or DOC wine would provide that. Imagine the difference it would make. A cluster of STE-awarded IGT wineries might one day elect to form a new DOC, but the flexibility of IGT and premium attracted by STE status should be sufficient to keep most wineries in the IGT system, thereby reducing any threat of a major expansion of the number of DOCs. And while the highest-flying STE-awarded DOCs should never be allowed to join the ranks of the DOCGs (all the best systems have something intrinsically unfair, yet inherently stable, built into them), they might well fetch the price of a top DOCG.

NORTHWEST ITALY

This area includes the great wine region of Piedmont as well as the regions of Liguria, Lombardy, and Valle d'Aosta. Generally, the wines are fuller and richer than those of northeastern Italy, which is a more mountainous area.

FEW AREAS ENCOMPASS such contrasting topographies as northwest Italy, from the alpine *pistes* of the Valle d'Aosta and the Apennines of Liguria to the alluvial plains of the Po River. Contrast is also evident in the character of its two most famous wines—the big, black, and tannic Barolo DOCG and the light, water-white, effervescent, and grapey-sweet Asti DOCG.

PIEDMONT (PIEMONTE)

Piedmont is dominated by two black grapes (Nebbiolo and Barbera) and one white (Moscato). Nebbiolo makes the magnificently rich and smoky Barolo and the elegant, more feminine, yet sometimes just as powerful, Barbaresco. The Barbera has a much greater yield than Nebbiolo but is potentially almost as fine. It is softer in tannin, at least as high in acidity, and

NORTHWEST ITALY, *see also p.263*
The presence of the Alps gives this largely hilly region a hot growing season and a long fall. The finest wines come from the foothills of Piedmont, which provide ideal growing conditions for the late-ripening Nebbiolo grape.

excels around Alba and, to a slightly lesser extent, around Asti. White Asti, made from Moscato, is Italy's most popular fine wine. Whether still, *frizzantino*, or *spumante*, Asti is light and succulently sweet, with a mesmerizing grapey character. Fully sparkling Asti is no longer called Asti Spumante because the term, like *mousseux*, has a cheap, low-quality connotation and Asti is undeniably the world's greatest dessert-style sparkling wine.

LOMBARDY (LOMBARDIA)

Northeast of Piedmont, Lombardy stretches from the flat plains of the Po Valley to snow-clad Alpine peaks. The region's finest wines

AVERAGE ANNUAL PRODUCTION

REGION	DOC PRODUCTION	TOTAL PRODUCTION
Piedmont	11 million cases (1 million hl)	44 million cases (4 million hl)
Lombardy	4 million cases (400,000 hl)	22 million cases (2 million hl)
Liguria	78,000 cases (7,000 hl)	4 million cases (400,000 hl)
Valle d'Aosta	5,550 cases (500 hl)	350,000 cases (30,000 hl)

Percentage of total Italian production: Piedmont, 5.2%; Lombardy, 2.6%; Liguria, 0.52%; Valle d'Aosta, 0.04%.

Legend

- Riviera Ligure di Ponente
- Colline Novaresi
- Monferrato
- Langhe
- Cinque Terre
- Colli di Luni
- Lambrusco Mantovano
- Barolo (1), Barbaresco (2), Nebbiolo d'Alba, Barbera d'Alba Docetto d'Alba
- Barbera d'Asti, Grignolino d'Asti Freisa d'Asti, Asti Spumante, Moscato d'Asti
- Carema (3)
- Erbaluce di Caluso, Caluso Passito
- Lessona (4), Bramaterra (5), Boca (6), Gattinara (7), Ghemme (8), Sizzano (9), Fara (10)
- Dolcetto di Ovada
- Gavi
- Oltrepò Pavese
- Franciacorta, Cellatica (16)
- Valcalepio
- Lugana
- Valtellina, Valtellina Superiore
- Rossese di Dolceacqua
- Colli Piacentini (11), Colli di Parma (12), Colli Tortonesi (13), Freisa di Chieri (14), Riviera del Garda Bresciano (15)
- *Provincia* boundary
- ▲ Height above sea level (meters)

0 10 20 30 40 50 miles
0 20 40 60 80 km

FACTORS AFFECTING TASTE AND QUALITY

LOCATION
Flanked to the north and west by the Alps and by the Ligurian Sea to the south, northwest Italy contains the provinces of Piedmont, Lombardy, Liguria, and Valle d'Aosta.

CLIMATE
The winters are severe with frequent inversion fogs rising out of the valleys. Summers are hot, though not excessively so, but hail can damage the grapes at this time of year. Long falls enable the late-ripening Nebbiolo grape to be grown very successfully.

ASPECT
This area covers mountains, foothills (*piedmont* means "foothill"), and the valley of Italy's longest river, the Po. Grapes are grown on hillsides that provide good drainage and exposure to the sun. In classic areas such as Barolo, every south-facing hillside is covered with vines, while in Lombardy many vineyards extend down to the rich, alluvial plains of the Po Valley.

SOIL
A wide range of soils with many local variations, the predominant type is calcarous marl (*see* p.18), which may be interlayered or intermingled with sand and clay.

VITICULTURE AND VINIFICATION
The great red wines of the region have suffered in the past from long aging in large wooden vats, as many growers bottled their wine only when they sold it. This practice dried up the fruit and oxidized the wine. However, many wines are bottled at the optimum time although there is still no consensus about the best aging vessels. The use of *cuve close* for sweet, grapey styles of wine from Asti has been very successful and these wines sell well internationally. Some of the same *spumante* houses have developed dry *spumante* from Pinot and Chardonnay grapes, using the traditional method, to produce fine-quality sparkling wines.

GRAPE VARIETIES
Primary varieties: Barbera, Muscat (*syn.* Moscato), Nebbiolo (*syn.* Chiavennasca).
Secondary varieties: Arneis, Blanc de Morgex, Bonarda, Brachetto, Brugnola, Cabernet Franc, Cabernet Sauvignon, Casalese, Chardonnay, Cortese, Croatina (*syn.* Bonarda in Lombardy, but not the true Bonarda of Piedmont), Dolcetto (*syn.* Ormeasco in Liguria), Erbaluce, Favorita, Freisa, Fumin, Gamay, Grenache, Grignolino, Gropello, Incrocio Terzi (Barbera x Cabernet Franc), Lambrusco, Malvasia, Marzemino, Mayolet, Merlot, Neyret, Petit Rouge (*syn.* Oriou), Petite Arvine, Pigato, Pignola Valtellina, Pinot Blanc (*syn.* Pinot Bianco), Pinot Gris (*syn.* Pinot Grigio, Malvoisie, not Malvasia), Pinot Noir (*syn.* Pinot Nero), Premetta, Riesling (*syn.* Riesling Renano), Rossese, Rossola, Ruché, Schiava Gentile, Syrah, Timorasso, Tocai Friulano (separate variety— neither Pinot Grigio nor Malvasia), Trebbiano (*syn.* Buzzetto), Ughetta, Uva Rara, Vermentino, Vespolina, Vien de Nus, Welschriesling (*syn.* Riesling Italico)

PERGOLA-TRAINED VINES
These Nebbiolo vines, grown near Carema in Piedmont, are trained on a Pergola Piemontese. They are made into a fragrant, medium-bodied wine.

include Franciacorta's full reds and its new DOCG for classic *brut* sparkling wines, plus the best of Valtellina's red Sassella. These wines are still relatively unknown compared with Piedmont's Barolo and Barbaresco and are good value.

LIGURIA
One of Italy's smallest regions, Liguria is more famous for its Riviera, which is set against the dramatic and beautiful backdrop of the Maritime Alps, than it is for its wines. Cinque Terre, which is the best-known Ligurian wine, is named after the *Cinque Terre*, or five villages, which are perched along the Ligurian coast, above which the steep, intricately terraced vineyards tower like some great Aztec pyramid. Other than the Cinque Terre, interesting wines include the soft, spicy Rossese di Dolceacqua and the vividly colored Albenga rosé of the Riviera Ligure di Ponente DOC. The Colli di Luni is almost Tuscan, and part of this DOC even overlaps that region, so it is not surprising that it is capable of producing a decent Sangiovese. However, most Ligurian wines belong to the category of pleasant vacation drinking, and some of the best potential vineyards have been grubbed up to accommodate the tourists who drink them.

VALLE D'AOSTA
If Liguria is a marginal wine region, then Valle d'Aosta is almost subliminal. High in the Alps, overlooked by Mont Blanc and the Matterhorn, the Valle d'Aosta looks at first as if it could as easily be a part of France or Switzerland as of Italy, but the only easy, natural access is from Piedmont along the Dora Baltea River. Italy's smallest and most mountainous wine region, the Valle d'Aosta has picturesque, high-altitude vineyards that produce some enjoyable wines, particularly Chambave, Nus, and Torrette, just three of the 20 wines within the Valle d'Aosta DOC. However, most are tourist wines; the best are easy-drinking and unpretentious.

VALLE D'AOSTA, *see also opposite*
The winters here are cold and snowy, but summers in the valley can be very hot with contrastingly cold nights, which should make for some exciting wines.

Morgex et La Salle
Enfer d'Arvier
Torrette
Nus
Chambave
Arnad-Montjovet
Donnaz
Provincia boundary
Valle d'Aosta DOC boundary
▲ Height above sea level (metres)

0   5   10   15 miles
0   10   20   30 km

THE APPELLATIONS OF
NORTHWEST ITALY

CLASSIC BRUT SPARKLING WINES

All these wines are made by the traditional method.

🍷 Upon purchase—for all regions

✓ **Lombardy** *Bellavista Cuvée Brut*
• *Bellavista Gran Cuvée pas Operé*
• *Berlucchi Brut Cuvée Impériale*
• *Berlucchi Brut Cuvée Impériale Millesimato* • *Berlucchi Brut Cuvée Impériale Max Rosé* • *Ca'del Bosco Franciacorta Pinot Brut* • *Ca'del Bosco Franciacorta pas Dose* • *Ca'del Bosco Franciacorta Crémant Brut* • *Doria Pinot Brut, Mirabella Franciacorta Brut* • *Villa Mazzucchelli Brut* • *Villa Mazzucchelli pas Dose*

Piedmont *Stefano Barbero, Luigi Bosca Brut Nature, Contratto Brut*

ALBENGA DOC
Liguria

Vividly colored, dry, and characterful, Liguria's best-known rosés are now classified as part of the Riviera Ligure di Ponente DOC. *See* Riviera Ligure di Ponente DOC.

ARENGO
Piedmont

A soft, light-bodied, fruity non-DOC Barbera red made by several Asti producers.

ARNAD-MONTJOVAT DOC
Valle d'Aosta

A red-only subappellation of the regional Valle d'Aosta DOC producing Nebbiolo-based red wines, with up to 30 percent Dolcetto, Freisa, Neyret, Pinot Noir, and Vien de Nus. *See* Valle d'Aosta DOC.

ARNEIS DI ROERO DOC
Piedmont

These wines are produced from the ancient Arneis grape grown in the hills north of Alba. Formerly a *vino da tavola*, the high price and reputation of these wines ensured they would eventually become part of the Roero DOC. The best are amazingly rich and full-flavored white wines, yet soft and deftly balanced with a fine *frizzantino*. Essentially dry wines, some renditions are, however, less dry than others and Deltetto's Bric Tupin has started a trend for a lusciously sweet style. *See* Roero DOC.

🍷 3–5 years

✓ *Ceretto* (Blangé) • *Carlo Deltetto* • *Bruno Giacosa* • *Castello di Neive* • *Vietti*

ASTI DOCG
Piedmont

Formerly sold as Asti Spumante, the *spumante* (which means "sparkling") has been removed because it has become tarnished by cheap products that also use the term. It is now known simply as Asti and has been promoted to full DOCG status, which the best wines deserve, but an increasing number of underperformers do not. Italy's finest sparkling wine, and one of the most famous wines in the world, Asti is made by *cuve close*, which is far superior to the traditional method when

producing an aromatic, sweet sparkling wine. The grapes used are grown in 52 communes throughout the provinces of Asti, Cuneo, and Alessandria.

The best Asti has a fine *mousse* of tiny bubbles, a fresh and grapey aroma, a luscious sweetness, and a light, delicately rich flowery-fruitiness that hints at peaches. Asti should be consumed as young as possible primarily because one of the most important compounds contributing to the Moscato aroma is geraniol, which is wonderful when fresh, but with bottle-age assumes a pungent geranium odor. Gancia's special selection *cuvée* called Camilo Gancia (no longer produced) was the best Asti I ever tasted. *See also* Moscato d'Asti DOCG.

🍷 Upon purchase

✓ *Barbero* (Conte di Cavour) • *Walter Barbero* (Acini Dolce) • *Batasiolo* • *Bersano* • *Capetta* • *Villa Carlotta* • *Cerutti* (Cesare) • *Conte di Cavour* • *Giuseppe Contratto* • *Romano Dogliotti* (La Selvatica) • *Fontanafredda* (Millesimato) • *Marenco* ⊙ • *De Miranda* • *Mondoro* • *Perlino* • *Sperone* • *Tosti* • *Cantina Sociale Vallebelbo*

BARBACARLO
Lombardy

Dry, *frizzante*, red *vin de garde* that was originally classified as part of the Oltrepò Pavese DOC. However, Lino Maga has been legally recognized as its exclusive producer and it has returned to being a *vino da tavola*.

BARBARESCO DOCG
Piedmont

Generally more feminine and elegant than Barolo, Barbaresco has a greater suppleness, softer fruit, and a more obvious charm, although some producers overlap the weightier Barolo style. Produced from Italy's greatest indigenous grape variety, Nebbiolo, these wines must be aged for a minimum of two years, one of which must be in oak or chestnut casks.

🍷 5–20 years

✓ *Produttori di Barbaresco* • *Ceretto* • *Pio Cesare* • *Fratelli Cigliuti* • *Giuseppe Cortese* • *Angelo Gaja* • *Bruno Giacosa* • *Piero Busso* • *Cantina del Glicine* • *Marchesi di Gresy* • *Moccagatta* • *Castello di Neive* • *Alfredo Prunotto* • *Bruno Rocca* • *Scarpa*

BARBERA
Piedmont

Although this grape can be a bit rustic, overly acidic, and may lack elegance if not grown in a suitable *terroir*, stunning *vini da tavola*, often aged in a *barrique*, are made in classic areas by producers who do not want to be restricted by the DOC and thus do not claim it.

✓ *Braida* (Bricco dell'Uccellone) • *Castello di Neive* (Rocca del Mattarello)

BARBERA D'ALBA DOC
Piedmont

Barbera is the most prolific Piedmont vine and, as such, has suffered unfairly from a somewhat lowly image. But in fact, it is one of Italy's great grapes and the best Barbera from Alba are magnificently rich and full of flavor, and quite

capable of challenging Barolo and Barbaresco very closely in terms of intrinsic quality. The production of Barbera d'Alba is very small, in fact often minute, in comparison with that of Barbera d'Asti.

🍷 5–12 years

✓ *Marziano Abbona* • *Pio Cesare* • *Fratelli Cigliuti* • *Clerico* • *Aldo Conterno* • *Giacomo Conterno* • *Conterno Fantino* • *Damonte* • *Franco Fiorina* • *Angelo Gaja* • *Gepin* • *Elio Grasso* • *Manzone* • *Giuseppe Mascarello* • *Prunotto* • *Renato Ratti* • *Bruno Rocca* • *Vajra* • *Vietti* • *Roberto Voerzio*

BARBERA D'ALBA COLLINE NICESI DOC
Piedmont

The lower yield of this proposed subzone of Barbara d'Alba is intended to lead the way to full DOCG status for part or all of the current Barbera d'Alba DOC classified wines.

BARBERA D'ASTI DOC
Piedmont

Similar in character to Barbera d'Alba, but softer and more supple, with simpler generic wines, but equally profound single-vineyard wines.

🍷 3–8 years

✓ *Marchesi Alfieri* • *Cascina la Barbatella* • *Bava* (Stradivario) • *Alfiero Boffa* • *Braida* (Bricco della Figotta) • *Cascina Castelet* (Passum) • *Chiarlo* (Valle del Sole) • *Coppo* • *Cossetti* (Cascina Salomone) • *Neirano* (Le Croci) • *Antica Casa Vinicola Scarpa* • *Zonin* (Castello del Poggio)

BARBERA DEL MONFERRATO DOC
Piedmont

Most of the wines produced by Barbera Del Monferrato are lesser versions of Barbera d'Asti. Semisweet or *frizzante* styles may also be made.

✓ *C. S. di Castagnole Monferrato* (Barbera Vivace)

BAROLO DOCG
Piedmont

Barolo is unquestionably Italy's greatest wine appellation and its finest wines are the ultimate expression of the Nebbiolo grape. All the best vineyards of Barolo are located on a small, raised area of mostly gentle, but occasionally steep, slopes surrounded by the hills of the Langhe. The soil is essentially calcareous marl (*see* p.18), the northwestern half high in magnesium and manganese, the southeastern half more iron-rich. This small difference is deemed to be the reason why Barolo wines from the northwest have more elegance, while those from the southeast are fuller in body.

The biggest factor in the quality of Barolo has, however, been due more to man than to soil, especially with the trend over the past 10 years to isolate the very best Barolo and market them under single-vineyard names. A vineyard name will not necessarily guarantee excellence, but hardly any of the very top Barolo are blended these days, and quality should continue to rise under the Goria Law (see p.263), which requires significantly lower yields from any wine claiming single-vineyard status.

Great Barolo is incomparable, but there are still poor Barolo wines, although not as many as in the late 1980s. But even then the emergence of a new wave of fruit-driven Barolo was fairly evident. Initially, this split Barolo: the modern style wines had more fruit, riper and more supple tannins, and were aged in small barriques of new oak, while the worst of the so-called traditionalists continued to produce thick, tannic, dried-out wines.

The popular belief that so many traditional Barolo are dried out because they are bottled late is only half right. The truth is that they are—or were—bottled to order. This meant that some of the shipments of the same vintage would be more dried-out than others. There is still a large number of producers who perceive themselves to be traditional, but this simply means that they eschew barriques and new oak. Most traditionalists now bottle their Barolo when the wines—not the orders—require it, which, in effect, is earlier than before. They also tend to pick later and began to drop their yields even before the Goria Law of 1992. Today, both the modern and traditional schools of producers make stunning Barolo.

Modern styles are riper and more creamy than traditional ones, supported by the vanilla of new oak, whereas the traditional styles are arguably more complex, with tobacco, tar, and smoky aromas replacing the clean-cut vanilla. The best of both, however, are deep, sometimes inky-deep, in color and share lashings of fruit. All Barolo should be powerfully built, even the more elegant, earlier-drinking styles, and they all have a surprising finesse for such weighty wines.

🍷 8–25 years

✓ *Marziano Abbona • Accomasso • Elio Altare • Abbazia dell'Annunziata • Azelia • Fratelli Barale • Giacomo Borgogno • Bricco Roche • Fratelli Brovia • Giuseppe Cappellano • Cavalotto • Ceretto • Clerico • Aldo Conterno • Giacomo Conterno*

• *Conterno-Fantino • Corino • Franco-Fiorina • Fratelli Oddero • Angelo Gaja • Bruno Giacosa • Manzone • Marcarini • Bartolo Mascarello • Giuseppe Mascarello • Alfredo Prunotto • Renato Ratti • Giuseppe Rinaldi • Luciano Sandrone • Antica Casa Vinicola Scarpa • Vietti • Roberto Voerzio*

BAROLO CHINATO DOCG
Piedmont

This Barolo, aromatized with quinine, is a DOCG, which is a bit like classifying Bordeaux's aperitif "Lillet" as a *cru classé*.

BLANC DE COSSAN
Valle d'Aosta

These are fresh, tart *blancs de noir* made by the Institut Agricole Régional from Grenache grapes grown at Cossan, just outside Aosta.

BOCA DOC
Piedmont

These are medium- to full-bodied, spicy red Nebbiolo wines. They are hard to find, but wines have been made here since Roman times and when found can be good value.

🍷 3–6 years

✓ *Antonio Vallana • Podere ai Valloni*

BOTTICINO DOC
Lombardy

Full-bodied, Barbera-based red wines with a good level of alcohol and a light tannic structure.

🍷 3–5 years

✓ *Miro Bonetti • Benedetto Tognazzi*

BRACHETTO
Piedmont

Sweet, red, non-DOC Brachetto is often made by Asti producers.

✓ *Batasiolo*

BRACHETTO D'ACQUI DOCG
Piedmont

Sweet, *frizzante* (semi-sparkling), and sparkling red wines that are grapey and Muscat-like.

BRAMATERRA DOC
Piedmont

Good value, full-bodied red wines produced primarily from Nebbiolo, but which may include Bonarda, Croatina, and Vespolina grapes.

🍷 3–6 years

✓ *Luigi Perazzi • Fabrizio Sella*

BUTTAFUOCO DOC
Lombardy

See Oltrepò Pavese DOC.

CABERNET FRANC
Lombardy

This grape is far more traditional in Lombardy than Cabernet Sauvignon is, although the latter steals the limelight today. Mostly used in blends.

CABERNET SAUVIGNON
Piedmont

Thrives in Piedmont where *vini da tavola* can be excellent in quality as well as in value.

✓ *Angelo Gaja* (Darmagi)

CABERNET-MERLOT
Lombardy

A relative newcomer to Lombardy, this classic Bordeaux mix has shown outstanding potential.

✓ *Bellavista* (Solesine) • *Ca'del Bosco* (Maurizio Zanella)

CALUSO PASSITO DOC
Piedmont

Fragrant yet full-bodied, sweet white wines made from *passito* Erbaluce grapes.

🍷 3–5 years

✓ *Vittorio Boratto*

CAPRIANO DEL COLLE DOC
Lombardy

Rarely encountered red wines made from the Sangiovese, which are blended with Marzemino, Barbera, and Merlot, and tart white wines made from the Trebbiano.

CAREMA DOC
Piedmont

Soft, medium-bodied Nebbiolo wines that are grown on the mountainous slopes close to the border with the Valle d'Aosta. They are good and reliable but rarely exciting.

🍷 2–5 years

✓ *Luigi Ferrando*

CASALESE
Piedmont

A local grape capable of light, delicately dry white wine with a characteristic bitter finish, both as DOC and *vino da tavola*.

CELLATICA DOC
Lombardy

This aromatic and flavorsome red wine has been made in the hills overlooking Brescia for 400 years. Permitted grapes are Barbera, Marzemino, Schiava Gentile, and Incrocio Terzi.

🍷 2–6 years

✓ *Barbi*

CHAMBAVE DOC
Valle d'Aosta

A subappellation of the regional Valle d'Aosta DOC, Chambave produces attractively scented, crisp red wines primarily from Petit Rouge grapes, plus up to 40 percent Dolcetto, Gamay, and Pinot Noir. Two white wines are also permitted; one sweet, long-lived, and *passito* in style, the other a highly perfumed, early drinking, dry- to off-dry white—both from the Moscato grape. *See* Valle d'Aosta DOC.

🍷 2–3 years (red and *passito*) • upon purchase (white)

✓ *La Crotta di Vegneron • Ezio Voyat*

CHARDONNAY
Lombardy, Piedmont, and the Valle d'Aosta

Most of the Chardonnay grown in Lombardy ends up in traditional method wines, many of no specific origin, or in the Franciacorta and Oltrepò Pavese DOCs. However, there are a growing number of excellent, pure varietal *barrique*-aged *vini da tavola*, many of which are surprisingly full and lusty in style.

In contrast to Valle d'Aosta below, pure Chardonnay *vini da tavola* are quite common in Piedmont. Although the quality is variable, when Piedmont Chardonnay is good, it is rich and lush, yet classically structured and of a quality that few other Italian wine regions can touch. Many will no doubt receive official DOC status in years to come.

A few *barrique*-aged examples have proved the worth of this grape in Valle d'Aosta, but it is not a frequently encountered varietal, even though it is recognized in the regional DOC.

✓ **Lombardy** *Bellavista* • *Ca'del Bosco* • *Cascina La Pertica* • *Tenuta Castello* • *Tronconero*

Piedmont *Angelo Gaja* • *Pio Cesare*

CINQUE TERRE *or* CINQUETERRE DOC
Liguria

These spectacular coastal vineyards produce good, though not exactly spectacular, delicately fruity dry white wines, and the somewhat more exciting Cinque Terre Sciacchetrà, which is a medium-sweet *passito* wine.

🍷— 1–3 years

✓ *Forlini Cappellini*

COLLI DI LUNI DOC
Liguria

Sangiovese-based reds and Vermentino whites from the eastern extremity of Liguria, bordering and even overlapping part of Tuscany.

🍷— 2–5 years (red) and 1–2 years (white)

✓ *La Colombiera*

COLLI MORENICI MANTOVANI DEL GARDA DOC
Lombardy

Although vines have been cultivated since ancient times in Lake Garda, today viticulture is one of the least important crops. The wines are dry, light-bodied, red, white, and rosé, produced from a mixture of grape varieties.

COLLI TORTONESI DOC
Piedmont

Robust and rather rustic, full-bodied Barbera reds, and crisp, dry, rather lightweight, and sometimes *frizzante* Cortese whites.

COLLINE NOVARESI DOC
Piedmont

A new DOC for red and white wines from the Novarese province northwest of Milan; the white is dry and made exclusively from the Erbaluce grape, whereas the red is a blend of at least 40 percent Uva Rara and 30 percent Nebbiolo, plus up to 30 percent Vespolina and Croatina.

CORTESE DELL'ALTO MONFERRATO DOC
Piedmont

Dry, crisp, still, *frizzante*, and fully sparkling white wines that often incline to a coarser style than expected for the Cortese grape.

CORTESE DI GAVI DOCG

See Gavi DOCG.

DIANO D'ALBA DOC

See Dolcetto di Diano d'Alba DOC.

DOLCETTO
Piedmont

Non-DOC Dolcetto can be excellent-value reds, gushing with soft, easy-drinking fruit.

✓ *Clerico* • *Corino* • *Marchesi di Gresy* • *Marcarini* • *Luciano Sandrone*

DOLCETTO D'ACQUI DOC
Piedmont

Dolcetto is a plump grape with a low acid content that is traditionally used to make cheerful, Beaujolais-type wines that are deep purple in color and best enjoyed young.

🍷— 1–3 years

✓ *Viticoltori dell'Acquese* • *Villa Banficut*

DOLCETTO D'ALBA DOC
Piedmont

Dolcetto d'Alba DOC produces some soft, smooth, juicy wines that should be drunk while they are young, fresh, and fruity.

🍷— 1–3 years

✓ *Elio Altare* • *Azelia* • *Batasiolo* • *Fratelli Brovia* • *Ceretto* • *Pio Cesare* • *Fratelli Cigliuti* • *Aldo Conterno* • *Cascina Drago* • *Franco Fiorina* • *Elio Grasso* • *Bartolo Mascarello* • *Pira* • *Roberto Voerzio*

DOLCETTO D'ASTI DOC
Piedmont

These wines are lighter than Dolcetto d'Alba.

DOLCETTO DELLE LANGHE MONREGALESI DOC
Piedmont

Rare wines produced in tiny quantities, reputed to have an exceptionally fine aroma.

DOLCETTO DI DIANO D'ALBA *or* DIANO D'ALBA DOC
Piedmont

Diano is a hilltop village just south of Alba, which produces wines that are slightly fuller and more grapey than most other Dolcetto wines.

🍷— 3–5 years

✓ *Alario* • *Casavecchia* • *Colué* • *Fontanafredda* • *Giuseppe Mascarello* • *Cantina della Porta Rossa* • *Mario Savigliano* • *Veglio & Figlio*

DOLCETTO DI DOGLIANI DOC
Piedmont

Most Dolcetto from Dogliani used to be made to drink young and fruity, but more is now being made in a *vin de garde* style. The best attain a lovely perfumed finesse with a few years in bottle.

✓ *Chionetti* • *Luigi Einaudi* • *Angelo Gaja* • *Pira* • *Roberto Voerzio*

DOLCETTO DI OVADA DOC
Piedmont

These are the fullest and firmest of Dolcettos.

🍷— 3–6 years (up to 10 for the very best)

✓ *Cascina Scarsi Olivi*

DOLCETTO-NEBBIOLO
Piedmont

When backed up by full, firm Nebbiolo, the soft, lush fruit of Dolcetto remains remarkably fresh for a considerable time in bottle.

✓ *Cascina Drago* (Bricco del Drago, especially Vigna le Mace)

DONNAZ *or* DONNAS
Valle d'Aosta

Formerly its own DOC, but now a subappellation of the regional Valle d'Aosta DOC, Donnaz produces soft, well-balanced, Nebbiolo-based red wines that have a pleasant, yet slightly bitter aftertaste. *See also* Valle d'Aosta DOC, p274.

ENFER D'ARVIER
Valle d'Aosta

Formerly its own DOC, but now a subappellation of the regional Valle d'Aosta DOC, Enfer d'Arvier is a low-key, medium-bodied red wine made primarily from the Petit Rouge grape, although Dolcetto, Gamay, Neyret, Pinot Noir, and Vien de Nus may also be used. *See also* Valle d'Aosta DOC, p274.

ERBALUCE DI CALUSO *or* CALUSO DOC
Piedmont

These are fresh, dry, light-bodied white wines made from the Erbaluce, which is a rather undistinguished grape. A far more interesting *passito* version exists and it is probably this that gave Erbaluce its overrated, albeit localized, reputation. *See also* Caluso Passito DOC.

🍷— 1–3 years

✓ *Luigi Ferrando*

FARA DOC
Piedmont

In the hands of someone like Dessilani, Fara DOC proves to be an underrated, enjoyable, Nebbiolo-based wine with lots of fruit combined with a spicy-scented character.

✓ *Luigi Dessilani* (Caramino)

FAVORITA
Piedmont

Descended from the Vermentino, this was once a popular table grape, but now makes dry, crisp white *vini da tavola* and, since 1995, DOC Langhe Favorita. The best varietal wines have a delicate floral aroma and refreshing acidity.

FLÉTRI
Valle d'Aosta

In this bilingual region, the French *flétri*, which means "shriveled," may be used in preference to the Italian *passito*.

FRANCIACORTA DOCG
Lombardy

The sparkling white and rosé wines made by Franciacorta were promoted to DOCG status in September 1995. Produced by the traditional method with 25 months' aging on the lees (or 37 if *riserva*), Franciacorta had already shown its potential for producing fine, biscuity, *brut*, and lightly rich rosé sparkling wines when this book was first published. It not only deserves its prestigious classification, it is an object lesson for the rest of the Italian wine industry for two reasons. First, the still wines have retained their former DOC status (*see* Terre di Franciacorta DOC), making it one of Italy's more prestigious appellations. Meanwhile, the selection of only sparkling wines for DOCG enhances this new classification, whereas promoting an entire DOC devalues it. Not every region has a supercategory to promote as Franciacorta has, but others could, for example, restrict production to the original *classico* area and a reduced yield. This would result in both a DOC and DOCG for the same region and, in the mind of the consumer, it would ensure that the "G" did guarantee an elevated quality equivalent to *grand cru*, for example. The second lesson is that as the first Italian wine to insist on bottle-fermentation, Franciacorta is currently the only Italian dry sparkling-wine appellation that can demand respect from the rest of the world. *See* Terre di Franciacorta DOC for still wines.

🍷— 2–5 years

✅ *Banfi • Bellavista • Fratelli Berlucchi • Bersi Serlini • Ca'del Bosco • Bredasole • Castelfaglia • Tenuta Castellino • Casteveder • Cavalleri • Cola • Ricci Curbastro • Faccoli • Lantieri de Paratico • Majolini • La Montina • Barone Pizzini • Lo Sparviere • Villa*

FREISA
Piedmont

The Freisa is a black grape of refreshing acidity, which makes ruby red wines with characteristic raspberry and rose-petal aromas for early drinking. Non-DOC wines abound, particularly around Alba, where this variety excels in quality, despite the lack of official recognition.

🍷— 3–6 years (up to 10 for the very best)

✅ *Clerico • Aldo Conterno • Coppo*

FREISA D'ASTI DOC
Piedmont

Known for centuries, and a favorite of King Victor Emmanuel, this is the original and most famous Freisa. These fruity red wines may be made fully sparkling, *frizzante*, or still, and in both dry and sweet styles.

🍷— 3–6 years (up to 10 for the very best)

✅ *Gilli*

FREISA DI CHIERI DOC
Piedmont

Freisa di Chieri produces the same styles of wine as Freisa d'Asti from just outside Turin.

FUMIN
Valle d'Aosta

Very little is known about this grape, which is usually blended with others but occasionally makes a robust red on its own under the Valle d'Aosta DOC or as a *vino da tavola*.

GABIANO DOC
Piedmont

The full-bodied, red Barbera wines of Castello di Gabiano seemed to make this a promising DOC, but the appellation has not taken off and these wines are seldom encountered.

GAMAY
Valle d'Aosta

The non-DOC wines of Gamay are light-bodied with an attenuated earthy fruitiness.

GAMAY-PINOT NERO
Valle d'Aosta

A light and fruity *passetoutgrains* style.

GATTINARA DOCG
Piedmont

From Nebbiolo and up to 10 percent Bonarda grown on the right bank of the Sesia River in northern Piedmont, Gattinara can be a fine, though not a great, wine, especially now that overcropping problems have been reduced since Gattinara attained DOCG status. When young, the fruit can be chunky and rustic when compared with Barbaresco or Barolo, but the best Gattinara wines develop a fine, silky-textured flavor and a graceful, violet-perfumed finesse when mature. Gattinara earned its DOC and then full DOCG status through the almost single-handed efforts of Mario Antoniolo, whose wines have always been among the greatest produced in the area. Others have followed his example, but have been too few and too slow to give Gattinara the sort of reputation that a world-class wine appellation ought to have.

🍷— 6–15 years

✅ *Mario Antoniolo • Le Colline • Travaglini*

GAVI *or* CORTESE DI GAVI DOCG
Piedmont

The quality and character of these highly fashionable wines is very uneven, although prices are uniformly high. At best, they are soft-textured, dry white wines with a slight *frizzantino* when young, and can develop a honey-rich flavor after a couple of years in bottle. Too many examples have all their character fermented out at low temperatures, which gives them an amylic peardrop aroma, and some are definitely *frizzante*.

🍷— 2–3 years

✅ *Nicola Bergaglio • Chiarlo* (Fior di Rovere) *• Carlo Deltetto • La Scolca*

GHEMME DOCG
Piedmont

A Nebbiolo-based wine produced on the bank opposite Gattinara, Ghemme is usually seen as the inferior of the two appellations, but it has never been as persistently overcropped and is generally more consistent. Although not capable of reaching the heights of Antoniolo's Gattinara, for example, most Ghemme has just as much color, body, and flavor as Gattinara in general, and starts off with a much finer bouquet and more elegant fruit. In addition to Nebbiolo, Vespolina and Bonarda may be used.

🍷— 4–15 years

✅ *Antichi Vigneti di Cantelupo • Le Colline • Luigi Dessilani*

GRIGNOLINO D'ASTI DOC
Piedmont

Grignolino d'Asti DOC produces lightly tannic red wines with a slightly bitter aftertaste.

GRIGNOLINO DEL MONFERRATO CASALESE DOC
Piedmont

These are light, crisp, fresh red wines made from Grignolino around the Casalese Monferrato.

GRUMELLO DOC
Lombardy

See Valtellina Superiore DOC.

INFERNO DOC
Lombardy

See Valtellina Superiore DOC.

LAMBRUSCO MANTOVANO DOC
Lombardy

Not all Lambrusco comes from Emilia-Romagna. This one is produced just across the border on the plains of Mantua (Mantova). Formerly a *vino da tavola*, Mantovano is red and *frizzante* with a pink foam and may be dry or sweet.

🍷— Upon purchase

✅ *C. S. di Quistello*

LANGHE DOC
Piedmont

This area overlaps the DOCs Barbaresco, Barolo, Nebbiolo d'Alba, Dolcetto d'Alba, and Barbera d'Alba and, if used sensibly, through selection, could ensure the highest quality in those wines. White, red, and six varietal wines are permitted: Dolcetto, Freisa, and Nebbiolo for red; and Arneis, Favorita, and Chardonnay for white.

✅ *Chionetti • Aldo Conterno • Angelo Gaja • Giuseppe Mascarello*

LESSONA DOC
Piedmont

These are red wines that can be delightfully scented, with rich fruit and some finesse.

LOAZZOLO DOC
Piedmont

From the village of Loazzolo, south of Canelli, this Moscato *passito* is aged for two years, including six months in *barriques*, to produce a golden-hued, richly flavored, lusciously textured, exotically sweet wine. A wine that can age, but which is best drunk young.

🍷— 2–4 years

✔ *Borgo Maragliano* • *Borgo Sambui*
• *Bricchi Mej* • *Giancarlo Scaglione*

LUGANA DOC
Lombardy

These are soft, smooth, dry white wines made from Trebbiano grown on the shores of Lake Garda, slightly overlapping Veneto in northeast Italy. There are many dullards, but the very best Lugana manage to transcend the lackluster level normally expected from this grape variety.

🍷 1–2 years

✔ *Cà dei Frati* • *Visconti*

MALVASIA
Lombardy

In many instances Malvasia, Malvoisie, and Pinot Gris are the same variety of grape, but the Malvasia of Lombardy is the true Malvasia and a very different grape from the Malvoisie of Valle d'Aosta. A dark-skinned grape, Malvasia makes both red and white wines, still and sparkling, dry and sweet, and, most puzzling of all, full- and light-bodied, and neutral and aromatic.

✔ *La Muiraghina*

MALVASIA DI CASORZO D'ASTI DOC
Piedmont

These are lightly aromatic, sweet, red, and rosé wines that may also be sparkling.

🍷 1–2 years

✔ *Bricco Mondalino*

MALVASIA DI CASTELNUOVO DON BOSCO DOC
Piedmont

The DOC of Malvasia di Castelnuovo Don Bosco produces attractive, lightly aromatic, sweet, red, still, and sparkling wines.

🍷 1–2 years

✔ *Bava*

MALVOISIE
Valle d'Aosta

The Malvoisie of Valle d'Aosta is in fact Pinot Gris, not Malvasia, and its dry, semisweet, and *passito* wines are, though not at all spicy, smooth and usually slightly bitter in both DOC and *vino da tavola* versions.

MONFERRATO DOC
Piedmont

This is a relatively new DOC, which was introduced in 1995 for red, white, and *ciaret* or *chiaretto* (rosé) Dolcetto, Casalese, and Freisa from a wide area overlapping the Asti region.

✔ *La Barbatella* • *Martinetti* • *Villa Sparina*

MORGEX ET LA SALLE DOC
Valle d'Aosta

A subappellation of the regional Valle d'Aosta DOC, the vineyards of these two communes reach as high as 4,265 feet (1,300 meters), which makes it one of the highest wine-growing areas in Europe. However, most vines in these two villages are grown between 2,952 and 3,280 feet (900 and 1,000 meters), although even this is remarkable as, in theory, grapes do not ripen above 2,625 feet (800 meters) in the Valle d'Aosta. However, in practice they ripen, and produce a fine, dry, *frizzantino* white. Brut, Extra Brut, and Demi Sec *spumante* versions are also made. *See also* Valle d'Aosta DOC.

🍷 1–3 years

✔ *Alberto Vevey*

MOSCATO
Lombardy and Piedmont

Good non-DOC is made in Lombardy and the Moscato di Scanzo is undoubtedly the best. In the Piedmont, non-DOC Moscato is prolific in many styles and formats, and even a crisp, dry version to challenge Alsace is available from Alasia (an alliance between the flying winemaker Martin Shaw and the Araldica consortium of cooperatives).

✔ **Lombardy** *Celinate Ronchello* • *Il Cipresso* • *La Cornasella*

Piedmont *Alasia* (especially Muscaté Sec)

MOSCATO D'ASTI DOCG
Piedmont

Wines similar in flavor to Asti, but with a minimum pressure of three atmospheres, as opposed to five. Still, slightly *frizzantino*, and positively *frizzante* examples of Moscato d'Asti exist. Those with some degree of effervescence are bottled without any *dosage*, while the first fermentation is still underway, as opposed to Asti plain and simple, which is made by the *cuve close* method. Compared with Asti, Moscato d'Asti is generally, though not necessarily, less alcoholic (5.5 to 8 percent instead of 7.5 to 9 percent) and almost always much sweeter. If there is any criticism of this luscious, heavenly nectar, it is the unfortunate trend to make these wines fizzier, as there is often little difference between modern Moscato d'Asti and Asti itself. Rarely does one find a still Moscato d'Asti with the barest prickle, as in the past. That said, this is the Asti DOC to pick. As there are fewer than 3 million bottles, as opposed to 85 million Asti, it is more expensive, and the best, such as Borgo Maragliano's La Caliera, which is in a completely different class from the rest, are definitely fine.

🍷 Upon purchase

✔ *Araldica* • *Castello Banfi* • *Alfiero Boffa* • *Borgo Maragliano* • *Redento Dogliotti* • *Gatti* • *Marchesi di Gresy* • *Villa Lanata* • *Luciana Rivella* • *La Spinetta-Rivetti*

NEBBIOLO
Piedmont

Most *vini da tavola* from this grape are relatively simple red wines, as the best areas for Nebbiolo have long been known and have become famous DOCGs. Exceptionally fine examples have, however, been made in great years by the best Barolo and Barbaresco producers. It remains to be seen whether or not they will continue to do so now that they also have the choice of Nebbiolo d'Alba and Langhe

Nebbiolo DOCs through which to sell such wines.

✔ *Elio Altare* • *Clerico* (Arté) • *Corino* • *Cascina Drago* • *I Paglieri* (Opera Prima)

NEBBIOLO D'ALBA DOC
Piedmont

Pure Nebbiolo wines come from between Barolo and Barbaresco. Most are fine, full, rich, and fruity. Sweet and sparkling versions are allowed.

🍷 4–10 years

✔ *Ascheri* • *Tenuta Carretta* • *Ceretto* • *Pio Cesare* • *Aldo Conterno* • *Giacomo Conterno* • *Franco Fiorina* • *Angelo Gaja* • *Bruno Giacosa* • *Hilberg-Pasquero* • *Giuseppe Mascarello* • *Val de Prete* • *Vietti*

NEBBIOLO-BARBERA
Piedmont

A strikingly successful *vino da tavola* blend that takes to *barrique*-aging like a duck to water, producing delicious yet classy red wines with plump, juicy fruit, held together by supple tannins and a touch of smoky-oak. Some wines, such as Conterno Fantino's Monprà, contain more Barbera than Nebbiolo. *See also* Petit Rouge.

✔ *Giacomo* (Bric Milieu) • *Chiarlo* (Barilot) • *Valentino Migliorini* (Bricco Manzoni) • *Conterno Fantino* (Monprà) • *Vietti* (Fioretto) • *Roberto Voerzio* (Vignaserra) • *Oriou* (Valle d'Aosta)

NUS DOC
Valle d'Aosta

A subappellation of the Valle d'Aosta DOC, Nus makes an interesting red from Vien de Nus, Petit Rouge, and Pinot Noir grapes. Dry and *passito* styles of white wine are made from Pinot Gris or Malvoisie de Nus. *See also* Valle d'Aosta DOC.

🍷 2–4 years

✔ *La Crotta di Vegneron*

OLTREPÒ PAVESE DOC
Lombardy

The Oltrepò Pavese covers 42 communes south of the Po River, although much of the production is not marketed under this DOC, but sold to specialized wineries in Piedmont. These wineries turn it into non-DOC *spumante* by the *cuve close* process or the traditional method. There used to be three geographical subappellations, but Barbacarlo has since been recognized as the exclusive product of Lino Maga, reverting to *vino da tavola* status. The two remaining subappellations are **Oltrepò Pavese Buttafuoco** ("sparks of fire"), a deep-colored, fruity, dry or semisweet *frizzante* red; and **Oltrepò Pavese Sangue di Giuda** (charmingly named "blood of Judas"), a soft, sweet, red *spumante*. Both wines are restricted to vineyards around the villages of Broni, Canetto Pavese, Castana, Cigognola, Montescano, Pietra de Giorgi, and Stradella. Aside from blended red, white, and rosé wines, Oltrepò Pavese permits 11 varietal wines: Barbera, Bonarda (made from Croatina), Cabernet Sauvignon, and Pinot Noir (still and *spumante*) for red; and Chardonnay, Cortese, Malvasia, Moscato (still, *spumante*, and *liquoroso*), Pinot Grigio, Riesling Italico, and Riesling Renano for white.

🍷 1–3 years (white, rosé, and sparkling)
   2–5 years (red)

✓ *Giacomo Agnes • Angelo Ballabio • Bianchina Alberici • Doria* (Pinot Nero) *• Lino Maga* (see also Barbacarlo) *• Monsupello • Piccolo Bacco dei Quaroni • Tronconero* (Bonarda) *• Zonin* (Moscato spumante)

ORMEASCO
Liguria

Ormeasco is the local Ligurian variant of Dolcetto, which can produce some deliciously easy-to-drink, soft, fruity red wines.

PETIT ROUGE
Valle d'Aosta

Deep, dark, and highly perfumed red wines from this low-yielding, local grape that can be met within both DOC and *vino da tavola* versions. There are many variants in the family of Petit Rouge, but they can all be traced back to the Oriou, which may in future be used for its varietal wines. Moves have been underway since the early 1990s to change the name of the Petit Rouge grape to Oriou owing to the supposedly belittling effect of *petit* in its name, even though this refers to the size of berry, not the quality of wine (most classic varieties have smaller, rather than larger, grapes and this should thus be seen as a positive attribute).

PIEMONTE DOC
Piedmont

Introduced in 1995, this DOC embraces all the other DOC areas in the Piedmont and, with the exception of Piemonte Moscato and Piemonte Moscato Passito, which must be made from 100 percent Moscato grapes, all wines claiming this appellation are required to contain at least 85 percent of the variety indicated. Permitted red wine varietals are Barbera, Bonarda, Brachetto, Dolcetto, and Pinot Noir, while in addition to the Moscato wines already mentioned above, white varietals include Cortese, Pinot Blanc, and Pinot Gris. The creation of this regional DOC probably explains why no IGT wines have been declared in Piedmont, and it is doubtful whether any IGT will be in the future.

PINOT NERO
Lombardy

Most Pinot Noir grown in northwest Italy goes into classic *brut spumante* wines. Still wines are made under the Oltrepò Pavese denomination (Doria being outstanding) and a small number of non-DOC examples are to be found. The two wines listed below are *barrique*-aged, and are exceptionally fine in quality.

✓ *Ca'del Bosco • Tenuta Mazzolino*

PREMETTA
Valle d'Aosta

Lightly tannic, bright cherry-red wines from this local grape, Premetta, can be encountered in both DOC and *vino da tavola* versions.

RIVIERA DEL GARDA BRESCIANO *or* GARDA BRESCIANO DOC
Lombardy

This area makes light, fruity, slightly bitter red wines that are no more interesting than the bulk of Valpolicella, produced on the opposite bank of Lake Garda. Most are blended from Gropello, Sangiovese, Marzemino, and Barbera, but some are pure varietal wines from the Gropello grape and these tend to be superior. Although the whites may be pure Riesling, this is taken to mean either Riesling Renano, which is true Riesling, or Riesling Italico, which is not. Furthermore, as up to 20 percent of other local grape varieties may be used, Garda Bresciano *bianco* has not been of much interest so far. The most successful wine here has been the rosé, or *chiaretto*, which, although it is made from exactly the same varieties as the *rosso*, can be much softer and easier to drink.

🍷— Upon purchase

✓ *Costaripa*

RIVIERA LIGURE DI PONENTE DOC
Liguria

Four former *vini da tavola* are grouped together under this appellation, which covers the western Riviera of Liguria. These are: *Ormeasco*, bright, cherry-red wines with juicy, raspberry, Dolcetto fruit; *Pigato*, full-flavored yet somewhat precocious red wines, *Rossese*, well-scented, characterful reds; and *Vermentino*, rich, full, and characterful dry white wines.

ROERO DOCG
Piedmont

This DOC covers light-bodied, easy drinking, inexpensive Nebbiolo reds and the highly regarded, highly priced Arneis whites from the Roeri hills north of Alba. *See* Arneis di Roero.

🍷— 1–2 years

✓ *Carlo Deltetto • Giovanni Almondo • Matteo Correggia • Monchero Carboni • Malvirà*

ROSSESE DI DOLCEACQUA *or* DOLCEACQUA DOC
Liguria

This DOC produces light, easy-drinking red wines that are capable of rich, lush fruit, a soft texture, and spicy-aromatic aftertaste.

🍷— 1–4 years

✓ *Giobatta Cane • Lupi • Antonio Perrino*

RUBINO DI CANTAVENNA DOC
Piedmont

A full-bodied red wine blend of mostly Barbera, Grignolino, and sometimes Freisa. It is made by a *cooperativa* called Rubino, which was solely responsible for creating this appellation, but failed to interest other producers. As a result, the DOC has not taken off.

RUCHÉ
Piedmont

The Ruché is a rather mysterious grape of unknown origin that generally makes a light ruby-colored wine with an aromatic twist, although, through reduced yields, much darker, weightier, richer wines can be achieved.

✓ *Scarpa*

RUCHÉ DI CASTAGNOLE MONFERRATO DOC
Piedmont

When grown on the vineyards overlooking Castagnole Monferrato, the Ruché grape is supposed to produce an aromatic red wine that ages like Nebbiolo. Up to 10 percent Barbera and Brachetto may be used in production.

🍷— 3–5 years

✓ *Piero Bruno • Ruché del Parrocco*

SAN COLOMBANO AL LAMBRO *or* SAN COLOMBANO DOC
Lombardy

Rich, robust, if somewhat rustic red wines made from Croatina, Barbera, and Uva Rara are produced by this DOC. San Colombano is the only DOC in the Milan province.

🍷— 2–5 years

✓ *Carlo Pietrasanta*

SAN MARTINO DELLA BATTAGLIA DOC
Lombardy

Dry, full-flavored white wine with a flowery aroma and slightly bitter aftertaste, and a sweet, *liquoroso* wine, made from the Tocai Friulano.

SANGUE DI GIUDA DOC

See Oltrepò Pavese DOC.

SASSELLA DOC
Lombardy

See Valtellina Superiore DOC.

SAUVIGNON BLANC
Piedmont

These wines are virtually unknown in the region, although the soil and climate seem favorable. Angelo Gaja's *barrique* aged pure Sauvignon Alteni di Brassica shows potential.

✓ *Angelo Gaja* (Alteni di Brassica)

SIZZANO DOC
Piedmont

These are good, full-bodied red wines that are produced from a Gattinara-like blend on a bank of the Sesia River, just south of Ghemme.

SPANNA
Piedmont

The local name for the Nebbiolo, Spanna merely represents the most basic wines from this grape variety, although in the hands of some specialists it can surpass many generic Barolo and Barbaresco.

✓ *Luciano Brigatti • Villa Era*

SYRAH
Valle d'Aosta

The Institut Agricole Régional has produced very interesting *barrique* wine from this grape, the Syrah, since the late 1980s.

TERRE DI FRANCIACORTA DOC
Lombardy

Part of the original Franciacorta appellation since 1967, the still wines were renamed Terre di Franciacorta in 1995 when the name in its singular form, Terra di Franciacorta, was reserved for the new DOCG. Produced northeast of Milan, on hilly slopes near Lake Iseo, the red wines are typically well colored, medium- to full-bodied, made from Cabernet Franc and Cabernet Sauvignon, with the possible addition of Barbera, Nebbiolo, and

Merlot. Many are richly flavored and show some finesse. The dry white wines, primarily from Chardonnay with a little Pinot Blanc permissible, have improved tremendously.

⌐— 3–8 years (red), 1–3 years (white)

✓ *Ca'del Bosco* • *Enrico Gatti* • *Ragnoli*

TIMORASSO
Piedmont

Tipped by some to be the next trendy white grape variety, Timorasso has until now been confined to *vini da tavola* and *grappa*, with more emphasis on the latter. Walter Massa in the upper Val Curone was the first to produce a varietal wine from Timorasso, almost by accident, when a *grappa* producer by the name of Antonella Bocchino became curious about this grape. She had seen it mentioned in 19th-century documents, but it was thought to be extinct until she tracked down a plot on Massa's estate. Since Bocchino was interested in making only *grappa* with the pressings, Massa was left with the wine on his hands and it turned out to be more than just a curiosity. Massa has supplied other estates with cuttings and several producers now make Timorasso, a varietal that could follow on the success of Gavi and Arneis.

TORRETTE DOC
Valle d'Aosta

A red-only subappellation of the regional Valle d'Aosta DOC, Torrette produces deep-colored wines of good bouquet and body from the Petit Rouge, plus up to 30 percent Dolcetto, Fumin, Gamay, Mayolet, Pinot Noir, Premetta, and Vien de Nus. *See also* Valle d'Aosta DOC.

✓ *Elio Cassol* • *Grosjean*

VALCALEPIO DOC
Lombardy

An up-and-coming appellation for well-colored, deeply flavored red wines made from a blend of Merlot and Cabernet Sauvignon, and for light, delicately dry white wines made from Pinot Blanc and Pinot Gris.

⌐— 1–3 years (white), 3–7 years (red)

✓ *Tenuta Castello*

VALGELLA DOC
Lombardy

See Valtellina Superiore DOC.

VALLE D'AOSTA *or* VALLÉE D'AOSTE DOC
Valle d'Aosta

A regional DOC encompassing 20 different styles of wine, Valle d'Aosta took under its wings the only two DOCs formerly recognized in the region: Donnaz and Enfer d'Arvier. These are now two of the seven subappellations within this DOC, the other five being Arnad-Montjovat, Chambave, Morgex et La Salle, Nus, and Torrette (*see* individual entries). The Valle d'Aosta DOC has revitalized this region's tiny production of somewhat low-key wines. Aside from blended red, white, and rosé, the following varietal wines are permitted: Fumin, Gamay, Nebbiolo, Petit Rouge, Pinot Noir, and Premetta for reds; and Chardonnay, Müller-Thurgau, Petit Arvine, and Pinot Gris for whites. There is also a Bianco di Pinot Nero, which you might see labeled as a Blanc de Noir de Pinot Noir, as all Valle d'Aosta wines have official alternative French designations.

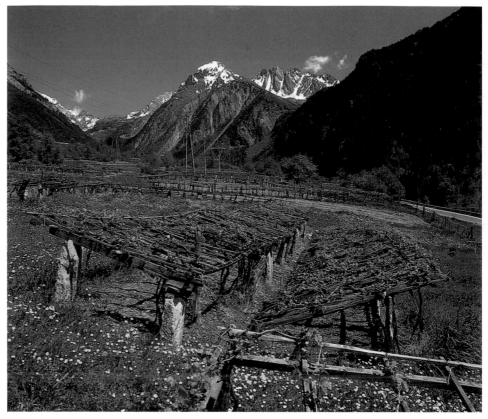

SPRINGTIME AT MORGEX, VALLE D'AOSTA
Grown at more than 3,000 feet (900 meters), these vines annually disprove the theory that grapes should not ripen above 2,600 feet (800 meters) in the Valle d'Aosta.

⌐— 1–3 years

✓ *Grosjean* • *La Crotta di Vegneron* • *Les Crêtes*

VALTELLINA DOC
Lombardy

Encompasses 19 communes of the province of Sondrio. Most are light-scented, medium-bodied red wines of simple, but pleasing, character. Many critics believe Valtellina to be very overrated, and the basic *appellation* certainly is, but the fine wines are virtually all classed as Valtellina Superiore. *See also* Valtellina Superiore DOC.

VALTELLINA SUPERIORE DOCG
Lombardy

The best wines of Valtellina are produced from a narrow strip of vineyards on the north bank of the Adda River near the Swiss border, and must contain a minimum of 12 percent alcohol, as opposed to the 11 percent required for Valtellina. Most of the wines come from four subdistricts: **Grumello** (the lightest), **Inferno** (supposedly the hottest, rockiest part of the valley), **Sassella** (the best), and **Valgella** (the most productive but least interesting). Essentially a Nebbiolo, but up to 10 percent Pinot Noir, Merlot, Rossola, Brugnola, and Pignola Valtellina may also be used. The richness of the best of these wines is belied by their elegance. They have good color and are capable of developing exquisite finesse after several years in bottle. *Sfursat* or *Sforzato*, which literally means "strained" and is made from shriveled grapes, is a dry, concentrated red wine that has a minimum of 14.5 percent alcohol (try Nino Negri's), which makes it the equivalent of *amarone*.

⌐— 5–15 years

✓ *Enologica Valtellinese* • *Sandro Fay* • *Fondazione Fojanini* • *Nino Negri* • *Conti Sertoli-Salis* • *Fratelli Triacca* • *Mamete Prevostini*

VIEN DE NUS
Valle d'Aosta

A very similar grape to the Petit Rouge, but whereas the Petit Rouge is widely planted throughout the Valle d'Aosta, cultivation of the Vien de Nus is restricted to the vineyards around Nus itself.

VIN DE CONSEIL
Valle d'Aosta

Perfumed dry white made by the Institut Agricole Régional from Petite Arvine.

NEW IGT WINES

The following Indicazioni Geografiche Tipiche wines were agreed to at the end of 1996, yet most have still to register with consumers, or establish any consistency of style or quality:

✓ **Liguria** *Colli Savonesi* • *Golfo del Tigullio* • *Val Polcevera*

Lombardy *Alto Mincio* • *Benaco Bresciano* • *Bergamasca* • *Collina del Milanese* • *Quistello* • *Ronchi di Brescia, Sabbioneta* • *Sebino* • *Terrazze Retiche di Sondrio*

Piedmont *none*

Valle d'Aosta *none*

NORTHEAST ITALY

Freshness, crisp acidity, and purity of varietal character personify the wines of the northeastern regions of Trentino-Alto Adige, Friuli-Venezia Giulia, and the Veneto; but beware the mass-produced wines, which are so clean and pure that they lack any fruit.

THIS IS A MORE MOUNTAINOUS area than the northwest (with the exception of that region's Valle d'Aosta), as just over half the land is occupied by the Dolomites and their precipitous foothills. Some of the finest wines are grown in the lush, verdant vineyards of the South Tyrol (Alto Adige), just over the border from Austria. A great deal of wine is exported; the bulk of it is unexciting Soave and Valpolicella. Locally there is much greater variety and value to be had—a number of French and German grapes are grown in addition to fascinating local varieties, and dedicated

TERMENO VINEYARDS, ALTO ADIGE
The town of Termeno, or Tramin, as it is also called, is situated between Bolzano and Trento, in the Alto Adige region. This is where the Traminer Aromatico, or Gewürztraminer, is supposed to have originated, but the local clone is far more restrained than the classic Alsace version, with hardly any spice to its character.

NORTHEAST ITALY, *see also* p.263
The variety of sites offered by the mountains and the hills of this area enables many grape varieties to be grown in addition to local ones. The most exciting wines come from the high vineyards of the South Tyrol, the hills of Friuli, and around Vicenza in the Veneto.

Valdadige

Casteller

Teroldego Rotaliano

Alto Adige encompassing Terlano, Santa Maddalena, Colli di Bolzano Lago di Caldaro, Valle Isarco (6)

Trentino, Casteller, Sorni

Bardolino, Bianco di Custoza, Bardolino Classico (7)

Valpolicella, Valpolicella Classico (8)

Soave

Lessini Durello

Gambellara

Colli Berici

Colli Euganei

Montello e Colli Asolani

Prosecco di Conegliano-Valdobbiadene

Lison-Pramaggiore

Friuli-Grave

Collio

Colli Orientali del Friuli

Carso

1 Breganze

2 Piave

3 Friuli-Latisana

4 Friuli-Aquileia

5 Isonzo

Provincia boundary

▲ Height above sea level (meters)

| 0 | 10 | 20 | 30 | 40 miles |
| 0 | 20 | 40 | 60 km |

AVERAGE ANNUAL PRODUCTION

REGION	DOC PRODUCTION	TOTAL PRODUCTION
Veneto	17 million cases (1.5 million hl)	110 million cases (10 million hl)
Trentino-Alto Adige	8 million cases (700,000 hl)	17 million cases (1.5 million hl)
Friuli-Venezia Giulia	5 million cases (5 million cases)	18 million cases (1.6 million hl)

Percentage of total Italian production: Veneto, 13%; Trentino-Alto Adige, 2%; Friuli-Venezia Giulia, 1.5%.

producers continue to experiment. Austria to the north and Slovenia to the east have influenced the styles produced.

TRENTINO-ALTO ADIGE

This is the most westerly and spectacular of the northeast's three regions, and more than 90 percent of its area is covered by mountainous countryside. It is made up of two autonomous provinces, the Italian-speaking Trento in the south and the German-speaking Bolzano, or South Tyrol, in the north. In Bolzano the wines may possess alternative German names and can carry a QbA (*Qualitätswein bestimmter Anbaugebiete*) designation. The generic Alto Adige DOC (*Südtiroler QbA*) is remarkably good and accounts for one-third of the region's total DOC output. There are also numerous fine wines produced in these cool, high vineyards.

THE VENETO

The Veneto stretches from the Po River to the Austrian border, between Trentino-Alto Adige to the west and Friuli-Venezia Giulia to the east, and most of the wines are grown on alluvial plains in the south. Once famous, but more recently infamous, for its Valpolicella and Soave, the Veneto is also one of the most exciting hunting grounds for some of Italy's best Bordeaux-type blends, and there are signs that even the aforementioned abused wine names are beginning to regain a little of their former respectability.

FRIULI-VENEZIA GIULIA

Situated in the northeastern corner of Italy, this predominantly mountainous region has grown many non-Italian varieties since phylloxera wiped out its vineyards in the late 19th century. The naturally innovative Friulians (and South Tyroleans) used the

BARDOLINO VINEYARDS
Ripening grapes adorn rows of vines in the Veneto's Bardolino area, which has a good reputation for light, dry red, and rosé wines.

opportunity to replant their vineyards with several better-quality foreign grape varieties, starting with the Merlot, which was brought to this region by Senator Pecile and Count Savorgnan in 1880. Over the past 100 years, the northeast has consistently demonstrated that the use of superior grape varieties and relatively lower yields can produce wines of dramatically improved quality. Friuli is the home of some of the country's finest wines, including many of its most complex Cabernet blends. Girolamo Dorigo's Montsclapade, which is the best of an exceptionally fine group of wines, is a typically Friulian blend of both Cabernets, Merlot, and Malbec. It is rare to find the Malbec variety on this side of the Alps, but it fares well in Friuli and might well be the key to the complexity of these wines. A few rather unconventional blends are found, the most unusual being Abbazia di Rosazzo's multinational Ronco dei Roseti, which mixes the four Bordeaux varieties with the German Limberger, the Italian Refosco, and the obscure Tazzelenghe. Another Abbazia di Rosazzo wine, Ronco delle Acacie, is a rare masterpiece in the new Italian school of "superdeluxe" *vini da tavola* white wines—a category of dry white Italian wine that is expensive but mostly disappointing.

The largest volume of fine wines produced in the northeast comes from Colli Orientali del Friuli, one of Friuli's two *colli*, or "hilly," areas. This one is situated close to the former Yugoslav border and encompasses many varietal wines. These wines are well worth looking out for—with the exception of the Picolit, which is a grossly overrated and horrendously overpriced sweet wine wherever it comes from. The Picolit produced in Colli Orientali del Friuli is the only one in Italy to have DOC status, but, in fact, the wine is no better than other examples to be found throughout the country.

FACTORS AFFECTING TASTE AND QUALITY

LOCATION
The northeast is bounded by the Dolomites to the north and the Adriatic Sea to the south.

CLIMATE
Similar to the northwest in that summers are hot and winters cold and harsh, but fog is less of a problem and hail more frequent. There are unpredictable variations in the weather from year to year so vintages are important, particularly for red wines.

ASPECT
Vineyards are found on a variety of sites ranging from the steep, mountainous slopes of Trentino-Alto Adige to the flat, alluvial plains of the Veneto and Friuli-Venezia Giulia. The best vineyards are always sited in hilly countryside.

SOIL
Most vineyards are on glacial moraine—a gritty mixture of sand, gravel, and sediment deposited during the Ice Age. Most are clayey or sandy clay and the best sites are often marly and rich in calcium. The light, stony soil in the South Tyrol is rapidly leached by weathering and fertilizers have to be added annually.

VITICULTURE AND VINIFICATION
The northeast has led Italy's move toward more modern vinification

techniques and experimentation with foreign grape varieties. It was the first area to use cold fermentation and, initially, the wines produced were so clean that they lacked natural character. There is now much experimentation into how to increase intensity of flavor through the use of new oak.

GRAPE VARIETIES
Blauer Portugieser (*syn. Portoghese*), Cabernet Franc, Cabernet Sauvignon, Chardonnay, Cortese (*syn. Bianca Fernanda*), Corvina (*syn. Corvinone or Cruina*), Durello, Franconia (*syn. Limberger*), Garganega, Gewürztraminer, Incrocio Manzoni 215 (*Prosecco x Cabernet Sauvignon*), Incrocio Manzoni 6013 (*Riesling x Pinot Blanc*), Kerner, Lagrein, Lambrusco a Foglia Frastagliata, Malbec, Malvasia, Marzemino, Merlot, Molinara (*syn. Rossara or Rossanella*), Mondeuse (*syn. Refosco or Terrano*), Muscat (*syn. Moscato*), Nosiola, Petit Verdot, Picolit, Pinella (*Pinello*), Pinot Blanc (*syn. Pinot Bianco*), Pinot Gris (*syn. Pinot Grigio*), Pinot Noir (*syn. Pinot Nero*), Prosecco (*syn. Serprina or Serprino*), Raboso (*syn. Friularo*), Ribolla, Riesling, Rossola (*syn. Veltliner*), Sauvignonasse (*syn. Tocai Friulano*), Sauvignon Blanc, Schiava (*syn. Vernatsch*), Schioppettino, Tazzelenghe, Teroldego, Tocai, Ugni Blanc (*syn. Trebbiano*), Verduzzo, Vespaiolo.

THE APPELLATIONS OF

NORTHEAST ITALY

THE BEST CLASSIC BRUT SPARKLING WINES

These wines all come from Trentino-Alto Adige and are made by the traditional method.

✓ *Equipe 5 Brut Riserva* • *Equipe 5 Brut Rosé* • *Ferrari Brut* • *Ferrari Brut de Brut* • *Ferrari Brut Rosé* • *Ferrari Nature* • *Ferrari Riserva Giulio Ferrari* • *Methius Brut* • *Methius Riserva* • *Spagnolli Brut* • *Vivaldi Brut* • *Vivaldi Extra Brut*

ALTO ADIGE *or* SÜDTIROLER DOC
Trentino-Alto Adige

This generic appellation covers the entire Alto Adige, or South Tyrol, which is the northern half of the Valdadige DOC.

There are seven red-wine varietals: Cabernet covers either Cabernet Sauvignon or Cabernet Franc, or both, and ranges from simple, but delightful, everyday wines to deeper-colored, fuller-bodied, richer wines that become warm, mellow, and spicy after five to 10 years; Lagrein Scuro, or *Lagrein Dunkel*, is made from an underrated, indigenous grape and can have a fine, distinctive character and good color; Malvasia, or *Malvasier*, is produced here as a red wine, although it would be better made into white or rosé; Merlot can be simply light and fruity or can attain greater heights, with a good spicy, sweet pepper aroma and a fine, silky texture; Pinot Noir, or *Blauburgunder*, is a difficult varietal to perfect, but those from Mazzon are good and a specialty of this region (they will have Mazzoner on the label); Schiava, or *Vernatsch*, accounts for one in five bottles produced under this appellation and is the most popular tavern wine; Schiava Grigia, or *Grauervernatsch*, has recently been added to the list, as have two red-wine blends of Cabernet-Lagrein and Cabernet-Merlot.

There are no fewer than 10 different white-wine varietals: Chardonnay can range from light and neutral to delicately fruity, and even *frizzantino* or verging upon *spumante*—the fuller versions can have recognizable varietal characteristics, but still lack the weight and intensity of flavor of even basic Burgundy; Moscato Giallo, or *Goldenmuskateller*, is made into delicious dessert wines; Pinot Bianco, or *Weissburgunder*, is the most widely planted of all the white grape varieties and produces most of Alto Adige's finest white wines; Pinot Grigio, or *Ruländer*, is potentially as successful as Pinot Blanc, but does not always occupy the best sites; Riesling Italico, or *Welschriesling*, is insignificant in both quantity and quality; Riesling Renano, or *Rheinriesling*, is fine, delicate, and attractive at the lowest level, but can be extraordinarily good in exceptional vintages; Riesling x Silvaner, or *Müller-Thurgau*, is relatively rare, which is a pity because it achieves a lively spiciness in this region; Sauvignon was very scarce in the early 1980s, but as the vogue for this grape spread so its cultivation increased and the crisp, dry, varietally pure Sauvignon is now one of the most successful wines of the Alto Adige; Silvaner is made mostly to be drunk young and fresh; Traminer Aromatico, or *Gewürztraminer*, is far more restrained than the classic Alsace version, even if, as some claim, the variety originated in the village of Tramin or Termeno, between Bolzano and Trento. If you can forget the full-blown spicy wine of Alsace, the delicate aroma and understated flavor of this wine can have a certain charm of its own.

Only three dry varietal *rosato*, or *Kretzer*, wines are allowed: Lagrein Rosato, or *Lagrein Kretzer*, is overtly fruity in a very round and smooth style; Merlot Rosato, or *Merlot Kretzer*, is a relatively recent addition and makes a curiously grassy or bell-pepper rosé; Pinot Nero Rosato, or *Blauburgunder Kretzer*, is more successful as a rosé than as a red.

Moscato Rosa, or *Rosenmuskateller*, are very flamboyant, deep-pink to scarlet-red, semisweet to sweet wines with an unusually high natural acidity, intense floral perfume, and an exaggerated Muscat flavor.

There is one sparkling-wine denomination for pure or blended Pinot Blanc and/or Chardonnay with up to 30 percent Pinot Gris and Pinot Noir, with both *cuve close* and the traditional method permissible.

In 1994 five former DOCs were incorporated into the Alto Adige, or Südtiroler, DOC as geographical subappellations. **Colli di Bolzano DOC**, or *Bozner Leiten*, for soft, fruity, early-drinking, Schiava-based red wines from the left bank of the Adige River, and both banks of the Isarco near Bolzano; **Meranese**, or **Meranese di Collina DOC**, or *Meraner Hügel*, from the hills around Merano, north of Bolzano, where the Schiava grape produces a light, delicately scented red wine, which may be labeled as Burgravio, or *Burggräfler*, if it comes from the part of the Meranese that was formerly part of the Contea di Tirol; **Santa Maddalena DOC**, or *Sankt Magdalener*, in the heart of the Colli di Bolzano (*see above*), where the Schiava-based red wines are just as soft and fruity, but fuller in body and smoother in texture—few Italian references today boast that Santa Maddalena was ranked by Mussolini (overoptimistically) as one of Italy's greatest wines; **Terlano DOC**, or *Terlaner*, which overlaps most of Caldaro DOC on the right bank of the Adige, running some 10 miles (16 kilometers) northwest of Bolzano to 15 miles (24 kilometers) south, and covers one blended, one *spumante*, and the following eight varietal white wines: Pinot Bianco (*Weissburgunder*), Chardonnay, Riesling Italico (*Welschriesling*), Riesling Renano (*Rheinriesling*), Silvaner, Müller-Thurgau, and Sauvignon; and, finally, **Valle Isarco DOC**, or *Eisacktaler*, which takes in both banks of the Isarco River from a few miles north of Bolzano to just north of Bressanone, where the vineyards are high in altitude and the vines trained low to absorb ground heat. Six white-wine varietals are produced: Kerner, Müller-Thurgau, Pinot Grigio, or *Ruländer*, Sylvaner, Traminer Aromatico, or *Gewürztraminer*, and Veltliner. Valle Isarco also includes a geographical blend called *Klausner Leitacher* for red wines from the villages of Chiusa (also known as *Klausen*), Barbiano, Velturno, and Villandro, which must be made from at least 60 percent Schiava plus up to 40 percent Portoghese and Lagrein. Furthermore, any Valle Isarco wine produced in Bressanone or Varna can be labeled "di Bressanone" or "*Brixner*."

🍷 2–10 years (red and rosé), 2–5 years (white), 1–3 years (sparkling)

✓ *Abbazia di Novacella* • *Cantina Gries-Bolzano* • *Cantina Terlano* • *Colterenzio* • *Cortaccia* • *Anton Gojer* • *Giorgio Grai* • *Franz Haas* • *Hofstätter* • *Kettmeir* • *Klosterkellerei Eisacktaler* • *Klosterkellerei Schreckbichl* • *Alois Lageder* • *Mazo Foradori* • *Muri-Gries* • *Nalles Niclara Magrè* • *Stiftskellerei Neustift* • *Niedermayr* • *Peter Pliger* • *Plattner-Waldgries* • *Prima & Nuova* • *Heinrich Rottensteiner* • *San Michele* (Sanct Valentin) • *Santa Margherita* • *Schloss Rametz* • *Schloss Sallegg* • *Schloss Schwanburg* • *Termeno* • *Tiefenbrunner* • *Elena Walch* • *Baron Georg von Widmann*

AMARONE DELLA VALPOLICELLA *or* RECIOTO DELLA VALPOLICELLA AMARONE DOC
Veneto

See Valpolicella DOC.

AQUILEA DOC
Friuli-Venezia Giulia

See Friuli-Aquilea DOC.

BARDOLINO SUPERIORE DOCG
Veneto

Bardolino DOC produces dry, sometimes *frizzante*, red and rosé (*chiaretto*) wines from the southeastern shores of Lake Garda. The reds, made from Corvina, Molinara, and Negrara, could be very interesting, but unfortunately most producers tend to make rather bland, lightweight wines.

🍷 1–3 years

✓ *Guerrieri-Rizzardi*

BIANCO DI CUSTOZA DOC
Veneto

Effectively the white wines of Bardolino, they can be scented with a smooth aftertaste and may sometimes be sparkling. Some critics compare Bianco di Custoza to Soave, which neatly sums up the quality. The grapes are Trebbiano, Garganega, Tocai Friulano, Cortese, and Malvasia.

BOZNER LEITEN *or* COLLI DI BOLZANO DOC
Trentino-Alto Adige

See Alto Adige DOC.

BREGANZE DOC
Veneto

This is one of Italy's unsung DOC heroes, largely due to the excellence of Maculan. As a generic red, Breganze is an excellent Merlot-based wine with the possible addition of Pinot Noir, Freisa, Marzemino, Gropello Gentile, Cabernet Franc, and Cabernet Sauvignon. As a white, it is fresh, zesty, and dry and made from Tocai Friulano, with the possible addition of Pinot Blanc, Pinot Gris, Welschriesling, and Vespaiolo. But it is mostly sold as a varietal, of which there are two red (Cabernet and Pinot Nero) and three white (Pinot Bianco, Pinot Grigio, and Vespaiolo).

⌐— 2–5 years (red), 1–2 years (white)

✓ *Bartolomeo da Breganze* • *Maculan*

CABERNET FRANC
Veneto

Most Cabernet wines are DOC, but a few non-DOC exist and are invariably well worth seeking out as they tend to be *barrique*-aged selections of ripe, not too grassy fruit.

✓ *Quintarelli* (Alerzo)

CABERNET SAUVIGNON
Veneto

Less traditional in Veneto than Cabernet Franc, pure varietal wines of any real quality or concentration are rarely encountered, but Cabernet Sauvignon from Anselmi and Le Vigne di San Pietro can be superb.

⌐— 3–6 years

✓ *Anselmi* (Realda) • *Le Vigne di San Pietro* (Refolà)

CABERNET-MERLOT
Trentino-Alto Adige and Veneto

There are so many Cabernet DOCs available in this region that few bother to produce a *vino da tavola*, but of those that do, the hellishly expensive San Leonardo is the very best. In the Veneto, with one notable exception, Cabernet-based blends are not as common as one imagines they might be.

✓ **Trentino-Alto Adige** *Tenuta San Leonardo* (Vallagrina)

Veneto *Conte Loredan-Gasparini* (Venegazzù della Casa, Venegazzù Capo di Stato)

CALDARO *or* LAGO DI CALDARO KALTERER KALTERERSEE DOC
Trentino-Alto Adige

As this overlaps the heart of the Terlano area, Caldaro might as well be yet another subappellation of the Alto Adige DOC, along with Terlano and the other former DOCs that have now been absorbed. Schiava-based red wines with the possible addition of Lagrein and Pinot Noir, they are usually soft and fruity, with a hint of almond, and easy to drink.

CARSO DOC
Friuli-Venezia Giulia

Carso Terrano must consist of at least 85 percent Terrano (also known as Mondeuse or Refosco), which makes a deep, dark, and full red wine that can be fat and juicy. Carso Malvasia is a rich and gently spicy, dry white wine.

⌐— 1–3 years

✓ *Edi Kante*

CASTELLER DOC
Trentino-Alto Adige

The thin strip of hilly vineyards that produces these wines is virtually identical to the Trentino DOC. Dry or semisweet, red and rosé wines for everyday drinking from Schiava, Merlot, and Lambrusco a Foglia Frastagliata grapes.

CHARDONNAY
Northeast Italy

A decade ago, only two pure Chardonnay DOCs existed in northeast Italy: Alto Adige and Grave del Friuli. Now it is one of the most ubiquitous varietals, but premium-priced non-DOC wines from this grape variety are still excellent quality.

✓ *Azienda Agricola Inama* (Campo dei Tovi) • *Jermann* (Where The Dreams Have No End)

COLLI BERICI DOC
Veneto

In addition to a sparkling Garganega-based white wine, this DOC includes three red varietals (Merlot, Tocai Rosso, and Cabernet) and five white (Garganega, Tocai Bianco, Pinot Bianco, Sauvignon, and Chardonnay). The Cabernet can be rich and grassy with chocolaty fruit, and the Merlot, in the right hands, is plump and juicy; the red Tocai is unusual and interesting, and the Chardonnay suffices as usual. However, the other wines from this area immediately south of Vicenza are less exciting.

⌐— 2–5 years (red), 1–2 years (white)

✓ *Castello di Belvedere* • *Villa dal Ferro*

COLLI DI BOLZANO *or* BOZNER LEITEN DOC
Trentino-Alto Adige

See Alto Adige DOC.

COLLI EUGANEI DOC
Veneto

Bordering Colli Berici to the southeast, this area produces soft, full-bodied, dry or semisweet red-wine blends (from Merlot plus Cabernet Franc, Cabernet Sauvignon, Barbera, and Raboso) and four red varietals: Cabernet, Cabernet Franc, Cabernet Sauvignon, and Merlot. There are dry or semisweet white-wine blends (from Prosecco, Garganega, and Tocai Friulano with the possible addition of Chardonnay, Pinot Blanc, Pinella, and Welschriesling) and seven white varietals: Chardonnay, Fior d'Arancio (from the Moscato Giallo grape in sweet *frizzantino*, *spumante*, and *liquoroso* styles), Moscato (sweet *frizzantino* and *spumante* styles), Pinella or Pinello, Pinot Bianco, Serprina or Serprino (dry

or sweet in still, *frizzantino*, *frizzante*, or *spumante* styles), and Tocai Italico.

⌐— 2–5 years (red), 1–2 years (white)

✓ *Villa Sceriman* ◉ • *Vignalta*

COLLI ORIENTALI DEL FRIULI DOC
Friuli-Venezia Giulia

Larger than neighboring Collio and initially more prestigious, both DOCs have now shown their excellent potential. In addition to a generic *rosato* blend, there are seven red varietals (Cabernet, Cabernet Franc, Cabernet Sauvignon, Merlot, Pinot Noir, Refosco, and Schioppettino); and 12 white (Chardonnay, Malvasia, Picolit, Pinot Bianco, Pinot Grigio, Ramandolo (dessert-style Verduzzo), Ribolla, Riesling Renano, Sauvignon Blanc, Tocai Friulano, Traminer Aromatico, and Verduzzo Friulano). The whites are especially outstanding, but the most famous, Picolit, is overrated and overpriced, even though this used to be the only Picolit in Italy to have its own DOC and should, therefore, have a reputation to maintain.

⌐— 3–8 years (red), 1–3 years (white)

✓ *Borgo del Tiglio* • *Girolamo Dorigo* • *Le Due Terre* • *Livio Felluga* • *Dorino Livon* • *Miani* • *Scubla* • *Le Vigne di Zamó* • *Volpe Pasini*

COLLIO *or* COLLIO GORIZIANO DOC
Friuli-Venezia Giulia

A large range of mostly white wines from a hilly area close to the Slovenian border, Collio now encompasses 19 different wines. With some top producers making very high-quality wines, this appellation is clearly in line for full DOCG status in the near future. As well as a blended dry white (primarily from Ribolla, Malvasia, and Tocai Friulano), which can be slightly *frizzantino*, and blended red (Merlot, Cabernet Sauvignon, and Cabernet Franc, plus Pinot Noir and possibly one or two others), there are five red varietals (Cabernet, Cabernet Franc,

Cabernet Sauvignon, Merlot, and Pinot Nero); and 12 white (Chardonnay, Malvasia, Müller-Thurgau, Picolit, Pinot Bianco, Pinot Grigio, Riesling Italico, Riesling Renano, Tocai Friulano, Ribolla, Sauvignon, and Traminer Aromatico). Jerman makes some of the very greatest wines, but now markets his wines under the IGT Delle Venezie. They are included below for completeness.

🍷 1–4 years (red), 1–3 years (white)

✓ • Borgo del Tiglio • Castello di Spessa • Josko Gravner • Jermann • Edi Keber • Dorino Livon • Dario Roccaro • Russiz Superiore • Schiopetto • Franco Toros • Venicia & Venicia • Villa Russiz

CORVINA
Veneto

Arguably the greatest grape in Veneto, Corvina is the key player in Bardolino and Valpolicella, particularly the recioto and amarone styles of the latter, but can also be found in a few premium vini da tavola.

✓ Allegrini (Pelara, La Poja)

EISACKTALER or VALLE ISARCO DOC
Trentino-Alto Adige

See Alto Adige DOC.

ETSCHTALER DOC
Trentino-Alto Adige

See Valdadige DOC.

FRANCONIA or BLAUFRANKISCH
Friuli-Venezia Giulia

Franconia is the synonym for the Limberger grape of Germany. The wine is made in a fuller, darker style than is possible in its homeland, yet it still possesses the same light, fruity flavor.

FRIULI-AQUILEA DOC
Friuli-Venezia Giulia

Formerly know simply as Aquilea, this is a wide-ranging appellation that covers five varietal red wines (Merlot, Cabernet, Cabernet Franc, Cabernet Sauvignon, and Refosco); eight white varietals (Chardonnay, Tocai Friulano, Pinot Bianco, Pinot Grigio, Riesling Renano, Sauvignon, Traminer, and Verduzzo Friulano); and a generic rosé of least 70 percent Merlot plus Cabernet Franc, Cabernet Sauvignon, and Refosco. There is also a Chardonnay spumante. All are generally light, crisply balanced wines, although some producers excel in better years.

🍷 1–4 years (red), 1–3 years (white, rosé, and sparkling)

✓ Zonin (Tenuta Cà Bolani)

FRIULI-GRAVE DOC
Friuli-Venezia Giulia

Formerly called Grave del Friuli, this massive appellation spreads out on both sides of the Tagliamento River between Sacile in the west and Cividale di Friuli in the east, and accounts for over half of the region's total production. It is a huge and complicated, but rapidly improving, multivarietal DOC in which several winemakers regularly produce fine wines. In addition to generic red and white blends, there are six red varietals (Cabernet, Cabernet Franc, Cabernet Sauvignon, Merlot, Refosco, and Pinot Noir); and eight white varietals (Chardonnay,

Pinot Bianco, Pinot Gris, Riesling Renano, Sauvignon, Tocai Friulano, Traminer Aromatico, and Verduzzo Friulano). There is a Chardonnay frizzante, Verduzzo frizzante, Chardonnay spumante, and a blended generic spumante.

🍷 1–4 years (red), 1–3 years (white, rosé, and sparkling)

✓ Borgo Magredo • Pighin • Vigneti le Monde • Vigneti Pittaro

FRIULI-LATISANA or LATISANA DOC
Friuli-Venezia Giulia

An area that stretches from the central section of the Friuli-Grave to the Adriatic coast at Lignano Sabbiadoro. In addition to a generic, blended rosé (Bordeaux varieties) and spumante (Chardonnay and Pinot varieties) there are five red varietal wines (Merlot, Cabernet Sauvignon, Franconia (Limberger), Pinot Nero, and Refosco); and nine white varietals (Chardonnay, Malvasia, Pinot Bianco, Pinot Grigio, Riesling Renano, Sauvignon, Tocai Friulano, Traminer Aromatico, and Verduzzo Friulano). Chardonnay, Malvasia, and Pinot Nero may also be produced in a frizzante style.

GAMBELLARA DOC
Veneto

Produces scented, dry, or sometimes semisweet white wines and fruity, semisweet, still, frizzante or fully sparkling white recioto. A smooth, sweet vin santo is also produced here.

🍷 2–5 years

✓ La Biancara

GARGANEGA
Veneto

The primary grape used for Soave— in skilled hands Garganega can produce a fabulously rich yet delicately balanced dry white, but it has a tendency to overcrop, and most Garganega wines turn out bland.

GRAVE DEL FRIULI DOC
Friuli-Venezia Giulia

See Friuli-Grave DOC.

ISONZO or ISONZO DEL FRIULI DOC
Friuli-Venezia Giulia

A small area south of Collio, producing a very good yet still improving quality wine. There are generic red- and white-wine blends, plus four red varietals (Cabernet, Merlot, Franconia (Limberger), and Refosco); and 10 white varietals (Chardonnay, Malvasia, Pinot Bianco, Pinot Grigio, Riesling Italico, Riesling Renano, Sauvignon, Tocai Friulano, Traminer Aromatico, and Verduzzo Friulano); and a Pinot spumante.

🍷 1–4 years (red), 1–3 years (white)

✓ Borgo Conventi • Lis Neris-Pecorari • Ronco del Gelso • Vie di Romans

KALTERER or KALTERERSEE DOC
Trentino-Alto Adige

See Caldaro DOC.

LAGREIN
Trentino-Alto Adige

An ancient Alto Adige variety, it was well known to Pliny, who called it Lageos. Although

it is by no means the greatest grape grown in the region, Lagrein does, however, produce one of Alto Adige's most original and expressive wines, with rich, chunky, youthful fruit of relatively high acidity, but capable of developing a silky, violety finesse after a few years in bottle.

LATISANA DOC
Friuli-Venezia Giulia

See Friuli-Latisana DOC.

LESSINI DURELLO DOC
Veneto

Dry white wine from just northeast of Soave, in still, frizzantino, and fully sparkling styles, from the Durello grape with the possible addition of Garganega, Trebbiano, Pinot Blanc, Pinot Noir, and Chardonnay.

✓ Marcato

LISON-PRAMAGGIORE DOC
Veneto and Friuli-Venezia Giulia

This DOC, which is in the very east of the Veneto, and overlaps a small part of Friuli, originally combined three former DOCs (Cabernet di Pramaggiore, Merlot di Pramaggiore, and Tocai di Lison) into one. However, it has since been expanded to encompass a total of seven white varietal wines (Chardonnay, Pinot Bianco, Pinot Grigio, Riesling Italico, Sauvignon, Tocai Italico, and Verduzzo), and four reds (Cabernet, Cabernet Franc, Cabernet Sauvignon, and Refosco dal Peduncolo Rosso). Cabernet and Merlot are still the best in a rich, delicious, chocolaty style.

🍷 3–8 years (red), 1–3 years (white)

✓ Santa Margherita • Russola • Tenuta Sant'Anna • Villa Castalda (Cabernet Franc)

LUGANA DOC
Veneto

See Lugana DOC (Lombardy) under Northwest Italy.

MARZEMINO
Trentino-Alto Adige

This grape variety was probably brought to Italy from Slovenia by the Romans. By the 18th century, it had achieved sufficient fame for Mozart to use it in his opera Don Giovanni as a preliminary to the seduction of Zerlina. A Marzemino cluster typically provides large, loosely bunched grapes, which make an aromatic, early-drinking red wine, either as DOC (Trentino) or vino da tavola.

MERANESE or MERANESE DI COLLINA MERANER HÜGEL DOC
Trentino-Alto Adige

See Alto Adige DOC.

MERLOT
Friuli-Venezia Giulia

A prolific grape in northeastern Italy, where it has been grown for almost 200 years. Far too many wishy-washy examples abound, but top producers achieve concentration and quality through low yields and strict selection. Although Merlot is a varietal wine in virtually all the DOCs of Friuli-Venezia Giulia, the only ones with any special reputation for it are Colli

Orientali, where the richest varietals are made, and Collio, which is less consistent, but the best are plump and juicy.

√ *Borgo del Tiglio (Rosso della Centa)*

MONTELLO E COLLI ASOLANI DOC
Veneto

From vineyards at the foot of the aptly named Mount Grappa, most of wines are varietals, comprising two reds (Merlot and Cabernet); four whites (Prosecco, Chardonnay, Pinot Bianco, and Pinot Grigio); and three *spumante* (Chardonnay, Pinot Bianco, and Prosecco). Any red wines that do not carry a varietal name will be primarily Cabernet-Merlot blends.

⌛ 1–3 years

√ *Fernando Berta • Abbazia di Nervesa*

NOSIOLA
Trentino-Alto Adige

Probably the least known of the Trentino's traditional grapes because it is mostly used for *vin santo*. However, dry white varietal wines are also made from this variety and, although it is best when blended with more aromatic varieties, as in Sorni DOC, it is even making a reputation as a premium *vino da tavola*.

√ *Pravis (Le Frate)*

PIAVE *or* VINI DEL PIAVE DOC
Veneto

A large area to the west of Lison-Pramaggiore producing five red varietals (Merlot, Cabernet, Cabernet Sauvignon, Pinot Nero, and Raboso); and five whites (Chardonnay, Tocai Italico, Pinot Bianco, Pinot Grigio, and Verduzzo). The Cabernet and Raboso can be particularly good.

⌛ 1–3 years

√ *Reichsteiner*

PICOLIT DOC
Friuli-Venezia Giulia

See Colli Orientali del Friuli DOC.

PROSECCO
Veneto

Although it is one of the most traditional of Veneto grape varieties, Prosecco originated in the village of that name in Friuli's Carso district. Latin-lovers adore the soft bubbly produced by this grape, but most of it is boring, and it will take a revolution in quality to convince me that this grape is suitable for dry sparkling wines.

PROSECCO DI CONEGLIANO-VALDOBBIADENE DOC
Veneto

Dry and semisweet fizzy white wines of passable quality, although most of them have large bubbles and a coarse, dull flavor. A still version is also produced.

⌛ Upon purchase

√ *Adami Adriano* (Vigneto Giardino) • *Fratelli Bartolin Spumante • Carpenè Malvolti*

RABOSO
Veneto

The indigenous Raboso grape has long made excellent-value red wines that are full of sunny fruit and capable of improving after two to three years in bottle. There are two distinct, localized clones—Raboso del Piave, most often used as a pure varietal, and the more productive Raboso Veronese, which does not have the richness or such a positive character, and is merely a blending component. Most of the wines produced are *vini da tavola* but DOC wines are available under the Piave appellation.

RAMANDOLO DOCG
Friuli-Venezia Giulia

Sweet Verduzzo dessert wine.

RECIOTO BIANCO DI CAMPOCIESA
Veneto

Soft, sweet, well-scented, golden-colored, non-DOC white wines made from *passito* grapes.

RECIOTO DELLA VALPOLICELLA *or* RECIOTO DELLA VALPOLICELLA AMARONE DOC
Veneto

See Valpolicella DOC.

RECIOTO DI SOAVE DOCG
Veneto

Naturally sweet Soave made from *passito* grapes, to produce wines that are either *liquoroso* or *spumante*. Most are too oxidative, but Pieropan is excellent and Anselmi is outstanding—both as pure as driven snow.

√ *Anselmi* (I Capitelli) • *Pieropan* (Le Colombare Vendemmia Tardiva)

REFOSCO
Friuli-Venezia Giulia

Known as Terrano in the Carso district, the Refosco is none other than the Mondeuse of France. It typically produces a deep-colored red wine with soft, juicy, low-acid fruit, which can be somewhat one-dimensional, but is at its best in the Colli Orientali and Friuli-Grave.

SANTA MADDALENA *or* SANKT MAGDALENER DOC
Trentino-Alto Adige

See Alto Adige DOC.

SCHIAVA
Trentino-Alto Adige

This is the most widely cultivated variety in the Alto Adige, where it accounts for 60 percent of the vines grown. In the Tyrol, where this grape is believed to have originated, it is known as Vernatsch, but most ampelographers refer to it as Schiava. There are four subvarieties: Schiava Grossa, Schiava Gentile, Schiava Grigia, and Schiava Meranese. Schiava wines are usually medium-bodied with an almond character to the fruit and a light bitterness on the finish.

SCHIOPPETTINO
Friuli-Venezia Giulia

An ancient Friulian variety, Schioppettino was nearly extinct until these wines suddenly became fashionable in the 1980s. It produces very ripe and round wines with a fine, spicy-scented bouquet and rich fruit flavor that attains great finesse only with maturity.

√ *Ronchi di Cialla • Ronco del Gnemiz • Giuseppe Toti*

SOAVE DOC
Veneto

Most Soave is still overcropped, thin, and acidic, and in 2000, Roberto Anselmi took his greatly admired wines out of the Soave appellation in protest. Top producers continue to make immensely enjoyable wines from Garganega and Trebbiano, when they are grown to restricted yields in the central, hilly, *classico* area. Anselmi's wines are included below for completeness. *See also* Recioto di Soave DOC.

⌛ 1–4 years

√ *Anselmi* (Capitel Foscarino, Capitel Croce) • *Bolla* (Castellaro, Vigneti di Froscà) • *Ca' Rugate* (Monte Alto) • *Cantina del Castello* (Monte Pressoni) • *Inama* (Vigneto du Lot) • *Pieropan* (Vigneto Calvarino, Vigneto la Rocca) • *Suavia* (Le Rive) • *Fratelli Tedeschi* (Monte Tenda)

SORNI DOC
Trentino-Alto Adige

This tiny DOC is situated just south of Mezzolombardo at the confluence of the Avisio and Adige rivers. Soft Schiava-based reds are often improved by the addition of Teroldego and Lagrein. Light, fresh, delicate Nosiola-based white wines are usually charged with a dollop of Müller-Thurgau, Silvaner, and Pinot Blanc.

⌛ 2–3 years (red), up to 18 months (white)

√ *Maso Poli*

SÜDTIROLER DOC
Trentino-Alto Adige

See Alto Adige DOC.

TACELENGHE *or* TAZZELENGHE
Friuli-Venezia Giulia

This grape variety takes its name from the local dialect for *tazzalingua* which means "a sharpness in the tongue," and is indicative of the wine's tannic nature. However, it does soften after five or six years in bottle.

TERLANO *or* TERLANER DOC
Trentino-Alto Adige

See Alto Adige DOC.

TEROLDEGO
Trentino-Alto Adige

An indigenous black grape with a thick bluish skin, Teroldego is productive and makes a dark-colored red wine with a distinctive aroma and a chewy, tannic raspberry richness that softens with age, attaining a silky-violety finesse. This has made it a very useful blending component in the past. However, more varietal wines are gradually being made and it has even started to be marketed as a premium *vino da tavola*.

✓ *Foradori (Granato)*

TEROLDEGO ROTALIANO DOC
Trentino-Alto Adige

Full-bodied red wines made from the Teroldego in the Rotaliano area, where the grape is said to have originated. There is also a fuller *Superiore* version and an attractive rosé.

⌇— 1–4 years

✓ *Foradori (Vigneto Morei)* • *Conti Martini*

TERRANO
Friuli-Venezia Giulia

See Refosco.

TREBBIANO
Veneto

The Trebbiano of Soave and Lugana are supposedly superior to the Trebbiano of Tuscany, but there is much dross produced in both DOCs, and it is the producer who makes the real difference.

TRENTINO DOC
Trentino-Alto Adige

This appellation represents the southern half of the Valdadige DOC and its wines are generally softer and less racy than those from Alto Adige to the north, although there is an equally bewildering number of varietal wines. If no variety is shown, white wines will be Chardonnay-Pinot Blanc blends and reds Cabernet-Merlot. There are seven red-wine varietals (Cabernet, Cabernet Franc, Cabernet Sauvignon, Lagrein, Marzemino, Merlot, and Pinot Nero); and nine white (Chardonnay, Moscato Giallo, Müller-Thurgau, Nosiola, Pinot Bianco, Pinot Grigio, Riesling Italico, Riesling Renano, and Traminer Aromatico). Furthermore, the Nosiola can be made in *vin santo* style, while all Pinot (Blanc, Gris, and Noir) may be fully sparkling. There is also a bright scarlet, lusciously sweet Moscato Rosa, and both Moscato Rosa and Moscato Giallo may be made in *liquoroso* style.

✓ *Barone de Cles* • *Cavit* • *Cesconi* • *LaVis* • *Longariva* • *Madonna del Vittoria* • *Conti Martini* • *Pojer & Sandri* • *Giovanni Poli* • *Tenuta San Leonardo* • *Armando Simoncelli* • *de Tarczal* • *Vallarom* • *Roberto Zeni*

VALDADIGE *or* ETSCHTALER DOC
Trentino-Alto Adige and Veneto

This huge generic denomination encompasses both the Alto Adige and Trentino DOCs, a myriad of subappellations, and extends well into the Veneto. Few producers bother to use what is generally considered to be Trentino-Alto Adige's lowest quality DOC. If the IGTs proposed by the Goria Law actually existed and worked, the size and location of Valdadige would make it an ideal candidate, as producers could select their best wines to go out under Alto Adige, Trentino, or another label, selling off the balance as an unpretentious Valdadige country wine. As it is already a DOC, nobody would dare suggest downgrading it to IGT, so the result is that hardly anyone uses it anyway. And, of the few who do, the dry and

semisweet white and red wines that they sell inevitably attract a poor reputation as DOCs, whereas underselling the same products as IGTs would make them honest, good-value introductions to the finer wines of Trentino-Alto Adige.

VALLE ISARCO *or* EISACKTALER DOC
Trentino-Alto Adige

See Alto Adige DOC.

VALPANTENA DOC
Veneto

See Valpolicella DOC.
Subappellation for Valpolicella, in *recioto*, *amarone*, *spumante*, and regular *rosso* styles.

VALPOLICELLA DOC
Veneto

In the first edition I agreed with Robert Parker, the American wine writer, when he described most Valpolicella as "insipid industrial garbage," but technology has changed things over the last 10 years. While most are still insipid and industrial, relatively few are as bad as garbage. Made from at least 80 percent Corvina with the possible addition of Rossignola, Negrara, Trentina, Barbera, and Sangiovese, most Valpolicella are simply light-red and light-bodied, with lackluster, attenuated fruit hinting of cherries, and a dry, slightly bitter finish. There are an increasing number of wines that are full of juicy cherry-fruit flavors, but they are still in a minority and for truly fine wines bearing the Valpolicella DOC you have to seek out exceptional wines from the tiny number of producers recommended below.

Valpolicella *recioto* is a bittersweet, yet very smooth, deep-colored, portlike wine made from *passito* grapes, although it may also be produced in a *spumante* style. *Amarone* is a derivative of *recioto*, with a similar deep color, but in a dry or off-dry style, which seems to make the flavors more powerful and chocolaty-spicy with a distinctly bitter finish. There is also something very specific that marks the fruit in *amarone* wines, which wine writer Oz Clarke once described—perfectly to my mind—as a "bruised sourness." This is an oxidative character that will not appeal to lovers of clean, precise, well-focused flavors, but its complexity is undeniable and such wines age wonderfully. Quintarelli is the most outstanding producer, with Allegrini hard on his heels.

⌇— Upon purchase for most, 2–5 years for recommendations

✓ **Valpolicella** *Allegrini (La Grola)* • *Bolla (Vigneti di Jago)* • *Guerrieri-Rizzardi (Villa Rizzardi Poiega)* • *Quintarelli* • *Le Ragose* •

Serègo Alighieri • *Fratelli Tedeschi (Capitel delle Lucchine, Capitel dei Nicalò)* • *Tommasi (Vigneto del Campo Rafael)*
Recioto della Valpolicella *Stefano Accordini (Acinatico)* • *Allegrini (Gardane)* • *Lorenzo Begali* • *Tommaso Bussola (TB)* • *Masi (Mazzanella)* • *Quintarelli* • *Serègo Alighieri (Casel dei Ronchi)* • *Fratelli Tedeschi (Capitel Monte Fontana)*
Recioto della Valpolicella Amarone *Allegrini (Fieramonte)* • *Bertani* • *Brigaldara* • *Tommaso Bussola* • *Masi (Mazzone)* • *Fratelli Pasqua (Vigneti Casterna)* • *Quintarelli* • *Romano Dal Forno (Vigneto di Monte Lodoletta)* • *Sant'Antonio (Campo de Gigli)* • *Serègo Alighieri (Vaio Armoron)* • *Speri (Vigneto Monte Sant'Urbano)* • *Fratelli Tedeschi (Capitel Monte Olmi)* • *Tommasi* • *Viviani (Casa de Bepi)*

VALPOLICELLA "RIPASSO"
Veneto

Ripasso ("re-passed") wine has long been traditional in the Veneto. The best young Valpolicella is put into tanks or barrels that still contain the lees of the *recioto* for which they were previously used. When mixed with the young wine, active yeast cells in this sediment precipitate a second fermentation. This increases the alcohol content and gives it some *recioto* character. After having undergone this process, the wines usually cannot carry the Valpolicella appellation and are therefore sold as *vino da tavola* under various brand names, although some Valpolicella wines are turbocharged by *ripasso* without any mention of it on the label.

⌇— 6–15 years

✓ *Allegrini (Palazzo alla Torre)* • *Boscaini (Le Cane)* • *Fratelli Tedeschi (Capitel San Rocco)* • *Masi (Campo Fiorin)*

VINI DEL PIAVE DOC
Veneto

See Piave DOC.

WILDBACHER
Veneto

This black grape seems to be restricted to the Veneto area and to Western Styria in Austria, where it is known as Blauer Wildbacher. Mostly used as a blending component, its distinctive, aromatic quality and high acidity are sometimes found in varietal form in non-DOC wines.

✓ *Le Case Bianche*

NEW IGT WINES

The following Indicazioni Geografiche Tipiche wines were agreed at the end of 1996, yet most have still to register with consumers, or establish any consistency of style or quality:

✓ **Friuli-Venezia Giulia** *Alto Livenza* • *Delle Venezie* • *Venezia Giulia*
Trentino-Alto Adige *Atesino* • *Delle Venezie* • *Vallagarina*
Veneto *Alto Livenza* • *Colli Trevigiani* • *Conselvano* • *Delle Venezie* • *Marca Trevigiani* • *Provincia di Verona or Veronese* • *Vallagarina* • *Veneto* • *Veneto Orientale*

WEST-CENTRAL ITALY

The heart of Italy is also the center of the country's most important quality-wine exports, which are dominated by famous red Sangiovese wines from the tiny Tuscan hills and valleys between Florence and the Umbria-Latium border.

TUSCANY (TOSCANA)

The home of traditional winemaking, Tuscany has also been the main focus of experimentation. Its powerful red Vino Nobile di Montepulciano was Italy's first DOCG, and has been followed by Brunello di Montalcino, Chianti, Carmignano, and Vernaccia di San Gimignano. But not all of its finest wines bear these famous appellations, a fact recognized by the Tuscan producers themselves, who, on the one hand, sought the ideal DOCG solution for Chianti, while on the other began to invest in premium wines that were not restricted by the DOC. It was the uncompromising quality of their Super-Tuscan wines that encouraged premium *vini da tavola* throughout the rest of Italy. Unfortunately, they were less successful with the DOCG of Chianti. The Tuscans had two sensible,

forward-thinking approaches: one was to apply DOCG to the Chianti Classico area and other isolated areas, such as parts of Rufina and the Colli Fiorentini, where most of the finest wines have traditionally been made, and to leave the rest as DOC Chianti; the other was to grant DOCG status to the best 10 percent, regardless of origin. Either would have made Chianti a success. But the biggest Chianti producers had more political clout than the best producers, and the new regulations gave DOCG status to the whole area and all Chianti wines, regardless of their origin or quality.

It is true that the Trebbiano Toscano, a localized clone, is an intrinsically high-class Trebbiano and, indeed, it can make some charming wines, but it is not a fine-wine grape. Currently, Tuscany has no white-wine sister for its red Sangiovese grape. Unfortunately, its best dry white-wine grape so far has been Chardonnay, a variety that excels in almost every half-decent wine area. Vermentino might be Tuscany's white-wine grape of the future, although it is really a Sardinian grape and currently mostly

Chianti including Carmignano (1), Rufina (2), Colli Fiorentini (3), Montespertoli (4), Colline Pisani (5), Vernaccia di San Gimignano (6), Vino Nobile di Montepulciano (7)

Chianti Classico

Bianco di Pitigliano

Montefalco

Orvieto

Est! Est!! Est!!! di Montefiascone

Colline Lucchesi

Montecarlo Bianco

Val di Cornia

Val d'Arbia

Bianco Vergine della Valdichiana

Colli Perugini

Colli Amerini

Colli Martani

Montalbano

Pomino

Aretini

Colli Senesi

Brunello di Montalcino

Candia dei Colli Apuani

Bianco della Val di Nievole

Bianco Pisano di San Torpe

Aleatico di Gradoli

Morellino di Scansano

8 Montescudaio

9 Bolgheri

10 Monteri di Massa Marittima

11 Moscadello di Montalcino

12 Elba

13 Maremma Toscana

14 Slovana

15 Parrina

16 Colli del Trasimeno

17 Colli Altotiberini

18 Torgiano

See page opposite

Provincia boundary

▲ Height above sea level (meters)

0   10   20   30   40   50 miles

0   20   40   60   80 km

WEST-CENTRAL ITALY, *see also* p.263
The hills of this area provide the best sites for vineyards, tempering the summer's heat and providing a variety of microclimates suitable for classic French grape varieties as well as traditional Italian ones.

FACTORS AFFECTING TASTE AND QUALITY

LOCATION
Located between the Apennines to the north and east and the Tyrrhenian Sea to the west.

CLIMATE
Summers are long and fairly dry and winters are less severe than in northern Italy. Heat and lack of rain can be a problem throughout the area during the growing season.

ASPECT
Vineyards are usually sited on hillsides for good drainage and exposure to the sun. Deliberate use is made of altitude to offset the heat, and black grapes grow at up to 1,800 feet (550 meters) and white grapes at up to 2,275 feet (700 meters). The higher the vines, the longer the ripening season and the greater the acidity of the grapes.

SOIL
These are very complex soils with gravel, limestone, and clay outcrops predominating. In Tuscany a rocky, schistose soil, known in some localities as *galestro*, covers most of the best vineyards.

VITICULTURE AND VINIFICATION
After much experimentation, particularly in Tuscany, with classic French grapes, the trend recently has been to develop the full potential of native varieties. Many stunning Cabernet-influenced,

super-Tuscan wines still exist, and always will, but top-performing producers are seeking clones, *terroirs*, and techniques to maximize the fruit and accessibility of their own noble grapes.

A traditional speciality is the sweet, white *vin santo*, which is made from *passito* grapes dried on straw mats in attics. It is aged for up to six years, often in a type of *solera* system.

GRAPE VARIETIES
Primary varieties: Sangiovese (*syn.* Brunello, Morellino, Prugnolo, Sangioveto, Tignolo, Uva Canina), Malvasia, Trebbiano (*syn.* Procanico)
Secondary varieties: Abbuoto, Aglianico, Albana (*syn.* Greco, but not Grechetto), Albarola, Aleatico, Barbera, Bellone, Bombino, Cabernet Franc, Cabernet Sauvignon, Canaiolo (*syn.* Drupeggio in Umbria), Carignan (*syn.* Uva di Spagna), Cesanese, Chardonnay, Ciliegiolo, Colorino, Gamay, Grechetto (*syn.* Greco, Pulciano), Inzolia (*syn.* Ansonica), Mammolo, Merlot, Montepulciano, Moscadelletto, Muscat (*syn.* Moscadello, Moscato), Nero Buono di Cori, Pinot Blanc (*syn.* Pinot Bianco), Pinot Gris (*syn.* Pinot Grigio), Roussanne, Sagrantino, Sauvignon Blanc, Sémillon, Syrah, Verdello, Vermentino, Vernaccia, Welschriesling

TRADITION AND INNOVATION
This tranquil landscape appears to have remained unchanged for many centuries, but, while Tuscan winemaking is steeped in tradition, the area is now also experimenting with different grape varieties and barrique *aging.*

restricted to Tuscany's coastal areas. It is time someone managed to rekindle an ancient, all-but-extinct Tuscan white grape and rescue it with commercial success, much as the *piemontesi* did with Arneis and, as I suspect, they will next try with Timorasso.

BIRTH OF THE SUPER-TUSCANS
Ten years ago the largest number of exceptional Tuscan wines were the then relatively new *barrique*-aged Super-Tuscans. Their story began in 1948 when the now famous Sassicaia wine was produced for the first time by Incisa della Rochetta using Cabernet Sauvignon vines reputedly from Château Lafite-Rothschild. This was an unashamed attempt to produce a top-quality Italian wine from Bordeaux's greatest grape variety, decades before the idea became old hat in the wine world. It became so successful that in the wake of the 1971 vintage, a new red called Tignanello was

ROME AND ITS ENVIRONS, *see also* opposite
The recent proliferation of appellations in the hills surrounding Italy's capital are evidence of a wine regime gone mad—this country's wines need cohesion, not further diversity.

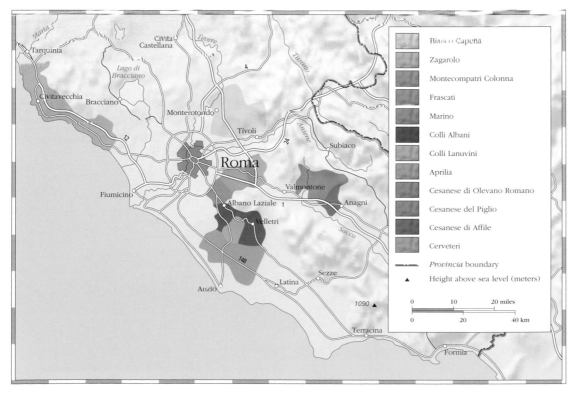

| Bianco Capena |
| Zagarolo |
| Montecompatri Colonna |
| Frascati |
| Marino |
| Colli Albani |
| Colli Lanuvini |
| Aprilia |
| Cesanese di Olevano Romano |
| Cesanese del Piglio |
| Cesanese di Affile |
| Cerveteri |

— — — *Provincia* boundary
▲ Height above sea level (meters)

0   10   20 miles
0   20   40 km

VERNACCIA VINES IN FALL
These vines grow exclusively around the medieval Tuscan town of San Gimignano, whose impressive towers can be seen here in the distance. When it comes from good producers, the white Vernaccia can be a deliciously crisp, fruity dry wine.

AVERAGE ANNUAL PRODUCTION

REGION	DOC PRODUCTION	TOTAL PRODUCTION
Tuscany	11 million cases (1 million hl)	44 million cases (4 million hl)
Latium	6 million cases (540,000 hl)	67 million cases (6 million hl)
Umbria	2 million cases (165,000 hl)	18 million cases (1.7 million hl)

Percentage of total Italian production: Latium, 7.8%; Tuscany, 5.2%; Umbria, 2.2%.

introduced by Piero Antinori with a Sangiovese base and 20 percent Cabernet Sauvignon, as a compromise between Tuscany and Bordeaux. Although Frescobaldi had used Cabernet Sauvignon in its Nipozzano Chianti for over a century and it grew in the Carmignano area in the 18th century, nobody had truly appreciated the harmony that could be achieved between the two grapes until Tignanello appeared. The blend was akin to the natural balance of Cabernet and Merlot, only the Cabernet added weight to the Sangiovese and provided balance through a more satisfying flavor. Tignanello thus sparked off a new wave of Super-Tuscan *vini da tavola*. However, as the numbers grew, so they became an embarrassment, as observers realized that very few of the region's greatest wines actually qualified for DOC. But at the same time, many of the winemakers responsible for these French-influenced Super-Tuscans were also working hard to make the Sangiovese stand alone. After extensive clonal and site selection, reduced yields, improved viticultural practices and vinification techniques, a new

breed of Super-Tuscan emerged; first as Sangiovese-dominated blends, such as Tignanello, then as pure Sangiovese wines. Now that the Goria Law has opened the door for Italy's greatest *vini da tavola*, many who had resorted to making wines outside the DOC system are using their experience in remolding the Sangiovese to reestablish the great old names of the past (Chianti, Brunello di Montalcino, Vino Nobile di Montepulciano) by making wines that are complete without the help of foreign varieties.

UMBRIA

Orvieto is Umbria's best-known and best-forgotten wine. Next to Frascati and Soave, it is the most used and abused name in the world's Italian restaurants. While there are a few good Orvieto wines, and tiny amounts of truly exciting *muffato* (a lusciously sweet botrytized version), they are in a lamentable minority. One of Umbria's few deservedly famous names is Lungarotti Rubesco Torgiano, whose reputation led to the Torgiano DOC and, more recently, to DOCG status for Torgiano Riserva. Lungarotti also leads in the production of Umbria's excellent new-wave wines. These use various grapes, both native and French, and are made in various styles, although nearly always aged in new-oak *barriques*.

LATIUM (LAZIO)

One of Italy's largest regions, Latium appropriately boasts one of its largest-selling wines, Frascati, the Latin Liebfraumilch, and Est! Est!! Est!!!, probably the blandest tourist wine in existence. For a region responsible for Falernum, a classic wine of antiquity, it can now boast only two truly fine wines, Boncompagni Ludovisi's Fiorano Rosso and Cantina Colacicchi's Torre Ercolana, both innovative Cabernet-Merlot blends, which are very good.

THE APPELLATIONS OF
WEST-CENTRAL ITALY

CLASSIC BRUT SPARKLING WINES

The best sparkling *brut* wines are made in Tuscany by the traditional method.

✓ *Brut di Capezzana* • *Falchini Brut* • *Villa Banfi Brut*

ALEATICO
Tuscany

These are rare, rich, sweet red wines.

ALEATICO DI GRADOLI DOC
Latium

Sweet, sometimes fortified, red wines, without the reputation of the Aleatico di Puglia DOC.

APRILIA DOC
Latium

This DOC has two red varietals, Merlot and Sangiovese, and one white, Trebbiano, which is uninspiring. The washed-out flavors indicate that official yields are far too high.

ASSISI
Umbria

Assisi produces some soft, satisfying red, and fresh, easy-drinking white wines.

✓ *Sasso Rosso* • *Fratelli* • *Sportoletti* • *Tili*

BARCO REALE DI CARMIGNANO DOC
Tuscany

After Carmignano became a DOCG, this appellation was adopted for easy-drinking, Sangiovese-dominated (with a touch of Cabernet) red wines in order to retain simple DOC status. This acted as a selection instrument to increase and maintain quality for the superior denomination. *See also* Carmignano DOC and Carmignano DOCG.

BIANCO CAPENA DOC
Latium

Bianco Capena is a large DOC northeast of Rome producing dry and semisweet Trebbiano-based white wines of modest quality.

BIANCO DELL'EMPOLESE DOC
Tuscany

This is an overrated, overpriced, and uninspiring dry white Trebbiano from the Empoli hills, west of Florence. A *passito* may be sold as *vin santo* under the same denomination.

BIANCO DELLA VAL DI NIEVOLE *or* BIANCO DELLA VALDINIEVOLE DOC
Tuscany

Dry, slightly *frizzante* white wines and soft, white *vin santo*, made primarily from Trebbiano grapes.

BIANCO DI PITIGLIANO DOC
Tuscany

This DOC produces delicate, refreshing, dry, and easy-drinking Trebbiano-based white wines, which are improved by the possible inclusion of Malvasia, Grechetto, Verdello, Chardonnay, Sauvignon, Pinot Blanc, and Welschriesling. A *spumante* version is also allowed.

⌛ 1–2 years

✓ *La Stellata*

BIANCO PISANO DI SAN TORPÉ DOC
Tuscany

These dry white wines and dry or semisweet *vin santo* are made from Trebbiano grown in a large area southeast of Pisa.

BIANCO VERGINE DELLA VALDICHIANA DOC
Tuscany

This DOC produces off-dry, Trebbiano-based white wines with a bitter aftertaste. The best have a more delicate, floral fragrance.

⌛ 1–2 years

✓ *Poliziano*

BOLGHERI DOC
Tuscany

Until recently this was a relatively anonymous, pleasant, but hardly exciting DOC, producing delicate, dry whites and dry, slightly scented, Sangiovese *rosato*. Reds were ignored, even though it was home to Sassicaia, one of Italy's greatest wines. Now that reds are allowed, Sassicaia has its own subappellation, and two varietal whites (Sauvignon and Vermentino) and a pink *vin santo*, Occhio di Pernice, have been added. Sassicaia will surely be upgraded to full DOCG status shortly, and will probably leave behind a much healthier, better-known Bolgheri DOC with, hopefully, a number of aspiring new wines aiming to replicate its success. Look out for Piero Antinori's new Vermentino, which promises to be Tuscany's first great white wine from a native variety, and for established wines, such as Lodovico Antinori's Ornellaia.

⊢— 1–3 years (white), 3–7 years (most reds), 8–25 years (Sassicaia and *vin santo*)

✓ *Antinori* (Guado al Tasso) • *Angelo Gaja* (Ca' Marcanda Camarcanda) • *Le Macchiola* (Paleo) • *Colle Massari* (Grattamacco) • *Enrico Santini* • *Michele Satta* • *Tenuta dell'Ornellaia* • *Tenuta San Guido* (especially Sassicaia)

BRUNELLO DI MONTALCINO DOCG
Tuscany

One of Italy's most prestigious wines, made from Brunello, a localized clone of Sangiovese. Many relatively unknown producers offer classic wines. The idea is that the wines should be so thick with harsh tannins that they must be left for at least 20 years. If they are ripe skin tannins and there is enough fruit, this can be a formula for a wine of classic stature. But too many are macerated for too long and are not destemmed, leaving the tannins in even the most expensive wines incapable of softening. The producers below make wines requiring at least 10 years' maturation, but packed with fruit that develops into layers of complex, smoky-spicy, plummy-fruit flavors. Look out for new Frescobaldi-Mondavi wines from the Solaria estate.

⊢— 10–25 years

✓ *Altesino, Tenuta di Argiano* • *Villa Banfi* (especially Poggio all'Oro) • *Fattoria dei Barbi* (Vigna del Fiore) • *Campogiovanni* • *Tenuta Caparzo* • *Tenuta Carlina* (La Torgata) • *Casanova di Neri* • *Case Basse* • *Castelgiocondo* • *Castello Romitorio* • *Cerbaiona* • *Col d'Orcia* • *Conti Costanti Frescobaldi* • *Eredi Fuligni* • *Fanti-La Palazzetta Fanti-San Filippo* • *Lisini* • *Mastrojanni* • *Pertimali* • *Podere Salicutti* • *La Poderina* (Poggio Banale) • *Poggio Antico Tenuta Il Poggione* • *Salvioni-La Cerbaiola* • *Tenuta Silvio Nardi* (Manachiara) • *Siro Pacenti* • *Solaria-Cencioni* • *Talenti* • *Uccelliera* • *Val di Suga*

CABERNET SAUVIGNON
Tuscany

Ideally suited to the Tuscan soil and climate.

✓ *Villa Banfi* (Tavernelle) • *Villa Cafaggio* (Cortaccio) • *Frescobaldi* (Mormoreto) • *Isole e Olena* • *Monsanto* (Nemo) • *Fattoria di Nozzole* (Il Pareto) • *Poliziano* (Le Stanze) • *Castello di Querceto* (Cignale)

CABERNET-MERLOT
West-central Italy

Cabernet-Merlot is a classic *bordelais* blend that is best suited to Tuscany.

✓ **Tuscany** *Il Paradis* (Saxa Calida) • *Villa di Capezzana* (Ghiaie della Furba) • *Podere Il*

Carnasciale • *Tenuta dell'Ornellaia* (Ornellaia)

Latium *Cantina Colacicchi* (Torre Ercolana), *Fiorano Rosso, Colle Picchioni* (Vigna del Vassello)

CABERNET-SANGIOVESE BLENDS
Tuscany

Most contain at least 80 percent Cabernet Sauvignon, 20 percent Sangiovese, and are the antithesis of the rising tide of Sangiovese blends.

✓ *Antinori* (Solaia) • *Tenuta di Bossi* (Mazzaferrata) • *Castellare di Castellina* (Coniale di Castellare) • *Castello di Gabbiano* (R e R) • *Lungarotti* (San Giorgio) • *Sette Ponti* (Oreno) • *Tenuta dell'Ornellaia* (Le Volte) • *Castello di Querceto* (Il Querciolaia) • *Poliziano* (Le Stanze) • *Castello dei Rampolla* (Sammarco, D'Alceo) • *Rocca delle Macie* (Roccato)

CANAIOLO
Tuscany

This is a native Tuscan grape, which is capable of soft, seductively fruity red wines.

CANDIA DEI COLLI APUANI DOC
Tuscany

Delicate, slightly aromatic, dry or semisweet whites from Vermentino and Albarola grapes.

CARMIGNANO DOC
Tuscany

Since Carmignano achieved DOCG status, the DOC has been used for *rosato*, *vin santo*, and *rosé vin santo*, called Occhio di Pernice (even though these styles were not allowed before the upgrading). The declassified Carmignano reds can now be sold as Barco Reale di Carmignano.

CARMIGNANO DOCG
Tuscany

Only traditional red Carmignano from this tiny appellation west of Florence may claim DOCG status. Other wines are classified as either Carmignano DOC or Barco Reale di Carmignano DOC. This DOCG is made from 45 to 65 percent Sangiovese, 10 to 20 percent Canaiolo Nero, 6 to 10 percent Cabernet Sauvignon, 10 to 20 percent Trebbiano, Canaiolo Bianco or Malvasia, and up to 5 percent Mammolo or Colorino. The result is similar to medium-bodied Chianti, but with less acidity, which, with its Cabernet content, gives a chocolaty-finesse to the fruit. *See also* Carmignano DOC and Barco Reale di Carmignano DOC.

⊢— 4–10 years

✓ *Fattoria di Ambra* • *di Artimino* • *Fattoria di Bacchereto* • *Contini Bonacossi* (Villa di Capezzana, Villa di Trefiano) • *Fattoria Il Poggiolo* • *Piaggia*

CASTELLI ROMANI
Latium

Castelli Romani are rarely exciting, dry and semisweet white, red, and rosé wines.

CERVETERI DOC
Latium

Rustic Sangiovese-based reds, dry and semisweet Trebbiano-Malvasia white wines of decent, everyday quality.

CESANESE
Latium

This local black grape variety makes medium-bodied red wines of no special quality in all styles from dry to sweet, and still to sparkling.

CESANESE DEL PIGLIO *or* PIGLIO DOC
Latium

This DOC covers a complicated range of basically simple red wines, from Cesanese grapes grown in a hilly area southeast of Rome. The styles include bone-dry, off-dry, medium-dry, semisweet, and sweet, and may be still, *frizzantino*, *frizzante*, or *spumante*.

CESANESE DI AFFILE *or* AFFILE DOC
Latium

This DOC produces the same styles as Cesanese del Piglio from a neighboring area.

CESANESE DI OLEVANO ROMANO *or* OLEVANO ROMANO DOC
Latium

Much smaller than the previous two nearby Cesanese DOCs, but covering the same styles.

CHARDONNAY
Tuscany and Umbria

The great, if ubiquitous, Chardonnay first squeezed into the official wines of Tuscany when it was adopted by the Pomino DOC, but the best renditions are still *vini da tavola*. In Umbria, although there are only a few great Chardonnay wines, it has great potential in the region, whether in the pure form, as made by Lungarotti, or blended with a little Grechetto, as in the case of Antinori's Cervaro della Sala.

✓ **Tuscany** *Castello di Ama* (Colline di Ama) • *Caparzo* (Le Grance) • *Villa Banfi* (Fontanelle) • *Felsina Berardenga* (I Sistri) • *Isole e Olena* • *Ruffino* (Cabreo Vigneto la Pietra)

Umbria *Antinori Castello della Sala* (Cervaro della Sala) • *Lungarotti* (Vigna I Palazzi)

CHIANTI & CHIANTI CLASSICO DOCG
Tuscany

When Chianti was granted DOCG status, its yields were reduced, the amount of white grapes allowed in Chianti Classico was cut, and up to 10 percent Cabernet Sauvignon was permitted in the blend. However, the DOCG was applied to the entire Chianti production area and thus has failed to be a guarantee of quality. Most Chianti is still garbage, albeit in a cleaner, more sanitized form than it used to be. The best basic Chianti, however, is full of juicy cherry, raspberry, and plummy fruit flavors, which makes an enjoyable quaffer, although it is not what DOCG should be about. Only the finest wines of Chianti deserve DOCG status and they are usually sold as *classico* (the original, hilly Chianti area), although Rufina (from a small area northeast of Florence, which should not be confused with Ruffino, the brand name) and Colli Fiorentini (which bridges the Classico and Rufina areas), which are both outside the *classico* district, also produce *classico*-like quality. Both also have lower yields than the rest of Chianti, with the exception of Classico, which demands the lowest yield of all.

Whatever the industrial bottlers do to continue debasing Chianti's reputation, readers must not forget that the best wines from these three areas rank among the greatest in the world. Rufina and Colli Fiorentini are, however, just two of six subappellations collectively known as the Chianti Putto, which covers the peripheral areas surrounding Chianti Classico itself. The other four are Colli Senesi (the largest and most varied, and so inconsistent that few wines claim this provenance, two portions of which are better known for Brunello di Montalcino and Vino Nobile di Montepulciano); Colli Pisani (lightest of all Chianti); Colli Aretini (young, lively Chianti); and Montalbano (in effect the second wine of Carmignano, although there are two of those, so maybe it is the third wine?).

All Chianti other than *classico* must contain between 75 and 90 percent Sangiovese plus the possibility of 5 to 10 percent Canaiolo Nero, 5 to 10 percent Trebbiano or Malvasia, and up to a maximum of 10 percent Cabernet or any other specified black grape varieties. This recipe applied to Chianti Classico until 1995, when it was changed to allow up to 100 percent Sangiovese, which should be a good move for those dedicated growers who are striving to get this difficult variety right. With the amount of Cabernet and other black grapes increased to 15 percent, this DOC is wide open to many of the so-called Super-Tuscans to be classified as Chianti Classico and thereby greatly enhance the reputation of this once great appellation.

⌐⊸ 3–5 years (inexpensive, everyday drinking), 4–8 years (more serious Chianti), 6–20 years (finest *classico*)

✓ *Antinori* (Peppoli) • *Badia a Coltibuono* • *Barone Ricasoli* (Castello di Brolio) • *Carobbio* (Riserva) • *Caparsa* (Doccio a Matteo Riserva) • *Castellare di Castellina* (Vigna Il Poggiale) • *Castellini Villa* • *Castello di Ama* • *Castello di Cacchiano* • *Castello di Fonterutoli* • *Castello Querceto* • *Castello di Rampolla* • *Castello di San Polo in Rosso* • *Castello di Volpaia* • *Felsina* (Rancia) • *Fontodi* • *Isole e Olena* • *La Massa* (Giorgio Primo) • *Monsanto* (Il Poggio) • *Podere Il Palazzino* (Grosso Sanese) • *Poggerino* • *Poggio al Sole* (Casasilia) • *Riecine* (Riserva) • *Rocca della Macie* (Roccato) • *San Fabiano Calcinaia* (Cellole Riserva) • *San Felice* (Poggio Rosso Riserva) • *San Giusto* (Gaio) • *San Vicente* (Riserva) • *Terrabianca* • *Uggiano* • *Vecchie Terre di Montefili* • *Villa Vignamaggio* (Mona Lisa Riserva)

COLLI ALBANI DOC
Latium

Soft and fruity, dry and semisweet white wines that can be *spumante*.

COLLI ALTOTIBERINI DOC
Umbria

An interesting DOC in the hilly upper Tiber Valley area, which produces dry white wines from Trebbiano and Malvasia, and firm, fruity reds from Sangiovese and Merlot. However, it is the crisp, fragrant rosés from the same red grape varieties that most people prefer.

COLLI AMERINI DOC
Umbria

Dry whites from Trebbiano with the possible addition of Grechetto, Verdello, Garganega, and Malvasia, with red and rosé from Sangiovese plus the possibility of Montepulciano, Ciliegiolo, Canaiolo, Merlot, and Barbera. A dry white pure Malvasia varietal may also be produced.

COLLI DEL TRASIMENO DOC
Umbria

A very large DOC area on the Tuscan border. The dry and off-dry whites are ordinary, but the reds, in which the bitter edge of Sangiovese is softened with Gamay, Ciliegiolo, Malvasia, and Trebbiano are more interesting.

⌐⊸ 2–5 years

✓ *La Fiorita*

COLLI DELL'ETRURIA CENTRALE DOC
Tuscany

The idea was fine, to provide an alternative appellation for lesser red, white, and rosé wines produced in the Chianti area and thus improve the DOCG through selection. But the name hardly trips off the tongue and one might be forgiven for thinking it was agreed to by producers who wanted any excuse not to use it and so keep churning out as much Chianti as possible. Red wines may be referred to as *vermiglio*, which has historical connotations with Chianti, and *vin santo* may also be made.

COLLI DI LUNI DOC
Tuscany

See Colli di Luni DOC (Liguria, Northwest Italy).

COLLI LANUVINI DOC
Latium

Smooth, white wines, either dry or semisweet.

COLLI MARTANI DOC
Umbria

This covers four varietal wines from a large but promising area encompassing the Montefalco DOC: Sangiovese, Trebbiano, Grechetto, and the single-commune Grechetto di Todi.

COLLI PERUGINI DOC
Umbria

Dry, slightly fruity, Trebbiano-based white wines, full-bodied red wines, and dry, fresh rosé wines, primarily from Sangiovese grapes. Produced in a large area between Colli del Trasimeno and the Tiber, covering six communes in the province of Perugia and one in the province of Terni.

COLLINE LUCCHESI DOC
Tuscany

This DOC produces light, soft, Chianti-like reds and bland, dry, Trebbiano-based whites.

CORI DOC
Latium

Little-seen and rarely exciting, dry, semisweet, or sweet white wines and smooth, vinous reds.

ELBA DOC
Tuscany

The range of wines from the vacation isle of Elba have been expanded to include 10 types: Trebbiano-based dry white; Sangiovese-based red, and *riserva* red; *rosato*; Ansonica dell'Elba (dry white from the Ansonica, better known as the Inzolia grape of Sicily); Ansonica Passito dell'Elba; Aleatico dell'Elba; Vin Santo dell'Elba; Vin Santo dell'Elba Occhio di Pernice; and a white *spumante*. However, these wines are mostly made for tourists.

⌐⊸ *In situ* only

✓ *Acquabona*

EST! EST!! EST!!! DI MONTEFIASCONE DOC
Latium

The name is the most memorable thing about these dry or semisweet white wines made from Trebbiano and Malvasia grapes grown around Lake Bolsena, adjacent to the Orvieto district. Traditionally, the name dates to the 12th century, when a fat German bishop called Johann Fugger had to go to Rome for the coronation of Henry V. In order to drink well on his journey, he sent his *majordomo* ahead to visit the inns along the route and mark those with the best wine with the word "Est," short for "*Vinum est bonum.*" When he arrived at Montefiascone, the *majordomo* so liked the local wine that he chalked "Est! Est!! Est!!!." Fugger must have agreed with him, because once he had tasted the wine he canceled his trip and stayed in Montefiascone until his death. The truth of the story is uncertain, for, although a tomb in the village church bears Fugger's name, whether it contains his 800-year-old body or not is unknown. As for the wine, Hugh Johnson has accurately described it as an unextraordinary white wine that trades on its oddball name.

FALERNO *or* FALERNUM
Latium

Falernum was the famous wine of Ancient Rome. Its modern equivalent is a typically dark and rustically rich Aglianico wine, the best of which is the Villa Matilde *riserva*, which has a full aroma and a better balance than most. A dry white wine is also produced.

FRASCATI DOC
Latium

Most Frascati used to be flabby or oxidized, but with recent improvements in vinification techniques they are now invariably fresh and clean, although many still have a bland, peardrop aroma and taste. The few exceptions come from virtually the same group of top-performing producers as they did a decade ago and these wines stand out for their noticeably full flavor, albeit in a fresh, zippy-zingy style. Frascati is made from Trebbiano and Malvasia grapes, primarily dry, but semisweet, sweet, and *spumante* styles are also made.

⌐⊸ 1–2 years

✓ *Colli di Catone* (especially Colle Gaio—other labels include Villa Catone and Villa Porziana) • *Fontana Candida* (Vigneti Santa Teresa) • *Villa Simone*

GALESTRO
Tuscany

This ultraclean, light, fresh, and delicately fruity, dry white wine is made by a *consorzio* of Chianti producers to agreed standards. It is shortly due to receive DOC recognition.

⌛ 1–2 years

✓ Bigi (Marrano)

GRECHETTO *or* GRECO
Umbria and Tuscany

Clean, fresh, dry and sweet white wines with a pleasant floral aroma that can make interesting drinking, but seldom excel, with the exception of Bigi's Marrano, which is aged in oak.

⌛ 1–2 years

✓ *Bigi* (Marrano)

MARINO DOC
Latium

A typically light and unexciting Trebbiano and Malvasia blend that may be dry, semisweet, or *spumante*. Paola di Mauro's deliciously rich and caramelized Colle Picchioni Oro stands out due to its relatively high proportion of Malvasia grapes, and the fact that it receives a prefermentation maceration on its skins and is matured in *barriques*.

⌛ 1–4 years

✓ *Colle Picchioni* (Oro)

MERLOT
Tuscany

There is only one classic Merlot produced in Tuscany, Masseto, and although it is one of the most expensive red wines in Italy, some vintages can stand shoulder to shoulder with Pétrus, which might make it look like a bargain, depending on your perspective.

⌛ 3–8 years

✓ *Villa Banfi* (Mandrielle) • *Tenuta dell'Ornellaia* (Masseto) • *Petrolo* (Galatrona)

MONTECARLO DOC
Tuscany

Some interesting dry white wines are starting to appear in this area situated between Carmignano and the coast. Although based on the bland Trebbiano, supplementary varieties (Roussanne, Sémillon, Pinot Grigio, Pinot Bianco, Sauvignon Blanc, and Vermentino) may account for 30 to 40 percent of the blend, thus allowing growers to express individual styles, from light and delicate to full and rich, either with or without *barrique*-aging. Red wines may be made from Sangiovese, Canaiolo, Ciliegiolo, Colorino, Syrah, Malvasia, Cabernet Franc, Cabernet Sauvignon, and Merlot. A white *vin santo* and a pink Occhio di Pernice *vin santo* are also allowed.

⌛ 4–10 years

✓ *Fattoria dell Buonamico* • *Carmignani* • *Fattoria Michi* • *Vigna del Greppo*

MONTECOMPATRI COLONNA *or* MONTECOMPATRI COLONNA DOC
Latium

These dry or semisweet, Malvasia-based white wines may bear the name of one or both of the above towns on the label.

MONTEFALCO DOCG
Umbria

There is a significant difference in quality between these basic red and white wines and the more interesting, characterful DOCG Sagrantino of Montefalco.

MONTEFALCO SAGRANTINO DOCG
Umbria

Upgraded to DOCG in 1992 and detached from the basic Montefalco denomination, these distinctive red wines in dry and sweet *passito* styles are made exclusively from the Sagrantino grape, which has the advantage of being grown on the best-exposed hillside vineyards southwest of Perugia. The *passito* wines are the most authentic in style, dating back to the 15th century, but the dry table-wine style, which hints of ripe, fresh-picked blackberries, is the best and most consistent.

⌛ 3–12 years

✓ *Fratelli Adanti* • *Antonelli* • *Villa Antico* • *Arnaldo Caprai* • *Colpetrone*

MONTEREGIO DI MASSA MARITTIMA DOC
Tuscany

These are red, white, rosé, *novello*, and *vin santo* from the northern part of the province of Grosseto. A dry white Vermentino varietal wine and a pink *passito* called Occhio di Pernice are also included within Monteregio di Massa Marittima DOC.

MONTESCUDAIO DOC
Tuscany

A Trebbiano-based dry white wine, a soft, slightly fruity, Sangiovese-based red, and a *vin santo* from the Cecina Valley.

⌛ 1–3 years

✓ *Poggio Gagliardo* • *Sorbaiano*

MORELLINO DI SCANSANO DOC
Tuscany

This DOC produces some good Brunello-like wines from 100 percent Sangiovese, which are thick with tasty, ripe fruit and can age well.

⌛ 4–8 years

✓ *Erik Banti* • *Poggio Argentiera* (Capa Tosta) • *Motta* • *Fattoria Le Pupille*

MOSCADELLO DI MONTALCINO DOC
Tuscany

An ancient style of aromatic, sweet Muscat that was famous long before Brunello. Fortified versions and sweet *frizzante* are also possible.

⌛ Upon purchase

✓ *Villa Banfi* (Vendemmia Tardiva) • *Col d'Orcia* • *Tenuta Il Poggione*

MOSCATO
Tuscany

There is just one Tuscan Moscato DOC, Moscadello di Montalcino, but a few delicately sweet rosé *vini da tavola* are made from the Moscato Rosa grape. It is an exquisite wine well worth searching out.

⌛ Upon purchase

✓ *Castello di Farnatella* (Rosa Rosae)

ORVIETO DOC
Umbria and Latium

The vineyards for this popular, widely exported, dry or semisweet, Trebbiano-based white wine are primarily located in Umbria. In general, Orvieto is still disappointing, although Bigi's Vigneto Torricella remains outstanding and the number of wines aspiring to a similar quality is growing. The best semisweet, or *abboccato*, style will include a small proportion of botrytized grapes. Fully botrytized, or *muffato*, Orvieto are extremely rare, but well worth tracking down as they offer a fabulous combination of elegance, concentration, and youthful succulence.

⌛ Upon purchase

✓ *Antinori* (Campogrande) • *Barberani* (Castagnolo) • *Bigi* (Torricella) • *Decugnano dei Barbi* • *Palazzone* (Terre Vineate)

PARRINA DOC
Tuscany

The dry whites of Parrina, the most southerly of Tuscany's DOCs, are the least interesting. The Sangiovese-based reds used to be merely soft, light, and attractive, but of late have become much darker, fuller, and richer, like an oaky Chianti, with just a touch of vanillin sweetness on the finish, and even an occasional wisp of mint on the aftertaste.

⌛ 3–7 years

✓ *Franca Spinola*

POMINO DOC
Tuscany

This wine dates back to 1716, and a Pomino was marketed as a single-vineyard Chianti by Marchesi de' Frescobaldi long before it was resurrected as its own DOC in 1983. The white is a blend of Pinot Blanc, Chardonnay, and Trebbiano, although Frescobaldi's Il Benefizio is pure Chardonnay. The red is a blend of Sangiovese, Canaiolo, Merlot, Cabernet Franc, and Cabernet Sauvignon. A semisweet *vin santo* is also made in both red and white styles.

⌛ 1–3 years (blended white) 3–7 years (red and Il Benefizio)

✓ *Frescobaldi* • *Fattoria Petrognano*

ROSATO DELLA LEGA
Tuscany

Rosato della Lega are dry, Tuscan rosé wines, which are produced by members of the Chianti Classico *consorzio*.

ROSSO DELLA LEGA
Tuscany

These are reasonable, everyday red wines, which are produced by members of the Chianti Classico *consorzio*.

ROSSO DI MONTALCINO DOC
Tuscany

This appellation is for lesser or declassified wines of Brunello di Montalcino or for wines made from young vines. Although there has been a tendency in recent years to produce deeper, darker, more concentrated wines, as a rule the biggest Rosso di Montalcino wines are much more accessible in their youth than Brunello, which some readers may prefer.

🍷— 5–15 years

✓ *Altesino • Castelgiocondo • Conti Costanti • Lisini • Tenuta Il Poggione • Val di Suga*

ROSSO DI MONTEPULCIANO DOC
Tuscany

This DOC is for the so-called lesser wines of Vino Nobile di Montepulciano and, like Rosso di Montalcino DOC, its wines are softer and more approachable when young.

🍷— 5–15 years

✓ *Avignonesi • Bindella • Podere Boscarelli • Le Casalte • Contucci • Fattoria del Cerro • Poliziano • Tenuta Trerose*

SAGRANTINO
Umbria

Another local variety that almost died out but has seen a revival, Sagrantino traditionally makes both dry and sweet, *passito* reds. Some people believe its name is derived from *sagra*, ("festival") and suggest that the wines it yields were originally reserved for feast days.

SANGIOVESE *or* SANGIOVESE-DOMINATED
Tuscany and Umbria

Although just 10 years ago no one believed that Sangiovese could stand alone, its success was merely a matter of reduced yields and a suitable *terroir*. With good, but not overstated, *barrique*-aging, and bottling at the optimum moment for fruit retention, Sangiovese can be rich, lush, and satisfyingly complete, with a succulent, spicy-cedary oak complexity. It is commonly found in Umbria, but exceptional Sangiovese-based wines are relatively rare.

✓ **Tuscany** *Altesino* (Palazzo Altesi) • *Avignonesi* (I Grifi) • *Badia a Coltibuono* (Sangioveto) • *Calcinaia* (Cerviolo Rosso) • *Castello di Cacchiano* (RF, Rocca di Montegrossi) • *Villa Cafaggio* (San Martino) • *Podere Capaccia* (Querciagrande) • *Castiglione* (Giramonte) • *Felsina* (Fontalloro) • *Fontodi* (Flaccianello della Pieve) • *Isole e Olena* (Cepparello) • *Monsanto* (Bianchi Vigneti di Scanni) • *Montepeloso* (Nardo) • *Podere Il Palazzino* (Grosso Senese) • *Poliziano* (Elegia) • *Castello di Querceto* (La Corte) • *Ruffino* (Cabreo Il Borgo) • *Guicciardini Strozzi* (Sodole) • *Terrabianca* (Campaccio, Piano del Cipresso) • *Monte Vertine* (Le Pergole Torte) • *Viticcio* (Prunaio)

Umbria *Lungarotti*

SANGIOVESE WITH OTHER ITALIAN GRAPES
Tuscany

✓ *Castellare di Castellina* (I Sodi di San Niccolò) • *Ricasoli-Firidolfi* (Geremia) • *Monte Vertine* (Il Sodaccio)

SANGIOVESE-CABERNET/MERLOT BLENDS
Tuscany

Cabernet Sauvignon was originally blended with Sangiovese to supply fruit and accessibility within a classic fine-wine structure.

✓ *Altesino* (Alte d'Altesi) • *Antinori* (Tignanello) • *Caparzo* (Cà del Pazzo) • *Castello di Bossi* (Corbaia) • *Colombaio* (Il Futuro) • *Fonterutoli* (Siepi) • *Monsanto* (Tinscvil) • *Querciabella* (Camartina) • *Castello di Volpaia* (Balifico)

SAUVIGNON
Tuscany

The Sauvignon does not really seem at home in Tuscany, although judging by the remarkable success of Ornellaia's Poggio alle Gazze, you wouldn't think this was the case.

✓ *Tenuta dell'Ornellaia* (Poggio alle Gazze)

SYRAH
Tuscany

This classic Rhône grape shows tremendous potential, but at equally tremendous prices.

✓ *Fontodi* (Case Vie) • *Isole e Olena* (L'Eremo) • *Varramista*

TORGIANO DOC
Umbria

This DOC was built on the back of the reputation of one producer, Lungarotti (*see also* Torgiano Riserva DOCG). As before, Torgiano DOC covers generic blends for red and rosé (Sangiovese, Canaiolo, Trebbiano, Ciliegiolo, and Montepulciano) and white (Trebbiano, Grechetto, Malvasia, and Verdello), but also sparkling (Pinot Noir and Chardonnay) and five varietals: Chardonnay, Pinot Grigio, Riesling Italico, Cabernet Sauvignon, and Pinot Noir.

🍷— 3–8 years (red), 1–5 years (white and rosé)

✓ *Lungarotti*

TORGIANO RISERVA DOCG
Umbria

Lungarotti's best *rosso*, the *riserva* is a model of how all DOCG denominations should work, and has deservedly been upgraded from DOC.

🍷— 4–20 years

✓ *Lungarotti*

VAL D'ARBIA DOC
Tuscany

A large area south of the Chianti Classico district, producing a dry, fruity, Trebbiano-based white wine boosted by Malvasia and Chardonnay, which may be dried prior to fermentation for dry, semisweet, or sweet *vin santo*.

VAL DI CORNIA DOC
Tuscany

A large area of scattered vineyards in hills east of Piombino and south of Bolgheri. Rarely seen Trebbiano dry whites and Sangiovese reds and rosés, with the subappellations of Campiglia Marittima, Piombino, San Vincenzo, and Surveto.

✓ *Russo* (Barbicone)

VELLETRI DOC
Latium

Rather uninspiring, dry or semisweet white wines and reds from the Castelli Romani area.

VERNACCIA DI SAN GIMIGNANO DOCG
Tuscany

This dry white wine was Italy's first-ever DOC, so DOCG status was inevitable, even if most are bland. The best have always been deliciously crisp and full of vibrant fruit, which makes them well worth seeking out, but not seriously worthy of DOCG status if this is supposed to signify one of the world's finest wines.

🍷— 1–3 years

✓ *Falchini • Panizzi • Teruzzi & Puthod*

VIGNANELLO DOC
Latium

This is a new and untested DOC for red, white, and rosé blends, plus pure Grechetto dry white wine in still and fully sparkling formats.

VIN SANTO
Tuscany and Umbria

A red or white *passito* wine that may be sweet, semisweet, or dry.

✓ *Avignonesi* (Occhio di Pernice)

VINO NOBILE DI MONTEPULCIANO DOCG
Tuscany

Made largely from Prugnolo Gentile, a clone of Sangiovese, plus Canaiolo and other local grapes, including white varieties, these wines come from Montepulciano. Most wines used to be overrated and overpriced, and a number still are, but a growing number of producers make wines that deserve DOCG status. The best resemble a fine *riserva* Chianti Classico, but have a more exuberant character, with generous ripe-fruit flavors hinting of cherry and plum.

🍷— 6–25 years

✓ *Avignonesi • Bindella • Podere Boscarelli • Le Casalte • Contucci • Fattoria de Cerro • Poliziano • Tenuta Trerose*

ZAGAROLO DOC
Latium

This DOC has a tiny production of dry or semisweet white from Malvasia and Trebbiano grapes, which are grown east of Frascati in an area more famed for its wines half a millennium ago than it is now.

NEW IGT WINES

The following Indicazioni Geografiche Tipiche wines were agreed to at the end of 1996, yet most have still to register with consumers, or establish any consistency of style or quality:

✓ **Latium** *Castelli Romani • Circeo • Civitella d'Agliano • Colli Cimini • Colli delle Sabina • Colli Etruschi Viterbesi • Frusinate or del Frusinate • Lazio • Nettuno*

Tuscany *Alta Valle Della Greve • Colli della Toscana Centrale • Maremma Toscana • Orcia • Toscana or Toscano • Val di Magra*

Umbria *Allerona • Assisi • Bettona • Cannara • Lago di Corbara • Narni • Spello • Umbria*

EAST-CENTRAL ITALY

This area comprises the regions of Emilia-Romagna, the Marches, the Abruzzi, and Molise. The best-quality wines come from the Marches and the Abruzzi, but the best-known is Emilia-Romagna's lollipop wine, Lambrusco, which is exported in vast quantities.

IF THIS REGION, which extends across almost the entire width of northern Italy into Piedmont, appears geographically to wander off its central-east designation, it certainly does not do so topographically, for every acre lies east of the Apennines on initially hilly ground that flattens out into alluvial plains stretching toward the Adriatic.

EMILIA-ROMAGNA

Emilia-Romagna is protected on its western flank by the Apennines, the source of seven major, and many minor, rivers.

FACTORS AFFECTING TASTE AND QUALITY

LOCATION
This area stretches along the Adriatic coast, from Molise in the south right up to Emilia-Romagna.

CLIMATE
The influence of the Mediterranean provides generally hot and dry summers, which become progressively hotter as one travels south, and cool winters. In hilly regions microclimates are created by the effects of altitude and aspect.

ASPECT
The best vineyards are invariably to be found on well-drained, foothill sites, but viticulture is spread across every imaginable type of terrain, with a heavy concentration on flat plains, particularly along the Po Valley in Emilia-Romagna, where grapes are produced in abundance.

SOIL
The soil is mostly alluvial, with some outcrops of granite and limestone.

VITICULTURE AND VINIFICATION
A wide variety of viticultural practices and vinification techniques are used here. Much bulk-blended

wine originates here, but some producers retain the most worthwhile traditions and augment them with modern methods.

GRAPE VARIETIES
Aglianico, Albana (*syn.* Biancame, Bianchello, Greco di Ancona, or Passerina), Ancellotta, Barbarossa, Barbera, Beverdino, Bombino Bianco (*syn.* Pagadebit or Pagadebito), Cabernet Franc, Cabernet Sauvignon, Chardonnay, Ciliegiolo, Croatina (*syn.* Bonarda), Fortana (*syn.* Fruttana or Uva d'Oro), Incrocio Bruni 54 (Verdicchio x Sauvignon), Lacrima (*syn.* Gallioppa or Galloppo), Lambrusco, Maceratino, Malvasia, Merlot, Mondeuse (*syn.* Cagnina, Refosco or Terrano), Montepulciano, Montuni (*syn.* Montù or Bianchino), Moscato (*syn.* Muscat), Ortrugo (*syn.* Altra Uva), Pecorino, Perricone (*syn.* Pignoletto), Pinot Bianco (*syn.* Pinot Blanc), Pinot Grigio (*syn.* Pinot Gris), Pinot Nero (*syn.* Pinot Noir), Sangiovese, Sauvignon (*syn.* Spergola), Toscano, Trebbiano (*syn.* Campolese, Ugni Blanc or Albanella), Verdea, Verdicchio, Vernaccia Nera, Riesling Italico (*syn.* Welschriesling)

The rich soil results in abundant grape production, the most prolific varieties being Lambrusco, Trebbiano, and Albana, which produce rustic white wines that, unaccountably, have been given Italy's first DOCG for a white wine. Emilia-Romagna does, however, have some genuinely outstanding *vini da tavola*, such as Fattoria Paradiso's Vigna del Dosso, a red from the Barbarossa, and, especially, a classy Sangiovese-Cabernet blend from Fattoria Zerbina, called Marzeno di Marzeno.

THE ABRUZZI (ABRUZZO)

Although its hills have a variety of soils and microclimates, and should be capable of producing many fine wines, the Abruzzi offers only one—Montepulciano d'Abruzzo. But winemakers are conservative here and only one producer, Santoro Corella, is experimenting with different grape varieties.

Map Legend:

- Colli Piacentini
- Colli di Parma
- Bosco Eliceo
- Cagnina di Romagna, Pagadebit di Romagna
- Montuni del Reno
- Bianchello del Metauro, Falerio dei Colli Ascolani
- Lacrima di Morro d'Alba
- Colli Maceratesi
- Albana di Romagna
- Sangiovese di Romagna
- Lambrusco
- Trebbiano di Romagna
- Verdicchio dei Castelli di Jesi
- Rosso Piceno
- Verdicchio di Matelica
- Montepulciano d'Abruzzo, Trebbiano d'Abruzzo
- Biferno
- 1 Bianco di Scandiano
- 2 Colli Bolognesi
- 3 Colli Pesaresi
- 4 Pentro
- 5 Vernaccia di Serrapetrona
- 6 Rosso Conero
- 7 Falerio dei Colli Ascolani
- 8 Rosso Piceno Superiore
- *Provincia* boundary
- ▲ Height above sea level (meters)

0 10 20 30 40 50 60 miles
0 20 40 60 80 100 km

EAST-CENTRAL ITALY, *see also* p.263
With the Apennines forming the region's western border, the eastern part of central Italy is dominated by their foothills and the plains.

THE MARCHES (MARCHE)

This region has a beautiful coastline where vacationers quench their thirst with the local white—the dry Verdicchio. But there are more exciting wines to be found in the exceptionally fine DOCs of Rosso Cònero and Rosso Piceno and, in a few circumstances, Sangiovese dei Colli Pesaresi, together with excellent *vini da tavola*, such as Rosso di Corinaldo and Tristo di Montesecco.

MOLISE

This poor region with high unemployment has a badly equipped wine industry. Until 1963 it was combined with the Abruzzi and only gained its first DOC in 1983. Italian-wine expert Burton Anderson believes that it may one day provide wines of real class.

AVERAGE ANNUAL PRODUCTION

REGION	DOC PRODUCTION	TOTAL PRODUCTION
Emilia-Romagna	6.6 million cases (600,000 hl)	122 million cases (11 million hl)
Molise	5 million cases (450,000 hl)	6 million cases (550,000 hl)
Marches	3 million cases (275,000 hl)	28 million cases (2.5 million hl)
Abruzzi	2.7 million cases (250,000 hl)	50 million cases (4.5 million hl)

Percentage of total Italian production: Emilia-Romagna 14%; Abruzzi 6%; Marches 3%; Molise 0.7%.

THE APPELLATIONS OF
EAST-CENTRAL ITALY

ALBANA
Emilia-Romagna

In theory, this must be Italy's greatest white-wine grape, as Albana di Romagna was Italy's first DOCG. In practice, this high-yielding grape makes a rather rustic, almost common wine.

ALBANA DI ROMAGNA DOCG
Emilia-Romagna

These straightforward, fruity, sometimes dry, occasionally semisweet white wines are still or sparkling and may be in a very sweet style, either by regular vinification or from *passito* grapes. This is the precise style, reputation, and quality that in 1987 became the first Italian white wine to receive DOCG status. From any angle, this occurred as a result of a political fudge. It's a bit like the French setting up a super-AOC and making Muscadet the first white to receive elite status. On the bright side, the producers of Albana di Romagna have had so much stick that they have had to work hard at improving their product, to good effect.

☙— *In situ* only

✓ *Fattoria Paradiso*

ANCELLOTTA
Emilia-Romagna

This is used to deepen the color of Lambrusco.

BARBAROSSA
Emilia-Romagna

This variety is unique to Emilia-Romagna and produces one of the region's best red wines.

✓ *Fattoria Paradiso* (Vigna del Dosso)

BERTINORO DOC
Emilia-Romagna

See Pagadebit di Romagna DOC.

BIANCHELLO DEL METAURO DOC
Marches

Dry, delicate white wines are made from the Bianchello grape (possibly with some Malvasia) which is grown in the lower Metauro Valley.

BIANCO DI SCANDIANO DOC
Emilia-Romagna

Full-bodied, dry and semisweet white wines that may also be *spumante* and *frizzante*.

BIFERNO DOC
Molise

Smooth, slightly tannic, red and fruity rosé wines from Montepulciano, Trebbiano, and Aglianico grapes; and dry, lightly aromatic, white wines from Trebbiano, Bombino, and Malvasia.

BOSCO ELICEO DOC
Emilia-Romagna

A large coastal region, separated from the major Emilia-Romagna viticultural areas in the northeast. There is a rustic red varietal from the mysterious Fortana grape, also called the Uva d'Oro, although I know nothing of it. Bosco Eliceo Fortan can be dry or sweet, has a slightly bitter tannic bite, is *frizzante,* and not dissimilar to Lambrusco. There is also a generic blended white (Trebbiano, Sauvignon, and Malvasia—may be *frizzante*); two pure varietals, a Merlot (sometimes *frizzantino*) and a Sauvignon (may also be *frizzantino*).

CAGNINA DI ROMAGNA DOC
Emilia-Romagna

Tannic but sweet and fruity red wines, with balancing high acidity.

COLLI BOLOGNESI DOC
Emilia-Romagna

Also known as Colli Bolognesi dei Castelli Medioevali or Colli Bolognesi di Monte San Pietro, this appellation covers an Albana- and Trebbiano-based generic white; three red varietals, Barbera, Cabernet Sauvignon, and Merlot; and five whites, Riesling Italico, Sauvignon (may be *frizzantino*), Pinot Bianco, Pignoletto, and Chardonnay. The last three are made still, *frizzante,* and *spumante.*

☙— 1–3 years

✓ *Terre Rosse*

COLLI DI PARMA DOC
Emilia-Romagna

Solid, slightly *frizzantino* red wines and two white varietals, Malvasia and Sauvignon, in dry, sweet, still, *frizzante,* or *spumante* styles.

COLLI MACERATESI DOC
Marches

This huge area produces a dry, white-wine blend that used to be Trebbiano-based, but now must contain at least 80 percent Maceratino, and Verdicchio, Malvasia, and Chardonnay if possible.

COLLI PESARESI DOC
Marches

Originally a Sangiovese DOC, Colli Pesaresi now includes four different wines, although the deeply flavored Sangiovese-based red still stands out, with the best showing real class. Focara may contain up to 15 percent Pinot Noir, but displays Sangiovese-like characteristics. There is also a Trebbiano-based dry white and a very similar wine called Roncaglia.

☙— 3–8 years

✓ *Tattà • Umani Ronchi • Vallone • Villa Pigna*

COLLI PIACENTINI DOC
Emilia-Romagna

Fourteen wines produced in the Piacenza hills, where Julius Caesar's father-in-law made a wine that was traditionally drunk from a vessel called a *gutturnium.* This is the origin of Gutturnio, the DOC's most famous wine, a Barbera-Bonarda blend. A red, it is usually dry and still, although a semisweet *frizzantino* or *frizzante* version is often made. There are two blended whites: an aromatic wine called Monterosso Val d'Arda (Malvasia, Moscato, Trebbiano, and Ortrugo, possibly with Beverdino and Sauvignon) in dry, sweet, still, *frizzantino,* or *frizzante* styles; and wine called Val Nur (Malvasia, Moscato, Trebbiano, and Ortrugo), which may be dry or sweet, still, *frizzante,* or *spumante.* The following whites may be *frizzantino, frizzante,* or *spumante*: Chardonnay, Trebbiano Val Trebba, Malvasia, Ortrugo, Pinot Grigio, and Sauvignon. The Chardonnay, Pinot Grigio, and Sauvignon must be dry, but the others may be dry or sweet. Three red varietals: Barbera, Cabernet Sauvignon, and Pinot Nero can be dry or sweet, still, *frizzantino, frizzante,* or *spumante.*

FALERIO DEI COLLI ASCOLANI DOC
Marches

Dry, lightly scented white wines made from a blend of Trebbiano, Passerina, Verdicchio, Malvasia, Pinot Blanc, and Pecorino.

☙— 1–3 years

✓ *Cocci Grifoni* (Vigneti San Basso)

FOCARA DOC
Marches

See Colli Pesaresi DOC.

GUTTURNIO *or* GUTTURNIO DEI COLLI PIACENTINI DOC
Emilia-Romagna

See Colli Piacentini DOC.

LACRIMA DI MORRO D'ALBA DOC
Marches

Nothing to do with the wine Lacryma Christi or the town of Alba in Piedmont, this is a soft, medium-bodied red from the mysterious Lacrima grape grown in and around Morro d'Alba, in the province of Ancona. A seemingly single-village wine, this DOC has the largest appellation of the Marches region. Montepulciano and Verdicchio may also be used.

LACRYMA *(or* LACRIMA*)* CHRISTI DOC
Campania

See Vesuvio DOC (Southern Italy and the Islands).

LAMBRUSCO
Emilia-Romagna

Non-DOC Lambrusco is not interesting and the DOC only occasionally so. Lambrusco is an off-dry, cherry-red, frothy wine, which is low in alcohol (although the DOC is higher) and tastes of ripe cherries; export wines are mostly sweet. White and rosé styles are made and the sparkle varies from barely *frizzantino* to *spumante*. Of the many subvarieties, Grasparossa, Salamino, and Sorbara make the most interesting wines.

LAMBRUSCO DI SORBARA DOC
Emilia-Romagna

Mostly dry, although sometimes semisweet, these are medium-bodied, *frizzantino* reds or rosés with more body and depth of flavor than most.

LAMBRUSCO GRASPAROSSA DI CASTELVETRO DOC
Emilia-Romagna

Dry or semisweet, vinous, *frizzantino* reds and rosés, usually better than non-DOC versions, but not quite matching the Lambrusco di Sorbara.

LAMBRUSCO REGGIANO DOC
Emilia-Romagna

Dry or semisweet, *frizzante* red and rosé wines that are the lightest DOC Lambruscos.

LAMBRUSCO SALAMINO DI SANTA CROCE DOC
Emilia-Romagna

These dry or semisweet, vinous, semi-*spumante* red and rosé wines are the most aromatic of the Lambruscos and can come up to the standard of the Lambrusco di Sorbara.

MONTEPULCIANO D'ABRUZZO DOCG
Abruzzi

This is the Abruzzi's only fine wine and there are two distinct styles. Made from Montepulciano with up to 15 percent Sangiovese, both are very deep in color, but one is full of soft, luscious fruit, the other firmer and more tannic. A lighter style called *cerasuolo* exists for cherry-pink wine with fresh fruit, but it is seldom as exciting.

🍷 4–8 or 8–20 years (red), 1–3 years

✓ *Illuminati* • *Gianni Masciarelli* • *Emidio Pepe* ◉ • *Tenuta del Priore* • *Valentini*

MONTEROSSO VAL D'ARDA DOC
Emilia-Romagna

See Colli Piacentini DOC.

MONTUNI DEL RENO DOC
Emilia-Romagna

Light, dry or sweet, still or sparkling white wine with a slightly bitter finish.

PAGADEBIT DI ROMAGNA DOC
Emilia-Romagna

Dry and semisweet, still or *frizzante* white wines from the Bombino Bianco grape, known locally as "Pagadebit." This DOC includes a single-village wine called Bertinoro, the characteristics of which are the same, although potentially finer.

PENTRO *or* PENTRO DI ISERNIA DOC
Molise

Smooth, slightly tannic reds and dry, fruity rosés from Montepulciano and Sangiovese; and dry, fresh whites from Trebbiano and Bombino.

PIGNOLETTO
Emilia-Romagna

Believed to be a distant relation of the Riesling.

RONCAGLIA DOC
Marches

See Colli Pesaresi DOC.

ROSSO CÒNERO DOCG
Marches

Fine Montepulciano-based wines that improve with *barrique* aging. Deep-colored and rich.

🍷 6–15 years

✓ *Garofoli* (Agontano) • *Umani Ronchi* (San Lorenzo) • *Marchetti* • *Mecvini* • *Monteschiavo* (Adeodato) • *Silvano Strologo* (Traiano)

ROSSO PICENO DOC
Marches

Small amounts of Trebbiano and Passerina may now be added to this excellent Sangiovese and Montepulciano wine. The best are firm and ruby-colored with smooth fruit. Often *barrique*-aged.

🍷 4–10 years

✓ *Saladini Pilastri* ◉

SANGIOVESE DI ROMAGNA DOC
Emilia-Romagna

These solid red wines rarely excite, unless from exceptional vineyards.

🍷 3–7 years

✓ *Fattoria Paradiso* (Vigneti delle Lepri) • *San Patrignano* (Avi Riserva) • *Stefano Berti* (Calisto)

SANGIOVESE-CABERNET
Emilia-Romagna

This blend is relatively rare in this region.

✓ *Fattoria Zerbina* (Marzeno di Marzeno)

TREBBIANO D'ABRUZZO DOC
Abruzzi

These are usually dry, neutral, and mediocre white wines, although they can sometimes be delicately scented and velvety in texture.

🍷 1–3 years

✓ *Emidio Pepe* ◉ • *Tenuta del Priore* • *Valentini*

TREBBIANO DI ROMAGNA DOC
Emilia-Romagna

This producer makes dry, neutral white wines that are also made in dry, sweet, and semisweet *spumante* versions.

VAL NUR *or* VAL NUR DEI COLLI PIACENTINI DOC
Emilia-Romagna

See Colli Piacentini DOC.

VERDICCHIO DEI CASTELLI DI JESI DOC
Marches

These are popular, lean, fresh, and mostly uninteresting dry white wines. *Spumante*, *frizzante*, and *frizzantino* versions are also produced.

🍷 1–4 years

✓ *Brunori* • *Bucci* • *Fazi Battaglia* (Le Moie) • *Garofoli* • *Monte Schiavo* • *Umani Ronchi* • *Zaccagnini*

VERDICCHIO DI MATELICA DOC
Marches

Made in a hilly area in the center of Macerata, these wines are slightly fatter than those of Castelli di Jesi, but most are just as uninteresting to drink.

🍷 1–4 years

✓ *Fratelli Bisci* • *La Monacesca*

VERNACCIA DI SERRAPETRONA DOCG
Marches

Made from Vernaccia grapes, Sangiovese, Montepulciano, and Ciliegiolo may be added to these semisweet to sweet *spumante* reds.

IGT WINES

The following IGT wines were agreed at the end of 1996, and yet most have still to register with consumers, or establish any consistency of style or quality.

✓ **Abruzzi** *Alto Tirino* • *Colli Aprutini* • *Colli del Sangro* • *Colline Frentane* • *Colline Pescaresi* • *Colline Teatine* • *Del Vastese or Histonium* • *Terre di Chieti* • *Valle Peligna*

Emilia-Romagna *Bianco del Sillaro* • *Bianco di Castelfranco Emilia* • *Colli Imolesi* • *Emilia or Dell'Emilia* • *Forli* • *Fortana del Taro* • *Modena or Provincia di Modena* • *Ravenna* • *Rubicone* • *Val Tidone*

Marches *Marche*

Molise *Molise* • *Osco or Terre degli Osci* • *Rotae*

SOUTHERN ITALY AND THE ISLANDS

Hot and largely hilly, with volcanic soils, southern Italy is an ancient and prolific wine-growing area. Overproduction continues to be a problem, but well-made wines were starting to clean up Italy's southern-plonk image over a decade ago, since when a host of flying winemakers have made some remarkably expressive wines utilizing local varieties.

JUTTING OUT INTO THE BLUE WATERS of the Mediterranean, the vineyards of southern Italy receive very little natural moisture and bake rather than bask in unrelenting sunshine. This explains the deep-colored wines with strong flavors and high alcoholic levels. Although these heavy wines do not suit modern tastes and southern Italy continues to produce a glut of these almost unsellable wines, the region is subtly changing course. Its

small but growing volume of cleaner, finer, more expressive wines may enable it to establish an identity capable of thriving in ever more sophisticated world-wine markets. In this respect it is being helped by foreign investment and flying winemakers, but the biggest obstacle to consolidating these isolated successes is the poverty that has for so long blighted southern Italy.

APULIA (PUGLIA)

Apulia's exceptionally fertile plains make it one of Italy's largest wine-producing regions, but until the 1970s most of its wines were seen as fit only for blending or for making Vermouth. Because of this, most Apulian producers chose to try to rid themselves of this lowly reputation, bringing about a radical transformation of their industry. A great number of very ordinary wines are still produced, but various changes have greatly improved the situation. Irrigation programs, the introduction of lower-yielding, higher-quality grape varieties (including many classic French ones), and a move away from the single-bush cultivation, known as *alberello*, to modern wire-trained systems, have led to both new wines gaining favor and some traditional ones showing renewed promise. The two most important grape varieties are now the Primitivo, which has been identified as the Zinfandel of California and is the earliest-ripening grape grown in Italy, and the Uva di Troia, which

ROME

Aleatico di Puglia	1	Falerno del Massico
Solopaca	2	Vesuvio
Taburno	3	Ischia
Greco di Tufo	4	Capri
Fiano di Avellino (A), Taurasi (B)	5	San Severo
Orta Nova	6	Cacc'e mmitte di Lucera
Rosso di Cerignola	7	Aglianico del Vulture
Rosso Barletta	8	Cilento
Ciro	9	Gravina
Moscato di Trani	10	Gioia del Colle
Martina	11	Primitivo di Manduria
Locorotondo	12	Rosso Canosa
Ostuni	13	Pollino
Brindisi	14	Donnici
Squinzano	15	Savuto
Salice Salentino	16	Melissa
Nardo	17	Sant'Anna di Isola Capo Rizzuto
Alezio	18	Lamezia
Leverano	19	Greco di Bianco
Matino		*Provincia* boundary
Copertino	▲	Height above sea level (meters)

0   20   40   60   80 miles
0   40   80   120 km

SOUTHERN ITALY, *see also p.263*
Southern Italy produces huge quantities of wine. Apulia makes distinguished wines, but aside from the Aglianico wines of Basilicata and Campania, the quality is patchy.

THE AMALFI COAST
These vines and citrus trees are terraced on cliffs typical to this area.

has no connection with the town of Troia in Apulia's northern province of Foggia, but refers to ancient Troy, whence the grape originates. It was brought to the region by the first Greeks to settle in the Taranto area.

CAMPANIA

The best-known wine of Campania Felix, as the Romans called this area, is Lacryma Christi (Tears of Christ), but the best quality is the lesser-known Taurasi DOCG made from the underrated Aglianico grape. Falerno del Massico is an up-and-coming Aglianico-based DOC, but aside from wines made by individual producers such as Mastroberardino and Antica Masseria Venditti, there is little else of interest produced here.

BASILICATA

Basilicata is a dramatic and wild region dominated by the extinct volcano Mount Vulture. Manufacturing industry is scarce here, accounting for less than one percent of the region's output, and the mountainous terrain makes mechanized agriculture extremely difficult. Lacking investment finance and with two in every three

AVERAGE ANNUAL PRODUCTION

REGION	DOC PRODUCTION	TOTAL PRODUCTION
Sicily	3 million cases (270,000 hl)	110 million cases (10 million hl)
Sardinia	2.8 million cases (260,000 hl)	28 million cases (2.5 million hl)
Apulia	2.2 million cases (198,000 hl)	2.5 million hl (11 million hl)
Calabria	367,000 cases (33,000 hl)	13 million cases (1.2 million hl)
Campania	139,000 cases (12,500 hl)	28 million cases (2.5 million hl)
Basilicata	70,000 casesx (70,000 cases)	4.7 million cases (0.42 million hl)

Percentage of total Italian production: Apulia, 14%; Sicily, 13%; Campania, 3.3%; Sardinia, 3.3%; Calabria, 1.6%; Basilicata, 0.6%.

inhabitants unemployed, Basilicata has not had the means nor the incentive to modernize its wine industry. Consequently, with the exception of the first-class, if idiosyncratic, Aglianico del Vulture, (Basilicata's solitary DOC), a wonderful non-DOC Aglianico called Canneto from Fratelli d'Angelo, and delicious Moscato and Malvasia from Fratelli d'Angelo and Paternosta, the fine-wine scene in Basilicata is as barren as the landscape, although it should make fertile pastures for flying winemakers.

CALABRIA

The decline in Calabria's viticultural output since the 1960s has been for the better in terms of quality. Since then, the most unsuitable land has been abandoned, and the 10 current DOCs, located in hilly and mountainous terrain, may eventually prove to be a source of quality wine. At the moment, however, improvement in wine technology is slow and, with the exception of Umberto Ceratti's succulent Greco di Bianco, a world-class dessert wine that is a relic of the past, and Odoardi's Vigna Vecchia, a fruity red from the obscure Gaglioppo variety, and a luscious Moscato *vino da tavola* from Guido Lojelo, this region also has little in the way of interesting wine.

SICILY (SICILIA)

Sicily is the largest island in the Mediterranean and, in terms of quantity, is one of Italy's most important wine regions, annually producing a quantity roughly equal to the Veneto or Emilia-Romagna. Much of this is produced at high yields deliberately to take advantage of the EU's intervention program, which takes the wine off the market and distills it. The ancient port of Marsah-el-Allah, built under Arab rule, gives its name to Sicily's once popular classic wine, Marsala. By the mid-19th century, Marsala had evolved into a style between that of Madeira and sherry, but now finds itself as popular as bread and dripping, and just as likely to come back into fashion. Indeed, until recently, Sicilian wines were generally unfashionable. Then in 1995, the Planeta family established its winery, the wines started to attract attention and growing respect in the early 2000s, and Planeta is now not only the island's top producer, but also one of Italy's greatest. The stunning quality of these

THE ISLANDS, *see also p.263*
Sicily and Sardinia are usually included with southern Italy because they are on the same latitude, but they had to be separated for mapping purposes in this edition because of the proliferation of new appellations, including the contentious DOCG status of Vermentino di Gallura in Sardinia.

- Moscato di Sorso Sennori
- Cagliari
- Vermentino di Gallura
- Malvasia di Bosa
- Vernaccia di Oristano
- Carignano del Sulcis
- Mandrolisai
- Campidano di Terralba
- Arborea
- Etna
- Alcamo
- Marsala
- Cerasuolo di Vittoria
- Moscato di Noto
- Moscato di Siracusa
- Faro
- Moscato di Pantelleria
- Malvasia delle Lipari
- ▲ Height above sea level (meters)

0   20   40   60 miles
0   40   80   120 km

wines encouraged some long-established wineries (such as Tasca d'Almerita and, when it was bought by Illva Saronno, Corvo) to raise standards, as well as investment from big mainland producers, such as Zonin, which established Feuda Principi di Butera.

SARDINIA (SARDEGNA)

Sardinia is the second-largest island in the Mediterranean and, while it produces virtually all styles of wine, the modernization its wine industry has undergone since the late 1970s has had a more radical effect on its white wines than on any other style. Although Sardinia produces no "fine" wines in the classic sense, the wines are generally well made and easy to enjoy, and a small number of top-performing wineries make interesting wines under the Carignano del Sulcis

and Cagliari DOCs, while exceptional Malvasia *vini da tavola* are made by Gian Vittorio Naitana. Vermentino di Gallura was another enjoyable DOC, but its controversial promotion was the most ludicrous abuse of DOCG status since Albana di Romagna. Gallura does offer potential for fine wines, but more for reds, than whites. Indeed, much of the hilly terrain on this island is naturally suited to lower-yielding, black grape varieties, which if harvested fully ripe could produce intensely flavored, age-worthy reds, such as Turriga from Antonio Argiolas, an excellent Cannonau-based blend.

FACTORS AFFECTING TASTE AND QUALITY

LOCATION
This area includes the southern mainland regions of Apulia, Campania, Basilicata, Calabria, the islands of Sicily farther south, and Sardinia, across the Tyrrhenian Sea to the west.

CLIMATE
The south is by far the hottest and driest region of Italy, although the coastal areas and islands are tempered by maritime winds.

ASPECT
Most of the region is either mountainous or hilly, although vineyards are to be found on the flat land and gentle slopes of Apulia. The best sites are always found on the north-facing, higher slopes of hillsides where the vines receive less sun and benefit from the tempering effect of altitude, thus ensuring a longer growing season.

SOIL
Soil is predominantly volcanic and granitic, but there are some isolated outcrops of clay and chalk.

VITICULTURE AND VINIFICATION
This area, together with the Midi in France, is the principal source of Europe's infamous "wine lake." Nevertheless, producers using better-quality grape varieties grown on higher sites are making wines of a standard and style that deserve wider recognition. Flying winemakers have helped enormously by showing what can be done.

GRAPE VARIETIES
Aglianico, Albana (*syn.* Greco, but this Greco is not Grechetto), Aleatico, Alicante Bouschet, Asprinio (*syn.* Asprino, Olivese, Ragusano, or Uva Asprina), Barbera, Bianco d'Alessano, Biancolella (*syn.* Biancolelle, Ianculillo, Ianculella,

Petit Blanche, or Teneddu), Bombino, Bombino Nero, Cabernet Franc, Calabrese (*syn.* Nero d'Avola or Niura d'Avola), Carignan (*syn.* Carignano or Uva di Spagna), Carricante, Catarratti (*syn.* Cataratto), Chardonnay, Cinsault (*syn.* Ottavianello), Coda del Volpe (Caprettone, Coda di Pecora, or Pallagrello Bianco), Damaschino, Falanghina, Fiano, Forastera, Francavidda (*syn.* Francavilla), Gaglioppo (*syn.* Arvino, Gaioppo, Lacrima Nera, Magliocco, Mantonico Nero, or Montonico Nero), Garganega (*syn.* Grecanico), Girò, Grechetto, Greco Nero, Grenache (*syn.* Cannonadu, Cannonatu, Cannonao, Cannonau, or Canonau), Grillo, Guarnaccia (*syn.* Cannamelu or Uarnaccia), Impigno, Incrocio Manzoni 6013 (Riesling x Pinot Blanc), Inzolia (*syn.* Ansolia, Ansonica or Nzolia), Malbec, Malvasia, Malvasia Nera,

Mantonico, Marsigliana, Monastrell (*syn.* Bovale or Muristrellu), Monica (*syn.* Monaca, Munica, Niedda, Pacali, Passale, or Tintilla), Montepulciano, Muscat (*syn.* Moscato), Nasco (*syn.* Nascu or Nusco), Negroamaro, Nerello (*syn.* Frappato), Nocera, Notar Domenico, Nuragus (*syn.* Abbondosa, Axina de Margiai, Axina de Poporus, Meragus, or Nuragus Trebbiana), Pampanuto (*syn.* Pampanino), Perricone (*syn.* Pignatello), Piedirosso (*syn.* Palombina Nera, Pedepalumbo, Per'e Palumme, Per'e Palummo, or Pied di Colombo), Pinot Blanc (*syn.* Pinot Bianco), Pinot Gris (Pinot Grigio), Pinot Noir (*syn.* Pinot Nero), Sangiovese, Sauvignon, Sciascinoso (*syn.* Olivella), Susumaniello, Torbato, Ugni Blanc (*syn.* Trebbiano), Uva di Troia, Verdeca, Vermentino, Vernaccia, Zibibbo (Moscato variant), Zinfandel (*syn.* Primitivo or Zagarese)

THE APPELLATIONS OF
SOUTHERN ITALY AND THE ISLANDS

AGLIANICO
Basilicata

Many people think that this black grape is not dissimilar to the Barbera, and it has been respected since Ancient Roman times, when it produced the famed wine of Falernum. One of Italy's two greatest Aglianico wines today is Basilicata's Aglianico del Vulture (the other is Campania's Taurasi). Its best producer, Fratelli d'Angelo, is also the greatest producer of a non-DOC Aglianico.

⌛ 6–20 years

✓ *Fratelli d'Angelo* (Canneto)

AGLIANICO DEL TABURNO DOC
Campania

See Taburno DOC.

AGLIANICO DEL VULTURE DOC
Basilicata

This is the only DOC in Basilicata to encompass the volcanic slopes of Mount Vulture and its surrounding hills, which make the best growing areas for the Aglianico grape. A big but balanced red wine of warm color, rich, chocolate-cherry fruit, and firm tannin structure, Aglianico del Vulture can be slightly rustic in youth, yet develops a true silky finesse with age.

Some would argue that it is the greatest Aglianico and will doubtless achieve DOCG status. If described as *vecchio* (old), Aglianico del Vulture will have been aged for a minimum of three years, while *riserva* will have had five; both will have been aged for two years in wood. Aglianico del Vulture may also be sold as semisweet and *spumante*.

⌛ 6–20 years

✓ *Fratelli d'Angelo* • *Paternosta*

ALCAMO *or* BIANCO ALCAMO DOC
Sicily

Dry, slightly fruity white wines from the Catarratto grape with the possible addition of Damaschino, Garganega, and Trebbiano. The soil is too fertile and yields far too high to produce wines of any real quality or character.

ALEATICO DI PUGLIA DOC
Apulia

Produced in tiny quantities throughout the region, this wine is rarely exported. Opulent and aromatic wines with a full, warming, smooth, and exotic flavour, ranging from very sweet and fortified (*liquoroso* or *liquoroso dolce naturel*) to medium-sweet and unfortified (*dolce naturel*). A *riserva* must be aged for at least three years from the date of harvest or, in the case of *liquoroso*, the date of fortification.

⌛ Upon purchase

✓ *Francesco Candido*

ALEZIO DOC
Apulia

A DOC since 1983 for red and *rosato* wines made from Negroamaro, with the possible addition of Sangiovese, Montepulciano, and Malvasia Nera. The red is alcoholic, slightly tannic, and not very interesting, but the dry rosé can be soft and flavorful with delicate fruit.

⌛ Upon purchase (rosé)

✓ *Michele Calò* (Mjère)

ARBOREA DOC
Sardinia

Three varietal wines: Sangiovese red, Sangiovese *rosato*, and a dry or semisweet Trebbiano white.

ASPRINIO
Basilicata

This grape is always grown on its own rootstock and produces a green, often mean, dry white that is often *frizzante*.

ASPRINIO DI AVERSA DOC
Campania

Fresh, crisp, Vinho Verde-look-alike dry white wine from Asprinio grapes grown on vines trained to trees. Usually still, *frizzantino*, or *frizzante*, but sometimes fully sparkling.

BIANCOLELLA
Campania

Almost exclusively grown on the island of Ischia where D'Ambra does a pure varietal bottling.

BRINDISI DOC
Apulia

Smooth, vinous red wines and dry, light, fruity rosés, both primarily from Negroamaro grapes, although Montepulciano, Malvasia Nera, Sangiovese, and Susumaniello may also be used.

⌛ 3–6 years (red)

✓ *Cosimo Taurino* (Patriglione)

CABERNET BLENDS
Calabria

Relatively few Cabernet-dominated wines stand out, but Gravello and Montevetrano are exceptionally fine.

✓ *Silvio Imparato* (Montevetrano) • *Librandi* (Gravello)

CACC'E MMITTE DI LUCERA DOC
Apulia

The name of this full-bodied red *uvaggio*, which is made from seven grape varieties, loosely means "knock it back" (*cacc'e* means "drink" and *mmitte* means "pour"), which aptly applies to this simple, easy-drinking red wine.

CAGLIARI DOC
Sardinia

Four varietals: Malvasia (a smooth, delicately scented red wine in dry, sweet, and *liquoroso* styles); Moscato (rich, succulently sweet white wines that may be fortified); Nasco (finely scented, delicate, dry and sweet white wines that can also be *liquoroso*); and Nuragus (a large production of dry, semisweet, and *frizzante* white wines from the Nuragus grape).

⌛ 1–2 years

✓ *Meloni* ❶

CAMPI FLEGREI DOC
Campania

Two generic blends: red (Piedirosso, Aglianico, and Sciascinoso) and white (Falanghina, Biancolella, and Coda del Volpe); plus one red-wine varietal: Piedirosso (dry or *passito* dry-to-sweet); and one dry white varietal Falanghina (still or *spumante*).

CAMPIDANO DI TERRALBA *or* TERRALBA DOC
Sardinia

Soft yet full-bodied reds from the Monastrell, known locally as Bovale.

CANNONAU DI SARDEGNA DOC
Sardinia

A DOC of variable quality that throws up the occasional gem, Cannonau, better known as the Grenache, encompasses dry, semisweet, or sweet red, rosé, and *liquoroso* styles.

CAPRI DOC
Campania

Easy-to-drink, dry white wines seldom seen beyond the Isle of Capri. The island's soil and climate suggests that these wines should be much finer, but the land for vines is scarce and expensive, encouraging growers to extract far too much from those vineyards that do exist.

CARIGNANO DEL SULCIS DOC
Sardinia

Promising red and rosé wines from the Carignan grape, to which may be added a little Monica, Pascale, and Alicante Bouschet.

⌛ 1–4 years

✓ *CS di Santadi* (Riserva Rocca Rubia, Terre Brune)

CASTEL DEL MONTE DOC
Apulia

The region's best-known wine is named after the 13th-century castle built by Emperor Frederick von Hohenstaufen. With the exception of a red *riserva* made by Rivera and called Il Falcone (The Falcon), the wines are less lofty than the name of this DOC suggests. In addition to the generic red and rosé, which are made from Uva di Troia and Aglianico grapes, and the basic dry white from Pampanuto and Chardonnay, there are two red varietals, Pinot Nero and Aglianico; four white varietals, Chardonnay, Pinot Bianco, Pinot Bianco da Pinot Nero, and Sauvignon; plus a rose, Aglianico.

🍷— 2–6 years (red, but 8–20 years for Il Falcone)

✓ *Rivera* (especially Il Falcone and Terre al Monte)

CASTEL SAN LORENZO DOC
Campania

A relatively new DOC covering several communes in the province of Salerno, Castel San Lorenzo encompasses generic red and rosé (Barbera and Sangiovese), white (Trebbiano and Malvasia), one red wine varietal (Barbera) and one sweet white varietal (Moscato, still or *spumante*).

CERASUOLO DI VITTORIA DOC
Sicily

Cherry-colored Nerello-Calabrese wines from the southeastern corner of Sicily.

✓ *Planeta*

CERDÈSER
Sicily

Red, white, and rosé wines produced in and around Cerda, close to Palermo.

CILENTO DOC
Campania

Vines struggle in the rocky vineyards of Cilento, where generic red and rosé are made from Aglianico, Piedirosso, and Barbera, and generic white from Fiano, Trebbiano, Greco, and Malvasia. An Aglianico varietal also exists, but has yet to prove itself.

CIRÒ DOC
Calabria

Strong, alcoholic Gaglioppo-based red and rosé, and Greco-based dry white wines that rely too heavily on the Cirò name, which was famous in ancient times.

CONTESSA ENTELLINA DOC
Sicily

Vigna di Gabri
DONNAFUGATA

This new DOC encompasses vineyards in the commune of Contessa Entellina in the province of Palermo for a delicate dry white blend of Inzolia, Catarratto, Garganega, Chardonnay, Sauvignon, and Müller-Thurgau; and three dry white-wine varietals, Chardonnay, Grecanico (Garganega), and Sauvignon.

COPERTINO DOC
Apulia

This appellation is named after the town of Copertino, although the wines that qualify for this DOC can also come from five other villages. These smooth, rich red wines and dry, finely scented rosés are made primarily from the Negroamaro grape with the possible addition of Malvasia Nera, Montepulciano, and Sangiovese.

🍷— 2–5 years

✓ *C. S. di Copertino* (riserva)

CORVO
Sicily

The brand name for red, white, *spumante*, and fortified "Stravecchio di Sicilia" wines of Duca di Salaparuta, Corvo has no DOC but is probably the most famous wine in Sicily. The full, smooth, fruity red is by far the most successful and consistent of the range.

CREMOVO ZABAIONE VINO *or* CREMOVO ZABAIONE VINO AROMATIZZATO DOC
Sicily

See Marsala DOC.

DONNICI DOC
Calabria

Fruity, cherry-colored red and rosé wines (traditionally *chiaretto*) from Gaglioppo and Greco Nero grapes grown in the province of Cosenza. They are best drunk young.

ELORO DOC
Sicily

This appellation straddles the provinces of Ragusa and Siracusa, where a generic red and rosé (Calabrese, Frappato, and Pignatello) are produced and, if the blend contains at least 80 percent Calabrese, it may be called Pachino. These grapes are also vinified separately to produce three varietal wines, the Calabrese being sold under its local synonym Nero d'Avola.

ETNA DOC
Sicily

According to Homer, this is the wine that Ulysses used to intoxicate the Cyclops. There are three basic styles: a full red and fruity rosé from the Nerello grape, and a soft but bland dry white from Carricante and Catarratto with the possible addition of Trebbiano.

✓ *Benanti* (Pietramarina)

FALERNO DEL MASSICO DOC
Campania

This appellation celebrates Falernum, the wine so enjoyed in Ancient Rome, which was made in the northwest of Campania and Latium. The deep-colored, full-bodied, and rustically robust red generic is a blend of Aglianico and Piedirosso with the possible addition of Primitivo and Barbera. The round, fruity dry white generic is, in fact, pure Falanghina. A red varietal Primitivo is also produced.

🍷— 3–7 years (red) Upon purchase (white and rosé)

✓ *Villa Matilde* • *Michele Moio* (Primitivo)

FARO DOC
Sicily

Ruby-colored, medium-bodied but firmly flavored red wines from Nerello and Nocera grapes grown around Messina. Calabrese, Gaglioppo, and Sangiovese may also be used.

🍷— 2–5 years

✓ *Bagni* • *Palari*

FIANO DI AVELLINO DOCG
Campania

Mastroberardino's Vignadora is the best wine in this unusual, but well above average, dry white wine DOCG, made from Fiano grapes grown in the hilly hinterland of Avellino.

🍷— 1–3 years

✓ *Mastroberardino*

GIOIA DEL COLLE DOC
Apulia

For this large DOC in the province of Bari there are generic red and rosé blends (Primitivo, Montepulciano, Sangiovese, Negroamaro, and Malvasia Nera); a dry white (Trebbiano and anything else that moves); and two varietals, a sweetish Primitivo and an intensely sweet Aleatico (which can be fortified).

GIRO DI CAGLIARI DOC
Sardinia

Smooth, alcoholic, dry and sweet red wines and dry and sweet fortified wines.

GRAGNANO DOC
Campania

See Penisola Sorrentina DOC.

GRAVINA DOC
Apulia

Dry or semisweet, blended white wines that may be still or *spumante*, made from Malvasia, Greco, and Bianco d'Alessano, with the possible addition of Bombino, Trebbiano, and Verdeca.

GRECO DI BIANCO DOC
Calabria

Made on the very tip of Calabria, around Bianco, from the Grechetto grape, known locally as Greco Bianco. With the exception of Umberto Ceratti's exceptional rendition, Greco di Bianco is a simple *passito* wine. Ceratti harvests tiny, already shriveled grapes and, apparently, plunges them into boiling water immediately after picking (to flash pasteurize the wine, which removes or reduces the need to use sulfur). His Greco di Bianco is deceptively strong, succulently sweet and smooth, with a vivacious bouquet, exuberant fruit, and a luscious silk finish.

🍷— 3–5 years

✓ *Umberto Ceratti*

GRECO DI TUFO DOCG
Campania

Delicate, dry, and soft white wines that may sometimes be *spumante*, from the true Greco grown north of Avellino.

🍷— Upon purchase

✓ *Mastroberardino* (Vignadangelo)

GUARDIA SANFRAMONDI *or* GUARDIOLO DOC
Campania

Located in the hilly terrain of the Benveneto, this DOC consists of a generic dry white (Malvasia and Falanghina plus up to 30 percent pick-and-mix), generic Sangiovese-based red and rosé, one dry white varietal (Falanghina), which may be *spumante*, and one red varietal (Aglianico).

ISCHIA DOC
Campania

Vinous, medium-bodied generic red (Guarnaccia and Piedirosso, plus 20 percent pick-and-mix); a lightly aromatic, generic dry white (Forastera and Biancolella), which may be *spumante*; two dry white varietal wines (Biancolella and Forastera); and one red varietal (Piedirosso), which can be either dry or *passito*.

🍷 2–4 years (red), upon purchase (white and rosé)

✓ *D'Ambra*

LAMEZIA DOC
Calabria

Originally a one-wine DOC for a light, delicately fruity, but otherwise unexceptional blended red wine (Nerello, Gaglioppo, Greco Nero, and Marsigliana), Lamezia has now been expanded to include a generic, full dry white (Grechetto, Trebbiano, and Malvasia) and a white varietal called Greco, the local name for Grechetto. The light red has been split into red and rosé.

LETTERE DOC
Campania

See Penisola Sorrentina DOC.

LEVERANO DOC
Apulia

Alcoholic red wines and fresh, fruity rosés (Negroamaro with the possible addition of Sangiovese, Montepulciano, and Malvasia Nera), and soft, dry white wines (Malvasia plus Bombino and Trebbiano). Conti Zecca's elegant red Vigna del Saraceno stands out.

🍷 3–7 years (red)

✓ *Conti Zecca* (Vigna del Saraceno)

LIZZANO DOC
Apulia

Negroamaro-based red and rosé, still or *frizzante* generic wines, which may be boosted by the addition of Montepulciano, Sangiovese, Bombino Nero, Pinot Noir, and Malvasia Nera. The rosé can also be fully *spumante*, as can the generic white blend of Trebbiano and Chardonnay (with the possible addition of Malvasia, Sauvignon, and Bianco d'Alessano), which also comes in still or *frizzante* styles. There are two red varietal wines, Negroamaro and Malvasia Nera; and one rosé varietal, Negroamaro—all three in straightforward, dry still-wine styles.

LOCOROTONDO DOC
Apulia

Fresh, lightly fruity, dry white wines of improving quality from Verdeca and Bianco d'Alessano, with the possible addition of Fiano, Malvasia, and Bombino, made in still and *spumante* styles.

🍷 Upon purchase

✓ *C. S. di Locorotondo*

MALVASIA
Basilicata and Sardinia

This grape plays a respectable second fiddle to Moscato in the *vini da tavola* stakes. Usually sweet, sometimes fizzy. In Sardinia, the wines are mostly fortified and DOC, but Malvasia della Planargia is still *vino da tavola*, although many rank it as the finest in Sardinia.

✓ **Basilicata** *Fratelli d'Angelo* • *Paternosta* **Sardinia** *Gian Vittorio Naitana* (Vigna Giagonia, Vigna Murapiscados)

MALVASIA DELLE LIPARI DOC
Sicily

Sweet, aromatic, *passito* white wines.

🍷 2–5 years

✓ *Carlo Hauner*

MALVASIA DI BOSA DOC
Sardinia

Rich, sweet and dry white wines, and sweet and dry *liquoroso* wines. Generally fuller-bodied than Malvasia di Cagliari.

MALVASIA DI CAGLIARI DOC
Sardinia

Rich, sweet or dry, white wines, and dry or sweet, *liquoroso* wines. They are lighter but finer and more elegant wines than Malvasia di Bosa and traditionally are drier.

MALVASIA NERA
Apulia

Dark-skinned Malvasia is commonly found in the Salento district, and traditionally complements the local Negroamaro grape, although it is sometimes made into a pure varietal wine, both as DOC and *vini da tavola*. Alone, this grape produces a vivid red wine with slightly aromatic fruit and a dry but velvety-smooth finish.

MANDROLISAI DOC
Sardinia

Red and rosé wines with a bitter aftertaste blended from Bovale (Monastrell), Cannonau (Grenache), and Monica.

MARSALA DOC
Sicily

This wine was conceived by John Woodhouse, who began shipping it in 1773. Its name is Arabic, deriving from *Marsah-el-Allah*, the old name of the port of Marsala. The grapes used include Grillo (the original Marsala variety and still considered the best), Catarratto, Pignatello, Garganega, Calabrese, Damaschino, Nerello, and Inzolia. The wine is fortified by the adding of neutral spirit and, where appropriate, sweetened with grape concentrate made locally. Marsala can be dry (*secco*), semisweet (*semi-secco*), or sweet (*dolce*); is further defined by color, gold (*oro*), amber (*ambra*), and red (*rubino*); and is made in four basic styles, *Fine, Superiore, Vergine*, and *Solera*.

Marsala Fine, the lowest category, is aged for just a year (not necessarily in wood) with at least 17 percent ABV. As Italian-wine expert David Gleave MW has put it, Marsala Fine is "usually anything but fine, being a cheap and rather nasty travesty of the name." Marsala Superiore is aged for at least two years in wood (four years if *riserva*), with a minimum 18 percent ABV. Marsala Vergine is aged for at least five years in wood, or 10 if *stravecchio* or *riserva*, is only *secco* (thus no grape concentrate allowed), and must have a minimum 18 percent ABV. Marsala Solera is also aged for at least five years in wood, or 10 years if *stravecchio* or *riserva*, is only *secco* (thus no grape concentrate allowed), and must have a minimum of 18 percent ABV. Some historical abbreviations are still found on labels: IP (stands for Italy Particular—Marsala Fine), LP (London Particular—Marsala Superiore), SOM (Superior Old Marsala—Marsala Superiore), GD (Garibaldi Dolce—Marsala Superiore). Flavored Marsala may be sold as Cremovo Zabaione Vino or Cremovo Zabaione Vino Aromatizzato (sickly sweet eggnog containing at least 80 percent Marsala wine, eggs, and a minimum of 200 grams of residual sugar per liter), Preparato con l'impiego di Vino Marsala (for other Marsala-based products containing not less than 60 percent Marsala wine), and you will find non-DOC Marsala-based concoctions with all sorts of flavorings (banana, chocolate, orange, etc.). I must confess that, except for rare old bottlings of Vergine or Solera, most Marsala leaves me cold and the flavored versions horrify me, but the best producers are well known.

🍷 Upon purchase

✓ *Cantina de Bartoli* • *Florio* • *Carlo Pellegrino*

MARTINA *or* MARTINA FRANCA DOC
Apulia

These dry white wines in still or *spumante* styles are very similar to those of Locorotondo.

MATINO DOC
Apulia

Dry, robust red and slightly vinous rosé wines made from Negroamaro with the possible addition of Malvasia Nera.

MELISSA DOC
Calabria

An appellation of full-bodied reds (Gagliopo, Greco Nero, Grechetto, Trebbiano, and Malvasia) and crisp, dry whites (Grechetto, Trebbiano, and Malvasia).

MENFI
Sicily

Decent red and white *vini da tavola* are made in and around Menfi at the western end of the south coast of the island.

METAPONTUM
Basilicata

Basic red and white *vini da tavola* are produced from the Ionian coastal plain either side of the Basento River around Metaponto in the eastern corner of Basilicata.

MOSCATO
Basilicata and Calabria

In Basilicata, the two best wine producers of these *vini da tavola* believe in the potential of Moscato, always sweet and usually fully *spumante*, from the Mount Vulture area. It is also grown all over Calabria, but is more often made into a *passito* wine than a *spumante* one.

✓ **Basilicata** *Fratelli d'Angelo* • *Paternosta* **Calabria** *Guido Lojelo*

MOSCATO DI CAGLIARI DOC
Sardinia

See Cagliari DOC.

MOSCATO DI NOTO DOC
Sicily

Still, *spumante*, or fortified semisweet and sweet Moscato wines.

MOSCATO DI PANTELLERIA DOC
Sicily

Sicily's best still, *spumante*, and fortified semi-sweet and sweet Moscato are made on the island of Pantelleria, closer to Tunisia than to Sicily.

✅ *De Bartoli* (Passito Bukkuram) • *Cantine Florio* (Morsi di Luce) • *Salvatore Murana*

MOSCATO DI SIRACUSA DOC
Sicily

These sweet, smooth white wines are made from semi-*passito* grapes.

MOSCATO DI SORSO-SENNORI DOC
Sardinia

Sweet, rich, white Moscato and sweet, aromatic *liquoroso*. The wines are fuller than either Moscato di Cagliari or Moscato di Sardegna.

MOSCATO DI TRANI DOC
Apulia

Tiny production of luscious, ultrasmooth, sweet white Moscato wines, which may be fortified. These wines are high quality and distinctive.

🍷 Upon purchase

✅ *Fratelli Nugnes*

NARDO DOC
Apulia

Cherry-red rosés from Negroamaro, with Malvasia Nera and Montepulciano permitted.

NASCO DI CAGLIARI DOC
Sardinia

See Cagliari DOC.

NEGROAMARO
Apulia

A productive grape, the Negroamaro makes dark, potentially bitter red wines that used to be sold in bulk for blending, but are starting to acquire their own reputation. It makes a good rosé under the Alezio DOC, but unless vinified with care, the red wine it produces tends to be too alcoholic, coarse, and bitter, although Calò's *barrique*-aged Vigna Spano and Vallone's *passito* Graticcia are *vino da tavola* exceptions.

✅ *Michele Calò* (Vigna Spano) • *Vallone* (Graticcia)

NEGROAMARO-MALVASIA NERO
Apulia

The traditional red-wine blend of Salento.

✅ *Cosimo Taurino* (Notarpanaro)

NURAGUS DI CAGLIARI DOC
Sardinia

See Cagliari DOC.

ORTA NOVA DOC
Apulia

These are full-bodied red and dry rosé Sangiovese-based wines from the villages of Orta Nova and Ordona in the province of Foggia.

OSTUNI DOC
Apulia

A delicate, dry white made from Impigno and Francavidda and a light-bodied red from the

THE MARSALA PLAINS, SICILY
Vines on the hot, arid plains of western Sicily grow on a low-yielding soil called sciari, producing the finest Marsala, while farther east, but still within the DOC, the soil is more fertile and the wines are of lower quality.

Cinsault grape, known locally as Ottavianello, with the possible addition of Negroamaro, Notar Domenico, Malvasia Nera, and Susumaniello.

OTTAVIANELLO DOC
Apulia

See Ostuni DOC.

PELLARO
Campania

Ottavianello DOC produces powerful Alicante-based *chiaretto* wines from just south of Reggio di Calabria on the very toe of Italy.

PENISOLA SORRENTINA DOC
Campania

This is a relatively new DOC for former *vini da tavola* from the Sorrento peninsula, including a generic red (Piedirosso with the possible addition of Sciascinoso, Aglianico, and other unspecified nonaromatic varieties), which can also be made in a purple-colored *frizzante* style, and a dry white generic (Falanghina with the possible addition of Biancolella, Greco, and other nonaromatic varieties). If the subzones Sorrento (for white and still red), Gragnano, or Lettere (red *frizzante*) appear on the label, the wines must conform to higher standards, including extraripe grapes.

PIEDIROSSO
Campania

An ancient variety identified by Pliny, Piedirosso is usually blended with more noble varieties, but has been produced as a varietal wine by D'Ambra on the island of Ischia, where the grape is commonly known as Per'e Palummo.

POLLINO DOC
Calabria

Full, fruity, *chiaretto* wines from Gaglioppo, Greco Nero, Malvasia, and Guarnaccia.

PRIMITIVO
Apulia

Now proven to be the Zinfandel, although it generally makes a wine that has nowhere near Zinfandel's character, let alone its quality.

PRIMITIVO DI MANDURIA DOC
Apulia

Dry to semisweet, full-bodied red wines which may also be fortified and naturally sweet, and fortified and dry. Until I tasted Giordano's 1993 vintage in 1996, no Primitivo had shown any class.

🍷 3–10 years (Giordano as from 1993)

✅ *Giordano* • *Vinicola Savese*

ROSSO BARLETTA DOC
Apulia

Medium-bodied, ruby-colored, everyday-quality red wines made from Uva di Troia with the possible addition of Montepulciano, Sangiovese, and a small amount of Malbec. Most Rosso Barletta is consumed locally when very young.

ROSSO CANOSA DOC
Apulia

Vinous, slightly tannic red wines made from Uva di Troia with the possible addition of Montepulciano and Sangiovese.

ROSSO DI CERIGNOLA DOC
Apulia

Rare, rustic reds from Negroamaro and Uva di Troia with the possible addition of Sangiovese, Barbera, Montepulciano, Malbec, and Trebbiano.

SALICE SALENTINO DOC
Apulia

Full-bodied reds and smooth, alcoholic rosés from Negroamaro with the possible addition of Malvasia Nera, and, more recently, two dry white wines: a Chardonnay, which may be *frizzante*, and a Pinot Bianco, which may be *spumante*; plus a sweet red Aleatico, which can be fortified. The Negroamaro-based red wines are still, however, the best wines in this DOC.

🍷 3–7 years

✅ *Francesco Candido* • *Leone de Castris* • *Cosimo Taurino* • *Vallone*

SAN SEVERO DOC
Apulia

Dry, vinous red and rosé wines made from Montepulciano and Sangiovese, and dry, fresh whites from Bombino and Trebbiano, with the possible addition of Malvasia and Verdeca.

SAN VITO DI LUZZI DOC
Calabria

A new DOC covering generic red, rosé (Gaglioppo and Malvasia with the possible addition of Greco Nero and Sangiovese), and dry white (Malvasia, Grechetto, and Trebbiano) wines produced in and near the village of Luzzi in the province of Conseza.

SANT'AGATA DEI GOTI DOC
Campania

Relatively new DOC for generic red, dry white, and rosé from Aglianico and Piedirosso (thus the white is a *blanc de noirs*); two red wine varietals, Aglianico and Piedirosso; and two white varietals, Greco and Falanghina.

SANT'ANNA DI ISOLA CAPO RIZZUTO DOC
Calabria

Vinous red and rosé wines from Gaglioppo, Greco Nero, and Guarnaccia grapes grown in the Ionian hills.

SARDEGNA DOC
Sardinia

This DOC is for wines made from grapes grown throughout the island, although in practice they are generally restricted to traditional areas. For Moscato, vines must not be grown above 1,476 feet (450 meters). Moscato di Sardegna is sweet and surprisingly delicate, usually in a natural still-wine style, although *spumante* is produced and the subappellations Tempio Pausania, Tempio, and Gallura are reserved for sparkling wines in the Gallura area. Monica di Sardegna is a fragrant red wine that may be dry or sweet, still or *frizzante*, but unlike Monica di Cagliari, is never fortified. Vermentino di Sardegna is a light-bodied, soft, clean, unexciting dry white wine that all too often has its flavors washed out by cool fermentation techniques.

SAVUTO DOC
Calabria

Fresh, fruity red or rosé wines from Gaglioppo, Greco Nero, Nerello, Sangiovese, Malvasia, and Pecorino grapes grown in Catanzaro province.

⟜ 1–3 years

✓ *Odoardi* (Vigna Vecchia)

SCAVIGNA DOC
Calabria

Generic red, rosé (Gaglioppo, Nerello, and Aglianico) and a fruity dry white (Trebbiano, Chardonnay, Grechetto, and Malvasia) from the communes of Nocera Terinese and Falerna.

⟜ 1–3 years

✓ *Abbazia Sant'Anastasia* (Passomaggio)

SICILIA IGT
Sicily

All—not just most—of the very best wines produced on this island are sold under this IGT, and considering Sicily's reputation up to now, the prices that some of these wines achieve should be an object lesson to all the odd, obscure IGTs on the mainland.

✓ *Cottanera* (Sole di Sesta) • *Corvo* (Duca Enrico) • *Cusumano* (Noà, Sagana) • *Fatascià* (Almanera) • *Feuda Principi di Butera* (Deliella) • *Firriato* (Camalot, Harmonium) • *Morgante* (Don Antonio), *Planeta* (Burdese, Cometa, Merlot, Syrah), *Santa Anastasia* (Litra) • *Tasca d'Almerita* (Contea di Sciafani, Cabernet Sauvignon), *Tenute Rapitala* (Hugonis, Solinero) • *Trapani* (Forti Terre Cabernet Sauvignon)

SOLOPACA DOC
Campania

Smooth generic red and rosé (Sangiovese and Aglianico with the possible addition of Piedirosso, Sciascinoso, and up to 30 percent pick-and-mix), generic dry white (Trebbiano, Falanghina, Malvasia, and Coda di Volpe), one red wine varietal (Aglianico) and one white varietal (Falanghina—still or *spumante*). Solopaca comes from the Calore Valley.

⟜ 1–4 years

✓ *Antica Masseria Venditti*

SORRENTO DOC
Campania

See Penisola Sorrentina DOC.

SQUINZANO DOC
Apulia

Full-bodied red wines and lightly scented rosé wines from Negroamaro with the possible addition of Sangiovese and Malvasia Nera, grown in Squinzano and the surrounding communes.

⟜ 2–4 years (red), upon purchase (rosé)

✓ *Villa Valletta*

TABURNO DOCG
Campania

This DOC started out life as Aglianico del Taburno in red and rosé, but it is one of those DOCs that just grows. It now includes a generic red (Sangiovese and Aglianico); white (Trebbiano and Falanghina, plus 30 percent pick-and-mix); a *spumante* (Coda di Volpe and Falanghina, plus 40 percent pick-and-mix); three white wine varietals (Falanghina, Greco, and Coda di Volpe); and one red (Piedirosso).

TAURASI DOCG
Campania

Red wines made primarily from Aglianico grapes (up to 15 percent in total of Barbera, Piedirosso, and Sangiovese may be added) that are grown in Taurasi and 16 nearby villages. It was elevated to DOCG status in 1993. Along with Basilicata's thicker tasting Aglianico del Vulture, it is one of the country's greatest wines from this underrated grape variety, in an equally age-worthy style. Mastroberardino's *riserva* excels.

⟜ 5–10 years (some may last for as long as 20)

✓ *Mastroberardino* • *Giovanni Struzziero* • *Antonio Caggiano*

TERRALBA DOC
Sardinia

See Campidano di Terralba DOC.

VERMENTINO DI GALLURA DOCG
Sardinia

Despite cool fermentation, this is the best Vermentino Sardinia offers, the hilly *terroir* of Gallura producing intense flavors. Although this wine was elevated to DOCG status in 1997, it could be much better quality and cheaper to make if fermented at slightly higher temperatures.

⟜ 1–2 years

✓ *Tenuta di Capichera* • *C. S. di Gallura* • *C. S. del Vermentino*

VERNACCIA DI ORISTANO DOC
Sardinia

The DOC of Vernaccia di Oristano makes dry and lightly bitter white wines, which are sherry-like in style. Also produced are *liquoroso* sweet and dry wines.

⟜ Upon purchase

✓ *Contini*

VESUVIO DOC
Campania

Restricted to vines on the volcanic slopes of Mount Vesuvius, a generic dry white (Coda di Volpe and Verdeca grapes, with the possible addition of Falanghina and Greco), and a generic rosé (Piedirosso and Sciascinoso with the possible addition of Aglianico) are produced by Vesuvio DOC. Those that are labeled Lacryma (or Lacrima) Christi del Vesuvio are usually dry white wines, but less commonly they may also be *spumante* or sweet and fortified.

NEW IGT WINES

The following IGT wines were agreed at the end of 1996, but we have yet to see what style, quality, or consistency each one will establish:

✓ **Apulia** *Daunia* • *Murgia* • *Puglia* • *Salento* • *Tarantino* • *Valle d'Itria*

Basilicata and Calabria *Arghilli* • *Bivongi* • *Calabria* • *Condoleo* • *Costa Viola* • *Esaro* • *Lipuda* • *Locride* • *Palizzi* • *Scilla* • *Val di Neto* • *Valdamato* • *Valle del Crati*

Campania *Colli di Limvara* • *Isola dei Nuraghi* • *Marmilla* • *Nurra* • *Ogliastro* • *Parteolla* • *Planargia* • *Provincia di Nuoro* • *Romangia* • *Sibiola* • *Tharros* • *Trexenta* • *Valle del Tirso*

Sicily *Camarro* • *Colli Ericini* • *Della Nivolelli* • *Fontanarossa di Cerda* • *Salemi* • *Salina* • *Sciacca* • *Valle Belice*

The WINES of
SPAIN

SPAIN CONTINUES TO OVERPERFORM,
providing more wines of real interest and quality
than the most optimistic critic could reasonably
hope for. Why do I say that? For a start, as
indigenous grape varieties go, Tempranillo is
Spain's only class act. Furthermore, although
most Spanish vineyards are not totally lacking
in potential (otherwise we would not have
witnessed the revolution in Spanish wines that
we have), there are no really world-class *terroirs*
to be found beyond parts of Rioja, Penedès, and
the Ribera del Duero. Yet the number of truly
fine Spanish wines continues to increase, with
at least as much excitement at the lower end of
the quality scale as at the higher end. As recently
as the 1980s, with the general exception of
Rioja, most Spanish wines were either oxidized
or oversulfured. Never has an established,
traditional winemaking nation got its act together
so quickly and thoroughly as Spain.

FALL VINES AT LAROCO, VALDEORRAS
*Until Rías Baixas came on the scene, Laroco was
Galicia's up-and-coming white-wine district.*

SPAIN

In the early 1970s, Spanish wines had such a bad reputation that, by comparison, Italian wines seemed preferable. By the late 1980s, however, the wines of Spain were being taken seriously, whereas those of Italy generally were not.

THAT SPAIN COULD ACHIEVE such a swift turnaround in the quality of its wines can be put down to its efforts to get out of the bulk wine market. The Spanish did not stop selling bulk wine altogether, but prevented this low-quality product from dominating exports. By its very volume, bulk wine dilutes and downgrades a country's winemaking reputation, and in the 1970s Spanish bulk wine was so bad that the country's worsening image threatened to undermine its share of global markets just as the culture of wine drinking was developing in the US, the UK, and other potentially lucrative markets. It was not as if there was a

CONSEJO REGULADOR STAMPS

Every current DO and DOCa possesses its own stamp, which usually appears somewhere on the label, offering a guarantee of authenticity.

SPANISH LABEL LANGUAGE

AÑEJO Aged for 12 months in cask or bottle
BLANCO White
BODEGA Literally a "wine cellar," commonly used as part of the name of a wine firm
CAVA A sparkling DO wine produced using the traditional method
CLARETE Midway between light red and dark rosé, synonymous with *tintillo*
COSECHA Means vintage, and indicates that a minimum of 85 percent of a wine thus labeled is produced in the year marked
COSECHERO A fresh, fruity, "new" or nouveau style wine, synonymous with *nuevo* and *vino joven*, and usually a *vino de mesa*
CRIADO Y EMBOTELLADO POR Blended and bottled by
CRIANZA A red *crianza* must be aged for a minimum of 2 years (of which at least 6 months must be in oak); a white or rosé *crianza* requires 1 year of aging, with at least 6 months in oak
CRIANZA CORTA Wines that have less than the legal minimum cask-age for any cask-age designation, synonymous with *sin crianza*.
DENOMINACIÓN DE ORIGEN (DO) Wine from a controlled-quality wine region
DENOMINACIÓN DE ORIGEN CALIFICADA (DOCA) The highest official classification, above *Denominación de Origen*
DOBLE PASTA This term refers to red wines that have been macerated with double the normal proportion of grape skins to juice during fermentation. Such wines are opaque, with an intense color, and may be sold in the bottle or for blending.
DULCE Sweet
EMBOTELLADO POR Bottled by
ESPUMOSO A sparkling wine made by any method
GENEROSO A fortified or dessert wine
GRAN RESERVA Wines from the very best years that are considered capable of even further aging. For red wines, the minimum is 5 years, of which at least 18 months must be in oak. White and rosé *gran reservas* require 4 years' aging, of which at least 6 months must be in oak

NOBLE Aged for 2 years in cask or bottle
NUEVO A fresh, fruity, "new" or nouveau style wine, synonymous with *cosechero* and *vino joven*, and usually a *vino de mesa*
RESERVA Wines from good years that are considered capable of even further aging. For red wines, the minimum amount of aging is 3 years, of which at least 1 year must be in oak. White and rosé *reservas* require 2 years' aging, of which at least 6 months must be in oak
ROSADO Rosé
SECO Dry
SEMIDULCE Medium-sweet
SIN CRIANZA A wine without wood-aging, including all cool-fermented, early-bottled white and most rosé wines. The term *sin crianza* is falling out of use, in favor of *vino joven*
TINTILLO Midway between light red and dark rosé, synonymous with *clarete*
TINTO Red
VIEJO A term that literally means "old." The use of this term was not controlled by law until 2005,

since which date a wine must be aged for at least 3 years
VIÑA OR VIÑEDO Literally "vineyard," but often merely part of a brand name, and nothing to do with a specific vineyard
VINO COMARCAL A regional wine, above *Vino de mesa* and below *Vino de la tierra*
VINO DE AGUJA A semi-sparkling, or *pétillant*, wine
VINO DE CALIDAD CON INDICACIÓN GEOGRÁFICA A stepping stone between *Vino de la tierra* and *Denominación de Origen*
VINO DE LA TIERRA Literally "country wine"
VINO DE MESA Literally "table wine"; likely to be seen on the labels of very ordinary, inexpensive wines
VINO DE PASTO An ordinary, inexpensive, and often light style of wine
VINO JOVEN Wine made to be drunk within the year. There are moves to replace the term *sin crianza* with *vino joven*, but while wines in both categories must be without any wood-aging, some *sin crianza* wines are made to age well in bottle, unlike *vino joven*

SPAIN, *see also* Canary Islands, p.304
The south of Spain has long been famed for its sherry, but the last 20 years have seen amazing progress in still and sparkling nonfortified, bottled wines.

Map legend:
- Rioja and Navarra *See also p312*
- Catalunya
- Jerez
- Cava
- Ribera del Duero
- La Mancha
- Valdepeñas
- Valencia
- Montilla
- Bullas
- Vinos de Madrid
- Campo de Borja
- Chacolí de Vizcaya (1), Chacolí de Getaria (2), Chacolí de Álava (3)
- Other DO areas
- • Small appellation
- — *Provincial* boundary
- ▲ Height above sea level (meters)

0   40   80   120 miles
0   50   100   150   200 km

---

meeting at which the entire Spanish wine industry took a vote to change things, but there must have been some sort of industry-wide determination to improve quality because the situation was reversed so quickly. Spain's reputation leapfrogged Italy's, despite having much less going for it in terms of native grape varieties and *terroirs*, establishing the country as one of the best-value sources in Europe.

ANCIENT ORIGINS

Vines were first planted in Spain *c.*1100 BC around Cádiz by, it is believed, the Phoenicians. The earliest wines were by all accounts rich, sweet, and heavy, the precursors of modern-day sherry. However, from the start of the 8th century until the end of the 15th, southern Spain was under the rule of the Moors, and being Mohammedans, wine production was not a priority. This is not to say that the Moors never drank wine; indeed, Al-Motamid, the last Moorish king of Seville, enjoyed wine so much that he publicly

mocked anyone who drank water. The Moors also enjoyed the grape as a fruit and for its fresh, unfermented juice, but under a theoretically abstemious rule, winemaking stagnated. So, while Spain can claim a 3,000-year history of wine, the diversity of its wine areas and styles did not commence until the 1490s, just 30 years before the Spanish planted the first vines in the Americas. Some parts of the Old and New Worlds are much closer in age, in terms of winemaking, than these terms imply.

SPAIN'S BEST WINES AND ITS APPELLATION SYSTEM

Vega Sicilia in the Ribera del Duero was once definitively Spain's most expensive wine, leading many to believe that it must be Spain's greatest. Others can now lay equal claim to be the most expensive and greatest of Spanish wines (Clos l'Ermita, Dominio de Pingus, and Cirsión are likely candidates), and many more are equal in quality if not quite as ridiculously priced, including

Pesquera, Rioja (Contino, Barón de Ley, Muga Prado Enea, Murrieta Castillo Ygay Gran Reserva), Penedés (Torres and Jean Léon), and even some nonappellation wines such as Marqués de Griñon.

The *Denominación de Origen* (DO) system is Spain's equivalent of the French *Appellation d'Origine Contrôlée* (AOC) or Italian *Denominazione di Origine Controllata* (DOC) systems. The only higher Spanish classification is *Denominación de Origen Calificada* (DOCa), and Rioja remains the only recipient of this superior status since its inception in 1981, although other high-quality wines may be promoted to DOCa in the future. Ribera del Duero, Navarra, Penedés, and Cava all spring to mind as candidates for such promotion. If there is a lesson the Spanish could learn from Italy, it is not to overlook outstanding nonappellation wines such as Marqués de Griñón's Cabernet Sauvignon and Syrah from south of Madrid. Indisputably two of Spain's great wines, they should jump from DO straight to DOCa status, if Spain's regime is to avoid the same fate as Italy's, whose best *vini da tavola* were forced to build up reputations at the expense of the official system.

RECENT SPANISH VINTAGES

2003 It might seem odd that Spain's baking-hot south fared better than the north of the country in this sweltering hot drought year, but as others have pointed out, the vineyards down there are prepared for the heat.

2002 Variable quality, mostly average to poor, with somewhat better quality in the south.

2001 Brilliant quality across the country and throughout the styles.

2000 Variable quality; best in Penedès, worst in Rioja.

1999 An unexciting year, most of which should have been consumed by now.

TRADITIONAL VERSUS MODERN STYLES

It used to be possible to speak of new-wave Spanish wines, as the tradition had been to leave wines in oak for longer than most modern winemakers consider wise and a younger generation of winemakers reacted by producing wines that were as fresh, clean, and unoaked as possible. However, although the old style for reds was dried-out and that for whites oxidized, the new style was so clean, it was clinical, and was no great improvement as such. The tendency now is to talk of modern style rather than new-wave, as the wines are much fruitier and the use of oak is not so much avoided, as restrained, with French casks more likely than American, and fermented rather than aged.

THE HILLTOP TOWN OF LAGUARDIA
Set against the majestic backdrop of the Sierra de Cantabria is the hilltop town of Laguardia, which boasts some of the finest vineyards of the Rioja Alava.

SAMPLING SHERRIES
USING A VENENCIA
The development of a cask of sherry is of crucial importance in determining its eventual style.

CANARY ISLANDS
The first of these appellations was established in 1992, but "Canary Sack" was famous in Shakespeare's time.

APPELLATIONS BELOW DENOMINACIÓN DE ORIGEN

A baffling oddity in Spain's wine regime is the hierarchy of country-wine classifications, all of which are similar to the French *vin de pays* appellation. *Vino de la tierra* (VdT) literally means "country wine," while *vino comarcal* (VC) means "local wine" and comes from a larger area, effectively adding regional status to a *vino de mesa*. A new appellation called *Vino de Calidad con Indicación Geográfica* (VCIG) has been introduced for wines that aspire to *Denominación de Origen* (DO) and is thus seen as a stepping stone to it, making VCIG similar to the French *Vin Délimité de Qualité Supérieure*.

ABANILLA VDLT
Murcia This flat, dry area has a scattering of vineyards whose wines have traditionally been blended with others in the Murcia region.

ALJARAFE VC
Andalucía These fortified wines are effectively an extension of the Condado de Huelva appellation.

ALTO JILOCA VC
Aragón Made mainly from Garnacha and Macabéo grapes, these wines were formerly sold with those of Daroca under the Alto Jiloca-Daroca appellation.

ANOIA VC
Catalonia Mostly soft, bland rosé wines from the Sumoll grape, as the whites are usually sold in bulk to Cava producers in Penedés.

BAGES VDLT
Catalonia Formerly the *vino comarcal* Artés, this area of Barcelona changed its appellation to Bages when it was upgraded to Catalonia's only *vino de la tierra*. Bages VdlT is now the DO Pla de Bages, although vintages of both are still available.

BAJO ARAGON VDLT
Aragón These wines are mostly *tinto* or *blanco* from red and white Garnacha grapes, although a fair amount of Macabéo, Mazuelo, and even Cabernet Sauvignon grow in this very large area.

BAJO-EBROE-MONTSIA VC
Catalonia Meseguera, known locally as Exquitxagos, is the widest-planted grape variety in this area.

BENAVENTE VC
Castilla-León This region was once quite famous for its *pétillant* rosé, but has yet to reestablish its historical reputation.

BENIARRÉS VC
Valencia This area produces robust, alcoholic reds and sweet Moscatel from Alicante.

BETANZOS VC
Galicia A small amount of crisp, light-bodied, "Vinho Verde"-style wines are produced here.

CADIZ VDLT
Andalucía These are light, white table wines of Jerez, pioneered and promoted by Barbadillo—they are fresh, but not special.

CAMPO DE CARTAGENA VDLT
Murcia Mostly oxidized whites, plus some rustic reds, although quality is apparently improving.

CAÑAMERO VDLT
Extremadura These rustic whites are produced in the foothills of the Sierra de Guadalupe. Now one of the six subregions of the DO Ribera del Guadiana, although some producers refused to join the DO and are still labeling their wines as Cañamero VdlT.

CASTILLA VDLT
Castilla-La Mancha This VdlT was inaugurated in 1999 after lobbying by "maverick" winemakers in Castilla-La Mancha, headed by Carlos Falcó. It is a "Vin de Pays d'Oc"-type classification allowing people to make the wines they want with minimal regulation throughout a vast region.

CEBREROS VDLT
Castilla-León A good source of cheap, fruity wines made from the Garnacha grape. Destined to achieve DO status.

CONCA DE TREMP VC
Catalonia A once-famous wine area at the foot of the Pyrenees, Conca de Tremp has a warmer microclimate than surrounding areas and could produce some interesting wines.

CONTRAVIESA-ALPUJARRA VDLT
Andalucía These rustic, fortified wines are from Granada and used to be called Costa-Albondón.

DAROCA VC
Aragón Made mainly from Garnacha and Macabéo grapes, these wines were formerly sold with those of Alto Jiloca.

FERMOSELLE-ARRIBES DEL DUERO VDLT
Castilla-León This is a large but shrinking viticultural area in which one of its secondary grape varieties, Juan Garcia, could prove to be the most interesting. Destined to become the Arribes del Duero DO.

GALVEZ VDLT
Castilla-La Mancha Grape varieties in this large area southwest of Toledo are Tempranillo and Garnacha.

GRAN CANARIA-EL MONTE VDLT
Canary Islands These wines are made from the Negra Común grape grown on Gran Canaria. Recently promoted to DO status under the appellation of Monte Lentiscal, but vintages of both are still available.

GRANDES PAGOS DE CASTILLA
Castilla-La Mancha & Castilla-León Literally meaning "Great Domains of Castile," this is a private designation utilized by an important group of producers throughout both parts of Castile. The wines they will make under this banner could be DO, VdlT, or without regulations, but the corporate designation will take pride of place. The founding members include Mariano García, formerly of Vega Sicilia, plus various local government dignitaries, and the wine writer Victor de la Serna. The president is Carlos Falcó. One to watch.

LA GOMERA VDLT
Canary Islands Wines made from Forastera and Palomino grapes grown on the steep hillsides of La Gomera.

LA RIBERA DEL ARLANZA VC
Castilla-León This is a declining viticultural area, but high-altitude vineyards growing Tempranillo vines show potential.

LA SIERRA DE SALAMANCA VC
Castilla-León This area has potential, but some 70 percent of its shallow granitic terraces overlooking the Alagón River are planted with Rufete, a high-yielding, low-quality Portuguese grape.

LAUJAR VC
Andalucía These are mostly rosé wines from an area better suited to the production of table grapes.

LOPERA VC
Andalucía These are unfortified Pedro Ximénez wines, sold in bulk.

LOS PALACIOS VC
Andalucía These wines are mostly *mistela* (a combination of unfermented grape juice and alcohol) made from the Mollar grape, or light, attenuated, white wines from Airen grapes.

MANCHUELA VDLT
Castilla-La Mancha These are effectively the lesser wines produced in the DO areas of Jumilla, La Mancha, and Utiel-Requena. This is now a DO, but vintages of both are still available.

MATANEGRA VDLT
Extremadura A very large area, Matanegra produces rather lackluster whites, but interesting Tempranillo-based reds.

MONTANCHEZ VDLT
Extremadura This is a sizeable area in the province of Cáceres, producing rustic reds and whites from a mixture of varieties.

MUNIESA VC
Aragón This area is planted mostly with Garnacha, and the wines tend to be dark and tough.

PLA I LLEVANT DE MALLORCA VDLT
Balearic Islands Mallorca is seeking to replicate the fame of Majorca's Binissalem, which itself is but local. This is now a DO, although vintages of both are still available.

POZOHONDO VDLT
Castilla-La Mancha The reds are made from Monastrell grapes, the whites from Airén. They have yet to achieve any reputation.

RIBEIRA DO ULLA VC
Galicia Albarella (syn. Albarello) is supposedly the best varietal to look for here.

RIBERA ALTA DEL GUADIANA VDLT
Extremadura There is promising potential here from both indigenous and foreign grape varieties.

SACEDÓN-MONDÉJAR VDLT
Castilla-La Mancha An area southwest of Madrid producing mostly young, Tempranillo-based reds that are deep in color and often sold in bulk. The area is also called Mondéjar-Sacedón. This is now the DO Mondéjar, although vintages of both are still available.

SAN MATEO VC
Valencia No reputation, not encountered, and no connection with the San Mateo festival in Rioja.

SIERRA DE ALCARAZ VDLT
Castilla-La Mancha No reputation, not encountered, but I hear that this area is starting to show some serious promise, mainly through Manuel Manzaneque, and could be a candidate for DO.

TIERRA BAJA DE ARAGON VDLT
Aragón These rough and ready Garnacha-dominated reds could well be improved over the next few years through increased cultivation of Tempranillo and Cabernet Sauvignon.

TIERRA DE BARROS VDLT
Extremadura Bodegas Inviosa is demonstrating this area's potential for inexpensive fruity reds.

TIERRA DEL VINO DE ZAMORA VDLT
Castilla-León This traditional winegrowing area between Toro and Zamora is best known for its Tempranillo-based reds.

VALDEJALÓN VDLT
Aragón This has a similar history to that of Calatayud, but lags behind and has not quite the same potential. This VdlT is about to become a DO.

VALDEVIMBRE-LOS OTEROS VDLT
Castilla-León Of all the VdlTs in Castilla-León, this area holds the most promise. Rocky-clay terraces either side of the Elsa River are planted with the Prieto Picudo grape, which produces wines that are similar to Tempranillo, but without the color. They are traditionally blended to good effect with Garnacha and the underrated Mencía grape.

VALLE DEL CINCA
Aragón Exciting new area being developed by Codorníu's high-tech Naviana winery and estate.

VALLE DEL MIÑO VDLT
Galicia These wines used to be sold as Ribeira del Sil prior to the best vineyards receiving DO status, while the remaining areas were relegated to this *vino de la tierra*.

THE APPELLATIONS OF
SPAIN

Note Regions or provinces in which appellations are located are given in bold beneath each heading. "DO" is short for *Denominación de Origen*. A synonym for a particular grape variety is indicated by "*syn.*"

ABONA DO
Canary Islands

This new appellation was established in 1996 for white wines made in the south of Tenerife, where the vines are grown on terraces that are also planted with potatoes. Before they gained DO status, these wines were sold under the names of Granadilla, San Miguel, and Vilaflor.

🍇 Listán, Malvasía

🍷 *Viña Peraza*

ALELLA DO
Catalonia

This is a tiny, predominantly white appellation just north of Barcelona, where grapes are traditionally grown on windy granite hills, but due to urban development the DO was extended in 1989 into the colder, limestone vallès of the Cordillera Catalana. The red wines of Alella have good color, medium body, and a soft, fruity flavor. White and *rosado* are pale-colored, fresh, and delicate, with good acidity when made with grapes from the best north-facing slopes.

🍇 Chardonnay, Chenin Blanc, Garnacha, Garnacha Blanca, Garnacha Peluda, Pansá Rosada, Tempranillo, Xarel-lo

🍷 1–5 years (red), 1–2 years (white and *rosado*), 1–4 years (sweet)

🍷 *Alta Alella Chardonnay • Alellasol • Marfil • Marqués de Alella*

ALICANTE DO
Valencia

These mild-climate red, white, and *rosado* wines are grown on dark, limey soil in the hills behind Alicante. The red wines are naturally deep in color and, when made in a *doble pasta* style, they can be ink-black and astringent, but younger, fruitier styles are emerging, as indeed they are among *rosados* and whites. Fortified Moscatels from this region are light and refreshing. A fortified wine of local repute called Fondillón is made from Monastrell grapes in a tawny port style.

🍇 Airén, Bobal, Garnacha, Garnacha Tinta, Meseguera, Moscatel Romano, Monastrell, Planta Fina, Tempranillo, Viura

🍷 6–12 years (reds)

🍷 *Enrique Mendoza • Hijo de Luís García Poveda* (Costa Blanca)

ALMANSA DO
Castilla-La Mancha

This red and *rosado* appellation, which lies north of Jumilla and Yecla, bridges the heights of the central plains of La Mancha and the lowlands of Valencia. The red wines produced here are full-bodied and richly colored, with the best examples being quite smooth and fruity. Good examples of *rosado* can be fruity and clean.

🍇 Airén, Garnacha, Meseguera, Monastrell, Tempranillo

🍷 3–10 years (red), 1–3 years (*rosado*)

🍷 *Alfonso Abellan • Carrion • Piqueras*

AMPURDAN-COSTA BRAVA DO
Catalonia

Lying at the foot of the narrowest section of the Pyrenees, this is the closest Spanish wine appellation to France. Most of the production is *rosado* and aimed at tourists, but the reds are much better, having a fairly deep, cherry-red color, medium to full body, and a crisp, plummy flavor. Whites are fruity and may be off-dry or slightly sweet, with a pale, often greenish-tinged color, and are sometimes *pétillant* (lightly sparkling).

🍇 Cariñena, Garnacha, Garnacha Blanca, Viura

🍷 2–5 years (red), 9–18 months (white and *rosado*)

🍷 *Cavas de Ampurdán • Convinosa • Oliveda*

BIERZO DO
Castilla-León

One of the more exciting of Spain's less traditional DOs, Bierzo includes red, white, and *rosado* wines. Young reds stand out, being made from a minimum of 70 percent Mencía, an underrated variety capable of attractively aromatic wines.

🍇 Doña Blanca, Garnacha, Godello, Malvasía, Mencía, Palomino

🍷 1–4 years (red), 9–18 months (white and *rosado*)

🍷 *Bodegas C. A. del Bierzo • Bodegas Palacio de Arganza* (non-DO wines) *• Pérez Caramés • Casa Valdaiga*

BINISSALEM DO
Balearic Islands

This appellation owes its existence primarily to just one man, José Ferrer, but there are at least two other producers of Majorca's best-known wine who are worth searching out. The white and *rosado* are simple, but the reds are slightly more serious and show some potential.

🍇 A minimum of 50% Manto Negro (for reds) or 70% Moll for whites, plus Callet, Monastrell, Parellada, Tempranillo, and Viura

🍷 Upon purchase

🍷 *José L Ferrer • Jaume Mesquida • Miguel Oliver*

BULLAS DO
Murcia

This is a large region just south of Jumilla where the soil is so poor that, aside from vines, only olives and almonds can survive. The young red wines here are made primarily from Monastrell grapes and seem to have the best potential, but white and *rosado* wines are also allowed. Bullas is, however, a new appellation that has yet to prove its quality.

🍇 Airén, Garnacha, Monastrell, Tempranillo

CALATAYUD DO
Aragón

A patchwork of vineyards, mostly planted with Garnacha vines, tussle with fruit trees for meager sustenance from the poor, buff-colored rocky soil. Increasing the amount of Tempranillo vines and temperature-controlled stainless-steel vats will eventually improve the potential here, but the best wines are still simple, fresh, fruity *rosados*.

🍇 Garnacha, Garnacha Blanca, Juan Ibáñez, Malvasía, Mazuelo, Miguel de Arco, Moscatel Romano, Monastrell, Tempranillo, Viura

🍷 Upon purchase

🍷 *Jalón • Langa*

CAMPO DE BORJA DO
Aragón

This name derives from the notorious Borgia family, who used to run things here at the height of their power in the late 15th century. The whites are fresh, but somewhat neutral. The reds and *rosados* are full, robust, and can be alcoholic, but are they improving. Their character is sometimes compared with that Navarra once had, and Campo de Borja is now experimenting with Cabernet Sauvignon in the same way as Navarra once did. This is a wine area to watch.

🍇 Garnacha, Garnacha Blanca, Viura

🍷 3–8 years (red), 9–15 months (white and *rosado*)

🍷 *Bordeje • Agrícola de Borja* (Borsao) *• C. A. del Campo Union • Agraria del Santo Cristo • C. A. del Campo San Juan Bautista*

CARIÑENA DO
Aragón

Cariñena's low rainfall accounted for the traditionally high alcohol content of these wines, but modern vinification now makes a fresher, lighter, fruitier, more aromatic style. Reds are the best of this appellation, especially from parcels of old Garnacha. Some deliberately maderized *rancio* wines are still produced.

🍇 Cabernet Sauvignon, Cariñena, Garnacha, Garnacha Blanca, Juan Ibáñez, Moscatel Romano, Monastrell, Parellada, Tempranillo, Viura

🍷 11–5 years (red), 9–18 months (white and *rosado*)

🍷 *Añadas • Covinca • Gran Ducay*

CATALUNYA DO
Catalonia

With all styles of red, white, *rosado*, and fortified wine allowed, this basic, regional appellation offers innovative winemakers more flexibility than the supposedly superior, smaller, more specific DOs.

🍇 Bobal, Cabernet Franc, Cabernet Sauvignon, Cariñena, Chardonnay, Chenin Blanc, Garnatxa Blanca, Garnatxa Negra, Garnatxa Tintorera, Gewürztraminer, Macabeu, Malvasia, Malvasia de Sitges, Mazuela, Merlot, Monastrell, Muscat d'Alexandrie,

Parellada, Pedro Ximénez, Peluda, Picapoll, Pinot Blanc, Pinot Noir, Riesling, Sauvignon Blanc, Syrah, Tempranillo, Ull de Llebre, Xarel-lo

√ *Mas Gil (Clos d'Agon)*

CAVA DO
See Penedés: Cava Country p.318

CHACOLÍ or TXAKOLINA DO
Cantabria

This appellation is split into three areas: Chacolí de Alava (or Getariako Alava), Chacolí de Guetaria (or Getariako Txakolina), and Chacolí de Vizcaya (or Bizkaiko Txakolina). The alternative names are Basque and, as this is Basque country, these spellings will probably take precedence. The wines are mostly white, dry, and slightly *pétillant*, although a little red is also produced. As is typical of wines in the northeastern corner of the Iberian peninsula, they are high in acidity and low in alcohol.

Hondarribi Beltza, Hondarribi Zuri

√ *Arretxondo • Txomin Etxaniz*

CIGALES DO
Castilla-León

This appellation is best known for fresh, fruity, light reds and *rosados*.

Albillo, Garnacha, Palomino, Tempranillo, Verdejo, Viura

√ *C. A. de Cigales* (Escogido del Año, Viña Torondos) • *Emeterio Fernández* (La Legua Capricho) • *Frutos Villa* (Conde Ansurez, Viña Calderona) • *González Lara* (Fuente del Conde Rosado)

CONCA DE BARBERA DO
Catalonia

This once little-known appellation for red, white, and *rosado* wines from the hilly hinterland of Penedés promises to be one of Spain's most exciting areas. Chardonnay is outstanding here, whether light and early-harvested as Ryman makes, or rich, serious, and potentially complex, as Torres demonstrates. Merlot is the most up-and-coming variety in the red department, but Trepat could mount a few surprises for fresh,

easy-drinking styles of both red and *rosado*.

Cabernet Sauvignon, Garnacha, Merlot, Parellada, Tempranillo, Trepat, Viura

1–5 years

√ *Torres* (Milmanda Chardonnay)

CONDADO DE HUELVA DO
Andalucía

The sweet dessert wines of this area, which is sandwiched between the sherry district of southwest Spain and the Algarve of Portugal, once had some fame, for they were mentioned by Chaucer in *The Canterbury Tales*. They ended up, however, as blending fodder for sherry. There are two basic types of fortified wine here: *pálido* (young, pale-straw color, dry, austere wines, of 14–17 percent alcohol) and *viejo* (solera-matured, mahogany-hued, in both dry and sweet styles that are deliberately oxidized, of 15–23 percent alcohol). Light, dry wines are a more recent phenomenon, and most are consumed locally.

Garrido Fino, Palomino, Zalema

Upon purchase

COSTERS DEL SEGRE DO
Catalonia

This is a top-performing appellation taking in four areas of different viticultural character in the province of Lérida: Les Garrigues and Valls de Riu Corb (primarily white-grape districts), Artesa (planted almost entirely with black grapes); and Raimat (dominated by foreign grape varieties and has quickly assumed classic status through Codorníu's innovative Raimat Estate).

Cabernet Sauvignon, Cariñena, Chardonnay, Garnacha, Garnacha Blanca, Merlot, Monastrell, Parellada, Trepat, Ull de Llebre, Viura, Xarel-lo

2–6 years (red), 1–4 years (white)

√ *Raïmat • Castell del Remei*

DOMINIO DE VALDEPUSA DO
Castilla-La Mancha

Owned by Carlos Falcó of Marqués de Griñón fame, Dominio de Valdepusa became Spain's first *Pago*, or single estate, appellation in 2001, recognizing 30 years of toil and extraordinary dedication. This vineyard was the first in Spain to use a new trellis system for training vines and the first to establish drip-irrigation, both as long ago as 1973. More recently, Dominio de Valdepusa became the first vineyard in Europe to adopt the Australian PRD technique, and one of the first in the world to deploy dendrometers (*see* Glossary). Over the years, Falcó has employed a veritable gaggle of gurus (Lichine, Peynaud), with Rolland and Smart his current advisors. According to Smart, the red clay over limestone at Dominio de Valdepusa is identical to the famous *terra rossa* soil of Coonawarra.

Cabernet Sauvignon, Petit Verdot, Syrah

√ *Marqués de Griñón* (Dominio de Valdepusa)

EL HIERRO DO
Canary Islands

This new appellation was established in 1996 for El Hierro, the smallest and most westerly island in the archipelago, yet the local cooperative is one of the most advanced in the Canary Islands. Before gaining DO status, these wines were sold under the local names of Frontera and Valverde. The best areas are Valle de Golfo, El Pinar, and Echedo. The Negramoll

grape is best for reds and *rosados*, while the Verijadiego is best for whites.

Listán, Malvasía, Moscatel, Negramoll, Pedro Ximénez, Verdello, Verijadiego

√ *Fontera*

FINCA ELEZ DO
Castilla-La Mancha

Located near the village of El Bonillo, in the heart of the Sierra de Alcaraz, this single-estate appellation was established in 2002 and is owned by Manuel Manzaneque, a theater director and producer.

Cabernet Sauvignon, Chardonnay, Merlot, Syrah, Tempranillo

√ *Finca Elez*

JEREZ or JEREZ-XÉRÈS-SHERRY DO
See Sherry Country p.321

JUMILLA DO
Murcia

The high, hilly vineyards of Jumilla have never been affected by phylloxera, and most of the vines are still ungrafted. Almost all the wines produced here are red, and until recently were lackluster, unless made in a *doble pasta* style, which produces wines so thick and intense that they are in great demand for blending purposes throughout Spain and also abroad. The best reds carry the Jumilla Monastrell varietal appellation and can be very smooth, fruity, and aromatic, tending to improve with age. With earlier picking and temperature-controlled fermentation, lighter, more accessible wines are now being made that are best drunk when young and juicy, including some soft, fruity whites as well as some *rosados*.

Airén, Garnacha, Meseguera, Monastrell, Pedro Ximénez, Tempranillo

1–3 years (red, but up to 6 years for wines made in *doble pasta* style), 9–15 months (white and *rosado*)

✓ *Bleda* (Castillo Jumilla) • *Julia Roch e Hijos*
• *Jumilla Union Vitivinícola* (Cerrillares,
Incunable) • *Señorío del Condestable*

LA MANCHA DO
Castilla-La Mancha

Although its output remains enormous,
accounting for some 40 percent of all Spanish
wines produced, the wine land of Don Quixote
has improved tremendously since the 1980s.
Many producers now harvest much earlier than
previously and ferment at cooler temperatures
(sometimes too cool), achieving fresher, lighter,
more aromatic wines. The best wines of La
Mancha used to be made in Valdepeñas DO,
and that appellation still boasts most of the
best, but the arrival of Alejandro Fernández
(El Vinculo) in 1999 has raised the stakes. Who
would have thought that any wine bearing "La
Mancha" could be considered up-and-coming?

🍇 Airén, Cabernet Sauvignon, Garnacha,
Merlot, Moravia, Pardina, Tempranillo, Viura

🍷 1–4 years (red), 9–15 months (white and
rosado)

✓ *Ayuso* (Estola Gran Reserva) • *Vinícola de
Castilla* (Castillo de Alhambra, Señorío de
Guadianeja) • *Jesús Diaz e Hijos* • *El
Vinculo* •*C. Españolas* (Fuente del Ritmo)
• *Hermanos Morales* (Gran Créacion) • *C. A.
del Campo Nuestra Señora de Manjavacas*
(Zagarrón) • *C. A. del Campo Nuestra Padre
Jesús de Perdon* (Casa la Teja, Lazarillo,
Yuntero) • *Rama Corta* • *Rodriguez y
Berger* (Viña Santa Elena) • *Julián Santos*
• *Torres Filoso* (Arboles de Castollejo)

LA PALMA DO
Canary Islands

This new appellation was established in
1995 for the island of La Palma. It was in
Fuencaliente, in the south of the island, that the
famed "Canary Sack" of Shakespeare's time was
produced, and the grape responsible, Malvasia,
still grows here, amid four smoking volcanoes,
in the same sort of craterlike depressions that
abound on Lanzarote. An oddity aged in pine
casks and curiously called Vino del Tea ("Tea"
being the local name for a particular species of
pine) is available in the north of the island, but
only the most ardent admirers of Retsina should
search it out.

🍇 Bujariego, Gual, Listán, Malvasia, Negramoll

✓ *Hoyo de Mazo*

LANZAROTE DO
Canary Islands

This new appellation was established in 1995
for the island of Lanzarote, where the lunar
landscape is dotted with vines in craterlike

depressions, protected by low stone walls.
The most spectacular example of this weirdly
beautiful form of viticulture can be viewed at
La Geria, an area west of Arrecife where no
fewer than 5,000 acres (2,000 hectares) of such
vineyards are to be found.

🍇 include: Caleta, Diego, Listán, Malvasia

MÁLAGA DO
Andalucía

Just northeast of Jerez in southern Spain, the
coastal vineyards of Málaga produce one of
the most underrated classic dessert wines in
the world. Most of this is matured by the *solera*
system, involving some six scales (*see* Sherry
Country, p.321) and may be blended in a
sherrylike manner using various grape-based
coloring and sweetening agents, such as *arrope*,
vino de color, *vino tierno*, and *vino maestro*.
The color of these fortified wines can range
from gold through tawny to brown and red,
depending on the style of Málaga, its age, and
method of maturation, its degree of sweetness,
and the grape variety used.

Málaga may be any one of the following.
Dulce Color is a dark, medium-bodied Málaga
that has been sweetened with *arrope*. Lágrima
is made from free-run juice only, and is the
most luscious of all Málaga styles. Moscatel is
a sweet, rich, raisiny, medium- to full-bodied
wine that is similar to the Jerez version, only
more luscious. Old Solera has the most finesse,
depth, and length of all Málagas and is capable
of complexity rather than lusciousness. It is
medium- to full-bodied, still sweet yet with a
dry finish. Oscuro is a dark, sweet Málaga that
has been sweetened with *arrope* and colored
by *vino de color*. Pajarette or Paxarete is
darkish in color, and less sweet, but more
alcoholic, than other Málagas. Pedro Ximénez
is a smooth, sweet, deliciously rich varietal
wine with an intense flavor that is similar
in character to the Jerez version. Seco is a
pale, dry, tangy wine with a distinctive creamy
hazelnut character.

🍇 Moscatel, Pedro Ximénez

🍷 Upon purchase (although it can last, but not
improve, for several years)

✓ *Scholtz Hermanos* • *Pérez Texeira* • *Larios*

MANCHUELA DO
Castilla-La Mancha

This is a very large region, encompassing La
Mancha, Ribera del Júcar, Utiel-Requena, and
Almansa, with cooperatives accounting for
two-thirds of the *bodegas*, and a quality that is
seldom better than an acceptable quaff. Much
is a lot worse. The delicious red wines of Finca
Sandova are, however, a class apart, and the
improving Gualberto may one day reach a
similar level.

🍇 Albillo, Bobal, Cabernet Sauvignon,
Cencibel, Chardonnay, Garnacha, Macabéo,
Merlot, Monastrell, Moravia Dulce,
Sauvignon Blanc, Syrah, Verdejo

✓ *Finca Sandoval* • *Gualberto*

MANZANILLA DO
See Sherry Country p.321

MÉNTRIDA DO
Castilla-La Mancha

Cheap wine, still mostly consumed locally, but
yields have dropped, and a number of *bodegas*
have improved their facilities, although it is too
early to confirm a similar improvement in

quality, as there are still too many deep-colored,
coarse reds and alcoholic *rosados*.

🍇 Garnacha, Tempranillo

MONDÉJAR DO
Castilla-La Mancha

Although fewer bulk wines are being produced
here since Mondéjar achieved DO status, the
wines are still mostly uninspiring, with Mariscal
the solitary producer that seems interested in
improving quality.

🍇 Airen, Cabernet Sauvignon, Garnacha, Jaén,
Macabéo, Malvar, Tempranillo, Torrontés

✓ *Mariscal*

MONSTANT DO
Catalonia

A new and potentially exciting appellation
clasping the eastern, western, and southern
edges of Priorat.

🍇 Cabernet Sauvignon, Cariñeña, Garnacha,
Merlot, Monastrell, Syrah, Tempranillo

✓ *Celler de Capéanes* (Mas Picosa) • *Fra
Guerau* • *Laurona*

MONTERREI DO
Galicia

This area was first awarded a provisional DO
in the early 1980s, but this was revoked when
too few of its growers showed any interest
in modernizing their estates. However, some
progress was made in the late 1980s, and
this appellation has now been granted full
DO status.

🍇 Alicante, Doña Blanca, Godello, Gran
Negro, Mencía, Mouratón, Palomino

✓ *Pazo Pondal* (Lenda Pondal)

MONTILLA-MORILES DO
Andalucía

The sherrylike wines of Montilla fall into
three categories: *generosos* (fortified *finos*,
amontillados, *olorosos*, and magnificent PX);
unfortified traditional wines (cream, medium,
and dry at 14.5 percent alcohol); and *jóvenes
afrutados* (ghastly).

🍇 Airén, Baladí, Moscatel, Pedro Ximénez,
Torrontés

🍷 Can be kept, but consume upon opening

✓ *Marqués de la Sierra* • *Alvear* • *Mora
Chacon* • *Gracia Hermanos* • *Perez
Barquero* • *Rodriguez Chiachio*

NAVARRA DO
See Rioja and Navarra p.312

PENEDÈS DO
See Penedès: Cava Country p.318

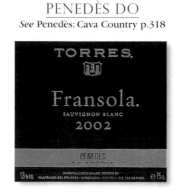

PLA DE BAGES DO
Catalonia

Winemaking is an old tradition in Bages, and yet this is an up-and-coming DO, with many newly planted vineyards and a small but growing band of modern *bodegas*, of which Massies d'Avinyó clearly leads the way. "Bages" is a derivative of Bacchus, the name of the Roman god of wine.

🍇 Chardonnay, Garnatxa, Macabéo, Malbec, Merlot, Picapoll, Pinot Noir, Sauvignon Blanc, Sumoll, Tempranillo

✓ *Massies d'Avinyó*

PLA I LEVANT DO
Mallorca

The island's newest appellation produces some of its best wines.

🍇 Cabernet Sauvignon, Callet, Chardonnay, Frogoneu, Manto Negro, Macabéo, Merlot, Moscatel, Parellada, Pinot Noir, Prensal Blanc, Syrah, Tempranillo

✓ *Miquel Geabert* • *Miquel Oliver*

PRIORAT DOCA
Catalonia

This area has a dry climate and poor soil, in which the vines' roots spread everywhere in search of moisture, the local saying being that Priorat vines can suck water out of stone. The best wines are currently being made around the hilltop town of Gratallops, by a group of young winemakers led by Bordeaux-trained Riojan oenologist Alvaro Palacios, who brought with him a wealth of experience from Château Pétrus to the Napa Valley. New-style reds are huge, serious, and stunningly rich, but those of the old style tend to be heavy, overalcoholic, and oxidized, although the best traditional wines fall somewhere in between. One of the country's oldest appellations, Priorat is one of the Spanish wine industry's superstars. The use of the spelling "Priorato" has been dropped on bottles in favor of the Catalan version "Priorat," and DOQ, the Catalan equivalent of DOCa, is now prevalent.

🍇 Cabernet Sauvignon, Cariñena, Garnacha, Garnacha Blanca, Merlot, Monastrell, Pedro Ximénez, Syrah, Viura

🍷 5–15 years (red)

✓ *Alvaro Palacios* 🅱 (Finca Dofi, Clos l'Ermita, Las Terrasses) • *René Barbier* (Clos Mogador) • *Clos Erasmus* • *Costers del Siurana* (Clos de l'Obac, Miserere) • *Masia Barril* • *De Muller* • *Scala Dei* (Cartoixa, El Cipres, Novell) • *Vinícola del Priorato* (Mas d'Alba, Onix)

RÍAS BAIXAS DO
Galicia

Spain's fastest-rising star in the DO firmament, the Rías Baixas appellation covers various red, white, and *rosado* wines, but the best-known and most enjoyable wines are the softly perfumed, zippy whites made from low-yielding Albariño grapes, which can have real depth and fruit, and a fresh, lively acidity. Although I have always admired the best of these wines, I did wonder whether they are worth what appeared to be an increasingly high price. At the table, however, they accompany fine food beautifully, which in my book makes even the most expensive Rías Baixas well worth the price demanded for it

🍇 Albariño, Brancellao, Caíño Blanco, Caíño Tinto, Espadeiro, Loureira Blanca, Loureira Tinta, Mencía, Sousón, Torrontés, Treixadura

🍷 1–3 years

✓ *Albariño do Salnes* • *Pazo de Barrantes* • *Cardallal* • *Lagar de Cervera* • *del Palacio de Fefiñanes* • *Granxa Fillaboa* • *Morgadio Agromiño* • *Pazo Pondal* • *de Vilariño Cambados* (Martín Códax, Organistrum) • *Santiago Ruíz*

RIBEIRA SACRA DO
Galicia

The most widely planted grape variety here is Palomino, but on the steep, terraced vineyards of Ribeira Sacra, Albariño is far more exciting, and the Mencía variety also shows promise for red wines.

🍇 Albariño, Brancellao, Caíño, Doña Blanca, Espadeiro, Ferrón, Godello, Garnacha, Loureira, Loureira Tinta, Mencía, Merenzao, Negrada, Palomino, Sousón, Torrontés

🍷 1–3 years

✓ *Adegas Moure* (Albariño Abadia da Cova)

RIBEIRO DO
Galicia

Due to the Atlantic-influenced climate of northwest Spain, the styles of Ribeiro's red and white wines reflect that of Portugal's Vinhos Verdes, except that they are somewhat more fruity and aromatic. The very best examples possess a wonderfully fresh, pure, vibrancy of fruit.

🍇 Albariño, Albillo, Brancellao, Caíño, Ferrón, Garnacha, Godello, Jerez, Loureira, Mencía, Sousón, Tempranillo, Torrontés, Treixadura, Viura

🍷 9–18 months

✓ *Alanis* • *Arsenio Paz* • *Rivera* • *C. A. del Ribeiro*

RIBERA DEL DUERO DO
Castilla-León

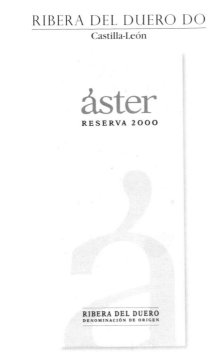

From the upper reaches of the Duero River (which becomes the Douro, once it crosses the Portuguese border), the *rosados* are fresh, dry, fruity wines of a *clarete* or *claro* style, but are nowhere near the class of the best reds, which have a truly dense, black color and are packed solid with rich, oaky sweet, plummy-blackcurrant fruit flavors.

Ribera del Duero DO built its reputation on "Vega Sicilia," formerly Spain's most expensive wine. In the first edition of this book, I categorically stated that contrary to the informed opinion of many other wine critics, this was not Spain's greatest red wine, although it was potentially the best. The problem was that 10 or more years in wood took its toll on the fruit in a way that would destroy many of the greatest wines of Bordeaux.

There was also no logic to the duration and mode of aging at Vega Sicilia, which occurred in different sizes and ages of wooden cask, the various vintages being transferred from one vessel to another simply to fulfill the logistical necessity of moving the wines around in order to accommodate the incoming harvest. Since the first edition, however, Vega Sicilia has given its wines no more than six years in wood and now has a more disciplined approach to how long wines spend in various types and ages of cask, including new oak *barriques*. It is once again one of Spain's greatest wines, but not necessarily the greatest Ribera del Duero, with a handful of *bodegas* capable of matching, sometimes surpassing, the quality of Vega Sicilia. These include Aalto, Vega Sicilia's own Alion, Alejándro Fernández's Pesquera, Condado de Haza (also owned by Fernández), Domino de Pingus, and Pago de los Capellanes, with a few others waiting in the wings.

🍇 Cabernet Sauvignon, Garnacha, Malbec, Merlot, Pardina, Tinto del País

🍷 3–8 years (modern red), 5–25 years (traditional red), 1–2 years (*rosado*)

✓ *Aalto* • *Abadía Retuerta* • *Alión* • *Arzuaga Condado de Haza* • *Dominio de Pingus* 🅱 • *Emelio Moro* • *Ismael Arroyo* • *Julio Cesar Conde Delgado y Otros* (Neo) • *Legaris* • *Mauro* • *Pago de Carraovejas* • *Pago de los*

Capellanes • Pagos del Rey • Pérez Pascuas (Viña Pedrosa) • Pesquera • Pomar Vinédos • Real Sitio de Ventosilla (Prado Rey) • Reyes • Sastre • Uvaguilera Aguilera • Vega Sicilia (including Valbuena)

RIBERA DEL GUADIANA DO
Extramadura

A group of six *vinos de la tierra* (Cañamero, Matanegra, Montanchez, Ribera Alta, Ribera Baja, and Tierra de Barros), which retain this classification, but also form subzones of the Ribera del Guadiana DO, entitling them to make wines under two different origins of quality.

Alarlje, Bobal, Borba, Cabernet Sauvignon, Cayetana Blanca, Chardonnay, Cigüente, Eva O Beba de Los Santos, Garnacha Tinta, Garnacha Tintorera, Graciano, Jaen Tinto, Macebéo, Malvar, Mazuela, Merlot, Monastrell, Montúa, Moscatel, Moscatel de Grano Menudo, Pardina, Parellada, Pedro Ximénez, Perruno, Pinot Noir, Sauvignon Blanc, Syrah, Tempranillo, Verdejo

✓ *La de Barros* • *Santa Mariña*

RIOJA DOCA
See Rioja and Navarra p.312

RUEDA DO
Castilla-León

This small district downriver from Ribeiro del Duero is known for fresh, crisp, dry white wines made almost entirely from Verdejo, but traditionally the wines were fortified *in fino* (Palido Rueda) and *rancio* (Dorado Rueda) styles, and these can still be found. A traditional method Rueda Espumoso is also allowed.

Palomino, Sauvignon Blanc, Verdejo, Viura

⌇— 1–2 years

✓ Agricola Castellana • Frutos Villa (Viña Morejona) • Marqués de Griñón • Marqués de Riscal

SHERRY *or* JEREZ-XÉRÈS-SHERRY DO
See Sherry Country p.321

SIERRAS DE MÁLAGA DO
Andalucía

Although Málaga is one of Spain's oldest DOs, this appellation was granted in 2001, for an area that is higher in altitude than Málaga, and for red and white wines that cannot be fortified.

Airén, Cabernet Franc, Cabernet Sauvignon, Chardonnay, Colombard, Doradilla, Garnacha, Macabeo, Merlot, Moscatel d'Alejandrie, Moscatel Morisco, Pedro Ximénez, Petit Verdot, Pinot Noir, Romé, Sauvignon Blanc, Syrah, Tempranillo

✓ *F. Schatz* ◉

SITGES
Catalonia

This is a famous, but rare, non-DO fortified Malvasia and Moscatel wine that is made just south of the outskirts of Barcelona, from grapes that are allowed to shrivel on the vine.

✓ *Cellers Robert*

SOMONTANO DO
Aragón

Set at the foot of the Pyrenees mountains, between the regions of Penedés and Navarra, Somontano is destined to become one of Spain's greatest wine regions. Chardonnay is by far the best grape grown here for serious, barrel-fermented white wines, but both Tempranillo and Cabernet Sauvignon show superb potential for making fragrant reds with a lively richness of fruit.

Alcañón, Cabernet Sauvignon, Chardonnay, Garnacha, Garnacha Blanca, Moristel, Parreleta, Tempranillo, Viura

⌇— 2–5 years (red), 1–3 years (white)

✓ *Aragonesa* • *Otto Bestué* • *Viñas del Vero* • *Enate* • *Lalanne* • *Pirineos*

TACORONTE-ACENTEJO DO
Canary Islands

Established in 1992, this is the oldest Canary Island appellation and, so far, it has proved to be the best, although it is too early to tell how the others will fare.

Castellano, Gual, Listán, Listán Negro, Malvasía, Marmajuelo, Moscatel, Negra Común, Negramoll, Pedro Ximénez, Tintillo, Torrontés, Verdello

✓ *El Lomo* • *Monje* • *Viña Norte*

TARRAGONA DO
Catalonia

This is the largest appellation in Catalonia, but its potential quality is modest compared with that of neighboring Penedés. Having said that, Australian winemakers Nick Butler and Mark Nairn have been quietly raising standards at Pedro Rovira, using hands-off methods to retain as much natural character in the wine as possible. The best red, white, and *rosado* from this region can all be fresh, fruity, and rewarding. Even the local fortified wine, which is sold as Tarragona Classico, can be worth looking out for.

Cariñena, Garnacha, Garnacha Blanca, Parellada, Tempranillo, Viura, Xarel-lo

⌇— 1–5 years (red), 1–2 years (white and *rosado*)

✓ *C. A. de Valls* • *José Lopez Beltrán* (Don Beltrán) • *Pedro Masana* (non-DO wines) • *De Müller* (Moscatel Seco, Parxete) • *Pedro Rovira*

TERRA ALTA DO
Catalonia

This slowly improving appellation lies in the highlands well away from the coast. It produces some good, everyday-drinking red and white wines, but the best sites are not always planted with the most suitable varieties and have to compete with Cava growers. It is advisable to avoid the local sweet, fortified *mistela*.

Cabernet Sauvignon, Cariñena, Garnacha, Garnacha Blanca, Merlot, Moscatel, Parellada, Tempranillo, Viura

⌇— 1–2 years

✓ *C. A. Gandesa* • *C. A. la Hermandad* • *Pedro Rovira* (Alta Mar, Viña d'Irto) • *Vinalba dels Arcs* (Vall de Berrús)

TORO DO
Castilla-León

The exciting quality of Toro wines today is a very recent phenomenon, built on a sudden influx of high-profile names, which has tripled the number of *bodegas* since 2000. When this DO was established in 1987, there were just four *bodegas*, the decrepit local cooperative dominated production, and the quality was really quite dire. By the mid-1990s, considerable improvements had occurred, notably at Farina, and British supermarket buyers began to import some of the better wines. However, there were still only 12 *bodegas* and the area obviously lacked the dynamics of a sufficient number of highly talented, ambitious, and competitive producers to push the quality envelope to anywhere near its full potential. In 2000, the number of *bodegas* had increased to 18, but, more importantly, the Álvarez family of Vega Sicilia fame had been purchasing land under an assumed name since 1997, and after this was announced in 2002, the floodgates opened, so that at the last count there were 40 *bodegas* Consequently, land prices have soared, and the battle for Toro's true quality has only just begun. Vega Sicilia's rival, Alejandro Fernández of Pesquera, followed suit in 1998, but the great wine produced under the Dehesa La Granja label is in fact made from vines growing just outside this DO, near Zamora. I suspect this may be a single-estate DO in waiting.

🍇 Garnacha, Malvasía, Tinta de Toro, Verdejo Blanco

⌛ 2–8 years (red), 1–3 years (white)

✓ *Alquiriz • Bajoz • Jacques & François Lurton (El Albar Excelencia, Campo Eliseo) • Numanthia • Farina (Gran Colegiata, Gran Colegiata Campus) • Maurodós*

TXAKOLINA DO
See Chacolí DO

UTIEL-REQUENA DO
Valencia

This large and important, essentially red-wine district is situated in the extreme west of the province of Valencia. Although distilling wine and the *doble pasta* process were once the area's forte, softer, more palatable reds are now being made, and the best dry *rosados* are fresh and delicate for such sunny climes.

🍇 Bobal, Garnacha, Meseguera, Tardana, Tempranillo, Viura

⌛ 2–5 years (red), 9–18 months (*rosados*)

✓ *Augusto Egli (Casa Lo Alto)*

VALDEORRAS DO
Galicia

Until Rías Baixas came on the scene, this was Galicia's most promising district. With vines planted on terraced, slaty hillsides flanking the Sil River and Valdeorras's northern, wet, Atlantic-influenced climate, these wines have never been overburdened with alcohol, as so much Spanish wine was once upon a time, and refreshing acidity is part of their charm. The best wineries have now been modernized and are even better than they used to be, particularly for white wines made from the Godello grape.

🍇 Doña Blanca, Garnacha, Godello, Gran Negro, Lado, María Ardoña, Mencía, Merenzao, Palomino

⌛ 1–4 years (red), 1 year (white and *rosado*)

✓ *Godeval • Guitián • Jesus Nazareno • Joaquín Rebolledo*

VALDEPEÑAS DO
Castilla-La Mancha

This is Castilla-La Mancha's solitary fine-wine area. Despite the torrid heat (the climate has been described as nine months of winter, three months of hell) and an apathetic attitude held by far too many producers, some terrific wines are being made here by a minority of wineries, and they represent very good value. The rich, red, stony soil hides a water-retentive limestone base that helps offset the lack of rainfall. The best reds are medium- to full-bodied, pure Tempranillo, with a wonderfully rich yet well-balanced flavor, and more and more new-oak influence. The *rosados* can be smooth and fruity, but it would take a complete overhaul of the vineyards, replanting them with something decent, to make the white wines appealing, although there is really no excuse for their not being fresh.

🍇 Airén, Tempranillo

⌛ 2–6 years (red), 9–18 months (*rosado*)

✓ *Miguel Calatayud • J. A. Megía • Los Llanos • Luis Megía (Marqués de Gastañaga) • Felix Solís (Viña Albali Reserva) • Casa de la Viña (Vega de Moriz)*

VALENCIA DO
Valencia

This area was once renowned for its heavy, alcoholic, and low-quality *vino de mesa* (table wine). However most modern wineries today produce much lighter wines than before, and they are at least fresh and drinkable. There are some good reds from the Monastrell grape, which are smooth and medium bodied, and these wines may sometimes be aged in oak. The deliciously sweet and raisiny Moscatel is consistently excellent value, often performing well under blind conditions against French Muscat de Beaumes de Venise that sells for twice the price.

🍇 Forcayat, Garnacha, Malvasía, Meseguera, Monastrell, Moscatel, Pedro Ximénez, Planta Fina, Tempranillo, Tortosí, Viura

⌛ 1–4 years (red), 9–18 months (white and *rosado*), upon opening (Moscatel)

✓ *C. A. de Villar • Vicente Gandía • Augusto Egli (particularly good-value Moscatel) • Schenk (Cavas Murviedro) • Tierra Hernández*

VALLE DE GÜIMAR DO
Canary Islands

This appellation was established in 1996 for wines from the eastern side of Tenerife, just south of downtown Santa Cruz. The vineyards here abut cultivated fields, which are irrigated and thus indirectly feed these vines. Before gaining DO status, these wines were not even sold locally, but consumed by the people who produced them.

🍇 Listán, Listán Negro, Negramoll

VALLE DE LA OROTAVA DO
Canary Islands

Established in 1996, this appellation covers wines produced on the lush, northern side of Tenerife, between the appellations of Tacoronte-Acentejo and Ycoden-Daute-Isora. Before they were granted DO status, these wines were sold under the *vino de la tierra* (literally "country wine") of La Orotava-Los Realos.

🍇 Listán, Listán Negro

VINOS DE MADRID DO
Madrid

Much admired by Casanova, who sought refuge in Madrid at a time when the capital was rapidly expanding at the expense of its vineyards, these wines probably assumed a rarity value that outshone their intrinsic quality. By extending the appellation well beyond its fast-disappearing 18th-century boundaries, Vinos de Madrid was resurrected in 1990, although you would have to be a greater lover of these wines than Casanova to declare your open admiration for them. There are, however, a couple of exceptions to the rule, and one of these, Jesús Díaz e Hijos, is exceptional by any standards

🍇 Airén, Albillo, Garnacha, Malvar, Tinto Fino

⌛ Upon purchase (2–3 years for recommended wines)

✓ *Francisco Figuero • Jesús Díaz e Hijos*

XÉRÈS *or* JEREZ-XÉRÈS-SHERRY DO
See Sherry Country p.321

YCODEN-DAUTE-ISORA DO
Canary Islands

This DO was established in 1995 for the wines that are produced on the northwestern corner of the island of Tenerife. In this area, the grapes are usually grown on terraces, which are often irrigated. Before they gained DO status, these wines were sold under the *vino de la tierra* of Icod de Los Vinos, a name that recalls their long-lost fame. After the Battle of Trafalgar, the Canaries were a favorite watering hole with the British Royal Navy, and the orange-tinged white wines of this area were apparently enjoyed by all ranks.

🍇 Listán, Listán Negro

YECLA CAMPO ARRIBA DO
See Yecla DO

YECLA DO
Murcia

You might think that these stony-limestone vineyards between Alicante and Jumilla should do rather well in terms of quality, but although some decent wines can be found, nothing special stands out.

The reds produced here are either ink-black, *doble pasta*-style wines, or are cherry-colored, generally with good body and fruit. Wines from the Campo Arriba zone in the north of this appellation are permitted to add this name to the Yecla DO if they are either red or *rosado*, and are made from 100 percent Monastrell grapes harvested at almost half the yield required elsewhere in Yecla. The white wines produced in Yecla are at their best fresh, clean, and pleasantly fruity, but, again, tend not to be remarkable.

🍇 Garnacha, Meseguera, Monastrell, Verdil

⌛ 2–5 years (red, but 3–6 years for Yecla Campo Arriba), 1–2 years (white and *rosado*)

✓ *Castaño (Pozuelo, Las Gruesas) • Ochoa Palao (Cuvée Prestige)*

RIOJA AND NAVARRA

The first wine to receive DOCa status, Spain's highest classification, Rioja is without doubt the country's greatest fine-wine region. Neighboring Navarra, which was once regarded as the country's best source of rosado *but little else, is slowly developing a reputation for other styles, having upgraded its vineyards and wineries.*

ONLY A SHORT DRIVE from the shabby suburbs of the commercial city of Bilbao, and the dramatic beauty of an upland valley becomes apparent, rich with architectural treasures of the 12th century, isolated hilltop *pueblos*, a philanthropic people, a generous tradition, and a hearty cuisine.

RIOJA

Rioja is oaky, and all attempts to rid the wine of oak are doomed to failure. Oak is the basis of its fame and the reason it became Spain's first and greatest red-wine success, and while critics who suggest that these wines are too oaky for today's more

sophisticated consumers may have a point, there is precious little left in most Rioja once you take away the oak.

It was the French who originally blessed the wines of this region with their unmistakable sweet-vanilla oak identity. As early as the 18th century, a few enlightened *Riojanos* had looked to France, Bordeaux particularly, to improve their winemaking skills. The transformation that resulted was subtle compared to the radical changes that occurred in Rioja in the 1840s and 1860s, after phylloxera, a louse that attacks vine roots, had wreaked havoc on French vineyards. A number of *vignerons*, mostly *Bordelais* but some Burgundian too, gave up hope of reviving their own vineyards and descended upon Rioja to set up new wineries. Their methods dramatically improved the quality and style of Rioja, while other Frenchmen, mostly merchants from Bordeaux, opened up an instantly lucrative trade for the wine, as they desperately sought to boost the dwindling produce of their own devastated vineyards.

Origins

Wine has been made in Rioja since at least the 2nd century BC, when the Romans conquered the area. Rioja was sufficiently well respected by 1560 that its producers forbade the use of grapes from outside the region, guaranteeing the authenticity of their

Map legend:

- Intensive vine-growing zone
- Rioja Alta
- Rioja/Alavesa
- Rioja Baja
- Navarra/Tierra Estella
- Navarra/Valdizarbe
- Navarra/Baja Montana
- Navarra/Ribera Alta
- Navarra/Ribera Baja
- Cava
- *Provincial* boundary
- Delimited DO Region
- ▲ Height above sea level (meters)

0   5   10   15   20 miles
0   10   20   30 km

RIOJA AND NAVARRA, *see also* p.303
Rioja consists of three distinct wine districts: Rioja Alta, Rioja Alavesa, and Rioja Baja, the first two of which are inherently superior. Navarra, which overlaps part of Rioja Baja, has a smaller area of vineyards, which are divided into five districts. A very small part of the Cava-producing area, most of which is in Catalonia, extends into Rioja and Navarra.

wines with a brand on the *pellejos* (goat skins) in which they were transported. Wooden barrels came into use in the 18th century, but were five times the size of casks today and it was not until 1860 at Marqués de Riscal that the first Bordeaux *barriques* were used (although there seems to be evidence that Manuel Quintano was the first, *c*.1800). One particularly influential Frenchman, Jean Pineau, was employed to teach French methods to local growers. In 1868, upon completion of his contract, Pineau was employed by Don Camilo Hurtado de Amezaga, the Marqués de Riscal, who was an admirer of Médoc wines and had lived in Bordeaux for 15 years. He had planted Cabernet Sauvignon on his estate in 1863 and wanted Pineau to develop his new *bodega* in the manner of the most advanced wine châteaux in the Médoc.

RIOJA'S CLASSIC WINE DISTRICTS
Rioja's vineyards are located along the Ebro Valley, between Haro and Alfaro, and throughout its hinterland, with vines clustered around many of the Ebro's tributaries, one of which, the Oja River, has given its name to the region. Most Rioja is red and blended from wines or grapes (primarily Tempranillo and Garnacha) originating from the region's three districts (Rioja Alta, Rioja Alavesa, and Rioja Baja), although many of the best-quality are single-district wines and a handful of single-estate Rioja have also emerged in recent years.

Rioja Alta
Logroño and Haro, the principal towns of Rioja, are both in the Rioja Alta. Logroño is a very big town by Spanish standards, but Haro, at the western edge of the region, is an enclosed hilltop community and a much smaller, far more charming, older, and traditional place. The area's wine is Rioja's fullest in terms of fruit and concentration, and can be velvety smooth. Bodegas Muga makes fine examples of pure Rioja Alta, as do CVNE (Compañia Vinícola del Norte de España) –in the form of their Imperial line– in nine years out of every ten.

Rioja Alavesa
There are no large towns in the Alavesa, a district that is similar in climate to the Alta. Wines produced here are Rioja's fullest in body and reveal a much firmer character than those of the Alta and the Baja, with greater acidity. It was to the Alavesa that Pedro Domecq came, after years of intensive research, to plant a vast estate of 988 acres (400 hectares), cultivating his vines on wires as opposed to

using the bush method traditional to the region. Aside from Bodegas Domecq, which produces mainly pure Alavesa wines, Remelluri and Contino, two single-estate Alavesas, are both typical of the district.

Rioja Baja
Baja is a semiarid area influenced by the Mediterranean, and is hotter, sunnier, and drier than the Alta and the Alavesa, with rainfall averaging between 15 and 17 inches (38 and 43 centimeters) per year, but falling as low as 10 inches (25 centimeters) at Alfaro in the south. Some 20 percent of the vines growing here come within, and can claim, the Navarra appellation. The wines are deep-colored and very alcoholic, some as strong as 18 percent, but lack acidity, aroma, and finesse, and are best used for blending.

NAVARRA
The wine-growing region of Navarra overlaps part of the Rioja Baja, but although not quite in the same league as Rioja in general, it is capable of producing some fine wines of exceptional value.

Recent marketing successes have halted the decline in Navarra's vineyards and encouraged various ambitious trials with foreign grapes such as Merlot, while previous experimental varieties such as Cabernet Sauvignon are now fully recommended. According to the Estación de Viticultura y Enología de Navarra (EVENA), Spain's most advanced viticultural and oenological research station, these Bordeaux varieties are ideally suited to Navarra's soil and climate.

A rosy past
Navarra was once virtually synonymous with *rosado* and this style still accounts for almost half of total production, but what has really held back the reputation of this area has been the Garnacha (*syn*, Grenache) grape. This modest-quality grape variety can make good *rosado*, but except as part of a blend, rarely excels in red wines. Garnacha makes up more than 65 percent of Navarra's vines, so the region is ill equipped to develop beyond its *rosado* horizon. Furthermore, Tempranillo, the grape upon which Rioja's success has been built and indubitably Spain's finest red-wine variety, represents just 15 percent of Navarra's vines. This proportion has, however, doubled in the last decade, and with Tempranillo and Cabernet Sauvignon making up 60 percent and 20 percent respectively of all new vines currently being planted, Navarra is set to achieve a tremendous boost in quality.

According to Javier Ochoa, former chief oenologist at EVENA, the perfect Navarra blend should be something in the order of

GRAPE VARIETIES IN RIOJA

Although there has been a recent trend toward pure varietal wines (particularly Tempranillo for *tinto* and Viura for *blanco*), most Rioja is blended, thus its character and quality depend to a large extent upon the producer's own house style. In addition to blending the strengths and weaknesses of different *terroirs*, there is usually an attempt to balance the various varietal characteristics of one or more of the seven grapes that are permitted in Rioja. These grape varieties are: Tempranillo, Garnacha, Graciano, Mazuelo, Viura, Malvasia, and the little-utilized Garnacha Blanca.

A TYPICAL RED RIOJA BLEND
Tempranillo 70 percent for its bouquet, acidity, and aging qualities. It ripens some two weeks before the Garnacha (*temprano* means "early") and is also known in Spain as the Cencibel, Tinto Fino, or Ull de Llebre. Tempranillo has a naturally low oxidizing enzyme content, giving its wines exceptional longevity.

Garnacha 15 percent for body and alcohol—too much can make the wine coarse. This is the Grenache of the Rhône, also known as the Lladoner and Aragonés. It is the major variety of the Rioja Baja, where it can produce wines of 16 percent alcohol.

Graciano 7.5 percent for freshness, flavor, and aroma. A singular variety with the unusual property of thin, yet tough, black skin.

Mazuelo 7.5 percent for color, tannin, and good aging characteristics. This is the Carignan of southern France and is also known in Spain as the Cariñena.

To the above a small proportion of white grapes, perhaps 5–10 percent of Viura, may sometimes be added, but this tradition is fading. Cabernet Sauvignon is not an authorized variety in Rioja, but is permitted by special dispensation for *bodegas* that have historically used the variety (such as Marqués de Riscal, which uses 15 to 60 percent) and those that are growing it on a trial basis. Although a number of *bodegas* have experimental plantations, Cabernet Sauvignon is not of any great significance for the vast majority of Rioja wines.

A TYPICAL WHITE RIOJA BLEND
Viura 95 percent for freshness and fragrance. This grape has reasonable acidity and a good resistance to oxidation. It is also known as the Macabéo and Alcañón in other parts of Spain, and is one of three major Cava varieties.

Malvasía 5 percent for richness, fragrance, acidity, and complexity. Also known as the Rojal Blanco and Subirat, this grape has a tendency to color a patchy red when ripe, so pressing must be quick to avoid tainting the juice.

Most white wines are pure Viura, although some contain up to 50 percent Malvasía. Some *bodegas* use a tiny amount of Garnacha Blanca, particularly in lesser years, to increase alcohol levels, but they do so at the expense of a certain amount of freshness and aroma.

50 percent Tempranillo, 30 percent Garnacha, and 20 percent Cabernet Sauvignon, but I wonder if even this is tempered by the large amount of Garnacha that will still exist when the replanting program has concluded.

NAVARRA'S DISTRICTS
The region is divided into five districts:

Baja Montaña
Situated in the Montaña foothills, Baja Montaña is the highest and wettest area of Navarra and the vintage is considerably later here than in the south of the region, hence the greater importance placed on early-ripening Tempranillo. Extra rain causes the grape yield to be between 50 and 100 percent higher than that of any of the other four areas. The district produces some of Navarra's best *rosados*, fresh and fruity in aroma and flavor.

Ribera Alta
With twice the number of vineyards as Baja Montaña and Tierra Estella, this is one of the two most important of Navarra's districts. Ribera Alta borders the Rioja Alta and produces some of the region's finest wines. The *rosados* are smooth and aromatic, and the reds soft and fruity, but with as much as 40 percent Viura planted, this is a major white-wine player and the style is soft, dry, and fresh.

TIERRA ESTELLA, NAVARRA
The picturesque village of Maneru is situated near Estella, southwest of Pamplona. Tempranillo is the main variety grown in the area's vineyards.

Ribera Baja
One of the two most important wine districts of Navarra, Ribera Baja is very hot and dry and includes approximately 20 percent of what is effectively the Rioja Baja district. The wines produced are mostly red, made principally from the Garnacha (Grenache) grape, and typically deep-colored, full, and robust. Muscat à Petits Grains accounts for 10 percent of the vines planted and produces a sweet Moscatel-style wine.

Tierra Estella
Viticulturally as important as Baja Montaña and climatically similar to Valdizarbe in the north, though gradually getting drier farther south, the Tierra Estella makes pleasant, fruity reds and *rosados* from the Tempranillo, which is heavily planted here. The Garnacha variety is less important since its wines tend to oxidize. Some crisp white wines from the Viura grape are also produced.

Valdizarbe
The smallest of Navarra's five districts, Valdizarbe has a slightly drier climate than the Baja Montaña and is an excellent source of good-value red and *rosado* wines, although some of these have an unfortunate tendency to oxidize.

FACTORS AFFECTING TASTE AND QUALITY

LOCATION
Situated in northern Spain in the upper valley of the Ebro River, Rioja and Navarra are bounded to the northeast by the Pyrenees and to the southwest by the Sierra de la Demanda. Navarra has the second-most northerly vineyards in Spain.

CLIMATE
The Cantabrian Mountains, a range that is modest in elevation yet impressive in structure, provide a major key to the quality of Rioja, protecting the region from the devastating winds whipped up over the Bay of Biscay and holding in precarious check the influence of the Atlantic and Mediterranean. That of the former is at its strongest in Navarra, and of the latter in the Rioja Baja. Temperature rises and rainfall decreases as one moves eastward to the Mediterranean. The Pyrenees also provide shelter from the north, but winters can be cold and foggy, particularly in Navarra. Rioja can suffer from hailstorms and the hot, dry *solano* wind.

ASPECT
Vineyards are variously located, from the highest in the foothills of the Pyrenees in Navarra to those on the flatter lands of the Rioja Baja in the southeast. Generally, the best vineyards are in the central hill country of the Rioja Alta and the Alavesa.

SOIL
Although soils do vary, the common denominator is limestone. In Navarra, limestone contains between 25 and 45 percent "active" lime, and is coated by a layer of silty-alluvium near the Ebro or by weathered limestone and sandstone topsoil in drier areas. Limestone with either sandstone or calcareous clay and slaty deposits dominate the Rioja Alavesa and Alta, while a ferruginous-clay and a silty-loam of alluvial origin cover a limestone base in the Rioja Baja.

VITICULTURE AND VINIFICATION
Most wines are a blend of at least three grapes from different areas within a single appellation; very few are 100 percent pure varietal or single-estate wines. The traditional vinification process, which is still used to produce the local *vino nuevo*, is a crude form of *macération carbonique* carried out in open vats; the grapes are trodden after the first few days of intercellular fermentation. This is much as Beaujolais wines used to be made, but the result here is much coarser, with a dark-damson color and lots of youthful tannin. Most wines are, however, vinified in the normal manner, but aged longer than other commercial wines. Although recent trends favor shorter oak-aging and longer bottle-maturation, the character of Rioja still relies heavily on oak, and it is essential for its future that it should remain so.

GRAPE VARIETIES
Primary varieties: Tempranillo, Viura (*syn.* Macabéo)
Secondary varieties: Cabernet Sauvignon, Carignan (*syn.* Mazuelo), Chardonnay, Cinsault, Garnacha (*syn.* Grenache), Garnacha Blanca (*syn.* Grenache Blanc), Graciano, Malvasia, Mourvèdre (*syn.* Monastrell), Muscat (*syn.* Moscatel)

RIOJA'S DISTRICTS AT A GLANCE

GRAPE VARIETIES GROWN (IN HECTARES)				
BLACK VARIETIES	**RIOJA ALTA**	**RIOJA ALAVESA**	**RIOJA BAJA**	**REGIONAL TOTAL**
Tempranillo	14,470	8,960	7,616	31,046
Garnacha	2002	171	6,980	9,153
Mazuelo	500	89	1,224	1,813
Graciano	93	52	250	395
Others	4	-	170	174
Experimental	28	52	92	172
TOTAL	17,097	9,324	16,332	42,753
WHITE VARIETIES	**RIOJA ALTA**	**RIOJA ALAVESA**	**RIOJA BAJA**	**REGIONAL TOTAL**
Viura	4,471	1,442	1,675	7,588
Malvasia	79	30	18	127
Garnacho blanco	28	-	16	44
Others	147	12	43	202
Experimental	4	4	9	17
TOTAL	4,729	1,488	1,761	7,978
TOTAL (ALL VINES)	21,826	10,812	18,093	50,731

WINE PRODUCED (IN HECTOLITERS) AND BY ROUNDED PERCENTAGE								
	RIOJA ALAVESA		**RIOJA BAJA**		**RIOJA BAJA**		**TOTAL**	
Red	836,000	74%	572,000	92%	339,000	80%	1,747,000	80%
White	150,000	13%	33,000	5%	18,000	5%	201,000	10%
Rosé	144,000	13%	19,000	3%	65,000	15%	228,000	10%
TOTAL	1,130,000	100%	624,000	100%	422,000	100%	2,176,000	100%

THE WINE PRODUCERS OF
RIOJA AND NAVARRA

Note Unless specifically stated otherwise, all recommendations (including "Entire range") are for red wine only. Reds from both regions are generally drinking well in their third year, but top *cuvées* often improve for up to 10 years, and exceptional ones can age gracefully for decades, while most white and *rosado* wines are best fresh and should thus be consumed when purchased. *See* p.304 for details of the wine styles mentioned.

BODEGAS AGE
Rioja

See also Campo Viejo and Marques del Puerto

Part of Bebidas (formerly Savin), this *bodega* is now better known as Bodegas & Bebidas or ByB, and is under the same ownership as Campo Viejo and Marques del Puerto. The basic quality is rather uninspiring, but top of the line wines are usually very good value indeed. Labels include Agessimo, Azpilicueta Martínez, Credencial, Don Ernesto, Marqués del Romeral (traditional style and the best), and Siglo (modern style).

 Reserva • *Gran Reserva*

BODEGAS ALAVESAS
Rioja

This makes some long-lived *reserva* and *gran reserva* of surprising quality and elegance. Labels include Solar de Samaniego (primary) and Castillo de Bodala (secondary).

✓ *Reserva* • *Gran Reserva*

FINCA ALLENDE
Rioja
★★

One of the fastest-rising stars on the Riojan firmament.

✓ *Entire range*

AMÉZOLA DE LA MORA
Rioja
★

I have encountered a couple of interesting wines from this Rioja Alta estate. One to watch.

✓ *Viña Amézola* • *Señorío de Amézola*

ARAEX
Rioja

Formed in 1993, ARAEX is a group of nine *bodegas* selling Rioja under the following labels: Bodegas Don Balbino, Bodegas Luís Cañas (some excellent *reservas* that benefit from aging 10 years or more in bottle), Viña Diezmo, Bodegas Larchago (voluptuous fruit), Viña Lur, Bodegas Heredad de Baroja (heaps of fruit, firm tannin structure), Bodegas Muriel, Solagüen, and Valserano.

BARÓN DE LEY
Rioja
★★★

See also El Coto

An exciting single-estate Rioja, produced by Barón de Ley using exclusively French, rather than American, oak. It is currently one of the two greatest Riojas in production (the other being Contino).

✓ *Entire range*

BARÓN DE OÑA
Rioja
★★⯪

See also La Rioja Alta

This small *bodega* at Paganos was established in the late 1980s but sold to La Rioja Alta in 1995, long before its wines had any chance of distribution in Spain, let alone abroad. With a high-tech, stainless-steel winery and use of 100 percent new French oak, Barón de Oña is a name to watch out for.

✓ *Entire range*

BODEGAS BERBERANA
Rioja
★⯪V

This producer can be disappointing at the lower end, but makes good to very good *reserva* and *gran reserva* wines that are full, fat, and sometimes even blowsy, with soft, oaky fruit. Berberana is also good value for older vintages. Labels include Preferido (*joven* style), Carta de Plata (younger style), Carta de Oro (bigger, richer), and Berberana *reserva* and *gran reserva* (best).

✓ *Reserva* • *Gran Reserva* • *Tempranillo* • *Dragon Tempranillo*

BODEGAS BERCEO
Rioja

Berceo has few vineyards and makes ordinary basic wines, but good *reservas* and *gran reservas*. Bodegas Berceo, located at Haro in Rioja Alta, has the same owners as Bodegas Luís Gurpegui Muga at San Adrián, where Rioja Baja overlaps Navarra.

✓ *Gonzalo de Berceo Gran Reserva*

BODEGAS BERONIA
Rioja

These are firm, oaky reds and fresh whites from Gonzalez Byass.

✓ *Reserva* • *Gran Reserva*

BODEGAS BILBAÍNAS
Rioja

Major vineyard owners, Bilbaínas are producers of traditionally styled Rioja. Labels include Viña Pomal (deep, dark, and well-oaked with plummy fruit), Viña Zaco (oakier), Vendimia Especial (excellent older vintages) and Royal Carlton (one of Rioja's Cava brands).

✓ *Reserva* • *Gran Reserva*

BODEGAS CAMPILLO
Rioja
★★V

See also Faustino Martínez

Touted by many as a new Rioja, Campillo has been around for some years, starting out as a second label of Faustino Martínez. Even at the time of the first edition of this encyclopedia in 1988, Campillo was "often better than the principal label." This was because these wines were used to break in Faustino's new barrels, a strategy that caused Campillo to outshine Faustino's flagship wines.

✓ *Entire range*

BODEGAS CAMPO VIEJO
Rioja
★V

See also Bodegas AGE and Marqués del Puerto

A large producer with major vineyard holdings under the same ownership as Bodegas AGE and Marqués del Puerto, Campo Viejo has a well-earned reputation for good-quality wines of exceptional value. Its *tinto* wines are typically full-bodied and marked by a fatness of ripe fruit and rich vanilla-oak. Labels include Albor (*joven* style), Viña Alcorta (wood-aged pure varietals), San Asensio (exuberantly fruity) and Marqués de Villamagna (created for bottle-aging, classic and fine rather than fat).

✓ *Reserva* • *Gran Reserva* • *Marqués de Villamagna Gran Reserva*

BODEGAS CARLOS SERRES
Rioja

Carlos Serres was founded by Charles (later known as Carlos) Serres in 1869, one year after his fellow Frenchman Jean Pineau went to Marqués de Riscal. The house style tends to be on the light side, but the *reserva* and *gran reserva* wines often have an elegant richness.

✓ *Carlomagno* (Reserva) • *Carlos Serres* (Gran Reserva)

BODEGAS CASTILLO DE MONJARDÍN
Navarra
★

An up-and-coming new *bodega* growing a high proportion of Tempranillo and French varieties. Fresh, creamy-rich red and white wines, both with and without oak. Exciting potential.

✓ *Chardonnay* • *Tinto Crianza*

CONTINO
Rioja
★★★⯪

Owned by CVNE and a group of growers (whose combined holdings comprise the vineyards of this single-estate Rioja), Contino was not the first single-vineyard Rioja, but its great success encouraged other boutique wineries to follow. It also stimulated interest in French oak as opposed to American.

✓ *Contino Rioja Reserva*

BODEGAS CORRÁL
Rioja

This improving *bodega* has relatively few vineyards and is best-known for its Don Jácobo line, although the underrated Corral Gran Reserva is by far its best wine.

✓ *Corral Gran Reserva*

COSECHEROS ALAVESES
Rioja
★⯪V

Perhaps one reason why this is one of Rioja's better cooperatives is that it is so small that it is hardly a cooperative in the commonly accepted definition of the term. The other reason is the excellent location of their vines around Laguardia in Rioja Alavesa. The style is always bright and fruity.

✓ *Artadi* (including blanco) • *Orobio* • *Valdepomares*

BODEGAS EL COTO
Rioja
★★⯪

See also Barón de Ley

These are wines of immaculate style, grace, and finesse, particularly the Coto de Imaz and, more recently, the single-vineyard Barón de Ley.

✓ *El Coto* • *Coto de Imaz Reserva*

CVNE
Compañía Vinícola del Norte de España Rioja
⯪

See also Contino

Also known as Cune (pronounced "coonay"), Compañía Vinícola del Norte de España Rioja was once the most old-fashioned and traditional of Rioja producers and its vintages were legendary, easily lasting 30 years or more. Ironically, these

PENEDÈS: CAVA COUNTRY

The worldwide popularity of Cava—Spain's only traditional method sparkling DO wine—together with the success of winemaking genius Miguel Torres, have made Penedès the most famous district in Catalonia, opening up the entire region's wine to export markets.

PRIOR TO PHYLLOXERA, which struck Penedès in 1876, more than 80 percent of the vineyards here were planted with black grapes. When the vines were grafted on to American rootstock, white varieties were given priority due to the growing popularity of sparkling white wines. It is easy to recognize the classic imported varieties in the vineyards because they are trained along wires, whereas traditional Spanish vines grow in little bushes.

THE DISTRICTS OF PENEDÈS
Penedès can be divided into three wine districts: Bajo Penedès, Medio Penedès, and Alta Penedès (also called Penedès Superior).

Bajo (or Baix) Penedès
The following grape varieties are grown in the Bajo Penedès: Monastrell, Malvasía, Grenache (*syn.* Garnacha), Cariñena, and various other, mostly black, grape varieties.

This area occupies the coastal strip and is the warmest of all three areas. The land of the Bajo Penedès is low and flat, with vines growing on limestone, clay, and sandy soil. This area produces more and more full-bodied red wines such as Torres's Sangredetoro.

Medio (or Mitja) Penedès
The grapes grown are mostly Xarello and Macabéo, but this is also the best area for Tempranillo, Cabernet Sauvignon, Merlot, and Monastrell.

The middle section of the Penedès is slightly hilly, occasionally flat land at an altitude of some 660 feet (200 meters) in the foothills west of Barcelona, on a soil of mostly limestone and clay. It has a cooler climate than the Bajo, with most areas equivalent to Regions II and III of the California Heat Summation System (*see* p.470). This is essentially Cava country, but it also produces the best of the new-style reds, including Torres's various Coronas wines.

Alta (or Alt) Penedès
Grape varieties grown in this district are almost exclusively white, being mostly Parellada, plus Riesling, Gewürztraminer, and Muscat. A little Pinot Noir is also grown.

This area is the farthest inland, and the grapes are grown on chalky foothills at an altitude of between 1,640 and 2,620 feet (500 and 800 meters). Climatic conditions are the coolest in Penedès, equivalent to Regions I and II. It is so cool that Cabernet Sauvignon will not ripen here and almost all wines produced are white, although Pinot Noir for Torres's Mas Borras is grown at San Marti. Most pure Alta Penedès wines are fresh, of the cool-fermented type, and can show remarkably fine aroma and acidity.

CAVA: SPAIN'S SPARKLING WINE
The first Spanish sparkling wine was made by Antoni Gali Comas some time prior to 1851, when he entered it in a competition in Madrid. He did not persevere, and the next milestone was with

PENEDÈS, *see also* p.303
Spreading out behind the coastal cities of Barcelona and Tarragona, this region has a flourishing Cava industry.

Intensive vine-growing zone
Penedès
Priorato
Tarragona
Monstant
Alella
Cava
Costers del Segre
Conca de Barbera
Terra Alta
Provincial boundary
▲ Height above sea level (meters)

0   5   10   15   20 miles
0   10   20   30 km

FACTORS AFFECTING TASTE AND QUALITY

LOCATION
Lying in the northeast corner of Spain, where Rioja's Ebro River enters the Mediterranean, Penedès is part of Catalonia, which also includes Alella, Tarragona, Priorato, and Terra Alta.

CLIMATE
A mild Mediterranean climate prevails in Penedès, becoming more continental (hotter summers and colder winters) moving westward and inland toward Terra Alta. In the same way, problems with fog in the northeast are gradually replaced by the hazard of frost toward the southwestern inland areas. In the high vineyards of Alta Penedès, white and aromatic grape varieties are cultivated at greater altitudes than traditional ones; since they benefit from cooler temperatures.

ASPECT
Vines are grown on all types of land, ranging from the flat plains of the Campo de Tarragona, through the 1,300-foot- (400-meter-) high plateaux of Terra Alta, to the highest vineyards in the Alta Penedès, which reach an altitude of 2,620 feet (800 meters). For every 330-foot (100-meter) rise in altitude, the temperature drops 0.56°F (1°C).

SOIL
There is a wide variety of soils, ranging from granite in Alella, through limestone-dominated clay, chalk, and sand in Penedès, to a mixture of mainly limestone and chalk with granite and alluvial deposits in Tarragona. The soil in Priorat is an unusual reddish slate with particles of reflective mica in the north, and schistose rock in the south.

VITICULTURE AND VINIFICATION
Catalonia is a hotbed of experimentation. Ultramodern winemaking techniques have been pioneered by Cava companies such as Codorníu and fine-wine specialists like Torres. Viticultural and vinification practices are generally quite modern throughout Catalonia. This is especially so at the Raimat Estate in Lérida, where the technology ranges from the latest and most efficient "Sernagiotto" continuous press for bulk production to the "Potter gravity crusher." Described as the simplest press ever designed, this extracts no more than 50–60 percent of the grape's potential juice.

GRAPE VARIETIES
Primary varieties: Cabernet Sauvignon, Carignan (*syn*. Cariñena, Mazuelo), Garnacha (*syn*. Lladoner, Aragonés), Mourvèdre (*syn*. Alcayata, Monastrell), Samsó, Tempranillo (*syn*. Ull de Llebre), Viura (*syn*. Macabéo); Xarel-lo (*syn*. Pansà Blanca)
Secondary varieties: Cabernet Franc, Chardonnay, Chenin Blanc, Gewürztraminer, Merlot, Muscat d'Alsace, Parellada, Pinot Noir, Riesling, Sauvignon, Subirat-Parent (*syn*. Malvasía Riojana)

internationally renowned grapes like Chardonnay can only dilute the wine's identity. However, as Codorníu has shown, blending with Chardonnay can fill out a Cava in a way that the traditional varieties (Macabéo, Parellada, and Xarel-lo) cannot.

At a Cava shippers' dinner in 1991, when Manuel Duran, the chairman of Freixenet, admitted that they were still undecided as to whether Cava's varieties were ideally suited to sparkling wine, he was challenged not simply to find an indigenous substitute for Chardonnay, but also to try to experiment with black Spanish varieties. Cava's traditionalists have, for some bizarre reason, always considered black grapes in a white Cava to be sacrilegious, yet Duran picked up the gauntlet, producing a Monastrell-Xarel-lo *cuvée* (the first release was too flabby, but the second release in 1997 was much better—the Catalonians are not used to handling black grapes for white wines, and I expect this Cava to continue improving). Prior to Freixenet's project, Codorníu was the only house to try black grapes in white Cava and succeeded in producing one of the most sumptuous Spanish sparkling wines ever using Pinot Noir.

Whether it is Monastrell, Grenache (*syn*. Garnacha), Trepat, Tempranillo, or some other Spanish grape, I believe that Cava will one day benefit from the use of indigenous black varieties and when that happens, Codorníu will, I am sure, use them, just as they will use any Spanish white variety that is discovered to be as useful in plumping up a *cuvée* as Chardonnay.

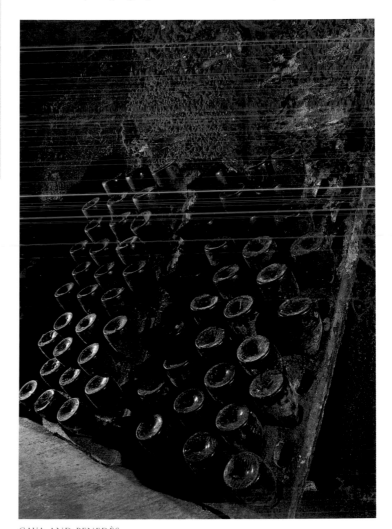

CAVA AND PENEDÈS
Although many Cava producers are either manual or computer-controlled girasols, *which enable* remuage *to be performed by the pallet-load, some of the more traditional houses, such as the family-owned firm of Juvé y Camps, still use* pupitres.

Luis Justo i Villanueva, the Laboratory Director at the Agricultural Institute of Sant Isidre in Catalonia. It was under Villanueva that all the earliest commercial producers of Spanish sparkling wine learned the Champagne process. In 1872, three of his former students, Domenec Soberano, Francesc Gil, and Augusti Vilaret, entered their sparkling wines in a Barcelona competition. All used classic Champagne grapes grown in Catalonia. Soberano and Gil were awarded gold medals, while Vilaret, who used raspberry liqueur in the dosage, received a bronze. Vilaret's firm, Caves Mont-Ferrant, is the only one of these enterprises to have survived.

The above facts are fully documented and thus contradict Codorníu's claim that it was first to produce Spanish sparkling wine in 1872. Codorníu did not, in fact, sell its first sparkling wines until 1879, and it would not be until 1893 that its production hit 10,000 bottles, a level that the three original firms achieved in the 1870s. What everyone seems agreed on, however, is that José Raventós i Fatjó of Codorníu was the first to make bottle-fermented sparkling wine out of Parellada, Macabéo, and Xarel-lo and that these grapes came to form the basis of the entire Cava industry.

CAVA'S SPANISH CHARACTER
The production of Cava is dominated by two firms: Codorníu and Freixenet. The latter has always been violently opposed to the invasion of Cava vineyards by foreign grape varieties. Freixenet's argument is certainly valid—that the introduction of foreign varieties could erode Cava's Spanish character. Cava is, after all, the only dry sparkling-wine appellation of any repute outside France and, of course, Spain has its own indigenous varieties, thus

3 feet (1 meter) and turns bluish after 16 feet (5 meters). It crumbles and is superabsorbent when wet, but extremely hard when dry. This is the key to the exceptional success of *albariza* as a vine-growing soil. Jerez is a region of baking heat and drought; there are about 70 days of rain each year, with a total precipitation of some 20 inches (50 centimeters). The *albariza* soaks up the rain like a sponge and, with the return of the drought, the soil surface is smoothed and hardened into a shell that is impermeable to evaporation. The winter and spring rains are imprisoned under this protective cap, and remain at the disposal of the vines, the roots of which penetrate some 13 feet (4 meters) beneath the surface. The *albariza* supplies just enough moisture to the vines, without making them too lazy or overproductive. Its high active-lime content encourages the ripening of grapes with a higher acidity level than would otherwise be the norm for such a hot climate. This acidity safeguards against unwanted oxidation prior to fortification.

OSBORNE,
PUERTO DE SANTA MARÍA
The Bajamar solera of Osborne was established in 1772.

The levante *and* poniente *winds*

The hot, dry *levante* is one of Jerez de la Frontera's two alternating prevailing winds. This easterly wind blow-dries and vacuum-cooks the grapes on their stalks during the critical ripening stage. This results in a dramatically different metabolization of fruit sugars, acids, and aldehydes, which produces a wine with an unusual balance peculiar to Jerez. Alternating with the *levante* is the wet Atlantic *poniente* wind. This is of fundamental importance, as it allows the growth of several *Saccharomyces* strains in the microflora of the Palomino grape. This is the poetically named sherry *flor* (*see* opposite), without which there would be no *fino* in Jerez.

SHERRY'S CLASSIC GRAPE VARIETIES

British sherry expert Julian Jeffs believes that as many as 100 different grape varieties were once traditionally used to make sherry and, in 1868, Diego Parada y Barreto listed 42 then in use. Today only

three varieties are authorized: Palomino, Pedro Ximénez, and Moscatel Fino. The Palomino is considered the classic sherry grape and most Sherries are, in fact, 100 percent Palomino, though they may be sweetened with Pedro Ximénez for export markets.

HOW GREAT SHERRY IS MADE
The harvest

Twenty or more years ago, it was traditional to begin the grape harvest in the first week of September. After picking, Palomino grapes were left in the sun for 12–24 hours, Pedro Ximénez and Moscatel for 10–21 days. Older vines were picked before younger ones, and Pedro Ximénez and Moscatel were picked first of all because they required longer sunning than Palomino. At night, the grapes were covered with *esparto* grass mats as a protection against dew. This sunning is called the *soleo*, and its primary purpose is to increase sugar content, while reducing the malic acid and tannin content. Although some producers still

THE SHERRY REGION,
see also p.303
The most important sector of the wine-producing areas of southern Spain is the sherry region of Andalucía, situated around Jerez de la Frontera, Sanlúcar de Barrameda, and Puerto de Santa María.

Intensive vine-growing zone
Sanlúcar de Barrameda
Trebujena
Chipiona
Rota
El Puerto de Santa María
Jerez de la Frontera
Cádiz
Puerto Real
San Fernando
Chiclana de la Frontera
- - - - Provincial boundary
———— Delimited Sherry-producing region
▲ Height above sea level (meters)

carry out the *soleo*, most harvest in the second week of September and forgo the *soleo* for all grapes but Pedro Ximénez and Moscatel, used in the sweetest sherry. The grapes are now left in the sun for far fewer than the traditional 10–21 days.

The yeso
Traditionally, prior to pressing the grapes, the stalks are removed and a small proportion of *yeso* (gypsum) is added to precipitate tartrate crystals. This practice, which is dying out, may have evolved when growers noticed that grapes covered by *albariza* dust produced better wine than clean ones. *Albariza* has a high calcium carbonate content that would crudely accomplish the task.

The pressing
Traditionally, four laborers called *pisadores* were placed in each *lagar* (open receptacle) to tread the grapes, not barefoot but wearing *zapatos de pisar*, heavily nailed cow-hide boots to trap the seeds and stalks undamaged between the nails. Each man tramped 36 miles (58 kilometers) on the spot during a typical session lasting from midnight to noon. Automatic horizontal, usually pneumatic, presses are now in common use.

Fermentation
Some sherry houses still ferment their wine in small oak casks purposely filled to only 90 percent capacity. After 12 hours, the fermentation starts and continues for between 36 and 50 hours at 77–86°F (25–30°C), by which time as much as 99 percent of available sugar is converted to alcohol; after a further 40 or 50 days, the process is complete. Current methods often use stainless-steel fermentation vats, and yield wines that are approximately 1 percent higher in alcohol than those fermented in casks due to an absence of absorption and evaporation.

THE MAGICAL FLOR
For the majority of sherry drinkers, *fino* is the quintessential sherry style. It is a natural phenomenon called *flor* that determines whether or not a sherry will become a *fino*. *Flor* is a strain of *Saccharomyces* yeast that appears as a gray-white film floating on a wine's surface, and it occurs naturally in the microflora of the Palomino grape grown in the Jerez district. It is found to one degree or another in every vat of sherry and Manzanilla, but whether or not it can dominate the wine and develop as a *flor* depends upon the strength of the *Saccharomyces* and the biochemical conditions. The effect of *flor* on sherry is to absorb remaining traces of sugar, diminish glycerine and volatile acids, and greatly increase esters and aldehydes. To flourish, *flor* requires:

- An alcoholic strength of between 13.5 and 17.5 percent. The optimum is 15.3 percent, the level at which vinegar-producing acetobacter is killed.
- A temperature of between 59 and 86°F (15 and 30°C).
- A sulfur dioxide content of less than 0.018 percent.
- A tannin content of less than 0.01 percent.
- A virtual absence of fermentable sugars.

CASK CLASSIFICATION AND FORTIFICATION
The cellarmaster's job is to sniff all the casks of sherry and mark on each one in chalk how he believes it is developing, according to a recognized cask-classification system. At this stage, lower-grade wines (those with little or no *flor*) are fortified to 18 percent to kill any *flor*, thus determining their character once and for all and thereafter protecting the wine from the dangers of acetification. The *flor* itself is a protection against the acetobacter that threaten to turn the wine into vinegar, but it is by no means invincible and will be at great risk until it is fortified to 15.3 percent, or above, the norm for *fino*, and is not truly safe until it is bottled. A fifty-fifty mixture known as *mitad y mitad*, *miteado*, or *combinado* (half

GRAPE-BASED SWEETENING AND COLORING AGENTS

The most traditional and most important sweetening agent in the production of sherry, although gradually giving way to other less expensive ones, is that made from pure, overripe, sun-dried Pedro Ximénez grapes, also known as PX. After the *soleo*, or sunning, of the grapes (*see* p.322), the sugar content of the PX increases from around 23 percent to between 43 and 54 percent. The PX is pressed and run into casks containing pure grape liquor. This process, known as muting, produces a mixture with an alcohol level of about 9 percent and some 430 grams of sugar per liter. This mixture is tightly bunged and left for four months, during which time it undergoes a slight fermentation, increasing the alcohol by about one degree and reducing the sugar by some 18 grams per liter. Finally, the wine undergoes a second muting, raising the alcoholic strength to a final 13 percent but reducing the sugar content to about 380 grams per liter. Other sweetening agents are:

MOSCATEL
This is prepared in exactly the same way as PX, but the result is not as rich and its use, which is always been less widespread than PX, is technically not permitted under DO regulations.

DULCE PASA
Preparation is as for PX and Moscatel, but using Palomino, which achieves up to a 50 percent sugar concentration prior to muting. Its use is on the increase. This must not be confused with *dulce racimo* or *dulce apagado*, sweetening agents that were once brought in from outside the region and are now illegal.

DULCE DE ALMIBAR OR DULCE BLANCO
A combination of glucose and levulose blended with *fino* and matured, this agent is used to sweeten pale-colored sherries.

SANCOCHO
A dark-colored, sweet, and sticky nonalcoholic syrup that is made by reducing unfermented local grape juice to one-fifth of its original volume by simmering over a low heat. It is used in the production of *vino de color* a "coloring wine."

ARROPE
This dark-colored, sweet, and sticky nonalcoholic syrup, made by reducing unfermented local grape juice to one fifth of its original volume, is also used in the production of *vino de color*.

COLOR DE MACETILLA
This is the finest *vino de color* and is produced by blending two-parts *arrope* or *sancocho* and one part unfermented local grape juice. This results in a violent fermentation and, when the wine falls bright, it has an alcoholic strength of 9 percent and a sugar content of 235 grams per liter. Prized stocks are often matured by *solera*.

COLOR REMENDADO
This is a cheap, commonly used *vino de color*, which is made by blending *arrope* or *sancocho* with local wine.

HOW THE FERMENTED SHERRY DEVELOPS

The larger *bodegas* like to make something of a mystery of the *flor*, declaring that they have no idea whether or not it will develop in a specific cask. There is some justification for this—one cask may have a fabulous froth of *flor* (looking like dirty soapsuds), while the cask next to it may have none. Any cask with good signs of dominant *flor* will invariably end up as *fino*, but others with either no *flor* or ranging degrees of it may develop into one of many different styles. There is no way of guaranteeing the evolution of the wines, but it is well known that certain zones can generally be relied upon to produce particular styles.

ZONE	STYLE	ZONE	STYLE
Añina	*fino*	Madroñales	*Moscatel/sweet*
Balbaina	*fino*	Miraflores	*fino/manzanilla*
Carrascal	*oloroso*	Rota	*Moscatel/sweet*
Chipiona	*Moscatel/sweet*	Sanlúcar	*fino/manzanilla*
Los Tercios	*fino*	Tehigo	*colouring wines*
Macharnudo	*amontillado*	Torrebreba	*manzanilla*

pure alcohol, half grape juice) is usually used for fortification. However, some producers prefer to use mature sherry for fortification instead of grape juice.

Further cask-classification
The wines are often racked prior to fortification, and always after. Two weeks later, they undergo a second, more precise classification,

but no further fortification, or other action, will take place until nine months have elapsed, after which they will be classified regularly over a period of two years to determine their final style.

CASK CLASSIFICATION IN THE CELLAR

FIRST CASK CLASSIFICATION

CHALK MARK	CHARACTER OF WINE	PROBABLE STYLE OF SHERRY	ACTION TO TAKE
una raya	light and good	*fino/amontillado*	fortify up to 15.5%
raya y punto	*slightly less promising*	undecided	fortify up to 15.5%
dos rayas	less promising	*oloroso*	*fortify up to 18%*
tres rayas	coarse or acid	–	usually distil immediately
vinegar	–	–	remove to avoid infection

SECOND CASK CLASSIFICATION

CHALK MARK	CHARACTER OF WINE	PROBABLE STYLE OF SHERRY	ACTION TO TAKE
palma	a wine with breeding	*has flor*	–
raya	fuller	*no flor*	–
dos rayas	tending to be coarse	*no flor*	–
gridiron	no good at all	*no flor*	–

FURTHER CASK CLASSIFICATION

CHALK MARK	CHARACTER OF WINE	PROBABLE STYLE OF SHERRY	ACTION TO TAKE
palma	Light and delicate	a *fino* sherry	–
palma cortada	Fuller than a fino	*Fino-amontillado* or *amontillado*	–
palo cortado	No flor, but exceptional, full-bodied, and delicate	*Palo cortado*	–
raya	Darker, fuller, not breeding flor	Medium-quality *oloroso*	–
dos rayas	Darker and fuller but coarser	Low-quality *oloroso*, for blending cheap sherries that are usually sweetened	–
pata de gallina	a *raya* that has developed the true fragrance of a fine *oloroso*	Top-quality *oloroso*, to be aged and kept dry	–

The solera blending system

Once the style of the sherry has been established, the wines are fed into fractional-blending systems called *soleras*. A *solera* consists of a stock of wine in cask, split into units of equal volume but different maturation. The oldest stage is called the *solera*; each of the younger stages that feed it is a *criadera*, or nursery. There are up to seven *criaderas* in a sherry *solera*, and up to 14 in a manzanilla *solera*. Up to one-third (the legal maximum) of the *Solera* may be drawn off for blending and bottling, although some *bodegas* may restrict their very high-quality, old *soleras* to one-fifth. The amount drawn off from the mature *solera* is replaced by an equal volume from the first *criadera*, which is topped off by the second *criadera*, and so on. When the last *criadera* is emptied of its one-third, it is refreshed by an identical quantity of *añada*, or new wine. This comprises like-classified sherries from the current year's production, aged up to 36 months, depending on the style and exactly when they are finally classified.

THE EVOLUTION OF SHERRY STYLES

The tree shows the course taken by each sherry to become one of the well-known styles by which it is sold.

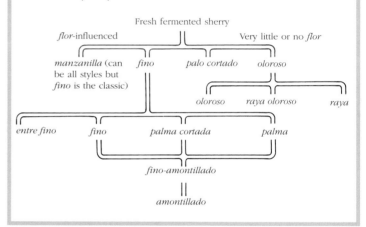

THE STYLES OF
SHERRY

The development of a sherry can be natural, so that a *fino* can, without the help of increased fortification, turn into an *oloroso* (thus a natural *oloroso* may have developed with the aid of *flor*, whereas the increased fortification usually used to turn a *fino* into an *oloroso* would prevent the development of *flor*). A *palo cortado* can develop from either an *amontillado* or an *oloroso*. A genuine old *fino* sherry can surprise everyone and turn into an *oloroso*.

ALMACENISTA *or* BODEGAS DE ALMACENADO

This is not a style, but a category of increasing interest among sherry enthusiasts. An *almacenista* is a private stockholder whose pure, unblended sherries are held as an investment for 30 years or more, after which they are in great demand by large *bodegas*, which use them to improve their commercial blends. Lustau, itself an *almacenista* until the 1950s (and now part of the Caballero group), was the first firm to market the concept, making these purest of sherries available to consumers

(and they registered "Almacenista" as a trademark in the process). All styles of sherry and *manzanilla* exist in *almacenista* form and are, almost by definition, guaranteed to be of extraordinary quality. Fractions on the label such as ⅛, ½, or ¼₀ indicate the number of barrels in the *solera* from which it was drawn, therefore, the lower the denominator (the number below the line), the greater the rarity of the wine and, consequently, the more expensive it will be.

✓ *Lustau*

AMONTILLADO

With age, a *fino* develops an amber color in cask and becomes a *fino-amontillado*, then, after at least eight years, a full *amontillado*, when it takes on a nutty character and acquires more body. A true *amontillado* is completely dry, with between 16 and 18 percent alcohol, but will often be sweetened to a medium style for export markets.

The term *amontillado* means "Montilla style"; it was originally used to distinguish a sherry with characteristics similar to those of Montilla

(then part of the Jerez region—*see* p.321). Ironically, it was illegal for producers of Montilla to use the term *amontillado* under the Spanish republic, thus sherry could be made in a montilla-style, but not Montilla! Under the EU, however, the law has changed and once again Montilla houses are shipping Montilla *amontillado*.

✓ *Domecq* (Botaina) • *Gonzalez Byass* (Duque) • *Sandeman* (Bone Dry Old Amontillado) • *Valdespino* (Coliseo, Don Tomás) • *Wisdom & Warter* (Very Rare Solera Muy Viejo)

BROWN

This sweetened *oloroso* is usually, but not always, of lesser quality than Oloroso. High-quality Brown sherries used to be very popular in Scotland.

✓ *Williams & Humbert* (Walnut Brown)

CREAM *or* DARK CREAM

An *oloroso* style that is usually sweetened with Pedro Ximénez, the quality of which can range from the commercial to extremely good.

✓ *Diego Romero* (Jerezana) • *Lustau* (Premium Solera, Vendimia)

EAST INDIA

Some sources believe that this rich, sweet, Madeira-like style of sherry dates back to as early as 1617, but the practice of shipping sherry to the Orient and back gradually disappeared during the 19th century with the advent of steam-driven ships. It was revived in 1958 by the owners of the Ben Line and Alastair Campbell, an Edinburgh wine merchant, when they sent a hogshead of Valdespino Oloroso on a 20,000-mile (32,000-kilometer) round trip to the Far East, but although the style survives, the effects of the sea voyage, as with Madeira, are now replicated in the cellar.

✓ *Lustau* (Old East India) • *Osborne* (India Rare Solera Oloroso)

FINO

A *palma* is the highest quality of *fino* sherry and may be graded in a rising scale of quality: *dos palmas*, *tres palmas*, *cuatro palmas*. A *palma cortada* is a *fino* that has developed more body, has a very dry, but smooth, almondy flavor, and is veering toward *amontillado*. An *entre fino* has little merit. Few *finos* remain *fino* with age in cask, which is why genuine Old Fino sherry is rare. A *fino* is light, dry, and delicate; its *flor* nose should overpower any acetaldehyde.

This style is best appreciated straight from the cask, when it is crisp and vital, as it quickly tires once bottled and further declines rapidly as soon as it is opened. Until producers are required to declare the bottling date on the label (fat chance), the only sensible advice is not to buy *fino* until the day you want to drink it and, once opened, consume the entire contents: don't keep it. The wines are invariably 100 percent Palomino with an alcoholic strength of between 15.5 and 17 percent.

✓ *Tomás Abad* • *Domecq* (La Ina) • *Gonzalez Byass* (Tio Pepe) • *La Riva* (Tres Palmas) • *Williams & Humbert* (Pando)

MANZANILLA

Sea winds in the Sanlúcar de Barrameda area create a more even temperature and higher humidity than those found in Jerez itself, which with the tradition of allowing more ullage (empty volume) in *manzanilla* casks, encourages the thickest, whitest, and most vigorous growth of *flor* in the region. *Fino* is, therefore, the most classic style, but *manzanilla*, too, has its *fino-amontillado*

(called *pasada*) and *amontillado*. *Oloroso* and various intermediary styles are also produced, but these are invariably sold as sherry, rather than *manzanilla*, even when they are exclusively composed of the latter.

MANZANILLA AMONTILLADA

Fuller than a *pasada*, but lighter and more fragrant than Jerez *amontillado*, this is less common than the previous two, but can be excellent.

✓ *Barbadillo* (Principe) • *Lustau* (Manuel Cuevas Jurado)

MANZANILLA FINA

Manzanilla (sherry made in Sanlúcar de Barrameda) is a relatively modern, early-picked *fino*. Its production differs from that of a traditional *fino* in that its fortification is lower and the *solera* system more complex. A true *manzanilla fina* is pale, light-bodied, dry, and delicate with a definite *flor* nose, a touch of bitterness on the palate, and sometimes even a slightly saline tang. *See* general *fino* style below about freshness and when to consume. These wines are usually 100 percent Palomino with an alcoholic strength of 15.5–17 percent.

✓ *Barbadillo* (Eva) • *Diez-Mérito* (Don Zoilo) • *Duff Gordon* (Cabrera)

MANZANILLA PASADA

When a *manzanilla* begins to age, it loses its *flor*, gains alcoholic strength, and becomes the equivalent of a *fino-amontillado*, known in Sanlúcar de Barrameda as a *pasada*. These wines are invariably 100 percent Palomino with an alcoholic strength of up to 20.5 percent.

✓ *Barbadillo* (Solcar) • *Delgado Zuleta* (Amontillado Fino, La Goya) • *Hidalgo* (Pasada)

MILK

Sweetened *amontillado*, usually of lesser quality.

MOSCATEL

Occasionally, releases of this wine can be rich, raisiny delights.

✓ *Lustau* (Las Cruzes, Solera Reserva Emelin)

OLOROSO

Oloroso means fragrant and, when genuinely dry, rich, and complex from age, I find it certainly has the greatest finesse, and is the most rewarding wine in Jerez. Much of its character is due to the relatively high fortification it receives and the generous glycerine content that develops without the aid of *flor*. The alcoholic strength of these wines

usually ranges between 18 and 20 percent. Some high-quality, sweeter, dessert-style *oloroso* wines are also produced.

✓ **Dry** *Barbadillo* (Oloroso Seco) • *Diez-Mérito* (Victoria Regina) • *Domecq* (Río Viejo) • *Gonzalez Byass* (Alfonso, Apostles) • *Hidalgo* (Oloroso Seco) • *Lustau* (Don Nuno, Emperatríz Eugenia, Principe Rio, Tonel) • *Osborne* (Bailén, Alonso el Sabio) • *Diego Romero* (Jerezana) • *Sandeman* (Dry Old Oloroso) • *Valdespino* (Don Gonzalo)

Dessert style *Gonzalez Byass* (Matúsalem) • *Sandeman* (Royal Corregedor) • *Valdespino* (Solera 1842)

PALE CREAM

Pale cream is sweetened, usually lesser-quality, *fino* sherry.

PALE DRY

This style is synonymous with *fino*.

PALO CORTADO

This wine cannot be deliberately made, nor even encouraged (a *palo cortado solera* is very difficult to operate); only one vat in a thousand turns into a true *palo cortado*. A law unto itself, it is a naturally dry wine with a style somewhere between *amontillado* (on the nose) and *oloroso* (on the palate), but this description does not by any means convey the stunning richness, nutty complexity, and fabulous finesse, which really must be experienced to be believed.

It should be totally dry, but some sweeter dessert-style *palo cortado* wines are produced and can be wonderful. Like *palma*, *palo cortado* may be graded: *dos cortados*, *tres cortados*, *cuatro cortados*.

✓ *Domecq* (Sibarita) • *Hidalgo* (Jerez) • *Lustau* (Peninsula) • *Rosario Fantante* (Dos Cortados) • *Sandeman* (Dry Old) • *Valdespino* (Cardenal) • *Williams & Humbert* (Dos Cortados)

Dessert style *Osborne* (Abocado Solera) • *Sandeman* (Royal Ambrosante) • *Wisdom & Warter* (Tizón)

PEDRO XIMÉNEZ

Although it is primarily produced as a sweetening agent, Pedro Ximénez is occasionally released in limited bottlings that are invariably very old and utterly stunning. These are huge, dark, deep, powerfully rich wines piled high with complex yet succulent, raisiny, Muscovado flavors. These bottlings of Pedro Ximénez can be compared in quality, weight, and intensity—though not in character—with only some of the oldest and rarest Australian liqueur Muscats.

✓ *Gonzalez Byass* (Noe) • *Lustau* (Murillo, San Emilio) • *Sanchez Romate* (Superior) • *Valdespino* (Solera Superior) • *Wisdom & Warter* (Viale Viejisimo)

PUERTO FINO

This is a *manzanilla*-type sherry that is produced in El Puerto de Santa Maria, where the winds are almost as legendary as those of Sanlúcar de Barrameda.

✓ *Burdon* (Puerto Fino Superior Dry) • *Osborne* (Coquinera Amontillado)

The WINES *of*
PORTUGAL

THIS COUNTRY IS SLOWLY BUT SURELY shaking off its image of tired white wines and dusty-dry reds. Thanks to a bonanza of grants during Portugal's honeymoon period of European Union membership, its wine industry underwent a massive technological upgrade in the 1990s, and we are only just beginning to reap the rewards. First came fresh, fruity, inexpensive red wines, then a whole raft of classy, upmarket reds hit the shelves. Over the next few years, we shall see similar improvements in Portugal's white wines. International varieties still have a role to play, but it will be this country's indigenous grapes that will establish its reputation in the third millennium. And while Madeira suffers the same woes as most other fortified wines, port remains by-and-large resistant to the modern trend of ignoring this style of wine.

VINEYARDS IN THE DOURO VALLEY
Vines grow on terraces overlooking the Douro River near Pinhão, a town in the port region.

PORTUGAL

Once devoid of anything interesting beyond its two classic fortified wines, port and Madeira, Portuguese winemakers have now woken up to the tremendous potential of the terroirs and native grape varieties that their country offers, making it a hotbed of innovation.

THE JOINT VENTURE BETWEEN Bruno Prats, the former owner and winemaker of Château Cos d'Estournel, and the Symington family of port fame to produce premium red wine in the Douro will put the icing on the cake for Portugal's fine wine reputation. This testament to the top-end potential of Portugal's wine industry follows close on the heels of the red wine revolution that started to materialize in its more inexpensive reds in the mid-1990s.

In the past, Dão had always typified the sort of wines we had come to expect from Portugal, with its dried-out, fruitless reds and dull, heavy, oxidized whites. But in 1995 deliciously fruity, easily accessible reds and fresh, crisp whites came on stream and, like a true revolution, the change started at the lowest levels, with wines such as Alta Mesa and Ramada from Estremadura. At the time these were, and still are, some of the cheapest wines in the world. They had already turned heads by being clean, easy-drinking wines from what was formerly considered a lackluster wine country but, with the vintages of 1994 and 1995, they suddenly had twice the fruit, which gave them instant gulpability and gained them international recognition.

VINEYARDS, SETÚBAL
The area's Moscatel vines (Muscat d'Alexandrie) produce a celebrated fortified wine that has its own Denominação de Origem Controlada.

PORTUGAL
It is in the north of the country that the most famous wines—port and Vinho Verde—are produced, along with the most upwardly mobile, those from Bairrada and Dão.

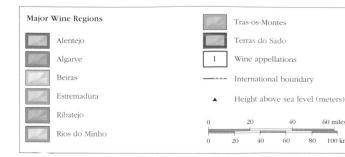

Major Wine Regions

- Alentejo
- Algarve
- Beiras
- Estremadura
- Ribatejo
- Rios do Minho
- Tras-os-Montes
- Terras do Sado
- 1 Wine appellations
- International boundary
- ▲ Height above sea level (meters)

0   20   40   60 miles
0   20   40   60   80   100 km

CURRENT TRENDS

The rush of fruit has only just begun to filter its way upward through the quality scale. This was in part due to the fact that more serious wines took longer to reach the market, thus while we were gulping 1994s and 1995s from Estremadura and other lesser-known Vinhos Regionals, such as Alentejo and Terras do Sado, the 1991s and 1992s from Dão and Bairrada were only just reaching the shelves. A few producers, such as Duque de Viseu in Dão, had got their act together by the early 1990s, but most had not and we still had to get through the dismal 1993 vintage before these more famous regions could show us what they were doing while the likes of Alta Mesa and Ramada were being knocked out.

Another reason for the delayed action in Portugal's fine-wine regions is that producers had until relatively recently been forced to buy wines. Quite extraordinarily, it was illegal for them to buy grapes. Most growers involved in the bulk market barely have a grasp of how to cultivate vines, let alone ferment wines, so being able to buy grapes has enabled firms like Sogrape (which makes Duque de Viseu) to have much greater control over the quality of

the final product. When and if the same growers ever learn to grow grapes properly, the recent surge in quality will seem nothing and Portugal's finest wine areas should be catapulted to superstardom.

RECENT PORTUGUESE VINTAGES

2003 Some excellent reds, and should be a very good vintage port year.

2002 A potentially outstanding red wine vintage destroyed by preharvest rain almost everywhere, the exception being in the Douro, both for still reds, and for single *quinta* port.

2001 A below-average year, due to a cool August and wet September, although a few fine single *quinta* ports might be released.

2000 Great for reds, particularly in the north, and a classic vintage port year.

1999 A vintage best forgotten, except for a number of exceptional single *quinta* ports.

PORTUGUESE LABEL LANGUAGE

ADAMADO Sweet

ADEGA Literally "cellar," and commonly used as part of the name of a company or cooperative, similar to the Spanish term *bodega*.

APERITIVO Apéritif

BRANCO White

BRUTO Portuguese adaptation of the French *brut*, used to describe a dry sparkling wine.

CARVALHO Oak

CASA Refers to the property or estate and may also indicate a single-vineyard wine.

CASTA Grape variety

CASTA PREDOMINANTE Refers to the major grape variety used in a wine.

COLHEITA This means vintage and is followed by the year of harvest.

CLARETE Bordeaux-style or deep rosé

CLARO New, or "nouveau," wine

DOCE Sweet

DENOMINAÇÃO DE ORIGEM CONTROLADA (DOC) Roughly equivalent to a French AOC.

ENGARRAFADO POR Bottled by

ENGARRAFADO NA ORIGEM Estate-bottled

ESCOLHA Choice or selection

ESPUMANTEA sparkling wine that may be made by any method unless qualified by another term.

GARRAFA Bottle

GARRAFEIRA This term may be used only for a vintage-dated wine that possesses an extra 0.5 percent of alcohol above the minimum requirement. Red wines must have a minimum of three years' maturation, including one year in bottle; white wines must have one year, with six months in bottle. The wine may come from a demarcated region, or be blended from various areas.

GENEROSO An apéritif or dessert wine rich in alcohol and usually sweet.

INDICAÇÃO DE PROVENIÊNCIA REGULAMENTADA (IPR) Roughly equivalent to a French VDQS

LICOROSO A fortified wine

MADURO Literally "matured"—it often refers to a wine that has been aged in a vat.

PALÁCIO Refers to the property or estate and may also indicate a single-vineyard wine.

PRODUZIDO E ENGARRAFADO POR Produced and bottled at or by

QUINADO Tonic wine

QUINTA Farm or estate

ROSADO Rosé

RESERVA A term that can be used only to qualify a vintage year of "outstanding quality," where the wine has an alcoholic strength of at least 0.5 percent above the minimum requirement. Wine may come from a demarcated region, but does not have to; it could be blended from different areas.

SECO Dry

SOLAR Refers to the property or estate and may also indicate a single-vineyard wine.

TINTO Red

VELHO Literally means "old" and, in the past, this term used not to have any legal definition. Now it can only be applied to wines with a strict minimum age: three years for red wines and two years for whites.

VINHA Vineyard

VINHO REGIONAL (VR) Similar to a large-sized *vin de pays*.

VINHO DE MESA The table wine equivalent to French *vin de table*. If the label does not state a specific DOC or Garrafeira, the wine will be a cheap blend.

THE APPELLATIONS OF
PORTUGAL

Note DOC stands for *Denominação de Origem Controlada*, Portugal's equivalent of France's AOC, Spain's DO, etc.

IPR stands for *Indicação de Proveniência Regulamentada*, roughly equivalent to VDQS or a "DOC in waiting", a number having been promoted to DOC status in recent years.

VR stands for *Vinho Regional*, a sort of large-sized *vin de pays*.

ALCOBAÇA IPR
Map (No. 1)

These wines from the hills surrounding the old monastic town of Alcobaça are predominantly white. Yields are unfavorably high, producing thin reds and light whites significantly lower in

alcohol than wines from surrounding areas.
🍇 For all wines: Arinto, Baga, Fernão Pires, Malvasia, Periquita, Tamarêz, Trincadeira, Vital

ALENQUER IPR
Map (No. 2)

The valley-side vineyards of Alenquer are well-suited to viticulture, ripening grapes easily and producing full, ripe-flavored reds, with peppery-spicy aromas and soft, easy-going, creamy-dry whites.

🍇 Arinto, Camarate (possibly the same as Castelão Nacional), Fernão Pires, Graciano (*syn.* Tinta Miuda), Jampal, Mortágua, Periquita, Preto Martinho, Vital

🍷 1–3 years (new-wave, fruity style) 2–5 years (others)

✓ *Quinta de Abrigada* • *Quinta de Plantos* • *Quinta do Carneiro*

ALENTEJO VR

Stretching up from the Algarve, the plains of Alto and Baixo Alentejo cover about one-third of Portugal. A sparsely populated area with large estates and a scattering of vines, Alentejo is better known for cork than vineyards, even though it has produced some of the country's most outstanding one-off wines and has achieved this with both indigenous and imported grape varieties.

ESPORÃO
Garrafeira 2000 - Alentejo - D.O.C.
Denominação de Origem Controlada-Reguengos
Vinho Tinto / Red Wine / Vin Rouge

Abundante, Alfrocheiro Preto, Alicante Bouschet, Antão Vaz, Arinto, Cabernet Sauvignon, Carignan, Chardonnay, Diagalves, Fernão Pires, Grand Noir, Manteudo, Moreto, Palomino (*syn.* Perrum), Periquita, Rabo de Ovelha, Tempranillo (*syn.* Aragonez), Trincadeira

1–3 years (new-wave, fruity style), 2–5 years (others)

Apostolo • *Cortes de Cima* • *Esporão* (other brands include Monte Velha) • *J. P. Vinhos* (Quinta da Anfora) • *Herdade de Mouchão* • *José de Sousa* • *Pêra Manca* • *A. C. de Reguengos* • *Quinta do Carmo* • *Sogrape* (Vinha do Monte) • *Tapada do Chaves*

ALGARVE VR

The downgrading of Algarve to Vinho Regional was just a smoke-screen to gain acceptance for its four new internal DOCs: Lagos, Portimão, Lagoa, and Tavira. Lagoa used to have a reputation for fortified whites, which is not surprising considering its proximity to Jerez, but although wine is still produced, none of any interest, fortified or not, is made in the Algarve these days. It is wise to remember that the tourist economy, not quality, regulates wine appellations in the Algarve.

Arinto, Bastardo, Diagalves, Moreto, Negra Mole, Periquita, Perrum, Rabo de Ovelha, Tamarêz d'Algarve (possibly the same as Roupeiro)

Adega do Cantor

ALMEIRIM IPR
Map (No. 3)

An up-and-coming area in the Ribatejo region, rapidly becoming known as a source for cheap, fruity red and white wines, often from the plains, known locally as *lezíria* and simply sold as *vinho de mesa*. Terraced vines on the left bank of the Tagus apparently have more potential.

Arinto, Baga (*syn.* Poeirinha), Castelão Nacional, Fernão Pires, Periquita, Rabo de Ovelha, Tinta Amarela (*syn.* Trincadeira Preta), Trincadeira das Pratas (*syn.* Tamarêz d'Azeitão), Ugni Blanc (*syn.* Tália), Vital

6–18 months

A. C. de Almeirim (including wines under Falcoaria and Quinta das Verandas labels)

ARRABIDA IPR
Map (No. 4)

This area on the Setúbal peninsula has well-drained limestone soil and great quality potential, particularly for reds, but whether it takes off as an appellation, when the much wider, more flexible

Terras do Sado VR is doing so well, remains to be seen.

Alfrocheiro, Arinto, Cabernet Sauvignon, Periquita (Castelão Francês), Fernão Pires, Muscat d'Alexandrie (*syn.* Moscatel de Setúbal), Rabo de Ovelha, Roupeiro

ARRUDA IPR
Map (No. 5)

From intensively cultivated hillsides surrounding the town of Arruda in the Estremadura region, come some of Portugal's cheapest, yet reliable, fruity reds.

Camarate (possibly the same as Castelão Nacional), Fernão Pires, Graciano (*syn.* Tinta Miuda), Jampal, Trincadeira, Vital

1–3 years (new-wave, fruity style), 2–5 years (others)

A. C. de Arruda

BAIRRADA DOC
Map (No. 6)

This area produces one of Portugal's two most important red wines and the best have a deep color with good tannin and fine, bell pepper-blackcurranty fruit. However, it is only just beginning to demonstrate its potential for white wines. Sogrape's Nobilis exemplifies Bairrada's fast-emerging rosé style, which really hits the spot with its freshness and depth of fruit.

Baga, Borrado das Moscas (*syn.* Bical), Castelão Francês, Fernão Pires (*syn.* Maria Gomes), Rabo de Ovelha, Tinta Pinheira

3–12 years (reds) 1–3 years (rosés and whites)

José Maria da Fonseca • *Gonçalves Faria* (Reserva) • *Luis Pato* (especially Quinta do Ribeirinho Vinhos Velhos) • *Quinta de Pedralvites* • *Casa de Saima* • *Caves São João* • *Sogrape* (Reserva, Nobilis Rosé) • *Terra Franca* (tinto)

BEIRAS VR

Located in the north of Portugal, encompassing the three Beira provinces of Alta, Baixa, and Litoral, containing the DOCs of Dão and Bairrada, plus the IPRs of Castelo Rodrigo, Cova de Beira, Lafões, Lamego, Pinhel, Varosa, Encostas da Nave, and most of Encostas d'Aire, Beiras produces virtually every imaginable style of wine made, but standards vary enormously.

Arinto, Baga, Bastardo, Borrado das Moscas (*syn.* Bical), Camarate (possibly the same as Castelão Nacional), Cerceal, Esgana Cão, Fernão Pires, Jaen, Malvasia, Marufo, Monvedro, Periquita, Rabo de Ovelha, Rufete, Tinta Amarela (Trincadeira Preta), Touriga Nacional, Verdelho, Vital

1–3 years (new-wave, fruity style) 2–5 years (others)

Bright Brothers (Baga) • *Buçaco* • *Conde de Santar* (Reserva) • *Entre Serras* • *João Pato* • *Quinta de Foz de Arouce*

BISCOITOS IPR
Map (No. 7)

Rarely encountered fortified wines produced on the island of Terceira in the Azores.

Arinto, Terrantez, Verdelho

BORBA DOC
Map (No. 8)

The first subappellation of the Alentejo region to gain recognition outside of Portugal itself,

especially for its inexpensive, juicy red wines.

Aragonez, Periquita, Perrum, Rabo de Ovelha, Roupeiro, Tamarêz, Trincadeira

1–3 years

A. C. de Borba (Reserva)

BUCELAS DOC
Map (No. 9)

The Arinto grape grows particularly well on the loam soil of this small district, but the antiquated winemaking methods are still holding back what is obviously a potentially fine white-wine appellation. Cool fermentation, early bottling, and a delicate touch of new oak would make this wine an international superstar, but so many wines are dried-out and overacidic. Quinta da Romeira is the most consistent Bucelas, and is recommended in this context, but has failed to live up to its promise.

Arinto, Esgana Cão

Upon purchase

Quinta da Romeira (Prova Régia)

CARCAVELOS DOC
Map (No. 10)

Famous in Portugal itself since the late 18th century when the Marquis of Pombal owned a large vineyard and winery here. This area's oldest surviving vineyard, Quinta do Barão, stopped production in 1991, but a relatively new one, Quinta dos Pesos, is trying desperately to rekindle interest in Carcavelos. Rarely seen on export markets, it is a topaz-colored, off-dry fortified wine with a nutty aroma, delicate almondy flavor, and a velvety texture.

Arinto, Boal, Galego Dourado, Negra Mole, Trincadeira, Torneiro

5–20 years

Quinta dos Pesos

CARTAXO IPR
Map (No. 11)

This flat, fertile area overlaps the Estremadura and Ribatejo regions, producing good, fruity, value-for-money reds and whites.

Arinto, Castelão Nacional, Fernão Pires, Periquita, Preto Martinho, Tinta Amarela (Trincadeira Preta), Trincadeira das Pratas (*syn.* Tamarêz d'Azeitão), Ugni Blanc (*syn.* Tália), Vital

1–3 years

Almeida

CASTELO RODRIGO IPR
Map (No. 12)

These full, spicy reds on the border with Spain, south of the Douro, in the Beiras region, show excellent potential, but have yet to establish an international reputation.

Arinto, Assario Branco (*syn.* Arinto do Dão), Bastardo, Codo, Fonte Cal, Marufo, Rufete, Touriga Nacional

1–3 years (new-wave, fruity style) 2–5 years (others)

Quinta do Cardo

CHAMUSCA IPR
Map (No. 13)

This subappellation of the Ribatejo region is adjacent to Almeirim and produces similar wines, but not quite of the same potential.

Arinto, Castelão Nacional, Fernão Pires,

Periquita, Tinta Amarela (Trincadeira Preta), Trincadeira das Pratas (*syn.* Tamarêz d'Azeitão), Ugni Blanc (*syn.* Tália), Vital

CHAVES IPR
Map (No. 14)

From the upper reaches of the Tâmega River in the Trás-os-Montes VR, this appellation tends to produce a similar but lighter style to that of the Douro DOC.

🍇 Bastardo, Boal, Codega (possibly the same as Roupeiro), Gouveio, Malvasia Fina, Tinta Carvalha, Tinta Amarela

COLARES DOC
Map (No. 15)

This small wine area is famous for its ungrafted Ramisco vines planted in trenches dug out of the sandy dunes of Sintra, which not only protects them from salt-blighting Atlantic winds, but also from the dreaded phylloxera louse. This is a historic wine, but should not be vinified in such an antiquated fashion if it is going to appeal to modern consumers. If the greatest Bordeaux châteaux have moved with the times, why not Colares? The reds are well-colored and full-bodied, but have so much tannin that they are mouth-puckeringly astringent, smoothing out to a silky finish only with great age, when there is no fruit left. If the grapes could be picked according to tannin-ripeness, rather than fruit-ripeness, and more careful fermentation techniques employed, Colares could be world class. The dry whites are traditional *maduro*-style and not recommended.

🍇 Arinto, Jampal, Galego Dourado, Malvasia, Ramisco

🍷 15–30 years (red)

✓ *Antonio Bernardino Paulo da Silva* (Chitas)

CORUCHE IPR
Map (No. 16)

This appellation covers wines made from sandy, well-irrigated plains covering the southern half of the Ribatejo region, but Coruche is seldom encountered and has yet to make its mark.

🍇 Fernão Pires, Periquita, Preto Martinho, Tinta Amarela (Trincadeira Preta), Trincadeira das Pratas (*syn.* Tamarêz d'Azeitão), Ugni Blanc (*syn.* Tália), Vital

COVA DE BEIRA IPR
Map (No. 17)

Located in the Beira Alta, between the Vinho Verde and Dão districts, Cova de Beira is the largest of Portugal's IPRs. As with the Beiras VR, every style of wine is produced in varying quality, but the area is best-known for its lightweight reds.

🍇 Arinto, Assario Branco (*syn.* Arinto do Dão), Jaen, Marufo, Periquita, Pérola, Rabo de Ovelha, Rufete, Tinta Amarela

DÃO DOC
Map (No. 18)

For 20 years there have been rumors that Dão wines have more fruit and less tannin, but only over the past five have we seen this promise fulfilled in the glass, as fruit-filled Dão have begun to emerge.

They have sufficient fruit to drink much earlier than the old-style Dão wines, but have a certain structure and dry, spicy-finesse that expresses their Portuguese origins. The best whites can be clean and fresh, but not yet truly special, although the Quinta de Saes branco is surprisingly good, especially when consumed with food.

🍇 Alfrocheiro Preto, Assario Branco (*syn.* Arinto do Dão), Barcelo, Bastardo, Borrado das Moscas, Cercial, Encruzado, Jaen, Tempranillo (*syn.* Tinta Roriz), Tinta Pinheira, Touriga Nacional, Verdelho

🍷 3–8 years (reds), 1–3 years (whites)

✓ *José Maria da Fonseca* (Garrafeira P) • *Campos da Silva Olivera* • *Casa da Insua* • *Duque de Viseu*

DOURO DOC
Map (No. 19)

Known principally for its port, the Douro Valley in fact makes as much table wine as fortified wine. Because the finest port is produced on schist soils, most table wines are relegated to areas of the region's other dominant soil, granite. I remain surprised that the Syrah, which thrives in the Northern Rhône's hot, granite soil, has not been tried here, even though it has been experimented with in the Alentejo, where there is much less potential for this variety. The Douro's table wine quality potential is highlighted by Barca Velha, Portugal's most expensive table wine, made by Ferreira at Quinta do Vale de Meão, although its second wine, Reserva Especial, is often just as good, if not better. Is it a coincidence that across the Spanish frontier, where the Douro becomes the Duero, Vega Sicilia, Spain's most expensive wine, grows on its banks? There is nothing porty about these table wines, which range from the lighter, claret types to the fuller, richer Burgundian style. New oak is almost *de rigueur* for premium quality wines.

🍇 Bastardo, Donzelinho Branco, Gouveio, Malvasia Fina, Rabigato (probably not the same as Rabigato *syn.* Rabo de Ovelha), Mourisco Tinto, Tempranillo (*syn.* Tinta Roriz), Tinta Amarela, Tinta Barroca, Tinta Cão, Touriga Nacional, Touriga Francesa, Viosinho

🍷 2–10 years (red, but up to 25 for Barca Velha), 1–4 years (white)

✓ *Bright Brothers* • *Ferreirinha* (Barca Velha, Reserva Especial) • *Niepoort* (Redoma and especially Charme Douro) • *Quinta do Côtto* (Grande Escolha) • *Quinta do Crasto* • *Quinta de Passadouro* • *Quinta de la Rosa* • *Quinta do Vale da Raposa* • *Ramos-Pinto* (Duas Quintas) • *Sogrape* (Reserva) • *Vale do Bomfim* (Reserva)

ENCOSTAS DA AIRE IPR
Map (No. 20)

Overlapping the Beiras and Estremadura region, the limestone hills of this appellation should produce some excellent wines, but most have so far been light and rather dried-out.

🍇 Arinto, Baga, Fernão Pires, Periquita, Tamarêz, Tinta Amarela (Trincadeira Preta), Vital

ENCOSTAS DA NAVE IPR
Map (No. 21)

Not to be confused with Encostas da Aire, this is a much smaller appellation, located entirely within the Beiras region, adjacent to Varosa, and its wines are much fuller, resembling those of the Douro immediately north, but have yet to establish themselves.

🍇 Folgosão, Gouveio, Malvasia Fina, Mourisco Tinto, Tinta Barroca, Touriga Francesa, Touriga Nacional

ESTREMADURA VR

From Lisbon, Estremadura stretches north to the Barrada region and encompasses the DOCs of Bucelas, Carcavelos, and Colares, plus the IPRs of Alenquer, Arruda, Óbidos, Torres Vedras, and, in part, Encostas d'Aire (which overlaps Beiras) and Cartaxo (which overlaps Ribatejo). This is Portugal's largest wine-producing region in terms of volume (although Beiras and Alentejo are much larger geographically) and, as such, Estremadura is often perceived as a source of cheap, uninteresting wine. While there are indeed cheap wines made here, they are good guzzlers and far from uninteresting, with a few *quintas* making much finer, more serious wines that are not remotely expensive.

🍇 Alfrocheiro Preto, Antão Vaz, Arinto, Baga, Bastardo, Borrado das Moscas (*syn.* Bical), Cabernet Sauvignon, Camarate (possibly the same as Castelão Nacional), Chardonnay, Esgana Cão, Fernão Pires, Graciano (*syn.* Tinta Miuda), Jampal, Malvasia, Moreto, Periquita, Rabo de Ovelha, Ramisco, Tamarêz, Tinta Amarela (Trincadeira Preta), Trincadeira das Pratas (*syn.* Tamarêz d'Azeitão), Ugni Blanc (*syn.* Tália), Vital

🍷 2–4 years (reds, 4–8 years for better wines), 1–3 years (whites)

✓ *A. C. do Arruda* (selected cuvées) • *A. C. de São Mamede da Ventosa* • *A. C. do Torres Vedras* (selected cuvées) • *Espiga* • *Quinta da Folgorosa* • *Quinta de Pancas* • *Palha Canas*

EVORA IPR
Map (No. 22)

This area of the Alentejo region is destined to be one of Portugal's most exciting appellations, especially for full-bodied, creamy-rich red.

🍇 Aragonez, Arinto, Periquita, Rabo de Ovelha, Roupeiro, Tamarêz, Tinta Caida, Trincadeira

🍷 2–5 years

✓ *Heredat de Cartuxa • Pêra Manca* (*branco*)

GRACIOSA IPR
Map (No. 23)

Rarely encountered light table wines produced on the island of Graciosa in the Azores.

🍇 Arinto, Fernão Pires, Terrantez, Verdelho

GRANJA AMARELEJA IPR
Map (No. 24)

The harsh climate and schistous soils of this subappellation of the Alentejo region can produce powerful, spicy reds, but it has yet to establish itself on export markets.

🍇 Manteudo, Moreto, Periquita, Rabo de Ovelha, Roupeiro, Trincadeira

LAFÕES IPR
Map (No. 25)

Light, acidic, red and white wines produced in a small area straddling the Vinho Verde and Dão regions.

🍇 Amaral, Arinto, Cerceal, Jaen

LAGOA DOC
Map (No. 26)

Formerly known for fortified white wines, which are still made, but are not of interest, this subappellation of the Algarve does not deserve its DOC classification.

🍇 Crato Branco, Negra Mole, Periquita

LAGOS DOC
Map (No. 27)

These Algarve wines do not deserve their DOC classification.

🍇 Boal Branco, Negra Mole, Periquita

MADEIRA DOC
Map (No. 28)

See The styles of Madeira, p.341

MOURA IPR
Map (No. 29)

Cool, red clay soil stretches out the grape's ripening period in this hot patch of the Alentejo, adding a certain finesse to the lush, plump fruit in these wines, which promise great things, but the appellation has not yet established itself.

🍇 Alfrocheiro, Antão Vaz, Fernão Pires, Moreto, Periquita, Rabo de Ovelha, Roupeiro, Trincadeira

OBIDOS IPR
Map (No. 30)

The white wines from this area have traditionally been distilled, but the firm, cedary-oaky reds might have potential.

🍇 Arinto, Bastardo, Camarate (possibly the same as Castelão Nacional), Fernão Pires, Periquita, Rabo de Ovelha, Tinta Miuda, Vital

PALMELA IPR
Map (No. 31)

The Palmela area was first made famous by the João Pires off-dry white made from early-picked Muscat grapes, but it is equally good for full-bodied reds and the inspired, high-volume João Pires now claims the much larger Terras do Sado appellation, as have others, hence there are no recommendations, despite the excellent wines made here.

🍇 Alfrocheiro, Arinto, Fernão Pires, Muscat d'Alexandrie (*syn.* Moscatel de Setúbal), Periquita, Rabo de Ovelha, Tamarêz, Tinta Amarela (*syn.* Espadeiro, but no connection with the Espadeiro of Vinho Verde)

PICO IPR
Map (No. 32)

Rarely encountered fortified wines produced on the island of Pico in the Azores.

🍇 Arinto, Terrantez, Verdelho

PINHEL IPR
Map (No. 33)

In the Beiras region, just south of the Douro, Pinhel makes dry, full, and earthy-tasting white wines, mostly sold to sparkling-wine producers.

🍇 Arinto, Assario Branco (*syn.* Arinto do Dão), Bastardo, Codo, Fonte Cal, Marufo, Rufete, Touriga Nacional

PLANALTO MIRANDÊS IPR
Map (No. 34)

In the Trás-os-Montes region, in the very northeastern corner of Portugal, Planalto Mirandês borders Spain, producing full-bodied reds and heavy whites.

🍇 Bastardo, Gouveio, Malvasia Fina, Mourisco Tinto, Rabo de Ovelha (*syn.* Rabigato), Tinta Amarela, Touriga Francesa, Touriga Nacional, Viosinho

PORT DOC

See The styles of port, p.337

PORTALEGRE DOC
Map (No. 35)

Powerful, yet elegant, spicy reds, and rather heavy, alcoholic whites produced in the Alentejo region, adjacent to the Spanish frontier.

🍇 Aragonez, Arinto, Assário, Fernão Pires, Galego, Grand Noir, Manteudo, Periquita, Roupeiro, Trincadeira

PORTIMÃO DOC
Map (No. 36)

These Algarve wines do not deserve their DOC classification.

🍇 Crato Branco, Negra Mole, Periquita

REDONDO DOC
Map (No. 37)

A subappellation within the progressive Alentejo region, Redondo shows promise for the sort of gushy, upfront, fruity reds that are popping up all over Portugal at grassroots level.

🍇 Aragonez, Fernão Pires, Manteudo, Moreto, Periquita, Rabo de Ovelha, Roupeiro, Tamarez, Trincadeira

🍷 1–3 years

✓ *A. C. de Redondo*

REGUENGOS DOC
Map (No. 38)

An up-and-coming DOC in the Alentejo, Reguengos is already producing both gluggy and much finer reds, plus increasingly good whites, making it an appellation to watch.

🍇 Aragonez, Manteudo, Moreto, Periquita, Perrum, Rabo de Ovelha, Roupeiro, Trincadeira

🍷 1–3 years (new-wave, fruity style), 2–5 years (others)

✓ *A. C. de Reguengos* (tinto) • *J. P. Vinhos* (Quinta da Anfora)

RIBATEJO VR

This large province is sandwiched between Estremadura and Alentejo, and includes the following IPRs: Almeirim, Cartaxo (in part), Chamusca, Coruche, Santarém, Tomar, and Valada do Ribatejo. The temperate climate and rich alluvial plains of the Tagus River encourage high yields, making this the second most important wine region in Portugal. Some very good wines are made by those who restrict yields, particularly by Peter Bright in collaboration with the Fuiza family's vineyards.

🍇 Arinto, Cabernet Sauvignon, Camarate (possibly the same as Castelão Nacional), Carignan, Chardonnay, Esgana Cão, Fernão Pires, Jampal, Malvasia Fina, Malvasia Rei (possibly the same as Palomino), Merlot, Periquita, Pinot Noir, Rabo de Ovelha, Sauvignon, Syrah, Tamarêz, Tinta Amarela (Trincadeira Preta), Tinta Miuda, Touriga Nacional, Trincadeira das Pratas (*syn* Tamarêz d'Azeitão), Ugni Blanc (*syn.* Tália), Vital

🍷 1–5 years (reds), 1–3 years (whites)

✓ *Bright Brothers • Falua • Fuiza • Quinta da Lagoalva • Terra de Lobos*

RIOS DO MINHO VR

A sort of *vin de pays* Vinhos Verdes, except that this appellation also allows for still table wines from foreign varieties. Predictably lightweight.

🍇 Alvarinho, Arinto (*syn.* Paderna), Avesso, Azal Branco, Azal Tinto, Batoca, Borracal, Brancelho (*syn.* Alvarelho), Cabernet Sauvignon, Chardonnay, Espadeiro, Loureiro, Merlot, Padreiro de Basto, Pedral, Rabo de Ovelha, Riesling, Trajadura, Vinhão (possibly the same as Sousão)

SANTARÉM IPR
Map (No. 39)

A new appellation for the area around the capital of the Ribatejo region, Santarém should begin to establish itself over the next few years.

🍇 Arinto, Castelão Nacional, Fernão Pires, Periquita, Preto Martinho, Rabo de Ovelha, Tinta Amarela (Trincadeira Preta), Trincadeira das Pratas (*syn.* Tamarêz d'Azeitão), Ugni Blanc (*syn.* Tália), Vital

SETÚBAL DOC
Moscatel de Setúbal
Map (No. 40)

This style of fortified Muscat wine is believed to have been created by José-Maria da Fonseca, the old-established company that still has a quasi-monopoly over its production today. There are various wood-aged styles (5- or 6-Year-Old is best for freshness and the grapey-apricoty varietal character, while 20- or 25-Year-Old is darker and far more complex with a raisiny-nutty-caramel-apricoty intensity), but single-vintage Setúbal is top of the range.

🍇 Muscat d'Alexandrie (*syn.* Moscatel de Setúbal), Moscatel do Douro, Moscatel Roxo plus up to 30 percent Arinto, Boais, Diagalves, Fernão Pires, Malvasia, Olho de Lebre, Rabo de Ovelha, Roupeiro, Tália, Tamarêz, Vital

🍷 Upon purchase (but will last many years)

✓ *J. M. Fonseca*

TAVIRA DOC
Map (No. 41)

These Algarve wines do not deserve their DOC classification.

🍇 Crato Branco, Negra Mole, Periquita

TERRAS DO SADO VR

Probably the most clever appellation the Portuguese could conjure up, Terras do Sado covers a fairly large area fanning out from the Sado estuary far beyond the Setúbal peninsula, where a good many innovative wines originated, but their development had been threatened by the urban sprawl south of Lisbon. If such wines take up the Terras do Sado appellation, they can be sourced from a much wider area. João Pires, Periquita, Quinta de Camarate, and Quinta da Bacalhôa have all claimed this humble VR status without it affecting the prices they command, which has made Terras do Sado an attractive appellation for future new wines.

🍇 **RED** At least 50 percent Aragonez, Cabernet Sauvignon, Merlot, Moscatel Roxo, Periquita (Castelão Francês), Tinta Amarela (Trincadeira Preta) and Touriga Nacional, plus up to 50 percent Alfrocheiro Preto, Alicante Bouschet, Bastardo, Carignan, Grand Noir, Monvedro, Moreto, Tinto Miuda

🍇 **WHITE** At least 50 percent Arinto, Chardonnay, Fernão Pires, Malvasia Fina, Muscat d'Alexandrie (*syn.* Moscatel de Setúbal) and Roupeiro, plus up to 50 percent Antão Vaz, Esgana Cão, Sauvignon, Rabo de Ovelha, Trincadeira das Pratas (*syn.* Tamarêz d'Azeitão), Ugni Blanc (*syn.* Tália)

🍷 1–3 years (new-wave style), 2–5 years (others)

✓ *J. M. Fonseca* (João Pires, Periquita, Quinta de Camarate Tinto) • *J. P. Vinhos* (Quinta da Bacalhôa, Cova da Ursa)

TOMAR IPR
Map (No. 42)

Red and white wines grown on limestone slopes of the right bank of the Tagus River in the Ribatejo region.

🍇 Arinto, Baga, Castelão Nacional, Fernão Pires, Malvasia, Periquita, Rabo de Ovelha, Ugni Blanc (*syn.* Tália)

TORRES VEDRAS IPR
Map (No. 43)

Originally called simply "Torres" until Miguel Torres objected, these high-yielding vineyards in the Estremadura region of Portugal have traditionally supplied the largest producers with bulk wines for their high-volume branded *vinho de mesa*.

🍇 Arinto, Camarate (possibly the same as Castelão Nacional), Fernão Pires, Graciano (*syn.* Tinta Miuda), Jampal, Mortágua, Periquita, Rabo de Ovelha, Seara Nova, Vital

TRÁS-OS-MONTES VR

The province of Trás-os-Montes is situated in northeastern Portugal, and encompasses the IPRs of Chaves, Valpaços, and Planalto-Mirandés. The style of wine ranges from light-bodied in the higher altitude vineyards to full-bodied and alcoholic in the south. But the most important wine made in terms of volume is semisweet, semi sparkling *rosado*.

🍇 Bastardo, Cabernet Franc, Cabernet Sauvignon, Chardonnay, Donzelinho, Gewürztraminer, Gouveio, Malvasia Fina, Merlot, Mourisco Tinto, Pinot Noir, Rabo de Ovelha (*syn.* Rabigato), Sauvignon Blanc, Sémillon, Tempranillo (*syn.* Tinta Roriz), Tinta Amarela, Tinta Barroca, Tinta Cão, Touriga Francesa, Touriga Nacional, Viosinho

🍷 1–3 years (new-wave style), 2–5 years (others)

✓ *Casal de Valle Pradinhos* • *Quintas dos Bons Ares*

VALPAÇOS IPR
Map (No. 44)

Firm reds and slightly *petillant* rosés from the upper reaches of the Tua, a tributary of the Douro, in the Trás-os-Montes region.

🍇 Bastardo, Boal, Codega (possibly the same as Roupeiro), Cornifesto, Fernão Pires, Gouveio, Malvasia Fina, Mourisco Tinto, Rabo de Ovelha (*syn.* Rabigato), Tempranillo (*syn.* Tinta Roriz), Tinta Amarela, Tinta Carvalha, Touriga Francesa, Touriga Nacional

VAROSA IPR
Map (No. 45)

Like Pinhel, this Beiras subappellation has yet to establish a reputation above that of being a traditional source of base wines for the sparkling-wine industry.

🍇 Alvarelhão, Arinto, Borrado das Moscas, Cercial, Chardonnay, Fernão Pires, Folgosão, Gouveio, Malvasia Fina, Pinot Blanc, Pinot Noir, Tempranillo (*syn.* Tinta Roriz), Tinta Barroca, Touriga Francesa, Touriga Nacional

VIDIGUEIRA DOC
Map (No. 46)

This appellation takes its name from one of three towns around which vineyards flourish on volcanic soils, while the name of the town itself is derived from the word *videira*, meaning "wine," illustrating how long vines have been growing in this part of the Alentejo.

🍇 Alfrocheiro, Antão Vaz, Manteudo, Moreto, Periquita, Perrum, Rabo de Ovelha, Roupeiro, Trincadeira

VINHO VERDE DOC

The vines literally grow on trees, up telephone poles, and along fences—on anything that takes them above the ground. Training the vine in such a way enables the smallholders—and there are more than 60,000 of them in the Minho—to grow the cabbages, corn, and beans that the families survive on, and to produce grapes, which are either sold to large wineries or made into wine locally and sold to tourists. Genuine Vinho Verde is sharp, may be slightly fizzy, but should always be totally dry, either delicately or raspingly dry, depending primarily on the grape varieties used. The best two grape varieties are Alvarinho and Loureiro. The Alvarinho is a low-cropping variety that is more at home in the northern part of the Minho, between the Lima Valley and the Spanish border. It produces the most substantial Vinhos Verdes, with alcohol levels of 12.5 percent ABV, compared to the norm of 9.5–10 percent. Palácio da Brejoeira is the yardstick for this grape, and widely considered to be a class apart from any other Vinho Verde. The Loureiro is a heavier-cropping variety, producing aromatic wines. Vinhão is the most successful grape for red Vinho Verde, followed by Azal Tinto and Espadeiro, and the best examples of these deep-purple wines have a peppery smack to them, even if it is quickly washed down the throat in a fizzy rush.

🍇 Alvarinho, Arinto (*syn.* Paderna), Avesso, Azal, Azal Tinto, Brancelho (*syn.* Alvarelho), Borracal, Espadeiro, Loureiro, Perdal, Trajadura, Vinhão (possibly the same as Sousão)

🍷 Upon purchase (9–18 months maximum)

✓ **Red single-quintas** *Casa do Valle* • *Ponte de Lima*

White single-quintas *Casa de Sezim* • *Morgadio de Torre* • *Palácio da Brejoeira* • *Ponte de Lima* • *Quinta de Azevedo* • *Quinta de Franqueira* • *Quinta da Tamariz* • *Solar de Bouças*

White commercial blends *Cepa Velha* (Alvarinho) • *Chello* • *Gazela* • *Grinalda*

PORT: THE DOURO VALLEY

*No two neighboring districts could produce wines
of more contrasting styles than the deep-colored,
rich, sweet, warm, and spicy fortified port of
Portugal's Douro Valley, and the light, water-
white, sharply dry, semi-sparkling Vinho Verde
of the Minho region.*

"IT SHOULD FEEL LIKE liquid fire in the stomach... it should burn
like inflamed gunpowder... should have the tint of ink... it should be
like the sugar of Brazil in sweetness and the spices of India in
aromatic flavor." Written in 1754 by the agents for the Association
of Port Wine Shippers, such vivid accounts of port remain a fair
description of the great after-dinner wine we know today.

THE ORIGIN OF PORT
It is hard to imagine how such a wonderful winter-warming drink
as port could ever have been conceived in such a hot and sunny
country as Portugal. Popular belief has it that it was not the
Portuguese but the British who were responsible for port;
however, this is not entirely accurate. We can thank the
Portuguese for dreaming up this most classic of fortified
wines; the British merely capitalized on their original idea.

In 1678, two Englishmen were sent by a Liverpool wine
merchant to Viana do Castello, north of Oporto, to learn the
wine business. Vacationing up the Douro River, they
were regally entertained by the Abbot of Lamego.
Finding his wine "very agreeable, sweetish,
and extremely smooth," they asked what
made it exceptional among all others
tasted on their journey. The Abbot

confessed to doctoring the wine with brandy, but the Englishmen
were so pleased with the result this had that they purchased the
entire stock and shipped it home.

THE ORIGIN OF THE PORT TRADE
The ancient house of C. N. Kopke & Co. had been trading in
Douro wines for nearly 40 years by the time the above encounter
took place. Eight years before they stumbled upon the Abbot of
Lamego, another Englishman named John Clark was busy building
up a business that would become Warre & Co. In 1678, the same
year as the encounter, Croft & Co. was established, and this was
followed by Quarles Harris in 1680 and Taylor's in 1692. By the
time the Methuen Treaty of 1703 gave Portuguese wines
preferential rates of duty in Britain, many British firms had set up
business in Oporto. Firms of other nationalities—Dutch, German,
and French—followed, but it was the British shippers who virtually
monopolized the trade, frequently abusing their power. In 1755, the
Marquis of Pombal, who had assumed almost dictatorial powers
over Portugal some five years before, put a curb on their activities
through the Board of Trade. The privileges enjoyed by British
merchants under two 100-year-old treaties were restricted. He also
established the Oporto Wine Company, endowing it with the sort
of powers to which the British had been accustomed.

This infuriated the British, but their protests were to no avail
and Pombal went on to instigate many worthy, if unpopular,
reforms, including limiting the Douro's production area
to the finest vineyards, the banning of elderberries for
coloring the wine, and the outlawing of manure, which
reduced yields but greatly improved quality.

THE DOURO AND THE MINHO. *see also* p.328
*These two northern areas produce the celebrated port and Vinho
Verde. The Douro River has long been crucial to the port trade.*

●	Quintas
	Intensive vine-growing zone
	Vinho Verde
	Port
–·–·–	International boundary
——	*Provincial* boundary
▲	Height above sea level (meters)

GRAPE PICKERS NEAR
AMARANTE, SOUTHERN MINHO
*Grape pickers use ladders with
buckets attached to them to harvest
the overhead bunches.*

PORT GRAPE VARIETIES

There are 48 grape varieties permitted in the production of port. This simple fact goes a long way to explaining the great variation in quality and character of ports within the same basic style. The official classification of the grapes is as follows:

VERY GOOD BLACK GRAPES
Bastardo, Donzelinho Tinto, Mourisco, Tinta Cão, Tinta Francisca, Tinta Roriz, Touriga Francesa, Touriga Nacional

GOOD BLACK GRAPES
Cornifesto, Malvasia Preta, Mourisco de Semente, Periquita, Rufete, Samarrinho, Sousão, Tinta Amarela, Tinta da Barca, Tinta Barroca, Tinta Carvalha, Touriga Brasileira

AVERAGE BLACK GRAPES
Alvarelhão, Avesso, Casculho, Castela, Coucieira, Moreto, Tinta Bairrada, Tinto Martins

VERY GOOD WHITE GRAPES
Donzelinho, Esgana Cão, Folgosão, Gouveio (or Verdelho), Malvasia Fina, Malvasia Rei, Rabigato, Viosinho

GOOD WHITE GRAPES
Arinto, Boal, Cercial, Côdega, Malvasia Corada, Moscatel Galego

AVERAGE WHITE GRAPES
Branco sem Nome, Fernão Pires, Malvasia Parda, Pedernã, Praça, Touriga Branca

THE SIX BEST PORT GRAPE VARIETIES
The six port grape varieties currently considered by growers and winemakers to be the best are:

Touriga Nacional
Almost universally agreed to be the very best of all port grapes, this has tiny berries and produces pitch-black wine with intense aromatic properties, great extract, and high tannin content. It prefers hotter situations, but is a poor pollinator and does not yield a large crop. Cloning is underway to increase production by 15 percent and sugar content by 10 percent, the most successful clone so far being R110.

Tinta Cão
This variety can add finesse and complexity to a blend, but it enjoys a cooler environment and requires training on wires to produce a decent crop. Since traditional cultivation methods make it a poor producer, growers are not overly eager to cultivate it; the grape's survival will depend upon the willingness of port shippers to maintain the variety on their large, managed estates.

Tinta Roriz
Not really a member of the Tinta family, this grape is sometimes simply called the Roriz. It is, in fact, the well-known Spanish variety, Tempranillo, the mainstay of Rioja. In the Douro it likes heat and fares best on the sunniest front rows of terraces cut into south- or west-

facing slopes. Its dark grapes have thick skins, high sugar content, and low acidity, providing great color, tannin, and succulence in a blend. Some believe this to be better than the Touriga Nacional.

Tinta Barroca
The wine produced by this grape variety is quite precocious and is therefore useful in younger drinking ports, or to dilute wines that are too tannic and distinctive. Like Tinta Cão, this grape variety prefers cooler situations and particularly enjoys north facing slopes.

Touriga Francesa
A member of the Touriga family, this grape has no connection with the similarly named Tinta Francisca, a member of the Tinta family. According to Bruce Guimaraens of Fonseca and Taylor's, this high-quality variety is useful for "filling in the gaps" in vineyards between those areas occupied by vines that like either hot or cool situations. It gives fruit and aroma to a blend.

Tinta Amarela
This grape variety is dark-colored and very productive. Its importance has been on the increase in recent years. As this high-quality vine is susceptible to rot, it performs best in the hottest, driest areas.

FACTORS AFFECTING TASTE AND QUALITY

LOCATION
Port is made in the Cima Corgo, Baixo Corgo, and Douro Superior districts of the Douro Valley in the north of Portugal.

CLIMATE
The summers are dry and hot, the winters mild and wet, becoming more continental in the upper Douro Valley, where the summers are extremely hot, rainfall is high—20½ inches (52 centimeters)—and winters can be very cold.

ASPECT
Vines are planted on generally hilly land that becomes very steep in some parts.

SOIL
The Douro is a patchwork of hard, sun-baked, granite, and schist soils, with the finest ports originating from the schist vineyards

that dominate upriver. Because of the importance of schist to port production, Douro table wines are relegated to granite soils.

VITICULTURE AND VINIFICATION
Terracing in the Douro is widespread to maximize the use of the land, although the current trend is to make wider terraces, thus enabling mechanization. Some of the less precipitous slopes are now cultivated in vertical rows. Steep terraces mean labor-intensive viticulture, and the hard Douro soil often requires blasting to enable planting. Port wines are made and fortified in the Douro, but most are blended and bottled at lodges in Vila Nova de Gaia.

GRAPE VARIETIES
See Port Grape Varieties, left

by the British. It is even possible to generalize about the stylistic difference between the wines of British- and Portuguese-owned port houses. The British tend to go for bigger, darker, sweeter, fruit-driven wines and have made vintage port their particular niche, while the Portuguese opt for lighter, elegant, more mellow styles, the best of which are exquisitely aged tawnies. At one time, some Portuguese houses rarely even declared a vintage, since they focused on tawny. When they did, the wines were so much lighter in style that export countries often dismissed them as inferior. Although a few were indeed inferior, many were just different. Now, of course, world markets demand that if they are to survive, the Portuguese houses must declare vintages as often as British-owned houses.

When considering stylistic differences between vintage port and the lighter, tawny styles, it is probably more accurate to categorize the fuller, fatter vintage port as North European, not simply British, because this style is also preferred by Dutch, German, and French port houses.

HOW PORT IS MADE
If any wine is perceived as having been "trodden," then it is port. This is perhaps because the pressing and winemaking traditionally takes place in the vineyards where, until relatively recently, affairs

The production of port had not been perfected at this time. Fifty years after the encounter with the Abbot of Lamego, the industry had widely accepted the practice of brandying, but the importance of when, and in what quantity, to administer the brandy had not been recognized. Ironically, the Abbot's wine was superior because he had added the brandy during, and not after, the fermentation, thus interrupting, or "muting," the process with the natural sweetness that had so attracted the two Englishmen. Even after several centuries, the port business is still dominated

THE HISTORIC BARCO RABELO
Based on the Viking warship, these flat-bottomed boats, loaded with pipes of port, would sail for Oporto on the hazardous journey from the upper Douro.

were conducted on farms in a rather rustic style. Today, few ports are trodden, although several houses have showpiece *lagars*—troughs used for crushing grapes—for tourists. Many houses have

THE QUINTA CLASSIFICATION

A *quinta* is a wine-producing estate or vineyard. The Douro Valley covers 600,000 acres (243,000 hectares), of which 82,000 acres (33,000 hectares) are cultivated. Within this area, there are approximately 80,000 individual vineyards or *quintas* owned by 29,620 growers. Each vineyard is classified according to a points system allocated for the categories listed below. The better the classification, the higher official price a vineyard receives for its grapes and the greater its permitted production.

CATEGORY	MINIMUM	MAXIMUM
Location	-50	+600
Aspect	1,000	+250
Altitude; lowest is best	(-900)	(+150)
Gradient; steepest is best	(-100)	(+100)
Soil	(-350)	(+100)
Schist	(N/A)	(+100)
Granite	(-350)	(N/A)
Mixture	(-150)	(N/A)
Microclimate; sheltered is best	0+	60
Vine varieties; official classification	-300	+150
Age of vines; oldest is best	0	+60
Vine density; lowest is best	-50	+50
Productivity; lowest is best	-900	+120
Vineyard maintenance	-500	+100
Total	**-3,150**	**+1,490**

Vineyards are classified from **A**, for best, to **F**, for worst, as follows: • **Class A** (1,200 points or more); **Class B** (1,001–1,199 points); **Class C** (801–1,000 points); **Class D** (601–800 points); **Class E** (400–600 points); **Class F** (400 points or below).

CLASS A

Aciprestes (Royal Oporto), *Atayde* (Cockburn), *Bomfin* (Dow), *Bom-Retiro* (Ramos-Pinto), *Carvalhas* (Royal Oporto), *Carvalheira* (Calem & Filho), *Boa vista* (Offley Forrester), *Corte* (privately owned, managed by Delaforce), *Corval* (Royal Oporto), *Cruzeiro St. Antonio* (Guimaraens), *Cavadinha* (Warre), *Eira Velha* (privately owned, managed by Cockburn), *Ervamoira* (Ramos-Pinto), *Fontela* (Cockburn), *Fonte Santa* (Kopke), *Foz* (Calem & Filho), *La Rosa* (privately owned), *Lobata* (Barros, Almeida), *Madalena* (Warre), *Malvedos* (Graham), *Mesquita* (Barroa, Almeida), *Monte Bravo* (privately owned, managed by Dow), *Nova* (privately owned, managed by Warre), *Panascal* (Guimaraens), *Passa Douro* (Sandeman), *Sagrado* (Càlem & Filho), *Santo Antonio* (Càlem & Filho), *Sibio* (Royal Oporto), *St Luiz* (Kopke), *Terra Feita* (Taylor's), *Tua* (Cockburn), *Vale de Mendiz* (Sandeman), *Vale Dona Maria* (Smith Woodhouse), *Vargellas* (Taylor's), *Vedial* (Càlem & Filho), *Zimbro* (privately owned, managed by Dow)

CLASS A-B

Aradas (Noval), *Avidagos* (Da Silva), *Casa Nova* (Borges & Irmao), *Ferra dosa* (Borges & Irmao), *Hortos* (Borges & Irmao), *Junco* (Borges & Irmao), *Leda* (Ferreira), *Marco* (Noval), *Meao* (Ferreira family), *Noval* (Noval), *Porto*

(Ferreira), *Roeda* (Croft), *Seixo* (Ferreira), *Silho* (Borges & Irmao), *Silval* (Noval), *Soalheira* (Borges & Irmao), *Urqueiras* (Noval), *Velho Roncao* (Pocas), *Vezuvio* (Symington family)

CLASS B

Carvoeira (Barros, Almeida), *Dona Matilde* (Barros, Almeida), *Laranjeira* (Sandeman), *San Domingos* (Ramos-Pinto), *Urtiga* (Ramos-Pinto)

CLASS B-C

Sta Barbara (Pocas)

CLASS C

Porrais (Ferreira family), *Quartas* (Pocas), *Valado* (Ferreira family)

CLASS C AND D

Sidro (Royal Oporto)

CLASS C, D AND E

Granja (Royal Oporto)

CLASS D

Casal (Sandeman), *Confradeiro* (Sandeman)

CLASS NOT DISCLOSED

Agua Alta (Churchill), *Alegria* (Santos), *Cachão* (Messias), *Côtto* (Champalimaud), *Crasto* (privately owned), *Fojo* (privately owned), *Forte* (Delaforce), *Infantado* (privately owned), *Rosa* (privately owned), *Val de Figueria* (Càlem & Filho), *Vau* (Sandeman)

"autovinificators"—rather antiquated devices that rely on the build-up of carbonic gas pressure given off during fermentation to force the juice up and over the *manta* (cap) of grape skins. The object is to extract the maximum amount of coloring matter from the skins, because so much is lost by fortification. It is possible also to achieve this using special vats and several have been installed throughout the port industry.

FERMENTATION AND FORTIFICATION

The initial fermentation phase of port differs little from that in the rest of the world, except that vinification temperatures are often as high as 90°F (32°C). This has no detrimental effect on port, and in fact probably accounts for its chocolaty, high-pH complexity. When a level of about 6 to 8 percent alcohol has been achieved, the wine is fortified, unlike sherry, for which the fermentation process is allowed to complete its natural course. Port derives its sweetness from unfermented sugars, whereas sweet sherries are totally dry wines to which a syrupy concentrate is added. The timing of the addition of brandy is dependent upon the sugar reading, not the alcohol level. When the sweetness of the fermenting juice has dropped to approximately 90 grams per liter of sugar , the alcoholic strength will normally be between 6 and 8 percent, but this varies according to the richness of the juice, which in turn is dependent upon the grape variety, where it is grown, and the year.

The use of the word "brandy" is somewhat misleading. It is not, in fact, brandy, but a clear, flavorless, grape-distilled spirit of 77 percent alcohol, known in Portugal as *aguardente*. It adds alcoholic strength to a port, but not aroma or flavor. *Aguardente* is produced either from wines made in southern Portugal or from excess production in the Douro itself. Its price and distribution to each shipper are strictly rationed. On average 29 gallons (110 liters) is added for every 116 gallons (440 liters) of wine, making a total of 145 gallons (550 liters)—the capacity of a Douro pipe, a specific size of cask used for shipping wine from the valley to the lodges at Vila Nova de Gaia. A drier port has a slightly longer fermentation and requires less than 26 gallons (100 liters) of *aguardente*, while a particularly sweet (or *geropiga*) port is muted with as much as 36 gallons (135 liters). If gauged correctly, the brandy which has been added to arrest the fermentation will eventually harmonize with the fruit and the natural sweetness of the wine. Our conception of balance between fruit, alcohol, and sweetness is, of course, greatly affected by what we are used to drinking. In deepest Douro a local farmer is likely to use a far higher proportion of alcohol for port he intends to drink himself than for the port he makes for export. Generally, British shippers prefer more fruit and less brandy, but all commercial shippers, British or Portuguese, would consider the domestic port of a Douro farmer to lack sufficient body to match the brandy.

MATURATION AND BLENDING

Until 1986, all port had by law to be matured and bottled at Vila Nova de Gaia on the left bank of the Douro estuary opposite Oporto. At some 47 miles (75 kilometers) from the region of production, this was like insisting that all Champagne be blended, bottled, and disgorged at Le Havre. The law bestowing Vila Nova de Gaia was made in 1756 and it was ostensibly created by and for the big shippers, as it effectively prevented small growers from exporting their wine, since they could not possibly afford the expense of a lodge at Vila Nova de Gaia. By the late 18th century, most of the famous port names were already established, and this restrictive law enabled them to maintain the status quo, especially on the lucrative international markets. All this has changed, and though most ports still come from the big shippers' lodges, many new ports now find their way on to the market directly from privately owned Douro *quintas*.

THE STYLES OF
PORT

Note With the exception of white port, there are just two basic styles from which all variants stem: ruby and tawny. What distinguishes these two styles is bottle-aging for rubies and cask-aging for tawnies.

WHITE PORT

Most dry white ports taste like flabby sherry, but there are some interesting sweet ones such as Ferreira's Superior White, which is creamy-soft and delicious. Truly sweet white port is often labeled Lagrima. Niepoort pure Moscatel can make an nice alternative to Moscatel de Setúbal.

🍷— Upon purchase

⋈/ *Ferreira's Superior White*

BASIC RUBY PORT

The cheapest red ports are rubies with less than a year in cask and often no time at all. Sold soon after bottling, they do not improve if kept. Inexpensive rubies have a basic, pepper-grapey flavor that can be quite fiery. Superior-quality wines are blended from various vintages with up to four years in cask, giving a more homogenous taste, though they should still have the fruity-spice and warmth of a young ruby.

🍷— Upon purchase

⋈/ *Cockburn's (Special Reserve)* • *Fonseca (Bin 27)* • *Graham's (Six Grapes)* • *Quinta de la Rosa (Finest Reserve)* • *Warre's (Warrior)*

CRUSTED PORT *or* CRUSTING PORT

The greatest nonvintage ruby port, this is a blend of very high-quality wines from two or more years, given up to four years in cask and, ideally, at least three years in bottle. Like vintage, it throws a deposit in bottle, hence the name. Ready to drink when purchased, providing it is carefully decanted, crusting port benefits from acclimatizing to new storage conditions, when it will shed further sedimentation before resuming the much slower process of maturation.

🍷— 1–10 years

⋈/ *Churchill's* • *Martinez* • *Smith Woodhouse*

LATE BOTTLED VINTAGE PORT (LBV)

A late-bottled vintage is a pure vintage port from a good, but not necessarily great, year. LBVs are usually made in lighter, generally undeclared years. Lighter, more precocious vintages are usually chosen for this less expensive category, and the wines are given between four and six years in cask to bring them on even quicker. LBVs are thus ready for drinking when sold, but will continue to improve in bottle for another five or six years.

🍷— 5–10 years

⋈/ *Burmester* • *Churchill's* • *Graham's* • *Quinta de la Rosa* • *Ramos-Pinto* • *Smith Woodhouse* • *Warre's*

SINGLE-QUINTA PORT

A wine from a single vineyard, this may be a classic vintage port from an established house or a special release from an undeclared vintage.

Most single-*quinta* ports are as accessible as LBV because, after bottling, the wines are stored until more or less ready to drink. Many single-*quinta* and LBV ports are the same age, although the former is aged longer *after* bottling, while the latter is aged longer *before*. With interest in these ports increasing, the change in the law allowing port to be matured at the *quintas*, and the fact that individual domaine wines are seen as more prestigious, this category could one day become more esteemed than vintage port itself.

🍷— 8–25 years

⋈/ *Cálem (Quinta de Foz)* • *Champalimaud (Quinta do Cotto)* • *Churchill's (Quinta de Agua Alta)* • *Ferreira (Quinta do Seixo)* • *Fonseca (Quinta do Panascal)* • *Niepoort (Quinta do Passadouro)* • *Quinta de la Rosa* • *Quinta de Vesuvio* • *Quinta do Noval* • *Quinta do Sagrado* • *Ramos-Pinto (Quinta da Urtiga)* • *Taylor's (Quinta de Vargellas)* • *Warre's (Quinta da Cavadinha)*

VINTAGE CHARACTER PORT

The suggestion that these wines, blended from various years and matured in cask for up to four years, have a "vintage" character is misleading. They may be fine ports, but the character is that of a genuine fine old ruby, not a vintage port.

🍷— Upon purchase

⋈/ *Cálem* • *Churchill's* • *Ferreira* • *Royal Oporto (The Navigator's)* • *Sandeman's (Signature)*

VINTAGE PORT

By law, a vintage port must be bottled within two years. Maturation in bottle is more reductive than cask-aging and the wine that results has a certain fruitiness that will not be found in any fine old tawny. When mature, a fine vintage port is a unique taste experience with a heady bouquet and a sultry flavor. A warming feeling seems to follow the wine down the throat—more an "afterglow" than an aftertaste. The grape and spirit are totally integrated and the palate is near to bursting with warm, spicy-fruit flavors.

🍷— 12–30 years (but see individual producers)

⋈/ *Churchill's* • *Champalimaud (Quinta do Cotto)* • *Ferreira* • *Fonseca* • *Fonseca Guimaraens* • *Gould Campbell* • *Niepoort* • *Quinta do Noval (especially Nacional)* • *Taylor's*

AGED TAWNY PORT

These 10-, 20-, 30-Year-Old and Over 40 Years Old ports are traditionally known as "fine old tawnies" (FOT), but like fine old rubies, there are no legal requirements. By constant racking over a period of 10, 20, or more years, port fades to a tawny color, falls bright, and will throw no further deposit. It assumes a smooth, silky texture, a voluptuous, mellow, nutty flavor, and complex after-aromas that can include freshly ground coffee, caramel, chocolate, raisins, nutmeg, and cinnamon. The years are merely an indication of age; in theory, a 20-Year-Old tawny could be just a year old, if it could fool the Port Wine Institute. In practice, most blends probably have an age close to that

indicated. Most tawny port experts find 20-Year-Old the ideal tawny, but 30- and Over 40 Years Old tawnies are not necessarily past it. The only relatively negative aspect of a good 30- or Over 40 Years Old is that it will be more like a liqueur than a port.

🍷— Upon purchase

⋈/ **10-Year-Old** *Cálem* • *Churchill's* • *Cockburn's* • *Croft* • *Dow's* • *Ferreira (Quinta do Porto)* • *Fonseca* • *Graham's* • *Niepoort* • *Offley (Baron Forrester)* • *Ramos-Pinto* • *Robertson's (Pyramid)* • *Smith Woodhouse* • *Taylor's* • *Warre's (Sir William)*

20-Year-Old *Barros Almeida* • *Burmester* • *Cálem* • *Cockburn's* • *Croft (Director's Reserve)* • *Dow's* • *Ferreira (Duque de Bragança)* • *Fonseca* • *Graham's* • *Niepoort* • *Noval* • *Offley (Baron Forrester)* • *Robertson's (Private Reserve)* • *Sandeman (Imperial)* • *Taylor's*

30-Year-Old *Cálem* • *Croft* • *Dow's* • *Fonseca* • *Niepoort* • *Ramos-Pinto*

Over 40 Years Old *Cálem* • *Fonseca* • *Graham's* • *Noval* • *Taylor's*

BASIC TAWNY PORT

These are often a blend of red and white ports. Some skillful blends can be very good and have even the most experienced port-tasters guessing whether they are tawny by definition or blending. On the whole it is wise to pay more to ensure you are buying an authentically aged product. The best tawnies are usually eight years old, although this is seldom indicated.

🍷— Upon purchase

⋈/ *Delaforce (His Eminence's Choice)* • *Dow's (Boardroom)* • *Warre's (Nimrod)*

SINGLE QUINTA TAWNY PORT

Although most single-vineyard ports are vintage and ruby in style, some are made as tawny, either with an indicated age or vintage-dated.

🍷— Upon purchase

⋈/ **10-Year-Old:** *Quinta do Sagrado* • *Ramos Pinto (Quinta da Ervamoira)*

20-Year-Old: *Ramos-Pinto (Quinta do Bom-Retiro)*

Vintage-Dated: *Borges' Quinta do Junco*

VINTAGE-DATED TAWNY *or* COLHEITA PORT

These excellent-value, often sublime, cask-aged wines are from a single vintage, and may have 20 or 50 years in cask. They must not be confused with the plumper, fruitier vintage ports. There should be an indication of when the wine was bottled or a term such as "Matured in Wood." Some vintage ports are simply labeled "vintage" and tawnies "Colheita." Other clues are "Reserve," "Reserva," or "Bottled in" dates.

🍷— Upon purchase

⋈/ *Barros Almeida* • *Burmester* • *Cálem* • *Offley (Baron Forrester)* • *Niepoort* • *Noval*

THE WINE PRODUCERS OF
THE DOURO VALLEY

Note The age range for "when to drink" refers to the optimal enjoyment of vintage ports and appears only when this style is recommended. When the entire range is recommended, this includes all wines with the exception of the most basic ruby and tawny or any white port, unless otherwise stated.

BARROS
Barros Almeida
★ ❷

Manuel de Barros started work as an office boy at Almeida & Co., ending up not only owning the company, but also building a port empire, as he and his descendants took over Douro Wine Shippers and Growers, Feist, Feuerheerd, Hutcheson, Kopke, Santos Junior, and Viera de Sousa. Only Kopke and Barros Almeida itself retain any form of independence, and the others have become little more than brands.

✓ *20-Year-Old Tawny • Vintage-Dated Tawny • Colheitas*

BORGES & IRMÃO
✖

Established in 1884, the Portuguese-owned house of Borges & Irmão is best known for its Soalheira 10-Year-Old and Roncão 20-Year-Old Tawnies, but the quality of their port has suffered under a lack of direction from Portuguese government ownership.

BURMESTER
★ ❷

Of Anglo-German origin, Burmester is an underrated house that is best for mature tawny styles, but also makes good vintage.

✓ *Late-Bottled • Vintage • 20-Year-Old Tawny • Colheitas • Vintage*

CÁLEM
★

Cálem was established in 1859 and today is still owned by the Cálem family, which consistently produces elegant tawny, single-*quinta*, and vintage port.

🍷 15–25 years

✓ *10-, 20-, 30-, and 40-Year-Old Tawny • Vintage Character • Quinta de Foz • Vintage*

CHAMPALIMAUD
Quinta do Cotto
★ ★

Although Miguel Montez Champalimaud can trace his family's viticultural roots in the Douro Valley back to the 13th century, he did not produce his first port until 1982, when it became the world's first estate-bottled single-*quinta* port, making him the fastest-rising star among the new wave of privately owned grower ports.

🍷 12–25 years

✓ *Quinta do Cotto*

CHURCHILL'S
★★★

Established in 1981 by Johnny Graham, a member of the Graham's port family who was married to Caroline (*née* Churchill), this was the first port shipper to be established in recent times, and it has quickly risen to the top.

🍷 12–25 years

✓ *Entire range*

COCKBURN'S
★★

Founded in 1815 by Robert Cockburn, who married Mary Duff, a lady much admired by Lord Byron, this house is still British-owned (Allied-Domecq). Although Cockburn's best-selling Special Reserve and Fine Old Ruby are produced in vast quantities, they are exceptionally good and consistent in quality as are the vintage ports also produced by Cockburn's. *See also* Martinez.

🍷 15–30 years

✓ *Entire range*

CROFT
★

To many people, Croft is best known for its sherries, yet it is one of the oldest port houses, having started production in 1678. Its elegant style best suits Fine old tawnies, more characteristic of a Portuguese-owned house than a British-owned one. In all but a few years, its vintage ports are among the lightest. *See also* Morgan.

✓ *10-, 20-, and 30-Year-Old Tawny*

CRUZ
✖

The lackluster quality of Cruz says a lot about the average Frenchman's appreciation of the world's greatest fortified wine. France takes nearly half of all the port currently exported and this is the best-selling brand. The French could be forgiven if they cooked with it, but they actually drink the stuff.

DELAFORCE
★

Although owned by IDV (Grand Met) since 1968, and thus a sister company to both Croft and Morgan, this house still retains a certain amount of independence, with fifth-generation David Delaforce very much in day-to-day control. The style of Delaforce is very much on the lighter-bodied side, which particularly suits His Eminence's Choice, an exquisite old tawny with a succulent balance as well as a lingering fragrance.

✓ *His Eminence's Choice Superb Old Tawny*

DIEZ
Diez Hermanos
❓

Interesting recent vintages make this low-key producer one to watch.

DOURO WINE SHIPPERS AND GROWERS
See Barros

DOW'S
Silva & Cosens
★★

Although the brand is Dow's, this firm is actually called Silva & Cosens. It was established in 1862 and James Ramsay Dow was made a partner in 1877, when his firm, Dow & Co., which had been shipping port since 1798, was merged with Silva & Cosens. Dow's is now one of the many brands belonging to the Symington family, but consistently makes one of the very greatest vintage ports. *See also* Gould Campbell, Graham's, Quarles Harris, Smith Woodhouse, Warre's.

🍷 18–35 years

✓ *Entire range*

FEIST
See Barros

FERREIRA
★★

This house was established in 1761 and was family-owned until 1988, when it was taken over by Sogrape, the largest wine-shipper in Portugal. The brand leader in Portugal itself, Ferreira did not establish its present reputation until the mid-19th century, when it was under the control of Dona Antonia Adelaide Ferreira, who was so successful that when she died she left an estate of $16.6 million, valued at 1896 rates. Ever mindful of its Portuguese roots, it is not surprising that elegantly rich tawny port is Ferreira's forte. Equally consistent is the style of its vintage port. While this wine is typically light, smooth, and mellow, it does age beautifully.

FEUERHEERD
See Barros

FONSECA
Fonseca Guimaraens
★★★

This house was originally called Fonseca, Monteiro & Co., but changed its name when it was purchased by Manuel Pedro Guimaraens in 1822. Although it has been part of Taylor, Fladgate & Yeatman since 1948, it operates in a totally independent fashion, utilizing its own *quintas* and contracted suppliers. Fonseca has always been the top-quality brand, but even its second wine, Fonseca Guimaraens, puts many port houses to shame.

🍷 15–30 years

✓ *Entire range*

GOULD CAMPBELL
★

Although at the cheaper end of the Symington group, Gould Campbell, which was established in about 1797, produces fine, sometimes stunningly fine, vintage ports. *See also* Dow's, Graham's, Smith Woodhouse, Quarles Harris, Warre's.

🍷 12–25 years

✓ *vintage*

GRAHAM'S
W. & J. Graham & Co.
★★★

Graham's was founded as a textile business and only entered the port trade when, in 1826, its Oporto office accepted wine in payment of a debt. Along the way, Graham's took over the firm of Smith Woodhouse and both of them became part of the Symington port empire in 1970. Although it is the vintage port that earned Graham's its reputation, the entire range is of an equally high quality, category for category. *See also* Dow's, Gould Campbell, Quarles Harris, Smith Woodhouse, Warre's.

🍷 18–40 years

✓ *Entire range, including basic Six Grapes Ruby*

GUIMARAENS
See Fonseca

HUTCHESON
See Barros

KOPKE
See Barros

MARTINEZ
Martinez Gassiot
★★ ❷

Martinez was founded in 1797 by Sebastian González Martinez, a

Spaniard, but became affiliated to Cockburn in the early 1960s. Rather underrated, it produces small quantities of high-quality vintage and great value crusted, and is also a source of extraordinarily good own-label port. *See also* Cockburn's.

🍷— 12–20 years

☑/ *Entire Range*

MORGAN
★☆ ❷

One of the oldest port houses, Morgan was purchased in 1952 by Croft (now part of IDV, thus Grand Met), and now produces plummy port, but is fast becoming known as an excellent source of good value, own-label ports, particularly the 10-Year-Old Tawny. *See also* Croft.

☑/ *Own-label Tawny*

NIEPOORT
★★

This small Dutch-owned firm is best known for its elegantly rich tawnies, especially the colheitas, but also makes fine, underrated vintage port.

🍷— 12–25 years

☑/ *Entire range*

NOVAL
Quinta do Noval
★★☆
Nacional ★★★

Originally a Portuguese house, having been founded in 1813 by Antonio José da Silva, Quinta do Noval was controlled by the Dutch van Zeller family for four generations until it was purchased by the French AXA group. Although the firm is officially known as Quinta do Noval, it has been careful to market most products under the Noval brand, reserving the *quinta* name for those ports made exclusively from the property itself.

🍷— 15–35 years (25–70 years for Nacional)

☑/ *Vintage • Nacional • 20- and 40-Year-Old Tawny*

OFFLEY
Offley Forrester
★★☆

Established in 1737, this firm once belonged to the famous Baron Forrester, but is now owned by Sogrape. Offley makes excellent quality colheitas, elegant vintage ports, and a deeper-colored single-quinta Boa Vista.

🍷— 12–25 years

☑/ *Vintage • Boa Vista • Colheita • 10- and 20-Year-Old Tawny*

POÇAS
Poças Junior

Established in 1918, like many Portuguese-owned firms, Poças Junior started declaring vintage ports relatively recently (1960s) and is primarily known for its tawnies and colheitas. Second labels include Lopes, Pousada, and Seguro.

QUARLES HARRIS

Established in 1680 and the second-largest port house in the 18th century, when it was taken over by Warre's, Quarles Harris is now one of the smallest port brands under the control of the progressive Symington Group. *See also* Dow's, Gould Campbell, Graham's, Quarles Harris, Smith Woodhouse, Warre's.

QUINTA DE LA ROSA
★

Promising new estate-bottled, Single-Quinta Port. Look out for the new 10-Year-Old tawny.

🍷— 8–25 years

☑/ *Finest Reserve • Late Bottled Vintage • Vintage*

QUINTA DO COTTO

See Champalimaud

QUINTA DO INFANTADO
❷

The vintage port from this estate-bottled single-*quinta* have been rather lightweight, but the 1991 late-bottled vintage was a real gem, so it might be worth keeping an eye on future releases from this independent producer.

QUINTA DO NOVAL

See Noval

QUINTA DO VESUVIO

This massive, 990-acre (400-hectare), former Ferreira property was considered to be the greatest *quinta* in the Douro when planted in the 19th century. Owned since 1989 by the Symington group, which has already established its vintage port as exceptional, but how exceptional remains to be seen.

🍷— 12–30 years

☑/ *Vintage*

RAMOS-PINTO
★★☆

Established in 1880 by Adriano Ramos-Pinto, when he was 20 years old, this firm remained in family ownership until 1990, when it was purchased by Champagne Louis Roederer. Ramos-Pinto always has produced excellent tawnies, particularly the single-*quintas* 10- and 20-Year-Old and its colheitas, but if the 1994 is anything to go by, vintage port could be its future *forte*.

🍷— 12–25 years

☑/ *Late-Bottled Vintage • Single-Quinta* (Quinta da Ervamoira 10-Year-Old, Quinta do Bom-Retiro 20-Year-Old) • *Colheitas • Vintage* (from 1994)

REBELLO VALENTE

See Robertson Brothers and Co.

ROBERTSON BROTHERS AND CO.
★

Established in 1881, this small port house is now a subsidiary of Sandeman and thus owned by

Seagram. Best known for its tawnies and, under the famous Rebello Valente label, very traditional vintage ports.

🍷— 12–25 years

☑/ *10- and 20-Year-Old Tawnies • Vintage*

ROYAL OPORTO
Real Companhia Velha
★☆ ❶

Founded in 1756 by the Marquis de Pombal to regulate the port trade, the future ownership of this firm looks uncertain at the time of writing, but its reputation as a good source of inexpensive tawny and vintage character ports should ensure its survival.

☑/ *Vintage Character* (The Navigator's)

ROZES
❷

Part of the giant Moët-Hennessy group, Rozes has yet to establish a reputation beyond the French market, but with Moët & Chandon's globe-trotting "wine doctor" Richard Geoffroy getting involved, anything could happen.

SANDEMAN
★

Also known for its sherry and Madeira, Sandeman was established in 1790 and took over Robertson's and Rebello Valente in 1881, after which it acquired Diez and Offley (now part of Sogrape), and is itself owned by Seagram. The quality of Sandeman's vintage port is variable and seldom blockbusting, but its tawnies are reliable, especially Imperial 20-Year-Old.

☑/ *20-Year-Old Tawny* (Imperial) • *Vintage Character* (Signature)

SANTOS JUNIOR

See Barros

SILVA & COSENS

See Dow & Co.

SILVA C. DA

Small Dutch house producing inexpensive ports; the tawnies can sometimes be very good value.

SMITH WOODHOUSE
★★☆ ❶

The products of this famous British port house are not as well known

in Portugal as they are on export markets, where they are much appreciated for tremendous value across the entire range, and also for some of the very greatest vintage ports ever made. *See also* Dow's, Gould Campbell, Graham's, Smith Woodhouse, Warre's.

🍷— 12–25 years

☑/ *Entire range*

SYMINGTON GROUP

The Symingtons are one of the most well-known and successful of all port families, owning six brands, yet not one of these boasts the family name. *See also* Dow's, Gould Campbell, Graham's, Quarles Harris, Smith Woodhouse, Warre's.

TAYLOR'S
Taylor, Fladgate & Yeatman
★★★

Founded in 1692 by Job Bearsley, this house underwent no fewer than 21 changes of title before adopting its present one, which derives from the names of various partners: Joseph Taylor in 1816, John Fladgate in 1837, and Morgan Yeatman in 1844. At one time the firm was known as Webb, Campbell, Gray & Cano (Joseph Cano was, as it happens, the only American ever to be admitted into the partnership of a port house). In 1744, Taylor's became the first shipper to buy a property in the Douro, but its most famous acquisition was Quinta de Vargellas in 1890, a prestigious property that provides the heart and soul of every Taylor's vintage port.

🍷— 20–40 years

☑/ *Entire range*

VIERA DE SOUSA

See Barros

WARRE'S
★★★

Only the German-founded house of Kopke can claim to be older than Warre's, which was established in 1670, although it only assumed its present name in 1729 when William Warre entered the business. This house, which now belongs to the entrepreneurial Symington family, normally vies with Graham's, another Symington brand, as the darkest and most concentrated vintage port after that of Taylor's. *See also* Dow's, Gould Campbell, Graham's, Quarles Harris, Smith Woodhouse.

🍷— 18–35 years

☑/ *Entire range*

WEISE & KROHN

Weise & Krohn port house was originally founded in 1865 by two Norwegians of German extraction, Theodore Weise and Dankert Krohn. It has been owned by the Portuguese Carneiro family since the 1930s. It makes rather insubstantial vintage port, and is best known for its tawnies.

☑/ *Colheitas*

MADEIRA

The island of Madeira gives its name to the only wine in the world that must be baked in an oven! This fortified wine is deliberately heated to replicate the voyages of old during which the wine accidentally underwent maderization at equatorial temperatures.

PRINCE HENRY THE NAVIGATOR sent Captain João Gonçalves in search of new lands in the 15th century. The Captain's nickname was Zarco, or "squinter," because he had been wounded in one eye while fighting the Moors. Although "squinter" seems an odd name for someone whose job it is to keep his eyes peeled for events on the horizon, particularly at that time, when every sailor was worried about falling off the edge of the world, this nickname is fact not fiction. Indeed, he was so proud of being called the "squinter" that he adopted it as a surname, becoming João Gonçalves Zarco. Despite this impediment to his sight, Zarco not only navigated his ship safely, but he actually managed to discover places. In 1418, for example, he found Madeira, although it must be admitted that he was searching for Guinea at the time. Zarco actually thought it was a cloud, but the more he squinted, the more suspicious he became: it was always in the same position.

One day he chased the cloud, sailed through it and bumped into an island. It was entirely covered in dense forest and the cloud was merely the mist of transpiration given off in the morning sun. The forest was impenetrable (Madeira means "island of woods"), so Zarco lit fires to denude areas of the island, sat back, and waited. By all accounts he had a long wait, as the fires raged for seven years and consumed every bit of vegetation, infusing the permeable volcanic soil with potash, which by chance rendered it particularly suitable for vine-growing.

THE ORIGIN OF MADEIRA'S DISTINCTIVE WINE

As a source of fresh food and water, the island soon became a regular port of call for east-bound ships, which would often transport barrels of Madeira wine for sale in the Far East or Australia. As the ships journeyed through the tropics, the wine was heated to a maximum of 113°F (45°C) and cooled again during the six-month voyage, giving it a very distinctive character. The winemakers of Madeira were totally unaware of this until one unsold shipment returned to the island. Since then, special ovens, called *estufas*, have evolved in order that this heating and cooling can be replicated in the *estufagem* process (cheaper wines do this in large concrete vats, while the casks of better-quality wines experience a much longer, gentler process in warm rooms). All Madeiras undergo a normal fermentation prior to the *estufagem* process. Drier wines are fortified prior to *estufagem*, the sweeter styles afterward.

THE FUTURE OF MADEIRA

Although sales of Madeira are growing, they are doing so from a relatively low base. Madeira has fallen a long way from its height of fame in the 19th century, when Russia was its greatest market and one Grand Duke alone purchased the equivalent of 76,000 cases a year. Far too much Madeira today is cheap, made from the lowly Tinta Negra Mole grape, and sold in bulk to France, Germany, and Belgium, where the natural impulse is to cook with it. If Madeira is to survive, it must concentrate on quality by replanting with classic varieties, encouraging a new wave of independent producers, banning bulk wines, and updating the concept of Vintage Madeira. Pushing Madeira upmarket is not merely required to reestablish its reputation, it is simple logic—viticulture on this precipitous island is so labor-intensive that cheap wine makes no economic sense.

COASTAL VIEW, MADEIRA
Terraced vineyards cling to Madeira's rocky terrain, where irrigation is accomplished via a network of aqueducts.

MADEIRA, *see also* p.328
The island of Madeira, in the Atlantic Ocean west of Morocco, is famed for its fortified wine. Funchal is the capital of the island, where many wine lodges are found.

Intensive vine-growing zone

▲   Height above sea level (meters)

0   5   10   15 km

0   2   4   6   8 miles

THE STYLES OF
MADEIRA

There have traditionally been four basic styles of Madeira, named after the following grape varieties: Sercial, Verdelho, Bual, and Malmsey. During the 20th century, however, the majority of Madeira produced was blended with a high proportion of Tinta Negra Mole (or its variant Complexa) or of American hybrids. Since 1990, however, no hybrids have been allowed, and since 1993, those wines made from Tinta Negra Mole may use only generic terms of sweetness (and not the stylistic terms listed below), such as *seco* (dry), *meio seco* (medium dry), *meio doce* (medium sweet), and *doce* (sweet), accompanied by descriptors such as pale, dark, full, or rich, while at least 85 percent of a varietal wine must be made from the grape indicated.

Note Madeira should be ready to drink when sold and good Madeira will keep indefinitely, so no optimal drinking periods are given below.

BASTARDO

Another rarity from Madeira's once glittering past, there is some question as to whether this black grape variety is related to the Douro variety of the same name, but there is no doubting its great potential quality, making it yet another golden oldie that is long overdue a revival.

BUAL

Definitely sweeter and darker than the styles above, Bual can often be recognized under blind conditions by its khaki-colored meniscus. This style has soft, gentle fruit with noticeable fatness and ripeness, underscored by a baked, smoky complexity. The legal limit for residual sugar is 78–96 grams per liter.

✓ *See* styles by age

EXTRA RESERVE *or* OVER-15-YEAR-OLD MADEIRA

This style is rarely encountered, but is always significantly richer and more complex than 10-Year-Old Madeira. The 15 years reference is excluded from some wines that are much older.

✓ *Barbeito* (25-Year-Old Bual) • *Cossart* (Malmsey 15-Year-Old Malmsey, Very Old Duo Centenary Celebration Bual, Very Old Duo Centenary Celebration Sercial)

FINEST *or* 3-YEAR-OLD MADEIRA

This, the lowest level of Madeira, will be the style of any Madeira whose age is not given. It consists primarily of Tinta Negra Mole, and some Moscatel. Three years is too short a time for any decent wine to evolve into a true Madeira and much is sold in bulk for cooking, and cannot be recommended.

MALMSEY

Made from both white and black varieties of Malvasia grown on the island's lowest and warmest regions, Malmsey is the ultimate Madeira and my own favorite. It is the most luscious, the sweetest, and most honeyed of all Madeira styles. Potentially the most complex and long-lived Madeira, Malmsey matures to an ultrasmooth, coffee-caramel succulence, which lasts forever in the mouth. The legal limit for residual sugar is 96–135 grams per liter.

✓ *See* styles by age

MOSCATEL

Madeira has made some interesting Moscatel, but only a few remain available for tasting today. However, with so many fortified Muscats of superb quality made throughout the world, Madeira's Moscatel should perhaps be reserved for blending purposes only.

RAINWATER

This is effectively a paler, softer version of a medium-dry Verdelho but, because varietal names are never used, making Rainwater with Verdelho would be a waste of this good-quality classic grape. Rainwater is more likely to be a paler, softer version of Tinta Negra Mole trying to emulate Verdelho. There are two theories about the origin of this curiously named Madeira style. One is that it came from the vines, which were grown on hillsides where it was impossible to irrigate, thus growers had to rely on rainwater. The other theory concerns a shipment that was bound for Boston in the US: even though the wine was accidentally diluted by rain en route, the Madeira house in question had hoped to get away with it, and were shocked when the Americans loved it so much they wanted more!

RESERVE *or* 5-YEAR-OLD MADEIRA

This is the youngest age at which the noble varieties (Sercial, Verdelho, Bual, Malmsey, Bastardo, and Terrantez) may be used, so if no single variety is claimed, you can be sure that it is mostly, if not entirely, Tinta Negra Mole. Five years was once far too young for a classic Madeira from noble grapes, but they are much better than they used to be and some bargain five-year-old varietals can be found.

✓ *Barbeito* (Malmsey) • *Blandy's* (Sercial, Bual, Malmsey) • *Cossart* (Sercial)

SERCIAL

This grape is known on the Portuguese mainland as Esgana Cão, or "dog strangler," and is grown in the island's coolest vineyards. Sercial is the palest, lightest, and driest Madeira, but matures to a rich, yet crisp, savory flavor with the sharp tang of acidic spices and citrus fruits. The legal limit for residual sugar is 18–65 grams per liter (the bottom end of this range tastes bone dry when balanced against an alcohol level of 17 percent in such an intensely flavored wine, and even 40 grams per liter can seem dry).

✓ *See* styles by age

SOLERA MADEIRA

Although an old *solera* will contain barely a few molecules from the year on which it was based and which it boasts on the label, the best examples of authentic Madeira *soleras* (there have been several frauds) are soft, sensuous, and delicious.

✓ *Blandy's Solera 1863 Malmsey* • *Blandy's Solera 1880 Verdelho* • *Cossart Solera 1845 Bual*

SPECIAL RESERVE *or* 10-YEAR-OLD MADEIRA

This is where serious Madeira begins, and even nonvarietals may be worthy of consideration because, although some wines in this style may be made with Tinta Negra Mole, producers will risk only superior wines from this grape for such extended aging.

✓ *Blandy's* (Sercial, Malmsey) • *Cossart* (Verdelho, Malmsey) • *Henriques & Henriques* (Sercial, Malmsey) • *Power Drury* (Malmsey) • *Rutherford & Miles* (Bual, Malmsey)

TERRANTEZ

This white grape variety is virtually extinct on the island, but the highly perfumed, rich, powerfully flavored, and tangy-sweet Madeira wine it produced is so highly regarded that old vintages can still attract top prices at auction. If and when the Young Turks ever reach Madeira, this is one variety they will be replanting in earnest.

VERDELHO

Some modern renditions of this style are almost as pale as Sercial, but Verdelho, both white and black varieties of which are grown on the island, traditionally produces a golden Madeira whose color deepens with age. It is, however, always made in a medium-dry to medium-sweet style, which gives it somewhat more body than Sercial, and this can make it seem softer and riper than it actually is, although its true astringency is revealed on the finish. The legal limit for residual sugar in these wines is 49–78 grams per liter.

✓ *See* styles by age

VINTAGE MADEIRA

All Madeira wines at one time bore a vintage, but this practice is unusual today, since most are blends or products of *solera* systems. Current regulations stipulate that vintage Madeira must spend at least 20 years in cask, but if Madeira is to prosper, this outdated approach must be discarded and a system similar to that used for vintage port must be adopted. This is not to suggest that vintage Madeira should not spend 20 years in cask, just that this rather lengthy process ought not to be mandatory. Consumers worldwide perceive vintage wines to be superior to nonvintage ones, and it does not seem to matter that the opposite is sometimes true: if Madeira is to reclaim the world stage and capture international imaginations, producers simply must put the spotlight on vintage Madeira, and the world is unlikely to wait 20 years for this to happen. Madeira must therefore release some of its vintages when they are much younger and put the onus on consumers to age the wines themselves. This would have the added advantage of feeding the auction circuit with a new investment and, as the different vintages are successively tasted and retasted, reported and discussed by critics, this would raise consumer awareness of these wines, thus very usefully enhancing the reputation of Madeira in general.

The WINES of
GERMANY, AUSTRIA, AND SWITZERLAND

CLASSIC GERMAN RIESLING IS INCOMPARABLE. No other wine can offer in a single sip as much finesse, purity of fruit, intensity of flavor, and thrilling acidity as a fine Riesling, yet it remains underrated. German Pinot Noir (Spätburgunder) is even more underrated. Few people have even heard of it. Yet, almost one-third of Germany's vineyards are planted with black grapes and, of that, one-third is Pinot Noir. Top Spätburgunder from the Ahr, Baden, and the Pfalz can be compared in quality with some of the best *premiers crus* in Burgundy. The only question is whether such wines can be produced at prices that do not make good Burgundy seem cheap by comparison! Austria also makes beautiful, underappreciated Riesling and Pinot Noir, in addition to which, top quality examples of one of its indigenous varieties, the highly distinctive Grüner Veltliner, are at last being taken seriously. And if German red wine is a surprise, nearly half of all Swiss wine is red, with smooth Pinot Noir and dense-yet-velvety Merlot the up-and-coming stars. These three countries will offer consumers some of the most exciting and diverse wine experiences of the new millennium.

THE RHEINGAU DISTRICT
A fall view of the quaint Hallgarten chapel, which lies between the Schönhell and Würzgarten vineyards.

GERMANY

The best German wines (Riesling and Pinot Noir) are better than ever, but the worst have never been as bad, and the German wine law passed in 1994 to replace the flawed law of 1971 has unfortunately not improved matters. On top of this, we now have a befuddled Großes Gewächs classification muddying the water at the very top end of the market, and wine labels with Anglicized fantasy names that are supposed to simplify labeling at the bottom end of the market, yet make some German wines look as if they were made in Eastern Europe.

EVERY GERMAN WINE is graded by the natural sugar content of its grapes; the more sugar, the higher the quality, therefore the greatest German wines are inevitably the sweetest. Although the philosophy that equates ripeness with greatness is misguided and has proved harmful to Germany's reputation, it is not an unreasonable one, for ripe grapes are required to make fine wine, and in Germany's northerly climate it is usually only the best sites that can fully ripen grapes. Nonetheless, taken to its ultimate conclusion, the German ideal implies, nonsensically, that a drier wine is inherently inferior to a sweeter wine. In the quest for sweetness and greater volume, the Riesling was gradually discarded in favor of German crosses such as Müller-Thurgau and Kerner, which easily ripened at much higher sugar levels and yielded far larger crops.

A GERMAN ESTATE-WINE REVIVAL?

In the 18th and 19th centuries, German wines from the Rhine were as famous and as expensive as the wines of Bordeaux, and Germany's system of aristocratic wine estates was on a par with the great wine châteaux of France. Today, almost every wine critic agrees that Germany's best estates must reassert their position, if this country wants to regain its reputation for quality. But this is not currently possible because each estate makes far too many wines to project any sort of unified image, let alone reputation.

SCHLOSS JOHANNISBERG
This historic, mansion-style schloss, *which dominates the Rheingau slope between Winkel and Geisenheim, was built in 1563.*

In Bordeaux one can speak of the style and quality of, say, Château Margaux *vis-à-vis* Château Latour, but what can be said about any top German estate, when the wines range from QbA, through *Kabinett, Spätlese, Auslese, Beerenauslese,* and *Trockenbeerenauslese* to *Eiswein* for each grape variety grown? At one time Germany's top wine estates did not market a vast number of *Prädikat* wines. Instead, they built their reputations on a single, flagship *cuvée*, which was invariably pure Riesling and, no matter how many times the vineyards were combed for

THE WINE REGIONS OF GERMANY

Viticulturally, Germany is made up of four large *Deutscher Tafelwein* regions encompassing eight *Tafelwein* subregions, within which there are separate infrastructures for 13 *Qualitätswein* and 20 *Landwein* regions. (The two *Qualitätswein* and two *Landwein* regions in former Eastern Germany fall outside the *Tafelwein* structure.) The *Qualitätswein* regions encompass 39 *Bereiche* (districts), containing 160 *Grosslagen* (collective sites), which in turn encapsulate 2,632 *Einzellagen* (single sites).

DEUTSCHER TAFELWEIN REGIONS	DEUTSCHER TAFELWEIN SUB-REGIONS	LANDWEIN REGIONS	QUALITÄTSWEIN REGIONS
Rhein-Mosel	Rhein	Ahrtaler Landwein	Ahr
		Starkenburger Landwein	Hessische Bergstrasse
		Rheinburgen Landwein	Mittelrhein
		Nahegauer Landwein	Nahe
		Altrheingauer Landwein	Rheingau
		Rheinischer Landwein	Rheinhessen
		Pfälzer Landwein	Pfalz
	Mosel	Landwein der Mosel	
	Saar	Saarländischer Landwein	Mosel
		Landwein der Ruwer	
Bayern	Main	Fränkischer Landwein	Franken
	Donau	Regensburger Landwein	
	Lindau	Bayerischer Bodensee Landwein	Württemberg
Neckar	–	Schwäbischer Landwein	
Oberrhein	Römertor	Südbadischer Landwein	Baden
	Burgengau	Unterbadischer Landwein	
		Taubertäler Landwein	
		Mitteldeutscher Landwein	Saale-Unstrut
		Sächsischer Landwein	Sachsen
Stargarder Land		Mecklenburger Landwein	

QUALITY STRUCTURE OVERVIEW

This is a simplistic overview because each category varies according to the grape variety and its area of origin. More detailed analyses are given under each region (*see* Quality Requirements and Harvest Percentages box, p.346).

QUALITY CATEGORY	MINIMUM OECHSLE	MINIMUM POTENTIAL ALCOHOL
Deutscher Tafelwein*	44–50°	5.0–5.9%
Landwein*	47–55°	5.6–6.7%
Qualitätswein bestimmter Anbaugebiete (QbA)*	50–72°	5.9–9.4%

QUALITÄTSWEIN MIT PRÄDIKAT (QmP):

Kabinett	67–85°	8.6–11.4%
Spätlese	76–95°	10.0–13.0%
Auslese	83–105°	11.1–14.5%
Beerenauslese	110–128°	15.3–18.1%
Eiswein	110–128°	15.3–18.1%
Trockenbeerenauslese (TBA)	150–154°	21.5–22.1%

*Chaptalization is allowed, and will be necessary if the wine has a potential alcoholic strength of less than 8.5 percent.

grapes, just one wine was produced. It would be like combining all the different *Prädikat* wines into one superrich blend today. In the days of Germany's illustrious wine estates, the wines were fermented more fully, rather than being arrested at artificially low alcohol levels in order to retain sweetness. Thus, these flagship *cuvées* were not just richer than today's wines, but drier, fuller-bodied, and more alcoholic. It was this sort of wine that made Germany's finest wine estates famous throughout the world, and

Tafelwein districts		3	Rheinburger Landwein
Rhein-Mosel		4	Nahegauer Landwein
Oberrhein		5	Altrheingauer Landwein
Bayern		6	Pfälzer Landwein
Neckar		7	Rheinischer Landwein
SAAR Tafelwein sub-regions		8	Landwein der Mosel
Qba Regions		9	Saarländischer Landwein
Ahr *See also p354*		10	Fränkischer Landwein
Mittelrhein *See also p356*		11	Regensburger Landwein
Mosel *See also p358*		12	Bayerischer Bodensee-Landwein
Nahe *See also p362*		13	Schwäbischer Landwein
Rheingau *See also p364*		14	Südbadischer Landwein
Rheinhessen *See also p368*		15	Unterbadischer Landwein
Pfalz *See also p371*		16	Landwein de Ruwer
Hessische Bergstrasse *See also p374*		17	Taubertäler Landwein
Baden *See also p381*		18	Mitteldeutscher Landwein
Franken *See also p376*		19	Sächsischer Landwein
Württemberg *See also p379*			State boundary
Landwein districts		▲	Height above sea level (meters)
1	Ahrtaler Landwein		
2	Starkenburger Landwein		

GERMANY
The country's winemaking zones are centered around its major rivers— the Rhine and Mosel, as well as the Neckar, Nahe, Saar, Ruwer, and Main.

Former East Germany (QbA Regions)

Saale-Unstrut   Sachsen

QUALITY REQUIREMENTS AND HARVEST PERCENTAGES

Germany is notorious for the variation of its vintages. Therefore, as a form of insurance, , most of the crop is harvested early. This secures a minimum income from Deutscher Tafelwein and QbA wines, with those grapes that remain on the vine providing a possibility of higher-quality wines from late harvests. If, when, and how much these grapes ripen is the most basic indication of the nature of any vintage. The degree of ripeness attained is expressed in degrees *Oechsle* and the minimum level for each QmP can vary according to the region and grape variety in question. Each degree of *Oechsle* is the equivalent of 2–2.5 per liter grams of sugar. The exact amount of sugar varies according to the level of unfermentable extract also present. (For a survey of each region, see the individual charts in the regional sections.)

only when they return to the same basic philosophy will they be able to rebuild their reputations.

THE 1971 GERMAN WINE LAW

In 1971 a wine law was established to take account of EEC legislation regulating wine production. The main aspect of the law was to reduce 30,000 *Einzellagen* (individually named vineyards) to 2,600. The law allowed the boundaries of each of the original *Einzellagen* to be extended in order to cover a minimum area of five hectares (12⅓ acres). The solution appeared efficient, but missed the point of why any plot of land evolves a name or reputation to distinguish it from neighboring vineyards: *terroir* (*see* pp.14–16). The enshrining of these amalgamated vineyards in law has duped the public into believing that highly priced wines come from specific, historical sites when in fact they may originate from the surrounding areas that, on average, are more than 10 times the size.

This was nothing less than legalized fraud, but the bureaucratic bungling did not end there. The lawmakers went on to create an entirely new geographical appellation called the *"Grosslage,"* which has turned out to be an even greater deception. In fact, once this law's capacity to deceive was fully understood, it became known on English-speaking markets as the "Gross lie." A *Grosslage,* or "collective site," is a very large area, not merely encompassing several *Einzellagen* (single sites as the term literally means) but many villages, each of which comprises a large number of *Einzellagen*. On average, each *Grosslage* consists of 17 post-1971 *Einzellagen* or 197 pre-1971 *Einzellagen*. Such wines are widely blended and of modest quality, but this in itself would not have been a problem had it been obligatory for the term *"Grosslage"* to appear on the label before the name of the

COMPARISON OF GERMAN HARVESTS 2000–2003

Production varies enormously in Germany—from as much as 171 million cases (15.4 million hectoliters) in 1982 to as little as 58 million cases (5.2 million hectoliters) in 1985—as does the spread of wines across the range of quality categories, shown by the table below:

QUALITY CATEGORY	2000	2001	2002	2003
Tafelwein to Landwein	2%	0.5%	0.5%	3%
QbA	54%	45.5%	43.5%	33%
QmP	44%	54%	56%	64%
SIZE OF HARVEST				
Millions of hectolitres	10.1	9.1	10.1	8.3
(Millions of cases)	112	101	112	92
Hectares under vine	101,546	99,714	98,772	98,270
(Acres)	250,926	246,399	244,071	242,830
Hectolitres per hectare	99.3	91.1	102.6	84.3

DECODING THE AP NUMBER

All QbAs and QmPs, including *Deutscher Sekt*, must carry an AP number (*Amtliche Prüfnummer*). This proves that a wine has undergone and passed various tasting and analytical tests and its origin has been established to the board's satisfaction. Each time a producer applies for an AP number, specially sealed samples of the approved wine are kept by both the board and the producer. Should there be a fault or a fraud enquiry, these samples are analyzed and checked against a sample of the product on the market that has given rise to complaint or investigation. This sounds foolproof, and it is indeed more stringent than the EU's Lot Number, which has been in operation since 1989. But like all systems it can be abused, which in this case would simply mean printing fictitious AP numbers on the label, although if noticed the penalty for this would be imprisonment, plus a ban from operating for the company, and a large fine. Understanding the AP number can be very useful. If the wine is a nonvintage QbA, it can give you some idea of how long it has been in bottle.

AP Nr. 5 174 079 16 03

2002 "Weingut Müller-Catoir" Riesling Spätlese Qualitätswein mit Prädikat (QmP)

5 = Examination Board number

174 = number of the commune where the wine was bottled

079 = the bottler's registered number

16 = the bottler's application number

03 = the year in which the bottler made the application

The communes' and bottlers' numbers run into thousands and are of the least significance to the consumer. It is the last two sets of numbers that provide the most useful information. In this instance, the 16 and 03 reveal that this is Weingut Müller-Catoir's 16th application made in 2003. The application numbers are sequential, but do not necessarily apply to the same wine, i.e., none of the 15 previous applications made by Weingut Müller-Catoir in 2003 need necessarily apply to its 2002 Riesling Spätlese QmP. You will find that some references state that the application number actually refers to a specific cask the wine came from (which in this case would be *fuder* 16), but although this is so in some cases (Fritz Haag, and Von Schubert's Maximin Grünhaus, for example), this is only because the producer in question will number his cask to coincide with the application number. What the last two sets of digits tell us is that if they are the same, then the wine is *exactly* the same. If you find two bottles of 2002 Weingut Müller-Catoir Riesling Spätlese QmP both bearing the AP number 5 174 079 16 03, then you know beyond any doubt that the contents of both bottles swam with each other before being bottled together. If you find two bottles of 2002 Weingut Müller-Catoir Riesling Spätlese QmP both bearing the AP number where either or both of the last two sets of digits are different, then you know that the contents are, at the very least, subtly different. They might simply be bottled on a different date, or from a different cask, but when the designation is as broad as Riesling Spätlese QmP, the grapes could have been grown miles apart, picked on different days, vinified in different tanks, with radically different sugar, alcohol, and acidity readings.

Grosslage itself, as *"Bereich"* (district) has to. Not only does the term *Grosslage* not have to appear anywhere on the label, but the name of the *Grosslage* appears after that of the village, in precisely the same way as the name of an *Einzellage* does, constantly leading consumers to believe that a *Grosslage* wine is from a single *Einzellage*. The criteria that originally established Germany as one of the great wine-producing countries of the world—the preeminence and defining quality of the Riesling grape, the famous villages or estates where it was grown, and the legendary quality of the individually named vineyards, or true *Einzellagen*—no longer applied after 1971.

THE 1994 WINE LAW

In 1994, when Germany was required to bring its wine law into line with those of other EU member states, it had a chance to remedy the flaws in the 1971 wine law. Those who cared about

GERMAN LABEL LANGUAGE

ABFÜLLUNG Bottling.

AUSLESE A category of German QmP wine that is very sweet, made from late-picked grapes, and which may also contain some botrytized grapes, *Auslese* is one step of sweetness above *Spätlese*, but one below *Beerenauslese*, and most of the best lean upward rather than downward.

BADISCH ROTGOLD A specialty rosé wine made from a blend of Ruländer and Spätburgunder, Badischer Rotgold must be of at least QbA level, and can be produced only in Baden.

BARIQUEWEIN Fermented or matured in new oak casks.

BEERENAUSLESE A category of German QmP wine that comes above *Auslese* in sweetness, but beneath *Trockenbeerenauslese* and is made from botrytized grapes. It has more finesse and elegance than any other intensely sweet wine, with the possible exception of *Eiswein*.

BEREICH If the wine carries the appellation of a *Bereich*, it will simply state this—"Bereich Burg Cochem," for example.

DEUTSCHER German.

DEUTSCHER QUALITÄTS-SCHAUMWEIN OR DEUTSCHER SEKT BESTIMMTER ANBAUGEBIETE A sparkling wine made by any method (but probably *cuve close*), from 100 percent German grapes grown in one specified region, although it may indicate an even smaller area of origin if at least 85 percent of the grapes come from that named area.

DEUTSCHER SEKT OR DEUTSCHER QUALITÄTSSCHAUMWEIN A sparkling wine made by any method (but probably *cuve close*), from 100 percent German grapes. It may indicate a maximum of two grape names and should be at least 10 months old when sold.

DEUTSCHER WEINSIEGEL An official seal of quality awarded to wines that receive a higher score than the minimum required for an AP number, Deutscher Weinsiegels use a color-coding system: *trocken* wines bear a bright yellow seal; *halbtrocken* a lime green seal, and sweeter wines a red seal.

EDELFÄULE The German term for noble rot.

EINZELLAGE A single-vineyard wine area; the smallest geographical unit allowed under German wine law.

EISWEIN A rare wine resulting from the tradition of leaving grapes on the vine in the hope of attracting *Botrytis cinerea*. The grapes are frozen by frost or snow, then harvested, and pressed while frozen. This is done because only the ice freezes and, as

this rises to the top of the vat, it can be scraped off to leave a concentrated juice that produces a wine with a unique balance of sweetness, acidity, and extract.

ERSTES LAGE *See* Grosses Gewächs

ERSTES GEWÄCHS *See* Grosses Gewächs

ERZEUGERABFÜLLUNG At one time this was considered to mean estate-bottled, but so many cooperatives use it (because, they claim, their members' estates are the cooperative's estates) that it now means no more producer-bottled, thus some estates now use *Gutsabfüllung*. See *Gutsabfüllung*

FLASCHENGÄRUNG A bottle-fermented *Sekt* that is not necessarily made by the traditional method.

FLASCHENGÄRUNG NACH DEM TRADITIONELLEN VERFAHREN A *Sekt* made by the traditional method, although it is not likely to show much autolytic character.

FÜDER A large oval cask that holds 1,000 liters (265 gallons); more prevalent in the Mosel than the Rhine.

FÜR DIABETIKER GEEIGNET Suitable for diabetics, the wines must be *trocken* (dry), contain less than 1.5 grams per liter of sulfur dioxide (as opposed to the legal maximum of 2.25 grams per liter), and no more than 12 percent alcohol.

GROSSES GEWÄCHS (Great Growth), **ERSTES GEWÄCHS** (First Growth—Rheingau only), and **ERSTE LAGE** (First Site—Mosel only) are reserved for wines from the most highly rated vineyards. Only *Auslese*, *Beerenauslese*, *Trockenbeerenauslese*, or *Eiswein prädikate* are allowed, except in Mosel, where *Kabinett* and *Spätlese prädikate* and various other designations may also be used. When not qualified by any *prädikat*, *Grosses Gewächs* must be a dry wine made from grapes with a minimum *Spätlese* must weight. In the Ahr, only dry Pinot Noir or Frühburgunder of a minimum *Auslese* must weight qualify for *Grosses Gewächs*. All *Grosses/Erstes Gewächs* and *Erste Lage* wines must be hand harvested to a maximum yield of 50hl/ha (220 cases/acre), subjected to a VDP taste test, and cannot be released until September of the year following that of the harvest (two years for red wines).

GROSSLAGE A *Grosslage*, or "collective site," is a large area under which name cheap, bulk-blended wines are sold.

GUTSABFÜLLUNG This term literally means "bottled on the property" and has been taken up by those who feel that *Erzeugerabfüllung* has been so debased by the the cooperatives that it no longer stands for a wine that is

truly estate-bottled. *Gutsabfüllung* can only be used by a winemaker who holds a diploma in oenology. This means any naturally gifted winemaker who has not sat the examination, but owns an estate and makes brilliant wines, has no legal way of indicating his or her wine is an authentic product that has been grown on, fermented at, and bottled on a individual wine estate.

GUTSWEIN AND ORTSWEIN (estate wine and commune wine) is applicable to wines observing the VDP's general standards, which include viticultural methods adhering to strict controls, regular inspection of vineyards, higher must weights than those prescribed by law, and a maximum yield of 75hl/ha (330 cases/acre).

HALBTROCKEN Literally "half-dry," although practically semisweet on most occasions, this wine does not contain more than 18 grams per liter of residual sugar and 10 grams per liter of acid .

JAHRGANG Vintage year.

KLASSIFIZIERTER LAGENWEIN (wine from a classified site) is restricted to wines from classified vineyards that impart site-specific traits, with a maximum yield of 65hl/ha (285 cases/acre).

KABINETT The predicate at the end of this wine's name (it can come either before or after the grape variety) reveals that it is the lightest and driest of the QmP wines.

LANDWEIN This Teutonic version of the French *vin de pays* is not only a failure in commercial terms (unlike its Gallic compatriot), but is also rather strange in that it may be produced in only *trocken* and *halbtrocken* styles

LIEBLICH Technically medium sweet, although nearer to the French *moelleux*, this wine may have up to 45 grams per liter of residual sugar.

ORTSWEIN *See* Gutswein

QUALITÄTSWEIN MIT PRÄDIKAT (QmP) The wine comes from the highest quality category of German wine and will carry one of the predicates that range from *Kabinett* up to *Trockenbeerenauslese*.

PERLWEIN Cheap, semi-sparkling wines made by carbonating a still wine. Mostly white, but may be red or rosé.

QbA *Qualitätswein bestimmter Anbaugebiete*, this is the theoretical equivalent of the French AOC.

QmP *Qualitätswein mit Prädikat*, this literally means a "quality wine with predication," and is a term used for any German wine above QbA, from *Kabinett* upward. The predication carried by a QmP wine depends upon the level of ripeness of the grapes used in the wine.

QUALITÄTSSCHAUMWEIN A "quality sparkling wine" can be produced by any member state of the EU, but the term should be qualified by the country of origin (of the wine). Only *Deutscher Qualitätsschaumwein* will necessarily be from Germany.

REBE Grape variety.

RESTUSSE Residual sugar.

ROSEWEIN OR ROSEEWEIN Rosé.

ROTLING A rosé wine that may be made from black grapes or a mixture of black and white. This designation must be indicated on the label of any category of *Tafelwein* up to and including *Landwein*, and must also be featured on the label of QbA wine, although it is optional for QmP.

ROTWEIN Red wine. This designation must be indicated on the label of any category of *Tafelwein* up to and including *Landwein*, and must also be featured on the label of QbA wine, although it is optional for QmP.

SCHAUMWEIN With no further qualification, such as *Qualitätsschaumwein*, this indicates the cheapest form of sparkling wine, probably a carbonated blend of wines from various EU countries.

SCHILLERWEIN A style of wine produced in Württemberg that is the same as a *Rotling*.

SEKT Sparkling wine.

SPÄTLESE A QmP wine that is one step of sweetness above *Kabinett*, but one below *Auslese*. It is fairly sweet and made from late picked grapes.

SÜSS A sweet wine with in excess of 45 grams per liter of residual sugar.

TAFELWEIN A lowly table wine or *vin de table*.

TROCKEN Literally "dry," a *trocken* wine must not contain more than 4 grams per liter of residual sugar, although up to 9 grams per liter is permitted if the acidity is 2 grams per liter or more.

TROCKENBEERENAUSLESE A wine produced from individually picked, botrytized grapes that have been left on the vine to shrivel, it is typically golden-amber to amber in color, intensely sweet, viscous, very complex and as different from *Beerenauslese* as that wine is from *Kabinett*.

VDP Verband Deutscher Prädikats-und Qualitätsweingüter, an association of top wine estates.

WEISSHERBST A single-variety rosé produced from black grapes only, the variety of which must be indicated.

WEISSWEIN White wine. This designation must be indicated on the label of any category of *Tafelwein* up to and including *Landwein*. It may also be featured on the label of QbA and higher-quality wines, but this is not mandatory.

SÜSSRESERVE

Süssreserve is sterilized grape juice that may have just one or two degrees of alcohol, but has none if processed before fermentation can commence. It not only contributes the grapey freshness and sweetness for which German wines are famous, but also provides the winemaker with a convenient last-minute ingredient with which he can correct the balance of a wine. The origin of *Süssreserve* must, in essence, be the same as the wine to which it is added. Its quality, or degree of ripeness, should by law be at least the equivalent of the wine itself. The quantity added is not in itself restricted, but is indirectly controlled by the overall ratio of sugar to alcohol.

QUALITY	GRAMS OF ALCOHOL FOR EVERY GRAM OF RESIDUAL SUGAR PER LITRE	EXECEPTIONS
Tafelwein	3g	Franconian red 5g
Qualitätswein	3g	Franconian red 5g
		Franconian white and rosé 3.5g
		Württemberg red 4g
		Rheingau white
Kabinett	no controls	Franconian red 5g
		Franconian white 3g and rosé

WEINGUT MAX FERD RICHTER, MÜLHEIM
A producer of great Riesling, particularly from Juffer Sonnenuhr in Braunberg, Dr. Richter is justly famous for his superb Eiswein.

quality bravely attempted reforms, but the large private and cooperative bottlers of inferior wine were too powerful, thus the bad law of 1971 was replaced by the even worse law of 1994. *Grosslagen* and *Bereiche* could and should have been disposed of because they are unnecessary appellations that do not enhance the reputation of German wines. But if such a simple yet radical move was too difficult to accomplish, then a temporary and perfectly adequate means of stopping the rot would have been to focus on reforming the *Grosslagen*, which are a deception as well as a distraction. This would have been easy to achieve simply by making it mandatory to print the term *Grosslage* on the label, in the same way that *Bereich* must appear. Until there is a consensus on the reform or eradication of the *Grosslagen*, there is no hope of reinstating the authentic names and boundaries of the *Einzellagen*, yet this is the only hope Germany has of reclaiming equal fine-wine status with France. Only a hierarchical classification of Germany's greatest vineyards will put this country back among the elite winemaking nations of the world, but it would be pointless to build one on the current tissue of lies. The number of *Einzellagen* was reduced to 2,600 in 1971 because, it was claimed, 30,000 was too confusing to contemplate;

but this claim was without justification. It does not matter whether there are 30,000 or 300,000—there are as many *Einzellagen* as there are; they all have the same right to exist, but only the outstanding ones will ever earn a reputation, so where is the potential for confusion? No one has suggested that all 30,000 should be classified. If the Germans ever conduct an official classification, and it is done properly, it would probably consist of no more than the best 250 *Einzellagen* and only the top 10 percent of these would need to create the sort of international reputation that Bordeaux's *premiers crus* have so effectively achieved.

VDP CLASSIFICATION

Without the will or authority to impose a legally recognized nationwide classification, this task has been left to voluntary, quality-conscious organizations. The earliest response was in 1983 in the Rheingau, where the late George Breuer pushed through the now famous Charta (pronounced "karta"), whereby vineyards were classified as *Erstes Gewächs* (First Growths), a designation that could only be used for wines that are essentially dry in style and comply with strict quality criteria. The most important aspect of the Charta, however, was its reclassification of the *Einzellagen*. It demonstrated that some famous sites had been inflated by as much as 806 percent under the 1971 wine law. It was hoped this example would be copied on a panregional basis by the largest organization of wine estates, the *Verband Deutscher Prädikatsweingüter* (VDP). Unfortunately, the VDP did not pick up the gauntlet until June 2002, when it announced its *Großes Gewächs* (Great Growths) classification for all regions, except the Ahr and Mosel (the Mosel having joined the scheme in March 2003, and the Ahr in August 2003).

RECENT GERMAN VINTAGES

2003 This was 1976 all over again, only the growers were given permission to irrigate the vines this time (water stress having turned that potentially great vintage into a hodgepodge of the good, bad, and the ugly). Only no one was set up for irrigation, and tanks were seen all over the vineyard, although what good they did is debatable. So 2003 is probably a slightly more successful version of 1976, and still they won't bother to waste money on irrigation.

2002 A truly great vintage that, despite rain at the beginning of the harvest, was perfect for everything from reds and QbAs to the upper end of the QmP scale.

2001 Brilliant quality, especially for Riesling. Outstanding *Eiswein*.

2000 Too much rain in July and October meant that 2000 was not as magical a year as some hoped it would be. Predominantly a Qualitätswein vintage with relatively small amounts of Prädikat wines produced. Definitely a year to stick to classic sites from top estates.

1999 With September rains, those who picked late rather than early turned out to be the winners, making the 1999 a high-quality vintage. Good ripeness levels in Riesling and Spätburgunder. Emphasis on *Kabinett* and *Spätlese* wines, although BA and TBA were produced.

A LITTLE GERMAN

Those who don't speak German may find it helpful to know that the plural of German words ending in "e" is achieved by adding an "n," thus, one *Grosslage*, two or more *Grosslagen*. For the plural of words ending with a consonant, an "e" is added, thus, one *Bereich*, two or more *Bereiche*.

The delay was much less of a worry than what had prompted the VDP into action in the first place. It was not so much vineyard classification, as the new dry wine designations of Classic and Selection. The VDP agreed with most of the criteria for the top Selection designation, which is restricted to *Einzellage* wines, but objected to the lack of any vineyard classification, other than the mostly bloated and thus meaningless *Einzellage* created by the 1971 wine law. It therefore withdrew its support of Classic and Selection designations and launched instead its *Grosses Gewächs* concept. Thus the whole *Grosses Gewächs* concept has become irrevocably and unnecessarily entangled in what wine should be produced using its designation, instead of setting out with blinding simplicity the true boundaries of Germany's greatest vineyards.

By not concentrating on a sense of place, the VDP became engrossed in ridiculous arguments as to what wine styles should be permitted to use the *Grosses Gewächs* classification, with definitions differing from region to region, not to mention the designation itself, which now accommodates the well-established *Erstes Gewächs* in the Rheingau, plus *Erstes Lage* (First Site) in the Mosel.

CHANGING IDEAS ABOUT GERMAN WINES

The modern idea of which German wines to drink, and how and when to drink them, is based on a tradition that is over a hundred years old. Outside Germany itself, the predilection for Rhine and Mosel is essentially a British one. Historically, this has always been so. Even two world wars failed to diminish the British fondness for these wines, and despite a 25 percent drop in exports in the early 1990s, Britain remains Germany's biggest customer.

At one time, the British, whose tastes influenced the rest of the world, drank only Hock, a name that originally applied only to the wines of Hochheim in Rheingau, but soon became generic for all white Rhine wines. Unlike the light, grapey Rhine wines we know today, the passion in the 19th century was for mature, full-flavoured, amber-colored wines. In fact, Hock glasses traditionally have brown stems because they were deliberately made to reflect the desired amber hue of age into the wine. The Christie's auction of May 1777 listed "Excellent Genuine Old Hock" of the 1719 vintage, and another London sale offered "Hock Hocheim" 1726 in August of 1792. How a modern Hock might taste in 60 years or so is anyone's guess, but mine is that it would not be very pleasant by today's standards—unless it happened to be a *Trockenbeerenauslese*.

FROM HOCK TO MOSEL

By the time Mosel wines became popular, the trend was for lighter, younger wines, hence traditional green-stemmed Mosel glasses were manufactured. The green stem reflected the verdancy of youth from the glass into the wine. (Incidentally, "Moselle" is the name of the river in France's most northerly wine area, producing VDQS Vins de Moselle, and as soon as the river crosses the border it becomes "Mosel." Surprisingly, too many English-labeled German wines mistakenly use the spelling "Moselle".) The brown- or amber-stemmed "Hock" glass was introduced in the 18th century, when it had become fashionable to drink Rhine of great maturity; the colored glass was intended to reflect the desired hues of honeyed-richness and maturity in the wine.

LIEBFRAUMILCH—NOT A WINE THE GERMANS DRINK OR EVEN KNOW!

More than one-third of all German wine exports are sold as Liebfraumilch, an inexpensive, bulk-blended product that few Germans have even heard of, let alone tasted. Less than 0.01 percent of the 12 million cases (1.1 million hectoliters) produced each year is consumed in Germany itself, and most of that is sold to foreign tourists and servicemen. Virtually 100 percent of all

PICKING GRAPES IN THE MOSEL
Harvesting the Riesling in this region's steep vineyards is labor-intensive, due to precipitous slopes and treacherous loose slate soil.

Liebfraumilch is consumed by non-Germans and, although it is no longer fashionable among the new generation of drinkers in the UK, it nevertheless remains the number one best-selling wine in Britain's largest supermarket groups. While the two largest markets, the UK and US, continue to consume such vast quantities of Liebfraumilch, I am duty bound to tell the full story.

Myriad theories surround the origin of the name Liebfraumilch (or Liebfrauenmilch), but many agree that it means "milk of Our Lady" and refers to the wine produced from one small and fairly indifferent vineyard in the suburbs of Worms that was once called Liebfrauenkirche, or "Church of Our Lady." This is now part of Liebfrauenstift-Kirchenstuck, which in turn is part of the 2,470-acre (1,000-hectare) *Grosslage* Liebfrauenmorgen. The single-vineyard wine that gave birth to the name of Liebfraumilch has no bearing whatsoever on the bulk-blended wine of today, nor, for that matter, any connection with the Liebfraumilch that was sold more than 100 years ago. What is interesting, however, is the nature of those early Liebfraumilch wines that gave the blended product of today its worldwide reputation and huge sales. The blurred and nonspecific character of this wine was officially classified by the Worms Chamber of Commerce in 1910, when it stated that Liebfraumilch was merely "a fancy name" that merchants "have made use of," applying it to "Rhine wines of good quality and character." The ill-defined use of this "fancy name" widened during the following 20 years. Even between 1945 and the advent of the new German wine laws in 1971, one-third of the wines blended into Liebfraumilch came from German regions other than the Rhine.

This should have ended when Liebfraumilch was granted *Qualitätswein* status under the 1971 German wine law because the law further stated that a *Qualitätswein* could come only from one specified region. However, the regulations also specified that

SEKT SWEETNESS CHART

SWEETNESS RATING	RESIDUAL SUGAR (GRAMS PER LITRE)
Extra Herb or Extra Brut	0–6
Herb or Brut	0–15
Extra Trocken or Extra Dry	12–20
Trocken* or Dry	17–35
Halbtrocken* or Demi-Sec	33–50
Süss, Drux, or Doux, or Sweet	50+

Not to be confused with still-wine limits, which are no more than 9 grams per liter for trocken and 18 grams per liter for halbtrocken.

BERNKASTEL-KUES, MOSEL
*Looking across the Mosel to Bernkastel-Kues, above which is the famous
Doctor vineyard, from which some of Germany's greatest wines come.*

Liebfraumilch could be made only from Rheinhessen, Pfalz, Rheingau, and Nahe grapes and, although few people doubted the spirit of the law, many producers interpreted this quite literally. They considered Liebfraumilch to be an umbrella designation that entitled the wine to come from any one or more of the four specified regions. Now, however, at least 85 percent of every Liebfraumilch has to come from just one region, which must be indicated on the label.

There have been many moves to reclassify Liebfraumilch as a *Tafelwein*, which would permit it to be blended with grape varieties from the much wider *Tafelwein* regions and this would be more in keeping with its quality, which is not poor or bad *per se*, simply unpretentious and of nonspecific character. However, Liebfraumilch producers disliked the idea of the *Tafelwein* classification—a misguided view in my opinion, not least because Liebfraumilch sells on its brand name. Although not intrinsically poor quality, far too many Liebfraumilch are bad wines, just as far too many cheap German wines in general are. Taken at its best, a decent Liebfraumilch should possess a fresh, flowery aroma and sweet, grapey taste. It has proved to be a good stepping-stone, with statistics showing that the vast majority of seasoned wine drinkers originally "cut their teeth" on this accessible wine, but there will always be some Liebfraumilch drinkers who never stray beyond it. Those drinkers, if honest, dislike the taste of alcohol, but enjoy the effect it has and most of them are not too fond of tannin, acidity, and the assertively dry taste found in most "real" wines. There is no reason why they should—it is all a matter of taste.

WHAT IS LIEBFRAUMILCH?
Ironically, Germany's most criticized wine is the only one to be defined by taste and sweetness in its wine laws. According to the regulations, the minimum residual sugar allowed is 18 grams per liter, equivalent to the maximum allowed for a *halbtrocken*, although few are actually this low, and some are twice as high. Producers have their own idea of what level of sweetness is right for the market and make their wines accordingly. Many buyers insist on a certain ratio of sugar to acidity; most brands contain between 22–35 grams per liter of sugar, with 27–28 grams per liter of sugar as a good average. Liebfraumilch labels must now show one of the four permitted regions; at least 85 percent of the wine must come from the region stated. On average, the Rheinhessen and the Pfalz produce more than nine out of every 10 bottles of Liebfraumilch, while the Nahe makes very little and the Rheingau virtually none. Any grape permitted for German QbA wine may be used for the production of Liebfraumilch, the only control being that at least 51 percent of the blend must be composed of one or more of the following varieties: Riesling, Silvaner, Müller-Thurgau, and Kerner. According to the present regulations, the wine should taste of these grapes, although I have so far met no expert who can either describe or detect a definitive blend of four such different varieties in the wine. What I have discovered, however, is that some of the best blends have actually been denied their AP numbers because they have received a beneficial *Süssreserve* of aromatic Morio-Muskat. The Liebfraumilch examining board apparently believes these eminently more attractive wines to be atypical of the appellation.

SEKT—GERMANY'S SPARKLING WINE
Germany's *Sekt* or sparkling wine industry is very important, producing almost half a billion bottles a year, more than twice that of Champagne. This is almost entirely made by *cuve close* and over 85 percent is not *Deutscher Sekt* at all, but *Sekt* plain and simple, made from imported wines. Despite a fourfold increase in exports over the past 15 years, foreign markets still represent barely 8 percent of sales. In general, Germans make *Sekt* for themselves and its bland, off-dry style with a very young tartness to it has a peculiarly domestic appeal that sparkling wine drinkers in most international markets cannot comprehend, whether they are used to Champagne or New World bubbly. *Deutscher Sekt* is little better, and the best *Deutscher Sekt* is seldom encountered. On those rare occasions when bottle-fermented wines are produced, *Sekt* will not appeal to most sparkling wine drinkers outside Germany itself because the grapes are too aromatic for the expected mellow biscuity character to develop. However, there are Pinot Noir-based *Sekt* rosés that cross the barrier, and the best mature Riesling *Sekt* can appeal to a niche market, just as Australia's sparkling Shiraz does.

HOW TO USE THE "APPELLATIONS OF..." SECTIONS

The entries that follow for each of Germany's wine regions are set out in a logical order. In each of these regions, or *Anbaugebiete*, every *Bereich* is listed and the wine styles are described; this is followed by the *Grosslagen* within that particular *Bereich*. Under each *Grosslage*, the best villages are listed where applicable and, within each of these, the finest *Einzellagen*, or vineyards, are named.

In Germany, vineyards are rarely owned only by one estate, as they are in Bordeaux, for example. It is therefore important to be aware of not only which are the top vineyards, but also who makes the best wines there, which is why I recommend growers and estates within each of the finest vineyards. The term "village" covers both *Gemeinden*—communes, which may be anything from a tiny village to a large, bustling town—and *Ortsteile*, which are villages absorbed within the suburbs of a larger *Gemeinde*. The term *"Grosslagenfrei"* refers to villages and *Einzellagen* within one *Bereich* that are not part of any of its *Grosslagen*.

Where it is stated that there are no outstanding villages, vineyards, estates, or growers in a particular *Grosslage*, excellent estates and growers might well own vineyards there, but the wine produced in these vineyards may not actually be of the highest standard.

All styles and descriptions of wines refer to Riesling, unless otherwise stated. The following sample entry is given from the Franken region.

BEREICH	# BEREICH STEIGERWALD
GROSSLAGE	## GROSSLAGE SCHLOSSBERG
BEST VILLAGE	**RÖDELSEE**
BEST VINEYARD AND/OR BEST GROWERS ...	✓ **Vineyard** *Küchenmeister* **Grower** *Juliusspital Würzburg* • **Vineyard** *Schwanleite* **Grower** *Johann Ruck*

THE WINE STYLES OF
GERMANY

Note From *Wein* to *Trockenbeerenauslese*, the categories below are in ascending order of quality, and not in alphabetical order, after which different styles are listed. Only the broadest character can be given for each category, since so much depends upon the grape variety. The grape variety can even determine the color of a wine, although some 90 percent of the production is white. Most grape varieties likely to be encountered, including all the most important crosses, are included in the Glossary of Major Grape Varieties (see pp.36–45).

The area of origin also has a strong influence on the type of wine a particular grape variety will produce. A winemaker can either make the most of what nature brings, or fail. For full details on these two aspects, see the regional chapters in which styles are described and growers recommended.

WEIN

The existence of this term without the qualification "Tafel-," indicates a cheap, blended wine made from grapes grown outside the EU.

TAFELWEIN

Table wine may be a blend from different EU countries or wine made in one member country from grapes harvested in another. Known as "Euroblends," these products are sometimes dressed up to look like German wines, but the wine beneath the Gothic writing and German language usually turns out to be an Italian or multistate blend. This practice, once prolific, now less so, is tantamount to deception and contrary to EU regulations. To be sure of drinking a genuine German product, check that "Tafelwein" is qualified by the all-important "Deutscher." The more successful of these wines are made in years when Germany is overburdened by such a huge yield of basic-quality wines that the wineries turn back the convoy of tankers from Italy and dump the excess production in their bulk-selling Euroblends. The best have a good dose of fresh and flowery Morio-Muskat *Süssreserve*.

🍷 Upon purchase

DEUTSCHER TAFELWEIN

This is the lowest grade of pure German wine, which about 10 years ago represented between 3 and 5 percent of the country's total production, but now, when added to *Landwein*, it accounts for between 1 and 2 percent. The quality of production has not dramatically improved at the bottom end of the German wine market and the cheapest QbAs have actually deteriorated in quality—now you know why.

This wine must be 100 percent German and, if at least 75 percent comes from any one of the *Tafelwein* regions or subregions indicated earlier in the table, the label is allowed to show that name. These regional names are the most specific geographic location permitted, although, prior to the introduction of *Landwein* legislation, it was permissible sometimes to include the name of a *Bereich*.

A *Deutscher Tafelwein* should convey the basic characteristics of the region from which it comes, so a Rhein, for example, might be expected to have a more flowery aroma, but less acidity than a Mosel. In practice, however, the wines are blended from such a hodgepodge of grape varieties, mostly crosses, that all one can hope for is something fresh and fruity in a medium-dry "Germanic" style!

🍷 Upon purchase

LANDWEIN

Landwein is a *Deutscher Tafelwein* from a specific region and the label must contain both terms. The major difference is that the former must be made either as *trocken*, with up to 9 grams per liter residual sugar, or as *halbtrocken*, with a maximum of 18 grams per liter.

Landwein was introduced in 1982 to parallel the French *vin de pays* system, although there are significant differences. The 153 or so *vins de pays* represent a group of wines that aspire to VDQS and, theoretically, AOC status, and it has become one of the most exciting categories of wine in the world (see p.248). The German category is not a transitional one, it consists of 20 fixed areas that have no hope of achieving anything more illustrious than a "dressed-up" *Tafelwein* status.

Although *Landwein* can never be the same as a *vin de pays*, it could and should serve a very useful, one might even say essential, purpose: to improve the quality of German wines in the QbA (primarily) and QmP categories through selection. By siphoning off the lesser elements of these wines of superior status, it could have improved not only their quality, but the quality of *Landwein* itself. It would be great to think that the biggest producers had taken this category to heart and, through a genuine desire to raise standards all round, reduced yields and used *Landwein* to mop-up 15 or 20 percent of total German production. However, the authorities have instead opted to use this category to increase yields, which is why the country's best winemakers have not been attracted to the notion of *Landwein* as a legitimate means to increase the quality of their other wines, thus there have been no special *Landweins* to attract critics and consumers. The wines have not taken off and, together with *Deutscher Tafelwein*, account for less than 2 percent of Germany's total production, which has not helped this country's wine reputation one iota.

🍷 Upon purchase

QUALITÄTSWEIN BESTIMMTER ANBAUGEBIETE OR QBA

A QbA is literally a quality wine from one of the 13 specified regions. These wines may be (and invariably are) chaptalized to increase the alcohol content, and sweetened with *Süssreserve*. The legal minimum potential alcoholic strength of a QbA is merely 5.9 percent, so it can be understood why the alcohol level is not increased for its own sake, but to give the wine a reasonable shelf life. The category includes Liebfraumilch and the vast majority of Niersteiner Gutes Domtal, Piesporter Michelsberg, and other generic wines. Most *Grosslage* and *Bereich* wines are sold as QbAs. There is no technical or legal reason why this is so, but it makes marketing sense if more specific wines, such as *Einzellagen* or estate-bottled wines, are sold as prestigious QmPs, as they can demand higher prices. Although a QbA has a lower *Oechsle* than a *Kabinett*, it is a more commercial product and therefore often distinctly sweeter.

🍷 1–3 years (up to 10 years for exceptional wines)

QUALITÄTSWEIN GARANTIERTEN URSPRUNGS OR QGU

Qualitätswein garantierten Ursprungs is a QbA from a specific district, vineyard or village that has a consistent taste profile associated with its appellation of origin. Such wines are subject to more stringent sensory and analytical requirements than QbAs generally. Some Mosel vintners near the Luxembourg border were the first to make use of QgU status with an Obermosel Elbling Trocken.

🍷 1–3 years

QUALITÄTSWEIN MIT PRÄDIKAT OR QMP

This means "a quality wine affirmed (predicated) by ripeness" and covers the categories *Kabinett*, *Spätlese*, *Auslese*, *Beerenauslese*, *Eiswein*, and *Trockenbeerenauslese*. The grower must give the authorities prior notice of his intention to harvest for any QmP wine and, whereas a QbA can be blended from grapes gathered from all four corners of an *Anbaugebiet*, providing it carries only the name of that region, the origin of a QmP must be a geographical unit of no greater size than a *Bereich*. A QbA can be chaptalized, but a QmP can not. A certain very highly respected estate owner who believes he could make much better QmP wines if he were allowed to chaptalize them, once made the interesting observation that the French chaptalize their best wines, while Germans chaptalize only their poorest! It is, however, permissible to add *Süssreserve*, although many growers maintain that it is not the traditional method and claim that sweetness is best achieved by stopping the fermentation before all the natural grape sugars have been converted to alcohol. (*See* the various QmP entries.)

KABINETT QMP

The term *Kabinett* once referred to wines that were stored for their rare and exceptional qualities, much as "Reserve" is commonly used today. In this context, it originated at Kloster Eberbach in the Rheingau in the early 18th century. The first documented existence of this word appeared as "Cabernedt" on an invoice from the Elville master cooper, Ferdinand Ritter, to the Abbot of Eberbach in 1730. Just six years later, another bill in Ritter's hand refers to the "Cabinet-Keller." (The meaning of "Cabinet" as a treasured store found its way into the French language as early as 1547, and is found in German literature in 1677.) *Kabinett* is the first of the predicates in the *Oechsle* scale. Its grapes must reach an *Oechsle* level of 67–85°, the exact minimum varying according to the grape variety concerned and its geographical origin. With no chaptalization, this means that the wine has a minimum potential alcoholic strength of between 8.6 and 11.4 percent by volume.

Although made from riper (thus sweeter) grapes than a QbA, a *Kabinett* is usually, though not necessarily, made in a slightly drier style. Some producers resolutely refuse to bolster the wine with *Süssreserve*. This makes *Kabinett* the lightest and, for some, the purest of German wine styles.

🍷— 2–5 years (up to 10 years in exceptional cases)

🏆 **Riesling** *Mittelrhein: Didinger • Rheingau: Leitz, Künstler • Mosel: Dr Loosen, Vollenweider • Nahe: Göttelmann, Kruger-Rumpf • Pfalz: Koehler-Ruprecht, Mosbacher • Rheinhessen: Kühling-Gillot, Manz • Baden: Bercher*

SPÄTLESE QMP

Technically, "*Spätlese*" implies that a wine is made from late-harvested grapes, but it is important to remember that "late" is relative to the normal (early) occurrence of a harvest in Germany. As both QbA and *Kabinett* are produced from grapes that have not fully ripened, *Spätlese* can more accurately be seen as the first level of German wine to be produced from ripe grapes. The minimum *Oechsle* level of 76–95°, which would give a minimum potential strength of between 10 and 13 percent by volume, is hardly an indication of overripe grapes. Although a *Spätlese* is made from grapes that merely have a modest degree of ripeness, the style of wine produced is traditionally sweet, with excellent balancing acidity.

🍷— 3–8 years (up to 15 in exceptional cases)

🏆 *Mittelrhein: Didinger, Weingart • Mosel: J. J. Prüm, Fritz Haag, Grans-Fassian, Molitor • Nahe: Dr. Crusius, Dönnhoff, Emrich-Schönleber • Rheingau: Künstler, Leitz • Rheinhessen: Gunderloch, Keller, Wittmann • Pfalz: A Christmann, Müller-Catoir • Baden: Andreas Laible • Württemberg: Graf Adelmann, Karl Haidle*

AUSLESE QMP

This predicated wine is made from bunches left on the vines after the *Spätlese* harvest and as such is truly late-harvested. The regulations state that bunches of fully ripe to very ripe grapes free from disease or damage must be selected for this wine – how this can be achieved by machine-harvesting, which has been permitted for *Auslese* since the new German wine laws of 1994, is beyond the imagination of every quality-conscious German winemaker I have spoken to.

Auslese must also possess an *Oechsle* reading of 83–105°, the exact minimum varying according to the grape variety concerned and its geographical origin. With no chaptalization, this means that the wine has a minimum potential strength of between 11.1 and 14.5 percent by volume.

Traditionally, this rich and sweet wine is made in exceptional vintages only. There may be some hint of *Edelfäule* (botrytis), especially if the wine comes from a top estate that has a policy of underdeclaring its wines, and thus an *Auslese* might be borderline *Beerenauslese*, but even without *Edelfäule*, an *Auslese* is capable of considerable complexity. It is possible to find totally dry *Auslese* wine and this may or may not be labelled *Auslese trocken*, depending on the whim of the winemaker. *Auslese* is the perfect ripeness level for *trocken* wines, but ideally a different designation should be found for these wines to distinguish them from their sweet counterparts.

🍷— 5–20 years

🏆 **Sweet style** *Franken: Horst Sauer • Rheingau: Leitz, Dr. Weil • Mittelrhein: Weingart • Mosel: Dr. Loosen, Fritz Haag, J. J. Prüm, Egon Müller, Molitor, Grans Fassian, Knebel • Nahe: Dönnhoff, Emrich-Schönleber • Pfalz: Bassermann-Jordan, Bürklin-Wolf, A. Christmann, Müller-Catoir • Rheinhessen: Gunderloch, Keller, Wittmann*

BEERENAUSLESE QMP

A very rare wine made only in truly exceptional circumstances from overripe grapes that have been affected by *Edelfäule*. According to the regulations, each berry should be shriveled, and be individually selected on a grape-by-grape basis. They must achieve an *Oechsle* level of 110–128°, the exact minimum varying according to the grape variety concerned and its geographical origin. With no chaptalization, this means that the wine has a minimum potential strength of between 15.3 and 18.1 percent by volume, but only 5.5 percent need actually be alcohol, with residual sugar accounting for the rest.

These intensely sweet, full-bodied wines are remarkably complex and elegant. I actually prefer *Beerenauslese* to the technically superior *Trockenbeerenauslese*—it is easier to drink and be delighted by the former, whereas the latter requires concentration and appraisal.

🍷— 10–35 years (up to 50 years in exceptional cases)

🏆 *Baden: Andreas Laible • Mosel: Molitor, Fritz Haag, J. J. Prüm, Dr. Loosen • Nahe: Dönnhoff, Emrich-Schönleber • Rheingau: Fritz Allendorf, August Kesseler, Dr. Weil • Rheinhessen: Keller • Pfalz: Müller-Catoir*

EISWEIN QMP

Until 1982 this was a qualification used in conjunction with one of the other predicates. It was previously possible to obtain *Spätlese Eiswein*, *Auslese Eiswein* and so on; but *Eiswein* is now a predicate in its own right, with a minimum *Oechsle* level for its grapes equivalent to *Beerenauslese*. An *Eiswein* occurs through extremely unusual circumstances whereby grapes left on the vine to be affected by *Edelfäule* are frozen by frost or snow. They are harvested, rushed to the winery, and pressed in their frozen state. Only the water inside the grape actually freezes; this either remains caked inside the press or rises to the top of the vat in the form of ice, which is then skimmed off. What remains available for fermentation is a freeze-condensed juice that is rich, concentrated, and capable of producing wines that are the equivalent of, but totally different from, *Beerenauslese* or *Trockenbeerenauslese*.

This icy harvest can be very late. It seldom occurs before December and often takes place in January of the following year (although it must carry the previous year's vintage). The *Oechsle* level of an *Eiswein*, which must be at least the equivalent of a *Beerenauslese*, can be every bit as high as a *Trockenbeerenauslese*. Its quality is also comparable, although of an entirely different character, due essentially to its far higher acidity balance. For me, it is the zippy, racy, tangy vitality of this acidity that makes it superior. The finest *Eiswein* has a finesse unequaled by other botrytis wine, but it remains to be seen what effect the 1994 German wine law will have on the reputation of these very special wines. The quality-minded wanted the new law to demand handpicking for *Eiswein*, which would bring it in line with *Auslese*, *Beerenauslese*, and *Trockenbeerenauslese*, but the industrial bottlers not only fended this off, but made it legal for it to be machine-harvested, although anyone who has made *Eiswein* will tell you this method is impossible.

🍷— 0–50 years

🏆 *Ahr: Deutzerhof • Mittelrhein: Didinger • Mosel: Molitor, Max Ferd Richter, Karthäuserhof (Ruwer), Egon Müller (Saar) • Nahe: Schlossgut Diel, Dönnhoff, Emrich-Schönleber, Schäfer-Fröhlich • Rheingau: Weil • Rheinhessen: Keller, Manz • Fürstlich Castellsches Domäneamt, Horst Sauer • Württemberg: Aldinger*

TROCKENBEERENAUSLESE QMP OR TBA

Germany's legendary TBA is produced from heavily botrytized grapes, left on the vine to shrivel into raisinlike berries that must be individually picked. These grapes must reach an *Oechsle* level of 150–154°. With no chaptalization, the wine will have a minimum potential strength of between 21.5 and 22.1 percent by volume, although only 5.5 percent need be alcohol, the rest being residual sugar.

Consulting charts, however, does little to highlight the difference in style that exists between a *Beerenauslese* and a TBA, which is every bit as great as that between a *Kabinett* and a *Beerenauslese*. The first noticeable difference is often the color. Going from *Auslese* to *Beerenauslese* is merely to progress from a light to a rich gold or buttercup yellow. The TBA color range extends from a raisin khaki through various shades of brown, to dark iodine, with some distinctly odd orange-tawny hues in between. The texture is very viscous and its liqueurlike consistency is just one of many reasons why it is impossible to drink TBA. Taking a good mouthful of TBA is about as easy as swigging cough syrup—one can merely sip it. Its intensity and complexity, and the profundity of its aromas and flavors really must be experienced. It demands attention and provokes discussion, but is not really a wine to enjoy, and is difficult to relax with.

🍷⏤ 12–50 years

🏆 *Mittelrhein: Weingart • Mosel: Fritz Haag, Egon Müller (Saar), Heymann-Löwenstein, Molitor • Nahe: Dönnhoff, Emrich-Schönleber • Rheingau: Weil • Franken: Horst Sauer, Staatlicher Hofkeller Würzburg • Rheinhessen: Gunderloch, Keller • Pfalz: A Christmann, Ökonomierat Rebholz, Müller-Catoir*

RED WINE

The most commonly encountered German red wines are Dornfelder, Regent, and Spätburgunder (Pinot Noir), and many of the best are sold simply as Qualitätswein or even Tafelwein, to allow producers a greater freedom of expression. Dornfelder is grown mostly in the Pfalz, Rheinhessen, and Württemberg and producers have developed three basic styles: *barrique*-aged for serious drinking, early-drinking Beaujolais-style, and an off-dry grapey style. Regent is a relative newcomer hybrid, grown for its fungus and mildew resistance and though mainly produced in a quaffing style can also yield wines with serious quality aspirations—a red wine equivalent of Müller-Thurgau. Spätburgunder is the widest-planted black grape variety in the country and over the past 15 years some talented winemakers have managed to produce truly beautiful, silky-smooth, well-colored red wines from this grape. A few growers have been almost as successful with Frühburgunder, a lighter mutation of Pinot Noir that has evolved in and around the village of Bürgstadt in the Franken, where it has been grown for at least 150 years. The Frühburgunder nearly became extinct in the 1970s because it was considered uneconomical due to its variable yields, but dedicated growers such as Rudolf Fürst have coaxed exquisitely elegant wines from this grape through very low yields. Red wines are generally at their best in southern Baden, the Pfalz, and the Ahr.

IMMACULATE VINEYARDS, BADEN
Baden's greatest wines are produced around the extinct volcano of Kaiserstuhl, in neat vineyards that are perfect examples of Flurbereinigung.

🍷⏤ 2–8 years

🏆 **Spätburgunder** *Ahr: Meyer-Näkel, Deutzerhof, Stodden • Pfalz: Friedrich Becker, Bernhart, A Christmann • Baden: Huber, Duijn, Johner • Rheingau: August Kesseler*

Frühburgunder *Franken: Fürst*
Dornfelder *Pfalz: Knipser*

SPARKLING WINE

The common method of production for this anonymous sparkling wine is *cuve close*, although when the industry was born in the 1820s, all *Sekt* was bottle-fermented. Today, not only is it an industrialized product, but most is made from grapes grown outside Germany, usually from Italy or the Loire Valley in France. Furthermore, until 1986, this Euro-fizz could be called *Deutscher Sekt*. This was because *Sekt* was considered to be a method of production and, so it was argued, if production took place in Germany, it must logically be German or *Deutscher Sekt*. As the vast majority of Germany's huge *Sekt* industry used imported grapes, juice, or wine (and still does), this was more a matter of lobbying by those with vested interests, than logic. However, much of the effort to dispose of this false logic came from honorable sectors within the German wine industry itself. Common sense finally won out on September 1, 1986, when an EU directive brought this appellation into line with the general philosophy of the EU's wine regime. There has been a noticeable upsurge in the numbers of what are now genuine German *Deutscher Sekt*, although *Sekt* plain and simple still dominates the market.

DEUTSCHER SEKT

Deutscher Sekt must be made from 100 percent German grapes. The best are usually Riesling-based and do not allow autolysis (the enzymatic breakdown of yeast) to interfere with the pure varietal aroma and flavor of the wine, characteristics that are held in the greatest esteem by its producers and the vast majority of its German consumers. Try Max Ferdinand. The best *Sekt* I have ever tasted was Wegeler-Deinhard Bernkasteler Doctor, but it is rarely produced and very expensive. See also Deutscher Qualitätsschaumwein bestimmter Anbaugebiete.

🍷⏤ 3–8 years

DEUTSCHER SEKT BESTIMMTER ANBAUGEBIETE OR DEUTSCHER SEKT BA

See Deutscher Qualitätsschaumwein bestimmter Anbaugebiete

DEUTSCHER QUALITÄTSSCHAUMWEIN BESTIMMTER ANBAUGEBIETE OR DEUTSCHER QUALITÄTSSCHAUMWEIN BA

This *Deutscher Sekt* must be made entirely from grapes grown within one specified wine region and may come from a smaller geographical unit, such as a *Bereich*, *Grosslage*, or *Einzellage*, providing that at least 85 percent of the grapes used come from the area indicated. An alternative appellation is Deutscher Sekt bestimmter Anbaugebiete.

🍷⏤ 3–8 years

TROCKEN/ HALBTROCKEN WINES

Wines of the *trocken* category must not contain more than 9 grams per liter of residual sugar, or 18 grams for the off-dry *halbtrocken* category. National demand for drier style wines really started to take off in the early 1990s and now accounts for more than 50 percent of all German wines produced, but some of these can be thin, weak, and disappointing. There are some terrific *trocken* wines, but to be any good, *trocken* really has to be made from grapes of Auslese ripeness. Only then does it have the body, structure, and weight that most dry wine drinkers are used to. The VDP's *Grosses Gewächs* classification considers *Spätlese trocken* ripe enough, but some of the wines released under this banner do not really meet the standard expected from a *grand cru* designation. The former practice of quality-conscious growers to make and sell *trocken* offerings as Deutscher Tafelwein has more or less ceased except for one or two producers of red wines.

🍷⏤ 2–6 years

🏆 **Riesling Trocken** *Baden: Dr. Heger, Bercher • Nahe: Emrich-Schönleber, Schlossgut Diel • Pfalz: Bürklin-Wolf, A. Christmann • Rheingau: August Eser, Breuer • Rheinhessen: Keller, Wittmann*

Riesling Halbtrocken *Mittelrhein: Matthias Müller, Weingart • Mosel: Knebel, Molitor • Nahe: Emrich-Schönleber, Kruger-Rumpf • Rheingau: Leitz, Künstler*

Grau- and Weissburgunder Trocken *Baden: Bercher, Huber, Johner, R. u C. Schneider • Franken: Fürst • Pfalz: Münzberg, Dr. Wehrheim, Ökonomierat Rebholz*

Gewürztraminer Trocken *Pfalz: Bernhart*

Silvaner Trocken *Franken: Horst Sauer*

THE AHR

It may seem surprising that black grapes can be cultivated here at all, considering the Ahr is one of Europe's most northerly wine regions, yet varieties such as Spätburgunder and Portugieser account for three-quarters of the Ahr's vines.

SPÄTBURGUNDER AND PORTUGIESER can grow here because the Ahr is a deep valley—protected by the Hohe Eifel hills— this captures sunlight in its rocky, slaty soil. The cumulative effect of the heat allows black grapes to ripen, but until recently few growers took advantage of these favorable conditions. Consequently the Ahr became known for mild, dilute red wines, popular with social clubs on weekend outings.

A change in winemaking philosophy, however, has propelled a good number of the region's Spätburgunders into contention for Germany's red wine crown. Unfortunately, quantities will always be too small to quench the international wine community's thirst, thus readers are unlikely to find the Ahr's best reds in their local wine store. These remain the preserve of knowledgeable consumers willing to put on walking boots and take a trip to the Ahr to buy them direct. Not that the wines are cheap. The likes of Meyer-Näkel, Deutzerhof, and Kreuzberg produce some of Germany's greatest Pinot Noirs, and the wines are priced accordingly. The region takes the name of the river that flows parallel to, and north of, the lower Mosel and joins the Rhine just south of Bonn. It is one of the world's most beautiful and serene viticultural landscapes, as anyone who has ever traveled along the *Rotweinwanderweg*, the Ahr's red-wine route, will verify.

FACTORS AFFECTING TASTE AND QUALITY

LOCATION
The Ahr is one of Germany's northernmost wine regions, with vineyards extending only 15 miles (24 km) along the lower reaches of the Ahr River, 6 miles (10 kilometers) south of Bonn.

CLIMATE
Despite its northerly position, the deep Ahr valley is sheltered by the surrounding Hohe Eifel hills and maintains temperatures that are favorable for viticulture, with a greenhouselike climate on some of the steeper sites.

ASPECT
The best vineyards of the Ahr are sited on steeply terraced rocky valley sides, with higher yielding vineyards on gentler slopes in the broader, eastern end of the valley.

SOIL
Deep, rich, loess soils in the lower Ahr valley (eastern) and basalt and slaty stone soils with some tufa in the upper Ahr valley (western).

VITICULTURE AND VINIFICATION
Three-quarters of vineyards are worked by part-time farmers, whose wines are sold by cooperatives. Most vines are cultivated under labour-intensive conditions, hence the wines are expensive to produce. Nearly all of the region's wine is consumed locally or sold to tourists. Pure varietal Weissherbst, usually Spätburgunder, is a speciality, but in terms of pure quality, this easy-drinking rosé has given way to fully red styles. As Riesling vines diminish, so the Spätburgunder is taking over as the classic Ahr variety.

GRAPE VARIETIES
Primary varieties: Portugieser, Riesling, Spätburgunder
Secondary varieties: Domina, Dornfelder, Frühburgunder, Kerner, Müller-Thurgau

RIESLING

Riesling grapes can produce fresh, racy, aromatic wines here, but over the years have given way to black grapes and now comprise just 8 percent of the region's vines. Given the healthy prices that Ahr reds command, Riesling is unlikely to regain its share.

HARVESTING IN THE AHR
These steeply sloping vineyards at Marienthal are planted with the black grape varieties Spätburgunder and a little Portugieser, and 80 percent of the region's wines are, in fact, red.

THE AHR, *see also p.345*
Formerly the most northerly of Germany's wine-producing regions, the Ahr is made up of districts close to the Ahr River, a tributary of the Rhine.

QUALITY REQUIREMENTS AND AVERAGE QMP PRODUCTION

AHR'S MINIMUM OECHSLE	QUALITY CATEGORY	HARVEST BREAKDOWN
44°	Deutscher Tafelwein	0.5%
47°	Landwein	0.5%
50–60°	* QbA	80%
67–73°	* Kabinett	12.5%
76–05°	* Spätlese	6%
83–88°	* Auslese	0.5%
110°	Beerenauslese	–
110°	Eiswein	–
150°	Trockenbeerenauslese	–

*Minimum Oechsle levels vary according to grape variety; those that have a naturally lower sugar content may qualify at a correspondingly lower level.

THE REGION AT A GLANCE

Area under vine
1,245 acres or 504 ha (decreasing)

Average yield
350 cases/acre or 81 hl/ha (increasing)

Red wine
82% (increasing)

White wine
18% (decreasing)

Dry & semidry wine
41% Trocken, 31% Halbtrocken

Most important grape varieties
59% Spätburgunder, 13% Portugieser, 8% Riesling, 20% Others

Infrastructure
Bereich 1; *Grosslage* 1; *Einzellagen* 43

Note: The vineyards of the Ahr straddle 11 *Gemeinden* (communes), the names of which may appear on the label.

THE APPELLATIONS OF
THE AHR

BEREICH WALPORZHEIM-AHRTAL

This is the only *Bereich* in the Ahr region. Walporzheim-Ahrtal produces many kinds of wines, from light, ruby-colored Portugiesers to Dornfelders with great intensity, but the real class is provided by some of Germany's finest Spätburgunders. Those areas in the *Bereich* with slaty soil give a vigorous wine, while those situated on rich loess soil produce a softer style. At one time, the wines used to be fairly sweet, but the trend today is for drier wines. The Weissherbst is a soft and fruity wine, and the Riesling fresh and racy. Try the Rotwein with *Rauchfleisch* (smoked meats), the Weissherbst with *Schinken* (ham), and the Riesling with trout or with the salmon that have recently been reintroduced into the river.

GROSSLAGE KLOSTERBERG

The only *Grosslage* in the *Bereich*, Klosterberg is thus identical to that of Walporzheim-Ahrtal.

AHRWEILER
✓ **Vineyard** *Silberberg* **Growers** *Kreuzberg* (red)

ALTENAHR
✓ **Vineyard** *Eck* **Growers** *Deutzerhof* (red and white), *Winzergenossenschaft Mayschoss-Altenahr*

DERNAU
✓ **Vineyard** *Pfarrwingert* **Growers** *Kreuzberg* (red), *Meyer-Näkel* (red)

MAYSCHOSS
✓ **Vineyard** *Moenchberg* **Grower** *Deutzerhof* (red)

NEUENAHR
✓ **Vineyard** *Schieferlay* **Grower** *Kreuzberg* (red) • **Vineyard** *Sonnenberg* **Growers** *Kreuzberg* (red), *W. G. Mayschoss-Altenahr* (red)

RECH
✓ **Vineyard** *Herrenberg* **Grower** *Jean Stodden* (red)

WALPORZHEIM
✓ **Vineyard** *Gärkammer* **Grower** *J. J. Adeneuer* (red) • **Vineyard** *Kräuterberg* **Grower** *Meyer-Näkel* (red) • **Premium Red Wine Blends: Growers** *Deutzerhof* (Melchior, Apollo, Grand Duc) • *Meyer-Näkel* (S, Goldkapsel) • *Nelles* (B48, B52, B59), *H. J. Kreuzberg* (Devonschiefer), *Winzergenossenschaft Mayschoss-Altenahr* (Ponsart, Selection XII), *J. J. Adeneuer* (No.1)

CERTIFIED ORGANIC WINEMAKERS

Christoph Bäcker (Mayschoss)
Ursula & Christoph Richter (Ahrweiler)

THE MITTELRHEIN

Possessing precariously perched vineyards that have declined by almost 50 percent since 1965, the Mittelrhein is a region that is all too often overlooked by serious wine drinkers. Yet it offers some of Germany's finest and most underrated wines.

IT WAS FROM THE MITTELRHEIN that the Celts spread out across Europe. With such ancient roots, it is not surprising that this region is so steeped in Germany's mythical history. It was at the Drachenfels in Königswinter, for instance, that Siegfried slew the dragon, and, in fact, the vineyards in this area produce a red Spätburgunder wine known as Drachenblut, or "Dragon's blood." The Rhine River, associated with many myths and fables, flows past numerous medieval castles and towers, and rushes through the Rhine Gorge, past the famous "Loreley" rock on to which the siren lured many ships to their final and fatal destination.

SHRINKING VINEYARDS, GROWING TOURISM

The difficulty of working the steepest of the Mittelrhein's vineyard slopes has encouraged many of the workforce to forsake them and seek higher wages for easier work in Germany's industrial cities. This has led to a decline in the number of vineyards, although the Mittelrhein is by no means deserted, as its dramatic beauty makes it one of Germany's favorite tourist spots. In this region, where many tiny tributaries provide valley vineyards of a superior natural aspect for viticulture than most others on the Rhine, there is much potential for producing high-quality Riesling on its slaty soil. There

QUALITY REQUIREMENTS AND AVERAGE QMP PRODUCTION

MITTELRHEIN'S MINIMUM OECHSLE	QUALITY CATEGORY	HARVEST
44°	Deutscher Tafelwein	1%
47°	Landwein	1%
50–60°	* QbA	68%
67–73°	* Kabinett	18%
76–85°	* Spätlese	4%
83–88°	* Auslese	2%
110°	Beerenauslese	2%
110°	Eiswein	2%
150°	Trockenbeerenauslese	2%

Minimum Oechsle levels vary according to grape variety; those that have a naturally lower sugar content may quality at a correspondingly lower level.

THE MITTELRHEIN, *see also p.345*
North and south of Koblenz, the Mittelrhein's vineyards run up toward the steep, rocky escarpments that closely border this stretch of the Rhine.

- ● Recommended wine village or town
- ▦ Intensive vine-growing zone
- — *Bereich* boundary
- — *Grosslage* boundary
- ▲ Height above sea level (meters)

| 0 | 2 | 4 | 6 | 8 | 10 miles |
| 0 | 4 | 8 | 12 | 16 km |

BERLIN ■

FACTORS AFFECTING TASTE AND QUALITY

LOCATION
A 100-mile (160-kilometer) stretch of the Rhine Valley between Bonn and Bingen.

CLIMATE
The benefits of the sun are maximized by the steep valley sides that afford protection from cold winds. The river acts as a heat-reservoir, tempering the low night and winter temperatures.

ASPECT
Vines on the steep valley sides benefit from any available sunshine. North of Koblenz the vineyards are on the east bank, while to the south most are on the west bank.

SOIL
Primarily clayish slaty soil and graywacke. There are also small, scattered deposits of loess and,

toward the north, some vineyards are of volcanic origin.

VITICULTURE AND VINIFICATION
Virtually all remaining vineyards have been *flurbereinigt* (modernized by abolishing terraces) and many slopes are a patchwork of steep vineyards. With a high proportion of Riesling giving an average yield that is very low by German standards, quality is generally high. About 80 percent of growers are part-time and a quarter of the harvest is processed by the coops using normal white-wine techniques.

GRAPE VARIETIES
Primary varieties: Riesling
Secondary varieties: Bacchus, Kerner, Müller-Thurgau, Optima, Portugieser, Scheurebe, Silvaner, Spätburgunder

THE REGION AT A GLANCE

Area under vine
1,260 acres or 510 ha (decreasing)

Most important grape varieties
71% Riesling (decreasing), 7% Müller-Thurgau (decreasing), 7% Kerner (increasing), 12% Others

Average yield
290 cases/acre or 66 hl/ha (decreasing)

Infrastructure
Bereiche 2; *Grosslagen* 11; *Einzellagen* 111

Red wine
7% (increasing)

White wine
93% (decreasing)

Note The vineyards of the Mittelrhein straddle 59 *Gemeinden* (communes), the names of which may appear on the label.

Dry & semidry wine
44% Trocken, 34% Halbtrocken

MITTELRHEIN VINEYARDS
The region's weekend winegrowers have plenty to do to maintain these slopes, which include some of the steepest vineyards in Germany.

are a few excellent estates making exciting wines that display a vigorous varietal character, intense flavor, and splendid acidity. The acidity, so prized that *Sekt* houses try to buy as much of the lesser quality and surplus wines as possible, makes the rare occurrence of *Auslese* and higher QmP wines something special.

THE APPELLATIONS OF
THE MITTELRHEIN

BEREICH LORELEY

This new *Bereich* is formed from the two former *Bereiche* of Bacharach (the very small but heavily cultivated southern end of the Mittelrhein, restricted to the west bank and named after the beautiful old market town of Bacharach) and Rheinburgengau (a very large, successful area bordering the Rheingau).

GROSSLAGE BURG HAMMERSTEIN

Starting just south of Königswinter and stretching along the right bank, almost as far as Koblenz, this long, scenic *Grosslage* comprises scattered vineyards, with the only unbroken stretch of fine Riesling vines at Hammerstein.

GROSSLAGE BURG RHEINFELS

A village-sized *Grosslage* on the west bank, with its best vineyards situated on the southeast-facing banks of a small tributary at Werlau, an *Ortsteil* of Sankt Goar.

GROSSLAGE GEDEONSECK

A top-performing *Grosslage* where a bend in the river allows for good east- and south-facing vineyards, the best of which are situated within an *Ortsteil* of Boppard.

BOPPARD HAMM
✓ **Vineyard** *Feuerlay* **Growers** *Didinger* (Oberspay), *Matthias Müller, Weingart* (Spay)* • **Vineyard** *Mandelstein* **Growers** *Matthias Müller, August Perll, Weingart* (Spay)* • **Vineyard** *Ohlenberg* **Growers** *Weingart* (Spay), *Matthias Müller*

GROSSLAGE HERRENBERG

The southeastern end of this *Grosslage* abuts the western edge of the Rheingau, but all of the *Einzellagen* are located in the north, between Dörscheid and Kaub, just downstream from Bacharach on the opposite bank.

GROSSLAGE LAHNTAL

There are no outstanding villages, vineyards, estates, or growers in this *Grosslage*, which has been in a state of decline for years.

GROSSLAGE LORELEYFELSEN

Some fine Riesling vineyards set amid dramatic scenery that includes the famous "Loreley" rock.

GROSSLAGE MARKSBURG

The vineyards on the Mittelrhein side of Koblenz have mostly been overtaken by urban sprawl, but one of the best remains in the *Ortsteil* of Ehrenbreitstein. The others in this *Grosslage* are located to the north and south of the city. There is a natural similarity between these wines and those of the lower Mosel.

GROSSLAGE PETERSBERG

The same area as *Bereich* Siebengebirge. There are no outstanding villages, vineyards, estates, or growers, although good wines are made in the Drachenfels vineyard of Königswinter.

GROSSLAGE SCHLOSS REICHENSTEIN

There are no outstanding villages, vineyards, estates, or growers in this *Grosslage* that faces the Rheingau across the river and neighbors the Nahe to the south, but good wines are made in the village of Niederheimbach, especially the vineyard of Froher Weingarten.

GROSSLAGE SCHLOSS SCHÖNBURG

The reputation of the fine Riesling vineyards in this *Grosslage* rests on two growers.

ENGELHÖLL
✓ **Vineyard** *Bernstein* **Grower** *Lanius-Knab*
OBERWESEL
✓ **Vineyard** *Römerkrug* **Growers** *Goswin Lambrich*

GROSSLAGE SCHLOSS STAHLECK

There is perhaps more potential here, in the south-facing vineyards that belong to tributaries of the Rhine, than in the east-facing vineyards on the great river itself. Yet it is wines from Hahn and Posten at Bacharach, with both easterly and southerly aspects, that excel.

BACHARACH
✓ **Vineyard** *Hahn* **Grower** *Toni Jost-Hahnenhof* • **Vineyard** *Kloster Fürstental* **Grower** *Ratzenberger* • **Vineyard** *Posten* **Grower** *Fritz Bastian* • **Vineyard** *Wolfshöhle* **Grower** *Ratzenberger*

WEINGUT TONI JOST
HAHNENHOF

MITTELRHEIN

Bacharacher Hahn
Riesling
Spätlese

alc 10%vol   Gutsabfüllung   750 ml

Qualitätswein mit Prädikat · A. P. Nr. 1698041001-095
Weingut Toni Jost · Hahnenhof · D-55422 Bacharach

SIEBENGEBIRG

A single-*Grosslage Bereich* covering the vineyards of Königswinter Siebengebirge.

CERTIFIED ORGANIC PRODUCERS

Dr. Randolph Kauer (Bacharach-Steeg) Edelfaul (Manubach); Gerd Lang (Rodenbach) Hof Wildeck (Urbar); Joachim Scherer (Manubach)

MOSEL

The greatest Rieslings grown along the Mosel River have an excruciating, but delightful, acidity that can only be relieved through a knife-edge balance of sweetness. Unlike in the warmer Rhine regions, the Riesling grape is at its best here in hot vintages.

IF ANY GRAPE IS INTRINSICALLY RACY, it is the vigorous Riesling; and if any region can be singled out for emphasizing this raciness, it must be Mosel. Grown on the steepest, slaty slopes, Riesling combines a relatively high acidity with an irrefutable suggestion of lightness and elegance. But a fine Mosel is never thin, as these wines have surprisingly high extract levels that, together with the acidity, intensify the characteristics of flavor.

In even the hottest vintages, the best *Auslesen* and *Beerenauslesen* remain racy, while those from the other regions appear fat and overblown by contrast. Even the most modest wines retain a freshness and vitality in sunblessed years that will be lacking in those from the warmer regions.

THE GOOD DOCTOR

There are many great vineyards in this region, but none so famous as the legendary Bernkasteler Doctor, which produces Germany's most expensive wine. The story is that Boemund II, Archbishop of Trier in the 14th century, was so ill that his doctors could do nothing for him. A winegrower from Bernkastel recommended the restorative powers of the wine from his vineyard. Boemund drank some, made a miraculous recovery, and declared "The best doctor grows in this vineyard in Bernkastel." More recently, the Doctor vineyard has been the subject of a lengthy court case. The original vineyard comprised 3⅓ acres (1.35 hectares), but in 1971 the new German wine law proscribed a ban on all vineyards of less than 12¼ acres (5 hectares). The authorities planned to expand the Doctor almost equally to the

west (into the *Einzellage* Graben) and to the east (into an area classified merely as Grosslage Badstube). This enabled 13 different producers to make and sell Bernkasteler Doctor, whereas only three owners of the true Doctor vineyards had existed before. It is not surprising that the owners of the original Doctor vineyard felt strongly enough to take their objections to court. The case continued until finally, in 1984, after an exhaustive study had

FACTORS AFFECTING TASTE AND QUALITY

LOCATION
This region follows the Mosel River, as it meanders for 150 miles (250 km) from Koblenz south to the border with France. It includes the vineyards of two major tributaries, the Saar and the Ruwer, that flow into the Mosel from the south.

CLIMATE
The moderate rainfall and rapid warming of the steep and protective valley sides provide ideal conditions for vines to flourish and produce grapes with high acidity, even when late harvested.

ASPECT
The Mosel has more loops and bends than any other German river, and most of the vines grow at an altitude of between 330 and 1,150 feet (100 and 350 meters). This valley provides slopes of every aspect, with many that are spectacularly steep, boasting gradients as high as 70 degrees.

SOIL
Soils in this region vary from sandstone, shell-limestone, and red marl in the upper Mosel, to Devon slate in the middle Mosel, Saar, and Ruwer, and clay slate and gray stony soil in the lower Mosel. Alluvial sand and gravel soils are also found in lower sites. Classic Riesling sites are slaty; the Elbling prefers limestone.

VITICULTURE AND VINIFICATION
Many of the greatest German wines come from the highest and steepest vineyards in this area, most of which are situated in the upper reaches of the valleys. In these notoriously difficult sites, each vine has to be tied to its own eight-foot wooden stake, and the slate soil that is washed down to the bottom of the slope by the winter rains has to be carried back up every year. Tending the vines is thus unavoidably labor-intensive and this, combined with a longer winter than experienced elsewhere in Germany, accounts for the higher prices asked for fine Mosel wines. The early onset of winter causes fermentation to take place at cool temperatures, and when the wines are bottled early they retain more carbonic gas, which emphasizes the crisp, steely character of the Riesling grape. There are about 13,750 growers owning very small plots of land. The regional cooperative in Bernkastel-Kues alone processes one-fifth of the entire crop, but much is sold on to the commercial wineries, which sell 60 percent of the total wine produced, whereas the cooperatives sell just 13 percent and this figure is declining. On the other hand, growers and estates account for 28 percent of sales, and are increasing their share.

GRAPE VARIETIES
Primary varieties: Müller-Thurgau, Riesling
Secondary varieties: Auxerrois, Bacchus, Elbling, Kerner, Optima, Ortega, Spätburgunder

Doctor (ex-Graben)	J. Lauerburg ⅓ acre (0.13 ha)
Doctor (Original)	Deinhard 2⅔ acres (1.06 ha)
Doctor (ex-Badstube)	Dr. H. Thanisch 4½ acres (1.81 ha)
Alte Badstube am Doctorberg	Hl Geist-Armenspende or Holy Spirit Charity Fund ⅔ acre (0.26 ha)

THE BERNKASTELER DOCTOR VINEYARD TODAY
The red outline encloses the area of the original vineyard (yellow) and those areas finally adopted in 1984 (light and medium green). The area excluded in 1984 is pink.

BERNKASTEL FROM THE DOCTOR VINEYARD
Bernkasteler Doctor wines are some of Germany's most prestigious and expensive. Bernkastel lies in the Badstube Grosslage.

QUALITY REQUIREMENTS AND AVERAGE QMP PRODUCTION

MOSEL'S MINIMUM OECHSLE	QUALITY CATEGORY	HARVEST BREAKDOWN
44°	Deutscher Tafelwein	1%
47°	Landwein	1%
50–60°	* QbA	72%
67–73°	* Kabinett	18%
76–85°	* Spätlese	4%
83–88°	* Auslese	1%
110°	Beerenauslese	1%
110°	Eiswein	1%
150°	Trockenbeerenauslese	1%

Minimum Oechsle levels vary according to grape variety; those that have a naturally lower sugar content may qualify at a correspondingly lower level.

MOSEL, *see also* p.345

Formerly known as the Mosel-Saar-Ruwer, the name of this region was simplified to Mosel in the wine legislation update that at the time of going to print was due to be passed in law sometime in 2005.

Legend

- Recommended wine village or town
- Intensive vine-growing zone
- *Bereich* boundary
- Grosslage boundary
- ▲ Height above sea level (meters)

0 2 4 6 8 10 12 miles
0 5 10 15 20 km

THE REGION AT A GLANCE

Area under vine
25,079 acres or 10,149 ha
(decreasing)

Average yield
395 cases/acre or 90 hl/ha
(decreasing)

Red wine
2% (increasing)

White wine
98% (decreasing)

Dry & semidry wine
15% Trocken, 11% Halbtrocken

Most important grape varieties
55% Riesling (increasing), 18% Müller-Thurgau (decreasing), 8% Elbling (decreasing), 7% Kerner (decreasing), 12% Others

Infrastructure
Bereiche 6; *Grosslagen* 19; *Einzellagen* 523

Note *The vineyards of Mosel straddle 192 Gemeinden (communes), the names of which may appear on the label.*

been made of the vineyard's *terroir*, the court decided that the Doctor vineyard could legitimately be stretched to include all the Graben element and a small portion of the Badstube, making a total of 8 acres (3.26 hectares). The main reason why the Doctor vineyard was primarily expanded westward, rather than eastward, is that these westerly exposures benefit from longer hours of sunshine. However, the 10 owners of the Badstube section excluded from the Doctor vineyard found themselves in possession of vineyards that, having for 13 years been accorded the status of Germany's most prestigious wine, were now nameless. They proposed that they should be allowed to use the *Einzellage* name of Alte Badstube am Doctorberg (Old Badstube on the Doctor's Hill) and, despite protests from the original owners, this was accepted by officials.

Not only was the expansion of the *terroir* open to question in this case, but the general directive that a single vineyard should be of a stipulated minimum size was sheer folly and illustrative of one of the fundamental flaws in the 1971 German wine law (*see also* p.346). It would have been much more effective to have amended the law to allow any genuine vineyard name the right to appear in small print on a label, and to establish a register of perhaps 100 or more (but certainly not 2,600) truly great vineyards that would have the right to appear on the label in a dominant size of print with an appropriate designation of elevated status. If the greatest German wines could trade on a reputation similar to that of the finest wines of France, the Mosel would probably have more *"grands crus"* than any other region, although the Rheingau would give it a good fight.

THE APPELLATIONS OF
MOSEL

BEREICH BERNKASTEL

This covers the entire Mittelmosel, encompassing all of the river's most famous villages and towns, and most of its best vineyards. Much wine is sold under this *Bereich* appellation, but unfortunately most of it is disappointing.

GROSSLAGE BADSTUBE

Badstube must be the grandest *Grosslage* in Germany, encompassing as it does the most famous of all *Einzellagen*, the Doctor vineyard, as well as the almost equally well-known Lay, the superb Graben, and six other good sites. The quality of even the surplus wine from such great vineyards is so high that it is practically impossible to find poor Badstube, and the *Grosslage* wines are especially good in relatively poor years when grapes from the Doctor vineyard fail to achieve *Kabinett* level and are included in these blends.

GROSSLAGE BLEND

⟋ **Grower** *Selbach-Oster*

BERNKASTEL

⟋ **Vineyard** *Doctor* **Growers** *Wwe. Dr. H. Thanisch-Erben Thanisch, Wegeler-Gutshaus Bernkastel* • **Vineyard** *Alte Badstube am Doctorberg* **Grower** *Dr. Pauly-Bergweiler/Peter Nicolay* • **Vineyard** *Lay* **Growers** *Dr. Loosen*

GROSSLAGE KURFÜRSTLAY

This includes the lesser wines of Bernkastel and the superior wines of Brauneberg, the best of which come from the fabulous vineyards on the south-southeast-facing Juffer hill that rises from the river opposite the village of Brauneberg. Its wines are remarkably racy considering their exceptional fullness of body and some prefer them to those of the Doctor, although I find it impossible to choose, and delight in their differences.

BRAUNEBERG

⟋ **Vineyard** *Juffer* **Growers** *Max Ferd Richter* • **Vineyard** *Juffer Sonnenuhr* **Growers** *Fritz Haag, Reichsgraf von Kesselstatt, Schloss Lieser, Max Ferd Richter, Paulinshof* • **Vineyard** *Mandelgraben* **Grower** *Markus Molitor*

LIESER

⟋ **Vineyard** *Niederberg Helden* **Grower** *Schloss Lieser*

MÜHLHEIM

⟋ **Vineyard** *Helenenkloster* **Grower** *Max Ferd Richter*

WINTRICH

⟋ **Vineyard** *Ohligsberg* **Grower** *Reinhold Haart*

GROSSLAGE MICHELSBERG

There are some great wines made in the village of Piesport in the Michelsberg *Grosslage*, but the thin, characterless Piesporter Michelsberg is not one of them. It is a *Grosslage* wine that comes not from steep, slaty slopes such as Goldtröpfchen or Domherr, but from very high-yielding, flat, alluvial land. No great grower would contemplate cultivating such fertile soil, the low-quality wines of which have unfairly debased the Piesporter village name to such a degree that its wine in the industry has become known as Piss-pot. The great wines of Trittenheim have not had to suffer from such great indignities, and the village of Dhron especially should not be forgotten for its produce.

PIESPORT

⟋ **Vineyard** *Domherr* **Growers** *Kurt Hain, Reinhold Haart* • **Vineyard** *Goldtröpfchen* **Growers** *Reinhold Haart, Kurt Hain, Grans-Fassian, Weller-Lehnert, Sankt Urbans-Hof, Vereinigte Hospitien* • **Vineyard** *Treppchen* **Grower** *Weller-Lehnert*

TRITTENHEIM

⟋ **Vineyard** *Apotheke* **Growers** *Ernst Clüsserath, Ansgar Clüsserath, Clüsserath-Eifel, Clüsserath-Weiler, Grans-Fassian, Josef Rosch, Milz Laurentiushof* • **Vineyard** *Altärchen* **Grower** *Franz-Josef Eifel*

GROSSLAGE MÜNZLAY

The three villages in this *Grosslage* may lack the fame of Bernkastel and the popularity of Piesport, but they possess truly superb Mosel vineyards and boast an incomparable number of great growers and estates.

GRAACH

⟋ **Vineyard** *Domprobst* **Growers** *Kees-Kieren, S. A. Prüm, Willi Schaefer, Philipps-Eckstein, Dr. Weins-Prüm* • **Vineyard** *Himmelreich* **Growers** *Kees-Kieren, Markus Molitor* (red)*, J. J. Prüm, S. A. Prüm, Max Ferd Richter, Selbach-Oster, Weins-Prüm, Philipps-Eckstein* • **Vineyard** *Josephshof* **Grower** *Reichsgraf von Kesselstatt*

WEHLEN

⟋ **Vineyard** *Sonnenuhr* **Growers** *Dr. Loosen, J. J. Prüm, S. A. Prüm, Dr. Weins-Prüm, Wegeler-Gutshaus Bernkastel*

ZELTINGEN

⟋ **Vineyard** *Sonnenuhr* **Growers** *Markus Molitor, Selbach-Oster* • **Vineyard** *Himmelreich* **Grower** *Selbach-Oster*

GROSSLAGE NACKTARSCH

The labels of this *Grosslage* are collectors' items because of the naked bottoms featured on many of them—reflecting not only the name but also the quality of most of the wine.

GROSSLAGE PROBSTBERG

There are no outstanding villages or vineyards, except at Longuic and Sweich, that face each other at the confluence with the Ruwer at Eitelsbach.

GROSSLAGE ST. MICHAEL

Popular but generally overrated wines come from Klüsserath these days, although the wonderful wines of Kirsten and Franz-Josef Regnery are bringing back the glory days. Detzem, Mehring, and Schleich all have good potential, but it is Leiwen that truly excels, especially in its steepest and sunniest vineyards of Laurentiuslay and Klostergarten, which stretch up above the village, exposing their superb southwesterly aspect.

KLÜSSERATH

⟋ **Vineyard** *Bruderschaft* **Growers** *Kirsten, Franz-Josef Regnery*

LEIWEN

⟋ **Vineyard** *Klostergarten* **Growers** *Heinz Schmitt, St. Urbanshof, Josef Rosch, Carl Loewen* • **Vineyard** *Laurentiuslay* **Growers** *Carl Loewen, Grans-Fassian, Josef Rosch*

MEHRING

⟋ **Vineyard** *Blattenberg* **Grower** *Heinz Schmitt*

GROSSLAGE SCHWARZLAY

Erden and Ürzig are two of the Mittelmosel's most underrated villages. Their spectacular vineyards cling to clifflike slopes in defiance of gravity and are capable of producing rich, racy wines of rapierlike acidity, stunning intensity, and immaculate style.

BURG

⟋ **Vineyard** *Wendelstück* **Grower** *Paul Knod*

ENKIRCH

⟋ **Vineyard** *Batterieberg* **Grower** *Immich-Batterieberg* • **Vineyard** *Steffensberg* **Grower** *Immich-Batterieberg*

ERDEN

⟋ **Vineyard** *Treppchen* **Growers** *Jos Christoffel Jun, Joh Jos Christoffel Erben, Stephan Ehlen, Dr. Loosen, Mönchhof-Robert Eymael, Dr. Weins-Prüm, Kees-Kieren, Andreas Schmitges, Klaus Lotz* • **Vineyard** *Prälat* **Growers** *Dr. Loosen, Mönchhof-Robert Eymael, Dr. Pauly Bergweiler/Peter Nicolay, Andreas Schmitges*

TRARBACH

⟋ **Vineyard** *Schlossberg* (red) **Grower** *Markus Molitor*

ÜRZIG

⟋ **Vineyard** *Würzgarten* **Growers** *J. J. Christoffel Erben, Jos Christoffel Jun, Dr. Loosen, Merkelbach, Mönchhof-Robert Eymael*

WOLF

✓ **Vineyard** *Goldgrube* **Grower** *Vollenweider*

GROSSLAGE VOM HEISSEN STEIN

There are two growers who excel in this otherwise modest *Grosslage*.

PÜNDERICH

✓ **Vineyard** *Marienburg* **Grower** *Clemens Busch* ◉

REIL

✓ **Vineyard** *Goldlay* **Grower** *Paul Knod*

BEREICH BURG COCHEM

Formerly Bereich Zell, this covers the lower Mosel and is generally regarded as an area of unexciting wines, yet there are some good ones to be found.

GROSSLAGE GOLDBÄUMCHEN

There are few outstanding villages, vineyards, or growers in this *Grosslage*, although good wines are made in the village of Eller at Pommern.

GROSSLAGE GRAFSCHAFT

Good wines are made in the villages of Alf and Bullay, but the Riesling of Neef stands out from the rest.

GROSSLAGE ROSENHANG

This is a promising *Grosslage*, which winds along the right bank of the Mosel downstream from *Grosslage* Schwarze Katz.

GROSSLAGE SCHWARZE KATZ

The village of Zell has some good *Einzellagen*, with officially classified slopes that can make fine and aromatic Riesling, but it is best known for its *Grosslage* label that carries the famous Schwarze Katz "Black Cat" logo. In 1863, three merchants from Aachen were selecting wines in cellar in Zell, but could not decide which of three casks to buy. When the grower tried to take a second sample of one of the wines, his black cat leaped on to the barrel, arched its back, and hissed. The merchants thought that the cat was perhaps defending the best wine, thus purchased it, returning each year for what they dubbed the "Schwarze Katz" wine. As this story spread, so it became customary for other producers in Zell to label their best wines with the insignia of the black cat, but since Merl and Kaimt have been merged with Zell, it has become merely a blended *Grosslage* wine.

GROSSLAGE WEINHEX

This *Grosslage* extends over both banks of the Mosel and into the suburbs of Koblenz, encompassing some very steep slopes planted entirely with Riesling. Three growers coax some world-class Riesling from this tourist-unfashionable end of the river.

WINNINGEN

✓ **Vineyard** *Uhlen* **Growers** *Heymann-Löwenstein, Knebel, Freiherr von Heddersdorf* • **Vineyard** *Röttgen* **Growers** *Knebel, Freiherr von Heddersdorf, Heymann-Löwenstein*

PREMIUM WHITES WITHOUT VINEYARD DESIGNATION

✓ **Growers** *Heymann-Löwenstein* (Schieferterassen, von blauem Schiefer)

BEREICH MOSELTOR

This is the most southerly *Bereich* on the Mosel. It encompasses the upper reaches of the river that flows from its source in the Vosges mountains of France through Luxembourg and into Germany, hence the name Moseltor or "Mosel gate." Its wines are very light and acidic, and of little significance except for the *Sekt* houses.

GROSSLAGE SCHLOSS BÜBINGER

Haven of the less than heavenly Elbling. While colleagues across the river in Luxembourg earn a good living out of wine and tourism, the acidic Elbling wines of this *Grosslage* do not make it easy for its growers to survive.

BEREICH OBERMOSEL

The Obermosel, or Upper Mosel, runs parallel to the Luxembourg border and is planted mostly with Elbling. The wines are thin, acidic, and mostly made into *Sekt*.

GROSSLAGE GIPFEL

No outstanding villages, vineyards, or growers, although respectable wines are made in the village of Nittel.

GROSSLAGE KÖNIGSBERG

No outstanding villages, vineyards, or growers.

BEREICH RUWERTAL

The northern half of the former Bereich Saar-Ruwer.

GROSSLAGE RÖMERLAY

This covers the vineyards of the Ruwer and incorporates the ancient Roman city of Trier, as well as a few scattered plots on the Mosel, including one on the left bank facing Trier. The Ruwer is much the smaller of the two tributaries, yet it has its share of exceptional vineyards owned by gifted growers who make very aromatic, vital wines that are as racy as any on the Mosel, but not quite as biting as those of the Saar. The quality is high and few wines are seen under the *Grosslage* appellation.

EITELSBACH

✓ **Vineyard** *Karthäuserhofberg* **Grower** *Karthäuserhof*

KASEL

✓ **Vineyard** *Kehrnagel* **Growers** *Karlsmühle* • **Vineyard** *Nieschen* **Growers** *Erben von Beulwitz, Reichsgraf von Kesselstatt,*

Karlsmühle

LORENZHOF

✓ **Non-Einzellage wines** • **Grower** *Karlsmühle*

MERTESDORF

✓ **Vineyard** *Maximin Grünhäuser Abtsberg* **Grower** *Gutsverwaltung von Schubert-Maximin Grünhaus*

BEREICH SAAR

The southern half of the former Bereich Saar-Ruwer.

GROSSLAGE SCHARZBERG

This covers the Saar and a small section of the Mosel between Konz and Trier to the north. These wines are so racy that they are positively biting and steely in their youth, but they age gracefully, harmonizing into exquisitely piquant flavors. Very modest Saar wines can be too thin and unripe to enjoy, but *Kabinett* and higher predicates from great growers are almost sure to please. Unlike the Ruwer's Römerlay, this *Grosslage* appellation is often used.

KANZEM

✓ **Vineyard** *Altenberg* **Grower** *Von Othegraven* • *Johann Peter Reinert*

OBEREMMEL

✓ **Vineyard** *Karlsberg* **Grower** *Reichsgraf von Kesselstatt* • **Vineyard** *Hütte* **Grower** *Von Hövel*

OCKFEN

✓ **Vineyard** *Bockstein* **Growers** *Weinhof Herrenberg* (Schoden) ◉ *St Urbanshof* (Leiwen)

SERRIG

✓ **Vineyard** *Schloss Saarstein* **Grower** *Schloss Saarstein*

SAARBURG

✓ **Vineyard** *Rausch* **Grower** *Forstmeister Geltz Zilliken*

SCHARZHOFBERG

✓ **Vineyard** *Scharzhofberger* **Growers** *Reichsgraf von Kesselstatt, von Hövel, Vereinigte Hospitien, Egon Müller*

SCHODEN

✓ **Vineyard** *Herrenberg* **Grower** *Weinhof Herrenberg*

WILTINGEN

✓ **Vineyard** *Klosterberg* **Grower** *Johann Peter Reinert* • **Vineyard** *Schlangengraben* **Growers** *Weinhof Herrenberg, Johann Peter Reinert* • **Vineyard** *Braune Kupp* **Grower** *Egon Müller*

OTHER CERTIFIED ORGANIC PRODUCERS

Biodynamic
Öko-Rita & Rudolf Trossen (Kinheim-Kindel)
Ulrich Treitz (Traben-Trarbach)

Organic
Ferienhof Josef Luy (Konz)
Alfred Cuy (Zell-Merl)
Artur Mentges (Kröv)
Christoph Rimmele (Zell/Kaimt)
Dr. Renate Wilkomm (Bernkastel-Kues)

Frank Brohl (Pünderich)
Gerhard Lönnartz (Ernst)
Günther (Wincheringen)
Hugo Schorn (Burg)
Joachim Deis (Senheim)
Johannes Schneider (Maring-Noviand)
Klaus Schweisel (Osann-Monzel)
Klaus Stülb (Zell/Kaimt)
Laurentiushof (Bremm)
Paul Schwarz (Neumagen)
Peter IG Frommer (Traben-

Trarbach)
Peter Mentges (Bullay)
Rudolf Holbach (Wincheringen)
Sekt und Karl Weber (Wincheringen)
Steffens-Keß (Steffens-Keß) (Reil)
Udo Wick (Kröv)
Volker Manz (Konz Kommlingen)
Weingut-Sektkellerei Uwe Kreuter (Alf)
zur Römerkelter (Maring-Noviand)

THE NAHE

In the Nahe region, a sunny microclimate and varied soils combine to produce wines that have the elegance of a Rheingau, the body of a light Rheinhessen, and the acidity of a Mosel. The perfumed aroma of a Nahe wine is unique, as are its extremely fragrant flavor and soft, smooth style.

DESPITE AN ABUNDANCE of Roman roads and villas, viticulture came relatively late to the Nahe, in the eighth century. As in the rest of Germany, the vineyards underwent expansion in the 12th and 13th centuries, and by the 19th century the Nahe was universally considered to be on a par with the Rheingau. Strangely, by World War II it had become Germany's least-known region. This had nothing to do with a loss of either quantity or quality: excellent vineyards such as Kupfergrube at Schlossböckelheim, today widely acclaimed as the greatest of all Nahe vineyards, did not even exist before 1900. The decline was probably due instead to the fact that the region was a relatively small area of scattered vineyards, and as such it was difficult to compete with larger, more compact ones. When those larger competitors also became industrialized, they prospered and developed sophisticated transportation systems, edging the Nahe further into the cold. As a region with an essentially rural, nonindustrialized, mixed-agricultural economy,

it looked inward. Its own population could consume most of its production with little trouble, and so the Nahe's wines adopted a lower profile on national and international markets.

SMALL COULD BE SO BEAUTIFUL

If the majority of the grape varieties cultivated in the Nahe were Riesling, the region would be able to capitalize on its limited size, and market the exclusive quality of its fine-wine production.

THE REGION AT A GLANCE

Area under vine
10,433 acres or 4,222 ha (decreasing)

Average yield
325 cases/acre or 74 hl/ha (decreasing)

Red wine
10% (increasing)

White wine
90% (decreasing)

Dry & semidry wine
23% Trocken, 11% Halbtrocken

Most important grape varieties
26% Riesling (decreasing), 18% Müller-Thurgau (decreasing), 9% Silvaner (decreasing), 31% Others

Infrastructure
Bereich 1; Grosslagen 7; Einzellagen 328

Note The vineyards straddle 80 *Gemeinden* (communes), the names of which may appear on the label.

QUALITY REQUIREMENTS AND AVERAGE QMP PRODUCTION

NAHE'S MINIMUM OECHSLE	QUALITY CATEGORY	HARVEST BREAKDOWN
44°	Deutscher Tafelwein	1%
47°	Landwein	1%
50–60°	* QbA	76%
67–73°	* Kabinett	17%
76–85°	* Spätlese	1%
83–88°	* Auslese	1%
110°	Beerenauslese	1%
110°	Eiswein	1%
150°	Trockenbeerenauslese	1%

Minimum Oechsle levels vary according to grape variety; those that have a naturally lower sugar content may qualify at a correspondingly lower level.

THE NAHE, *see also p.345*
Between Rheinhessen and the Mittelrhein nestles the self-contained wine-producing region of the Nahe. Its namesake river has many tributaries running between spectacular overhanging cliffs.

- •   Recommended wine village or town
- ▨   Intensive vine-growing zone
- —   *Grosslage* boundary
- ▲   Height above sea level (meters)

0   1   2   3   4   5   6 miles
0   2   4   6   8   10 km

FACTORS AFFECTING TASTE AND QUALITY

LOCATION
The region balloons out from between Rheinhessen and Mittelrhein around the Nahe River, which runs parallel to, and 25 miles (40 kilometers) southeast of, the Mosel.

CLIMATE
A temperate, sunny climate with adequate rainfall and no frosts. Local conditions are influenced by the Soonwald forest to the northeast and heat-retaining, rocky hills to the east. Protected south-facing vineyards enjoy microclimates that are almost Mediterranean.

ASPECT
Vineyards are found on both the gentle and steep slopes of the Nahe and its hinterland of many small tributary river valleys. Vines grow at altitudes of between 330 and 985 feet (100 and 300 meters).

SOIL
Diverse soils ranging from quartzite and slate along the lower reaches to porphyry (hard rock poor in lime), melaphyry (hard rock rich in lime), and colored sandstone in the middle and upper reaches. Near Bad Kreuznach, weathered

clay, sandstone, limestone, loess, and loam soil may also be found. The greatest Riesling wines grow on sandstone.

VITICULTURE AND VINIFICATION
Since the mid-1960s, cultivation of Riesling and Silvaner has declined by 20 and 15 percent respectively, yet Riesling is still the most widely planted variety, accounting for some 26 percent of the Nahe's vineyards. This is due to the increased cultivation of crosses such as Kerner, Scheurebe, and Bacchus. In the cellar, methods

remain traditional but very efficient, with technically up-to-date cooperatives processing just 20 percent of the crop. As much as 40 percent of all Nahe wine is processed by small growers who sell directly to passing customers, with the remaining 40 percent belonging to the traditional industrial and export houses.

GRAPE VARIETIES
Primary varieties: Müller-Thurgau, Riesling, Silvaner
Secondary varieties: Bacchus, Faberrebe, Kerner, Scheurebe, Ruländer, Weissburgunder

---

THE APPELLATIONS OF
THE NAHE

BEREICH NAHETAL

This region-wide *Bereich* replaces the former *Bereich* of Kreuznach, which covered the area once called Untere Nahe, or Lower Nahe, and Schlossböckelheim, which is the most famous.

GROSSLAGE BURGWEG

Not to be confused with the *Grosslagen* of the same name in the Rheingau and Franken, this Burgweg produces the Nahe's greatest range of fine Riesling wines. For many years Schlossbockelheimer Kupfergrube was regarded as the best of all, but today the Oberhäuser Brücke gets most of the rave reviews.

NIEDERHAUSEN
✓ **Vineyard** *Hermannshöhle* **Grower** *Hermann Dönnhoff, Gutsverwaltung Niederhausen-Schlossböckelheim* • **Vineyard** *Hermannsberg* **Growers** *Gutsverwaltung Niederhausen-Schlossböckelheim*

NORHEIM
✓ **Vineyard** *Kirschheck* **Grower** *Dr. Crusius, Hermann Dönnhoff* • **Vineyard** *Kafels* **Grower** *Staatsweingut Bad Kreuznach*

OBERHAUSEN
✓ **Vineyard** *Brücke* **Grower** *Hermann Dönnhof*

SCHLOSSBÖCKELHEIM
✓ **Vineyard** *Kupfergrube* **Grower** *Gutsverwaltung Niederhausen-Schlossböckelheim, Hermann Dönnhoff* • **Vineyard** *Felsenberg* **Grower** *Dr. Crusius, Hermann Dönnhoff*

TRAISEN
✓ **Vineyard** *Bastei* **Grower** *Dr. Crusius* • **Vineyard** *Rotenfels* **Grower** *Dr. Crusius*

GROSSLAGE KRONENBERG

This is not a branded beer, but one of the best *Grosslagen* in the Nahe, although all its finest wines, invariably Rieslings with a magical blend of perfumed fragrance and soft yet racy acidity, carry *Einzellage* names.

BAD KREUZNACH
✓ **Vineyard** *Paradies* **Grower** *Korrell-Johanneshof* • **Vineyard** *St. Martin* **Grower** *Korrell-Johanneshof*

GROSSLAGE PARADIESGARTEN

This *Grosslage* consists of many scattered vineyards of very variable quality. Aside from Oberndorf, all its finest wines come from the very eastern edge of the Nahe. One grower, Emrich-Schönleber, has raised the Rieslings of Monzingen from relative obscurity to cult status.

MEDDERSHEIM
✓ **Vineyard** *Rheingrafenberg* **Grower** *Hexamer*

MONZINGEN
✓ **Vineyard** *Frühlingsplätzchen* **Grower** *Emrich-Schönleber* • **Vineyard** *Halenberg* **Grower** *Emrich-Schönleber, Schäfer-Fröhlich*

SOBERNHEIM
✓ **Vineyard** *Marbach* **Grower** *Hexamer*

GROSSLAGE PFARRGARTEN

Although the *Grosslage* of Pfarrgarten is relatively small, it is intensively cultivated. Grosslage Pfarrgarten lies west and slightly north of Bad Kreuznach. Wallhausen wines are the best.

WALLHAUSEN
✓ **Vineyard** *Johannisberg* **Grower** *Prinz zu Salm* ⊙ • **Vineyard** *Felseneck* **Grower** *Prinz zu Salm* ⊙

GROSSLAGE ROSENGARTEN

The true, original, and famous Rüdesheimer Rosengarten is a great Rheingau Riesling from an *Einzellage* called Rosengarten. The Nahe version may be honest enough, but it is not particularly special, being merely a modest *Grosslage* wine and, in all probability, a blend of Müller-Thurgau and Silvaner.

BOCKENAU
✓ **Vineyard** *Felseneck* **Grower** *Schäfer-Fröhlich*

ROXHEIM
✓ **Vineyard** *Berg* **Grower** *Prinz zu Salm*

GROSSLAGE SCHLOSSKAPELLE

In this *Grosslage* there are a number of attractive, good-quality wines from Münster-Sarmsheim and Dorsheim that are excellent value. In addition to some full and rich Riesling, the Weisser and Grauer Burgunder are also making a name for themselves.

DORSHEIM
✓ **Vineyard** *Burgberg* **Grower** *Schlossgut Diel* • **Vineyard** *Goldloch* **Grower** *Schlossgut Diel, J. B. Schäfer* • **Vineyard** *Pittermännchen* **Grower** *J. B. Schäfer, Schlossgut Diel*

LAUBENHEIM
✓ **Vineyard** *Karthäuser* **Grower** *Tesch* • **Vineyard** *St. Remigiusberg* **Grower** *Tesch*

WINDESHEIM
✓ **Vineyard** *Rosenberg* **Grower** *Rudolf Sinß* (red) **Non-Einzellagewein Grower** *Lindenhof* (red)

MÜNSTER (-SARMSHEIM)
✓ **Vineyard** *Dautenpflänzer* **Growers** *Göttelmann • Kruger-Rumpf* • **Vineyard** *Rheinberg* **Grower** *Göttelmann* • **Vineyard** *Pittersberg* **Grower** *Kruger-Rumpf* • **Non-Einzellagen wine** *Kruger-Rumpf*

GROSSLAGE SONNENBORN

Sonnenborn is a one-village *Grosslage* and at least one grower in Langenlonsheim produces some interesting and fulsome wines.

LANGENLONSHEIM
✓ **Vineyard** *Löhrer Berg* **Growers** *Tesch*

OTHER CERTIFIED ORGANIC WINEMAKERS

Biodynamic
Fuchs Jacobus (Waldaubersheim)
Im Zwölberich (Langenlonsheim)
Klaus Krost (Waldlaubersheim)
Wolfgang Hermes/Hermeshof (Bretzenheim)

Organic
Aloys Müller (Pfaffen-Schwabenheim)
Anke Eckes (Windesheim)
Anni & Hermann Steitz (Dielkirchen)
Brühler Hof (Volxheim)
Georg Forster (Rümmelsheim)
Gutshöfe FVA Ernst Anhauser (Bad Kreuznach)
Hans-Gerhard Hamann (Guldental-Heddenheim)
Hanmühle (Mannweiler-Cölln)
Häussling (Laubenheim)
Konrad Knodel (Windesheim)
Rheinhold Grossmann (Windesheim)
Schillingshof (Waldlaubersheim)

THE RHEINGAU

There can be no doubt that Riesling, the king of Germany's grapes, is more at home in and around the village of Johannisberg in the Rheingau than anywhere else in the world. Nowhere else can it produce such lush, juicy-ripe wines with distinctive, silky-smooth peach fruit.

MANY COUNTRIES OF THE WORLD use the synonym "Johannisberg Riesling" to distinguish the true Riesling grape variety from the many false and inferior Rieslings that claim the name. There can be no doubt that the Riesling grape luxuriates on this single sun-blessed slope of the Johannisberg vineyard in a most unique way.

Even at QbA level, the relaxed and confident style of a good Rheingau wine will leave a soft, satisfying, and elegant taste of peaches in the mouth. This gradually merges into a youthful, honeyed character that has nothing to do with *Edelfäule* (botrytis,

VITICULTURE IN THE RHEINGAU
Just under 80 percent of the vines are Riesling, and it is here that Riesling has historically ripened to such perfection that the wines have a juicy peachiness.

THE REGION AT A GLANCE

Area under vine
8,125 acres or 3,129 ha (decreasing)

Average yield
295 cases/acre or 67 hl/ha (increasing)

Red wine
12% (increasing)

White wine
88% (decreasing)

Dry & semidry wine
66% Trocken, 22% Halbtrocken

Most important grape varieties
79% Riesling (decreasing), 12% Spätburgunder (increasing), 2% Müller-Thurgau (decreasing), 7% Others

Infrastructure
Bereich 1; *Grosslagen* 10; *Einzellagen* 118

Note The vineyards of Rheingau straddle 28 *Gemeinden* (communes), the names of which may appear on the label.

or noble rot), overripeness, or bottle-aging. One can prefer other stylistic renditions of the Riesling grape, but it is impossible to find finer, more graceful examples.

THE RHEINGAU'S INITIAL CHARTA FOR QUALITY

In the midst of the excitement generated by Germany's new *trocken* wines, it became evident to various top Rheingau estates that most of the wines exported were bulk blended and of low commercial quality. Since these properties had traditionally produced naturally drier wines, they believed that a continuance

Recommended wine village or town

Intensive vine-growing zone

Grosslage boundary

Height above sea level (meters)

0 1 2 3 4 5 6 miles
0 2 4 6 8 10 km

THE RHEINGAU, *see also* p.345
This region's vineyards cling to the northern banks of the Rhine and Main rivers, in the area that curves gently between the towns of Mainz and Wieshaden.

QUALITY REQUIREMENTS AND AVERAGE QMP PRODUCTION

RHEINGAU'S MINIMUM OECHSLE	QUALITY CATEGORY	HARVEST BREAKDOWN
44°	Deutscher Tafelwein	0.5%
53°	Landwein	0.5%
57–60°	* QbA	70%
73–80°	* Kabinett	20%
85–95°	* Spätlese	5%
95–105°	* Auslese	1%
125°	Beerenauslese	1%
125°	Eiswein	1%
150°	Trockenbeerenauslese	1%

Minimum Oechsle levels vary according to grape variety; those that have a naturally lower sugar content may qualify at a correspondingly lower level.

of poor *trocken* wines could damage their own image, so they banded together to protect it. In 1983, the Association of Charta (pronounced "karta") Estates was launched to "further the classic Rheingau Riesling style, to upgrade the quality of Rheingau wines, and to make them unique among wines from other growing areas." Although this could not have succeeded without the active support of almost all the best Rheingau producers, the engine that relentlessly drove the Charta organization was, until his untimely death, Georg Breuer. Under his direction, Charta became the antithesis of any official quality-control system, as it aspired to the highest possible quality, rather than succumbing to the lowest

common denominator. When first drawn up, the Charta's rules were uncommonly stiff; yet every few years, Breuer would tighten the ratchet a bit more by issuing even tougher rules.

TROCKEN WINES

One in every five bottles of German wine is *trocken,* or dry, but many of these are thin and short. The intrinsically riper grapes grown by the Rheingau's Charta estates produce a fatter, fuller style of wine that adapts naturally to the *trocken* style, especially with food; but *trocken* wines produced in other regions have come on in leaps and bounds since the early 1990s. They are now well balanced, with an elegance that was missing from even the best of the best in the late 1980s. Due to the botrytis found in *Spätlese* and *Auslese* grapes used, they also possess a level of youthful complexity that is seldom encountered in other wines. They are very accessible when young, but rarely improve after their first flush of youth.

SCHLOSS VOLLRADS
This famous wine schloss was built circa 1300 by the Knights of Greiffenclau.

THE CHARTA RULES

I have tasted many Charta wines and am convinced that they are indeed superior to other Rheingau wines. It must be emphasized, however, that it is only dry styles that are subject to the Charta organization's regulations—great QmP Rheingau wines of sweet styles from *Auslese* upward are not affected. A Charta wine may be recognized by the traditional tall, slim, brown bottle typical of the Rheingau region and by the distinctive "Charta capsule" consisting of a Romanesque double-arch on a white background. There is also a label on the back with the same insignia.

Charta wines are examined organoleptically (using only the senses of taste, smell, and sight) before and after bottling. There is a second examination to check the authenticity of the original sample. Wines destined to receive the Charta imprimatur must be accompanied by official analysis documents and must also satisfy certain criteria laid down by the Association of Charta Estates, as follows:

The wines that are submitted for examination must be made in a "dry" style and conform to the following:

• 100 percent own estate production

• 100 percent Riesling grapes

• Grapes handpicked by *tries*

• Minimum of 12 percent potential alcohol

• Maximum production of 50 hl/ha (220 cases/acre)

• No *Prädikat* may be mentioned*

The wines must have the true characteristics of a Riesling, of the specific vintage, and of the vineyard where the grapes were grown.

Registration has to be made four weeks prior to the date of examination, indicating the vintage and category.

*Older vintages of Prädikat wines may be encountered. These will not have been produced according to the above rules if only for the simple reason that they have not been made in a dry style, but they will have undergone the same exhaustive tasting and, if selected, become "Charta Designated," rather than "Charta Approved."

As a control, normal wines of comparable location and category are tasted blind alongside wines submitted for examination. Charta wines have to surpass the quality of these standard wines in each of the required aspects. The wines provided for the second tasting, as well as being a control, have to be accompanied by the analysis of the AP number (see p.346). The results of these tests are lodged with the association and can be used in the eventuality of any subsequent claim that a member is passing off an inferior wine as a Charta wine.

Charta capsule   Back label

CAPSULE AND BACK LABEL
All wines that have passed the Charta examination are sealed with a capsule bearing the organization's logo consisting of a Romanesque double-arch that also appears on the back label.

CHARTA BOTTLE
Originally all bottles were embossed with the Charta logo similar to the example here. However, the cost of embossing proved prohibitive for some of the smaller producers, and it is now optional.

Charta bottle

BERG SCHLOSSBERG VINEYARDS, RÜDESHEIM
*These south-facing vineyards on the slopes of Berg Schlossberg
are blessed with perfect exposure to the sun's rays.*

FACTORS AFFECTING TASTE AND QUALITY

LOCATION
The Rheingau is a compact region only 22 miles (36 kilometers) long, situated on the northern banks of the Rhine and Main rivers between Bingen and Mainz.

CLIMATE
Vines are protected from cold by the tempering effect of the rivers and the shelter provided by the Taunus Mountains. The region receives above-average hours of sunshine during the growth period of May to October.

ASPECT
The vines grow at an altitude of 330 to 985 feet (100 to 300 meters) on a superb, fully south-facing slope.

SOIL
Quartzite and weathered slate-stone in the higher situated sites produce the greatest Riesling, while loam, loess, various types of clay, and sandy gravel soils of the lower vineyards give a fuller, more robust style. The blue phyllite-slate around Assmannshausen is traditionally thought to favor the Spätburgunder.

VITICULTURE AND VINIFICATION
In contrast to other German regions, the Rheingau consists of a large number of independent wine estates (500 odd) in a relatively compact area. There are approximately 2,600 private growers, many of whom make and market their own wines, while others supply the region's 10 cooperatives. The Riesling grape variety represents almost 80 percent of the vines cultivated and it is traditional in this region to vinify all but the sweetest wines in a drier style than would be used in other regions. Assmannshausen is famous for its red wine, one of Germany's best.

GRAPE VARIETIES
Primary varieties: Riesling
Secondary varieties: Ehrenfelser, Kerner, Müller-Thurgau, Silvaner, Spätburgunder, Weissburgunder

THE CHARTA'S NEW CLASSIFIED VINEYARD WINES

Look out for Charta *Einzellage* wines with a black bottom border bearing not one but three Romanesque double-arches on the front label. This is verification that the wine comes not from the grossly inflated official *Einzellagen*, but from the original, authentic site, which Charta has called *Erstes Gewächs* or First Growths. They must conform to the same rules (i.e., dry style with no mention of *Prädikat*), although new regulations to cover botrytis and even Spätburgunder *Erstes Gewächs* are under study. The difference between official and authentic *Einzellage* size can be, as you can see, quite enormous. In fact, the 1971 German wine law is nothing less than the promotion of legalized fraud on a massive and widespread scale.

VILLAGE	EINZELLAGE	VINEYARD SIZE		1971 EXPANSION
		Official	Charta	
Lorch	Bodenthal-Steinberg	28.1	12.3	128%
Lorch	Kapellenberg	56.9	17.9	218%
Lorch	Krone	14.5	7.5	93%
Assmannshausen	Höllenberg	43.4	20	117%
Rüdesheim	Berg Schlossberg	25.5	23.2	10%
Rüdesheim	Berg Roseneck	26.7	16.2	65%
Rüdesheim	Berg Rottland	36.2	32.3	12%
Geisenheim	Fuchsberg	44.4	5.6	693%
Geisenheim	Rothenberg	26.8	9	198%
Geisenheim	Kläuserweg	57.6	14.3	303%
Geisenheim	Mäuerchen	32.6	3.6	8.60%
Johannisberg	Schloss Johannisberg	21.9	16.6	32%
Johannisberg	Klaus	2	2	0%
Johannisberg	Hölle	20.9	6.2	237%
Johannisberg	Mittelhölle	6.5	6.5	0%
Winkel	Jesuitengarten	31.2	26	20%
Winkel	Hasensprung	103.8	19.9	421%
Winkel	Schloss Vollrads	37.7	15	151%
Mittelheim	St Nikolaus	44.8	6.7	569%
Oestrich	Lenchen	130.6	35.8	265%
Oestrich	Doosberg	137.9	38.4	259%
Hattenheim	Engelmannsberg	14.1	10.5	34%
Hattenheim	Mannberg	8.1	8.1	0%
Hattenheim	Pfaffenberg	6.6	6.6	0%
Hattenheim	Nussbrunnen	10.8	10.8	0%
Hattenheim	Wisselbrunnen	16.9	9.7	74%
Hattenheim	Steinberg	36.7	26.9	36%
Hallgarten	Schönhell	52.1	18.9	176%
Erbach	Marcobrunn	5.2	5.2	0%
Erbach	Steinmorgen	28.2	8.6	228%
Erbach	Siegelsberg	15.1	13.7	10%
Erbach	Hohenrain	17.1	5.8	195%

VILLAGE	EINZELLAGE	VINEYARD SIZE		1971 EXPANSION
		Official	Charta	
Erbach	Schlossberg	28.1	12.3	128%
Kiedrich	Gräfenberg	56.9	17.9	218%
Kiedrich	Wasseros	14.5	7.5	93%
Eltville	Sonnenberg	43.4	20	117%
Rauenthal	Baiken	25.5	23.2	10%
Rauenthal	Gehrn	26.7	16.2	65%
Rauenthal	Rothenberg	36.2	32.3	12%
Rauenthal	Nonnenberg	44.4	5.6	693%
Rauenthal	Wülfen	26.8	9	198%
Rauenthal	Wildsau	57.6	14.3	303%
Martinsthal	Langenberg	32.6	3.6	806%
Wallut	Walkenberg	21.9	16.6	32%
Wiesbaden	Neroberg	2	2	0%
Hochheim	Domdechaney	20.9	6.2	237%
Hochheim	Kirchenstück	6.5	6.5	0%
Hochheim	Hölle	31.2	26	20%
Hochheim	Königin Victoria Ber	103.8	19.9	421%

THE APPELLATIONS OF
THE RHEINGAU

BEREICH JOHANNISBERG

This *Bereich* covers the entire Rheingau. Trading off the famous village of Johannisberg, situated behind Schloss Johannisberg, lesser wines sell well under it. However, some producers have started using *Grosslage* names on labels and because they do not use the word "*Grosslage*," this implies the wine might be from one specific site, and perhaps of better quality.

GROSSLAGE BURGWEG

This is the westernmost *Grosslage*. If a wine bears its name on the label and clearly shows "Riesling," it may well be good, but it will not in any way compare with Burgweg's superb *Einzellage* wines that are produced by the great estates or small growers.

GEISENHEIM
✓ **Vineyard** *Rothenberg* **Grower** *Wegeler-Gutshaus Oestrich*

RÜDESHEIM
✓ **Vineyard** *Berg Roseneck* **Grower** *Josef Leitz, August Kesseler* • **Vineyard** *Berg Rottland* **Growers** *Georg Breuer, Johannishof, Josef Leitz, Wegeler-Gutshaus Oestrich* • **Vineyard** *Berg Schlossberg* **Growers** *Georg Breuer, August Kesseler* (red and white), *Josef Leitz* • **Vineyard** *Bischofsberg* **Growers** *Georg Breuer, August Kesseler* • **Premium Red Wine Blends Growers** *Breuer* (Spätburgunder "S")

GROSSLAGE DAUBHAUS

The best vines of Daubhaus, which is the most easterly *Grosslage* in *Bereich* Johannisberg, grow in just one tiny, isolated, but excellent strip at Hochheim. The wines are firm and full, but do not quite match the elegance of the Rheingau's very best.

HOCHHEIM
✓ **Vineyard** *Domdechaney* **Grower** *Domdechant Werner'sches Weingut* • **Vineyard** *Kirchenstück* **Grower** *Domdechant Werner'sches Weingut, Franz Künstler* • **Vineyard** *Hölle* **Growers** *Franz Künstler* • **Vineyard** *Reichestal* **Grower** *Franz Künstler* (red)

WICKER
✓ **Vineyard** *Mönchsgewann* **Grower** *Joachim Flick*

GROSSLAGE DEUTELSBERG

Grosslage Deutelsberg encompasses the great Erbach vineyards as well as the rather underrated wines of Hattenheim, which have great strength and longevity. It also includes the famous Kloster Eberbach and Mariannenau Island vineyard, where there is a little Chardonnay grown.

HATTENHEIM
✓ **Vineyard** *Pfaffenberg* **Grower** *Domäne Schloss Schönborn* • **Vineyard** *Wisselbrunnen* **Growers** *Josef Spreitzer, Hans Lang, Schloss Reinhartshausen*

GROSSLAGE ERNTEBRINGER

The most often-seen of the Rheingau's *Grosslagen*, Erntebringer is also its best, although not comparable to the *Einzellagen*, particularly the legendary Schloss Johannisberg and the grossly underrated Klaus.

GEISENHEIM
✓ **Vineyard** *Klaus* **Grower** *Prinz von Hessen*

JOHANNISBERG
✓ **Vineyard** *Hölle* **Grower** *Johannishof* • **Vineyard** *Schloss Johannisberg* **Grower** *Schloss Johannisberg* • **Vineyard** *Klaus* **Growers** *Prinz von Hessen*

WINKEL
✓ **Vineyard** *Hasensprung* **Grower** *Prinz von Hessen* • **Vineyard** *Schloss Vollrads* **Grower** *Schloss Vollrads*

GROSSLAGE GOTTESTHAL

It is strange that this *Grosslage*, sandwiched between the superb Deutelsberg and Honigberg, should be disappointing in the wines it produces. However, some excellent, long-lived Riesling can be found.

OESTRICH
✓ **Vineyard** *Lenchen* **Growers** *Wegeler-Gutshaus Oestrich, Peter Jakob Kühn, Josef Spreitzer*

GROSSLAGE HEILIGENSTOCK

The best product of this small *Grosslage* is the fabulous, peach-and-honey Riesling of Kiedrich, often culminating in some of the world's most noble sweet wines. The *Grosslage* wine can also be good.

KIEDRICH
✓ **Vineyard** *Gräfenberg* **Grower** *Robert Weil*

GROSSLAGE HONIGBERG

Wines of great vitality, finesse; all the elegant, mouthwatering, peachy fruit, and youthful honey you could expect from top Rheingau wines.

ERBACH
✓ **Vineyard** *Hohenrain* **Grower** *Jakob Jung* • **Vineyard** *Marcobrunn* **Growers** *Schloss Schönborn* • *Schloss Reinhartshausen* ◉ • **Vineyard** *Michelmark* **Grower** *Jakob Jung* • **Vineyard** *Steinmorgen* **Grower** *Heinz Nikolai* • **Vineyard** *Schlossberg* **Grower** *Schloss Reinhartshausen*

WINKEL
✓ **Vineyard** *Hasensprung* **Growers** *Prinz von Hessen* • **Vineyard** *Jesuitengarten* **Growers** *Prinz von Hessen, J. Wegeler Erben*

GROSSLAGE MEHRHÖLZCHEN

The *Grosslage* of Mehrhölzchen, on higher, steeper slopes than the rest of the Rheingau, is tucked up beneath the Taunus hills. The area is planted almost entirely with Riesling, and the wine is fat, almost heavy. It is sometimes full of fruit, displaying a unique spicy aroma.

HALLGARTEN
✓ **Vineyard** *Jungfer* **Grower** *Prinz*

GROSSLAGE STEIL

The tiny *Grosslage* of Steil divides the *Grosslage* of Burgweg. Steil is famous for the red wines of Assmannshausen. These are soft and delicate, and have a pure varietal style, but possess neither the body nor the tannin one is accustomed to finding to some degree in any red wine, whatever its grape variety or provenance. The majority of the vineyards in Grosslage Steil are situated on steep, southwest-facing slopes, but those of Höllenberg, which notably produce the best wine, are situated on a tiny, south-facing tributary.

ASSMANNSHAUSEN
✓ **Vineyard** *Höllenberg* **Growers** *August Kesseler* (red), *Staatsweingüter Assmannshausen, Robert König* (red), *Weingut Krone* (red)

GROSSLAGE STEINMÄCHER

The vineyards of Grosslage Steinmächer are less intensively cultivated than those situated in the main body of the Rheingau's vine-growing area, but this does not mean that the wines they produce are in any way less impressive.

WALLUF
✓ **Vineyard** *Walkenberg* **Grower** *J. B. Becker*

OTHER CERTIFIED ORGANIC WINEMAKERS

Organic
Altenkirch & Schmidt (Lorch im Rheingau)
Asbach-Kretschmar (Rüdesheim)
Bernd J Richter (Hochheim)
Graf von Kanitz (Lorch im Rheingau)
Hans-Josef Engelmann (Kiedrich)
Hirt-Albrecht (Eltville)
Jakob Hamm (Oestrich-Winkel)
Rheinhard Glassner (Lorch im Rheingau)
Stefan Muskat (Geisenheim)
Troitzsch-Pusinelli (Lorch)

RHEINHESSEN

Rheinhessen is the most heavily cultivated of all Germany's Qualitätswein regions. The diversity of its soils and grape varieties makes it impossible to convey a uniform impression of its wines. Riesling is planted in just eight percent of its vineyards. These vineyards produce cheap, unpretentious wines, ranging from mild Silvaner to aromatic Müller-Thurgau, but some truly fine wines are to be found.

RHEINHESSEN IS INDISPUTABLY LINKED with the ubiquitous Liebfraumilch. This is partly because the area is responsible for producing one in every two bottles, partly because of the famous Liebfraumilch-Kirchenstück in Worms, where the Liebfraumilch story began; and partly because Sichel & Co. brews up perhaps the most famous Liebfraumilch ("Blue Nun") in sleepy Alzey. Nierstein carries a similar stigma to that of Liebfraumilch in the minds of many experienced drinkers,

FACTORS AFFECTING TASTE AND QUALITY

LOCATION
This region is situated between the towns of Bingen, Mainz, and Worms, immediately south of the Rheingau.

CLIMATE
Rheinhessen enjoys a temperate climate and is protected from cold winds by the Taunus hills to the north and the Odenwald forest to the east. Vineyards that slope down to the river are protected by the Rhine terrace itself.

ASPECT
On the river slopes of the Rhine Terrace vines grow on east- and southeast-facing slopes at an altitude of between 330 and 660 feet (100 and 200 meters), while those in Rheinhessen's hinterland are found at various heights and with every possible aspect.

SOIL
Mainly loess deposited during interglacial sandstorms, but also limestone, sandy-marl, quartzite, porphyry-sand, and silty-clay. Riesling growers favor heavier marl soil, except near Bingen, where there is an outcropping of quartzite-slate. A red, slaty-sandy clay soil known as *rotliegendes* is found on the best, steep riverfront vineyards of Nackenheim and Nierstein.

VITICULTURE AND VINIFICATION
Due to the large number of part-time growers, much of the wine is made from vast vineyard yields and bulk-blended into cheap generic wines such as Bereich Nierstein, and, of course, Liebfraumilch. At the other extreme, small quantities of some fine wines are produced on the best estates.

GRAPE VARIETIES
Primary varieties: Müller-Thurgau, Silvaner, Riesling
Secondary varieties: Bacchus, Faberrebe, Huxelrebe, Kerner, Morio-Muskat, Portugieser, Scheurebe

due to the huge quantities of the cheap Bereich Nierstein and Niersteiner Gutes Domtal that flood the market and which downgrade the reputation of the high-quality Niersteiner *Einzellagen*.

THE RHINE TERRACE

Despite the high volume of indifferent wines, there are many great growers and estates producing good wine in this region. If you are looking for an initial increase

Legend:
- Recommended wine village or town
- Intensive vine-growing zone
- *Bereich* boundary
- *Grosslage* boundary
- ▲ Height above sea level (meters)

0　2　4　6　8 miles
0　2　4　6　8　10　12 km

RHINE TERRACE VINEYARDS AT NIERSTEIN
Nierstein is one of the nine member villages of the "Rhein Terrasse" group, which offers good-value, quality wines. New grape crosses are a feature of this area.

RHEINHESSEN, see also p.345
One of Germany's largest regions in terms of acres under vine, this is an area of great variety where several different grapes are grown.

in quality for a modest price, look out for the "Rhein Terrasse" sticker on bottles of Rheinhessen wine.

The Rhine Terrace comprises nine villages on the slopes that descend from Rheinhessen's plateau to the Rhine River. These villages and their *Grosslagen* are as follows: Bodenheim in the St. Alban *Grosslage*; Nackenheim in the Gutes Domtal *Grosslage*; Nierstein, which is shared by the *Grosslagen* of Gutes Domtal, Spiegelberg, Rehbach, and Auflangen; Oppenheim in the *Grosslagen* of Güldenmorgen and Krötenbrunnen; Dienheim, also in the Krötenbrunnen *Grosslage*; Guntersblum and Ludwigshöhe, both of which are in the Krötenbrunnen and Vogelsgarten *Grosslagen*; and Alsheim and Mattenheim, in the *Grosslage* of Rheinblick.

LIEBFRAUMILCH COUNTRY IN THE SPRING
The village of Grau-Heppenheim, near Alzey, the home of Blue Nun, in the large Petersberg Grosslage.

QUALITY REQUIREMENTS AND AVERAGE QMP PRODUCTION

RHEINHESSEN'S MINIMUM OECHSLE	QUALITY CATEGORY	HARVEST BREAKDOWN
44°	Deutscher Tafelwein	0.5%
53°	Landwein	0.5%
60–62°	* QbA	69%
73–76°	* Kabinett	17%
85–90°	* Spätlese	8%
92–100°	* Auslese	1%
125°	Beerenauslese	2%
125°	Eiswein	1%
150°	Trockenbeerenauslese	1%

Minimum Oechsle levels vary according to grape variety; those that have a naturally lower sugar content may qualify at a correspondingly lower level.

THE REGION AT A GLANCE

Area under vine
62,269 acres or 25,199 ha (decreasing)

Average yield
415 case/acre or 95 hl/ha (increasing)

Red wine
13% (increasing)

White wine
87% (decreasing)

Dry & semidry wine
22% Trocken, 8% Halbtrocken

Most important grape varieties
20% Müller-Thurgau (decreasing), 11% Silvaner (decreasing), 10% Riesling (increasing), 8% Dornfelder (increasing), 8% Kerner (decreasing), 7% Portugieser (increasing), 6% Scheurebe (decreasing), 6% Bacchus (decreasing), 24% Others

Infrastructure
Bereiche 3; Grosslagen 24; Einzellagen 434

Note The vineyards of Rheinhessen straddle 167 *Gemeinden* (communes), the names of which may appear on the label.

THE APPELLATIONS OF
RHEINHESSEN

BEREICH BINGEN

Abutting the Nahe region to the west and separated by the Rhine from the Rheingau to the north, Bereich Bingen is the smallest of Rheinhessen's three *Bereiche* and the least important in terms of both the quantity and quality of the wine produced.

GROSSLAGE ABTEY

The *Grosslage* of Abtey does not have any outstanding villages, vineyards, or growers, although good-quality wines are produced in the village of St. Johann.

GROSSLAGE ADELBERG

Some good value wines can be found in the small town of Wörrstadt, but in terms of quality no vineyards or growers stand out.

GROSSLAGE KAISERPFALZ

Kaiserpfalz is a *Grosslage* consisting mainly of Bingen and Mainz, with vineyards facing to both the east and west. This *Grosslage* produces some of the region's most promising red wines from the Portugieser and Spätburgunder grapes. The village of Ingelheim is one of the places that claim to be the birthplace of the emperor Charlemagne.

INGELHEIM

✓ **Vineyard** *Steinacker* **Grower** *Arndt F. Werner* ❂ (red and white)

GROSSLAGE KURFÜRSTENSTÜCK

Gau-Bickelheim is the home of Rheinhessen's huge central cooperative, but it has been the good growers or excellent *Staatsdomäne* from the *Einzellage* of Kapelle that have produced superior wines in the past.

GROSSLAGE RHEINGRAFENSTEIN

Some exciting efforts from a new shooting star demonstrate the potential of this *Grosslage*.

SIEFERSHEIM

✓ **Vineyard** *Heerkretz* **Grower** *Wagner-Stempel* • **Vineyard** *Höllberg* **Grower** *Wagner-Stempel* • **Premium Red Wine Blend Grower** *Wagner-Stempel* (Spaetburgunder "R")

GROSSLAGE SANKT ROCHUSKAPELLE

Bingen is often thought to belong more to the Nahe region than to Rheinhessen, but 14 of its

18 *Einzellagen* belong to this Rheinhessen *Grosslage*, which is among the best in *Bereich* Bingen.

HORRWEILER

✓ **Vineyard** *Gewürzgärtchen* **Grower** *Huf-Doll*

BEREICH NIERSTEIN

Although this is a famous *Bereich* with many superb sites and great growers, most wines sold under its label include some of the most dull, characterless, and lackluster in all of Germany. Wine enthusiasts will find it best to choose the great *Einzellagen* and leave these *Grosslage* products alone.

GROSSLAGE AUFLANGEN

This is the best of the three *Grosslagen* that encompass some parts of Nierstein (the other two are Rehbach and Spiegelberg). Its vineyard area actually begins in the center of the town, then stretches west to include the south- and southeast-facing vineyards of the tiny tributary of the Rhine that flows through Schwabsburg, and then north to the Kranzberg, which overlooks the Rhine itself.

NIERSTEIN

☑ **Vineyard** *Oelberg* **Growers** *Heyl zu Herrnsheim* ⊙ • *St. Antony, Seebrich*

GROSSLAGE DOMHERR

Once forming ecclesiastical vineyards (Domherr means "Canon of the Cathedral") this *Grosslage* has good vineyards on steep slopes, but there are few outstanding growers.

GROSSLAGE GÜLDENMORGEN

Güldenmorgen was once a fine-quality *Einzellage* belonging to Oppenheim, but now encompasses three villages. The best wines come from the Sackträger site. Please note that although the village of Uelversheim is clearly situated in the *Grosslage* of Krötenbrunnen, the eastern tail end of its vineyards actually overlaps Güldenmorgen.

OPPENHEIM

☑ **Vineyard** *Sackträger* **Grower** *Manz* • *Kühling-Gillot*

GROSSLAGE GUTES DOMTAL

This district covers a vast area of Rhine hinterland behind the better *Grosslagen* of Nierstein. Although it encompasses 15 villages, most is sold under the ubiquitous Niersteiner Gutes Domtal (sometimes Domtal) name. Much is decidedly inferior and cheapens the reputation of Nierstein's truly great wines. The most famous village is Dexheim, because of its so-called Doktor, named after the old spelling of the great Bernkasteler Doctor vineyard. But neither Dexheim generally, nor Dexheimer Doktor specifically, warrant the attention.

WEINOLSHEIM

☑ **Vineyard** *Kehr* **Grower** *Manz*

GROSSLAGE KRÖTENBRUNNEN

This district encompasses those parts of Oppenheim's vineyards that are not included in the *Grosslage* Güldenmorgen, and the wide-ranging vineyards of Guntersblum.

GROSSLAGE PETERSBERG

This *Grosslage* lies behind Gutes Domtal and is wedged between the *Bereiche* of Bingen and Wonnegau. Although large, this *Grosslage* has few, if any, exciting sites or growers.

GROSSLAGE REHBACH

Rehbach is one of the greatest *Grosslagen* in Rheinhessen, consisting of a long, thin strip of very steep terraced slopes overlooking the Rhine, just north of Nierstein. Riesling wines produced by these vineyards are aromatic, intense, and delightfully mellow, yet have a definite raciness on the finish.

NIERSTEIN

☑ **Vineyard** *Hipping* **Growers** *Georg Albrecht Schneider, St. Antony* • **Vineyard** *Pettenthal* **Growers** *Heyl zu Herrnsheim* ⊙, *St. Antony, Gunderloch, Kühling-Gillot*

GROSSLAGE RHEINBLICK

This district produces better-than-average Grosslage wines.

GROSSLAGE ST. ALBAN

Named after the St. Alban monastery, which once owned most of the land in this underrated *Grosslage* situated between Mainz and Nierstein.

The *Einzellage* wines have fine, positive character and usually represent excellent value for money.

GROSSLAGE SPIEGELBERG

The largest of Nierstein's riverside districts, its vineyards stretch to the north and south of both the famous town and the Grosslage Auflangen. Ignore the ubiquitous, mild, and neutral-flavored *Grosslagen* wines and choose the wines of the finer *Einzellagen* that are situated between Nierstein and Oppenheim.

NACKENHEIM

☑ **Vineyard** *Rothenberg* **Grower** *Gunderloch*

GROSSLAGE VOGELSGARTEN

This is not, in fact, one of the best Rheinhessen districts, although Weingut Ohnacker makes fine, rich, sometimes powerful wines that are well worth seeking out.

BEREICH WONNEGAU

The least-known of Rheinhessen's three *Bereiche*, Wonnegau contains the world-famous (although not world-class) Liebfrauenstift *Einzellage*, which had the rather dubious honor of giving birth to Liebfraumilch. Wonnegau means "province of great joy."

GROSSLAGE BERGKLOSTER

Some of Germany's top dry Riesling comes from Westhofen.

WESTHOFEN

☑ **Vineyard** *Aulerde* **Grower** *Wittmann* ⊙ • **Vineyard** *Morstein* **Grower** *Wittmann, Gerhard Gutzler* (red), *Keller* • **Vineyard** *Kirchspiel* **Grower** *Wittmann K. F. Groebe* • **Premium red wine blends Growers** *Gerhard Gutzler* ("GS" *barrique*)

GROSSLAGE BURG RODENSTEIN

A large proportion of the wines made in the Grosslage Burg Rodenstein district are sold under its *Grosslage* name. Most of it is well above average quality, although not in the same class as its best *Einzellage* wines. Since the mid-1990s Keller has been considered by many critics to be Germany's top wine estate.

DAHLSHEIM (an *Ortsteil* of Flörsheim-Dalsheim)

☑ **Vineyard** *Hubacker* **Grower** *Keller*

Vineyard *Bürgel* (red) **Growers** *Keller* **Non-Einzellage Premium White Grower** *Keller* (G-Max, varietals)

NIEDERFLÖRSHEIM (an *Ortsteil* of Flörsheim-Dalsheim)

☑ **Vineyard** *Frauenberg* **Growers** *Scherner-Kleinhanns*

GROSSLAGE DOMBLICK

There are few outstanding growers here, although good wines are made in the village of Monsheim, and the *Grosslage* label usually offers sound value.

MONSHEIM

☑ **Vineyard** *Silberberg* **Grower** *Keller* (Flörsheim-Dalsheim)

OFFSTEIN

☑ **Non-Einzellage Premium Red Grower** *Georg Jakob Keth*

GROSSLAGE GOTTESHILFE

A tiny district encompassing the excellent wine village of Bechtheim. Very little wine is seen on export markets under the *Grosslage* label.

BECHTHEIM

☑ **Vineyard** *Geyersberg* **Grower** *Riedenbacher Hof-Spiess* (red)

GROSSLAGE LIEBFRAUENMORGEN

This familiar sounding *Grosslage* includes the famous Liebfrauenstift-Kirchenstück vineyard in Worms, the birthplace of Liebfraumilch.

WORMS

☑ **Vineyard** *Liebfrauenstift-Kirchenstück* **Grower** *Gerhard Gutzler*

GROSSLAGE PILGERPFAD

This *Grosslage* stretches from the lesser vineyards of Bechtheim to the large Petersberg district in Bereich Nierstein.

GROSSLAGE SYBILLENSTEIN

There are no outstanding villages, vineyards, or growers in this *Grosslage*, although some valid efforts with Silvaner can be reported from the Kappellenberg vineyard. Alzey is the location of Sichel & Co., master blenders of "Blue Nun" Liebfraumilch.

WEINHEIM

☑ **Vineyard** *Kapellenberg* **Grower** *Meiser*

OTHER CERTIFIED ORGANIC WINEMAKERS

Biodynamic
Armin Ackermann (Mettenheim)
Helmut and Walfried Sander (Gau-Odernheim)
Volker Feth (Flörsheim-Dalsheim (Ortsteil Dalsheim)

Organic
Adam Schmitt (Mommenheim)
Albrecht Schütte (Alsheim)
Axel (Ober-Hilbersheim)
Bardo Kneib (Zornheim)
Berthold Ferstl (Zwingenberg)
Birkenhof (Armsheim)
Brüder Dr. Becker (Ludwigshöhe)
Dieter Klein (Offstein)
Dr. Helmut Scholl (Bornheim)

Dr. Schnell (Guntersblum)
E. Weidenbach (Ingelheim)
Eckhard (Ingelheim)
Eckhard Weitzel (Ingelheim)
Eugen Schönhals (Bieblenheim)
Gerhard Huf (Ingelheim)
Gerhard Sander (Mettenheim)
Goldberg (Osthofen)
Hans L. Spanier (Hohen-Sülzen)
Harald Scholl (Gau-Heppenheim)
Haxthäuser Hof (Ingelheim (Wackernheim)
Heinz-Walter Metzler (Bermersheim)
Helmut Kloos (Worms-Horchheim)
Hirschof (Westhofen)
Hollerhof (Fürfeld)

Jakob Neumer (Uelversheim)
Jutta & Raimund Huster (Ingelheim-Grosswinternheim)
Klaus Knobloch (Ober-Flörsheim)
Lehnerhof (Mettenheim)
Lunkenheimer (Ingelheim-Groswinternheim)
Marienhof (Dienheim)
Reh Kendermann (Bingen am Rhein)
Rösch-Spies (Guntersblum)
Rothes (Aspisheim)
Schäfer (Armsheim)
Villa Sachsen (Bingen)
Villa Waldorf Schulz (Biebelsheim)
Wambolderhof (Stadecken-Elsheim)

THE PFALZ

Germany's rising star, the Pfalz, or Rheinpfalz, as it was called until recently, has always been capable of producing world-class wines, but it has only just started doing so on any widespread scale. The best winemakers of the Pfalz now tend to make rich, powerful, spicy wines that are more reminiscent of Alsace than those of Alsace's mirror image, Baden.

RARE PHYSICAL EVIDENCE of ancient German wines exists in the Pfalz at the wine museum in Speyer. Here, a glass amphora contains genuine, golden 1,600-year-old wine, made by the Romans. By the 12th century, the Bishop of Speyer owned the best vineyards in the Pfalz and they remained the property of the Church until acquired by Napoleon.

After the great Corsican emperor somewhat reluctantly left the region, the socioeconomic composition of the Pfalz changed dramatically and irrevocably. With the restructuring came a considerably less monopolistic form of land ownership.

THE PFALZ TODAY

Sometimes referred to as the Palatinate, the Pfalz covers 50 miles (80 kilometers) of the sun-blessed vineyards of the Haardt Mountains and the Pfalz forest. It has some 25,000 smallholders, each of whom works less than about two-and-a-half acres (one hectare) on average; most are part-time. Many sell their grapes to cooperatives, who process about 25 percent of the Pfalz's output. There is, however, still a minority of estates that have larger land-holdings. The vast

THE REGION AT A GLANCE

Area under vine
54,967 acres or 22,244 ha (decreasing)

Average yield
440 cases/acre or 102 hl/ha (increasing)

Red wine
21% (increasing)

White wine
79% (decreasing)

Dry & semidry wine
46% Trocken, 16% Halbtrocken

Most important grape varieties
21% Riesling (static), 15% Müller-Thurgau (decreasing), 11% Portugieser (increasing), 10% Dornfelder (increasing), 8% Kerner (decreasing), 5% Silvaner (decreasing), 5% Spätburgunder (increasing), 25% Others

Infrastructure
Bereiche 2; Grosslagen 25; Einzellagen 335

Note: The vineyards straddle 170 communities, the names of which may appear on the label.

THE PFALZ, *see also p.345*
Over 2,000 years ago the Romans built a palace in this region. The German word "Pfalz" is derived from palatium, *Latin for "palace."*

numbers of growers, grapes, soil types, and microclimates combine to create a diversity of wine styles, from close to half of all Liebfraumilch produced (Rheinhessen accounts for most of the other half) to a wealth of expressive pure varietals. This region yields more wine than any other in Germany, and it is the smallest growers who make it such a great one.

QUALITY REQUIREMENTS AND AVERAGE QMP PRODUCTION

PFALZ'S MINIMUM OECHSLE	QUALITY CATEGORY	HARVEST BREAKDOWN
44°	Deutscher Tafelwein	1%
50–53°	Landwein	0.5%
60–62°	* QbA	70%
73—76°	* Kabinett	19.5%
85–90°	* Spätlese	5%
92–100°	* Auslese	1%
120°	Beerenauslese	1%
120°	Eiswein	1%
150°	Trockenbeerenauslese	1%

Minimum Oechsle levels vary according to grape variety; those that have a naturally lower sugar content may qualify at a correspondingly lower level.

FACTORS AFFECTING TASTE AND QUALITY

LOCATION
The second-largest German wine region, stretching 50 miles (80 km) from Rheinhessen to Alsace, bounded by the Rhine on the east and Haardt Mountains on the west.

CLIMATE
The Pfalz is the sunniest and driest wine-producing region in Germany, sheltered by the Haardt Mountains and Donnersberg hills.

ASPECT
Vineyards are sited mainly on flat land or gentle slopes, at an altitude of between 330 and 820 feet (100 and 250 meters).

SOIL
Although loam is prevalent, it is often interspersed with a wide range of other soils, from loess, sand, and weathered sandstone to widely dispersed "islands" of limestone, granite, porphyry, and clayish slate.

VITICULTURE AND VINIFICATION
The Pfalz vies with Rheinhessen as the largest wine producer among Germany's wine regions. The leading estates have a relatively high proportion of Riesling in their vineyards and produce wines of the very highest quality, although specialty Gewürztraminers and Muskatellers can be extraordinarily good when vinified dry. One-third of Pfalz wine is sold directly to consumers, and half is marketed through large commercial wineries and two dozen or so cooperatives.

GRAPE VARIETIES
Primary varieties: Müller-Thurgau, Riesling
Secondary varieties: Bacchus, Dornfelder, Gewürztraminer, Huxelrebe, Kerner, Morio-Muskat, Muskateller, Portugieser, Ruländer, Scheurebe, Silvaner, Spätburgunder

THE APPELLATIONS OF
THE PFALZ

Note In the Pfalz wine region, each *Grosslage* can be prefixed only by a specified village name. The village name has been listed here under the name of the *Grosslage*.

BEREICH MITTELHAARDT-DEUTSCHE WEINSTRASSE

The quality of wines from this *Bereich* is so high, few are sold as anything less than *Einzellagen*.

GROSSLAGE FEUERBERG
Bad Dürkheim

A versatile *Grosslage*, producing a wide range of wines from full, spicy Gewürztraminers to soft, velvety Spätburgunders.

BAD DÜRKHEIM

✓ **Premium Red Wine Blends: Grower** *Egon Schmitt* (Taurus, Thur, Duca XI)

ELLERSTADT

✓ **Vineyard** *Kirchenstück* **Grower** *Klaus Schneider* (also red and white *cuvées*)

GROSSLAGE GRAFENSTÜCK

Producer Ludi Neiss stands out with some excellent Spätburgunder and Frühburgunder.

KINDENHEIM

✓ **Non-Einzellagen red wines: Grower** *Ludi Neiss*

MÜHLHEIM

✓ **Vineyard** *Sonnenburg* **Grower** *Matthias Gaul*

GROSSLAGE HOCHMESS
Bad Dürkheim

This is a small, but high-performance *Grosslage*. It includes the best vineyards of Bad Dürkheim, although some fine wines are also produced within the boundaries of the two neighboring *Grosslagen* of Feuerberg and Schenkenböhl. The attractive wines of Grosslage Hochmess display a perfect harmony of full flavor and flowery fragrance.

BAD DÜRKHEIM

✓ **Vineyard** *Michelsberg* **Growers** *Karl Schaefer* • **Vineyard** *Spielberg* **Growers** *Karl Schaefer*

GROSSLAGE HOFSTÜCK
Deidesheim

Grosslage Hofstück produces homogeneous, noble, and elegant wines. The outstanding quality of these wines owes a great deal to the vineyard's favorable soil conditions.

DEIDESHEIM

✓ **Vineyard** *Nonnenstück* **Growers** *Bürklin-Wolf, Reichsrat Von Buhl*

RUPPERTSBERG

✓ **Vineyard** *Gaisböhl* **Grower** *Bürklin-Wolf* • **Vineyard** *Reiterpfad* **Growers** *Bassermann-Jordan, Bergdolt, A. Christmann, Dr. Deinhard, Bürklin-Wolf*

GROSSLAGE HÖLLENPFAD
Grünstadt

Produces a range of wines that are full and substantial in body but lack finesse.

GROSSLAGE HONIGSÄCKEL
Ungstein

This is a small *Grosslage* composed of varied soil and making full-bodied wines of intense flavor, especially Scheurebe.

UNGSTEIN

✓ **Vineyard** *Herrenberg* **Grower** *Pfeffingen-Fuhrmann-Eymael* • **Vineyard** *Weilberg* **Grower** *Pfeffingen-Fuhrmann-Eymael*

GROSSLAGE KOBNERT
Kallstadt

A single vineyard prior to the 1971 wine law, this is now a *Grosslage*, but a very good one.

KALLSTADT

✓ **Vineyard** *Saumagen* **Growers** *Koehler-Ruprecht, Koehler-Ruprecht* (Philippi), *Landshaus Kronenberg-Familie Bender*

GROSSLAGE MARIENGARTEN
Forst an der Weinstrasse

Nowhere in the Pfalz can Riesling wines of such incomparable finesse and intensity be found.

DEIDESHEIM

✓ **Vineyard** *Kalkofen* **Growers** *Dr. Deinhard* • *Bassermann-Jordan, Bürklin-Wolf* • **Vineyard** *Kieselberg* **Growers** *Josef Biffar, Georg Mosbacher* • **Vineyard** *Herrgottsacker* **Grower** *Dr. Deinhard* • **Vineyard** *Leinhöhle* **Grower** *Bassermann-Jordan* • **Vineyard** *Hohenmorgen* **Growers** *Bassermann-Jordan, Bürklin-Wolf, A. Christmann* • **Vineyard** *Langenmorgen* **Grower** *Dr. Deinhard*

FORST

✓ **Vineyard** *Freundstück* **Grower** *Georg Mosbacher* • **Vineyard** *Ungeheuer* **Growers** *Bassermann-Jordan, J. L. Wolf, Lucashof, Georg Mosbacher, Eugen Müller, Dr. Deinhard* • **Vineyard** *Jesuitengarten* **Growers** *Bassermann-Jordan, von Buhl, Bürklin-Wolf, Dr. Deinhard* • **Vineyard** *Kirchenstück* **Growers** *Bassermann-Jordan, Bürklin-Wolf* • **Vineyard** *Pechstein* **Growers** *Bassermann-Jordan, von Buhl, Bürklin-Wolf, J. L. Wolf*

WACHENHEIM

✓ **Vineyard** *Gerümpel* **Growers** *Bürklin-Wolf, Karl Schaefer, Josef Biffar, J. L. Wolf* • **Vineyard** *Goldbächel* **Growers** *Josef Biffar, Bürklin-Wolf* • **Vineyard** *Rechbächel* **Grower** *Bürklin-Wolf*

GROSSLAGE MEERSPINNE
Neustadt-Gimmeldingen

These climatically pampered vineyards, on the sheltered slopes of the Haardt Mountains, produce some of the very finest Pfalz wines.

GIMMELDINGEN

✓ **Vineyard** *Mandelgarten* **Growers** *A. Christmann, Müller-Catoir* • **Vineyard** *Schlössel* **Growers** *Müller-Catoir*

HAARDT

✓ **Vineyard** *Bürgergarten* **Grower** *Müller-Catoir* • **Vineyard** *Herrenletten* **Growers** *Müller-Catoir* • **Vineyard** *Mandelring* **Growers** *Müller-Catoir*

KÖNIGSBACH

✓ **Vineyard** *Idig* **Growers** *A. Christmann* (red and white) • **Vineyard** *Ölberg* **Grower** *A. Christmann* (red)

MUSSBACH

✓ **Vineyard** *Eselshaut* **Grower** *Müller-Catoir* • *A. Christmann* (red)

NEUSTADT

✓ **Vineyard** *Mönchgarten* **Grower** *Müller-Catoir*

GROSSLAGE PFAFFENGRUND
Neustadt-Diedesfeld

This is not an exceptional *Grosslage*.

DUTTWEILER

✓ **Vineyard** *Kalkberg* **Grower** *Bergdolt* (red and white)

GROSSLAGE REBSTÖCKEL
Neustadt-Diedesfeld

No outstanding villages, vineyards, or growers.

GROSSLAGE ROSENBÜHL
Freinsheim

No outstanding villages, vineyards, or growers.

GROSSLAGE SCHENKENBÖHL
Wachenheim

The third *Grosslage* to share the vineyards of Bad Dürkheim

WACHENHEIM

✓ **Vineyard** *Königswingert* **Grower** *Emil Zimmermann*

GROSSLAGE SCHNEPFENFLUG AN DER WEINSTRASSE
Forst an der Weinstrasse

Except for a small part of Forst's vineyards (the rest belong to Grosslage Mariengarten), few outstanding growers are to be found here.

FORST

✓ **Vineyard** *Stift* **Grower** *Georg Mosbacher*

GROSSLAGE SCHNEPFENFLUG VOM ZELLERTAL
Zell

No outstanding villages, vineyards, or growers.

GROSSLAGE SCHWARZERDE
Kirchheim

Mediocre Silvaner-based wines are standard here, but there are a couple of excellent growers in obscure villages that offer good value.

DIRMSTEIN

✓ **Vineyard** *Mandelpfad* **Grower** *Knipser*

GROSSKARLBACH

✓ **Vineyards** *Burgweg* (red and white)

Grower *Knipser*

LAUMERSHEIM

✓ **Vineyards** *Kirschgarten* (red) **Grower** *Knipser, Philipp Kuhn*

BEREICH SÜDLICHE WEINSTRASSE

Dominated by rather dull and neutral Müller-Thurgau, but younger winemakers are beginning to excel.

GROSSLAGE BISCHOFSKREUZ
Walsheim

Improving quality.

BURRWEILER

✓ **Vineyard** *Schlossgarten* **Grower** *Herbert Messmer*

WALSHEIM

✓ **Vineyard** *Silberberg* **Grower** *Karl Pfaffmann*

GROSSLAGE GUTTENBERG
Schweigen

When is a German wine not German? When it's grown in France, of course, where 321 acres (130 ha) of Schweigen's "sovereign" vineyards are located. Every year the growers pick their grapes in France and trundle across the border to vinify them. Weird as it might sound, the grapes are German if pressed in Germany, but French if pressed in France! The *terroir* of this *Grosslage* is most suited to the Burgunder varietals and Gewürztraminer, reflecting the area's northern extension of the Alsace vineyards.

SCHWEIGEN

✓ **Vineyard** *Sonnenberg* **Growers** *Friedrich Becker* (red and white), *Bernhart* (red and white) • **Premium Red Wine Blend Grower** *Friedrich Becker* (Tafelwein Reserve)

GROSSLAGE HERRLICH
Eschbach

An area easily capable of producing good QmP wines. The *Auslese* can be astonishingly cheap.

LEINSWEILER

✓ **Vineyard** *Sonnenberg* **Grower** *Siegrist* • **Non-Einzellagen red and white wines Grower** *Siegrist*

GROSSLAGE KLOSTER LIEBFRAUENBERG
Bad Bergzabern

One grower is beginning to break the mold.

PLEISWEILER-OBERHOFEN

✓ **Premium red wine Grower** *Wilker* (Frühburgunder)

GROSSLAGE KÖNIGSGARTEN
Godramstein

This *Grosslage* consists of some excellent wine villages and several talented winemakers.

ALBERSWEILER

✓ **Vineyard** *Latt* **Grower** *Ökonomierat Rebholz*

BIRKWEILER

✓ **Vineyard** *Kastanienbusch* **Growers** *Ökonomierat Rebholz, Dr. Wehrheim* (red and white) • **Vineyard** *Mandelberg* **Growers** *Schneider, Albersweiler* (red), *Dr. Wehrheim*

GODRAMSTEIN

✓ **Vineyard** *Münzberg* **Growers** *Münzberg* **Vineyard** *Schlangenpfiff* **Grower** *Münzberg*

SIEBELDINGEN

✓ **Vineyard** *Im Sonnenschein* **Growers** *Ökonomierat Rebholz* (red and white), *Wilhelmshof* (red and white) • **Premium Red Wine Blend Grower** *Ökonomierat Rebholz* (Tradition)

GROSSLAGE MANDELHÖHE
Maikammer

Some pleasant, attractive Rieslings.

KIRRWEILER

✓ **Vineyard** *Mandelberg* **Grower** *Bergdolt*

MAIKAMMER

✓ **Vineyard** *Heiligenberg* **Grower** *Ullrichshof-Familie Faubel* • **Vineyard** *Kapellenberg* **Grower** *Ullrichshof-Familie Faubel*

GROSSLAGE ORDENSGUT
Edesheim

Rising red wine star!

HAINFELD

✓ **Vineyard** *Kapelle* **Grower** *Gerhard Klein* **Premium red wines Grower** *Gerhard Klein* ("B," "S," Theatrum Vinum "R")

GROSSLAGE SCHLOSS LUDWIGSHÖHE
Edenkoben

No outstanding villages, vineyards, or growers.

GROSSLAGE TRAPPENBERG
Hochstadt

Few outstanding vineyards in this *Grosslage*.

ESSINGEN

✓ **Non-Einzellagen wines: Grower** *Weingut Frey & Soehne*

CERTIFIED ORGANIC PRODUCERS

Andreas Kopf (Landau)
Brigitte Hohl (Freinsheim)
Dr. Helmut Scholl (Bornheim)
Feitig-Richter (Siebeldingen)
Fippinger-Wick (Zell)
Franz Braun (Ranschbach)
Franz Krahl (Heinfeld)
Friedrich Graf (Edesheim)
G. Schwarztrauber (Mußbach)
Georg Siben Erben (Deidesheim)
Hans Clödy (Niederotterbach)
Hans Manck (Freinsheim)
Hans Pflüger (Bad Dürkheim)
Hartmut Risser (Kerzenheim)

Hartmut Stauch (Kallstadt)
Heiner Sauer (Böchingen)
Helmut Krauss (Zellertal/Zell)
Hoffmann (Göcklingen)
Isegrim-Hof, Klaus Wolf (Bad Dürkheim-Ungstein)
Janson Bernhard (Zellertal-Harxheim)
Karin Deutscher (Klein-Bockenheim)
Klaus Hohlreiter (Göcklingen)
Kurt Weber (Böchingen)
Lebenshilfe (Bad Dürkheim)
Ludwig Seiler (Weyher)

Martinshof (Böbingen)
Marzolph (Landau-Wollmesh)
Rudolf Eymann (Gönnheim)
Rummel (Landau-Nussdorf)
Schneider-Beiwinkel (Edenkoben)
Spinnrädel (Kaiserslautern)
Stefan Kuntz (Landau)
Stephanshof (St Martin)
Walbacherhof (Contwig)
Walter Merk (Ellerstadt)
Winfried Seeber (St Martin)
Wöhrle (Bockenheim)

THE HESSISCHE BERGSTRASSE

Situated between the Rheinhessen and Franken, the northern tip of Baden's vineyards is the Hessische Bergstrasse. This is the smallest and least-known of Germany's Qualitätswein regions, and its fruity wines are marked by a pronounced earthy acidity, with almost 60 percent made in a dry style.

THIS REGION CORRESPONDS to the northern section of the old Roman *strata montana*, or "mountain road," hence Bergstrasse. This ancient trade route ran from Darmstadt to Wiesloch, which is south of Heidelberg in what is now the Baden region. The Romans brought viticulture to this area, but without the monasteries, which developed, spread, and maintained the vineyards throughout the medieval period, the tradition of winemaking would have ceased long ago.

The vineyards of the Hessische Bergstrasse are dotted among orchards in a strip of foothills along the western edge of Odenwald. Protected by the Odenwald, the fragrance of fruit trees in full bloom hangs noticeably over these hills in springtime. Indeed, Odenwald's forested mountains offer such effective protection that the sun-trap vineyards of Bensheim boast the

THE HESSISCHE BERGSTRASSE, *see also p.345*
This area is called the " spring garden," because of the early flowering of its fruit and almond orchards, between which vineyards are planted.

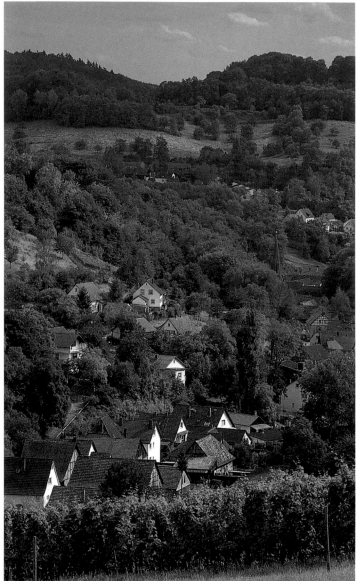

UNTERHAMBACH
A vineyard above Unterhambach, where small-scale winemaking is the norm. The cooperative in nearby Heppenheim receives 70 percent of the region's grapes.

THE REGION AT A GLANCE

Area under vine
1,087 acres or 440 ha (decreasing)

Average yield
315 cases/acre or 72 hl/ha (static)

Red wine
8% (increasing)

White wine
92% (decreasing)

Dry & semidry wine
58% Trocken, 29% Halbtrocken

Most important grape varieties
53% Riesling (decreasing), 10% Müller-Thurgau (decreasing), 8% Grauburgunder (increasing), 29% Others

Infrastructure
Bereiche 2
Grosslagen 3
Einzellagen 22

Note The vineyards of the Hessische Bergstrasse straddle 10 *Gemeinden* (communes), the names of which may appear on the label.

highest annual mean temperatures in Germany. This exceptional heat is, of course, relative to Germany's cool northern climate, and the wines produced here have an excellent level of acidity, but there is a definite peachiness to the finest Rieslings, which is an indication of their ripeness. The Hessische Bergstrasse is planted with a relatively high proportion of Riesling, particularly in the *Bereich* Starkenburg, where the best wines are grown.

The vines, which grow on relatively rich soils, produce very fruity wines that have a typical and easily recognized, earthy acidity, with a style that is richer than most Rheinhessen wines and more reminiscent of a somewhat rustic Rheingau. The Müller-Thurgau is not Germany's best, but it can be fragrant; the Silvaner lacks the assertive character found in Franken to the east; but the Gewürztraminer can have a fine, subdued style.

The vineyards are farmed by more than 1,000 individual growers with the average-sized plot being barely more than four-fifths of an acre (one-third of a hectare). Most of these growers are part-timers who tend their plots on the weekends. This helps to explain the anonymity of the area's wines, and this will remain until a number of large, quality-minded estates are established.

FACTORS AFFECTING TASTE AND QUALITY

LOCATION
Between Darmstadt and Heppenheim, beside the Odenwald Mountains, with the Rhine to the west and the Main to the north.

CLIMATE
The vineyards on the southern slopes of the valleys flanking the Bergstrasse benefit from an average temperature of over 48°F (9°C). Combined with an annual rainfall of 30 inches (75.5 centimeters), this produces ideal conditions. Bensheim is supposed to be the hottest place in Germany.

ASPECT
The best vineyards are generally on southwest-facing slopes in the *grosslagen* of Schlossberg and Wolfsmagen (particularly Kalkgasse in Bensheim and Centrericht in Heppenheim). The terrain is more one of hilly hinterland than steep valleys.

SOIL
Most of the soil consists of varying amounts of light, finely structured loess and basalt.

VITICULTURE AND VINIFICATION
The vineyards are not contiguous, but are planted rather haphazardly, sometimes on old-established terraces among orchards. Although a great many individuals grow grapes, more than half the crop is processed by the regional cooperative in Heppenheim. Müller-Thurgau is giving way to Grauburgunder, and almost 60 percent of the total wines produced in this region are technically dry (*trocken*). The State Wine Domain in Bensheim is the region's largest vineyard owner, but given the small size of this region, almost all of its wines are consumed locally.

GRAPE VARIETIES
Primary varieties: Müller-Thurgau, Riesling
Secondary varieties: Ehrenfelser, Gewürztraminer, Grauburgunder, Kerner, Ruländer, Scheurebe, Silvaner, Weissburgunder

GRONAU HESSISCHE BERGSTRASSE
Looking down the south-facing slopes of the Hemsburg vineyard toward Gronau, an Ortsteil of Bensheim.

QUALITY REQUIREMENTS AND AVERAGE QMP PRODUCTION

HESSISCHE BERGSTRASSE'S MINIMUM OECHSLE	QUALITY CATEGORY	HARVEST BREAKDOWN
44°	Deutscher Tafelwein	0.5%
53°	Landwein	0.5%
57–66°	* QbA	68%
73–80°	* Kabinett	23%
85–95°	* Spätlese	6%
95–105°	* Auslese	1%
125°	Beerenauslese	1%
125°	Eiswein	–
150°	Trockenbeerenauslese	–

Minimum Oechsle levels vary according to grape variety; those that have a naturally lower sugar content may qualify at a correspondingly lower level.

THE APPELLATIONS OF
THE HESSISCHE BERGSTRASSE

BEREICH STARKENBURG

This is the larger of this region's *Bereiche*, and the best in terms of quality. Riesling is planted in most of its vineyards.

GROSSLAGE ROTT

The largest of Starkenburg's three *Grosslagen*, this includes the northern section of Bensheim, one of the region's two best communes. The finest wine comes from its south-facing Herrnwingert vineyard.

GROSSLAGE SCHLOSSBERG

This *Grosslage* covers part of Bensheim and three villages to the south, with Heppenheim the most highly rated. A unique peachiness is associated with the sun-drenched Stemmler and Centgericht vineyards.

HEPPENHEIM
✓ **Vineyard** *Centgericht* **Grower** *Staatsweingut Bergstrasse*

GROSSLAGE WOLFSMAGEN

This includes the southern section of Bensheim with the two *Ortsteile* of Zell and Gronau.

BENSHEIM
✓ **Vineyard** *Kalkgasse* **Grower** *Staatsweingut Bergstrasse, Weingut der Stadt Bensheim*

BEREICH UMSTADT

There are no remarkable villages, vineyards, or *Grosslagen* in this *Bereich*.

ZELL VINEYARD
Vineyard in the Streichling Einzellage at Zell, near Bensheim, Hessen.

FRANKEN

Classic Franconian Silvaner wine is distinctly dry with an earthy or smoky aroma and is bottled in the traditional flask-shaped Bocksbeutel. *In this region, the Silvaner grape variety has, to a certain extent, given way to Müller-Thurgau, among others, although this trend is now being reversed.*

THERE IS ALMOST twice as much land under vine in Franken as there is in the Rheingau, for instance, but the vineyards are scattered over a far greater area and they are interspersed with meadows and forests. Franken is also a beer-producing region, and many say that more pleasure can be had from a Stein of

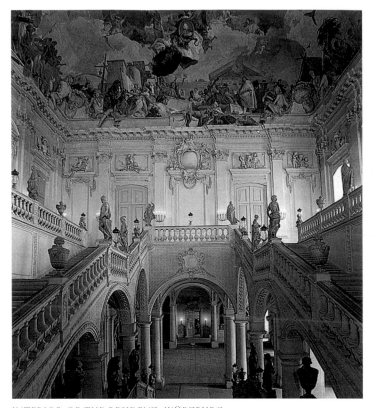

INTERIOR OF THE RESIDENZ, WÜRZBURG
The Residency in Würzburg, with its Baroque grand staircase, is now part of the Bavarian State Domain.

QUALITY REQUIREMENTS AND AVERAGE QMP PRODUCTION

FRANKEN'S MINIMUM OECHSLE	QUALITY CATEGORY	HARVEST BREAKDOWN
44°	Deutscher Tafelwein	1%
50°	Landwein	1%
60°	* QbA	69%
76–80°	* Kabinett	21%
85–90°	*Spätlese	4%
100°	*Auslese	1%
125°	Beerenauslese	1%
125°	Eiswein	1%
150°	Trockenbeerenauslese	1%

*Minimum Oechsle levels vary according to grape variety; those that have a naturally lower sugar content may qualify at a correspondingly lower level.

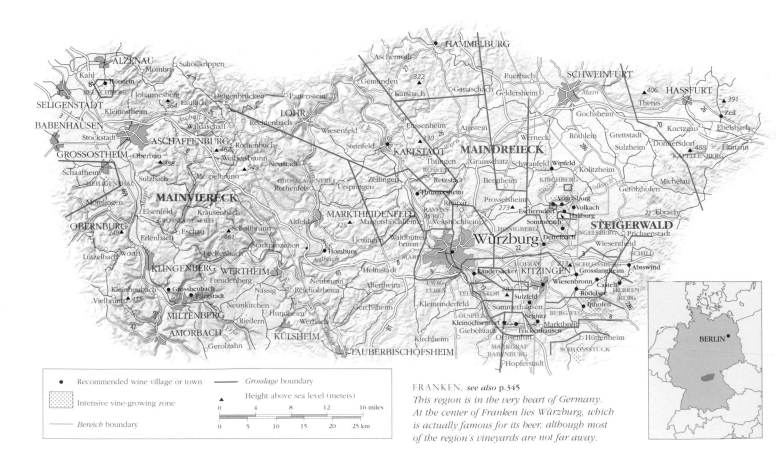

Map legend

- • Recommended wine village or town
- Intensive vine-growing zone
- Bereich boundary
- Grosslage boundary
- ▲ Height above sea level (meters)

0   4   8   12   16 miles
0 5 10 15 20 25 km

FRANKEN, *see also p.345*
This region is in the very heart of Germany. At the center of Franken lies Würzburg, which is actually famous for its beer, although most of the region's vineyards are not far away.

THE REGION AT A GLANCE

Area under vine
5,907 ha or 14,597 acres (decreasing)

Average yield
75 cases/acre or 85 hl/ha (static)

Red wine
8% (increasing)

White wine
92% (decreasing)

Dry & semidry wine
55% Trocken, 34% Halbtrocken

Most important grape varieties
39% Müller-Thurgau (decreasing), 21% Silvaner (increasing), 12% Bacchus (increasing), 28% Others

Infrastructure
Bereiche 3; *Grosslagen* 20; *Einzellagen* 171

Note: The vineyards of Franken straddle 125 *Gemeinden* (communes), the names of which may appear on labels.

THE CELLAR AT THE RESIDENZ, WÜRZBURG
The magnificent cellar under the Baroque Residency at Würzburg has been state run since 1803.

Würzburger beer than from a glass of Würzburger Stein, Franken's most famous wine. Exported wine invariably comes from the better estates and it is relatively expensive, particularly if bottled in the traditional *Bocksbeutel*.

Wines made from this region's Silvaner grape have a full taste and an earthy bite, sometimes attaining smoky complexity, making it far more interesting than most examples of this variety. However, my favorite Franconian wine is Riesling, because,

although it accounts for less than 3 percent of the vines grown and often fails to ripen here, it can be made into exceptional wines in sunny years. Rieslaner (Riesling x Silvaner cross), Bacchus, and Kerner are all successful, particularly as QmP, although it is rare to find a wine above *Auslese* level.

FACTORS AFFECTING TASTE AND QUALITY

LOCATION
Situated in Bavaria, Franken is the most northeasterly of the wine regions of former West Germany.

CLIMATE
The most continental climate of Germany's wine regions, with dry warm summers and cold winters. Severe frosts affect yields.

ASPECT
Many vineyards face south and are located on the slopes of the valleys of the Main and its

tributaries, as well as on sheltered sites of the Steigerwald.

SOIL
Franken's three *Bereiche* have different soil structures: Mainviereck has predominantly weathered colored sandstone; Maindreieck limestone with clay and loess; and Steigerwald, weathered red marl.

VITICULTURE AND VINIFICATION
The classic Franconian vine, the Silvaner, has become less widely

planted than the Müller-Thurgau, although the pendulum has started to swing back the other way. Rieslaner is something of a local specialty. Franken wines generally are usually drier than most in Germany and accompany food well. There are 6,000 growers, allowing for a great range of styles, although 40 percent of the wines are processed by the regional cooperative in Kitzingen and smaller cooperatives. Exports are insignificant, with four out of

every five bottles of Franken wine consumed within a 150 mile radius of where they were produced.

GRAPE VARIETIES
Primary varieties: Müller-Thurgau, Silvaner
Secondary varieties: Bacchus, Kerner, Ortega, Perle, Rieslaner, Riesling, Scheurebe, Spätburgunder, Traminer

THE APPELLATIONS OF
FRANKEN

Note In Franken, certain *Grosslagen* can be prefixed only by a specified village name, which is listed immediately beneath the relevant *Grosslage* name.

BEREICH MAINDREIECK

Most of the vineyards in this *Bereich* are in the vicinity of Würzburg. Grapes grown on the limestone soils can produce exceptional wines.

GROSSLAGE BURG
Hammelburg

Robust, earthy Silvaners and the lighter, fragrant Müller-Thurgaus are the main attractions.

GROSSLAGE ENGELSBERG

A new *Grosslage*, God forbid, encompassing part of two *Einzellagen* formerly in the

Grosslage Kirchberg, the Sommeracher vineyards of Katzenkopf and Rosenberg.

SOMMERACH
☑ **Vineyard** *Katzenkopf* **Grower** *Glaser-Himmelstoss*

GROSSLAGE EWIG LEBEN

This *Grosslage* contains the greatest concentration of fine vineyards in Franken and some fine wines are available under its generic designation. Ewig Leben has the advantage of a particularly favorable microclimate, which helps create wines of a rare harmony. Rieslings from this area possess an original natural charm complemented by a bouquet often reminiscent of peaches.

RANDERSACKER
☑ **Vineyard** *Sonnenstuhl* **Growers** *Schmitt's Kinder, Schloss Sommerhausen* • **Vineyard** *Marsberg* **Growers** *Schmitt's Kinder*

GROSSLAGE HOFRAT
Kintzingen

This is one of Franken's few relatively large *Grosslagen*, where the *Einzellagen* seldom excel, except for the vineyards on the lazy bend of the Main River north and south of Sulzfeld.

SULZFELD
☑ **Vineyard** *Cyriakusberg* **Grower** *Zehnthof Theo Luckert*

WEINGUT ZEHNTHOF THEO LUCKERT
Qualitätswein mit Prädikat
Sulzfelder Cyriakusberg
Riesling Spätlese trocken
Amtl. Prüf. Nr. 4050.026-94
GUTSABFÜLLUNG
D-97320 SULZFELD FRANKEN KETTENGASSE 3-5
12,5% vol   0,75 l

GROSSLAGE HONIGBERG

In this *Grosslage* there are no particularly
outstanding villages, vineyards, or growers,
although a few good wines are made in the
village of Dettelbach.

GROSSLAGE KIRCHBERG
Volkach

Grosslage Kirchberg contains some of the finest
vineyards in all of Franken. After years of
mediocrity the full potential offered by the land
is now being realized by a number of growers.

ESCHERNDORF

✓ **Vineyard** *Fürstenberg* **Grower** *Horst Sauer*
• **Vineyard** *Lump* **Growers** *Juliusspital,
Horst Sauer, Egon Schäffer, Rainer Sauer*

NORDHEIM

✓ **Vineyard** *Vögelein* **Growers** *Waldemar
Braun, Glaser-Himmelstoss*

VOLKACH

✓ **Vineyard** *Karthäuser* **Grower** *Rudolf Fürst*
(red) • *Juliusspital*

GROSSLAGE MARIENBERG

This has been created as a new *Grosslage* for
the previously *Grosslagenfrei* vineyards north
and west of Würzburg.

WÜRZBURG

✓ **Vineyard** *Stein* **Growers** *Am Stein-Ludwig
Knoll, Bürgerspital Würzburg, Juliusspital
Würzburg* • **Vineyard** *Innere Leiste*
Growers *Juliusspital, Am Stein-Ludwig
Knoll* • **Vineyard** *Abtsleite* **Growers**
Juliusspital Würzburg • **Red and White
Premium Blends Grower** *Am Stein-
Ludwig Knoll* (Montania)

GROSSLAGE
MARKGRAF BABENBERG

There are no outstanding villages, vineyards, or
growers in this *Grosslage* although some very
good wines are made in Frickenhausen.

GROSSLAGE OELSPIEL

This *Grosslage*'s main feature is a fine strip
of vineyards on the right bank of the Main,
southeast of Würzburg. Schloss Sommerhausen
has emerged as the district's leading producer.

SOMMERHAUSEN

✓ **Vineyard** *Steinbach* **Growers** *Schloss
Sommerhausen*

GROSSLAGE RAVENSBURG
Thüngersheim

Grosslage Ravensburg is situated downstream
from Franken's best vineyards, but some of the
wines here can still be quite attractive.

GROSSLAGE ROSSTAL
Karlstadt

One grower who has shown promise in this
otherwise lackluster *Grosslage* is the Weingut
Am Stein in Stetten.

STETTEN

✓ **Vineyard** *Stein* **Grower** *Am Stein-Ludwig
Knoll*

GROSSLAGE TEUFELSTOR

The *Grosslage* of Teufelstor is a continuation of
Ewig Leben, but the quality of the wines it
produces is not as good.

EIBELSTADT

✓ **Vineyard** *Kapellenberg* **Grower** *Schloss
Sommerhausen*

GROSSLAGENFREI

Many vineyards in this *Bereich* are
Grosslagenfrei (composed of individual
Einzellagen that are not grouped under any
Grosslagen).

HOMBURG

✓ **Vineyard** *Kallmuth* **Grower** *Fürst
Löwenstein*

BEREICH
MAINVIERECK

Mainviereck is the smallest of the *Bereiche*, as
well as being the most westerly, and the wines
it produces are modest.

GROSSLAGE HEILIGENTHAL

This *Grosslage* comprises one village,
Grossostheim, with just two *Einzellagen*, most
vineyards in the area being *Grosslagenfrei*.

GROSSLAGE REUSCHBERG

This *Grosslage* comprises one village, Hörstein,
and just two *Einzellagen*, most vineyards in the
area being *Grosslagenfrei*.

GROSSLAGENFREI

Most of Mainviereck's vineyards are
Grosslagenfrei (individual *Einzellagen* not
grouped under any *Grosslage*). Standards have
been rising over the past two decades and there
is potential for excellent red wines on sites
featuring red sandstone soils.

BÜRGSTADT

✓ **Vineyard** *Centgrafenberg* **Grower** *Rudolf
Fürst*

BEREICH
STEIGERWALD

The distinctive, earthy character of Franconian
wine is evident in *Bereich* Steigerwald, where
heavier soils result in fuller-bodied wines.

GROSSLAGE BURGWEG

This *Grosslage* contains one of Franken's
greatest wine villages, Iphofen.

IPHOFEN

✓ **Vineyard** *Julius-Echter Berg* **Growers**
*Johann Ruck, Hans Wirsching, Juliusspital
Würzburg* • **Vineyard** *Kalb* **Grower** *Hans
Wirsching* • **Vineyard** *Kronsberg* **Grower**
Hans Wirsching

GROSSLAGE HERRENBERG

There are a number of south-facing vineyards in
Herrenberg, yet it is the northwest-facing ones
in Castell that yield the exceptional wines.

CASTELL

✓ **Vineyard** *Kugelspiel* **Grower** *Castellsches
Domänenamt* • **Vineyard** *Schlossberg*
Grower *Castellsches Domänenamt* ◉

GROSSLAGE KAPELLENBERG

There are no outstanding villages, vineyards, or
growers in Grosslage Kapellenberg, although a
number of good wines are often produced in
the village of Zeil.

GROSSLAGE SCHILD

This *Grosslage* has no outstanding villages,
vineyards, or growers, although good wines are
made in the village of Abtswind.

GROSSLAGE SCHLOSSBERG

Underrated, with excellent, sheltered vineyards.

RÖDELSEE

✓ **Vineyard** *Schwanleite* **Grower** *Johann
Ruck*

GROSSLAGE SCHLOSSTÜCK

No outstanding villages, vineyards, or growers,
although good wines are made in Ippesheim.

CERTIFIED ORGANIC PRODUCERS

Organic	Geier (Königheim)	Manfred Schwab (Iphofen)
Anton Hell (Wiesenbronn)	Gerhard Roth (Wiesenbronn)	Rainer Zang (Nordheim am Main)
Bausewein (Iphofen)	Helmut Christ (Nordheim)	Roland Hemberger (Rödelsee)
Erwin Christ (Nordheim)	Hermann Kramer (Simmershofen)	Wille Gebrüder (Esselbach)
Fred Ruppert (Prichstenstadt-Kirch)	Lauerbach (TBB-Impfingen)	Willert-Eckert (Müdersheim)
	Mainstockheim (Mainstockheim)	

WÜRTTEMBERG

Württemberg is not well known as a wine region, principally because the wines produced in the area (a light red wine and a rosé called "Schillerwein") are not styles that are much in demand outside the region itself.

WÜRTTEMBERG IS GERMANY'S red-wine-producing region. But this is not red wine as most non-German wine drinkers would perceive it. Black grape varieties grow in over half the vineyards in Württemberg, and half of these are planted with Trollinger, a grape that produces a light, fresh, and grapey wine with none of the body, tannin, or other characteristics associated with a true red wine. The most concentrated Trollinger wines are made between Heilbronn and Winnenden, just northeast of Stuttgart, but they do not compare with reds produced in nearby Baden.

Red Lemberger is enjoyed locally, but until recently it produced unimpressive neutral-flavored wines. A few growers have begun to get more out of this variety, but it is never going to make waves.

The rosé Schillerwein is a specialty and usually has more character than red wines made from other black grapes grown here, such as Schwarzriesling (Pinot Meunier), which makes a better white wine than red or rosé.

WHITE WINES

White Württemberg wines are usually of modest quality, although there are exceptions, such as robust, intensely flavoured Riesling, with pronounced acidity. The region's other white grape varieties make very ordinary wines, unless harvested at one of the higher QmP categories. One of these white grapes—Kerner—deserves a mention as this Trollinger x Riesling cross was created at the Württemberg Weinsberg viticultural institute and named after the local 19th-century doctor and poet Justinus Kerner.

WÜRTTEMBERG, *see also p.345*
Most of the region's vineyards, in fertile districts near the Neckar River, are interspersed with farmland.

● Recommended wine village or town

▨ Intensive vine-growing zone

— *Bereich* boundary

— *Grosslage* boundary

▲ Height above sea level (meters)

```
0        4        8        12       16 miles
0     5      10      15      20     25 km
```

THE REGION AT A GLANCE

Area under vine
27,264 acres or 11,033 ha (decreasing)

Average yield
465 cases/acre or 105 hl/ha (increasing)

Red wine
58% (increasing)

White wine
42% (decreasing)

Dry & semidry wine
22% Trocken, 52% Halbtrocken

Most important grape varieties
23% Trollinger (increasing), 21% Riesling (decreasing), 17% Schwarzriesling (increasing), 11% Lemberger (increasing), 7% Spätburgunder (increasing), 5% Kerner (decreasing), 16% Others

Infrastructure
Bereiche 6; *Grosslagen* 17; *Einzellagen* 206

Note The vineyards of Württemberg straddle 230 communes, the names of which may appear on the label.

QUALITY REQUIREMENTS AND AVERAGE QMP PRODUCTION

WÜRTTEMBERG'S MINIMUM OECHSLE	QUALITY CATEGORY	HARVEST BREAKDOWN
40°	Deutscher Tafelwein	1%
50°	Landwein	1%
57–63°	*QbA	84%
72–78°	*Kabinett	9%
85–88°	*Spätlese	3%
95°	*Auslese	0.5%
124°	Beerenauslese	0.5%
124°	Eiswein	0.5%
150°	Trockenbeerenauslese	0.5%

Minimum Oechsle levels vary according to grape variety; those that have a naturally lower sugar content may qualify at a correspondingly lower level.

FACTORS AFFECTING TASTE AND QUALITY

LOCATION
Württemberg is situated between Frankfurt to the north and Lake Constance to the south.

CLIMATE
Sheltered by the Black Forest to the west and the hilly Swabian Alb to the east, this area has an especially warm growing season.

ASPECT
Vineyards are widely scattered either side of the Neckar River.

SOIL
Soils vary, but red marl, clay, loess, keuper and loam dominate, with scatterings of shell-limestone in the Neckar Valley area. Topsoils are deep and well drained, producing full wines with a firm acidity.

VITICULTURE AND VINIFICATION
Most of Württemberg's 16,500 growers own tiny plots and tend them part-time, taking their grapes to the cooperatives for processing. Most of the production is consumed locally. Trollinger has overtaken Riesling as the leading grape, while Lemberger and Spätburgunder are the fastest expanding. Another major

variety, Schwarzriesling, is the same as Pinot Meunier. Over half the wine is made in *halbtrocken* style.

GRAPE VARIETIES
Primary varieties: Lemberger, Riesling, Schwarzriesling, Trollinger
Secondary varieties: Kerner, Müller-Thurgau, Pinot Meunier, Portugieser, Ruländer, Silvaner, Spätburgunder

THE APPELLATIONS OF
WÜRTTEMBERG

BEREICH BAYERISCHER BODENSEE

Climatic conditions are not suited to Riesling.

GROSSLAGE LINDAUER SEEGARTEN

Politically part of Bavaria (QbA Franken), but classified by wine law as part of Württemberg.

BEREICH KOCHER-JAGST-TAUBER

White wines that rarely excel.

GROSSLAGE KOCHERBERG

Modest wines are made in Criesbach.

GROSSLAGE TAUBERBERG

Some good Rieslings, Traminers, and Muscats.

BEREICH OBERER NECKAR

A tiny *Bereich* with no outstanding vineyards.

BEREICH REMSTAL-STUTTGART

The second-largest *Bereich*.

GROSSLAGE HOHENNEUFFEN

Good wines are made in Metzingen.

GROSSLAGE KOPF

Improvements in a once uninspiring *Grosslage*.

WINTERBACH
✓ **Vineyard** *Hungerberg* **Grower** *Ellwanger*
✓ **Non-Einzellagen premium blends: Growers** *Ellwanger* ("Hades," red and white), *Albrecht Schwegler* ("Saphir," "Granat," both red)

GROSSLAGE SONNENBÜHL

No outstanding villages, vineyards, or growers.

GROSSLAGE WARTBÜHL

Superior wines from between the unremarkable *Grosslagen* of Kopf and Sonnenbühl.

STETTEN
✓ **Vineyard** *Pulvermächer* **Growers** *Karl Haidle, Beurer* • **Premium red blends Grower** *Karl Haidle* ("Ypsilon," and *trocken barrique* wines)

GROSSLAGE WEINSTEIGE

An up-and-coming *Grosslage*.

UNTERTÜRKHEIM
✓ **Vineyard** *Herzogenberg* (red and white) **Grower** *Wöhrwag* • **Non-Einzellagen premium red blends Grower** *Wöhrwag* (*cuvées* "X" and "Philipp"), *Weinmanufaktur Untertürkheim*

BEREICH WÜRTTEMBERGISCH BODENSEE

A one-*Einzellage Bereich* on Lake Constance.

BEREICH WÜRTTEMBERGISCH UNTERLAND

This *Bereich* encompasses more than 70 percent of Württemberg's vineyards.

GROSSLAGE HEUCHELBERG

Some of Württemberg's finest wines.

NEIPPERG
✓ **Vineyard** *Schlossberg* **Grower** *Graf zu Neipperg* • **Premium red wine blend Grower** *Graf zu Neipperg* (Cuvee SE)
PFAFFENHOFEN
✓ **Vineyard** *Hohenberg* **Grower** *Wachtstetter* (also Cuvée Ernst Combe premium red and white wines)
SCHWAIGERN
✓ **Vineyard** *Ruthe* **Grower** *Graf zu Neipperg*

GROSSLAGE KIRCHENWEINBERG

Pinot Meunier dominates in this area.

GROSSLAGE LINDELBERG

A small, scattered area east of Heilbronn.

GROSSLAGE SALZBERG

Sandwiched between Heilbronn and Lindelberg.

GROSSLAGE SCHALKSTEIN

Käsberg vineyard is the finest in this *Grosslage*. It specializes in full, dark red wines.

GROSSLAGE SCHOZACHTAL

Mostly white wines, including fine Riesling, but also some encouraging *barrique*-matured Lemberger and Spätburgunder.

GROSSLAGE STAUFENBERG

This covers the town of Heilbronn, its *Ortsteile*, and several outlying villages.

HEILBRONN
✓ **Non-Einzellagen wines: Grower** *Drautz-Able* (red and white varietals)
WEINSBERG
✓ **Non-Einzellagen wines: Grower** *Staatsweingut Weinsberg* ◉ (red and white varietals and *cuvées*)

GROSSLAGE STROMBERG

A predominantly black-grape area.

BÖNNIGHEIM
✓ **Vineyard** *Sonnenberg* **Grower** *Ernst Dautel* • **Premium red wine blend: Grower** *Ernst Dautel* (Kreation)

GROSSLAGE WUNNENSTEIN

For many years now Graf Adelmann has carried the torch for an area that could otherwise be regarded as vinous hinterland.

KLEINBOTTWAR
✓ **Vineyard** *Süssmund* **Grower** *Graf Adelmann*

OTHER CERTIFIED ORGANIC PRODUCERS

Biodynamic
Ernst-Friedrich Haller (Remshalden-Rohrbronn)
Siegfried Setzer (Vaihingen)
Werner Gienger (Illingen)
Werner und Bernd Lieberherr (Kirchheim am Neckar)

Organic
Andreas Stutz (Heilbronn)
Gen Brackenheim (Brackenheim)
Häberlen (Weinsberg)
Häusser (Bönnigheim)
Hermann Schmalzried (Korb)
Jürgen Winkler (Brackenheim)
Klaus Halter (Neckarsulm)

Muck (Bietigheim)
Reiner Döbler (Brackenheim)
Schäfer-Heinrich (Heilbronn)
Schloßgut Hohenbeilsten/ Hartmann Dippon (Beilstein)
Siglinger (Weinstadt-Grossheppach)
St. Urban (Ilsfeld-Schozach)
Stromberg Kellerei (Bönnigheim)

BADEN

Often described as Germany's southernmost wine-producing region, Baden is not so much one region as a hadgepodge of politically diverse districts that once produced wine in the now defunct Grand Duchy of Baden.

THE MOST NORTHERLY SECTION OF BADEN is parallel with the Mosel, bridging Franconia and Württemberg, while south from Baden-Baden, the vineyards are the mirror-image of Alsace across the border, and three pockets of vines on the shores of Bodensee are almost the most southerly in Germany; that dubious honor goes to Württemberg's nearby *Grosslage* of Lindauer Seegarten.

This variation of geographical, geological, and climatic conditions produces a wide range of wines, from mild Silvaner, through light, spicy Gutedel, to the full-bodied Ruländer, the attractive pink-colored Weissherbst, a specialty of the region, and

QUALITY REQUIREMENTS AND AVERAGE QMP PRODUCTION

BADEN'S MINIMUM OECHSLE	QUALITY CATEGORY	HARVEST BREAKDOWN
50–55°	Deutscher Tafelwein	0.5%
55°	Landwein	0.5%
60–72°	* QbA	81%
76–85°	* Kabinett	10%
86–92°	* Spätlese	5%
100–105°	* Auslese	1%
128°	Beerenauslese	1%
128°	Eiswein	–
154°	Trockenbeerenauslese	1%

Minimum Oechsle levels vary according to grape variety; those that have a naturally lower sugar content may qualify at a correspondingly lower level.

THE REGION AT A GLANCE

Area under vine
37,906 acres or 15,340 ha (decreasing)

Average yield
335 cases/acre or 76 hl/ha (increasing)

Red wine
32% (increasing)

White wine
68% (decreasing)

Dry & semidry wine
55% Trocken, 26% Halbtrocken

Most important grape varieties
33% Spätburgunder (increasing), 24% Müller-Thurgau (decreasing), 9% Grauerburgunder (static), 8% Riesling, 7% Gutedel (decreasing), 7% Weissburgunder, 12% Others

Infrastructure
Bereiche 8; *Grosslagen* 16; *Einzellagen* 306

Note The vineyards of Baden straddle 315 *Gemeinden* (communes). Their names may appear on the label.

BADEN, *see also p.345*
The vineyards of this huge wine-producing region are mostly spread along a strip extending beside the western boundary of the Black Forest, between it and the border with France. Inset (right) is the northerly area of the Bereich of Tauberfranken, while inset (above) is the Grosslage of Vulkanfelsen, which has been magnified to reveal all the recommended wine villages of this first-class wine district.

RIESCHEN VINEYARD
The old and new castles above the Rieschen vineyard,
on the north shore of the Bodensee at Meersburg.

a good deal of Germany's best red wines. If, however, anything can be said to be the mark of a Baden wine it must be a certain warmth, roundness, and mellowness.

Baden is considered to be one of Germany's newest wine regions, yet by 1800 it had become its largest, possessing more than 66,700 acres (27,000 hectares) of vines, almost twice the amount grown today. Ironically, it was when Germany acquired a wealthy and viticulturally prolific Alsace in 1871, as one of the spoils of the Franco-Prussian War, that Baden's vineyards began to decline. The downward trend continued, despite the formation of the Baden Wine Growers' Association, founded by the priest and winemaker Heinrich Hansjakob in Hagnau in 1881. Even after the return of Alsace to French sovereignty in 1918, Baden's wine production continued to decline, primarily through lack of investment. In the 1920s wine production was adversely affected by inheritance laws that split Baden's vineyards into smaller and smaller units. By 1950, with barely 14,800 acres (6,000 hectares) of vines, Baden's wine industry was at its lowest ebb.

The eventual resurgence of Baden's wine industry began in 1952 with the formation of the Zentralkellerei Kaiserstuhler Winzergenossenschaften (Central Winery of Kaiserstuhl), which two years later expanded into the Zentralkellerei Badischer Winzergenossenschaften (Central Winery of Baden), or ZBW for short. ZBW built a $120 million vinification and storage plant at Breisach that helped to raise quality standards throughout the

region and adopted an aggressive marketing policy on the domestic scene. Baden established itself as Germany's third-largest wine producing region, yet its wines were virtually unknown outside the country until ZBW made a serious effort to export its products in the early 1980s. Sadly, Baden is now a victim of its own success, for ZBW, which accounts for some 90 percent of the region's output, has established such a clear-cut identity for its wines that Baden is generally perceived to produce one style of well-made, but rather basic, characterless wine. The truth is that while this one style represents the bulk of ZBW's, and thus Baden's, production, both ZBW and the region's independent producers have a wealth of other wines that are seldom seen or spoken about outside their locality. It is now time for ZBW to turn its marketing expertise to the relatively small number of very high-quality wines within its region, and promote them as independent wine estates for the benefit of all.

FACTORS AFFECTING TASTE AND QUALITY

LOCATION
The longest *Anbaugebiete*, Baden stretches for approximately 250 miles (400 km), from Franken in the north, past Württemberg and the Badische Bergstrasse to Bodensee, or Lake Constance, some of Germany's most southerly vineyards.

CLIMATE
Compared with the rest of Germany, the bulk of Baden's vineyards have a sunny and warm climate, due in part to the shelter afforded by the Black Forest and the Odenwald Mountains.

ASPECT
Most vineyards are on level or gently sloping ground. Some, however, are to be found higher up the hillsides, and these avoid the frosts of the valley floors.

SOIL
Baden's soils are rich and fertile, varying from heat-retaining gravel near Lake Constance, through limestone, clay, marl, loam, granite, and loess deposits to limestone and keuper, a sandy-marl, in the Kraichgau and Taubergrund. Volcanic bedrock forms the main subsoil structure throughout most of the region.

VITICULTURE AND VINIFICATION
The relatively flat and fertile vineyards of this region are easily mechanized. Although the geographical spread and variety of soils has led to a large number of different, traditional styles of wine, they are overshadowed by the mild and neutrally fruity, bulk-produced Baden QbA marketed by ZBW. More than 90 percent of the winemaking in Baden is conducted by its 54 cooperatives, but there are several independent and top-quality estates among the region's 26,000 growers. Spätburgunder has now officially taken over from Müller-Thurgau as Baden's most important grape, and more than half the wines produced from all varieties in this region are made in a dry or *trocken* style. A specialty that is unique to Baden is Badisch Rotgold, a soft, delicately-flavored rosé made from pressing Ruländer and Spätburgunder grapes together.

GRAPE VARIETIES
Primary varieties: Müller-Thurgau, Ruländer, Spätburgunder
Secondary varieties: Gutedel, Kerner, Nobling, Riesling, Silvaner, Traminer, Weissburgunder

BODENSEE (LAKE CONSTANCE)
These vines are in the south of Baden, at Meersburg, the best village of the
Sonnenufer Grosslage, with some of the most southerly vineyards in Germany.

THE APPELLATIONS OF
BADEN

BEREICH BADISCHE BERGSTRASSE-KRAICHGAU

This *Bereich* has four *Grosslagen*, two in the Badische Bergstrasse, north and south of Heidelberg, and two in the Kraichgau, a larger but sparsely cultivated area farther south. Only one *Grosslage*, Stiftsberg, in the Kraichgau, has any reputation at all. Half the *Bereich* is planted with Müller-Thurgau grapes, but it makes mostly dull and lackluster wine. When successful, the best wines are Ruländer and Riesling.

GROSSLAGE HOHENBERG

In this *Grosslage* there are no outstanding villages, vineyards, or growers, although good wines are made in the village of Weingarten.

GROSSLAGE MANNABERG

This *Grosslage* is situated just southeast of Mannheim and it encompasses the historic university town of Heidelberg, which has some fine steep vineyard slopes overlooking the Neckar River.

HEIDELBERG

✓ **Vineyard** *Herrenberg* (red and white) **Grower** *Seeger/Leimen* • **Premium red wine blends: Grower** *Seeger* (Leimen— "R," "S," "RR")

GROSSLAGE RITTERSBERG

There are no outstanding villages, vineyards, or growers here, although good wines are made in the villages of Leutershausen, Lützelsachen, Schriesheim, and Weinheim.

GROSSLAGE STIFTSBERG

Situated in the Kraichgau, this is the *Bereich's* most successful *Grosslage*. Nearly half of its vineyards are classified as "steep," which officially means sloping at more than 20 degrees, and this contributes to the extreme fruitiness of the Ruländer and the relatively racy character of the Riesling.

SULZFELD

✓ **Non-Einzellagen premium red: Growers** *Burg Ravensburg*

BEREICH BODENSEE

In the Hochrhein of Bodensee, or the Upper Rhine of Bodensee (known in English as Lake Constance), the wines are not great, but can be very acceptable. They range from the fruity and lively Müller-Thurgau to Rotwein and Weissherbst, both produced from Spätburgunder.

GROSSLAGE SONNENUFER

The steep sides of Lake Constance around Meersburg are the most spectacular vineyards here. The brothers Aufricht have brought a new dimension to the wines of this district, taking over the lead from Winzerverein Meersburg, Germany's first state domain (since 1802).

MEERSBURG

✓ **Vineyard** *Sängerhalde* **Grower** *Aufricht*

BEREICH BREISGAU

Strangely, the old city of Breisach is not part of the *Bereich* that takes its name; it is, in fact, situated in the *Bereich* of Kaiserstuhl-Tuniberg to the south. The wines of *Bereich* Breisgau have narrowed the gap on the better-known Kaiserstuhl-Tuniberg, with fruity, off-dry Müller-Thurgau balanced by some excellent Weiss-burgunder, Grauburgunder, and Spätburgunder.

GROSSLAGE BURG LICHTENECK

Besides those of the villages recommended below, good wines are also made in Altdorf.

MALTERDINGEN

✓ **Vineyard** *Bienenberg* **Grower** *Bernhard Huber* ◎ • **Premium red wine blends: Grower** *Bernhard Huber* (R, S, Alte Reben)

GROSSLAGE BURG ZÄHRINGEN

There are no outstanding villages, vineyards, or growers in this *Grosslage*, although good wines are made in the village of Glottertal.

GROSSLAGE SCHUTTER-LINDENBERG

There are no outstanding villages, vineyards, or growers in this *Grosslage*, although good wines are made in the village of Friesenheim.

BEREICH KAISERSTUHL

Formerly part of Kaiserstuhl-Tuniberg, this *Bereich* is dominated by the extinct volcano of Kaiserstuhl, whose immaculate slopes are textbook examples of *Flurbereinigung* (growing vines in rows up and down slopes).

In this, Germany's warmest and driest *Bereich*, there are microclimates that favor certain sites protected by the volcano. Some of Baden's best wines come from these *Einzellagen*, although most of the wine is sold under the *Bereich* name, usually with the grape name attached; Bereich Kaiserstuhl Müller-Thurgau dominates. But it is the very full white Ruländer and the assertive Weissherbst Ruländer that made the reputation of the *Bereich*. Some fine, rich Spätburgunder wines enhance this reputation.

GROSSLAGE VULKANFELSEN

Vulkanfelsen is the largest and most successful of the two *Grosslagen* that belonged to the now defunct Kaiserstuhl-Tuniberg. As its name implies (Vulkanfelsen means volcano rock), it covers the superior, high volcanic vineyards of the Kaiserstuhl mound itself. Above all else, it is the full, fiery intensity of Ruländer wines from the Kaiserstuhl that give this district its reputation.

ACHKARREN

✓ **Vineyard** *Schlossberg* **Growers** *Dr. Heger* (red and white), *Michel* (red and white) • **Non-Einzellagen Premium red and white wines Grower** *Johner* (SJ)

BURKHEIM

✓ **Vineyard** *Feuerberg* **Grower** *Bercher* (red and white), *Winzergenossenschaft Burkheim*

ENDINGEN

✓ **Grower** *Reinhold und Cornelia Schneider*

IHRINGEN

✓ **Vineyard** *Winklerberg* **Growers** *Dr. Heger* (red and white), *Stigler*

JECHTINGEN

✓ **Vineyard** *Fichert* **Grower** *Bercher*

KÖNIGSSCHAFFHAUSEN

✓ **Vineyard** *Steingrüble* **Grower** *Winzergenossenschaft Königschaffhausen* (red)

NIMBURG-BOTTINGEN

✓ **Vineyard** *Steingrube* **Grower** *Fischer*

OBERBERGEN

✓ **Vineyard** *Bassgeige* **Grower** *Winzergenossenschaft Oberbergen* • **Premium red and white blends Grower** *Franz Keller-Schwarzer Adler* (Selection A and S)

OBERROTTWEIL

✓ **Vineyard** *Eichberg* **Growers** *Freiherr von Gleichenstein, Salwey* (red and white) • **Vineyard** *Kirchberg* **Grower** *Salwey* (red and white)

SASBACH

✓ **Vineyard** *Limburg* **Grower** *Bercher* • **Vineyard** *Rote Halde* **Grower** *Winzergenossenschaft Sasbach*

SCHELINGEN

✓ **Vineyard** *Kirchberg* **Grower** *Schätzle*

BEREICH MARKGRÄFLERLAND

This is the second-most important *Bereich* in Baden. The principal grape variety is, unusually, Gutedel, which makes a light, dryish, and neutral wine that benefits from a slight spritz and can be most attractive when very youthful. Other prominent varieties include Nobling, an up-and-coming cross between Gutedel and Silvaner that makes a more characterful wine than the light Müller-Thurgau. The latter can be attractive nevertheless. Spätburgunder can be full and successful, and Gewürztraminer also fares well.

GROSSLAGE ATTILAFELSEN
Not enough is made of the potential for good wines at this small volcanic outcrop of the Tuniberg.

GROSSLAGE BURG NEUENFELS
The vast majority of vineyards in this *Grosslage* are on steep ground. These vineyards make some of Germany's most delicious Gutedel, although the greatest potential lies in the Burgunder varietals.

BADENWEILER
✓ **Vineyard** *Römerberg* **Grower** *Winzergenossenschaft Britzingen*

LAUFEN
✓ **Non-Einzellagen wines: Grower** *Schlumberger* (red and white)

MAUCHEN
✓ **Vineyard** *Sonnenstück* **Grower** *Lämmlin-Schindler* ◉ • **Vineyard Frauenberg Grower** *Lämmlin-Schindler*

GROSSLAGE LORETTOBERG
A cooperative, a part-time asparagus grower and a Chardonnay specialist have brought some credibility to a long-underestimated Grosslage.

PFAFFENWEILER
✓ **Vineyard** *Oberdürrenberg* **Grower** *Winzergenossenschaft Pfaffenweiler*

SCHERZINGEN
✓ **Vineyard** *Batzenberg* **Grower** *Heinemann*

SCHLATT
✓ **Vineyard** *Maltesergarten* **Grower** *Martin Wassmer* (red and white)

GROSSLAGE VOGTEI RÖTTELN
Although much wine is sold under this *Grosslage*, its exceptional vineyards are known for Gutedel and, to a lesser extent, Spätburgunder.

BEREICH ORTENAU
Sheltered by the Black Forest, the two *Grosslagen* in this *Bereich* produce some of Baden's greatest wines. They are generally full, fruity, and often very spicy. The Riesling, known locally as Klingelberger, is extremely fine for such a powerful and spicy variation of this normally racy variety. Müller-Thurgau is particularly good and full, and a successful Ruländer-Spätburgunder blend called Badisch Rotgold is also produced. Confusingly, the Gewürztraminer is often called Clevner, which is usually a synonym for Pinot Blanc.

GROSSLAGE FÜRSTENECK
This *Grosslage* sports some of Baden's finest estates. The range of grape varieties is greater here than anywhere else within Baden and the wines include Rieslings that range from firm and spicy to fine and delicate; powerful Gewürztraminer; some of Germany's best Müller-Thurgau; and some extraordinary Gutedel. Many of the wines are made in increasingly drier styles, although some estates are famous for their sweeter, late-harvested products.

DURBACH
✓ **Vineyard** *Schloss Grohl* **Grower** *Gräflich Wolff Metternich'sches Weingut* • **Vineyard** *Schlossberg* **Growers** *Gräflich Wolff Metternich'sches Weingut* • **Vineyard** *Plauelrain* **Growers** *Andreas Laible, Durbacher Winzergenossenschaft*

ORTENBERG
✓ **Non-Einzellagen wines: Grower** *Schloss Ortenberg*

GROSSLAGE SCHLOSS RODECK
For many years Schloss Neuweier was the undisputed number one in this *Grosslage*, but a Dutch newcomer has propelled himself to the forefront of developments with Spätburgunder in *barriques*.

BÜHL
✓ **Non-Einzellagen premium red wines Grower** *Duijn*

NEUWEIER
✓ **Vineyard** *Mauerberg* **Grower** *Schloss Neuweier* • **Vineyard** *Schlossberg* **Grower** *Schloss Neuweier*

BEREICH TAUBERFRANKEN
The most northerly of Baden's vineyards, Bereich Tauberfranken bridges Franken and Württemberg. The wines have a similar style to those produced in both regions. If anything, the crisp, dry, aromatic, and slightly earthy Müller-Thurgau and Silvaner wines bear more resemblance to Franken wines rather than to Württemberg wines. Only that part of the *Bereich* outside Franken itself is allowed to use Franken's famous *Bocksbeutel* bottle.

GROSSLAGE TAUBERKLINGE
As well as at Reicholzheim, good wines are also made in the villages of Beckstein, Königshofen, and Tauberbischofsheim.

REICHHOLZHEIM
✓ **Vineyard** *First* **Grower** *Konrad Schlör*

BEREICH TUNIBERG
Formerly part of Kaiserstuhl-Tuniberg, this *Bereich* is to the south of the mighty Kaiserstuhl and it is the far less awesome sight of the Tuniberg, another volcanic outcrop, that provides the only other topographical and viticultural relief. The Tuniberg's steeper, west-facing slopes are cultivated, but neither its reputation nor its bulk can match those of Kaiserstuhl's fabulous recommendations above.

OTHER CERTIFIED ORGANIC PRODUCERS

Biodynamic
Alfons Schüber (Sasbach-Jechtingen)
Breitehof Hubert Schies (Vogtsburg-Burkheim a Kaiserstuhl)
Christoph Brenneisen (Sulburg-Laufen)
Guido Friderich (Sasbach)
Josef u Klara Vögtle (Sasbach-Jechtingen a Kaiserstuhl)
Josef Wörner (Durbach)
Markus Bürgin (Fischingen)
Max und Alice Schneider (Sasbach)

Organic
Andrea und Heiner Renn (Hagnau)
Andreas Fritz (Bühlertal)
Bettina Beck (Bahlingen)
Daniel Feuerstein (Heitersheim)
Edmund Eisele/Schelb (Ehrenkirchen)
Eduard Mannsperger (Sinsheim-Dühren)
Erwin Mick (Nimburg)
Freiburg (Heiliggeist Freiburg im Breisgau)
Friedhelm Rinklin (Eichstetten)
Friedrich & Bärbel Ruesch (Buggingen)
Fritz Lampp (Heitersheim)
Gallushof/Hügle (Teningen-Heimbach)
Geier (Königheim)
Gerd Köpfer (Staufen-Grunern)

Gerhard Aenis (Binzen)
Gretzmeier (Merdingen)
Gudrun Lauerbach (Tauberbischofsheim-Impfingen)
Günther Kaufmann (Efringen-Kirchen)
H. & J. Sprich (Weil-Haltingen)
Hans Hardt (Herbolzheim)
Harald Süssle (Merdingen)
Harteneck (Schliengen)
Hermann Helde & Sohne (Jechtingen)
Hermann Neuner-Jehle (Immenstaad)
H. P. & Helmut Grether (Laufen-Sulzburg)
Hubert Lay (Ihringen)
Jette Krumm (Auggen)
Joachim Netzhammer (Klettgau-Erzingen)
Johannes Haug (Nonnenhorn)
Kirchberghof (Kenzingen-Bombach)
Klaus Benz (Ballrechten-Dottingen)
Klaus Bischoff (Kelltern)
Klaus Vorgrimmler (Freiburg-Munzingen)
Koehly-Harteneck (Bad Bellingen)
Kuckuckshof (Karlsbad-Ittersbach)
Kurt Breisacher (Riegel)
Langwerth Öko-Wein (Esselbach)
Ludwig Missbach (Ebringen)
Manfred & Eva Maria Schmidt (Vogtsburg-Bischoffingen)
Manfred Dannmeyer (Bamlach)
Markgräfler Wyhus (Efringen-

Kirchen)
Martin Hämmerlin (Buggingen)
Martin Küchlin (Buggingen-Betberg)
Martina Heitzmann (Bahlingen)
Matthias Höfflin/Schambachhof (Bötzingen)
Matthias Seywald (Ballrechten-Dottingen)
Matthias Wolff (Riedlingen)
Peter Kaiser (Bahnbrücken)
Philip Isele (Achkarren)
Pix (Ihringen A. K.)
Rabenhof (Vogtsburg-Bischofingen)
Reblandhof (Sulzfeld)
Reinhard Burs (March)
Richard G Schmidt (Eichstetten)
Siegfried Frei (Wasenweiler)
Sonnenbrunnen (Freiburg-Opfingen)
Stadt Lahr (Lahr/Schwarzwald)
Stränglehof (Leiselheim)
Thomas Schaffner (Bötzingen am Kaiserstuhl)
Thomas Selinger (Merdingen)
Tobias Kehnel (Broggingen)
Trautwein (Bahlingen)
Ulrich Klumpp (Bruchsal)
Walter J Schür (Vogtsburg-Oberrotweil)
Wendelin Brugger (Laufen)
Wilhelm Zähringer (Heitersheim)
Willi Frey (Freiburg-Tiengen)
Winzerhof Leber (Vogtsburg-Schelingen)
Wolfgang Ibert (Wallburg)

SAALE-UNSTRUT AND SACHSEN

These two eastern outposts of viticulture are the most northerly in Germany. Even though their terraced vineyards are being renovated and replanted, and modern vinification facilities installed, their wines can never be more than a tourist curiosity.

PARADOXICALLY THIS LIMITATION may be the saving grace for the wines of Saale-Unstrut and Sachsen because they are far too small and rustically structured to stand any chance of competing with the large volumes of cheap plonk churned out by cooperatives in Germany's more intensively cultivated wine regions. Furthermore, as Meissen and Dresden are lucrative tourist areas, the wines must adhere to a certain standard if they are to satisfy tourists with far more sophisticated palates than those who consumed them under former GDR mismanagment. Most of the vineyards are between Dresden and Diesbar-Seusslitz, with a few vineyards that have been restored on the southern outskirts of Dresden itself. The state-owned cellars in historic Schloss Wackerbarth in Radebeul and the region's oldest (and privately owned) estate at Schloss Proschwitz are Sachsen's largest estates. The largest estate in Saale-Unstrut is Kloster Pforta, which was named after the 12th-century monastery between Bad Kösen and Naumburg.

THE FUTURE—VARIETAL EVOLUTION

When Germany was reunified in 1989, the most commonly cultivated grape variety in the former GDR's rundown vineyards was Müller-Thurgau, and although it remains an important grape, it is on the decline, and its days must be numbered. Riesling has increased from five to seven percent of the vines grown, but it is Germany's greatest variety, thus more will be planted, if only for the sake of national pride. The area is, however, more suited to the full, rich, and distinctively earthy wine produced by Silvaner and, perhaps surprisingly for such a northerly, frost-prone region, also to red wine grape varieties. But of all the varieties to choose from, who would have predicted the rise of Weisserburgunder when the Berlin Wall came down? Very few, I think, but it is the best placed to succeed Müller-Thurgau as this region's more important variety, although it will take a few years yet.

THE REGION AT A GLANCE

Area under vine
2,656 acres or 1,075 ha (increasing)

Average yield
185 cases/acre or 42 hl/ha (decreasing)

Red wine
14% (increasing)

White wine
86% (decreasing)

Dry & semi-dry wine
86% Trocken, 10% Halbtrocken

Most important grape varieties
25% Müller-Thurgau (decreasing), 14% Weissburgunder (increasing), 7% Riesling (increasing), 6% Silvaner (decreasing), 48% Others

Infrastructure
Bereiche 5; *Grosslagen* 8; *Einzellagen* 35

Note The vineyards of Saale-Unstrut and Sachsen straddle 63 *Gemeinden* (communes), the names of which may appear on the label.

Saale-Unstrut

Sachsen

Bereich boundary

Grosslage boundary

▲ Height above sea level (meters)

• Recommended wine village or town

miles 5   10   15
km 5 10 15 20 25

SAALE-UNSTRUT AND SACHSEN,
see also p.345
More than 2,500 acres (1,000 hectares) of vines grow in these areas, formerly part of East Germany. Production is centered in Bad Kösen, Freyburg, and near the confluence of the Saale and Unstrut rivers at Naumberg.

FACTORS AFFECTING TASTE AND QUALITY

LOCATION
The most northerly wine regions in Germany, Saale-Unstrut is equidistant between Berlin and the Franken region, while Sachsen is about 80 miles (128 kilometers) east, around Dresden, close to the border with the Czech Republic.

CLIMATE
Despite their northerly position, the continental climate ensures high summer temperatures. However, winters are long and very cold, resulting in a short and dry growing season compared with other German regions. Spring and fall frosts are a particular danger, often cutting yields by 20–70 percent in Saale-Unstrut and as much as 90 percent in Sachsen.

ASPECT
Vineyards are on south and southeast facing valley slopes, but much of the terracing has deteriorated under Communist rule and the current reconstruction will take some time to complete.

SOIL
Limestone and a tiny amount of sandstone in Saale-Unstrut, with loam and loess over granite and volcanic subsoils in most of Sachsen, and weathered granite and gneiss on its steepest slopes.

VITICULTURE AND VINIFICATION
Many of the small parcels are planted on steep, labor-intensive stone terraces, most of which are cultivated by part-time growers who deliver their crop to Saale-Unstrut's regional cooperative in Freyburg or Sachsen's regional cooperative in Meissen. Yields were very low prior to reunification, but although production has since increased, yields remain very low due to the northerly situation. There are problems such as decimation of production by fierce attacks of frost, decaying terracing, dead vines, and rustic production methods, but it would be a pity if old vines were replaced and if the hardy but highest-yielding characterless crosses were introduced in place of classic varieties. Weissburgunder and Riesling are the fastest expanding grape varieties. Mostly dry wines are produced, with only four percent of the production sweeter than *Halbtrocken*, and as much as 86 percent sold as *Trocken*.

GRAPE VARIETIES
Primary varieties: Müller-Thurgau, Weissburgunder
Secondary varieties: Bacchus, Dornfelder, Elbling, Gewürztraminer, Grauburgunder, Gutedel, Kerner, Morio-Muscat, Portugieser

THE APPELLATIONS OF
SAALE-UNSTRUT AND SACHSEN

ANBAUGEBIET SAALE-UNSTRUT

Wines have been produced in this area for nearly 1,000 years, but it took the GDR less than 50 years to erase these once-well-known names from the memory of wine drinkers. This region comprises two *Bereiche*, and Müller-Thurgau is the most important grape variety. It accounts for some 35 percent of the vines planted and black grapes account for some 10 percent.

BEREICH SCHLOSSNEUENBURG

By far the largest of Saale-Unstrut's two *Bereiche*, Schloss Neuenburg encompasses all but a tiny section in the very south of the Saale-Unstrut region, plus the island of vines just west of Halle.

GROSSLAGE BLÜTENGRUND

Some respectable wines have appeared on the market under the designation of this *Grosslage*.

GROSSLAGE GÖTTERSITZ

Previous expectations in this Grosslage have not been quite fulfilled.
NAUMBURG
✓ **Vineyard** *Steinmeister* **Grower** *Gussek*

GROSSLAGE KELTERBERG

No outstanding villages, vineyards, or growers.

GROSSLAGE SCHWEIGENBERG

Two growers have made this the most respected *Grosslage* of the Saale-Unstrut region.
FREYBURG
✓ **Vineyard** *Edelacker* **Grower** *Pawis*
KARSDORF
✓ **Vineyard** *Hohe Gräte* **Grower** *Weingut Lützkendorf*

BEREICH THÜRINGEN

The southern tip of the Saale-Unstrut region does not contain any *Grosslagen*, just two *Einzellagen*, one in Grossheringen, the other in Bad Sulza.

BEREICHEFREI AND GROSSLAGENFREI MARK BRANDEBURG

Mark Brandenburg covers the vineyards around Werder, from which no outstanding wines have so far been made.

ANBAUGEBIET SACHSEN

Incorporating Dresden and Meissen, this *Aubaugebiet* produces wines that are grown along the Elbe River (Sachsen was formerly known as Elbethal). The area is even more prone to frost damage than Saale-Unstrut, with Riesling relatively more important (13 percent as opposed to Saale-Unstrut's 5 percent). The quantity of black grapes is minuscule.

BEREICH DRESDEN

This *Bereich* covers most of the southern half of Sachsen.

GROSSLAGE ELBHÄNGE

Continuous efforts have finally paid off for one grower in this otherwise unremarkable *Grosslage*.
PILLNITZ
✓ **Vineyard** *Königlicher Weinberg* **Grower** *Klaus Zimmerling*

GROSSLAGE LÖSSNITZ

There are no outstanding villages or vineyards, and no remarkable growers to be recommended in this *Grosslage*.

BEREICH ELSTERTAL

This is a *Bereich* consisting of three villages at the southern end of Sachsen. There are relatively few vines and, so far, no village has produced any outstanding wines.

BEREICH MEISSEN

The northern end of the Sachsen region, Meissen itself will always be more well known for the porcelain it once produced than its wine. This area, however, did have something of a name for producing fine wine at the beginning of the 19th century. Wine drinkers can only wait and see if there is sufficient potential for that reputation to be recaptured sometime in the future.

GROSSLAGE SCHLOSS-WEINBERG

North of Meissen, some decent wines can come from a bend in the Elbe at Diesbar-Seusslitz where the vineyards face south.
SEUSSLITZ
✓ **Vineyard** *Heinrichsburg* **Grower** *Schloss Proschwitz*

GROSSLAGE SPAARGEBIRGE

Substantial investments have helped to bring at least one estate's shine back to this *Grosslage*.
PROSCHWITZ
✓ **Vineyard** *Schloss Proschwitz* **Grower** *Schloss Proschwitz*

CERTIFIED ORGANIC PRODUCERS

Organic
Hof Loessnitz (Dresden)

AUSTRIA

Austria used to be seen as a winemaking clone of Germany, but over the past decade, Austria has slowly but surely begun to establish its own unique wine identity, and it now produces some exceptionally fine red wines.

IN THE LATE 1970S, Austrian wine production increased as domestic consumption declined, resulting in the largest wine lake outside the EC. Austria's wine industry was designed chiefly for exports to Germany, traditionally its only significant customer. After a succession of bumper harvests in both Germany and Austria, sales to Germany dried up, but overproduction in Austria continued. With hindsight, the so-called "antifreeze" scandal that took place in 1985 can be seen as a godsend for Austrian wine. Call it a scam or a scandal, but it was not the health

Weinbauregion Niederösterreich

- Wachau
- Kremstal
- Kamtal
- Weinviertel
- Traisental
- Donauland
- Carnuntum
- Thermenregion

Weinbauregion Wien

- Wien

Weinbauregion Burgenland

- Neusiedler See
- Neusiedler See-Hügelland
- Mittelburgenland
- Südburgenland

Weinbauregion Steiermark

- Weststeiermark
- Süd-Oststeiermark
- Südsteiermark
- Intensive vine-growing zone
- ● Best wine villages
- Provincial boundary
- International boundary
- ▲ Height above sea level (meters)

0   5   10   15   10   25 30 miles

0   10   20   30   40   50 km

AUSTRIA
Austria produces Riesling to compete with the greatest in Germany; botrytized wines to match those of Sauternes; and the unique, incomparable Grüner Veltliner.

THE WACHAU
Much of Austria is very picturesque, making it a popular vacation destination; here the lush vineyards complement this typical Lower Austrian landscape.

scare it was made out to be. It did, however, have the effect of putting the Austrian government under enormous pressure to tighten up controls, with the result that Austria now has the most strictly controlled, safest wine industry in the world.

WHAT WAS THE ANTI-FREEZE SCANDAL?
In 1985, a handful of Austria's 40,000 wine producers used diethylene glycol to sweeten their wines artificially. The media throughout the world claimed that Austrian wines had been poisoned with antifreeze, but it was not antifreeze, of course (ethylene glycol is). Diethylene glycol is, in fact, less toxic than alcohol, so adding it actually made the wines less poisonous.

AUSTRIA VERSUS GERMANY
Both countries operate wine regimes that base levels of quality on degrees of ripeness by measuring the amount of sugar found in the grapes at the time of harvest. As in Germany, Austrian wines range from *Tafelwein*, through *Qualitätswein*, to *Trockenbeerenauslese*. The overview below shows that most Austrian wines conform to higher minimum standards than their German counterparts. More significant, however, is the fact that the minimum level for each category is rigid, so it has a distinctive style. This gives the consumer a clear idea of what to expect, whereas a German category varies according to the variety of grape and its area of origin. In Germany, only experience can reveal that a Mosel *Auslese*, for example, tastes no sweeter than a *Spätlese* from other regions. Also, *Süssreserve* is not allowed for any *Prädikat* wines, whereas in Germany this is permitted for *Kabinett*.

MINIMUM OECHSLE LEVELS

QUALITY CATEGORY	AUSTRIA	GERMANY
Tafelwein	63°	44–50°
Landwein	63°	47–55°
Qualitätswein	73°	50–72°
Kabinett	83.5°	67–85°
Spätlese	94°	76–95°
Auslese	105°	83–105°
Beerenauslese	127°	110–128°
Eiswein	127°	110–128°
Ausbruch	138°	N/A
Trockenbeerenauslese	156°	150–154°

FACTORS AFFECTING TASTE AND QUALITY

LOCATION
The vineyards are in the east of the country, north and south of Vienna, bordering the Czech Republic, Hungary, and Yugoslavia.

CLIMATE
The climate is warm, dry, and continental, with annual rainfall between 23 to 31 inches (57 and 77 centimeters). The hottest and driest area is Burgenland, where in the warm falls, mists rising from the Neusiedlersee help promote *Botrytis cinerea* (the "noble rot" beloved by winegrowers).

ASPECT
Vines are grown on all types of land, from the plains of the Danube to its valley sides—which are often very steep and terraced—and from the hilly Burgenland to the slopes of mountainous Styria.

SOIL
Soils vary from generally stony schist, limestone, and gravel (though occasionally loamy) in the north, through predominantly sandy soils on the shores of the Neusiedlersee in Burgenland, to mainly clay with some volcanic soils in Styria.

VITICULTURE AND VINIFICATION
Not surprisingly, Austria's methods are similar to those of Germany, but, although modern techniques have been introduced here, far more Austrian wine is produced by traditional methods than is the case in Germany. More than 85 percent of the country's vines are cultivated by the Lenz Moser system. This is a method of training vines to twice their normal height, thereby achieving a comparatively higher ratio of quality to cost, by enabling the use of mechanized harvesting. This system brought fame to its Austrian inventor, Lenz Moser, and has been adopted by at least one grower in most winemaking countries. Harvesting is traditionally accomplished in *tries*, particularly on steeper slopes and for sweeter styles.

GRAPE VARIETIES
Blauberger, Blauer Portugieser, Blauer Wildbacher, Blaufränkisch, Bouviertraube, Cabernet Franc, Cabernet Sauvignon, Chardonnay, Frühroter Veltliner (*syn.* Malvasia), Furmint, Gewürztraminer, Goldburger, Grüner Veltliner, Pinot Blanc, Pinot Noir, Merlot, Müller-Thurgau, Muskateller, Muskatottonel, Neuburger, Pinot Gris, Roter Veltliner, Rotgipfler, Sauvignon Blanc, Scheurebe, St. Laurent, Silvaner, Trollinger, Riesling, Welschriesling, Zierfandler, Zweigelt

THE MODERN WINE TRADE
Enthusiasts have always known that Austria produces some of the greatest botrytized wines in the world, yet just how electrifying these wines can be became clear when Willy Opitz, one of the smallest, but truly greatest, dessert wine producers, took the trouble to tour world markets and speak to people about his products.

Over the past few years, Austria has produced Cabernet Sauvignon and Chardonnay to a very high standard, and even St. Laurent, an obscure local variety of grape, has proved to be quite stunning. What Austria must do now is to promote its greatest Riesling wines, which can compare with the best from Germany, and export its top Grüner Veltliner, and keep pushing these wines onto the international markets.

AUSBRUCH—A RELIC OF THE AUSTRO-HUNGARIAN EMPIRE
Ausbruch is a still-popular style of wine that harks back to the days of the Austro-Hungarian Empire (and is also still produced in Hungary). At 138° *Oechsle* (*see left*), *Ausbruch* falls between the sweetness levels of *Beerenauslese* (127°) and *Trockenbeerenauslese* (156°). In terms of character, however, *Ausbruch* should be totally different from either a *Beerenauslese* or *Trockenbeerenauslese*. The name means "to break up"; the wine is made traditionally from the richest and sweetest botrytized grapes that are so shriveled and dried-out that to press them is virtually impossible without first moistening the mass (breaking it up) with a more liquescent juice (the regulation stipulates *Spätlese* quality). A true *Ausbruch* is overwhelmed by an intensely raisiny aroma and flavor that may be even more botrytized than a *Trockenbeerenauslese*, yet the wine itself need not necessarily be as rich.

THE WINE STYLES OF
AUSTRIA

BLAUBURGER

RED A Blauer Portugieser/Blaufränkisch cross that produces a well-colored wine of little distinction, but tends to improve in bottle.

⌛ 1–3 years

🏆 *Weingut Schützenhof Fam Korpe • Willi Opitz*

BLAUER PORTUGIESER

RED This used to be Austria's most widely planted black grape variety and is still commonly found in Lower Austria, particularly Paulkautal, Retz, and the Thermen region, where it makes a light-bodied but well-colored red wine with a mild flavor, hinting of violets.

⌛ 1–2 years

🏆 *Johann Gipsberg • H. V. Reinisch*

BLAUER WILDBACHER

RED/ROSÉ Otherwise known as Schilcher, this variety traditionally produces a light, dry, crisp, and fruity, pale rosé wine.

⌛ 1–2 years

🏆 *E. & M. Müller*

BLAUFRÄNKISCH

RED Known as Lemberger in Germany and Kékfrankos in Hungary, this variety is popular in Neusiedlersee-Hügelland Burgenland, where it produces tart, fruity wine with good tannin and an underlying hint of cherries and spice. The best examples of Blaufränkisch are fat and sometimes given time in oak.

⌛ 2–4 years

🏆 *Weingut Gessellmann (Creitzer) • Feiler-Artinger • Weingut Fam Igler • Weingut H. und M. Krutzler*

BOUVIER

WHITE An early-ripening table grape that has a low natural acidity and is often used for high-quality *Prädikatswein*.

⌛ 1–3 year (*Qualitätswein*), 2–8 years (*Prädikatswein*)

🏆 *Willi Opitz*

CABERNET SAUVIGNON

RED Very little of this variety used to be grown in Austria. Until 1982 the only commercial cultivation of Cabernet Sauvignon was by Schlumberger at Bad Vosläu. Then Lenz Moser received special permission to cultivate 6 acres (2.5 hectares) at Mailberg, and the first Cabernet Sauvignon was grown in 1986 in Lower Austria. Today, everyone seems to be growing Cabernet Sauvignon.

⌛ 5–6 years (*Qualitätswein*), 10–15 years (*Prädikatswein*)

🏆 *Lenz Moser (Siegendorf Prestige) • Weingut Fam Igler • Weingut Gessellmann*

CHARDONNAY

WHITE Also known in Austria as Feinburgunder, this grape variety has been grown for decades in Styria, where it is known as Morillon. Cultivation of this grape has risen rapidly since the early 1990s, producing some fat, rich wines.

⌛ 2–5 years

🏆 *Weingut Bründlmayer (Kabinett) • Juris-Stiegelmar (Classic) • H. V. Reinisch • Andreas Schafler • Weingut Gottfried Schellmann • Weingut Tement*

FRÜHROTER VELTLINER

WHITE Sometimes labeled Malvasia, this dry Frühroter Veltliner has more alcohol and body than Austria's most widely grown white wine, Grüner Veltliner.

⌛ 1–2 years

🏆 *Weingut Leth*

FURMINT

WHITE This is a rarely encountered Hungarian dry, medium- to full-bodied, rich, and fruity varietal that does well at Rust in Burgenland.

⌛ 3–5 years

🏆 *Weinbau Ladislaus und Robert Wenzel*

GEWÜRZTRAMINER

WHITE Usually labeled Traminer or Roter Traminer, the wines from this variety range from light and floral to intensely aromatic. They may be dry or have one of various shades of sweetness. They are the fullest, richest, and most pungent of *Trockenbeerenauslesen*.

⌛ 3–6 years

🏆 *Weingut Rheinhold Polz • Andreas Schafler (Traminer)*

GOLDBURGER

WHITE This is a Welschriesling/Orangetraube cross that produces white wines that are used for blending purposes.

⌛ 1–3 years

GRÜNER VELTLINER

WHITE The Danube is the best area for great Grüner Veltliner, the finest examples of which have a fiery flavor that delivers a burning sensation reminiscent of freshly ground pepper. It certainly is not the bland *vin ordinaire* made by this grape in virtually every other area.

⌛ 1–4 years (*Qualitätswein*), 3–10 years (*Prädikatswein*)

🏆 *Weingut Bründlmayer (Langenloiser Berg Vogelsang Kabinett, Ried Lamm, Spätlese Trocken) • Freie Weingärtner Wachau (Weissenkirchner Achleiten "Smaragd") • Graf Hardegg (Dreikreuzen Kabinett, Maximilian Kabinett) • Weingut Hirtzberger (Rotes Tor "Smaragd," Spitzer Honifogl)*

• *Lenz Moser (Knights of Malta) • Weingut Mantlerhhof (older vintages) • Metternich-Sandor (Princess) • Weingut Franz Prager • Weingut Wieninger (Ried Herrenholz)*

JUBLINÄ UMSREBE

WHITE A Blauer Portugieser/Blaufränkisch cross, this is allowed for *Prädikatswein* only, as its mild character is transformed by botrytis.

⌛ 3–7 years

MERLOT

RED Small amounts are grown in Krems, Mailberg, and Furth in Lower Austria, plus in a few scattered plots in Burgenland. This variety has potential in Austria, as it can produce richly colored red wines with soft, spicy-juicy fruit, but has been underexploited until quite recently.

⌛ 1–3 years (*Qualitätswein*), 3–5 years (*Prädikatswein*)

🏆 *Hofkellerei des Fürsten von Liechtenstein (Herrenbaumgärtner Spätlese)*

MÜLLER-THURGAU

WHITE Often labeled as Riesling x Silvaner, this is Austria's second most prolific grape variety. Austrian exporters should realize the value of Müller-Thurgau for adding fat to their Grüner Veltliners, most of which do not have the bite found in the best examples and lack a depth of fruit—outside Austria, the international taste is for a less peppery and more fruity style. The best of Austria's pure varietal Müller-Thurgaus have a fine, spicy character that is superior to the average German version.

⌛ 1–2 years

🏆 *Weingut Hirtzberger • Weingut Schützenhof Fam Korper*

MUSKATELLER

WHITE This is an underexploited variety that makes some of Burgenland's best *Prädikatswein* and excels in the sheltered sites of Styria.

⌛ 1–3 years (*Qualitätswein*), 2–10 years (*Prädikatswein*)

🏆 *Weingut Leth • Weinhof Platzer • Weinbau Ladislaus und Robert Wenzel*

MUSKAT-OTTONEL

WHITE Less weighty than the Muskateller, the Muskat-Ottonel variety has more immediate aromatic appeal and is best drunk when young.

⌛ 2–4 years

🏆 *Willi Opitz*

NEUBURGER

WHITE An Austrian variety that excels on chalky soil, making full-bodied wines with a typically nutty flavor in all categories of sweetness.

⌛ 2–4 years (*Qualitätswein*), 3–8 years (*Prädikatswein*)

🏆 *Dip-Ing Kasl Alpart • H. V. Reinisch*

PINOT BLANC

WHITE Often called Klevner or Weisser Burgunder, this produces a fresh, light-bodied, easy-to-drink wine at lower quality levels. In exceptional years, it can develop a fine spicy-richness in the upper *Prädikatswein* categories.

🍴 2–4 years (*Qualitätswein*), 3–8 years
(*Prädikatswein*)

🍷 *Weingut Skoff* (Kabinett)

PINOT GRIS

WHITE Sold in Austria as Ruländer or Grauer
Burgunder, this is a fuller, spicier version of
Pinot Blanc, but it has a typical nutty richness.

🍴 2–4 years (*Qualitätswein*), 3–8 years
(*Prädikatswein*)

🍷 *Weingut Tement*

PINOT NOIR

RED Labeled Blauer Burgunder, Blauer Spätburgunder, or Blauburgunder in different parts
of Austria, the wines are often disappointing,
although there are a few growers that excel.

🍴 1–3 years

🍷 *Weingut Bründlmayer* • *Johann Gipsberg*
• *Juris-Stiegelmar* • *H. V. Reinisch*

RIESLING

WHITE In Austria the wines from this grape
should be sold as Weisser Riesling or
Rheinriesling, in order to distinguish it from
Welschriesling. Wachau and Kremser Riesling
can be compared with fine German examples.

🍴 2–6 years (*Qualitätswein*), 4–12 years
(*Prädikatswein*)

🍷 *Weingut Bründlmayer* (Spätlese) • *Freie
Weingärtner Wachau* (Weissenkirchner
Achleiten "Federspiel" and "Smaragd")
• *Weingut Hirtzberger* (Spitzer Steinterrassen
"Federspiel") • *Hofkellerei des Fürsten von
Liechtenstein* (Spätlese) • *Weingut Thiery-
Weber* (Kremser Sandgrube)

ROTER VELTLINER

WHITE This grape makes a rather neutral white
wine that is usually blended in light, dry styles.

🍴 1–3 years

ROTGIPFLER

WHITE This makes a robust, full-bodied, spicy
wine of not dissimilar character to the Zierfandler,
which is often made into a dry style, although
the semisweet Rotgipfler of Gumpoldskirchen
may be the most famous rendition of this grape.

🍴 3–7 years

🍷 *Weinbau Franz Kurz* • *Weingut Hoffer*
• *Weingut Gottfried Schellmann*

ST. LAURENT

RED This variety typically produces a light, mild-
flavored wine of quaffing character. St. Laurent
is thought to be related to Pinot Noir, and it has
to be said that some producers can craft lovely,
velvety wines of Pinot-like quality and style.

🍴 1–3 years

🍷 *Weingut Gessellmann* • *Johann Gipsberg*
• *Weingut Umathum* (Vom Stein)

SAUVIGNON BLANC

WHITE Called Muskat-Silvaner (or occasionally
Weisser Sauvignon), this variety grown in Styria
normally makes an austere, dry style, but can
excel at the higher levels of *Prädikatswein*.

🍴 2–4 years (*Qualitätswein*), 4–10 years
(*Pradikatswein*)

🍷 *Weingut Fam Kollwentz* (Römerhof) •
Weingut • *Rheinhold Polz* • *Weingut Skoff*
(Gamlitz Eckberg Edel Kabinett) •
Weingut Tement

SCHEUREBE

WHITE This is not very pleasant at *Qualitätswein*
level, but develops a beautiful aromatic
character at higher levels of *Prädikatswein*.

🍴 2–4 years

🍷 *Weingut Gessellmann* • *Willi Opitz*

SILVANER

WHITE Seldom seen, tomato-tasting varietal.

🍴 1–2 years

🍷 *Weingut Sonnhof Josef Jurtschitsch*

WELSCHRIESLING

WHITE Austria's third most prolific variety,
making very ordinary dry wines, but can be rich
and stylish at upper levels of *Prädikatswein*.

🍴 1–3 years (*Qualitätswein*), 2–8 years
(*Pradikätswein*)

🍷 *Weingut Bründlmayer* • *Willi Opitz*
• *Weinhof Platzer* • *Weingut Tement*

ZIERFANDLER

WHITE Also known as Spätrot, this variety
makes full-bodied and well-flavored dry wine.

🍴 2–6 years

🍷 *Weinbau Franz Kurz* • *Weingut Hoffer*
• *Weingut Gottfried Schellmann*

ZWEIGELT

RED Another mild red wine variety, Zweigelt is
sometimes given the name Blauer Zweigelt or
Rotburger. The best examples have a structure
that is suited to food, with big, peppery fruit,
but the norm is rather light and lackluster.

🍴 1–3 years

🍷 *Johann Gipsberg* • *Weingut Walter Glatzer*
(Dornenvoge) • *Weingut Maria Magdalena
Romer* (Schweizerreid)

BLENDED RED

The finest of these blended reds are usually
oak-aged in new *barriques* and Cabernet-
Sauvignon-based for backbone, with
Blaufränkisch, St. Laurent, and sometimes
Zweigelt added for fruit and softness.

🍴 2–8 years

🍷 *Weingut Gessellmann* (Opus Eximium) •
Weingut Igler (Cuvée Vulcano) • *Weingut Josef
Pöckl* (Admiral) • *H. V. Reinisch* (Cabernet-
Merlot) • *Schlossweingut Malteser Ritterorden*
(Cabernet Sauvignon-Merlot) • *Weingut
Umathum* (Ried Hallebühl Cuvée Rot)

BLENDED WHITE

Cheap, commercial white wine blends are
commonly found in Austria, whereas finer
examples of the blender's art are thin on the
ground. However, Franz Mayer produces an
intriguing blend of Grüner Veltliner, Müller-
Thurgau, Riesling, Silvaner, and Zierfandler.

🍷 *Weingut Franz Mayer* (Grinzinger Reisenberg)

BOTTLE-FERMENTED
SPARKLING

Austria's best-known sparkling wine is the
bottle-fermented Schlumberge, produced in
Vienna, but it seldom excels in quality.

🍷 *Weinhof Platzer* (Pinot Cuvée)

THE APPELLATIONS OF
AUSTRIA

BURGENLAND

Austria's easternmost region is also its warmest.
It consistently provides overripe grapes, almost
guaranteeing a substantial production of
Prädikatswein each year. The Mittelburgenland
and Südburgenland are Austria's most important
red wine areas, with black varieties accounting
for some 75 percent of the vines cultivated.

MITTELBURGENLAND

Mittelburgenland was originally part of the old
Rust-Neusiedlersee, but it is physically separated
from the Neusiedlersee by the Sopron wine area
of Hungary. Mittelburgenland wines are more
passerillage than botrytized in character. This is
a red wine district, with some 75 percent of
the production coming from varieties such as
Blaufränkisch and Zweigelt. The wines from this
region do not have the body, tannin, and

acidity balance that is associated with even the
most modest red wines.

🥂 **Villages** *Deutschkreuz* • *Horitschon*
• *Neckenmarkt*

    Growers *Johann Heinrich* • *Igler*
• *Weninger*

NEUSIEDLERSEE

These vineyards and those of Neusiedlersee-
Hügelland are within the area of influence of
Neusiedlersee, a vast, shallow pan of water
barely 6½ feet (2 meters) deep. Its microclimate
produces more botrytized grapes than any other
wine area in the world.

🥂 **Villages** *Apetlon* • *Frauenkirchen* • *Gols*
• *Illmitz* • *Podersdorf*

    Growers *Juris* • *Heinrich* • *Alois Kracher*
• *Willi Opitz* • *Umathum* • *Velich*

NEUSIEDLERSEE-HÜGELLAND

The western side of Neusiedlersee produces a
similar range of wines to those on the eastern
side, although more red wine is produced here,
and this is also the home of *Ausbruch* wines.

🥂 **Villages** *Donnerskirchen* • *Grossböflein*
• *Rust*

    Growers *Feiler-Artinger* • *Kollwentz*
• *Schandl* • *Schröck* • *Triebaumer* • *Wenzel*

SÜDBURGENLAND

The red wines, mainly Blaufränkisch, are
generally uninspiring. Some surprisingly fine
Prädikatswein from the modest Welschriesling
are also made.

🥂 **Villages** *Deutsch Schützen* • *Eisenberg*
• *Rechnitz*

    Grower *Krutzler*

KÄRNTEN

The wines of Kärnten are confined to a small area immediately to the west of Weststeiermark, comprising a few vineyards scattered between the towns of Klagenfurt and St. Andrä (not the St. Andrä in Südsteiermark). Red, white, Schilcher, and Bergwein wines of modest quality are produced and sold by one or two small firms.

NIEDERÖSTERREICH

This is Austria's premier dry wine region. It is famous for its peppery Grüner Veltliners and the elegance of its Rieslings. Top Rieslings can be light and airy in their youth, but they attain a richness after a few years in bottle and they can achieve a fine, racy balance comparable to that of some of the best German Rieslings. *Kabinett* is the style that dominates the classic wines of this region, although *Spätlese* and, occasionally, *Auslese* wines are made in the hottest years.

CARNUNTUM

Part of Donauland-Carnuntum until 1994, this appellation consists of vineyards on the banks of the Danube, and its hinterland, between Vienna and the Slovakian border. Although a mixed cast of white grapes dominate (with Chardonnay and Grüner Veltliner standing out), red wines have proved most successful, resulting in more black varieties being planted.

✓ **Village** *Göttelsbrunn*

Growers *Glatzer • Markowitsch • Pitnauer*

DONAULAND

Donauland, or land of the Danube, houses the world's oldest viticultural college at Klosterneuburg. Best for Grüner Veltliner.

✓ **Villages** *Kirchberg • Klosterneuburg • Wagram*

Growers *Josef Bauer • Leth • Ott • Söllner*

KAMTAL

North of Kremstal, this region produces some of Austria's finest Riesling, and is the home to some of the country's most gifted, innovative, and expressive winemakers.

✓ **Villages** *Langenlois • Strass*

Growers *Brandl • Bründlmayer • Jurtschitsch Sonnhof • Schloss Gobelsburg*

KREMSTAL

Part of the old Kamtal-Donauland region, this relatively small area north and south of a short stretch of the Danube was singled out in 1994, due to the fame of Krems, which is renowned for its high-quality Grüner Veltliner. Some good Rieslings are also produced. Zweigelt can do well, and there are occasional international varietal highlights from Chardonnay, Cabernet Sauvignon, and even Pinot Noir.

✓ **Village** *Krems*

Growers *Angerer • Buchegger • Mantler • Nigl • Salomon*

THERMENREGION

Named after the hot springs, Thermenregion is also, coincidentally, one of Austria's warmest regions. Wines produced are both red and white, with the Blauer Portugieser and Neuburger grape varieties dominating. Zierfandler and Rotgipfler are specialties of Gumpoldskirchen.

✓ **Villages** *Bad Vöslau • Gumpoldskirchen*

Growers *Alphart • Hartl • Reinisch • Andreas Schafler • Gottfried Schellmann*

TRAISENTAL

Formerly the southwestern half of Donauland, Traisental achieved independence as a regional appellation in 1994.

✓ **Village** *Hertzogenburg*

Grower *Neumayer*

WACHAU

Lower Austria's top-performing district, Wachau makes many fine varietals, including Grüner Veltliner, the most important, and Riesling, definitely the best.

✓ **Villages** *Durnstein • Loiben • Spitz*

Growers *Alzinger • Donabaum • Gritsch • Hirtzberger • Hollmüller • Knoll • Jameh • Lagler • Nikolaihof • Pichler • Franz Prager • Wess*

WEINVIERTEL

This large area combines two former districts of Retz (the hinterland of Kamtal and Donauland) and Falkenstein, which is a totally separate area north of Vienna. Both extend northwards to the border with the Czech Republic. Some reds but mostly white wines are made here. Although few could be said to have any class, they are well made, drinkable, and represent great value for money.

✓ **Villages** *Falkenstein • Mailberg • Retz*

Growers *Graf Hardegg • Pfaffl • Malteser Ritterorden*

OBERÖSTERREICH

This is a large region to the west of the Wachau, but with just 210 acres (85 hectares) of vineyards in the vicinity of Linz. To my knowledge, all the wines are sold under the Weinbauer brand in a *gasthof* at Hofkirchen.

STYRIA *or* STEIERMARK

Situated in the southeastern corner of Austria, this region has a high level of rainfall interspersed with exceptional levels of sunshine and warmth. The region makes red and very dry white wines and, although few particularly fine-quality wines are encountered, there are many interesting local specialties. The most famous is Schilcher. Made from the obscure Blauer Wildbacher grape, Schilcher is a sort of blush-wine that results from the briefest maceration on the grape skins. There are three wine districts in this region.

SÜD-OSTSTEIERMARK

The Müller-Thurgau and Welschriesling are surprisingly successful in the Süd-Oststeiermark,

and the Gewürztraminer can be the most expressive in Austria. Gräflich Stügkh'sches is the oldest, best-known, and most traditional producer, but the wines of Manfred Platzer are more expressive.

✓ **Village** *Kloch*

Growers *Neumeister • Platzer • Winkler-Hermaden*

SÜDSTEIERMARK

The very best wines of this area have Styria's naturally high acidity, but this is combined with delicate and pure fruit flavors, making for exceptional finesse, particularly in varieties such as Gewürztraminer, Chardonnay (known locally as Morillon), and Riesling.

✓ **Villages** *Gamlitz • Leibnitz • Leutschach*

Growers *Gross • Maitz • Polz • Sattler • Skoff • Tement*

WESTSTEIERMARK

Made of some 70 percent Schilcherwein, Zwicbelschilcher is an onionskin-colored Schilcher, which is grown on the slopes above Stainz. Another specialty is Sauvignon Blanc, known locally as Muskat-Silvaner, a somewhat mystifying synonym since the searingly dry wines it produces in these vineyards (and elsewhere for that matter) have absolutely no hint of either Muskat or Silvaner, and the parentage of the Sauvignon Blanc vine has, of course, no connection with either of these grape varieties.

✓ **Village** *Stainz*

Growers *Müller*

TIROL

The Zirler Weinhof produces some 1,500 cases (135 hectoliters) of very ordinary wine from less than 4 acres (just 1.5 hectares) of Müller-Thurgau, Blauer Portugieser, and Zweigelt at Zirl. This might seem an unlikely place to plant a vineyard, if not for the fact that it is conveniently placed on the tourist route to the popular resort of Seefeld.

VIENNA *or* WIEN

Until Madrid recently revived its ancient appellation, Vienna was the only capital city in Europe to have its own winegrowing region. Most of the wines are sold by the pitcher as Wiener Heuriger, in the city's many bars called Heurigen (also known as Buschenschanken). The wine is less than one year old when sold. As much as 28 percent is blended, but pure varietals of classic grapes are on the increase. There are no inner districts, but there are several wine villages within the city limits, of which the most famous is Grinzing.

✓ **Growers** *Franz Mayer • Wieninger*

VORARLBERG

Vorarlberg is the westernmost region of Austria. It used to boast 247 acres (100 hectares) of vines, but only 15 acres (6 hectares) exist today, strung out between Bregenz, on Lake Constance (Bodensee), and Frastanz, which is close to Liechtenstein. The quality of the wine produced here is unremarkably ordinary, and there are only about half a dozen growers who sell their wines commercially.

SWITZERLAND

*At their best, Swiss wines are as fresh and clean
as the Alpine air. Although many grape varieties
are cultivated in Switzerland, the most famous
grape grown here is the Chasselas. In France this
variety is perceived as a table grape, yet the Swiss
make it into a light, dry, spritzy, and delicately
delicious wine that is the perfect partner to the
Swiss cheese fondue.*

THE CHASSELAS CAN BE FOUND under the guise of the Dorin
in the Vaud region, the Perlan in Geneva, and, most famous of
all, the Fendant in the Valais. However, although this country's
most popular grape variety represents 40 percent of the vines
cultivated, nearly half of all Swiss wine produced is, rather
surprisingly, red.

There is, in fact, as much as 27 percent Pinot Noir, 14 percent
Gamay, and, nowhere near as important, but very much on the
increase, Merlot, which currently accounts for 6 percent, leaving
all the other varieties just 13 percent of the vineyards.

The quality of Swiss wines has certainly improved over the last
decade, but yields have always been much too high in general
(350 cases per acre/80 hectoliters per hectare on average, with some
cantons producing as much as 530 cases per acre/120 hectoliters per
hectare) for Switzerland to achieve a serious international reputation
as a quality wine-producing country.

Producers who keep their yields low make some splendid wines,
but, unfortunately, they are at present too few to change the
reputation of the country as a whole. The accepted wisdom on
this issue is that the value of the Swiss franc and the high cost of
living inevitably makes these wines expensive in international
terms, especially the very best wines. Since the Swiss drink twice
as much wine as they can produce and are conditioned to high
prices, there is no need to export and little incentive, therefore, to
develop better-value wines. Price aside, the finest Swiss whites
can be delightful, and the best reds are getting deeper and more
velvety by the vintage.

SWITZERLAND
*Switzerland is divided into three basic areas: French-
speaking, German-speaking, and Italian-speaking. Some
of the wine-producing cantons cross these "international"
boundaries and possess alternative names, with most
vineyards concentrated around the country's lakes and rivers.*

Intensive vine-growing zone

Swiss Romansch

French-speaking Switzerland

German-speaking Switzerland

Italian-speaking Switzerland

1 — Mandement
2 — Arve-et-Lac
3 — Vully
4 — Lavaux
5 — Chablais
6 — Bielersee
7 — Limmattal
8 — Klettgau
9 — Weinland
10 — Thurtal
11 — Oberland
12 — Sopraceneri
13 — Sottoceneri
14 — Misox
15 — Untersee
16 — Zürichsee
17 — Züricher Unterland
18 — Rheinthal
19 — Neuchâtel
20 — Bonvillars
21 — La Côte
22 — Côtes de l'Orbe
23 — Überland
24 — Bündner Herrschaft
‒ ‒ ‒   Canton boundary
▬▬▬   International boundary
▲   Height above sea level (meters)

0   10   20   30   40   50 miles
0   20   40   60   80 km

FACTORS AFFECTING TASTE AND QUALITY

LOCATION
Situated between the south of Germany, north of Italy, and the central-east French border.

CLIMATE
Continental Alpine conditions prevail, with local variations due to altitude, the tempering influence of lakes, and the sheltering effects of the various mountain ranges. An Alpine wind called the Foehn raises, rather than lowers, temperatures in some valleys. Rainfall is relatively low, and a number of areas, such as the Valais in the south, are very dry indeed. Spring frosts are a perennial threat in most areas.

ASPECT
Vines are grown in areas ranging from valley floors and lake shores to the steep Alpine foothill sites, which have an average altitude of 2,460 feet (750 meters), although just south of Visp, they reach nearly 3,940 feet (1,200 meters) and are reputedly the highest vineyards in Europe. The best sites are found on south-facing slopes, which maximize exposure to sun, and where the incline is too steep to encourage high yields.

SOIL
Mostly a glacial moraine (scree) of decomposed slate and schist, often with limestone over sedimented bedrock of limestone, clay, and sand. In the Vaud, Dézaley is famous for its "pudding stones," Chablais has limestone and marl, and Ollon and Bex both benefit from gypsum deposits.

VITICULTURE AND VINIFICATION
Terracing is required on the steeper sites, and so too is irrigation (with mountain water) in dry areas such as the Valais. Most vineyard work is labor-intensive, except in a few more gently sloping vineyards such as those around Lake Geneva (Lac Léman), where mechanical harvesting is practical. Careful vinification produces remarkably high yields. The last three decades have seen a growth in the production of red wine in what is generally a white-wine-dominated region.

GRAPE VARIETIES
Aligoté, Amigne, Ancellotta, Bacchus, Bonarda, Bondola, Cabernet Franc, Cabernet Sauvignon, Chardonnay, Charmont, Chasselas (syn. Dorin, Fendant, Gutedel, Perlan), Chenin Blanc, Completer, Cornalin (syn. Landroter), Diolinoir, Doral, Elbling (syn. Räuschling), Freisa, Freishamer (syn. Freiburger), Gamaret, Gamay, Gewürztraminer (syn. Païen), Gouais (syn. Gwäss), Himbertscha, Humagne Blanc, Humagne Rouge, Kerner, Lafnetscha (possibly the same variety as Completer), Malbec, Marsanne (syn. Ermitage), Merlot, Müller-Thurgau (syn. Riesling x Sylvaner), Muscat à Petits Grains, Petite Arvine, Pinot Blanc, Pinot Gris (syn. Malvoisie, Ruländer), Pinot Noir (syn. Blauburgunder, Clevner), Rèze, Riesling, Sauvignon Blanc, Seibel (syn. Plantet), Sémillon, Seyval Blanc, Sylvaner (syn. Silvaner), Syrah, Traminer (syn. Heida, Païn, Savagnin).

THE APPELLATIONS OF
SWITZERLAND

Note Under the federal appellation system, all cantons have the right to their own appellation and each winemaking village within each canton can register its own appellation. Geneva was the first canton to comply in 1988, followed by Valais in 1991, Neuchâtel in 1993, and Vaud in 1995. Along with these village appellations, each canton may also designate generic district and stylistic appellations, the number of which is increasing all the time.

FRENCH-SPEAKING SWITZERLAND

Cantons *Fribourg, Gea, Jura, Neuchâtel, Valais, Vaud*

District appellations *Vully* (part in Fribourg, part in Neuchâtel); *Arve-et-Lac, Arve-et-Rhône, Mandement* (Geneva); *Bonvillars, Chablais, La Côte, Côtes de l'Orbe, Lavaux* (Vaud)

French-speaking Switzerland represents only 16 percent of the country by area, yet manages to boast more than 80 percent of its vineyards. Two-thirds of the wines are white, with Chasselas accounting for 90 percent, while the Pinot Noir and Gamay together represent 99 percent of the black grapes planted. Valais is the longest-established, most famous, and by far the most intensively cultivated of Switzerland's cantons, with vineyards stretching along 30 miles (50 kilometers) of the Rhône, from Lac Léman (Lake Geneva) to Brig (in the German-speaking sector). The Valais canton accounts for more than one-third of the country's wines, and even its lowliest wine villages are at least as good as the best villages of other Swiss cantons. The Vaud canton encompasses almost one-quarter of Switzerland's vineyards, which makes it the second most intensively cultivated canton in the country. The village of Salgesch is a fast-rising star for red wines—everything from elegant Pinot Noir to muscular Syrah.

✓ **Villages** *Auvernier, Cortaillod* (Neuchâtel) • *Salgesch* • *St.-Léonard, Vétroz* (Valais) • *Calamin* • *Dézaley* (Vaud)

Growers *Adrian Mathier* • *Alain Gerber, Albert Mathier & Söhne* • *Alphonse Orsat* • *André Ruedin* • *Antoine et Christophe Bétrisey* • *Cave de Champ de Clos* • *Cave de la Madelaine/André Fontannaz* • *Cave Emery* • *Cave Saint-Pierre* • *Caves Cidis* • *Caves de Riondaz* • *Caves du Château d'Auvernier* • *Caves Fernand Cina* • *Chanton* • *Charles Bonvin* • *Charles Favre* • *Château d'Allaman* • *Château de Vaumarcus* • *Château de Vinzel* • *Château Lichten* • *Château Maison Blanche* • *Christine & Stéphanie Delarze-Baud* • *Claudy Clavien* • *Clos de la George* • *C. V. Bonvillars* • *Denis Mercier* • *Didier Joris* • *Domaine de la Lance* • *Domaine E. de Montmollin Fils* • *Domaine de Riencourt* • *Domaine des Abeilles d'Or* • *Domaine des Graves* • *Domaine des Muses* • *Domaine du Martheray* • *Domaine du Mont d'Or* • *Domaine Saint-Raphaël* • *Dominique Passaquay* • *Dubuis et Rudaz* • *François et Dominique Giroud* • *Frédéric Dumoulin* • *Gérald Besse* • *Gérard Pinget* • *Germanier-Balavaud* • *Gilles & Joell Cina* • *Hammel* • *Henri Badoux* • *J. & P. Testuz* • *Jean-René Germaner* • *Jean-Michel Novelle* • *Jean-Pierre Walther* • *Jean-Yves Crettenand* • *Kuntzer & Fils* • *Louis Bovard* • *Louis Vuignier* • *Madeleine et Jean-Yves Mabillard-Fuchs* • *Marie-Thérèse Chappaz* • *Maurice Dupraz* • *Maurice Gay* • *Maurice Zufferey* • *Pierre-Alain Meylan* • *Philippe Rossier* • *Raphaël Vergère* • *René Favre* • *Robert Isoz* • *Roger Burgdorfer* • *Romain Papilloud* • *Rouvinez* • *Stéphane Clavien* • *Vincent Favre*

GERMAN-SPEAKING SWITZERLAND

Cantons *Aargau, Basel, Bern, Graubünden* (part), *St.-Gallen, Schwyz, Schaffhausen, Thurgau*

District appellations *Bielersee, Uberland* (Bern); *Bündner Herrschaft* (Graubünden); *Oberland, Rheinthal* (St.-Gallen); *Klettgau* (Schaffhausen), *Thurtal, Untersee* (Thurgau); *Flaachtal, Limmattal, Rafzerfelder, Zürcher Unterland, Weinland* (Zürich)

By far the largest of the three cultural divisions, German-speaking Switzerland (eastern Switzerland) covers almost two-thirds of the country, yet encompasses only one-sixth of its total viticultural area. Aargau is best known for its red wines, but also produces off dry, light, fragrant white wines of low alcohol content. Basel is a producer of white wine only. Although some rather thin and mean red wines are produced in Bern, the majority of grapes grown are white and produce wines that are fragrant and lively, with refreshing acidity. In Graubünden vineyards on the upper reaches of the Rhine, the Pinot Noir ripens well and provides wines made from it with comparatively good color and body. Saint-Gallen also encompasses the upper reaches of the Rhine and produces mostly red wine. The southern fringes of Graubünden fall within the Italian-speaking sector of Switzerland, where the canton is referred to locally as Grigioni. The vines of Schaffhausen grow within sight of the famous falls of the Rhine. Thurgau is, of course, home of the famous Dr. Müller, who left his mark on world viticulture with his prolific Müller-Thurgau cross, and inevitably the grape grows there, although more than 50 percent of the vines are Pinot Noir and the fruity wine that grape produces is far superior. Zürich is the most important canton in German-speaking Switzerland, but it produces some of the most expensive, least impressive wines in the entire country, although Pinot Noir grown on sheltered slopes with a good exposure to the sun can produce attractive fruity wines.

✓ **Villages** *Brestenberger* • *Goldwand* • *Netteler* (Aargau) • *Schafis* (Bern) • *Fläsch, Jenins, Maenfeld* • *Malans* (Graubünden) • *Leutschen* (Schwyz)

- *Hallau* • *Schaffhausen* (Schaffhausen)
Growers *Adelheid von Randenburg* • *Adolf Boner* • *Daniel & Martha Gantenbein* • *Georg & Ruth Fromm* • *Christian Hermann* • *Graaf von Spiegelberg* • *Hans Schlatter* • *Schlossgut Bachtobel/ Hans Ulrich Kesselring* • *Peter & Rosi Hermann* • *Peter Graf, Peter Wegelin* • *Urs Pircher Stadtberg* • *Weingut am Worrenberg* • *Weingut Picher*

ITALIAN-SPEAKING SWITZERLAND

Cantons *Ticino, Grigioni* (part)
District appellations *Misox* (Grigioni); *Sopraceneri, Sottoceneri* (Ticino)

Italian-speaking Switzerland consists of the cantons of Ticino (also known as Tessin) and the southern fringes of Graubünden (known in Italian as Grigioni) and more than 80 percent of the vineyards are planted with the Merlot grape

variety. Merlot del Ticino is consistently one of the best wines produced in Switzerland. Labor costs are nowhere near as high as they are in the rest of the country, which also makes Merlot del Ticino the least expensive of Switzerland's finest wines.

✓ **Village** *Misox* (Grigioni)
Growers *Adriano Kaufmann* • *Agriloro, Carlo Tamborini* • *Christian Zündel* • *Huber Vini* • *Johanniterkeller* • *Luigi Zanini* • *Tamborini* • *Werner Stucky*

THE WINE STYLES OF
SWITZERLAND

AMIGNE

WHITE Old Valais variety mostly grown at Vétroz, the Amigne usually makes a full, rustic, smooth, dry white, although Germanier-Balavaud makes a sweet, luscious, late-harvest style.

🍷— 1–2 years

🏆 *Cave de la Madelaine/André Fontannaz* • *Germanier-Balavaud* (Mitis)

ARVINE

WHITE Another old Valais variety that makes an even richer, dry white, with a distinctive grapefruit character and good acidity. The Petite Arvine (to distinguish it from the lesser-quality Grosse Arvine) adapts well to late-harvest styles and is highly regarded by Swiss wine lovers in both dry and sweet styles.

🍷— 1–3 years

🏆 *François et Dominique Giroud* • *Jean-Yves Crettenand* • *René Favre*

BONDOLA

RED An indigenous grape producing rustic reds on its own, Bondola is at its best in a wine called Nostrano, in which it is blended with Bonarda, Freisa, and other local varieties.

BONVILLARS

WHITE Restricted to Chasselas grown around Lac de Neuchâtel in the villages of Côtes de l'Orbe and Vully, Bonvillars is lighter and more delicate and lively than Vaud wines of this variety grown farther south.

🏆 *C. V. Bonvillars* (Vin des Croisés)

CABERNET SAUVIGNON

RED A relatively new variety that does well in the Chablais district and Ticino, both pure and blended.

🍷— 2–6 years

🏆 *Christine & Stéphanie Delarze-Baud* • *Pierre-Alain Meylan*

CHARDONNAY

WHITE Just what the world needs, another Chardonnay, and at Swiss prices! However, the very best are worth a try.

🍷— 1–4 years

🏆 *Caves Cidis* • *Gilles & Joell Cina* • *Johanniterkeller* • *Kuntzer & Fils* • *Peter Graf*

CHASSELAS

WHITE Called Fendant in the Valais, Dorin in the Vaud, and Perlan in Geneva, this is the most

important Swiss grape variety and can be nicely flavored, often having a charming *pétillance*. When grown on light, sandy soils it may have a lime-tree blossom aroma. The grape is sensitive to soil, with different characteristics depending on whether the soil is limestone, flint, gypsum, marl, schist, or whatever. Although it is possible to find relatively full, potentially long-lived wines from this variety, it is a wine best enjoyed young.

🍷— 1–3 years

🏆 *Henri Dadoux* (Cuvée Prestige) • *Louis Bovard*

CLASSIC RED BLEND

RED Although Ticino grows Switzerland's best Merlot and up-and-coming Cabernet Sauvignon, it also makes the best Bordeaux-style blends.

🍷— 3–10 years

🏆 *Huber Vini* (Montagna Magica)

COMPLETER

WHITE The Completer is rare grape variety of ancient origin that makes a fascinating, rich, *Auslese*-style of wine from scattered plots found in Graubünden.

🍷— 3–7 years

🏆 *Adolf Boner* • *Peter & Rosi Hermann*

CORNALIN

RED Most vines of this indigenous Swiss variety are very old, and restricted to the Valais, where they make dark, powerful red wines that are rich and concentrated, with a full, spicy complexity.

🍷— 3–7 years

🏆 *Denis Mercier* • *Maurice Zufferey*

DÔLE

RED A light red comprised of at least 50 percent Pinot Noir plus up to 50 percent Gamay, Dôle is the Swiss (Valais) equivalent of Burgundy's Passetoutgrains.

🍷— 1–3 years

🏆 *Dubuis et Rudaz*

DÔLE BLANCHE

WHITE The *blanc de noirs* version is popular, but does not carry its own appellation.

ERMITAGE

WHITE A synonym for the Marsanne used in the Valais, where it makes a delicately rich, dry white wine that is often aged too long in bottle by its aficionados.

🍷— 1–4 years

🏆 *Adrian Mathier* • *Marie-Thérèse Chappaz*

FENDANT

WHITE This Chasselas synonym is used in the Valais, where it produces a fleshy-styled, dry white wine, the best of which can have a flinty, lime-tree-blossom aroma and a crisp, minerality of fruit. Ideal with cheese fondue.

🍷— 1–3 years

🏆 *Adrian Mathier* • *Dubuis et Rudaz* • *Frédéric Dumoulin* (L'Orpailleur) • *Raphaël Vergère*

GAMAY

RED Until recently, this Beaujolais grape rarely made red wines of distinction in its pure varietal form, and was much more successful when blended with Pinot Noir (*see* Dôle).

🍷— 1–3 years

🏆 *Gérald Besse* • *Madeleine et Jean-Yves Mabillard-Fuchs*

GEWÜRZTRAMINER

WHITE Rarely encountered.

🍷— 1–5 years

🏆 *Dominique Passaquay* (Passerillé) • *Maurice Dupraz*

HEIDA

WHITE Fresh, lightly aromatic, dry and off-dry wine made from the Savagnin (Traminer) grape.

🍷— 1–2 years

🏆 *Chanton*

HUMAGNE BLANC

WHITE The Humagne Blanc is a wine with a relatively high iron content, which could be the reason it used to be given to babies, although it is probable that the dear little things cried when allowed to suck on Humagne Blanc. It has a green bean or capsicum aroma, hints of exotic fruit on the palate, and a touch of bitterness on the finish.

HUMAGNE ROUGE

RED An old Valais variety, this dark-skinned grape hails from Italy's Valle d'Aosta and makes big, rich, rustic reds that traditionally go well with feathered game.

⊩⟶ 1–4 years

🏆 *Jean-René Germaner*

JOHANNISBERG

WHITE This is not the Johannisberg Riesling, but the official synonym for Sylvaner in the Valais, where it is supposedly musky, although they are usually sappy and savory with some sweetness.

⊩⟶ Upon purchase

🏆 *Adrian Mathier • Albert Mathier & Söhne • Claudy Clavien • Domaine du Mont d'Or • François et Dominique Giroud*

LA CÔTE

RED & WHITE Grown exclusively at La Côte (which encompasses the villages of Aubonne, Begnins, Bursinel, Coteau de Vincy, Féchy, Luins, Mont-sur Rolle, Morges, Nyon, Perroy, and Vinze, as well as La Côte itself), where the Chasselas grape is at its most floral and aromatic, and fruity reds are often blended from two or more varieties, including Gamay, Gamaret, and Garanoir.

⊩⟶ 1–2 years

🏆 *Caves Cidis* (Gamaret/Garanoir/Gamay, Garanoir) • *Philippe Rossier* (Aubonne Merlot)

LAVAUX

WHITE Grown exclusively at Lavaux (which encompasses the villages of Calamin, Chardonne, Dézaley, Epesses, Lutry, Saint-Saphorin, Vevey-Montreux, and Villette, as well as Lavaux itself), the Chasselas is at its softest yet fullest.

⊩⟶ 1–2 years

MERLOT DEL TICINO

RED The Merlot grape accounts for more than 80 percent of the vines planted in Italian-speaking Switzerland, where it produces red wines that range from young and light-bodied to fuller, better-colored wines that have a nice varietal perfume and are often aged in *barriques*. The VITI classification on a bottle of Merlot del Ticino used to be seen as a guarantee of superior quality, but now merely indicates the wine has had one year's aging before being bottled.

⊩⟶ 2–4 years (lighter styles), 3–10 years (*barrique* wines)

🏆 *Adriano Kaufmann • Carlo Tamborini • Christian Zündel • Huber Vini • Luigi Zanini • Werner Stucky*

MÜLLER-THURGAU

WHITE This most prolific (supposedly) *Riesling\Sylvaner* cross was created in 1882 by Dr. Hermann Müller, who hailed from the canton of Thurgau, hence the name, which makes it rather ironic that the Swiss should call this grape *Riesling* x *Sylvaner* rather than by the name that honors its Swiss origins! However, the mild, grapey wine this variety produces even in its home canton is no more exciting than it is elsewhere, although relatively superior examples are produced in Aargau.

⊩⟶ 1–2 years

🏆 *Schlossgut Bachtobel/Hans Ulrich Kesselring*

MUSCAT

WHITE The Muscat à Petits Grains is traditionally grown in the Valais, in small quantities. It makes wines of very light body, with the grape's unmistakable varietal flowery aroma. Some interesting late-harvest styles are beginning to emerge.

⊩⟶ 2–4 years

🏆 *Cave Emery* (Grains Nobles de la Saint Nicolas—Séduction) • *Domaine des Muses • Stéphane Clavien* (Coteaux de Sierre)

NOSTRANO

RED This used to be an inexpensive blend of *vin ordinaire* quality, produced from grapes that failed to reach appellation standard, but now it has its own official classification and the quality has certainly improved. Nostrano means "our" and literally refers to the local varieties used, as opposed to American hybrids.

OEIL DE PERDRIX

ROSÉ Oeil de Perdrix, which literally means "partridge eye," is a French term for pale, dry rosé wines made from free-run Pinot Noir.

⊩⟶ Upon purchase

🏆 *Alain Gerber • Cave de Champ de Clos*

PERLAN

WHITE In the canton of Geneva the Chasselas makes a slightly spritzy flowery wine that is sold as Perlan. Geneva must be mentioned on the label, or a village name: L'Allondon, Bardonnex, Dardagny, Jussy, Lully, Peissy, Russin, or Satigny.

PINOT BLANC

WHITE Recently planted, fashionable variety, but few wines stand out.

⊩⟶ 1–3 years

🏆 *Domaine des Abeilles d'Or • Domaine Saint-Raphaël*

PINOT GRIS

WHITE This famous Alsace grape is becoming quite fashionable in Switzerland, where it makes more of a Pinot Grigio style, with some very successful *vendange tardive* emerging.

⊩⟶ 1–3 years

🏆 *Cave Saint-Pierre • Caves du Château d'Auvernier* (Vendange Tardive) • *Domaine E. de Montmollin Fils* (Vendange Tardive) • *Schlossgut Bachtobel/Hans Ulrich Kesselring • Urs Pircher Stadtberg* (Egfisauer Stadtberger)

PINOT NOIR

RED In a country like Switzerland, which adores Burgundy, it is not surprising that top producers make some of Switzerland's most serious wines with this grape variety—well colored, velvety, with soft, cherry fruit and a touch of oak. Although this wine is sold as Blauburgunder in German-speaking Switzerland, and Pinot Nero in Italian-speaking Switzerland, there are moves toward harmonizing under the internationally recognizable Pinot Noir name.

⊩⟶ 3–6 years (up to 10 years in exceptional cases)

🏆 *Agriloro • Caves Fernand Cina • Christian Hermann • Daniel & Martha Gantenbein • Georg & Ruth Fromm • Peter Wegelin • Weingut am Worrenberg*

RÄUSCHLING

WHITE This rarely seen variety is in decline and is now found only along the shore of Lake Zurich, where it is appreciated for its very fresh scents and fine acidity.

⊩⟶ Upon purchase

🏆 *Weingut Picher*

RIESLING

WHITE Aside from exceptional botrytized wines, Swiss Riesling does not have the quality or varietal intensity of Germany or Austria.

SALVAGNIN

WHITE A light, supple red-wine blend of Pinot Noir and Gamay, this is the Vaud's equivalent of the more famous Dole.

⊩⟶ 1–3 years

🏆 *Jean-Pierre Walther*

SÜSSDRUCK

ROSÉ A soft, fresh, dry rosé produced in eastern Switzerland from free-run Pinot Noir.

SYRAH

RED This grape is at home in the heat and exposure of the northern Côtes du Rhône, and in Valais the Rhône River is as northerly as it gets. Peppery black fruits distinguish these fast-improving, increasingly fashionable wines.

⊩⟶ 3–10 years

🏆 *Antoine et Christophe Bétrisey • Caves Fernand Cina • Domaine des Graves • Dubuis et Rudaz • François et Dominique Giroud • J. & P. Testuz* (Les Oenocrates) • *Jean-René Germaner • Roger Burgdorfer* (Diable) • *Romain Papilloud*

VIN DE PAIN

WHITE A fresh, gently aromatic, dry white wine made from the Traminer in the Valais.

VIN DU GLACIER

Valais

Although Switzerland's equivalent of Germany's Eiswein tends to be oxidative, this rare product does have its enthusiastic followers.

CERTIFIED ORGANIC PRODUCERS

Biodynamic
Ca di Ciser (Mergoscia)
Domaine de Beaudon (Fully)
Liesch-Hiestand (Malans)

The WINES of
NORTHWESTERN
EUROPE

IF ENGLISH WINE COMES AS A SURPRISE TO SOME, then the thought of commercial vineyards in Belgium, the Netherlands, and even on a Danish island north of Poland will beggar belief—yet they exist. Their scope will always be limited because of the combination of northerly latitude and the uncertain climatic effect of the northern Atlantic. However, sparkling wines produced by Nyetimber and Ridgeview demonstrate that world-class quality can be achieved in England. The success enjoyed by these producers has encouraged the English wine industry to focus its efforts on perfecting sparkling wines, and other countries in northwestern Europe would be well advised to follow this lead.

VINEYARDS IN THE WINTER, SURREY, BRITISH ISLES
While winters can sometimes be cold, vineyards in southeastern England generally enjoy a relatively mild climate and soil types that range from clay to chalk.

THE BRITISH ISLES

The future of British wine literally is sparkling. Forget the Müller-Thurgau, Seyval Blanc, and other odd-sounding French hybrids and German crosses that have provided local consumers with mostly forgettable wines. Nyetimber and Ridgeview are world-class sparkling wine producers, and as such represent a blueprint for all quality-conscious English and Welsh winemakers.

ANY ENGLISH OR WELSH VINEYARD owner who does not have the courage to grow more popular grape varieties will eventually be doomed. This country's winemaking efforts are destined to remain a cottage industry, but this is not because England and Wales lack serious or successful producers, rather it is due to two simple facts: British vineyards are a very recent phenomenon and Britain is a densely populated island. It will always be difficult to find suitable land for vineyards, so the potential growth of English and Welsh wine is severely limited. Furthermore, if any *grand cru* sites ever existed, they would be under concrete or asphalt today. It is a bit like starting up the French wine industry from scratch in a country half the size and twice as densely populated with a severely unfavorable climate.

ANCIENT BRITONS

Winemaking in Britain is not new, but dates back to 43 CE, when every important villa had a garden of vines. It was not until 1995, however, when a 20-acre (8-hectare) Roman vineyard was excavated at Wollaston in Northamptonshire, that the true scale of this early viticulture was realized. The Domesday Book reveals the existence of some 40 vineyards of significance during the reign of William the Conqueror, and by medieval times, the number had risen to 300, most of which were run by monks. The Black Death took its toll in the mid-14th century and, almost 200 years later, the dissolution of the monasteries virtually brought an end to English winemaking. Aside from a couple of vineyards in the mid-18th century and two more in the late 19th century, winemaking on a commercial scale was almost non-existent until Hambledon was established in 1951. English vineyards began to boom in the late 1960s and peaked in the early 1970s. Since then, almost 500 have been planted, although just over 300 survive today, and only 109 of these have their own winery.

THE DELL ON DENBIES, DORKING, SURREY
Set amid Surrey countryside, Denbies Estate is the largest winery in Great Britain, surrounded by more than 250 acres (100 hectares) of vineyards.

Few vineyards in the UK can reasonably expect more than an average of 1,440 degree-days Fahrenheit (800 degree-days Celsius), which is well below the accepted minimum for winemaking of 1,800 degree-days Fahrenheit (1,000 degree-days Celsius), so even the best-situated vineyards risked failure when they were first established. Some vineyards were unsuccessful, but those in existence today have proved the theoretical minimum conditions to be just that—theoretical.

FUTURE TRENDS

Although English wine will remain forever a cottage industry, this does not mean it cannot earn a reputation for quality. High duty rates do mean, however, that it is difficult for the smallest vineyards, which have the highest overheads, to establish sales of a new product. Initially, this problem was overcome by contract winemaking, with virtually all the oldest and largest vineyards providing a service for small vineyards where a winery was not a viable option. Since the early 1990s, however, cooperative groups have formed to produce large volumes of relatively inexpensive wines by blending wines from their members, all of whom also make and market their own single-vineyard products.

The next step in the development of English wine is to rid the country of most of its crosses and hybrids. This has nothing to do with the European ban on hybrid grapes or the ill-informed view that they are somehow intrinsically inferior. Indeed, exceptionally fine wines can on occasions be made from some hybrids, and it is relatively easy to make passable wines from such grapes. On the other hand, in a country such as this, it is hard to make decent wines from *vinifera* varieties, and the winemaker is severely punished for every mistake. No, the reason why these funny grapes with funny names must go is because they have a negative impact on most serious wine consumers. Wine drinkers are attracted to classic varieties and even willing to dabble with more obscure *vinifera* grapes, particularly when indigenous to the wine-producing area of origin, but they either do not understand hybrids or find them a turn-off. As for German crosses, how can producers expect to establish an English or Welsh wine reputation with names like Reichensteiner or Siegerrebe?

English vineyard owners should learn from Ontario, British Columbia, and New England in the United States, all of which faced climatic hazards at least as great as those in the British Isles. They were seen as a joke, the hicks of the wine world, by consumers of fine wine. Only when they started growing *vinifera* varieties did they gain respect. Owners of vineyards in climatically challenged regions must learn the unpleasant truth: that it is not possible to build a serious reputation on hybrid grapes. There is only one consistently high-quality product of a hybrid grape and that is Canada's Icewine, and the lesson to be learned there is that it has built its reputation on the connotation of the word Icewine. It would never have been sold on Vidal, the hybrid name.

HERE COMES THE CAVALRY!

It took two Americans, Stuart and Sandy Moss, the original owners of Nyetimber, to shake the English out of their lethargy. The Mosses were the true pioneers. They had a crazy ambition to make a top-quality English fizz from classic Champagne varieties, but when they sought "expert" advice, they were told that there was no way that Chardonnay would ripen in the English climate, and Pinot Noir would simply rot. With no such thing as an indigenous grape variety in Britain, they were advised to play

it safe and plant hardy hybrids. This was never an option for the Mosses, who knew it would be impossible to establish a worthwhile reputation with grapes that are not even taken seriously by the majority of wine drinkers in Britain, let alone on major international markets. They stopped listening to the English, most of whom were trained at Geisenheim, where many of the crosses occupying English vineyards originated, and did the unthinkable—they asked the French for help. The *champenois* arrived, examined the soil, advised which clones should be planted and how they should be trained, and they helped make the wine. Within 18 months of the first release, Nyetimber had created such a stir that it was chosen for the Queen's Golden Anniversary lunch. Certainly proof that bottle-fermented sparkling wine represents Britain's greatest potential for quality, especially in southeastern England, where even the chalk subsoil is exactly the same as that found in the Champagne region.

RECENT BRITISH VINTAGES

2003 The greatest potential vintage since that other Year of the Drought, 1976, but, this time around, English winemakers certainly had the experience to take full advantage of the conditions. This year not only produced the best reds, but also some of the finest dry white and sparkling wines.

2002 A very good all-around vintage.

2001 In general, wines were above average in quality, with white wines performing better than reds.

2000 A fairly average-quality vintage, with white wines performing the best.

1999 Above-average quality, with both red and white wines performing well.

THE WINE REGIONS OF
THE BRITISH ISLES

Regional characteristics have not yet been established in the wine regions of the British Isles, and I am not sure that they ever will be, but it is very difficult to build up a proper spatial awareness of where English vineyards are located without first breaking them down into a small number of workable areas.

The following regions are all officially recognized by the United Kingdom Vineyard Association, or UKVA (which took over from the English Vineyard Association in 1996) and it would help if more vineyard owners were to utilize these regions on their labels in addition to a more specific location. Until they do, British consumers will be less informed about their own wines than they are about those of France or Australia.

EAST ANGLIA
Bedfordshire, Cambridgeshire, Essex, Hertfordshire, Norfolk, Suffolk

The flattest and most exposed of all the regions, East Anglia is subject to bitterly cold easterly and northeasterly winds, but has fertile soils, which can encourage significantly higher yields than in some areas of England. Quite often this has the effect of trading off quality for an attempt to preserve consistency.

MERCIA
Cheshire, Derbyshire, Lancashire, Leicestershire, Lincolnshire, Northamptonshire, Nottinghamshire, Rutland, Shropshire, Staffordshire, Warwickshire, West Midlands, West Yorkshire

This is a very large and naturally diverse region, with vineyards planted both on flat ground and slopes, with soils ranging from light sand to heavy clay. About the only common factor is Madeleine Angevine, which seems to be the most reliable variety. At the time of writing, another ten vineyards have been planted, but are not yet in production.

SOUTHEAST
East and West Sussex, Kent, Surrey

This region covers the "Garden of England," which probably says it all. It is not as wet as the West Country, and milder than East Anglia, but not as warm as Thames and Chiltern. Soils range from clay to chalk. The latter forms the same basin that creates the chalk cliffs at Dover and goes under the Channel to rise in Champagne.

SOUTHWEST
Bristol, Cornwall, Devon, Gloucestershire, Herefordshire, Isles of Scilly, Republic of Ireland, Somerset, South Wales, Worcestershire

Geographically the largest region, with vineyards as far apart as Cornwall, where the Gulf Stream has its greatest effect, but there is also a tendency to wet weather, and North Wales, which takes the brunt of weather systems from the Atlantic. Although prevailing westerly winds make conditions difficult in the west of Cornwall and Wales, the region is generally milder than the east coast. The topography of the region ranges from mountainous to flat, with some areas below sea level. Soils vary tremendously from limestone through shale, clay, and peat to granite.

THAMES AND CHILTERN
Berkshire, Buckinghamshire, Oxfordshire

This large area is the warmest of all the regions, and most vineyards are located on slopes of moisture-retaining soils. There are also many aquifers in the area, which prevent stress during drought conditions.

WESSEX
Channel Islands, Dorset, Hampshire, Isle of Wight, Wiltshire

The major factor linking these counties together is the interesting pattern of isotherms that form south of the Isle of Wight and provide a more temperate climate than the surrounding regions.

THE WINE PRODUCERS OF
THE BRITISH ISLES

1 ADGESTONE
Adgestone, Isle of Wight (Wessex)

Estate-bottled wines from a south-facing chalk slope that was first planted in 1962.

2 ASTLEY
Stourport on Severn, Worcestershire (Southwest)
★ V

An award-winning vineyard established in 1979 by Jonty Daniels and Janet Baldwin.

✓ *Classic white blend* (Dry Reserve) • *Late Harvest*

3 BEARSTED
Beardsted, Kent (Southeast)

Small boutique winery with 4 acres planted in the late 1980s by former research chemist John Gibson.

✓ *Sparkling* (Brut Vintage)

4 BEAULIEU
Nr Brockenhurst, Hampshire (Wessex)

This enthusiastic, aristocratic venture has been running since 1958.

5 BEECHES HILL
Upton Bishop, Herefordshire (Southwest)

Established in 1991, Beeches Hill grows Madeleine Angevine and Seyval Blanc grapes, but the wines are made by Three Choirs.

6 BIDDENDEN
Biddenden, Kent (Southeast)
★ V

A former orchard on a gentle south-facing slope in a shallow, sheltered valley, Biddenden is principally known for its Ortega. Wines produced in part or whole from grapes grown elsewhere are sold under the Gribble Bridge label.

✓ *Ortega* • *Rosé* (Gribble Bridge) • *Sparkling* (Gribble Bridge Vintage)

7 BINFIELD
Wokingham, Berkshire (Thames and Chiltern)

A dry white wine and a light red are produced here, but the emphasis is on a fizz under the Champion label, which is linked to the Bob Champion Cancer Fund, a charity that receives a percentage of the price of every bottle sold.

8 BOOKERS
Bolney, Sussex (Southeast)
★ V

The first vines were planted in 1973, but initially the Pratt family sold their grapes, and only started making their own wine in 1983, with red wine unusually accounting for as much as half the output.

✓ *Classic red blend* (Dark Harvest)

9 BOTHY
Frilford Health, Oxfordshire (Thames and Chiltern)
★ V

The most successful wine produced by new owners Sian and Richard Liwicki is their Oxford Dry. Although from a typically English hodgepodge of grape varieties, it is a refreshing dry white that anyone partial to Sauvignon Blanc would enjoy.

✓ *Oxford Dry*

10 BOZE DOWN
Whitchurch-on-Thames, Oxfordshire (Thames and Chiltern)

Established in 1985 by Dick and Sandra Conn, Boze Down Vineyard lies on the sheltered southern slopes of the Chiltern Hills overlooking the Thames River between Reading and Oxford.

✓ *Classic white blend* (Skippetts)

11 BOW-IN-THE-CLOUD
Malmesbury, Wiltshire (Wessex)

Bow-in-the-Cloud vineyard was planted in 1992 and has been producing wine since 1995. Pure varietal wines are sold under the Arkadian label, while blends are sold under the Cloud Nine label.

12 BREAKY BOTTOM
Northtease, Sussex (Southeast)
★ V

Peter Hall used to release his Seyval-based fizz far too young, but now he is running the risk of holding on to them for too long. The two *cuvées* below are best to buy and drink when Hall offers them at 5–6 years of age.

✓ *Müller-Thurgau* • *Seyval Blanc* • *Sparkling* (Cuvée Maman Mercier, Cuvée Remy Alexandre)

13 CAMEL VALLEY
Nanstallon, Cornwall (Southwest)
★ V

Former RAF pilot Bob Lindo gave up the high life for the more down-to-earth task of working the soil on the sunny slopes of the Camel River valley, midway between the Atlantic and Channel coasts. Local celebrity chef Rick Stein so enjoyed eating Lindo's Reichensteiner grapes off the vine that he renamed the variety "Ricksteiner" on his television program. Cornwall Brut is a rather too easy to drink sparkling wine with a potted history of Christopher Merret on the back label.

✓ *Bacchus* • *Seyval Blanc* • *Pinot Noir* • *Sparkling* (Cornwall Brut)

14 CANTERBURY CHOICE
Ash, Kent (Southeast)
★ V

The label under which the wines from Barnsole Vineyard are sold.

✓ *Dry Reserve* • *Pilgrim's Harvest*

15 CARR TAYLOR
Westfield, Sussex (Southeast)

Established in 1971 by David and Linda Carr Taylor, with Alexander Carr Taylor the second-generation winemaker.

✓ *Reichensteiner* (Alexis)

16 CHATEAU LE CATILLON
Jersey, Channel Islands (Wessex)

Chateau le Catillon has been bought by La Mare.

17 CHIDDINGSTONE
Chiddingstone, Kent (Southeast)

This vineyard was established by the late Dudley Quirk, whose two sons run Chiddingstone today.

18 CHILFORD HUNDRED
Linton, Cambridgeshire (East Anglia)
★ V

This large vineyard was established in 1972, but it did not produce its first sparkling wine until 1994.

✓ *Sparkling* (Aluric de Norsehide)

19 CHILTERN VALLEY
Hambledon, Oxfordshire (Thames and Chiltern)

Also known as Luxters, because owner David Ealand established his winery on the site of Old Luxters pig farm. Has produced some interesting wines in the past, although they have a lower profile these days.

20 COACH HOUSE
Romsey, Hampshire (Wessex)

This vineyard is owned by Roger Marchbank, who is better known as the chairman of UKVA, and cannot be accused of using his position to promote his wine, as I have never tasted Coach House wine, and seldom heard mention of it!

21 COURT LANE
Alresford, Hampshire (Wessex)

Stephen Flook must have broken a record when he took 12 years to plant just over one acre of vines.

22 DANEBURY
Stockbridge, Hampshire (Wessex)

Anne Bishop named her fizz Cossack after the controversial winner of the 1847 Derby.

23 DAVENPORT
Rotherfield, East Sussex & Horsmonden, Kent (Southeast)
O ★ V

Will Davenport is a graduate of Roseworthy College in Australia, and has worked for wineries in Alsace, California, and South Australia before setting up in England in 1990. He has a still wine vineyard at Horsmonden in Kent, but his Rotherfield vineyard is primarily for sparkling wine. Planted in 1993 with Pinot Noir and Auxerrois, Davenport's Rotherfield vineyard came into production in 1997. His 1999 Limney Brut was brilliant, and the 2000 almost as good, suggesting that Davenport will soon be a third force to reckon with in the establishment of world-class English wine from a dedicated sparkling wine estate, following in the footsteps of Nyetimber and Ridgeview.

✓ *Limney Brut* • *Limney Fumé* • *Red wine* (Pinot Noir)

24 DENBIES WINE ESTATE
Dorking, Surrey (Southeast)
★ V

With 265 acres (106 hectares) of vines, Denbies Wine Estate is the largest English vineyard. Its Tesco-looking winery is also designed and equipped to receive tourists by the bus-load; consequently Denbies is also the most visited of English vineyards. Capable of producing award-winning wines, but not consistent throughout the range.

✓ *Rosé* (Rose Hill)

25 EGLANTINE
Costock, Nottinghamshire (Mercia)

Readers might think that Tony Skuriat's vineyard is northerly enough, without deliberately freezing his grapes, but this is how he produces his award-winning wine North Star.

✓ *Dessert wine* (North Star)

26 FAWLEY
Henley-on-Thames, Oxfordshire (Thames and Chiltern)

Nick and Wendy Sargent are just beginning to establish a reputation for Bacchus.

✓ *Bacchus*

27 GIFFORD'S HALL
Hartest, Suffolk (East Anglia)

John and Jeanie Kemp claim to tread their grapes, and they also produce a variety of homemade liqueurs, but Gifford's Hall was up for sale in 2004.

28 GREAT STOCKS
Stock, Essex (East Anglia)

This vineyard was established between 1993 and 1999 by Brian and Gillian Barnard, who are hoping that Rondo will provide good red wine.

29 HALE VALLEY
Boddington, Buckinghamshire (Thames and Chiltern)

Sparkling wine has been Antony and Carol Chapman's most successful wine so far.

✓ *Sparkling* (Brut Vintage)

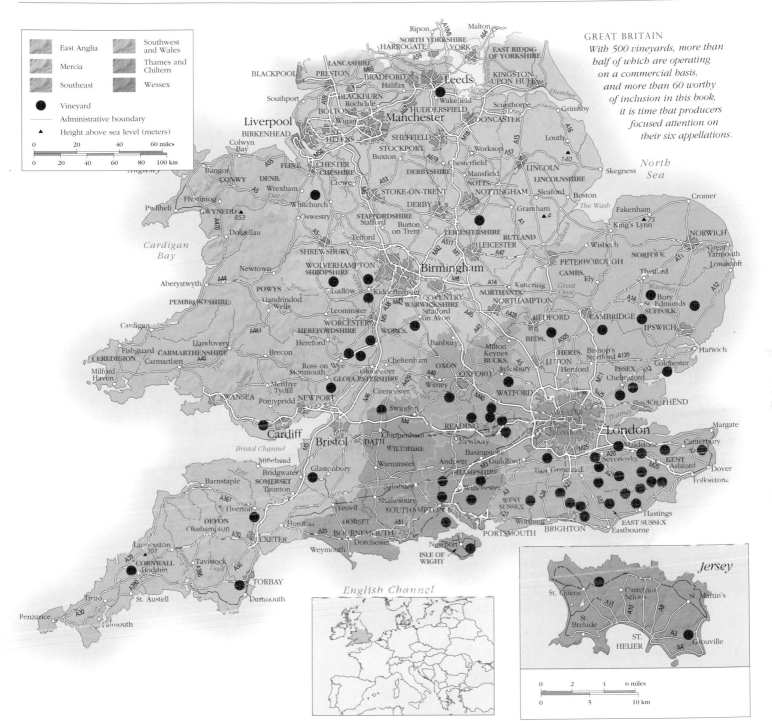

GREAT BRITAIN
With 500 vineyards, more than half of which are operating on a commercial basis, and more than 60 worthy of inclusion in this book, it is time that producers focused attention on their six appellations.

Map legend:
- East Anglia
- Mercia
- Southeast
- Southwest and Wales
- Thames and Chiltern
- Wessex
- ● Vineyard
- — Administrative boundary
- ▲ Height above sea level (meters)

Scale: 0 20 40 60 miles / 0 20 40 60 80 100 km

English Channel

Jersey (inset map) — St. Ouens, Carrefour Selous, St. Martin's, St. Brelade, St. Helier, Grouville

Scale: 0 2 4 6 miles / 0 5 10 km

30 HALFPENNY GREEN

Halfpenny Green, Staffordshire (Mercia)
★ V

Just over 22 acres (9 hectares) were planted between 1983 and 1991, then a winery was built in 1994. As with most northerly English vineyards, Madeleine Angevine has proved the most reliable variety.

✓ *Classic white blend* (Penny Black) • *Huxelrebe* • *Madeleine Angevine*

31 HEART OF ENGLAND

Welford-on-Avon, Warwickshire (Mercia)
★ V

David Stanley planted this vineyard in "Shakespeare Country" in 1995

but did not achieve his first commercial harvest until 2000.

✓ *Classic red blend* (Oberon)

32 HIDDEN SPRINGS

Horsham, Sussex (Southeast)
★ V

Although Martyn Doubleday and Chris Cammel make some trophy-winning wines, devotees would kill for Hidden Springs Art Deco labels, even if they put nothing inside the bottles!

✓ *Classic red blend* (Dark Fields) • *Classic white blend* (Decadence) • *Rosé* (Sussex Sunset) • *Sparkling wine* (Vintage Brut)

33 LA MARE

Jersey, Channel Islands (Wessex)
★ V

The Channel Islands' first vineyard and the only one open to visitors, La Mare now also owns Chateau le Catillon. Also produces a Norman-style cider and has installed a small Calvados pot still for apple brandy.

✓ *Classic white blend* (Domaine de La Mare) • *Sparkling wine* (Brut, Lily)

34 LAMBERHURST

Lamberhurst, Kent (Southeast)
★

Merged with Chapel Down in 2001 to form English Wines Plc.

✓ *Classic white blend* (Fumé)

35 LEVENTHORPE VINEYARD

Woodlesford, West Yorkshire (Mercia)
★

Established by chemist-turned-winemaker George Bowden in 1986, Leventhorpe vineyard is just a stone's throw away from the historic stately home of Temple Newsome. This is the country's most northerly vineyard and it is no mere curiosity, since it crops ripe grapes every year, and has its own winery.

36 LLANERCH VINEYARD

Hensol, Vale of Glamorgan, Wales (Southwest)
★ V

Wines are sold under the Cariad label. The fizz is improving.

✓ *Classic white blend* (Cariad Celtic Dry) • *Sparkling* (Cariad Blush)

37 LUDLOW VINEYARD
Clee St. Margaret, Shropshire (Mercia)
★ V

An up-and-coming, new vineyard, Ludlow might have struck it lucky with 2003 as its inaugural vintage, but it was an impressive start nonetheless. Clee Moonlight is a blend of Madeleine Angevine, Seyval, and Phoenix with a slight hint of oak. Only 200 bottles were made.

✓ *Clee Moonlight*

38 MEOPHAM
Wrotham, Kent (Southeast)

Part organic production, including an organic medium-sweet Pinot Noir.

39 MERSEA
Mersea Island, Essex (East Anglia)

On an island 9 miles (15 kilometers) south of Colchester, halfway between West Mersea and East Mersea, this vineyard and winery also boasts a microbrewery.

40 MOORLYNCH
Bridgwater, Somerset (Southwest)

This vineyard is located on a sunny south-facing hillside that has, surprisingly for England, a somewhat dry microclimate. Owner-winemaker Peter Farmer's most successful wine so far has been his 1996 Vintage Reserve Brut sparkling wine.

41 NEW HALL
Purleigh, Essex (East Anglia)

Established by the Greenwood family in 1969, this 91-acre (37-hectare) vineyard is one of the oldest and largest English wine producers, and the first to be planted in Essex.

42 NEW WAVE WINES
Tenterden, Kent (Southeast)
★ V

One of the country's four largest wine producers, this company was formed in early 2001, when Chapel Down Wines at Tenterden Vineyard merged with Lamberhurst Vineyard. Also referred to as English Wines Plc, the multi-award-winning New Wave Wines still has the feel of a large and expanding winery that is finding its way, which indeed it is, but the quality and consistency has greatly improved since the merger. Improvements continue under Owen Elias, who was named Winemaker of the Year in 2002 and 2003.

✓ *Bacchus* (Curious Grape)
• *Ortega* (Curious Grape)
• *Pinot Blanc* (Curious Grape)
• *Pinot Noir* (Curious Grape)
• *Schönburger* (Curious Grape)
• *Sparkling* (Chapel Down Pinot Reserve)

43 NORTHBROOK SPRINGS
Bishop Waltham, Hampshire (Wessex)

Owner-winemaker Brian Cable Young has made some good-value fizz and noble rot dessert wines in the past.

44 NYETIMBER
Pulborough, Sussex (Southeast)
★★

Established in 1988 by American couple Stuart and Sandy Moss, who achieved their ambition of creating a world-class English sparkling wine, and sold it on to English songwriter Andy Hill, who appears to be every bit as serious about maintaining the very highest of standards. The secret here is not so much the determination or money that have been put into the project (although both help greatly), but the topography of the vineyard, which has not changed since Nyetimber was mentioned in the Domesday Book. The vineyard is south-facing, with a modest slope, which acts as a frost drop, allowing the vines to be trained close to the ground and in a high density of 2,500 per acre (6,200 per hectare). Nyetimber makes classic sparkling wine from traditional Champagne varieties (Chardonnay, Pinot Noir, and Pinot Meunier), which have exceptional longevity, and show remarkable finesse.

✓ *Entire range*

45 PARVA FARM
Tintern, Monmouthshire, Wales (Southwest)
★ V

Emerging Pinot Noir potential from steep vineyards set within a working farm environment with sheep, cattle, and ponies.

✓ *Pinot Noir*

46 PENSHURST
Penshurst, Kent (Southeast)

First planted in 1972 on a south-facing slope, the first crop was promising, and some excellent wines have been produced here. The picturesque label is charming and very English, except for the hidden kangaroo!

47 PLUMPTON COLLEGE
Plumpton, East Sussex (Southeast)

The only educational facility in the UK to provide courses in all aspects of wine, Plumpton College also possesses a well-equipped, commercial winery.

48 RIDGEVIEW ESTATE
Ditchling, Sussex (Southeast)
★★ V

Owned by Christine and Mike Roberts, this 16-acre (6-hectare) vineyard did not come into full production until 1997, yet quickly started snapping at the heels of Nyetimber for the English sparkling wine crown, and some *cuvées* are superior. In honor of Christopher Merret, the first person to document the process that eventually became known as the traditional method, all Ridgeview wines are marketed as "Cuvée Merret," a name the Roberts have registered. Furthermore, to maintain Merret's association with London, each style of "Cuvée Merret" is named after an area of London.

✓ *Entire range*

49 SANDHURST VINEYARDS
Sandhurst, Kent (Southeast)

A 25-acre (10-hectare) vineyard established in 1988 by the Nicholas family on Hoads Farm.

50 SEDLESCOMBE
Robertsbridge, Sussex (Southeast)
◉

In 1994 Sedlescombe became Britain's first organic vineyard, and in this rain-swept country, there have not been many brave enough to follow.

✓ *Classic white blend* (Dry White)

51 SHARPHAM
Asprington, Devon (Southwest)
★ V

Sharpham makes and markets wine from Beenleigh Manor Vineyard in Harbertonford, which was Britain's first "real" red wine in the 1980s. Since then, it has become a multi-award-winning wine.

✓ *Classic red blend* (Beenleigh)
• *Classic white blend* (Dart Valley Reserve) • *Madeleine Angevine* (Barrel Fermented Dry) • *Pinot Noir*

52 SHAWSGATE
Framlingham, Suffolk (East Anglia)
★ V

One intriguing offer from this vineyard, which was established in 1973, is the chance to rent a row of vines, from which wine will be made for you—because they are "your" vines, the wine will be tax-free!

✓ *Rosé*

53 TENTERDEN
Tenterden, Kent (Southeast)
★ V

Originally planted and owned by Stephen Skelton, Tenterden is now the home of New Wave Wines, as well as one of its better labels.

✓ *Classic white blend* (Tenterden Estate)

54 THREE CHOIRS
Newent, Gloucestershire (Southwest)
★ V

One of the country's four largest wine producers, Three Choirs has always had potential, but was disappointing until the 2002/03 vintages.

✓ *Bacchus* (Estate Reserve)
• *Desert* (Estate Reserve Noble Rot) • *Siegerrebe* (Estate Reserve)

55 THROWLEY
Throwley, Kent (Southeast)
★ V

A southwest-facing slope of the North Downs that is developing a reputation for Ortega.

✓ *Ortega* (Reserve)

56 TILTRIDGE
Upton-on-Severn, Worcestershire (Southwest)
★ V

Peter and Sandy Barker have not been very successful with their Elgar

sparkling wine, the grapes for which obviously have more potential for still wines.

✓ *Schönburger* (Cello) • *Seyval* (Oaked)

57 VALLEY VINEYARDS
Stanlake Park, Berkshire (Thames and Chiltern)
★ V

Owner Jon Leighton and his business partner, Australian-trained winemaker John Worontschak, have done much to put a fresh, affordable face on the reputation of English wine.

✓ *Classic white blend* (Fumé)
• *Rosé* (Pinot Blush)
• *Schönburger* (Hinton Grove)
• *Sparkling* (Ascot Brut, Heritage Rose)

58 WARDEN ABBEY
Biggleswade, Bedfordshire (East Anglia)

Established in 1986 by Jane Whitbread at the Abbey of Warden, which was founded by Cistercian monks in 1135 as the "daughter abbey" to Rievaulx Abbey in Yorkshire.

✓ *Bacchus*

59 WORTHENBURY
Worthenbury, Wrexham, Wales (Southwest)

The most northerly cultivation of Chardonnay, Pinot Noir, and Sauvignon Blanc, the grapes have to be trucked 170 to 260 miles (272 to 420 kilometers) (depending on the destination winery) to be vinified.

✓ *Classic white blend* (Chardonnay/Sauvignon)

60 WYKEN
Stanton, Suffolk (East Anglia)

Established in 1988, Carla and Ken Carlisle have been winning awards for their Bacchus since the inaugural 1991 vintage.

✓ *Bacchus*

61 YEARLSTONE
Bickleigh, Devon (Southwest)

Originally established by the late, lamented Gillian Pearkes, who planted her first vineyard in 1963 at the age of 18, and whose pioneering book *Growing Grapes in Britain* (1969) was used as a blueprint by many of today's vineyards. Yearlstone vineyard in the Exe Valley was taken over by Roger White, a BBC presenter, when Pearkes died in 1993.

✓ *Classic white blend* (Number 5)
• *Avalon* (Pennard) • *Carter's Vineyards* (Colchester)

OTHER CERTIFIED ORGANIC PRODUCERS

Avalon (Pennard)
Carter's Vineyards (Colchester)

THE WINE STYLES OF
THE BRITISH ISLES

AUXERROIS

This grape variety is capable of producing fresh, creamy-rich wine that adapts well to oak and can also be a useful blending component for classic bottle-fermented sparkling wine.

BACCHUS

Fat and grapey with rich, Muscatlike fruit when ripe, this grape provides high sugar levels even in cool climates, making it one of Great Britain's more successful German crosses. It does, however, develop an intensely herbaceous, elderflower style in cooler years and is downright catty when unripe.

Y *Camel Valley* • *New Wave* (Curious Grape)

CABERNET

Grown with Merlot in plastic tunnels at Beenleigh, this has promised deep, plummy fruit but has always been ruined during vinification.

CHARDONNAY

Mostly planted for sparkling wine, but some still wine versions are beginning to emerge. Winemakers need to look to Champagne for the best clones (95, 96, 75, and 121) and to New Zealand for advice on how to handle this variety in a maritime-influenced growing environment.

Y *Nyetimber* (Premier Cuvée)

EHRENFELSER

Penshurst specializes in this grape, which is the darling of British Columbia in Canada, but to my mind it performs much better in Kent, where in warm years it is soft and ripe with a Riesling-like peach-stone intensity that develops well.

GAMAY

The climate in Great Britain might not have the warmth to make good red wine from this grape, but if Thames Valley's effort in 1992 (Clocktower Gamay) was not an anomaly, it could well be one of the most useful grapes for bottle-fermented sparkling wine.

HUXELREBE

Easy-going fruit that sometimes has a herbaceous-grapefruit bite and can become elderflower-tasting or catty in poor years.

KERNER

More aromatic in Great Britain than in Germany, where it was developed, Kerner is unsuitable for oak and is often grown for its late budding (thus frost avoidance) and high sugar level.

MADELEINE ANGEVINE

This grape has a light, floral aroma and after-perfume, and can have apricoty fruit, but often fights against an elderflower pungency.

Y *Halfpenny Green* • *Sharpham* (Barrel Fermented Dry)

MÜLLER-THURGAU

Müller-Thurgau is a typically German style that can become elderflower-tasting or catty, although wines of real flavor are possible.

Y *Breaky Bottom*

ORTEGA

Fat and jammy when ripe, becoming herbaceous in cooler years, with an elderflower, white currant character when unripe.

Y *Biddenden* • *New Wave* (Curious Grape) • *Throwley*

PINOT BLANC

Can be delicious, easy-drinking, and reminiscent of what Alsace does with this variety.

Y *New Wave* (Curious Grape)

PINOT GRIS

England's Pinot Gris is not the spiciest in the world, but it does offer richer fruit per ounce of acidity than either Pinot Blanc or Chardonnay. It can be successfully oaked, although the best-known example, Denbies 1995 Special Release, was over-oaked and would have been better if blended with another variety.

PINOT NOIR

Some vineyard owners fear that English weather and this variety's susceptibility to rot will not mix, but those growers who have chosen the right clone (115, 114, 779, and 927) have been successful. In a good year, this grape is capable of making an elegant English red with a very attractive cherry and raspberry flavor. In less ripe years, color extraction can be a problem, and a school of thought reckons that such grapes should be used for sparkling wine, but Pinot Noir that cannot produce a light red will not make good fizz, and would be better used making off-dry, New World-style *blanc de noirs*.

Y *Hidden Springs* (Dark Fields) • *New Wave* (Curious Grape) • *Parva Farm* (Rosé)

REICHENSTEINER

Appreciated by growers for its resistance to rot and by winemakers for its high sugar levels, but its neutral character is seldom enjoyed by wine enthusiasts, although exceptions exist.

SCHÖNBURGER

Soft and peachy when ripe, good examples should have at least a light spiciness. There is nothing worse than a dry Schönburger from a cool year, when it smells like a tomcat's spray.

Y *New Wave* (Curious Grape) • *Valley Vineyards* (Hinton Grove)

SEYVAL BLANC

Relatively neutral and capable of oak-aging, but classic English style is crisp and unoaked, with a grassy-elderflowery intensity that is very tangy and almost Sauvignonlike, although unlike Sauvignon, good Seyval ages well in bottle. However, it can be catty with less ripeness.

Y *Breaky Bottom* • *Camel Blanc*

SIEGERREBE

A Madeleine Angevine/Gewürztraminer cross that can produce fat wines with tangy fruit.

Y *Three Choirs* (Estate Reserve)

TRIOMPHE

Triomphe is a red-wine hybrid with a hint of foxiness on the aftertaste, but this can be hidden in a clever blend.

OTHER STYLES

BOTRYTIS *or* LATE-HARVEST

There's no doubt that the UK can guarantee sufficiently damp mornings to encourage rot, but it requires a strong burn-off from mid-morning sun for two weeks to encourage noble rot, which is not that common. When it occurs, however, these wines can have a stunning piquance of mouthwatering fruit and acidity.

Y *Three Choirs* (Estate Reserve Noble Rot)

BOTTLE-FERMENTED SPARKLING WINE

The best wines use nonaromatic varieties, preferably classic Champagne grapes. Nyetimber has shown that these varieties can succeed.

Y *Nyetimber* • *Ridgeview*

CLASSIC RED BLENDS

Most English red wines are light and insubstantial, but New World influence has encouraged softer, more upfront, fruity styles.

Y *Sharpham* (Beenleigh) • *Hidden Springs* (Dark Fields)

CLASSIC WHITE BLENDS

One way to ignore the funny-sounding grape names of hybrids and crosses is to blend them into a wine sold under a proprietary label.

Y *Hidden Springs* (Decadence) • *Sharpham* (Dart Valley Reserve) • *Valley Vineyards* (Fumé)

OAKED WHITES

As in the US, some producers have adopted the term *fumé* to indicate oak-aging. Marginal climatic conditions produce wines of leaner structure than those of Europe or the New World, thus oak can easily overwhelm, and winemakers tend to restrain its use. Normally only nonaromatic varieties such as Seyval Blanc are oaked.

Y *New Wave Wines* (Curious Grape Ortega) • *Sharpham* (Madeleine Angevine Barrel Fermented Dry) • *Valley Vineyards* (Fumé)

ROSÉ

Although the British climate makes it difficult to produce a true red wine year in and year out, the viticultural fringe should be ideal for making crisp, ultrafresh, off-dry rosés and a few vineyards are beginning to realize the potential.

Y *Denbies* (Rose Hill) • *Hidden Springs* (Sussex Sunset) • *Valley Vineyards* (Pinot Blush)

LUXEMBOURG

A small but varietally diverse wine-producing country on the northern cusp of commercially viable viticulture, Luxembourg's best vineyards consistently produce wonderfully fresh and pure dry white wines that are delicious to drink with food or without, and they fit conveniently into the niche vacated by so many Alsace producers as they make sweeter and sweeter wines.

LUXEMBOURG DERIVES ITS NAME from Lucilinburhuc, or "Little Fortress," which is the Saxon name for a defensive position originally built by the Romans on a rocky promontory around which the city of Luxembourg was destined to grow. Under the Romans, this area held no geopolitical identity, but was part of the Trier region, where vines were grown 2,000 years ago. Today, the vineyards are scattered around and between 28 towns and villages, stretching from Wasserbillig in the north to Schengen in the south. This viticultural area is the mirror image across the Moselle River of the German *Bereiche* of Obermosel and Moseltor, which are located on the right bank, and generally produce less exciting wines than those from Luxembourg's vineyards opposite. It is from the German side of the river that the topography of Luxembourg's vineyards can best be observed, especially when the river bends north and south. This strip of the Moselle's left bank is officially designated *Appellation Moselle Luxembourgoise Contrôlée*, and vines are not allowed to be planted anywhere else in Luxembourg.

TERROIR?

These vineyards are at their narrowest in the northern half of Luxembourg's Moselle valley, where the dolomite limestone subsoil has resisted erosion, leaving a narrower valley with steeper slopes. This pinkish-brown bedrock can be seen overhanging the old Caves St. Martin—now owned by the firm of Gales—which were carved out of the dolomite in 1919–21. Going south from Remich, much softer marly and clayey soils dominate; consequently, the area has been prone to erosion, which has widened the valley, leaving a softer landscape of gently rolling hills. It is said in Luxembourg itself that the wines in the south are soft, mellow, and best drunk young, whereas those in the north are crisper and finer, requiring

LUXEMBOURG
A country united by other tongues: French is used by its government and courts, with most newspapers published in German, leaving the national dialect with no official role.

THE LIEUX-DITS—LUXEMBOURG'S BEST-KEPT SECRET

The *lieux-dits* represent Luxembourg's richest source of fine, expressive wines, and a joint project between the Institut Viti-Vinicole (IVV) and the German Weather Institute could be this country's key to international success. This project is identifying the best areas in each *lieu-dit* according to meteorological criteria (rain, sunshine, heat, etc.), which some believe could be the basis of a future *grand cru*-type classification. Weather is an infinitely better way of discerning which *parts* of a vineyard (rather than vineyards *per se*) should be classified than the French system. The French claim to isolate an individual *terroir* by its geological homogeneity compared with the surrounding area within a historically established

named site. As the relatively recent classification of Alsace's *grands crus* illustrates, not only does the geological homogeneity fly out of the window in the process, but so does the extent of the historically established named site. As growers on the periphery of a historically established named site realize the premium that can be demanded by a wine with *grand cru* on the label, they ask, "If his plot is going to be classified *grand cru*, why not mine?" And, of course, once they are allowed, their own neighbors—who were previously separated by unclassified land—want in. Thus it was that *grands crus* like Brand in Turckheim grew from less than 7 acres to almost 143! Such corrupt behavior would kill Luxembourg's

fledgling reputation. This is the one area where the IVV needs a firm hand. Its hardest task will be to establish in law the true historical boundary of every *lieu-dit*, after which the meteorological data cannot be argued with—growers cannot claim to have more or less rain, sunshine, or heat than the records show. So it should be possible, not merely to use this data to classify *grands crus*, but also to subdivide each *lieu-dit* so that, for example, parts of the *lieu-dit* of Greiveldange Fels are officially designated Greiveldange Fels *grand cru* and Greiveldange Fels *premier cru*, while the rest remains Greiveldange Fels *lieu-dit* plain and simple, albeit a single-vineyard wine in its own right.

is definitely on the decline. Twenty years ago, every other bottle of wine produced in the Grand Duchy was made from Rivaner. This grape is grown at very high yields and turned into a sweetish, Liebfraumilch-type wine, making it Luxembourg's least interesting variety, but one that enjoys high-volume sales. Rivaner prices are low, and the popularity of this style of wine extends beyond the domestic market to Belgium, where it accounts for more than half of global exports of Vins Moselle Luxembourgeoise. As long as the cultivated area of this variety continues to decline, there seems little point in getting high-minded about its yield. It will eventually bottom-out, and lowering yield will hardly produce a noticeably finer quality of wine.

🍾 Upon purchase

🏆 *Aly Duhr* (Sélection Ahn Hohfels)

OTHER GRAPE VARIETIES

**Minimum natural ripeness (2003):
63° Oechsle (8%ABV)
Maximum yield: 528 cases/acre.**

Gamay did not impress me, although the three Muscats demonstrated that it might be worth persevering with this variety, especially Charles Decker's Muscat Ottonel (deliciously creamy 2001, and evocatively strawberry 1997).

🍾 1–4 years

🏆 *Charles Decker* (Muscat Ottonel, Remerschen Kreitzberg)

OTHER STYLES

CRÉMANT DE LUXEMBOURG
Maximum yield: 528 cases/acre.

Champagne—real Champagne—was in fact produced in Luxembourg by Mercier from 1886 up to almost the beginning of World War II.

During this time, Mercier was known as "Champagne Mercier, Epernay-Luxembourg," and both establishments were famous for being completely powered by 19th-century electricity. Today, of course, Champagne is a prohibited term, and the Crémant de Luxembourg appellation was created as part of the deal with Champagne not to use the term *méthode champenoise*. Curiously, it gets lumped in with French Crémant appellations (Alsace, Bordeaux, Bourgogne, Die, Jura, Limoux, Loire, and Luxembourg) at the annual Concours des Crémants. Most Crémant de Luxembourg encountered outside the country is boring, but the general standard is much higher, primarily because it is much fresher, and these sparkling wines are a delight to drink young. The style is fresh, soft, and elegant, with good acids providing a crisp, fruity finish. The only exception is Domaine Alice Hartmann Brut, which is crammed full of flavor and character, perhaps at the expense of finesse, and could be criticized for being too big and too oaky, but has to be admired, and is currently Luxembourg's greatest sparkling wine. However, it's a style that I would not like to see more than two or three other producers emulate, as Luxembourg is more naturally attuned to the Gales style of freshness and finesse. Whereas Crémant de Luxembourg must be made exclusively from grapes grown within the appellation Moselle Luxembourgeoise, readers should be aware that any Luxembourg wines labelled Vin Mousseux, Vin Pétillant, Perlwein, or sold as "boissons effervescents à base de vin" may be blended from imported grapes, juice, or wine.

🍾 1–2 years

🏆 *Domaine Alice Hartmann* (Brut) • *Gales* (Heritage) • *Gales* (Jubilée) • *Gales* (Cuvée Premier Rosé) • *Vinsmoselle* (Poll-Fabaire Cuvée Art Collection)

VENDANGE TARDIVE
Only Auxerrois, Pinot Blanc, Pinot Gris, Riesling, and Gewürztraminer are authorized. The minimum ripeness level of 243 grams per liter (220 for Riesling) of natural sugar content, is as tough as the *vendange tardive* law introduced in Alsace in 1984, and raising ripeness levels is more difficult in Luxembourg's colder, more northerly climate. Alsace raised the bar in 2001 (to 235–257 grams per liter), and Luxembourg should do likewise, confident in the knowledge that its vineyards are nothing like the suntraps in Alsace, thus the Grand Duchy will never be in danger of losing its primary crop of dry wine grapes. Vendange Tardive is a new, emerging category of wine, and too many of the wines are noticeably high VA, with a bitter finish. This will change, as producers get used to the style. Some, like Domaine Thill Frères, already are.

🍾 1–8 years

🏆 *Domaine Thill* (Château de Shengen Riesling)

VIN DE GLACE OR ÄISWÄIN
Only Pinot Blanc, Pinot Gris, and Riesling are authorized. The minimum ripeness level is 292 grams per liter of natural sugar content. Luxembourg would seem to be more climatically adept at *vin de glace* than *vendange tardive*, but it is a style that generally attracts a high VA level and the Grand Duchy is no exception.

🍾 1–8 years

🏆 *Charles Decker* • *Domaine Gales*

VIN DE PAILLE
Only Auxerrois, Pinot Blanc, Pinot Gris, and Gewürztraminer are authorized. The minimum ripeness level is 317 grams per liter of natural sugar. Only one outstanding example so far.

🍾 1–8 years

🏆 *Caves Sunnen-Hoffmann* 🔴 🔵 (Auxerrois)

THE APPELLATIONS OF
LUXEMBOURG

Due to the varying usage of all three languages (Luxembourgish, German, French, and sometimes Dutch/Low German), spellings of some villages and *lieux-dits* can vary. The most common variations are shown below. To list all the villages and all the *lieux-dits* in use today in all languages, not to mention the odd variant in each language, would confuse more than it would inform. It is obvious that Luxembourg must clean up its labelling act, obliging everyone to use the same nomenclature, and most observers would agree that Luxembourgish should be the dialect of choice.

AHN
Lieux-dits *Palmberg, Vogelsang, Elterberg, Hohfels/Houfels, Göllebour, Pietert, Nussbaum*

Warmer vineyards enable Gewürztraminer to succeed in exceptionally hot years. It is said that Luxembourg's first Traminer and Muscat vines were grown here at the beginning of the 20th century. Also good for Pinot Gris, Auxerrois, Riesling, and occasionally Crémant de Luxembourg. Domaine Viticole Mme Aly Duhr & Fils is the most famous producer here, but I have been at least as pleased by Schmit-Fohl,

followed by Steinmetz-Duhr. Other Ahn wines that have impressed me on occasions have been Clos du Rochers (Bernard-Massard) and Jean Ley-Schartz.

BECH-KLEINMACHER
Lieux-dits *Enschberg, Jongeberg, Falkenberg, Naumberg, Fuusslach, Gaalgeberg, Brauneberg, Gottesgôf, Kurschels, Rëtschelt*

Two villages, Bech and Macher, merged 100 years or so ago, when they built a communal church. Just two producers resident in the town (Krier-Bisenius and Schram et Fils), but growers sell most grapes to the cooperative at Wellenstein and Caves Gales for their sparkling wine (they also grow their own grapes here). Naumberg has been the most successful *lieu-dit* in my tasting, with fine Pinot Gris from Krier Welbes and the cooperative at Wellenstein. Schram makes a very good Pinot Blanc on both Falkenberg and Kurschells.

BOUS
Lieux-dits *Johannisberg, Fels*

Just one local producer (Caves Beissel) and nothing outstanding so far.

EHNEN
Lieux-dits *Kelterberg, Meschteschberg, Ebnerberg/Einerberg, Rousemen, Bromelt, Wousselt*

Ehnen is one of the prettiest villages on the Luxembourg wine route. I have enjoyed wines from Jean Linden-Heinisch and M Kohll-Reuland. Pinot Gris and Auxerrois fare well, with Mesteschberg and Kelterberg among the most successful *lieux-dits*.

ELLINGEN/ELLANGE
Lieux-dits *None*

Two very good producers are located here, Caves Gales and Krier Welbes, but no mono-cru wines produced. Growers either deliver their grapes to the cooperative or sell them to one of the six commercial wineries.

ELVANGE/ELVINGEN
Lieux-dits *None*

No producers are located here. Although there is one grower who owns three plots within this village that are delimited for the production of

Appellation Moselle Luxembourgoise Contrôlée, and have been exploited in the recent past, there are no vines growing here at the moment.

ERPELDINGEN
Lieux-dits *None*

No producers are located here. Growers either deliver to the cooperative or sell to one of the six commercial wineries.

GOSTINGEN
Lieux-dits *Bocksberg, Häreberg*

Just one local producer (Caves Fernand Rhein) and nothing outstanding so far.

GREIVELDANGE/ GREIWELDIGEN
Lieux-dits *Hutte/Hëtt, Dieffert, Herrenberg/Häreberg, Hëttermillen*

The village is one mile from the Moselle, but the vineyards extend down to the river's banks. Of the two local producers, Beck-Franck and Stronck-Pinnel, the latter makes one of Greiveldange's best Rieslings from the Hëtt *lieu-dit*, while the former makes better wines from other villages. However, most of the growers belong to the village cooperative, and Vinsmoselle makes most of the best wines here, especially Dieffert Pinot Gris and Herrenberg Auxerrois.

GREVENMACHER
Lieux-dits *Fels, Rosenberg/Rouseberg, Leitschberg/Leiteschberg, Pietert, Groaerd/Groärd*

The best-known producer here is Bernard Massard, one of Luxembourg's truly international exporters. The Fels *lieu-dit* is for Riesling, Leitschberg, and Pietert for Pinot Blanc. Steinmetz-Jungers, Vinsmoselle's Caves de Grevenmacher, and Fédération Viticole make the finest local wines.

LENNINGEN
Lieux-dits *Häreberg*

Just one local producer (Caves Fernand Rhein) and nothing outstanding so far.

MACHTUM
Lieux-dits *Alwengert, Hohenfels, Ongkâf, Goellebour/Göllebour, Widdem*

Matchum is supposedly known for its Ongkâf Riesling, but it produces better Pinot Gris, and to be truthful, Göllebour vies with Ongkâf as the top *lieu-dit* in the village. Matchum also makes good Pinot Blanc. The Riesling is good, but no better than Auxerrois and, in hotter years, Gewürztraminer. The two local producers, Jean Schlink-Hoffeld and Pundel-Hoffeld, are both very good, with Vinsmoselle and Cep d'Or the best producers from outside the village.

MERTERT
Lieux-dits *Bocksberg, Herrenberg/Häreberg*

The best *lieu-dit* in this ugly, industrial port is Herrenberg, which thankfully is closer to Wasserbillig. Pinot Gris is Herrenberg's most successful variety, with Häremillen and the local Vinsmoselle Caves de Grevenmacher the top-performing producers.

MONDORF
Lieux-dits *None*

No producers are located here. Growers either deliver to the cooperative or sell to one of the six commercial wineries.

NIEDERDONVEN
Lieux-dits *Fels, Gölleberg, Diedenacker*

No producers are located here. Growers either deliver to the cooperative or sell to one of the six commercial wineries.

OBER-WORMELDINGEN
Lieux-dits *None*

No producers are located here. Growers either deliver to the cooperative or sell to one of the six commercial wineries.

OBERDONVEN
Lieux-dits *None*

No producers are located here. Growers either deliver to the cooperative or sell to one of the six commercial wineries.

REMERSCHEN
Lieux-dits *Jongeberg, Kräitchen, Kreitzberg, Rodernberg/Roudeberg, Reidt*

Charles Decker is the award-winning producer here; many of his medals are for wines that were denied the most lowly appellation, having been rejected by the IVV. In the best years, Decker can produce good Muscat Ottonel and Gewürztraminer on the Kreitzberg *lieu-dit*, while Krier Frères has made good Riesling on Jongeberg.

REMICH
Lieux-dits *Fels, Goldberg, Gaalgeberg, Hélwéngert, Hôpertsbour, Primerberg, Scheuerberg*

Primerberg is the most important *lieu-dit* here, and Riesling its best variety, with Krier Frères and Mathis Bastian the top producers, but this vineyard also makes fine Pinot Blanc and Auxerrois (St Remy Desom), and Pinot Gris (Gales). Overall Remich is most successful for Pinot Blanc, with Mathis Bastian (Coteau de Remich) and Krier Frères (Hôpertsbour) both vying with St. Remy Desom.

ROLLING
Lieux-dits *None*

No producers are located here. Growers either deliver to the cooperative or sell to one of the six commercial wineries.

ROSPORT
Lieux-dits *None*

Everyone in the Luxembourg wine trade will tell you that Wasserbillig is the very northern limit of *Appellation Moselle Luxembourgois Controlée*, yet I found these vines seven miles further north, and they are officially within the delimited region, even though they are not on the Moselle or even in its hinterland, but located on a tributary called the Sauer.

SCHENGEN
Lieux-dits *Fels, Markusberg*

Although Fels Riesling is supposed to be best known, this most southerly of Luxembourg's wine villages is definitely Pinot country (Blanc and Gris), with Vinsmoselle dominating, though A Gloden & Fils also makes some fine wines.

SCHWEBSINGEN/ SCHWEBSANGE
Lieux-dits *Letscheberg, Steilberg, Hehberg, Kolteschberg*

Supposedly good for Gewürztraminer, but I have yet to confirm that. The best *lieu-dit* is

Kolteschberg, where Vinsmoselle Caves de Wellenstein and Laurent & Benoît Kox produce some good Pinot Gris and Riesling.

STADTBREDIMUS
Lieux-dits *Primerberg, Goldberg, Dieffert, Fels*

Only Wormeldingen produces more top-quality Luxembourg wines than Stadtbredimus. Most of the best come from Vinsmoselle Caves de Stadtbredimus and and Cep d'Or, but some also from Gales and Laurent & Benoît Kox. The largest *lieu-dit* is the Primerberg, but Dieffert and Fels are the best, producing some of the finest Rieslings in the country. Pinot Gris is the second best variety in Stadbredimus, and Primerberg, Goldberg, and Fels the most successful *lieu-dit* for this grape.

WASSERBILLIG
Lieux-dits *Bocksberg, Häreberg*

Supposedly the most northerly of Luxembourg's main drag of vineyards, but not strictly so (*see* Rosport).

WELLENSTEIN
Lieux-dits: *Foulschette, Kurschels, Veilchenberg, Roetchelt, Brauneberg, Knipp, St Annaberg*

Kurschels stands out as the best *lieu-dit*, and the best *lieu-dit* for Riesling. Foulschette is the second-best *lieu-dit*, and the best *lieu-dit* for Pinot Gris. Krier Welbes and Gales are the top producers in this region, followed closely by Mathis Bastian and Vinsmoselle (Série Limitée Art).

WINTRANGE/WINTRINGEN
Lieux-dits *Hommelsberg, Felsberg*

Felsberg is the best-known *lieu-dit*, with its statue of St. Donatus crowning the hill, where Pinot Gris and Riesling are supposed to be among the best in Luxemboug, although I have tasted only one wine that matches up to that sort of reputation (and that is Vinsmoselle Caves de Remerschen Riesling Grand Premier Cru Wintrange Felsberg).

WORMELDANGE/ WORMELDINGEN
Lieux-dits *Elterberg, Heiligenbäuschen, Koeppchen/Köppchen, Moorberg, Nidert, Nussbaum, Péiteschwengert, Pietert, Weinbour, Woussell*

Wormeldingen is the superstar of Luxembourg's wine villages, Koeppchen its greatest *lieu-dit*, Domaine Alice Hartmann its best producer, and Riesling its king of grapes. Domaine Alice Hartmann is by no means the only top producer making wines from this village. I have also been impressed by Wormeldingen wines from Aly Duhr, Fédération Viticole, Häremillen, Jean Schlink-Hoffeld, Mathes, Pundel-Hoffeld, Schumacher-Lethal, St. Remy Desom, Steinmetz-Jungers, and Vinsmoselle Caves de Wormeldange. I have tasted some good Pinot Gris, Pinot Blanc, and Auxerrois from these producers, but with one exception (Aly Duhr), they have all been from other *lieux-dits*. If I have learned anything about the wines of Luxembourg, it is that the best parts of Koeppchen produce the country's finest Riesling, and it would be a great shame to plant this *terroir* with any other variety.

OTHER WINEMAKING COUNTRIES OF NORTHWESTERN EUROPE

In the northern hemisphere, the farther north a vine grows, the fewer hours of daylight it receives and the greater the angle at which the sunlight is spread out, thus the longer it takes to ripen grapes. Factor in the wet, windy, and uncertain climes of the Atlantic, and it may seem surprising that these countries do in fact manage to produce wine.

THERE ARE ONLY TWO WAYS of looking at these frontier wine countries—outside looking in or inside looking out.

Those with a purely quality-oriented perspective and who are fascinated by expressive wines would be highly sceptical of the value of planting vineyards in the south of England, let alone in Belgium and even farther north. They would argue that growing conditions are less favorable in Belgium than in the Pas de Calais, and more tricky in Ireland than Finistère—and they would be right. They would point out that there are no vines growing in the Pas de Calais or in Finistère, and that the French would think anyone who suggested planting them there out of their mind—and they would be right.

However, if you are on the inside looking out, you probably think, why not? Such is the attitude that makes this page in the encyclopedia possible. Irrational, unnecessary, and half-crazy, almost certainly, but nevertheless possible.

BELGIUM
Appellations: *Côtes de Sambres et Meuse VQPRD, Hagelandse or Hageland VQPRD, Haspengouwse or Hespaye VQPRD, Vin de Pays des Flandres, Vin de Pays du Walloon*
In Belgium, winegrowing dates back to Roman times. Today, over 250 acres (100 hectares) of vineyards are cultivated by more than 100 growers. Most of these growers are part-time or hobbyists, although there are around 20 who could be described as commercial to one extent or another.

Chardonnay has proved most successful, even if the best wines are too oaky and decidedly international in style. Müller-Thurgau, Auxerrois, and Pinots (Blanc, Gris, and Noir) are also grown, but some observers believe that the hardier crosses such as Optima, Kerner, and Würzer actually produce superior wines in Belgium. The Hagling-Bio estate in Hageland is organic.

Genoels-Elderen (Chardonnay Goud), *Peter Colemont* (Chardonnay Clos d Opleeuw)

DENMARK
Amazingly, there are 62 acres (25 hectares) of vines in this country. Even more amazingly, the European Union has limited growth to no more than 245 acres (99 hectares). There are nine commercial producers, the oldest of which is Domain Aalsgaard, which was established in 1975. Chateau Lille Gadegard produced its first vintage in 2003 on Bornholm, a Danish island in Eastsee, to the north of Poland.

IRELAND
Better suited to stout and whisky, Ireland had absolutely no winemaking history when, in 1972, Michael O'Callaghan planted Müller-Thurgau vines at Mallow in County Cork. O'Callaghan has just over 2.5 acres (1 hectare) of exclusively Reichensteiner vines nowadays, and his wine is sold exclusively in the restaurant of his country house hotel, Longueville House. Just 3 miles (5 kilometers) away from Mallow is another Irish vineyard, called Blackwater Valley, where owner Dr. Christopher has 12 acres (5 hectares), growing Reichensteiner, Madeleine Angevine, and Seyval Blanc. Another venture, West Waterford Vineyards at Cappoquin, was not in production at the time of writing.

LIECHTENSTEIN
Located between Germany and Switzerland, Liechtenstein is a tiny principality of 62 square miles (160 square kilometers), with just 37 acres (15 hectares) of planted vines. They are primarily Pinot Noir and Chardonnay varieties, and are mostly owned by the Crown Prince through his private winery, the Hofkellerei Fürsten von Liechtenstein.

NETHERLANDS
Although the Netherlands is north of Belgium, and therefore would seem an even more unlikely location for growing vines, almost all of its vines grow east of Maastricht, so they are actually located further south than the Belgian vineyards of Brabant. There are over 100 growers farming 124 acres (50 hectares) of vines, primarily consisting of Riesling, Müller-Thurgau, Auxerrois, and the inevitable German crosses.

Apostelhoeve (Riesling)

SWEDEN
Two vineyards have been established recently in the Skåne region of southern Sweden: the Kullabygden Vingård near Helsingborg in 2000 and the Nangijala Vingård near Malmö in 2001. No pesticides or fungicides are used in these vineyards. The first crop of grapes was in 2003, when 85 gallons of red wine, and 21 gallons of mixed dry white, sweet white, and sparkling white wine were produced.

A VINEYARD IN LIECHTENSTEIN
The Prince of Liechtenstein's vineyards in Vaduz, the capital of this tiny European principality.

The WINES of
SOUTHEASTERN
EUROPE

ALMOST ALL THE COUNTRIES IN Southeastern Europe have the capacity to become major players in the global wine market, but Hungary has the lead and, probably, the most potential of all. It has the lead because Tokaji is already regarded as one of the world's greatest classic wines and because its government had been dabbling in a mixed-market economy long before the collapse of Communism, whereas the other countries in the Eastern Bloc and former USSR were—and still are—struggling. Tokaji gives Hungary instant status in the wine world and this attracts international investors, but the role of a botrytized wine is very small in the scheme of things. Red wine is Hungary's future, and it has a long way to go in honing regional styles and developing markets for this wine. Indeed, all the countries in this region should be exploiting their red wine potential, as their various *terroirs* are better suited to it than to white wine, whatever they happen to be making at the moment.

4,750-GALLON BARRELS IN SUHINDOL WINERY, BULGARIA
The Suhindol Winery started the Bulgarian wine bandwagon rolling in the mid-1970s with cheap but reliable Cabernet Sauvignon.

BULGARIA

Once the most dependable wine-producing state in Eastern Europe, Bulgaria was fashionable in the West for its cheap Cabernet Sauvignon as early as 1975, but by the mid-1990s, this country was no longer a consistent source of reliable quality. The privatization of the industry has not been as successful as hoped, partly due to an inefficiently large number of tiny plots that have been mismanaged, and partly because arguments over their ownership have dragged on while the vines have been left to wither. Some foreign investment has helped, but more is needed to buy up thousands of these ailing vineyards and consolidate them into a smaller number of larger, well-maintained estates. Unfortunately, much of the investment already at work has gone into faux New World brand names such as Blueridge and Stork Nest. Such Anglicized names undermine Bulgaria's identity and do nothing for its reputation, whatever the quality of the individual wines.

FACTORS AFFECTING TASTE AND QUALITY

LOCATION
Located in the center of the Balkan Peninsula, Bulgaria's eastern border is formed by the Black Sea, while its neighbors to the north, west, and south are respectively Romania, Serbia/Macedonia, and Greece/Turkey.

CLIMATE
The climate is warm continental, although it is cooler in the north and more temperate toward the east due to the influence of the Black Sea. Annual rainfall averages between 19 and 38 inches (47 and 95 centimeters).

ASPECT
Vines are grown largely on the flat valley floors and coastal plains.

SOIL
Predominantly fertile alluvium in the valleys, with dark-gray and brown forest soils in the northern region, and rich, black carbonate soils in the southern region, becoming sandy in the vineyards of the southeast coastal area.

VITICULTURE AND VINIFICATION
Most vineyards are concentrated in the valleys of the Danube and Maritsa Rivers. The disruption of privatization has not been a positive factor for Bulgaria, whose vineyards are highly fractured, with many that are poorly maintained. The wineries are comparatively well equipped, and vinification methods have been updated; there is a state-of-the-art facility at Sliven (Blueridge).

GRAPE VARIETIES
Primary varieties: Cabernet Sauvignon, Gamza, Mavrud, Merlot, Pamid, Rkatsiteli, Red Misket, Ugni Blanc, Welschriesling
Secondary varieties: Aligoté, Bolgar, Cabernet Franc, Chardonnay, Dimiat, Fetjaska, Gamay, Mavrud, Melnik (also called Shiroka Melnishka loza), Muskat Ottonel, Pinot Gris, Pinot Noir, Rubin (Nebbiolo x Syrah), Sylvaner, Syrah, Riesling, Sauvignon Blanc, Tamianka, Traminer

ALTHOUGH BULGARIANS HAVE been cultivating vines for more than 3,000 years, winemaking came to a halt when the Turks imposed Muslim rule between 1396 and 1878. It was not until 1918 that winemaking began again in earnest, and it was only in the 1970s that the Bulgarians made any real effort to export their wines. Bizarrely, it was PepsiCo who started this export drive. The company wanted to open up sales of its cola and, not interested in Bulgarian currency, needed something marketable in exchange. Wine seemed a good idea, so PepsiCo supplied the Sliven Winery with expertise from UC Davis to bring the domestic product up to modern standards. During the mid-1970s, the economic depression that was affecting most Western countries meant that consumers were on the look-out for cheaper alternatives to Bordeaux, and Bulgaria was suddenly in a position to oblige, thanks to PepsiCo.

EXPORTING WINE
Cabernet Sauvignon from Bulgaria's Suhindol region was not simply cheap in the 1970s, it was extraordinarily well made, had a deep color, full body, soft fruit, rich blackcurrant varietal flavor, and just a hint of wood-aging on the finish.

Spurred on by the success of Cabernet Sauvignon, Bulgaria soon became the world's fourth-largest exporter of wine, and state subsidies ensured that prices remained attractive. For many years, Bulgarian wine was well known for its consistency and value for money, but Gorbachov's alcohol reforms in the mid-1980s resulted in the uprooting of many vineyards, which was the first factor to have a detrimental effect on quality. Ironically, the second factor was democracy, as this was the precursor to privatization, which denied many of the largest former state-owned wineries some of their best sources of grapes. The result has been a rather mixed bag, as some wineries have gone completely private, while most remain local cooperatives, and a large number of private growers have put their products (grapes now, but surely single-vineyard wines in the future) on the market for the very first time. In 1991, Domaine Boyar in Sofia became the first private wine company to be established in Bulgaria since 1947, and this has put it one step ahead of the rest in terms of sourcing by enabling it to forge links with ten of the best wineries in the country.

BULGARIAN LABEL LANGUAGE

BJALO VINO White wine
BUTILIRAM To bottle
CHERVENO VINO Red wine
CONTROLIRAN These wines constitute just 2 percent of the total production of quality wines, and are made from grapes that originate from strictly defined and controlled microregional vineyards, with a limited maximum yield of grapes per acre and defined minimum sugar content.
COUNTRY WINE Inexpensive blended wine on a par with French *vins de pays*.
DESERTNO Dessert or sweet wine

ISKRIASHTO VINO Sparkling wine
KOLEKTZIONO Reserve
LOZIA Vineyard
LOZOVA PRACHKA Vine or vine variety
NATURALNO Natural
SLADKO VINO Sweet wine
RESERVE This term is restricted to DGO and Controliran wines, and indicates ageing in oak of at least three years for white and four for red, although after an intitial, indeterminate period the wines may be transferred from small *barriques* to large wooden vats.

SOSTATACHNA ZAKAR Semidry or medium wine
SUHO VINO Dry wine
TRADITZIONI REGIONALNI Vino Country Wine
VINO KONTROLIRANO NAIMENOVANIE ZA PROIZHOD Controliran wine (*see Controliran*)
VINO OT DEKLARIRAN GEOGRAFSKI OR DGO Wine of Declared Geographical Origin. This category constitutes 70 percent of all Bulgarian quality wines, those made from selected grapes originating from a particular geographical region.
VINOPROIZUODITEL Wine producer

RECENT BULGARIAN VINTAGES

2003 An excellent red and white wine vintage yielded very ripe grapes with relatively high acidity levels.

2002 Poor-quality vintage for both red and white wines.

2001 A variable year in which well-maintained vineyards in cooler areas produced some exceptional red wines, but the vines' metabolism shut down in hotter areas and in poorly maintained vineyards.

2000 Excellent-quality reds.

1999 Variable quality, although some good-quality wines were made in the best-maintained vineyards.

NEW LAWS

On November 14, 2000, the Association of Producers and Merchants of Wines and Spirits of Bulgaria (APMWSB) was disbanded and, in line with the new Bulgarian Wine Law, its role was transferred to the newly established National Vineyard and Wine Chamber (NVWC), which is aligned with European Union structures, and is designed to facilitate European integration in 2007, if economic and other factors are met. The new Bulgarian Wine Law has been described by its opponents in Bulgaria as "French law" and, not unreasonably, they claim that a more flexible law would enable them to compete with New World rivals. By flexible, they do not mean anything underhand or corner-cutting, simply the sort of "truth in labelling" philosophy that their New World opponents tend to adopt. If a Bulgarian wine states that it is from a particular grape grown in a specific area, then that is what should be in the bottle. Eminently sensible, but if Bulgaria is to be a part of the European Union, then it must obey its wine regime, which is indeed very much based on French wine law at present. Once in the Union, Bulgarians can argue for fundamental changes to the pan-European wine regime until they are blue in the face. That will be their right. And they will discover that it is a very minor cog in a vast machine called the Common Agricultural Policy, which itself has such a history of corruption and kick-backs that there are far too many vested interests, both open and shadowy, to have a hope in hell of changing, as so many other, far more powerful, countries have found out.

There are other good producers in Bulgaria, of course, and, although many more dull wines exist than before, and handling of oak by some wineries has been very clumsy indeed, there has also been much progress. The introduction of young, unvatted Cabernet and Merlot at the behest of a certain British supermarket group has shown what these wines can be like if bottled before the first flush of wonderfully fresh fruit is lost in vat. For all those who still like a lot of oak, some of the top Reserve wines are very good indeed. And huge strides have been made in white winemaking, thanks to Australian flying winemakers.

This internationalization of Bulgarian wine was already well underway before Domaine Boyar launched its Blueridge export brand. Blueridge was designed to lull supermarket shoppers into a false sense of New World security; as they scanned the shelves, consumers would not realize that they had strayed out of familiar territory. The new Blueridge Winery in Sliven cost over 5 million euros in 1999, but it has contributed nothing to the world's awareness of Bulgarian wine. Its balance sheets might look fine now, but ultimately the value of its wines and the profitability of its operation will depend on the public's perception of its geographical origin. If its Anglicized abomination of a name is kept and customers continue to have their attention diverted from the wine's true origin, Blueridge might as well move to India, where costs are even cheaper, and make wines from imported grape concentrate. Domaine Boyar's Blueridge is not alone in its Westernization of Bulgarian wine. In 2003, a group of Australian investors purchased the Svichtov Winery and renamed it Stork Nest. The Australians are performing miracles in the vineyard, but doing nothing to promote Bulgarian wine *per se*.

It is about time that Bulgarians realize there is a difference between international input and internationalization. Thanks to international input, there is absolutely no doubt that Bulgaria can make world-class wines, but its winemakers must look to their roots. There is no reason to forsake international varieties such as Cabernet Sauvignon and Merlot, but they should also experiment intensively with indigenous varieties. The obvious strategy would

BULGARIA

Located in the center of the Balkan Peninsula, Bulgaria has an extremely varied landscape, many different soil types, and an attractive climate.

be to work with clones of Gamza, Mavrud, and Melnik, all easy enough to pronounce on export markets, planting them in the best *terroirs*, at high densities, pruning them to ultra-low yields to remove the leafy character, and building these grapes into Bulgaria's flagship wines. Utilizing the same practices, other intrinsically Bulgarian grapes could rise above their current reputation. For example, is Pamid the simple, light-bodied variety we imagine it to be, or is that merely the result of high-yield production? The new governing body, the National Vineyard and Wine Chamber, should use its honeymoon period to institute strong measures to combat the deterioration of Bulgaria's vineyards. A three-year ban, perhaps, on grapes from poorly maintained vineyards being allowed

in any wine other than an anonymous table wine. The threat of such a severe reduction in earnings would either force real changes in vineyard practices, or the sale of vineyards to more quality-conscious estates. Ironically, although too many vineyards are allowed to produce very high yields, poor standards of vineyard maintenance has reduced overall output, and some wineries are operating at less than half capacity. When vines are not looked after properly and allowed to bear a greater burden of fruit, they become vulnerable to climatic excesses and diseases throughout the growing season. However, above all, Bulgarians must take back their individuality, treating the use of New World technology as a means to carve out a unique Bulgarian identity.

THE APPELLATIONS OF
BULGARIA

Note Bulgaria's quality wines are divided into two categories: wines of Declared Geographical Origin, or DGOs, which carry subregional, district, town, or village appellations, and *Controliran* wines, the highest-quality category, which have to be made from specified grape varieties grown in certain DGOs.

EASTERN REGION (TSCHERNOMORSKI RAION)

DGO regions *Burgas, Razgrad, Targovischte, Tolbukin*

DGO villages *Ajtos, Bjala, Dragoevo, Euxinograd, Kabelskovo, Kavarna, Kamen Brjag, Kubrat, Medovetz, Pliska, Pomorie, Popovo, Preslav, Prosenik, Provadija, Sabla/Shabla, Shumen/Sumen, Silistra, Tutraken, Zarev Dol*

Controliran wines *Jujen Briag* (South Coast), *Khan Krum, Kralevo, Novi Pazar, Varna*

This region accounts for 30 percent of Bulgaria's vineyards and includes four regional DGOs. The Schumen district has long been noted for white wines, particularly those from Khan Krum, but it was only recently that they rose to international standards, thanks to Australian expertise. Other well-known Schumen Chardonnays come from Novi Pazar and Preslav. Preslav now makes good, gluggy Chardonnay-Sauvignon blends. Khan Krum is also known for its Riesling and Dimiat, which has become very fresh and tangy. South Coast Rosé is an off-dry Cabernet Sauvignon blush wine from Burgas, an underrated district that produces many inexpensive yet very drinkable Country Wines.

🍇 Aligoté, Bolgar, Cabernet Sauvignon, Chardonnay, Dimiat, Gewürztraminer (*syn* Traminer), Pamid, Rkatsiteli, Red Misket, Riesling (*syn* Rheinriesling), Sauvignon Blanc, Tamianka, Ugni Blanc, Varneski Misket, Welschriesling (*syn* Italian Riesling)

✓ *Domaine Boyar • Pomorie • Shumen • Targovischte*

NORTHERN REGION (DUNAVSKA RAUNINA)

DGO regions *Pleven, Vidin*

DGO districts *Aleksandrovo, Bjala, Bjala Cerkva, Bjala Slatina, Dimca, Dve Mogili, Dolni Dâbnik, Elena, Kamen, Komarevo, Krivodol, Levski, Lom, Magura, Mihajlovgrad, Nikopol, Orahovo, Polski Trâmbes, Resen, Rupci, Sevlievo, Strakika, Trojan, Varbovka, Vraca*

Controliran wines *Lyaskovetz, Lositza, Novo Selo, Pavlikeni, Russe, Suhindol, Svichtov*

This region accounts for 35 percent of Bulgaria's vineyards, encompassing two subregional DGOs. Suhindol's reputation is based on Bulgaria's best-selling Cabernet Sauvignon, but two others from the district are worth trying: the grapey-oaky Gamza, which is a *Controliran* wine, and the interesting, soft-textured Merlot-Gamza blend, which is of equal quality but only a DGO. Russe has produced gorgeously fruity, so-called "unvatted" reds and, under the guidance of winemaker Kym Milne, Lyaskovetz is now making easy-drinking, inexpensive blended whites.

🍇 Cabernet Sauvignon, Chardonnay, Gamza, Gamay, Muskat Ottonel, Pinot Noir, Red Misket, Rkatsiteli, Sauvignon Blanc, Traminer, Vrachanski Misket

✓ *Stork Nest* (formerly Svichtov winery) *• Maxima • Tellish* (Merlot)

SOUTHERN REGION (THRAKIISKA NIZINA)

DGO regions *Cirpan/Chirpan, Dolinata na Maritza, Haskovo, Iambol, Pazardzik, Plovdiv, Stara Zagora, Strandja*

DGO villages *Blatec, Brestovica, Brezovo, Dalboki, Elhovo, Gavrilovo, Granit, Kalugerovo, Korten, Liubimec, Nova Zagora, Perustica, Septemvri, Sivacevo, Svoboda, Vetren, Vinogradec, Zlatovrah*

Controliran wines *Assenovgrad, Brestnik, Oriachovitza, Sakar, Stambolovo*

This region accounts for 22 percent of Bulgaria's vineyards and encompasses eight regional DGOs. Assenovgrad is justly famous for its dark, dry, plummy-spicy Mavrud wine, which can age well for 10 or more years. Plovdiv makes fine, firm, blackcurranty Cabernet Sauvignon, as does Stara Zagora, a district that boasts a superb Cabernet Sauvignon-Merlot *Controliran* wine from Oriachovitza. Oriachovitza also makes a classy Cabernet Sauvignon Reserve. From the Strandja region comes Sakar Mountain Cabernet, one of the first wines to establish a reputation on export markets, although it is the Merlot from this area that has *Controliran* status. East of Stara Zagora is Iambol, which produces a very rich Cabernet Sauvignon Reserve in which the oak can take on a spicy-caramel complexity, while in the southeast, Elhovo churns out a much cheaper Cabernet with obvious coconutty aromas that should suit budget-conscious oak-lovers. Bessa Valley is an exciting joint venture between the Damianitza Winery, Count von Neipperg of Pomerol fame, French oenologist Mark Dworkin, and a couple of investors, who are building a Bordeaux-type

wine estate with over 250 acres (100 hectares) of grapes (Malbec, Merlot, Petit Verdot, and Syrah).

🍇 Aligoté, Cabernet Sauvignon, Dimiat, Gamay, Malbec, Mavrud, Merlot, Pamid, Petit Vardot, Pinot Noir, Red Misket, Sauvignon Blanc, Syrah

✓ *Assenovgrad • Bessa Valley • Domaine Saker • Ententa • Haskovo • Iambol • Korten • Oriachovitza • Todoroff* (Terres) *• Yamantievs* (King Leo, Parallel 41)

SOUTHWESTERN REGION (JOLINAKA NA STRUMA)

DGO regions *Blagoevgrad, Kjustendil, Molina Dolina, Petric*

DGO villages *Bobosevo, Damjanica, Melnik, Sandanski*

Controliran wines *Harsovo*

This region accounts for 6 percent of Bulgaria's vineyards and includes four regional DGOs. The most famous wine is Melnik, which is generally well-colored, rich, and warm, and may be tannic or soft, depending on how it is made. Damianitza Melnik is very smooth and rich. No Mans Land is pure Cabernet Sauvignon. Re Dark is aptly named for a dense-colored, super-premium wine made from Merlot. Uniquato is made from a unique early-ripening clone of Melnik known locally as Shiroka Melnishka Loza.

🍇 Cabernet Sauvignon, Chardonnay, Melnik, Merlot, Shiroka Melnishka Loza, Tamianka

✓ *Damianitza* (No Man's Land, Re Dark, Uniquato) *• Santa Sarah Estate*

SUB-BALKAN REGION (PODBALANSKI RAION)

DGO regions *Sliven*

DGO villages *Banja, Cernica, Hissar, Karnobat, Kasanlak, Pâderevo, Straldza* Controliran wines *Karlovo, Rozova Dolina* (Rose Valley), *Slaviantzi, Sungurlare*

This region accounts for 7 percent of vineyards and encompasses one regional DGO. The Rozova Domina Misket is made in the Karlovo district, and Sungurlare Misket in Slaviantzi. Both are light-golden, floral-scented, musky wines. Sliven makes one of the world's cheapest Merlot blends, using Pinot Noir to add a touch of elegance to what is a very gluggy wine indeed.

🍇 Cabernet Sauvignon, Chardonnay, Merlot, Red Misket, Riesling, Ugni Blanc

✓ *Blueridge • Slaviantzi • VINI*

HUNGARY

Although potentially the most exciting winemaking country among the former Iron Curtain states, and despite there being a quality-focused movement afoot in some quarters, Hungary has a long way to go if it is to become a serious world player. Even in Tokaj, undisputably one of the greatest botrytis regions in the world, improvements since the collapse of Communism have been sporadic, despite the example set by foreign investors, and local hero István Szepsy. If every wine producer in every region was as gifted and as committed as Szepsy, Hungary would be the greatest wine-producing country in the world. Perhaps the Hungarian government should give Szepsy prime sites in every single wine region in the country?

WHEN DEMOCRACY ARRIVED in 1989, Hungary had a clear advantage over other former Eastern Bloc countries because even under Communist rule, it had long been dabbling with a mixed economy. Exploiting this to the full, the transition from a centrally planned economy to a market-driven one has been relatively smooth, with the private sector now accounting for more than 80 percent of Hungary's economic output, and foreign investment totaling in excess of $23 billion. This provides most Hungarian industries with the economic success and stability required to attract further investment to expand and improve, but although

FACTORS AFFECTING TASTE AND QUALITY

LOCATION
Hungary is sandwiched between Austria and Romania, north of Yugoslavia, in the Carpathian basin south of Slovakia.

CLIMATE
Generally a continental climate, with some Mediterranean influence in the southern wine districts. The annual mean temperature is 51°F (10.5°C), with an average rainfall of 23 inches (60 centimeters). In the Carpathian foothills of Tokaj, in northeastern Hungary, long misty autumns encourage botrytis.

ASPECT
Almost half of the country's vines are grown on the Great Plain, where the land is flat or gently undulating river plains. The rest of the country is hilly.

SOIL
Slate, basalt, clay, and loess in the west, through the sandy soils of the Great Plain, to the clay, loess, and volcanic rock in the northeast, and volcanic, slate, and sandy soils in the south.

VITICULTURE AND VINIFICATION
Tokaji necessitates the harvesting and sorting of botrytized grapes. Otherwise, all Hungarian red and white wines are produced using standard vinification techniques, with no exceptional practices. However, a steady modernization of winemaking facilities has taken place since the 1990s.

GRAPE VARIETIES
Cabernet Franc, Cabernet Sauvignon, Chardonnay, Ezerjó, Furmint, Hárslevelű, Irsai Olivér, Kadarka, Kékfrankos (Limberger), Kékporto (Portugieser), Leányka, Olaszrizling (Welschriesling), Pinot Blanc, Pinot Gris, Sauvignon Blanc, Tramini (Traminer), Zweigelt

DID YOU KNOW?

- Tokaj is the place, Tokaji is the wine, and Tokay is the old, Anglicized spelling, which is no longer used.
- *Szamorodni* is Polish, not Hungarian, for "the way it comes" and indicates a wine to which *aszú* (overripe grapes for sweetening) has not been added.

HUNGARY
A country that has great potential for red wine, although this is overshadowed by the history and fame of Tokaji, one of the world's classic botrytized wines.

Map legend:
- Sopron
- Aszár-Neszmély
- Etyek-Buda
- Balatonmellёke
- Balatonboglár
- Tolna
- Mecsekalja
- Kunság
- Csongrád
- Mátraalja
- Bükkalja
- Tokaj-Hegyalja
- Other areas
- Intensive vine-growing areas
- International Boundary
- Height above sea level (meters)

0   20   40   60   80 miles
0   50   100 km

THE DANGER OF INTERNATIONALIZED BRANDS

As with other former Eastern Bloc wine-producing countries, Hungary has more than its fair share of Anglicized brand names, each of which has been concocted to attract Western wine consumers who might not otherwise consider buying Hungarian wines, but should feel comfortable with the New World style of labelling. Whatever reputation the likes of Chapel Hill and Hilltop (including Riverview and Woodcutters White) earn, they do nothing to establish an identity for Hungarian wines, except perhaps the wrong one.

TOKAJI TABLE

Pre-1991 criteria are provided because many vintages from that era are still available on primary (retail) and secondary (auction) markets.

| | PRE-1991 WINE ACT | | | POST-1991/7 WINE ACT | |
| | | MINIMUM | | | MINIMUM |
WINE STYLE	RESIDUAL SUGAR	AGING IN WOOD	ALCOHOL	RESIDUAL SUGAR	AGING IN WOOD
Varietal wines (*Furmint, Hárslevelű Sárga Muskotály, Zéta*)	N/A	N/A	N/A	N/A	1
Máslás	N/A	N/A	13%	N/A	1
Fordítás	N/A	N/A	13%	N/A	1
Száraz Szamorodni	0–4 g/l	2 years	13%	N/A	1
Edes Szamorodni	20–50 g/l	2 years	13%	30 g/l	1 year
Aszú 2 puttonyos[2]	50–60 g/l	2 years	N/A	N/A	2 years
Aszú 3 puttonyos	60–90 g/l	3 years	N/A	60 g/l	2 years
Aszú 4 puttonyos	90–120 g/l	4 years	N/A	90 g/l	2 years
Aszú 5 puttonyos	120–150 g/l	5 years	N/A	120 g/l	2 years
Aszú 6 puttonyos	150–180 g/l	6 years	N/A	150 g/l	2 years
Aszúesszencia (7–8 puttonyos)	200–240 g/l	7–8 years	N/A	180 g/l	2 years
Esszencia or Natúresszencia	N/A	N/A	N/A	250 g/l	2 years

Notes

[1] Aging in wood allowed, and normal practice, but no prescribed minimum.

[2] Aszú 2 *puttonyos* is allowed, but for some reason has not been made since 1938.

---

the wine industry has enjoyed some foreign investment, it has not expanded and improved across the board. Why? Because finance alone cannot create a range of fine wines. It takes quality-conscious growers and inspirational winemakers, something that Hungary does not appear to have in any great number at the moment. It is probably a symptom of the country's past, and it might take a complete generation born in and bred under the ideals of a free, democratic state to nurture the sort of spirit needed to make something as decadent as fine wine. Certainly, there is no one who comes within a mile of István Szepsy's genius for winemaking. My suggestion, in the introduction, that the Hungarian government should give him prime sites in every single wine region in the country was only partly in jest. It would at least demonstrate the quality that is ultimately possible in each wine region, and that would attract foreign investors to those parts of the country.

INVESTMENT IN TOKAJ

The first area that received investment was Tokaj. This is understandable, as Tokaji is the only classic wine of authentic historical reputation in all Eastern Europe. Hugh Johnson and the Australian-trained, Anglo-Danish maestro winemaker Peter Vinding-Diers (no longer involved) purchased the Royal Tokaji Wine Company in Mád and 156 acres (63 hectares) of vineyards. Interestingly, the Royal Tokaji vineyards have never been state-owned (all other investors have been forced to buy vineyards from Borkombinat, the State Wine Farm), and almost 60 percent are classified (dating back to 1700), including three first growths (Nyulaszo, Szt Tamas, and Betsek) and one second growth (Birsalmas). After this dynamic duo came a number of others:

• **Chateau Dereszla** Established in 1992 by CANA (France), but bought by the d'Aulan family (former owners of Champagne Piper-Heidsieck) in 1999, Chateau Dereszla has 37 acres (15 hectares) in Henye, and 49 acres (20 hectares) in Csirke, processing another 370 acres (150 hectares) of bought-in grapes.

• **Disznókõ** A new winery built by AXA, the most prominent French investor, led at the time by the redoubtable Jean-Michel Cazes, who purchased 320 acres (130 hectares) of vineyards.

• **Királyudvar** A joint venture funded by Philippine-born American businessman Anthony Hwang, with the winemaking talents of István Szepsy, who is also involved with Hwang in the purchase of Huet in the Loire. This renovated historic winery owns 222 acres (90 hectares) spread over 12 vineyards, mostly in Heyne, Lapis, and Danczka.

• **Chateau Megyer** Purchased in 2000 by Jean-Louis Laborde of Chateau Pajzos, Chateau Megyer comprises 193 acres (78 hectares) of vineyards.

• **Chateau Pajzos** Established in 1991 as a French-funded joint venture between Jean-Louis Laborde and the late Jean-Michel Arcaute, with Michel Rolland consulting. Chateau Pajzos owns 198 acres (80 hectares) of vineyards.

• **Tokaj Classic** A joint venture between Hungarian and German investors, Tokaj Classic was established in 1998, and consists of just over 17 acres (7 hectares) of vineyards, mostly in Betsek.

• **Tokaj Oremus** Spanish-owned by the famous Vega Sicilia, Tokaj Oremus own 272 acres (110 hectares) of vineyards, mostly in Mandúlas, Kútpatka, Budaház, Heyne, Máriássy, and Deák.

HUNGARIAN LABEL LANGUAGE

ASZTALI BOR Table wine, the lowest quality of wine.

ASZÚ Overripe grapes for sweetening Tokaji, equivalent of German *Auslese*

BOR Wine

BORKÜLÖNLEGESSÉGE SZÖLÖGAZDASÁGÁNAK A speciality from the vineyards of the region named

BORVIDÉK Wine region

DŰLŐ Vineyard   check

ÉDES Sweet

FEHÉR White

FORDÍTÁS A sweet Tokaji produced from reused *aszúpaste*, drained from a *gönc* of *aszú* wine, rekneaded and macerated in fresh must. The result is comparable to a 4 or 5 *puttonyos* in

sweetness, but more tannic. They say that a Fordítás from a very good year is often better than an *aszú* from a poor vintage, but I have yet to see this difference demonstrated by the same Tokaji producer.

HABZÓ Sparkling

HORDÓ Cask or barrel

JEGBOR Ice wine, or Eiswein

KÉSÖI SZÜRETELÉSŰ Late harvest

KÍMERT BOR Ordinary wine

KÖTNYÉKI BOR Country wine

KÜLÖNLEGES MINÖSÉGŰ Official denomination denoting "special quality," placing it above Minösegi bor.

MÁSLÁS A dry version of Fordítás

(*see* Fordítás above), but fermented on the unpressed lees of an *aszú* wine, with much less lees to wine ratio. Máslás literally means "copy."

MINÖSEGI BOR Quality wine, equivalent to French AOC.

ORSZÁGOS BORMINÖSITŐ BIZOTTSÁG OR OBB National Wine Qualification Board

ORSZÁGOS BORMINÖSITŐ INTÉZET OR OBI State Wine Qualification Institute

PALACK Bottle

PALACKZÁS Bottling

PALACKOZOTT Bottled

PEZSGO Sparkling

PINCE Cellar

SILLER A dark rosé or light red

SZAMORODNI Literally "as it comes," the term often refers to Tokaji that has not been specially treated with *aszú* and is therefore usually dry, though it can be used for other wines.

SZÁRAZ Dry

SZŐLŐ Grapes

SZŐLŐBIRTOK Wine estate

SZŐLŐSKERT Vineyard

TÁJBOR Country wine, equivalent to a French *vin de pays*

TERMELŐ Production

TŐKE Vine

TÖPPEDT SZŐLŐBŐL KÉSZÜLT Botrytis selection

VÖRÖS Red

The one thing these investors have in common is a change in the methods used to produce Tokaji. It was suggested that the French were intent on making Sauternes in Hungary, and this rankled local pride, with some critics wondering "whether Tokaji should not legitimately remain an oxidative wine." Old-style Tokaji was not, however, merely oxidative; it was deliberately oxidized. The only possible comparison is sherry and *vin jaune*, since they are the only wines that are deliberately left in part-filled barrels to oxidize, as Tokaji producers did in the Communist era. However, sherry and *vin jaune* casks are part-filled for a purpose: the ullage allows for the growth of *flor*, a froth of rare yeast that is responsible for the particular character and style of those wines. In the Tokaji process, there is no guarantee of *flor* and thus no justification for exposing the wine to the air—in which it merely oxidizes.

Tokaji old and new

It would be wrong to divide old and new style between Hungarian and foreign producers. Firstly, old style is only as old as the Communist era. There is no evidence of half-filled casks in the 19th century; this practice is not mentioned in the meticulously detailed *Tokaj-Hegyaljai Album* (1867). Secondly, not all foreign-funded ventures are successful at the new style. Some have not gone the full distance—or they have old-style stocks they are gradually disposing of by fractional blending. Even those who went the full distance reined back on new style in the 1990s, when too many of their wines were refused the Tokaji appellation because of lack of typicity. And it is wrong to suggest that only foreign winemakers pioneered new-wave Tokaji. The first and the best by far was István Szepsy. No one has ever made Tokaji with the purity, precision, and finesse that Szepsy can manage.

So what is the difference between the so-called new and old styles? Most importantly, it is no longer a requirement to leave Tokaji Aszú in barrels for up to a decade with at least one-third air-space. This is still permitted for those who believe that oxidation is Tokaji's most essential character, but it is no longer obligatory. However, fortification was banned, even for those who persist with the old style. Fortification was common practice when Hungary was part of the Eastern Bloc (as was pasteurization), but the Communists cannot be blamed, as it was originally a late 19th-century "innovation," and officially recognized in law in 1936. Two years is the minimum aging period in wood under the new law, but although there is a lot of new or relatively new oak in use today, it has not so much been a conscious move as a necessity to replace ancient, leaking, and often diseased wood.

The other major change that has occurred since the decentralization of Tokaji cellars is the emergence of two fundamentally different, but mutually admirable, production philosophies—those who make wine based on a single estate (the Bordeaux concept), and those who make single-vineyard wines, which might or might not belong to the winery in question (the Burgundian route).

The official tasting committees should have changed their decision-making process after the 1991 Wine Act, or at least by the changes introduced in 1997, but they had difficulty shaking off the old ways. A number of new wineries were frustrated as their more pristine products were rejected throughout the 1990s for their lack of typicity (i.e., no "sherrylike" character). After a decade of stylistic debate, the authorities caught up with the times in 2000.

How Tokaji is made today

As with all great sweet wines, Tokaji owes its quality and character to semidried, extremely rich grapes (Furmint and Hárslevelű) that have been affected by *Botrytis cinerea*, or "noble rot." These shriveled grapes, called *aszú* (pronounced "ossu") are put into a wooden hod called a *puttony* for six to eight days, and under their own weight a highly concentrated, thick, syrupy juice slowly drains out of holes at the bottom of the container into glass vessels called balloons. This is pure Esszencia, also called *nectar*. Each *puttony* holds 50 lb (25 kilograms) of *aszú* grapes but yields only a quarter of a pint (0.2 liters) of pure Esszencia. After the Esszencia has been removed, the *puttony* of *aszú* grapes is kneaded into a paste and added to a 36-gallon cask called a *gönc*, or a stainless-steel vat, of unfermented must or dry base wine. This is made from a blend of nonbotrytized Furmint and Hárslevelű grapes (though wines labelled Muskotály Aszú contain 100 percent Muskotály grapes). The sweetness of the wine depended upon how many *puttonyos* (plural of *puttony*) were added to the must or dry base wine, and wines are still marketed with *puttonyos* designations.

Tokaji Aszúesszencia is the equivalent of at least seven *puttonyos*, whereas Esszencia or Natúresszencia is pure Esszencia, and is the closest thing to the legendary drink of the tsars. It is so rich in sugar (up to 850 grams per liter) that it requires a special strain of yeast to ferment it, and even then it can take many decades to reach 5 or 6 percent of alcohol. Until privatization, it was made only for sweetening, and even now it is extremely rare and expensive (Oremus 1997 Esszencia was over $750 per bottle in 2005). I will never forget the first pure Esszencia, back in the days of Communist rule, at the state cellars at Tolcsva. It had been fermenting for 13 years, yet had achieved less than 2 percent of alcohol. With 640 grams of residual sugar per liter, it poured like oil, and had the most incredible bouquet, like the scent of a fresh rose in full morning bloom. It was intensely sweet and very grapey, but with a clean, almost crisp, finish thanks to an astonishing 38 grams per liter of acidity.

BEYOND TOKAJI

Hungary is generally recognized as a potentially exciting red wine country, yet only 25 percent of its vineyards are planted with black grapes. One of Hungary's biggest problems is that its flagship wine, Tokaji, is an intensely sweet wine, and it is very difficult to promote any winemaking region on the back of a wine that is consumed very occasionally by a tiny minority of consumers. It will be essential, therefore, for the industry to concentrate its efforts on improving, experimenting with, and expanding the quality and styles of wines of Eger, Villány, Hajós-Baja, Szekszárd, and Sopron, the areas where the greatest red wine promise exists.

THE APPELLATIONS OF
HUNGARY

ASZÁR-NESZMÉLY

Area under vine: *3,460 acres*
Subregions *Aszár, Neszmély*

Winemaking traditions date back to the Middle Ages. Vineyards were cultivated along the lines of large estates as from the 18th century, with the famous Esterházi Csákvári estate considered to be a model vineyard and cellars in the 19th century. Most soils are loess-based. The climate is milder than the surrounding Great Plains area, with less risk of spring and fall frost. Mostly fresh, fragrant, lively white wines. The internationally known Hilltops winery produces over 50 different wines every year in Neszmély.

🍇 Chardonnay, Cserszegi Fûszeres, Királylányka, Irsai Olivér, Olaszrizling, Pinot Gris, Sauvignon Blanc, Szürkebarát

✓ *Hilltops* (Cserszegi Fûszeres, Riverview Cabernet Sauvignon, Virgin Vintage Chardonnay, Virgin Vintage Sauvignon Blanc)

BADACSONY

Area under vine: *4,000 acres*

With its south-facing volcanic slopes on the northerly shores of Lake Balaton, Europe's largest lake, Badacsony is noted for its own indigenous grape called Kéknyelú. This increasingly rare white variety has excellent potential for full-bodied white wines, with a fiery palate, fine acids, and an intensive, aromatic bouquet, but often produces a disappointing quality.

🍇 Kékfrankos, Kéknyelu, Olaszrizling, Szürkebarát

✓ *Szent Orbán Pince* (Szőlősgyöröki Olaszrizling) • *Szeremley* (Kéknyelu, Szürkebarát, Tihanyi Kékfrankos)

BALATONBOGLÁR

Area under vine: *6,400 acres*
Subregions *Csáfordi, Szentgyörgyvári, and Muravidéki*

The winemaking potential of Lake Balaton's south shore was seldom fulfilled until the early 1990s, when Australian flying winemaker Kym Milne started producing extremely rich, oak-aged Chardonnay at the Balatonboglár Winery under the Chapel Hill label. With Master of Wine Milne still in charge, ably assisted by Kiwi Clive Hartnell, and fellow Australian Richard Smart advising in the vineyard, the quality at Chapel Hill has strengthened in the 2000s. Other products from the Balatonboglár Winery are far less exciting, and some producers churn out a lot of very second-rate wines, particularly in the semisweet Olaszrizling category.

🍇 Chardonnay, Cserszegi Fûszeres, Kékfrankos, Királyleányka, Merlot, Olaszrizling, Rizlingszilváni, Szürkebarát, Sauvignon Blanc

✓ *Chapel Hill* (Chardonnay, Chardonnay-Pinot Noir Brut, Merlot, plus entire Winemaker's Selection and Single Vineyard Selection ranges) • *Ottó Légli* (Szőlőskislaki Barrique Chardonnay)

BALATONFELVIDÉK

Area under vine: *6,200 acres*
Subregions *Cserszeg, Kál, Balatonederics-Lesence*

With its hot, sunny, Mediterranean climate, and the extraordinary beauty of this area, it is no surprise that so many artists have set up home here. The best wines are full-bodied, with a fine fragrance and crisp acidity.

🍇 Chardonnay, Olaszrizling, Szürkebarát

BALATONFÜRED-CSOPAK

Area under vine: *4,200 acres*
Sub-regions *Balatonfüred, Csopak, Zánka*

On the northern shore of Lake Balaton, viticulture and winemaking have prospered here since Roman times. The wines are full-bodied yet fragrant, with fine acidity.

🍇 Cabernet Sauvignon, Chardonnay, Merlot, Olaszrizling, Rizlingszilváni, Tramini

✓ *Isván Jásdi* (Csopaki Olaszrizling)

BALATONMELLÉKE

Area under vine: *5,400 acres*
Subregions *Balatonmellék, Muravidéki*

On the eastern and northeastern flank of Lake Balaton. The Zalla hills are known for their so-called harrow-cellars, made in the 19th century from timbers and plastered inside and out with clay. The Balatonmelléke, with its brown forest soils and mild, wet climate, has been revived as a wine region as recently as 1998.

🍇 Chardonnay, Kékfrankos, Müller-Thurgau, Olaszrizling, Oportó, Rizlingszilváni, Tramini, Zöld Veltelini (Veltliner), Zweigelt

✓ *László Bussay* (Csörnyeföldi Szürkebarát)

BÜKKALJA

Area under vine: *2,400 acres*

Grown on the southern and southwestern slopes of the Bükk Mountains, where Kékfrankos and Leányka are the major varieties, but produce wines that are lighter than those of neighboring Eger. As in Eger and Tokaj further east, cellars have long been hewn out of rhyolite-tuffa rock, with more than 1,000 such cellars carved out of the slopes of Avas.

🍇 Cserszegi Fûszeres, Kékfrankos, Olaszrizling, Leányka

CSONGRÁD

Area under vine: *4,600 acres*
Sub-regions *Csongrád, Kistelek, Mórahalom, Pusztamérges*

This Great Plain wine region is the warmest and sunniest part of the country during the vegetation period of the vine. Principally, the red and rosé wines are renowned. The white wines of the region contain moderate acids and are rich in fragrance and aroma. The red wines are characterized by richness in coloring agents, pleasant acerbity, and excellent aroma.

🍇 Kadarka, Kékfrankos, Olaszrizling, Zweigelt

EGER

Area under vine: *7,900 acres*
Subregions *Debrő, Eger*

Located halfway between Budapest and Tokaj is Eger, a region famous for the legend of Egri Bikavér, or "Bull's Blood of Eger." The story dates from 1552, when the fortress of Eger, fiercely defended by István Dobó and his Magyars, was besieged by the numerically superior force of the Turkish army, led by Ali Pasha. It is said that, throughout the battle, the Magyars drank copious quantities of the local wine and that when the Turks saw the beards of their ferocious enemies stained red with wine, they ran in terror, thinking that all Magyars gained their strength by drinking the blood of bulls. Hence the name of this wine was born. Other regions produce Bikavér, but Egri Bikavér is the Bull's Blood that is most famously associated with the legend. It was never a pretentious wine, but it was traditionally a robust, Kadarka-based red of firm structure and fiery flavor. Since the early 1980s, however, Bull's Blood has been notoriously variable in both quality and character, as indeed has its varietal composition, with Kékfrankos now the most dominant grape, and others such as Cabernet Franc, Cabernet Sauvignon, Kékoportó, and Merlot playing minor roles. Hungary will never earn a reputation for the depth and breadth of its wines until the quality and consistency of its second most famous wine is something to write home about. Egri Bormives Céh, a group of quality-conscious Bikavér producers, are trying to raise standards, but they have had trouble with the largest producers of the most mediocre Egri Bikavér.

Leányka can make a decent gold-colored, medium-sweet white wine, but it is too soft and understated to grab the headlines, and Eger is really red wine country. The successes here with Merlot and Cabernet Sauvignon, even Pinot Noir, should encourage producers to explore their own red wine grapes. Before his untimely death in February 2005, Tibor Gál was the best local producer. He teamed up with Antinori to produce good-value, international-style wines under the GIA label, but his own wines—especially his single-vineyard Pinot Noirs and Bikavér Reserve—were superior.

🍇 Cabernet Franc, Cabernet Sauvignon, Kékfrankos, Kékoportó, Leányka, Merlot, Olaszrizling

✓ *GIA* (Bikavér, Cabernet Sauvignon, Chardonnay) • *István Balla* (Barrique Olaszrizling) • *József Hagymási* (Cabernet Sauvignon) • *Thummerer* (Bikavér, Kékfrankos, Vili Papa Cuvee) • *Tibor Gál (Bikavér)* • *Béla Vincze* (Cabernet Franc)

ETYEK-BUDA

Area under vine: *4,400 acres*
Subregions *Etyek, Buda*

Etyek-Buda is supposedly Hungary's sparkling wine region, but the quality of its largest producer, Törley, leaves much to be desired, and more vineyards are moving over to still, dry white wines from individual estates, but since this region overlaps the prettier, hilly half of Budapest, it receives a lot of attention. The vines grow on a black loess soil over a limestone base, in a dry, sunny, but windy climate.

🍇 Chardonnay, Királyleányka, Olaszrizling, Pinot Blanc, Pinot Gris, Sauvignon Blanc

✓ *Nyakashegy* (Budai Chardonnay)

HAJÓS-BOAJA

Area under vine: *3,500 acres*
Subregions *Hajós, Baja*

The white wines of this Great Plains region are rich in fragrance and aroma, while the reds rival the highly ranked wines produced in hilly regions.

🍇 Cabernet Franc, Cabernet Sauvignon, Kadarka, Kékfrankos, Merlot, Olaszrizling, Riesling

KUNSÁG

Area under vine: *63,300 acres*

Subregions *Bácska, Cegléd, Dunamente, Izsák, Jászság, Kecskemét-Kiskunfélegyház, Kiskőrös, Kiskunhalas Kiskunmajsa, Monor, Tiszamente*

This Great Plain wine region is the largest wine region in Hungary. The wines of this region can be rich in fragrance and flavors. Some good Kadarka.

🍇 Ezerjó, Cserszegi Fûszeres, Kékfrankos, Olaszrizling

MÁTRAALJA

Area under vine: *18,000 acres*

At Gyöngyös, the first truly excellent Hungarian dry white wine was produced in the early 1980s, and no prizes for guessing that it was made from Chardonnay. But it was essential to demonstrate what could be done with grapes of a certain quality and the right technology. That particular Chardonnay steadily improved until 1995, when it jumped up another notch in quality, and Sauvignon Blanc can be almost as successful, but nowadays, winemakers are looking at achieving at least the same general quality with local varieties, such as Chardonnay, Hárslevelû, and Muskotály.

🍇 Chardonnay, Hárslevelû, Kékfrankos, Müller-Thurgau, Muscat Ottonel, Muskotály, Olaszrizling, Tramini, Rizlingszilváni, Zweigelt

MECSEKALJA

Area under vine: *1,200 acres*
Sub-regions *Pécs, Szigetvár, Versend*

Vineyards here scattered over more than 50 miles (80 kilometers) of warm slopes around the historic city of Pécs, which has long been noted for Olaszrizling, although the traditional Furmint and Cirfandli vines are giving way to international varieties.

🍇 Cabernet Franc, Cabernet Sauvignon, Chardonnay, Cirfandli, Furmint, Merlot, Olaszrizling, Pinot Noir, Riesling, Rizlingszilváni, Sauvignon Blanc

✓ *Ebner Andreas* (Cosmo Cuvée)

MÓR

Area under vine: *2,200 acres*

Ezerjó is the best grape variety suited to this region, where it makes one of Hungary's most distinctive dry white wines.

🍇 Ezerjó, Leanyka, Olaszrizling, Rizlingszilvani, Tramini

PANNONHALMA-SOKORÓALJA

Area under vine: *1,600 acres*
Subregions *Pannonhalma, Sokoróalja*

Viticulture here dates back to 996, when Benedictine monks settled on Saint Martin Mountain, and established Hungary's first monastery at Pannonhalma. Hungary's first document mentioning vinegrowing is the deed of foundation of the Pannonhalma Monastery. The fresh, crisp, varietally pure Pannonhalmi Sauvignon Blanc from Szőllősi Mihály Pricészette winery is the best dry Hungarian white wine I have tasted.

🍇 Chardonnay, Cserszegi Fûszeres, Irsai Olivér, Királyleányka, Müller-Thurgau, Olaszrizling, Riesling, Tramini

✓ *Szőllősi Mihály Pricészette* (Sauvignon Blanc)

SOMLÓ

Area under vine: *1,200 acres*
Subregions *Kissomlyó-Sághegy, Somló*

This is the smallest wine region of Hungary. Its wines are fiery, with a heavy, masculine character, and they have high acid and alcohol content. The long aging in wooden barrels produces a fine, elegant harmony of fragrance, taste, and aroma. According to popular memory, in the imperial court of Vienna, the newlyweds drank Somló wines on their wedding night to promote the birth of a male heir to the throne.

🍇 Chardonnay, Furmint, Hárslevelû, Juhfark, Olaszrizling, Tramini

✓ *Béla Fekete* (Chardonnay) • *József Laposa* (Bazalt Borhaz Olaszrizling)

SOPRON

Area under vine: *3,400 acres*
Subregions *Kőszeg, Sopron*

One of the most ancient wine regions of Hungary, the Sopron lies on the foothills of the Alps in the northwestern corner of the country. For centuries, the city of Sopron itself enjoyed thriving trade and, surprisingly, until the 18th century Sopron was reputedly the largest wine-trading center in central Europe. Sopron is a potentially fine wine region, where the Kékfrankos grape is most famous, although the quality in the vineyard and the bottle could and should be significantly superior to the light, everyday-drinking wines that are commonplace in this region. Although essentially a red wine region, Sopron does also produce some interesting whites.

🍇 Cabernet Franc, Kékfrankos, Leányka, Sauvignon Blanc, Zöld Veltelini, Zweigelt

✓ *Franz Weninger* (Kékfrankos, Merlot, Rosé, Syrah) • *Hilltop* (Soproni Sauvignon Blanc)

SZEKSZÁRD

Area under vine: *4,700 acres*

The Szekszárd vineyards have been noted for their wines since Roman times and for red wines since the 15th century. In this sunny wine region with its greater Mediterranean influence, excellent red wines can be produced,

which are known for their velvety texture, and often show more elegance than the red wines of Villány. The Szekszárdi Bikavér (Bull's Blood of Szekszárd) is ranked outstandingly high. The indigenous Kadarka variety gives excellent flavored, deep red wine, plus a local speciality, Nemes Kadar, made from botrytized grapes. Very good Kékfrankos, Cabernet Sauvignon, and some stunning Merlot are also produced.

🍇 Cabernet Sauvignon, Kadarka, Kékfrankos, Merlot, Olaszrizling, Rizlingszilváni

✓ *Dúzsi Tamás* (Kékfrankos Rozé) • *Péter Vida* (Cabernet Franc-Merlot) • *Szent Gaál Kastély* (Merlot) • *Takler Pince* (Cabernet Sauvignon Selection, Primarius Merlot, Regnum Monarchia Gold Selection) • *Vesztergombi* (Cabernet Sauvignon)

TOKAJ-HEGYALJA

Area under vine: *13,000 acres*
Subregions *Tokaj, Hegyalja*

For full details about the classic sweet wines and other styles of wine produced in Tokaj, please see the main text on pp416–417.

🍇 Furmint, Hárslevelû, Sárga Muskotály, Zeta (formerly Oremus)

✓ *Arvay és Társa* • *Borok Úri* • *István Szepsy* • *Királyudvar* • *Oremus* • *Pajzos*

TOLNA

Area under vine: *5,300 acres*
Subregions *Tamási, Tolna, Völgység*

Although Tolna became a wine region in its own right as recently as 1998, winemaking traditions go back centuries, and were strengthened in the 16th century, when the area was settled by Germans.

🍇 Chardonnay, Grüner Veltliner, Kadarka, Kékfrankos, Müller-Thurgau, Olaszrizling

VILLÁNY SIKLÓS

Area under vine: *4,000 acres*
Subregions *Villány, Siklós*

Vines have been growing here since this region was part of the Roman province of Pannonia. In Villány, the more Mediterranean climate produces some of Hungary's best red wines, including dark, spicy Kadarka and more velvety Bordeaux varietals. The red wine potential of Villány is probably the greatest of all of the 22 Hungarian wine regions. At the time of writing, a new two-tier appellation system called Hungaricus Districtus Controllatus (HDC for short), created for and by Villány, was due to be in place as from the 2005 vintage. HDC will have two superior quality levels, Classic and Premium, with stricter maximum yields and quality controls that will be monitored by a committee. Some growers in Villány still train their vines to a single pole, instead of along wires, which is four times as labor-intensive, and yields are reduced to as little as 413 or 550 cases per acre, rather than the normal 1,650. The wines of Siklós are white and fiery, including those that have been produced from late-harvested grapes, although they are more *passerillé* in style than botrytized.

🍇 Cabernet Sauvignon, Cabernet Franc, Kékporto, Olaszrizling, Hárslevelû, Zweigelt

✓ *Attila Gere* (Kopár Villanyi Cuvée, Merlot Solus) • *Gere Tamás Pincészet* (Gere Tamás Cuvée) • *Tiffán* (Villányi Cuvée) • *Vylyan Pincészet* (Kadarka, Merlot, Zweigelt)

ROMANIA

Romania has at least as much potential as any other Eastern European winemaking country. It has a growing reputation for Pinot Noir, particularly from the Dealul Mare region, but has received a fraction of the foreign investment that Hungary has enjoyed, and needs both financial and technical expertise to compete internationally.

THE BIGGEST PROBLEM IN ROMANIA has been a lack of consistency. Since the early 1990s, we have seen flashes of promise—from exciting Gewürztraminer from Transilvania to deep, dark, brooding Cabernet Sauvignon from Dealul Mare, only to see some of these wines followed up by vintages of barely *vin de table* quality. Only a handful of wineries have received significant foreign investment and expertise, and it is no coincidence that they generally make the best wines in Romania today.

MORE IMPORTANT THAN RUSSIA

Viticulture and winemaking is an old tradition in Romania, dating back 4,000 years. In Europe, only France, Italy, Spain, and Germany are bigger wine-producing countries. Romania is significantly more important than Hungary or Russia in winemaking terms. As in Bulgaria, there was a massive planting program in the 1960s, when the country was geared up to supply Comecon states with bulk-blending fodder, but most wine today is purchased and consumed on the home market. After the fall of Ceausescu in December 1989, the area under vine increased, going against the trend of other Eastern Bloc wine-producing countries. However, much of the replanting saw *vinifera* varieties being replaced with

LOW-TECH VINEYARDS
Rickety pergolas providing support for vines and old thatched-roofed buildings reflect the conditions that most of Romania's agricultural industry has survived on since medieval times.

hybrids, as the new private owners did not know how to look after their vineyards—or if they did, they could not care less—and hybrids are much hardier, yielding the highest volumes for the least effort. This expansion continued until 1995, when it started to decline. Both new planting and the replanting of old vineyards now represent less than two percent of the total area under vine, with a staggering amount of land planted with hybrids (estimates vary

ROMANIA

The main winemaking areas in Romania are scattered throughout the country: in the Carpathian foothills, on the plateau lands of Dobrudja, and on the plains.

	Vine-growing Zone
	Crisana
	Maramures
	Transilvania
	Moldova
	Banat
	Oltenia
	Mutenia
	Dobrudja
Red wine	White wine

- - - - International Boundary
▲ Height above sea level (meters)

0   20   40   60   80   100 miles
0   50   100   150 km

RECENT ROMANIAN VINTAGES

2003 Severely reduced yields, due to spring frosts and summer droughts, but excellent quality, especially in reds.

2002 Variable quality; mostly average to poor, with the excellent white wines of Transilvania the exception.

2001 Generally good quality.

2000 A great year across the country for both red and white wines.

1999 A very good year for red wines, and not bad for whites, although most should have been consumed before now.

FACTORS AFFECTING TASTE AND QUALITY

LOCATION
The main wine-producing areas in Romania spread from Iaşi in the northeast of the country down through the Carpathian foothills to the Danube river.

CLIMATE
A continental climate, with hot summers and cold winters, which are tempered only in the southeast by the Black Sea.

ASPECT
Vines are grown on all types of land—from the plains through the plateau land of Dobrudja to the slopes of the foothills of the Carpathian Mountains.

SOIL
A wide variety of soil types, including the generally sandy-alluvial plains and the stony, hillside soils of Banat; the limestone of Dobrudja; the oolitic limestone of Mutenia's Pietroasele vineyards; and the stony fringes of the Carpathian Mountains.

VITICULTURE AND VINIFICATION
Although some modernization of facilities has taken place since the 1990s, and a few new wineries have been established, at least half the wines are produced in antiquated conditions, and almost two-thirds must be made from hybrids, whatever the official statistics state.

GRAPE VARIETIES
Hybrids plus Băbeaskă, Băbcaskă Neagră, Cabernet Sauvignon, Fetească Albă, Fetească Neagră, Fetească Regălă, Galbenă, Grasă, Merlot, Pinot Gris, Pinot Noir, Riesling, Tămaîoasă, Welschriesling

wildly between the official 75,000 acres and external observers' 297,500 acres). Furthermore, despite privatization, almost 23 percent of the vineyards still belong to the Romanian state. There are now eight wine regions encompassing 37 winegrowing districts, and vineyard registration is slowly coming into operation in preparation for Romania's EU membership in 2007–2010. The two largest wine-producing regions, Moldova and Mutenia, together account for more than 60 percent of all Romanian wines.

THE FUTURE

Despite the difficulties of the past and accession to the EU, which will present the growers with as many problems as solutions, Romania has an excellent future—if it can be grasped. According to pre-membership agreements between Romania and the EU, all hybrids must be removed by 2014; although, on past experience, this will no doubt be extended. And extended. And extended. Far more important than replanting hybrid vines with *vinifera* is to ensure that only the best vineyards are replanted and that an emphasis is put on growing the best indigenous varieties, such as those of the Fetească family: Fetească Albă, Fetească Neagră, and Reglă. Other potentially interesting local varieties include Băbeaskă, Busuioaca, Francusa, Galbenă, Grasă, and Tămaîoasă. Most wines currently produced from these grapes are a bit rustic, but they do show promise. Once the clones are sorted out; the vines are grown in the best-suited sites, at low yields; and skilful winemakers are employed to hone the style of the wines they produce, there will be no stopping Romania taking its rightful place in the world of wine.

NEW VINEYARDS IN DEALUL MARE
A vineyard is staked out, waiting to support new vine growth in the Dealul Mare district of Mutenia.

ROMANIAN LABEL LANGUAGE

CULES LA ÎNNOBILAREA BOABELOR (CIB) Equivalent to *Beerenauslese* or above (a minimum of 112° *Oechsle*)
CULES LA MATURIATE DEPLINA (CMD) Similar to a high *Spätlese* (a minimum of 95° *Oechsle*)
CULES LA MATURIATE ÎNNOBILAREA (CMI) Similar to a high Auslese (a minimum of 100° *Oechsle*)
DULCE Sweet
EDELBEERENLESE Equivalent to *Beerenauslese* or above (a minimum of 112° *Oechsle*)
EDELREIFLESE Equivalent to *Auslese* or above (a minimum of 100° *Oechsle*)
IMBUTELIAT Bottled
IVV This stands for cooperative and should be followed by its name or location.
PIVNITĂ Cellar
RECOLTA Vintage
SEC Dry
SPUMOS Sparkling
STRUGURE Grape
VIE Vine
VIILE Vineyard
VIN ALB White wine

Hariton
PRODUCE OF ROMANIA

FETEASCA NEAGRA
VIN ROŞU DEMIDULCE
DOCC · CEI VANJU MARE · OREVITA

VIN DE MASĂ Table wine
VIN ROSE Rosé wine
VIN ROSU Red wine
VIN SUPERIOR Superior wine
VIN USOR Light wine
VOLLREIFLESE Similar to a high *Spätlese* (a minimum of 95° *Oechsle*)
VSO Basic quality-wine designation
VSOC Categorized-quality wine designation similar to Germany's QmP and covering *Edelbeerenlese* (CIB), *Edelreiflese* (CMI) and *Vollreiflese* (CMD)

RIESLING DE BANAT
VINURI DE CALITATE SUPERIOARA VSO.
70 cl (e)   Alc. 10,5% by Vol.
TEREMIA MARE   Produce of RUMANIA
MEDIUM WHITE WINE
Bottled by: VINOROMAN D 8000 München 82

THE APPELLATIONS OF
ROMANIA

BANAT

Wine districts *Buzias, Dealul Tirolului, Moldova Noua, Recaş, Teremia*

Although Banat is one of the better known wine regions in Romania—and has been since the 1980s—it is the smallest by a large margin, representing less than two percent of the country's vineyards. The sandy plain of the Teremia district is best known for its large production of eminently drinkable white wines, while the mountain slopes of Recaş-Tirol produce Valea Lunga, a pleasant, light-bodied red wine.

🍇 Cabernet Sauvignon, Cadarca, Fetească Regălă, Merlot, Mustoasă, Pinot Noir, Riesling

✓ *Recaş*

CRIŞANA

Wine districts *Minis-Maderat*

Formerly part of the Banat region, the hilly Minis-Maderat area provides excellent, inexpensive reds from Cadarca, Pinot Noir, Cabernet Sauvignon, and Merlot grapes grown on stony terraces.

🍇 Cabernet Sauvignon, Cadarca, Fetească Regălă, Merlot, Mustoasă, Pinot Noir, Riesling

DOBRUDJA

Wine districts *Babadag, Istria, Murfatlar, Saricia-Niculitel*

Murfatlar is the most important and oldest winemaking district in Dobrudja (or Dobrogea), with well-organized vineyards on hills close to the Black Sea and an experimental state research station that has introduced many classic western varieties. Once reliant on the region's prestigious past, the wines used to be too old, oxidized, and heavy, but they are beginning to receive the attention they deserve now that they are clean and well balanced; the lovely, late-picked, softly sweet, and stylish Gewürztraminer is a good example of this style.

🍇 Cabernet Sauvignon, Chardonnay, Gewürztraminer, Muscat Ottonel, Pinot Gris, Pinot Noir, Riesling

✓ *The Carpathian Winery • Murfatlar* (Ferma Noua, Trei Hectare)

MARAMURES

Wine districts *Diosig, Silvania, Valea lui Mihai*

A breathtakingly wild and beautiful mountainous area full of rather strange but friendly people living a folksy, arts-and-crafts life in a place that time forgot. Maramures is a white-wine-only region. Diosig produces acidic wines that are ideal for brandy distillation.

🍇 Burgund Mare, Cabernet Sauvignon, Cadarca, Fetească Regălă, Merlot, Muscat Ottonel, Pinot Noir, Welschrieling

MOLDOVA

Wine districts *Catchiest, Cotesti, Cotnari, Dealurile Bujorului, Dealurile Moldovei, Husi, Iaşi, Ivesti, Nicoresti, Odobesti, Panciu, Zeletin*

The vineyards of Odobesti surrounding the industrial town of Focsani produce quantities of rather ordinary red and white wine. There are, however, exceptions: Cotesti, for example, has a good reputation for Pinot Noir and Merlot, while Nicoresti is known for its full-colored,

spicy red wine produced from the Băbeaskă grape. The vineyards of Cotnari are the most famous in Romania; their reputation dates back to the 15th century. The wine is a rich dessert wine, not unlike Tokaji but not as complex. The Bucium hills of Visan and Doi Peri overlook the city of Iaşi and the cool conditions are reflected in Cabernet Sauvignon wines that have crisp, leafy characteristics.

🍇 Băbeaskă, Cabernet Sauvignon, Fetească Albă, Fetească Neagră, Grasă, Merlot, Pinot Noir, Welschriesling

MUTENIA

Wine districts *Dealul Mare, Dealurile Suzaului, Pietroasele*

Dealul Mare is located to the north of Bucharest, stretching across the lower, southeast-facing slopes of the Carpathian Mountains. It is famous for Pinot Noir, Cabernet Sauvignon, and Merlot. There is a small area of chalky soil within this district that has a special microclimate best suited to the production of sweet white wines with fine, balancing acidity. It is here that the vineyards of Pietroasele are located. The area's Tămaîoasă or "Frankincense" grape is a Muscat-related variety that makes a lusciously sweet, gold-colored wine of very expressive quality. One of the most remarkable Romanian wines I have tasted was a beautiful, botrytized rosé

Edelbeerenlese version of the normally lackluster Fetească Neagră grape.

🍇 Băbeaskă Neagră, Cabernet Sauvignon, Fetească Neagră, Fetească Regălă, Galbenă, Merlot, Pinot Gris, Pinot Noir, Riesling, Tămaîoasă

✓ *Prahova Valley* (Cabernet Sauvignon, Merlot)
 • *S E R V E* (Cuvée Charlotte, Terra Romana)
 • *Vinarte* (Castel Bolovanu, Villa Zorilor)

OLTENIA

Wine districts *Drăgasăni, Plaiurile Drincei, Podguria Dagilor, Sadova Corabia, Samburesti/ Simburesti, Severinului, Segarcea, Stefănesti, Vanju Mare*

Simburesti in the Drăgasăni district produces Oltenia's best reds. It is also known for a full, dry red wine from the Fetească Neagră grape, as well as for Cabernet Sauvignon. The Segarcea district also produces red wines. The Pinot Noir produced here is good, although it is not as well known as the Cabernet Sauvignon. Interesting sweet wines are found on the west side of the River Oltul.

🍇 Cabernet Sauvignon, Fetească Neagră, Fetească Regălă, Muscat Ottonel, Pinot Noir, Riesling, Sauvignon Blanc, Tămaîoasă

TRANSILVANIA

Wine districts *Aiud, Albă, Iulia-Aiud, Bistrita, Lechinta, Sebes-Apold, Tarnave*

Of all the winegrowing regions of Romania, Transilvania is perhaps the most exciting. The crisp fruit and good acidity of its white wines lies somewhere between the styles of Alsace and South Tyrol. The steep Tirnave vineyards produce good-quality white wines with more than just a hint of Germanic style and delicacy. Not surprisingly, German settlers in Transilvania introduced many of their own grape varieties to the region. The native Fetească grape is also successful.

🍇 Fetească Albă, Fetească Regălă, Muscat Ottonel, Pinot Gris, Riesling, Sauvignon Blanc, Traminer, Welschriesling

✓ *Carl Reh • Vinarte* (Terasse Danubiane)

SLOVAKIA AND THE CZECH REPUBLIC

Slovakia has twice as much area under vine as the Czech Republic, even though it is much smaller. However, Slovakia's vineyards are in a state of decline, and the Czech Republic is rightly better known for its beer than its wine.

ALTHOUGH THE FIRST VINES were planted in Moravia (now part of the Czech Republic) by the Romans as early as the third century CE, and winemaking in Slovakia is supposed to date back 3,000 years, none of the wines from anywhere encompassed by the borders of these countries today has ever gained sufficient repute to warrant significant exports, let alone worldwide fame. And, as with the rest of the former Eastern Bloc wine producing countries, the period of centralized processing under Communist rule obscured whatever local reputations there were and cast a gray shadow over any individual efforts, as the vineyards were replanted high and wide for mass production.

SLOVAKIA

Most Slovakian wine is classified as lowly table wine, which would be a good thing if this were the result of a quality-conscious culling of the total production to produce stunning quality top wines, but that is not the case—the wines are naturally of a dismal quality. Potentially the quality of Slovakian wine is greater than that of the Czech Republic, but the decline in the state of the Slovakian wine industry is greater, so it will be an even tougher job to turn around. More than 85 percent of Slovakian wine is white, with Müller Thurgau, Ryzlink Vlašsky (Welschriesling), and Veltlinske Zelene (Gruner Veltliner) together accounting for over 60 percent of all the vines growing in this country. Sparkling wines have been made since 1825 at Sered and are still marketed under the "Hubert" brand, but quality is not high.

CZECH AND SLOVAK LABEL LANGUAGE

BIELE VÍNO White wine
ČERVENÉ VÍNO Red wine
DEZERTNÉ KORENENÉ VÍNO Aromatized dessert wine
DEZERTNÉ VÍNO Dessert wine
DIA Suitable for diabetics (in other words, sugar-free)
JAKOSTNÍ VÍNO The equivalent of a *vin de pays*, must have a natural alcoholic potential of 8–11%
KABINET Equivalent to the German term Kabinett; must have a natural alcoholic potential of 11–12%
LEDOVÉ VÍNO The equivalent of Eiswein, which not only must have a natural alcoholic potential of at least 16%, but the grapes must be picked at below 21°F and must remain frozen throughout pressing
ODRODOVÉ VÍNA Grape variety
OBSAH CUKRU Sugar content
POLOSLADKÉ Semi-sweet
POZDNÍ SBĚR Literally "late harvest;" must have a natural alcoholic potential of 12–14%
RUŽOVÉ VÍNO Rose wine
SLADKÉ Sweet

SLÁMOVÉ VÍNO Literally a "straw wine," which not only must have a natural alcoholic potential of at least 16%, but, for 3 months prior to being pressed, must also be stored on straw or reeds or hung in a well-aired place
STOLNÍ VÍNO Table wine, the lowest quality; must have a natural alcoholic potential of 5.5–8%
SUCHÉ Dry
ŠUMIVÉ VÍNO Sparkling wine
VÍNA S PŘÍVLASTKEM A wine of appellation, thus the equivalent of a French AOC
VINÁRSKYCH ZÁVODOV Wine producer
VÍNO Wine
VÝBĚR A wine predicated by selection; must have a natural alcoholic potential of at least 14%
VÝBĚR Z HROZNŮ A wine predicated by selection of individual grapes; must have a natural alcoholic potential of at least 16%
ZVYŠKOVYM CUKROM Residual sugar

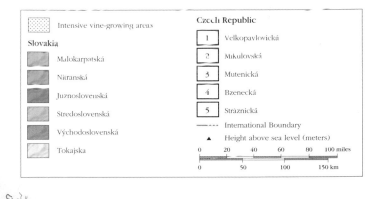

	Intensive vine-growing areas	Czech Republic
	Slovakia	**1** Velkopavlovická
	Malokarpatská	**2** Mikulovská
	Nitranská	**3** Mutenická
	Juznoslovenská	**4** Bzenecká
	Stredoslovenská	**5** Stráznická
	Východoslovenská	- - - International Boundary
	Tokajska	▲ Height above sea level (meters)

0   20   40   60   80   100 miles
0   50   100   150 km

SLOVAKIA AND THE CZECH REPUBLIC
Most of this region's vineyards are found in Slovakia, along the border with Austria and Hungary.

CZECH VINES
A vineyard at Ratískovice, near Hodonin in the Czech Republic.

The most intriguing wine from this country is Slovakian Tokaji, produced in the small part of the world-famous district that falls within Slovak borders. The same grapes are grown as in the rest of the Tokaji-producing region (Furmint, Hárslevelű, and Muscat), and the wine is supposedly made in a very similar style to the great Hungarian version. In truth they do not compare, but there is no reason why, with properly maintained vineyards, adequately equipped producers of Slovakian Tokaji should not compete with their famous neighbors. With a little imagination, this wine has the potential to be so lucrative that it must surely be the door-opener for that much-needed foreign investment.

THE CZECH REPUBLIC

Most Czech wines are produced in Moravia, where the majority of the vineyards are located. The two major areas of production are Hustopěce-Hodonin on the Morava River and Znojmo-Mikulov on the Dyje River. Around 80 percent of all the wine produced is white, with a good level of winemaking expertise for light, elegant, and aromatically fresh whites. Although the climate does not generally suit red-wine production, some interesting reds (such as the Cabernet Sauvignon from Pavlovice) are produced. Sparkling wines are made in the towns of Mikulov and Bzenec by *cuve close* and continuous methods. Since the 1995 Czech Wine Law was introduced, wines are categorized according to the grapes' sugar contents: effectively table wine, *vin de pays*, and AOC equivalents, followed by German-style predicated wines: Kabinet, Pozdní sběr, Výběr z hroznů, Výběr z bobulí, Ledová vína, and Slámová vína (*see* label language, p423).

FACTORS AFFECTING TASTE AND QUALITY

LOCATION
The Czech Republic is an inland central European country north of Austria and its vines are mostly located in Moravia. There are also vineyards in Bohemia, mainly to the north and northeast of Prague. Slovakia is located south of Moravia.

CLIMATE
Generally a continental climate with occasional maritime influences from the Atlantic. In the Czech Republic, Moravia is significantly sunnier (1,760 hours) than Bohemia (1,450 hours), but Slovakia is even more favorable (2,000 hours), with less precipitation.

ASPECT
In the Czech Republic, vines are grown on rolling hills in Bohemia, and on mountain foothills in Moravia. Generally steeper and hillier in Slovakia.

SOIL
The primarily loess topsoils found in most Czech vineyards cover the acidic crystalline slate of the Bohemian Massive, the exception being in the Bohemian limestone basin around Prague. Sandy or rocky soils, with scattered alluvial deposits, dominate Slovakia.

VITICULTURE AND VINIFICATION
Although some modernization of facilities has taken place in the Czech Republic since the 1990s, and a few new wineries have been set up, at least half the production occurs under antiquated conditions, and far too much wine is made from hybrids for the country to be able to build a reputation. While the situation in Slovakia is worse, the potential quality is greater.

GRAPE VARIETIES
Slovakian Primary Grape varieties: Chardonnay, Devín, Frankovka Modrá (Limberger), Ryzlink Vlašsky (Welschriesling), Sauvignon Blanc, Svätovavrinecké (St-Laurent), Veltlinske Zelene (Grüner Veltliner)
Slovakian Secondary Grape varieties: Cabernet Sauvignon, Dievčie Hrozno, Furmint, Lipovina (Hárslevelű), Rulandské Bílé (Pinot Blanc), Ryzlink Rýnsky (Riesling), Silvánske Zelené (Sylvaner)
Czech Primary Grape varieties: Frankovka (Limberger), Müller-Thurgau, Rulandské Bílé (Pinot Blanc), Ryzlink Rýnsky (Riesling), Ryzlink Vlašsky (Welschriesling), Veltlínské Červene (Roter Veltliner), Svatovavřineké (St-Laurent)
Czech Secondary Grape varieties: André, Chardonnay, Modrý Portugal (Portugieser), Muskat Moravské, Neuburské (Neuburger), Rulandské Modrý (Pinot Noir), Rulandské Šedé (Pinot Gris), Sauvignon Blanc, Tramín (Savagnin), Zweigeltrebe

RECENT CZECH VINTAGES

2003 The best Czech vintage in living memory. Also excellent in Slovakia, particularly for reds and late-harvest whites.

2002 Variable quality, with some good white wines in the Czech Republic, but rain during the harvest affected some Slovak wines.

2001 Extremely variable; careful selection required.

2000 Very good for reds and late-harvest whites in Slovakia.

1999 Some elegant wines produced in both the Czech Republic and Slovakia.

THE APPELLATIONS OF
SLOVAKIA AND THE CZECH REPUBLIC

SLOVAKIA
JUŽNOSLOVENSKÁ
Internal regions: *Dunajskostredský, Galantský, Hurbanovský, Komárňanský, Palárikovský, Šamorínsky, Strekovský, Stúrovský*

The Južnoslovenská or Southern Slovak region is warm and sunny; rich clay soils encourage late-harvest whites and well-colored reds.

🍇 Cabernet Franc, Cabernet Sauvignon, Frankovka Modrá, Muškat Moravsky, Ryzlink Rýnsky, Rulandské, Rulandské

Bílé, Rulandské Modré, Tramín Červný (Red Traminer)

✓ *Château Belá • Karpatská Perla • Vino-Masaryk*

MALOKARPATSKÁ
Internal regions: *Bratislavský, Dolanský, Hlovecký, Modranský, Orešanský, Pezinský, Senecký, Skalický, Stupavský, Trnavský, Vrbovský, Záhorský*

The Malokarpatská or "Little Carpathian" region has a winemaking tradition of almost 3,000 years. Riesling from Limbach has the greatest reputation,

followed by Modrý Portugal (Blauer Portugieser) from Oresany.

🍇 Chardonnay, Modrý Portugal, Veltlinske Zelene, Ryzlink Rýnsky, Ryzlink Vlašsky

✓ *Karpatská Perla • Mrva & Stanko*

NITRANSKÁ
Internal regions: *Nitranský, Pukanský, Radošinský, Šintavský, Tekovský, Vráhel'ský, Željezovský, Žitavský, Zlatomoravský*

This region produces a mixed bag of red and white, dry and sweet, still, and sparkling wines.

🐝 Cabernet Sauvignon, Frankovka Modrá, Müller-Thurgau, Pálava, Ryzlink Vlašsky, Rulandské Modré, Svätovavřinecké, Veltlinske Zelene

✓ *Mrva & Stanko • Vinanza*

STREDOSLOVENSKÁ

Internal regions: *Fiľakovský, Gemerský, Hotiansky, Ipeľský, Modrokamenský, Tornaľský, Vinický*

In the Stredoslovenská, otherwise known simply as the Central Slovakian wine region, Tramín is considered to be the best variety.

🐝 Cabernet Sauvignon, Chardonnay, Ryzling Vlašsky, Svätovavřinecké, Tramín, Veltlinske Zelene

✓ *Mrva & Stanko*

TOKAJSKÁ

This tiny region is surrounded on three sides by the Východoslovenská region, and on one by the Tokaj region in Hungary. Slovakian Tokajské is made from the same varieties as Hungarian Tokaji (Furmint, Lipovina, or Hárslevelů, and Muškát Žltý or Sárga Muskotály). Wines made from other varieties are not sold as Tokajské.

🐝 Devín, Furmint, Lipovina, Muškát Žltý, Rulandské Bílé, Tramín Červený (Red Traminer)

✓ *J. & J. Ostrožovič*

VÝCHODOSLOVENSKÁ

Internal regions: *Kraľovskochlmecký, Michalovský, Moldavský, Sobranský*

The heavy clay soils of the Východoslovenská, or Eastern Slovakian, wine region are mostly thought to be suitable for white grapes, although red wines are made.

🐝 Frankovka Modrá, Müller-Thurgau, Ryzling Vlašsky, Svätovavřinecké, Tramín, Veltlinske Zelene

THE CZECH REPUBLIC

BRNĚNSKÁ

With two basic soil types, white grapes are mostly grown on lighter sandy soils, with black grapes grown on gravelly soils. Dolní Kounice is the most important wine town.

🐝 Frankovka, Modrý Portugal, Müller-Thurgau, Muskat Moravské, Palava, Svatovavřineké, Tramín, Veltlinske Zelene

BZENECKÁ

Orechov, Bzenec, Polesovice, and Vracov are the most important wine villages in Bzenecká, the Czech Republic's smallest wine region. Clayey, sandy, and gravelly soils predominate. The local specialty is Bzenecká Lipká, made from Ryzlink Rýnsky. Olsava and Vitra are new varieties created by Cultivation Station at Polesovice.

🐝 Frankovka, Muskat Moravské, Olsava, Rulandské Bílé, Ryzlink Rýnsky, Svatovavřineké, Veltlinske Zelene, Vitra

CÁSLAVSKÁ

A small enclave of vines growing at the foot of the Kutna Hora Mountain.

🐝 Modrý Portugal, Müller-Thurgau, Svatovavřineké, Sylvanske Zelene

KYJOVSKÁ

The best wines are made from vines grown at Vresovice, on south-facing slopes, at 1,800 feet

in altitude; the grapes produced in this region have a pronounced acidity.

🐝 Müller-Thurgau, Svatovavřineké, Veltlinske Zelene

MĚLNICKÁ

The largest wine region in Bohemia, Mělnická has a certain reputation for oak-aged reds, but produces better Chardonnay.

🐝 Chardonnay, Rulandské Bílé, Rulandské Modré, Rulandské Šedé, Ryzlink Rýnsky, Svatovavřineké, Zweigeltrebe

MIKULOVSKÁ

With 6,180 acres (2,500 hectares) under vine, Mikulovská is the largest wine region in the country. Most wines produced are white, with the best coming from limestone soils, although sandy and marly soils are also quite common. The new Palava variety (Tramin x Müller-Thurgau) was developed here.

🐝 Chardonnay, Müller-Thurgau, Neuburské, Palava, Ryzlink Vlašsky, Silvánske Zelené, Tramin, Veltlinske Zelene

✓ *Sklepy • Tanzberg*

MOSTECKÁ

This region has an extremely dry climate and volcanic (basalt) soils. A significant portion of the wine is traditionally produced under strictly Kosher conditions.

🐝 Müller-Thurgau, Ryzlink Rýnsky, Svatovavřineké, Zweigeltrebe

MUTĚNICKÁ

The vines grow on various clayey, sandy soils, with the best on calcareous clay. Although Mutěnická encompasses 14 communes, almost 90 percent of the vineyards are located in Cejkovice, where the wines have pronounced acidity. Most of the rest of the vines are located in Mutěnice, the location of Moravia's premier viticultural research station.

🐝 Frankovka, Müller-Thurgau, Ryzlink Vlašsky, Svatovavřineké, Veltlinske Zelene

PODLUŽÍ

The vines grow in mineral-deficient clayey, sandy, and gravelly soils on frost-prone sites in this small region bordering Austria and Slovakia. The best wines are made from Veltlinske Zelene and originate in the clayey soils of Prušánsky.

🐝 Frankovka, Rulandské Bílé, Rulandské Šedé, Ryzlink Rýnsky, Ryzlink Vlašsky, Svatovavřineké, Veltlinske Zelene, Zweigeltrebe

PRAŽSKÁ (PRAGUE)

Although this is the smallest region in the Czech Republic, Prague used to be the largest wine-producing town in Bohemia in centuries past. Modrý Portugal is the most widely planted variety, but the best wines are made from Riesling and Pinot Blanc, while colder, less-suitable sites are planted with Kerner and Müller-Thurgau.

🐝 Chardonnay, Modrý Portugal, Müller-Thurgau, Muskat Moravské, Rulandské Šedé, Ryzlink Rýnsky, Tramín, Svatovavřineké, Zweigeltrebe

ROUDNICKÁ

Once famous for Sylvaner, Roudnická now grows a considerable amount of Müller-Thurgau, and has had some success with red wines produced on the valley slopes, with gold medal Rulandské Modré (Pinot Noir) giving short-lived hope in the mid-1990s. Most vines are grown on a marly limestone and chalk plateau, covered by loess and gravelly sand, near the Elbe river.

🐝 Modrý Portugal, Müller-Thurgau, Rulandské Modre, Svatovavřineké

STRÁZNICKÁ

The vineyards in this region are located on the heavy clay slopes of the Bílé Karpaty, where red wines can be hard. Growers therefore mainly grow white-wine varieties.

🐝 Müller-Thurgau, Rulandské Šedé, Veltlinske Zelene

USHERSKOHRADIŠTSKÁ

Vines grow on the banks of the Morava river and in its hinterland, on sandy and gravelly sand slopes of Chirby and Bílé Karpaty. Primarily white wines.

🐝 Müller-Thurgau, Rulandské Šedé

VELKOPAVLOVICKÁ

The best wines are made from Neuburské and Veltlinske Zelene grown in the north of Velkopavlovická, the Czech Republic's second-largest wine region (5,810 acres/2,350 hectares).

🐝 Frankovka, Modrý Portugal, Müller-Thurgau, Neuburské, Ryzlink Vlašsky, Veltlinske Zelene

✓ *Vinum*

ZERNOSECKÁ

Typical of Bohemia's sporadic viticultural character today, Zernosecká has just 16 wine producers (owning in total just 175 acres of vineyards spread over five wine villages), whereas the village of Litoměřice alone was once surrounded by more than 1,235 acres (500 hectares) of vines.

🐝 Müller-Thurgau, Rulandské Bílé, Rulandské Modré, Ryzlink Rýnsky, Svatovavřineké

ZNOJEMSKÁ

This region's best wines come from Znojmo, which is not so much a city as two cities in one. Znojmo resides above its own underground city, comprising 19mi of interconnecting catacombs.

🐝 Müller-Thurgau, Ryzlink Rýnsky, Sauvignon Blanc, Veltlinske Zelene

✓ *Znovín*

THE WESTERN BALKANS

Few regions in the world have undergone so much political turmoil and human tragedy over such a relatively short period as the Western Balkans. Until the early 1990s, the entire region was supposedly just one country—Yugoslavia. However, Yugoslavia comprised at least seven one-time sovereign nations and was populated by five ethnic groups.

FOLLOWING THE DEATH OF TITO, and the general collapse of Communism, it was inevitable that this artificial edifice would start to unravel, and the powder-keg of centuries of resentment would one day explode into bloody conflict. In these more peaceful times, newly independent countries at least have a chance to establish their own wine reputations. The fact that Slovenia, which for the most part avoided the skirmishes of war, is already competing on the world market with its wines should encourage other states that they could be equally successful once their wine industries return to their peacetime potential.

ALBANIA

Winemaking in Albania dates back to pre-Roman times. However, since most Albanians are Muslim, wine production has not been of great importance in recent historical terms, and, under a xenophobic Communist government for 46 years, there were no exports. Thus the potential for this country's wine industry has been severely restricted. Since democracy was established between 1990 and 1992, successive governments have sought viticultural expert advice from the West, but the area under vine in Albania is now less than 14,800 acres (6,000 hectares), which is actually less than one-fifth of the area that was planted under Communist rule. Only a small fraction of vines are grown for wine, and they are located around the capital of Tirana, and in five surrounding disctricts: Durres, Berät, Korcë, Skoder, and Lushnje. Although well-known varieties such as Cabernet Franc, Mavrud, Merlot, and Welschriesling are to be found, indigenous varieties such as Shesh i Zi, Shesh i Barhe, and Kalmet (otherwise known as Kadarka) represent almost 60 percent of all Albanian vines, and three other local grapes (Vlosh, Serine, and Debine) account for most of the rest.

BOSNIA-HERZEGOVINA

Vines are restricted to the south, in the Brotnjo hills around Mostar, where the climate and rocky soil favor two indigenous varieties, Zilavka for white wine and Blatina for red. There are currently 3,460 acres (1,400 hectares) planted. Other significant varieties grown are Bena, Dobrogostina, Krkoshia, Podbil, and Rkaciteli for white wines, and Alicante Bouschet, Cabernet Sauvignon, Gamay, Merlot, Plavka, Trnjak, and Vranac for reds.

CROATIA

Prior to hostilities, Croatia was one of the two most prosperous states in Yugoslavia. Although it is today in a relatively stable

WESTERN BALKANS
Historically one of the world's political hotspots, the Western Balkans possess an impressive combination of indigenous grape varieties and terroirs where they can be exploited.

condition, many vineyards were destroyed during the worst
upheavals of the Croatian war, when one million landmines
were sown, and it will take until 2020 to clear them all. Massive
replanting programs created new vineyards in the late 1990s.
There are two main regions: Continental Croatia and the
Dalmatian Coast. Watch out for the emergence of this wine
country as it rides tail-winds of Dalmatia's newly found fame
as home of the Zinfandel grape (which was originally known
as Crljenak Kastelanski).

Inland Croatia
More than 90 percent of the production is white wine, with
over half of the vineyards planted with Graševina (Welschriesling).
Of the few black grape varieties, Frankova (Lemberger) is
probably the most important. Other grapes grown here include
Chardonnay, Gewürztraminer, Muscat Ottonel, Riesling, Traminer,
and Sauvignon Blanc.

Coastal Croatia
White wine is also important here, accounting for no less than
70 percent of total production. The grape varieties grown are
more diverse, with Malvasia the most widely planted, yet accounting
for less than 10 percent of the vineyards. Other grape varieties
include Debit-Grk (Ugni Blanc), Marastina, Plavać Mali, Pošip
(Furmint), Vugava (Viognier), and Zlahtina (Chasselas). New
plantations in this region include Cabernet Sauvignon and
Merlot, and there have been serious attempts to revive Crljenak
Kastelanski (Zinfandel).

√ *Grgić Vina Winery*

MACEDONIA
Following the secession of Slovenia and Croatia in 1991,
Macedonia received full international recognition in 1993. The
grape varieties grown in this country include Grenache, Kadarka,
Kratošija, Plovdina, Prokupac, Temjanika, and Vranac. Phylloxera,
which devastated European vineyards in the late 19th century, did
not reach Macedonia until 1912.

The most popular Macedonian wine is Kratošija, which is a
deep colored red made from native Vranac and Kratošija varieties.
It has a distinctive taste and aroma, full body, and a smooth
flavor. It is bottled in its second year, when the bouquet is at its
fullest, and is best drunk when very young. Prokupac and
Kadarka make interesting reds, Belan produces a neutral white
Grenache wine, and Temjanika an aromatic white.

SERBIA AND MONTENEGRO
Although the Federal Army made abortive attempts to put down
independence in Slovenia and Croatia, and supported the Bosnian
Serbs, it did not fight any battles on its home ground until the
Kosovo conflict. Most Serbian vineyards thus remain unaffected.
There are four major viticultural regions: Kosovo, Vojvodina,
Montenegro, and Serbia itself.

Kosovo
Although part of Serbia, Kosovo is governed by the United Nations
Interim Administration Mission, and this is set to continue until its
future status has been confirmed by the international community.
Until the conflict, the Rahovic winery had a lucrative contract to
supply the German Racke group with over 5–7 million gallons of
light red Kosovar wine, which was sold under the Amselfelder
brand, but due to the uncertain political situation, production was
transferred elsewhere. In these more peaceful times, Kosovo finds
itself with a substantial wine industry, but no ready market.

Montenegro
There are three winegrowing districts in Montenegro: Crnogorsko,
Titogradski, and Primorje. The main grape varieties grown here

DALMATIAN VINES PROTECTED BY DRY-STONE WALLS, CROATIA
*Many vineyards built on the stony coastal hillsides of Croatia are protected
by low dry-stone walls. These walls are painstakingly constructed by peasant
farmers to protect low-growing vines from the cold north winds and to keep
them cool in the heat of summer. Without such techniques, it would be
impossible to cultivate this difficult ground.*

are Kratošija, Krstač, Merlot, and Vranac. The best-known
vineyards of this region are those that are located on the terraced
southern slopes of Lake Skadar. The Vranac and Merlot wines can
be good, but Montenegro is better known for its grape brandy
than for its wine.

Serbia
I think that the best potential here is for Cabernet Sauvignon
and Merlot when grown in Južna Morava and, possibly, Timok,
but the best level of quality currently being achieved is by
producers of the snappy, fresh Sauvignon Blanc from Kruševac
in Zapadna Morava.

√ *Rubin* (Sauvignon Blanc)

Vojvodina (Voivodina)
North of Serbia, bordering Croatia, Hungary, and Romania, the
vines grown include Ezerjó, Graševina (Welschriesling), Kadarka,
Merlot, Riesling, Sauvignon Blanc, Sémillon, and Traminer. The
Traminer is a more interesting alternative and the soft, fruity
Merlot a good buy for red-wine drinkers.

SLOVENIA
By far the wealthiest part of former Yugoslavia, with per capita
income close to that of Austria, Slovenia is the rising star among
the winemaking countries of the Western Balkans.

Inland Slovenia (Kontinentalna Slovenija)
Squeezed between Austria, Hungary, and Croatia are two
winegrowing districts, each comprising several smaller areas:
Podravina (Bela Krajina, Haloze, Lutomer-Ororske, Maribor,
Prekmurje, Radgona-Kapela, Slovenske) and Posavina (Belakrajina,
Bizeljsko-Sremic, Dolenjska, Smarje-Virstajn).

√ *Curin* (Sauvignon) • *Meranovo* (Sauvignon) • *Jožef Prus* (Ledeno Vino
Renski Rizling)

Coastal Slovenia (Primorska Slovenija)
This region is close to the Italian border and consists of four
winegrowing districts: Brda, Karst, Koper, and Vipava. The
climate of Coastal Slovenia is of a mild Mediterranean type,
except in Vipara and Briški Okoliš, which come under the
moderating influence of the Alps.

√ *Movia* (Veliko Belo) • *Simčič* (Teodor Rdeče Reserve) • *Stojan Ščucrek*
(Stara Brajda—white) • *Vipava* (Lathieri Sauvignon Zemono)

THE BLACK AND CASPIAN SEAS

Although Russia is the largest wine producing country in this region, the wines of Moldova are better known internationally, while the legendary wines of Krym in the Ukraine boast the most illustrious history.

GEORGIA AND ARMENIA have at least equivalent winemaking potential as these countries, but they are at the back of the line when it comes to heavy-duty international investment, and that is what it will take to upgrade the wine industries in this region. Without a radical overhaul of the technologies deployed in the vineyards and wineries, none of these countries will be able to produce wines of export quality.

ARMENIA

At the height of the Soviet Union's hegemony, Armenia's vineyards covered 90,150 acres (36,500 hectares), but this declined following the collapse of Communism, and by 2003 amounted to just 29,650 acres (12,000 hectares). More than 200 grape varieties are grown here, many of them indigenous, but only 30 are wine grapes, and these include Adisi, Anait, Areni, Azateni, Dmak, Garan, Kahet, Karmrayut, Megrabuir, Mskhali, Muscat (various), Nerkeni, Rkatsiteli, Tokun, and Voskeat. The Ararat Valley is the most important winegrowing region, claiming up to 60 percent of the country's vineyards, but as with Armenian wine in general, most of the production is distilled. High-strength table wines and strong dessert wines are made, but grape brandy is this country's most important alcoholic product.

AZERBAIJAN

Official statistics for the area under vine are notoriously inaccurate, having gone from 447,000 acres (181,000 hectares) in 1990 to less than 29,650 acres (12,000 hectares) in 2001. In 2004 the French Castel Group was hired to consult on expanding these vineyards, in the hope of exporting an improved quality of Azerbaijan wine to Russia. Azerbaijan has yet to resolve its conflict with Armenia over the largely Armenian-populated Azerbaijani Nagorno-Karabakh enclave, where vines are also planted.

GEORGIA

Georgia has one of the oldest winemaking traditions in the world. There is evidence that the first vines could have spread from here or, at least, been preserved in this area during the last major ice age. Georgia has numerous valleys, each with its own favorable microclimate, and it is said that they contain 1,000 indigenous grape varieties. This should one day propel this country to the forefront of the East European wine scene, but isolated pockets of enthusiasm have yet to be translated into a solid range of quality wines on the shelf.

KAZAKHSTAN

This is the country made famous by Borat, a character played by British comic genius Sacha Baron Cohen, who claims that in Kazakhstan, wine is made from horses' urine! The wine is not in fact that bad, but if any Kazakh entrepreneur decided to sell a wine labelled "Horses' Urine" (not too far away from the New Zealand "Cat's Pee"), they would probably double their country's exports overnight. The largest concentration of Kazakhstan's vineyards is in the extreme east, between Chimkent and Alma-Ata, in the foothills of the Tien Shan Mountains.

BLACK AND CASPIAN SEAS
This region in general, and Georgia in particular, is thought to have provided a safe haven for the vine during the last ice age.

MOLDOVA

A small country the size of Belgium, Moldova is, in fact, an extension of Romania's Moldova and, historically, the two parts were one. There are six winemaking districts: Pucari, Balti, Ialoveni, Stauceni, Hincesti, Romanesti, and Cricova.

Pucari is 100 miles (160 kilometers) south of the capital in the heart of red wine country. Negru de Pucari is a deep-colored and firm-structured red wine blended from Cabernet Sauvignon and Saperavi; Purpuruiu de Pucari is a softer Pinot-Merlot blend; and Rosu de Pucari is a dark rosé made from Cabernet Sauvignon, Merlot, and Malbec. Romanesti's vineyards lie 30 miles (50 kilometers) farther north. Romanesti was named after the Romanov Tzar Alexander I, who restarted the Moldovan wine industry by establishing his own winery here. Vines include Aligoté, Cabernet Sauvignon, Malbec, Merlot, Pinot Noir, and Rkatsiteli, but it is the Bordeaux varieties that tend to fare best.

Halfway between Kishinev and Romanesti is Cricova, where unremarkable and often faulty sparkling wines are made in the most remarkable and elaborate underground city. Its entrance is a massive pair of steel doors in a rock face, through which the largest eighteen-wheelers can drive, winding their way 262 feet (80 meters) below the surface, where a city has been hewn out of solid rock. Its size corresponds to the area covered by 25 villages on the surface and it is serviced by 40 miles (65 kilometers) of underground roads, complete with stop lights and road signs. In addition to these roads, there are 75 miles (120 kilometers) of galleries, which almost equals the entire storage capacity of the Champagne region of France. Why, I asked myself, is this workplace equipped with opulent reception halls, a dining room the like of which I have not seen anywhere else during the Eastern Bloc era, and a cellar containing priceless old vintages of Mouton Rothschild, Latour, Romanée-Conti, and so on? I had absolutely no doubts that this was where the Politburo would head in a nuclear exchange.

Atu Vin (Firebird) • *Cricova-Acorex* • *Dioysis Mereni*

RUSSIA

Climate is something of an obstacle to vinegrowing in Russia, as winters are generally very cold indeed, often -22°F (-30°C), and the vines in many regions have to be buried in the earth to survive the bitterly cold months. Summers are very hot and dry and, but for the tempering effect of the Black and Caspian Seas, climatic conditions would probably be impossible for viticulture. There are five major winegrowing districts in Russia: Checheno-Ingush, Dagestan, Krasnodar, Rostov-na-Donu, and Stavropol, with grape varieties that include Aligoté, Cabernet, Muscatel, Pinot Gris, Pinot Noir, Plechistik, Pukhljakovsky, Rizling, Rkatsiteli, Sylvaner, and Tsimlyansky. In general, Russian producers concentrate on white and sparkling wines in the north and west, and red in the south and east.

In the mid-1950s, a system that has become known as the "Russian Continuous Flow Method" was developed for producing sparkling wine cheaply, easily, and quickly by a natural second fermentation. Krasnodar's most reputable vineyards are on southwest-facing coastal slopes overlooking the Black Sea. Abrau is known for its dry Rizling (Riesling), Cabernet, and Durso sparkling wine. Anapa, just along the coast to the north, also makes Rizling, while down the coast at Gelendzhik, Aligoté is the local specialty. To the east of Krasnodar and north of the Caucasus, Stavropol is known for its dry Rizling and Silvaner, as well as the Muscatel Praskoveiski dessert wines. Other dessert wines include the spicy Mountain Flower; and Rostov-na-Donu, located around the confluence of the rivers Don and Kan and the Taganrogskiy Zaliv estuary, is famous for its rich Ruby of the Don dessert wines. Plechistik is a grape variety that is used to lend backbone to Tsimlyansky and, throughout the state, it also makes decent, dry red wines.

On the east-facing slopes of the Caucasus Mountains, overlooking the Caspian Sea, are the vineyards of the Republic of Dagestan. This is a black grape area that is known for the full body and flavor of its dry red wines; the best come from Derbent in the south. Checheno-Ingush is another republic with vineyards on the Caucasus, but these are found inland, along its northern slopes, to the southeast of Stavropol. Most of the wines produced in this area are of the port type.

Château le Grand Vostock

UKRAINE

As viticulture represents one-fifth of this recently re-established nation's agricultural economy, it will be instrumental in building up overseas trade. This is necessary to replace Ukraine's trade with Russia, upon which it is still dependent. The state's wine industry is mainly concerned with producing still white wines, although red wines and white sparkling wines are also produced in the Crimea, and dessert wines are a local specialty. Crimea (Krym) is the peninsula that encloses the Sea of Azov. Sparkling "Krim" is a traditional method wine made in five styles, from Brut through to Sweet, and in a semi-sweet red version. The grapes used include Chardonnay, Pinot Noir, Rizling, Aligoté, and Cabernet. The wines are coarse, and the traditional addition of brandy does not help, but the Brut and Demi-Sec Red are widely available on export markets and sell on novelty value. The Ruby of Crimea, which is a blend of Saperavi, Matrassa, Aleatika, Cabernet, and Malbec, is a robust, rustic, full-bodied red that is quite commonly encountered in various countries.

Nikolayev-Kherson, just northeast of Crimea, and Odessa, near the Moldova state border, produce various white, sparkling, and dessert wines. The best known local wines are dry white wines such as Perlina Stepu, Tropjanda Zakarpatja, and Oksamit Ukrainy.

That this region is capable of not merely good but great wines of exceptional longevity is beyond doubt. In 1990, David Molyneux-Berry MW brought back some extraordinary wines for auction at Sotheby's in London. These came from the famous Massandra cellars, which were built on the outskirts of Yalta in the Crimea for the Russian Imperial court at the end of the 19th century. This was not a winery, merely an aging facility acting as the central hub to a complex of 25 satellite wineries. The wineries were in the surrounding hills of Krymskiye Gory, where the vineyards were located, thus the grapes did not have to be transported, and almost every ounce of their potential quality was retained. This would be an ambitious project even by today's standards.

The wines Molyneux-Berry showed at a pre-auction tasting were nothing less than sensational. The Massandra Collection, as it has become known, consisted of fortified wines and I do not mean to be disparaging when I say that their maker deliberately mimicked classic styles such as Madeira, port, and so on. How could you put down a 1932 white-port-style wine that had more class, fragrance, and finesse at almost 60 years old than anything white and fortified that has ever been made in Oporto? The 1940 was let down by a spirity nose, but I would not keep a genuine white port five years, let alone 50, and it blew away the 1932 on the palate anyway. The 1929 Muscat had as much toffee, caramel, and exotic fruit as the best Australian Muscats, but a balance that undeniably placed it in the northern hemisphere. The best Massandra wines I tasted that day were both Madeiras, a 1937 and a 1922 (No.31), but although I would like to see such wines made again (fortified wines are still made, but not of comparable quality), I do not for one moment suggest that the entire Crimea should be turned over to the production of classic-quality fortified wines. What I do mean, however, is that great wines can be made in the Ukraine, in certain parts, given the right vines, yield, and proper winemaking expertise.

The WINES of
THE EASTERN
MEDITERRANEAN

WHEN THIS ENCYCLOPEDIA WAS FIRST PUBLISHED IN 1988, you could count the recommended wine producers in Greece on the fingers of one hand. There was general despair at how the first civilization to develop viticulture and winemaking could be reduced to such a pathetic state. Now it is one of Europe's most exciting wine-producing countries and, with thousands of unidentified ancient grape varieties preserved in its nurseries, it should be able to delight and surprise wine lovers for centuries to come. Turkey has the potential to rival Greece, but its political and religious constraints will not allow that to happen in our lifetime. The two most up-and-coming wine-producing countries are Lebanon and Israel; wines from here have flourished since the new millennium, as new boutique wineries have started to blossom—quite miraculously, all things considered. There is even improvement in the quality of Egyptian wine, not that it could have become much worse!

VINEYARDS ON THE ISLAND OF CEPHALONIA, GREECE
The wines of origin produced in this appellation range from fresh and fruity dry whites to sweet red liqueur wines.

GREECE

The speed with which the best boutique wineries in this country have turned around the reputation of Greek wines is nothing less than breathtaking. And the future promises to be even better, as they start experimenting with more than 300 untested, but possibly very exciting, indigenous grapes.

THIS IS GOOD NEWS, of course, but it used to be so easy when friends went to Greece for a vacation and asked what they should drink—"If it hasn't got Boutaris, Tsantalis, or Porto Carras on the label," I would say, "don't drink it. And if it's Retsina, pour it down the toilet as a pine disinfectant." While wines from these three producers are still worth drinking, there are now a lot of new boutique wineries to watch out for—and even most of the cooperatives, once the scourge of the Greek wine industry, are making clean, drinkable wines these days. Mind you, Retsina is still more useful as a disinfectant!

ANCIENT GREEK WINES
Between the 13th and 11th centuries BCE, long before a single vine existed in what are now the most famous wine regions of the world, Greek viticulture was at its peak and, along with wheat and olives, was of fundamental importance to the economy. The classic wines of ancient Greece were great wines indeed, relative to their era, and worthy of note in the writings of Hippocrates, Homer, Plato, Pliny, Virgil, and many others. Sources such as these show how sophisticated the viticulture at that time was. Vines were trained in parallel rows, just as they are today, with care taken to ensure proper spacing between each plant, and at least six different methods of pruning and training were employed, depending upon the variety of grape, type of soil, and strength of the wind.

The Greeks taught the Romans all they knew about viticulture, and the Romans took this knowledge to France, Germany, and other parts of the Empire. Wine was the economic foundation of Greek civilization, but with the decline of this civilization went the famous wines of antiquity, and Greek wines now represent a mere two percent of the nation's gross national product.

GREEK WINE TODAY
Over 15 years ago, in the first edition of this encyclopedia, I told a story about the occasion on which I asked Yannis Boutaris, then one of the country's few decent wine producers, why Greek wines were invariably oxidized, maderized, or sometimes just plain bad. Boutaris stretched, raised a gentle smile, and replied that most Greeks actually liked oxidized wines—and that if most Greek producers made fresh, clean wines, they would not be able to sell them on the domestic market and would have to export them. He doubted this would work because most foreigners considered Greek wines to be either dross or Retsina, so no one would buy them.

He was probably right: Greek wines have improved so much over the last decade, yet exports have made little progress. Consumption in Greece has declined sharply, as is the trend in other European countries, as younger consumers refuse the oxidized products their fathers still guzzle; instead they drink less, but better, wine. In such circumstances, the only way the Greek wine industry has survived an influx of new producers has been by reducing production, which, with the help of EU grants to uproot vineyards, is down a third in the last ten years.

FACTORS AFFECTING TASTE AND QUALITY

✶ LOCATION
Greece is located halfway between southern Italy and Turkey. Vines grow throughout the mainland and its many islands, but most are in Macedonia and Peloponnisos.

☼ CLIMATE
Mild winters followed by sub-tropical summers, during which the heat in many vineyards is tempered by sea breezes called *meltemi* and they are bathed in around 3,000 hours of sunshine. Extremes are mountain vineyards in Macedonia, where grapes sometimes fail to ripen, and on Crete, where the summer brings 5 months of intense heat and drought.

⊠ ASPECT
Vines grow on all types of land, from flat coastal sites on the mainland, through rolling hills and river valleys, to mountain slopes. The best sites are north-facing (to avoid the sun) slopes up to 2,000 ft (610 meters) above sea level.

▦ SOIL
Mainland soils are mostly limestone, while those on the islands are rocky and volcanic.

⊞ VITICULTURE AND VINIFICATION
The Greek cooperatives have long been in possession of thermostatically controlled stainless-steel vats as well as other modern equipment, but they have only started to take advantage of this technology since the mid-1990s. The majority of the best Greek wines on the market today are made by small, high-tech, boutique wineries.

🍇 GRAPE VARIETIES
Primary varieties: Agiorgitiko, Assyritiko, Liatiko, Limnio, Malvasia, Mandeleria, Mavrodaphne, Muscat (various subvarieties), Rhoditis, Robola, Xynomavro
Secondary varieties: Cabernet Franc, Cabernet Sauvignon, Chardonnay, Syrah

It was the shipping magnate and multimillionaire John Carras who established the first boutique winery, with the ambition of making the best wine in Greece. Not a great ambition in those days, but he believed that Greek viticulture could recapture its former glory. He built the winery quite close to his luxurious Porto Carras vacation complex on Sithonia, the middle prong of the three peninsulas that jut into the Aegean Sea from the Macedonian mainland. With advice from Professor Émile Peynaud, Carras surrounded the hilly terrain of his winery with 142 acres (350 hectares) of vineyards, including a large proportion of Bordeaux

HARVEST TIME
Harvesting the vineyards of Domaine Porto Carras, which were bulldozed out of the slopes of Sithonia, the middle prong of Halkidiki's three peninsulas.

GREECE
The mainland areas and islands that form modern-day Greece provide a plethora of wine regions. Cooler northern regions produce the best wines, while the island of Samos produces great sweet wines.

varieties. When Peynaud said that some of the hills were in the wrong place or not the right shape, Carras ordered bulldozers to rectify the problem. The first vintage was 1972, but the Greek winemaker made mistakes and was fired; Peynaud poured away most of the wine. The few barrels he retained were mixed with the next vintage, which was processed by Evangelos Gerovassiliou, who had trained in Bordeaux as one of Peynaud's oenology students.

Château Porto Carras became a legend and Gerovassiliou made the wine for many years. He has also set up his own boutique winery, which is equally excellent, and he is involving himself in other quality-led ventures. Other newcomers include Nicholas Cosmetatos of Cephalonia, who was one of the first Greeks to wonder why his fellow countrymen drank oxidized wines.

GREEK LABEL LANGUAGE

ΑΦΡΩΔΗΣ ΟΙΝΟΣ, ΗΜΙΑΦΡΩΔΗΣ
Αφρώδης Οίνος, Ημιαφρώδης
Sparkling wine, semi-sparkling
ΕΛΛΗΝΙΚΟ ΠΡΟΙΟΝ Ελληνικό Προϊόν
Produce of Greece
ΕΠΙΤΡΑΠΕΖΙΟΣ ΟΙΝΟΣ Επιτραπέζιος Οίνος
Table wine
ΕΡΥΘΡΟΣ, Ερυθρός
Red
ΗΜΙΓΛΥΚΟΣ Ημιγλύκος
Sweet, semi-sweet
ΗΜΙΞΗΡΟΣ Ημιξηρός
Dry, semi-dry
ΛΕΥΚΟΣ Λεύκος
White
ΞΗΡΟΣ Ξηρός
Dry

ΟΙΝΟΣ Οίνος or **ΚΡΑΣΙ** Κρασί
Wine
ΟΝΟΜΑΣΙΑ ΚΑΤΑ ΠΑΡΑΔΟΣΗ Ονομασία κατα παράδοση
Traditional appellation (reserved for Retsina only)
ΟΝΟΜΑΣΙΑ ΠΡΟΕΛΕΥΣΕΩΣ ΑΝΩΤΕΡΑΣ ΠΟΙΟΤΗΤΟΣ Ονομασία Προελεύσεως Ανώτερας Ποιότητος
Appellation of Origin of High Quality (listed as AO on pp434–436). Although there are still many wines of ordinary quality bearing this so-called "high quality" appellation, there are no longer any that are actually poor quality, and there are an increasing number that do actually live up to its claim.
ΟΙΝΟΠΟΙΕΙΟΝ Οινοποιείον
Winery

ΠΑΡΑΓΩΓΗ ΚΑΙ ΕΜΦΙΑΛΩΣΕΙΣ
Παραγωγή και Εμφιαλώσεις
Produced and bottled by
ΡΕΤΣΙΝΑ Ρετσίνα
Retsina. May carry no appellation of origin and may therefore be blended
ΡΕΤΣΙΝΑ ΑΤΤΙΚΗΣ Ρετσίνα Αττικής
Retsina with appellation of origin from Attica
ΡΕΤΣΙΝΑ ΕΥΒΟΙΑΣ Ρετσίνα Ευβοίας
Retsina with appellation of origin from Evia
ΡΟΖΕ Ροζέ
Rosé

VINTAGE As Greece belongs to the European Union, the vintage on the label should mean that at least 85 percent of the wine comes from the year indicated.

antiseptic effect of resin, the aroma and flavor of which quickly tainted the stored wine. It was, of course, a false assumption, but in the absence of Pasteur's discoveries (then some twenty-five centuries in the future), it appeared to be supported by the fact that the more resinous the wine, the less it deteriorated. Within a short time, the resin was being added directly to the wine and the only difference between modern and ancient Retsina is that the resin is now added directly to the wine during fermentation, rather than after. The best Retsina is said to come from three areas, Attica, Evia, and Viota, and the best resin, which must be from the Alep or Aleppo pine, comes from Attica.

Strictly speaking, Retsina is not wine. It would be if its pine character were the result of maturation in pine casks, but having pine resin added makes it an aromatized wine, like vermouth. In the first edition, I joked about the possibility of a wine matured in pine casks, but I have since discovered on La Palma "Tea Wine," which is exactly that. Insignificant in volume—and oddity though it is—if it can be done in the Canary Islands, why not in Greece?

Perhaps understandably, his first wine, Gentilini, started out so clean it was clinical, but it has moved on to become one of the country's finest, zippiest whites. Squeaky-cleanliness was a problem for Calligas, too, but its top white, Château Calligas, has been fatter since the early 1990s and this has been lifted by a nifty touch of residual gas. In recent years, numerous small wineries of exceptional talent have cropped up. Some have been around for a while, others are very new, but the best of these include names such as Aidarinis, Antonopoulou, Castanioti, Chrisohoou, Emery, Hatzimichali, Château Lazaridi, Mercouri, Oenoforos, Papaioannou, Château Pegasus, Semeli, Sigalas, and Skouras, with many others, no doubt, waiting in the wings.

RETSINA—BOON OR BURDEN?
Retsina is wine (usually white) to which pine resin is added during fermentation. This practice dates back to antiquity, when wine was stored in jars and amphorae. As they were not airtight, the wines rapidly deteriorated. In the course of time, people learned to seal the jars with a mixture of plaster and resin and the wines lasted longer. This increased longevity was attributed to the

DOMAINE PORTO CARRAS
Looking out across the blue waters of the Aegean to the fishing village of Maramas from the vineyards of Domaine Porto Carras, which also consists of a luxurious leisure and sports complex.

THE APPELLATIONS OF
GREECE

AO = Appellation of Origin
TA = Traditional Appellation
TI = Topikos Inos (Regional Wine, similar to the French *vin de pays*)

AMYNDEO AO *or* AMYNTAION AO
Macedonia

One of the most exciting, up-and-coming wine regions in Greece, Amyndeo is also the most northerly of this country's appellations, with vines growing at an altitude of 2,046 to 2,343 feet (620 to 710 meters). Until relatively recently, virtually all the output has been from the Amyntaion cooperative, and although the quality has been sporadic, the occasional gem has given hope of what might be. That hope has now been realized by the brilliant, *terroir*-driven Alpha Estate, which planted 11 international and indigenous grape varieties in the late 1990s, using the latest partial rootzone drying techniques and low yields to produce some beautifully structured wines. Most of

these wines are not pure Xinomavro, thus cannot claim the Amyndeo appellation, but are all outstanding. The non-appellation reds are particularly impressive, although I have a feeling that the wines released so far offer only an inkling of the quality that is to come. Yannis Boutaris is also trying hard at the Vegoritis winery, established in 1997.

🍇 Xinomavro

⌛ 2–12 years (non-AO whites 1–3 years)

✓ *Alpha Estate* (Unfiltered Xinomavro)

ANCHIALOS AO *or* ANHIALOS AO
Thessaly

This is a medium-bodied, dry white wine from the Nea Anchialos area on the Gulf of Pegassitikos near Volos. The local cooperative wine is clean, though unexciting. Babatzim wines are clean, acceptable, and improving.

🍇 Savatiano, Rhoditis, Sykiotis

⌛ 1–2 years

ARCHANES AO *or* ARHÁNES AO
Crete

The local cooperative makes the usual range of clean but unexceptional table wines, including a very ordinary red under the Archánes appellation. Vangelis Lidakis's non-appellation blend of Kotsifáli and Cabernet is the stand-out in this region.

🍇 Kotsifáli, Mandilariá

⌛ 2–7 years

✓ *Boutari* (Domaine Fantaxometocho) • *Vangelis Lidakis*

CÔTES DE MELITON AO *or* PLAYIES MELITONA AO
Macedonia

This appellation covers the red, white, and rosé wines of Sithonia, the middle of Halkidiki's three peninsulas, and was established by Domaine Porto Carras, the brainchild of the late

John Carras. Although secondary to the tourist resort of Porto Carras, the winery was profitable, whereas the tourist resort swallowed all the money, eventually bankrupting both ventures, which were sold to the Technical Olympic group in 2000. In the early 1980s, Domaine Porto Carras and, in particular, its flagship Château Porto Carras, became the first Greek wines of modern times to establish a truly international reputation. This was thanks to the aspirations of John Carras, which urged him to hire Bordeaux consultant Professor Peynaud, and Peynaud's choice of his ex-pupil Evangelos Gerovassiliou (*see* Epanomi TI, *below*) as winemaker. With the exception of the rich, classy Syrah, the Domaine wines are generally light, and are best enjoyed young, whereas the top-of-the-range Château Porto Carras has always been a rich-flavored, full-bodied, deep-colored red wine of true *vin-de-garde* quality.

🍇 Assyrtico, Athiri, Cabernet Franc, Cabernet Sauvignon, Cinsault, Grenache, Limnio, Petite Sirah, Rhoditis, Sauvignon Blanc, Savatiano, Ugni Blanc, Xinomavro

🍷 1–2 years (Château Porto Carras: 5–8 years for lighter vintages; 10–20 years for bigger)

✓ *Domaine Porto Carras*

DAFNÉS AO
Crete

Douloufakis is the best-known producer of these red wines, which may be dry or sweet.

🍇 *Liatiko*

DRAMA TI
Macedonia

Huddled between the Falakro, Menekio, and Peggio mountains, this regional appellation is grabbing attention primarily due to the huge investment in two of its wineries—Domaine Constantin Lazaridi (also known as Kosta or Kostas Lazaridis) at Adriani and Château Niko Lazaridi (also known as Nico or Nicos Lazaridis) at Agora—and the excellent, sometimes superb, wines that they have produced. But they are by no means the only excellent producers in this exciting new area.

🍇 Agiorgitiko, Assyrtico, Cabernet Sauvignon, Chardonnay, Limnio, Merlot, Rhoditis, Sauvignon Blanc, Semillon, Ugni Blanc

🍷 2–7 years (red), 1–2 years (white)

✓ *Kostas Lazaridis* (Cava Amethystos) • *Château Nico Lazaridi* (Maghiko Vuono red & white) • *Pavlidis* (Assyrtico) • *Wine Art Estate* (Idisma Drios Merlot, Techni Alipias Chardonnay and roze)

EPANOMI TI
Macedonia

This wine region has been put on the map single-handedly by Evangelos Gerovassiliou, the winemaker who made the first great Greek wine of modern times: Château Porto Carras. Gerovassiliou planted experimental vines on his family's property in 1981, while still working for Domaine Porto Carras, and has had no formal relationship with that winery since the Carras family relinquished ownership (*see* Côtes de Meliton AO) in 1999. The low, hilly land of Epanomi might not be the greatest place in Greece to grow wine grapes, but under Gerovassiliou, it definitely produces some of the country's greatest wines, both red and—particularly—white. The outstanding red is Syrah, while excellent whites include Fumé,

Malagousia, and Viognier, but all Domaine Gerovassiliou wines come highly recommended.

🍇 Negoska, Xinomavro

🍷 3–8 years

✓ *Gerovassiliou*

GOUMENISSA AO
Macedonia

A light-bodied red wine from the Goumenissa district, northeast of Naoussa. Usually a wine of good fruit and a certain elegance, the best undergo a light maturation in cask and can be relatively rich in flavor.

🍇 Negoska, Xinomavro

🍷 3–8 years

✓ *Aidarini* • *Boutari* (Filliria)

KEFALONIA AO *or* CEPHALONIA AO
Ionian Islands

There are three wines of origin in this appellation: Kefalonia or Robola of Kefalonia, Mavrodaphne of Kefalonia, and Muscat of Kefalonia. Kefalonia or Robola of Kefalonia is a dry white wine that can be fresh and floral, with an almost racy nose and a tangy, lightly rich, delicate-lemon fruity flavor. In the past, this wine has all too often been spoiled by sloppy winemaking, but most producers have cleaned up their act. The Mavrodaphne of Kefalonia is a sweet red liqueur wine similar in character to the Mavrodaphne of Patras (but not quite in the same class), while Muscat of Kefalonia is one of the lesser-known, sweet liqueur wines from the Muscat grape. Gentilini's non-appellation Syrah is probably the best single wine produced here.

🍇 Mavrodaphne, Muscat Blanc à Petits Grains, Robola

🍷 1–2 years (Robola), 1–10 years (Mavrodaphne), upon purchase (Muscat), 2–7 years (Syrah)

✓ *Gentilini* ◉

KRANIA TI
Thessaly

Dimitrios Katsaros produces a godlike Cabernet-Merlot blend and a very good, improving Chardonnay from vines growing on the slopes of Mount Olympus.

🍇 Cabernet Sauvignon, Chardonnay, Merlot

🍷 2–7 years (reds), 2–4 years (whites)

✓ *Katsaros*

LIMNOS AO *or* LEMNOS AO
The Aegean

There are two wines of origin produced in this appellation: Limnos and Muscat of Limnos. Limnos is an unfortified Muscat wine that may be made in dry, off-dry, and semi-sweet styles. It is usually soft and flowery, with an attractive Muscat aroma, followed by clean fruit. Muscat of Limnos is a superior liqueur Muscat wine that is richer and sweeter than Patras, though not in the class of Samos. So-called Muscat of Limnos Grand Cru is its sweetest style.

🍷 Upon purchase

✓ *Limnos Cooperative* • *Tsantali*

MANTINÍA AO
Peloponnese

This is a dry white wine from mountain vineyards in the center of the Peloponnese. The vines grow at an altitude of 2,130 feet (650

meters) and there are some very fresh, young wines with nice, lively fruit. Tselepos's non-appellation wines, such as Vareli, Cabernet-Merlot blend, and Merlot, are at least as good as its Mantinia.

🍇 Minimum of 85% Moschophilero, plus optional Asproúdes

🍷 Upon purchase

✓ *Antonopoulos* • *Cambas* • *Spyropoulos* • *Tselepos*

MESSENIKOLA AO
Peloponnese

This appellation was introduced in 1994, but has not exactly taken off. The primary variety, Mavro Messenikola, is grown at between 825 and 990 feet (250 and 300 meters).

🍇 70% Mavro Messenikola, 30% Carignane and Syrah

NAOUSSA AO
Macedonia

These generally reliable wines are grown west of Thessalonika, at a height of 1,150 feet (350 meters) on the southeastern slopes of Mount Velia. Although I give only rock-solid recommendations, I cautiously suggest that almost any Naoussa could be worth the gamble; the growers took a pride in their wine long before their peers did elsewhere. Good Naoussa is well-colored, rich, and aromatic, with heaps of spicy fruit and a long finish. Great Naoussa is world class. Yannis Boutaris's Kyr-Yanni is one of Naoussa's greatest, up-and-coming wineries, and his Yanakohori—a Xinomavro-Merlot blend—is at least as good as his excellent Xinomavro Ramnistas.

🍇 Xinomavro

🍷 4–15 years

✓ *Chrisohoou* • *Dalamaras* • *Karydas* • *Kyr-Yanni* (Xinomavro Ramnistas)

NEMEA AO
Peloponnese

This is a relatively reliable appellation and there is a local pride similar to that in Naoussa. Grown in the Corinth district at an altitude of between 820 and 2,620 feet (250 and 800 meters), the Agiorgitiko grape provides a deep-colored, full, and spicy red wine that can be spoiled by dried-out fruit, or by a lack of fruit. Known locally as the Blood of Hercules, because his blood was shed when he killed the Nemean lion, this wine has been produced for 2,500 years. Kokotos's *vins de pays* under his Château Semeli label are even better than his Semeli Nemea, and Skouras's Megas Oenos (*see* Other Wines, p436) is at least as classy as its Nemea.

🍇 Agiorgitiko

🍷 5–20 years

✓ *Gaia* (Estate) • *Kokotos* (Semeli) • *Kourtakis* (Kouros) • *Papaïoannou* (Palea Klimata) • *Parparoussis* (Epilegmenos) • *Skouras* (Aghiorghitiko, Grande Cuvée)

PANGEON TI
Macedonia

This regional wine area is south of Drama, in an ocean-influenced, mountainous microclimate, the elevation and weather of which result in a significantly longer growing season. Pangeon was effectively discovered and established by Vassilis Tsaktsarlis and Evangelos Gerovassiliou (*see* Côtes de Meliton AO and Epanomi TI), who started planting their vineyard at Kokkinohori as recently as 1999. Pangeon promises an even more exciting quality than Drama.

🍇 Agiorgitiko, Cabernet Sauvignon, Chardonnay, Merlot, Sémillon, Syrah

🍷 3–8 years

✓ *Biblia Chora*

PAROS AO
The Cyclades

This is a deep-colored, light-bodied red wine from the Mandilaria grape, which I have tasted only once. My notes record a very strange, but difficult to describe, taste. A rich, dry, white wine from the Monemvassia grape (which some believe to be the original Malvasia), is also produced, but I have not tasted it.

🍇 *Mandilaria, Monemvassia*

PATRAS AO
Peloponnese

There are four different wines of origin produced in this appellation in the hilly hinterland of Patras in the Peloponnese: Patras, Mavrodaphne of Patras, Muscat of Patras, and Muscat Rion of Patras. Patras plain and simple is a light, dry white wine made exclusively from the Rhoditis grape. These wines were once dull and flabby, but are now clean and crisp, although seldom excite, with Antonopoulos's Alepou about as good as it gets (and nowhere near the quality of its non-appellation Cabernet-Nea Dris; *see* Other Wines, below). Mavrodaphne of Patras is a rich, sweet, red liqueur wine with a velvety smooth, sweet-oak finish. Often compared to a Recioto della Valpolicella, a good Mavrodaphne is in my opinion far better, although it does have a similar raisiny-sherry oxidative aroma. One delightful aspect of this wine is that it can be drunk with equal pleasure when it is either young and fruity or smooth and mature. Muscat of Patras is a gold-colored, sweet, liqueur Muscat wine that can be delicious in its typically raisiny way, as can the Muscat Rion (or Rio) of Patras, which comes from Rion/Rio in Patras.

🍇 Mavrodaphne, Muscat Blanc à Petits Grains, Rhoditis

🍷 1–2 years (Patras), 1–20 years (Mavrodaphne), upon purchase (Muscat)

✓ **Patras** *Antonopoulos* (Adoli Ghis) • *Oenoforos* (Asprolithi) **Muscat of Patras** *Achaia Clauss* (Collector Series) **Muscat Rion (or Rio) of Patras** *Parparousis*

PEZA AO
Crete

The white wines are made from the Vilána grape and lack crispness, and the red wines, which are made from the Kotsifáli and Mandilaria grapes, are usually dried-out and could be fresher.

🍇 Kotsifali, Mandilaria, Vilána

RAPSANI AO
Thessaly

Uninspiring dry red wines from flat, uninspiring land in the vicinity of Mount Olympus.

🍇 Krasáto, Stavrotó, Xinomavro

RETSINA TA
Central Greece

Although rosé is not unknown, Retsina is almost invariably white, with 85 percent of the blend coming from the Savatiano grape. It may be blended from various areas or can have a specific, usually superior, origin, but in every case, Retsina carries the unique Traditional Appellation. This designation recognizes the ancient practice of resinating wine and the EU has confined its use to Greece.

There are degrees of resination, ranging from relatively light to heavy, and the quality of the pine resin itself can range from poor to fine; the better-quality pine resin makes better-quality Retsina. Despite its penetrating aroma and flavor, pine resin cannot hide a tired, flabby, oxidized, or simply bad wine. Personally, I do not like Retsina, but I have to admit that the aroma of fine pine resin is refreshing and I also agree that this aromatized wine has a useful cutting quality when drunk with oily Greek food.

🍇 Rhoditis, Savatiano

🍷 As young and as fresh as possible

✓ **Appellations** *Attica • Evia • Thebes • Viota* **Brands** *Gaia* (Ritinitis Nobilis)

RODOS AO *or* RHODES AO
The Dodecanese

Reds are 100 percent Mandilaria, whites are 100 percent Athiri; neither of which has so far amounted to much. The best wines are the sweet, golden, liqueur Muscat, the best of which are on a par with the Muscat of Patras. Other non-appellation wines produced on this island include the *méthode champenoise* wines of CAIR, the local cooperative, but they are rather coarse with an overly assertive mousse.

🍇 Amorgiano (aka Mandilaria), Athiri, Muscat Blanc à Petits Grains, Trani Muscat

🍷 Upon purchase

✓ *CAIR* (Muscat of Rhodes)

SAMOS AO
The Aegean

One of the great sweet wines of the world, the local cooperative's Samos, Samos Grand Cru, Samos Nectar, and Samos Anthemis, in order of increasing complexity and sweetness, are all superb, perfectly-balanced, rich, and mellifluous wines. The cooperative also produces a deliciously dry and fresh non-appellation version called Doryssa, and two that are off-dry: Samena and Samena Gold, which are both as clean as a whistle with a

delightful orange flower-water aroma and delicate fruit.

🍇 Muscat Blanc à Petits Grains

🍷 Upon purchase

✓ *Cambas • Samos cooperative*

SANTORINI AO
The Cyclades

This full-bodied, dry white wine can have an intriguing combination of high natural alcohol and a high acidity level. Sweet *vin de liqueur*, *vin doux naturel*, and *vin de paille* styles are also produced. Sigalas makes the best quality, most complete range within this appellation.

🍇 Aidani, Assyrtiko

🍷 2–5 years

✓ *Boutaris* (Nyhteri) • *Gaia* (Thalassitis) • *Kostas Antoniou* (Vareli, Vinsanto) • *Sigalas* (Bareli)

SITIA AO
Crete

The red wines in this appellation can be dry or sweet, fortified or not. White wines must be dry and cannot be fortified. They have traditionally been somewhat rustic in character, but the Sitia cooperative has improved out of all recognition, and Yannis Economou has been working hard since the mid-1990s to bring some elegance and finesse to his wines.

🍇 80% Liatiko plus 20% Mandilaria (reds), minimum 70% Vilána plus optional Thrapsathíri (whites)

✓ *Economou • Sitia cooperative*

ZITSA AO
Epirus

Dry and semi-sweet, slightly spritzy, clean, and fruity white wine from six villages around Zitsa, northwest of Ioánnina, where the vines grow at an altitude of 1,970 feet (600 meters). Most of this appellation's production is processed by the cooperative.

🍇 Debina

🍷 Upon purchase

✓ *Ioánninan cooperative* (Orion)

OTHER WINES
Some of the country's best wines do not claim any of the above appellations.

RED

✓ *Alpha Estate* (Ktima Alpha) • *Antonopoulos* (Cabernet Nea-Dris) • *Boutaris* (Grande Reserve) • *Calligas* (Nostos) • *Evharis* (Estate Red, Merlot) • *Hatzimichali* (Cava) • *Mercouri* (Antaris, Cava) • *Parparoussis* (Oenofilos) • *Skouras* (Mega Oenos) • *Tsantalis* (Merlot) • *Tselepos* (Kokkinomylos Merlot) • *Voyatzis* (Erythros)

WHITE

✓ *Alpha Estate* (Ktima Alpha, Sauvignon Blanc) • *Antonopoulos* (Chardonnay) • *Chrisohoou* (Prekniáriko) • *Gentilini* (Fumé) • *Oenoforos* (Asprolithi, Lagorthi) • *Papaïoannou* (Chardonnay) • *Tsantali* (Ampelonas) • *Voyatzi* (Malvasia)

DRY ROSÉ

✓ *Emery* (Granrosé) • *Gentilini* (Rosé) • *Oenoforos* (Esperitis)

SPARKLING WHITE

✓ *Spiroloulos* (Oude Panos) • *Tselepos* (Villa Amalia)

THE LEVANT

In 1988, when this encyclopedia was first published, I wrote that aside from two wineries in Lebanon and one in Israel, "fine wine is nonexistent in the Levant." Who would have thought that after all the bloody troubles those two war-torn countries have been through since, we would find such growth, diversification, and exhilarating promise in the wines from Lebanon and Israel as we do today? But we do, and, essentially, this is down to the boom in boutique wineries in these two countries over the past decade.

WINE WAS FIRST PRODUCED in Mesopotamia (an area roughly equivalent to modern-day Iraq) circa 4000 BCE. In recent times, most vineyards throughout this region have been used for the production of table grapes, raisins, and currants. The 1960s were a golden age for Lebanese wine and, indeed, Lebanon in general, but the outside world did not really know anything about wines from the Levant until the early 1980s. It was the success of Serge Hochar at Château Musar in Lebanon that drew our attention to the wine potential of this region. In the 1960s, Hochar's wines had been the favorite of certain French colonial officers, attracting them away from Château Ksara, their previous Lebanese favorite; but 1979 was the seminal year, as it was then that he showed his wines at the Bristol Wine Fair in England. In the late 1980s, Yarden put Israel on the wine map, but it was not until the early 2000s that more than a hundred boutique wineries gave these two pioneering Levant wine-producing countries real credibility.

CYPRUS

Wine districts: *Marathassa Afames, Pitsilia, Maheras Mountains, Troödos Mountains, Mesaoria*
Total area under vine: *4,520 acres (18,300 hectares)*
Wines have been made on this beautiful island for at least 4,000

Intensive vine-growing zone

Turkey
- Thrace-Marmara
- Aegean Coast
- Ankara
- Central Anatolia
- Mediterranean Coast
- Black Sea Coast
- Eastern Anatolia

Syria
- Aleppo
- Homs
- Damascus

Lebanon
- Bekaa Valley
- Other winemaking areas of the Levant

Israel
1. Galilee
2. Shomron
3. Samson
4. Negev
5. Judean Hills

- - - International boundary
▲ Height above sea level (meters)

0   50   100   150   200 miles
0   100   200   300 km

THE LEVANT
Among the disparate group of countries that form the area known as the Levant, Lebanon and Israel currently produce the finest wines.

years and Cyprus's historically famous wine, Commanderie St John, is one of a handful that claim to be the world's oldest wine. It can be traced back to 1191, when Richard the Lionheart, King of England, acquired the island during the Crusades. He subsequently sold it to the Order of the Knights of the Temple, who established themselves as Commanderies and later became known as the Knights of the Order of St. John. Commanderie St John is a *solera*-matured, sweet dessert wine, which is made from a blend of black and white grapes that have been left in the sun for between 10 and 15 days after the harvest to shrivel and concentrate the grape sugars. It used to be rich and luscious with a fine, toasty fullness, but there is nothing special about the wine produced today. Those privileged enough to taste rarities dating back to the turn of the 20th century will recognize just how great these wines once were.

In recent years, early harvesting, temperature-controlled stainless-steel vats, and various modern vinification techniques have revolutionized Cypriot winemaking, producing much lighter, cleaner, and crisper wines. The large cooperative producers are cutting down the time taken to get the harvest to the winery, delays which were detrimental to the quality of their wines at one time. KEO, the island's largest and most advanced winery, is making the greatest strides toward improving quality, while the emergence of small, independent wineries since the early 1990s is only just beginning to offer consumers real choice.

Fikardos (Achillas, Chardonnay Xilogefiro) • *K & K Vasilikon* (Ayios Onoufrios, Xynisteri) • *KEO* (Domaine d'Ahera, Fino, Heritage, Othello, Rosella)

EGYPT

Wine district: *Abu Hummus*
Total area under vine: *165,490 acres (67,000 hectares)*
When traveling to the Nile Delta, it has always been advisable to refuse the ice, and until very recently, the same advice should also have applied to the foul-tasting Egyptian wine. This was not only because of poor winemaking, but also due to the temperature of the storage facility at the sole winery, Gianaclis, which was a mind-boggling 104°F (40°C). The Gianaclis Winery was offered for privatization by the Egyptian government in 1999, and the successful bidder was the Al-Ahram Beverages Company (ABC), which in theory had a virtual monopoly on both wine and (far more importantly) beer, but had no time to enjoy this before it was challenged by the El Gouna Beverages Company. Although Egyptian wine has not been of sufficient quality to export, and attracts a 100 percent tax on the domestic market, foreign imports face a 300 percent tax, thus sales to tourists are potentially very lucrative. El Gouna started up in 1999, and immediately began to undercut ABC's prices, marketing its products so aggressively that it quickly captured 15 percent of domestic beer sales and 40 percent of domestic wine sales. ABC could not compete, so it took over El Gouna in 2001, and the fat profits from its monopoly of the tourist drinks trade attracted its own take-over by the Dutch brewing group Heineken.

The good news is that ABC began to plant classic grape varieties and to modernize the winemaking facilities from the moment it took over Gianaclis. The bad news is that the government has withdrawn start-up incentives offered to both ABC and El Gouna, and as long as there is no competition, there is little incentive to improve quality beyond a basic, acceptable, clean product. And just how authentic is Egyptian wine, in any case, when there are tales of the Gianaclis Winery buying in 200 tons of (mainly) Cinsault and Cabernet Sauvignon grapes from Lebanon in 2004?

ISRAEL

Wine districts: *Galilee/Galil, Shomron/Samaria, Samson/Shimshon, Judean Hills, Negev*
Total area under vine: *14,820 acres (6,000 hectares)*
Over the last five years, we have seen a raft of small, independent wineries come on stream, forcing the biggest producers, notably Golan Heights (Yarden), Carmel (including the new Yatir winery), and Barkan, constantly to raise their game. This boutique boom started in the 1990s, and by the turn of the new millennium, there were 70 or so small new wineries on the scene, but by 2005 this had increased to no fewer than 140. Yet, paradoxically, while this is the most exciting time ever for the quality and diversity of Israeli wines, it is also financially the most precarious period in the wine industry's history, with huge losses incurred by a number of wineries, large and small. However, a series of sell-outs and mergers should see the Israeli wine industry settle down over the next five years.

Castel (Grand Vin) • *Chateau Golan* (Eliad, Merlot, Syrah) • *Flam* (Cabernet Sauvignon Reserve) • *Yarden* (Cabernet Sauvignon, Cabernet Sauvignon Elrom Vineyard, Katzrin Red, Merlot Ortel Vineyard) • *Yatir* (Forest)

JORDAN

Wine district: *Amman-Zarqua*
Total area under vine: *9,880 acres (4,000 hectares)*
A country where the vine once flourished, Jordan's fast-diminishing vineyards now cover barely more than one-quarter of the area they did as recently as the late 1990s, and only a small percentage of these vines produce wine, averaging just 67,000 cases (6,000 hectoliters) a year. Jordanians are not wine drinkers, preferring Arrack, the aniseed-flavored spirit ubiquitous in the Levant.

FACTORS AFFECTING TASTE AND QUALITY

LOCATION
Technically, the Levant comprises the countries along the eastern Mediterranean shores, which for practical reasons this encyclopedia has extended northwest to Turkey, southwest to Egypt, east to Jordan, and this necessitates that Cyprus is also included.

CLIMATE
Hot and dry for the most part, with a minority of cooler microclimates due to their proximity to the Mediterranean, or high altitude. Vines in Lebanon's Bekaa Valley receive an amazing 300 days of sunshine per year and no rain during the harvest.

ASPECT
Vines grow on all types of land from coastal plains to higher mountain slopes.

SOIL
Soils vary greatly from volcanic origin on Cyprus, through the alluvial river and sandy coastal plains to the Bekaa Valley's gravel over limestone.

VITICULTURE AND VINIFICATION
Better-quality vineyards are being planted on higher mountain slopes,
grapes are being harvested at lower sugar levels, and the resulting wines are being fermented at cooler temperatures, with increasing use of new French oak for top-of-the-range wines.

GRAPE VARIETIES
Cypriot Grape Varieties:
Cabernet Sauvignon, Chardonnay, Grenache, Maratheftiko, Mavro, Opthalmo, Xineisteri
Israeli Grape Varieties:
Cabernet Franc, Cabernet Sauvignon, Carignan, Chardonnay, Colombard, Merlot, Riesling, Sauvignon Blanc
Note The Argaman, an Israeli *Souzão* x *Carignan* cross of disappointing quality, is being removed
Lebanese Grape Varieties:
Cabernet Sauvignon, Carignan, Chardonnay, Chasselas, Cinsault, Clairette, Gamay, Grenache, Muscat (various), Obaideh, Pinot Noir, Riesling, Sémillon, Syrah, Ugni Blanc
Turkish Grape Varieties:
Adakarasi, Ak Dimrit, Alicante Bouschet, Beylerce, Boğazkere, Burdur Dirmiti, Cabernet Sauvignon, Calkarasi, Carignan, Clairette, Dökülgen, Emir, Gamay, Kalecik Karası, Misket, Narince, Oküzgözü, Semillon, Sultaniye

LEBANON

Wine district: *Bekaa Valley*
Total area under vine: *37,000 acres (15,000 hectares)*
Although Lebanon's vineyards have shrunk from 66,690 acres (27,000 hectares) since the mid-1990s, the vines used for winemaking are on the increase. Only 10 percent of Lebanon's vineyards are used for wine, and they are mostly confined to the Bekaa Valley, where there is a ten-fold potential for expansion. The Bekaa Valley was put on the wine map by Serge Hochar, owner of Château Musar, during the 15-year civil war when he had to contend with Syrian tanks, Israeli jets, and all sorts of militia to get his grapes from the vineyards to his winery. At one time, Musar and Lebanese wine were synonymous, but its high volatile-acidity (VA) style makes Musar a yesterday wine. I have read that Hochar reduced VA levels in 1995, yet when tasting with him in 2001, he admitted that he has actually given instructions that the wines must have high minimum VA levels! The Hochar second wine is said to be new-style, but it is still old-style and fails to impress. It would be sad if Serge Hochar, who has been such a great ambassador for Lebanese wine, learns the hard way that reputations do not last forever and are easier to lose than gain. In the meantime, there are a number of more modern producers, with numerous new ventures in the pipeline.

✓ *Chateau Belle-Vue* (La Renaissance) • *Chateau Kefraya* (Chateau Kefraya, Comte de M) • *Chateau Ksara* (Chardonnay, Cuvee de Printemps, Vin Gris) • *Clos St. Thomas* (Chateau St. Thomas) • *Massaya* (Selection) • *Wardy* (Private Selection)

SYRIA

Wine districts: *Aleppo, Homs, Damascus*
Total area under vine: *185,250 acres (75,000 hectares)*
In ancient times, wine was second only to olives in terms of agricultural production in Syria. However, since Muslims now account for 90 percent of the country's population, the vines planted are mostly used for table grapes, raisins, and currants, with wine production rarely exceeding 90,000 cases (8,000 hectoliters) a year. The above-mentioned winegrowing districts are located on lower mountain slopes.

It was, apparently, French troops stationed in the country during World War II who were the catalyst for the wine industry that does exist today—because the French, being French, demanded wine. And if you want to taste Syrian wines, visit France, where an increasing number of Syrian-made "Lebanese" wines are finding their way onto Lebanese and North African restaurant wine lists!

TURKEY

Wine districts: *Thrace-Marmara, Ankara, Mediterranean Coast, Black Sea Coast, Central Anatolia, Central-South Anatolia, East Anatolia*
Total area under vine: *1,383,200 acres (560,000 hectares)*
This country has the fourth-largest area under vine in the world (after Spain, Italy, and France), but because its population is predominantly Muslim, most vines produce table grapes, raisins, or currants. Just 2.5 percent of Turkish vineyards produce wine. Perhaps surprisingly, there are over 100 wineries in Turkey, but their wines are generally flabby, too alcoholic, heavy, over-sulfured, and all too often oxidized. The best known are Trakya (dry white Sémillon from Thrace), Trakya Kirmisi (a red blend of native grapes that also comes from Thrace), and the amusingly named Duo Hosbag (red Gamay, from Thrace) and Buzbag (red wine made from native grapes grown in southeast Anatolia), but

RECENT LEVANT VINTAGES

2003 Excellent reds and good whites produced in Lebanon, which benefited from a wet winter, providing water reserves, and a dry harvest. Israeli vines also benefited from an abundance of winter rain, and Israel was even more successful than Lebanon for both reds and whites.

2002 Another excellent year for Lebanon, particularly the reds, but below-average quality and quantity in Israel, where the best wines are merely early drinking.

2001 Below average in quality for Lebanese wines, although reds are better than whites. Above average in Israel, with reds also having the edge over whites.

2000 Good to average quality in Lebanon, good to very good in Israel, where whites were slightly more successful than reds.

1999 A truly great vintage for Lebanon, especially for red wines, but only above average in Israel.

despite local fame, these wines should be avoided. The right varieties in well-selected sites could have a much greater potential in Turkey than the same grapes grown in either Lebanon or Israel, and with sufficient investment, technology, and passion, Turkey could even compete with Greece in terms of quality. There has been some investment since the second half of the 1990s, but media claims in early 2005 that Turkish wine production had enjoyed a "20 percent year-on-year growth" over the previous 10 years were a case of gross exaggeration. The latest reliable statistics available at the time of writing show a 27 percent decline between 1996 and 2001.

Political and religious considerations make significant foreign investment unlikely in the near future. However, it is worth noting that the best Turkish wine boasting any track record is Villa Doluca, and until the firm of Doluca was founded in 1926 by Nihat Kutman, the entire wine industry in this country was non-Muslim. Obviously, the religious dimension is not the brick wall that some might think. Kutman's son, Davis-trained Ahmet Kutman, teamed up with his old school buddy Güven Nil to establish Sarafin, a project involving the establishment of Sauvignon Blanc, Chardonnay, Cabernet Sauvignon, and Merlot vineyards at Saroz Bay on the Gallipoli Peninsula. That these wines have set new standards in Turkish winemaking is just a hint of what might lie in store.

✓ *Doluca* (Kav, Villa Doluca) • *Safarin* (Chardonnay, Merlot)

CYPRIOT VINEYARDS
One of the island's thriving winemaking areas is located in the foothills of the Troödos Mountains.

The WINES of
THE AFRICAS

THE OLD WORLD MEETS THE NEW WORLD
on the African continent, although they are
thousands of miles apart. There is no interest, let
alone excitement, in the former French colonies
of Algeria, Morocco, or Tunisia. The wine
industries in these increasingly fundamentalist
Islamic countries face difficult times, but if they
can survive, there is certainly potential and it is
only a matter of time before a flock of flying
winemakers arrives to exploit it. If and when this
happens, our perception of North African wine
could change profoundly. There are a number of
commercial wineries on Madagascar and a few
curiosities found in Ethiopia, Kenya, Namibia,
and Tanzania. The French even have a *vins de
pays* on the island of Réunion. But the class act
in Africa is, of course, South African wine. We
saw its exports soar in the Mandela years, but
that was merely filling the void created by its
isolation under apartheid. Sales of South African
wine in the second half of the 1990s were little
more than an international expression of
solidarity with the new Rainbow State. Since
2000, however, a technological revolution has
transformed the quality and diversity of Cape
wine, putting this country on a firm footing as
a New World player that is second to none.

FRANSCHOEK VALLEY IN THE PAARL REGION, SOUTH AFRICA
*An aerial view of vineyards that are higher and steeper than most
of the Paarl region, and well suited to red wines.*

SOUTH AFRICA

As export markets opened up in the mid-1990s, so the quality of South African wine started to blossom, but by the turn of the millennium it had gone into overdrive, as new vineyards got on board, and winemakers grasped every opportunity to hone their skills in the full glare of international attention. Some observers have called on South Africa to focus its attention on those varieties it grows best, but this country has only just come in from the cold, and the next couple of decades will see plenty of experimentation.

AT FIRST, BETTER QUALITY simply meant stricter selection and, where appropriate, a massive investment in new oak, but an increasing amount of South Africa's growing export income has been plowed into the industry's Vine Improvement Programme (VIP). Phase one of VIP concentrates on clonal selection and rootstock improvement, while phase two analyzes the suitability to specific *terroirs* of various combinations of the clones and rootstocks the plan develops. It is so ambitious that the project will probably never end, but after such a lengthy period of international isolation it was essential to revitalize the country's vineyards. However, VIP has already manifested itself in wines of richer varietal character and greater complexity than ever before, and South Africa, which was once 10 years behind the rest of the world, is now at the forefront of viticultural research.

IN THE BEGINNING

Virtually all South Africa's vineyards are found within 100 miles (160 kilometers) of Cape Town. The first vines were planted in 1655 and the wines were not, by all accounts, particularly successful. Simon van der Stel, who arrived in 1679, complained about the "revolting sourness" of the local wines. He proceeded to remedy the situation by founding Constantia, the most illustrious wine farm in the country's history (this has since split into three properties: Groot Constantia, Klein Constantia, and Buitenverwachting).

RECENT SOUTH AFRICAN VINTAGES

2004 An excellent vintage for both reds and whites, due to a long, drawn-out ripening period, providing ripe grapes with exceptional extract and acidity. However, the delayed maturity of early-ripening varieties meant that they were picked at the same time as some late-ripening varieties, which caused a congestion in many wineries.

2003 Very good quality across the board, with some standout reds, but some late-ripening varieties proved difficult.

2002 A vintage of variable quality that succeeded in separating the wheat from the chaff, as the most carefully tended vineyards produced winning wines.

2001 Some great wines, both red and white. However, others from this vintage are just good to very good, and far too many are rather big and alcoholic.

2000 The third in a trio of fiercely hot and dry vintages, in which those producers with water dams that did not run dry made good, but alcoholic, red wines.

Three centuries of winemaking

The arrival of French Huguenots, with their viticultural and winemaking expertise, greatly improved the quality of Cape wines, and by the early 1700s they were beginning to be held in high esteem. When French Revolutionary forces entered the Netherlands in 1806, the British occupied the Cape and, cut off from supplies of French wines, began exporting South African wines to the many corners of their empire, enhancing the wines' growing reputation there.

By 1859, the export of Cape wines to Britain alone had reached 1 million gallons (45,000 hectoliters) per year. However, in Britain, Richard Cobden (the "apostle of the free market") and William Gladstone secretly negotiated a commercial treaty with the French that had a devastating effect on this wine industry. In 1860, Cape wine exports fell to 22,000 hectoliters; the next year this dropped to 5,700 hectoliters; and by 1865 as little as 4,200 hectoliters were being exported.

FACTORS AFFECTING TASTE AND QUALITY

LOCATION
South Africa is on the southernmost tip of the African continent.

CLIMATE
The climate is generally mild Mediterranean, but coastal areas have a much higher rainfall and are cooler than inland parts in spring and fall. All coastal areas are cooled by sea breezes chilled by the icy Benguela current from Antarctica. The coolest, Constantia, like Stellenbosch, rates as low Region III. Klein Karoo, Tulbagh, Olifants River, and parts of Paarl (Dal Josaphat) are the hottest, falling between high Region IV and low Region V (*see* p.470).

ASPECT
Most vines are cultivated flat on gently undulating valley floors. More recently, higher slopes have been increasingly cultivated and Klein Constantia, Thelema Mountain Vineyard, Bellingham, and Boschendal all have very steep vineyards.

SOIL
Soils range from gravel and heavy loams of sandstone, shale, and granitic origin on the coastal plain, to the deep alluvial, sandy, and lime-rich, red-shale soils of Klein Karoo and other river valleys.

VITICULTURE AND VINIFICATION
Contrary to popular belief, Cape vineyards sometimes fail even to ripen their grapes, although there are, of course, many hot areas where vines may suffer from heat-stress and grapes can quickly overripen. Irrigation is often necessary in Robertson, Worcester, and Vredendal, where successful cultivation depends on the availability of water. Where the heat factor is critical, some estates may conduct the harvest at night, under floodlight. South Africa has a history of overproduction, due to having too great an area under vine, too little emphasis on high-quality varieties, poor clones, and undesirably high yields, but is quickly upgrading its vineyards, and is now at the forefront of research on new clones and rootstock. Yields are also being lowered to appeal to export markets. Until the early 1990s, estates were slow to cultivate higher, cooler slopes, but this has changed, especially with emergence of a new breed of winery that buys in from single vineyards, often over a large area. There is a trend for each estate or winery to develop one "flagship" wine, usually a classic red blend.

GRAPE VARIETIES
Primary varieties: Cabernet Franc, Cabernet Sauvignon, Chardonnay, Chenin Blanc (*syn.* Steen), Cinsault, Colombard, Crouchen, Merlot, Muscat à Petit Grains (*syn.* White Muscadel), Muscat d'Alexandrie (*syn.* Hanepoot), Pinot Noir, Pinotage, Riesling (*syn.* Rhine Riesling, Weisser Riesling), Ruby Cabernet, Sauvignon Blanc, Sémillon, Syrah (*syn.* Shiraz)

Secondary varieties: Barbera, Bukettraube, Carignan, Chenel (*syn.* Chenin Blanc x Trebbiano), Emerald Riesling, Fernão Pires, Gamay, Gewürztraminer, Grenache (*syn.* Rooi Grenache), Hárslevelü, Malbec, Mourvèdre, Muscat Rosé à Petit Grains (*syn.* Red Muscadel), Nebbiolo, Petit Verdot, Pinot Gris, Sangiovese, Souzão, Tinta Barocca, Touriga Nacional, Ugni Blanc, Viognier, Zinfandel

SOUTH AFRICA

The Cape area, which produces the vast majority of South Africa's wines, has an ideal climate for viticulture. However, heat stress can be a problem in some areas, and irrigation may be crucial. Most quality wine areas lie in the Coastal and Breede River Valley Wine of Origin regions, but other outlying districts are also interesting.

Reivilo
Blikfontein
Hartswater
Andalusia
Jan Kemp
Hartswater
Warrenton

Olifantshoek
Danielskuil
Delportshoop

Langklip
UPINGTON
Postmasburg

Lower Orange
Augrabies
▲1682
Bermolli
▲1615
Schmidtsdrif
KIMBERLEY

Kakamas
Keimoes
N O R T H E R N   C A P E
Modderrivier
FREE
STATE

Bitterfontein
Griquatown
Riet
Douglas
▲1338

Nuwerus
N7
1556▲
Abrahamsdam
Higg's Hope
Rooipan

Koekenaap
Vredendal
Vanrhynsdorp
Boegoeberg
Dam
Niekerkshoop
Hopetown

Lutzville
Spruitdrift
Klawer
Marydale

Lamberts
Bay
Graafwater
Doring
Doringbos
Strydenburg

Clanwilliam
Prieska

Citrusdale
Mountain

Velddrif
Citrusdal
▲2013
Cedarberg
Vinkekuil
W E S T E R N   C A P E
▲1436

Vredenburg
Citrusdale
Valley
Tulbaghkloof
Groot

Saldanha
Piketberg
Berg
Prince Albert
2152▲
De Rust

Porterville
▲1370
Hottentotskloof
Laingsburg
N1
2326▲

Riebeeckberg
Gouda
Matjiesfontein

Darling
Wolseley
Ceres
▲2251
Touwsrivier
Anysberg
Ladismith
Calitzdorp
OUDTSHOORN

Groenekloof
MALMESBURY
Wellington
Slanghoek
Goudini
De Doorns
Olifants
Uniondale

Voor Paardeberg
WORCESTER
Wolwefontein
Groot
Prince Albert Valley
▲1500
GEORGE

Durbanville
Simonsberg-
Paarl
Montagu
Montagu
Brak
▲1520
Knysna

Cape Town
PAARL
Robertson
Barrydale
Tradouw
Muiskraal
Herbertsdale

Bottelary
Franschhoek
11
15
Swellendam
Heldelberg
Riversdale
MOSSELBAAI

Constantia
Devon
Valley
STELLENBOSCH
9
13
SWELLENDAM
Mossel Bay

Simon's Town
Helderberg
▲1104
N2
Riviersonderend
Breë
Port
Beaufort

Elgin
Caledon

Cape of
Good Hope
Hermanus
Walker
Bay
Bredasdorp
PRETORIA

Elim
Elim

Cape
Agulhas

Legend

— Olifants River	Piketberg	Overberg	5 Nuy	14 Boesmansrivier	
— The Coastal Region	Swartland	Swellendam	6 Scherpenheuvel	15 Bonnievale	
— The Breede River Valley	Tulbagh	Calitzdorp	7 Eilandia	★ Smaller wine wards	
— The Boberg Region	Paarl	Wine wards	8 Vinkrivier	Cape (on small map showing all of Africa)	
— Klein Karoo	Tygerberg	1 Simonsberg - Stellenbosch	9 Le Chasseur		
Orange River Valley	Stellenbosch	2 Papegaaiberg	10 Riverside	Provincial boundary	
Douglas	Cape Point	3 Jonkershoek	11 Agterkliphoogte	▲ Height above sea level (meters)	
Lutzville Valley	Worcester	4 Aan-de-Doorns	12 Klaasvoogds		
Darling	Robertson		13 McGregor		

0   20   40   60 miles
0 20 40 60 80 100 km

A time of struggle for South African wine

Despite this setback to the wine nidstry, production was not checked. In fact, the large influx of immigrants, attracted by the discovery of gold and diamonds in the late 19th century, prompted a rapid expansion of vineyards in anticipation of a vastly increased demand. This increase in demand was realized, but the sudden wealth of these immigrants sparked off the Boer War, and sales of wine decreased at home and abroad. Yet unsellable wine continued to be made.

In 1905, the Cape government encouraged the formation of cooperatives, but nothing constructive was done either to reduce production or stimulate demand. Thus, when the Koöperatiewe Wijnbouwers Vereniging, or KWV, as it is now known, was formed in 1918 with government-backed powers, its decision to distill half the country's annual wine production into brandy immediately and very effectively improved the quality of Cape wines. Its policy of blending the rest of the surplus into marketable export products did no less than save the South African wine industry.

NEW AREAS AND BETTER WINES

Stellenbosch and Paarl are traditionally viewed as the country's two greatest wine districts. With the establishment of Hamilton Russell's top-performing vineyard at Hermanus, however, the Walker Bay area of Overberg to the southeast is now seen by many as potentially as fine for winemaking. Although there are just two wine estates in Hermanus at the moment, Elgin has developed into another startlingly good wine area. Elgin is the Cape's apple-growing capital, and, as Washington State in the United States quickly learned, wherever apple growers choose to go, fine-quality wine grapes will follow. With Neil Ellis currently sourcing excellent Sauvignon Blanc from Elgin, this area is certainly another feather in Overberg's cap. Most surprising of all is the even more recent establishment of Buitenverwachting and Klein Constantia, in 1985 and 1986 respectively, for these two estates have completed the cycle of exploration and development in South Africa's winelands. Constantia, once merely the site of an historic wine, is now one of the most exciting white wine areas in all South Africa. Outside of the mainstream vineyard regions, Mossel Bay in the extreme east of the Cape district is a potentially fine wine area, offering great hopes for aromatic white wine varieties such as Riesling and Sauvignon Blanc—some even think Pinot Noir will do well there.

In 1995, South African wine estates were allowed for the first time to buy in grapes from other areas; these were not to blend with their own grapes, but to enable them to extend their range by offering single-vineyard wines from other locations. Thus, instead of struggling to produce, for instance, Sauvignon Blanc in red wine territory (because customers demand the style), an estate may now source these grapes from a more ideal *terroir*, dig up their own Sauvignon vines, and replant with more suitable varieties. This should lead to a certain polarizing of varieties in the areas where each performs best, which ties in with the second phase of the Vine Improvement Programme, and the results can only be good for the future of South African wine.

SOUTH AFRICAN LABEL LANGUAGE

Although an increasing number of South African wine labels are in English or in English and Afrikaans, Afrikaans-only terms may be found on labels.

CAPE DATED TAWNY PORT Wine of a single year which must have the character of a tawny port, and the label must include the year of vintage, the words "matured in wood" and the words "Tawny Port"..

CAPE LATE BOTTLED VINTAGE (LBV) PORT Should be a port-style of a single year of quality, be dark and full-bodied with signs of going tawny in color. The main label could indicate the year of bottling as well as the vintage, and the description "Late Bottled Vintage" or "LBV" must appear on the label. The port will be aged for three to six years, of which at least two years in oak, before bottling.

CAPE RUBY PORT A blend of young, full-bodied, round, and fruity port-style wine. Components could be aged in wood for up to three years, depending on the size of wood used, but no components should be aged for less than six months. The average age should not be less than one year.

CAPE TAWNY PORT A blend of wine that has been wood matured, this port-style wine must be amber/orange (tawny) in color and must have acquired a smooth, light, slightly nutty flavor. Blending of white and red Port for tawny port is not allowed.

CAPE VINTAGE PORT A port-style wine from one harvest, dark and full-bodied, aged in wood of any size. The words "Vintage Port" and date of vintage may appear on the label.

CAPE VINTAGE RESERVE PORT A port-style wine from one harvest, produced in a year of recognized quality, with exceptional organoleptic characteristics, dark and full-bodied, with very fine aroma and palate. The producer can be assisted by a tasting panel set up by the Association. The wine must preferably be aged for an average of at least one year or more in wood of any size. The wine must be sold exclusively in glass. The words "Vintage Reserve Port" and date of vintage must appear on the label.

CAPE WHITE PORT Made from a non-Muscat white cultivar, aged in wood of any size for a minimum period of six months.

CULTIVAR Cultivar derives from a shortened form of "cultivated variety" and is the South African term for grape variety.

EDEL LAAT-OES Noble late harvest. Botrytized grapes must be used for this style, which must have a minimum of 50 grams of residual sugar per liter.

EDELKEUR This literally means "noble rot."

FORTIFIED WINE, LIQUEUR WINE This style of wine must have an alcoholic strength of no less than 16.5 percent by volume and no more than 22 percent. This category includes port and sherry, plus such uniquely South African wines as Jerepigo or Jerepiko.

GEBOTTEL IN... Bottled in...

GEKWEEK EN GEMAAK OP... Grown and made on... (i.e., but not bottled on).

GEKWEEK, GEMAAK EN GEBOTTEL OP... Grown, made, and bottled on... (i.e., estate-bottled).

GEPRODUSER EN GEBOTTEL IN... Produced and bottled in...

GEPRODUSER EN GEBOTTEL IN DIE REPUBLIEK VAN SUD-AFRICA Produced and bottled in the Republic of South Africa.

GRAPE VARIETY A wine must contain at least 75 percent of the grape variety or varieties indicated (85 percent for exported wines).

JEREPIGO OR JEREPIKO A very sweet liqueur wine with at least 160 grams per liter of residual sugar. Jerepigo Muscadel is very popular among old-timers and heavy drinkers.

KOÖPERATIEWE, KÖPERATIEVE, KOÖPERASIE, KOÖPERATIEF Cooperative.

LAAT-OES Late harvest, with natural alcoholic strength of at least 10 percent and 10–30 grams of residual sugar per liter.

LANDGOEDWYN Estate wine.

MÉTHODE CAP CLASSIQUE A general term that is used to describe a bottle-fermented sparkling wine.

MOSKONFYT Concentrated grape paste.

OESJAAR Vintage.

ORIGIN OF THE WINE (WO) The Wine of Origin (or *Wyn van Oorsprong*) is South Africa's equivalent of *Appellation d'Origine Contrôlée*. WO wines must be 100 percent from the appellation area indicated.

SEMI-SOET The Afrikaans term for "semisweet."

SPESIALE LAAT-OES Special late harvest. This usually, but not necessarily, implies that some botrytized grapes have been used; there is a minimum natural alcoholic strength of 10 percent by volume, and between 20 and 50 grams per liter of residual sugar.

STEIN A semisweet style of wine that is normally Chenin-based.

VINTAGE A vintage must contain at least 75 percent of the year indicated or 85 percent for exported wines (the balance must come from either the preceding or succeeding vintage).

WYN VAN OORSPRONG (WO) Dutch for Wine of Origin, South Africa's equivalent of *Appellation d'Origine Contrôlée*. WO wines must be 100 percent from the appellation area indicated.

THELEMA MOUNTAIN VINEYARDS
These beautifully tended vineyards on the Simonsberg in Stellenbosch belong to Thelema Mountain, one of South Africa's youngest and most exciting wineries.

Pinotage and the "Cape Blend"

There are those who think that a "Cape Blend" with an obligatory Pinotage component should become the flagship of South Africa's export drive in the 21st century. And then there are those who are less than enamored with the Cape's adopted grape. It might be possible to play down this grape's typically high-toned, estery character and, in particular, iron out its high acetate (often incorrectly referred to as acetone) content with appropriate vinification techniques. And if it is cultivated on the Cape's higher slopes, it should be possible to utilize extended hang-time to harvest Pinotage on tannin ripeness without running the risk of producing wines that are big and cumbersome, with too much alcohol. In this way, Pinotage does not have to have its rough edges, green tannins, or the banana and nail-polish aroma of acetate-laden fruit. But, as its detractors inside South Africa point out, they will still be left with a rustic 1920s cross that has not attracted anyone to plant the variety widely anywhere else in the world—there are 232 acres (94 hectares) in New Zealand, but that is as good as it gets, because outside of that country it is found only in the US, Canada, and Germany, where it is grown in such minuscule quantities that there are no official statistics.

Is Pinotage as bad as it is made out to be, and are they right not to want South Africa's reputation to depend on a blend that must contain this grape? Yes and no. Of course, Pinotage has a poor track record, otherwise South Africa's Pinotage diehards would be right, and the rest of the world wrong, but blending it is a good idea. Pinotage is a good team player. With the right support, it is better at improving some blends than intrinsically finer grapes would be. We can see this in everything from sparkling wine *cuvées*, such as Villiera Tradition Brut, to some of South Africa's most stunning classic red blends, including Flagstone Dragon, Kaapzicht Steytler Vision, and Meinert Synchronicity. And who knows, perhaps they will make a prince out of this pauper's grape in the process. It is not as if there are absolutely no fine-quality pure Pinotage wines. Although I am a declared sceptic when it comes to this variety, you will find a number of excellent Pinotage wines listed on the following pages. And in my humble opinion, most Pinotage vineyards are on the wrong sites, so these successes must be encouraging. Diverting the bulk of this variety's production into blends while truly objective winemakers trial Pinotage on higher, cooler slopes for longer hang-times, to ripen its notoriously harsh tannins without increasing alcohol levels, can only be good for the long-term reputation of the Cape's own cultivar.

THE APPELLATIONS OF
SOUTH AFRICA

Note Wine wards are the most specific type of WO (Wine of Origin) appellation. One or more WO wards may be contained in a larger WO district, and one or more WO districts may be contained in a WO region.

BOBERG WO
Wine districts *Paarl WO, Tulbagh WO*
This regional WO is restricted to fortified wine except for the Paarl and Tulbagh districts.

BREEDE RIVER VALLEY WO
Wine districts *Robertson WO, Swellendam WO, Worcester WO*

Wine wards *Agterkliphoogte WO, Bonnievale WO, Boesmansrivier WO, Eilandia WO, Hoopsrivier WO, Klaasvoogds WO, Le Chasseur WO, McGregor WO, Vinkrivier WO, Aan-de-Doorns WO, Goudini WO, Nuy WO, Scherpenheuvel WO, Slanghoek WO, Buffeljags WO, Stormsvlei WO*

The vineyards in this region, situated east of the Drakenstein Mountains, depend on irrigation, and mostly produce white or fortified wines. Although Robertson is known as "the valley of vines and roses," its hot climate relegated this region to largely bulk-produced wine until the emergence of fine-wine hotspots on its lime-rich soils. It now has a number of top-performing estates with well-established reputations for white wines, particularly Chardonnay and sparkling wines, and an emerging one for reds, including several up-and-coming Syrahs. Swellendam is just east of Robertson, in an area where few wineries and vineyards exist, although it is suited to Muscadel and other fortified wines, and plantations of Chenin Blanc can be found. Worcester is on the western edge of Little Karoo, adjoining the eastern border of Paarl, in the Breede River catchment area, which is intensively cultivated with vines. The hot climate is tempered in the west by high rainfall, while in the east rainfall is very low, with soils that are derived from Table Mountain sandstone and the fertile red shale of Little Karoo. Although there are some good wine estates in Worcester, including the excellent Bergsig, the real stars of this district are the high-performing cooperatives (Du Toitskloof, Goudini, and Nuy), which make exceptionally fine white and fortified wines.

CEDERBERG WO
This up-and-coming ward comprises the Cederberg Wilderness Area, which lies within

the Cape's famous "fynbos" region, one of the world's six floral kingdoms, an outlying area just east of the southern part of the Olifants River region. Cederberg Cellars (formerly a cooperative, but now owned by the Nieuwoudt family) is one of the South African wine industry's fastest-rising superstars, with vineyards planted at an altitude of 3,300 feet (1,000 meters), the highest in the country, producing a raft of recently award-winning wines, including a coveted Veritas Double Gold.

COASTAL REGION WO

Wine districts *Cape Point WO, Darling WO, Paarl WO, Stellenbosch WO, Swartland WO, Tulbagh WO, Tygerberg WO*

Wine wards *Bottelary WO, Constantia WO, Devon Valley WO, Durbanville WO, Franschhoek Valley WO, Groenekloof WO, Jonkershoek Valley WO, Paardeberg WO, Papegaaiberg WO, Philadelphia WO, Riebeekberg WO, Simonsberg-Paarl WO, Simonsberg-Stellenbosch WO, Voor Malmesbury WO, Wellington WO*

The most frequently encountered appellation, the Coastal Region comprises two external wards (Constantia WO and Durbanville WO) in addition to the above seven districts and their wards. Cape Point is a challenging new cool-climate district on the western and southern slopes of the Cape Peninsula that has demonstrated its potential for white wines, although the jury is still out for its red. Darling was part of Swartland, but its vineyards, particularly in the higher Groenkloow area, are too good not to have their own appellation. The Paarl district embraces the fertile Berg River valley and vineyards surrounding the towns of Franschhoek, Wellington, and Paarl itself. The vineyards are located on three main types of soil: granite in the Paarl district, Table Mountain sandstone along the Berg River, and Malmesbury slate to the north. The climate is Mediterranean, with wet winters and hot, dry summers. Average annual rainfall is about 26 inches (65 centimeters), but this declines toward the northwest of the district. Although this used to be a white-wine area, it is now more of a red-wine area, with high-lying vineyards that are well suited to the production of fine-quality reds. The Stellenbosch district is located between False Bay to the south and Paarl to the north. This is where the greatest concentration of South Africa's finest wine estates have traditionally been situated. There are three types of soil: granite-based in the east (considered best for red wines), Table Mountain sandstone in the west (favored for white wines), and alluvial soils around the Eerste River. With warm, dry summers, cool, moist winters, and an average annual rainfall of 20 inches (50 centimeters), irrigation is usually unnecessary, except in some situations at the height of the summer season. Helderberg is the current hot spot. The Swartland district replaced Malmesbury WO. Of the vast area covered by Swartland, most is arable land, with viticulture being

confined to the southern section around Darling, Malmesbury, and Riebeek. The soils are Table Mountain sandstone and Malmesbury slate, and the rainfall is light, at around 9 inches (24 centimeters), which makes irrigation generally necessary, although some vineyards surprisingly manage without it. Within the Swartland district, Philadelphia is the latest, most exciting wine ward to emerge, with the reds from Havana Hills grabbing the headlines. Tulbagh is bordered to the south by the Riversonderend Mountains and to the north by Langeberg Range. Soil, climate, and topography are – for the most part – similar to those of the Karoo, although somewhat more temperate. Readers may not have heard of the Tygerberg district, but most will know Meerendal Estate, which sits on the southeastern slopes of the Tygerberg, where rich, red soils combine with moderated temperatures and airflow from the cool summer winds to provide the vines with an excellent growing environment. The vineyards of Constantia are situated on the eastern, red-granitic slopes of Constantia Mountain, south of Cape Town. Bordered by sea on two sides, the climate is very moderate, of Mediterranean character, but it is quite wet, with up to 47 inches (120 centimeters) of annual rainfall. Durbanville is located in the lowlands of the Tygerberg hills and, although the rainfall is less than half that of Constantia, the deep, well-weathered, red, granite-based soils have a particularly good water retention, and the vines are cooled and dried by the sea breezes coming in from Table Bay.

KLEIN KAROO WO

Wine districts *Calitzdorp WO*

Wine wards *Montagu WO, Outeniqua WO, Tradouw WO, Upper Langkloof WO*

This appellation is a long, narrow strip that stretches from Montagu in the west to De Rust in the east. The vineyards require irrigation to survive the hot and arid climate. The famous red, shale-based Karoo soil and the deep alluvium closer to the various rivers are very fertile and are well suited to growing grapes to make the Jerepigo, Muscadel, and other dessert wines for which this area is well known. Calitzdorp is a semi-arid desert region, with summer temperatures of up to 104°F (40°C). These temperatures are moderated by afternoon sea breezes and cool nights, providing a beneficial diurnal effect of ensuring better acidity levels than would otherwise be found in such a hot climate. Calitzdorp's Boplass Estate is famous for its port-style fortified wines, and is arguably South Africa's finest producer of such wines.

NORTHERN CAPE

Wine districts *Douglas WO*

Wine wards *Hartswater WO, Lower Orange WO, Rietrivier* (Free State) *WO*

Formerly known as Orange River, this region encompasses Hartswater, South Africa's northernmost viticultural area, which is 50 miles (80 kilometers) north of Kimberley, encompassing the town of Jan Kempdorp, which was formerly known as Andalusia. Northern Cape is totally divorced from the rest of the country's vineyards. No fine wines as such are produced in this region, but there are good fortified wines and an improving quality of good-value, fruity varietal wines being made at Hartswater Wine Cellar, Landzicht, Oranjerivier Wine Cellars, and Douglas Winery.

OLIFANTS RIVER

Wine districts *Citrusdal Mountain WO, Citrusdal Valley, Lutzville Valley WO*

Wine wards *Bamboes Bay, Koekenaap WO, Piekeniersloof WO, Spruitdrift WO, Vredendal WO*

The vines in this long, narrow district grow on sandstone or lime-rich alluvial soil. The climate is hot and dry, with rainfall averaging just 10 inches (26 centimeters) per year and decreasing closer to the coast. This is a large region where you will find few wineries, but two of those wineries are huge. Westcorp's Vredendal is South Africa's largest wine producer, and Lutzville, the country's second-largest winery, is now bigger than KWV, Fleur du Cap, and Nederburg, the former colossi of the Cape wine industry, put together.

OVERBERG WO

Wine districts *Douglas WO, Walker Bay WO*

Wine wards *Elgin WO, Elim WO, Kleinrivier WO*

Overberg WO replaced Caledon WO, and consists of a huge, recently cultivated area southeast of Paarl and Stellenbosch. Fifteen years ago, there was only one estate here, Hamilton Russell Vineyards in Walker Bay, but this was obviously one of South Africa's most potentially exciting wine districts. Walker Bay is now one of the hottest spots on South Africa's wine map. Hottest meaning coolest, of course. This is considered the benchmark district for South Africa's Chardonnay and Pinot Noir, Hamilton Russell's success having attracted several highly reputed wineries to set up here, the highest flyers of which include Bartho Eksteen, Bouchard Finlayson, Newton Johnson, Sumaridge, and Whalehaven. Many more wineries are, at the time of writing, about to begin production in both areas.

PICKETBERG

Wine wards *none*

This large district lies between Swartland and Tulbagh to the south and Olifants River district to the north. With very hot temperatures and annual rainfall as low as 7 inches (17.5 centimetrers) in places, it is really not suited to viticulture, yet is starting to produce some interesting fruit.

WESTERN CAPE WO

A vast multiregional appellation covering all South African WO appellations except Northern Cape WO.

OTHER ISOLATED WINE AREAS

Wine wards *Ceres WO, Herbertsdale WO, Prince Albert Valley WO, Ruiterbosch WO, Swartberg WO*

Ceres is located just east of the Tulbagh WO; Herbertsdale is 28 miles (45 kilometers) northwest of the potentially exciting Mossel Bay area, just south of the Klein Karoo, and contains two wineries, Die Poort and Nietverloren; Prince Albert Valley is a 12-mile-(20-kilometer-) long valley at the foot of the Swartberg Mountain Nature Reserve, north of Klein Karoo, in an area previously better known for its olives than for its wine, although it has attracted considerable investments recently, including the Dutch-funded Bergwater Winery, which is irrigated by pure mountain water; Boplass produce wines under the Ruiterbosch; and Swartberg is a promising wine ward that overlooks Prince Albert Valley.

THE WINE STYLES OF
SOUTH AFRICA

CABERNET SAUVIGNON

Traditional, firm, assertive styles are made here, but the trend is toward more up-front wines driven by ripe, juicy *cassis* fruit with cedary, spicy-vanilla oak complexity. New-wave wines are often enjoyable when young, but some also develop in bottle. Cabernet blends rank as one of South Africa's finest red wine styles. Other constituents are usually Cabernet Franc and Merlot, but may include Malbec, or, in the case of Boschendal Lanoy, even a dash of Shiraz (Shiraz-dominated blends are dealt with below).

⌛ 3–7 years (modern style), 5–10 years (traditional style, exceptional modern style)

🏆 *Boekenhoutskloof* • *Cederberg* (V Generations) • *Kanonkop* • *Le Riche* (Reserve) • *Morgenhof* (Reserve) • *Neil Ellis* (Jonkershoek) • *Rustenberg* (Peter Barlow) • *Thelema* • *De Trafford* • *Vergelegen*

CHARDONNAY

Although this is South Africa's most improved varietal, it was originally so bland that it could only get better. The trouble was that as soon as new oak became widely available for the first time, many winemakers went over the top, producing heavy, overwooded Chardonnays. These wines also suffered from poor raw material, but this situation improved with clonal selection and matching this variety to more suitable *terroirs*. The best oaked Chardonnays are often barrel-fermented, rather than just oak-aged, with just a kiss of creamy new oak, although some less refined, if just as lip-smacking, wines dominated by yummy, coconutty-oak are also to be found. The top unoaked Chardonnays are very pure and exquisitely balanced, and they often belie their hot-climate origins.

⌛ 1–3 years (unoaked), 1–5 years (oaked)

🏆 *Bouchard Finlayson* (Kaaimansgat, Missionvale) • *Durbanville Hills* (Rhinofields) • *Eikendal Vineyards* • *Hamilton Russell* • *Jordan* • *Mulderbosch* (Barrel Fermented) • *Rustenberg* (Five Soldiers) • *Thelema* (Ed's Reserve) • *Vergelegen* (Reserve) • *De Wetshof* (Bateleur)

CHENIN BLANC

Not so long ago this grape covered almost one-third of South Africa's vineyards. Yields were very high, producing wines that were generally off-dry to semisweet and considered cheap and cheerful for their day. Now it accounts for just over 17 percent, and most of the wines produced are still cheap, but although the

quality is generally the same, "cheerful" translates more as "dull, boring, and mediocre" by today's standards. In recent years, as this country's wines have come on by leaps and bounds, there has been much hype about the special quality of South African Chenin Blanc, and very little fulfillment in the bottle. It should be possible for the best sites of oldest vines to produce bone-dry wines of greater intensity than commonly found in the Loire, but truly special Chenin Blanc, such as Jean Daneel's Signature (I am thinking of the 2003 here), are few and far between.

⌛ Upon purchase

🏆 *Avontuur* (Barrel Select) • *Boland* • *Cederberg* (V Generations) • *Fort Simon Estate* (Barrel Fermented) • *Jean Daneel* (Signature) • *Kanu* (Wooded) • *Ken Forrester* • *Old Vines* • *Spice Route* • *Villiera*

MERLOT
Pure and blended

Cape winemakers are following in California's footsteps, having started with pure Cabernet Sauvignon, they then moved on to Cabernet blends and then pure Merlot wines. Cape Merlot is often spoiled by green tannins, but the best have a persistence of flavor that belies their softness. This softness can be anything from the simple, fruit-driven delight of, say, a Veenwouden Merlot to the very classy, silky smoothness of Du Plessis Havana Hills.

⌛ 2–5 years

🏆 *Avondale* (Les Pleurs) • *Du Preez* (Reserve) • *Havana Hills* (Bisweni) • *KWV* (Cathedral Cellar) • *Morgenhof* (Reserve) • *Overgaauw* • *Spice Route* (Flagship) • *Thelema* (Reserve) • *De Trafford* • *Vergelegen*

PINOT NOIR

South Africa is not likely to challenge Burgundy or, for that matter, California, Oregon, or New Zealand when it comes to this fussy variety, but a few highly talented winemakers are crafting some elegant exceptions.

⌛ 2–5 years

🏆 *Bouchard Finlayson* (Galpin Peak Tête de Cuvée) • *Cabrière* (Haut Cabrière) • *Flagstone* (The Poetry Collection) • *Glen Carlou* • *Hamilton Russell* • *Meerlust* • *Newton Johnson*

PINOTAGE

This Cinsault x Pinot Noir cross is to South Africa what Zinfandel is to California and Shiraz to Australia. Or at least it should be. The problem is that it does not have half the potential of either of the other two grapes, but if anyone has the audacity to criticize this grape on its home turf, the South Africans become very touchy indeed. Yet, even after all these years, this country's winemakers still seem to be in a bit of a quandary about how it should be produced and that, if nothing else, puts Pinotage in the same league as Zinfandel because the Americans produce a hodgepodge of styles from that grape too. South African Pinotage can be found in all shades between the big, baked, earthy brews with volatile aromas, to the Beaujolais look-alikes with a touch of bubble-gummy oak. The trend for the best wines seems to be leaning toward the bigger styles, but too many are overly big or spoiled by green phenolics. Although the development of this cross was supposed to provide Burgundy-like elegance in the baking-hot vineyards of North Africa, the genes have transmitted more Cinsault than Pinot Noir. This is not a bad thing, as South Africa produces some fine wines from authentic Pinot Noir grapes anyway, and old-vine Cinsault can be interesting in its own right. However, rather than baking-hot vineyards, I would like to see Pinotage grown in places like Cederberg, where the altitude can draw out the hang-time, resulting in full physiological (tannin) ripeness without the high levels of sugar found in top examples of this grape today.

⌛ Upon purchase

🏆 *Bellevue Estate* (PK Morkel) • *Clos Malverne* (Basket pressed) • *Diemersfontein* (Carpe Diem) • *Graham Beck* (The Old Road) • *Kaapzicht* (Steytler) • *KWV* (Cathedral Cellar) • *Morgenhof* • *Môreson* • *Neil Ellis* (Stellenbosch) • *Thelema*

RIESLING

Unless produced in a late-harvest or botrytized style, Riesling in South Africa just does not seem to have the fruit-acidity elegance I expect from this variety, but I find that I am similarly picky about Riesling throughout most of the New World. Others find far more satisfaction in these wines than I do, so perhaps I am being too harsh in my judgment, but where we do agree, I think, is on the exceptional style and quality of the wines below.

🏆 *De Wetshof* (Rhine Riesling) • *Klein Constantia* (Rhine Riesling) • *Thelema* (Rhine Riesling)

SAUVIGNON BLANC

This is not this country's most successful varietal, despite the number of recommendations that are listed below. Their success is, however, disproportionate to the intrinsic quality Sauvignon that has established in South Africa. The reason for this is that much of the industry seems to be committed to trying every which way in order to master this grape variety and, although the results show there are many overachievers out there, I had to drink my way through a sea of dross to find them. There are too many overherbaceous wines from those who are trying too hard with this varietal, and a great many dull wines from those who are jumping on the Sauvignon bandwagon.

Most of these wines will never hold a candle to your average New Zealand Sauvignon Blanc, although if there is such a thing as South Africa's answer to Marlborough, it could be Elgin. Note that "Fumé Blanc" or "Blanc Fumé" is used for barrel-fermented or oak-aged Sauvignon Blanc; Le Bonheur is the one exception to this, and honors the term's original French meaning, which is simply a synonym for the grape variety.

⌐ Upon purchase

☐ *Bellevue* (Morkel) • *Boschendal* (Jean de Long) • *Cederberg* • *Mulderbusch* • *Neil Ellis* (Groenekloof) • *Nitida Cellars* (Club Select) • *Springfield* (Life from Stone) • *Steenberg* (Reserve) • *Vergelegen* (Schaapenburg Reserve) • *Villiera* (Traditional Bush Vine)

SÉMILLON

Sémillon has great potential in South Africa, where it can produce rich yet refined wines on to which skilled winemakers can graft a lovely leesy complexity. However, the number of recommendations below is meager because few producers take the potential of this grape seriously. If the industry applied half the effort to this variety that they have to Sauvignon Blanc, Sémillon would quickly become one of South Africa's most fashionable wines.

⌐ 18 months to 5 years

☐ *Boekenhoutskloof* • *Boschendal* (Jean de Long) • *Constantia Uitsig* (Reserve) • *Fairview* (Oom Pagel) • *Rihk's* • *Nitida* • *Steenberg* • *Stellenzicht* (Reserve)

SYRAH
Pure and blended

Syrah is planted far less widely than in Australia, but it is South Africa's second fastest expanding red wine variety. It has come from virtually nothing in the 1990s to equal-sixth most widely planted black grape, placing it on a par with the Cape's beloved Pinotage, and not only do the best examples knock the socks off the best Pinotage, but they can give most Australian Shiraz a run for their money. This must now be regarded as South Africa's most exciting red wine variety.

⌐ 2–8 years

☐ *Avondale* (Les Pleurs) • *Boekenhoutskloof* • *Cederberg* (Shiraz) • *Fairview* (Solitude) • *Graham Beck* (The Ridge) • *Rust en Vrede* (Shiraz) • *Sentinel* • *Stellenbosch* (Genesis Shiraz) • *Stellenzicht* • *Vergelegen* (Shiraz)

OTHER REDS

This section lists the best examples I have found of South Africa's less frequently encountered red wine varietals, some of which will no doubt become more widely established in this country one day.

☐ **Barbera** *Altydgedacht*

Cabernet Franc *Bellingham* (Spitz) • *Neethlingshof* (Lord Neethlingshof) • *Warwick Estate*
Carignan *Fairview* (Pegleg)
Malbec *Bellevue* (Limited Release)
Nebbiolo *Steenberg*
Petit Verdot *Du Preeze* (Hendrik Lodewyk) • *Signal Hill* • *Simonsig* (Auction Reserve)
Ruby Cabernet *Flagstone* (Ruby in the Dust)
Tinta Barocca *Allesverloren*
Zinfandel *Blaauwklippen* (Vineyard Selection)

OTHER WHITES

This section lists the best examples I have found of South Africa's less frequently encountered white wine varietals, some of which will no doubt become more widely established in this country one day.

☐ **Grenache Blanc** *Signal Hill*
Viognier *Backsberg* (Babylons Toren) • *Bellingham* (Maverick) • *Fairview* • *Spier* (Private Collection)

OTHER WINE STYLES
CAP CLASSIQUE

This is South Africa's own term for "traditional method." Sparkling wine is generally less exciting here than in most other New World countries, which is probably due to the longer learning curve these wines demand. Most are merely in the fruity-fizz category, and only those recommended below show promise of anything more serious, but we could well see a revolution for sparkling wines as we have for Chardonnay. Two wines that should be represented below are Graham Beck's Synergy (a 70 percent Pinot Noir *cuvée* that I previewed in 2003, but have never seen on sale, although it is one of the two greatest sparkling wines produced in this country) and Graham Beck's Sparkling Pinotage (which was discontinued after the first release was not understood locally).

⌐ Upon purchase

☐ *Graham Beck* (Blanc de Blancs) • *J. C. Le Roux* (Pinot Noir) • *Twee Jonge Gezellen* (Private Vintners Limited Release Pinot Noir) • *Villiera* (Brut Natural Chardonnay)

CLASSIC RED BLENDS

These blends, particularly the Bordeaux-style red blends, are gradually establishing a solid superiority over their pure varietal counterparts in this country.

⌐ 3–10 years

☐ *De Toren* (Fusion V) • *Grangehurst* (Nikela) • *Havanah Hills* (Du Plessis Reserve) • *Kanonkop* (Paul Sauer) • *Meerlust* (Rubicon) • *Morgenhof* (Première Sélection) • *Rust en Vrede* (Estate Wine) • *Rustenberg* (John X Merriman) • *Vergelegen* (Vergelegen V) • *Warwick* (Trilogy)

CLASSIC WHITE BLENDS

This category encompasses white wine blends that are made from too many permutations of grapes to be able to record them all here. However, Sémillon, Chardonnay, Chenin Blanc, and Sauvignon Blanc are the most commonly featured grape varieties.

⌐ Mostly upon purchase (exceptional examples 2–3 years)

☐ *Constantia Uitsig* (Sémillon-Sauvignon Blanc) • *Dornier* (Donatus White) • *Hamilton Russell* (Chardonnay-Sauvignon Blanc) • *Stellenbosch* (VVS) • *Vergelegen* (Vergelegen White) • *Zevenwacht* (Tin Mine White)

FORTIFIED WINES

Other high-performance fortified wine styles include red and white Muscadel, which is often called Hanepoot when made from Muscat d'Alexandrie (also in red and white styles). Jerepigo (or Jerepiko) is the South African equivalent of *vin de liqueur*, in which grape spirit is added to grape juice before fermentation can begin (as opposed to *vin doux naturel*, in which the grape spirit is added after fermentation has achieved an alcohol level of between 5 and 8 percent). Red styles range in color from cherry-bright to orange-gold and grow lighter with age, whereas white styles deepen with age (venerable vintages of both styles can become indistinguishable if they both assume an old-gold hue). Authentic port is made only in the Douro Valley of northern Portugal, but port-type fortified wines are made the world over, and South Africa has proved itself to be particularly adept at this style.

☐ **Red** *Boplass* (Red Muscadel) • *Nuy* (Red Muscadel) • *Du Preez* (Hanepoot) • *Du Toitskloof* (Hanepoot Jerepigo) • *KWV* (White Muscadel) • *Rietvallie* (Muscadel 1908) • **White** *De Wetshof* (Muscadel) • *Jonkheer* (Muscatheer Family Reserve Muscat de Frontignan) • *KWV* (Red Muscadel) • *Monis* (Muscadel) • *Nuy* (White Muscadel) • **Port** *Allesverloren* • *Axehill* (Vintage) *Boplaas* (Vintage Reserve) • *KWV* (Tawny) • *Monis* (Very Old Tawny) • *Overgaauw* (Cape Vintage Reserve) • *Vergenoegd* (Old Cape Colony Vintage Port)

LATE HARVEST

There are various categories of this style: Late Harvest must contain between 10 and 30 grams per liter of residual sugar; Special Late Harvest contains between 20 and 50 grams and usually, but not necessarily, implies that some botrytized grapes have been used; Noble Late Harvest contains a minimum of 50 grams of residual sugar, from botrytized grapes. Other naturally sweet, unfortified, non-botrytis dessert-style wines exist, including such marvelous oddities as Klein Constantia's Vin de Constance and Boschendal's Vin d'Or. All these styles will be seductive as soon as they are released, yet most will gain complexity over a great period of time.

⌐ Upon release and up to 20 years for Late Harvest; possibly 50 years or more for richer styles

☐ *Boekenhoutskloof* (Noble Late Harvest Sémillon) • *Fleur du Cap* (Noble Late Harvest Riesling) • *Ken Forrester* (T Noble) • *Robertson Winery* (Wide River Reserve) • *Vergelegen* (Sémillon Noble Late Harvest) • *De Wetshof* (Edeloes) • **Other unfortified dessert wines** *Fairview* (La Beryl Blanc) • *Klein Constantia* (Vin de Constance) • *Signal Hill* (Mathilde Aszú 6 Puttonyos) • *Signal Hill* (Vin de Glacière) • *Signal Hill* (Vin de l'Empereur)

SPARKLING WINES

☐ *See Cap Classique.*

THE WINE PRODUCERS OF
SOUTH AFRICA

AGUSTA
Franschhoek
★★☆

One of Franschhoek's newest and finest wineries.

✓ *Cabernet Sauvignon*
• *Chardonnay*

ALLESVERLOREN
Swartland
★★

Traditionally one of the Cape's greatest port producers, the latest generation owner-winemaker Danie Malan has stepped up a gear over the last few years.

✓ *Cabernet Sauvignon •
Fortified* (Port) • *Syrah*
(Shiraz) • *Tinta Barocca*

ALTO
Stellenbosch
★★☆

All it took to turn around this estate was a new viticultural consultant (Professor Eban Archer), a replanting program, a new winemaker since 2000, and a new winemaking consultant (Pascal Chatonnet).

✓ *Cabernet Sauvignon • Classic red blend* (Alto Estate) •
Syrah (Shiraz)

ALTYDGEDACHT
Durbanville
★

This property is owned by John and Oliver Parker, who learned their winemaking skills in California and New Zealand. Barbera and Tintoretto (a Barbera Shiraz blend) are the most interesting wines here.

✓ *Barbera • Pinotage • Syrah*
(Shiraz)

ASARA
Stellenbosch
★★☆

I might have tasted these wines before now, but although in existence since 1970, this is the first time I have noticed Asara.

✓ *Cabernet Sauvignon •
Chardonnay • Classic red
blend* (Bell Tower, Cape
Blend, Carillon) • *Late Harvest*
(Noble Late Harvest Chenin
Blanc) • *Syrah* (Shiraz)

L'AVENIR
Stellenbosch
★★☆♥

This property has shot to fame since François Naudé became the winemaker in 1992. The style is creamy, rich and accessible, yet not without considerable complexity in some of the wines.

✓ *Cabernet Sauvignon*
• *Chardonnay • Chenin Blanc*

• *Classic red blend* (Black Label Reserve) • *Fortified* (Cape Port) • *Pinotage*

AVONDALE
Stellenbosch
◐★★

One of South Africa's few organic producers, Avondale has shown that organic wines from this country can be award-winners from almost the very start. The first vintage here was 1999, and the 2000 classic red blend won a double gold at the Veritas Awards.

✓ *Cabernet Sauvignon • Classic red blend* (Avondale) • *Merlot* (Les Pleurs) • *Sauvignon Blanc* • *Syrah* (Les Pleurs)

AVONTUUR
Stellenbosch
★☆♥

This is the winery that gave the world pink Chardonnay. Avontuur wines used to be very much in the quaffing style, but now include a number of very serious wines.

✓ *Chardonnay* (Luna de Miel) • *Chenin Blanc* (Barrel Select) • *Classic red blend* (Baccarat)

BACKSBERG
Paarl
★★

This estate is owned by Michael Back and it produces some of South Africa's most consistent and classy wines, combining richness, finesse, and complexity with great success.

✓ *Chardonnay* (Babylons Toren) • *Classic red blend* (Babylons Toren Cabernet Sauvignon Merlot, Klein Babylons Toren) • *Viognier* (Babylons Toren)

BARTHO EKSTEEN
Walker Bay
★★☆

One of the fast-rising stars of the up-and-coming Walker Bay district.

✓ *Sauvignon Blanc • Syrah* (Shiraz)

GRAHAM BECK
Robertson & Franschhoek
★★★☆♥

Graham Beck's senior winemaker is Pieter Ferreira, one of South Africa's top sparkling winemakers. This fact was confirmed at the Diners Club Winemaker Awards in 2004, its Cap Classique year, when Ferreira received the much coveted Winemaker Award. But he's a genius with other styles too. Charles Hopkins is the brilliant winemaker at Graham Beck's Franschhoek winery.

✓ *Classic red blend* (The Joshua, The William) • *Pinotage* (The Old Road) • *Sparkling wine* (Blanc de Blancs, Brut Rosé) • *Syrah* (Shiraz, The Ridge Syrah)

BELLEVUE ESTATE
Stellenbosch
★★☆

Long-time grape farmers, the Morkel family released the first wines under its own label as recently as the 1999 vintage. These wines have enjoyed a resounding success.

✓ *Classic red blend* (Tumara) • *Malbec* (Limited Release) • *Pinotage* (P. K. Morkel) • *Sauvignon Blanc* (Morkel) • *Syrah* (Shiraz)

BELLINGHAM
Paarl
★★♥

Owned by Graham Beck, Bellingham is a totally separate, stand-alone operation that makes some pretty remarkable wines.

✓ *Cabernet Franc* (Spitz) • *Cabernet Sauvignon* (Maverick) • *Chardonnay* (Spitz) • *Chenin Blanc* (Maverick) • *Merlot* (Spitz) • *Syrah* (Founder's Shiraz, Maverick Syrah) • *Viognier* (Maverick)

BILTON
Stellenbosch
★★☆

Another name to watch, Mark Bilton established this operation on the Helderberg with his first vintage in 1998.

✓ *Cabernet Sauvignon • Merlot • Syrah* (Shiraz)

BLAAUWKLIPPEN
Stellenbosch
★

These days Blaauwklippen seems a rather traditional winery, yet it was a pioneer of maturation in new oak, and one of the Cape's first great innovators. If you thought that Zinfandel was relatively new to South Africa, you should think again—Blaauwklippen has been making it since the 1970s.

✓ *Cabernet Sauvignon* (Vineyard Selection) • *Zinfandel* (Vineyard Selection)

BOEKENHOUTSKLOOF
Franschhoek
★★★☆

This rapidly rising star continues to make good. Entry-level wines are also sold under the Porcupine Ridge label, with the Syrah punching well above its weight.

✓ *Cabernet Sauvignon • Classic red blend* (The Chocolate Box) • *Late Harvest* (Noble Late Harvest Sémillon) • *Syrah* • *Sémillon*

BOLAND WINE CELLAR
Paarl
★★☆♥

This former cooperative has greatly improved since going private.

✓ *Cabernet Sauvignon* (No. 1 Reserve) • *Chardonnay* (No. 1 Reserve) • *Chenin Blanc • Fortified* (Red Muscadel) • *Pinotage* (Winemaker's Selection) • *Syrah* (Shiraz No. 1 Reserve)

BOPLAAS
Klein Karoo
★♥

Lurking in a large range of commercially acceptable products are a number of extremely fine fortified wines, including one, the Vintage Reserve Port, one of South Africa's very greatest "ports."

✓ *Fortified* (Cape Tawny Port, Red Muscadel, Vintage Reserve Port)

BOSCHENDAL
Paarl
★

Although this large producer is best known as the Cape's pioneering traditional method producer, Boschendal Estate also makes a large range of still wines, many of which, particularly the reds, are much more exciting than the sparkling ones.

✓ *Cabernet Sauvignon* • *Chardonnay* (Reserve) • *Merlot • Sauvignon Blanc* (Jean de Long) • *Sémillon* (Jean de Long) • *Sparkling* (Boschendal Brut) • *Syrah*

BOUCHARD-FINLAYSON
Overberg
★★★½

This small, deluxe enterprise was started by Hamilton Russell's winemaker Peter Finlayson, who was joined by Paul Bouchard from Burgundy. In 2001, however, controlling interest in the winery was taken over by Bea and Stanley Tollman. Bouchard remains a partner and Finlayson continues as winemaker. Finlayson is a bit of a gentle giant, and his wines reflect that, building quietly in the mouth to a remarkable elegance and depth of flavor. Galpin Peak Pinot Noir and Galpin Peak Tête de Cuvée Pinot Noir are the standouts here.

✓ *Chardonnay* (Kaaimansgat, Missionvale, Sans Barrique) • *Classic red blend* (Hannibal) • *Pinot Noir*

J. P. BREDELL
Stellenbosch
★★½

This "port" specialist has always made varietal wines, but these have improved of late, particularly the Merlot.

✓ *Fortified* (Port: Late Bottled Vintage, Cape Vintage Reserve) • *Merlot*

BUITENVERWACHTING
Constantia
★★

Part of the historical Constantia estate, Buitenverwachting was renovated and replanted in the 1970s. It produced its first vintage in 1985, and was already showing promise by 1988. Throughout the 1990s it has been outstanding in virtually every style produced.

✓ *Cabernet Sauvignon* • *Chardonnay* • *Classic red blend* (Christine) • *Late Harvest* (Rhine Riesling Noble Late Harvest) • *Merlot* • *Sauvignon Blanc*

CABRIÈRE
Paarl
★★½

This estate belongs to Achim von Arnim, formerly the winemaker at Boschendal, and, not surprisingly, he has carved out his initial reputation by specializing in Cap Classique, but also produces a very good Pinot Noir.

✓ *Sparkling wine* (Pierre Jourdan: Blanc de Blancs, Brut, Cuvée Belle Rose, Cuvée Reserve) • *Pinot Noir* (Haut Cabrière)

CEDERBERG
Cederberg
★★

South Africa's highest-altitude vineyards produce wines of great length and finesse, rather than heavy in weight and alcohol.

✓ *Cabernet Sauvignon* •

Chenin Blanc • *Classic red blend* (Cederberger) • *Sauvignon Blanc*

CLOOF
Darling
★★½ Ⓥ

Too big for me, but these massively structured, high-alcohol wines are highly regarded award-winners within South Africa.

✓ *Pinotage* • *Syrah* (Crucible Shiraz)

CLOS MALVERNE
Stellenbosch
★★½

Noted for its deep-colored, powerful, slow-developing wines.

✓ *Cabernet Sauvignon* • *Classic red blend* (Auret Cape Blend, Cabernet Sauvignon Pinotage Cape Blend, Cabernet Sauvignon Shiraz) • *Pinotage* (Reserve)

PAUL CLUVER
Elgin
★★½

Pioneering Elgin wines from the first vintage in 1997.

✓ *Cabernet Sauvignon* • *Chardonnay* • *Late Harvest* (Weisser Riesling Noble Late Harvest) • *Pinot Noir* • *Riesling* (Weisser Riesling)

CONSTANTIA UITSIG
Constantia
★★½

Owned by Dave and Marlene McCay, Constantia Uitsig makes some of South Africa's most lush red wines.

✓ *Chardonnay* (Reserve) • *Classic red blend* (Cabernet Sauvignon-Merlot) • *Classic white blend* (Sémillon-Sauvignon Blanc) • *Sémillon* (Reserve)

CORDOBA
Stellenbosch
★★½

These high mountain vineyards produce some of South Africa's

finest reds, showing great length and finesse.

✓ *Classic red blend* (Crescendo) • *Merlot*

JEAN DANEEL
Napier
★★

A promising start for the former Morgenhof winemaker, who has just started releasing small volumes of exceptionally expressive wines from his own winery.

✓ *Chenin Blanc* (Signature) • *Classic red blend* (Cabernet Sauvignon-Merlot)

DARLING CELLARS
Darling
★★½ Ⓥ

Abé Beukes produces increasingly fine wines at this former cooperative, although the alcohol levels can be alarmingly high.

✓ *Cabernet Sauvignon* (Onyx) • *Classic red blend* (Onyx Croon) • *Late Harvest* (Noble Late Harvest Chenin Blanc) • *Pinotage* (Onyx) • *Syrah* (DC Black Granite Shiraz)

DELAIRE
Stellenbosch
★★½

Established by John Platter, South Africa's best-known wine writer; has since changed hands a couple of times. Delaire seems most consistent with Bordeaux-style blends and scintillating botrytized Riesling.

✓ *Chardonnay* • *Desert* (Edeloes)

DELHEIM
Stellenbosch
★★½ Ⓥ

Always good value, but until recently the quality is more good than great, and more consistent than outstanding. In recent years, however, Delheim has shown a dramatic improvement in quality.

✓ *Cabernet Sauvignon* (Grand Reserve) • *Merlot* • *Late Harvest* (Edelspatz) • *Syrah* (Vera Cruz Estate Shiraz)

DEVON HILLS
Stellenbosch
★★½

An up-and-coming winery, Devon Hills was established in 1997, with Erhard Roux taking over as winemaker in 2002.

✓ *Classic red blend* (Blue Bird) • *Syrah* (Shiraz)

DIEMERSDAL
Durbanville
★★½ Ⓥ

Although the 14 percent-plus alcoholic strength of these wines is not unusual for a premium South African producer, the surprisingly elegant style is.

✓ *Cabernet Sauvignon* • *Chardonnay* • *Classic red blend* (Private Collection) • *Pinotage*

DIEMERSFONTEIN
Wellington
★★½ Ⓥ

Full-throttle Pinotage in the style adored by South Africans.

✓ *Pinotage* (Carpe Diem)

DISTELL
Caledon

Created in 2000 by the merger of Stellenbosch Farmers' Winery (SFW) and Distillers Corporation, bringing together Fleur du Cap and Nederburg (two competing, high-quality wine brands), making this South Africa's largest wine and spirit group. Another excellent-value brand owned by Distell is Zonnenbloem. It also owns the good-value Drosdy-Hof wines; the successful, fast-selling sparkling wines of J. C. Le Roux; and the award-winning fortified wines of Monis. Chateau Libertas is viewed as one of the Cape's largest-volume, "quality" red wines, and figures prominently in the turnover of this group. Distell has sole ownership of Plaisir de Merle, its flagship wine estate, and joint ownership of Durbanville Hills, Hill & Dale, and Tukulu (a black empowerment project). Five wine estates owned jointly with German industrialist Hans Schreiber—through Lusan Holdings—are Alto, Le Bonheur, Neethlingshof, Stellenzicht, and Uitkyk. Recently launched good-value brands, which are essentially export-oriented but also available on the home market, include African Skies, Obikwa, Oracle, Table Mountain, and Two Oceans. Other good-value Distell brands include Grünberger, Kupferberger Auslese, and Ship Sherry. And there are dozens of decent, if run-of-the-mill, commercial wine brands, including Autumn Harvest, Capenheimer, Cellar Cask, Graça, Grand Mousseux, Kellerprinz, Oom Tas, Overmeer Cellars, Sedgewick's, Tassenberg, and Taverna. Jacobsdal and Theuniskraal are often associated with Distell, but are both privately owned estates, with Distell merely providing exclusive distribution.

DORNIER
Paarl
★★½

Dornier shows astonishing quality and consistency for a winery whose first vintage was 2002.

✓ *Classic red blend* (Donatus) • *Classic white blend* (Donatus White)

DURBANVILLE HILLS
Durbanville
★★½

Apparently, it is so cold during the harvest that the Durbanville Hills pickers have to wear thick woolen sweaters. No doubt this is the explanation for the excellent, bracing quality of the white wines at this up-and-coming joint venture between Distell and seven leading Durbanville growers.

✔ *Chardonnay* (Rhinofields) • *Classic red blend* (Caapmans Cabernet Sauvignon-Merlot) • *Sauvignon Blanc*

EIKENDAL
Stellenbosch
★★½

This Swiss-owned producer is perhaps best known on export markets for its blockbuster Chardonnay, but it actually produces finer reds, and even manages to make a fine-quality Cinsault-dominated blend. Its second wines are made under the Duc de Berry label.

✔ *Cabernet Sauvignon* (Reserve) • *Chardonnay* • *Classic red blend* (Classique, Rossini) • *Sémillon*

NEIL ELLIS
Stellenbosch
★★

The Cape's first and foremost winemaker-négociant, Ellis's uncanny skill in sourcing grapes from cutting-edge viticultural areas, and equal expertise in crafting some of South Africa's classiest wines from them, has sparked off a whole raft of wineries that buy in from selected vineyards.

✔ *Cabernet Sauvignon* (Stellenbosch, Jonkershoek) • *Classic red blend* (Cabernet Sauvignon-Merlot) • *Chardonnay* (Aenigma, Elgin) • *Pinotage* (Stellenbosch) • *Sauvignon Blanc* (Groenekloof) • *Syrah* (Jonkershoek Shiraz)

FAIRVIEW
Paarl
★★★½

This estate is run by Charles Back, one of the most innovative wine producers in South Africa, offering a large and constantly expanding range of wine styles. The poorest wines here are good, and the best are sensational.

✔ *Carignan* (Pegleg) • *Chardonnay* (Akkerbos) • *Classic red blend* (Caldera) • *Desert* (La Beryl Blanc) • *Pinotage* (Primo) • *Sauvignon Blanc* • *Sémillon* (Oom Pagel) • *Shiraz* (Cyril Back, Solitude) • *Viognier*

FLAGSTONE
Somerset West
★★½

Owner-winemaker Bruce Jack was quick off the block with a stunning quality range of wines from his first vintage in 1999. A master at classic red blends.

✔ *Cabernet Sauvignon* (Berrio)

• *Classic red blend* (Bowwood, Dragon Tree, Foundation Longtitude, Mary Le Bon) • *Pinot Noir* (The Poetry Collection) • *Ruby Cabernet* (Ruby in the Dust) • *Sauvignon Blanc* (Berrio)

FLEUR DU CAP
Stellenbosch
★★★ Ⓥ

Made and marketed by the Bergkelder at Stellenbosch, Fleur du Cap has established a high standard of quality for its basic wines, but has reinvented itself with spectacular success with its "Unfiltered" range.

✔ *Cabernet Sauvignon* (Unfiltered) • *Chardonnay* (Unfiltered) • *Chenin Blanc* • *Classic white blend* (Unfiltered Viognier-Chardonnay Sauvignon Blanc-Sémillon) • *Late Harvest* (Noble Riesling) • *Merlot* (Unfiltered) • *Sauvignon* (Unfiltered Limited Release) • *Sémillon* (Unfiltered)

KEN FORRESTER
Stellenbosch
★★½

This property dates back to 1689, when the farm was called Zandberg, and by 1692 some 12,000 vines had been planted. But the first wine in modern times was produced in 1994, when owners Ken and Teresa Forrester pressed a small quantity of Sauvignon Blanc grapes to produce a Blanc Fumé. They also own the wonderful restaurant opposite the vineyard called 96 Winery Road.

✔ *Chenin Blanc* • *Classic red blend* (Gypsy) • *Late Harvest* (T Noble)

FORT SIMON
Stellenbosch
★★½

Since its first vintage in 1998, Fort Simon Estate has impressed with the elegance of its wines.

✔ *Chardonnay* • *Chenin Blanc* (Barrel Fermented)

THE FOUNDRY
Stellenbosch
★★

Although made at Meerlust, this is the private label of Chris Williams and his business partner James Reid of Kumala fame. In 2004 Chris Williams took over from the legendary Giorgio Dalla Cia, as Meerlust's winemaker, and brought The Foundry label with him.

✔ *Classic red blend* (Double Barrel) • *Syrah*

GLEN CARLOU
Paarl

Donal Hess of The Hess Collection in Napa was the co-owner, until he bought out David Finlayson. Finlayson remains as winemaker, continuing to produce some of South Africa's finest Chardonnay.

✔ *Chardonnay* • *Classic red blend* (Grand Classique) • *Pinot Noir* • *Syrah*

GOEDE HOOP
Stellenbosch
★ Ⓥ

Under owner Pieter Bestbier, this former Bergkelder estate offers an expanded range of wines of improving quality.

✔ *Cabernet Sauvignon* • *Classic red blend* (Merlot-Cabernet Sauvignon)

GRANGEHURST
Stellenbosch
★★

One of the new breed of winemakers who source grapes from various other growers, Grangehurst makes exciting, well-crafted, elegant yet substantive wines.

✔ *Cabernet Sauvignon* (Chairman's Reserve) • *Classic red blend* (Cabernet Sauvignon-Merlot, Nikela) • *Pinotage*

GROOT CONSTANTIA
Constantia
★½

This property is part of the original Constantia farm, the oldest and most famous of Cape estates, and is currently being run with passion and great skill.

✔ *Classic red blend* (Gouverneurs Reserve) • *Merlot* (Gouverneurs) • *Syrah* (Gouverneurs Shiraz)

HAMILTON RUSSELL
Overberg
★★★½

Established by Tim Hamilton Russell, this was once Africa's most southerly vineyard. Now there are many this far south and some farther still. No expense was spared to ensure that this would become one of the finest wineries in the Cape, and winemaker Peter Finlayson helped make that dream come true. Finlayson left to establish his own winery, Bouchard-Finlayson (which is just next door), but his replacement, Kevin Grant, continued to make some of the Cape's most spell-binding Burgundian varietals. Hannes Storm became the new winemaker at the Hamilton Russell vineyard in 2004.

✔ *Chardonnay* • *Pinot Noir*

HARTENBERG
Stellenbosch
★★

Some stunning wines, but what a pity they ripped out the Zinfandel!

✔ *Cabernet Sauvignon* • *Chardonnay* • *Merlot* • *Syrah* (Shiraz)

HAVANA HILLS
Philadelphia
★★½

The winery that has single-handedly established the reputation of the new Philadelphia wine ward for top-performing red wines.

✔ *Cabernet Sauvignon* (Du Plessis Reserve) • *Classic red blend* (Du Plessis Reserve) • *Merlot* (Du Plessis Reserve) • *Shiraz* (Du Plessis Reserve)

HILLCREST
Durbanville
★★½ Ⓥ

The Hillcrest estate's first vintage was as recent as 2002, yet the deftly sculptured wines scream out for attention.

✔ *Classic red blend* (Merlot-Cabernet Sauvignon) • *Sauvignon Blanc*

JONKHEER
Stellenbosch
★★½ Ⓥ

The Madonna of the Cape wine industry, Jonkheer was established as long ago as 1912, and was known as Jonkheer Boere Wynmakery, when they were known for semisweet white wines called Edelweiss, but they have not only economized their trading name, but have also reinvented their wines, which are exemplary by any standards.

✔ *Chardonnay* (Dead Frogge, Family Reserve) • *Classic red Blend* (Cobblers Hill) • *Fortified* (Bakenskop White Muscadel, Muscatheer Family Reserve Muscat de Frontignan)

JORDAN
Stellenbosch
★★

This property is now a Cape front-ranker, especially for Cobblers Hill classic red wine blend (a three-barrel selection called Jordan Sophia is sold exclusively at the CWG Auction), but its primary reputation is for rich and vibrant white wines.

✔ *Chardonnay* (Nine Yards) • *Classic red Blend* (Cobblers Hill) • *Sauvignon Blanc* • *Merlot*

KAAPZICHT
Stellenbosch
★★ Ⓥ

Established in 1984, Kaapzicht Estate has only just awoken to provide a number of exciting wines in recent years. Although the Pinotage is usually a big wine, it is so well balanced that it belies its 15 point something of alcohol.

✓ *Cabernet Sauvignon* • *Classic red blend* (Steytler Vision) • *Pinotage* (Steytler) • *Shiraz*

KANONKOP
Stellenbosch
★★

Winemaker Beyers Truter is generally considered to be one of the greatest Stellenbosch red wine exponents, and more specifically the king of Pinotage.

✓ *Cabernet Sauvignon* • *Classic red blend* (Paul Sauer) • *Pinotage*

KANU
Stellenbosch
★✫ⓥ

Delightful, easy-drinking, good-value standard range, and serious to stunning Limited Release wines from this winery that has captured much attention since it was established in 1998.

✓ *Cabernet Sauvignon* (Limited Release) • *Chardonnay* (Limited Release) • *Chenin Blanc* (Wooded) • *Classic red blend* (Keystone) • *Merlot* (Limited Release)

KLEIN CONSTANTIA
Constantia
★★✫

This property was part of Simon van der Stel's original Constantia Estate, but after centuries of neglect it was replanted as recently as 1982. Note that Vin de Constance is not a botrytis wine, nor is it fortified; it is supposedly a faithful replication of the famous Constantia of old.

✓ *Cabernet Sauvignon* (Reserve) • *Desert* (Vin de Constance) • *Late Harvest* (Noble Late Harvest Sauvignon Blanc) • *Riesling* (Rhine Riesling) • *Sauvignon Blanc*

KLEINE ZALZE
Stellenbosch
★ⓥ

This former Gilbeys property was purchased by Kobus Basson and Jan Malan in 1996, since when its wines have been put on the map and its reputation has been rising fast.

✓ *Cabernet Sauvignon* (Barrel Matured) • *Chardonnay* (Barrel Fermented) • *Merlot* (Barrel Matured, Cellar Selection)

KWV
Paarl
★★ⓥ

This was a supersized cooperative that controlled the entire South African wine industry until 1995, when it was stripped of its legislative powers, and privatized. Extraordinary as it might seem to external observers, KWV wines

were not allowed to be sold in South Africa itself. However, with legal and structural changes, this was due to change in 2001, although certain obstacles prevented these wines from reaching the shelf locally until 2004. As it turned out, 2004 was a year when the KWV hit the headlines for reasons its management would rather forget—it was discovered that two of its winemakers had added illegal (but harmless) flavorants to two Sauvignon Blanc wines (2004 Laborie and 2004 KWV Reserve). They were dismissed, and 16,000 gallons (60,000 liters) of wine had to be destroyed. Looking on the bright side, the quality and value of KWV wines (especially in the Cathedral Cellar and Reserve ranges) have never been higher, and if such trickery were to occur anywhere else in South Africa, the one thing we can be sure about is that it will not be at KWV. There are just too many official eyes looking at everything it does.

✓ *Cabernet Sauvignon* (Cathedral Cellar, KWV Reserve, Labourie) • *Chardonnay* (Cathedral Cellar) • *Classic red blend* (Cathedral Cellar Triptych) • *Classic white blend* (Robert's Rock Chardonnay-Sémillon) • *Fortified* (Tawny Port, Vintage Port, Vintage Red Muscadel) • *Merlot* (Cathedral Cellar, KWV Reserve) • *Pinotage* (Cathedral Cellar) • *Sauvignon Blanc* (Labourie, KWV Reserve) • *Syrah* (Cathedral Cellar Shiraz, Labourie Cabernet Merlot Reserve, Labourie Jean Taillefert)

LAIBACH
Stellenbosch
★

This farm was called Good Success until it was purchased by Swiss-based German businessman Friedrich Laibach, who built a new cellar and bottled these wines for the first time in 1997. Almost 15 percent of the Laibach vineyard is farmed organically.

✓ *Classic red blend* (Friedrich Laibach, The Ladybird) ◉ • *Pinotage*

LANDSKROON
Paarl
★✫ⓥ

This is a very large estate at 148 acres (600 hectares), of which 74 acres (300 hectares) are under vine.

✓ *Cabernet Sauvignon* • *Port* • *Shiraz* (Paul de Villiers)

LONGRIDGE WINERY
Stellenbosch
★✫

Longridge Winery is now part of the Australian wine group Winecorp, which also owns Savanha and Spier. Longridge constitutes one of the largest of the Cape's quality-oriented producers.

✓ *Cabernet Sauvignon* • *Chardonnay* • *Merlot* • *Pinotage*

LOUISVALE
Stellenbosch
★

Louisvale offers a solid range of well-made wines, but is best known for its big, leesy Chardonnay.

✓ *Chardonnay* • *Classic red bend* (Dominique)

MEERLUST
Stellenbosch
★★✫

For more than 30 years this has been one of the Cape's most consistent wine estates. Meerlust is owned by the Myburgh family, who have been assisted from the very start by the visionary winemaker Giorgio Dalla Cia. Dalla Cia retired in 2004, handing over to Chris Williams, who worked with Michel Rolland, and was Dalla Cia's assistant winemaker between 1995 and 2000, when he set up The Foundry. All wines produced are among the very best in the country for their particular styles, but with eighth generation Hannes Myburgh in overall charge, and such a talented, inquisitive new winemaker at the helm, Meerlust is set to go from top gear into overdrive.

✓ *Chardonnay* • *Classic red blend* (Rubicon) • *Merlot* • *Pinot Noir*

MEINERT
Stellenbosch
★★

Since 1997, Ken Forrester's winemaking partner Martin Meinert has made some splendid wines under his own label.

✓ *Classic red blend* (Devon Crest, Synchronicity) • *Merlot*

MIDDELVLEI
Stellenbosch
★

This estate made its reputation with Pinotage, but has recently been producing stunning Syrah.

✓ *Pinotage* • *Syrah* (Shiraz)

MONIS
Paarl
★✫ⓥ

This famous old Cape fortified brand belongs to Distell (*see* separate entry).

✓ *Fortified* (Cream Sherry, Muscadel, Very Old Tawny Port)

MOOIPLAAS
Stellenbosch
★✫ⓥ

After making and selling wine in bulk for 30 years, the owners started selling wines under their Mooiplaas label in 1995.

✓ *Cabernet Sauvignon* • *Pinotage* • *Syrah* (Shiraz)

MÔRESON
Stellenbosch
★✫

Acquired by Richard Friedmann in 1985, this estate initially developed a reputation for its white wines, although it is its reds that have shone out in recent vintages.

✓ *Cabernet Sauvignon* • *Chardonnay* (Premium) • *Classic red blend* (Magia) • *Pinotage* • *Sauvignon Blanc*

MORGENHOF
Stellenbosch
★★★ⓥ

This historic wine estate is owned by Anne Cointreau-Huchon, whose *cognaçais* family own Champagne Gosset. Morgenhof makes some truly stylish wines, with excellent-value entry-level wines sold under the Fantail label. I have not tasted New Cap Classique, but I would be surprised and disappointed if it is not one of the country's best.

✓ *Cabernet Sauvignon* (Reserve) • *Chardonnay* • *Classic red blend* (Première Sélection) • *Merlot* (Reserve) • *Pinotage* • *Sauvignon Blanc*

MORGENSTER
Stellenbosch
★★

Another new name to watch, Morgenster was established in 1993, but did not produce any wine under its own label until the 1998 vintage. Morgenster grows just four Bordeaux varieties (Merlot, Cabernet Sauvignon, Cabernet Franc, and Petit Verdot), and specializes in classic red blends. Pierre Lurton consults.

✓ *Classic red blend* (Lourens River Valley, Morgenster)

LA MOTTE
Paarl
★★

Owned by Hanneli Koegelenberg, the daughter of Anton Rupert, the second richest man in South Africa, La Motte's wines have been made by Edmund Terblanche since 2001.

✓ *Classic red blend* (Shiraz-Viognier) • *Syrah* (Shiraz)

MULDERBOSCH
Stellenbosch
★★

These are top-flight wines from superbly sited mountain vineyards, with moves toward organic viticulture, and crafted by skillful winemaking.

✓ *Chardonnay* • *Chenin Blanc* (Steen-op-Hout) • *Classic red blend* (Beta Centauri, Faithful Hound) • *Sauvignon Blanc*

MURATIE
Stellenbosch
★✫

Owned by the Melck family, which has made some brilliant wines since 2000. Guillaume Nell is the new winemaker since 2003.

✓ *Cabernet Sauvignon • Classic red blend* (Ansela) • *Fortified* (Cape Vintage) • *Syrah* (Shiraz)

NEDERBURG
Stellenbosch
★☆ⓥ

Owned by Distell. As with Fleur du Cap, the consistency is remarkable for such a commercial range, on top of which the quality improves with each year. The entire 20-plus range of Private Bin wines sold exclusively at the annual Nederburg Auction is recommended, but they become available only should a retailer successfully bid for a lot, and later decide to market them.

✓ *Cabernet Sauvignon* (Private Bin) • *Classic red blend* (Edelrood) • *Classic red blend* (Prelude) • *Late Harvest* (Noble Late Harvest) • *Sauvignon Blanc* (Private Bin) • *Shiraz* (Private Bin)

NEETHLINGSHOF
Stellenbosch
★☆ⓥ

Owned by Lusan Holdings, this vineyard's wines have greatly improved in quality since the 1990s.

✓ *Cabernet Franc* (Lord Neethlingshof) • *Cabernet Sauvignon* (Lord Neethlingshof) • *Chardonnay* (Lord Neethlingshof) • *Classic red blend* (Cape Blend, Lord Neethlingshof Laurentius) • *Late Harvest* (Weisser Riesling Noble Late Harvest) • *Syrah* (Shiraz)

NELSON
Paarl
★☆

Established in 1993 by the Nelson family, this estate has moved up a gear since the new millennium.

✓ *Classic red blend* (Cabernet Sauvignon Merlot) • *Chardonnay • Syrah* (Shiraz)

NEWTON JOHNSON
Walker Bay
★★ⓥ

One of the brightest new stars in the exciting Walker Bay wine scene.

✓ *Cabernet Sauvignon • Chardonnay • Classic red blend* (Shiraz-Mourvèdre) • *Pinot Noir • Sauvignon Blanc*

NITIDA CELLARS
Durbanville
★☆ⓥ

Small, up-and-coming boutique in the Durbanville Kloof, where there is a distinct intensity to the wines.

✓ *Cabernet Sauvignon • Sauvignon Blanc • Sémillon*

NUY WINE CELLAR
Worcester
★ⓥ

South Africa's best cooperative has a more private-sounding name these

days, but the secret of its success is the same—it selects just 3 percent of the 10,000 tons processed every year to sell under its own label.

✓ *Colombard* (Dry) • *Fortified* (Red Muscadel, White Muscadel)

THE OBSERVATORY
Malmesbury
★★

The Lubbe family has made an indelible impact with minuscule releases from vines growing on the slopes of the Paardeberg.

✓ *Classic red blend* (Carignan-Syrah) • *Syrah*

OLD VINES
Rosebank
★☆ⓥ

South Africa's only women's empowerment winery, Old Vines was established in 1995 by mother and daughter, Irina von Holdt and Françoise Botha, whose primary goal is to raise awareness of Chenin Blanc as the Cape's white-wine flagbearer.

✓ *Chenin Blanc*

L'ORMARINS
Paarl
★☆

Restored by the late Toni Rupert, son of Anton Rupert. With virtually unlimited finance at his disposal, Toni quickly established L'Ormarins at the very top of Cape winemaking. L'Ormarins is now owned by Toni's brother, Johann.

✓ *Cabernet Sauvignon • Classic red blend* (Optima) • *Merlot*

OVERGAAUW
Stellenbosch
★☆

This is a technically superior operation that produces exciting wines. With lots of class and very little sulfur dioxide, Overgaauw has been a pioneering wine estate for a quarter of a century.

✓ *Cabernet Sauvignon • Chardonnay • Classic red blend* (Shiraz-Cabernet Sauvignon, Tria Corda) • *Fortified* (Cape Vintage, Cape Vintage Reserve) • *Merlot*

PLAISIR DE MERLE
Stellenbosch
★★

Grapes from Plaisir de Merle formed the heart of many Nederburg wines until 1993, when with the help of consultant Paul Pontallier of Château Margaux, owner-winemaker Niel Bester launched a range of estate-bottled wines that are worthy of Distell's flagship domaine.

✓ *Classic red blend* (Grand Plaisir) • *Merlot • Sauvignon Blanc*

DU PREEZ
Goudini
★☆ⓥ

An up-and-coming new star from an unlikely part of the Breede River

Valley, with less expensive wines sold under Rockfields and Dry Creek labels.

✓ *Classic red blend* (Polla's Red) • *Fortified* (Hanepoot) • *Merlot* (Reserve) • *Petit Verdot* (Hendrik Lodewyk)

REMHOOGTE
Stellenbosch
★★☆

A rapidly improving winery whose inaugural vintage was 1995. Michel Rolland consults.

✓ *Classic red blend* (Bonne Nouvelle)

RHEBOKSLOOF
Paarl
★★☆

My my, how the quality here has rocketed since the late 1990s.

✓ *Cabernet Sauvignon • Chardonnay* (Grand Reserve) • *Classic red blend* (Cabernet Sauvignon-Merlot)

LE RICHE
Stellenbosch
★★

The first vintage was 1997 for this small, up-and-coming winery that has focused on making a limited range of highly polished reds.

✓ *Cabernet Sauvignon • Cabernet Sauvignon-Merlot*

RIETVALLEI
Robertson
★

Classic Muscadel.

✓ *Chardonnay • Fortified* (Muscadel 1908, Red Muscadel) • *Syrah* (Shiraz)

RIJK'S PRIVATE CELLAR
Tulbagh
★☆

Fast-rising, potential star winery, Rijk's inaugural vintage was as recent as 2000.

✓ *Classic red blend* (Bravado) • *Sémillon*

ROBERTSON WINERY
Robertson
★☆ⓥ

For a cooperative that could be relied upon for little more than fortified wine, the Robertson Winery has developed an exciting range of

modern, finely honed table wines, and these have been on a roll since the early 2000s.

✓ *Chardonnay* (Kings River) • *Classic red blend* (No. 1 Constitution Road) • *Late Harvest* (Wide River Reserve) • *Syrah* (Wolfkloof Shiraz)

J. C. LE ROUX
Stellenbosch
★

This Bergkelder label was originally used exclusively for sparkling wines, but various still wines have since been added.

✓ *Sparkling* (Pinot Noir)

RUDERA
Robertson
★★

With his first vintage as recent as 2001, owner-winemaker Teddy Hall has rapidly established a broad and convincing reputation as one of the names to watch in the future of South African wine, particularly for Chenin Blanc.

✓ *Cabernet Sauvignon • Chenin Blanc • Late Harvest* (Noble Late Harvest Chenin Blanc) • *Syrah*

RUST EN VREDE
Stellenbosch
★

Owned by Jannie Engelbrecht, a former Springbok, who produces only wines he likes to drink—rich, red, dense, well balanced, and not sold until they are ready.

✓ *Cabernet Sauvignon • Classic red blend* (Estate Wine) • *Merlot • Syrah* (Shiraz)

RUSTENBERG
Stellenbosch
★★☆

Once heralded as the very best of South Africa's top growths, the quality at Rustenberg Estate faltered in the early 1990s, only for it to be picked up as from the 1996 vintage, and pushed higher than it has ever been. Rustenberg Estate is now under the direct control of Simon Barlow, who installed a brand new winery and has done everything necessary to ensure that Rustenberg's reputation remains impeccable. Wines sold under the entry-level Brampton label sometimes rival Rustenberg at its best.

✓ *Cabernet Sauvignon* (Peter Barlow) • *Chardonnay* (Five Soldiers, Stellenbosch) • *Classic red blend* (John X Merriman) • *Late Harvest* (QF)

SAXENBURG
Stellenbosch
★★

This Swiss-owned winery has been a rising star for wines of increasingly high quality and complexity since the late 1990s.

✓ *Cabernet Sauvignon* (Private Collection) • *Chardonnay* (Private Collection) • *Classic red blend* (Gwendolyn, Manuel) • *Merlot* (Private Collection) • *Pinotage* (Private Collection) • *Sauvignon Blanc* (Private Collection) • *Syrah* (Shiraz Select)

SEIDELBERG
Paarl
★ ½

Brilliant wines since the early 2000s.

✓ *Classic red blend* (Un Deux Trois) • *Fortified* (Red Muscadel) • *Merlot* (Roland's Reserve) • *Syrah* (Roland's Reserve)

SENTINEL
Stellenbosch
★ ★

Established by Rob Coppoolse, Walter Finlayson, and Viv Grater in 1995, the quality of these wines really began to take off with the 2002 vintage.

✓ *Merlot* • *Pinotage* • *Syrah* (Shiraz)

SIGNAL HILL
Stellenbosch
★ ½

Jean-Vincent Ridon is in the process of planting a vineyard on Signal Hill, next to Table Mountain, by renting every square inch he can find. Until these vines come on stream, he buys in grapes to produce a mostly splendid range of wines.

✓ *Chardonnay* (Corsaire) • *Classic red blend* (Frans Malan, Tiara) • *Desert* (Mathilde Azú 6 Puttonyos, Vin de Glacière, Vin de l'Empereur) • *Grenache Blanc* • *Late Harvest* (Muscat d'Alexandrie Noble Late Harvest) • *Petit Verdot* • *Pinotage* (Malwenn) • *Sparkling* (Kaapse Vonkel) • *Syrah* (Merindol)

SIMONSIG
Stellenbosch
★ ★

This winery has a huge production, and its wines range from the

---

sensational down to pretty standard stuff, with an increasing proportion of the former.

✓ *Classic red blend* (Frans Malan, Tiara) • *Late Harvest* (Vin de Liza) • *Petit Verdot* (Auction Reserve) • *Sparkling* (Kaapse Vonkel) • *Syrah* (Merindol)

SPICE ROUTE
Malmesbury
★ ★

This estate was originally owned by a consortium of Charles Back, Jabulani Ntshangase, John Platter, and Gyles Webb, but it is now solely owned by Back. Spice Route excels at red wines, and its signature style is typically deep, dark, rich, and spicy, with masses of black fruit. Its Flagship Syrah is still one of the best I have tasted from South Africa.

✓ *Chenin Blanc* • *Classic red blend* (Malabar) • *Merlot* (Flagship) • *Syrah* (Flagship)

SPIER
Stellenbosch
★ ★

A winery has been added to this deluxe, classy hotel complex, which Winecorp originally established in 1976. The first vintage to be produced here was in 1996. The very best wines are sold under Spier's Private Collection label (which is considerably better quality than is found among most of their basic range).

✓ *Cabernet Sauvignon* (Private Collection) • *Chenin Blanc* (Private Collection) • *Late Harvest* (Noble Late Harvest) • *Merlot* (Private Collection) • *Pinotage* • *Sauvignon Blanc* (Private Collection) • *Viognier* (Private Collection)

SPRINGFIELD
Robertson
◉ ★ ½

Owner-winemaker Abrie Bruwer is considered a bit of an eccentric in his own country, but virtually all of his practices merely represent an organic approach, with even a touch of biodynamics, to farming and winemaking.

✓ *Cabernet Sauvignon* (Méthode Ancienne, Whole Berry) • *Chardonnay* (Méthode Ancienne, Wild Yeast) • *Classic red blend* (The Work of Time) • *Sauvignon Blanc* (Life From Stone)

STARK-CONDÉ
Stellenbosch
★ ★

Condé wines are named after the winemaker José Conde, and are single-vineyard wines made from Stark-Condé's best blocks. Stark wines are named after Franciska Stark, the late family matriarch, and are blended from more than one of Stark-Condé's vineyard blocks; given the same hand treatment as the Condé wines, they differ simply by being blends of multiple vineyard blocks.

✓ *Cabernet Sauvignon* (Condé, Stark) • *Shiraz* (Stark)

STEENBERG
Constantia
★ ★

From small quantities of gorgeously fresh Sauvignon Blanc to a fabulous range of stunning wines in a myriad of styles, including the country's best Sémillon.

✓ *Classic red blend* (Catharina) • *Nebbiolo* • *Sauvignon Blanc* • *Sémillon*

STELLENBOSCH
Stellenbosch
★ ★ ◐

The Eersterivier Vineyards and Helderberg cooperatives consolidated with Bottelary, Hoelenhof, and Welmoed to become Stellenbosch. They then reinvented themselves as a private cellar by converting their members into shareholders.

✓ *Cabernet Sauvignon* (Genesis) • *Chardonnay* (Genesis) • *Classic red blend* (Kumkani Merlot-Cabernet Franc) • *Classic white blend* (Kumkani VVS) • *Merlot* (Genesis) • *Syrah* (Genesis Shiraz) • *Sauvignon Blanc* (Kumkani)

STELLENZICHT
Stellenbosch
★ ★ ½

Under the same ownership as Neethlingshof, Stellenzicht's mountain vineyards produce some of the finest new arrivals on the South African fine-wine scene.

✓ *Classic red blend* (Stellenzicht) • *Sémillon* (Reserve) • *Syrah*

THABANI
KwaZulu-Natal
❓

Despite promises of black empowerment, this is the first and only wholly black-owned (Jabulani Ntshangase and Trevor Steyn) wine company in South Africa. This is definitely a name to watch, not because of any condescending, pseudo-liberal hype, but because of Jabulani Ntshangase, a mover and shaker in every sense. Once met, never forgotten, Ntshangase was one of the original partners in Spice Route, and I will be extremely surprised if Thabani does not rival that operation when its soon-to-be-built boutique winery is in operation.

THELEMA MOUNTAIN
Stellenbosch
★ ★ ★ ½

Under the steady hand of owner-winemaker Gyles Webb, Thelema Mountain has become one of the country's most exciting producers, producing stunningly rich, refined, and complex wines.

✓ *Cabernet Sauvignon* • *Cabernet Sauvignon-Merlot* • *Chardonnay* • *Merlot* • *Pinotage* • *Riesling* (Rhine Riesling) • *Sauvignon Blanc* • *Syrah* (Shiraz)

DU TOITSKLOOF WINERY
Worcester
★ ½ Ⓥ

The Du Toitskloof Winery, a cooperative, has a long record of award-winning table wines and now produces top-flight dessert wines.

✓ *Fortified* (Hanepoot Jerepigo, Red Muscadel)

DE TOREN
Stellenbosch
★ ★

Although this winery's first vintage was as recent as 1999, it already has a cult following for its stunningly successful Fusion V, a classic blend of five varieties (Cabernet Sauvignon, Cabernet Franc, Merlot, Malbec, and Petit Verdot).

✓ *Classic red blend* (Diversity Beta, Fusion V)

DE TRAFFORD
Stellenbosch
★ ★

This ultrasmall boutique winery has established a reputation for beautifully crafted Cabernet, with whispers in the wind of things to come, including serious, *barrique*-fermented Chenin Blanc.

✓ *Cabernet Sauvignon* • *Merlot*

TUKULU
Groenkloof
★ ★ ½ Ⓥ

This is a black empowerment joint venture with Distell, which will divest itself of its shareholding as the start-up capital is repaid through the sale of grapes in about 12 years' time (from 1998, its date of establishment).

✓ *Chenin Blanc* • *Pinotage*

TWEE JONGEGEZELLEN
Tulbagh
★ Ⓥ

Having endured horrendous bottle quality problems, Nicky Krone's

Krone Borealis is back on track, particularly because he is now giving it greater bottle-age. His greatest Cap Classique wine is, however, Private Vintners Limited Release 1995 Pinot Noir.

✓ *Sparkling wine* (Krone Borealis, Private Vintners Limited Release)

VEENWOUDEN
Paarl
★★☆ ⓥ

This boutique winery enjoyed its first vintage in 1993. Since then it has built up a compact range of increasingly fine quality.

✓ *Chardonnay* (Special Reserve) • *Classic red blend* (Classic, Vivat Bacchus) • *Merlot* • *Veenwouden* (Cabernet blend)

VERGELEGEN
Stellenbosch
★★★☆

This immaculately restored, historic wine estate must be everyone's choice as the leading South African wine producer, thanks to the meticulous efforts of its winemaker André van Rensburg.

✓ *Cabernet Sauvignon* • *Chardonnay* • *Classic red blend* (Vergelegen, Vergelegen V) • *Merlot* • *Sauvignon Blanc* • *Syrah* (Shiraz)

VERGENOEGD
Stellenbosch
★★☆ ⓥ

Owner-winemaker John Faure has gradually focused the quality of these wines since the 1990s.

✓ *Cabernet Sauvignon* • *Classic red blend* (Vergenoegd) • *Fortified* (Old Cape Colony Vintage Port) • *Merlot* • *Syrah* (Shiraz)

VILLAFONTÉ
Paarl-Simonsberg
★★ ⓥ

This is a brand-new joint venture between winemaking guru Zelma Long, viticulturist Phillip Freese, Warwick Estate's Mike Ratcliffe, and Bartholomew Broadbent, the American wine merchant son of Michael Broadbent. Villafonté is taken from the name *villafontes*, the gray, sandy soil on the property, which its owners believe to have a significant impact on the flavor profile and development of their wines. The vineyards are in Paarl-Simonsberg district, on the northern side of the Simonsberg Mountains, and planted in high density with four Bordeaux varieties (Cabernet Franc, Cabernet Sauvignon, Malbec, and Merlot). All of the farming is performed with four-wheel-drive motorcycles to reduce soil compaction. Series C is Cabernet Sauvignon-based, whereas Series M is Merlot-based.

✓ *Classic red blend* (Series C, Series M)

VILLIERA
Paarl
★★ ⓥ

VILLIERA INSPIRATION

Villiera Estate was a rapidly rising star when the first edition of this encyclopedia was published 17 years ago, and it is now a well-established producer by current Cape wine standards.

✓ *Chenin Blanc* • *Classic red blend* (Monro) • *Classic white blend* (Down to Earth) • *Late Harvest* (Chenin Blanc Noble Late Harvest) • *Sparkling* (Brut Natural Chardonnay, Monro Brut, Tradition Brut, Tradition Rosé) • *Sauvignon Blanc* (Traditional Bush Vine)

WARWICK
Stellenbosch
★★

Michael Ratcliffe is doing a masterly job of filling his father's shoes, following Stan Ratcliffe's untimely death. Innovations include moving away from some varietals into the classic red "flagship" blend, and holding back five cases of every wine for rerelease five years later. I can't help wondering why other wineries around the world do not hold back limited quantities like this, particularly for those wines in the range that tend to sell out well before their prime.

✓ *Cabernet Franc* • *Chardonnay* • *Classic red blend* (Three Cape Ladies, Trilogy)

WATERFORD
Stellenbosch
★★☆

The first Waterford vintage was in 1998, and already this winery promises to be one of South Africa's star wineries.

✓ *Cabernet Sauvignon* • *Chardonnay* • *Classic red blend* (Cape Winemaker's Guild Blend) • *Syrah* (Kevin Arnold Shiraz)

WELGEMEEND
Paarl
★★☆

A small, high-quality red wine specialist that was established in the 1970s, Welgemeend was one of the first boutique wineries in South Africa. The winemakers at Welgemeend are aiming more for finesse and length than they are for alcohol and weight.

✓ *Classic red blend* (Douelle, Estate Reserve, Pinotage Shiraz)

WELTEVREDE
Robertson
★★☆

Weltevrede means "well satisfied," which I am glad to say is still an apt description of anyone who has sampled the wines.

✓ *Chardonnay* (Poet's Prayer) • *Riesling* (Rhine Riesling) • *Sauvignon Blanc* (The Travelling Stone)

DE WETSHOF
Robertson
★★☆

Quite how Danie de Wet can make such exquisite Chardonnay wines when you can cook an egg on the rocks in his vineyard is a mystery; such mysteries are part of the eternal fascination that wine holds for enthusiasts.

✓ *Riesling* (Rhine Riesling) • *Chardonnay* • *Fortified* (Muscadel) • *Edeloes* (botrytis)

THE WINERY
Stellenbosch
★★

With partners from the Rhône, Barossa, and the Cape, The Winery has crafted some of South Africa's most stylish wines since its inception in 1998.

✓ *Cabernet Sauvignon* (Vinum) • *Chardonnay* (Radford Dale) • *Chenin Blanc* (Vinum) • *Classic red blend* (Radford Dale Gravity) • *Merlot* (Radford Dale) • *Syrah* (Radford Dale Shiraz)

WOOLWORTHS
No fixed region
★★

Readers should be aware that Woolworths in South Africa does not have any of the connotations of the Woolworths chain of stores in the US. This winery produces wines that are stylish and generally good value. Much of the extraordinary in Woolworths' range can be attributed to Allan Mullins, who is one of this country's good guys, and possessor of a gifted palate. In addition to those wines recommended below, the Limited Release range can stand out, but the producer for each wine tends to change more often than those in other ranges. There is also a decent-quality organic range of wines here.

✓ *Cabernet Sauvignon* • *Chardonnay* (Limestone Hill, Reserve, Signature) • *Chenin Blanc* (Barrel) • *Classic red blend* (Cabernet Sauvignon-Merlot Reserve, Signature Cabernet Sauvignon) • *Pinotage*

(Reserve) • *Sauvignon Blanc* (Reserve) • *Sparkling wine* (Vintage Reserve Brut) • *Syrah* (Groenkloof Shiraz)

YONDER HILL
Stellenbosch
★

Yonder Hill produces a couple of beautifully crafted wines made from grapes grown in mountain vineyards on the Helderberg. The name of its classic red blend, iNanda, is Zulu for "beautiful place."

✓ *Classic red blend* (iNanda) • *Merlot*

ZANDVLIET
Robertson
★

Zandvliet is famous for its Syrah, and its new Hill of Eon wine is certainly the best yet. Astonvale is its second label.

✓ *Shiraz*

ZEVENWACHT
Stellenbosch
★☆ ⓥ

Zevenwacht grew rapidly in the 1980s, making wines that were fresh, frank, and aromatic, but perhaps not all that exciting. Recently, however, there have been considerable improvements in quality, and these wines can represent great value.

✓ *Classic white blend* (Tin Mine White) • *Merlot* • *Sauvignon Blanc* • *Syrah*

ZONNEBLOEM
No fixed region
★★☆ ⓥ

Although Zonnebloem, Distell's upmarket range, has always been strong on reds, they have noticeably more "oomph" in recent vintages and even the Chardonnay has become quite exciting.

✓ *Cabernet Sauvignon* • *Chardonnay* • *Classic red blend* (Lauréat) • *Merlot* • *Pinotage* • *Syrah* (Shiraz) • *Rozendal* (Stellenbosch) • *Stellar Winery* (Olifants River)

OTHER CERTIFIED ORGANIC WINE PRODUCERS

Rozendal (Stellenbosch)
Stellar Winery (Olifants River)

NORTH AFRICA

The wine industries of Algeria, Morocco, and Tunisia, and the appellation systems within which they work, are all based on the structure left behind by the colonial French. Although some good wines can be found, and a trickle of foreign investment exists, the development of wine industries in these countries has been held back by their governments, which do not promote alcohol in Islamic states. Furthermore, their laws do not allow direct sales by wineries to the public, making wine tourism impossible, cutting out an important source of revenue and feedback.

CULTIVATION OF THE VINE flourished in Algeria, Morocco, and Tunisia as far back as 1000 BC, and winemaking was firmly established by at least the 6th century BC. Under French rule, North Africa was one of the most important winemaking regions

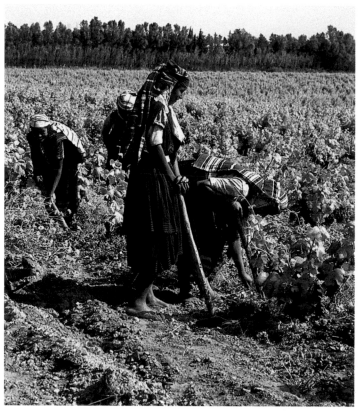

BERBER WOMEN WORKING IN A TUNISIAN VINEYARD
The best and most reliable AOC wines in Tunisia are Muscats, although rosé enjoyed an ephemeral fashion just after World War II.

AVERAGE ANNUAL PRODUCTION

COUNTRY	VINEYARDS TOTAL Acres	VINEYARDS WINE GRAPES Acres	WINE PRODUCTION Cases	Hectoliters	MAJOR GRAPE VARIETIES
Algeria	40,000	10,000	5.0m	450,000	Alicante Bouschet, Carignan, Cinsault, Grenache, Muscat d'Alexandria
Morocco	20,000	4,000	3.3m	300,000	Alicante Bouschet, Cabernet Sauvignon, Carignan, Cinsault, Grenache
Tunisia	10,000	6,000	4.6m	412,000	Alicante Bouschet, Carignan, Cinsault, Grenache, Sangiovese

NORTH AFRICA
Morocco, Algeria, and Tunisia are all wine-producing countries. Most vineyards are concentrated along the coastal belts.

in the world. Yet today it is difficult to see how the quality of wine can progress in any of these countries, where wine production is at best tolerated, and even that level of forbearance is often undermined by government officials who would personally like to see a total ban.

ALGERIA

Wine districts of the *Département* of Oran *Coteaux de Mascara, Coteaux de Tlemcen, Monts du Tessala, Mostaganem, Mostaganem-Kenenda, Oued-Imbert*

Wine districts of the *Département* of Alger *Aïn-Bessem-Bouïra, Coteaux du Zaccar, Coteau de Médéa, Dahra*

Other wine areas of note *Alicante d'Oranie, Fontaine du Genie, Khayyam, Montagne des Lions, Nadim, Trappe*

In 1830, Algeria became the first North African country to be colonized by the French, which gave it a head start in viticulture over other North African countries. Algeria has always dominated North African viticulture in terms of quantity, if not quality. The demise of the country's wine industry after it gained independence in 1962 made it clear that cynical remarks about the use of its wine in bolstering Burgundies were true, but the ironic fact is that both the Algerian and the Burgundian wines benefited from being blended together. It was not the best Burgundies that were enhanced with dark Algerian red, but the poorest, thinnest, and least attractive wines. After the blending, they were not Burgundian in character, but were superior to the original Burgundy. By 1938 the Algerian wine

KHEMIS MILIANA, ALGERIA
Gently undulating vineyards south of Cherchell in the Alger region, just west of Haut-Dahra district.

industry had reached a peak of 988,000 acres (400,000 hectares) and 244 million cases (22 million hectoliters). Since independence, these vineyards have shrunk, and the number of wineries has plummeted from more than 3,000 to fewer than 50. Algeria has never known phylloxera, thus its varieties retain their own rootstock. Of the few reds that can honestly be recommended, the best are from Château Tellagh in Coteaux de Médéa and Cave de Bourkika in Coteaux de Mascara. Other wineries that produce reasonably good wine include: Coteaux de Mascara (Domaine El Bordj, Domaine Mamounia, Domaine Beni Chougrane); Coteaux de Tlemcen (Domaine de Sebra); Coteaux du Zaccar (Chateau Romain); and Dahra (Domaine de Khadra). Algeria has dropped further behind its wine-producing neighbors, but with the recent involvement of Jabulani Ntshangase, South Africa's only black winery owner (Thabani), and a real mover and shaker, it could be a sign that the future might be brighter than anticipated.

MOROCCO

Wine districts *Berkane, Boufekrane, El Jadida, Les Coteaux de l'Atlas, Meknès-Fez, Mjat, Rabat-Casablanca, Marrakech, Sidi-Slimane, Skhirate*

Wines were made here during Roman times, but after more than 1,000 years of Muslim rule, viticulture died out. In 1912, however, most of Morocco came under either French or Spanish control (with an international zone encompassing Tangiers) and it once more became an active winemaking country. When Morocco gained independence in 1956, the new government introduced a quality-control regime similar to the French AOC (*Appellation d'Origine Contrôlée*) system and, in 1973, it nationalized the wine industry. However, few wines carry the official *Appellation d'Origine Garantie* designation. In 1998, the first *Appellation d'Origine Contrôlée* was created, Les Coteaux de l'Atlas, encompassing the districts of Sidi-Slimane, Mjat, and Boufekrane, on the cool slopes of the Atlas Mountains, where

Intensive vine-growing zone

Algeria

Oran

Alger

Tunisia

Bizerte-Mateur-Tébourba

Kélibia-Cap Bon

Thibar

Grombalia

International boundary

Height above sea level (meters)

0   50   100   150 miles
0 50 100 150 200 250 km

OLD MUSCAT VINES
Vineyards at Bizerte in the Bizerte-Mateur-Tébourba region at the northern tip of Tunisia.

on the home market, and much of this is at undeservedly high prices, to tourists who are not willing to pay the even more exorbitant prices demanded for heavily taxed imported wines. Poor storage conditions inevitably spoil both Moroccan and imported wines. Moroccans themselves do drink wine, although there is a notable discrepancy between international per capita consumption figures (one quart) and Morocco's own religiously sensitive official estimation (zero!).

TUNISIA

Wine districts *Grombalia, Bizerte-Mateur-Tébourba, Kélibia-Cap Bon, Thibar*

Wines were first made around the Carthage area in Punic times, but production was forbidden for 1,000 years under Muslim rule. After French colonization in 1881, viticulture resumed, and by Tunisian independence in 1955, the foundations of a thriving wine industry had been laid. At this time two basic appellations had been established—*Vin Supérieur de Tunisie*, for table wines, and *Appellation Contrôlée Vin Muscat de Tunisie*, for liqueur Muscat. These designations did not, however, incorporate any controls to safeguard origin, and in 1957 the government introduced a classification system that established four levels as follows: *Vins de Consommation Courante, Vins Supérieurs, Vins de Qualité Supérieure*, and *Appellation d'Origine Contrôlée*.

The best traditional Tunisian wines are those made from the Muscat grape, ranging from the lusciously sweet, rich, and viscous Vin de Muscat de Tunisie, to fresh, delicate, dry Muscats such as the Muscat de Kelibia. There are also a small number of good red wines, such as Château Feriani, Domaine Karim, and Royal Tardi, with Carignan and Cinsault the most important black grape varieties. The finest new-wave wines are made by the partly German-owned Domaine Magon, which is working proficiently with Cabernet Sauvignon, Merlot, Pinot Noir, and Syrah. There is also encouraging news of progress from research scientist Amor Jaziri, who produces organic wines under the Almory label, from his 35-acre (14-hectare) vineyard near Jedeida.

the lime-rich clayey soils over dry, siliceous subsoil is particularly suitable for viticulture. Here we find Cabernet Sauvignon, Chardonnay, Merlot, and Syrah growing, and the wines produced by Les Celliers de Meknès, particularly the classic red blend, are the finest that Morocco currently has to offer. The country's more tradtional wines are made from Carignan, Cinsault, and Grenache, usually in a pale rosé style, and often sold as *vin gris*. These can be pleasant when served chilled, but the best of even the traditional wines are red, and the most successful of these are also produced by Les Celliers de Meknès, but sold under the Les Trois Domaines label. Owned by Reda Zniber, who is regarded as something of a "godfather" in Morocco, Les Celliers de Meknès produces 90 percent of the country's wine, and most of it is at least drinkable. Or it is when it leaves the cellars. Most is sold

---

OTHER WINEMAKING COUNTRIES OF

AFRICA

ETHIOPIA

Grape-growing in Ethiopia? In fact, viticulture has existed here for many centuries. This country converted to Christianity in the 4th century, and locally grown Communion wine has been used by the Ethiopian Orthodox Church since at least the 12th century. So entrenched is grape-growing in Ethiopian history that it has entered the language as a specific term. Ethiopians distinguish three altitude-defined climatic zones: dega, wayna-dega, and kola. Dega means "cold" and indicates areas that are higher than 8,200 feet (2,500 meters) above sea level. Kola means "hot place," and applies to areas below 5,900 feet (1,800 meters). Wayna-dega literally means "grape elevation," or "place where you grow grapes," and refers to areas between 5,900 and 8,200 feet (1,800 and 2,500 meters) in height.

Ethiopia's largest vineyard is located at Awash, 100 miles (160 kilometers) east of Addis Ababa, in the Harar province, where some 74 acres (30 hectares) of Aleatico, Barbera, Chenin Blanc, Grenache, Petit Sirah, and Ugni Blanc are grown. There are also 185 acres (75 hectares) of so-called "local" varieties, including Debulbul Attere, Key Dubbi, Nech Debulbul, and Tiku

Weyn. There are two harvests each year, and the grapes are trucked to the Awash Winery in the outskirts of Addis Ababa, where reasonable-quality red and white wines are produced. The most commonly encountered wines are Axumite (sweetish white), Crystals (dry white), Dukam (red), and Gouder (Ethiopia's best red, from the Gouder vineyard, 84 miles (135 kilometers) west of Addis Ababa). However, the Awash Winery is located next to the Awash River, which irrigates the Awash vineyards 100 miles (160 kilometers) downstream, and in 1998 researchers from the University of Turku found the Awash River to be polluted downstream from the winery's own effluent discharge, but not upstream. This situation will have to be rectified before any serious thoughts of export can be entertained, as will its practice of using rehydrated imported raisins in some of the wines. Currently, the most exported wine is made from honey, not grapes. Called Tej, it is made all over the country, and is much more famous than its grape-based counterparts. The Awash Winery exports Tej to Sweden and the US, but Ethiopia is not really wine country, whether from honey or grapes. It is coffee country, to the point of giving the world the name itself—the province of Kaffa was the etymological origin of the word "coffee."

KENYA

Lake Naivasha Vineyards are located on volcanic soils beside Lake Naivasha, situated 6,200 feet (1,900 meters) above sea level in the Rift Valley. The Rift Valley is the Flower Garden of Africa, the blooms of which are flown to florists all over the world. In fact, you can grow absolutely anything here, and grow it twice a year too. You can certainly grow grapes, as John and Elli D'Olier did between 1982 and 1992, with cuttings they brought back from California. They ripped out most of the vines in 1992 when overnight hikes in local taxes made Kenyan wine economically unviable, making just the odd wine for home consumption, only to replant in earnest in 2002. The economics are not much better now than they were in 1992, but the d'Oliers just cannot give up on the idea of Kenyan wine.

Richard Leakey is famous for finding a 2.5-million-year-old human skull in Kenya, but he is also one of this country's newest winemakers. He might have lost both legs below the knee in a plane crash, and have only one kidney (and that the gift of Philip Leakey, his younger brother and sometime political foe), but this anthropologist, paleontologist, bruised politician, great African patriot, and tireless warrior against the ivory trade is still game for a new challenge. Leakey is not the sort of person to settle for Kenyan Carignan or Cardinal, but who would have thought that he, or anyone else in this country, could set their sights on Pinot Noir, the Holy Grail of winemaking? Well Leakey has, and by 2001 he had succeeded in cropping Pinot Noir at his Ol Choro Onyore vineyard in Ngong, and putting it (and Sauvignon Blanc) in bottle.

MADAGASCAR

Affectionately known as "Mad" to Anglo-Saxon inhabitants of the African continent, Madagascans have been growing grapes and making wine since the 19th century. Most of the vines growing on the island today are hybrids. With not a little tongue in cheek, John and Erica Platter write in *Africa Uncorked* (2002) that Stéphane Chan Foa Tong's sparkling Grand Cru d'Antsirabe is "Unquestionably the best sparkling wine in all Madagascar. Probably the finest Couderc Blanc *méthode champenoise* in the world!" and certainly it seems better than his still wines. The clean and decent, but hardly exciting, wines of Clos Malaza in the Ambatomena area are generally agreed by the locals to be the best that Madagascar currently produces, from 74 acres (30 hectares) of well-trained Chambourcin, Couderc Blanc, Petit Bouchet, Villardin, Varousset, and Villard Noir vines. From an outsider's point of view, the Chan brothers in Ambalavao produce more promising wine under the Côte de Fiana appellation (their best wine is sold as an exclusivity under the Tsara Be label). Domaine Manomisoa is also known as Soavita Estate, and even more confusingly, its best wine is sold as Château Verger. Other wines are produced under the following labels: Clos de la Maromby (from the Masina Maria monastery, near Fiana) and Lazan'i Betsileo (a small cooperative in Fiana). Nothing really stands out among these wines, but with better grape varieties growing at altitude on the drier, eastern side of the island, and pruned to yield less than half the current average crop, Madagascar does have the potential to produce very much more interesting wines.

MAURITIUS

Beware Mauritian-looking wine sold under the Oxenham label, which is made from imported grape concentrate. While there is nothing wrong with that, the fact should be made clear.

NAMIBIA

Commercial Namibian wine is a very recent phenomenon, dating back to 1994, when Helmuth Kluge established Kristall Kellerei at Omaruru, on the periphery of the Namib desert. All wines are clean and well made, with fresh, zesty Colombard the best.

RÉUNION

This African island is, believe it or not, the most far-flung of all French wines areas: Vin de Pays de Cilaos. Created as recently as 2004, the *vin de pays* regulations forced the removal of the hybrids that used to grow here. Hybrids are still the mainstay of viticulture on Madagascar, which arguably offers greater potential, but the performance of the classic *vinifera* varieties growing on Réunion (Chenin Blanc, Pinot Noir, and Malbec) could well change the mind of those "Mad" people. There are plans to plant Gros Manseng, Pinotage, Syrah, and Verdelho. The styles produced are red, white, rosé, and, because the tendency is for grapes to overripen rather too easily, Moelleux. The only wine producer currently is the local cooperative, Chais du Cilaos, which harvested just 28 tons of grapes in 2004. The vines grow at an altitude of 3,930 feet (1,200 meters) on volcanic soil, cropping in January. The wines are fresh, crisp, and well-made, fermented in new, temperature-controlled, stainless-steel vats.

TANZANIA

There is only one winery, Tanganyika Vineyards, in Tanzania but two harvests a year, producing a decent, but not exciting, Chenin Blanc, and a Makutupora red and white.

ZIMBABWE

Although the first production of wine began in the early 1950s under the labels of Worringham and Lorraine, these semisweet wines were made from table grapes. It was not until UDI that this most beautiful country in Africa gave birth to a

truly commercial wine industry. During the mid-1960s, when sanctions bit deep, and anything that could be produced locally was produced locally, Rhodesian farmers grew the grapes to make the wines they could no longer import. In the 1990s, many low quality grape varieties were ripped up, and replaced by classic *vinifera*, with drip irrigation. The grape varieties grown in Zimbabwe today include Bukettraube, Cabernet Sauvignon, Cinsault, Clairette Blanche, Colombard, Chenin Blanc, Cruchen, Gewürztraminer, Merlot, Pinotage, Pinot Noir, Riesling, Ruby Cabernet, Sauvignon Blanc, and Seneca (*Lignan Blanc x Ontario* hybrid), but many wine farms have been occupied by "war vets." Worringham still exists, both as a wine farm (111 acres; 45 hectares) and as a brand, and is owned by African Distillers (also known as Stapleford Wines), but other familiar wine names from the early days, such as Philips and Monis, no longer exist, having been absorbed by the Mukuyu Winery. Export brands such as Flame Lily, which made an ephemeral appearance on the UK market, have also fallen by the wayside. Meadows Estate used to be a shining example of cutting-edge viticulture in the 1980s, growing Gewürztraminer, Riesling, Chardonnay, and Pinot Noir, but it is a rose farm now, although Mukuyu still sell wines under the Meadows Estate brand. The 1990s also witnessed the installation of cool fermentation technology, and internationally trained winemakers deployed on flying visits, with New Zealander Clive Hartnell (of Hungary's Chapel Hill renown) currently winging his way around the wineries of African Distillers. The late Peter Raynor and his son Humpfrey established Zimbabwe's largest private vineyard near Wedza, but its once impeccably trained vines have been unattended since the Raynor family was evicted by Minister of Youth Brigadier Ambrose Mutinhiri in December 2004. The family had been forcibly removed in July of that year, only to be herded back three weeks later and told to produce a crop. They are trying to get back in, but sadly the current situation seems ominously more permanent. In addition to the human tragedy, this sadly marks the end of the brief promise shown by Zimbabwe's first and, now, only single-vineyard, pure varietal wines—Fighill 2002 Chardonnay and Fighill 2003 Shiraz, which the Raynors made from a superselected five percent of their own production. Most of their crop used to be split 50/50 between African Distillers (which bottled their domain wines) and Mukuyu (which is 65 percent government-owned, thus escaped its threatened compulsory acquisition in December 2001). Private farms have been so vulnerable to compulsory acquisition (i.e., occupation by "war vets") that African Distillers and Mukuyu are now the only producers here.

The WINES of
THE AMERICAS

ALL OF THE MOST FAMOUS WINE REGIONS—
California, Washington, Oregon, and Chile—are
found on or inland from the western coast. This is
because eastern seaboards are generally too humid
and prone to severely cold winters. Of the famous
regions in the Americas, California is, of course, the
most important. It is staggering to think that the 25
largest wineries in this state on their own produce
twice the output of Argentina (which itself is the
fifth-largest winemaking country in the world).
However, California is actually more about quality
than quantity. It produces some of the world's
greatest Cabernet Sauvignon, Merlot, Zinfandel,
Pinot Noir, and Chardonnay wines. Although
Washington has always been a considerably
larger wine-producing state than Oregon, from
an international perspective it used to live in the
shadow of the latter's excellent-but-overhyped
Pinot Noir. Well, no more. Washington is now justly
famous for powerful *bordelais* varietals, not to
mention its up-and-coming Syrah. British Columbia
has far more in common with Washington state
than it does with Ontario, and is creating at least
as much of a buzz in the wine world. Chile still
rules in South America, but a small number of
quality-conscious Argentinian producers are
giving their old rival a good run for its money.

MUSTARD FLOWERS IN CARNEROS, NAPA, CALIFORNIA
*Mustard planted near vines provides a habitat for predators of
vine pests and also prevents the evaporation of moisture.*

NORTH AMERICA

The US is the fourth-largest wine-producing country in the world, and the output of California alone is more than double that of the fifth-largest wine-producing country (Australia), yet almost every state in this vast country produces wine. And, of course, North America does not consist of just the US; it also encompasses the viticultural areas of Ontario and British Columbia in Canada (see also pp.532–7), and the Baja California and Sierra Madre in Mexico (see also pp.538–9).

IN 1521, WITHIN ONE YEAR of invading Mexico, the Spanish planted vines and set about making the first North American wines. Fourteen years later, when French explorer Jacques Cartier sailed down the St. Lawrence to New France, he discovered a large island overrun by wild vines and decided to call it the Île de Bacchus. He had second thoughts, however, and later renamed it the Île d'Orléans, a calculated move in view of the fact that the then Duke of Orléans was the son of King Francis I of France. It is assumed that, circa 1564, the Jesuit settlers who followed in the wake of Cartier's explorations were the first winemakers in what was to become Canada. The earliest wines made in what is now the United States of America came from Florida. Between 1562 and 1564, French Huguenot settlers produced wines from native Scuppernong grapes on a site that would become Jacksonville.

JEKEL VINEYARDS, CALIFORNIA
An irrigation pipe skirts rows of vines in one of the drier parts of Monterey County. Conditions are a far cry from those around the Finger Lakes, New York.

NATIVE NORTH AMERICAN GRAPE VARIETIES

All classic grape varieties belong to one species, *Vitis vinifera*, but North America's native varieties belong to several different species, not one of which happens to be *Vitis vinifera*. There were plenty of native vines growing wild wherever the early settlers traveled, and so they came to rely on them for their initial wine production. Settlers in Australia, on the other hand, were forced to wait for precious shipments of classic European vines before they could plant vineyards. Although various European varieties were taken across the Atlantic in the 19th century, nearly all North American wines, aside from California ones, remained products of native varieties until relatively recently.

The most common native North American species, *Vitis labrusca*, has such a distinctive aroma and flavor that it seems truly amazing that those pioneers who were also winemakers did not pester their home countries for supplies of more acceptable vines. The *labrusca* character, commonly referred to as "foxy," is so exotic, it cloys at the back of the throat, and is generally not appreciated by European and antipodean palates.

PROHIBITION IN THE UNITED STATES

Although total Prohibition in the United States was confined to 1920–1933, the first "dry legislation" was passed as early as 1816, and the first state to go completely dry was Maine, in 1846. By the time the 18th Amendment to the Constitution was put into effect in 1920, forbidding "the manufacture, sale, or transport of intoxicating liquors," more than 30 states were already totally dry.

The result of Prohibition was chaos. It denied the government legitimate revenue and encouraged bootleggers to amass fortunes. The number of illicit stills multiplied quicker than the authorities could find and dismantle them, and the speakeasy became a way of life in the cities. Not only did the authorities often realize that it was much easier to turn a blind eye to what was going on, but the federal government actually found it useful to open its own speakeasy in New York! Many vineyards were uprooted, but those grapes that were produced were often concentrated, pressed, and sold as "grape bricks." These came complete with a yeast capsule and instructions to dissolve the brick in one gallon of water, but warned against adding the yeast because it would start a fermentation! This would turn the grape juice into wine "and that would be illegal," the warning pointed out.

Prohibition and the wine industry

By the mid- to late 19th century, the California wine industry had such a reputation that great French wine areas, such as Champagne, began to form syndicats to protect themselves, in part, from the potential of California's marketing threat. However, the 13 years of Prohibition coincided with a vital point in the evolution of wine, and set the California wine industry back a hundred years, since other wine regions had just recovered from the effects of phylloxera (*see* p.471), and were busily reestablishing their reputations and carving out future markets. In Europe, World War I had robbed every industry of its young, up-and-coming generation, but the rich tradition of the wine industry enabled it to survive until the arrival of a new generation. The early 1900s were also the era of the foundation of the French *Appellation Contrôlée* laws, a quality-control system that many other serious winemaking countries would eventually copy.

The United States also lost much of one generation in World War I, but it had less of a winemaking tradition to fall back on and, by 1920, there was virtually no wine industry whatsoever to preserve. After Prohibition came one of the worst economic depressions in history, followed by World War II, which took yet

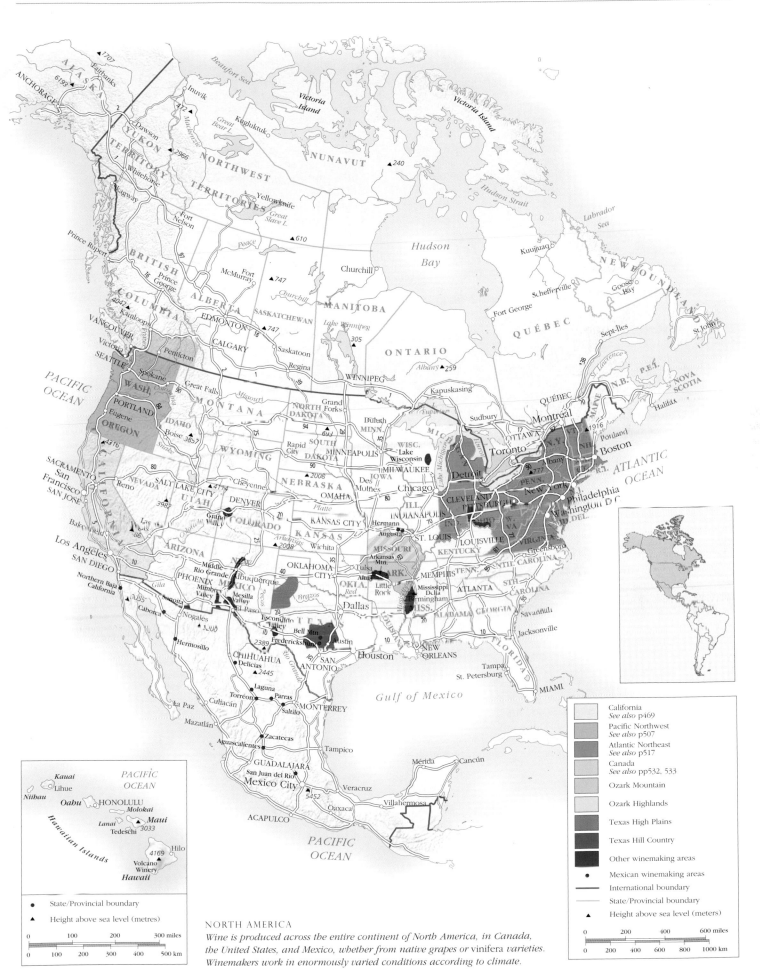

NORTH AMERICA

Wine is produced across the entire continent of North America, in Canada, the United States, and Mexico, whether from native grapes or vinifera varieties. Winemakers work in enormously varied conditions according to climate.

MOUNT PLEASANT VINEYARDS
These vineyards in Augusta, Missouri, were the first Approved Viticultural Area in the United States.

another generation of bright young minds. It was, therefore, little wonder that by the late 1940s the wine industry of the United States was so out of date. It had lost touch with European progress and resorted to the production of awful *labrusca* wines that had been the wine drinker's staple diet in pre-Prohibition days. California produced relatively little *labrusca* compared to the eastern states, but its winemakers also resorted to old-fashioned styles, making heavy, sweet, fortified wines.

The fact that Californian wine today is a match for the best of its European counterparts and that its industry is healthy, growing fast, and looking to compete on foreign markets, clearly proves that in the United States opportunity is boundless.

THE APPELLATION SYSTEM OF THE UNITED STATES

The older generation of appellations of the United States is based on political boundaries such as counties or states, and still exists. However, during the mid-1970s, the Department of Treasury's Bureau of Alcohol, Tobacco, and Firearms (BATF) considered the concept of specific controlled appellations based on geography and climate, and in September 1978 BATF published its first laws and regulations designed to introduce a system of Approved Viticultural Areas (AVAs), to supplement the old system, which is now run by the Alcohol and Tobacco Tax and Trade Bureau (TTB). Every state, from Hawaii to Alaska, and the counties they contain, are recognized in law as their own individual appellations of origin, but other generic appellations are also recognized:

American or United States This appellation classifies blended and varietal wines from anywhere in the US, including the District of Columbia and the Commonwealth of Puerto Rico. These wines, like *vins de tables* in France, are not allowed to carry a vintage, which is, in my opinion, irrational. It is the only appellation allowed for wines shipped in bulk to other countries.

Multistate Appellation This appellation is used to classify a wine from any two or three contiguous states. The percentage of wine from each state must be clearly indicated on the label.

State Appellation A wine from any state may use this appellation; at least 75 percent of grapes must come from grapes grown within the one state indicated (except for Texas, which is 85 percent, and California, which is 100 per cent). Thus, wine claiming the appellation of Oregon may contain up to 25 percent produce of other states. The grapes can be shipped to a neighboring state and

still be given the originating state name, but not to any state that does not share a border. Grapes can therefore be shipped from California to Oregon, where they are turned into wine, and may be called California wine (as long as the wine is at least 75 percent from those grapes), but the same grapes cannot be shipped to Washington State and be called California wine (although such a wine could be labeled California-Oregon-Washington, if it contained grapes from all three states, see Multistate Appellation). The same principles apply to County Appellations and Multicounty Appellations.

Multicounty Appellation This appellation classifies a wine from any two or three contiguous counties. The percentage of wine from each county must be clearly indicated on the label.

County Appellation A wine from any county within any state may use this appellation: at least 75 percent of the wine must come from grapes grown within the one county indicated.

DID YOU KNOW?

- America's third president, Thomas Jefferson, was the country's greatest wine connoisseur, and even tried to grow vines at Monticello.

- There is a winery in every state of the US, even Alaska (though the grapes have to be trucked in, of course).

- Although almost every state in the US grows wine grapes, California accounts for more than 90 percent of the wines produced.

- It is legal to produce and sell American Champagne or Burgundy, but not American Bordeaux or Rhône.

- There are still "dry" counties in some US states.

- The oldest winery in the US is the Brotherhood Winery (1839) at Washingtonville in the foothills of the Catskills of New York State.

THE SEMI-GENERIC SAGA

It is not only easy to understand how the misuse of famous European wine names started in the US, it is also perfectly understandable. As European immigrants poured into this land, some brought vines with them and when they made different styles of wine, it was inevitable that they would use the only wine names they knew to distinguish between them. Names like Burgundy, Chablis, Champagne, *et. al.* There is nothing to forgive. Until now, that is. Ever since the California wine industry became a significant exporter, opening the door for other wine-producing states, it was incumbent upon the US to respect all other legitimate geographical appellations, however well entrenched the usage might have become within the US itself. However, in 1978, well after California wines had stepped onto the international stage, the director of the Department of Treasury's Bureau of Alcohol, Tobacco, and Firearms (BATF) legally enshrined the concept of semi-generic wine names within Federal Regulations, citing, but not restricting itself to, 14 such examples: "Burgundy, Claret, Chablis, Champagne, Chianti, Madeira, Malaga, Marsala, Moselle, Port, Rhine Wine, Sauterne, Sherry, Tokay." The regulations state that these so-called semi-generic names must be qualified by their true place of origin: American Chablis, California Champagne, and so on. However, American regulations are not only unfair, they are decidedly quirky. While it is perfectly legal for US wineries to sell wines labeled as Champagne or Chablis, the name Liebfraumilch is protected by the full might of Federal Law. And whereas Burgundy is permitted, Bordeaux or Rhône are not. Where is the logic? As the most abused wine names were French, it was left initially to that country to redress the situation, but they got nowhere and, frankly, were not helped by their own antics in South America, where the *champenois* were abusing the Champagne appellation. The French were also chronically shortsighted when turning down an under-the-table deal that would have seen "Champagne" dropped in favor of "Champagne Style." Since then, the production of American wine sold under famous Italian appellations has become a substantial industry in itself, which with the use of other European wine names has seen the European Union take up the fight. Its negotiators have been hammering away at the US through the World Trade Organization, but they have not been any more successful than the French. What they have failed to understand is that they have nothing to bring to the negotiating table that the US is in the slightest bit bothered about, but when they recognize this, it should provide the European authorities with the obvious solution. If the French, Italians, Spanish, Portuguese, and Hungarians officially created a few new appellations, like Napa Valley, Sonoma County Green Valley, and, to catch the attention of the East Coast elite, North Fork of Long Island and Northern Neck George Washington Birthplace, the EU would soon find that it had something to bargain with, and the US might at least understand why Europeans are so protective of their appellations. The irony is that should such appellations be formally adopted and the wines put into distribution in their country of origin, they would be automatically eligible for sale in the US, where the law defines an acceptable foreign appellation on an imported wine to be "a delimited place or region the boundaries of which have been recognized and defined by the country of origin for use on labels of wine available for consumption within the country of origin." Perhaps the wine-producing countries who feel that they have been treated unfairly by the US will realize that sometimes it does take a wrong to right another wrong. Virtually all self-respecting, quality wine producers in the US will be on their side because they are proud of their own products, which do not need any famous European names as a crutch.

AMERICAN WINE LABEL LANGUAGE

ALCOHOL It is obligatory to indicate the alcoholic strength of a US wine, and this is expressed as a percentage by volume.

ANGELICA An authentic American fortified wine style of 17–24 percent, traditionally made from Mission grapes, typically blended 50/50 wine and brandy, with the liquor added after fermentation has achieved just 5 percent alcohol, resulting in excess of 100g/l of residual sugar. If the strength is less than 18 percent, the wine must be labeled "Light Angelica." Other grapes that are sometimes used include Grenache, Muscat, and Palomino. The quality can be extremely high. Angelica was named after Los Angeles by Spanish Missionary winemakers in the 18th century, when the city was just a town and its name in full was El Pueblo de Nuestra Señora Reina de los Ángeles de la Porciuncula.

BOTTLE FERMENTED A sparkling wine derived through a second fermentation in "glass containers of not greater than one (US) gallon capacity." Usually refers to a wine that, after second fermentation, is decanted and filtered under pressure before rebottling.

BURGUNDY A semi-generic name allowed under US Federal Law for a red wine of legally undefined "Burgundy-style," such products today are inevitably of basic quality and made from almost anything, although high-yielding Carignane, Grenache, and Zinfandel are traditional. American Burgundy is typically dark in color, and full in body, but with some residual sweetness to give an impression of softness.

CARBONATED WINE Still wine made bubbly through the addition of carbon dioxide from a bottle of gas, the method used to produce carbonated drinks such as lemonade or cola.

CHAMPAGNE A semi-generic name allowed under US Federal Law for a wine rendered sparkling through a second fermentation in "glass containers of not greater than one (US) gallon capacity."

CHIANTI A semi-generic name allowed under US Federal Law for a red wine of legally undefined style, American Chianti is generally medium-bodied, falling somewhere between American claret and American Burgundy in color, character, and residual sweetness, with a more pronounced fruitiness, but is equally basic in quality.

CLARET A semi-generic name allowed under US Federal Law for a red wine of legally undefined style, American claret is a very basic wine that is generally drier than American Burgundy, as well as being somewhat lighter in color and in body.

CRACKLING WINE A sparkling wine derived through a second fermentation in "glass containers of not greater than one (US) gallon capacity," thus the same as for American "Champagne," although with less effervescence. This type of wine may also be called *pétillant, frizzante,* or *crémant.*

CRACKLING WINE—BULK METHOD I have not actually seen "Bulk Method" on a wine label, but it does exist, and it means the same as for "Crackling Wine" but made by the *cuve close* method.

DESSERT WINE A wine, usually fortified, with an alcohol content of 14–24 percent. If less than 18 percent, the wine must be labeled "Light Dessert Wine."

FERMENTED IN THE BOTTLE A simple and smart way of describing a wine made by the *méthode champenoise.*

FUMÉ BLANC Widely used term for oak-aged Sauvignon Blanc.

GRAPE VARIETY If a single grape variety is mentioned on a label, the wine must contain at least 75 percent of the grape variety indicated (90 percent in Oregon). Although the potential of varietal labeling was recognized in Alsace in the 1920s, the international marketing phenomenon these wines represent today was brought about by the widespread application of the concept by California wineries.

HAUTE SAUTERNE (*sic*) Rarely encountered, highly questionable, semi-generic name allowed and misspelled under US Federal Law for medium-sweet and sweet variants of Sauterne (*sic*).

HEALTH WARNING Health warnings are required by federal law, yet none of the proven health advantages are permitted on the label (*see* p.634).

HOCK A semi-generic name allowed under US Federal Law for an undefined style of wine that, curiously, is light and dry, rather than vaguely approximating some sort of German Rhine wine. The grapes used are often the same as for American Chablis, but are blended to produce something lighter (which is correct) and drier (which is not).

LIGHT WINE A wine with an alcohol level not in excess of 14 percent (synonymous with Table Wine).

MADEIRA A semi-generic name allowed under US Federal Law for any fortified wine of 17–24 percent, made in a legally undefined "Madeira-style" that is usually sweet to some degree. If it contains less than 18 percent alcohol, the wine must be labeled "Light Madeira." This slowly diminishing style of wine is primarily Californian and is traditionally produced by blending American sherry with Angelica.

MALAGA A semi-generic name allowed under US Federal Law for any fortified wine of 17–24 percent, made in a legally undefined "Malaga-style" that is usually sweet to some degree. If it contains less than 18 percent alcohol, the wine must be labeled "Light Malaga." Made primarily from Concord grapes, American Malaga is often a kosher product and is used for sacramental rites.

MARSALA A semi-generic name allowed under US Federal Law for any fortified wine of 17–24 percent, made in a legally undefined "Marsala-style" that is amber or brown in color, usually sweet to some degree, and sometimes flavored with herbs. If it contains less than 18 percent alcohol, the wine must be labeled "Light Marsala."

MOSELLE A semi-generic name allowed under US Federal Law for an undefined style of wine that is traditionally made from Chenin Blanc and Riesling grapes.

American Moselle is light in body, pale in color, medium sweet to taste, and sometimes very lightly *pétillant.* It is softer and lighter than American hock.

MUSCATEL Generally a more basic quality version of sweet Muscat wine (which is usually sold varietally as Muscat Frontignan or Muscat Canelli), Muscatel is usually a blend of two or more of the following: Aleatico, Malvasia Bianca, and Muscat (Alexandria, Canelli, and Frontignan). Black Muscatel is a blend of Aleatico and Black Muscat (also known as Muscat Hamburg).

NATURAL WINE A wine may be called "natural" only if it has not been fortified with grape brandy or alcohol.

PORT A semi-generic name allowed under US Federal Law for any fortified wine of 17–24 percent that has been made in a legally undefined "port style." If it contains less than 18 percent alcohol, the wine must be labeled "Light Port." Zinfandel, Petite Sirah, and Cabernet Sauvignon are the most common grapes to be declared on a label, but others widely used include Alicante Bouschet, Carignane, Grenache, and Mission. Additionally, there is a small but growing category of quality ports, blended and varietal, that are made from various Portuguese varieties such as Tinta Madeira, Tinta Cão, Alvarelhão, Touriga, and Bastardo or Trousseau. When blended from different Portuguese varieties, the wine is often sold as a Tinta port. Whichever grapes are used, the wines are usually sweet to some degree, and often qualified by traditional port terminology such as Ruby, Tawny, and Vintage. Some examples can be very good indeed, particularly from specialists.

RHINE WINE Synonymous with American hock.

SAUTERNE (*sic*) A semi-generic name allowed and misspelled under US Federal Law for a wine that is usually of basic quality, less sweet than genuine Sauternes, and with no hint of botrytis. A few better-quality Sauterne wines are made, usually from Semillon and Sauvignon Blanc, but most Sauterne are nothing more than bland blends of Palomino, Sauvignon Vert, Thompson Seedless, and other even less respectable varieties. Amazingly for a semi-generic wine that should by definition be intensely sweet, Sauterne wines range from dry to very sweet, and are often qualified by "Dry" or "Sweet," with "Chateau" weirdly used for the sweetest styles. The cheapest dry Sauterne wines are not dissimilar to American Chablis. Some California producers spell Sauternes correctly, but it is difficult to work out which spelling constitutes the worst insult.

SEMI-GENERIC A semi-generic name is a geographical designation that has, in the opinion of the Director of the Department of Treasury's Alcohol and Tobacco Tax and Trade Bureau (TTB), become at least as well known for a specific style of wine, wherever it might happen to be produced, and is thus allowed under US Federal Law to be used by any wine producer in the US.

Thus, it is entirely legal within the borders of the US to abuse the appellations of Burgundy, Chablis, Champagne, Chianti, and many others.

SHERRY A semi-generic name allowed under US Federal Law for any fortified wine of 17–24 percent that has been made in a legally undefined "sherry style," usually sweet to some degree. If the alcohol content is less than 18 percent, the wine must be labeled "Light Sherry." Palomino is the favored variety for high-class sherries, and is also known in California as the Golden Chasselas or Napa Golden Chasselas. Palomino is the only varietally labeled sherry that is likely to be encountered, since the other grapes used (Mission, Thompson Seedless, and *labrusca*) are hardly worth shouting about. Although legally undefined by Federal Law, the best sherries will often involve the use of flor and will be blended under a solera system. However, the most common production method is to heat the wines for several months in order to replicate sherry's oxidative style, and some efforts are worse than others. Whatever method of production used, there are numerous substyles produced. Some sherries are actually labeled Dry, Medium, or Sweet, in addition to which there are Pale Dry (closer to fino) or Cocktail sherries, which are dry; Golden or Amber sherries, which are medium sweet; and Cream, which is sweet. The best American sherries can be very fine indeed.

SPARKLING WINE This term may be used to describe "carbonated," *cuve close,* "bottle-fermented," or *méthode champenoise* wine. If the label bears no other information, the consumer should fear the worst (carbonated or *cuve close*). However, the label may indicate any of the following terms: Champagne, Bottle Fermented, Fermented in this Bottle, Crackling Wine (including Crackling Wine—Bulk Method), and Carbonated Wine.

SULFITES It is obligatory for all American wines to state "Contains sulfites" or "Contains sulfiting agent/s" when sulfur dioxide or a sulfuring agent can be detected at a level of 10 or more parts per million.

TABLE WINE A wine with an alcohol level not in excess of 14 percent (synonymous with Light Wine).

TOKAY All-American blend of Angelica, Dry Sherry (to reduce the sweetness), and a dash of port to provide its characteristic tawny-pink color, Tokay is a medium-sweet dessert wine with a slightly nutty flavor, and 17–24 percent in strength. If less than 18 percent, the wine must be labeled "Light Tokay."

VINTAGE At least 95 percent of the wine must be from the vintage indicated. Until the early 1970s, federal regulations demanded that the figure was 100 percent, but winemakers, particularly those producing higher-quality wines aged in small oak barrels, petitioned for a limited margin to enable topping off, and this was granted.

VOLUME This must be stated somewhere on the bottle by law.

Approved Viticultural Areas There are no AVA rules governing the varieties grown, the methods of vine-training employed, the yields allowed, or the style of wines produced, and AVAs are all the better for it. Although some have evolved to a point where they can be said to favor certain grape varieties and produce identifiable styles, many have not and probably never will. America's AVAs are much maligned by various American critics, yet they are the healthy product of New World free enterprise. The *raison d'être* of the AVA system is truthful labeling: a wine comes from where it says it comes from (or, at least, a minimum of 85 percent must). The AVA process merely establishes the boundary of what must be demonstrated to be a fairly homogenous growing zone, whether small or large. Unfortunately, the law does not insist that the AVA name should be immediately followed by the term "Approved Viticultural Area." As a result, who is to know if a geographical area (or a seemingly geographical area) on a wine label has any official connotation whatsoever?

HEALTH WARNINGS ON AMERICAN WINE LABELS

The following "Government Warning" must appear on every bottle of wine sold in the United States: 1. According to the Surgeon General, "women should not drink alcoholic beverages during pregnancy because of the risk of birth defects"; 2. "Consumption of alcoholic beverages impairs your ability to drive a car or operate machinery and may cause health problems." In my opinion, however, the warning is grossly misleading and contains half-truths and unsubstantiated claims, while proven health benefits are not included on the label.

As to the first part of the warning, women alcoholics can give birth to children deformed by "fetal alcohol syndrome," but a study of 2,000 Australian women concluded (in line with other reports) that "there is no significant relationship between light and moderate maternal alcohol intake and fetal growth effect." There can be no argument with the first part of the second warning because the "consumption of alcoholic beverages" does "impair" the ability to "drive a car or operate machinery," but, while the second part is true—that alcohol may cause health problems—it is grossly misleading because it does not put into context the word "may." The US government was forced to use this word because only excessive alcohol consumption is a potential health hazard, whereas tests and studies throughout the world, many of them carried out by America's most respected institutions, have shown various benefits to health of drinking alcohol in moderation (*see* Health Benefits of Wine, p.634).

THE AVAS OF THE UNITED STATES

The very first AVA was, strangely enough, not Napa, but Augusta in Missouri, which was established in June 1980. There are now 149 AVAs and the number continues to rise, with another 15 waiting in the wings: Alexandria Lakes (Douglas County, Minnesota), Bennet Valley (Sonoma County, California), Chehalem (Willamette Valley, Oregon), Columbia Gorge (Oregon and Washington), Dundee Hills (Yamhill County, Oregon), Eola Hills (Willamette Valley, Oregon), McMinnville (Yamhill County, Oregon), Oak Knoll (Napa County), Red Hills (Lake County, California), Ribbon Ridge (Yamhill County, Oregon), Salado Creek (Stanislaus County, California), San Bernabe (Monterey County, California), Southern Oregon (encompassing the Applegate, Rogue, and Umpqua Valleys, Oregon), Trinity Lakes (Trinity County, California),

Yamhill-Carton District (Willamette Valley, Oregon). Although the establishment of these AVAs cannot be taken for granted, very few are likely to be rejected, if the growers making the proposals have done their homework. The only denial in recent memory was for a proposed California Coast AVA, which was not only 650 miles (1,050 kilometers) long, but also penetrated inland, encompassing interior basins and valleys, 5,000-foot- (1,500-meter-) high mountain ranges, as well as shorelines and coastal plains, thus providing no homogeneity of climate. Most applications are, however, more sensibly prepared, and there will, no doubt, be many more AVA proposals to come. For an explanation of why this encyclopedia uses "Approved Viticultural Areas" rather than "American Viticultural Areas," see "AVA" in the Glossary.

Alexander Valley, California
Established November 23, 1984
Altus, Arkansas
Established June 29, 1984
Anderson Valley, California
Established September 19, 1983
Applegate Valley, Oregon
Established February 12, 2001
Arkansas Mountain, Arkansas
Established October 27, 1986
Arroyo Grande Valley, California
Established February 5, 1990
Arroyo Seco, California
Established May 16, 1983
Atlas Peak, California
Established January 23, 1992
Augusta, Missouri
Established June 20, 1980
Bell Mountain, Texas
Established November 10, 1986
Ben Lomond Mountain, California
Established January 8, 1988
Benmore Valley, California
Established October 18, 1991
California Shenandoah Valley,
California
Established January 27, 1983
Capay Valley, California
Established February 18, 2003
Carmel Valley, California
Established January 15, 1983
Catoctin, Maryland
Established November 14, 1983
Cayuga Lake, New York

Established March 25, 1988
Central Coast, California
Established November 25, 1985
Central Delaware Valley,
Pennsylvania and New Jersey
Established April 18, 1984
Chalk Hill, California
Established November 21, 1983
Chalone, California
Established July 14, 1982
Chiles Valley, Caliornia
Established April 19, 1999
Cienega Valley, California
Established September 20, 1982
Clarksburg, California
Established February 22, 1984
Clear Lake, California
Established June 7, 1984
Cole Ranch, California
Established March 16, 1983
Columbia Valley, Oregon and
Washington
Established December 13, 1984
Cucamonga Valley, California
Established March 31, 1995
Cumberland Valley, Maryland and
Pennsylvania
Established August 26, 1985
Diablo Grande, California
Established August 21, 1998
Diamond Mountain District,
California
Established July 31, 2001
Dry Creek Valley, California

Established September 6, 1983
Dunnigan Hills, California
Established May 13, 1993
Edna Valley, California
Established June 11, 1982
El Dorado, California
Established November 14, 1983
Escondido Valley, Texas
Established May 15, 1992
Fair Play, California
Established April 27, 2001
Fennville, Michigan
Established October 19, 1981
Fiddletown, California
Established November 3, 1983
Finger Lakes, New York
Established October 1, 1982
Fredericksburg, Texas
Established December 22, 1988
Grand River Valley, Ohio
Established November 21, 1983
Grand Valley, Colorado
Established November 25, 1991
Guenoc Valley, California
Established December 21, 1981
Hames Valley, California
Established March 27, 1994
Herman, Missouri
Established September 10, 1983
Howell Mountain, California
Established January 30, 1984
Hudson River Region, New York
Established July 6, 1982
Isle St. George, Ohio

Established September 20, 1982
Kanawha River Valley, West
Virginia
Established May 8, 1986
Knights Valley, California
Established November 21, 1983
Lake Erie, New York, Pennsylvania,
and Ohio
Established November 21, 1983
Lake Michigan Shore, Michigan
Established November 14, 1983
Lake Wisconsin, Wisconsin
Established January 5, 1994
Lancaster Valley, Pennsylvania
Established June 11, 1982
Leelanau Peninsula, Michigan
Established April 29, 1982
Lime Kiln Valley, California
Established July 6, 1982
Linganore, Maryland
Established September 19, 1983
Livermore Valley, California
Established October 1, 1982
Lodi, California
Established March 7, 1986
Long Island, New York
Established July 16, 2001
Loramie Creek, Ohio
Established December 27, 1982
Los Carneros, California
Established September 19, 1983
Madera, California
Established January 7, 1985
Malibu-Newton Canyon, California

What truly amazes me is that a country regarded by the rest of the world as litigation-crazy has a wine industry that does not have the conviction to stand up for itself. I am informed that it would be impossible to prove the Surgeon General's unsubstantiated claim about birth defects in a court of law, so why not hire the largest firm of first-rate lawyers in the country and sue the Surgeon General for $50 billion in lost revenue? Instead, they welcomed with open arms the recently won (1999) right to put the following message on a bottle of wine: "The proud people who made this wine encourage you to consult your family doctor about the health effects of wine consumption." Such is the unempowered state of the US wine industry that some of its members have been absolutely euphoric about this statement, declaring it a small victory in the quest to redress the negative effect of the health warning, but what does it actually say? Wine is so good for you that you should consult your doctor? That sounds more like a warning than a benefit to me. No wonder the Surgeon General approved it.

VINEYARDS, UPSTATE NEW YORK
Rows of vines combine to form an emerald-green patchwork on the gently sloping countryside near Hammondsport. In the distance is Keuka Lake, one of the finger-shaped lakes that have a moderating influence on the area's climate.

Established June 13, 1996
Martha's Vineyard, Massachusetts
Established February 4, 1985
McDowell Valley, California
Established January 4, 1982
Mendocino, California
Established July 16, 1984
Mendocino Ridge, California
Established December 26, 1997
Merritt Island, California
Established June 16, 1983
Mesilla Valley, New Mexico and Texas
Established March 18, 1985
Middle Rio Grande Valley, New Mexico
Established February 2, 1988
Mimbres Valley, New Mexico
Established December 23, 1985
Mississippi Delta, Louisiana, Mississippi, and Tennessee
Established October 1, 1984
Monterey, California
Established July 16, 1984
Monticello, Virginia
Established February 22, 1984
Mt. Harlan, California
Established November 29, 1990
Mt. Veeder, California
Established March 22, 1990
Napa Valley, California
Established February 27, 1981
North Coast, California
Established October 21, 1983
North Fork of Long Island, New York
Established November 10, 1986
North Fork of Roanoke, Virginia
Established May 16, 1983
North Yuba, California
Established August 30, 1985
Northern Neck—George Washington Birthplace, Virginia
Established May 21, 1987
Northern Sonoma, California
Established June 17, 1985
Oakville, California
Established July 2, 1993
Ohio River Valley, Indiana, Ohio,

West Virginia, and Kentucky
Established October 7, 1983
Old Mission Peninsula, Michigan
Established July 8, 1987
Ozark Highlands, Missouri
Established September 30, 1987
Ozark Mountain, Arkansas, Missouri, and Oklahoma
Established August 1, 1986
Pacheco Pass, California
Established April 11, 1984
Paicines, California
Established September 15, 1982
Paso Robles, California
Established November 3, 1983
Potter Valley, California
Established November 14, 1983
Puget Sound, Washington
Established October 4, 1995
Red Mountain, Washington
Established June 11, 2001
Redwood Valley, California
Established December 23, 1996
River Junction, California
Established July 9, 2001
Rock Pile, California
Established April 29, 2002
Rocky Knob, Virginia
Established February 11, 1983
Rogue Valley, Oregon
Established February 22, 1992
Russian River Valley, California
Established November 21, 1983
Rutherford, California
Established July 2, 1993
San Benito, California
Established November 4, 1983
San Francisco Bay, California
Established March 22, 1999
San Lucas, California
Established March 2, 1987
San Pasqual Valley, California
Established September 16, 1981
San Ysidro District, California
Established June 5, 1990
Santa Clara Valley, California
Established March 28, 1989
Santa Cruz Mountains, California
Established January 4, 1982

Santa Lucia Highlands, California
Established June 15, 1992
Santa Maria Valley, California
Established September 4, 1981
Santa Rita Hills, California
Established July 30, 2001
Santa Ynez Valley, California
Established May 16, 1983
Scald Valley, California
Established June 20, 1994
Seneca Lake, New York
Established September 2, 2003
Shenandoah Valley, Virginia and West Virginia
Established January 27, 1983
Sierra Foothills, California
Established December 18, 1987
Solano County Green Valley, California
Established January 28, 1983
Sonoita, Arizona
Established November 26, 1984
Sonoma Coast, California
Established July 13, 1987
Sonoma County Green Valley, California
Established December 21, 1983
Sonoma Mountain, California
Established February 22, 1985
Sonoma Valley, California
Established January 4, 1982
South Coast, California
Established December 23, 1985
Southeastern New England, Connecticut, Rhode Island, and Massachusetts
Established April 27, 1984
Spring Mountain District, California
Established May 13, 1993
St. Helena, California
Established September 11, 1995
Stag's Leap District, California
Established January 27, 1989
Suisun Valley, California
Established December 27, 1982
Temecula Valley, California
Established November 23, 1984

Texas Davis Mountain, Texas
Established May 11, 1998
Texas High Plains, Texas
Established March 2, 1992
Texas Hill Country, Texas
Established November 29, 1991
The Hamptons, Long Island, New York
Established June 17, 1985
Umpqua Valley, Oregon
Established April 30, 1984
Virginia's Eastern Shore, Virginia
Established January 2, 1999

Walla Walla Valley, Washington and Oregon
Established March 7, 1984
Warren Hills, New Jersey
Established August 8, 1988
West Elks, Colorado
Established May 7, 2001
Western Connecticut Highlands, Connecticut, Est. February 9, 1988
Wild Horse Valley, California
Established November 30, 1988
Willamette Valley, Oregon
Established January 3, 1984
Willow Creek, California
Established September 9, 1983
Yadkin Valley, North Carolina
Established February 7, 2003
Yakima Valley, Washington
Established May 4, 1983
York Mountain, California
Established September 23, 1983
Yorkville Highlands, California
Established June 8, 1998
Yountville, California
Established May 18, 1998

AMERICA'S LARGEST WINE GROUPS

When the New York-based Canandaigua group merged with Australia's BRL Hardy to form Constellation Brands, it replaced E. & J. Gallo as the world's largest wine producer, but it is nowhere near the biggest producer of American wines.

1. E. & J. GALLO
Accounting for more than one-quarter of all US wine sales, this company was founded by Ernest and Julio Gallo, who were driven by tragedy, division, and a legendary zeal for hard work to create—in their own words—the "Campbell Soup Company of the wine industry." Elder brother Ernest became head of the family in 1933, after his father, a grape grower, inexplicably killed Ernest's mother, then shot himself. With the end of Prohibition, the brothers began winemaking, selling in bulk until 1940, when the first wines to carry the Gallo label appeared. The Gallo brothers had achieved their ambition by the 1960s, when theirs was easily the most popular wine brand in the US, but they wanted to conquer the world, and the only way to do that was with a profusion of inexpensive brands. By the 1980s, Gallo was the world's largest wine producer, churning out more wine than the annual output of countries like Australia. Ernest and Julio divided everything. Ernest ran the business and marketing, while Julio looked after the production. Julio died in a car crash in May 1993, but Ernest was still going, at the ripe old age of 95, in 2004.

Production is estimated at 75 million cases, mostly under penny-pinching labels such as Ernest & Julio Twin Valley Vineyards, Totts, Carlo Rossi, Ballatore, André, Gossamer Bay, Livingston Cellars, Peter Vella, and Wild Vines. Brands sold exclusively to hotels and restaurants (Burlwood, Copperridge, Liberty Creek, and William Wycliff) also represent a significant proportion, whereas midpriced wines such as Indigo Hills, Turning Leaf, and Redwood Creek do not. The combined turnover of Gallo of Sonoma and the following other authentic wineries (as opposed to "homeless" brands) belonging to E. & J. Gallo is relatively tiny: Anapamu Cellars, Bridlewood, Frei Brothers, Louis Martini, MacMurray Ranch, Marcelina Vineyards, Mirassou Vineyards, and Rancho Zabacca.

2. CONSTELLATION BRANDS
Formed by the merger between Canandaigua Wine and BRL Hardy, Constellation Brands produces 85 million cases worldwide, some 50 million of which are made by American wineries. Almost 19 million are inexpensive wines from the Mission Bell Winery, 7 million from Canandaigua, 7 million under Turner Road Vintners, 2.5 million from Widmer Wine Cellars, and 1.8 million from Batavia Wine Cellars. The balance is Mondavi, taken over by Constellation in November 2004, and Columbia Winery, Covey Run, Dunnewood Vineyards, Franciscan Vineyards, Paul Thomas Winery, Simi Vineyards, Ste. Chapelle Winery, and Viña Santa Carolina (Chile).

3. THE WINE GROUP
The annual production of this San Francisco-based group is estimated to be over 25 million cases by the following wineries: Colony, Concannon, Corbett Canyon, Franzia, Glen Ellen, Golden State Vintners (Pacific Peak and numerous other brands), Lejon, M. G. Vallejo, Morgan David, Summit, and Alamonte (Argentina).

4. JFJ BRONCO
This is the company that gave the world "Two Buck Chuck" and it did so through one of its wineries, Charles Shaw, which accounts for about 5 million of Bronco's 9-million-case

production. While other groups were uprooting vineyards, Charles Shaw was siphoning off the excess production from Bronco's other wineries (C. C. Vineyard, Coastal Ridge, Forest Glen, Hacienda, JFJ, and Napa Ridge), feeding it on to the market exclusively through Trader Joe's in a brilliant marketing coup. Bronco still has its assets in the ground, and instead of paying money out, it has raked it in. Other Bronco brands include: Albertoni Vineyards, Antares Cellar, Bear's Lair, Black Mountain, The California Winery, Cedar Brook, Domaine Napa, Douglas Hill, Estrella, Forestville, Fox Hollow, Gibson Winery, Grand Cru, JJJ, Laurier, J. W. Morris, Montpellier, Salmon Creek, and Silver Ridge.

5. VINCOR
A fast-expanding, Canada-based group, with recent acquisitions in California, Washington, and Australia, Vincor produces 8 million cases in the Americas. Wineries include Inniskillin, Hawthorne Mountain, Jackson-Triggs, Sumac Ridge, Hogue Cellars, and R. H. Phillips.

6. DIAGEO
This UK-based group is the largest spirit company in the world. It has a 7-million-case wine portfolio, 90 percent of which is US-based, with wineries that include Beaulieu Vineyards, Blossom Hill, Painted Hills, Sterling Vineyards, and The Monterey Vineyard. In December 2004, Diageo acquired the Chalone Group, which, in addition to Chalone Vineyards itself, includes the Californian wineries of Acacia Vineyard, Provenance Vineyards, Hewitt Vineyard, Jade Mountain, Moon Mountain Vineyard, Dynamite Vineyards, Orogeny Vineyards, and Echelon Vineyards. Chalone is also joint owner of Edna Valley Vineyard and, in Washington, owns Sagelands Vineyard and Canoe Ridge Vineyard.

7. BROWN-FORMAN
Generally perceived to be a Kentucky-based wine and spirits company, Brown-Forman is in fact much more than that, manufacturing everything from china and crystal, through stainless-steel and pewter products, to leather and luggage. Its American wine production totals some 6 million cases from the following wineries: Bel Arbor, Bonterra, Fetzer (including the Jekel brand), Korbel, Mariah, One.9, and Sonoma-Cutrer.

8. BERINGER BLASS
The wine division of Fosters, the Australian beer group, Beringer Blass's global wine production amounts to 17 million cases, although just 5.5 million are American. Wineries include Beringer Vineyards, Chateau St. Jean, Chateau Souverain, Etude, Meridan Vineyards, Stag's Leap Winery, St. Clement, and Windsor.

9. JACKSON WINE ESTATES
With interests in Australia, Italy, and Chile as well as the US, annual sales are just over 4 million cases, and the vast majority are under Jess Jackson's core brand, Kendall-Jackson. Other American wineries in this group include Edmeades, La Crema, Stonestreet, and Calina (Chile).

10. ALLIED-DOMECQ
This Anglo-Spanish group is the second-largest beverage group in the world, but its strength is in spirits. Its wine division includes Domecq, Harvey's, and Cockburns, plus G. H. Mumm and Perrier-Jouët (France), and Montana (New Zealand), and is more focused on fine wines than high volumes. Just over 3 million cases come from its American wineries, including Atlas Peak Vineyards, Bodegas Balbi (Argentina), Buena Vista, Callaway Coastal, Clos du Bois, J. Garcia, Haywood Estate, Mumm Napa, and William Hill Winery.

CALIFORNIA

California's finest wines have become a victim of their own success. Ignoring the ridiculously priced iconic wines, the vast majority of California's greatest wines can stand shoulder-to-shoulder with equivalently priced wines from the classic regions of France, yet while the international market is willing to pay such prices for famous names from Bordeaux, Burgundy, and the Rhône, it is either unwilling or lacks the knowledge to pay the same price for the California wines. This has resulted in midpriced California wines filling the top end of the available line on even the most open-minded export markets. Thus, what is perceived to be the best that California has to offer is not really its best at all.

CALIFORNIA WAS FIRST SETTLED by the Spanish in 1769 and formed part of Mexico until 1848, when it was ceded to the United States, becoming a state of the Union in 1850. The first California wine was made in 1782 at San Juan Capistrano, by Fathers Pablo de Mugártegui and Gregorio Amurrió. Mission grapes, from vines brought to California by Don José Camacho on the *San Antonio*, which docked at San Diego on May 16, 1778, were used to make the wine. However, it was not until 1833 that *Bordelais* Jean Louis Vignes established California's first commercial winery. He was the first California winemaker to import European vines and, in 1840, he also became the first to export California wines.

THE AMAZING HARASZTHY

Eight years before California passed from Mexican to American sovereignty, a certain Hungarian political exile called Agoston Haraszthy de Mokesa settled in Wisconsin. Haraszthy was a colorful, flamboyant entrepreneur in the mold of Barnum or Champagne Charlie. Among other things, he founded a town in Wisconsin and modestly called it Haraszthy (it was later renamed

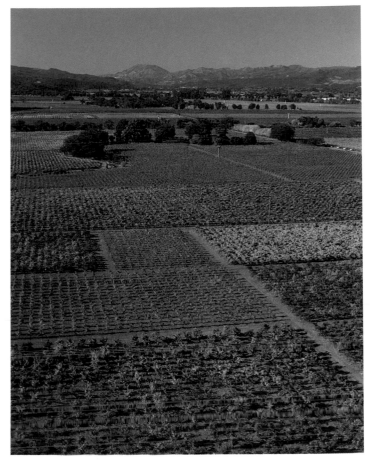

NAPA VALLEY VINEYARDS
Of all California's winemaking regions, the Napa Valley is perhaps the best known, and its wines are the most sought after. The first vines were planted here in 1838, and today the valley boasts a vast area under vine, with a bewildering array of grape varieties.

Sauk City), ran a Mississippi steamboat, and cultivated the first vineyard in Wisconsin—all within two years of beginning a new life in a strange country.

In 1849, Haraszthy moved to San Diego, leaving his business interests in the hands of a partner, who promptly took advantage of a rumor that he had perished during his transcontinental trek, sold all the business and properties, and vanished with the money. Haraszthy was broke, yet within six months he was farming his own 160-acre (65-hectare) fruit and vegetable ranch. Such rapid success followed by disaster then an even greater triumph was to become Haraszthy's trademark. Within a few months of acquiring his ranch, he also became the owner of a butcher's shop and a livery stable in Middleton, a part of San Diego that still boasts a Haraszthy Street. In addition, he ran an omnibus company, started a construction business, was elected the first sheriff of San Diego, was made a judge, and became a lieutenant in the volunteer militia. He also began importing cuttings of numerous European vine varieties.

The Buena Vista Winery

Having imported no fewer than 165 different vine varieties from Europe, in 1857 Haraszthy purchased 560 acres (230 hectares) of land near the town of Sonoma, in an area called the Valley of the Moon. Here, he built a winery, which he named Buena Vista, and dug six cellars out of the sandstone hill. With north California's

Less than 2,500 degree days
(eg) Bordeaux, France 2,390
Reims, Champagne, France 1,820

2,501–3,000 degree days (eg)
Asti, Piemonte, Italy 2,930
Auckland, New Zealand 2,540

3,001–3,500 degree days (eg)
Querateo, Mexico 3,400 Milan,
Piemonte, Italy 3,310

3,500–4,000 degree days (eg)
Cape Town, South Africa 3,720
Florence, Tuscany, Italy 3,530

More than 4,000 degree days
(eg) Zaccar, Algeria 5,200
Perth, Australia 4,010

CALIFORNIA'S CLIMATIC REGIONS
*California has five categories of vine-growing
region, graded from Region I (the coolest)
to Region V (the hottest) by a heat
summation system (see Glossary)
that measures in "degree days"
the amount of heat useful for
vine growth a region has
each year. The research
helps growers predict
which grape varieties
will thrive in
which areas.*

Benmore Valley

San Lucas

North Coast
See also p479, p481, p487

Central Valley
See also p502

Sierra Foothills

San Francisco Bay

South Coast

Central Coast
See also p495, p498

Other delimited AVA wine areas

International boundary

State boundary

County boundary

▲ Height above sea level (meters)

0   50   100 miles
0   50   100   150 km

CALIFORNIA,
see also p.463
*The best wines of California
are produced in areas cooled by
the sea, bay winds, and the great
coastal fog bank. The hot Central
Valley yields most of the region's jug-
wine, mass-produced vin ordinaire, which,
with cool fermentation, is clean and fruity.*

THE SECOND COMING

Because phylloxera, a root-feeding insect, came from the US to destroy European vineyards, which were saved only when the vines were grafted on to phylloxera-resistant native American varieties, there is a widespread belief that California's vineyards have always been safe. Nothing could be further from the truth. Phylloxera's home was east of the Rockies, where over eons native vines, such as *Vitis berlandieri* and *V riparia*, developed a natural resistance to phylloxera. When European *vinifera* vines were introduced to California, phylloxera was bound to follow, via the wagon trains across the Rockies or on the vines themselves, and *vinifera* varieties proved to be as vulnerable in California as anywhere else.

THE ANTI-BEAST

Phylloxera was first identified at Sonoma in 1873, coincidentally at the same time as another native American bug, *Tyroglyphus*, was deliberately being shipped to France. The idea of using *Tyroglyphus*, which was harmless to the vine but a deadly enemy of phylloxera, to infect phylloxera-infested vineyards was an imaginative one. Unfortunately, unlike phylloxera, *Tyroglyphus* did not care for the European climate and failed to settle.

In California, the effect of phylloxera was devastating. By 1891, Napa could boast 18,000 acres (7,200 hectares) of vines, but phylloxera multiplies at a terrifying rate (one female bug can be responsible for one billion offspring in twelve, 30-day generation cycles every year) that this had been reduced to a mere 3,000 acres (1,200 hectares). Under the auspices of Professor Hilgard, Head of Agriculture at the Department of Viticulture and Enology in the University of California at Berkeley (established in 1880, moved to Davis in 1906), California's growers eventually adopted the same method as the Europeans to control the pest, grafting *vinifera* vines on to phylloxera-resistant varieties. Ironically, it was some time before Californians realized these wonder vines originated from eastern American states and initially imported them from France! Only half the vineyards had been grafted when they were hit by another, even more lethal, plague—Prohibition. By the late 1940s, UC Davis had assembled one of the most formidable teams of viticultural and oenological experts in the world. Headed by such legendary figures as Amerine, Olmo, and Winkler, the university was primarily responsible for making California the wine force it is today. Along the way, however, they made some errors, such as placing too much emphasis on volume and technical correctness, but the biggest mistake of all was to recommend the widespread use of AxR#1 rootstock.

ROOT CAUSE

Despite warnings from various European sources about its susceptibility to phylloxera (all acknowledged but brushed aside by numerous university textbooks), UC Davis recommended AxR's use on fertile valley floors, such as Napa, because of its ability to increase yields. As Winkler *et. al.* put it in *General Viticulture*: "This is a case where the choice of (root) stock cannot be based entirely on its resistance to phylloxera."

These words came back to haunt the faculty at Davis in the 1980s, when, slowly but inexorably, vineyards grafted on to AxR failed and the culprit, phylloxera, was identified. Three out of every four vines in California will have to be replaced, which will bring financial ruin to many, although for the California wine industry as a whole, it will ultimately be recognized as a blessing in disguise as undesirable grapes will not only be replaced by selected clones of better-quality varieties, but will also be grafted on to less productive rootstocks and planted at higher densities. The estimated cost of replanting the Napa and Sonoma districts alone is $1.2 billion. Napa was the worst hit, but has tackled the problem far more quickly and effectively than has Sonoma.

SHARPSHOOTERS

Just as California's growers were counting the cost of dealing with phylloxera, so their vineyards were being invaded by another, possibly more dangerous, bug—*Homalodisca coagulata*, or the Glassy-Winged Sharpshooter. This leaf-hopper is not harmful in itself, but it carries the bacterium that infects vines with Pierce's disease. This disease is considerably faster-acting than phylloxera, killing vines in just one to five years, but what really frightens the industry is that there is no known cure. With no way to defeat Pierce's disease, most efforts have been focused on trying to control its vector, the Glassy-Winged Sharpshooter. In August 2000, David Morgan, a post-doctoral research scientist at the Riverside campus of the University of California, began a program to control the spread of Sharpshooters by releasing their natural enemy, *Gonatocerus triguttatus*. This tiny, stingless wasp had been effective in reducing populations in Texas and Mexico, but has yet to turn the tide in the Golden State, the southern and central counties of which are already infected. Despite Morgan's efforts, it is still predicted that the Glassy-Winged Sharpshooter will probably become a "permanent part of various habitats throughout northern California."

first significant wine estate, Haraszthy won several awards, and he attracted much publicity for both his vineyard and his wine. This venture drew so much attention that, in 1861, the governor of California commissioned Haraszthy to visit Europe and report on its winegrowing areas. Haraszthy's trip took him to every wine region in France, Germany, Italy, Spain, and Switzerland, where he interviewed thousands of winegrowers, took notes, consulted foreign literature, and so accumulated a library of reference material. He returned to the US with a staggering 100,000 cuttings of 300 different vine varieties, only to have the state Senate plead poverty when he presented them with a bill for $12,000 for his trip, although the cuttings alone were worth three times that amount. He was never reimbursed for his trouble and many of the cuttings, which he had expected to be distributed among the state's other winegrowers, simply rotted away.

CALIFORNIA WINERIES

There are at least 1,050 wineries in California, over half of which sell less than 5,000 cases each, while the largest 25 account for 90 percent of all California wine sold on markets worldwide. According to the TTB, there were as many as 1,689 wineries in California in 2004, but there are various reasons why several different winery names might be located at the same physical address, whereas the Wine Institute's list below is a reliable source of bricks and mortar wineries on a county-by-county basis.

COUNTY	1990	2004	DIFFERENCE
Alameda	19	24	5
Amador	17	25	8
Butte	3	4	1
Calaveras	5	12	7
Contra Costa	6	1	-5
El Dorado	11	32	21
Fresno	19	11	-8
Humboldt	4	8	4
Kern	7	4	-3
Lake	8	11	3
Lassen	0	1	1
Los Angeles	16	7	-9
Madera	5	6	1
Marin	8	8	0
Mariposa	0	3	3
Mendocino	41	46	5
Merced	1	1	0
Modoc	1	0	-1
Monterey	20	25	5
Napa	211	204	13
Nevada	3	5	2
Orange	1	2	1
Placer	1	7	6
Riverside	16	22	6
Sacramento	5	3	-2
San Benito	6	6	0
San Bernardino	5	3	-2
San Diego	7	13	6
San Francisco	10	0	-10
San Joaquin	22	32	10
San Luis Obispo	40	98	58
San Mateo	10	5	-5
Santa Barbara	24	50	26
Santa Clara	35	28	-7
Santa Cruz	23	20	-3
Shasta	1	3	2
Siskiyou	0	1	1
Solano	9	2	-7
Sonoma	160	210	50
Stanislaus	6	5	-1
Trinity	1	1	0
Tulare	4	4	0
Tuolumne	3	4	1
Ventura	5	5	0
Yolo	8	6	-2
Yuba	1	2	1
Total	808	1,050	242

Haraszthy was not deterred: within seven years he managed to expand Buena Vista to 6,000 acres (2,430 hectares). In doing so, he totally changed the course of Californian viticulture, transferring the focus of attention from the south of the state to the north. At the height of its fame Buena Vista had offices in San Francisco, Philadelphia, Chicago, New York, and London. However, this success was purely superficial, for the vineyard was described in 1864 as "the largest wine-growing estate in the world and the most unprofitable." Haraszthy also suffered a number of losses on the stock exchange and was faced with a new tax on brandy, which resulted in further loss of income. A fire at the winery then destroyed much of his stock and the bank proceeded to cut off his credit.

Enough was enough, even for Agoston Haraszthy de Mokesa. He left California for Nicaragua, where he was successful in obtaining a government contract to distill rum from sugar. An enigmatic character to the end, Haraszthy disappeared altogether in 1869, presumed drowned while trying to cross an alligator-infested stream on his plantation.

LEARNING CURVE

With California's natural abundance of sun and what to most Europeans seems like America's preoccupation with size, it was perhaps inevitable that the 1950s and early 1960s saw a series of massive, ink-black, tannic Cabernet Sauvignon blockbusters hitting the shelves. The late 1960s witnessed the introduction of high-tech wineries and the use of 100 percent new oak, and the precision of style and focus of fruit that resulted were welcomed at the time, as were the supple tannins that replaced harsh ones. The mid-1970s saw the irresistible rise of Chardonnay, but the wines were blatantly too rich and oaky. Sidetracked by the quest for finesse, the wines went too far in the wishy-washy vintages of 1982 and 1983, when overacidified, tart, and downright stingy wines were made. Some winemakers wanted to sacrifice the voluptuousness that is inherent in this sunny state in a fruitless bid to fabricate some sort of European-styled, slower-developing, longer-lived wine (a number still pursue this misguided idea), but the truly magnificent 1985 vintage, the best year since 1974, was a turning point for California's wine industry. Virtually everyone got it right. Since then, the wines of all those who sought elegance without stripping away their natural expression have deliciously demonstrated that the original quest for finesse was no folly.

This learning curve has established in California, as it has elsewhere, that the secret of fine wine is merely a matter of balance. The difficulty is in achieving it, for perfect balance is by definition a natural state that can be achieved only in the vineyard, not in the winery.

SPRING MUSTARD FLOWERS IN THE NAPA VALLEY
This bright yellow carpet of mustard seed in full bloom will soon be plowed in as a "green manure" to feed the vines.

LONGEVITY

Now that most of California's makers of fine wines have found their direction, the only obstacle to prevent them from achieving their full potential (aside from the vagaries of vintage and occasional overzealousness), is the problem of cellarage temperature. Air conditioning is vital in California, but few people seem to realize that at 57°F (14°C), which seems to be the norm here, potentially fine white wines will fall over after two or three years and the longevity of even the best-quality red wines will be halved. The additional cost of maintaining a temperature just a few degrees lower can be considerable, but once the bottle maturation process has set in, it can only be speeded up, not slowed down, so it is a cost that cannot be cut. The *champenois* know this more than anyone else, since even their cheapest products must spend years in their cellars prior to distribution, which is why they are stored at between 50 and 52°F (10 and 11°C). Once most California cellars are kept at no more than 53.5°F (12°C), the notion that these wines rapidly mature will be shown to be a myth.

TOO MUCH OF A GOOD THING?

Investors overestimated public demand for sparkling wines in the 1980s, when they copied Domaine Chandon in a number of new dedicated sparkling wine operations (Piper-Sonoma in 1980, Maison Deutz in 1981, Freixenet's Gloria Ferrar in 1982, Roederer Estate in 1982, Mumm Napa in 1985, Taittinger's Domaine Carneros in 1987, and Codorníu in 1991), only to release their products onto a market plateau, sparkling off a bubbly war, as they tried to grab a slice of the shrinking pie. The only real winner was Domaine Chandon, which had already recouped its capital outlay and was the only one that could afford to play the discount game and still make a profit. Also Roederer Estate, which refused to participate, and has subsequently built up a reputation as one of the greatest sparkling wine producers outside of Champagne itself. Domaine Carneros and Mumm Napa have both survived by discounting their entry-level wines, while creating awareness for some of their higher-quality *cuvées*, but Piper-Sonoma is just a label operating out of a small corner of what was once its own proud winery, but was purchased by Judy Jordan for the production of her premium-quality "J" sparkling wine. Maison Deutz has been defunct since 1997, and Codorníu was renamed Artesa and now specializes in upmarket still wines.

History repeated itself on a grander scale at the turn of the 21st century. In the mid-1990s, California was riding on the crest of the French Paradox wave, which started with the *60 Minutes* television program in 1991 and increased per capita wine consumption in the US by almost one third. In 1995, California experienced the largest growth in its wine sales for 20 years, when the industry was hit by a small crop. Sales continued to soar in 1996, and that year's crop was also down. Faced with the prospect of increasing sales and diminishing crops, growers commenced planting new vineyards at such a rate that by 2001 the acreage under vine had increased by more than 60 percent—then global economic decline was heightened by September 11. Wine drinking did not slow down, but consumers became more sensitive to price points. This resulted in $10 wines being discounted to $6, and cheaper wines being sold off anonymously. The ripple effect caused tens of thousands of acres to be grubbed up. This may not have been such a bad thing, since they were mostly fit for little more than blending, but it did seem a bit backward that while vines were being planted at the fastest rate ever in marginal areas like the Atlantic Northeast, vineyards were actually disappearing in sunny California. There was even talk that California's wine glut was affecting sales of its ultrapremium products, but although their prices have dropped, this was not the result of a general sensitivity to price points. The minuscule tip of the California wine market had become overcrowded with $100-plus wines, and their primary patrons, California's new money, eventually realized the value of scarcity.

CALIFORNIA'S GRAPE VARIETIES

The area under vine in California has increased by almost 165,000 acres since 1995, but obscured by a modest increase in table grapes, and the fact that raisin varieties have actually decreased, this includes an even larger expansion of wine grapes (nearly 175,000 acres). The breakdown of vines in 2003 was as follows:

VINE TYPE	1995 ACRES	2003 ACRES	INCREASED ACREAGE	PERCENTAGE GROWTH
Wine grape varieties	354,417	529,000	174,583	49%
Raisin grape varieties	277,190	260,000	-17,190	-6%
Table grape varieties	85,539	93,000	7,461	9%
TOTAL	717,146	882,000	164,854	23%

From the breakdown below of wine grape varieties by color, the swing from red to white wine varieties continues to gather pace. In the 1980s, when the demand for Chardonnay was at its height and most people in the US believed that lighter meant healthier, white wine grapes accounted for as much as 57 percent, but the dominance of white wine sales in the US changed that fateful day in November 1991, when the so-called "French Paradox" (see Glossary) was much publicized on CBS television's *60 Minutes* program. It now appears clear that growers took advantage of the costly replanting of phylloxera-ravaged vineyards to swing the pendulum from white grape varieties to black.

GRAPE COLOR	1995 ACRES	%	2003 ACRES	%	INCREASED ACREAGE	PERCENTAGE GROWTH
Black	142,546	55%	287,075	61%	144,529	101%
White	116,979	45%	185,373	39%	68,394	58%
TOTAL	259,525	100%	472,448	100%	212,923	82%

CALIFORNIA'S WHITE GRAPE VARIETIES

In 2003 there were 185,373 acres of white grapes growing in California, with just 12 varieties accounting for almost 96 percent of this total. Again, no surprise which white grape is the fastest growing in the state, but it is strange to see the Burger (a.k.a. Monbadon) coming back into favor, having once been a very widely planted alternative to the Mission grape. It is good to see so much interest in Pinot Gris, even if the imported clones bear very little varietal relation to the spice-laden *selection massal* from the best established vineyards in Alsace. Latin lovers should be interested to note an almost 7,000% increase (albeit from a minuscule base) in plantings of Catarratto, the prolific Sicilian grape.

LE5	FG5	GRAPE VARIETY	1995 ACREAGE	2003 ACREAGE	INCREASED ACREAGE	PERCENTAGE GROWTH
1.		Chardonnay	53,228	97,680	44,452	84%
		French Colombard	31,325	31,865	540	2%
2.		Sauvignon Blanc	7,122	15,308	8,186	115%
		Chenin Blanc	12,658	13,416	758	6%
3.	2.	Pinot Gris	590	5,908	5,318	901%
		Muscat of Alexandria	3,213	3,775	562	17%
4.		Viognier	547	2,089	1,542	282%
		Malvasia Bianca (Vermentino)	1,616	1,857	241	15%
		Riesling	1,399	1,844	445	32%
5.		Burger	716	1,500	784	109%
		Gewürztraminer	832	1,358	526	63%
		Semillon	610	1,255	645	106%
		Muscat Canelli	638	970	332	52%
		Pinot Blanc	461	627	166	36%
		Palomino	573	623	50	9%
		Symphony	372	612	240	65%
		Ugni Blanc	274	275	1	0%
		Emerald Riesling	267	267	0	0%
	5.	Sauvignon Musque	41	184	143	349%
	3.	Roussanne	18	176	158	878%
		Muscat Orange	83	163	80	96%
		Tocai Friulano	110	128	18	16%
	1.	Catarratto	1	70	69	6900%
		Marsanne	39	68	29	74%
	4.	Grenache Blanc	7	64	57	814%
		Other	239	3,291	3,052	1277%
		WHITE WINE TOTAL	116,979	185,373	68,394	58%

CALIFORNIA'S BLACK GRAPE VARIETIES

In 2003 there were 287,075 acres of black grapes growing in California, with just 15 varieties accounting for more than 96 percent of this total. It is amazing to think that Zinfandel, which has been the most widely planted classic black variety for decades, could increase acreage by 36 percent, yet be nudged down to third place. Little surprise, however, to see that Cabernet Sauvignon is the fasting-growing black grape in the state, widening the gap between it and Merlot, despite the fashionability of softer-styled red wines from the latter variety. Interesting to note that Primitivo is listed separately from Zinfandel (see Zinfandel under The Wine Styles of California, p.478), although combining the two would not affect its positioning, despite the relatively small gap between second and third largest planted black varieties. However, Syrah looks as if it could be the dark horse, expanding from barely more than 2,000 acres to over 17,000 in just eight years.

LE5	FG5	GRAPE VARIETY	1995 ACREAGE	2003 ACREAGE	INCREASED ACREAGE	PERCENTAGE GROWTH
1.		Cabernet Sauvignon	27,385	75,154	47,769	174%
2.		Merlot	26,605	51,973	25,368	95%
5.		Zinfandel	37,032	50,199	13,167	36%
3.		Pinot Noir	6,096	23,950	17,854	293%
4.	3.	Syrah	2,206	17,140	14,934	677%
		Rubired	7,039	12,467	5,428	77%
		Barbera	8,164	8,851	687	8%
		Grenache	7,057	8,668	1,611	23%
		Ruby Cabernet	4,972	7,472	2,500	50%
		Petite Sirah	1,738	5,166	3,428	197%
		Carignane	5,033	5,132	99	2%
		Cabernet Franc	1,435	3,547	2,112	147%
		Sangiovese	881	2,603	1,722	195%
		Carnelian	882	1,637	755	86%
	4.	Petit Verdot	144	1,096	952	661%
		Alicante Bouschet	755	1,074	319	42%
	5.	Malbec	161	1,065	904	561%
		Tempranillo	380	767	387	102%
		Mission	447	656	209	47%
		Mataro (Mourvèdre)	288	644	356	124%
		Salvador	554	555	1	0%
		Gamay	474	539	65	14%
		Royalty	479	480	1	0%
		Gamay Beaujolais	362	403	41	11%
		Centurion	236	305	69	29%
	1.	Primitivo	18	240	222	1233%
		Meunier	163	207	44	27%
		Nebbiolo	113	177	64	57%
		Cinsaut	57	144	87	153%
		Lambrusco	103	103	0	0%
		Dolcetto	47	89	42	89%
		Lagrein	60	86	26	43%
		Charbono	40	81	41	103%
		Touriga Nacional	19	81	62	326
	2.	Counoise	5	51	46	920%
		Souzão	16	51	35	219%
		Other	1,100	4,222	3,122	284%
		RED WINE TOTAL	142,546	287,075	144,529	101%

Notes

LE5 = Five largest-expanding varieties by increased acreage.

FG5 = Five fastest-growing varieties by percentage difference.

THE WINE STYLES OF
CALIFORNIA

BARBERA

This Italian grape is mostly cultivated in the Central Valley, where its high natural acidity makes it useful for blending purposes. This said, it is cultivated on a much smaller scale in fine-wine areas, particularly Sonoma, Mendocino, and Sierra Foothills, where a number of wineries produce a pure varietal Barbera in one form or another. Although L'Uvaggio di Giacomo's best Barbera is La Pantera, its Il Gufo is extraordinarily good for a Central Valley wine.

🍷 *3–6 years* (up to 10 in exceptional cases)

🏆 *Eberle • Kunde Estate • L'Uvaggio di Giacomo* (La Pantera) • *Palmina • Preston • Renwood* (Sierra Series) • *Thornton* (Curran Ranch)

BOTRYTIZED AND LATE HARVEST STYLES

Some of the world's most succulent botrytized and late-harvest wines are made in California. The "sunshine state" brings a wonderfully ripe peachiness to Riesling and mouthwatering tropical fruit freshness to Chenin and Muscat. Several excellent Icewines have been made, including one from Bonny Doon's irrepressible Randall Grahm, even though he openly admits to storing the grapes in his freezer before pressing them! I cannot write this section without mentioning the legendary wines of Sine Qua Non in the Edna Valley, which I have never visited because it is between Pinot Noir wineries, and I have always feared that a stop there could very well kill my dry wine palate for a couple of days. However, it would be unfair to suggest anything other than that its wines should be included on this page.

🍷 *Ready when released* (but last well in bottle)

🏆 *Arrowood* (Riesling Owl Hoot) • *Beringer* (Nightingale) • *Bonny Doon* (Muscat Vin de Glaciere) • *Dolce • Domaine de la Terre Rouge* (Muscat à Petits Grains) • *Château St. Jean* (Special Late Harvest Johannisberg Riesling) • *J. C. Cellars* (Ripken Late Harvest Viognier) • *Martinelli* (Jackass Hill) • *The Ojai Vineyard* (Late Harvest Viognier)

BOTTLE-FERMENTED SPARKLING WINES

California used to be notorious for its cheap sparkling wine until Schramsberg and Domaine Chandon led the way in the early 1970s. Then in 1991, by dint of tasting back, it could be discerned that a number of houses had come of age with the wines that were made only four years earlier. Roederer Estate, in particular, was in a class of its own, and still is, but so many other producers dramatically improved the style and finesse of their wines that the quality of California sparkling wine in general had quadrupled by 1995.

🍷 *2–5 years* (up to 10 in very exceptional cases)

🏆 *Domaine Carneros* (Le Rêve) • *Gloria Ferrer* (Royal Cuvée) • *Handley* (Vintage Blanc de Blancs, Vintage Brut, Vintage Rosé) • *Robert Hunter* (Vintage Brut de Noirs) • *Iron Horse* (Classic Vintage Brut) • *J* (magnums) • *Mumm* (DVX) • *Roederer Estate*

CABERNET FRANC

California's cultivation of this Bordeaux variety tripled between 1983 and 1988. At that time, it was primarily used for effecting better-balanced Cabernet Sauvignon blends, and the only pure varietal versions readers were likely to encounter were rosés from the North Coast area. Since then, the area occupied by Cabernet Franc vines has doubled and pure varietals will shortly become commonplace. Top California Cabernet Franc seems to have a fragrance and finesse not dissimilar to the way it performs in the best St.-Émilion vineyards.

🍷 *1–4 years*

🏆 *Detert Family Vineyards • Nevada City Winery • Peju • Pride • Rancho Sisquoc • Raymond Burr Vineyards • Reverie • Gainey Vineyard* (Limited Selection) • *Titus*

CABERNET SAUVIGNON

California's most widely planted, and probably potentially its finest, black grape variety. In areas that are too cool, Cabernet Sauvignon wines can have bell-pepper character, or even green bean, but in most other areas they tend to produce saturated, purple-hued wines with a smooth texture, deliciously ripe blackcurrant fruit, and oak-derived notes of vanilla, mocha, cedar, and spice. Oak is now used intelligently and some of the most exciting Cabernet wines are blended with Merlot, Cabernet Franc, and/or Petit Verdot, although not to the extent of a classic blend (*see* Classic Red Blends, and Meritage). At their best, these wines are a match for all but the very greatest vintages of Bordeaux *premiers crus*. Indeed, California is so blessed with Cabernet Sauvignon that it is impossible to come up with a definitive top 10, just 10 of the best, and in compiling the list below I have tried not to go overboard on too many fabulously expensive, virtually unobtainable iconic wines.

🍷 *3–5 years* (inexpensive), *5–12 years* (top wineries), *8–25* (or more) *years* (exceptional wines)

🏆 *Abreu • Atalon • Behrens and Hitchcock • Caymus* (Special Selection) • *Colgin* (Tychson Hill) • *Duckhorn* (Estate Grown) • *Dunn • Lewelling Vineyards • Lokoya • Robert Mondavi* (Reserve)

CARIGNANE

Surprisingly, this rarely sighted varietal is the 11th most widely grown black grape in California, well ahead of more prestigious varieties such as Cabernet Franc. Carignan, or Carignane as it is spelled in the US, provides a high yield of well-colored, strongly flavored wine that can be quite coarse and tannic. It is useful for blending both in California and in its native south of France, where it is one of the 13 grapes permitted in Châteauneuf-du-Pape. It has a less harsh character in California's coastal districts, where some wineries produce a pure varietal version, and very old vines can lose the coarse character, yielding wines of extraordinary depth and quality.

🍷 *3–6 years* (up to 10 years in exceptional cases)

🏆 *Cline* (Ancient Vines) • *Jessie's Grove* (Ancient Vine) • *Ravenswood • Ridge • Windsor* (Oat Valley Vineyards)

CHARBONO

This variety is the Corbeau, an almost extinct French variety that is also known as the Charbonneau. It produces a wine with vibrant cherry fruit and tingling ripe acidity, in a not dissimilar style to Barbera. Indeed, Inglenook Vineyards, which was the first winery to make a pure varietal wine from this grape, labeled it Barbera until Dr. Winkler of the UC-Davis nursery identified it properly as Charbono.

🍷 *2–4 years*

🏆 *Duxoup • Robert Foley • Turley* (Tofanelli)

CHARDONNAY

California might be awash with dreadful Chardonnay, but it also boasts more great-quality and/or great-value Chardonnay than ever. Although massive, blockbusting Chardonnays still abound, the best have improved and there have never been so many Chardonnay wines showing as much finesse as they do today. It is at the bottom end of the market where much of the dregs exists. Unlike the readers of this and other wine books, most consumers are no more interested in learning about wine than most drivers are in understanding cars. There is no reason why they should be, but this has resulted in most consumers budgeting for Chardonnay as they would canned goods, and within this price-banding they have come to think of Chardonnay as a brand with recognizable characteristics like butter and vanilla. They do not realize that butter is diacetyl produced by malolactic or that the vanilla is vanillin from oak. Because Chardonnay was the first, biggest, and, for a long time, practically the only wine that most American consumers drank, the signature notes of methods used at that time have become mistaken in consumer psyche as Chardonnay's varietal character. This misconception has prevented Chardonnay as a whole from progressing, particularly at the bottom end of the market. This phenomenon is not unique to the US, but it does seem to be stronger and longer lasting. If the country could only go through a trend for zippy, zingy, unoaked Chardonnay, then it would help raise standards from the basement upward, and this would percolate through to even the most expensive Chardonnay wines, in which it would then become commercially acceptable to allow more fruit to show through. It has to be said that far too many of the most widely acclaimed California Chardonnay wines betray their production techniques on the nose long before they express their fruit or origin. Beware, also, the residual sugar level in some of these wines. There could be dozens of top 10 best California Chardonnays, all of them arguably correct, thus when I have had to make a choice, I have opted for the wine with the most harmonious acidity balance, which provides the longest, most beautifully focused, and graceful finish.

⌐ 2–8 years (15 or more years in very exceptional cases)

⏏ Au Bon Climat (Harmony Nuits-Blanches au Bouge) • Beringer (Sbragia) • Blackjack Ranch • Brewer-Clifton (Sweeney Canyon) • Cuvaison (Carneros Estate) • Du Mol (Chloe) • Hartford Court (Three Jacks) • Kistler (Vine Hill Road) • Martinelli (Three Sisters Vineyard) • Walter Hansel (Cahill Lane)

CHENIN BLANC

This Loire Valley grape is famous for wines such as the sweet, honey-rich Vouvray and the very dry, searingly flavored Savennières. In California it is the fourth most widely planted white wine grape, yet it is seldom spoken of. Although the recent trend to improve the acidity balance has raised the standard of California Chenin Blanc, it fares less well in this state than it does in France. Since I am not a fan of any but the greatest Chenin Blancs, it is hard for me to work up much enthusiasm for the Chenin Blanc in California. I have long wondered about the veracity of all those books that carry the same spiel—that Clarksburg is the only area to produce a regionally identifiable Chenin Blanc, especially as finding wines with any Central Valley AVA is something of a quest. The now defunct R. & J. Cook winery used to be the most prolific producer of wines bearing the Clarksburg appellation, but produced better Petite Sirah than Chenin. Dry Creek Vineyard is considered by some to produce the best Chenin Blanc, but it used to blend Clarksburg with Sonoma fruit until relatively recently, thus it was never possible to assess Dry Creek Clarksburg Chenin Blanc in its own right. Now we can, of course, and the quality is at least as good as it ever was, so more than 20 years after the Clarksburg AVA was established, we are finally

seeing this appellation make a name for itself. However, although Dry Creek is one of California's best Chenin Blanc wines, collecting more awards for this variety than any other winery in the US, it is not always that special, and others can make much finer wines on occasions. Furthermore, because of the lack of consistency for this varietal and, indeed, the small number of producers, it is sometimes worth checking out the following: Callaway Coastal, Chapellet, Foxen Vineyard, Meador Estate, Sutter Home. All the best wines below are dry or off-dry. See Botrytized and Late-Harvest Wines for sweeter styles.

⌐ 1–4 years

⏏ Baron Herzog (Clarksburg) • Beringer • Casa Nuestra • Chalone • Dry Creek (Clarksburg) • Husch (La Ribera) • Windsor Vineyards

CINSAUT

Until the Rhône-style wine revolution in California, this variety was better known as the Black Malvoisie. There is precious little Cinsault or Cinsaut in the state, even though plantings have increased by more than 150 percent since 1995, and what does exist is mostly used in blends, although Frick continues to make a statement with 30-year-old Cinsaut vines in Sonoma's Dry Creek. There are very few pure Cinsaut wines produced in California; the only others I have come across are Castle (Sonoma), Domaine de la Terre Rouge, and Preston.

⌐ 2–5 years

⏏ Frick

CLASSIC RED BLEND

On balance I would say that Bordeaux-style blends are more successful in California than pure Cabernet Sauvignon varietals. However, it has proved very difficult to persuade California wine drinkers that they should pay the same price, let alone a premium, for such wines. For this reason the Meritage Association was formed (see Meritage), but not all wineries are members and some of the greatest Bordeaux-style blends do not actually use the portmanteau. Therefore, many of the best Bordeaux-style blends recommended here and under the producer profiles do not necessarily carry the Meritage designation. Furthermore, this encyclopedia's definition of a Classic Red Blend is not restricted to Bordeaux varieties, and California has experienced a substantial growth in Rhône-style blends since the mid-1990s. In American usage, this encyclopedia's Classic Red Blend can be taken as synonymous with a "Proprietary" red blend, but only from a certain classic quality and upward.

⌐ 3–5 years (inexpensive), 5–12 years (top wineries), 8–25 (or more) years (exceptional wines)

⏏ Beringer (Alluvium) • Blackjack Ranch (Harmonie) • Colgin (Cariad) • Dalla Vale (Maya) • Harlan • L'Aventure (Cuvée) • Lewis (Cuvée L) • Peter Michael (Les Pavots) • Niebaum-Coppola (Rubicon) • Pride Mountain Vineyards (Reserve Claret)

CLASSIC WHITE BLEND

The combination of Sauvignon and Sémillon is a good one, the traditional view being that the Sauvignon provides the aromatics, freshness, acidity, and crispness, while the Sémillon adds the necessary fat, weight, depth, and

complexity. In some New World areas, however, including California, the Sauvignon is too soft and neutral for this philosophy to work successfully and is much better used to play the Sémillon's role, whereas a small quantity of that grape can, if harvested early enough, provide a grassy herbaceousness that is more like Sauvignon than Sauvignon. The effect is similar, but the reasoning somewhat back to front. This category includes all high-quality white wine blends, not just Bordeaux-style (see Meritage). Having found it difficult to whittle down the Classic Red Blends below 30-odd wines, all arguably top-10 material, it is clear that California is far better blessed for its red blends than its whites, as I have failed to find 10 worthy inclusions!

⌐ 2–4 years

⏏ Andrew Murray (Enchanté) • Beringer (Alluvium) • Luna Vineyards (Bianco) • Ojai (Vin du Soleil) • Signorello (Seta) • St Supéry (Virtú)

COLOMBARD

Amazingly, this is the second most widely planted white grape in California, and it is not even shrinking, having seen another 540 acres (200 hectares) planted since 1995. Colombard, also known as French Colombard, has always been more than adequate, but its true potential was realized only with the advent of cool fermentation techniques. A pure-varietal Colombard is not a fine-quality wine, but it can be superb value in a totally unpretentious and absolutely delicious way, if it is consumed young and fresh.

⌐ Upon purchase

⏏ De Loach

FORTIFIED STYLES

A small number of California wineries are fast catching up with Australia in the fortified wine category. Port is the most successful style. Long before its demise, Inglenook used to be the yardstick for California Palomino Sherry.

⌐ Ready when released (but last well in bottle)

⏏ Bellow Wine Company (Touriga Nacional Vintage Reserve Port) • Cedar Mountain (Chardonnay del Sol) • Ficklin (Vintage Port) • Geyser Peak Winery (Henry's Reserve Shiraz Vintage Port) • Guenoc (Vintage Port) • Joseph Filippi (Angelica Elena) • Joseph Filippi (Oloroso Sherry Library Reserve) • V. Sattui (Madeira) • Windsor (Distinguished Cream Sherry)

FUMÉ BLANC

This term was first coined by Mondavi in the 1970s, who stole and transposed two words from the French appellation Pouilly Blanc Fumé. It was very simple, yet very clever, and by fermenting the wines in oak barriques, he was able to sell what was then a very unfashionable grape variety under a new and catchy name. Fumé Blanc is now used as a generic name for a Sauvignon Blanc wine that has been fermented and/or aged in oak, with the results ranging from a subtle, barrique-fermented influence to a heavily oaked character. See also Sauvignon Blanc.

⌐ 1–3 years

⏏ Château St. Jean (La Petite Étoile) • De Loach (Russian River Valley) • Grgich Hills

Cellar (Estate Grown) • *Robert Mondavi* (To Kalon I Block) • *Murphy-Goode* (Reserve)

GEWÜRZTRAMINER

Although by no means one of California's commonly encountered varietal wines, Gewürztraminer must be one of its most overrated. The hype surrounding California's Gewürztraminers baffles me—most of them lack not only the varietal definition I expect of any classic grape, but their winemakers will insist on acidifying what is an intrinsically low-acid variety. The only way to extract the true pungency of spice that admirers of this varietal expect is through a prefermention maceration. The spice will not be immediately apparent when bottled, but requires additional aging for the terpene-laden bottle-aromas to develop. The phenolics picked up from the skins during the preferment maceration are essential to the balance and length of such low-acid wines, providing a tactile impression that literally sears the spice on to the palate in its later life. It also gives such wines surprising longevity. The problem is that virtually every winemaker in California has been brainwashed into avoiding phenolics in white wine as if they were the plague. In case American readers should think I am taking an unreasonably European viewpoint, I quote Robert Parker: "Anyone who has tasted fine French Gewürztraminer must be appalled by what is sold under this name in California." About the only thing most California Gewürztraminer has in common with its French counterparts is that classic dry renditions are equally rare.

🕰 *1–3 years*

🍷 *Claiborne & Churchill* (Dry Alsatian Style) • *Fetzer* (Echo Ridge) • *Navarro* • *Windsor Vineyards*

GRENACHE

Although cultivation of this variety has been in decline in recent years, it still accounts for some 10 percent of California's black grapes and, despite being traditionally associated in this state with medium-dry rosé and tawny-port-type dessert wines, some truly delicious, high-quality pure varietals have surfaced.

🕰 *1–3 years*

🍷 *Alban Vineyards* • *Bonny Doon* (Clos de Gilroy) • *Epiphany* (Revelation Rodney's Vineyard) • *Holly's Hill* (El Dorado) • *Wild Horse* (Equus James Berry Vineyard)

MALBEC

Although a few wineries are now making good pure varietals from this grape, it has never really caught on in California, where, if it is not ignored entirely, Malbec is merely regarded as a blending component, much as it is in Bordeaux. Perhaps California's winemakers should look more to the 19th-century Black Wines of Cahors than to Bordeaux when considering this variety. When grown ungrafted or on low-yield rootstock, Malbec can produce excellent deep-colored red wines with soft, chewy fruit and has demonstrated the capability of developing much individuality and complexity in most warm climes, particularly when grown on gravelly-clay and marly-clay soils.

🕰 *2–5 years*

🍷 *Arrowood* • *Benzinger* • *Clos du Bois* (L'Étranger) • *Rancho Sisquoc* (Flood Family Vineyard) • *River Run* (Mannstand Vineyard)

MERITAGE

Concocted from "merit" and "heritage," the term "Meritage" was devised as a designation for upmarket Bordeaux-style blends in 1988, and trademarked the following year. Meritage was first coined by Neil Edgar, who was one of 6,000 entrants in an international contest to come up with a name. There are no rules or regulations governing wines that use this trademark, other than that the wineries must be paid-up members of the Meritage Association, and the blends conform to very simple rules of varietal content. Such blends must consist of two or more of the following varieties: Cabernet Sauvignon, Merlot, Cabernet Franc, Petit Verdot, St. Macaire, Gros Verdot, Carmenère, and Malbec for reds; and Sauvignon Blanc, Sémillon, Muscadelle, Sauvignon Vert, and Sauvignon Musque for whites; with no single variety making up more than 90 percent of the blend. Certainly not the most inspired of American marketing terms, it has nevertheless been adopted by a wide range of wineries and restaurants, which often list these wines separately. The most outstanding, plus the many first-class blends that are not marketed as Meritage, are recommended under the Classic Red Blend and Classic White Blend categories.

MERLOT

It has always been obvious that Merlot possessed everything required to make it one of California's most fashionable and sought-after

varietals, and that is exactly what it became in the early 1990s. Its lush fruit and velvety texture are tailormade for this sunshine state, although up to 25 percent Cabernet Sauvignon may be blended into supposedly pure varietals in order to give the wines added structure (25 percent if exported to EU countries).

🕰 *3–8 years*

🍷 *Beringer* (Founders' Estate) • *Blackjack Ranch* (Billy Goat Hill) • *Cosentino* (Reserve) • *Gainey Vineyards* (Limited Edition) • *Hartwell* • *Havens Wine Cellar* (Reserve) • *Napa Cellars* • *Newton* (Epic) • *Paloma* • *Pride* (Mountaintop Vineyard)

MOURVÈDRE

Sometimes known as Mataro, this is one of the most underrated Rhône varieties, and can produce dark, silky-soft, smooth wines that compare to the Syrah, but are not as rich or dense. In California, Mourvèdre can easily acquire a raspberry-jam flavor, which is fine for inexpensive wines and even better as a blending component, although it is possible to find some exciting pure varietals.

🕰 *2–5 years*

🍷 *Bonny Doon* (Old Telegram) • *Cline Cellars* (Ancient Vines) • *Jade Mountain* (Evangelho Vineyard) • *Joseph Filippi* (Library Reserve) • *Ridge* (Mataro) • *Rosenblum Cellars* (Continente Vineyard) • *Sean Thackrey* (Taurus)

MUSCAT BLANC

See Muscat Canelli.

MUSCAT CANELLI

Also known as Muscat de Frontignan, Muscat Blanc, and Moscato Canelli, this grape is in fact the Muscat Blanc à Petits Grains, and it is surprisingly successful in California, producing some delightfully perfumed, flowery-flavored wines in off-dry through to very sweet and dessert styles. *See* Botrytized and Late-Harvest Wines for even sweeter styles.

🕰 *Upon purchase*

🍷 *Bonny Doon* (Vin de Glaciere) • *Eberle* • *Fresno State Winery* (John Diener Vineyard) • *Maurice Car'rie* • *Rosenblum* (Muscat de Glacier) • *Robert Pecota* (Muscato di Andrea) • *St. Supéry* (Moscato)

OTHER VARIETALS

This section lists the best examples found of California's rarely encountered varietals, some of which will no doubt become more widely established one day.

🍷 **Albariño** *Havens* • *Verdad*
Alicante Bouschet *Topolos*
Dolcetto *Mosby*
Grignolino *Emilio Guglielmo* (Santa Clara Valley Reserve)*
Nebbiolo *Palmina* • *Santa Barbara Winery* (Stolpman Vineyard) • *Thornton* (Curran Ranch)
Negrette *De Rose* (Cienega Valley)*
Orange Muscat *Quady* (Electra) • *Renwood*
Pinot Meunier *Domaine Chandon*
Sémillon *St. Supéry* (Dollarhide Ranch)
Sylvaner *Rancho Sisquoc*
Symphony *Ironstone*
Teroldego *Mosby*
Tempranillo *Clos du Bois* (Alexander Valley Reserve) • *Gundlach-Bundschu* (Rhinefarm Vineyard) • *Verdad*

(Santa Ynez Valley)
Trousseau *Fanucchi Vineyards* (Wood Road Vineyard Gris)*

*Wineries not featured in the following pages.

PETITE SIRAH

In the first edition I suggested that ignorance was perhaps bliss in the case of California's Petite Sirah. Although California growers had referred to this grape as Petite Sirah since the 19th century, it was unknown to consumers until the 1960s, when varietal wines began to take off. Petite Sirah quickly gained in popularity on the back of the Rhône's Syrah, only for prices to plummet ridiculously in the 1970s, when it was identified as the Durif, a lowly French variety. It was the same wine, but its humble origins obviously lacked cachet for budding new wine consumers of that era. In 1997, Dr. Carole Meredith used DNA "fingerprinting" to determine that only four of the seven Petite Sirahs in the UC Davis collection were in fact Durif, and that one was identified as true Syrah. As consumers began to wonder if their favorite Petite Sirah might not in fact be Syrah, the prestige and price of this varietal began to soar. But while 10 percent of Petite Sirah is indeed Syrah, the mix is found on a vine-by-vine basis. Rather than find one vineyard of Syrah for every nine vineyards of Durif, growers find they have 10 percent Syrah in their Petite Sirah vineyards. And not just Syrah. Petite Sirah vines are mostly found in old vineyards, planted with perhaps the odd Peloursin, Carignane, Grenache, Barbera, or Alicante Bouschet, in what is known as a "field blend." Despite increased prices, the purple-colored wine made by Petite Sirah, with its floral, blackfruit aromas, is not considered the equal of a true Syrah (although Switchback Ridge and Turley Cellars Petite Syrah—*sic* definitely are), thus it remains one of California's most underrated varietals.

4–8 years

♟ *Biale* (Thomann Station) • *Delectus* • *Girard Winery* • *J. C. Cellars* (Frediani Vineyard) • *Jeff Runquist* ("R" Enver Salmon Vineyard) • *La Jota* • *Lava Cap* • *Rosenblum* (Rockpile) • *Switchback Ridge* • *Turley Cellars* (Petite Syrah)

PINOT BLANC

When grown with care and barrel-fermented, it is virtually impossible to tell Pinot Blanc from a Chardonnay, particularly the examples from Napa, Monterey, and Sonoma. There are some excellent, very serious makers of pure varietal Pinot Blancs, but essentially this is one of California's most underexploited varieties.

1–3 years

♟ *Arrowood* (Saralee's Vineyard) • *Chalone* • *Etude* (Carneros) • *Michel-Schlumberger* (Dry Creek Valley) • *Navarro* • *Steele* (Santa Barbara)

PINOT GRIS

Even at its best, California Pinot Gris is not at all the spicy heavyweight of Alsace fame, but more like a superior Pinot Grigio, with riper, purer fruit. Many of these wines are in fact sold as Pinot Grigio, which is preferable, as Pinot Gris implies a definite spicy element to the fruit and that is almost impossible to find outside of Alsace.

Upon purchase

♟ *Etude* (Carneros Pinot Gris) • *Gallo of*

Sonoma (Sonoma Coast Pinot Gris) • *Luna* (Pinot Grigio) • *Monteviña* (Pinot Grigio) • *Navarro* (Pinot Gris) • *Palmina* (Alisos Vineyard Pinot Grigio)

PINOT NOIR

Beyond all expectations, this Burgundian grape has found a natural home in parts of California, most notably in Sonoma's Russian River Valley, the Carneros area straddling Sonoma and Napa, and the Santa Ynez Valley in Santa Barbara. Santa Barbara does, I think, have the greatest potential of all; equally fine Pinot Noir will be made elsewhere, but the largest number of Pinot Noir producers will eventually be seen to come from this southerly district. Other areas also show promise, particularly San Benito, Monterey, and the Arroyo Grande.

2–5 years

♟ *Au Bon Climat* (La Bauge Au-dessus) • *Brewer-Clifton* (Melville) • *Gary Farrell* (Rochioli-Allen Vineyards) • *Gainey Vineyards* (Limited Edition) • *Kistler* (Occidental Vineyard Cuvée Elizabeth) • *Martinelli* (Blue Slide Ridge) • *J. Rochioli* (West Block) • *Siduri* (Pisoni Vineyard) • *Talley Vineyards* (Rosemary's Vineyard) • *Williams Selyem* (Rochioli Riverblock Vineyard)

RIESLING

Also known as Johannisberg Riesling and White Riesling, this grape covers more than 10 percent of California's white-grape vineyards. Aside from a small, but increasing number of sensational, tangy-dry exceptions, most wines are made in a slightly sweet, commercial style to placate consumer demand. I have tried, wherever possible, to shortlist only the drier styles below, as the sweeter ones are found elsewhere. *See* Botrytized and Late-Harvest Wines for sweeter styles.

1–3 years

♟ *Château Montelena* (Potter Valley) • *Claiborne & Churchill* (Dry Alsatian Style) • *Fetzer* (Echo Ridge) • *Kendall-Jackson* (Vintner's Reserve) • *Navarro* • *Rancho Sisquoc* (Flood Family Vineyard) • *Robert Mondavi* (Private Selection) • *Sanford Winery* (Vin Gris Santa Rita Hills) • *Windsor Vineyards* (California)

ROSÉ OR BLANC DE NOIRS

One of the most overlooked wine styles in California, its well-made, unpretentious rosés can be delicious. All the wines recommended below are dry or off-dry.

Upon purchase

♟ *Bonny Doon* (Vin Gris de Cigare) • *Eberle* (Syrah Rosé) • *Heitz* (Grignolino Rosé) • *Thornton* (Grenache Rosé) • *V. Sattui* (Gamay Rouge—*sic*) • *Verdad*

SANGIOVESE

Cultivation of this variety has increased over 20-fold since the late 1980s, and much of this is due to the number of winemakers and grape-growers who have Italian ancestry. Its success will depend on the choice of site, where the vine should struggle, so there is no need to employ labor-intensive methods to reduce yields through green pruning.

3–7 years (15 years or more in exceptional cases)

♟ *Atlas Peak* • *Beringer* (Knights Valley) •

Coturri (Jessandre Vineyard) • *Luna* (Riserva) • *Pride Mountain Vineyards* • *Saddleback* (Penny Lane Vineyard) • *Seghesio* • *Silverado Vineyards*

SAUVIGNON BLANC

Also known as the Fumé Blanc, a synonym now adopted for an oaked style that is dealt with separately. Many wines labeled Sauvignon Blanc rather than Fumé Blanc are also oaked, but it would be too confusing to list them in this category, so all recommended wines are listed according to their labels, whether they adhere to that style or not. A straight California Sauvignon Blanc should have a crisp style, with the vibrancy of its varietal fruit picked up by, and highlighted with, abundant ripe acidity. California Sauvignon Blanc has, however, an identity problem, as most are soft and neutral, and some are downright wishy-washy. Although there has been a move toward better, more racy acidity by California's best winemakers, the greatest wines from this grape definitely lean more toward a Graves style than varietal purity. There is none of the turbocharged vibrancy of fruit found in New Zealand's Marlborough Sauvignon Blanc, let alone any gooseberry or passionfruit intensity, yet that country built its reputation on the UCD1 clone imported from the US, and until recently, UCD1 was the only clone available for planting in the US. It is about time that Davis reimported UCD1 back from New Zealand, performed comparative trials with the UCD1 motherstock, and made available the Kiwi-evolved UCD1 to growers in the US.

Upon purchase

♟ *Araujo Estate* (Eisele Vineyard) • *Artesa* (Napa Valley Reserve) • *Atalon* • *Gary Farrell* (Redwood Ranch) • *Geyser Peak Winery* (Block Collection) • *Lail* (Georgia) • *Peter Michael* (L'Après-Midi) • *Peju Province* • *J. Rochioli* • *Spottswoode*

SYRAH

This classic Rhône grape illustrates how quickly things move in California. In the first edition I mentioned how surprised I was that the Syrah was not more widely planted. Since then it has increased from a modest 110 acres (45 hectares) to a massive 14,934 acres (6,403 hectares), making it the fourth most widely planted variety in California. There is a sumptuousness about California Syrah that makes it a totally different wine from either French Syrah or Australian Shiraz, although when full and ripe all three versions share the silky-*cassis* fruit and have the potential to develop a fine smoky-spicy complexity. From the top Syrahs listed below, it is obvious that this grape can be successfully grown in several areas of California.

⌁— *3–10 years*

🏆 *Alban* (Lorraine Vineyard) • *Araujo* (Eisel Vineyards) • *Arrowood* (Saralee's Vineyard) • *Blackjack* (Maximus) • *Du Mol* (Eddie's Patch) • *J. C. Cellars* • *Kongsgaard* (Hudson Vineyard) •*Martinelli* • *The Ojai Vineyard* (Thompson Vineyard) • *Pax* (Adler Springs The Terraces)

VIOGNIER

This great Rhône white-wine grape was nonexistent in California until 1985, when the first vines were planted by Joseph Phelps, thus when the first edition of this book was published in 1988 they were not even bearing fruit. At that time, just 11 acres (4.5 hectares) of these vines existed. Now there are more than 2,000 acres (800 hectares), and it is the fourth largest-expanding white varietal in the state. While the vine seems to thrive in California, the wines seldom capture its elusive character. The same could be said about Château Grillet, of course, but if Condrieu has been able to overcome Viognier's inherent difficulties, there was no reason why more California winemakers could not follow suit. And in a way they have, as it is one of California's most successful white wines. What does bother me, however, is that the notoriously difficult Viognier should thrive so well in the golden state: not only is there no problem with flowered vines failing to fruit, but the yield is exceptionally high even by the greediest French grower's standard. This leads me to suspect the authenticity of the vines being sold as Viognier in California. Or, if indeed they are genuine, to wonder what else might have been eradicated during the eight years it took UC Davis to remove the virus from its Viognier bud stock before release. Perhaps the exquisiteness that makes

the best Viognier wines great can be achieved only through debilitated vines? Because, although very successful, far too many are overtly floral, instead of being peachy-floral or, at least, fruity-floral, with too much residual sweetness (aside from those that are made in a Late-Harvest style, and should be sweet), and too little acidity, making them flabby. Authentic Viognier is not overblessed with acidity, but when it is grown at low yields, and harvested physiologically ripe, rather than sugar-ripe, there is a certain acid balance that, together with the proper fruit structure, will provide sufficient grip and length to avoid any connotation of flabbiness.

⌁— *Upon purchase*

🏆 *Alban* (Alban Estate Vineyard) • • *Alan Murray* (Calzada Vineyard) *Arrowood* (Saralee's Vineyard) • *Calera* • *Cold Heaven* • *Eberle* (Mill Road Vineyard) • *Failla* (Alban Vineyard) • *Foxen* (Rothberg Vineyard) • *J. C. Cellars* (Ripken Vineyard) • *Pride Mountain Vineyards*

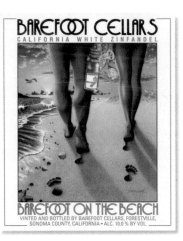

ZINFANDEL

This was once thought to be America's only indigenous *Vitis vinifera* grape, but was later positively identified by Dr. Carole Meredith as the Primitivo grape of southern Italy by Isozyme "fingerprinting," a method of recording the unique pattern created by the molecular structure of enzymes found within specific varieties. However, this led to a conundrum because the earliest records of Primitivo in Italy date from the late 19th century, whereas the Zinfandel name appears in the nursery catalog of William Prince of Long Island, dated 1830. One clue was that Italian growers often referred to their Primitivo as a foreign variety. This led Meredith farther afield and, with the help of Croatian researchers, she was able to announce in 2002 that the Zinfandel and Primitivo are in fact an obscure variety called Crljenak Kastelanski (pronounced Sirl-YEN-ak Kastel-ARN-ski). Referred to as Crljenak, for short, this grape was once widely planted throughout Dalmatia and on more than 1,000 islands, but has mostly been replaced by Croatia's best-known variety, Plavac Mali (the result of a cross-pollination of Crljenak and Dobricic). Nothing special has been produced so far by Crljenak in its homeland, but there will no doubt be efforts to see what can be achieved with it in the future. In the meantime, UC Davis has imported Crljenak and when it has gone through the regulated clean-up process

(possibly by 2008), they intend growing it side by side with Primitivo and Zinfandel, to see which local characteristics these "localized clones" of the same variety might possess. Since the Crljenak gave way to Plavak Mali in Croatia because its tight grape clusters attracted rot, it would seem to be much closer to the tight-clustered Zinfandel than Primitivo, which has much looser fruit clusters. It is not unreasonable to surmise that the Primitivo clone probably adapted to the much hotter, drier local conditions in southern Italy by developing looser-hung berries.

Some growers have already started to vinify Primitivo separately from Zinfandel, and one day we shall probably see the emergence of California Crljenak. When this happens, it would make sense also to develop a blend of all three, and it strikes me that the new UC Davis classication for these grapes—ZPC—would be the ideal name for such *cuvées*. Depending on the way it is vinified, Zinfandel produces many different styles of wine, from rich and dark to light and fruity, or *nouveau* style, from dry to sweet, white to rosé, dessert wine or sparkling. The reason for such a variation in styles is that it is virtually impossible to harvest Zinfandel when all the grapes have an even ripeness. When most of the bunch achieves perfect ripeness, some grapes are green, but if the grower waits for these to ripen, the shoulder clusters quickly raisin. There are several ways to overcome this, but they are all labor-intensive, seemingly wasteful, and inevitably costly, which is why great Zinfandel is never cheap. Great Zinfandel is as rich and deep-colored as only California could produce, with ripe, peppery-spicy fruit, liquorice intensity, and a chocolate-herb complexity. When young, such wines are chewy and have classic berry-fruit flavors, which can swing toward black-cherry or simply have a gluggy-jamminess. It is the only varietal that positively demands the coconutty aromas of American oak, and it is often improved when blended with Petite Sirah for increased backbone. This is a wine that requires a certain amount of bottle-aging to bring out the dried-fruit spiciness.

Zinfandel is not one of California's longest-lived wines, but without sufficient time in bottle, the wine will merely have a richness of oak and berry fruits, and lack complexity. Massive, black, opaque Zinfandels with 16.5 percent plus of alcohol are on the increase, but they are grotesque abominations, and certainly do not stir my soul as they obviously do those of numerous American critics. I don't know what difference in style Crljenak might possess on California soil, but when Primitivo is vinified by the same winemaker, it is usually less alcoholic (just a 0.5 percent reduction), and a little softer, with less berry fruit and less "sweet and sour" flavor.

⌁— *2–5 years* (good but inexpensive wines), *5–15 years* (expensive, more serious styles)

🏆 *DeLoach* (OFS) • *Edmeades* (Zeni Vineyard) • *Gary Farrell* (Maple Vineyard) • *Hartford Court* (Hartford Vineyard) • *Martinelli* • *Nalle* (Reserve) • *Rosenblum* • *Storybook Mountain* (Estate Reserve) • *Turley Cellars* (Hayne Vineyard) • *Williams-Selyem* (Forchini Vineyard)

MENDOCINO COUNTY

The best vineyards here are located on the fork of the Navarro and Russian rivers in the south of Mendocino, a district that has become a byword for top-quality California sparkling wine since the emergence of Roederer Estate. Such is the climatic variation here that some excellent Zinfandel is made, and aromatic varieties may also do very well.

IN THE EARLY 1980s, Champagne Louis Roederer sunk some $15 million into a 500-acre (200-hectare) vineyard and winery in the Anderson Valley, where the climate is considerably cooler than that of surrounding areas. A nonvintage wine in the *champenois* tradition, the first, 1986-based release was nothing special and has not improved over the years, yet the 1987-based release was the best sparkling wine produced anywhere in the world outside of Champagne itself, a quality that has been maintained ever since. The diversity of *terroir* within the sparkling-wine growing areas of Mendocino provides a fascinating contrast of styles, for Scharffenberger, just around the corner from Roederer, could hardly make a wine more different from Roederer. Whereas Roederer is rich, well-structured, and potentially complex in a style that leans decidedly toward Champagne, Scharffenberger is all lightness and elegance with a purity of fruit that gains in finesse every year. There are lots of reasons for this over and above that of *terroir*, including the good old joker in the pack—man—but it does suggest that we are witnessing the very earliest stages of development in California's sparkling-wine industry. In 20 years' time there is every chance that the state's best sparkling-wine areas will be known, planted, and exploited to the extent that each will have many producers making contrasting styles from neighboring vineyards.

GROWTH OF MENDOCINO'S WINE INDUSTRY

Because parts of Mendocino are too hot for classic wine production, there has been a tendency in the past to plant highly productive vines for jug-wine blends. However, the county has a complex climate, and there are some areas where coastal influences dominate and cooler Region I and II climates (*see* p.470) prevail. This has been recognized by the substantial amount of premium quality varietals that were planted in the late 1970s, and by the rise in the number of wineries in the area, from 16 in 1981 to 29 in 1985 and 41 in 1995.

FACTORS AFFECTING TASTE AND QUALITY

LOCATION
100 miles (160km) northwest of San Francisco, Mendocino is the most northerly of the major viticultural coastal counties.

CLIMATE
The mountain ridges surrounding the Upper Russian and Navarro rivers climb as high as 3,500ft (1,070m) and form a natural boundary that creates the reputed transitional climate of Mendocino. This climate is unusual in that either coastal or inland influences can dominate for long or short periods, although it generally has relatively warm winters and cool summers. This provides for a growing season with many warm, dry days and cool nights. The Ukiah Valley has the shortest, warmest growing season north of San Francisco.

ASPECT
Mainly flat ground on valley bottoms or gentle, lower slopes at a height of 250 to 1,460ft (76 to 445m), with some rising to 1,600ft (490m). The vines generally face east, though just south of Ukiah they face west.

SOIL
Deep, diverse alluvial soils in the flat riverside vineyards, gravelly-loam in parts of the Russian River Valley, and a thin scree on the surrounding slopes.

VITICULTURE AND VINIFICATION
The average growing season is 268 days, compared with 308 in Sonoma (bud-break is 10 days earlier here), and 223 days in Lake County.

GRAPE VARIETIES
Primary varieties: Cabernet Sauvignon, Carignan, Chardonnay, Chenin Blanc, Colombard, Sauvignon Blanc, Zinfandel
Secondary varieties: Barbera, Burger, Cabernet Franc, Charbono, Early Burgundy, Flora, Folle Blanche, Gamay, Gamay Beaujolais, Gewürztraminer, Grenache, Gray Riesling, Green Hungarian, Malvasia Bianca, Merlot, Muscat Blanc, Palomino, Petite Sirah, Pinot Blanc, Pinot Noir, Ruby Cabernet, Sauvignon Vert, Sémillon, Sylvaner, Syrah, White Riesling

MENDOCINO, *see also* p.470
This area's northerly location need not mean harsher microclimates. Inland regions are protected by the mountains, although the Anderson Valley is cooler.

THE APPELLATIONS OF
MENDOCINO COUNTY

ANDERSON VALLEY AVA

Of some 57,600 acres (23,300 hectares) in this area, a mere 600 acres (240 hectares) have been planted with vines. Anderson Valley's coastal-influenced microclimate is cooler than in the rest of Mendocino. This is seen as one of California's coolest wine-growing areas, but temperatures do rise the frther southwest that vines are grown. The valley's soil consists of more than 20 alluvial soils, providing the diversity required for wineries such as Roederer Estate and Scharffenberger to produce a variety of base wines, the building blocks of any fine-quality sparkling wine. This area is also suitable for aromatic varieties such as Gewürztraminer and Pinot Gris, and farther inland Cabernet Sauvignon and Zinfandel are possible.

COLE RANCH AVA

Situated in a small, narrow valley, this appellation consists of just 62 acres (25 hectares) of Cabernet Sauvignon, Chardonnay, and Johannisberg Riesling vineyards, all owned by the Cole family. Soils range from gravelly-clay loam to gravelly-silty clay.

MCDOWELL VALLEY AVA

The McDowell Valley enjoys the protection of the mountains encircling it. Its vineyards are restricted to the gravelly-loam soils at around 1,000 feet (300 meters), other soils being unsuitable for vines. The microclimate here warms up when other areas are having spring frosts, although it is slightly cooler in the growing season.

MENDOCINO AVA

This may only be used for wines produced from grapes that are grown in the southernmost third of the county. It encompasses four other smaller AVAs plus surrounding vineyards.

MENDOCINO COUNTY AO

This appellation (not an AVA) covers the wines from anywhere within the county of Mendocino.

POTTER VALLEY AVA

This appellation consists of 27,500 acres (11,130 hectares) situated northwest of Clear Lake, some 11,000 acres (4,450 hectares) of which are under vine. Vines grow on the valley floor and are protected by the surrounding hills.

REDWOOD VALLEY AVA

This area is where the first Mendocino vines were planted. It has been known as Redwood Valley since it was settled in the mid-1850s and covers 35 square miles (90 square kilometers), with some 2,300 acres (930 hectares) of area under vine already in existence. The grapes ripen later than in the hotter and drier Ukiah area, providing higher acidity, color, and tannin.

YORKVILLE HIGHLANDS AVA

Geographically, but not topographically, this appears to be an extension of the Anderson Valley AVA. Yorkville Highlands has a rocky soil with high gravel content, and a cool climate that is comparable to the middle of the Anderson Valley. Sauvignon Blanc does well here, and this AVA could also favor red Bordeaux varieties.

THE WINE PRODUCERS OF
MENDOCINO COUNTY

BONTERRA
Ukiah
❶✪★☆Ⓥ

Part of the Brown-Forman group, but its organic philosophy proves that big business can be good guys too.

☑ *Chardonnay • Merlot*

EDMEADES VINEYARDS
Philo
★☆

Part of the Kendall-Jackson group.

☑ *Zinfandel*

FETZER VINEYARDS
Redwood Valley
★Ⓥ

Owned by Brown-Forman, Fetzer produces value-for-money wines..

☑ *Cabernet Sauvignon • Gewürztraminer • Merlot • Pinot Noir* (Ben Nacido Vineyard Reserve, Five Rivers Ranch) *• Syrah • Zinfandel*

FREY
Redwood Valley
❸☆

The oldest and largest fully organic winery in the US, Frey was set up in 1980 and was the first US winery to produce biodynamic wines. Just over 10 percent of its wine is biodynamic.

☑ *Petite Sirah ❸ • Sangiovese • Syrah*

GREENWOOD RIDGE VINEYARDS
Philo
☆Ⓥ

An underrated winery best-known for its Riesling, particularly its Late Harvest, although other varieties are well worth a look.

☑ *Cabernet Sauvignon • Classic red blend* (Home Run Red) *• Pinot Noir • White Riesling* (Late Harvest)

HANDLEY
Philo
★Ⓥ

An excellent, underrated *méthode champenoise* specialist. Handley's crisp Vintage Brut has creamy-vanilla richness, but he also makes flavorful Pinot Noir and Sauvignon Blanc of increasing elegance.

☑ *Pinot Noir* (Estate Reserve) *• Sauvignon Blanc* (Handley Vineyard) *• Sparkling wine* (Vintage Brut)

HUSCH VINEYARDS
Philo
☆Ⓥ

Founded by Tony Husch, this winery was sold in 1979 to Hugo Oswald, the current owner and winemaker, who also has large vineyard holdings in the Anderson and Ukiah Valleys, from which his unpretentious white-wine varietals always stand out.

☑ *Chardonnay • Chenin Blanc* (La Ribera) *• Muscat Canelli* (La Ribera) *• Sauvignon Blanc* (La Ribera)

NAVARRO VINEYARDS
Philo
★Ⓥ

Some critics believe these vineyards produce some of California's best Gewürztraminer, although I think they have the potential to do much better. If I had to name the worst varietal for a sparkling wine, it would probably be Gewürztraminer, and I've only come across four producers stupid enough to try. Yet Navarro is the exception that proves the rule. It has nothing to do with classic sparkling wine as we generally perceive it, but there are far more spicy bottle-aromas in Navarro's fizzy Gewürztraminer than there are in its regular still wine. If you can appreciate the finest Riesling Sekt and sparkling Shiraz, then you really should try Navarro Sparkling Gewürztraminer. Otherwise, it's the purity of fruit found in the Pinot wines that most attracts me to this producer at the moment.

☑ *Pinot Blanc • Pinot Gris • Pinot Noir • Riesling* (Riesling Cluster Select) *• Sparkling wine* (Gewürztraminer)

PARDUCCI WINE CELLARS
Ukiah
☆Ⓥ

Parducci is a large winery, with over 351 acres (142 hectares), which was founded in Sonoma in 1918 and moved to Ukiah in 1931, where a new winery was built in preparation for the end of Prohibition. The wines are clean and fruity, and possess a good depth of flavor for their price.

☑ *Petite Sirah • Zinfandel* (Zingaro)

ROEDERER ESTATE
Philo
★★★☆Ⓥ

The first New World venture to achieve a quality of sparkling wine comparable not just to Champagne, but to very good Champagne, Roederer Estate (or Quartet as it is known on export markets) ages like no other California sparkling wine. L'Ermitage is the greatest wine here, but the standard nonvintage Brut can be almost as stunning. A bottle of the 1994-based nonvintage, which was disgorged in February 1997 and matured in my own cellar until 2002, still displayed beautifully pristine fruit of great finesse, when most California sparkling wines of a similar age would be as dead as a dodo.

☑ *Entire range*

SCHARFFENBERGER CELLARS
Ukiah
★☆Ⓥ

Founded by John Scharffenberger in 1981 and part-owned by Pommery until it was transferred to Veuve Clicquot. After it was decided to change the name to Pacific Echo, a soulless name with no sense of place, the writing was on the wall. Veuve Clicquot did nothing to encourage exports and even thwarted efforts to promote the brand abroad. It came as no surprise when Pacific Echo was purchased in July 2004 by the Roederer-owned Maisons Marques & Domaines USA, and announced that it would drop Pacific Echo in favor of a return to the original Scharffenberger name. The company has retained Tex Sawyer, who has been the winemaker from the start; he has slowly and consistently increased the elegance and finesse of these sparkling wines.

☑ *Sparkling wine* (Blanc de Blancs, Rosé)

SONOMA COUNTY

Six fertile valleys combine to make Sonoma County California's most prolific wine-producing area, with an output comprising equal quantities of red and white wine, and a reputation for quality now fast approaching that of Napa County.

BECAUSE OF THE VOLUME of its production, Sonoma County was classed as little more than a source of blending wine until the late 1960s. It produced better-quality blending wine than the Central Valley, admittedly, but that wine was still nothing more than pep-up fodder for the bulk-produced anonymous generics. Then, in 1969, Russell Green, a former oil mogul and owner of a fast-growing vineyard in the Alexander Valley, purchased Simi, a once-famous winery founded in 1876, but at the time in decline. Green had great plans for Simi, many of which he successfully carried out, but soaring costs forced him to sell up in 1973. During those four brief years, however, he managed to restore the pre-Prohibition reputation of the old winery by creating a new genre of high-quality varietal Sonoma wines. With this achievement, he made other winemakers in the district ambitious to improve the quality of their own wines.

Not only did this result in a very pleasing plethora of interesting vinous delights, but Green's activity also attracted new blood to the area. By 1985 there was a remarkable total of 93 wineries, and since then the number has increased to a staggering 210.

FACTORS AFFECTING TASTE AND QUALITY

LOCATION
North of San Francisco, between Napa and the Pacific.

CLIMATE
Extremes of climate range from warm (Region III, *see* p.470) in the north of the county to cool (Region I, *see* p.000) in the south, mainly due to ocean breezes. Fog is prevalent around Petaluma.

ASPECT
Sonoma Valley creek drains into the Russian River, and the Russian River flows directly into the Pacific. The vines grow at an altitude of approximately 400 feet (120 meters) on flatland, or on the gentle lower slopes. Steeper slopes are being cultivated in the Sonoma Valley.

SOIL
The soil situation varies greatly, from low-fertile loams in the Sonoma Valley and Santa Rosa areas, to highly fertile alluvial soils in the Russian River Valley, with limestone at Cazadera, a gravelly soil in Dry Creek, and vent-based volcanic soils within the fallout vicinity of Mount St. Helena.

VITICULTURE AND VINIFICATION
Bulk winemaking is no longer important in the Russian River Valley; boutique wineries specializing in premium varietals have taken over.

GRAPE VARIETIES
Primary varieties: Cabernet Sauvignon, Chardonnay, Chenin Blanc, Colombard, Gewürztraminer, Merlot, Petite Sirah, Pinot Noir, Pinot Blanc, Sauvignon Blanc, White Riesling, Zinfandel
Secondary varieties: Aleatico, Alicante Bouschet, Barbera, Cabernet Franc, Carignan, Chasselas Doré, Folle Blanche, Gamay, Gamay Beaujolais, Grenache, Malbec, Malvasia, Muscat Blanc, Palomino, Pinot St. George, Ruby Cabernet, Sauvignon Vert, Sémillon, Sylvaner, Syrah

Wineries
Intensive vine-growing areas
Sonoma Mountain
Dry Creek Valley
Alexander Valley
Knights Valley
Russian River Valley
Chalk Hill
Sonoma County Green Valley
Sonoma Valley
Los Carneros
Northern Sonoma
Sonoma Coast
County boundary

Belvedere
Chalk Hill Winery
Christopher Creek
Duxoup Wine Works
Ferrari-Carano
Field Stone Winery
Foppiano Vineyards
Hop Kiln Winery
Marietta Cellars
Michel-Schlumberger
Nalle
Quivira
Rabbit Ridge
A. Rafanelli
J. Rochioli Vineyards
Simi Winery
Stonestreet

Arrowood Vineyards
Benzinger
B.R. Cohn
H. Coturri & Sons Ltd.
Glen Ellen Winery
Laurel Glen Vineyard

Cline Cellars
Richard Cuneo
Gloria Ferrer
Hartford Court
Robert Hunter
Robert Stemmler
Viansa

▲ Height above sea level (metres)

0 2 4 6 8 10 miles
0 5 10 15 km

DRY CREEK VALLEY
Sonoma's Dry Creek lies close to the Russian River, of which Dry Creek is a tributary. Moist and fertile, the valley has a gravelly soil unique to the area, enabling it to claim AVA status.

SONOMA COUNTY *See also p.470*
One of California's most important wine regions, Sonoma has a varied climate with different soils, which produce a broad spectrum of wines. It is perhaps aptly named, as Sonoma is derived from the local Wintun Native American word for "nose."

THE APPELLATIONS OF
SONOMA COUNTY

ALEXANDER VALLEY AVA

Located in the northeast of the county, this appellation extends from the banks of the Russian River into the foothills of the Mayacamas Mountains. In 1986 its boundaries were extended so that it overlapped the Russian River AVA, and were further extended in 1990 to incorporate Sir Peter Michael's Gauer Ranch and Ellis Alden's Chestnut Springs vineyards in the foothills east of Geyserville. Cabernet Sauvignon and Merlot are ideally suited to this area, where very fine Nebbiolo, Sangiovese, and Chardonnay can also be produced. Formerly part of Dry Creek AVA, the Gill Creek watershed area was reclassified as Alexander Valley AVA in 2001.

CHALK HILL AVA

This appellation covers 33 square miles (85 square kilometers) and encompasses 1,600 acres (650 hectares) of vineyards rising in altitude from 200 to 1,300 feet (60 to 400 meters). There is no chalk here; the soil's whiteness is in fact derived from volcanic ash with a high quartzite content. Emitted by Mount St. Helena over many centuries, the ash has mixed with local sandy and silty loams to provide a deep soil that is not particularly fertile. This area is protected by a thermal belt that promotes a September harvest, compared with October in surrounding areas.

DRY CREEK VALLEY AVA

This appellation faces that of the Alexander Valley across the Russian River. Its climate is generally wetter and warmer than surrounding areas, with a longer growing season than the Russian River appellation to the south, and varietal suitability is very flexible, stretching from Sauvignon Blanc to Zinfandel. The Gill Creek watershed area was declassified as Dry Creek in 2001, and reclassified under the Alexander Valley AVA.

KNIGHTS VALLEY AVA

Knight's valley covers an area of approximately 55 square miles (140 square kilometers) containing 1,000 acres (400 hectares) of vineyards. The vines grow on rocky and gravelly soil of low fertility at altitudes that are generally higher than those in the adjacent AVAs, making it ideal Cabernet country.

LOS CARNEROS AVA

The Los Carneros, or simply Carneros, appellation covers an area of low, rolling hills that straddle the counties of Sonoma and Napa. This was originally sheep country, but the cool sea breezes that come off San Pablo Bay to the south provide an excellent fine-wine growing climate, especially for Chardonnay, Pinot Noir, and sparkling-wine varieties.

NORTHERN SONOMA AVA

The large appellation of Northern Sonoma completely encapsulates six other AVAs, those of Alexander Valley, Chalk Hill, Dry Creek Valley, Knights Valley, Russian River Valley, and Sonoma County Green Valley, and is separated from the Sonoma Valley appellation to the south by the city of Santa Rosa.

RUSSIAN RIVER VALLEY AVA

The name Russian River began appearing on wine labels as recently as 1970, although vineyards in this region date from the 19th century. The early-morning coastal fog provides a cooler growing season than that of neighboring areas, making the Russian River Valley very well suited to Pinot Noir—and indeed it produces some of California's finest Pinot Noir wines. In September 2003, this AVA was expanded to include 767 acres (307 hectares) south of Fulton.

SONOMA COAST AVA

An appellation covering 750 square miles (1,940 square kilometers), Sonoma Coast AVA is made up of the area directly inland from the length of Sonoma's Pacific coastline—the AVA's western boundary. It is significantly cooler than other areas because of the persistent fog that envelops the Coast Ranges, the mountains that are within sight of the Pacific Ocean.

SONOMA COUNTY GREEN VALLEY AVA

Originally it was proposed that this area within the Russian River Valley AVA be called, simply, Green Valley, but to avoid confusion with Solano County's Green Valley appellation, it was decided to add "Sonoma County." The climate here is one of the coolest in the Russian River Valley and the soil is mostly fine sandy loam, well suited to sparkling wine.

SONOMA MOUNTAIN AVA

This tiny appellation is within the Sonoma Valley AVA. Sonoma Mountain AVA has a thermal belt phenomenon that drains cold air and fog from its steep terrain to the slopes below, creating a climate that is characterized by more moderate temperatures than the surrounding areas.

SONOMA VALLEY AVA

The first vines were planted here in 1825 by the Mission San Francisco de Sonoma. Rainfall is lower than elsewhere in the county and fog rarely penetrates the Sonoma Mountains. It is red-wine country; particularly for Cabernet Sauvignon and Zinfandel.

THE WINE PRODUCERS OF
SONOMA COUNTY

A. RAFANELLI
Healdsburg
★

It was always said that Americo Rafanelli, who died in 1987, made wine "as they used to in the olden days." Well, he would be proud of the blockbusters made by his son David from this small, unirrigated, hillside vineyard.

✓ *Zinfandel*

ALEXANDER VALLEY VINEYARDS
Healdsburg
★ V

An underrated winery built on the original homestead of Cyrus Alexander, who gave his name to the Alexander Valley, now a famed AVA. Most products are well worth buying as value-for-money, everyday drinking wines, but some are much finer than that, despite their modest prices, and the Cyrus comes precariously close to making the top 10 classic red blends in California.

✓ *Cabernet Sauvignon •
Chardonnay* (Wetzel Family Estate) • *Classic red blend*
(Cyrus) • *Merlot • Pinot Noir*

ARROWOOD VINEYARDS
Glen Ellen
★ ★ V

Ex-Château St. Jean winemaker Richard Arrowood makes very stylish wines and the quality gets better each year, as he hones down his varietals. Excellent-value second label (Grand Archer).

✓ *Cabernet Sauvignon* (Grand Archer, Réserve Spéciale) • *Chardonnay* (Cuvée Michel Berthod) • *Merlot* (Grand Archer, Réserve Spéciale) • *Pinot Blanc • Riesling* (Special Select Late Harvest Riesling Hoot Owl) • *Syrah • Viognier*

B R COHN
Glen Ellen
★

Sometimes you have to spit the splinters out of these wines, but you cannot deny the quality and have to admire the enthusiasm.

✓ *Cabernet Sauvignon* (Olive Hill) • *Merlot* (Sonoma Valley)

BELVEDERE
Healdsburg
★ V

Large vineyards enable owner Bill Hambrecht to make a wide range of wines. He used to excel at Chardonnay, but his best and most consistent wines are now Merlot and Zinfandel.

✓ *Merlot* (Healdsburg Ranches) • *Zinfandel* (Healdsburg Ranches)